D1481060

REFERENCE

THE NEW INTERPRETER'S® BIBLE

IN TWELVE VOLUMES

VOLUME ELEVEN

THE SECOND LETTER TO THE CORINTHIANS

THE LETTER TO THE GALATIANS

THE LETTER TO THE EPHESIANS

THE LETTER TO THE PHILIPPIANS

THE LETTER TO THE COLOSSIANS

THE FIRST AND SECOND LETTERS TO
THE THESSALONIANS

THE FIRST AND SECOND LETTERS TO
TIMOTHY AND THE LETTER TO TITUS

THE LETTER TO PHILEMON

EDITORIAL BOARD

THE NEW INTERPRETER'S BIBLE

GENERAL ARTICLES
&
INTRODUCTION, COMMENTARY, & REFLECTIONS
FOR EACH BOOK OF THE BIBLE
INCLUDING
THE APOCRYPHAL / DEUTEROCANONICAL BOOKS
IN
TWELVE VOLUMES

VOLUME
XI

ABINGDON PRESS
Nashville

THE NEW INTERPRETER'S® BIBLE
VOLUME XI

This book is printed on recycled, acid-free paper.

Library of Congress Cataloging-in-Publication Data

The New Interpreter's Bible: general articles & introduction,
    commentary, & reflections for each book of the Bible, including the
Apocryphal/Deuterocanonical books.
        p. cm.
    Full texts and critical notes of the New International Version and
the New Revised Standard Version of the Bible in parallel columns.
        Includes bibliographical references.
        ISBN 0-687-27824-4 (v. 11: alk. paper)
        1. Bible—Commentaries. 2. Abingdon Press. I. Bible. English.
New International. 1994. II. Bible. English. New Revised
Standard. 1994.
BS491.2.N484 1994
220.7'7—dc20   94-21092
                                                                                    CIP

The Hebraica® and Graeca® fonts used to print this work are available from Linguist's Software, Inc., PO Box 580, Edmonds, WA 98020-0580 tel (206) 775-1130.

PUBLICATION STAFF

President and Publisher: Neil M. Alexander
Editorial Director: Harriett Jane Olson
Project Director: Jack A. Keller, Jr.
Reference Resources Senior Editor: Michael R. Russell
Production Editors: Linda S. Allen
                    Joan M. Shoup
Hebrew and Greek Editor/Assistant Editor: Emily Cheney
Production and Design Manager: Walter E. Wynne
Designer: J. S. Laughbaum
Copy Processing Manager: Sylvia S. Street
Composition Specialist: Kathy M. Harding
Publishing Systems Analyst: Glenn R. Hinton
Prepress Manager: Billy W. Murphy
Prepress Systems Technicians: Thomas E. Mullins
                                J. Calvin Buckner
                                Phillip D. Elliott
Director of Production Processes: James E. Leath
Scheduling: Laurene M. Martin
            Tracey D. Craddock
Print Procurement Coordinator: Martha K. Taylor

00 01 02 03 04 05 06 07 08 09 —10 9 8 7 6 5 4 3 2 1

MANUFACTURED IN THE UNITED STATES OF AMERICA

CONSULTANTS

NEIL M. ALEXANDER
President and Publisher
The United Methodist Publishing House
Nashville, Tennessee

OWEN F. CAMPION
Associate Publisher
Our Sunday Visitor
Huntington, Indiana

MINERVA G. CARCAÑO
Director
Mexican American Program
Perkins School of Theology
Southern Methodist University
Dallas, Texas

V. L. DAUGHTERY, JR.
Retired Pastor
South Georgia Conference
The United Methodist Church

SHARON NEUFER EMSWILER
Pastor
First United Methodist Church
Rock Island, Illinois

JUAN G. FELICIANO VALERA
Director
Development Office
Evangelical Seminary of Puerto Rico
San Juan, Puerto Rico

CELIA BREWER MARSHALL
Lecturer
University of North Carolina at Charlotte
Charlotte, North Carolina

NANCY C. MILLER-HERRON
Attorney and clergy member of the
Tennessee Conference
The United Methodist Church
Dresden, Tennessee

ROBERT C. SCHNASE
Pastor
First United Methodist Church
McAllen, Texas

BILL SHERMAN
Pastor Emeritus
Woodmont Baptist Church
Nashville, Tennessee

RODNEY T. SMOTHERS
Pastor
Ousley United Methodist Church
Lithonia, Georgia

WILLIAM D. WATLEY
Pastor
St. James African Methodist Episcopal Church
Newark, New Jersey

TALLULAH FISHER WILLIAMS[†]
Superintendent
Chicago Northwestern District
The United Methodist Church
Chicago, Illinois

SUK-CHONG YU
Superintendent
Nevada-Sierra District
The United Methodist Church
Reno, Nevada

[†] *deceased*

CONTRIBUTORS

ELIZABETH ACHTEMEIER
  Adjunct Professor of Bible and Homiletics
  Union Theological Seminary in Virginia
  Richmond, Virginia
  (Presbyterian Church [U.S.A.])
    Joel

LESLIE C. ALLEN
  Professor of Old Testament
  Fuller Theological Seminary
  Pasadena, California
  (Baptist)
    1 & 2 Chronicles

GARY A. ANDERSON
  Associate Professor of Religious Studies
  University of Virginia
  Charlottesville, Virginia
  (The Roman Catholic Church)
    Introduction to Israelite Religion

DAVID L. BARTLETT
  Lantz Professor of Preaching and
    Communication
  The Divinity School
  Yale University
  New Haven, Connecticut
  (American Baptist Churches in the U.S.A.)
    1 Peter

ROBERT A. BENNETT, PH.D.
  Cambridge, Massachusetts
  (The Episcopal Church)
    Zephaniah

ADELE BERLIN
  Robert H. Smith Professor of Hebrew Bible
  Associate Provost for Faculty Affairs
  University of Maryland
  College Park, Maryland
    Introduction to Hebrew Poetry

BRUCE C. BIRCH
  Dean and Woodrow W. and Mildred B. Miller
    Professor of Biblical Theology
  Wesley Theological Seminary
  Washington, DC
  (The United Methodist Church)
    1 & 2 Samuel

PHYLLIS A. BIRD
  Professor of Old Testament
    Interpretation
  Garrett-Evangelical Theological Seminary
  Evanston, Illinois
  (The United Methodist Church)
    The Authority of the Bible

C. CLIFTON BLACK
  Otto A. Piper Professor of Biblical Theology
  Princeton Theological Seminary
  Princeton, New Jersey
    1, 2, & 3 John

JOSEPH BLENKINSOPP
  John A. O'Brien Professor of Biblical Studies
  Department of Theology
  University of Notre Dame
  Notre Dame, Indiana
  (The Roman Catholic Church)
    Introduction to the Pentateuch

M. EUGENE BORING
  I. Wylie and Elizabeth M. Briscoe Professor of
    New Testament
  Brite Divinity School
  Texas Christian University
  Fort Worth, Texas
  (Christian Church [Disciples of Christ])
    Matthew

WALTER BRUEGGEMANN
William Marcellus McPheeters Professor of Old
Testament
Columbia Theological Seminary
Decatur, Georgia
(United Church of Christ)
Exodus

DAVID G. BUTTRICK
Professor of Homiletics and Liturgics
The Divinity School
Vanderbilt University
Nashville, Tennessee
(United Church of Christ)
The Use of the Bible in Preaching

RONALD E. CLEMENTS
Samuel Davidson Professor of Old Testament
King's College
University of London
London, England
(Baptist Union of Great Britain and Ireland)
Deuteronomy

RICHARD J. CLIFFORD, S.J.
Professor of Old Testament
Weston Jesuit School of Theology
Cambridge, Massachusetts
(The Roman Catholic Church)
Introduction to Wisdom Literature

JOHN J. COLLINS
Professor of Hebrew Bible
The Divinity School
University of Chicago
Chicago, Illinois
(The Roman Catholic Church)
Introduction to Early Jewish Religion

ROBERT B. COOTE
Professor of Old Testament
San Francisco Theological Seminary
San Anselmo, California
(Presbyterian Church [U.S.A.])
Joshua

FRED B. CRADDOCK
Bandy Distinguished Professor of Preaching
and New Testament, Emeritus
Candler School of Theology
Emory University
Atlanta, Georgia
(Christian Church [Disciples of Christ])
Hebrews

SIDNIE WHITE CRAWFORD
Associate Professor of Hebrew Bible
and Chair of the Department of Classics
University of Nebraska—Lincoln
Lincoln, Nebraska
(The Episcopal Church)
Esther; Additions to Esther

JAMES L. CRENSHAW
Robert L. Flowers Professor of Old Testament
The Divinity School
Duke University
Durham, North Carolina
(Baptist)
Sirach

KEITH R. CRIM
Pastor
New Concord Presbyterian Church
Concord, Virginia
(Presbyterian Church [U.S.A.])
Modern English Versions of the Bible

R. ALAN CULPEPPER
Dean
The School of Theology
Mercer University
Atlanta, Georgia
(Southern Baptist Convention)
Luke

KATHERYN PFISTERER DARR
Associate Professor of Hebrew Bible
The School of Theology
Boston University
Boston, Massachusetts
(The United Methodist Church)
Ezekiel

ROBERT DORAN
Professor of Religion
Amherst College
Amherst, Massachusetts
1 & 2 Maccabees

THOMAS B. DOZEMAN
Professor of Old Testament
United Theological Seminary
Dayton, Ohio
(Presbyterian Church [U.S.A.])
Numbers

JAMES D. G. DUNN
Lightfoot Professor of Divinity
Department of Theology
University of Durham
Durham, England
(The Methodist Church [Great Britain])
1 & 2 Timothy; Titus

ELDON JAY EPP
Harkness Professor of Biblical Literature
and Chairman of the Department of Religion
Case Western Reserve University
Cleveland, Ohio
(The Episcopal Church)
*Ancient Texts and Versions of the New
Testament*

KATHLEEN A. ROBERTSON FARMER
Professor of Old Testament
United Theological Seminary
Dayton, Ohio
(The United Methodist Church)
Ruth

CAIN HOPE FELDER
Professor of New Testament Language
and Literature
The School of Divinity
Howard University
Washington, DC
(The United Methodist Church)
Philemon

TERENCE E. FRETHEIM
Professor of Old Testament
Luther Seminary
Saint Paul, Minnesota
(Evangelical Lutheran Church in America)
Genesis

FRANCISCO O. GARCÍA-TRETO
Professor of Religion and Chair of the
Department of Religion
Trinity University
San Antonio, Texas
(Presbyterian Church [U.S.A.])
Nahum

CATHERINE GUNSALUS GONZÁLEZ
Professor of Church History
Columbia Theological Seminary
Decatur, Georgia
(Presbyterian Church [U.S.A.])
*The Use of the Bible in Hymns, Liturgy,
and Education*

JUSTO L. GONZÁLEZ
Adjunct Professor of Church History
Columbia Theological Seminary
Decatur, Georgia
(The United Methodist Church)
*How the Bible Has Been Interpreted in
Christian Tradition*

DONALD E. GOWAN
Robert Cleveland Holland Professor of Old
Testament
Pittsburgh Theological Seminary
Pittsburgh, Pennsylvania
(Presbyterian Church [U.S.A.])
Amos

DANIEL J. HARRINGTON, S.J.
Professor of New Testament
Weston Jesuit School of Theology
Cambridge, Massachusetts
(The Roman Catholic Church)
Introduction to the Canon

RICHARD B. HAYS
Professor of New Testament
The Divinity School
Duke University
Durham, North Carolina
(The United Methodist Church)
Galatians

THEODORE HIEBERT
Professor of Old Testament
McCormick Theological
Seminary
Chicago, Illinois
(Mennonite Church)
Habakkuk

CARL R. HOLLADAY
Professor of New Testament
Candler School of Theology
Emory University
Atlanta, Georgia
*Contemporary Methods of Reading the
Bible*

MORNA D. HOOKER
Lady Margaret's Professor of Divinity, Emeritus
The Divinity School
University of Cambridge
Cambridge, England
(The Methodist Church [Great Britain])
Philippians

DAVID C. HOPKINS
Professor of Old Testament
Wesley Theological Seminary
Washington, DC
(United Church of Christ)
Life in Ancient Palestine

LUKE T. JOHNSON
Robert W. Woodruff Professor of New
Testament and Christian Origins
Candler School of Theology
Emory University
Atlanta, Georgia
(The Roman Catholic Church)
James

WALTER C. KAISER, JR.
President and Colman M. Mockler
Distinguished Professor of Old Testament
Gordon-Conwell Theological Seminary
South Hamilton, Massachusetts
(The Evangelical Free Church of America)
Leviticus

LEANDER E. KECK
Winkley Professor of Biblical Theology, Emeritus
The Divinity School
Yale University
New Haven, Connecticut
(Christian Church [Disciples of Christ])
Introduction to The New Interpreter's Bible

CHAN-HIE KIM
Professor of New Testament and Director of
Korean Studies
The School of Theology at Claremont
Claremont, California
(The United Methodist Church)
Reading the Bible as Asian Americans

RALPH W. KLEIN
Christ Seminary-Seminex Professor of
Old Testament
Lutheran School of Theology at Chicago
Chicago, Illinois
(Evangelical Lutheran Church in America)
Ezra; Nehemiah

MICHAEL KOLARCIK, S.J.
Associate Professor of Old Testament
Regis College
Toronto, Ontario
Canada
(The Roman Catholic Church)
Book of Wisdom

ANDREW T. LINCOLN
Portland Chair in New Testament Studies
School of Theology and Religious Studies
Cheltenham & Gloucester College of Higher
Education
Cheltenham, England
Colossians

J. CLINTON MCCANN, JR.
Evangelical Professor of
Biblical Interpretation
Eden Theological Seminary
St. Louis, Missouri
(Presbyterian Church [U.S.A.])
Psalms

ABRAHAM J. MALHERBE
Buckingham Professor of New Testament
Criticism and Interpretation, Emeritus
The Divinity School
Yale University
New Haven, Connecticut
(Church of Christ)
*The Cultural Context of the New Testament:
The Greco-Roman World*

W. EUGENE MARCH
Dean and Arnold Black Rhodes Professor
of Old Testament
Louisville Presbyterian Theological Seminary
Louisville, Kentucky
(Presbyterian Church [U.S.A.])
Haggai

JAMES EARL MASSEY
Dean Emeritus and
Distinguished Professor-at-Large
The School of Theology
Anderson University
(Church of God [Anderson, Ind.])
*Reading the Bible from Particular Social
Locations: An Introduction;
Reading the Bible as African Americans*

J. MAXWELL MILLER
Professor of Old Testament, Emeritus
Candler School of Theology
Emory University
Atlanta, Georgia
(The United Methodist Church)
Introduction to the History of Ancient Israel

PATRICK D. MILLER
Charles T. Haley Professor of Old Testament
Theology
Princeton Theological Seminary
Princeton, New Jersey
(Presbyterian Church [U.S.A.])
Jeremiah

PETER D. MISCALL
Adjunct Faculty
The Iliff School of Theology
Denver, Colorado
(The Episcopal Church)
Introduction to Narrative Literature

FREDERICK J. MURPHY
Professor
Department of Religious Studies
College of the Holy Cross
Worcester, Massachusetts
(The Roman Catholic Church)
Introduction to Apocalyptic Literature

CAROL A. NEWSOM
Professor of Old Testament
Candler School of Theology
Emory University
Atlanta, Georgia
(The Episcopal Church)
Job

GEORGE W. E. NICKELSBURG
Professor of Christian Origins and Early Judaism
School of Religion
University of Iowa
Iowa City, Iowa
(Evangelical Lutheran Church in America)
*The Jewish Context of the New
Testament*

IRENE NOWELL, O.S.B.
Community Formation Director
Mount St. Scholasticas
Atchison, Kansas
(The Roman Catholic Church)
Tobit

KATHLEEN M. O'CONNOR
Professor of Old Testament Language,
Literature, and Exegesis
Columbia Theological Seminary
Decatur, Georgia
(The Roman Catholic Church)
Lamentations

GAIL R. O'DAY
Almar H. Shatford Professor of Preaching and
New Testament
Candler School of Theology
Emory University
Atlanta, Georgia
(United Church of Christ)
John

BEN C. OLLENBURGER
Professor of Biblical Theology
Associated Mennonite Biblical Seminary
Elkhart, Indiana
(Mennonite Church)
Zechariah

DENNIS T. OLSON
Associate Professor of Old Testament
Princeton Theological Seminary
Princeton, New Jersey
(Evangelical Lutheran Church in America)
Judges

CAROLYN OSIEK
Professor of New Testament
Department of Biblical Languages
and Literature
Catholic Theological Union
Chicago, Illinois
(The Roman Catholic Church)
Reading the Bible as Women

SAMUEL PAGÁN
President
Evangelical Seminary of Puerto Rico
San Juan, Puerto Rico
(Christian Church [Disciples of Christ])
Obadiah

SIMON B. PARKER
Professor of Hebrew Bible and
Harrell F. Beck Scholar in Hebrew Scripture
The School of Theology
Boston University
Boston, Massachusetts
(The United Methodist Church)
*The Ancient Near Eastern Literary
Background of the Old Testament*

PHEME PERKINS
Professor of New Testament
Boston College
Chestnut Hill, Massachusetts
(The Roman Catholic Church)
Mark; Ephesians

DAVID L. PETERSEN
Clifford E. Baldridge Professor of
Biblical Studies
The Iliff School of Theology
Denver, Colorado
(Presbyterian Church [U.S.A.])
Introduction to Prophetic Literature

CHRISTOPHER C. ROWLAND
Dean Ireland's Professor of the Exegesis
of Holy Scripture
The Queen's College
Oxford, England
(The Church of England)
Revelation

ANTHONY J. SALDARINI
Professor of Biblical Studies
Boston College
Chestnut Hill, Massachusetts
(The Roman Catholic Church)
Baruch; Letter of Jeremiah

J. PAUL SAMPLEY
Professor of New Testament and
Christian Origins
The School of Theology and The Graduate Division
Boston University
Boston, Massachusetts
(The United Methodist Church)
1 Corinthians; 2 Corinthians

JUDITH E. SANDERSON
Associate Professor of Hebrew Bible
Department of Theology and Religious Studies
Seattle University
Seattle, Washington
*Ancient Texts and Versions of the Old
Testament*

EILEEN M. SCHULLER, O.S.U.
Professor
Department of Religious Studies
McMaster University
Hamilton, Ontario
Canada
(The Roman Catholic Church)
Malachi

FERNANDO F. SEGOVIA
Professor of New Testament and
Early Christianity
The Divinity School
Vanderbilt University
Nashville, Tennessee
(The Roman Catholic Church)
Reading the Bible as Hispanic Americans

CHRISTOPHER R. SEITZ
Professor of Old Testament and Theological
Studies
The Divinity School
University of St. Andrews
Fife, Scotland
(The Episcopal Church)
Isaiah 40–66

CHOON-LEONG SEOW
Henry Snyder Gehman Professor of Old
Testament Language and Literature
Princeton Theological Seminary
Princeton, New Jersey
(Presbyterian Church [U.S.A.])
1 & 2 Kings

MICHAEL A. SIGNER
Abrams Professor of Jewish Thought and
Culture
Department of Theology
University of Notre Dame
Notre Dame, Indiana
*How the Bible Has Been Interpreted in
Jewish Tradition*

MOISÉS SILVA
Professor of New Testament
Westminster Theological Seminary
Philadelphia, Pennsylvania
(The Orthodox Presbyterian Church)
*Contemporary Theories of Biblical
Interpretation*

DANIEL J. SIMUNDSON
Professor of Old Testament
Luther Seminary
Saint Paul, Minnesota
(Evangelical Lutheran Church in America)
Micah

ABRAHAM SMITH
Associate Professor of New Testament
Andover Newton Theological School
Newton Centre, Massachusetts
(The National Baptist Convention, USA, Inc.)
1 & 2 Thessalonians

DANIEL L. SMITH-CHRISTOPHER
Associate Professor of Theological Studies
Department of Theology
Loyola Marymount University
Los Angeles, California
(The Society of Friends [Quaker])
Daniel; Bel and the Dragon; Prayer of Azariah; Susannah

ROBERT C. TANNEHILL
Academic Dean and Harold B. Williams
Professor of Biblical Studies
Methodist Theological School in Ohio
Delaware, Ohio
(The United Methodist Church)
The Gospels and Narrative Literature

GEORGE E. TINKER
Professor of American Indian Cultures and
Religious Traditions
The Iliff School of Theology
Denver, Colorado
(Evangelical Lutheran Church in America)
Reading the Bible as Native Americans

W. SIBLEY TOWNER
The Reverend Archibald McFadyen Professor of
Biblical Interpretation
Union Theological Seminary in Virginia
Richmond, Virginia
(Presbyterian Church [U.S.A.])
Ecclesiastes

PHYLLIS TRIBLE
Professor of Biblical Studies
The Divinity School
Wake Forest University
Winston-Salem, North Carolina
Jonah

GENE M. TUCKER
Professor of Old Testament, Emeritus
Candler School of Theology
Emory University
Atlanta, Georgia
(The United Methodist Church)
Isaiah 1–39

CHRISTOPHER M. TUCKETT
Rylands Professor of Biblical Criticism
and Exegesis
Faculty of Theology
University of Manchester
Manchester, England
(The Church of England)
Jesus and the Gospels

RAYMOND C. VAN LEEUWEN
Professor of Religion and Theology
Eastern College
Saint Davids, Pennsylvania
(Christian Reformed Church in North America)
Proverbs

ROBERT W. WALL
Professor of Biblical Studies
Department of Religion
Seattle Pacific University
Seattle, Washington
(Free Methodist Church of North America)
Acts; Introduction to Epistolary Literature

DUANE F. WATSON
Associate Professor of New Testament Studies
Department of Religion and Philosophy
Malone College
Canton, Ohio
(The United Methodist Church)
2 Peter; Jude

RENITA J. WEEMS
Associate Professor of Hebrew Bible
The Divinity School
Vanderbilt University
Nashville, Tennessee
(African Methodist Episcopal Church)
Song of Songs

LAWRENCE M. WILLS
Associate Professor of Biblical Studies
The Episcopal Divinity School
Cambridge, Massachusetts
(The Episcopal Church)
Judith

VINCENT L. WIMBUSH
Professor of New Testament and
Christian Origins
Union Theological Seminary
New York, New York
(Progressive National Baptist Convention, Inc.)
The Ecclesiastical Context of the New Testament

N. THOMAS WRIGHT
  Canon of Westminster
  Westminster Abbey
  London, England
  (The Church of England)
    Romans

GALE A. YEE
  Associate Professor of Old Testament
  Department of Theology
  University of Saint Thomas
  Saint Paul, Minnesota
  (The Roman Catholic Church)
    Hosea

FEATURES OF
THE NEW INTERPRETER'S® BIBLE

The general aim of *The New Interpreter's Bible* is to bring the best in contemporary biblical scholarship into the service of the church to enhance preaching, teaching, and study of the Scriptures. To accomplish that general aim, the design of *The New Interpreter's Bible* has been shaped by two controlling principles: (1) form serves function, and (2) maximize ease of use.

General articles provide the reader with concise, up-to-date, balanced introductions and assessments of selected topics. In most cases, a brief bibliography points the way to further exploration of a topic. Many of the general articles are placed in volumes 1 and 8, at the beginning of the coverage of the Old and New Testaments, respectively. Others have been inserted in those volumes where the reader will encounter the corresponding type of literature (e.g., "Introduction to Prophetic Literature" appears in Volume 6 alongside several of the prophetic books).

Coverage of each biblical book begins with an "Introduction" that acquaints the reader with the essential historical, sociocultural, literary, and theological issues necessary to understand the biblical book. A short bibliography and an outline of the biblical book are found at the end of each Introduction. The introductory sections are the only material in *The New Interpreter's Bible* printed in a single wide-column format.

The biblical text is divided into coherent and manageable primary units, which are located within larger sections of Scripture. At the opening discussion of any large section of Scripture, readers will often find material identified as "Overview," which includes remarks applicable to the large section of text. The primary unit of text may be as short as a few verses or as long as a chapter or more. This is the point at which the biblical text itself is reprinted in *The New Interpreter's Bible*. Dealing with Scripture in terms of these primary units allows discussion of important issues that are overlooked in a verse-by-verse treatment. Each scriptural unit is identified by text citation and a short title.

The full texts and critical notes of the New International Version and the New Revised Standard Version of the Bible are presented in parallel columns for quick reference. (For the Apocryphal/Deuterocanonical works, the NIV is replaced by The New American Bible.) Since every translation is to some extent an interpretation as well, the inclusion of these widely known and influential modern translations provides an easy comparison that in many cases will lead to a better understanding of a passage. Biblical passages are set in a two-column format and placed in green tint-blocks to make it easy to recognize them at a glance. The NAB, NIV, and NRSV material is clearly identified on each page on which the text appears.

Immediately following each biblical text is a section marked "Commentary," which provides an exegetical analysis informed by linguistic, text-critical, historical-critical, literary, social-scientific, and theological methods. The Commentary serves as a reliable, judicious guide through the text, pointing out the critical problems as well as key interpretive issues.

The exegetical approach is "text-centered." That is, the commentators focus primarily on the text in its final form rather than on (a) a meticulous rehearsal of problems of scholarship associated with a text, (b) a thorough reconstruction of the pre-history of the text, or (c) an exhaustive rehearsal of the text's interpretive history. Of course, some attention to scholarly problems, to the pre-history of a text, and to historic interpretations that have shaped streams of tradition is important in particular cases precisely in order to illumine the several levels of meaning in the final form of the text. But the *primary* focus is on the canonical text itself. Moreover, the Commentary not only describes pertinent aspects of the text, but also teaches the reader what to look for in the text so as to develop the reader's own capacity to analyze and interpret the text.

Commentary material runs serially for a few paragraphs or a few pages, depending on what is required by the biblical passage under discussion.

Commentary material is set in a two-column format. Occasional subheads appear in a bold green font. The next level of subdivisions appears as bold black fonts and a third level as black italic fonts. Footnotes are placed at the bottom of the column in which the superscripts appear.

Key words in Hebrew, Aramaic, or Greek are printed in the original-language font, accompanied by a transliteration and a translation or explanation.

Immediately following the Commentary, in most cases, is the section called "Reflections." A detailed exposition growing directly out of the discussion and issues dealt with in the Commentary, the Reflections are geared specifically toward helping those who interpret Scripture in the life of the church by providing "handles" for grasping the significance of Scripture for faith and life today. Recognizing that the text has the capacity to shape the life of the Christian community, this section presents multiple possibilities for preaching and teaching in light of each biblical text. That is, instead of providing the preacher or teacher full illustrations, poems, outlines, and the like, the Reflections offer *several* trajectories of possible interpretation that connect with the situation of the contemporary listeners. Recognizing the power of Scripture to speak anew to diverse situations, not all of the suggested trajectories could be appropriated on any one occasion. Preachers and teachers want some specificity about the implications of the text, but not so much specificity that the work is done for them. The ideas in the Reflections are meant to stimulate the thought of preachers and teachers, not to replace it.

Three-quarter width columns distinguish Reflections materials from biblical text and Commentary.

Occasional excursuses have been inserted in some volumes to address topics of special importance that are best treated apart from the flow of Commentary and Reflections on specific passages. Set in three-quarter width columns, excursuses are identified graphically by a green color bar that runs down the outside margin of the page.

Occasional maps, charts, and illustrations appear throughout the volumes at points where they are most likely to be immediately useful to the reader.

CONTENTS
VOLUME XI

THE SECOND LETTER TO THE CORINTHIANS

INTRODUCTION, COMMENTARY, AND REFLECTIONS
BY
J. PAUL SAMPLEY

THE SECOND LETTER TO THE
CORINTHIANS

INTRODUCTION

Nowhere else in Paul's letters can we observe his enduring relationship with a particular church. In the documents called 1 and 2 Corinthians, Paul relates to the Corinthian believers across a number of years. In those two works scholars have found references to five—and text of at least three—letters Paul wrote to the believers at Corinth and one they wrote to him. When the letters or letter fragments are arranged in a sequence, they portray Paul's relations to the Corinthians as ranging from good times to times not so good. Though we know that Paul had enduring relations with other churches, such as the one at Philippi (Phil 1:5; 4:15-16), we have no such detailed evidence anywhere but with the Corinthians.

In the letters redacted into 2 Corinthians, personal relations, modest goals and purposes, and even what some might consider rather petty matters are the occasion for grand theological reflections. A near-fatal disaster elicits a rumination about the God of consolation and comfort (1:3-11). Paul's poor scheduling and failure to make a promised trip generate a profound reflection on the faithfulness of God (1:15-22). Paul's desire to recement relations with the Corinthians gives him the opportunity to reflect on his ministry to them in three original constructions, depicting himself as minister of the new covenant, as minister through affliction and comfort, and as minister of reconciliation (2:14–6:10). His commitment to the collection for the saints in Jerusalem generates powerful reflections on God's grace and the generosity it inspires (chaps. 8–9). Paul's strife with his opponents in chapters 10–13 provides striking ruminations regarding the Pauline paradox of (divine) strength in (human) weakness.

Discussions of Corinth as a city, its character, the history of Paul's establishing a church

The Aegean Region

there, and the socioethnic makeup of that congregation are all detailed in the Introduction of the Commentary on 1 Corinthians.[1]

LITERARY INTEGRITY OF 2 CORINTHIANS

The literary integrity of 2 Corinthians has proved a problem for scholars. Though most agree that the text is made up of more than one letter fragment,[2] much disagreement remains over the number, scope, and even sequence of the fragments. Absolutely no textual variations or manuscript evidence supports any of the partition theories. The lack of such evidence, however, does not necessarily argue against partition; it could simply be that the editing together of available fragments was done before the oldest extant manuscripts were written. Persons who want to pursue varying theses regarding the partition and sequencing of the segments of 2 Corinthians are invited to see the section of this Introduction entitled "Deliberations Concerning Fragmentation and Sequence Within 2 Corinthians."

Events and Circumstances Connecting the Fragments. Before he wrote what we now call 1 Corinthians, Paul had written the Corinthians what has come to be called the "previous" letter (1 Cor 5:9-11), his first to them (*Letter A,* lost). After some time he wrote his second letter to them—now labeled 1 Corinthians (*Letter B*)—in part because of apparent confusion regarding what he meant about holiness in the previous letter.

Sometime after Paul had written and sent 1 Corinthians, he went to Corinth, as 1 Cor 16:5-7 promised. During that visit, one of the Corinthian believers made a verbal attack on Paul, and, to his chagrin, no one came to his defense (2 Cor 2:3; see the Commentary on 2:3 for details of this interpretation). Mortified, Paul left. Although he had promised another visit to the Corinthians, he rethought it (1:23) and instead sent a letter of rather harsh frank speech (*Letter C,* lost; see "Frank Speech," below), calling them to task for the "one who did the wrong," chastizing them for their abandonment of him, and calling them back into "obedience" to him (2 Cor 7:8-16).

The frank speech letter achieved considerable success, as reported by Titus, though it is probably fair to say not quite as much as Paul had wished (2 Cor 6:11-13; 7:2-3*a*). The majority of the Corinthians embraced Paul and disciplined the man who had attacked him (2:6-11; 7:8-16).

When Paul found Titus in Macedonia and got the report on the results of the frank speech letter, he also learned that Titus had been very successful among the Macedonians in gathering the collection for the saints at Jerusalem. The Macedonians had embraced the collection with considerable zeal (8:1-5; 9:2), thinking themselves emulating the Corinthians and the other Achaians. Paul thus found that his earlier plans for the collection

---

1. See J. Paul Sampley, "The First Letter to the Corinthians," in *The New Interpreter's Bible,* vol. 10 (Nashville: Abingdon, forthcoming).

2. For the interpretation that 2 Corinthians is one letter, see B. Witherington III, *Conflict and Community in Corinth: A Socio-Rhetorical Commentary on 1 and 2 Corinthians* (Grand Rapids: Eerdmans, 1995).

(gather it in Macedonia, sweep through Achaia, go to Jerusalem; 2 Cor 1:16) were well under way in Macedonia and that a group was ready to leave for Corinth. Paul was in a bind: The Corinthians, in their recent hithers and fros with Paul, had lost their zeal for the collection. One group, ready and eager (the Macedonians), was about to encounter another group, reticent and unprepared (the Corinthians).

In this context, Paul writes his fourth letter to the Corinthians (*Letter D,* 2 Corinthians 1–9). Several tasks confront him: (1) He must try to build beyond his recently stressed relations with the Corinthians; in particular, he must account for his dependability, even though he broke his promise about a scheduled visit, and he must account for his having resorted to a harsh letter instead of the projected visit. (2) He needs to recognize, and sign off as satisfied by, the Corinthian punishment of the one who did the wrong. (3) He must consolidate his fresh gains with the Corinthians to the point that (4) he can appeal to them for full participation in the collection for the Jerusalem saints. Paul tries to accomplish these goals (1) by accounting for his relatively recent decisions and whereabouts (2 Cor 1:8–2:13; 7:5-16); (2) by an extended initial, *indirect* appeal for a fuller Corinthian embrace of him and his ministry as refracted through a series of powerful, thoughtful lenses (2:14–6:10), followed by a brief, *direct* request for what he has just indirectly sought— namely, more affection—and (3) by moving to an open discussion of his plans for the collection and for their participation in it.

So the letter fragment 2 Corinthians 1–9 reflects complex motives and goals on Paul's part. He has personal incentives: He wants more affection from the Corinthians and thinks that, as the one who was their father in the faith (2 Cor 6:13), he deserves it; and he wants to avoid the embarrassment of having bragged about the Corinthians' enthusiasm regarding the collection (9:2), only to have the Macedonians discover, on their projected arrival in Corinth, apathy and perhaps even dissension. He has public motivations as well: The collection is the crown jewel of his ministry because, more than anything else, it demonstrates the unity of believers in the midst of their social and ethnic diversities, and his desire to bring the Corinthians into a more affectionate relationship is not simply self-serving but also accords with his conviction that the Corinthians' destiny depends on their close adherence to his gospel.

A fragment of Paul's fifth letter to the Corinthians is found in 2 Corinthians 10–13 (*Letter E*). Several developments, none of them positive, have muddied the waters for Paul and the Corinthians since his writing of 2 Corinthians 1–9. The letter-commended intruders, whose presence was only a minor matter in 2 Cor 3:1-3, have become a major force because they aligned with some currents of resentment that have been building in Corinth for some time.

The exact dynamics between the outsiders and the Corinthians escape us, but they cannot be ignored because the lines of initiative could have come from disaffected believers or from the rival intruders—but more likely from some combination of the two. Whichever the source, some Corinthians have come to believe that Paul's fiduciary relations are problematic. First, by his refusal to receive support, he has openly shamed some Corinthian believers who bid to become his patrons (12:13). Among this group may be some who had long-standing resentment over his rebuke of their having taken poorer believers to court (1 Cor 6:1-8) and of their having been insensitive to the poor believers who came to the Lord's supper in their houses (1 Cor 11:21-22, 33-34). Second, some Corinthians think he is two-faced, preaching a gospel "free of cost" (1 Cor 9:18) and then drumming up a collection. Third, some Corinthians note Paul's inconsistencies in refusing to accept support from them while receiving help from the Macedonians and raise questions of his probity and motives.[3] Fourth, some Corinthians believe that Paul's insistence on working with his hands is inconsistent with his status as apostle—and they see in the rival intruders the pattern they wish was Paul's. Finally, Paul's letter of frank speech (*Letter C,* the third, lost one) probably also exacerbated some old irritations to which he likely added another when, in his next letter (*Letter D,* 2 Corinthians 1–9), he used frankness as a means of asking for more affection, a culturally problematic use of frank speech (see the Commentary on 2 Cor 6:13).

The ultimate blow comes when (some of) the Corinthians, sensitive about the differences between Paul and his rival intruders, want to "test" Paul, apparently with regard to his apostleship (2 Cor 13:3, 5-10). Paul can no longer avoid confrontation. He projects a third visit, a showdown encounter in which he and they can sort out their differences and he can reassert his authority. The letter fragment 2 Corinthians 10–13 (*Letter E*) announces this visit, warns the Corinthians of the stakes involved, and, by heavy use of irony and under the guise of the fool's weakness, rehearses some of his disputed credentials.

Deliberations Concerning Fragmentation and Sequence Within 2 Corinthians. Possible Fragments Within 2 Corinthians 1–9. With regard to the literary unity of 2 Corinthians 1–9, interpreters have varied widely. Some hold that these chapters all belong to the same letter fragment, but different scholars have posited within those same chapters at least four distinct letter fragments, as listed below.[4]

2 Corinthians 2:14–7:4 Within 2 Corinthians 1–7. Although least convincing on its face, 2 Cor 2:14–7:4 is sometimes argued as a separate letter fragment by scholars who are struck by what they perceive as the lack of a link back to 2:13 and the preceding verses and forward to 7:5-16.[5] The supposed fragment 2:14–7:4 has been placed, on one construction, within a travel narrative, sometimes identified as yet another fragment—beginning in 1:8 (cf. 1:15-17), running through 2:12-13, and finding its completion in 7:5-16—whose travel plans have no clear connection, as these advocates see it, with what

---

3. Though it may have looked to the Corinthians as if the Macedonian support of Paul was patronage, Paul's understanding of it seems quite different. See Sampley, *Pauline Partnership in Christ: Christian Community and Commitment in Light of Roman Law* (Philadelphia: Fortress, 1980) 55-77.

4. D. Georgi, *The Opponents of Paul in Second Corinthians* (Philadelphia: Fortress, 1986) 16-18, holds for five fragments. See M. E. Thrall, *The Second Epistle to the Corinthians* (Edinburgh: T. & T. Clark, 1994) 1:47-49, for a chart of various theories.

5. For the issues and an argument for the continuity of 2 Cor 2:12-13 to the section that opens with 2:14, see A. C. Perriman, "Between Troas and Macedonia: 2 Cor 2:13-14," *ExpTim* 101 (1989) 39-41. D. A. DeSilva, "Measuring Penultimate Against Ultimate Reality: An Investigation of the Integrity and Argumentation of 2 Corinthians," *JSNT* 52 (1993) 57, argues that the "latter section [2:14–7:3] develops themes which are introduced in the former [1:1–2:13]."

they consider the more theological reflections in 2:14–7:4. An alternative construction, but presuming the same intrusion of 2:14–7:4 into chapters 1–7, takes the framing material in 1:1–2:13 and 7:5-16 as a distinct "letter of reconciliation."[6]

2 Corinthians 6:14–7:1. Scholars are divided over whether 6:14–7:1 is a separate Pauline letter fragment that a later redactor has inserted into Paul's appeal for more affection, dividing the latter into two sections (6:11-13; 7:2-4).[7] Further, some declare that these verses are not even authentically Pauline.[8]

2 Corinthians 8 and 2 Corinthians 9. Chapters 8 and 9 both deal with Paul's collection for the saints in Jerusalem, but the opening words of 9:1 (περὶ μὲν γάρ *peri men gar,* "So concerning"; hidden in the NRSV and NIV translations) can be argued to introduce a new item and thereby to suggest that the two chapters once stood alone;[9] 9:2 features the Achaians as models for the Macedonians, while 8:1-5 runs the modeling in the opposite direction, and the accompanying "brothers" in 8:18-20 are a safeguard against accusations against Paul, whereas in 9:3-5 they are supposed to get the donation together before Paul arrives.[10]

2 Corinthians 10–13. Most scholars who admit to any fragmentation recognize that 2 Corinthians 10–13 is a literary unit distinct from what precedes it. If nothing else, its tone is so different, signaling a time of mutual distress between Paul and the Corinthians. Whether this letter fragment should be considered to have originated earlier or later than any other possible fragment is another matter and will receive its treatment below.

Sequence of the Letter Fragments. To compound matters, scholars who hold for the same partition theories do not always agree on the historical sequence of the fragments. Most of the permutations have their advocates. Chapter 9 was written before chapter 8;[11] chapter 8 preceded chapter 9.[12] Chapters 10–13 were written before chapters 1–9 or parts thereof;[13] and chapters 10–13 were written last.[14]

Possible Missing Letter. All of these reckonings are further complicated by Paul's unequivocal declarations (2 Cor 2:9; 7:8-12) that he has earlier written to the Corinthians a letter that has come subsequently to be denominated by scholars as "painful" (so described because of its effect on the Corinthians, 7:8-11) or "tearful" (so named because of Paul's description of his demeanor in writing it, 2:4).

6. G. Bornkamm, "Die Vorgeschichte des sogennanten Zweiten Korintherbriefes," in *Gesammelte Aufsätze* IV, BEvT (München: Evangelischer) 53, 179-90, 192-94.

7. See J. C. Hurd, Jr., *The Origin of I Corinthians* (London: SPCK, 1965) 235-39.

8. See J. Fitzmyer, *Essays on the Semitic Background of the NT,* SBLSBS 5 (Missoula, Mont.: Scholars Press, 1974) 217.

9. So H. D. Betz, *2 Corinthians 8 and 9* (Philadelphia: Fortress, 1985) 90-91; countered decisively by S. K. Stowers, *"Peri men gar* and the Integrity of 2 Corinthians 8 and 9," *NovT* 32 (1990) 340-48.

10. For detailed examination of these and other arguments and their limitations, see V. P. Furnish, *II Corinthians,* AB 33 (Garden City, N.Y.: Doubleday, 1984) 429-33.

11. R. K. Bultmann, *The Second Letter to the Corinthians,* trans. R. A. Harrisville (Minneapolis: Augsburg, 1985) 18.

12. H. Windisch, *Der zweite Korintherbrief* (Göttingen: Vandenhoeck & Ruprecht, 1924) 287.

13. F. Watson, "2 Cor X-XIII and Paul's Painful Letter to the Corinthians," *JTS* (1984) 346.

14. Furnish, *II Corinthians,* 38, 44-46.

The question naturally arises as to whether any of the letter fragments that reputedly make up 2 Corinthians are part of that painful letter. The most obvious candidate is chapters 10–13 because it is the type of letter—indeed, the only extant candidate—that could aggrieve or bring pain to the recipients (7:8).[15] However, chapters 10–13 fail to qualify as the painful letter on every other count; most important, they make no mention of the one who "did the wrong" (2:3-11; 7:8-12); even though Paul sent the painful letter in place of a visit that he spares them (2 Cor 1:23–2:1), chapters 10–13 allude to no failed visit, but rather invite preparation for an impending visit. Finally, Paul's exuberant description of the Corinthians' change of heart (7:11) does not fit the problem of intruding rivals that pervades chapters 10–13. So we must conclude that the painful letter, though surely written before 2 Corinthians 1–9, is lost in its entirety. Because no fragments of it survive, its content can only be deduced from Paul's description of it in chapters 2 and 7.[16]

The Definition and Sequence of Fragments. This commentary assumes that 2 Corinthians 1–9 is the fragment of one letter, that 2 Corinthians 10–13 is a section of another, and that the sequence in which we find the fragments reflects their actual historical order. The change in tone and in the relation of Paul to the Corinthians in chapters 10–13 indicates that it is a distinct fragment and not a continuation of chapters 1–9. The reasons for adopting this sequence as historical will become clear in the detailed arguments.

The case for further fragmentation of 2 Corinthians 1–9 is not compelling. The purported break between 2 Cor 2:13 and 2:14 is an interpretive failure to see Paul's own connection between details of his travel plans—in particular his having decided not to come when he promised—and 2:14ff., where Paul depicts himself as a prisoner whom God leads around as *God*, not Paul, wills. Scholars' resistance to see 2 Corinthians 8–9 as a continuation of 2 Corinthians 1–7 rests in their failure to comprehend that Paul dare not make explicit mention of the collection, a matter for which they have lost their earlier zeal, until he has recemented his relations with the Corinthians, precisely the initial burden of his efforts in 2 Cor 2:14–7:16. The Commentary will show how well Paul has laid the groundwork in 2:1–7:16 for his treatment of the collection in 2 Corinthians 8–9. As will also be evident in the Commentary, Paul's rhetorical purposes in 2 Corinthians 8–9 tie the two chapters together as a literary unit that caps off 2 Corinthians 1–9 as a single letter.

Methodological Caution. Although all five letters to the Corinthians were written by the same apostle to the same general group of believers in the same city, each letter has a singularly distinctive dynamic that must be honored and not read into or affected by the interpretation of any of the others. For that reason we must exercise great care not to import a conflict or problem from a later letter into an earlier one. The primary clues

15. So Watson, "2 Cor X-XIII and Paul's Painful Letter to the Corinthians," 345-46, and L. L. Welborn, "The Identification of 2 Corinthians 10–13 with the 'Letter of Tears,' " *NovT* 37 (1995) 153.
16. Furnish, *II Corinthians*, 37-38.

for determining the relation to Paul in any given letter or fragment must be generated from the document in question.

Taking the Temperature of Paul's Relations with the Corinthians in the Different Letters. The "previous" letter (*Letter A,* lost) leaves us in the dark except for the references to it in 1 Cor 5:9-10. The Corinthians have asked Paul for clarification about holiness and living in the world—a clear indication that they were interested to understand and follow his counsel.

First Corinthians (*Letter B*) manifests the Corinthians in good relations with Paul; they ask his counsel on a series of issues, and he openly seeks to guide and lead them even though their fractiousness with each other shows him that they are nearer being babies in the faith than adults—and are overly engaged in status seeking. Although the Corinthians are in disharmony with one another, they are in good relations with Paul, and no problems or persons impinge from outside the community of believers.

The painful letter (*Letter C,* lost), by the descriptions of it and references to it in 2 Corinthians 1–9, reveals that relations between Paul and the Corinthians have hit some problems. His response in that letter is to call the Corinthians to task; Titus's report reassures Paul that the letter has brought the Corinthians into fidelity to Paul again (2 Cor 7:6-16).

Second Corinthians 1–9 (*Letter D*) tries to build on the success of the painful letter and shows Paul striving to elaborate and to enhance his own ministry for and with them in ways that invite and increase Corinthian allegiance—with the ultimage goal of encouraging and assuring their full participation in the collection for the saints in Jerusalem. Outsiders are noted (2 Cor 3:1-3) but are not considered the threat that they will become by chapters 10–13; Paul's epistolary efforts are focused on the Corinthians and their relationship to him, and not on any intruders.

A ground shift of considerable proportions must be supposed as a context for 2 Corinthians 10–13 (*Letter E*). Paul and the Corinthians have never been in more contentious relations; some of them want to put Paul to the test regarding his apostolic standing and, therefore, authority. The intruders have been established among (at least some of) the Corinthians as rival authorities. Of course, Paul detracts from his rivals, but his attention is focused on the Corinthians and on a final effort to bring them into allegiance. The letter does two things: It addresses some of the differences from the rivals that Paul wants to claim as distinctive for himself, and it lays the groundwork for a personal visit in which the matters may be resolved.

The following table graphs Paul's relations with the Corinthians. The left vertical is a graduated scale depicting the quality of their relationship, ranging from excellent down to poor. Across the bottom is a time line depicting Paul and the Corinthians at the moment of each letter or letter fragment.

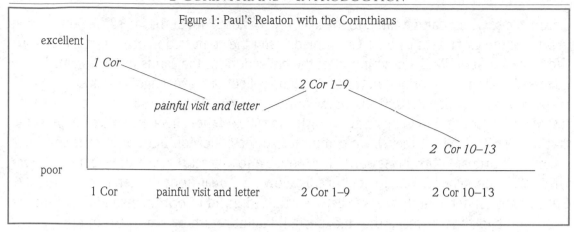

Figure 1: Paul's Relation with the Corinthians

excellent

1 Cor

2 Cor 1–9

painful visit and letter

2 Cor 10–13

poor

| 1 Cor | painful visit and letter | 2 Cor 1–9 | 2 Cor 10–13 |

While honoring the methodological caution about keeping Paul's letters and letter fragments from affecting the interpretation of each other, we can observe certain continuities in the Corinthian community of believers. The same socioethnic makeup prevails from letter to letter fragment: A few rich people are part of the community, but most members are not wealthy (1 Cor 1:26); the affluent made a clear impact in taking cobelievers to court (1 Cor 6:1-8) and at the Lord's supper (1 Cor 11:17-34); in 2 Corinthians the wealthy seek to become Paul's patrons, but he refuses them (11:7-10, 20-21; 12:13); and most of the believers are Gentiles (1 Cor 8:1, 7; 12:2). Throughout the Corinthian correspondence, believers have been susceptible to status grasping, envy, fractiousness, and the lure of wisdom and fine speech (1 Cor 1:18-25; 2 Cor 10:10; 11:6).

DATES OF COMPOSITION OF THE LETTERS

The dates of the letters can only be estimated in general terms. The reckoning of dates must be interlaced with Paul's projected and actual visits. Starting from what we can know, Paul wrote 1 Corinthians from Ephesus (1 Cor 16:8) in the fall or winter (53 or 54 CE) and expected to stay there until Pentecost (spring). He promises a visit to Corinth, perhaps to stay for the winter, after he makes the land journey through Macedonia (1 Cor 16:5-6).

When he wrote 2 Corinthians 1–9 from Macedonia, he had only recently made the long-projected visit to Macedonia—but then only because he was desperate to find Titus and to know the Corinthian response to his letter of frank speech (lost to us). Timothy, as the co-author of the current letter fragment (2 Cor 1:1), has returned from Corinth (1 Cor 16:10-11) and accompanied Paul from Asia, where Paul (and Timothy, perhaps, since the plural is used) has recently been spared a threat to his life (2 Cor 1:8-11).

Between the writing of 1 Corinthians and 2 Corinthians 1–9, Paul has made a visit to Corinth that turned bad (with the one who "did the wrong," 2 Cor 2:1-3; 7:12), and, instead of the promised subsequent visit, he wrote them the (lost) letter of harsh frank speech (2 Cor 2:1-4; 7:8-16). What length of time transpired between the writing of 1

Corinthians, which can be dated to the fall or winter of 53 (or at the latest the same period in 54; see the Commentary on 1 Corinthians), and the composition of 2 Corinthians 1–9? We have a clue in Paul's description of the collection for the saints in Jerusalem. Twice he mentions that the Corinthians had begun the collection "a year ago" or "since last year" (πέρυσι *perysi*, 2 Cor 8:10; 9:2). First Corinthians 16:1-4 seems to have been a Pauline response to a Corinthian inquiry regarding the logistics of the collection, so we can presume that in fall 53 or fall 54 they were committed to the collection but not certain how they might best prepare. On this ground, it is possible to project that 2 Corinthians 1–9 was written by the fall of 54 CE (or fall of 55, allowing a year from the range of dates for 1 Corinthians). In the year that passed between the writing of 1 Corinthians and 2 Corinthians 1–9, Paul had time to make the unexpected, fateful return by sea to Corinth (spring or summer), to return to the Roman province of Asia (probably Ephesus), and to write and have Titus deliver his frank speech letter instead of a promised further visit.

Second Corinthians 10–13 requires sufficient time after chapters 1–9 for the following to have occurred: First, the logistics of the collection dictate a certain time lag. As Paul lays it out in 2 Cor 8:16-24, he sends ahead Titus and the two brothers, with the apparent expectation that they will oversee the Corinthians' preparedness before Paul's and some Macedonians' arrival (9:5). Paul's projected visit must have taken on different proportions when he heard for the first time the extent to which the intruders had captured the fancy of at least some of the Corinthians, subverting Paul's authority. The two-stage visit to Achaia would have required some time (during which Paul discovers the seriousness of the threat represented by the intruding rivals). Finally, the itinerary supposes that the sea passages must be opened after the winter and early spring for the projected trip to Judea.

Second, we do not know who informed Paul that matters in Corinth were much worse than he had suspected, but candidates aplenty suggest themselves: Titus, the two selected brothers (8:18, 22), and any of the Macedonians who may have accompanied them with the collection. Each of these people could be expected to be devoted to Paul and sensitively ready to report remonstrations against him. In any case, the writing of 2 Corinthians 10–13—one of whose major burdens is to announce and prepare for Paul's imminent showdown visit to Corinth—need not be more than a few months after the composition of 2 Corinthians 1–9. Accordingly, we can posit that 2 Corinthians 10–13 was also written from Macedonia, probably in the spring or early summer of 55 (or of 56, allowing for the same time range noted for 1 Corinthians).

PAUL'S OPPONENTS AT CORINTH

The identification of Paul's opponents has become a growth industry, often with more conjecture and speculation than certainty or substance emerging.[17] Truth be told, we know

---

17. See J. L. Sumney's laudable methodological caution and circumspection in *Identifying Paul's Opponents: The Question of Method in 2 Corinthians,* JSNTSup 40 (Sheffield: Sheffield Academic, 1990) 15-67. He categorizes the traditional options for identifying Paul's opponents: Judaizers (led by Baur, followed by Barrett, Gunther, Lüdemann), Gnostics (Schmithals), divine men (Georgi and Friedrich), and pneumatics (Käsemann).

very little about Paul's opponents in 2 Corinthians. The Corinthians knew their identity; at some point Paul knew enough about them to be or become concerned about them, so he had no need to rehearse it for us as interlopers. Second, we must acknowledge that our primary source for knowing anything about the opponents is Paul, who is biased against them and who has no interest in being fair or what we might call objective in his representations of them. In any search for clues regarding the opponents' identity, we must expect that Paul depicts them in an unfavorable light—that was how opponents were treated in those days[18]—but we can suppose that he did not totally misrepresent them, if not because of his moral values, surely for fear that the Corinthians would dismiss him and all his argumentation if he were too out of line with reality. Exaggeration and distortion cannot be ruled out, however, because Paul's purpose is to overthrow them, to prevail—and to do that he must establish himself as the *sole* legitimate apostle for the Corinthians.

Third, and along the same line, Paul's knowledge about his opponents is always secondhand (only in 2 Cor 2:5 do we see Paul knowing firsthand a Corinthian opponent). His agents or his other supporters, themselves persons biased in favor of Paul, are the sources of what he knows about the opponents. That means that any knowledge we today have of Paul's opponents in Corinth is thirdhand. Fourth, mirror reading—that is, taking items in the text and assuming that in them Paul is responding to some criticism or to some claim of the opponents—has been overused in the study of Paul's letters.[19] Not every denial or distinction of him can be read as reflecting a charge.[20] Neither is every Pauline theological affirmation a response to something his opponents have said.

Finally, Paul's (indeed, the culture's) predisposition for indirect or figured speech has been underestimated. In such rhetoric one does not take issues head-on but chooses an alternate, less-heated matter, issue, or topic and, by treating it, leaves the hearers to make the application to the question at hand.[21] Paul's original hearers would bring enough information to the hearing of his letters so that they could readily distinguish what we can only surmise—namely, when Paul is speaking directly and when indirectly.

Two Stages of Opposition. For the purpose of identifying Paul's opposition, this commentary distinguishes between two distinct stages of Paul's struggle with the Corinthians as reflected in 2 Corinthians. The two stages correspond to the two letter fragments. The reckoning about Paul's opponents must be different regarding each letter fragment, because Paul's relation to the Corinthians is distinct at the two different times of writing.

---

18. See J. Paul Sampley, "Paul, His Opponents in 2 Corinthians 10–13, and the Rhetorical Handbooks," in *The Social World of Formative Christianity and Judaism,* ed. J. Neusner, P. Borgen, E. S. Frerichs, R. Horsley (Philadelphia: Fortress, 1988) esp. 165-67.

19. So G. Lyons, *Pauline Autobiography: Toward a New Understanding* (Atlanta, Scholars Press, 1985).

20. Cf. A. J. Malherbe's compelling interpretation of 1 Thess 2:1-12 not as a denial of a charge against Paul but as Paul's distinguishing of himself from itinerant sages, in "Gentle as a Nurse," *NovT* 12 (1970) 216-17.

21. See Demetrius *On Style* 5.294-296. For a fuller discussion of indirect speech and its canons, see J. Paul Sampley, "The Weak and the Strong: Paul's Careful and Crafty Rhetorical Strategy in Romans 14:1–15:13," in *The Social World of the First Christians: Studies in Honor of Wayne A. Meeks,* ed. L. M. White and O. L. Yarbrough (Minneapolis: Fortress, 1994) 43-46.

When he wrote 2 Corinthians 1–9, intruders were of little consequence. They had come to Corinth with their letters of commendation (3:1-3), but Paul does not treat them as a major problem. Paul is not unaccustomed to having other believers pass through his work sites (Gal 2:4, 11-12; cf. 1 Cor 9:5), so at first the appearance of these people might not have caused him great concern. At that point he has his own special issues with the Corinthians and has just recently heard that his letter of harsh frank speech (*Letter C*) has effected a rapprochement of the Corinthians to him. The lofty theological constructions that he struts before them in 2:14–6:10 are not a reflection of anything his opponents have said, but simply his own creative self-portrayal of his ministry as seen in three grand perspectives.

The exigence of 2 Corinthians 10–13 is starkly different. Now the outsiders, who were merely noted in 3:1-3, have become rivals who have bid with some success for Corinthian allegiance at the expense of Paul's status and authority. So here the central struggle is one of rivalry, of contested authority between Paul and his opponents—and, therefore, of fractured Corinthian allegiance. Much of past scholarship on Paul's Corinthian opponents has assumed, arguably anachronistically, that the central issues between Paul and his opponents were doctrinal—that is, disputes over theological ideas. In Paul's differences with the Corinthians, not ideas but practices, comportment, and standing are in contention.[22] Paul's theological assertions are not at dispute; Paul's authority is.[23] Paul's theological claims are adduced by him as a way of authenticating his authority.

Paul's standing and competence are at issue across all of 2 Corinthians; this fact has led interpreters to bleed what they see and know most clearly from 2 Corinthians 10–13, a distinct and subsequent letter (see elsewhere in the Introduction), back onto 2 Corinthians 1–9. If we resist that simplification and importation, we can distinguish between the way Paul's standing and competence are treated in the two letter fragments.

When the focus is restricted to 2 Corinthians 1–9, then the questions of Paul's adequacy as an apostle, as *their* apostle, are best understood as a Pauline advocacy of himself as the very apostle who brought the gospel to them and who deserves their full adherence by dint of his work with and among them. Paul thus champions himself and his cause as the apostle, as their apostle, whom they should embrace more fully. Paul's rich self-portraits as minister of the new covenant (3:1–4:6), as minister sustained through affliction and mortality (4:7–5:10), and as minister of reconciliation (5:11-21) overlap and reinforce one another, identifying Paul as their apostle who is worthy of their full devotion. Why is Paul led to such a self-promotion? There are two prominent reasons, one directed toward the immediate past, the other targeted toward the immediate future. As to the past, Paul must overcome any residual reticence among the Corinthians not only because of his failure to visit them as he had promised, but also because he had upbraided them harshly with a

---

22. Theirs was not an "intellectual confrontation." See A. J. Malherbe, "Antisthenes and Odysseus, and Paul at War," *HTR* (1983) 143-73, esp. 168, 172.

23. So C. J. A. Hickling, "Is the Second Epistle to the Corinthians a Source for Early Church History?" *ZNW* 66 (1975) 287, argued powerfully a quarter-century ago.

letter of frank speech (*Letter C*). As to the future, he has to prepare the Corinthians for the Macedonians' imminent and enthusiastic arrival with the collection for the Jerusalem saints when he has learned that the Corinthians have lost their zeal for it. His success with healing the past wounds and with avoiding embarrassment regarding the collection both demand that his ethos, his character and his standing with the Corinthians, be strong—the ultimate goal of 2:14–6:10, the central portion of 2 Corinthians 1–9. Only when his ethos has been sufficiently refurbished can and does he turn explicitly to the touchy question of the collection (2 Corinthians 8–9).

In 2 Corinthians 10–13, Paul's adequacy and standing as an apostle are certainly directly under question and attack. Paul's response is different also—even though some self-commendation continues to be present. Here, in his defense, he is drawn onto the grounds of the opposition: He boasts and references visions and revelations, signs and wonders, but only as a fool. Then he rejects visions and revelations as a basis of authority and puts in their place the standard of day-in-day-out performance—that is, what he has done among them across the years (12:6). Whereas in chapters 1–9 Paul's ethos was burnished by three grand theological ruminations about ministry and how Paul enacted each of them, in chapters 10–13 we see Paul, God's warrior, ironically embracing weakness as his shield and engaging, in turn, in accusation, reproach, apology, and appeal. Finally, in chapters 10–13 we see him declare guidelines for how he and the Corinthians will resolve their differences when he arrives in Corinth.

In order to reconstruct what we can know about Paul's opponents at Corinth, we start from the text, the only evidence we really have, and distinguish three categories: more certain evidence; less certain, but plausible, evidence; and possible evidence.[24] Identification of certain clues regarding the opponents is the more difficult because it is not always easy to tell when Paul is speaking directly and when he is using indirect speech (see the Introduction to 1 Corinthians) as an oblique way of relating to or describing his opponents.

More Certain Indices of Opponents. Nothing is clearer than this: By the time of 2 Corinthians 10–13, the intruders have become Paul's rivals for the leadership of the Corinthian believers. In significant ways they claim to be like Paul, but it is equally important that they distinguish themselves from him. *They* have made the comparison, and Paul finds it odious (10:12); he wants to remove any pretext they have for claiming that they are "just like us" (11:12). But they also move beyond parity, alleging to be superior to Paul (see Paul's mocking designation of them as "super apostles," 11:5; 12:11). This is at the heart of the rivalry.

Inherent in their comparative assessment of Paul is a critique of him at several points. It is impossible to tell just how much or how many of the following points the outsiders generated or how many they simply seized upon and focused sentiments already present

---

24. Sumney, *Identifying Paul's Opponents,* 118, distinguishes "five levels of *certainty of reference*," beginning with "explicit statements" and moving through two levels of "proposed allusions."

among the Corinthians. Either way, however, the Corinthian soil was ready for the planting and harvest.

Paul's bearing and performance are not up to par for a person in such a position of authority, they claim (and appear to have convinced at least some Corinthians). Paul has provided them abundant evidence across the years; the Corinthians will remember that Paul did not come among them with "lofty words of wisdom" but simply preached the cross (1 Cor 2:1-2); that he likened himself, in an ironically self-deprecating way, to leftover dishwater (1 Cor 4:13); that his speech amounts to nothing (2 Cor 10:10); that he has a proclivity to find himself in humble, if not humiliating, circumstances (1 Cor 4:11-12; cf. 2 Cor 4:7-12; 6:1-10; 11:21 b-29); that he made no credible defense when he was with them and that one of their own attacked him (2 Cor 2:1-11); and that he has steadfastly eschewed the perquisites appropriate to his status, insisting instead on supporting himself via demeaning hand work (1 Cor 4:12a; 9:4-14). Further, 2 Cor 10:10 suggests that Paul's opponents have derisively labeled him "weak" in bodily presence.

The intruders, on the other hand, at least by Paul's implications, share the status of being "apostles" in some sense (2 Cor 11:5, 13-15; 12:11), though they, in contrast to Paul, seem ready to relish the entitlements of status and honor (11:20; cf. 11:7-12; 12:17). Accordingly, they do not work to support themselves (11:20; cf., perhaps obliquely, 11:7-12; 12:13-16). Clearly the wealthier Corinthians who were eager to patronize Paul would have found ready recipients in his rivals.

Paul counters on several fronts. With regard to himself, his opening insistence is key: "Look at what is before your eyes" (2 Cor 10:7; 12:6b). The Corinthians' long (and mostly) good history with him should reassure them that he is dependable and faithful. He has never accepted support from them, so why should he start now? On the contrary, he has always worked for their benefit, never his own (12:19; 13:7-9). Absent or present, he has continually been the same Paul (10:11). He brought the gospel all the way to them (10:13-15), and he has stuck by them through thick and thin. Further, he embraces the charge of his weakness as a badge of ironic honor and portrays his weakness over and over as a positive sign of God's abundant power working through him for the gospel and *for them* (2 Cor 11:6a, 23–12:10).

Paul understands that God designated him to take the gospel to the Corinthians, that they are, therefore, part of his divinely appointed "sphere of influence/province" (κανών *kanōn* ; see the Commentary on 10:13-16) and that he has paternal responsibilities with the Corinthians because God has given him responsibility for recruiting believers in that area. Others, such as Apollos, may be of assistance to him (1 Cor 3:5-9), but the Corinthians can have only one father (2 Cor 11:2; cf. 1 Cor 4:15). Paul's 2 Corinthians intruders have moved beyond being helpful; they bid to supplant Paul and have wrongly moved into Paul's *kanōn*.

More important, Paul does not directly counsel the Corinthians about what they should do toward the rivals (unless 2 Cor 6:14–7:1 is regarded as authentic and the "unfaithful" in 6:14-16 are dubiously deemed the opponents). Rather, his attention is focused on a call for the Corinthians to reassess their own standing in the faith, to return to their roots in his preaching and to his leadership, and to accord one another the proper attention that love demands.

Less Certain, but Plausible, Indices of Opponents. It is less sure that the opponents are Jewish, though Paul's question, "Are they Hebrews?" and his detailing of his high-caliber Jewish credentials surely point in that direction. Curiously, however, no problems between Paul and the Corinthians are traceable to Jewish issues such as one can see, by contrast, in Galatians, with its concern for circumcision and the place of the law. The two-covenant discussion in 2 Cor 3:1–4:6, which some scholars credit, at least in some measure, to Paul's opponents,[25] is hardly part of a dispute; rather, it is Paul's creative elaboration and enhancement—in a typical Pauline "not this, but that" form—of his own ministry as an appeal for increased Corinthian fidelity.[26] If Paul's adversaries are Jews, allowing for that reading of 11:22, then one can equally argue that Paul credits them with being "ministers of Christ" (διάκονοι Χριστου *diakonoi Christou*, 11:23), though Paul is quick to claim superiority for himself.

We cannot be exactly certain what is behind the letters of recommendation mentioned in 2 Cor 3:1, though the practice is a commonplace in the Greco-Roman world, and it is plausible that the outsiders came to Corinth armed with supporting documents that credited them with a measure of ready-made authority (see 2 Cor 2:17). Whether those letters came from some of the original apostles and/or from some in leadership positions in Jerusalem we simply cannot know.[27] It is attractive to make such connections because the drama is enhanced and we can drift into the timeworn Peter-versus-Paul conundrum for which there is no other evidence in 2 Corinthians.

Paul resorts to telling about his heavenly transit (12:2-5) as if forced. Did his rivals (or even worse for Paul, some of the Corinthians) credit visions and revelations as an indicator of status and authority? We know that the Corinthians have a long-standing attraction for silver-tongued speech (1 Cor 2:1), but Paul values "knowledge" over "speech" (2 Cor 11:6) as an assessment of apostolic credentials. Curiously, after telling of his extraordinary transport to paradise (12:2-5), Paul effectively rejects visions as an apostolic index, preferring instead what one sees and hears in him (2 Cor 12:6, an echoing refinement of 10:7*a*). Whether it was the intruders or the Corinthians,[28] visions and revelations bid to play too great a role in estimating status, for Paul's values.

Unclear Indices of Opponents. What are we to make of the reference in 11:4 to

25. The most extreme example is D. Georgi, *Paul's Opponents in 2 Corinthians* (Philadelphia: Fortress, 1986) 229-83; cf. J. J. Gunther, *St. Paul's Opponents and Their Background,* NovTSup 35 (1973) 276.

26. Hickling, "Is the Second Epistle to the Corinthians a Source for Early Church History?" 286. L. L. Belleville, "Tradition or Creation? Paul's Use of the Exodus 34 Tradition in 2 Corinthians 3:7-18," in *Paul and the Scriptures of Israel,* ed. C. A. Evans and J. A. Sanders (Sheffield: JSOT, 1993) 185, shows that Paul's creativity comes not in his use of Exodus 34 and his portrait of Moses' fading glory, but in tying the fading glory to the "waning of the covenant."

27. So also J. L. Sumney, *Identifying Paul's Opponents. The Question of Method in 2 Corinthians,* JSNTSup 40 (Sheffield: Sheffield Academic, 1990) 177.

28. C. K. Barrett, "Paul's Opponents in II Corinthians," *NTS* 17 (1971) 244-45, holds it is the latter.

"another Jesus," "another spirit," and "another gospel"? Or should that be translated "another Spirit," indicating the Holy Spirit, as the expression could equally well be read? Have the outsiders offered these alternatives, or is this a dramatic rhetorical move on Paul's part? Nowhere in 2 Corinthians is there evidence of a dispute over Jesus or the Spirit (or spirit, for that matter). The Spirit is associated with the second covenant and with Paul's ministry (2 Cor 3:8, 17), as we would fully expect, because Paul sees the Spirit and its reception as the hallmark of the life of faith (see 1 Cor 12:13; Gal 3:2). But Paul does not treat his claims about the Spirit as if they are being defended or advocated over against competing claims about the Spirit.

Paul is given to stark antitheses, especially when he wants to distance an alternative from himself. Paul knows there is only one gospel (Gal 1:7*a*), but that gospel can be perverted (Gal 1:7*b*). Paul apparently has a commonplace saying to the effect that anyone who preaches a gospel different from his own is anathema (Gal 1:9: "As I said before, so now again I say"), and he may have recycled that saying here—with elaboration—as a way of setting himself antithetically over against his rivals. In his categories, Paul's rivals represent another gospel if they differ from him—whether the differences are in ideas or in practices. Finally, the Jesus whom Paul proclaims is "Christ Jesus as Lord, with ourselves as your slaves for Jesus' sake" (2 Cor 4:5). Paul's humble, weak demeanor is grounded in the Jesus he preaches, the Jesus who is Lord. So his comportment is, as always, fundamentally christologically based (e.g., 1 Cor 11:1).

Two passages in 2 Corinthians 1–9 have been mirror-read as references to Paul's opponents. Paul's disclaimer that "we are not, like many, hucksters of God's word" in 2:17 may be a reference to opponents. If it is, then we learn nothing in particular about them. Paul's differentiation may, however, be considered a patterned reference to others who preach the gospel out of different (and less noble) motives (see Phil 1:15-18). Interpreters have similarly read 4:2 to mirror Paul's opponents, but it may just as well be Paul's *via negativa* magnification of his own ethos and exemplary comportment (cf. 2:17). Without reinforcement from 2 Corinthians 10–13, a document from a later time and with different dynamics, the two references in 2:17 and 4:2 do not give any certain picture of opponents; accordingly, in the commentary they are not treated as clear indices of opponents.

In sum, we can be sure that Paul's opponents include some intruders who have appeared in Corinth with letters of commendation from some unidentifiable, but putatively powerful, persons. Although the intruders have arrived in Corinth by the time of Paul's writing 2 Corinthians 1–9, their impact is not certain to be major until the time of his composition of chapters 10–13. By then, the intruders have surely found a hearing among some (but we cannot be certain how many) Corinthians and been accorded status and authority by them. When favorable to them, these outsiders claim to be like Paul; but in certain key matters they distinguish themselves from him: They do not act below their station; they do not stoop to menial labor to support themselves; they readily count on patronage from others as part of their apostolic perquisites.

Pauline opposition *among the Corinthians* may no longer be ignored, and the commentary will be assiduous in detailing the sources of Corinthian discontent signaled in the text of 2 Corinthians. At issue between Paul and his opponents (intruders and allied Corinthians alike) is Paul's status and authority with the Corinthians. All else in the contention takes its place around that central pillar. Whether the intruders are also Jews is plausible but is not necessary to determine for the interpretation of any part of 2 Corinthians.

Whatever else one may discern about Paul's opponents, it is clear that he wrote 2 Corinthians 10–13 with the major purpose of setting up the terms and conditions under which he expected to make an imminent, showdown visit to Corinth. He puts the Corinthians, supporters and opponents together, on notice that he expects to bring about Corinthian obedience. In doing so, he must be able to assume that the intruders will have been served a warning as well. In 2 Corinthians, Paul has no direct engagement or contention with his intruding rivals. Like silent third parties as Paul relates to the Corinthians, his rivals are an important part of what amounts to a triangle. And Paul's attention is devoted to regaining the affection and allegiance of the Corinthians; nowhere in 2 Corinthians does he engage the outsiders directly.

For a reasoned estimate of Paul's success or failure in the encounter that 2 Corinthians 10–13 signals, see the Overview to chapters 10–13 in the Commentary.

PAUL'S USE OF "WE" IN 2 CORINTHIANS

Paul employs the plural in self-reference more in 2 Corinthians than in any other letter. Before detailing Paul's goals in doing so, we must note that 2 Cor 1:1 does credit Timothy with co-authorship, so the plural may refer to Timothy as well. Other letters are jointly authored (Gal 1:2; Phil 1:1; 1 Thess 1:1; Phlm 1), however, without such heavy use of plural self-references. So the proliferation of the plural in 2 Corinthians demands an accounting.

By using plural pronouns so often in referring to himself, Paul accomplishes a variety of goals that are important for his rhetorical task of persuading the Corinthians to ally themselves (more fully) with him. First, with the plural self-references, Paul regularly invites the Corinthians to think of themselves as one with him—a major objective in all of 2 Corinthians.

Second, by using plural pronouns Paul encourages the Corinthians to think that Paul does not stand alone, that he has widespread support, and that he is part of a larger group—his rhetoric suggests the mainstream—who advocate the gospel as he does. Among those who can be associated in the plurals are Timothy, the co-author (1:1), the Achaians (i.e., the Corinthians' provincial neighbors, who are also named as addressees; 1:1), the Macedonians (9:2, 4; 11:9), Silvanus (1:19), Titus (2:13; 7:6, 13-14; 8:6, 16, 23; 12:18), and the "brother" praised by all the churches (8:18). All of these people, explicitly mentioned in 2 Corinthians, are allied with Paul.

Third, while some Corinthians might question that Paul was a minister of the gospel, Paul's regular description of his ministry in the plural "we" leaves them no room to deny that God has commissioned ministers such as he and must make it more difficult to deny that Paul is one of them. Fourth, the plural allows Paul to depict himself in rather grand fashion, with diminished risk of his being thought to be boasting inordinantly.[29]

Fifth, specifically in regard to the collection for the saints in Jerusalem, Paul's use of plural self-references suggests broad support for him and for the collection while also depicting him as the leader of such a larger movement (with which the Corinthians hopefully will want to ally themselves). Finally, his pervasive use of the plural as a way of referring to himself makes it all the more striking and powerful rhetorically when he explicitly invites the Corinthians into the picture that is otherwise described by the plurals (cf. 3:18; 5:10).

WHAT WE LEARN ABOUT PAUL IN 2 CORINTHIANS

Paul the Person. Paul was a passionate man, given to a wide range of emotions. We observe his anger and distress in 2 Corinthians 10–13 not only as Corinthian opposition hardens against him, but also as some of his beloved drift away under outside influences. Also visible, though, is his heartfelt affection, his sense that he loves the more and is loved less (12:15). Clear as well is his anxiety over whether his painful letter might have proved too painful for the Corinthians (7:6-16); equally clear and powerful are his expressions of relief and joy when he receives Titus's report of their return to filiation with him (7:6-7, 13-14). Professions of his love for them (11:11) fit well with other expressions of friendship, such as his preparedness to spend and be spent for them (12:15), his readiness to live and to die with them (7:3), and his willingness to speak frankly as a friend to them (6:11).

As reflected in 2 Corinthians, Paul's experiences range from the most sublime to the most precarious. What can surpass his being caught up into the third heaven, into paradise (12:2-6)? It is almost as difficult to imagine anyone having more hardships than Paul (4:8-12; 6:4-10; 11:23-27), including his thorn or stake in the flesh (12:7-9) and his Damascus escape (11:30-33). In fact, the letter fragment 2 Corinthians 1–9 opens with Paul's disclosure of a recent experience in Asia (roughly modern western Turkey), where he feared for his life; he refers to it as a virtual death sentence (1:8-11). Even if we allow for some inflation as part of a rhetorical appeal for pity, the experience must have been traumatic.

Paul's self-descriptions are illuminating because they show a Paul not always victorious, not always triumphant, but often vexed, put upon, and, at times, almost overwhelmed.

29. See Plutarch *On Praising Oneself Inoffensively* 542B-543F, where speakers can praise and, as in the case at hand, positively associate themselves with others "whose aims and acts are the same as . . . [one's] own and whose general character is similar."

His Asian affliction left him with no resource other than to trust in "God who raises the dead" (1:9). Regarding that situation, he describes himself, in evocative terms, as being utterly, beyond measure weighed down, as despairing of living (1:8). Elsewhere in the same letter he depicts himself as being pushed almost to the brink: afflicted, perplexed, persecuted, and struck down—to each of those powerful verbs he adds a codicil of grace-filled limitations: "but not crushed . . . not driven to despair . . . not forsaken . . . not destroyed" (4:8-9). A similar self-portrait acknowledges a fundamental dissonance between the way he is treated or perceived and how he thinks he truly is: "treated as impostors, and yet are true; as unknown, and yet are well known; as dying, and see—we are alive; as punished, and not yet killed; as sorrowful, yet always rejoicing; as poor, yet making many rich; as having nothing, and yet possessing everything" (6:8c-10 NRSV). Another powerful self-description shows him with "conflicts on the outside, fears within" (7:5 NIV). Some important insights into Paul are available here. First, what one sees and experiences is, thanks be to God, not the whole picture. Second, as strong in faith as Paul was, he never expected his faith or his God to shelter him from the vicissitudes and vagaries of life. He did expect God to be present for him *in whatever circumstance;* indeed, that was Paul's experience.

Paul was a person of incredible theological imagination and resources. Second Corinthians 1–9 is a showcase of his reflections because in those chapters he projects three portraits of his ministry as a means of enhancing his ethos and Corinthian affiliation with him (see the Commentary on 2:14–6:10). Not only does he have his Scriptures as a potent resource and stimulus for his thoughts and for their expression, but he also has pre- and para-Pauline Christian formulations and the conventions of the Greco-Roman world to draw upon and to weave together with his own reflections. Throughout 2 Corinthians, and indeed across all his correspondence, he has no interest in theological notions for their own sake, but only as they engage life, as they bear on the way people comport themselves. His theologizing, therefore, is never abstract or abstruse; instead it is always engaged, always linked to life as real people—he and his hearers—are experiencing it.

Paul's Fiduciary Relations. Paul's flexible financial practices got him into difficulty with some Corinthians—perhaps not early on, but surely by the time 2 Corinthians was written. Although Paul clearly accepted support from the Philippians (Phil 1:5; 2:25; 4:10-16) and even had a Macedonian delivery of support to him while he was at Corinth (2 Cor 11:8-9), he resolutely and stubbornly persisted in his refusal to accept assistance from the Corinthians, even though some Corinthians apparently sought to become his patrons. It is not difficult to imagine, given the cultural suppositions of the time, that Paul refused to become client to some of the wealthy Corinthians because he could not allow himself either to be indebted to them or to be obligated to pay them honor in return for their favor.

Further, Paul regularly expects to be assisted on his journeys by local congregations as he pursues his itinerary (see Rom 15:24), and he does not count that aid as making him a client with its culturally assumed obligations. Even with the Corinthians he distinguishes between accepting their support and their helping him along in his travel (cf. 1 Cor 16:6; 2 Cor 1:16). We may suppose, therefore, that Paul distinguishes clientage from all forms of "hospitality" (see Rom 12:13; 15:24).

Finally, Paul's embrace of the collection for the poor at Jerusalem, an outgrowth of the Jerusalem conference (Gal 2:1-10), may not have created any early Corinthian confusion about his motives (1 Cor 16:1-4), but surely by the time of 2 Corinthians it had become a ground of contention. Witness Paul's extraordinary care to secure reputable representatives to accompany the delivery of the collection (2 Cor 8:18-23) in order to avoid any charges of fiscal abuse.

Unique Information from the Hardship Lists. For the most part, the hardship catalogs detail what we know about Paul from other texts and sources. He often was in danger and experienced great obstacles and problems in his efforts to advance the gospel. We might take special note of how frequently he experienced certain difficulties or the severity of them: "countless floggings, and often near death" (11:23 NRSV) or "afflicted . . . but not crushed . . . struck down" (4:8-9 NRSV).

Two details, however, shed unique light on Paul. First, five times he received the Jewish punishment of thirty-nine lashes (11:24). This discipline, founded on Deut 25:3, was enforced by the synagogues in Paul's time.[30] His submission to this penalty suggests that even after he became an apostle he continued to maintain his ties to Jewish synagogue worship and practice; otherwise, he would neither have been judged out of order or needed to allow himself to be thus chastened. Of course, we cannot tell at what points across his ministry he received the thirty-nine lashes, but five times suggests a longer rather than shorter period. That he kept contact with fellow Jews is also clear from passages like 1 Cor 9:20, but such a passage does not indicate as clearly that he submitted to synagogue authority.

Second, he reports that he was three times beaten with rods (11:25), a Roman punishment (see Acts 16:22-23, 37-39) that was not supposed to be administered to Roman citizens, as Acts 16:37 affirms. Josephus reports, however, that such propriety was not always honored everywhere.[31] Thus Paul's report of having been beaten with rods does not rule out his having been a Roman citizen, as Acts 16:37 declares he was.

PAUL'S THOUGHT WORLD

Although Paul spends much of his time in these letter fragments either commending or defending himself, his way of doing so yields a view of several basic convictions that structure his thought world.

The Cosmic Purposes of God. God is ultimately in control, and, with what has been begun in Christ, God's plan is nearing completion. Paul has been captured and put

---

30. See Josephus *Antiquities of the Jews* 4.238; *Mishnah Makkot* 3.
31. Josephus *The Jewish War* 2.308.

on display in God's triumphal victory procession as God's power sweeps across the world (2:14-16). The plan and the power belong solely to God. To be sure, Satan has plans (and agents), but he poses no real threat to believers if they stay alert and remember that they have been made privy to Satan's design (2:11). The conclusion of God's purposes is near, so all opposing power is doomed.

Across both letter fragments, Paul uses references to end-time considerations as leverage on the Corinthians. Believers are going to face Christ's judgment for the way they have comported themselves (5:10). The panoply of God's power is marshaled behind Paul as he promises to vanquish all foes and render their defenses useless (10:3-6). God's purpose, in Christ, is the reconciliation of the entire cosmos (5:19), with everyone included, to God; that is why Christ "died for all" (5:14-15). This grand portrait of purpose, sketched out across the letter fragments of 2 Corinthians, utterly transcends and renders foolishly impotent any opposition to God, and derivatively to Paul. Captured by and now the agent of this overwhelming divine power, Paul dismisses any rival claims to the Corinthians' fealty and announces himself ready, with God's power, to induce (2:9; 7:15; 10:6; 13:5-10), if not enforce, obedience (13:4).

The Life of Faith as Process, as Growth, as Being Transformed. Paul understands that believers, as a part of God's new creation (5:17), are works in process, that God is working in them to transform them from one degree of glory to another (3:18). The new creation starts when, by God's grace, a person dies with Christ and, in dying, is brought to newness of life (Rom 6:4). At the outset of faith, believers are called babies (1 Cor 3:1-2; Phlm 10) or "weak with respect to faith" (Rom 14:1). As believers progress in the faith, Paul thinks of them as more mature, more like adults (1 Cor 2:6; 14:20; Phil 3:15). Every believer is given a measure of faith by God (Rom 12:3), and they, like their paradigmatic father Abraham, are to grow strong in faith (Rom 4:20). The resurrection at the last day, featured so prominently in 1 Corinthians 15, is confidently expected by Paul to be the capstone, the zenith at which the life of faith is brought to its fulfillment.

Here in 2 Corinthians Paul several times makes clear his anthropological assumption that believers are being transformed, but nowhere clearer or more powerfully than in his declaration: "And all of us . . . are being transformed . . . from one degree of glory to another" (2 Cor 3:18 NRSV; see the Commentary on 3:18). In sharp contrast with "those who are perishing," Paul sees believers—those who are already justified and reconciled (Rom 5:9-10)—as "those who *are being saved*," who are going "from life to life" (2 Cor 2:15-16, italics added). In a passage where he uses three different terms for "house" as a means of referring to human life, he depicts believers as currently living in what he imaginatively describes as "this tent" and as longing for a transformed, heavenly dwelling (5:1-2). With a shift of metaphor, he again describes the anticipated permutation as an expectation of being "further clothed" (5:4). Believers have died with Christ; God, who "raised the Lord Jesus will raise us also with Jesus" (4:14). Believers have received the Holy Spirit, but that is only a down payment of all that is to come (1:22; 5:5; cf. Rom

8:11). Believers' outer selves are wasting away, but their inner selves are being renewed day by day (4:16). That which is transitory is being replaced by what is eternal (4:18). What is mortal will be swallowed up without remainder by life (5:4). Paul's explicit hope for the Corinthians is that their faith may grow (10:15; cf. 13:9).

Change, growth, and development are presupposed by Paul across the letters. Compare his own self-portrait in 1 Corinthians 13, where he looks back to his life as a child and forward to a time not yet here when he will "see face to face . . . and know fully" (1 Cor 13:11-12). He works with the Philippians for their "progress and joy in faith" (Phil 1:25). He labors with the Thessalonians "to complete what is lacking in your faith" (1 Thess 3:10).

Believers' Proper Care for One Another. Although Paul's overriding concern in 2 Corinthians is a return of the Corinthians to full, proper relationship to him, he does not lose sight of their need to be concerned about each other. Ever the model, Paul presents himself as the one who cares in an exemplary way about the Corinthians. In his most dramatic representation of his caring, reserved for the confrontational 2 Corinthians 10–13 fragment, he portrays himself as ready to fail personally if doing so will ensure their doing "what is right" (13:7). He is eager to spend and be spent for them in his effort to secure them in the faith (12:15; cf. similar sacrificial imagery in Phil 2:17). In another instance, he models compassion when he urges the Corinthians to restore to fellowship the one they have dismissed: "pardon and console him, lest he be overwhelmed by excessive grief . . . decide in favor of love for him" (2:7-8). Though the individual had aggrieved Paul and the community (2:5), the communal rebuke must not be so severe or so sustained that the person is permanently lost from the fellowship; even someone who has wronged the community must be cared for in love.

Paul's reflections about the collection provide other windows onto how he thinks believers are or should be related to one another. First, believers should pattern themselves after the best they see in other believers: The Macedonians were spurred to contribute by the reports of the Corinthians (9:2); now the Corinthians should renew their commitment when they see how readily and fully the Macedonians have embraced the collection (8:1-7). Second, one's bounty provides for the need of another, without anyone's being disadvantaged in the giving or lacking in the receiving (8:12-14). Instead, Paul sees that among believers generosity and need are so correlated that, when proper concern for one another is present, a fundamental equality should result among the believers (ἰσότης *isotēs*, "fairness/equality," 8:13-14; cf. another idealized portrait of believing community in Acts 2:43-47; 4:32–5:11).

Reassessment of Contemporary Values. Profoundly grounded in Paul's gospel and observable across 2 Corinthians are ideas that are at least contrary—and may even be properly deemed subversive—to the culture and to its impact on at least some of the Corinthians. Paul thinks that judgments made simply on what is seen, on what appears, on surface observations, are bound to be wrong. He employs various means to advocate that fundamental skepticism. He distinguishes walking by faith—that is, by trusting God—from walking by sight (5:7); he eschews reckoning from what can be seen in favor of "the things that cannot be seen" (4:18); and he distinguishes what appears on one's face from what is in one's heart (5:12). In embracing this perspective, Paul reaffirms to the Corinthians the same conviction expressed elsewhere in his letters: "Hope that is seen is not hope" (Rom 8:24); "Now we see in a mirror, enigmatically; then face to face; now we know partially; then we shall know completely just as we have been known" (1 Cor 13:12).

Paul acknowledges the same ambiguity in human estimations of other people. To consider another person "according to the flesh" (κατὰ σάρκα *kata sarka*)—that is, according to standard ways of reckoning, is certain to be misleading (5:16). Paul develops the thought christologically, saying that he no longer regards Christ *kata sarka;* to do so would be to view him wrongly, incompletely, without the resurrection that establishes his identity as Lord. Along these same lines, we must understand Paul's later self-description as not walking   that is, comporting himself—*kata sarka* (10:2), and his related assertion that the warfare he is prepared to prosecute against any opposition should not be confused with theoretically defeatable—that is, *kata sarka*—power (10:3).

The same undercutting of traditional cultural values is present in the hardship list of 2 Cor 6:4-10 but is packed especially into the verses at its end. As to the list, Paul's self-commendation comes not in the number of victories he can boast of or in his grand accomplishments or wealth, but is grounded instead in afflictions, hunger, and even disrepute (6:4ff.). The catalog concludes, however, with three couplets, each of which begins with cultural disvalues—"sorrowful," "poor," and "having nothing"   and turns each one of them radically, distinctly on its head—"rejoicing," "enriching many," and "possessing everything" (6:10). By doing this Paul depicts himself, and all those associated with him in the living of the gospel, as being shored up in joy even in the midst of sorrow, as showering riches where poverty seems to prevail, and as possessing everything while others might (wrongly) think the opposite is true. Believers possess everything because, as those who through Christ belong to God, believers share all that God possesses (1 Cor 3:21 *b*-23).

Paul's fundamental critique of conventional values in 2 Corinthians should not have come as a surprise to the Corinthians. In an earlier letter to them, Paul had argued that, in the light of God's concluding purposes in reclaiming the cosmos, believers should comport themselves "as-if-not"; that is, they should live in the world so as to practice detachment from the values and entanglements it offers (1 Cor 7:30-31; see the Commentary on 1 Corinthians). As a predominantly Gentile congregation, the Corinthians will have been exposed to such Stoic reflection about "indifferent matters" (ἀδιάφορα *adiaphora*). Paul's inversion of values in 2 Cor 6:10 fits such a context and reinforces a certain distancing from cultural norms.

In a similar way, but focused on the cultural category of rich/poor, Paul's christological claim about Christ's having been rich and submitting himself to poverty for the believers so that by his poverty they might become rich offers a critique of riches and poverty and indirectly provides a model for Paul's relinquishing the accoutrements that some might think appropriate to apostleship (2 Cor 8:9). In this christological formulation, Paul does not offer an escape from poverty to riches as seen in the categories of the world; instead, Paul imparts a perspective that answers the question of what is truly valuable, of where real wealth resides.

Paul's basically contrary-to-culture outlook is also aimed, with great irony, at anyone among the Corinthians who is enamored of the intruders and their values. In focus is the way the intruders have inveigled the Corinthians into according to themselves grand status and support, both of which Paul has assiduously refused. Paul mocks the intruders, their Corinthian allies, and their values with an ironic parody: "You put up with it if someone enslaves you, if someone exploits you, if someone takes advantage of you, if someone is presumptuous, if someone slaps you in the face. With what shame I must say we were too weak to do that!" (11:20-21). Likewise, when acknowledging that, though he accepted support from other churches, he persisted in not burdening the Corinthians, he again feigns shame: "Forgive me this wrong" (12:13 NRSV).

All of Paul's subversion of cultural norms, every bit of his revaluation of values, is grounded in his christological conviction that Christ's resurrection overthrows not only death but also the structures of meaning by which people previously reckoned. If, in Christ, the fundamental antinomy of life and death has been cashiered from its governance of human encounters and significance, then indeed there is a "new creation" and truly "everything has become new" (5:17 NRSV). After Christ's death and resurrection, the norms of conduct have to be revised or newly invented, as the Corinthians have learned already from Paul in 1 Corinthians.

Because Paul's contention with the intruders and their Corinthian adherents comes to focus on his too humble status and demeanor, Paul moves his counter onto the weakness/power antinomy and grounds it in Christ, whom Paul claims "was crucified in weakness but lives by the power of God" (13:4 NRSV). So for Paul crucifixion/life and weakness/power are directly correlated.

By means of the weakness/power doublet, Paul at once defends himself and puts perspective on not only what is truly important, but also where the ultimate power resides. Paul's weakness/power critique has long been known to the Corinthians (see 1 Cor 1:20-25; 15:43), but it probably emerges once again when some unidentified persons are reported to be claiming about Paul that "his letters are weighty and strong, but his bodily presence is weak" (2 Cor 10:10 NRSV). In 11:21, Paul, brimming with irony, embraces the description of himself as "too weak" to take advantage of the Corinthians as the intruders have. From that point in the letter, weakness becomes a major, positive theme of Paul's self-identification; having just recounted a list of hardships and sufferings (11:23-28), he pledges to boast of nothing but his weaknesses (11:30). And so he does, detailing how, in Damascus, he recently managed to escape with his life (11:31-33) and capping it off with a recounting of how he earnestly desired to have the stake or thorn in the flesh removed from him (12:7b-10). Paul depicts his weakness as a perfect avenue for God's power. Although he is not allowed to disclose the message that he received when he was in the third heaven (12:4), he readily recounts the word he received from the Lord in response to his failed petition for the removal of the thorn: "My grace is sufficient; my power is perfected in weakness" (12:9). It is in God's nature to display power in weakness, to place divine treasures in earthen vessels (4:7). God's power is perfectly suited to human weakness. So the culturally generated complaint against Paul, that he does not display the proper perquisites of power and status of a true apostle (12:12), is critiqued and rejected by Paul, who suggests indirectly that the complainers do not understand even the basics regarding the gospel and, by implication, about how God works.

Paul taps a widespread, popular contemporary notion of the inner and outer person and overlays it with a related contrast of temporary and permanent (4:16-18; see the Commentary on 4:16-18), as a part of his sustained argument that what one sees on the surface or outside is not predictably indicative of inner or permanent reality. In so doing he sets the stage for its amplification in the following, kindred antinomies between "face" and "heart" (5:12) and between knowing someone "according to the flesh" and as being related to the new creation (5:16-17).

The Importance of Works. With the classical emphasis on justification by faith we have sometimes lost Paul's perspective on works and their place in the life of faith. Much of 2 Corinthians is directed at the issue of how people behave, at what their conduct is. Paul's own comportment is a continuing topic, sometimes defined positively in terms of what he has done, sometimes delineated negatively as to how he has refrained from behaving (e.g., 2 Cor 1:12, 17; 2:17; 4:2; 11:7-9; 12:6, 14-18).

In 2 Corinthians, Paul is also attentive to the Corinthians' behavior, reminding them that they, like he, will have to face the judgment before Christ at the last day (5:10). Then and there, Paul holds, all believers will be accountable for what they have done (2 Cor 5:10), for their thoughts (Rom 2:16), and for their purposes of heart (1 Cor 4:5). The judgment will be based on "the things done while in the body" (2 Cor 5:10 NIV), whether for good or for bad. Satan's ministers also face an end (τὸ τέλος *to telos*) that will correspond to their works (2 Cor 11:15).

In Romans, Paul develops the final judgment motif more fully. There, using commercial terminology, Paul declares that God will "pay back to each person according to that one's works" (2:6): eternal life, glory, honor, and peace to those who patiently do good and seek immortality; wrath and fury to those who do evil (2:7-10). The repayment is reckoned in terms of the deeds one does (cf. 1 Cor 3:12-15), how one comports oneself in the body, and not whether one has faith, because faith is a gift (χάρισμα *charisma*) given by God to each believer (cf. 1 Cor 12:9-11) and, therefore, not the subject of judgment.

Judgment regarding works has sometimes not been given adequate attention in studies of Paul because interpreters rightly recognize that, for Paul, one does not come to faith by means of works, but by God's grace freely given. Faith—that is, right relation to God—does express itself in works, in deeds of love (Gal 5:6; 1 Thess 1:3). Paul consistently decries any attempt to attain right relation with God by performance of works, by dint of one's own efforts (cf. Rom 3:27-28; 9:30–10:3).

The topic of judgment according to works comes up in 2 Corinthians because Paul feels the need to defend his comportment, his works, among the Corinthians, and he is concerned about their works as expressed in relation to him. At several points in 2 Corinthians 1–9 Paul has reminded the Corinthians that he and they must live and behave in such a way as to be ready for the completion of God's purposes (2 Cor 3:18; 4:17-18; 5:4-5; 6:1-2). The eschatological, end-time references are designed to leverage the Corinthians into closer affiliation with Paul, who, in exemplary fashion, declares himself as aiming to please God in all that he does (5:9) precisely because he knows that "all of us" will have to appear before Christ's tribunal for judgment (5:10).

Continuity/Discontinuity Between Past and Present. On the one side, Paul is convinced that all of God's promises find their "yes," their fulfillment, in Christ (2 Cor 1:20; cf. Rom 1:3; 9:5). Christ is the confirmation of the promises granted the patriarchs (Rom 15:8). Likewise, the gospel was declared already to Abraham (Gal 3:8), and Abraham becomes the type of faithful person whose unconditional trust in God is the model for all believers who follow (Romans 4; Galatians 3). In 2 Corinthians as well, the first covenant shares with the second one, no matter how distinctive they may be in other respects, the fundamental characteristic of "glory," presumably a glory that is in both cases derived or reflected from God, who grants the covenants (2 Cor 3:7-11). So the new covenant is, like the first, still covenant, still made by God, and still manifests the glory from God so that some fundamental continuity between past and present is affirmed.

Driven by a desire to make absolutely clear to the Corinthians that their current relation to God stems from their relation to the gospel through Paul and his ministry, Paul ties his own ministry to a "new" covenant, which he affirms that he represents. To distinguish himself and his ministry from all others, he distances the new covenant from its predecessor in significant ways. He radicalizes the distinction between what he labels as two "ministries" and pictures these ministries as having distinctive covenants. In each instance his ministry and its covenant are distinguished by contrasts or described as surpassing the other one: written on stone/on hearts (3:3), with ink/with the Spirit of the living God (3:3), old/new (3:6, 14), death (stated)/life (implied; 3:7), letter/spirit (3:6), and fading away/permanent (3:11, 13). Indeed, Paul's eagerness to interpret his own ministry and its covenant as being of singular importance for the Corinthians leads him to an oxymoronic position: He knows that the old covenant had glory, but, being convinced that the new covenant's glory (and, therefore, his ministry) so exceeds the earlier glory, he says that the new glory is so dazzling as to make the earlier glory seem to be no glory at all (3:10).

Reconciliation. Reconciliation as a term presupposes a familial or friendship setting in which, after enmity has been overcome, relationships are restored to amicability. So it is also in Paul. All of creation was made by God for association with God's own self. Sin intervened and led creation, humans included, into alienation and even enmity with God (Rom 5:10). By a freely given gift—that is, grace in Christ—God overcame the enmity and established peace (Rom 5:1), another term for reconciliation.

Among the seven undisputed letters, Paul's most powerful delineation of reconciliation is found in 2 Cor 5:11-21, where the reconciliation is at once cosmic, communal, and personal. It is cosmic in that as surely as the world—that is, all of creation—has been subjected to futility and is in bondage to decay (Rom 8:20-21), in Christ God "was reconciling the world to himself" (2 Cor 5:19 NRSV). In Romans 8, Paul describes in more detail how he views God's ultimate rehabilitation of the entire created order: God's newly reclaimed children already experience the "freedom of the glory" for which the rest of creation still longs, much as a pregnant woman experiences her labor pains just prior to delivery (Rom 8:19-23). It is communal in that when Paul describes reconciliation it always has a plural object, "us" or the world in its collectivity (Rom 5:10-11; 2 Cor 5:18-19). Reconciliation is also personal because it takes place "in Christ," precisely the locus where individual believers become members of Christ's body and are given into one another's care (1 Cor 12:12-26). Further, as the commentary shows, in 2 Cor 5:11-21 Paul *explicitly* calls for reconciliation to God, but *the encoded message* is that he wants more filiation from the Corinthians and a heightened sense of reconciliation with them—*to him* as the one who brought the gospel of reconciliation to them in the first place. He is personally concerned that their already established reconciliation to God wash over onto him with new enthusiasm on their part (cf. 2 Cor 6:12-13; 7:2).

SOCIAL AND RHETORICAL CONVENTIONS: EPISTOLARY STYLE

Thoroughly at home in the Greco-Roman world, Paul employs the practices and conventions of the time as a means of engaging with and relating to the Corinthians.

Frank Speech. Frank speech (παρρησία *parrēsia*)[32] was, along with indirect or figured speech and flattery, one of the three ways that a person in Paul's time could attempt to influence deliberation regarding proper behavior. Without ever mentioning it explicitly from 2 Cor 1:3 through 2 Cor 6:10, Paul *indirectly* bids for increased filiation from the Corinthians; in 6:11-13, however, he shifts to frankness and appeals *directly* for increased affection (see also 7:2). Indirect speech treats an issue or problem obliquely, in a roundabout fashion, never head-on, and often without even expressly mentioning the main concern; in 1:3–6:10, Paul strives in a variety of ways to cement his newly restored relations with the Corinthians, though, properly abiding by the canons of indirect speech, he never explicitly states in those verses his concern to do so.

Frankness has friendship as its locus. It is the highest "office of a friend" to call a friend

---

32. For the conventions and practice of frank speech, see J. Paul Sampley, "Paul's Frank Speech with the Galatians and the Corinthians," in *Philodemus and the New Testament World,* ed. J. T. Fitzgerald, G. S. Holland, and D. Obbink, NovTSup (Leiden: E.J. Brill, 2001).

to task, to encourage the friend to reach for the best and to perform at the optimum.[33] Frank speech ranges from "the gentlest sting," on the one extreme, where one pleasantly nudges the friend toward improvement, across a continuum of increasing degrees to the other, harshest extreme: a rebuke. The success of frank speech depends on many considerations, among which are the timing, the proportionality of the severity to the situation, the ethos or character of the frank speaker, and the care to mix in varying, appropriate degrees of praise. In some sense and degree, the friendship is always placed in hazard by the undertaking of frank speech, but true friendship, genuine caring for the other one, sometimes leaves no alternative but to take that risk.

Paul employs a range of frank speech in the correspondence reflected in 2 Corinthians. In the painful letter, he uses harsh frank speech and reports himself appropriately anxious about how the Corinthians have received it (2 Cor 7:5-7, 12-13). In 6:11-13 and 7:2, Paul uses a milder form of frank speech as he calls for the Corinthians to open their hearts to him.

Self-commendation. Modern readers often have great difficulty with Paul's persistent reminders to the Corinthians of his considerable efforts toward them. Similarly, his boasting seems extravagant; he even acknowledges as much in 2 Cor 11:16-17, 21 *b;* 12:1. In that culture, friends commended each other, wrote letters of commendation for each other, and put in good words for each other at critical times.

Further, Paul's contemporaries were, as Paul shows himself to be also, not reticent to commend themselves as a part of the self-promotion that was so prevalent culturally. Encomiastic practices regularly expected that a speaker or writer detail, as Paul does here, his deeds that benefited others. Goodwill is earned when one details what one has done for others, when we "refer to our own acts and services without arrogance."[34] *Ad Herennium,* a contemporary rhetorical handbook, wrongly attributed to Cicero, concurs and urges the speaker to reveal "also our past conduct toward the republic, or toward our parents, friends, or the audience."[35] Paul has no interest in the republic; he is totally focused on his audience, the Corinthians, as he recites his good works and diligence in service of the gospel to the Corinthians[36] and hopes thereby to garner their increased goodwill.

Ideally, one should not be totally dependent on self-commendation. One's clients or dependents should rally. In one context where outsiders show up with letters of commendation, Paul assumes that he should not need any such letters of support from his followers (3:1). Later, when his relations with the Corinthians have deteriorated once again, Paul contends that the Corinthians should have met his opponents with commendations, with boasting about him and about what he has meant to them: "You forced me [to be a fool and commend myself], for I ought to have been commended by you" (12:11). When his Corinthian allies failed to commend him, he saw no option other than to commend himself.

33. Philodemus *On Frank Criticism* col. XIXb.
34. Cicero *De inv.* 1.16.22.
35. Cicero *Ad Herennium* 1.5.8.
36. S. H. Travis, "Paul's Boasting in 2 Cor 10–12," *Studia Evangelica,* ed. F. L. Cross (Berlin: Akademie, 1973) 6:529-30; 554-55.

Therefore, he boasts, but he tempers his boasting with irony and by adopting a fool's pose (11:16, 21 *b*, 23; 12:11). Had the Corinthians come to his defense, he would not have felt the need to engage in self-commendation.

Paul openly embraces a certain type of self-commendation: "In every way we commend ourselves as ministers of God" (6:4). The hardship list that follows shows that Paul's self-commendation is grounded in his difficulties and distress, an ironic testimony to the power of God working through and sustaining him in whatever circumstances he encounters. In 6:4-10 irony functions as did the fool's mantle and thus places Paul's self-commendation in perspective.

Epistolary expressions of self-confidence such as we see in 2 Corinthians (1:12-14; 5:11; 11:5; 13:6; cf. Heb 13:18) are an accepted part of persuasion and are necessary when the writer wants "to create or restore a good relationship between" the readers/hearers and himself.[37] In 2 Corinthians 1–9, Paul is especially eager to rehearse their grounds for mutual pride, so he mixes praise of them and self-commendation of himself (see 1:13 *b*-14). The goal of self-commendation is to shape the way the audience thinks of the speaker. Paul's self-commendation lays out the picture he wants the Corinthians to have of him.[38]

Patron/Client, Honor/Shame. The culturally pervasive categories of patron and client, of honor and shame, continue to make their marks on Paul's communication with the Corinthians. (For a treatment of honor and shame, see the Introduction of 1 Corinthians.)

In the Greco-Roman world a gift or benefaction establishes or maintains a patron/client relationship and places the recipient under obligation. Seneca says it clearly: "The giving of a benefit is a social act, it wins the good will of someone, it lays someone under obligation."[39] For the one who receives a benefit, gratitude is merely the "first installment of his debt."[40] Epictetus deems the one who "repays a favour without interest" an ingrate.[41] In that world, patronage was the glue that bound every level of society to their benefactors. Not simply a political tool as we know it in modern times, patronage was omnipresent, in all relations, where one person's favor binds the recipient(s) to honor the donors and, in cases of money or possessions, allows the recipients to confer beneficence and, therefore, obligation, on persons beneath them in status.

In 2 Corinthians, patronage is a matter of great importance because some Corinthians seek to become Paul's patrons and thereby support his ministry. These Corinthians, who may reasonably be supposed to include some of the wealthy, are spurred to move in that direction by two forces that we can identify. First, they have seen the Macedonian believers arrive with support for Paul and him accept it (11:9). Given the prevalent cultural patterns, they have every superficial reason to view that transaction as a patron/client relationship between the Macedonians and Paul, exactly the association they seek with him. Second, they seem to have been encouraged by the intruders to think that real apostles did not do menial work (as Paul insisted on doing) as a means of self-support (11:7; 12:16).

37. S. N. Olson, "Epistolary Uses of Expresssions of Self-Confidence," *JBL* 103 (1984) 588.
38. Ibid., 593.
39. Seneca *Of Benefits* 5.11.5.
40. Ibid., 2.22.1.
41. Epictetus *Epistles* 81.18; cf. 81.9-10.

Paul, however, rejects their bid of patronage. In strong language he avers that his boast of self-support will not be silenced anywhere in the environs of Corinth (11:10). With an oath as to his truthfulness, he preempts any claim that his refusal of patronage is a sign that he does not love them (11:11). Further, he declares that he is not about to change his long-standing pattern of self-support with them. By refusing their offer of patronage, Paul has avoided being obligated to them, probably an important personal consideration, but, in the categories of the culture, he has rebuked and shamed them by his refusal. In that setting, as in many to this day around the world, patronage and its gifts cannot be refused without shame attaching itself to the would-be donors. Shame produces enmity.[42] No doubt a part of Paul's problems with the Corinthians is attributable to his contravention of the traditional cultural patterns of patronage.

The Types of Rhetoric in 2 Corinthians. In the Greco-Roman world, all rhetoric could be divided into three classes. *Judicial rhetoric,* the most common, addresses questions of culpability regarding the past. *Deliberative rhetoric* attends to questions of what a person or group will do in the (perhaps even imminent) future. *Epideictic rhetoric* focuses on praise and blame, usually of a person, though events may also be the subject. All of Paul's letters are deliberative, at least in part if not completely, because each of them at some point calls for the hearers to reflect on their comportment and to consider emending their current practices. Both letter fragments contained in 2 Corinthians do that, though 2 Corinthians 10–13, with its rehearsal of Paul's past behavior and its preparation for a confrontational showdown, may at times also be judicial. Both letter fragments, insofar as they shower praise or cast blame, engage in some epideictic rhetoric as well.

Epistolary Style. Much attention is properly placed on categorizing the Pauline letters as to type or literary style.[43] For 2 Corinthians, two determinations are necessary, one for chapters 1–9, another for chapters 10–13. Chapters 1–9 are "a letter of apologetic self-commendation."[44] As noted already, the primary burden of 2 Corinthians 1–9 is Paul's recovery of Corinthian filiation after he has subjected them to a frank rebuke.

Chapters 10–13 are an "excellent example of a mixed letter type."[45] Their legal overtones are prompted not only by Paul's eagerness to counter charges made against him, but also by his determination to put the Corinthians on warning of his imminent arrival when he expects to confront his accusers. But the letter is truly a hodgepodge as to style or type, containing as it does not only accusations, self-defense, and reproaches, but also self-commendation and apologies.

Frank speech, discussed above, is, along with indirect speech and flattery, a mode of

---

42. Peter Marshall, *Enmity in Corinth: Social Conventions in Paul's Relations with the Corinthians,* WUNT44 (Tübingen: J. C. B. Mohr, 1987) 242-47.

43. See L. L. Belleville, "A Letter of Apologetic Self-recommendation: 2 Cor 1:8–7:16," *NovT* 31 (1989) 150.

44. Belleville establishes this identification quite clearly by comparing 2 Corinthians 1–9 with examples from Sophists. See ibid., 158-59.

45. J. T. Fitzgerald, "Paul, the Ancient Epistolary Theorists, and 2 Corinthians 10–13: The Purpose and Literary Genre of a Pauline Letter," in *Greeks, Romans, and Christians: Essays in Honor of Abraham J. Malherbe,* ed. D. L. Balch, E. Ferguson, W. A. Meeks (Minneapolis: Fortress, 1990) 200.

the speaker's relating to the hearers and can be employed in any of the types of rhetoric noted above and in any epistolary style.

CONCLUDING NOTES

Although we know that chapter designations were added to the biblical texts only in the Middle Ages and that subdivisions into verses came about even later, nevertheless in the Commentary chapters and verses are used as a means of handy reference. The reader of this commentary will note, however, that occasions are cited in which the relatively modern division of the text into chapters and paragraphs and verses does not reflect the sections and turning points in Paul's argument.

The Scripture translations in the Commentary and in the Reflections are my own, unless otherwise indicated. In order to make clear to modern readers the semantic range of a given Greek term, additional possible translations of the same term by different English words separated by a slash are given—for example, Paul's mention of παράκλησις (*paraklēsis*), "so also our encouragement/comfort/consolation abounds through Christ" in 1:5. The hope is that such a translation will provide the readers with additional information by which they can appreciate the different nuances of *paraklēsis* in that verse—and indeed in 1:3-10, where the term or some form of it occurs ten times.

In this commentary the recipients of 2 Corinthians are frequently referred to as "hearers" or "auditors" because the majority of the Corinthians were surely illiterate (1 Cor 1:26) and, therefore, dependent upon someone else to read the letter to them. So most Corinthian believers experienced these letters as a heard communication.

The term "Christian" is lacking in the Commentary sections because Paul and his readers did not employ this term as a self-description. It was a later development.[46]

46. Thanks to you, Sally Backus Sampley, love of my life, for your hours of research, for your helpful, insightful critiques, and most of all for your love. Thanks also to Suzanne Webber for her editorial suggestions throughout the commentary.

BIBLIOGRAPHY

Belleville, L. L. "A Letter of Apologetic Self-Commendation: 2 Cor 1:8–7:16." *NovT* 31 (1989). Significant for her classification of the letter and for her understanding of self-commendation.

Danker, F. W. "Paul's Debt to the *De Corona* of Demosthenes: A Study of Rhetorical Techniques in Second Corinthians." In *Persuasive Artistry: Studies in New Testament Rhetoric in Honor of G. A. Kennedy.* Edited by D. F. Watson, JSNTSup 50. Sheffield: Sheffield Academic, 1991. Helpful in understanding Paul's rhetorical techniques.

DeSilva, D. A. "Measuring Penultimate Against Ultimate Reality: An Investigation of the Integrity and Argumentation of 2 Corinthians." *JSNT* 52 (1993). A helpful use of rhetorical traditions for understanding some of Paul's transitions and purposes.

Fitzgerald, J. T. *Cracks in an Earthen Vessel: An Examination of the Catalogues of Hardships in the Corinthian Correspondence.* Atlanta: Scholars Press, 1988. An illuminating window on Paul's adaptation of a social convention.

Furnish, V. P. *II Corinthians.* AB 33. Garden City, N.Y.: Doubleday, 1984. This thoughtful, careful, thorough commentary was a landmark.

Georgi, D. *The Opponents of Paul in Second Corinthians.* Philadelphia: Fortress, 1986. A tendentious study whose methodology and suppositions have carried a disproportionate weight in the study of 2 Corinthians.

Marshall, Peter. *Enmity at Corinth: Social Conventions in Paul's Relations with the Corinthians.* WUNT 44. Tübingen: J. C. B. Mohr, 1987. One of the early looks at Paul's relation to the Corinthians in the light of the way social practices and conventions affected human relations.

Savage, T. B. *Power Through Weakness: Paul's Understanding of the Christian Ministry in 2 Corinthians.* New York: Cambridge University Press, 1996. A competent and suggestive appreciation of Paul's ironic vision.

Sumney, J. L. *Identifying Paul's Opponents: The Question of Method in 2 Corinthians.* JSNTSup 40. Sheffield: Sheffield Academic, 1990. Signal for its cautions about the problems it addresses.

Thrall, M. E. *A Critical and Exegetical Commentary on the Second Epistle to the Corinthians 1–7.* Edinburgh: T. & T. Clark, 1994. Thorough, cognizant of competing interpretations, this commentary exhibits detailed, balanced, insightful illumination of chaps. 1–7.

OUTLINE OF 2 CORINTHIANS

II. 2 Corinthians 10:1–13:13, Paul's Preparation for a Showdown Visit

A. 10:1-6, Paul's Readiness to Do Battle

B. 10:7-11, Consider What You Know

C. 10:12-18, Boasting Within Limit

D. 11:1-15, Betrothal and Betrayal: Paul and the Opponents

E. 11:16–12:10, The Fool's Speech: Paul's Boastful Comparison
  11:16-21*a*, Bearing with Fools
  11:21*b*-29, So to Boast
  11:30-33, Boasting and Deliverance Through the Damascus Wall
  12:1-10, The Man in Paradise with a Thorn/Stake in His Flesh

F. 12:11-13, Apostolic Commendation and Confirmation

G. 12:14-18, Paul's Final Self-defense

H. 12:19-21, Preliminary Assessment and Differing Expectations

I. 13:1-10, Ground Rules and Challenge

J. 13:11-13, Concluding Admonitions and Grace

2 CORINTHIANS 1:1–9:15

AN APPEAL FOR AFFECTION AND FOR FUNDS FOR THE JERUSALEM CHURCH

OVERVIEW

In 2 Corinthians 1–9 Paul has written a powerful letter in which he makes every attempt to put himself forward as the apostle fully worthy of the Corinthians' embrace and obedience. This letter is bracketed on the front by Paul's severe disappointment that the Corinthians did not rally to his side when he was done "wrong" by one of them and by a painful letter of harsh frank speech that he wrote to them subsequent to the "wrong" and prior to what we now call 2 Corinthians 1–9. These chapters were written after Titus's reassurances that the Corinthians had come around and shown themselves ready for a fuller reassociation with Paul. Titus must also have been the one who told Paul that his failure to make a promised trip had generated grumblings among the Corinthians about Paul's dependability; so that becomes one of the first issues treated explicitly in the letter and, we can safely say, referenced indirectly in subsequent defenses of his comportment. The letter is bracketed on the other end by Paul's discovery that the Macedonians have successfully, even cheerfully, gathered the collection and are ready to pursue the itinerary with it that Paul had earlier set out: through Corinth to Jerusalem.

So from the first verse of the letter, Paul knows that he has two overriding concerns to deal with: He must conciliate and reassure the Corinthians that their inclination to realign with him is sound and proper, and he must lay the groundwork—by giving the Corinthians cause to embrace him and by establishing the hooks on which he will hang his final appeal—for persuading the Corinthians to regain their earlier zeal for him *and* to partake wholeheartedly in the collection. Paul cannot settle for just one of the two goals because they are inextricably bound together.

He surely cannot, however, tackle the collection issue until he thinks he has given the Corinthians grounds for full reassociation with him; so the collection is only hinted at in the opening seven chapters. When he does turn explicitly to the collection, he can then capitalize, as he does, on many of the preceding claims and themes that he has so powerfully argued.

That 2 Corinthians 1–9 was not successful on every front will be painfully clear in chapters 10–13. Romans, written after all of the Corinthian correspondence and written from Corinth (Rom 16:23), does depict that Achaia took part in the collection for the saints in Jerusalem (Rom 15:26). "The saints in all of Achaia" were, along with the Corinthians, recipients of 2 Corinthians 1–9 (see 1:1), so Paul's epistolary efforts at encouraging participation in the collection did bear fruit, when seen in the light of Rom 15:26. Whether Achaia's cooperation included Corinthian participation, however, is beyond our capacity to know, but we may ponder that when we take into account the tone of 2 Corinthians 10–13, a subsequent Pauline fragment of a later letter sent to the Corinthians.

2 CORINTHIANS 1:1-2, SALUTATION

NIV

1 Paul, an apostle of Christ Jesus by the will of God, and Timothy our brother,

To the church of God in Corinth, together with all the saints throughout Achaia:

²Grace and peace to you from God our Father and the Lord Jesus Christ.

NRSV

1 Paul, an apostle of Christ Jesus by the will of God, and Timothy our brother,

To the church of God that is in Corinth, including all the saints throughout Achaia:

²Grace to you and peace from God our Father and the Lord Jesus Christ.

COMMENTARY

A comparison of this salutation with that of 1 Corinthians offers some parallels and some significant differences. In both letters Paul describes himself as "apostle of Christ Jesus by God's will" (1:1). In 2 Corinthians, however, Paul names a different person as his co-authoring "brother." Missing is Sosthenes (1 Cor 1:1; cf. Acts 18:17). In his place is Timothy (2 Cor 1:1). Timothy, whom Paul elsewhere describes as his "soul mate" (ἰσόψυχος *isopsychos*, Phil 2:20), has had a long, positive relationship with the Corinthians. He is the one whom Paul had sent to the Corinthians in the early days to teach them "my ways in Christ" (1 Cor 4:17), apparently successfully, and 1 Corinthians closes with Paul, who is detained in Ephesus, sending Timothy once again to work with them (1 Cor 16:10-11). Timothy's continued good standing with the Corinthians is signaled by Paul's inclusion of him (with Silvanus) as one of those who, along with Paul, have faithfully preached Jesus Christ among the Corinthians (2 Cor 1:19). Paul's association of himself with Timothy as co-author bids to co-opt for himself the goodwill Timothy has garnered with the Corinthians over the years. Thus, from the very outset of this letter, Paul works to enhance his own standing with the Corinthians.

The addressees are once again called "the church of God which is in Corinth," as they were in 1 Cor 1:2. Whereas 1 Corinthians stopped with that, the audience for this new letter fragment is significantly widened to include "all the saints who are in the whole of Achaia," the Roman province that includes Corinth and the entire Peloponnese. This enlargement of the audience is

a bit like inviting a third party, no doubt favorable to Paul, into the deliberation with the Corinthians. We do not know a great deal about other Pauline churches in Achaia, but we are aware that Phoebe, whom Paul describes to the Romans as one of his patrons and as a deacon of the church at Cenchreae (Rom 16:1), a town at Corinth's eastern shore, is a strong advocate for Paul. It is not unreasonable to suppose that the other believers in her church are also positively related to Paul. If Phoebe is any index, Paul's including other believers in Achaia brings into the circle of letter recipients more people who are favorably attentive to Paul. Already, two details in the salutation—Paul's choosing Timothy as co-author and the inclusion of the Achaians among the addressees—are tilted positively toward enhancing Paul's relations with the Corinthians, a matter of enormous concern throughout 2 Corinthians 1–9.

The salutation concludes exactly as all of Paul's other salutations: with a wish—indeed, a blessing delivered with apostolic bearing—for grace and peace (from God and Jesus Christ; 1:2). Grace, the freely given, unmerited favor of God, is appropriately the greeting among believers because the very life of faith and the basis of their having community together come about as a direct result of God's grace poured into their lives. Grace is not only actively present at the beginning of the life of faith, but it is also the enduring ground of all of life, from start to finish. Peace, no doubt for Paul out of his rich Jewish heritage, is the *shalom* that comes about by God's reclamation and righting of people and their social circumstances.

Peace, the end of enmity between people and God (Rom 5:1), is a Pauline code word for the reconciliation that brings alienated persons back into fellowship and into accord with one another and, as we shall see in this letter fragment, between the Corinthians and Paul (2 Cor 5:14-21; cf. 1 Cor 7:15; 14:33; 2 Cor 13:11).

REFLECTIONS

Paul signals an important consideration in these opening verses: Christians are never isolated from one another. They always live their lives of faith in connection with one another. The creedal affirmation "I believe in the communion of the saints" could just as well have derived from Paul, who believes that the saints—that is, all of us whom God has claimed, are given to one another. How matters go for any of God's people is important to all of us. Christian community does not allow any to be left out or behind. The insularity of modern life threatens Christian community and sometimes clouds the visibility of those in need.

2 CORINTHIANS 1:3-11, BLESSING OF GOD

NIV

[3]Praise be to the God and Father of our Lord Jesus Christ, the Father of compassion and the God of all comfort, [4]who comforts us in all our troubles, so that we can comfort those in any trouble with the comfort we ourselves have received from God. [5]For just as the sufferings of Christ flow over into our lives, so also through Christ our comfort overflows. [6]If we are distressed, it is for your comfort and salvation; if we are comforted, it is for your comfort, which produces in you patient endurance of the same sufferings we suffer. [7]And our hope for you is firm, because we know that just as you share in our sufferings, so also you share in our comfort.

[8]We do not want you to be uninformed, brothers, about the hardships we suffered in the province of Asia. We were under great pressure, far beyond our ability to endure, so that we despaired even of life. [9]Indeed, in our hearts we felt the sentence of death. But this happened that we might not rely on ourselves but on God, who raises the dead. [10]He has delivered us from such a deadly peril, and he will deliver us. On him we have set our hope that he will continue to deliver us, [11]as you help us by your prayers. Then many will give thanks on our[a] behalf for the gracious favor granted us in answer to the prayers of many.

[a]11 Many manuscripts *your*

NRSV

3Blessed be the God and Father of our Lord Jesus Christ, the Father of mercies and the God of all consolation, [4]who consoles us in all our affliction, so that we may be able to console those who are in any affliction with the consolation with which we ourselves are consoled by God. [5]For just as the sufferings of Christ are abundant for us, so also our consolation is abundant through Christ. [6]If we are being afflicted, it is for your consolation and salvation; if we are being consoled, it is for your consolation, which you experience when you patiently endure the same sufferings that we are also suffering. [7]Our hope for you is unshaken; for we know that as you share in our sufferings, so also you share in our consolation.

8We do not want you to be unaware, brothers and sisters,[a] of the affliction we experienced in Asia; for we were so utterly, unbearably crushed that we despaired of life itself. [9]Indeed, we felt that we had received the sentence of death so that we would rely not on ourselves but on God who raises the dead. [10]He who rescued us from so deadly a peril will continue to rescue us; on him we have set our hope that he will rescue us again, [11]as you also join in helping us by your prayers, so that many will give thanks on our[b]

[a] Gk *brothers*   [b] Other ancient authorities read *your*

NRSV

behalf for the blessing granted us through the prayers of many.

COMMENTARY

Where we might expect to find a thanksgiving in Paul's letters (cf. Rom 1:8-15; 1 Cor 1:4-9; Phil 1:3-11; 1 Thess 1:2-12; Phlm 4-7), we see a "Blessed be God" (NIV, "Praise be") formula, which Paul adopts and adapts from his Jewish heritage. Throughout the literature of Israel and of the early churches the "blessed be" formula is used only of God (1 Kgs 1:48; 2 Chr 2:12; 6:4; Pss 34; 72:18[71:18]; Mark 14:61; Luke 1:68; cf. Eph 1:3; 1 Pet 1:3).

A brief look at the formula in Israel's Scriptures is instructive for understanding it in 2 Corinthians 1. David, near his death, uses the expression to praise God's faithfulness in granting that David's son Solomon will sit on the throne God gave to David (1 Kgs 1:48). Even the king of Tyre invokes the formula because the God who made heaven and earth has faithfully granted David a wise son who will build God a temple (2 Chr 2:12). Solomon cites the exodus from Egypt and the selection of Jerusalem as the site for the Temple as the signs that "the LORD has fulfilled his promise that he made" (2 Chr 6:10 NRSV) and on that basis says "Blessed be God" (2 Chr 6:4).

At the heart of one's blessing of God, therefore, is a thankful appreciation of *God's faithfulness,* of God's steadfastness in making good on what God has promised. Even more directly in view for Paul may be the kind of expression exemplified in Psalm 34, where God is blessed explicitly for deliverance from trouble and difficulty, precisely the connection Paul pursues in the verses directly following the "blessed be" formula. The writer of that psalm, like Paul, recognizes that the faithful are beset by distress and afflictions, but the Blessed One (God) delivers the righteous "out of them all" (Ps 34:19).

Others of Paul's letters show that he has clearly appropriated the expression of God's blessedness and occasionally uses it in doxological settings where he finds himself moved to praise and give thanks to God (Rom 1:25; 9:5), in effect for God's

faithfulness, for God's coming through on what has been promised, or in a place where Paul vows his own truthfulness and calls God as his witness (2 Cor 11:31). Blessing God is giving thanks to God; when one believer blesses God, others are expected to join in the affirmation of thanksgiving by saying, "Amen" (1 Cor 14:16). So Paul opens 2 Corinthians with a "blessed be God" formula and thereby anticipates, and indeed sets the context for, his note of the faithfulness of God that explicitly surfaces in 2 Cor 1:18-20 and that associates Paul's faithfulness and dependability with God's. Significantly also, Paul's blessing of God invites the Corinthian auditors to join with him.

Paul's blessing of God opens a passage that begins with God's consolation in the face of afflictions and distress and concludes with a note of hope and thanksgiving. The blessing itself (v. 3) names God as "Father of our Lord Jesus Christ," an echo of the grace that closes the salutation (v. 2; cf. a similar association in 11:31). The sequence "God" and "Father" of vv. 2 and 3*a* is, in v. 3*b,* reversed, forming a small chiasmus (ABB′A′), and allowing Paul an opportunity further to characterize the God who is blessed.

As any proemium or exordium, the classic opening of a speech in Paul's time, was expected to do, vv. 3-10 set the tone and lay down certain themes that will suffuse the passages that follow.[47] The verses are loaded with passion and emotion. Charged rhetoric of extremes flashes before us. The lexicon of difficulties (including θλῖψις *thlipsis,* vv. 4, 8; παθήματα *pathēmata,* vv. 5-7; θλίβω *thlibō,* v. 6; and πάσχω *paschō,* v. 6) contributes to the tone and introduces a major theme of affliction and distress that will lace through the entire letter fragment. A second theme, even more pro-

---

47. F. W. Hughes, "The Rhetoric of Reconciliation: 2 Corinthians 1.1–2.13 and 7.5–8.24," in *Persuasive Artistry: Studies in New Testament Rhetoric in Honor of G. A. Kennedy,* ed. D. F. Watson, JSNTSup 50 (Sheffield: Sheffield Academic, 1991) 250-51.

nounced in these opening verses, is God's compassion (οἰκτιρμός *oiktirmos,* v. 3) and comfort/consolation (παρακαλέω *parakaleō,* παράκλησις *paraklēsis,* repeated ten times in vv. 3-10 and fourteen times in the remainder of the letter fragment). A third theme, that of abundance, expressed in the term περισσεύω (*perisseuō*), appears twice in the proemium (v. 5) and seven times in the rest of the letter fragment (3:9; 4:15; 8:2, 7; 9:8, 12; cf. 8:2, 14) and ties the two already noted themes together.

These verses depict "suffering/misfortune" (*pathēmata,* vv. 5-6) and "affliction/distress" (*thlipsis;* NIV, "troubles" [v. 4] and "hardships" [v. 8]) as the context in which God's "encouragement/comfort/consolation" (*paraklēsis*) finds its proper expression. Much as in Romans, where Paul said that as sin abounds, grace abounds all the more (Rom 5:20), here in these verses he suggests that God's *paraklēsis* meets human *pathēmata* and *thlipsis* in a superabounding fashion; God's *paraklēsis* overflows people's *pathēmata* and *thlipsis.* Human suffering or misfortune and affliction must not be confused with sin, however—quite the opposite. Identifying with God, with the gospel, assures one of encountering distress and suffering, and that very affliction becomes the locus where God's consolation, comfort, and encouragement find abundant expression.

Paul's use of "we" and "us" throughout this passage invites the Corinthian hearers to picture themselves in solidarity with Paul before their compassionate God, whose comfort meets them in every distress (vv. 3-4). Paul further encourages his listeners to identify with him by his reference to *Christ's* suffering flowing over into "our lives" (v. 5a NIV). A christological identification underlies this subpart of his argument (vv. 5, 9). In quite parallel constructions, Paul ties together the sufferings of Christ, which abound to "our" benefit, with our consolation, which abounds on account of Christ. The two are directly linked for Paul. Paul's eschatological frame of reference and his confidence upon which it is based lead him to affirm that as surely as "we" share Christ's sufferings, "we" are assured that our consolation/comfort abounds because of Christ (v. 5). The Corinthians had heard this confidence in an earlier letter from Paul (cf. 1 Cor 15).

In v. 6, however, although the "we" expression continues in the first verb, the hearers will find that Paul now inserts himself and his own experience directly into the picture. For the first time he mentions "your consolation and salvation" and shows by that expression that he has begun to talk primarily about himself, even though he continues to use the plural pronoun "we."

For Paul, association with the gospel guarantees one's being at cross purposes with the world, whose structures are dominated by sin. Witness Paul's telling the Thessalonians that, as they face the opposition of their unbelieving neighbors, they are experiencing precisely what he had forecast for them while he was with them (1 Thess 3:3). Or consider his own self-depiction at the end of 1 Corinthians, where he reports a huge door opened for his evangelizing at Ephesus, "and there are many opponents" (1 Cor 16:9). So affliction, distress, and opposition are expected for those who are claimed by the gospel.

At the heart of Paul's opening engagement of the Corinthians in this letter is his foundational conviction that God comes to the aid of those who are afflicted, who are down-and-out. God dependably meets human suffering with overflowing comfort (cf. the same confidence for those who mourn in Matt 5:4). God faithfully meets the affliction of believers with comfort and with consolation or encouragement.

God, as the source of pity, mercy, and compassion, is known throughout Israel's Scriptures (2 Sam 24:14; Ps 24:6; Isa 63:15; cf. *T. Jos.* 2:3), and we find elsewhere in the letters that Paul affirms God's mercy (cf. Rom 12:1). God is not merely sometimes or occasionally merciful; God is continually and faithfully merciful. God's mercy and compassion are attributes that consistently characterize God.

God's comfort and compassion are not given to believers as a personal possession. Recipients of God's merciful encouragement become the channels through whom God's comfort is made available to others who are themselves "in any affliction" (v. 4). Paul finds a certain logic to this: Those who experience the abundance of Christ's sufferings by their exposure to affliction in this world experience a corresponding abundance of comfort (v. 5).

As soon as Paul has established that God's

comfort/encouragement/consolation overflows in the face of distress and affliction (vv. 3-5), he tells the Corinthians, in the most general and sweeping way, that any affliction he has suffered has been for their "comfort and salvation"; any comfort he has received is for their comfort, which they experience as they share his sufferings (v. 6). Several important rhetorical moves converge here. First, Paul seeks to secure Corinthian identification with him; his suffering is at once benefiting them, and they should identify with his suffering, as he had already told them in an earlier letter: "If one member suffers, all the members suffer together" (1 Cor 12:26). The form of Paul's formulation is a *sorites*, or chain, each element picking up and reaffirming the previous one: A leads to B; B leads to C; and so forth. Such rhetorical structures are designed to make the strongest connection between the first and the last element in the chain,[48] in this case "afflicted" (v. 6*a*) and "suffering" (v. 6*d*). In v. 7 Paul explicitly and powerfully calls them and himself *"partners in suffering . . . and encouragement"* (κοινωνοι . . . τῶν παθημάτων . . . τῆς παρακλήσεως *koinōnoi . . . tōn pathēmatōn . . . tēs paraklēseōs*). Second, he seeks to elicit goodwill from the Corinthians toward himself because the rhetorical tradition trained persons to generate goodwill by references to themselves and to their service in behalf of the ones who can return the favor with goodwill.[49] Third, by linking their ultimate "salvation" with "patient endurance" (ὑπομονη *hypomonē*, v. 6), Paul bids them to stay the course even though their relation with Paul has been somewhat stormy of late (see the Introduction).

Because the Corinthians are his partners (he now additionally enforces that identification by calling them ἀδελφοί [*adelphoi*], "brothers and sisters," v. 8)[50] in suffering and comfort (v. 7), and because he has already established that any distress of his is also theirs (v. 6), he makes certain that they learn immediately of the adversity he has recently experienced in Asia, the Roman province that roughly corresponds to the western part of modern Turkey. The Corinthians do not learn what this calamity was, but they surely are told of its enormity. Paul describes his own state in hyperbolic categories: "beyond measure" or "beyond our ability" (καθ' ὑπερβολήν *kath' hyperbolēn*, v. 8; NRSV, "utterly" [ὑπὲρ δύναμιν *hyper dynamin*]). He was so weighed down that he "despaired of life" (v. 8); he felt as if he had received a death sentence (v. 9). Twice more he refers to "the dead" and the "deadly" (vv. 9-10). Clearly, Paul identifies what happened to him in Asia as life threatening. Paul's desperate scenario is surely designed to elicit pity, and therefore support, from his audience.[51]

Stripped of any pretention of personal power, Paul found himself trusting in the God who not only comforts, consoles, and encourages, but also "raises the dead" (v. 9; cf. Rom 4:17, where God is depicted as the one "who raises the dead and calls into being the things that are not"). In his overwhelming distress, Paul relied upon the truth encapsulated in a christological dictum: In raising Christ from the dead, God showed power over death. Paul, despairing of life itself, counted on God, on God's power, a power demonstrated and warranted in Christ's having been raised. If the Corinthians did not know the identity of Paul's Asian crisis from some other source, such as the person who delivered the letter, then they, like we, are left to imagine it.

Paul vests his hope in God because of God's faithfulness in deliverance, the very reason why Paul blessed God at the start of this letter (v. 3). The God who raises the dead (present description, v. 9) is the same God who has delivered Paul (credit from the past, v. 10), presumably from this most recent, dreadful crisis in Asia, and is the identical God on whom Paul counts (twice, v. 10) to deliver (confidence toward the future) yet again. References to hope have bracketed Paul's report of his brush with death in Asia (vv. 7, 10). Paul's hope is not some wishing against the odds. Hope is based on the very character of God, a steadfast, trustworthy character built across history. Accordingly, Paul looks at the future with confidence that God will bring matters to a fruitful end, and in like fashion, Paul can look death in the face and have confidence that God is the one

---

48. H. A. Fischel, *Rabbinic Literature and Greco-Roman Philosophy* (Leiden: Brill, 1973) 77, 151-52n. 126.

49. See *Ad Herennium* 1.5.8, a roughly contemporary rhetorical handbook.

50. L. L. Belleville, "A Letter of Apologetic Self-recommendation: 2 Cor 1:8–7:16," *NovT* 31 (1989) 147-48, argues that the body of the letter fragment begins with this verse.

51. Ibid., 149: "The central concern of the body opening is thus that of reciprocity." See also *Ad Herennium* 2.31.50.

who delivers/saves/preserves/rescues (ῥύομαι *ryomai*; 3 times in v. 10).

The passage concludes with Paul's request for intercessory prayer, that the Corinthians join in helping (συνυπουργέω *synypourgeō*) by their prayers, which Paul construes as thanksgivings for the favor (χάρισμα *charisma*; NRSV, "blessing") that has been bestowed upon him—namely, his deliverance. The proemium opens with a blessing of God, who, like the grandest of patrons (on patrons and clients, see the Introduction), has, in the context of abundant intercession of others, done a favor for the distressed client named Paul. It closes with Paul expecting his own deliverance to generate many persons' thanksgivings to that same patron (v. 11; cf. Rom 12:15). Their prayers—and Paul's call for prayers for himself—affirm a reciprocity between Paul and the Corinthians that mirrors the reciprocity that God as divine patron deserves from the believing clientele (v. 11).

Curiously, though many of the openings in Paul's letters *begin* with a thanksgiving (cf. Rom 1:8-15; 1 Cor 1:4-9; Phil 1:3-11; 1 Thess 1:2-10; Phlm 4-7), the opening section of 2 Corinthians *ends* with a thanksgiving that yet once more invites the Corinthians to make common cause with Paul. In vv. 3-11 we have heard only of God's deliverance of Paul from his Asian perils, but this grand thanksgiving for personal deliverance surely serves as a background for Paul's upcoming celebration of his deliverance from tough times with the Corinthians.

REFLECTIONS

1. Blessing God is strange to our ears. We are more likely to think of—or at least to hope for—God's blessing of us. But here Paul has it going the other way. For Paul, blessing God is another way of giving thanks, but the blessing of God is especially to be employed when we hit hard times. It is a way of remembering, a way of reminding ourselves, and one another, that God has delivered us in the past—indeed, that God's nature is to deliver. The God of the exodus is our God. Our recitation of God's faithfulness, via our blessing of God, should not only help us to remember God's deliverance in the past, but also assist our trusting—and even eager—expectation that God's comfort will somehow find us in our present distress. Our God delivers and comforts. The very act of looking for deliverance or comfort is the first faithful response, which itself may help us to see the exodus that is perhaps already graciously before our eyes.

2. We tend to think of comfort as a feeling, as in a comfortable chair or of feeling good about something. In such a conception, the "God of comfort" would help us to feel good. Paul opens a different window onto the understanding of comfort: It is more like a gift that God gives or a door that God opens to us for a way out of affliction.

3. Deep-seated in our culture is the notion that prosperity is a signal of God's favor and that adversity, affliction, or suffering is a sure sign of God's displeasure and judgment. Jesus did not think that suffering or physical problems were a sign of sin (John 9:1-2). Neither does Paul here in this text—or anywhere. Paul's laudation of affliction is not an elevation of suffering for its own sake; neither must it be taken as a prescription so that to be a Christian is to be miserable. Paul thinks distress happens to people along two patterns: in part because people who live by faith are at odds with the world, whose structures are under the power of sin and therefore caustic to Christians, and in part because fragile, finite human beings experience distress and loss as ingredient to life (see 2 Cor 4:16-18).

4. Distress and all the rites of passage that mark great changes or signal the extremities of life (e.g., death, divorce, adverse medical prognoses) provide occasions that may break through human pretense. That is why persons who are dying, or who are around those who are, sometimes find themselves moved to forgive and to overcome previous hostilities and misunderstandings. Just as human distress and change provide occasion for God's abundant comfort, according to Paul, so also we can generously console those we find in adversity. God's comfort is our model and our inspiration. Have you ever been around an older person who, facing death, finds a serenity and peacefulness that is absolutely infectious? That person knows the comfort Paul is describing. Is there any reason why those of us who are not at death's door might not also understand and celebrate that comfort in the junctions of our lives?

5. We may find it easier to show comfort and concern when another person is suffering and more difficult to celebrate his or her deliverance. No jealousy leaches into our thoughts when a friend or acquaintance is experiencing some affliction, but when a friend gets a new, better job, a better car, is admitted into a prestigious college, gets a raise, or has a better harvest, can we be genuinely thankful that person has done well? Another person's deliverance or boon is an occasion for thanksgiving. If we could genuinely rejoice over other people's deliverance and good fortune, then we could contagiously share their joy.

6. Seeing Paul at the end of his rope—indeed, near death—can provide us with a model for dealing with affliction. By all the evidence of his letters, he had innumerable hardships and difficulties (see 2 Cor 6:4-10; 11:23-28; 12:10). As down and out as he was sometimes, he received comfort from God and trusted that God would not let distress have the last word. Too often we romanticize biblical characters, making them distant from us and less like us. Maybe the next time we reflect on our own distresses, failures, and disappointments, we might try to picture ourselves as like Paul and wonder how he found joy in the midst of suffering. Reading some of his passages about joy experienced in the midst of suffering might be a good place to start that reflection (see Romans 8; Phil 1:12-26).

2 CORINTHIANS 1:12-14, PAUL'S PRINCIPLED CONDUCT

NIV

[12]Now this is our boast: Our conscience testifies that we have conducted ourselves in the world, and especially in our relations with you, in the holiness and sincerity that are from God. We have done so not according to worldly wisdom but according to God's grace. [13]For we do not write you anything you cannot read or understand. And I hope that, [14]as you have understood us in part, you will come to understand fully that you can boast of us just as we will boast of you in the day of the Lord Jesus.

NRSV

12Indeed, this is our boast, the testimony of our conscience: we have behaved in the world with frankness[a] and godly sincerity, not by earthly wisdom but by the grace of God—and all the more toward you. [13]For we write you nothing other than what you can read and also understand; I hope you will understand until the end— [14]as you have already understood us in part—that on the day of the Lord Jesus we are your boast even as you are our boast.

[a]Other ancient authorities read *holiness*

COMMENTARY

In the previous section, Paul described the distress he recently experienced in service of the gospel, a conventional move in that time, designed to engender goodwill on the part of auditors. Here he characterizes his conduct, again by reference to a conventional form, an expression of self-confidence.[52] In all of his correspondence, these verses rank as some of his most thorough self-reflections of how he has conducted his life according to certain principles (ἀναστρέφω *anastrephō*, v. 12). Consistency is the subtext: Paul has comported himself well everywhere (ἐν τῷ κόσμῳ *en tō kosmō*, "in the world," v. 12) as he has with the Corinthians; if anything, he suggests, he has been even more scrupulous with them (περισσοτέρως δὲ πρὸς ὑμᾶς *perissoterōs de pros hymas*, v. 12; cf. similar expressions of Paul's superabounding concern for and commitment to the Corinthians, 2 Cor 2:4; 7:15). Verse 12, with its declarations of his exemplary comportment and of his commitment to the Corinthians, introduces the twin themes that will ground everything Paul writes through 6:10.

Paul presents his self-portrait as a boast (καύχησις *kauchēsis*, v. 12). Paul writes about boasting in two very distinct ways. If one's boasting is a showing off, a gloating, a suggestion that one's actions are one's own achievement and, therefore, an index of status, then Paul rejects it as inappropriate. (Examples of Paul's view of improper boasting can be seen in 1 Cor 3:21; 4:7; 5:6.) On the contrary, however, one can properly boast of the gospel, of God (Rom 5:11; 1 Cor 1:31; cf. Jer 9:24), and of God's power. In an ancillary fashion, as here, one can boast of one's labors in service of the gospel because that boasting does not simply and unequivocally point to one's own power and accomplishment, but rather places one's own work in the larger picture of God's work (see the discussion of "work" in the Commentary on 1 Cor 15:58). Paul regularly boasts of his preaching the gospel and, as here, of his work in advancing it (Rom 15:17; 1 Cor 9:15; Gal 6:14; Phil 1:26; 2:16; cf. 1 Cor 9:16 for Paul's own sense of the ambiguity of boasting). Proper boasting is always grounded in God's grace-filled, preemptive working and is, therefore, always fundamentally responsive; it points more to God than to oneself.

Boasting and self-commendation do, however, play quite an extensive role in the letter fragments that make up 2 Corinthians and emerge here for first consideration. Self-commendation is used when one wants to recover good relations between the speaker or writer and the audience. This will become an apparent need in the next topic because Paul has failed to make a promised visit to the Corinthians (vv. 15-22). Among the topics that are frequently featured in self-commendations are one's comportment and character, as here in v. 12 (cf. 4:2), one's past efforts in behalf of the hearers, as in 4:5 and 5:13, or the hope that speaker and hearers may be mutually proud of one another, as in 1:14 and 5:12.

Paul introduces his boast with the clause "our conscience bears witness" and thus declares that his accompanying self-commendation has been subjected to the scrutiny of his moral consciousness that confirms its veracity and propriety (v. 12). Thus Paul certifies that what he here declares about his conduct regarding the Corinthians is not lightly or casually advanced. The Corinthians can remember from an earlier letter hearing Paul's view that all believers have moral consciousness or consciences, as the term συνείδησις (*syneidēsis*) may variously be translated, and that some will have weaker and others stronger moral consciousness (1 Cor 8:7, 10, 12). Further, he expects all believers to weigh matters with their consciences (1 Cor 10:23-30), as he has done here in what he now says to them.

He structures his conscience-vetted boast—about how he has conducted himself—in a positive-negative-positive form. Both positive statements give ultimate credit to God as the source of power behind not only Paul's comportment, but also his boast. Paul's frank speech (which the Corinthians have experienced most recently in the no longer extant letter; see the Introduction; reading ἁπλότης [*haplotēs*] instead of ἁγιότης [*hagiotēs*], "holiness," "moral purity") and his sincerity or purity of motive (εἰλικρίνεια *eilikrineia*) are nec-

---

52. S. N. Olson, "Epistolary Uses of Expressions of Self-Confidence," *JBL* 103 (1984) 596-97. Cf. 2 Cor 5:11; 11:5; 13:6.

essarily related. To speak in frankness effectively with friends requires that the speaker have an established ethos founded on sincerity or purity of motive.[53] Paul's choice of words expresses his understanding of his relationship with the Corinthians as one of friendship in which Paul, the friend in question, assures his friends that they have been able to count on him as a dependable, consistent associate whose probity of motive and practiced frankness are indispensable indices of friendship. In v. 12, Paul declares that both his frankness and his sincerity cohere in and ground his conduct. In a classical antithetical construction, Paul declares that his comportment has been guided not by mundane wisdom, but by the grace of God. Paul lays bare his conviction that there are two rival ways of being in the world: One can take primary guidance from what one can figure out about the world on one's own; or one can be guided, and from Paul's perspective energized, by God's grace (cf. the upcoming alternatives "outer/inner," 4:16; "seen/unseen," 4:18; "face/heart," 5:12).

Paul's reference to what and how he has written to the Corinthians is given as evidence of his sincerity and of his eagerness for them to under-

stand. No doubt the *immediate* focus of the understanding is centered on solidifying the Corinthians' relation to Paul (as expressed by the NIV's insertion of "us" as the object of the understanding Paul hopes for in v. 14). Although the Greek does not explicitly make that connection, Paul's readers are free to do so. Paul does not stop, however, with the immediate. Rather, he transposes the whole question of understanding into an eschatological issue, into whether the Corinthians will *finally* understand as they should so that at the last day, at the judgment, at the return of Christ, they will be found acceptable and that Paul and they can boast of one another (then boasting becomes equivalent once again to thanksgiving) on the day of our Lord Jesus Christ (v. 14). Subtly, Paul elides the Corinthians' understanding of what he writes, and therefore of himself, with their understanding of their place in God's cosmic purposes, which will come to a conclusion in the day of Christ. The ambiguity that resides already in the Greek phrase ἕως τέλους (*heōs telous*), which can mean simply "completely" or "fully" (NIV) or "until the end" (NRSV), is precisely the ambiguity that resides in the entire passage.

53. See Plutarch *How to Tell a Flatterer from a Friend* 71E.

REFLECTIONS

1. Boasting has earned a bad reputation—and rightly so when it involves self-puffery and self-service—but we might wonder if boasting is of necessity always to be avoided. It may be difficult for some persons to read Paul, partly because he had a certainty about his faith that many today find beyond their reach, and partly because his boasting sometimes slips beyond what seems to be good taste. When Paul's boasting is clearly in what God is doing, we probably have an easier time. But there is a problem in our reticence to boast: How can we properly celebrate what God is doing in our lives? Must we not tell others about it so that we can celebrate it together? Paul presumes so. Restraint in boasting about God's grace in our lives further privatizes faith and limits community.

2. Consistency of conduct is the foundation of trust in human relations. Friendship can go nowhere if there is not confidence that the other person can be counted on regularly and completely. Trust is built one brick at a time. The structure we build by our day-in/day-out dependability is the house where we live and into which we invite our friends. When it comes to building or destroying trust, there are no little failures of dependability, no little slights of each other. All of our peccadilloes corrode trust. Failing to take the trash out as promised may not seem like such a big thing, but it subtly raises the question of what all our promises mean.

3. Paul's setting of "worldly wisdom" over against the "grace of God" should not be understood as a disparagement of wisdom per se. Neither should it be understood as an advocacy for Christians' not thinking. Clearly, Paul believes the conscience and its moral reflection are important in daily comportment (1:12b). Paul probes here the question of where believers begin their reasoning, where they ground it. Paul's answer: Believers start with the grace of God as their reasoning point—that is, they take God's freely given love as the cardinal point, the magnetic north, of their moral compass. Then they reckon from there what shape and direction their own life and loving ought to take. Christians do not start their reckoning from the world and its values.

2 CORINTHIANS 1:15–2:4, PAUL'S TRAVEL PLANS AND HIS PAINFUL LETTER

NIV

[15]Because I was confident of this, I planned to visit you first so that you might benefit twice. [16]I planned to visit you on my way to Macedonia and to come back to you from Macedonia, and then to have you send me on my way to Judea. [17]When I planned this, did I do it lightly? Or do I make my plans in a worldly manner so that in the same breath I say, "Yes, yes" and "No, no"?

[18]But as surely as God is faithful, our message to you is not "Yes" and "No." [19]For the Son of God, Jesus Christ, who was preached among you by me and Silas[a] and Timothy, was not "Yes" and "No," but in him it has always been "Yes." [20]For no matter how many promises God has made, they are "Yes" in Christ. And so through him the "Amen" is spoken by us to the glory of God. [21]Now it is God who makes both us and you stand firm in Christ. He anointed us, [22]set his seal of ownership on us, and put his Spirit in our hearts as a deposit, guaranteeing what is to come.

[23]I call God as my witness that it was in order to spare you that I did not return to Corinth. [24]Not that we lord it over your faith, but we work with you for your joy, because it is by faith you stand firm. [2:1]So I made up my mind that I would not make another painful visit to you. [2]For if I grieve you, who is left to make me glad but you whom I have grieved? [3]I wrote as I did so that when I came I should not be distressed by those who ought to make me rejoice. I had confidence in all of you, that you would all share my joy. [4]For I wrote you out of great distress and

a19 Greek Silvanus, a variant of Silas

NRSV

[15]Since I was sure of this, I wanted to come to you first, so that you might have a double favor;[a] [16]I wanted to visit you on my way to Macedonia, and to come back to you from Macedonia and have you send me on to Judea. [17]Was I vacillating when I wanted to do this? Do I make my plans according to ordinary human standards,[b] ready to say "Yes, yes" and "No, no" at the same time? [18]As surely as God is faithful, our word to you has not been "Yes and No." [19]For the Son of God, Jesus Christ, whom we proclaimed among you, Silvanus and Timothy and I, was not "Yes and No"; but in him it is always "Yes." [20]For in him every one of God's promises is a "Yes." For this reason it is through him that we say the "Amen," to the glory of God. [21]But it is God who establishes us with you in Christ and has anointed us, [22]by putting his seal on us and giving us his Spirit in our hearts as a first installment.

[23]But I call on God as witness against me: it was to spare you that I did not come again to Corinth. [24]I do not mean to imply that we lord it over your faith; rather, we are workers with you for your joy, because you stand firm in the faith. [2:1]So I made up my mind not to make you another painful visit. [2]For if I cause you pain, who is there to make me glad but the one whom I have pained? [3]And I wrote as I did, so that when I came, I might not suffer pain from those who should have made me rejoice; for I am confident about all of you, that my joy would be the joy of all of you. [4]For I wrote you out of much

a Other ancient authorities read pleasure   b Gk according to the flesh

NIV	NRSV
anguish of heart and with many tears, not to grieve you but to let you know the depth of my love for you.	distress and anguish of heart and with many tears, not to cause you pain, but to let you know the abundant love that I have for you.

COMMENTARY

The previous two pericopes have set the context for these verses. In the first passage, Paul established God's faithfulness as the ground for the blessing of God (1:3-11). In the second, Paul pictured himself as a dependable, steadfast friend whose consistent moral probity is his hallmark (1:12-14). Now, in 1:15-22, he has to account for what has no doubt seemed to some Corinthians as a contradiction of his self-portrait in 1:12-14: Paul has not made the visit to Corinth that he had promised (2:1). Instead, he has sent them a letter (2:3), which he (later) describes as "painful" for them and for himself (7:8-12). Paul supposes himself vulnerable to a complaint of vacillation—and he responds to it.

1:15-16. In these verses Paul lays out the itinerary he had wanted (the term βούλομαι [*boulomai*, "wish/want/desire"] appears four times) to follow. The proposed route would have involved two trips through Corinth, which Paul calls a "double favor" (δευτέραν χάριν *deuteran charin*), continuing the language of friendship as well as of patron/client and giving pride of place to Corinth. If this letter fragment was written from Ephesus (see the Introduction), Paul had projected a sea voyage on the Aegean to Corinth, from which he would make his way north overland to Macedonia, the Roman district where Paul had established churches, at least in Thessalonica and in Philippi. From there he had expected to return to Corinth (the doubled favor) and had hoped that they would provide "help on our journey to Judea," the southern part of ancient Palestine where Jerusalem lies (1:16). The Macedonians' plans to go to Corinth with their part of the collection show that they also knew this projected itinerary (9:1-5).

But none of this happened as touted. Paul decided not to go to Corinth. In a refinement, he uses rather formal terminology of rendering a carefully considered choice: "I reached a decision [ἔκρινα δὲ ἐμαυτῷ τοῦτο *ekrina de emautō touto*; 2:1] not to come to you *again* painfully [ἐν λύπῃ *en lypē*]" (2:1, italics added).

1:17. A fuller picture of Paul's increasingly troubled relations with the Corinthians is now possible. Since he wrote what we call 1 Corinthians, Paul (1) has made what must have been a disastrous visit to them (Paul describes it as having been "painful," 2:1; more on that follows), (2) has written them what he dubs a "painful" letter instead of making a promised visit (2:2-3), and (3) has thereby left himself open to a charge of vacillation, that he runs hot and cold (1:17-18). Each of these events no doubt caused problems between Paul and the Corinthians, but now they have come together, and Paul addresses them collectively; further, he is concerned for the harm the two events have caused to the Corinthians' relation with him.

The "painful" visit and the "painful" letter are connected to each other in this fashion: Timothy, the co-author of 2 Corinthians 1–9 and who, according to Acts 18:5, was, along with Paul and Silvanus (Silas), present for the founding of the Corinthian church, was first sent back to Corinth by Paul to "explain my ways" (1 Cor 4:17). Next Timothy was dispatched to Corinth, perhaps as bearer of 1 Corinthians to them (1 Cor 16:10-11). From there the matter is not crystal clear, but events seem to have fallen this way: After some time, Timothy apparently returned to Paul in Ephesus with a report that the situation at Corinth had deteriorated. Clearly once again, Paul, in an effort to bring things back into line, went to Corinth for what he now dubs a "painful" visit (2:1); and later, when faced with the prospect of another painful visit, Paul scrubbed his planned trip to Corinth and sent a stern letter instead (7:8). All these problems, addressed first here, will make their impact at later points in the letter fragment as well (cf. 7:8-12).

With that background, we return to Paul's first engagement of this mare's nest of problems: the possible charge that he vacillates, or to put it most directly, that he is not dependably a man of his word in the conduct of his life. This is a serious challenge to the very underpinning not only of Paul's authority, but also of the most essential ingredient to friendship—namely, the dependable, steadfast, trustworthy character of the individual. In two questions formed in the Greek so as to expect a negative answer, Paul tries to distance himself from anyone whose plans and actions are subject to whim and caprice (1:17).[54]

1:18-22. By contrast, Paul is about to present himself—and significantly Silvanus and Timothy—as subject to God. In these verses Paul transposes the challenge of his trustworthiness from the question of his recent change of itinerary, which apparently is an issue with some Corinthians, first, to a claim about God (1:18), then to an assertion about Christ (1:19-20), and then to a longer claim about God (1:21-22). The theological declarations, rich as they are, affirm that it is God, and by implication *not* Paul, who is in charge, a theme that will be explicitly addressed in 2:14-17. Paul takes an oath on God's faithfulness that he, Paul, has not been wishy-washy, "Yes and No," with them regarding his word to them (1:18). In the same way, Christ, God's Son, whom Paul, Silvanus, and Timothy preached among the Corinthians, is not "Yes and No, but always Yes" (1:19). Likewise, God, as seen in connection with past promises, is always faithfully "Yes." Finally, in refinement, Paul has one of his longest descriptions of God, which in the Greek literally reads: "*The* confirming-us-with-you-in-Christ-and-who-sent-us *God*." This God is not to be denied by Paul (1:21); the implication is that Paul goes as God sends.

Just as quickly as Paul places himself under the shield of God's choosing and sending, he opens up the "we" statement so that each of the Corinthians can understand themselves as also being the recipients of God's claiming and calling action. Paul makes common cause with his Corinthians when he speaks of God's marking "us" with a

seal, signifying ownership and protection by God, and giving "us" into "our" hearts the Holy Spirit as a down payment that ensures the full payment in due time, as earnest money that secures the deal (ἀρραβών *arrabōn*)—another eschatological note, echoing the one of 1:14.

Silvanus (Acts shortens the name to Silas) and Timothy (cf. 1:1) are fittingly mentioned in 1:19 because Paul is taking the Corinthians back to the time when those two and Paul brought the gospel to the Corinthians (cf. Acts 18:5). Silvanus is described by Acts as a prophet, as an authority associated with the Jerusalem Christians (Acts 15:22, 32; cf. 1 Pet 5:12), and as a cohort with Timothy on several occasions (Acts 17:14-15; 18:5; 1 Thess 1:1; 2 Thess 1:1).

Windows onto Paul's theological claims here include, first, his assertion of God's faithfulness (1:18). God's faithfulness and trustworthiness are bedrock Pauline convictions, and the Corinthians have heard this important Pauline claim several times before (1 Cor 1:9; 10:13; cf. 1 Thess 3:3). In its appearance in 1:18, God's fidelity becomes a cloak with which Paul eagerly shrouds himself. Second, Paul's claim that the promises of God find their "Yes" in Christ is a profound interpretation of history. For Paul, God's promises have been made to Abraham (Rom 4:13, 21-22; Gal 3:16-18, 29) and to his offspring (Rom 4:16; Gal 3:16) and to all believers (2 Cor 7:1; Gal 3:21-22). And in Christ, Paul declares, all of God's promises find their exclamatory "yes."

1:23–2:1. Just as Paul's conscience was earlier cited as a witness to his probity of conduct (1:12), so also Paul now escalates his rhetoric and calls God as a witness upon his soul. Paul decided to "spare" (φείδομαι *pheidomai*, "refrain from," 1:23) them another visit from him. His choice of words here suggests that consideration *of them* motivated his decision not to go again to Corinth. Perhaps 1:24 should be understood to represent the two options Paul saw before him: He could either go there and endeavor to force his way with them regarding their faith ("not that we lord it over your faith"), or he could attempt to relate to them as "fellow workers for your joy" (1:24).

In a curiously ironic way, the situation as Paul reflects on it here is somewhat similar and a bit different from the option he gave the Corinthians in 1 Cor 4:21. There he told them he was ready

---

54. L. L. Welborn, "The Dangerous Double Affirmation: Character and Truth in 2 Cor 1,17," *ZNW* 86 (1995) 41-48, argues that the doubled yes and no in 1:17 was recognizable in Paul's time as implying an oath to one's truthfulness.

to come to them and that they could have either the harsh Paul or the gentle Paul, depending on whether they continued as they were or changed their ways. The current situation is similar because Paul, had he come when he had planned, would have been the harsh Paul; there would have been no escaping it, and neither would there have been any joy. It is different because now Paul has decided that he would not go to Corinth because he knew he would find them as he would not like them. In either option, whether he had come to them or not, Paul knows and reaffirms with the Corinthians that "you stand by faith" (1:24). Remembering that "to stand" or "to be confirmed/validated" (ἵστημι *histēmi*) is generally for Paul eschatological, hinting as it does about standing before God's judgment at the end time (cf. Rom 11:20; 1 Cor 10:12), we can see that this little statement at the end of 1:24 is a third in a series of notes hinting that the Corinthians will have to account for themselves before God (1:14, 21-22). And the hearers have just been reminded that the faith by which they do stand and will stand before God is the very faith that Paul brought to them under God's commission (1:19).

Paul pulls together his thoughts, really his defense, on these matters by linking together the aborted visit and the painful letter he sent instead. With the mention of joy in 1:24 and "grief/pain/affliction/sorrow" (λύπη *lypē*) in 2:1, Paul establishes the antithetical frame on which his argument is structured in the opening verses of chap. 2. He has sought to minimize the grief/pain; that consideration ruled out a trip to Corinth ("I reached a decision," 2:1) because, had he come with things as they were, he would have had no alternative but "to come in grief" (ἐν λύπη *en lypē*)—a wonderfully ambivalent expression, available in neither the NRSV or NIV, allowing the hearers to understand that his having come to them as projected would have been painful for both them (developed in 2:2) and him (developed in 2:4).

2:2-4. These verses, an oblique bid for them to gladden him, contain a verbal flow chart mapping grief/pain and joy/gladness between Paul and the Corinthians over the aborted visit and its substituted letter. The Corinthians should be a source of joy for Paul; his joy should be a well-spring of joy for them—and so it should go round and round. But what if he should aggrieve them? Will it not interrupt the joyous reciprocity that should be in place between himself and the Corinthians? Paul and enough of the Corinthians had drifted into mutual suspicion that some clearing of the air was necessary. Paul's choice of a letter instead of personal presence is depicted in 2:3-4, which describes the letter as being generated not from a desire to cause them distress but to let them know the abundant love he has (ἔχω *echō*, "I have," present tense; 2:4) for them.

Paul's description of this letter makes clear it was an exercise in frank speech (παρρησία *parrēsia*); that is, it took the Corinthians to task for what they had done and the way they had behaved (see the Commentary on 1:12). People in Paul's day often used medical analogies to describe the effects of frank speech:

> The true frankness such as a friend displays applies itself to errors that are being committed; the pain which it causes is salutary and benignant; and, like honey, it causes the sore places to smart and cleanses them too.[55]

Accordingly, Paul's use of *lypē* ("pain") to refer to the Corinthians' reception of his frank speech is appropriate. The "cure" sometimes has accompanying "pain."

Paul describes himself as having had no choice but to write a letter he knew would cause pain to the very persons who ought to be cheering up, gladdening him. His decision to administer the painful reproof by letter rather than in person—thereby minimizing his self-exposure—may have been an exercise in wishful thinking as Paul imagines a future visit of real joy beyond the painful frank speech (2:3).

Paul's emotive description of his disposition when he wrote the painful letter overflows with heightened details about his own distress in writing: "Out of much affliction and distress of heart . . . with much weeping" (2:4). Of course, his purpose was not to cause grief or pain—frank speech, properly done, is never undertaken with pain or grief as its *goal*! Paul was driven to write to them as he did so that they "might know the especial love I have toward you" (2:4; the Greek clause is constructed so that "the love" appears

---

55. Plutarch *How to Tell a Flatterer from a Friend* 59D.

at the start, for even further emphasis). By careful construction of 2:4, Paul assures the Corinthians that he did not lightly decide to write them what turned out to be a painful letter for them. Neither was it easy for him. But his abundant love for them compelled him to undertake it and to hope for an amelioration such as the rest of the letter fragment confirms.

REFLECTIONS

1. God as witness against us (1:23) is a radical way of averring our truthfulness. It would be best if we never had to resort to such a radical claim and if our truthfulness were always obvious. But the complexities of life and, indeed, the post-Freudian capacities we all have for second-guessing ourselves often leave us on less certain ground than Paul vaunts here. Because God is the ultimate judge and alone knows the secrets of the heart (1 Cor 4:5), we can never achieve absolute certainty regarding another person's truthfulness; nor can we expect others simply to take our word regarding our truthfulness. Much more impressive than claims and assertions are a proven track record of being found truthful.

2. In Paul's time, being marked with a seal was a sign of ownership for animals and slaves and of identity for devotees of a cultus (cf. the "mark of the Beast, Satan" in Rev 19:20). The seal not only signified ownership or identity, but also guaranteed safekeeping. Paul declares that believers are sealed by the Holy Spirit. Belonging to the Holy Spirit means receiving one's identity from the Holy Spirit,[56] and the best clue in Paul's letters of what that means is that those sealed would bear what Paul calls "the fruit of the Spirit": love, joy, peace, patience, kindness, generosity, faithfulness, gentleness, and self-control (Gal 5:22). People today may have problems with the notion of "belonging" to or being "owned" by another. In the Greco-Roman world it was a reality for all slaves and a practicality for everyone as they always found themselves somewhere in the patron/client chain that structured society. We might wonder whether our vaunted independence from one another is not a collective illusion.

3. Doors frequently open and close with the "yes" and "no" we hear from those around us. Relations are problematic with persons whose "yes" and "no" seem random and inconsistent. Children whose parents' "no" and "yes" do not dependably stick lose their moorings and often think themselves unloved. Parents' thoughtful "nos" can at times be the surest sign of love for their children. Elsewhere Paul pays attention to God's "no" (2 Cor 12:8-9). Here, however, Paul's picture of God is focused on God's faithfulness, so the issue is God's "yes" and Christ's representation of God's "yes" to all of God's promises.

4. Frankness can be abused. Some take pride in telling whatever is "on their mind" and construe that as a virtue, but the ancients knew better. They understood that the right to use frank speech had to be earned, and only those of high moral character, those who are faithful and dependable, have the right to speak with frankness. Even then, frank speech must be appropriately timed and dispensed in carefully measured doses. Frankness can be overused. Each of us has a finite reservoir of the goodwill necessary to sustain frank speech, and care must be taken not to draw it down too far or too fast. On the other side, however, not to speak frankly to a person with whom we have a special relationship can let the other person down at a significant moment. Prayerful reflection, a self-examination of whether you are genuinely seeking the good of the other person, and a trust that God will use your efforts creatively should precede any use of frank speech.

56. L. L. Belleville, "Paul's Polemic and Theology of the Spirit in Second Corinthians," *CBQ* 58 (1996) 303, concludes: "Enlightenment (3:16-18), regeneration (3:6), and the ongoing and progressive transformation of mortality into immortal existence are attributed to the Spirit (5:1-5; cf. 4:10-11, 16-17)."

5. Just as the genie cannot be put back into the bottle once it has been freed, trust cannot be restored once it is splintered. What might be casually dubbed "a little indiscretion" in a marriage can take years to overcome—and even then may leave a lifelong scar. Trustworthiness, the coin of all relationships (whether marriage, friendship, work, or whatever), is destroyed easier and quicker than it is built. So protecting and caring for trust are not only a priority, but also a day-in/day-out, moment by moment enterprise.

6. In 2 Cor 1:18 Paul takes an oath on God's faithfulness. Clearly what Paul does there has no connection with what we today call cursing or swearing. We are warned against taking oaths in Matt 5:34-37 and Jas 5:12, which argue, as Paul perhaps echoes in 2 Cor 1:18, that one's yes should be simply yes and one's no directly no. Yet Paul is given to calling God as *witness* to his veracity (cf. Rom 1:9; Phil 1:8; 1 Thess 2:5, 10). It is a sure sign of dubiety if one needs to say more than a simple "yes" or "no" in order to be believed. The same may be said for having to repeat ourselves before someone believes us.

2 CORINTHIANS 2:5-11, THE ONE WHO CAUSED THE PAIN AND PAUL'S FORGIVENESS

NIV

⁵If anyone has caused grief, he has not so much grieved me as he has grieved all of you, to some extent—not to put it too severely. ⁶The punishment inflicted on him by the majority is sufficient for him. ⁷Now instead, you ought to forgive and comfort him, so that he will not be overwhelmed by excessive sorrow. ⁸I urge you, therefore, to reaffirm your love for him. ⁹The reason I wrote you was to see if you would stand the test and be obedient in everything. ¹⁰If you forgive anyone, I also forgive him. And what I have forgiven—if there was anything to forgive—I have forgiven in the sight of Christ for your sake, ¹¹in order that Satan might not outwit us. For we are not unaware of his schemes.

NRSV

⁵But if anyone has caused pain, he has caused it not to me, but to some extent—not to exaggerate it—to all of you. ⁶This punishment by the majority is enough for such a person; ⁷so now instead you should forgive and console him, so that he may not be overwhelmed by excessive sorrow. ⁸So I urge you to reaffirm your love for him. ⁹I wrote for this reason: to test you and to know whether you are obedient in everything. ¹⁰Anyone whom you forgive, I also forgive. What I have forgiven, if I have forgiven anything, has been for your sake in the presence of Christ. ¹¹And we do this so that we may not be outwitted by Satan; for we are not ignorant of his designs.

COMMENTARY

In 2:5-11 we can see what Paul and the Corinthians already know: At Paul's most recent visit, at the meeting he described as "painful" in v. 1, and which he wished not to repeat (1:23), someone distressed him (εἰ δέ τις λελύπηκεν *ei de tis lelypēken*, "if someone has caused pain") and, therefore, Paul maintains, by indirection, the rest of the Corinthians. We cannot recover the particulars, though this fellow is probably the same one who is mentioned again later in 7:12 as "the one who did the wrong" (τοῦ ἀδικήσαντος *tou adikēsantos*). The importance of this person for Paul and for his relationship with the Corinthians may be observed first in the space devoted to him (2:5-11; 7:5-16) and second in the location of Paul's discussion of him (as an inclusio, as rhetorical bookends, so to speak, for all that falls within). Clearly Paul's chagrin over this person and the Corinthians' failure to take Paul's side played into his travel plans, which are discussed before 2:5-11 (cf. 1:15–2:4) and mentioned after 7:5-16 (cf. 9:4).

What we can know is that the person "who did the wrong" is a man (vv. 5-8; 7:12). Whatever he did was directed primarily at another man ("the one who was wronged," 7:12), but, Paul is at pains to argue, the whole community was grieved in this one occasion (v. 5). Paul acknowledges that he was himself grieved (v. 5). The majority of the believers have punished the man (v. 6), and Paul counsels the community to pardon and console the offender (vv. 6-8). Finally, Paul emphatically reports himself ready to join his pardon to that of the community "for their sake" (v. 10). Of course, the Corinthians and Paul know the details and the identities.

Several observations support the surmise that Paul was the offended one: because he mentions his own personal grief/suffering (v. 5); his visit was so painful that he chose not to return but to write instead (1:23); and he announced his readiness to forgive/pardon (i.e., the person who had wronged him, v. 10). It is Paul's interpretation—with his apologetic "not to overstate"—that enlarges the sense of the wrongdoer's impact from merely himself to the entire community (v. 5). If the offense had been to the Corinthians directly Paul would not have had to venture into such an explanation. That the grief is not just his fits his otherwise commonplace assertion that when one member of the community suffers or stumbles, all do; and its positive counterpart, that when one member rejoices, all share in that joy (Rom 12:15; 1 Cor 12:26; 2 Cor 11:28). His later reference to "the one who was wronged" (7:12) as if it might not be him is a rhetorically delicate self-reference designed, at least in part, to make more emphatic his distancing of his reason for having written from the event of his having been wronged. Finally, Paul's celebration that the Corinthians have reembraced him and his leadership—as reported by Titus, they have experienced godly grief, indignation, and alarm over the event (7:11); have punished the man (2:6); and have recovered their zeal and longing for Paul (7:11)—confirms that Paul had very painfully experienced

their abandonment of him in the face of the wrong done him by the man during his painful visit (1:23–2:1).

Some scholars have tried to identify the person who did the wrong with the man who slept with his father's wife (1 Cor 5:1-8), whom Paul encouraged the Corinthians to dismiss from the fellowship. But the match is not compelling on several counts. No concern for a person who was wronged is exhibited in 1 Cor 5:1-8 (cf. 2 Cor 7:12). Further, Paul's rhetoric in 2 Cor 2:5 acknowledges that a person aggrieved Paul directly by something he had done during Paul's visit; that wrong (2 Cor 7:2) hurt Paul. What is worse, the Corinthians did not rally around Paul; they did not defend him as he felt they should have done. His distress over the visit and their failure to come to his support prompted his writing the painful letter: "For this reason, I wrote, so that I might know your being 'tried and true' [δοκιμη *dokimē*], whether in every respect you are obedient" (sense: "whether . . . you are allied or aligned with me," 2 Cor 2:9; cf. 7:12).

By the time Paul wrote 2 Corinthians 1–9, his sources, among them most assuredly Titus (7:7), had reported that the Corinthians had punished the wrongdoer and reaffirmed their allegiance to Paul. Paul's painful letter had the desired effect, and he is now in the position to practice and to model the reconciliation and forgiveness (2:10) that he so eagerly wants increased between himself and the Corinthians. So he counsels the Corinthians to "forgive" or "pardon" (χαρίζομαι *charizomai*, 2:7; cf. 12:13) the offender and, picking up the strong theme of the opening verses of this letter fragment, to "comfort/console/encourage" (παρακαλέω *parakaleō*) the one who was disciplined by their punishment or "censure" (ἐπιτιμία *epitimia*, 2:6-7). In pardoning one whom they have censured, the believers reflect their God, who, as Paul has already written eloquently in chap. 1, comforts and consoles those who suffer (1:3-11).

"Forgiveness" (χάρις *charis*) is a term whose understanding is grounded in God's giving freely and graciously to people who do not deserve it. Sometimes Paul expresses that free gift as reconciliation of people to God, a theme that will surface just ahead in 5:14-21. In the context of a community and one of its disciplined members, however, the term functions to describe the restoration of relationships between or among people (see a similar function for μετάνοια [*metanoia*] in 7:9). Nowhere in the seven undisputed Pauline letters does Paul write about "forgiveness of sins" (cf. Eph 1:7; Col 1:14). Paul's lexicon for restored relations to God includes "justification" and "reconciliation" (cf. Rom 5:6-9; 2 Cor 5:19-20), but not forgiveness of sins. For Paul, forgiveness and pardon are reserved for failed relations between human beings, as here in chap. 2.

Paul's mention of rebuke or punishment "by the majority" suggests that, even when the determination was finally made that the wrongdoer should be punished, not everyone came to Paul's defense against the one who had committed the wrongful act (v. 6). Such a reservoir of resentment against Paul may help to account later for Paul's urging an increase in the Corinthians' affection toward him (6:11-13; 7:2), even in the same letter fragment where he celebrates a restoration of good relations with the Corinthians (7:11-12).

The risk in not forgiving a person is here noted: "lest such a one be swamped/engulfed by extreme sorrow" (v. 7*b*). In all of Paul's letters we have only two instances of someone's being dismissed from fellowship. In both cases, Paul voices some desire that the person not be totally lost. Paul hopes that at least the spirit of the fellow mentioned in 1 Corinthians 5 "might be saved on the day of the Lord" (1 Cor 5:5). In 2 Cor 2:5-11 Paul wants the man to be restored because he has suffered sufficiently already and Paul does not want to see him lost (vv. 6-7). Paul's summary appeal is succinctly put and may be translated richly in two ways: "Decide in favor of love for him"; "Confirm love for him" (κυρῶσαι εἰς αὐτὸν ἀγάπην *kyrōsai eis auton agapēn*, v. 8). Through

his advice to the Corinthians, Paul models love in action. For Paul, believers in the God who comforts, redeems, restores, and reconciles cannot look the other way when one of their brothers or sisters is suffering or has been suffering. They must extend to that person the same love and acceptance and consolation and comfort they have received (cf. Rom 15:7).

In v. 7 Paul encourages them to forgive and console the one who did the wrong. In v. 9 Paul takes the Corinthians into his confidence and identifies with them by telling them, "Whomever you forgive, I also forgive." The statement also assures the Corinthians that when they do grant forgiveness to the one who did the wrong, Paul will join them in it. Paul thereby accomplishes several important things: He shares his authority with the Corinthians, he encourages them to follow through, and he indirectly reassures the one who did the wrong that Paul is ready for him and the community to move beyond the problems they had earlier. "In the face of Christ" (ἐν προσώπῳ Χριστοῦ *en prosōpō Christou*, v. 10; NEB, "as the representative of Christ"; NRSV, "in the presence of Christ") is a metaphorical expression and thus open to several lines of interpretation, but all of them must suggest that Paul's act of forgiving is in some sense appropriate to or generated from Christ. The expression could be Paul's way of saying that, standing before or in the presence of Christ, one could do nothing less than proffer forgiveness. Paul does see a loathsome alternative to forgiveness: He and the Corinthians could let Satan outwit them by robbing them of one of their own. But, using the plural very effectively to incorporate the Corinthians, Paul says, in effect, "That is not about to happen because *we* know Satan's plots" (v. 10, italics added).

REFLECTIONS

1. "Decide in favor of love," Paul's counsel to the Corinthians in 2:8 regarding the man who had been disciplined, is actually a good moral guideline for all of life. When we are torn in our deliberation between two choices, as we often are, one way to weigh out the two alternatives is to explore which one more fully or more directly favors love—love for God, love for others, and even (proper) love for ourselves. The latter may seem very difficult to imagine, but needs to be considered because Jesus' reaffirmation of Lev 19:18—"You shall love your neighbor as yourself" (NRSV)—assumes a proper self-love as the basis for reckoning what will count as love of neighbor.

2. Forgiveness is the indispensable condition of life (before God and with others). No one decides in favor of love each time; sometimes it is even too complex to reckon what favors love the most. Forgiveness is the turning to a clean page, a chance to start afresh, a readiness to let bygones be bygones. Forgiveness is made easier when two things are kept in mind. First, each of us has been forgiven by God—and has needed it! Second, forgiveness without a change in behavior, without subsequent actions and deeds that in fact show a different pattern of life from that which generated the need for repentance, cannot be counted as genuine. Genuine repentance moves beyond words of apology to deeds—indeed, to patterns of performance—that amount to what John the Baptist calls "fruits that befit repentance" (Luke 3:8).

2 CORINTHIANS 2:12-13, PAUL'S ANXIETY OVER TITUS THE LETTER BEARER

NIV

[12]Now when I went to Troas to preach the gospel of Christ and found that the Lord had opened a door for me, [13]I still had no peace of mind, because I did not find my brother Titus there. So I said good-by to them and went on to Macedonia.

NRSV

12When I came to Troas to proclaim the good news of Christ, a door was opened for me in the Lord; [13]but my mind could not rest because I did not find my brother Titus there. So I said farewell to them and went on to Macedonia.

COMMENTARY

This letter fragment is laced with accountings of Paul's travels, in part no doubt because Paul's promised, but failed, visit has heightened sensitivity about Paul's plans and how trustworthy he is (1:15-16; 2:1; 7:5). In the text at hand, Paul describes how he went to Troas, the Aegean seaport on northwest Asia. Not incidentally, he says he went there "on account of the gospel of Christ," subtly reaffirming his ethos or character as the one who is regularly focused on the gospel.[57] Also, predictably, Paul reports success: "A door was opened to me in the Lord" (2:12). The metaphor of a door being opened describes for Paul a challenging occasion for preaching the gospel (cf. 1 Cor 16:9). This pattern of Paul's going to a new place and proclaiming the gospel is his signature. The Corinthians know that is who he is. So when they hear his next claim—namely, that he was so anxious to hear from Titus that

he picked up and moved to Macedonia, where he would meet Titus (7:6)—they have a clear index of his deep concern for them. Without Titus to report on how things went with the Corinthians when they received Paul's painful letter, Paul reports that he had no "rest/relief" (ἄνεσις *anesis*), a term the opposite of θλῖψις (*thlipsis*), and a subtle, indirect echo of the affliction with which he opened the letter (2:13). Once again, he depicts himself as the one who is very deeply and properly concerned about the Corinthians. This little detail reinforces all his other claims in this letter to be consistently devoted to them and contributes to his ethos as a dependable friend.

Titus, like Timothy, is one of Paul's doubles who provides crucial liaisons with Pauline communities. Titus, a Gentile convert, was with Paul at the conference at Jerusalem and was not compelled to be circumcised (Gal 2:1, 3). When Paul chose not to make his projected visit to Corinth and sent his harsh letter to the Corinthians, it was

57. For a good treatment of ethos and its importance in relationships in Paul's time, see M. M. DiCicco, *Paul's Use of Ethos, Pathos, and Logos in 2 Corinthians 10–13* (Lewiston: Mellen Biblical, 1995) 36-112.

probably Titus who actually delivered the letter to the Corinthians. This supposition is supported by Paul's linking Titus so closely to the report of how the Corinthians responded to the letter (7:5-16; cf. 8:6, 16, 23; 12:18).

REFLECTIONS

Should we always take biblical characters to be examples worthy of imitation? Not likely! Cain slays his brother Abel. David has Bathsheba. Judas has his thirty pieces of silver. Peter denies Jesus. It is worth wondering whether Paul is a good example for emulation here. He leaves behind an "open door" to evangelize, which is his calling, and, because of intense anxiety, he seeks word about how the Corinthians have responded to his painful letter. If you had been in Paul's shoes, would you have done that or would you have stayed in Troas? Why?

2 CORINTHIANS 2:14–6:10, A MULTIFACETED TREATMENT OF PAUL'S MINISTRY

OVERVIEW

Alhough interpreters of this extended section understandably often mine it for its profound and rich theological claims, every portion of it is aimed by Paul not only at enhancing the Corinthians' understanding of his ministry among and for them, but also especially at binding them more closely to himself as their apostle. Given his recent experiences with them and their umbrage over his changed plans, a direct request for increased affection from the Corinthians would be far too risky a rhetorical move at this point. Rather than hazard further alienation of the Corinthians, Paul avails himself of the rhetorical option called *insinuatio,* which features a subtle approach and seeks to lay the ground for an affirmative response to himself that will be sought explicitly and directly only later in the letter (6:12-13; 7:2-4).[58]

The opening section (2:14-17) is rich with imagery that points to one end: Paul is the agent of God's powerful and triumphant gospel; Paul is part of a victory processional across the Mediterranean world that would make the Romans proud; and Paul is part of a vast sacrifice whose fragrance, though it is being offered up to God, is manifest to everyone around.

Then, in what amounts to a series of three complementary depictions that together make up the heart of this letter fragment, we see (1) Paul's as a ministry of a new covenant (3:1–4:6), (2) Paul's as a ministry sustained through affliction and mortality (4:7–5:10), and (3) Paul's as a ministry of reconciliation (5:11-21). The entire section closes with a primary appeal for the Corinthians not to receive the grace of God in vain (6:1-2) and, once more, a defense of Paul's apostolic probity and an insistence, yet once again, that Paul is worthy of exemplification and honor (6:3-10). The integrity and rectitude of Paul's ministry is *the* issue that laces together everything from 2:14 to 6:10.

58. So D. A. DeSilva, "Measuring Penultimate against Ultimate Reality: An Investigation of the Integrity and Argumentation of 2 Corinthians," *JSNT* 52 (1993) 57.

2 Corinthians 2:14-17, Paul's Place in God's Purposes

NIV

[14]But thanks be to God, who always leads us in triumphal procession in Christ and through us spreads everywhere the fragrance of the knowledge of him. [15]For we are to God the aroma of Christ among those who are being saved and those who are perishing. [16]To the one we are the smell of death; to the other, the fragrance of life. And who is equal to such a task? [17]Unlike so many, we do not peddle the word of God for profit. On the contrary, in Christ we speak before God with sincerity, like men sent from God.

NRSV

14But thanks be to God, who in Christ always leads us in triumphal procession, and through us spreads in every place the fragrance that comes from knowing him. [15]For we are the aroma of Christ to God among those who are being saved and among those who are perishing; [16]to the one a fragrance from death to death, to the other a fragrance from life to life. Who is sufficient for these things? [17]For we are not peddlers of God's word like so many;[a] but in Christ we speak as persons of sincerity, as persons sent from God and standing in his presence.

[a]Other ancient authorities read *like the others*

COMMENTARY

Shifting to the plural again and employing a formula of thanksgiving (cf. 8:16; 9:15), "Thanks be to God," Paul places himself among the wider group of his colleagues—that is, his coworkers and perhaps even other apostles who, in Christ, are put on display by God in triumph. "Thanks be to God" (τῷ δὲ θεῷ χάρις *tō de theō charis*) is a Pauline expression that he evokes when he wants to honor the great power of God to transform and redeem; so the phrase appears in passages where Paul is recognizing transformation—that is, where God's own "grace" (χάρις *charis*) toward believers is honored by a reflection of the grace back to God in thankfulness. Accordingly, former "slaves of sin" become, "thanks to God," "slaves of righteousness" (Rom 6:17-18) in Christ Jesus (Rom 6:23) and are delivered from death, "thanks to God," through Jesus Christ (Rom 7:24-25). A similar "thanks be to God" is sounded at the climax of Paul's discourse on resurrection, where he celebrates the gift of God's victory (in 1 Cor 15:57, τὸ νῖκος *to nikos*, a military motif like that of 2:14; cf. Col 2:15) over death through Jesus Christ (1 Cor 15:57). All of these "thanks to God" formulations, including the one that opens v. 14, are therefore eschatological acknowledgments of God's great power to deliver in Christ.

In v. 14 Paul portrays himself as a vanquished captive who is put on display along with others, as caught up by God's triumphant march of the gospel. Two further textual clues, the one temporal, the other spatial, evince Paul's desire to associate himself with the one and only comprehensive action by God; the claim "always" (πάντοτε *pantote*) stresses God's—and by indirection, Paul's also—faithfulness and dependability; the assertion "in every place" (ἐν παντὶ τόπω *en panti topō*) ties Paul's known travels for the purpose of spreading the gospel prominently into God's overall effort.

All of Paul's communities will have been familiar with the Roman military's victory processions,[59] and Paul's rhetoric in vv. 14-16 would have called to his auditors' minds those processions in which defeated leaders were paraded in shame and disgrace. Just a few years earlier, in 44 CE, Claudius had defeated the southern Britons and came back home to stage a monumental triumph.[60] At least some of the Corinthians, as

59. Peter Marshall, "A Metaphor of Social Shame: ΘΡΙΑΜΒΕΥΕΙΝ in 2 Cor 2:14," *NovT* 25 (1983) 304, reckons that Greek and Roman literature record some 350 triumphs, many of which recount processionals. See S. J. Hafemann, *Suffering and the Spirit: An Exegetical Study of II Cor. 2:14–3:3 Within the Context of the Corinthian Correspondence* (Tübingen: Mohr, 1986) 22-31, for details of triumphal processions in that time.

60. Suetonius *Life of Claudius* 17.

residents of an official Roman colony city and, therefore, especially attuned to Rome, would have Claudius's triumphal procession in memory. In such processionals, "aromatic substances were also carried."[61]

Paul's use of θριαμβεύω (thriambeuō), though it most often is associated with military processions led by the victorious leaders as just suggested, may also call to mind an epiphany procession of deities such as Dionysus and Isis, who were regarded as victors and were thus honored with processions.[62] Likewise, the fragrance noted in vv. 15-16 may evoke memories of the triumphal incense burned in those very processions.[63] Paul co-opts established conceptions and practices as a way of describing God's awe-inspiring purposes and Paul's place in them.

The imagery of aroma (ὀσμη osmē, 2:14, 16) and fragrance (εὐωδία euōdia) probably evinces Paul's deep sense of life before God as a sacrifice of thanksgiving, as seen most clearly elsewhere in Rom 12:1: "I appeal to you, therefore, brothers and sisters, on account of the mercies of God, to present your bodies as a living sacrifice [θυσίαν ζῶσαν thysian zōsan], holy and pleasing to God." When the Philippians respond in partnership with Paul and send him support via their agent, Epaphroditus, Paul construes their backing as a "fragrant aroma [ὀσμὴν εὐωδίας osmēn euōdias], a sacrifice acceptable and pleasing to God" (Phil 4:18). Paul uses this terminology when he contemplates persons who, out of grateful thankfulness to God, consecrate themselves to God and act in loving service to others (see Phil 2:17 as an extreme personal example). Paul understands his own ministry in categories of Israel's sacrifices in Rom 15:16; on account of the grace given to Paul by God, he has become "a minister of Christ Jesus to the Gentiles, with the priestly service to the gospel of God, so that the offering of the Gentiles may be acceptable, sanctified in the Holy Spirit."

In all these instances the sacrifice is a thanksgiving offering to God, but in v. 14 its fragrance makes itself known to all those whom the procession passes as it journeys through the world. In vv. 14-17, Paul views those who represent the gospel, himself included, as the ones who make known the presence of God, much as the fragrance of Wisdom announces her presence in the world (Sir 24:15).

In a refinement of the fragrance imagery, Paul boldly and directly identifies himself as "the fragrance of Christ among the ones who are being saved and among the ones who are perishing" (v. 15). This antithetical construction is basic to Paul's rival two-way view of how people relate to God (cf. 1 Cor 1:18 and the Commentary there; cf. Matt 7:13-14; 2 Cor 4:3; 2 Thess 2:10). The contrast is stark, allowing no middle ground. One is either counted among the ones who are in process toward salvation or among the ones who are cut off from God and are, therefore, perishing. The Corinthians can hear an encoded message: Paul *is* the aroma of Christ; his gospel is *the* gospel; *they* came to faith—that is, they were included among those who are being saved—through *his* spreading of the gospel, the aroma of Christ; the alternative, stark as it is, awaits them if they turn their backs on Paul.

His even further elaboration of the fragrance imagery—"to the ones an aroma from death to death, to the others, an aroma from life to life" (v. 16)—emphasizes that the ones who are being saved are in process, moving from life to (even more and permanent) life, a thought that will receive confirmation and development in 4:16–5:5. Similarly, those who are perishing have death as their current status, and their future is (permanent) death. Seeing these mutually exclusive alternatives, whose choice dictates not only present status, but also eternal fate, the Corinthians do well to cleave to Paul.

The whole picture is so grand, the choices so final, that Paul throws up his hands in awe at his role in God's eternal purposes, asking, "Who is sufficient/competent [ἱκανός hikanos] for these things?" (v. 16c). By this gesture Paul affirms several claims. He has not chosen this role for himself, but has been selected by God, as the Corinthians well know (cf. 1 Cor 1:1, 17; 4:1; 9:16-17); he does not now arrogantly overreach

---

61. H. S. Versnel, *Triumphus: An Inquiry into the Origin, Development, and Meaning of the Roman Triumph* (Leiden: Brill, 1970) 95.

62. P. B. Duff, "Metaphor, Motif, and Meaning: The Rhetorical Strategy Behind the Image 'Led in Triumph' in 2 Corinthians 2:14," *CBQ* 53 (1991) 83, details literary and pictorial evidence. Duff takes συνέχω (synechō) in 2 Cor 5:14 to mean "to take or hold captive" and reads it to mean that the love of Christ, not a deity's vengeance, as 2:14 might wrongly be taken to suggest, has led Paul captive.

63. Incense was also used in epiphany processions as a manifestation of the deity. See ibid., 91. See also K. A. Plank, *Paul and the Irony of Affliction* (Atlanta: Scholars Press, 1987) 77.

but modestly and beyond his own comprehension finds himself playing this role in God's drama; and he lays the ground for his refinement of this notion a bit later when he will declare that competence or sufficiency rests not on human claims, but on God's graceful pleasure (3:4-6).

What starts out as a contrast between the ones who respond to the gospel positively and negatively (vv. 15-16) concludes with a contrast between "the many who huckster the word of God" and those who, like Paul, speak with moral sincerity and purity of motive (εἰλικρίνεια *eilikrineia*, v. 17*a;* this term echoes its earlier appearance in 1:12 as a Pauline attribute) and sets the stage for 3:1–4:6, where the contrast will be elaborated. The Greek of Paul's self-description is dense and powerful: Unlike those people, "the many" (οἱ πολλοὶ *hoi polloi*), Paul says, "We speak as *from* [ἐκ *ek*] God, *before* [κατέναντι *katenanti*] God, *in* [ἐν *en*] Christ" (v. 17*b*, italics added). With these prepositions Paul affirms that he is solidly among those commissioned by or sent from God, that he makes his proclamation as one who understands himself to be responsibly standing in God's presence, and finally that he knows himself firmly established in Christ. Though not daring to claim his worthiness to be entrusted with such a responsibility by God, Paul boldly affirms that by God's grace he does stand where he stands and does speak what he says as a part of God's plan. No wonder the next section questions whether Paul is again commending himself (3:1). Paul begins vv. 14-17 with the plural, clearly placing him alongside those others who are (also) God's proper agents. He closes it, still using the plural, but obviously thinking primarily of himself, as 3:1-3 makes clear.

Paul's distinction of himself (and those like him) from the "many who huckster the word of God" is difficult to assess. Has *he* been accused of doing so? He does not credit others with saying that (cf. 10:10*a*). For someone who has been so scrupulous as Paul at Corinth in insisting on self-support, Paul might be a difficult, hardly credible, target for such a charge. Is Paul deriding some specific people, perhaps the ones just about to be mentioned in 3:1-3, who have shown up in Corinth with letters of commendation? Of course, that is possible, but the sparseness of the evidence gives little ground for certainty. Also

possible, and at least as likely, Paul could be using a cultural commonplace about itinerant philosopher types—whom he superficially resembles in some ways, but who were also notorious for bilking their clients and moving on—as a foil for a more elaborate confirmation of his credentials and performance standards.[64]

We may wonder how Paul's self-description as one who by God, in Christ, is "always" being led[65] in triumph accords with his self-portrait in chap. 1, where he reports not only a scrape with death but also the sense of being "so utterly, unbearably crushed that we despaired of life itself" (1:8 NRSV). First, Paul is able to construe the same or similar circumstances in very different lights, depending on what angle of vision he takes on the matter. For example, in 1:8-11, he views his personal distress as something from which he hopes to be delivered; in Gal 4:12-15, he effectively credits illness with causing him to stay still long enough to preach to the Galatians. Second, and probably more germane, Paul's dramatic description of his Asian peril is an indirect appeal for pity and, at the same time, an effort to enhance his ethos with the Corinthians. Accordingly, he paints his distress in sensational proportions ("we despaired of life itself"; "In ourselves we had received the death sentence," 1:8-9). But those descriptions serve the theological point that follows them: "But this happened that we might not rely on ourselves but on God, who raises the dead" (1:9*b* NIV), a motif that resurfaces later in this letter fragment (cf. 4:7-12).

Finally, the Roman practice of triumphal parades had the victors leading the vanquished, so Paul's picture in vv. 14-17 does not portray him, and the representatives with whom he there counts himself, as *themselves* triumphing always. To the contrary, Paul here describes himself and his fellow ministers of the gospel as the conquered captives who, in the practices and according to the cultural values of his time, would normally

---

64. A. J. Malherbe, "Gentle as a Nurse," *NovT* 12 (1970) 203-17. M. E. Thrall, *The Second Epistle to the Corinthians* (Edinburgh: T. & T. Clark, 1994) 217, declares: "Paul's aim here is apologetic, not polemical."

65. Hafemann states that such a use of θριαμβεύω (*thriambeuō*) "*always* refers to the one having been conquered and subsequently led in the procession, and never to the one having conquered." See S. J. Hafemann, *Suffering and the Spirit: An Exegetical Study of II Cor. 2:14–3:3 Within the Context of the Corinthian Correspondence* (Tübingen: Mohr, 1986) 33.

be counted failures, who, at the parade's conclusion, would be slaughtered.

It is *God* who always triumphs; those who are led are not themselves triumphalists—a picture that accords very well with what Paul says about himself and the other apostles in a passage he had earlier written to these Corinthians: "For it seems to me that God has put us apostles on display at the end of the procession, like men condemned to die in the arena" (1 Cor 4:9-13 NIV).[66]

How does this august processional portrait of God's triumphing and leading Paul (and the others represented by the use of plurals) fit into the context of Paul's leaving Troas and going to Macedonia to hear about the Corinthians? Paul pictures himself as the one who, like captives on display, are led along by God in God's processional, captives who nevertheless are the ones through whom God is spreading the fragrance of God's salvific presence across the world. It is at once a humble and an exalted portrait of Paul and his ministry; Paul is not in charge, and yet through him God spreads the gospel. Paul may be so distracted by his concern for the Corinthians that he leaves an open door in Troas, but God does not abandon him or allow any place to miss the fragrance (see v. 14c). In v. 14 Paul celebrates the fact that God is triumphing whether or not Paul is as focused on his evangelizing as he should be.[67]

---

66. P. B. Duff, "Metaphor, Motif, and Meaning: The Rhetorical Strategy Behind the Image 'Led in Triumph' in 2 Corinthians 2:14," *CBQ* 53 (1991) 91, says that Paul's self-portrait as a defeated person embraces the image that his opponents have propagated; it may just as well have played into their hands.

67. So A. C. Perriman, "Between Troas and Macedonia: 2 Cor 2:13-14," *ExpTim* 101 (1989) 40.

REFLECTIONS

1. Life is not static, for Paul or for us. Witness the youth who thinks the world is his oyster, or the older woman who finds herself suddenly alone when her loved one has died. Changes can be for the better or for the worse. In the text before us ("from life to life," 2:16), Paul sees the life of faith as one of progress or growth. When we test our own lives against a pattern of constant enhancement as the desideratum, we are likely to be disappointed and may even become despondent. But Paul nowhere says that this progress is experienced in a straight line. As noted in the Commentary, even Paul's life is not always one of success and progress, but *over time* one's faith, no matter how weak or strong, should grow or improve (Rom 4:20; 14:1; 2 Cor 10:15; 13:9; Phil 1:25).

2. Paul's clear picture of two antithetical groups (one progressing toward salvation and the other in the process of perishing) may seem harsh, and it can even be foolish if we go around trying to sort people into opposing groups. Behind the description of the two groups is a Pauline conviction that one either trusts or believes God or one does not. There is no Pauline middle ground of being just a little bit wicked. Paul probably comes by that understanding from his Scriptures, in which the choice between blessing, life, and prosperity, on the one side, is balanced by curse, death, and adversity on the other side (cf. Deut 30:15-20; Prov 11:19; 14:27; Jer 21:8).

3. It is often said that actions speak louder than words. Paul offers a slight adaptation here: He thinks that the life of faith, in which one offers oneself as a sacrifice of thanksgiving to God (Rom 12:1), has a fragrance that is noticeable and that commends itself to others. For yet another variation on the same theme, see the depiction of believers as letters of commendation written on the hearts and legible by all in 3:2-3. Maybe a helpful way to order things is to worry first about your deeds and whether they are manifestations of love for others and then trust that the proper oral expressions of your convictions or faith will come whenever they are ready.

2 Corinthians 3:1–4:6, Paul's Ministry of a New Covenant

NIV

3 Are we beginning to commend ourselves again? Or do we need, like some people, letters of recommendation to you or from you? [2]You yourselves are our letter, written on our hearts, known and read by everybody. [3]You show that you are a letter from Christ, the result of our ministry, written not with ink but with the Spirit of the living God, not on tablets of stone but on tablets of human hearts.

[4]Such confidence as this is ours through Christ before God. [5]Not that we are competent in ourselves to claim anything for ourselves, but our competence comes from God. [6]He has made us competent as ministers of a new covenant—not of the letter but of the Spirit; for the letter kills, but the Spirit gives life.

[7]Now if the ministry that brought death, which was engraved in letters on stone, came with glory, so that the Israelites could not look steadily at the face of Moses because of its glory, fading though it was, [8]will not the ministry of the Spirit be even more glorious? [9]If the ministry that condemns men is glorious, how much more glorious is the ministry that brings righteousness! [10]For what was glorious has no glory now in comparison with the surpassing glory. [11]And if what was fading away came with glory, how much greater is the glory of that which lasts!

[12]Therefore, since we have such a hope, we are very bold. [13]We are not like Moses, who would put a veil over his face to keep the Israelites from gazing at it while the radiance was fading away. [14]But their minds were made dull, for to this day the same veil remains when the old covenant is read. It has not been removed, because only in Christ is it taken away. [15]Even to this day when Moses is read, a veil covers their hearts. [16]But whenever anyone turns to the Lord, the veil is taken away. [17]Now the Lord is the Spirit, and where the Spirit of the Lord is, there is freedom. [18]And we, who with unveiled faces all reflect[a] the Lord's glory, are being transformed into his likeness with ever-increasing glory, which comes from the Lord, who is the Spirit.

[a]18 Or *contemplate*

NRSV

3 Are we beginning to commend ourselves again? Surely we do not need, as some do, letters of recommendation to you or from you, do we? [2]You yourselves are our letter, written on our[a] hearts, to be known and read by all; [3]and you show that you are a letter of Christ, prepared by us, written not with ink but with the Spirit of the living God, not on tablets of stone but on tablets of human hearts.

[4]Such is the confidence that we have through Christ toward God. [5]Not that we are competent of ourselves to claim anything as coming from us; our competence is from God, [6]who has made us competent to be ministers of a new covenant, not of letter but of spirit; for the letter kills, but the Spirit gives life.

[7]Now if the ministry of death, chiseled in letters on stone tablets,[b] came in glory so that the people of Israel could not gaze at Moses' face because of the glory of his face, a glory now set aside, [8]how much more will the ministry of the Spirit come in glory? [9]For if there was glory in the ministry of condemnation, much more does the ministry of justification abound in glory! [10]Indeed, what once had glory has lost its glory because of the greater glory; [11]for if what was set aside came through glory, much more has the permanent come in glory!

[12]Since, then, we have such a hope, we act with great boldness, [13]not like Moses, who put a veil over his face to keep the people of Israel from gazing at the end of the glory that[c] was being set aside. [14]But their minds were hardened. Indeed, to this very day, when they hear the reading of the old covenant, that same veil is still there, since only in Christ is it set aside. [15]Indeed, to this very day whenever Moses is read, a veil lies over their minds; [16]but when one turns to the Lord, the veil is removed. [17]Now the Lord is the Spirit, and where the Spirit of the Lord is, there is freedom. [18]And all of us, with unveiled faces, seeing the glory of the Lord as though reflected in a mirror, are being transformed into the same image from one degree of glory to another; for this comes from the Lord, the Spirit.

[a]Other ancient authorities read *your*   [b]Gk *on stones*   [c]Gk *of what*

NIV

4 Therefore, since through God's mercy we have this ministry, we do not lose heart. [2]Rather, we have renounced secret and shameful ways; we do not use deception, nor do we distort the word of God. On the contrary, by setting forth the truth plainly we commend ourselves to every man's conscience in the sight of God. [3]And even if our gospel is veiled, it is veiled to those who are perishing. [4]The god of this age has blinded the minds of unbelievers, so that they cannot see the light of the gospel of the glory of Christ, who is the image of God. [5]For we do not preach ourselves, but Jesus Christ as Lord, and ourselves as your servants for Jesus' sake. [6]For God, who said, "Let light shine out of darkness,"[a] made his light shine in our hearts to give us the light of the knowledge of the glory of God in the face of Christ.

[a]6 Gen. 1:3

NRSV

4 Therefore, since it is by God's mercy that we are engaged in this ministry, we do not lose heart. [2]We have renounced the shameful things that one hides; we refuse to practice cunning or to falsify God's word; but by the open statement of the truth we commend ourselves to the conscience of everyone in the sight of God. [3]And even if our gospel is veiled, it is veiled to those who are perishing. [4]In their case the god of this world has blinded the minds of the unbelievers, to keep them from seeing the light of the gospel of the glory of Christ, who is the image of God. [5]For we do not proclaim ourselves; we proclaim Jesus Christ as Lord and ourselves as your slaves for Jesus' sake. [6]For it is the God who said, "Let light shine out of darkness," who has shone in our hearts to give the light of the knowledge of the glory of God in the face of Jesus Christ.

COMMENTARY

Paul must walk a fine line. He is chosen by God to be an apostle, and he is their apostle, as the Corinthians surely realize (cf. 1 Cor 9:2). That divine commission places Paul solidly in God's august plan, which is sweeping the known world. The Corinthians, however, have just been through a time when they did not think very highly of Paul—surely not as highly as he would have preferred. And even now he is working to cement their relation to him. So his boasting about the gospel has built into it the risk that some Corinthians will think he is blowing his own horn.[68]

Paul employs syncrisis, the rhetorical mode of comparison, in this section of his letter.[69] He has described most others besides himself as "huckstering" the gospel, an image suggesting that, unlike himself, they are in it for what they can get out of it as they hawk the gospel around the Mediterranean (2:17). Now he further contrasts himself with those few who need letters of rec-

ommendation to enhance their status (3:1). In the highly stratified Roman society of Paul's time, letters of commendation were commonplaces.[70] The bearers of such letters came with the stamp of approval of someone of standing whose recommendation the letters' recipients would be expected to honor. Typically such letters praised and endorsed the subject person;[71] sometimes they even requested a favor or the granting of special status to the one named in the letter (see Rom 16:1-2).

Paul does not operate that way. He does not depend on such sycophantic catering. He prefers to have his work speak for itself—and that is exactly what he thinks the Corinthians, who are indisputably his work in the gospel (1 Cor 9:1d), should do. So he turns the Roman practice of commendatory letters on its head and avers that

68. For a thoughtful reflection on Paul's boasting, see C. K. Barrett, "Boasting (καυχάομαι.κτλ.) in the Pauline Epistles," in *L'Apôtre Paul*, ed. A. Vanhoye (Leuven: University of Leuven Press, 1986) 363-68.

69. C. Forbes, "Comparison, Self-Praise and Irony: Paul's Boasting and the Conventions of Hellenistic Rhetoric," *NTS* 32 (1986) 2-8.

70. L. L. Belleville, "A Letter of Apologetic Self-recommendation: 2 Cor 1:8–7:16," *NovT* 31 (1989) 152, treats commendation letters in an informative way. See also J. White, "The Greek Documentary Letter Tradition, Third Century B.C.E. to Third Century C.E.," *Semeia* 22 (1981) 96; S. K. Stowers, *Letter Writing in Greco-Roman Antiquity* (Philadelphia: Westminster, 1986) 154-55; and W. Baird, "Letters of Recommendation: A Study of II Cor 3 1-3," *JBL* 80 (1961) 168.

71. Stowers, *Letter Writing in Greco-Roman Antiquity*, 79-80.

the Corinthians themselves are his letters, "written on human hearts" (3:3) and available for all to know and read (3:2). This note will reappear, with more Pauline distress, in 12:11, where Paul will have come to realize that those who have shown up in Corinth with letters of recommendation threaten his standing with the Corinthian believers.

The idea that Paul's commendatory letters have been written on flesh-and-blood hearts (καρδίαις σαρκίναις *kardiais sarkinais*) echoes Jeremiah's prophecy of a new covenant, not like the old one "with their ancestors . . . a covenant that they broke" (Jer 31:31-32 NRSV), but one written "on their hearts" (Jer 31:33; cf. Jer 38:33 LXX). This structures a fundamentally antithetical set of claims that appear from 3:1 through 4:6.

The first antithesis is between letters of commendation that some self-servingly carry with them and letters written on hearts (it matters not much whether the writing is on the Corinthians' hearts or on Paul's; the point is that what is written there can be read and understood by "all people" [ὑπὸ πάντων ἀνθρώπων *hypo panton anthrōpōn*]), which when read reveal that the Corinthian believers are, indeed, "a letter from Christ" (3:3). The contrast is carried even further: The letter has been cared for (one can imagine "written and delivered"; the Greek term is a form of διακονέω [*diakoneō*], which will appear very importantly in the following verses in the nominal form διακονία [*diakonia*], when Paul will characterize his own "ministry") by Paul and was written not with ink, but "by the Spirit of the living God" (cf. 1 Thess 1:9). The Jeremiah echo emerges most clearly in the last contrast: "Not in stone tablets, but in tablets of flesh-and-blood hearts" (3:3; cf. Jer 31:33).

The second antithesis, a refinement of the first, is between competence established by human claim or accomplishment and competence declared by God. God is the ground of Paul's confidence and competence. The claim that Paul's confidence comes through Christ is shorthand for a huge convictional base in Paul. Association with Christ, with his death and suffering, is the ground for Paul's assurance that he will ultimately overcome death and move beyond suffering into joyful, perpetual presence with God, just as Christ, the firstfruits and the firstborn of many brothers

and sisters, has (already) been raised (Rom 8:29; 1 Cor 15:20, 23). It is Christ, himself raised, who makes it possible for Paul to rely not on himself "but on the God who raises the dead" (2 Cor 1:9).

Paul has continued to use plurals throughout the section that deals with his own competence and, therefore, authority. By that choice he has reduced the opportunity for any disgruntled Corinthians to deny that God has commissioned ministers of the gospel such as Paul. Paul's case does not rest on their judgment about him alone, but about all those with whom Paul associates himself as the ones who preach the gospel as it should be, without any personal gain and without any self-aggrandisement. To deny Paul any divinely given competence would require that all other ministers and apostles also be discredited.

Paul credits the Holy Spirit, here called "the Spirit of the living God" (3:3), with having done the writing on human hearts. When he recalls the Roman believers' beginnings of their faith, Paul reminds them that the Spirit joined with their spirits and enabled them to articulate the response of babies calling upon their father: *Abba ho Pater* (ἀββα ὁ πατήρ; Rom 8:15-16).

At the heart of this very complex two-covenant passage (3:1–4:6) lies a quite simple point:[72] Paul's ministry, governed by the Spirit, producing life, and worthy of Corinthian embrace, is radically contrasted with what he dramatically characterizes as the "ministry of death."[73]

To understand what Paul has done in 3:1–4:6, we must know the biblical passages he interlaces, in chain-of-association form,[74] into his own text. Although there are allusions to other biblical texts,

---

72. B. Wagner, "Alliance de la lettre, alliance de l'esprit: essai d'analyse de 2 Corinthiens 2:14 à 3:18," *ETR* 60 (1985) 65, rightly argues against construing this text as "un exposé doctrinal" where every term must be mined.

73. Once again, Paul's purpose is apologetic, not polemical. See Thrall, *The Second Epistle to the Corinthians*, 237. However, on 297-318, she construes 4:1-6 as a "defence of ministry" and does not see the overarching apologetic purpose argued for in this commentary.

74. E. Richard, "Polemics, Old Testament, and Theology: A Study of II Cor., III,1-IV,6," *RB* 88 (1981) 342-44, affirms Paul's associative flow of thought but questions the appropriateness of using the term "midrash" (cf. his good history of recent research). Fitzmyer states that Paul's argument flows by "the free association of ideas which runs through the entire passage" so that, for example, epistle of recommendation becomes epistles written on the heart, and so on. See J. A. Fitzmyer, "Glory Reflected on the Face of Christ (2 Cor 3:7–4:6) and a Palestinian Jewish Motif," *TS* 42 (1981) 631-32. R. B. Hays, *Echoes of Scripture in the Letters of Paul* (New Haven: Yale University Press, 1989) esp. 125-49, sensitively examines Paul's linking of scriptural passages through 2 Corinthians 3.

Paul builds primarily from two, one about Moses and the other about Jeremiah's prophecy of a new covenant.[75] Like his Jewish coreligionist contemporaries, Paul relates to both passages freely, highlights what interests him, ignores what does not, and weaves his own message through the old accounts.[76] The two primary texts are the story of Moses and the stone tablets (Exod 34:29-35) and Jeremiah's new covenant promise (Jer 31:31-34). A rehearsal of both, highlighting Paul's salient interests in them, will aid the interpretation of Paul's own composition.

Central to the first account is Moses' encounter with God, or more particularly with God's glory, in the giving of the commandments and the covenant expressed through them. On Moses' second trip up Mt. Sinai (the first ended in the broken stone tablets [Exod 32:19] when Moses saw that the people were unfaithful while he was gone), Moses is assured that God's "face will go with you," a way of guaranteeing God's presence and favorable disposition (Exod 33:14). Moses beseeches God, "Show me your glory, I pray" (Exod 33:18). God responds by pledging divine presence and graciousness (Exod 33:19), but cautions Moses that "no one shall see my face and live" (Exod 33:20, 23). God then details all the steps that will be taken to protect Moses on the mountaintop while God's fearsome and awe-filled glory passes by (Exod 33:22; cf. 1 Kgs 19:11-12; Hab 3:3-4).

The reader of Exodus has been prepared to understand that God's glory is not to be taken lightly. God's glory is a sign of divine presence in the cloud that led the Israelites in the exodus from Egypt (Exod 16:10; Num 16:42). God's glory is "like a devouring fire" (Exod 24:17 NRSV). When the Lord looked down directly upon the Egyptian army, they were thrown into panic (Exod 14:24); the splendor of God's face, "no longer veiled by cloud, 'panics' the Egyptians, who recognize him."[77]

When Moses comes down off the mountain with the stone "tablets of the covenant" (Exod 24:12; 31:18; 34:1; Deut 4:13; 5:22; 9:10), he does not realize that his face shines as a reflection of God's glory. But Aaron and the Israelites do, and their response of fear is exactly appropriate as a response to God's glory (Exod 34:30). When Moses has called them to him and finished telling them of the Lord's commands, Moses puts a veil over his face (Exod 34:33), much as the cloud had covered God's glory earlier (Exod 24:16). In the verses that follow, Moses is depicted as alternating between meeting with God ("whenever Moses went in before the LORD," Exod 34:34 NRSV) without a veil and covering his face "again" (Exod 34:35) with a veil when the Israelites again see his face, whose "skin was shining" (Exod 34:34-35).

In two powerful ways, Paul interlaces the Jeremiah passage with the one about Moses. First there is the shared reference to covenant (Exod 34:27-28; Jer 31:32-33). Second, Paul makes an implicit contrast of Jeremiah's "I will write it on their hearts" (Jer 31:33 NRSV) with the old covenant, whose statutes, according to the first passage and widely in Israel's Scriptures, were written or cut into stone (implied, but not stated in Jeremiah 31).

Paul weaves these two scriptural accounts throughout his own passage (3:1–4:6), sometimes taking over a detail of the story as is, other times dwelling on one particular, and in other instances changing the detail or taking advantage of it for his particular application. Within Paul's construction, though, he adopts the stance that is present in Jeremiah's depiction of the promised new covenant. In part, the new is described as an alteration of the older, previous covenant.

The passage (3:1–4:6) is like a tapestry that merits close examination first of the most obvious pattern of the weave, the weft, which is cast from one side to the other.[78] This left-to-right fabric is conspicuous because Paul has a fundamentally antithetical message to communicate by it to the Corinthians. Later we will explore the warp, those lines that move vertically down through the pas-

---

75. T. B. Savage, *Power Through Weakness: Paul's Understanding of the Christian Ministry in 2 Corinthians* (New York: Cambridge University Press, 1996) 106-10, demonstrates considerable elite and popular contemporary Gentile interest in Moses as well as remarkable contemporary Jewish regard for him.

76. Using the "poetic function of dissimile," Hays rightly suggests that "it becomes unnecessary to postulate a pre-Pauline source for Paul's midrash on Exodus 34 in order to account for the internal tensions of the passage." See Hays, *Echoes of Scripture in the Letters of Paul,* xii.

77. E. L. Greenstein, *The HarperCollins Study Bible,* ed. W. A. Meeks (New York: HarperCollins, 1989) 105.

78. On the literary unity of 3:1–4:6, see E. Richard, "Polemics, Old Testament, and Theology: A Study of II Cor., III,1-IV,6," *RB* 88 (1981) 363-64.

sage and express continuity between the old and the new.

The texture across the passage is structured predominantly on an "A, not B" type of argumentation. Paul's primary interest is to depict himself and his ministry (*diakonia*)[79] positively, and he builds, *via negativa*, from that positive depiction to contrast the ministry that is not his. He evinces no genuine concern for any other ministry; his descriptions of the alternate ministry, as indeed of all the contrasts in this passage, are of interest to him solely as they illuminate, elucidate, and enhance his own ministry, *via negativa*. Understandably, he is trumpeting his own ministry and should not be mistaken for advertising an alternative. It is irrelevant, therefore, to wonder if there are people who would embrace Paul's alternative ministry as their own. The negative parts of Paul's rhetoric are not descriptive of anyone but are there simply and solely to amplify himself and his ministry.

The following table features the contrasts that are structured through the passage:

79. J. N. Collins, "The Mediatorial Aspect of Paul's Role as *diakonos*," *AusBR* 40 (1992) 36, takes the term to mean "messenger of the divine" in Paul's self-application.

Figure 2: The Two Ministries and Their Consequences

letter versus Spirit

not of letter (3:6)	but new covenant of Spirit (3:6)
letter kills (3:6)	Spirit gives life (3:6)

rival ministries

diakonia of death (3:7)	*diakonia* of Spirit (3:8)
diakonia of condemnation (3:9)	*diakonia* of righteousness (3:9)
perishing/transitory (3:11)	permanent (which remains [τὸ μένον *to menon*]) (3:11)

rival representatives

not like Moses (3:13)	Paul (3:12)

rival consequences

	advantages of Paul's ministry
minds hardened (3:14)	
veil over heart (3:15; "minds," NRSV)	we all with unveiled face, contemplating the glory of the Lord, are being transformed (3:18)

Paul's own comportment illuminated by contrast with its opposite

hidden things of darkness (4:2)	
walking in craftiness	with disclosure of truth not falsifying God's word

reason for this behavior

God of this age blinded the minds of the unbelievers (4:4)	mercifully God has granted this ministry (4:1)

By the starkest of contrasts, Paul depicts his own ministry, still using the plural as a way of identifying himself with the mainstream, as having been granted by God (4:1),[80] as powered by the Holy Spirit (3:6), as generating righteousness among believers (3:9), as permanent (3:11), and as efficacious (Paul and his adherents are in the process of being transformed, 3:18). Confirmation for the Corinthian believers—and an encouragement for them to identify with Paul as they hear or read this passage—is secured by Paul's radically negative portrayal of the alternative ministry and of its negative results for discernment and moral reasoning. The rival ministry is governed by the concern with the letter, which kills (3:6), and so it is a ministry whose result is death (3:7), in which minds are hardened (3:14) and hearts are veiled over (3:15; "minds," NRSV). Its adherents are counted among the unbelievers who serve the god of this age, Satan,[81] who has blinded their

80. Collins, ibid., 37-41, gives ample evidence that in the Greco-Roman world a *diakonos* was a "go-between" or "message-bearer."

81. S. R. Garrett, "The God of This World and the Affliction of Paul: 2 Cor 4:1-12," in *Greeks, Romans and Christians: Essays in Honor of A. J. Malherbe*, ed. D. Balch, W. A. Meeks, and E. Ferguson (Minneapolis: Fortress, 1990) 104.

minds (4:4; darkness and blindness characterize Satan's reign: Luke 22:53; Acts 13:4-12; 26:18; 2 Cor 6:14-15; Eph 6:12; Col 1:13; *T. Sim.* 2:7; *T. Levi* 19:1).

Romans 8:2 has the same antinomy and the same rhetorical purpose, striving as it does to depict the "law of the Spirit of life in Christ Jesus" as prevailing over the negatively portrayed alternative, the "law of sin and death." The Spirit always prevails over death for Paul.

It would be misleading, however, to construe the entire passage as being structured simply antithetically. Indeed, 3:1–4:6 does begin with strong adversatives: letter versus Spirit; kills versus gives life; and ministry of death versus ministry of Spirit and righteousness. Translations and other interpretations have taken that set of contrarieties and wrongly transposed them into a sort of schema of history. For example, the RSV translated *diakonia* into "dispensation" and thus encouraged interpreters to read Paul as taking these two contrasts as sequential, supersessionist covenants, with the latter *superseding* and replacing the former.[82] It was then easy for an interpreter to claim that Paul has here a view of history, an *Heilsgeschichte* or sacred history, in which the new covenant and its "dispensation" have replaced the old.[83]

To correct such a view, we need to follow the way Paul has formulated the tapestry of his argument along the warp of the fabric. What began as a plain contrast, because Paul was justifying his own ministry over against any other ministry—so he set up an opposite that by contrast illuminated and made his own ministry more appealing—moves in 3:7-11 into a threefold use of a widespread Hellenistic and Jewish rhetorical pattern of argument "from the lesser to the greater."[84]

(1) A verse-long protasis, whose condition-of-fact statement affirms that the ministry that ended in death (taking διακονία τοῦ θανάτου [*diakonia tou thanatou*] as a genitive of result or direction,

"that brought death," NIV) came, indeed, in "glory/splendor" (δόξα *doxa*, 3:7), sets up an apodosis, or conclusion, that argues, "How much more shall the ministry of Spirit [a genitive of origin or quality] be in glory?" (3:8). So both ministries have glory. Comparison has taken the place of absolute contrast;[85] distinction with a desire to laud the second glory now replaces antithesis.

(2) In the succeeding verse, Paul continues the same reasoning from the lesser to the greater: "If there was glory in the ministry that resulted in condemnation, how much more the ministry of righteousness abounds in glory" (3:9). Once again, Paul assumes that glory is present in *both* ministries, but the glory of the one mentioned second—namely, the one Paul is privileged to be a part of—surpasses the glory of the one mentioned first. Indeed, in the very next verse Paul refines his view of the relationship of the two glories and their respective ministries, arguing that "in this case" the "surpassing glory" associated with Paul's ministry so overwhelms the previous glory as to suggest that the former had no glory at all (3:10).

Paul's oxymoronic construction—"what was glorified has no glory" (καὶ γὰρ οὐ δεδόξασται το δεδοξασμένον *kai gar ou dedoxastai to dedoxasmenon*)—must be considered carefully. With this expression, Paul is trying to provide perspective and proportion that adequately honor the incredible glory associated with God's "new creation," as he will call it just ahead (5:17). Its glory is so prodigious as to reduce to naught anything compared to it. That is not the same as denying glory to the other ministry.[86] The old ministry is critiqued *by comparison with the ministry of the Spirit* and *for the results that it delivered:* condemnation and ultimately death. In his argument here Paul finds himself very much in a situation similar to that reflected in his argument in Romans 7: The law, even though through it people found death (Rom 7:8-10), is nevertheless holy, and its commandments are "holy, just and good" (Rom 7:12). The thing itself, whether a ministry or the law, can be said to have been good even though people derived negative results from it.

---

82. See R. B. Hays, *Echoes of Scripture in the Letters of Paul* (New Haven: Yale University Press, 1989) 156-60, for a thoughtful critique of supersessionist readings of 2 Corinthians 3.

83. Another RSV translation facilitated this misinterpretation. Taking γράμμα (*gramma*) in 3:6 not simply as "letter" but as "written code" could mislead one to think of the entirety of Israel's Scriptures as alien to the Spirit, a position Paul nowhere embraces; the problem with the writings of the "old covenant" is simply that they cannot be read and understood apart from the Lord (3:14), not that they should be jettisoned (cf. Rom 7:12; 2 Cor 1:20).

84. Quintillian *Inst.* 5.11.9-12.

85. So E. Richard, "Polemics, Old Testament, and Theology: A Study of II Cor., III,1-IV,6," *RB* 88 (1981) 353.

86. Contra S. Hafemann, "Paul's Argument from the Old Testament and Christology in 2 Cor 1–9," in *The Corinthian Correspondence,* ed. R. Bieringer (Leuven: University of Leuven Press, 1966) 292, in an otherwise insightful interpretation.

(3) The same general perspective is reflected in Paul's next verse (3:11), where he once again confirms that there was glory before ("For if what is passing away came in glory . . ." 3:11*a*) and avers "how much more has the permanent come in glory" (3:11*b*).

Because "glory" (δόξα *doxa*) is such a major theme in 3:1–4:6 (used 14 times), we must examine Paul's usage of it. From Israel's Scriptures, Paul derives the notion of glorification in two ways: (1) God is known to manifest an awe-inspiring glory, and, in connection with Moses and the mountain (cf. Exod 33:19-22), God assures Moses that he will recognize God because God's glory will pass by and the Lord's name will be called (Exod 33:19). (2) Paul recalls the story about Moses' face glowing with glory after the latter had met with God on the mountain and received the stone tablets of the covenant (Exod 34:29, 35).

Among other confirmations that Paul is primarily focused on his own ministry are these: The rhetorical target is (twice) expressed in the expression "present day" (σήμερον *sēmeron*, 3:14-15), whereby Paul brings his message to bear on his Corinthian hearers; Paul's explicit inclusion of his Corinthian hearers in the expression "we all" (ἡμεῖς δὲ πάντες *hēmeis de pantes*, 3:18); throughout 3:1–4:6 Paul is much more detailed about the new covenant and its characteristics; and Paul's concluding description of his comportment in this new-covenant ministry (4:1-6).

The key to understanding Paul's interest in the two-covenant passage lies in 3:18 where, for the first time, he *explicitly* invites his Corinthian hearers to make a direct identification with what he is writing: "And we all, with unveiled face, looking at the glory of the Lord as in a mirror, are being transformed into his image, from glory to glory, for this comes from the Lord, the Spirit."

As has been noted throughout this commentary, Paul's use of "we" formulations occasionally challenges the interpreter, but in the passage at hand the usage is straightforward. He opens 3:1 with "we" formulations because he wants to depict his own ministry as a part of the one he will magnify by contrasting and comparing it with Moses. From 3:1 until 3:18 Paul's "we" references function primarily as self-descriptions, though secondarily they also cast him as being in the mainline with the others with whom he

happily identifies. But with 3:18 and its *hēmeis de pantes* ("we all," "ourselves"), Paul explicitly widens his scope to include the Corinthians (and all believers) and bids them to associate with his multifaceted portrait of them (and of himself), which is contained in this verse.

The verse defines—that is, describes—*who* the believers are, and positions the Corinthians (again, along with Paul) by describing *where* they are in God's unfolding purposes. In good Pauline fashion, the latter always involves depicting where they are now (which Paul elsewhere describes by "already" statements) and where they will be in God's larger plan (which Paul in other places sketches under the rubric "not yet").[87]

The first two items of the verse—"with unveiled face" and "looking at the glory of the Lord as in a mirror"—are woven together out of what has preceded. The notion of veiling goes through three distinguishable phases in this passage. First, the veiling of the face comes from Paul's adaptation of the Moses story in the preceding verses. Paul builds from his recitation of the pattern of Moses' covering his face as it reflects the glory of God (2 Cor 3:7, 13). Moses' facial glory was derived from his being in God's presence, but Paul treats it almost like a tan that, without further and renewed exposure, fades.[88] The account in Exod 34:29-35, if it gives a motive for Moses' veiling his face, may suggest that he did it to alleviate the Israelites' fear that he of shiny face looked like a deity (Exod 34:30). Paul provides a very different motive: Moses covers his face "so that the children of Israel should not look intently at the finish of what [the glory, understood] was passing away" (3:13); but this motive rests on Paul's distinctive interpretation that the glory associated with Moses is "passing away" (καταργέω

87. J. Paul Sampley, *Walking Between the Times: Paul's Moral Reasoning* (Minneapolis: Fortress, 1991) 11-20.

88. L. L. Belleville, "Tradition or Creation? Paul's Use of the Exodus 34 Tradition in 2 Corinthians 3:7-18," in *Paul and the Scriptures of Israel,* ed. C. A. Evans and J. A. Sanders (Sheffield: JSOT, 1993) 165-84, gives ample evidence to suggest that Paul's interpretation of Moses' fading glory was not unique among contemporary Jews; it need not be understood as having been generated by Paul's opponents. V. P. Furnish, *II Corinthians,* AB 33 (Garden City: Doubleday, 1984) 203, rejects the interpretation of fading and prefers annulment, writing of a "glory which, because it is part of the old covenant, is to be annulled as is that covenant." This view is followed by N. T. Wright, "Reflected Glory: 2 Corinthians 3:18," in *The Glory of Christ in the New Testament: Studies in Christology in Memory of George Bradford Caird,* ed. L. D. Hurst and N. T. Wright (Oxford: Clarendon, 1987) 144. M. D. Hooker, "Beyond the Things That Are Written? St. Paul's Use of Scripture," *NTS* 27 (1981) 291, 303-4, dismisses annulment.

katargeō). The term *katargeō* plays a big role in this passage, appearing four times (3:7, 11, 13, 14), and its interpretation is critical. Its semantic range includes "make ineffective, powerless," "nullify," "wipe out, abolish," "set aside"; in the passive, as here, it may mean "cease," "pass away" (3:7, 14), and in the substantive (3:11, 13), "what is transitory."[89]

Second, Paul shifts ground and takes the veiling motif into new, metaphorical territory when he moves the discussion so that it bears on time contemporary with himself and his audience (σήμερον ἡμέρας *sēmeron hēmeras*, "this day/to-day," 3:14-15) and declares that contemporary, non-believing Jews have hardened minds (τὰ νοήματα αὐτῶν *ta noēmata autōn*) when they read the "old covenant" because "a veil lies over their heart" (3:15)—that is, they do not readily see and understand ("heart" is here a Pauline rhetorical variation for "minds/thoughts" of 3:14; the NRSV translates καρδία [*kardia*] as "minds").[90] "Reading the old covenant" is parallel to "reading Moses" (3:15), which is another way of referring to the Torah, or Pentateuch (the first five books), as having been written by Moses (Acts 15:21; cf. 2 Chr 25:4; Neh 13:1; Mark 12:26).

Until the present day, Paul avers, the veil of non-understanding remains unremoved (3:14), "since only in Christ is it set aside" (3:14 NRSV). This fits Paul's understanding of Scripture and the law elsewhere in his letters. The law and Scripture are brought into focus, are understood clearly only as those "in Christ" look back at it from the standpoint of grace's having claimed them and set them right with God. Apart from one's being "in Christ," the law, which is holy (and its commandments just and good; Rom 7:12, 16) and "spiritual" (Rom 7:14), becomes the vehicle through which sin wreaks havoc and ultimately death (Rom 7:13) so that the very commandment that pointed toward life ends up, courtesy of sin's effective hijacking of it, in death.[91] Paul puts the same argument another way: Israel, seeking a righteousness of their own (for Paul there is

no such thing, though its non-existence has not slowed people from living by its fiction) through attempts to perform the law have not found it. Why? Because they have not truly understood the law and accepted righteousness, which is a right relationship as what it can only be: a gift from God (Rom 9:30–10:4; see esp. Rom 9:31 and 10:3).

As Paul depicts it to the Corinthians, Moses put a veil over his face so that the children of Israel would not see the end (τέλος *telos*) of what was fading—namely, the glory reflected on his face (3:13). Paul's affirmation that "in Christ" the veil is set aside (3:14) is shorthand that those who are "in Christ," his favorite expression for those who have already been restored to right relationship to God, are given eyes to see and minds and hearts to understand not only what is going on in God's plan, but also that Moses and all of Scripture still disclose God's purpose and God's will and provide guidance to all God's people. As he put it earlier to the Corinthians, "These things happened as an example for those people, but they are written for our instruction" (1 Cor 10:11).

Third, by contrast with unbelievers (cf. 4:4), Paul describes all believers, but especially featuring himself and his Corinthian dependents, as having an "unveiled face" (collectively their hoped-for unity is expressed in their having *one* face, and it unveiled; the NIV and the NRSV change to the plural, "faces") so that they can, indeed, be described as "gazing into the glory of the Lord as in a mirror" (3:18). The identity of "Lord" here as everywhere in Paul's letters must be determined by context and Paul's patterns.[92] When Paul references Scripture, as he does in this passage with its indebtedness to Exodus 33–34, he often adopts κύριος (*kyrios*) as the title for God from his Greek translation of "Yahweh" (cf. Rom 9:28-29; 1 Cor 14:21). The context, from 2:14 (where Paul gives thanks to *God,* who through Christ leads Paul and others), to 3:4 (where Paul's confidence is through Christ to *God*), to 3:5 (where Paul's confidence is from *God*), to the conclusion of the section in 4:6 (where it is *God* who has caused "the light of the glory of God" to shine [φῶς λάμψει *phōs lampsei*; cf. Isa 9:1 LXX] into the hearts of believers)—all of these

---

89. *BAGD* 417.

90. Rhetorical handbooks advised avoiding the needless repetition of the same term. See *ad Herennium* 4.12.18.

91. See L. E. Keck, "The Absent Good: The Significance of Rom 7:18*a,*" in *Text und Geschichte: Facetten theologischen Arbeitens aus dem Freundes- und Schülerkreis Dieter Lührmann zum 60. Geburtstag,* ed. S. Maser and E. Schlarb (Marburg: Elwert, 1999) 66-70, who states that sin is the "real culprit."

92. Following Furnish, *II Corinthians,* 211-12.

encourage the reading of "Lord" in 3:18 as referring to God.[93]

Throughout the passage, the references to Christ express means or agency, but the primary relationship is regularly between people and God. Further, the reference in 4:6 is unambiguously to *God's* glory, so that the "glory of the Lord" of 3:18 ought to be taken also as pointing to God. Finally, the image of contemplating the glory of the Lord "as in a mirror" (κατοπτρίζομαι *katoptrizomai*) invites the identification of Christ as the mirror reflecting the glory of God.[94] Taking Christ as the mirror is reinforced at the conclusion of the passage, where once again the glory of God is said to be visible "in the face of Christ," meaning reflected in Christ.[95]

With the notion of gazing indirectly at God's glory, Paul honors his Scriptures' general view, indeed the particular outlook of the Exodus account, that he has employed as a ground for his two-covenant exposition: Humans cannot bear to look directly at God. In the original story, Moses asks God for assurances (Exod 33:12-16) and is promised by God: "I will pass by before you with my glory [τῇ δόξῃ μου *tē doxē mou*]" (Exod 33:19 LXX). The story goes on to detail the care God takes in protecting Moses from the full effect of God's glory by placing Moses in a hole in the rock and covering him with God's hand (Exod 33:22). God's mercy precludes Moses' looking directly at God's face because God's majesty and power are so great that God declares, "No one shall see me and live" (Exod 33:20 NRSV; see also Judg 6:22-23; 13:22; cf. Isa 6:5).

For Paul, Jesus Christ is the clear, visible reflection of God. Believers, "through Christ" (2 Cor 3:14), experience the removal of the veil, so "with unveiled face" they can gaze intently upon God's glory as in the mirror that Christ provides. With this note, Paul distances the glory of God from direct vision, but at the same time celebrates that

believers, in and through Christ, have access to God.

Paul's conception of glory is eschatologically freighted. Because all have sinned, all "have fallen short of the glory of God" (Rom 3:23); but because of God's grace manifested in Christ and because of the from-God redemption of all creation begun in Christ's death and resurrection, those identified with Christ now are confidently assured of the end-time "glory about to be revealed to us" (Rom 8:18)—a glory that in some measure the "children of God" already have received and that the rest of creation longs to achieve (Rom 8:21).

The next part of 3:18 ("being transformed into the same image from glory to glory") parallels and is set contemporaneously with "gazing into the glory of the Lord as in a mirror" so that those who are permitted to contemplate God's glory are the very ones who are being transformed. A well-documented Hellenistic notion holds that to look upon the deity is to be changed and conformed to that deity (or to its image).[96]

For Paul, the beginning of the life of faith is variously described, sometimes using birth or adoption images (Romans 8), other times using conversion terminology (ἐπιστρέφω *epistrephō*, "to turn toward," "to turn around"; see Gal 4:9). Here the language of radical change, fundamental transformation, is needed: from death to life, from sin to righteousness. The expression "new creation," which Paul uses in chap. 5, suggests what a fundamental alteration is involved in the inauguration of the new aeon that God has begun in Christ's death and resurrection (5:17; cf. Gal 6:15).

But Paul's interest is not simply focused on what people today might call "the moment of conversion"; he is at least equally profoundly interested in an ongoing transformation that he considers fundamental to and characteristic of the life of faith. Evidence for this view is found widely in the Pauline corpus. Note his critical depiction of the Corinthians as still being babies when they should have been ready for solid food (1 Cor 3:1-2); the positive counterpart is what Paul calls the "spiritual person," who understands and discerns what is important (1 Cor 2:13-15). Ones-

---

93. So also S. Hafemann, "Paul's Argument from the Old Testament and Christology in 2 Cor 1–9," in *The Corinthian Correspondence,* ed. R. Bieringer (Leuven: University of Leuven Press, 1966) 300.

94. Alan Segal, "Paul and Ecstasy," SBLSP (1986) 574, 575n. 71, interprets the "glory of God" as "the technical term for the *Kābôd* (כבוד), the human form of God appearing in biblical visions" and takes the reference in 3:18 to the "glory of God" as in a mirror as another "mystical theme," which he traces back to Ezekiel 1.

95. N. T. Wright, "Reflected Glory," 145, argues suggestively, if not convincingly, that the " 'mirror' in which Christians see reflected the glory of the Lord is . . . *one another"* (italics added).

96. Cf. Furnish, *II Corinthians,* 240, who cites Apuleius *Metamorphoses* XI.15 and *Corpus Hermeticum* IV.11b.XI.15.23-24.

imus, the runaway slave mentioned in the Letter to Philemon, became Paul's child in the faith (Phlm 10). At the other extreme of the life of faith, Paul imagines the mature, the adult, the person whose faith has grown strong and whose related judgment has correspondingly become more trustworthy—as he states in the first person in the heart of his hymn of love: "When I was a child, I spoke as a child, thought as a child, reasoned as a child; when I became a man, I set aside the things of a child" (1 Cor 13:11). On two other occasions he summons his hearers to identify with adults, with mature people (1 Cor 2:6; Phil 3:15). In another instance, he pictures himself as not having attained maturity, but assiduously seeking it: "Not that I have already received this or am already mature, but I pursue it to make it my own, because Christ Jesus has made me his own" (Phil 3:12). Paul, ever the model of faith for his followers, depicts himself as the ideal: the believer who presses on toward maturity because Christ has claimed him.

Believers are works in progress; they should be moving from their infancy at the beginning of faith toward maturity, toward adulthood in the faith. Paul expresses that conviction in a variety of ways beyond the baby-to-adulthood motif. He writes to the Philippians that he has chosen to stay with them "for your progress [προκοπη prokopē, "advancement/furtherance"] and joy in the faith" (Phil 1:25). Using a different Greek term, he makes the same point in his conclusion of the very last letter he writes the Corinthians: "This is what I pray for, your being made complete [κατάρτισις katartisis, "completion"]" (2 Cor 13:9). Along this same line, he writes to the Romans about the person who is "weak with respect to faith" (Rom 14:1; see also Rom 15:1; cf. the statements about weaker and stronger consciences, which may reflect the same pattern, 1 Cor 8:7-13). And he expresses his deep wish to visit the Thessalonians so that he may "complete what is lacking in your faith" (1 Thess 3:10).

Another index of Paul's interest in the progress of individuals in the life of faith is his insistence that all things be done for edification, for "building up" (οἰκοδομη oikodomē). Granted, sometimes it is the church that is built up (1 Cor 14:4-5, 12), at other times it is clearly individuals (Rom 14:19; 15:2; 1 Cor 14:3, 17). Even where the edification is of the church, Paul clearly is not thinking of growth in numbers of members, but in the growth of members collectively in the faith.[97]

So when Paul writes to the Corinthians about "we all" being "transformed" (μεταμορφούμεθα metamorphoumetha), stated in the passive as a way of crediting God as the transformer, he is expressing, in the tersest scope, a strong conviction about the nature of the believing life. Believers are works in progress; they are being transformed. The rhetorical climax of the Letter to the Romans grounds its appeal for a life appropriate to the gospel by affirming a metamorphosis (using the same Greek term found in 2 Cor 3:18), a transformation, which in this case focuses on a renewal of the mind so that the Roman hearers can make appropriate moral decisions such that God is properly honored (Rom 12:1-2).

Two particular features of the transformation claim in 2 Cor 3:18, however, are the pithy little expressions τὴν αὐτὴν εἰκόνα (tēn autēn eikona, "into the same image") and ἀπὸ δόξης εἰς δόξαν (apo doxēs eis doxan, "from glory to glory").[98] The reference to εἰκών (eikōn; "image/likeness," "icon") functions on at least two levels. First, it is a reflection of the mirror supposed in the construction that has preceded it: "we all . . . gazing upon the glory of the Lord as reflected in a mirror" (2 Cor 3:18a; cf. Wis 7:26). Second, interpreting "Lord" to be God and the mirror to be Christ, the eikōn as image or reflection continues to be Christ. Paul explicitly confirms this identification four verses later: "Christ, who is the eikōn of God" (4:4; cf. Col 1:15). Thus the transformation Paul here celebrates is that all believers are (ideally) becoming ever more Christlike.

Imitation of Christ is a theme of massive proportions in the Pauline letters and is evinced here. In Paul's view, God's plan includes believers' being "conformed to the image [eikōn] of God's

97. Just as Paul is interested in the growth of invidivual believers' faith, so also he views his congregations collectively and recognizes that some communities are more mature in faith than are others. See J. Paul Sampley, "Reasoning from the Horizons of Paul's Thought World: A Comparison of Galatians and Philippians," in *Theology and Ethics in Paul and His Interpreters; Essays in Honor of Victor Paul Furnish*, ed. E. H. Lovering Jr., and J. L. Sumney (Nashville: Abingdon, 1996) 114-31.

98. M. D. Hooker, "Adam in Romans 1," *NTS* 6 (1960) 305, affirms that Paul frequently associates εἰκών (eikōn) and δόξα (doxa; Rom 8:29-30; 1 Cor 15:42-49; cf. Col 4:4).

son" (Rom 8:29). Paul is convinced that believers will "wear the image of the one from heaven," Christ (1 Cor 15:49). In all these passages, 2 Cor 3:18 included, Paul regularly thinks of believers as being conformed to Christ, but the expression "from glory to glory" indicates, as the NIV translation has rightly rendered it, that this association with Christ involves an "ever-increasing" glorification, or "from one degree of glory to another" (NRSV).[99] The faithful life begins with the restored glory of God from which people had fallen short via sin (Rom 3:23), and it will end in the full, cosmic refurbishment wherein God's glory is once again fully manifest (Rom 8:18-21). So "from glory to glory" expresses, once more, in the most cryptic fashion, Paul's larger picture that the life of the Spirit is a life ever growing and increasing.[100] As believers gaze upon the glory of the Lord, therefore, they actually look to their source and at the same time to their goal to which, gradually, as they become more like Christ, God's glory reflected, they become more identified with the glory of God.

An enigmatic construction ends 3:18 that may be understood to relate to all the elements in the verse in a most general, correlative way and be translated "as from the Lord, the Spirit" (καθάπερ ἀπὸ κυρίου πνεύματος *kathaper apo kyriou pneumatos*). From the outset, we must acknowledge that Paul does not have a clearly formulated trinitarian view of matters divine;[101] in fact, one could argue that he contributes to the situation that forced the later church to inquire more carefully about the relationship among God, Spirit, and Christ. As already noted, it is sometimes difficult in Paul's letters to know whether "Lord" refers to God or to Christ. In 3:18, κύριος (*kyrios*) is taken to refer to God. At times, however, *kyrios* is applied to Christ (e.g., Rom 1:7 and parallels in the other salutations; Rom 14:9; 1 Cor 12:3; Gal 1:19). At other times, *kyrios*,

though standing alone, probably refers to Christ (e.g., 1 Cor 7:10; Gal 5:10; Phil 4:1, 10; 1 Thess 1:6). Again, at times *kyrios* clearly refers to God (e.g., Rom 4:8; 9:28; 10:12). And some references to *kyrios* leave the reader open to think of God or Christ (Rom 12:11; 2 Cor 5:11).

The relation of the Spirit to God and to Christ is even more problematically and variously represented within Paul's letters. Sometimes the Spirit is directly linked to God: Once it is the Spirit from God (1 Cor 2:12); more frequently it is described with the genitive construction, which can denote "source" or "belonging" (πνεῦμα θεοῦ *pneuma theou*) to the Spirit of God (Rom 8:9, 11, 14; 1 Cor 2:11, 14; 3:16; 6:11; 7:40; 12:3). At other times the Spirit is immediately connected to Christ as in the expressions "the Spirit of God's Son" (Gal 4:6), "the Spirit of Jesus Christ" (Phil 1:19), and "the Spirit of Christ" (Rom 8:9). And there are the ambiguous references such as in 2 Cor 3:17-18, where "Spirit of the Lord" requires the hearer to ponder whether "the Lord" refers to God or to Christ.

Perhaps it is our post-Chalcedonian longing for neatness that drives us to distinguish and compartmentalize what obviously for Paul was a more fluid mix. A glance at Rom 8:9-11 may be instructive. The burden of that passage is to stress the immanence of Spirit-Christ-God in the believers. Note the many ways it stresses the indwelling: "dwells in you" (3 times: Rom 8:9, 11); "in you" (once: Rom 8:10); and "has" as in "possesses" (ἔχει *echei*; once: Rom 8:9). A closer look shows that *what* or *who* dwells or is in persons is diversely expressed: It is the "Spirit of God" in Rom 8:9, "the Spirit of the one who raised Jesus from the dead" and "the Spirit of the one who raised from the dead Christ Jesus and who will make alive your mortal bodies" in Rom 8:11; and "Christ" in Rom 8:10. Finally, the Spirit, mentioned so frequently, is three times the Spirit of God (Rom 8:9, 11) and once the "Spirit of Christ" (Rom 8:9). In this Romans passage, Paul's primary interest is to affirm in as many ways as possible the divine presence with believers as that which defines them and gives them meaning. Accordingly, he risks redundancy and even some fuzzing of categories for the larger purpose of accentuating presence and immanence.

In 2 Cor 3:1–4:6, Paul chooses to accentuate

---

99. J. D. G. Dunn, "A Light to the Gentiles: The Significance of the Damascus Road Christophany for Paul," in *The Glory of Christ in the New Testament: Studies in Christology in Memory of G. B. Caird,* ed. L. D. Hurst and N. T. Wright (Oxford: Clarendon, 1987) 261, correctly writes of the "process of salvation."

100. J. Lambrecht, "Transformation in 2 Cor 3:18," *Bib* 64 (1983) 246, 251-54, agrees.

101. Though Richard argues that Paul is "developing a trinitarian theme, not on an ontological but on a soteriological and functional level" and rightly observes: "The turning to God is achieved through Christ and remains the work of the Spirit." See E. Richard, "Polemics, Old Testament, and Theology: A Study of II Cor., III,1-IV,6," *RB* 88 (1981) 35.

the Spirit and its work through him and in the lives of all believers. He cannot simply dwell on the Spirit, however, because he has structured his argument around the story of Moses and God, and his Greek version of the Scriptures has used *kyrios*, "Lord," as the translation for the term "Yahweh." He can and does strengthen the link between Lord and Spirit by an earlier note (2 Cor 3:17, "The Lord [just mentioned] is the Spirit") in which he identifies the Lord of the Exod 34:34 citation in 2 Cor 3:16 with the Spirit, anticipating and setting the stage for the conclusion of 3:18. So Paul has bound up his primary interest—namely, to write about the Spirit's work through him—with his secondary interest: structuring a comparison of himself and Moses that features *kyrios*, "Lord" (meaning "God"). Hence, when he comes to the capstone of his argument in 3:18, he composes a generalizing statement ("as from the Lord, the Spirit") that affirms both "Lord," understood as God, and Spirit as the source, the power behind the ministry of the new covenant that he has just described and which he personally represents so directly in the lives of the Corinthians, his addressees.

In the two-covenant passage Paul references the Spirit seven times (3:3, 6 [twice], 8, 17 [twice], 18). Rhetorically this mention of a term and a frequent returning to it is called *refining*. Refining requires dwelling on a topic while seeming to move into new material; it usually involves a degree of repetition and a finding of alternate ways to make and elaborate the same point.[102] The first mention of the Spirit ("Spirit of the living God," 3:3), very much in line with Paul's claims in Romans 8 about the Spirit joining with human spirits to enable people to become God's children (Rom 8:15-16), credits the Spirit with working, indeed writing, on human hearts. It is not until a few verses later that the "new covenant" is said to be based on Spirit, not letter (*pneuma*, not γράμμα *gramma*, 3:6); and the rhetorically refining link becomes clear when Paul affirms, in contradistinction from the letter that kills, the "Spirit which makes alive" (3:6c), a clear echo of the "Spirit of the living God" (3:3). The ministry with which Paul readily identifies is characterized by him as ἡ διακονία τοῦ πνεύματος (*hē*

diakonia tou pneumatos), "the ministry of the Spirit," which, as in such Greek genitives, can be understood as a ministry driven by the Spirit (genitive of source, origin) and as a ministry that deals in Spirit (and in righteousness, 3:9, and in reconciliation, 5:18; these are genitives of quality).[103] Then, as noted, when the passage moves toward its climax: The Spirit references cluster and ground all of this—ministry, new covenant, freedom—in the Lord God and the Spirit.

Paul's mention of freedom in 3:17 merits attention. The claim that "where the Spirit is, there is freedom" seems gratuitously inserted; but there can be no doubt that Paul very positively associates the Spirit and the life of the Spirit with freedom. Once again Romans 8 is a strong parallel:

Rom 8:2-3	2 Cor 3:1-18
"Spirit of life" (8:2)	"Spirit of the living God" (3:3)
	"the Spirit makes alive" (3:7)
"has set you free" (8:2)	"Where the Spirit of the Lord is, there is freedom." (3:17)

Where the Romans 8 passage sets one νόμος (*nomos*, "law"; in Rom 8:2 signifying a way of being or of living) over against another *nomos* ("the *nomos* of the Spirit of life" versus "the *nomos* of sin and death," Rom 8:2), the 2 Corinthians 3 passage has a similar contrast of life and death, a similar insistence on the work of the Spirit associated with life, and a similar resultant freedom. The focus is not on rival notions of *nomos*, however, but on "old" and "new" covenants (2 Cor 3:6, 14). Likewise, the discussion of freedom in Galatians 5 grounds the peroration that follows: "Let us be in line with the Spirit" (Gal 5:25).

Paul's remark about Spirit-founded freedom, however, is not a call for the Corinthians to celebrate *their* freedom. Paul has had his problems with the Corinthians' zeal for their new freedom in Christ, as a glance over 1 Corinthians readily shows. In fact, his purposes in 2 Cor 3:1-18 are anything but freedom for the Corinthians; he works here assiduously instead to bind them ever more fully to himself. It is *his own* Spirit-inaugu-

---

102. See *Ad Herennium* 4.42.54.

103. V. P. Furnish, *II Corinthians*, AB 33 (Garden City: Doubleday, 1984) 204.

rated freedom that he has in view. Paul's assertion of Spirit-grounded freedom is a subtle move on his part because he has used his Spirit-based freedom to upbraid the Corinthians in the "painful" letter of frank speech (παρρησία *parrēsia*) about which Paul will have much more to say later in this letter fragment. In fact, in the passage at hand Paul has adumbrated once before to his use of *parrēsia* in his previous letter: "Having such hope [because he is grounded in the ministry of permanent glory] we have used much frank speech" (3:12),[104] *not like Moses,* who dealt gingerly with the Israelites when he came down off the mountain with his fading glory. Because of Paul's solid grounding in the Spirit and its ministry (3:8), Paul has exercised his freedom—"Where the Spirit of the Lord is, there is freedom"—in his relation to the Corinthians. Accordingly, he was not "out of line" to have written them using frank speech, even though the letter proved painful to them and to him. In 3:12 and 17 Paul has laid the foundation for further and more explicit reflections about his resort to *parrēsia,* frank speech (2 Cor 7:5-16).

Without the term's being used, Paul has been writing about grace, God's freely given, unmerited disposition working through his ministry. His insistence that his "competence" (ἡ ἱκανότης ἡμῶν *hē hikanotēs hēmōn*) comes not from himself but from God (3:5) affirms that it is God's grace and power, not Paul's own skills or performance, that sustain his association with this ministry of new covenant. Along this same line, Paul uses passive constructions, a notorious Pauline way of stressing God's grace: In Christ the veil is taken away (3:14, 16), and we are being transformed (3:18).

It is impossible to overstate the importance of the Holy Spirit for Paul's understanding of the life of faith.[105] To be sure, receiving the Spirit is the hallmark of belonging to the new people of God; Spirit reception is associated with the beginning of faith (Rom 8:15-16) and, therefore not surprisingly, with baptism (1 Cor 12:13). When Paul takes the Galatians back to the origin of their faith, he asks about their reception of the Spirit (Gal 3:2). In fact, "spiritualist" or "Spirit-person" (πνευματικός *pneumatikos*) seems to be Paul's basic descriptor for those who today would be called "Christian," a term not available to Paul (1 Cor 2:15; 3:1; Gal 6:1).

In 2 Cor 3:1-18, Paul has attempted two goals. First and most prominent, Paul has tried to overcome any objection that he might have been boasting too much when he identified himself with those whom God, like a victor, always leads around and in whom God manifests life and death (2:14-17). Paul's response lies in his depiction of himself as part of a coterie of especially designated ministers of the new covenant of Spirit, righteousness, and life. His second goal, admittedly quite minor in proportion to the first, is to incorporate his having used *parrēsia* with the Corinthians in his most recent letter—the lost, "painful" one—as an appropriate action for someone of his standing and ethos. The next segment of 2 Corinthians, 4:1-6, the conclusion to the argument begun in 3:1, elaborates how Paul's performance among and toward the Corinthians is appropriate—to the gospel and, by insinuation, to them.

The passage 4:1-6, addressing Paul's comportment in this very ministry, opens with a strong link to what has just preceded: "because of this" (διὰ τοῦτο *dia touto*), referring to the ministry of the new covenant that Paul has been graced to be a part of (4:1). What follows is a characterization, presented alternately in positive and negative forms and thereby echoing the antithetical structure of the opening of 3:1-18, of the way Paul has comported himself. And 4:1-6 confirms that Paul's primary concern in 3:1-18 was to advance his own standing with the Corinthians. The terminology of the section is charged; strong words provide emphasis to his claims. He has not just "set aside" certain ways of behaving; he has "renounced/disowned" (ἀπεῖπον *apeipon*) them (4:2). He does not "adulterate/falsify" (δολόω *doloō*) the word of God (4:2; perhaps echoing a complaint seen in 2:17). His scrupulousness regarding the way he handles himself and the gospel is of one piece and should serve to

104. Some scholars, such as Furnish, *II Corinthians,* 206, 230, take *parrēsia* in 3:12 to refer to Paul's psychological demeanor—i.e., Paul acted boldly. John Chrysostom (c. 40–120 CE) knew the rhetorical conventions of frank speech and recognized it as such here. See *Hom.* 7 in 2 Cor. 2. See also J. Migne, *Patrologica graeca* 61.444.

105. Other functions of the Spirit, not relevant to 2 Corinthians 3, include its producing fruit in the lives of believers (Gal 5:22) and its giving χαρίσματα (*charismata*), "spiritual gifts," to believers (Rom 12:6-8; 1 Cor 12:4-11). See G. D. Fee, *God's Empowering Presence: The Holy Spirit in the Letters of Paul* (Peabody, Mass.: Hendrickson: 1994) 870-95.

commend him not only to the Corinthians, but also to everybody's conscience everywhere (4:2).

In this context, "conscience" (συνείδησις *syneidēsis*, 4:2) functions as a synonym for "minds" (τὰ νοήματα *ta noēmata*), which he uses on either side, in 3:14 and 4:4. Conscience and mind are the human capacities that people must use in moral reasoning as they deliberate how they should live their lives, and in this case as they weigh out how, as Paul hopes for it, they ought to reaffirm their relation to him as the one who has faithfully and truthfully brought them the gospel.

Twice in 4:1-6 Paul, by his careful, and arguably clever, use of rhetoric, leaves the Corinthians no place to turn other than himself. The first is wily; the second is subtle. In the first, Paul picks up on the image of veiling from the previous pericope and takes up what might have been an objection of some Corinthians or even of some outsiders: "If [really, as some believe or perhaps say] our gospel is veiled, it is veiled [only, understood] for those who are perishing" (4:3; cf. 2:15, where Paul divided all human beings into two categories, "those who are being saved" and "those who are perishing"). Paul refines his description of those "who are perishing": "the god of this aeon has blinded the minds of unbelievers so that they do not see the light" (4:4; cf. the "hardened minds" of 3:14). So persons at Corinth who would distance themselves from Paul and his leadership leave themselves open to the charge of being "unbelievers" who really should be counted among "those who are perishing" and that their reasoning capacities are blinded by their deity, the "god of this age" (αἰών *aiōn*, 4:4a). Paul, who mentions Satan occasionally (cf. 1 Cor 5:5; 7:5; 2 Cor 2:11; 11:14; 12:7), quite likely has Satan in view, though he pointedly uses the more dramatic "god of this aeon," an expression that neither he nor any other NT writer uses elsewhere (cf. John 14:30; 1 Cor 2:6-8; 8:5; Eph 2:2).

The second rhetorical move is attached to Paul's claim that he preaches not himself but Christ Jesus as Lord: "and ourselves as your slaves for Jesus' sake" (4:5). Already in chaps. 1–9 Paul has anticipated that his lofty claims about himself and his gospel, somewhat muffled as they may be by his insistence on using the plural to include himself with all others who represent the same

gospel, may cause some of the Corinthians to bridle (cf. 1:12, 21-22; 3:1-2). In 4:5, therefore, his claim that, no matter how lofty the ministry to which he has been called, he has made himself a slave to the Corinthians—using the term "slave" to translate δοῦλος (*doulos*), for its shock rather than the NIV's milder "servant." The posture of servitude reflects Paul's relation to the Corinthians as expressed elsewhere (e.g., 1 Cor 4:8-13; 9:19) and should help to counteract any Corinthian offense at his lofty self-claims.

But his is not simply a rhetorical strategy to depict himself as a servant or a slave; it accords with his picture of Christ and is, therefore, a Pauline imitation of Christ, who, as the *eikōn* ("image/reflection") of God (4:4), has just been mentioned as the focus of the gospel that Paul propounds. So Paul, like the Christ he proclaims at the heart of his gospel, takes the role of the servant/slave (cf. "the form of a slave," Phil 2:7) in his relation to the Corinthians.

In this lofty ministry to which, by God's mercy (4:1), Paul has been called, he does not despair (an echo from 1:8-10 and a note that will reappear in 4:16), though the hardship list just ahead in 4:7-12 will suggest that he has had plenty of reasons not only to lose heart but also to lose hope (cf. 3:12). Neither does he resort to shameful, hidden ways. Nor does he walk as one prepared to do just anything (πανουργία *panourgia*, "trickery/[unfavorable] craftiness," 4:2; this will reemerge as a charge with some currency in 12:16). By contrast, he operates with full disclosure of the truth (another oblique reference to his having spoken frankly to them through his "painful" letter) and by so doing expects to "commend himself to everyone's conscience before God" (4:2). This practice of open, truthful disclosure, as Paul views it, "shines forth the light of the gospel, the glory of Christ who is the image of God" (4:4).

Although the discussion earlier has been of the glory of Moses' face (3:7) and of the Lord God (3:18), Paul now identifies the glory as "the glory of Christ" (τῆς δόξης τοῦ Χριστοῦ *tēs doxēs tou Christou*), who, as the "image" or "reflection" (εἰκὼν τοῦ θεοῦ *eikōn tou theou*) of God, reflects the glory that ultimately is God's, just as Paul suggested already in 3:18. The notion of the glory of Christ is refined in 4:6 to be "the light of the knowledge of the glory of God in the face of Christ" (ἐν προσώπῳ Χριστου *en prosōpō Christou*, or "in the presence of Christ"). Ultimately, the glory belongs to God. Glory is known by believers in Christ, whose face, whose presence, reflects that glory like light. The redemptive light, construed as analogous to God's calling forth "light out of darkness" at creation by the powerful and glorious utterance of the word (Gen 1:3), now shines forth (4:4; cf. Gen 1:3; Isa 9:2 LXX) through the luminous gospel Paul preaches and that he has preached from the start in Corinth.

Paul's claims in 4:2*a* about *how he did not act* have been taken by some as an attack on and a denigration of the outsiders who have come into Corinth (see 3:1-3).[106] But they may just as well be amplifications *via negativa* of Paul's own exemplary comportment, which the rest of 4:2 details quite positively.[107]

Apart from any consideration of Paul's rhetorical goals with the Corinthians in the two-covenant passage (3:1–4:6), we gain some fundamental insight into Paul's convictions. Though engaged with predominantly Gentile audiences in his correspondence, Paul shows clearly here that he thinks covenantally about God's relations to people. Ritually grounded in the Lord's supper, Paul thinks of the renewed relationship made possible through Christ's death ("blood" in 1 Cor 11:25) as a covenant; indeed, it is of that "new covenant" that Paul has been made a minister (3:6).

Scholarship has not always adequately placed Paul's justification/righteousness claims—which are so important to him and to his proclamation of the gospel—within a covenant context. Covenant terminology does not have to be explicit in a given text before we can consider that Paul may have had it as a part of his own framework. Surely

Gentiles who were unfamiliar with covenant conceptions could readily have understood that Paul's claim of justification or righteousness suggested a sort of judicial vindication, or, to put it differently, that the charges brought against one had been dropped. This forensic semantic possibility is significant and must be retained regarding Paul's usage. Nevertheless, the richness of detail and interpretive insight reflected in 2 Cor 3:1–4:6 shows that Paul understands his own ministry as a part of God's new covenant, opening full participation to all who are claimed by the Spirit, whether Jew or Gentile.

Because the covenant framework is so pronounced here, our reading of *all of* Paul's claims about justification (or righteousness, which is also based on the same Greek root), no matter where they occur in his letters, must adequately interpret that term within a covenant context. The eighth-century BCE prophets, such as Amos, Hosea, Isaiah, and Micah, take their readers to task for their failure to seek justice, to pursue covenant righteousness, "that quality of life in relationship with others in the community that gives rise to justice"[108] (see Isa 1:17; Hos 10:12; Amos 5:24; Mic 6:6-8). Paul is quite thoroughly aligned with those prophets when he expects his followers, who are "justified" or "made righteous" with God, by God's grace, to live in love, and to care for others for whom Christ has died. In 3:9 Paul described his work as a "ministry of righteousness," which can readily be understood as a genitive of content or focus: a ministry dedicated to righteousness. For Paul, to live the justified, righteous life is to live in proper (new) covenant relationship to God, to show the appropriate care and concern for others who are also part of that (new) covenant, and to share in the reception of peace and mercy, along with the Israel of God (Gal 6:16).

---

106. Peter Marshall, *Enmity in Corinth: Social Conventions in Paul's Relations with the Corinthians,* WUNT 44 (Tübingen: J. C. B. Mohr, 1987) 272, 321.

107. M. E. Thrall, *The Second Epistle to the Corinthians* (Edinburgh: T. & T. Clark, 1994) 218, 221-22, also considers this to be apologetic, and not polemical.

108. G. M. Tucker, "Notes on Amos," in *The HarperCollins Study Bible,* 1364.

❖   ❖   ❖   ❖

EXCURSUS: PAUL'S DISCUSSION OF MULTIPLE COVENANTS

Three times in the undisputed Pauline corpus (and also Eph 2:12), Paul refers to more than one covenant. First, 2 Cor 3:1–4:6 mentions more than one covenant, as has been observed. Second, Galatians has the allegorical representation of Abraham's children by the two women, one by the "free woman" (Sarah), and the other by the slave, Hagar (Gal 4:21-31). There the two covenants "correspond . . . to the covenant of promise and the covenant of law,"[109] and in Paul's view the Galatians are "children of the promise, like Isaac" (Gal 4:28 NRSV). Clearly, one of the two covenants in Galatians is positive and is associated with freedom and inheritance; the other is negative and is linked to slavery: The children of the one inherit; the children of the other do not.

The third instance is found in his Letter to the Romans, where Paul acknowledges that the Israelites have many advantages, among which he lists "the covenants" (αἱ διαθῆκαι *hai diathēkai*, Rom 9:4). In Rom 9:4, Paul does not declare how many covenants he has in mind; he simply uses the plural. The textual evidence of that verse suggests that some copyists have thought Paul must have meant "the covenant," and accordingly have reduced it to the singular. But many patristic writers, and even Augustine, know the text as reflecting the plural designation, "the covenants." For one simple reason—namely, that the entire list of the Israelites' advantages in Rom 9:4 is positive, its plural "covenants" cannot be the two covenants depicted in 2 Cor 3:1–4:6; neither can the Rom 9:4 covenants be equated with Paul's Galatians allegorical representation of two rival covenants, one representing the free woman and one representing the slave woman.

Because Rom 9:4 makes positive mention of "the covenants," we cannot import for its interpretation either Galatians' rival covenants or 2 Corinthians' partially contrasted covenants. Scholars have never adequately pursued the issue of how, apart from Paul's dual-covenant construction in 2 Corinthians and the rival covenant depiction in Galatians, a plural of covenants might fit positively within Paul's thinking. An attempt to do so will be made here in an effort to reconstruct the broadest possible backdrop against which modern readers can assess Paul's 2 Corinthians claims about the two covenants. Because Paul nowhere lays out his thought on this matter, the following is admittedly constructive and suggestive and is offered for reflection and deliberation, not as established or completely verifiable.

Israel has two types of covenant: the ברית עולם (*běrît 'ôlām*), or "perpetual covenant," and the suzerainty type, or conditional covenant. The perpetual covenant is exemplified in David and in Abraham and rests solely on God's faithfulness (cf. also the covenant with Noah, Genesis 9). It is granted by God, simply out of God's mercy and commitment. No special performance is expected or required by the recipients of this type of covenant. As its name suggests, the perpetual convenant is everlasting. God's covenant with David is a good example. God says of David: "I will establish the throne of his kingdom forever . . . I will not take my steadfast love from him . . . your throne shall be established forever" (2 Sam 7:13-16 NRSV). The warrantee of this covenant is the faithfulness of God. The covenant with Abraham is of this same type. Abraham is simply chosen by God as the one to receive God's commitment of beneficence; he is given God's promise. The covenant is granted not because of something Abraham has done to merit consideration, but simply because God has selected Abraham, and the covenant is for all time (Genesis 15; 17).

---

109. R. B. Hays, "Notes on Galatians," in *The HarperCollins Study Bible*, 2189.

The suzerainty type of covenant is granted by the superior, or by analogy God, on the condition of certain performance by the recipients. For example, "These are the statutes and ordinances that you must diligently observe in the land that the LORD, the God of your ancestors, has given you to occupy all the days that you live on the earth" (Deut 12:1 NRSV). This text introduces the conditions on which covenant continuance is predicated. Failure of the covenant recipients to maintain performance can lead to curse rather than blessing (cf. Deuteronomy 27–28); and, if the covenant granter wishes, can lead to termination of the covenant altogether.

Although he never uses the technical term "covenant" to describe it, Paul knows and takes delight in God's special relationship with Abraham (Romans 4; Galatians 3). In fact, Abraham becomes the type of the faithful person, exemplifying complete trust in God's promises, simultaneously glorying in God and growing in faith, and being reckoned righteous by God for his faith. God's commitment to Abraham is unbounded; God's faithfulness grounds that commitment.

Paul creatively incorporates features of both covenant types in his letters and, therefore, in his understanding of the gospel. Central to Paul's connections with the perpetual covenant is his repeated insistence on God's inerrant faithfulness, already affirmed in 2 Cor 1:18 and long since familiar to the Corinthians from 1 Cor 1:9 and 10:13 (cf. 1 Thess 5:24).

The most striking reflection on God's faithfulness, however, comes precisely in Rom 3:1-4, where Paul asks, "What advantage has the Jew?" This is a key passage in the structure of Romans because, although it begins a list of prerogatives ("they were entrusted with God's oracles," Rom 3:2), the list breaks off and is resumed only in the already mentioned Rom 9:4, where he speaks of the Israelites' having the advantage, among other things, of "the covenants." So as to highlight the centrality of God's faithfulness, Paul takes the argument to extremes: "If some were unfaithful, will not their unfaithfulness nullify the faithfulness of God?" (Rom 3:3). Paul's answer is a striking affirmation of God's covenant faithfulness: "No way! Let God be true even if every person is a liar" (3:4, which he supports by citing Ps 51:6). Clearly, God's commitment to the Jews does not rest on *any consideration* of their performance. The worst-case scenario that Paul proposes—let them all be unfaithful—does not unhinge the faithfulness of God. This is unquestionably covenant talk on Paul's part, as the mention of circumcision in 2 Cor 3:1 shows—and of the perpetual covenant type.

At the same time that he affirms God's faithful covenant commitment to people, however, Paul holds that people are responsible to God. Paul declares that believers will be held accountable for their actions (see the Commentary on 5:10). At the end-time judgment, people will be judged regarding their works of obedience (Rom 2:6-10, 16; 14:10). Paul expects believers to be engaged in the labor of love, in behalf of the gospel (1 Cor 15:58; 16:10, 16; 1 Thess 1:3). To do works of love (Gal 5:6) is not merely an option for believers. Those in Christ are expected to experience the love of Christ controlling and extending them toward each other (2 Cor 5:14).

Curiously, like no other early Christian writer, Paul creatively weaves together elements of both types of covenants, the perpetual and the conditional. From the former he grounds his gospel in the unchanging faithfulness of God, and from the latter he expects believers to perform the conditions appropriate to the covenant commitment God has made to them. Romans 9:4, with its mention of "the covenants," lets us see that when Paul thinks of multiple covenants, he does not always set one covenant against another, as in Galatians, nor does he always have a mixed picture of some continuity and some discontinuity, as in 2 Cor 3:1–4:3. In the larger picture, Paul can think of more than one covenant quite positively and embrace elements of both the perpetual and the conditional covenants in his larger understanding of God's purposes.

❖   ❖   ❖   ❖

REFLECTIONS

1. Basic to Paul's construction here is the notion that the glory of God is reflected, not seen directly. How true of life, that God's surprises break out in the most unexpected ways and places: in that little moment where someone reaches out to you in a time of need; where you have joy over being of assistance to someone; or where a baby shows up in a manger and changes lives and history. Maybe God has to surprise us in order to get our attention sometimes. The problem with that, however, is that we might not notice the reflections of God's glory that are happening around us. Part of the task of worship is the rehearsing of how we learn not only to look for God's surprises in life, but also how to recognize them.

2. When our culture uses the term "freedom," it generally means something people achieve through power or cunning or win with luck. Freedom, for Paul, is not something we generate for ourselves, not something we achieve by our own maneuvering or decisions. Freedom is a gift that liberates us to be what God created us to be. Luther had a sense of that when, following Paul, he said that true freedom is found in service to others. Imagine our culture's calling as service of others' freedom! But God's gift of acceptance and love of us as we are affirms who we already are, so we do not need to scrap and fight to earn personal status. God has already given us the only status we need: God's acceptance. With that in mind, we can reach out to others in service.

3. Paul's two-covenant account has prompted both a denigration of Israel as having an inadequate covenant and an accompanying claim of Christian superiority. But Paul's message is at once more complex than inferior/better and at the same time designed to bind the Corinthians to him and his ministry; Paul has no apparent interest here in reflecting on Israel or Jews. Marcion, a second-century heretic who believed there were two Gods and that the God of Jesus was superior to the God of Israel, may be alive in the hearts of some when they read Paul's two-covenant thought here as supersessionist, as replacing the old with the new, without any continuity. In the Middle Ages, cathedral statuary represented this supersessionist view through carved stone figures of two women, "Church" and "Synagogue." On the south transept portal of the Strasbourg Cathedral, for example, lady "Church" stands tall and looks out confidently, carrying a staff topped by a cross and holding a chalice representing Christ's blood. Lady "Synagogue" stands opposite, head bowed and blindfolded, signifying moral ignorance. Often such representations of her also include a crown falling from her head or depict her as dropping the stone tablets of the law. Such characterizations are misrepresentations of Paul's view of the two covenants.

4. Paul's antithesis—what fades versus what persists—is a way for him to distinguish what is important from what is indifferent (for a similar point expressed in other categories, cf. 1 Cor 2:6 and 13:13). In a society so defined by its throwaway character, where items are made not to be repaired but replaced, we are captivated by the latest fashion. Paul, on the other hand, is interested in what remains, what is dependable, what is trustworthy.

5. God is not finished with us as we are. We are works in progress. With its double depiction of the life of faith as being changed into the image of Christ and as moving from one degree of glory to another, 2 Cor 3:18 is a powerful affirmation that the Christian life is one of growth and improvement. That thought, of course, raises for any modern reader the question of whether our faith shows such growth or improvement. Paul thinks one can test oneself in that regard (see the Commentary on 1 Cor 11:28-29 and on 2 Cor 13:5-10).

6. Change is not always a welcome experience; it is at times unsettling. But it is in the nature of grace and of one of its primary expressions, the Holy Spirit, to bring about change, to intercept and interrupt the neat calculus that we like to make between the A's and B's of life by which we attempt to control and understand the way life comes to us. Animosity does not always have to lead to hatred; a wrong step is not always followed by a slap on the wrist. Perhaps we need to discuss with each other how we can embrace change that bids to bring us good or, to put it differently, that moves us to a new place.

7. Paul suggests that a certain comportment is inappropriate to the gospel: The secretive ways of shame and deception are simply ruled out. Jesus' attacks on hypocrites (see Matthew 23) are on the same wavelength. Our English term "hypocrite" is a virtual transliteration of a Greek term (Latin picked it up from the Greek) that refers to a stage actor—that is, someone who puts on a front, who in effect wears a face that is not his or her own, who acts the part of someone else. Dissembling is alien to the gospel.

8. The expression "god of this age" is daring because it risks misunderstanding what Paul knows clearly—namely, that there is only one God (cf. 1 Cor 8:4). But Paul also knows that there are "many gods and many lords" that, in fact, bid to hold sway over our lives (1 Cor 8:5). Whatever is at the center of our lives, whatever governs our decisions and bears on all our actions—that is our god, our true lord. "Idolatry" is the technical term of Israel and of the early churches for putting some thing or purpose other than God at the determining center of our lives. Modern gods/lords that bid for our fealty are legion: job, status, money, happiness, acceptance, and you fill in the blank. Even good things, when our desire for them gets out of proportion, can assume lordship over us and become a "god of this age."

9. In the creation narratives of Israel's traditions, Adam is said to have been created in the image of God (Gen 1:26). All of us, as Adam and Eve's descendants, also share God's image. Paul invites us to think about that christologically: Christ represents and reveals God to us. When we act with love and clemency toward others, we reflect Christ to them (2 Cor 10:1) and, at least in some little measure, re-present Christ to them. The idea behind this notion is that God's love is a powerful agent in every life it engages, so when God's love is imaged or reflected through and beyond us, we reflect not ourselves but Christ through us. When we have to be in the middle of the picture, Christ is not being reflected well (or perhaps at all).

2 Corinthians 4:7–5:10, Paul's Ministry Sustained Through Affliction and Mortality

NIV

⁷But we have this treasure in jars of clay to show that this all-surpassing power is from God and not from us. ⁸We are hard pressed on every side, but not crushed; perplexed, but not in despair; ⁹persecuted, but not abandoned; struck down, but not destroyed. ¹⁰We always carry around in our body the death of Jesus, so that the life of Jesus may also be revealed in our body. ¹¹For we who are alive are always being given over to death for Jesus' sake, so that his life may be revealed in our mortal body. ¹²So then, death is at work in us, but life is at work in you.

¹³It is written: "I believed; therefore I have

NRSV

7But we have this treasure in clay jars, so that it may be made clear that this extraordinary power belongs to God and does not come from us. 8We are afflicted in every way, but not crushed; perplexed, but not driven to despair; 9persecuted, but not forsaken; struck down, but not destroyed; 10always carrying in the body the death of Jesus, so that the life of Jesus may also be made visible in our bodies. 11For while we live, we are always being given up to death for Jesus' sake, so that the life of Jesus may be made visible in our mortal flesh. 12So death is at work in us, but life in you.

13But just as we have the same spirit of faith

NIV

spoken."[a] With that same spirit of faith we also believe and therefore speak, [14]because we know that the one who raised the Lord Jesus from the dead will also raise us with Jesus and present us with you in his presence. [15]All this is for your benefit, so that the grace that is reaching more and more people may cause thanksgiving to overflow to the glory of God.

[16]Therefore we do not lose heart. Though outwardly we are wasting away, yet inwardly we are being renewed day by day. [17]For our light and momentary troubles are achieving for us an eternal glory that far outweighs them all. [18]So we fix our eyes not on what is seen, but on what is unseen. For what is seen is temporary, but what is unseen is eternal.

5 Now we know that if the earthly tent we live in is destroyed, we have a building from God, an eternal house in heaven, not built by human hands. [2]Meanwhile we groan, longing to be clothed with our heavenly dwelling, [3]because when we are clothed, we will not be found naked. [4]For while we are in this tent, we groan and are burdened, because we do not wish to be unclothed but to be clothed with our heavenly dwelling, so that what is mortal may be swallowed up by life. [5]Now it is God who has made us for this very purpose and has given us the Spirit as a deposit, guaranteeing what is to come.

[6]Therefore we are always confident and know that as long as we are at home in the body we are away from the Lord. [7]We live by faith, not by sight. [8]We are confident, I say, and would prefer to be away from the body and at home with the Lord. [9]So we make it our goal to please him, whether we are at home in the body or away from it. [10]For we must all appear before the judgment seat of Christ, that each one may receive what is due him for the things done while in the body, whether good or bad.

[a]13 Psalm 116:10

NRSV

that is in accordance with scripture—"I believed, and so I spoke"—we also believe, and so we speak, [14]because we know that the one who raised the Lord Jesus will raise us also with Jesus, and will bring us with you into his presence. [15]Yes, everything is for your sake, so that grace, as it extends to more and more people, may increase thanksgiving, to the glory of God.

16So we do not lose heart. Even though our outer nature is wasting away, our inner nature is being renewed day by day. [17]For this slight momentary affliction is preparing us for an eternal weight of glory beyond all measure, [18]because we look not at what can be seen but at what cannot be seen; for what can be seen is temporary, but what cannot be seen is eternal.

5 For we know that if the earthly tent we live in is destroyed, we have a building from God, a house not made with hands, eternal in the heavens. [2]For in this tent we groan, longing to be clothed with our heavenly dwelling— [3]if indeed, when we have taken it off[a] we will not be found naked. [4]For while we are still in this tent, we groan under our burden, because we wish not to be unclothed but to be further clothed, so that what is mortal may be swallowed up by life. [5]He who has prepared us for this very thing is God, who has given us the Spirit as a guarantee.

6So we are always confident; even though we know that while we are at home in the body we are away from the Lord— [7]for we walk by faith, not by sight. [8]Yes, we do have confidence, and we would rather be away from the body and at home with the Lord. [9]So whether we are at home or away, we make it our aim to please him. [10]For all of us must appear before the judgment seat of Christ, so that each may receive recompense for what has been done in the body, whether good or evil.

[a]Other ancient authorities read *put it on*

COMMENTARY

Paradox and incongruity characterize Paul's second of three complementary portraits of his ministry (4:7–5:10). Antinomies are played off against one another throughout, as the following list shows.

not our power	God's power (4:7)
outer	inner (4:16)
seen	not seen (4:18)
temporal	eternal (4:18)
earthly tent	heavenly dwelling (5:1)
be at home	get away (5:6-9)

4:7. Paul's opening metaphor—"We have this treasure in earthenware vessels"—is a powerful cue to what follows in this section, and it will become the theme of "power through weakness," which dominates chaps. 10–13. Continuing to write in the plural, signifying his belonging to the mainstream, Paul adverts to his just-described new-covenant ministry and the glory of God represented within it with his generalizing phrase "this treasure" (θησαυρός *thēsauros*). So grand a treasure borne in such a menial, frail, seemingly inept container makes it unmistakable that the power enabling the whole enterprise is "from God and not from us" (4:7).

4:8-11. The hardship list that follows (4:8-10) is presented as proof that the entire endeavor is from God. Paul wears each of the difficulties as an ironic badge of honor. The verbs are a lexicon of adversity, structured in an "A not B" form. The first, θλίβω (*thlibō*, "hard pressed, afflicted," 4:8) is a repetition of the same verb that inaugurated the *sorites* (form: A leads to B; B leads to C; etc.) in 1:6 and, therefore, invites the hearers to link Paul's early and later delineations of the suffering he has endured for the gospel (and for the Corinthians). The "A not B" form (4:8-9) is designed to paint a picture of considerable, but not totally overwhelming, hardship. The ready conclusion is that the aforementioned "power of God" (4:7) is what has kept the difficulties from being overwhelming so that Paul does not "lose heart" or "despair" (ἐγκακέω *enkakeō*, 4:1, 16).

Hardship lists (*peristasis* catalogs) are a common feature of the Roman world of Paul's time. Sages often employed such recountings of difficulties to show that they were imperturbable and not governed by externals. Paul does the same.[110] The list in 4:8-9 is but the first of several in 2 Corinthians (cf. 6:4-10; 11:23-29).

At the end of the catalog (4:10), Paul makes a double connection with Jesus: In his own body,

Paul carries "hither and yon" (περιφέρω *peripherō*) the death of Jesus (symbolizing Paul's sufferings and afflictions as reflections of Christ's death), so that the life of Jesus (a reference to Jesus Christ's resurrection, which is the very basis of hope) may be shown forth (φανερόω *phaneroō*; an echo of 2:14, where the NIV and the NRSV translate "spreads"), again in his body. The term for "death" here (νέκρωσις *nekrōsis*) is used in contemporary medical writings to describe dead or dying tissue;[111] Paul employs it for dramatic effect (cf. elsewhere in the NT only in Rom 4:19) as a way of emphasizing the difficulties he has experienced for the gospel. Paul's missionizing, despite all his troubles and setbacks, is itself a witness to Christ's resurrection because the perdurance of his mission says nothing more clearly than that the power indeed rests with God. This interpretation is made explicit by Paul when, again using a dramatic term that as a legal technical word has the overtones of being "handed over" or given into the custody of someone, he declares about himself that "we the living are always being bound over [παραδίδωμι *paradidōmi*] to death for Jesus' sake" (4:11; cf. a parallel with Judas's pact to "hand over" Jesus, Matt 26:15; Mark 14:10; note also Paul's receiving a death sentence, 2 Cor 1:9). The expression "for Jesus' sake" (διὰ Ἰησοῦν *dia Iēsoun*) specifies that it is not just any handing over that is being described. It is, instead, a life lived in service of Jesus and in conformity to the gospel;[112] those persons, Paul prominent among them, are the ones who are being given over into the custody of death.

Both 4:10 and 4:11 have opening clauses that identify the death of Jesus with the daily life of new-covenant ministers like Paul; and both sentences conclude with purpose clauses tied up with parallel expressions of "the life of Jesus," once again a reference to the resurrection. Both the death (i.e., crucifixion) and the life (i.e., resurrection) of Jesus are seen in Paul's body, a note to

---

110. J. T. Fitzgerald, *Cracks in an Earthen Vessel: An Examination of the Catalogues of Hardships in the Corinthian Correspondence* (Atlanta: Scholars Press, 1988) 47-116.

111. Fitzgerald, *HarperCollins Study Bible* 2170n. J. Lambrecht, "The Nekrōsis of Jesus' Ministry and Suffering in 2 Cor 4,7-15," in *L'Apôtre Paul: personalité, style et conception du ministère,* ed. A. Vanhoye (Leuven: University of Leuven Press, 1986) 120 and n. 2.

112. N. M. Watson, "'The Philosopher Should Bathe and Brush His Teeth': Congruence Between Word and Deed in Graeco-Roman Philosophy and Paul's Letters to the Corinthians," *AusBR* 42 (1994) 12, asserts that this hardship list is not presented to prove "his own fortitude" but as "the sign that his life is being conformed to the pattern of Christ crucified." Cf. 4:11.

which Paul returns for refinement beginning in 4:16 with a "therefore" (διό *dio*) and with reflections about the "inner" and "outer" person.

4:12. Paul does not resist the temptation to pursue this image for further, personal purposes. Up until 4:12, both the death and the life of Jesus have been present in Paul and in his leadership colleagues (4:10-11). Now, however, Paul turns to a more explicit set of reflections that bear on himself and the Corinthians and alters the picture so that now only *death* is at work *in him* (and in his ubiquitous cohorts) while *life* is at work *in the Corinthians* (4:12). In this direct appeal for sympathy from the Corinthians, Paul seeks to turn his suffering and hardship into a source of increased goodwill from them.

4:13-14. Just as he did in the heart of the two-covenant passage, so also now Paul adverts to the frank speech (see the Introduction) that he employed with the Corinthians in his most recent correspondence with them, the painful letter (4:13). Using a quotation from Ps 115:1 LXX (cf. Ps 116:10), Paul justifies the way he has spoken (harshly) to them in the painful letter, but, at the same time, he accounts for his current self-promotion.

Paul's confidence then and now is grounded in his faith ("Having the same spirit of faith" as the psalmist, 4:13), which contains at its heart the conviction ("we know," 4:14) of how the rest of the salvation story is going to play out—namely, that God, the understood subject of all the verbs in the declaration, "who raised the Lord Jesus will raise us with Jesus and will present us [before himself, understood] along with you" (4:14). This pithy statement encapsulates the heart of the gospel for Paul, providing the basis for his hope and, indeed, for his perduring in the world (stated in other categories, for his not giving up), where he experiences so much affliction and distress.

In one short sentence Paul scans from the past (4:14*a*) to the future (4:14*b*), affirms that all is based on the character of God (whom Paul aptly describes elsewhere as the one who brings into existence the things that do not exist and who brings life out of death, Rom 4:17), and includes the Corinthians ("along with you") with himself as being destined to be "presented" before God (4:14). The NRSV translation of 4:14 hides what is for Paul a technical term of the judgment day

at the parousia: παρίστημι (*paristēmi*), "to present/offer/bring before a judge."

Throughout the corpus of his letters, Paul displays his view that believers will be presented for a last-day accounting of themselves and of their works (see esp. 2 Cor 5:10, where the notion will be reprised and refined). Even later in 2 Corinthians the same idea is garbed in bridal imagery when Paul, depicting himself as the father of the bride, writes of his having betrothed the Corinthians to Christ "in order to *present* you to Christ [ὑμᾶς... παραστῆσαι τῷ Χριστῷ *hymas ... parastēsai tō Christō*] as a pure bride to her one husband" (11:2, italics added; cf. Rom 6:13; 14:10; 1 Cor 8:8). Of course, the death and resurrection of Jesus Christ are at the heart of Paul's gospel. Because Christ was raised from the dead, believers who are one with Christ and who have died with Christ and shared his sufferings already have newness of life and are assured that, at the end times, they will have a resurrection like his (Rom 6:4; Phil 3:10-11). Christ has died and been raised; believers currently share his death and confidently expect to share his resurrection at the end time, at the parousia.[113] At the center of this gospel is Paul's affirmation of God's grace, by which he means God's freely given, unmerited gift of new life in Christ. So it is not surprising that Paul brings this little subsection of his argument to a climax by mentioning grace (4:15), a grace that by its very inner power means that it abounds to more and more people. And how does it do that? The answer is only implied: At least in part, it is by Paul's doing what he is called to do—spread the gospel just as he has done to the Corinthians.

4:15. "All of this is for your sake" (4:15). One may wonder just what the hearers are to include in "all of this" (τὰ πάντα *ta panta*). Immediately in the text it could be that they know, along with Paul, that God is working in them through Christ to present them before God at the end time (4:14). But the "all of this" expression could very well be interpreted not only to mean that immediate affirmation, but also to include Paul's extraordinary experiences of affliction and distress in bringing the gospel to the Corinthians.

"All of this" is also "unto the glory of God."

---

113. Cf. Eph 2:5-6 and Col 2:13, letters from the Pauline school that affirm the resurrection in the present, removing the Pauline tension.

Paul expects "the grace that is reaching more and more people" (4:15 NIV) to "cause thanksgiving to abound, to the glory of God" (4:15, echoing 1:11 in part) because grace, when it transforms a life, generates glorification of God. That is the way grace works, and glorification of God is the fruit of grace at work. The goal of human life, transformed by God's grace, is to glorify God (Rom 1:21; 15:6, 9; 1 Cor 6:20; 2 Cor 9:13), to give thanks to God (Rom 14:6; 1 Thess 5:18), and to bless God (see 1:3 and the Commentary on 1:3-11).

4:16-17. Because of God's grace and the hope founded upon it, Paul reaffirms (διο *dio* "therefore") that he does not "lose heart" (*enkakeō*, "despair/become weary," 4:16), a reprise of 4:1. Using categories no doubt familiar to his predominantly Gentile congregation at Corinth,[114] Paul speaks indirectly about himself by referring to an "inner man" (ὁ ἔσω *ho esō),* as distinguished from an "outer man" (ο ἔξω ἄνθρωπος *ho exō anthrōpos,* 4:16). Anyone who goes simply by appearances, by what is seen on the outside, would surely err, Paul argues, because what they would accurately see is that the "outer man" is indeed "wasting away," being destroyed (διαφθείρω *diaphtheirō,* 4:16). By his repeated references to his afflictions, persecutions, and hardships (1:8-11; 4:7-11), Paul has openly embraced the "external" picture of himself as wasting away, as being destroyed. But the external vista does not disclose the whole story or even the most important part; further, it is not a reliable indicator of the full picture.

By contrast, the internal portrait is the one to be taken seriously, and about that Paul avers: "But our inner self [lit., man] is being renewed day by day" (4:16). The renewal day by day is a clear pointer, once again, toward the eschatological time when days and renewal will reach their goal. From that end-time perspective, Paul takes a third look at his afflictions (θλῖψις *thlipsis,* 1:8-11; 4:7-11, 17) and characterizes them as "momentary" (παραυτίκα *parautika*), "light/insignificant/slight" (ἐλαφρός *elaphros*); seen from this perspective, the afflictions are understood as "pro-

ducing for us an eternal weight of glory beyond all proportion" (4:17). Elsewhere Paul makes that same association of present affliction or suffering leading to and ensuring a future glory of major proportions (Rom 8:17). Paul has an abiding conviction: Afflictions are part of the life of faith; they are signposts that one is proceeding as should be expected, a claim he made to the Thessalonians (1 Thess 3:3-4; cf. Rom 5:3-5). So his hardship catalogs also serve to document that he is on the right track and, therefore, to enhance his ethos[115] as their proper leader who is due their full adherence.

4:18. There is a slight cautionary note in Paul's development of the idea that appearances can be misleading. He goes ahead to describe himself and the rest of the mainstream as "not looking to the things that are seen, but to the things that are not seen" (4:18). Not only are appearances misleading, but, he says, they are also temporary; they last only for a time (πρόσκαιρα *proskaira*), whereas the unseen things are eternal (αἰώνια *aiōnia,* 4:18). The things that are seen, paralleling his portrayal of his "outer man," are not as reliable a guide as the things that are not seen, or as his "inner man." Any Corinthian hearers who might take Paul's sufferings, afflictions, and hardships to be failures are here implicitly put on notice that they could be foolishly misled. Paul, and by implication from the plurals all other ministers like him, take their reckonings from the inner self, from eternals, and from the things that are not seen.

5:1-4. In the verses directly ahead, this same image resurfaces for refinement when Paul writes that "we walk by faith, not by sight" (5:7). This fits also his earlier assertion to these Corinthians that now believers have partial knowledge and will have full knowledge only at the parousia, only at the end of the ages (1 Cor 13:12). The whole section (4:7–5:10) opened with the image of Paul and his associates having divine (and we now know "eternal" as well as "inner") treasures in earthenware vessels (4:7).

The passage concludes in a multiple refinement where the images of inner and outer (4:16),

---

114. H. D. Betz, "The Concept of the 'Inner Human Being' (ὁ ἔσω ἄνθρωπος *ho esō anthrōpos*) in the Anthropology of Paul," presidential address, *SNTS* (1999). Paul uses Platonic categories but accommodates them to his own non-dualistic anthropology.

115. See J. T. Fitzgerald, *Cracks in an Earthen Vessel: An Examination of the Catalogues of Hardships in the Corinthian Correspondence* (Atlanta: Scholars Press, 1988) 203; M. M. DiCicco, *Paul's Use of Ethos, Pathos, and Logos in 2 Corinthians 10–13* (Lewiston: Mellen Biblical, 1995) 60n. 101.

temporal and eternal (4:17), what is seen and what is not seen (4:18), are developed around a series of further, related antinomies: earthly tent/heavenly dwelling (5:1-2), being clothed/being naked (5:3-4), mortal/life, and being at home/taking a journey (5:6-8). Because refinement develops the same points by appearing to be talking about something else, we should not be surprised that twice Paul states, in a slightly different form, that he is "confident/courageous" (5:6, 8; earlier he wrote of "not despairing/losing heart," 4:1, 16).

When Paul introduces a statement with οἴδαμεν (*oidamen*), "we know," he draws on material that he assumes his auditors know and embrace. Therefore, his statement, "If the earthly tent . . . is destroyed, we have a building from God" (5:1 NIV), buttresses what he has previously said about not being misled by externals and appearances (5:1). For emphasis, Paul dwells on the topic. He contrasts an earthly, temporal tent (σκῆνος *skēnos*) with an eternal, heavenly edifice (οἰκοδομή *oikodomē*) and, because his interest is more on the latter, he elaborates it in more detail: It is from God, and not made by hands (5:1). Although the tent is mentioned once more in 5:4, the terminology shifts to vestment with additional clothes (5:3-4).

Recognizing that believers sigh or groan in their earthly existence (5:2), a position thoroughly consonant with Paul's treatment of his hardships and afflictions (4:8-12), and reaffirming that believers groan in this tent (5:4), Paul's choice is not the gnostic one—that is, to escape the body by sloughing it off. Neither is Paul the least bit interested in how people are changed from the tent to the building. On the contrary, his choice is that "we might be further clothed, so that the mortal might be swallowed up without remainder by life" (5:4). For Paul, the alternative is not bodily existence versus life without a body, because life is always bodily. In 1 Cor 15:35-44, Paul makes a similar point by arguing that life now and in God's redemptive future is and will be bodily. Humans do not *have* bodies that can be "taken off," leaving some untarnished inner entity (e.g., the soul, as in much of second-century and some modern versions of Christianity). No, life is bodily. Afflicted, suffering human beings,

like earthenware vessels, are the very place where God's treasure is borne.

In 5:4, with his imagery of being further clothed and of life's swallowing up what is mortal, Paul instructs his hearers that his earlier antinomies, such as inner/outer, are not to be taken as completely divorced from one another.[116] In fact, Paul affirms that a process not unlike the transition "from glory unto glory" of 3:18 is under way. Paul has utter confidence that life is "swallowing up" (καταπίνω *katapinō*; the verb is emphatic, "without remainder/completely") what is mortal. What a perspective that gives on what he calls "this slight, momentary affliction" (4:17)! Harking back to 4:17, Paul avers that "the one who is producing [a repeat of the term κατεργάζομαι (*katergazomai*) from 4:17] this very thing [i.e., life's swallowing up of death without remainder] is God who is giving us the down payment of the Spirit" (5:5; cf. 1:22).

5:5. Within this segment of the letter, Paul periodically reaffirms his strong eschatological convictions, which so powerfully inform his view of life in the present. In 5:5, his end-time conviction that death as the last enemy will be overcome (1 Cor 15:26) is recast as a process that God begins with the granting of the Holy Spirit, which all believers experience at the initiation of their life of faith (Rom 8:15-16). To make his point Paul employs a legal technical term with which his hearers should be acquainted: The Spirit is the ἀρραβών (*arrabōn*, "down payment" or "earnest money"), whose initial payment ensures that the one making it (in this case no less than God) will make good on the rest of the obligation (5:5). So the Spirit is here adduced as the guarantee that what God has begun in the afflicted, mortal lives of believers (i.e., life's swallowing up of death) will be finished because God is faithful to do what God has promised (1:20; Phil 1:6).

How could Paul not have "confidence" or "courage" (θαρρέω *tharreō*) when he not only believes God's transforming work is under way but also knows that the Holy Spirit is the down payment of it all? Ever the realist, though, Paul knows that "being at home in the body" inevitably entails, in some measure, "being away from the

---

116. P. Grelot, "De la maison terrestre à la maison céleste (2 Corinthiens 4,16-5,10)," 344-45, engagingly argues that throughout this passage Paul sets actual experience over against that for which one hopes.

Lord" (5:6). In other words, the present circumstances, which include suffering and affliction, are not the ideal arrangement or the final picture, the goal. Paul knows that to remain in the world is necessarily to experience distraction and divided devotion. When writing to the Corinthians earlier, he acknowledged that daily concerns of life and the needs of spouses, for example, could divide one's attention and devotion to the Lord (1 Cor 7:32-35).

5:6-10. Verses 6-9 are a complex passage. Using a term sometimes associated with exile (ἐκδημέω *ekdēmeō*),[117] Paul sets up a rhetorical figure (form: ABBAAB) with the A's representing "being at home" (ἐνδημέω *endēmeō*) and the B's meaning "being away from home" (*ekdēmeō*). First, Paul takes "being at home" and "being away from home" in a metaphorical sense and treats that alternative in Stoic categories of *adiaphora,* indifferent matters. Second, he distinguishes being at home in the body from being with the Lord. Finally, the text is framed by two very strongly eschatological claims (5:5, 10).

Being at home/away and adiaphora. To unpack the construction with the "at home" and "away from home" statements, we begin with 5:9 because there Paul subjugates his preferences with regard to being "at home" or "away" to a matter of infinitely greater importance: that he be one of those "pleasing the Lord" (5:9). In fact, the need to please the Lord trumps any personal preference (5:8) Paul may have. Paul's audience would have understood this deliberation as a Stoic-like sorting out of what is important from what is non-essential (*adiaphora,* "indifferent matters"; cf. 1 Corinthians 7). At many points in his letters, Paul employs this concept of indifferent matters as he relates to his predominantly Gentile audiences (cf. Rom 8:35-39; 14:8; Gal 3:28; Phil 1:10 ["discern what really matters"]; 4:10-13). In the scattered passages just referenced one finds quite a list of unimportant matters, including one's gender, social status, ethnic background, the way life comes to be, and even life and death themselves.

One might ask, then, what really matters to Paul and will find many ways he expresses it: "Jesus Christ, and him crucified" (1 Cor 2:2 NRSV); that his hearers will be "blameless at the

coming of our Lord Jesus Christ" (1 Thess 5:23 NRSV); that his auditors maximize their devotion to their Lord (1 Cor 7:32-35); and in the passage at hand that believers "please the Lord" (2 Cor 5:9; cf. 1 Cor 7:19; Gal 5:6; 6:15).

Among the indifferent matters, Stoics did recognize that there were "preferreds" and "not preferreds." For example, it mattered not whether one ate sumptuously, but if one were given the opportunity to choose in such a way as not to compromise one's own integrity, then why not eat well? In 2 Cor 5:6-9, the indifferent matters are whether one is "at home" or "away from home." Clearly, Paul has a preference that would move him beyond his affliction and hardships: "I would prefer rather to be away from the body and at home with the Lord" (5:8). But, like his thorn in the flesh to which he refers in the next letter fragment (12:7*b*-10), his preferences are not always granted to him—or even always chosen by him (Phil 1:23-26).

A similar passage in Philippians is instructive because the same options and assumptions are also present there.[118] Writing to the Philippians from prison (Phil 1:12-14), Paul declares the options he is considering: "to depart and be with Christ" versus "to remain in the flesh" (Phil 1:23-24 NRSV). The former is "much better" and is what he prefers (1:23); yet, the latter is what he chooses out of consideration for the Philippians and their need for him.

These alternatives, as stated in both passages, do not assume the absence of Christ in one's worldly life. Paul realizes that, for the present, believers cannot escape being in the world, where sin, though its power has been broken in Christ's death and resurrection, controls the structures of the world, and where to be associated with Christ is also to experience tribulation with this aeon and its residual powers. Apart from such negative forces, there are also goals or goods that compete with others for one's time, energies, and commitment; for example, caring for one's spouse properly attenuates one's "undivided devotion to the Lord" (1 Cor 7:35). As long as Paul is at home in the world, he will have anxiety over his

---

117. See Plato *Leg.* 9.864E.

118. Thus we are dealing with a Pauline commonplace of being at home and being away, not some slogan of his opponents as J. Murphy-O'Connor argues in "Being at Home in the Body We Are in Exile from the Lord (2 Cor 5:6*b*)," *RB* 93 (1986) 216-17.

churches (2 Cor 11:28); as often as someone in the faith suffers or stumbles, Paul will suffer or be indignant (1 Cor 12:26; 2 Cor 11:29). As long as he represents the gospel in the world, he will experience opposition and suffer affliction. Of course, he would prefer to be delivered from all such distress—and that is what he voices in 2 Cor 5:8. Faith, not sight, enables him to recognize God's power positively at work through these afflictions, bringing about ever-greater glory and having life triumph over the mortal.

The overriding concern in 5:6-9 to "please the Lord" renders "indifferent" whether one is alive (in the earthly body) or beyond life in the earthly body. Paul's rumination that he chooses to transcend his preference and to stay the course with the Corinthians as a way of pleasing the Lord has the added effect of appealing for sympathy and, therefore, stands a chance of winning him some measure of goodwill from them.

Being in the body/away from the Lord. Being in the body is at the same time being with the Lord for Paul. He has no confusion about this; he is being dramatic and forceful. Some modern interpreters have a problem because they do not recognize that Paul is free to set his rhetorical opposites in any way he chooses. His hearers know that they and Paul are "in Christ," that Christ is even "in them." They are members of Christ. They are part of Christ's body. All that is clear to them and is never a point of dispute in any of Paul's considerable correspondence with the Corinthians. Without any prejudice to any other conviction Paul has, he has simply made a rhetorical decision to write about daily life and has chosen the expression "in the body" to describe that experience; he chooses to write about leaving that daily life and has used going away "to the Lord" to designate that. This interpretation is confirmed when the phrase "in the body" is used to describe the deeds that will be weighed in the final judgment: One's life's works "in the body" will be assessed (5:10).

The eschatological frame. Paul encases 5:6-9 between two strong eschatological assertions (5:5, 10). On the one side is his declaration that receipt of the Holy Spirit is the "earnest money" that, having been "paid," assures God's finishing up of the "contract" (5:5). On the other side, Paul reminds the Corinthians that "all of us" must appear before the "judicial bench" (βῆμα *bēma*) of Christ, where everyone will receive recompense for what he or she has done "in the body" (5:10). So, as curious as the passage is, its interpretation must be guided in every particular by the eschatological framework Paul has given it. For example, Paul's three-time use of *ekdēmeō* (5:6, 8-9), "to leave one's country," "take a journey," "leave home" is surely each time a reference to what happens beyond life in this world, which he twice characterizes in 5:6-9 with the expression "in the body" (5:6, 8), a setup for the phrase's appearance in 5:10. Accordingly, in Paul's stated preference to "be away from the body" and to "be at home with the Lord" (ἐνδημῆσαι πρὸς τὸν κύριον *endēmēsai pros ton kyrion*, 5:8) he is not disclosing any metaphysics of resurrection, but is using "in the body" to express everyday life.

We should not read 1 Corinthians 15 into this discussion. There Paul used the notion of the "resurrection of the body" as a means of countering a *Corinthian* misunderstanding of resurrection, a misunderstanding for which there is no further clue in any of the subsequent Pauline correspondence with the Corinthians. So here he is not denying "resurrection of the body"; he has no interest in the "how" of resurrection here because his focus is on the way people, specifically himself and the Corinthians, live in their present daily lives. Far from diminishing the importance of "body" in Paul's thought, he carries through the instinct reflected in the opening of 4:1, where he expresses his wonder that God has placed all "this treasure" in such earthenware vessels as humans.

Actually, as 5:10 shows, Paul's attention is focused on the way believers must live their lives in the daily give-and-take of the world so that, when the judgment does come, when the fullness of what the Spirit guaranteed is present, when believers are given the opportunity to be "with the Lord" full-time, then they will pass muster at the judgment seat of Christ. Paul, ever the exemplar, declares in these verses that he has no hesitance to look forward to that day because he knows that he endeavors to live every day of his life in such a fashion that the judgment of "what he has done in the body"—that is, "in his life"—will be found acceptable and that his "recompense" (κομίζω *komizō*, "receive a recompense") will be "good" (ἀγαθός *agathos*), not "worthless" or "bad" (φαῦλος *phaulos*, 5:10).

The picture of the last judgment is intriguing. For the first time since 3:18, Paul explicitly invites the Corinthians ("For we, all of us" [γὰρ πάντας ἡμᾶς *gar pantas hēmas*]) into his frequent use of the plurals by which he for the most part depicts himself in the context of mainstream faith and practice. Not just he, but they also, will have to appear before the tribunal of Christ (cf. Rom 14:10, where it is the βῆμα [*bēma*] of God), so that "each one can receive a recompense for what he or she has done in the body, whether good or evil" (5:10). The term translated as "receive a recompense" (*komizō*) is often used of wages, so the judgment is a sort of payback (cf. the "wages of sin is death," Rom 6:23). This glimpse is supported by other references in the Pauline letters. In 2 Cor 11:15, Paul describes false apostles, whom he associates with Satan, who claim they are Paul's equals; he dismisses them with the cryptic "their end will be according to their works" (ὧν τὸ τέλος ἔσται κατὰ τὰ ἔργα αὐτῶν *hōn to telos estai kata ta erga autōn*, 11:15). The same outlook is reflected in Romans, where, in part, he cites Prov 24:12 in saying that God "will render to each according to his or her works"; the text goes on to detail not only the types of actions honored and punished but also the ultimate rewards and punishments (Rom 2:6-10).

Paul expects a final assessment regarding what we have done in the day-to-day transactions of life. The judgment will not be on what one believes or on whether one has the right ideas. The judgment will not be levied on one's faith, because faith is the free gift from God of right relationship to God (cf. 1 Cor 12:9). Faith, the right relationship with God, expresses itself, works itself out, in love, in acts of love concretely expressed in daily life (Gal 5:6, πίστις δι᾽ ἀγάπης ἐνεργουμένη *pistis di' agapēs energoumenē*). So justification—being made right with God, which comes on the basis of God's grace freely given—is indeed on the basis of grace through faith. But the judgment Paul expects is focused on the works faith has produced in the individual's life, just as Rom 2:6-10 also indicates.

Taking this insight back to the understanding of the rhetorical transactions Paul is attempting to make with the Corinthians, he stresses human responsibility for daily comportment. His self-portrait throughout chaps. 1–5 has shown him to be exemplary as he has fully lived out his call to be an apostle despite problems, hardships, and afflictions. His stated preference to "be at home with the Lord" (2 Cor 5:8), his acknowledgment that Christ's judicial bench awaits (5:10), and his implied readiness for it all suggest that his repeated avowals of his apostolic probity (1:23-24; 2:17; 4:2, 5, 8-12) are grounded in his understanding that his conduct has, indeed, been appropriate to his call and to the gospel that he proclaims.

REFLECTIONS

1. "Treasure in earthen vessels" is a powerful double metaphor that recognizes the awesome trust God bestows upon each of us and at the same time honors our fragility as bearers of God's grace and might. The image allows Paul and us to celebrate the awesome blessing of life and joy in tribulation, limitation, and difficulty. Because we are God's chosen vessels, we do not need to build cathedrals or make pilgrimages, to engage in extraordinary actions to prove our faith. Instead, we simply need to live our lives each day in ways that love and honor one another. Jesus' parable of the sheep and the goats (Matt 25:31-46) makes the same point: Those who simply and humbly go about each day caring for the ill, visiting the imprisoned, and so forth are so naturally dedicated to caring for one another that there is no room for religious calculation in them. They can honestly ask, "When, Lord, did we see you thus?"

2. Those curious expressions about the death and life of Jesus being in our bodies may help us to reflect on our physical limitations and problems. We are accustomed to thinking of our bodies as having problems, getting fat, or not working as we wish they would. Paul thinks that physical problems are everyday reminders of Christ's death and of our association with it. Likewise, our moments of joy and delight, forgiveness and reconciliation, are windows onto the life of Jesus (i.e., resurrection), making its way into our very corporeal existence. The life of Jesus "in our mortal flesh" (not "body" as in 4:11 NIV) honors the fleshliness of existence as a proper locus for the life of faith. Gnostics denigrated the flesh and fleshliness, and redemption was for them always depicted as an escape from corporeality. Paul embraces human fleshliness and declares, with all its foibles and limitations, that the very life of Jesus comes to expression precisely there. Thus it is not strange that Paul should see in the cross, that earthy, crude instrument, the very ground of hoping and being.

3. We tend to glorify biblical characters and paint them in colors alien to our experiences and lives. It is not one of our better moves. We surmise that they do not suffer, that they have no doubt, that they do not struggle as we do. But note well that Paul describes himself (much as he did in chap. 1) as being near the brink of what he can bear, as about to fall over the edge. Maybe we extol biblical characters out of self-doubt; perhaps, worse, our doing so may be driven by self-loathing or self-pity. As downtrodden and crushed as Paul was, however, he was convinced that God would never let him go.

4. Are you not often taken aback when you meet someone again after several years have passed? "How they have aged!" you might think. Paul takes it for granted that what people see about us, the externals, is wasting away like rust eats into iron. But he also believes that is not the whole story; inside we are being renewed day by day. From inside, the Spirit is working to express its fruit—love, joy, peace, patience, kindness, goodness, faithfulness, gentleness, self-control (Gal 5:22)—in us. Perhaps we should be making every effort to get out of the Spirit's way and let these fruit show through from our inner selves to those around us.

5. "We walk by faith, not by sight" (5:7)—a refinement of Paul's earlier comments about looking to things that are not seen (4:18). This is one of Paul's great pieces of wisdom. Where should we get our clues about purpose and direction, about what to make of what is around us? Fueled by his apocalyptic outlook, Paul knew that to reckon from what is seen, from appearances, is a sure way to be misled about what is really important and about what is truly going on. We all know how easily people can misunderstand when they know just the externals or when they make assumptions from superficial knowledge. Yet, that awareness does not keep us from doing the same thing regarding others. So it is with God's purposes: Imagine how far astray you might go if you made your own decision about Jesus on the basis of his being born out of wedlock; of his keeping company with prostitutes, lepers, and tax collectors; and of his being killed in that culture's most shameful manner (the equivalent of the electric chair or the gas chamber or lethal injection). Paul's care to distinguish between externals and internals should caution us about making superficial, snap judgments regarding the truth about someone. Conclusions and conjectures based on external, superficial information or impressions will more often prove wrong than right—and can do a great disservice, if not injustice, to others.

6. Most popular representations of the final judgment have the smell of sulfur and the sounds of Armageddon about them. Too often the last-day judgment is presented as a fearsome event. Some writers and speakers even use it as a means of frightening their followers into compliance. Note that Paul does not have even the slightest hint of a fearful understanding of the last judgment. It is worth thinking about why Paul does not stoop to fear-mongering when he thinks of the last judgment and of giving an account of his life, of his decisions, of his actions, of his "deeds done in the body." Two reasons for this suggest themselves: First, he knows that the love he is supposed to show toward others is generated by the Holy Spirit (Gal 5:22), so it is quite present if he will simply let the Spirit do its work in his life. Second, in his everyday life Paul always aims for love and seeks to glorify God.

2 Corinthians 5:11–6:10, Paul's Ministry of Reconciliation

NIV

[11]Since, then, we know what it is to fear the Lord, we try to persuade men. What we are is plain to God, and I hope it is also plain to your conscience. [12]We are not trying to commend ourselves to you again, but are giving you an opportunity to take pride in us, so that you can answer those who take pride in what is seen rather than in what is in the heart. [13]If we are out of our mind, it is for the sake of God; if we are in our right mind, it is for you. [14]For Christ's love compels us, because we are convinced that one died for all, and therefore all died. [15]And he died for all, that those who live should no longer live for themselves but for him who died for them and was raised again.

[16]So from now on we regard no one from a worldly point of view. Though we once regarded Christ in this way, we do so no longer. [17]Therefore, if anyone is in Christ, he is a new creation; the old has gone, the new has come! [18]All this is from God, who reconciled us to himself through Christ and gave us the ministry of reconciliation: [19]that God was reconciling the world to himself in Christ, not counting men's sins against them. And he has committed to us the message of reconciliation. [20]We are therefore Christ's ambassadors, as though God were making his appeal through us. We implore you on Christ's behalf: Be reconciled to God. [21]God made him who had no sin to be sin[a] for us, so that in him we might become the righteousness of God.

6 As God's fellow workers we urge you not to receive God's grace in vain. [2]For he says,

"In the time of my favor I heard you,
  and in the day of salvation I helped you."[b]

I tell you, now is the time of God's favor, now is the day of salvation.

[3]We put no stumbling block in anyone's path, so that our ministry will not be discredited.

[a]21 Or be a sin offering   [b]2 Isaiah 49:8

NRSV

11Therefore, knowing the fear of the Lord, we try to persuade others; but we ourselves are well known to God, and I hope that we are also well known to your consciences. [12]We are not commending ourselves to you again, but giving you an opportunity to boast about us, so that you may be able to answer those who boast in outward appearance and not in the heart. [13]For if we are beside ourselves, it is for God; if we are in our right mind, it is for you. [14]For the love of Christ urges us on, because we are convinced that one has died for all; therefore all have died. [15]And he died for all, so that those who live might live no longer for themselves, but for him who died and was raised for them.

16From now on, therefore, we regard no one from a human point of view;[a] even though we once knew Christ from a human point of view,[a] we know him no longer in that way. [17]So if anyone is in Christ, there is a new creation: everything old has passed away; see, everything has become new! [18]All this is from God, who reconciled us to himself through Christ, and has given us the ministry of reconciliation; [19]that is, in Christ God was reconciling the world to himself,[b] not counting their trespasses against them, and entrusting the message of reconciliation to us. [20]So we are ambassadors for Christ, since God is making his appeal through us; we entreat you on behalf of Christ, be reconciled to God. [21]For our sake he made him to be sin who knew no sin, so that in him we might become the righteousness of God.

6 As we work together with him,[c] we urge you also not to accept the grace of God in vain. [2]For he says,

"At an acceptable time I have listened to you,
  and on a day of salvation I have helped you."

[a]Gk according to the flesh   [b]Or God was in Christ reconciling the world to himself   [c]Gk As we work together

NIV

[4]Rather, as servants of God we commend ourselves in every way: in great endurance; in troubles, hardships and distresses; [5]in beatings, imprisonments and riots; in hard work, sleepless nights and hunger; [6]in purity, understanding, patience and kindness; in the Holy Spirit and in sincere love; [7]in truthful speech and in the power of God; with weapons of righteousness in the right hand and in the left; [8]through glory and dishonor, bad report and good report; genuine, yet regarded as impostors; [9]known, yet regarded as unknown; dying, and yet we live on; beaten, and yet not killed; [10]sorrowful, yet always rejoicing; poor, yet making many rich; having nothing, and yet possessing everything.

NRSV

See, now is the acceptable time; see, now is the day of salvation! [3]We are putting no obstacle in anyone's way, so that no fault may be found with our ministry, [4]but as servants of God we have commended ourselves in every way: through great endurance, in afflictions, hardships, calamities, [5]beatings, imprisonments, riots, labors, sleepless nights, hunger; [6]by purity, knowledge, patience, kindness, holiness of spirit, genuine love, [7]truthful speech, and the power of God; with the weapons of righteousness for the right hand and for the left; [8]in honor and dishonor, in ill repute and good repute. We are treated as impostors, and yet are true; [9]as unknown, and yet are well known; as dying, and see—we are alive; as punished, and yet not killed; [10]as sorrowful, yet always rejoicing; as poor, yet making many rich; as having nothing, and yet possessing everything.

COMMENTARY

5:11-12. In the third of his complementary reflections of his ministry, Paul describes himself, along with all the others in the mainstream, as being guided by the "fear of the Lord" as he "persuades" (a euphemism for effectively preaching the gospel and a description of what he is doing as he writes; 5:11). "Fear of the Lord" is a traditional phrase, deeply grounded in Paul's Scriptures (cf. Deut 6:2, 13; 10:20; 28:58; Job 28:28; Ps 111:10; Prov 1:7; Isa 11:2; Jer 32:39). Far from a psychological description or some physical manifestation, "fear of the Lord" in biblical tradition describes post-exilic faithfulness. The ones who "fear the Lord" are the devotees of Yahweh. As Paul has adopted the phrase, it also betokens his sense of the majesty and power, the *mysterium tremendum,* of God, who promotes justice, opposes all wickedness, and expects accountability (cf. Rom 1:18; 3:18-19). Accordingly, appearing before the tribunal of Christ is taken with utmost seriousness, and the "fear of the Lord" means that Paul makes certain that "what he does in the body" is appropriate to the gospel and "pleasing to the Lord" (5:9).

Paul affirms that he is known by God (5:11*b*).

God already knows the secrets of peoples' hearts (Rom 2:16; 8:27; 1 Cor 14:25), and at the end time the heart's plans will be revealed (1 Cor 4:5; 1 Thess 2:4). Paul is more confident about God's understanding of him, and less sure about the Corinthians' understanding. His appeal to their consciences is a subtle request that they employ their moral reasoning to bring themselves more fully into conformity with him (5:11).[119] The Corinthians, who should function as letters of commendation for Paul (3:2-3), are now described as those who should be able to boast about Paul because they ought to be competent to distinguish between "appearances" and "realities" (Paul's contrast is literally between "face" ["what is seen," NIV; "outward appearance," NRSV] and "heart," 5:12), harking back to and capitalizing on his earlier differentiation between things seen and not seen and between his "inner" and "outer" self (4:16-18).

5:13. Alongside the contrast between "face" and "heart" (5:12) he lodges another: "out of one's mind" versus "in one's right mind" (5:13).

119. J. Paul Sampley, *Walking Between the Times: Paul's Moral Reasoning* (Minneapolis: Fortress, 1991) 57-58.

With this pair of enigmatic statements, Paul gives an invaluable, though concise, self-portrait: "If we are out of our mind, it has to do with God; if we are in our right mind, it has to do with you" (5:13). As the Corinthians surely know, Paul is prone to visions and revelations (1 Cor 2:10; 2 Cor 12:7; Gal 1:12; 2:2) and ecstatic speech (glossolalia; 1 Cor 14:18), and they are soon to learn that he was once even transported to paradise (12:1-4). His being "out of his mind" (ἐξίστημι *existēmi*) as between himself and God probably refers to his manifestation of such well-known personal characteristics because his description of glossolalia in 1 Cor 14:2 is congruent; glossolalia, without interpretation, relates the individual to God alone, not to others (1 Cor 14:2).

The verb σωφρονέω (*sōphroneō*), "being in right mind" (5:13), is used one other time in the Pauline corpus in a context where Paul describes balanced, thoughtful, purposeful evaluation of the self that does not overreach the measure of faith meted out by God (Rom 12:3). Applying that sense here, we see that Paul, in effect, says, "When I think in a reasoned, appropriate way about myself, it is for your advantage."

What does Paul's self-portrait in 5:13 reveal about him? It shows that, even though he would delight to depart and be with the Lord unfettered, a part of his life is between himself and God (1 Cor 14:2, 4a) and is distinguishable from his relation to believers. When it is just between an individual and God, as in glossolalia, for example, one's own edification benefits from the special relationship to God (cf. 1 Cor 14:4a). In that same sphere belong revelations, heavenly transit, and any other such ecstatic experiences; there one is dealing fully and only with God, as Paul says in 5:13a.

In the other sphere, where one walks in part by sight, where the outer is wasting away, and where things are transitory, Paul's call as apostle to the Gentiles must be exercised in relation to other believers. There, Paul must honor his relationship with the Corinthians by acting in a reasoned way that serves their interests—which is precisely what he says he is doing (5:13b).

Sōphroneō ("to be right-minded," 5:13b) and συνείδησις (*syneidēsis*, "moral consciousness," "conscience," 5:11) are both primary terms in Paul's moral reasoning, as one might suspect the

Corinthians would already know from their long exposure to him and his teachings. In 5:11 he subtly urges them to use their moral consciousnesses (consciences) in making a proper, not superficial, assessment of him; in 5:13 he describes himself as *continuing* to relate to them with the best of his right-mindedness "for their sakes," just as love always does. Though the term "love" is not mentioned in 5:13, Paul's description of himself as always acting in their interest is tantamount to using the term, which surely is close to his mind, judging from its appearance in the very next verse (5:14).

5:14-21. The terminology and the claims of 5:14-21 are dense and laconically compressed. Much of Paul's richness developed in much more detail in other places is here suggested by the slightest clue. For example, the idea that believers should live not for themselves (5:15) is a tacit reaffirmation of self-commendatory claims that Paul has made about himself previously in this letter (4:2, 12, 15; 5:8-9). But beyond that, the idea of living for Christ (the one "who died and was raised for them," 5:15) subtly suggests the slave market and its practices, which Paul has found so useful in writing elsewhere about how believers are "bought with a price" (1 Cor 6:20; 7:23) and now have a new Lord who deserves their full obedience and service ("You are not your own," 1 Cor 6:19-20; 7:23; Gal 2:20).

5:14-15. In 5:14-21, Paul portrays himself—still using the plural to identify with the mainstream—as the one who has advanced the gospel, whose focus is now depicted as being reconciliation. In fact, 5:14a—"for the love of Christ impels us"—is a refinement of 5:13b, crediting love as the force that drives Paul's care for the Corinthians. The mention of the love of Christ triggers from Paul a rather set formulation, a Pauline commonplace (signaled by the formulaic κρίναντας τοῦτο ὅτι [*krinantas touto, hoti*, "being convinced of this, that . . ."]) about God's great purpose begun in the death of Christ "for all" (5:14-15).

Paul's employment of the genitive construction ἡ γὰρ ἀγάπη τοῦ Χριστοῦ (*hē gar agapē tou Christou*, "the love of Christ") leaves the hearers and the interpreter to decide whether Paul intends "Christ's love" (for us, understood) or believers' love for Christ. The other place where Paul uses the same Greek expression is Rom 8:35: "Who shall separate us from the love of Christ?" The parallel with Rom 8:39 ("Nothing . . . can separate us from the love of God in Christ") suggests that the phrase in 5:14 ought to be read as subjective, indicating that the direction of the love is from Christ. The flow of love in Paul's thought world seems regularly to be *from* God or Christ *to* human beings. This love establishes, in turn, the right relation to God that Paul calls by the code word "faith." Faith, when it functions as it should, expresses itself in love of others (Gal 5:6).

Most often in the Pauline corpus the term "love" is used to describe how believers relate to one another; less frequently, Paul speaks of God's love for humans (Rom 5:5, 8; 8:39; 2 Cor 13:14). Taking it as Christ's love for believers has the further merit of honoring Paul's deep conviction that, no matter the topic, the initiative, expressed in terms of grace, rests not with people but with God, through Christ.

The verb translated "compels" (NIV) or "urges on" (NRSV; συνέχω *synechō*) has a semantic range from "impels" to "hold within bounds/control." Given the larger context of this letter fragment, Paul can be understood to claim that Christ's love drives him on, affirming what he has repeatedly said earlier in the letter about not despairing (4:1, 16; cf. 2:14-17). In the verses that lie ahead, with the assertions about ambassadorship, for example, further support will be found for the notion that Christ's love impels believers (in particular, Paul) out into the world (5:19).

For Paul elsewhere, however, love just as surely holds a believer within bounds. For example, in a chapter that begins by affirming that love builds up (1 Cor 8:1), Paul writes that he will not eat meat if doing so would cause a brother or sister in Christ to stumble (1 Cor 8:13). On account of love, Paul resists commanding Philemon what to do about Onesimus, but supposes love will set the borders of Philemon's response (Phlm 8-9).

In the set piece to which Paul adverts (in 5:14-21), the foundational claim is that "one [Christ] has died for all" (5:14). The same assertion is stated in slightly different ways in the corpus: "Christ died for the ungodly" (Rom 5:6 NRSV); "Christ died for us" (Rom 5:8 NRSV; cf. 1 Cor 8:11; 15:3; 1 Thess 5:10). And because he assumes that believers die *with* Christ, which also

can be expressed in different fashions (Rom 5:15; 6:3-8), Paul postulates that "therefore all have died" (5:14).

The claim that Christ died "for all" (ὑπὲρ πάντων *hyper pantōn*, 5:14) is repeated for refinement in 5:15 and should be taken, not in a substitutionary manner in the sense of Christ's taking everybody's place at his death, but in the sense of Christ's being for—that is, siding with—people.[120] Christ's death shows that God is "for them," as can be seen unmistakably in Rom 8:31: "If God is for us [ὑπὲρ ἡμῶν *hyper hēmōn*], who can be against us?" (NIV; see the same outlook reflected in Paul's Lord's supper traditions, 1 Cor 11:24). Christ's death broke the power of sin as lord over people's lives (Rom 6:11). People were reconciled to God by Christ's death (Rom 5:10). Jesus' death provides deliverance (1 Thess 1:10). Redemption in Christ's death leads to adoption as God's children (Gal 4:5) and newness of life (Rom 6:4).

The "ones who are living" (οἱ ζῶντες *hoi zōntes*, 5:15) are a subset refinement of the "all" for whom Christ died (5:14; cf. Rom 6:4). So Christ died for everyone (5:14-15). Some of those whom Paul now calls the living ones, have, by sharing his death, been brought to newness of life (cf. Rom 6:4); they are part of what Paul is about to describe as the "new creation" (5:17).

5:16. Christ's death is the transformative event for all of life. Nothing is the same after that. First among the radical changes brought about by Christ's death is the way people should live: no longer for themselves but for the one who died and was raised for them (5:15). The transformations begun in Christ's death and resurrection will be expanded until they encompass the entire universe (κόσμος *kosmos*, 5:19, which fits the Romans 8 pattern, where the whole of creation longs for the freedom the children of God already experience; see Rom 8:21-23). Another constitutive change involves how believers now view others: no longer κατὰ σάρκα (*kata sarka*), literally, "according to the flesh." Paul's lead up to this passage has established how this phrase must be understood: Believers must look to what is not seen (4:18; 5:7); they must look to the inner person and not take primary clues from the outer

---

120. E. P. Sanders, *Paul and Palestinian Judaism: A Comparison of Patterns of Religion* (Philadelphia: Fortress, 1977) 463-72.

person (4:16); they must consider the heart and not the face (5:12).

In this letter, Paul has been practicing what he preaches. Now Christ is set forth as his example: "Even though we once knew Christ *kata sarka,* but now we no longer do so" (5:16). To know Christ *kata sarka* is, in part as Paul recognizes elsewhere, to know him as descended from David according to the flesh (Rom 1:3). "Now"—that is, *this* side of, after, Christ's resurrection—Paul no longer contents himself with that apprehension of Christ. Just as he no longer considers Christ as if he had not been raised from the dead, so also he now asserts that "we can no longer consider anyone" simply from the flesh (*kata sarka*), with that phrase standing now for regarding people from all the misleading, inadequate ways that offer themselves and that Paul has been careful to reject in the previous paragraphs, from 4:7 forward.

To consider anyone simply from the flesh (*kata sarka*) is to view that person as if the fundamentally transformative resurrection of Christ had not taken place—and as if the norms or standards of judgment had not therein been radically altered. Believers are not simply offered a new perspective they may or may not adopt as and when they see fit; rather, something so fundamental has changed in such a profound fashion that the old ways of looking, perceiving, understanding, and, more profoundly, evaluating, have to be let go and replaced with a new way of seeing and understanding.

5:17. Paul accounts for this transformative shift: "If one is in Christ," and all believers by definition are, "he or she is a new creation." Much of Paul's letter before us wrestles with the way people, particularly the Corinthians, see and understand him, Paul, too much from externals. Those who are part of the new creation can no longer be considered *kata sarka,* according to the standards of the world.

The phrase "new creation" (καινὴ κτίσις *kainē ktisis*) is evocative and enigmatic. It is used only one other time in Paul's letters: "For neither circumcision is anything not uncircumcision, but new creation is" (Gal 6:15). A classic Pauline *adiaphora* (indifferent matters) statement, Gal 6:15 is a refinement of the same general expression found earlier in that very letter: "In Christ Jesus, neither circumcision nor uncircumcision means anything, but faith working through love

does" (Gal 5:6). These two Galatians statements, with the same indifferent-matters construction (i.e., neither A nor B matters, but C does), conclude by affirming that what really counts in life is "faith working through love" and "new creation." The similarity of form for the first and second A's and B's suggests that the two C's are in some deep sense mutually interpretive. So "new creation" must allow within it rather definitionally "faith"—that is, the right relationship with God—"expressing itself in love," in the right relationships among those whom God loves. This identification of "new creation" (Gal 5:16) with "faith expressing itself in love" (Gal 5:6) fits equally well with Paul's description elsewhere of believers' "walking in newness of life" (ἐν καινότητι ζωῆς *en kainotēti zōēs,* Rom 6:4).

Finally, Paul's concern with "new creation" in 2 Cor 5:17 parallels the sublime picture in Romans 8, where the whole of creation that was subjected to purposelessness and decay (Rom 8:20-21) because of sin's corrosive power (cf. Rom 1:18-23) is groaning, like a woman in childbirth, toward its own redemption (Rom 8:21-22). Throughout 2 Corinthians 1–5, Paul has shown the capacity to encapsulate in a few sentences, and once even in a single sentence (2 Cor 3:18), much of the gospel—and the life appropriate to it. Here in the two-word construction "new creation," Paul captures the whole of the gospel he represents.

The last part of 2 Cor 5:17 is pithy and subject to very different interpretations, whose viability cannot be judged simply within the immediate context. Where one lands on the hermeneutical issues here depends on how one understands Paul's entire outlook. First, the Greek of the first clause, τὰ ἀρχαῖα παρῆλθεν, ἰδοὺ γέγονεν καινα (*ta archaia parēlthen, idou gegonen kaina*), is readily translatable: "the old things have gone/passed away." The second clause presents the problems. The demonstrative pronoun ἰδού (*idou*) grabs attention by expressing "behold" or "see."

The puzzle rests on how to construe the two terms *gegonen kaina* and on determining their relationship to the rest of the sentence. *Gegonen,* the verb, is the perfect tense, signifying "the *continuance* of *completed action,*"[121] of γίνομαι

---

121. *BDF* 340, italics added.

(*ginomai*), which has the semantic range "come to be," "become," "made." The term *kaina* ("new") with a verb like *ginomai* can be construed as either the subject or the object of the verb. The most prevalent interpretation, as may be seen readily in the NIV and in the RSV, takes *kaina* as the subject: "the new has come." The NRSV achieves its translation, "everything has become new," by honoring, in effect, a variant that specifies the subject as τὰ πάντα (*ta panta*, "all things," "everything") and by assuming, very reasonably, that the singular verb *gegonen* can have a neuter, plural subject.[122] In the NIV and in the RSV, *kaina*, "new," is taken as the subject; in the NRSV it functions as an object or a predicate adjective.

A third interpretation, however, is equally possible, and without resort to any textual variants. The verb *gegonen* can take as its subject τὰ ἀρχαῖα (*ta archaia*, "the old") from the preceding clause, with the resulting translation: "The old things have passed away; see, they [the old things] have become new" (5:17).

The Greek leaves itself open to either translation: "the new has come" or "it [the old] has become new." The consequences of the choice are considerable.[123] The former makes a stronger demarcation between "the old" and "the new," and discontinuity is stressed. The latter recognizes a difference, a transformation, but allows more continuity. We have already seen these issues played out in the two-covenant passage (2 Cor 3:1-18). And one can see it in a comparison of Romans and Galatians, where, for rhetorical purposes of engaging very different audiences, the former emphasizes continuity and the latter stresses discontinuity.[124]

Paul sometimes accents the continuity of God's purposes. In those places the faithfulness of God is affirmed, and what has happened in Christ is understood as the carrying out of God's plans and promises (see Rom 3:3-4; 15:8-13; 1 Cor 1:9; 10:13; 2 Cor 1:20). When Paul features contrast or discontinuity, however, he usually is trying to

help auditors understand how much their lives have changed (see Gal 3:1-5, 22-24) or will yet change before God has finished with them (1 Cor 15:35-50).

What would it mean if Paul were understood to say that "the old things have passed away; see, they have become new" (5:17)? Paul is quite capable of looking at a single phenomenon from two different perspectives and making quite distinctive claims about them. For the most mundane sort of example of this Pauline capacity, Epaphroditus is Paul's "brother, fellow worker, and fellow soldier" and is the Philippians' "apostle and servant" (Phil 2:25). Paul can also abide the complexity in matters where statements in some tension with each other must be made so that the larger picture can be served. Witness the treatment of the two covenants in 2 Cor 3:1–4:6, where Paul employs contrast and antithesis to make his points, but not to the extent of denying value and glory to the first covenant. Paul's picture in the two-covenant passage is much more complex than "out with the old" and "in with the new."

In many of his letters, Paul has an intricate, nuanced view of the relation of past and present, old and new. Paul's choice of the phrase "new creation" (*kainē ktisis*) itself exemplifies the complexity of his thinking. It expresses redemption as a kind of creation renewed, made over. It is a new thing that recaptures, not jettisons, the old, much as Deutero-Isaiah, one of Paul's favorites, projects (see Isa 42:9; 43:19-20).

In some senses, for Paul the old things have passed—especially when Paul wants to appreciate the changes faith has wrought. Paul frequently uses "no longer" expressions to describe how things were apart from faith (Rom 6:9; 2 Cor 5:16; Gal 2:20; 3:25; 4:7); believers do walk in "newness of life" (Rom 6:4). Old patterns of living have also passed; believers are not supposed to walk as they formerly did (cf. Gal 4:8-9; Phil 3:13-14).

On other occasions, however, especially when he takes the long view of God's purposes, Paul thinks of continuity. God's promises are finding their fulfillment in Christ (Rom 15:8-13; 2 Cor 1:20). The Scriptures foresaw certain things (Gal 3:8) and were written for the instruction of Paul and his contemporaries (1 Cor 10:6, 11). Christ

---

122. *BDF* 133.
123. See the reflections on this issue by a variety of authors in *Interpreting 2 Corinthians 5:14-21: An Exercise in Hermeneutics,* ed. J. P. Lewis (Lewiston: Edwin Mellen) 116-18, 136-37, 148-50, 173-74.
124. J. Paul Sampley, "Romans and Galatians: Comparison and Contrast," in *Understanding the Word: Essays in Honor of B. W. Anderson,* ed. J. T. Butler, E. W. Conrad, and B. Ollenberger, JSNTSup 37 (Sheffield: JSOT, 1985) 315-39.

became a minister to the circumcised in order to confirm the promises given to the patriarchs (Rom 15:8).

5:18-20. "All of this"—the "new creation" that begins in Christ's death—is from God (5:18). Romans 5:6-11 parallels 2 Cor 5:14-21 in instructive ways. Both mention reconciliation as the defining act of God. Both credit love as the defining force (God's, Rom 5:8; Christ's, 2 Cor 5:14). Romans uses the passive as a subtle way of ascribing the reconciliation to God: "For if while we were enemies, we were reconciled to God through the death of his son" (Rom 5:10 NRSV). Here in 2 Corinthians, Paul, in line with his purposes throughout this letter to credit God as working *in him* (cf. 2:17; 3:5; 5:1), openly avers that "all of this is from God who . . . *has given us the ministry of reconciliation*" (5:18, italics added).

Whereas Romans links justification with reconciliation as equivalent and interchangeable terms (Rom 5:9-10), Paul, in 2 Corinthians, lacking any problem with the Corinthians' relationship to the law, does not mention justification (but note 5:21, where the same root term, "righteousness," does cap off the argument). Justification has its social setting in the law or in the courts, and so it does not have any pertinence here in 2 Corinthians; reconciliation has its social setting in a familial or friendship environment where there has been a restoration of a broken relationship, precisely Paul's recent and somewhat continuing problem with the Corinthians.

Paul's statement, still in the plural, that God has "reconciled us to himself through Christ" (5:18) offers a slight invitation to the Corinthians to think of themselves as being included, because that is as true of them as it is of Paul. But as the passage goes on, Paul's plural becomes restrictive to himself once again: "and has given us the ministry of reconciliation" (καὶ δόντος ἡμῖν τὴν διακονίαν τῆς καταλλαγῆς *kai dontos hēmin tēn diakonian tēs katallagēs*, 5:18). Once more he makes an explicit connection between the grand theological tradition and his problems with the Corinthians.

Before he pursues that link with the Corinthians, however, he returns to the tradition yet one more time to affirm that God's work in Christ was cosmic in scope, that it involved a divine forbearance toward human trespasses (which Paul worked hard to communicate as also imitatively operative for him with the Corinthians, 2:5-11; cf. 7:5-12) and, possibly echoing Ps 104:27 LXX, that God has "entrusted to us the word of reconciliation" (5:19).

The twice-stated claim that God selected Paul for this ministry and message of reconciliation (5:18-19) provides him the base to make a not too subtle address to the Corinthians. Paul, who has been made "ambassador for Christ," is now the one through whom God's appeal is made in behalf of Christ: "be reconciled to God" (5:20). The verb πρεσβεύω (*presbeuō*, "to be an ambassador/envoy") places Paul in a lofty position of responsibility, as one who must, in all his activities, represent the one in authority and, as here, speak for him[125] (cf. Paul's use of δοῦλος [*doulos*, "slave"] to the Corinthians as a self-description in 4:5). Paul's call to the Corinthians to "be reconciled to God" is at the same time an encouragement of them to associate themselves more closely with Paul, who is so clearly a major part of God's plan for reconciliation.

Uncharacteristically, 5:20 is the only place in the Pauline corpus where the reconciling is to be done by people. In the other instances, Paul either uses the passive, such as "we were reconciled" (Rom 5:10 NRSV), where God is the understood actor or directly states that God is the reconciling one (2 Cor 5:18). We may understand this anomaly because the Corinthians are, at the time of his writing of 2 Corinthians 1–9, the people Paul most needs to reconcile with. The statement explicitly calls for them to "be reconciled to God," but the encoded message is that they should thereby be reconciled to Paul, the ambassador who has brought the reconciliation gospel to them in the first place and thereby been the occasion for the end of their enmity with God (cf. Rom 5:1, 10).

5:21. Rather than let the appeal for reconciliation conclude the tradition and its application, Paul makes a christological development that is very reminiscent of the "story" that structures the

<hr />

125. M. M. Mitchell, "New Testament Envoys in the Context of Greco-Roman Diplomatic and Epistolary Conventions: The Example of Timothy and Titus," *JBL* 111 (1992) 649-70. J. N. Collins, "The Mediatorial Aspect of Paul's Role as *diakonos*," *AusBR* 40 (1992) 36, 44, sees in 5:20 a confirmation that Paul's earlier use of (διακονία *diakonia*) must be read with overtones of "ambassador" and "messenger."

Christ hymn in Phil 2:5-11 and that reappears later in the letter fragment before us. The "story" goes like this: (phase 1) The exalted (rich) one assumes lowly (poor) status, becoming like us (phase 2), so that we can become exalted (rich) like him (phase 3). In the other two places in his letters where Paul tells this story (2 Cor 8:9; Phil 2:5-11), his interest resides in the hearers' move with Christ from the second phase to the third. The three phases are represented in 5:21: Phase 1 is the portrait of Christ as the one who did not know sin; phase 2 is Christ's being made (by God) sin on behalf of believers; and phase 3 is expressed in the purpose clause "in order that we might become the righteousness of God in him."

In the Rom 5:6-11 parallel to 2 Cor 5:14-21, Paul puts justification (the same root term as "righteousness" and "justice") alongside reconciliation as a functional synonym. For Paul, to be reconciled to God is to be justified or made righteous or, as Paul puts it elsewhere, to receive the righteousness of God (Rom 9:30–10:4). In Rom 10:3, precisely as in 2 Cor 5:21, the expression "righteousness of God" can be understood as the righteousness that comes from God or that is a characteristic of God. It is no surprise, then, when Paul writes so eloquently of reconciliation as he does in 2 Cor 5:14-21, that the passage should conclude in a claim about righteousness. From the clues one can see widely in the Pauline corpus, being reconciled to God implies some responsibilities to represent the righteousness ("justice" is also in the semantic range of δικαιοσύνη [dikaiosynē]) of God to others. That connection of reconciliation and righteousness/justice manifests itself explicitly in Paul's treatment of the collection for the saints in Jerusalem in 2 Cor 9:9-10.

In 2 Cor 5:21 Paul's chief interests in this particular recasting of the old story lie in getting the hearers to identify with Christ—as Christ identified with them by becoming one with them in their sin—and with the change represented in the purpose clause "our becoming the righteousness of God in [Christ]." Paul is not concerned to get into a theological deliberation about the "sinfulness" or "sinlessness" of Christ. Instead, he is eager to remind the Corinthians of their having been brought from sin to righteousness in Christ by God's grace (this term appears in 6:1) *and by*

Paul's having been given the ministry of reconciliation.

Paul's closing tradition celebrates that "in Christ" the believers have been made right with God by God's doing—which is the only way it can happen (cf. Rom 9:30–10:3). This is yet another time in this letter fragment that Paul has brought a section to a climax with what amounts to a concise summary of the gospel (5:21; cf. 3:14, 18).

6:1-3. In 6:1, Paul moves to relate his ministry of reconciliation more explicitly, and he opens with a delightful ambiguity in the participle συνεργοῦντες (*synergountes*, "working together with/cooperating with"). With whom is he cooperating? The Corinthians? God? (Both the NIV, inserting "God's" as the modifier of "fellow workers," and the NRSV, inserting "with him," hide the ambiguity of the Greek.) Paul's history has shown him working together with God; the Corinthians know that about him. What is left open is that the Corinthians could hear this participle as describing themselves as working together with Paul, a goal we have seen Paul pursue by insinuation and innuendo at every possible point in the letter. So Paul, working together at least with God and hoping for the Corinthians' cooperation, appeals to them not to receive the grace of God (which Paul has just been describing and of which Paul was given the ministry of reconciliation) in vain. The formulation "not in vain" (εἰς κενόν *eis kenon*) is a commonplace with Paul that always reckons with whether the person's life has honored the life-governing grace of God (1 Cor 15:10; Gal 2:2; Phil 2:16; 1 Thess 2:1; 3:5).

Paul's citation of Isa 49:8 provides him with a rallying call for the Corinthians: "Now is the acceptable/favorable time . . . now is the day of salvation" (6:2). It has been Paul's pattern throughout this letter fragment to highlight the eschatology, to emphasize that the Corinthians are near the time of fulfillment and must act accordingly, and he does so here again. Paul's intensity suggests little room for error and later recovery. The Corinthians risk everything if they stray or, as he puts it here, if they receive God's grace in vain.

Paul offers his own self-assessment as to how he, still using the plural and depicting himself as part of the mainstream, has comported himself blamelessly in his ministry (cf. 5:18). Negatively stated, he has given "no one in any way" (μηδεμίαν ἐν μηδενί *mēdemian en mēdeni*) an occasion for making a misstep (6:3). Stated positively, "in everything" he has commended himself as one of God's "ministers" (διάκονοι *diakonoi*, echoes of 3:6–4:1).

6:4-10. To unpack the commendatory "everything," Paul launches into an elaborate hardship list, longer and more stylized than the one in 4:7-12. Its length is designed to overwhelm any remaining opposition and to burnish Paul's ethos. In a list so extensive, overlap and, therefore, intensification must be expected. Also, what comes first and last in a series is always worth special notice because rhetoricians of Paul's time taught that those were the places of supreme emphasis.[126] It can be no surprise that Paul leads off the list with ὑπομονή (*hypomonē*, "patience/endurance/fortitude/perseverence") and θλῖψις (*thlipsis*, "affliction/tribulation/distress," 6:4). To reinforce the *hypomonē* of 6:4, μακροθυμία (*makrothymia*, "steadfastness/forbearance/endurance") shows up two verses later (6:6). Both these terms buttress Paul's self-depiction in this letter as not losing heart, but instead pressing on.

The last two constructions in the list—"as poor, but enriching many" and "as not having, but possessing everything" (6:10)—relate to Paul's economic patterns and to his special perspective on what really matters. Paul's apostleship has been one of service to others, not self-service and self-aggrandizement, perhaps to the chagrin of some Corinthians who see in him a person of attenuated status, too diminished to be considered a true apostle.

The hardship catalog has an intricate structure. Its repeated elements give it grandeur and suggest a limitless list.[127] The catalog opens with eighteen instances of the preposition ἐν (*en*, "in") constructions that describe (1) situations and circumstances in which Paul has found himself (6:4-5) and (2) his *modus operandi* in those circumstances (6:6). Then Paul shifts prepositions to διά (*dia*, "through") three times, probably to avoid monotony, but he continues through the first *dia* to develop his *modus operandi* (6:7). The other

two *dia* constructions (6:8) introduce a section that is finished with seven instances of ὡς (*hōs*, "as") structures (6:9-10), all nine of which (the *dia* and *hōs*) sketch out extremes within which Paul's apostolic ministry has been exercised.

These nine constructions share the outlook that has been developed formerly in this letter fragment where Paul cautions the Corinthians against being deceived by looking simply at the surface and not seeing to the heart of things, and admonishes them not to confuse what is important with what are truly *adiaphora*, "indifferent matters." The other Pauline passage that is most like 6:9-10 in outlook is 1 Cor 7:29-31, where ὡς μη (*hōs mē*, "as-if-not") becomes an eschatological lens through which one sees a way of living within this world without being governed by its values.

The entire hardship list shows Paul exposed to the vagaries of life, to the extremes of shame and honor, from slander to good report, being understood and misunderstood—yet steadfastly dependable through it all. All the quotidian challenges are put in perspective, once again (4:7, 10-12, 16; 5:4), by the ultimate couplet: "as dying, and, see, we live" (6:9).

With this hardship catalog, Paul brings to a conclusion the long section (2:14–6:10) in which he has advanced, along three complementary lines (3:1–4:6; 4:7–5:10; 5:11-21), his apostolic ministry and has attempted to give the Corinthians added reasons for adhering to him and for embracing him more fully. The location of the hardship list (6:1-10) at the end of this huge section is fitting; it serves to demonstrate that Paul is tried and true (δόκιμος *dokimos*; see 10:18; 13:7), that he has been and is for the Corinthians through thick and thin, and that he is worthy of their affirmation and affection. So it should not surprise us that Paul turns to press immediately and explicitly (6:11-13) for such an increase of affection.

Apart from Paul's rhetorical purposes with the Corinthians in his sublime affirmations about reconciliation (5:14-21), we should note that the conception is near the heart of his gospel.[128] The term "reconciliation" is a functional equivalent for "justification," as the parallelism of Rom 5:9-10 shows. We have seen in the Commentary on

---

126. See *Ad Herennium* 3.10.17-18; Demetrius, *On Style* 2.63; 5.249.
127. See Demetrius *On Style* 2.63.

128. R. P. Martin, *Reconciliation: A Study of Paul's Theology* (Atlanta: John Knox, 1981), argues that it is the center of Paul's gospel.

3:1–4:6 that "justification" and its related term, "righteousness," are for Paul covenant terms that often in the letters have a judicial tone; the provenance of these terms is covenant (where the ones made right with God do what is right) and law court (where the charges formerly lodged against one are dropped). The social setting of reconciliation is distinct; it relates to the restoration of relationships, the end of hostility and enmity, and the overcoming of alienation.

Paul writes of reconciliation in two aspects, one treating of the relation to God and the other detailing relations between human beings. Briefly, Paul's view is that sin, with its lordship power in effect, has alienated people from their proper filiation with God (Rom 1:18–3:20). Enmity has resulted. As Rom 5:1 expresses it, believers have been granted peace with God through Jesus Christ; the enmity between people and God is ended by a decisive act on God's part (Rom 5:10). "Reconciliation" is Paul's term for describing that restored relationship with God.

Equally important to Paul, and a consequence of the divine reconciliation, is the reconciliation of people to each other in Christ. Because God has properly reestablished relations with people, they can no longer carry animosity or grudges or resentments toward one another. The common denominator seen in several letters, and expressed most directly in 2 Cor 5:14-15 ("one has died for all . . . he died for all"), is that in human relations the baseline consideration regarding any human being is that Christ died for that person. Moral deliberation must take care that decisions and choices not harm one for whom Christ has died (Rom 14:15; 1 Cor 8:9-12; cf. Eph 2:11-22; Phil 2:1-5).

REFLECTIONS

1. The most basic fact for Christians is this: People have value because Christ has died for them. People, whoever they are, whether they have responded to Christ or not—Christ died for everyone (2 Cor 5:14-15)—are treasured by God. From the moment of Christ's death, everyone, *everyone,* has value. The problem rests with us. We often want to establish hurdles that others must jump before *we* will grant them value. They must think the way we do, act the way we do, vote the way we do, land on our issues the way we want them to—and the list could go on and on. No, each person's value has *already* been established by Christ's death for them, not by their response to that death. So we do not need to inquire whether persons are fellow Christians before we know that they deserve to be treated with respect. They are valuable because Christ has died for them.

2. Reconciliation is at the heart of life's business. If the most important single factor about any of our lives is God's having reconciled us to God's very self, then the proper celebration of our reconciliation is to share it with others by fostering reconciliation and atonement wherever and whenever we can. (If that is not the most significant single factor in your life, you might consider engaging in some deep reflection about idolatry.) Reconciliation as a ground of life would mean that when your friend makes some negative or judgmental comment about a neighbor, you will resist joining in. Indeed, instead you might respond by noting something you have appreciated about the same neighbor. Thus you may help two of your acquaintances come to understand each other better.

3. Related are Paul's observations that we may experience some difference between our outer and inner selves. Renewal of life can take place in the presence of huge problems that bear externally on us. Paul's is a way of thinking about life as being governed or defined not by what is happening around us—or even to our bodies—but by what God is doing from the inside. Similarly, Paul's contrast between face and heart (5:12) diminishes the definitional power of externals and emphasizes instead what is happening in our hearts.

4. Consider the first time you thought you were in love with someone. Odds are you could not contain yourself—or better yet, you could not contain the love you felt. Christ's love for us is not different in its effect. Christ's love not only claims us for God but also pushes us out toward others. The rubric goes like this: We-who-are-loved love others. Love of others is not an option for which we may or may not decide. Love generates love—that is true among humans most of the time. At the same time that love pushes us toward others, however, it also sets borders on the actions that are fitting or appropriate. Love scrutinizes the options for action and rules out those that are not advantageous or beneficial for others.

5. When Paul contemplates that the Corinthians may have accepted God's grace in vain (6:1), he acknowledges that believers can fall out of faith. You may have heard the expression "Once saved, always saved." It is not Pauline. Paul believed that we can turn away from God (cf. Gal 4:9). It is a powerful testimony to how much God loves us that God's grace at work in our lives frees us to say no to God. There is a delicacy about love: It is fullest and richest when it is freest, when all the trappings of compulsion are gone. Something like that is true also of grace: God's grace does claim us—no mistake about that. But it claims us in a way that enables us fully and freely to embrace it. Grace is perhaps better thought of as a stewardship rather than as a possession.

6. Why do bad things happen to good people? That may be our question, but it is not Paul's. Faith does not function as a protection from hard times or from difficulties. Problems and tribulations are not a sign of God's disfavor. The gospel and its grace do not work as a hermetic seal against difficulties. Paul's hardship lists show that he frequently encounters problems and tribulations. Rather, faith—that is, our trust in God—becomes the assurance that God is "for us," that God is on our side through tough times and good times. Read Rom 8:35-39 and see Paul's powerful assertion that nothing, no matter how bad or how terrifying, can separate us from God's love. Challenging times and situations are occasions for us to trust in "the one who strengthens me" (Phil 4:13); with every predicament, God also provides an exodus (1 Cor 10:13).

7. The last items in the hardship list (6:10) provide what we might describe as an eschatological window on suffering and possessions. Seen from the vantage point of God's ultimate redemptive purposes, sorrow and grief do not have the last word; joy and rejoicing do. Paul's encoded affirmation is that God will not leave us in grief and sorrow (cf. Jesus' beatitude in Matt 5:4; Luke 6:21*b*). As to possessions, Paul raises the question as to what makes a person truly rich and what it means to possess something. Paul's view, expressed elsewhere, is that God freely gives us what counts, so boasting about possessions is voided; so also is valuing life based on what we own (1 Cor 4:7). Paul's notion that believers "possess everything" may seem strange to us, but Paul thinks that God, to whom everything belongs by virtue of divine creation and preservation, shares everything with believers (1 Cor 3:21-23).

8. Paul's new perspective that, after Christ's death and resurrection, we regard no one according to the flesh is not applied solely to our brothers and sisters in Christ. Paul's text does not say, "From now on we regard no *fellow believers* according to the flesh." It says *no one.* So even unbelievers must be considered and related to differently now because Christ has died for them, whether they have responded to that death-for-them or not. All of our relationships, with everyone, must be governed by the fact that Christ has died for all; because of that death, they are valued and must be treated accordingly.

2 CORINTHIANS 6:11–7:4, PAUL'S DIRECT APPEAL FOR MORE AFFECTION

NIV

[11]We have spoken freely to you, Corinthians, and opened wide our hearts to you. [12]We are not withholding our affection from you, but you are withholding yours from us. [13]As a fair exchange—I speak as to my children—open wide your hearts also.

[14]Do not be yoked together with unbelievers. For what do righteousness and wickedness have in common? Or what fellowship can light have with darkness? [15]What harmony is there between Christ and Belial[a]? What does a believer have in common with an unbeliever? [16]What agreement is there between the temple of God and idols? For we are the temple of the living God. As God has said: "I will live with them and walk among them, and I will be their God, and they will be my people."[b]

[17]"Therefore come out from them
   and be separate,

                              says the Lord.

Touch no unclean thing,
   and I will receive you."[c]
[18]"I will be a Father to you,
   and you will be my sons and daughters,
                    says the Lord Almighty."[d]

7 Since we have these promises, dear friends, let us purify ourselves from everything that contaminates body and spirit, perfecting holiness out of reverence for God.

[2]Make room for us in your hearts. We have wronged no one, we have corrupted no one, we have exploited no one. [3]I do not say this to condemn you; I have said before that you have such a place in our hearts that we would live or die with you. [4]I have great confidence in you; I take great pride in you. I am greatly encouraged; in all our troubles my joy knows no bounds.

[a]15 Greek *Beliar*, a variant of *Belial*   [b]16 Lev. 26:12; Jer. 32:38; Ezek. 37:27   [c]17 Isaiah 52:11; Ezek. 20:34,41   [d]18 2 Samuel 7:14; 7:8

NRSV

[11]We have spoken frankly to you Corinthians; our heart is wide open to you. [12]There is no restriction in our affections, but only in yours. [13]In return—I speak as to children—open wide your hearts also.

[14]Do not be mismatched with unbelievers. For what partnership is there between righteousness and lawlessness? Or what fellowship is there between light and darkness? [15]What agreement does Christ have with Beliar? Or what does a believer share with an unbeliever? [16]What agreement has the temple of God with idols? For we[a] are the temple of the living God; as God said,

"I will live in them and walk among them,
   and I will be their God,
   and they shall be my people.
[17] Therefore come out from them,
   and be separate from them, says the Lord,
and touch nothing unclean;
   then I will welcome you,
[18] and I will be your father,
   and you shall be my sons and daughters,
says the Lord Almighty."

7 Since we have these promises, beloved, let us cleanse ourselves from every defilement of body and of spirit, making holiness perfect in the fear of God.

[2]Make room in your hearts[b] for us; we have wronged no one, we have corrupted no one, we have taken advantage of no one. [3]I do not say this to condemn you, for I said before that you are in our hearts, to die together and to live together. [4]I often boast about you; I have great pride in you; I am filled with consolation; I am overjoyed in all our affliction.

[a]Other ancient authorities read *you*   [b]Gk lacks *in your hearts*

COMMENTARY

6:11-13. What was certainly persistent but always subtle, indirect, and encoded in the text before 6:11 is now explicit and direct: Paul yearns for increased affection from the Corinthians. For the first time in the letter since the salutation, he directly addresses them: "you, Corinthians" (6:11). He retains for himself, however, the plural in 6:11-12 and thereby continues to cast himself as part of the larger, mainstream group of believers. Even that ruse breaks down, however, and Paul, expressing his affection, emerges in the singular as he plays the paternal role: "I speak as to children" (6:13; cf. 1 Cor 4:14-16). Paul's address of them as children, as *his* children, is a subtle attempt to recapture some of the familial affection he and they have enjoyed in the past.

Paul is swept up into emotive expressions. He writes of his mouth's being open to them, surely a euphemism for the "frank speech" (παρρησία *parrēsia*), the highest sign of friendship, he has recently used with them in his painful letter (6:11; cf. 3:12; 4:13). He declares that his "heart is open" to them and thus signifies his capacious commitment to them; by contrast, he thinks them restricted in their "affections" (6:12), translating the quite affecting term σπλάγχνα (*splagchna*, "inward parts/entrails/gut") to express the very center of one's being as the locus of the deepest commitment (cf. Phil 1:8; 2:1; Phlm 12, 20). The little subsection 6:11-13 closes with Paul emphatically urging the Corinthians: "You yourselves, open up [your narrowness, your hearts, understood, as the NIV and NRSV have supplied from 6:11]."

7:2-4. Paul's urgings in 6:11-13 have their reprise in 7:2-4, where, using a different verb (χωρέω *chōreō*), he refines his call for them to open up: "make room [in your hearts, understood] for us" (7:2). Just as in 6:11-12 he began in the plural, so also in 7:2 he starts in the plural and, sounding like he has in earlier sections of this letter, he once again asserts his apostolic probity; so the plural, which pictures him as being in line with other believers, works quite appropriately for him. With the rhetorically repetitive "no one" leading the Greek constructions for heavy emphasis, Paul says the Corinthians have no excuse not to embrace him more openly: "No one have we wronged; no one have we corrupted; no one have we defrauded" (7:2). Unrelenting in his emotional appeal, Paul, exonerating the Corinthians for any doubts along this line, reminds ("I said before," 7:3; cf. 6:11) them that "you are in our hearts."

But the refinement continues significantly: They are in his heart "to live together and to die together," a phrase that has probably been more overinterpreted than many. Paul simply promises that nothing, not even death, can confine his love for them. This is the ultimate pledge of friendship in which Paul sketches out his and the Corinthians' scope of commitment (see similar reflections of love's extent by Paul in Rom 5:7; 9:3). In no sense is Paul here casting any doubt on the resurrection; rather, he is being dramatic and affecting in his depiction of the magnitude of his togetherness with them and, therefore, inscribes related signs of friendship.[129]

As a second index of that devoted friendship, he once again mentions his recent frank speech in the painful letter (7:4*a*; cf. 6:11; 3:12; 4:13) and, as the refining continues, adds yet another sign of his boasting about them (7:4*b*). Saying positive things about one's friends is a fundamental duty of friendship; such commendations may redound to the extoller's benefit with the opening of unexpected doors.[130]

The next sentence (7:4*c*), building from the report of his bragging about them, caps off Paul's request for more affection and telegraphs Paul's final return to the theme of affliction with which he began the letter. Using terms redolent of surfeit, he pictures himself as being sated with encouragement (παράκλησις *paraklēsis*, "comfort/consolation," harking back to the heavy concentration of that term and its root in chap. 1) and as overflowing with joy while he is in the middle of all his afflictions (7:4*c*). This sentence exhibits once again Paul's ebullient affirmation of life in the midst of suffering, hardship, distress,

---

129. K. A. Plank, *Paul and the Irony of Affliction* (Atlanta: Scholars Press, 1987) 1-7, depicts Paul as "a kind of poet" of the affections, using emotive and affecting speech powerfully.

130. J. T. Fitzgerald, "Philippians in the Light of Ancient Friendship," in *Friendship, Flattery, and Frankness of Speech*, ed. J. T. Fitzgerald (Brill: Leiden, 1996) 147.

and affliction, a theme used throughout this letter and, indeed, a hallmark of his gospel (cf. the direct association of joy and suffering in Phil 2:17-18 and 1 Thess 1:6; for the connection of boasting and joy, see Phil 1:25-26).

Given the cultural presuppositions of his time, Paul's direct call for the Corinthians to respond to him with more affection (6:13; 7:2) falls once again under the category of *parrēsia*, "frank speech." Conventionally, frank speech is expected to be used rarely; when employed, it can range from harsh to what Philodemus, a roughly contemporary rhetorician, calls the "slightest sting"[131] from the shouted warning as someone courts disaster, to the gentle urging for a change of decision or behavior. In that culture, any call for an emendation of behavior is understood as frank speech. Paul's painful letter was certainly an example of harsher frank speech (see the Commentary on 2 Cor 7:7-13*a*). Now, just a little later and in his very next communication with them, Paul once again employs frank speech in 6:13 and repeats it in 7:2; these two instances are certainly on the "slight sting" end of the scale, but they are frank speech nonetheless.

The material from 2 Cor 1:1–6:10 was not frank speech, though throughout those chapters Paul repeatedly hinted at and indirectly attempted to induce greater allegiance and affection for himself; in those places it was indirect or figured speech.[132] Paul's speech became frank when he directly urged them to "open" their hearts to him (6:12) and "make room for us" (7:2).[133] That he writes, in 2 Corinthians 1–6, *about* his frank speech that he used in the previous, painful letter does not make 2 Corinthians 1–6 frank speech.

When, however, Paul directly asked them to change, to become more affectionate toward him, he violated two canons of frank speech in that culture. Paul's immediate reassurance that what he says is not a condemnation (κατάκρισις *katakrisis*, 7:3) shows that he knows he may have pushed matters too far. First, he followed frank

speech in one letter (the painful letter that grieved them into repentance, 7:8-9) with new frank speech in 2 Cor 6:11-13 and 7:2-4. Rhetoricians warn against using frank speech a second time with someone who may be stinging from an earlier "hit," as the Corinthians clearly are. Plutarch, a relatively contemporary moralist, recognizes that persistent hits of frank speech, if not smoothed over, build further and enduring problems in a relationship. Perhaps Paul has now become the recipient of some negative fallout along these lines: "But the man who has been hard hit and scored by frankness, if he be left rough and tumid and uneven, will, owing to the effect of anger, not readily respond to an appeal the next time."[134]

For what amounts to five chapters, Paul seems to have resisted the temptation to be directly frank with them about his desire for more solidarity and affection from them, settling instead for hints and insinuations, a socially acceptable pattern. Then in the sixth chapter he moves to direct, frank speech. One of the problems with literary frank speech is that its writer is not on hand to see how the recipients are responding. No wonder Paul was "restless" until he heard from Titus's firsthand report regarding his earlier employment of frankness (7:5-7). Paul writes the present letter with only Titus's assessment and word as to how his earlier frank speech was received. Was everyone at Corinth changed by Paul's frank speech in his "painful" letter? Fully? Equally? The odds are that there was some residual sensitivity, if not resentment, among at least some of the Corinthians; frank speech always risks building residual anger.[135] Into that context Paul now launches more frank speech. Granted, it is gentle frankness. At best this is hazardous; at worst, it is foolish. If some people are still irritated, they may experience this gentle frankness as severe even though Paul probably thinks of himself as being affectionate.

The second mistake is Paul's using frank speech in an effort to modify affection or to alter emotions. Frank speech, the rhetoricians know, is designed for deliberative circumstances where an individual (or group) is weighing which direction to go or whether to do something. Frank speech is not to be used in matters of fondness and

131. See Philodemus *On Frank Criticism*.

132. J. Paul Sampley, "The Weak and the Strong: Paul's Careful and Crafty Rhetorical Strategy in Romans 14:1–15:13," in *The Social World of the First Christians: Studies in Honor of Wayne A. Meeks,* ed. L. M. White and O. L. Yarbrough (Minneapolis: Fortress, 1994) 43-46.

133. This is Paul's "response to a lack of reciprocity in a relationship" and therefore a "mild form of censure." See Stowers, "Letters of Praise and Blame," in *Letter Writing in Greco-Roman Antiquity* (Philadelphia: Westminster, 1986) 86.

134. Plutarch *How to Tell a Flatterer from a Friend* 74E.

135. See Philodemus *On Frank Criticism* fragment 70.

allegiance. Frank speech employs "the thinking and reasoning powers," not the emotions.[136] A further problem is that love and affection are resistant to command, even the most modest command.

Beyond this, Paul probably did not help his case when he called his auditors "children" (ὡς τέκνοις *hōs teknois*) when he wrote, "I am speaking as to children" (6:13). Although there is no clue that he intends the reference in 6:13 as anything other than affectionate, some Corinthians may have heard annoying echoes of earlier unpleasantries; Paul had condescendingly addressed them as "babies" (ὡς νηπίοις *hōs nēpiois*) who were not mature and not ready for meat (1 Cor 3:1-2; though the image is refined to τέκνα [*tekna,* "children"] in 1 Cor 4:14, 17). And Paul has already said that he writes to them nothing beyond what they can read and understand (2 Cor 1:13), which may have struck some of them as similarly haughty on Paul's part.

The two violations of the culturally accepted guidelines for frank speech and his calling them "children" may have contributed to the breakdown of relations between Paul and the Corinthians that is reflected in nearly every sentence of the letter fragment 2 Corinthians 10–13, which was written subsequently to this frank speech in 6:11-13 and 7:2-4 (see the Introduction). If there was residual resentment toward Paul from the frankness in his painful letter, this new frank speech will have made Paul a ready target for increased animosity and perhaps even enmity such as must be supposed is the context for 2 Corinthians 10–13.

6:14–7:1. Between the two interlocked frank speech passages lies 2 Cor 6:14–7:1, a six-verse conundrum. It does not fit well in its immediate context.[137] Certain of its features do not square well with the rest of the letter fragment. It has some otherwise unknown expressions for Paul. It is about ten degrees off from what we expect from him in several of its claims, but, as we shall see, not alien to Paul in others.

The structure of 6:14–7:1 is rather clear. It opens with a command not to be unevenly yoked

(ἐτεροζυγέω *heterozygeō*, 6:14a)—a term referring to yoking together two unalike draft animals, such as an ox and an ass—with unbelievers[138] and follows with five rhetorical questions (6:14b-16a) that are cast in such direct antithetical form that the hearer is compelled, on the basis of common sense, to answer to each of them with something like, "Nothing whatsoever!" These questions set the ground for the central declaration of the passage, the "for/because" statement that grounds why they should not be yoked with unbelievers: "for we ourselves are the temple of the living God" (6:16b). Immediately following is a catena of scriptural citations that, without using the precise terms of the central declaration, nevertheless affirm and in a multifaceted way extend the truthfulness not only of the central claim but also of the opening command not to be misyoked to unbelievers.

A circular argumentation unpacks the central notion of 6:14–7:1. The hearers are God's temple; God does dwell among those who *therefore* become God's people who should *therefore* come out, separate, from those who in 6:14a are called unbelievers[139] and not touch anything unclean, and *therefore* God will receive them as God's sons and daughters. The passage concludes with another *therefore* ("having these promises"), which gains expression in the admonition "let us cleanse ourselves" (7:1). Because God dwells among people, they must separate and not touch anything unclean, and the resulting holiness, cleanness, and abstinence prompt God to welcome them as children. God's residence claims, defines, a people who must live and comport themselves appropriately and distinctively; when they do so, God welcomes them as sons and daughters. This circularity of God's claiming a people who then live appropriately and are embraced by God as children is what the author refers to collectively as "these promises" (7:1). The passage concludes with a call for the auditors to join with the writer to "cleanse" themselves "from every defilement of the flesh and spirit" (7:1).

The passage 6:14–7:1 is strange to the imme-

---

136. Plutarch *How to Tell a Flatterer from a Friend* 61E.

137. Scott argues that 6:14–7:1 "explains *how they are to open their 'heart.'* "See J. M. Scott, "The Use of Scripture in 2 Corinthians 6:16c-18 and Paul's Restoration Theology," JSNT 56 (1994) 96, italics added.

138. See also Philo *On the Special Laws* 4:204.

139. These ἄπιστοι (*apistoi,* "unbelievers") have been identified as Paul's opponents. See N. A. Dahl, *Studies in Paul: Theology for the Early Christian Mission* (Minneapolis: Augsburg, 1977) 69. But M. E. Thrall, *The Second Epistle to the Corinthians* (Edinburgh: T. & T. Clark, 1994) 473, argues against it.

diate context. First, the dynamic in 2 Corinthians 1–9 is between Paul their apostle who, associating himself with a larger group of believers, defends his actions and comportment among and toward the auditors and who for most of the letter implicitly bids for greater esteem and only toward its climax openly asks for greater affection from those to whom he has brought the gospel. Paul's encoded focus is on the Corinthians' relationship to him; prior to 6:14–7:1 there has not been the slightest inkling of concern for *their behavior.* Any attention to behavior has been on Paul, because he has been so determined to show that he has lived and worked in absolute accord with the gospel he has brought to them. Further, though no textual traditions or variants support excising 6:14–7:1, the passage does separate the materials on both sides that, as we have seen, together urge the Corinthians to be more affectionate to Paul. So if the passage were non-Pauline and thus inserted later into the Pauline text, as some have argued,[140] then it would probably have been done early on, perhaps by the person(s) who edited fragments of more than one letter into the document that we now call 2 Corinthians.

When considered in the light of Paul's earlier correspondence with the Corinthians, 2 Cor 6:14–7:1 appears strange. In these verses, the believers must be on guard against association with unbelievers; they must not be misyoked to them (6:14); they must "come out from them and be separate" (6:17); and they must (protect and) perfect their holiness via a self-cleansing of body and spirit (7:1). The closest Paul comes to such a picture elsewhere in his correspondence with the Corinthians is in the "previous" letter where he warned them about associating with immoral persons (πόρνοι *pornoi*) and later clarifies that he meant immoral persons within the community of believers because, he argues, one simply cannot avoid contact with immoral persons in the world (see the Commentary on 1 Cor 5:9-13).

From many details in 1 Corinthians, however, Paul's hearers will have a dramatically different picture of how holiness is lived in the world. Whether one takes the misyoking in 2 Cor 6:14 to refer to marriage or not, Paul has written quite positively in 1 Corinthians about believers' asso-

ciation with unbelievers. Paul's auditors will know that he condones believers' being married to unbelievers (1 Cor 7:12-16). But 1 Cor 7:12-16 goes beyond condoning marriage to unbelievers; it even speculates that the holiness of the believing spouse may, in fact, positively affect the unbelieving spouse and certainly has affected any children (1 Cor 7:14, 16). In 2 Cor 6:14–7:1, however, Paul expects believers to preserve holiness through separation and withdrawal, a position not unlike what he has *opposed* among some Corinthians (cf. 1 Cor 7:5-7, 12-13, 27-28, 36). In 1 Cor 7:12-16, Paul credits holiness with its own power to cross over the border and influence so as to change unbelievers. The one protects holiness; the other assumes that holiness has its own divinely inspired power. The one fears that holiness may be lost by association with unbelievers; the other assumes that holiness may change the unbelievers.

Elsewhere in 1 Corinthians Paul readily condones believers' having social involvement with unbelievers. In an imagined scene, he contemplates that an unbeliever invites a believer to dinner, and he finds absolutely no problem with a believer's going (1 Cor 10:27). Further, Paul anticipates that unbelievers may venture in when the church gathers and is not the least concerned; in fact, he contemplates that such a circumstance may ultimately be the occasion for what we might call a conversion (1 Cor 14:23-25).

In all three instances in 1 Corinthians, associations with unbelievers are viewed quite positively by Paul, and in two of them the relationship is positively infectious. In yet one more passage from 1 Corinthians, Paul depicts believers as living in a world whose structure (σχῆμα *schēma*), tainted by sin, is passing away (1 Cor 7:31; see also Rom 1:18-25); that world is where believers transact their lives. So Paul thinks they live directly in that world, but ὡς μὴ (*hōs mē*, "as-if-not") doing so (1 Cor 7:29-31). There Paul advocates an eschatological reserve in which believers do not take their clues or values from the world in which they perforce live. They live in that world, but not by it.

The notion that believers can be enjoined to "cleanse themselves" is unfamiliar in the Pauline corpus. For Paul it is God who sanctifies, who washes, who claims people and makes them ap-

---

140. For details and propounders of those arguments, see V. P. Furnish, *II Corinthians,* AB 33 (Garden City: Doubleday, 1984) 375-83.

propriate as a new creation, for restored relationship. Even the Pauline school, in letters written after Paul's death, maintains the conviction that it is not the believers but Christ who cleanses and purifies (Eph 5:26; Titus 2:14). The temple is *already* made holy (cf. 1 Cor 3:17), and believers honor that holiness as a sort of stewardship given into their care. Writing earlier to these same Corinthians, Paul declares, "But you were washed, you were made holy, you were justified" (1 Cor 6:11). Though the first verb is ἀπολούω (*apolouō*), rather than the καθαρίζω (*katharizō*) of 2 Cor 7:1, the semantic overlap is sufficient to warrant two contrasts: In 1 Cor 6:11 Paul uses the aorist form of the verbs to signify completed, finished action in the past—the Corinthians were washed and made holy, with their baptism probably being the point of reference (cf. the baptismal phrase "in the name of the Lord Jesus Christ"). Each of the three verbs in 6:11 is in the passive, with God, not the believers, as the one who is understood to have done the washing and the making holy. Also, the term μολυσμός (*molysmos*, "defilement"; NIV, "everything that contaminates," 2 Cor 7:1) occurs nowhere else in Paul, or in the NT for that matter, though Paul uses the verbal form of the term to describe the defilement that he thinks waits for the person who eats meat offered to idols despite his weak conscience, which does not allow it (1 Cor 8:7). The use of the term in 2 Cor 7:1 fits well with the notion of uncleanness mentioned in 6:17.

In other respects, however, 2 Cor 6:14–7:1 is not so alien to Paul's view of things. Paul is quite capable of setting up antithetical pairings as those in 6:14*b*-16. For example, he describes fidelity to Christ with one's body—that is, with one's whole self (cf. Rom 12:1)—as proscribing any rival relationship. He uses an image as old as Israel's prophets, prostitution, to express an alternative, totally unacceptable rival relationship (Jeremiah 2–3; Ezek 16:15-34; Hosea 2): Your bodies, which are members of Christ, cannot also be members of a prostitute (1 Cor 6:15-16). Similarly, while in some circumstances Paul condones eating meat that has been offered to idols (1 Cor 8:4-6; 10:25-27; cf. Rom 14:17), in the cultic setting he cannot and does not approve of it (1 Cor 10:17-21).

Paul readily affirms that Christ, or the Holy Spirit, resides or dwells in or among believers (Christ: Rom 8:10; Gal 2:20; Spirit: Rom 8:9-11; 1 Cor 3:16; 6:19; 1 Thess 4:8; God: 1 Cor 3:16-7 possibly) and even uses the image of the Temple to develop that notion (1 Cor 3:16-17; 6:19), as in 2 Cor 6:16. The expression "the living God" (θεοῦ ζῶντος *theou zōntos*) employs a divine descriptor that, though not frequent in Paul, is represented in the corpus (2 Cor 3:3; 1 Thess 1:9) and is much more widespread in Jewish tradition as a way of describing that God is not subject to death (Deut 5:26; 2 Kgs 19:4, 16; Ps 42:2; Isa 37:4, 17; Jer 10:10; 23:36; Hos 1:2 LXX).[141]

Likewise, the reference to βελιάρ (*Beliar*, or Belial; in Hebrew meaning "worthlessness"), is a derisive way contemporary Jews referred to Satan[142] or to the antichrist.[143] Satan is mentioned often in the Corinthian correspondence: Satan has power to destroy the flesh of those in sin's thrall (1 Cor 5:5), tests self-control (7:5), has plans (2 Cor 2:11), takes on disguises, and has agents who pretend to be like believers (11:14-15). Satan even tests Paul via the thorn or stake in his flesh (2 Cor 12:7). *Beliar* is the antithesis of Christ (2 Cor 6:15).

The antithetical listing provides a virtual lexicon of Greek synonyms for sharing: "partnership" (μετοχη *metoche*), "fellowship" (κοινωνία *koinōnia*, 6:14*b*-c), "agreement" (συμφώνησις *symphōnēsis*), "part/share" (μερίς *meris*), "union" (συγκατάθεσις *sygkatathesis*). All these terms function, in a reinforcing way, to distinguish, to mark off boundaries between the life of faith and its opposite—boundaries that provide the basis for the subsequent call for separation, the avoidance of contact (6:17-18), and ultimately the need for cleansing (7:1).

The use of Scripture citations—"as God said" (6:16), "says the Lord" (6:17), and "says the Lord Almighty" (6:18)—is noteworthy in certain respects. Nowhere else in Paul's works is Scripture introduced with "as God said" (6:16).[144] Nowhere else in Paul is the title "Almighty" (παντοκράτωρ

---

141. See also Philo *Dec* 67.
142. See *T. Reub.* 2, 4, 6; *Jub.* 15:33; CD 6, 9.
143. See *T. Dan* 5; *Sib. Or.* 2.167; 3.63; 73; *Ascension of Isaiah* 4.2.
144. J. Fitzmyer, *Essays on the Semitic Background of the NT,* SBLSBS 5 (Missoula, Mont.: Scholars Press, 1974) 216, notes that the "as God said" formula is absent from Hebrew Scriptures and the Mishnah but has a "Qumran counterpart in CD 6:13; 8:9."

pantokratōr) used, though it is found frequently in the Septuagint and in Revelation (e.g., Rev 1:8; 4:8; 11:17). The Scripture citations themselves are at times difficult to identify as to source and occasionally are significantly changed from early manuscripts. The first quotation—"I shall dwell in them," 6:16—is nowhere in the Scriptures of Israel. In fact, nowhere in the Septuagint is God ever the subject of the verb "dwell" (ἐνοικέω *enoikeō*).[145] This citation is probably a free rendition of Lev 26:11 because Lev 26:12 is heavily used in 2 Cor 6:16: (1) "and I will walk about among them" shares with Lev 26:12 LXX, in the same declension, ἐμπεριπατήσω (*emperipatēsō*), and (2) the promise of God, shifted from the direct address of Lev 26:12 to a third-person declaration, is that God will be their God and they will be God's people. Paul has taken Lev 26:11 LXX, "I shall put my tent among you," and transformed it in 2 Cor 6:16 from direct address and increased the immediacy by dropping the tent and having God dwell directly.

The next quotation (2 Cor 6:17) is introduced with διό (*dio*, "therefore") to link it as a consequence of God's indwelling. The key elements in 6:17*a-c*, including "and do not touch the unclean thing," may all be found in Isa 52:11-12 LXX, though in the original text the exiles were called to leave Babylon in a new exodus, whereas in 2 Cor 6:14–7:1 the call is for the hearers to separate themselves from the corrupting influence of unbelievers. By its insertion of "says the Lord," 2 Cor 6:17 gives special emphasis to the call not to touch any unclean thing (Isa 52:11) and to the appended promise, which may well come from Ezek 20:34 LXX, "and I will take you out/receive you," cropping off the rest of the construction that appeared in the Scripture—"from the lands where you have been dispersed"—which does not fit the scope of 6:14–7:1.

Linked to God's promise to receive them (2 Cor 6:17 referencing Ezek 20:34) is another scriptural promise—"and I will be your father" (6:18)—which has been taken from its context of God's promise

always to keep a son of David available to Israel (2 Sam 7:14: "I will be a father to him, and he shall be a son to me," NRSV) and has been applied, adaptively and directly, to God's whole people: "and you *yourselves* shall be to me sons *and daughters*" (εἰς υἱοὺς καὶ θυγατέρας *eis huious kai thygateras*, 6:18, italics added to indicate the alterations the author has made).

The section 2 Cor 6:14–7:1 uses Scripture, two passages that originally had an exodus motif and one text that had to do with Davidic inheritance, for distinctive purposes: to call the hearers to recognize God's dwelling and being among them, to exhort them to separate themselves from contamination, and to promise them that they will be received by God and constituted as sons and daughters before God their Father. Then, focusing on the promises (see 7:1*a*), the author urges the hearers to "cleanse themselves," an exhortation that refines the Isa 52:11 command, "Do not touch an unclean thing" (2 Cor 6:17).

If 6:14–7:1 is neither written by Paul nor inserted where it is by him, we must ask on what principles a redactor might have placed these verses in this place. The question remains a difficult one for many of the reasons cited above. One suggestion, however, merits consideration.[146] In the Greco-Roman world, processions often went through the city and ended at a temple. A herald preceded the procession, alerted people to prepare the route, and demanded that the temple be readied. Paul's Letter to the Corinthians (chaps. 1–9) has the ingredients for a redactor to connect 6:14–7:1, with its call for preparation of the "temple of the living God," to the triumphal processional mentioned in 2:14-16, with its fragrance "of the knowledge of God." The redactor would have put 6:14–7:1 between the calls for the Corinthians to "open wide" or "make room" (πλατύνω *platynō*, 6:13; χωρέω *chōreō*, 7:2) and would have understood that appeal to be that they prepare themselves as God's temple.

---

145. Furnish, *II Corinthians*, 363.

146. The following thesis is propounded by P. B. Duff, "The Mind of the Redactor: 2 Cor 6:14–7:1 in Its Secondary Context," *NovT* 35 (1993) 178-80.

REFLECTIONS

1. Frankness, now as then, is best suited for strong friendship relations. Outside of friendship, frank speech is likely to be perceived as meddlesome at best. But even among friends, speaking frankly is a delicate undertaking that requires caution as well as a sense of timing and proportion. Furthermore, the speaker needs to be of good character and should not have the same log in his or her own eye (cf. Matt 7:1-5). Frank speech can easily slip into abuse, and no excuse can be made for that. There are times, however, when frankness (short of abuse) may be unavoidable, even if the friendship may be lost in the process (cf. Gal 4:16).

2. Open professions of love and affection such as Paul uses are appropriate, even fundamental, to human well-being. Expressions of love are not signs of wimpiness but are absolutely necessary for good rapport among people. Note the number of times when, after someone has suddenly died, the survivors lament that they did not have the chance to say good-bye or "I love you." Simple statements of love are seldom misunderstood.

3. We may be able to resonate with Paul's eagerness for a fuller friendship with the Corinthians. At times we may want or expect more of our friends than they are either willing to give or perhaps even capable of giving. In such circumstances, we might ask whether we are the ones cloaking ourselves and not sharing ourselves fully. If we find that we are doing that, then we might realistically ponder that genuine friendship requires an opening up and a giving from both sides.

4. How should Christians relate to the world around them? Is association with unbelievers inappropriate? There are very different answers in the New Testament. In fact, there are even different answers in Paul's letters. At times Paul knows—and condones—that believers are married to unbelievers (1 Cor 7:12-16). Likewise, he knows that unbelievers may wander into worship (1 Cor 14:24). Yet here in 2 Cor 6:14–7:1 the lines are drawn ever so sharply. These verses emphasize the importance of human responsibility, stressing as they do our obligations to honor our relation to God by examining all other associations in the light of that one, central relationship with God. Any compromise of our being God's temple is inappropriate. Because this passage is not about marriage, these verses probably should not be construed as having any counsel one way or the other about whether a believer should marry an unbeliever.

5. The living God has determined to dwell among us as a temple. People in Paul's world would have known that temple maintenance was a consequence of God's indwelling. The issue would immediately be one of keeping the temple ready and fit for God to dwell there. If we knew that God was bent on living with us, what would we want to change? What associations, what habits, and what patterns of behavior would we need to stop? Temples require cleaning and polishing, and that on a regular and consistent basis.

2 CORINTHIANS 7:5-16, REPRISE OF CONCERN AND REASSURANCES OF CONFIDENCE

NIV

⁵For when we came into Macedonia, this body of ours had no rest, but we were harassed at every turn—conflicts on the outside, fears within. ⁶But

NRSV

⁵For even when we came into Macedonia, our bodies had no rest, but we were afflicted in every way—disputes without and fears within. ⁶But

NIV

God, who comforts the downcast, comforted us by the coming of Titus, [7]and not only by his coming but also by the comfort you had given him. He told us about your longing for me, your deep sorrow, your ardent concern for me, so that my joy was greater than ever.

[8]Even if I caused you sorrow by my letter, I do not regret it. Though I did regret it—I see that my letter hurt you, but only for a little while— [9]yet now I am happy, not because you were made sorry, but because your sorrow led you to repentance. For you became sorrowful as God intended and so were not harmed in any way by us. [10]Godly sorrow brings repentance that leads to salvation and leaves no regret, but worldly sorrow brings death. [11]See what this godly sorrow has produced in you: what earnestness, what eagerness to clear yourselves, what indignation, what alarm, what longing, what concern, what readiness to see justice done. At every point you have proved yourselves to be innocent in this matter. [12]So even though I wrote to you, it was not on account of the one who did the wrong or of the injured party, but rather that before God you could see for yourselves how devoted to us you are. [13]By all this we are encouraged.

In addition to our own encouragement, we were especially delighted to see how happy Titus was, because his spirit has been refreshed by all of you. [14]I had boasted to him about you, and you have not embarrassed me. But just as everything we said to you was true, so our boasting about you to Titus has proved to be true as well. [15]And his affection for you is all the greater when he remembers that you were all obedient, receiving him with fear and trembling. [16]I am glad I can have complete confidence in you.

NRSV

God, who consoles the downcast, consoled us by the arrival of Titus, [7]and not only by his coming, but also by the consolation with which he was consoled about you, as he told us of your longing, your mourning, your zeal for me, so that I rejoiced still more. [8]For even if I made you sorry with my letter, I do not regret it (though I did regret it, for I see that I grieved you with that letter, though only briefly). [9]Now I rejoice, not because you were grieved, but because your grief led to repentance; for you felt a godly grief, so that you were not harmed in any way by us. [10]For godly grief produces a repentance that leads to salvation and brings no regret, but worldly grief produces death. [11]For see what earnestness this godly grief has produced in you, what eagerness to clear yourselves, what indignation, what alarm, what longing, what zeal, what punishment! At every point you have proved yourselves guiltless in the matter. [12]So although I wrote to you, it was not on account of the one who did the wrong, nor on account of the one who was wronged, but in order that your zeal for us might be made known to you before God. [13]In this we find comfort.

In addition to our own consolation, we rejoiced still more at the joy of Titus, because his mind has been set at rest by all of you. [14]For if I have been somewhat boastful about you to him, I was not disgraced; but just as everything we said to you was true, so our boasting to Titus has proved true as well. [15]And his heart goes out all the more to you, as he remembers the obedience of all of you, and how you welcomed him with fear and trembling. [16]I rejoice, because I have complete confidence in you.

COMMENTARY

Like a ring structure or, as rhetoricians would call it, an inclusio, Paul now reaches back to the beginning of the letter to revisit some themes and dwell on them. First, Paul, returning to the plural again as a way of continuing to associate himself with the majority of believers, picks up his journey narrative. Earlier (2:12-13), Paul had detailed his arrival in Troas (northeast shore of the Aegean Sea, in the Roman province of Asia, modern Turkey), his distress because Titus was not there (to inform him about how the Corinthians received his painful letter), and how he was so concerned that he ended his preaching in Troas and went on to Macedonia. As if nothing in the intervening chapters had broken his train of thought, Paul returns to the travel narrative in

7:5: "And, coming into Macedonia, our flesh found no relief" (ἄνεσις *anesis*, "rest," "relief," 7:5; the antonym of θλῖψις *thlipsis*, "affliction," "distress," 7:4).

Second, Paul opened the letter with a self-description grounded on the verb θλίβω (*thlibō*), depicting him as "pressed upon/oppressed/afflicted" (1:6). In 7:5 he uses the same verb and now adds the emphatic and all-encompassing phrase ἐν παντί (*en panti,* "in every way"), which he then elaborates even further with an extension that describes internal and external distress (7:5), an echo of his description of the inner and outer person in 4:16.[147] Paul's portrait (7:5-7) is that of his being so anguished that, once again, he had to be rescued by God's consolation—this time in the form of Titus, whose message about the Corinthians reassured Paul that his rebuke of the Corinthians had not caused them to turn against him.

Third, Paul's letter-opening rumination about the God who comforts and consoles the afflicted, Paul among them (1:3-11), is reaffirmed in 7:6, where God is poignantly described as "the one who is comforting the downhearted" (using the present participle to denote continued action and a characteristic of God), who now comforts Paul. Just as the theme of consolation/comfort pervaded 1:3-11 (occurring ten times), so also it dominates 7:5-16 (occurring five times).

Finally, only in 7:8-16 do we fully see what was the nature of the painful letter Paul already acknowledged he wrote them (2:3-4) and what connection that had to his distress at not finding Titus at Troas (2:12-13). As noted, adversions to the painful letter and to Paul's use of παρρησία (*parrēsia,* "frank speech") in it have been scattered occasionally within the letter (1:12; 2:4, 17; 3:12; 4:2, 13; 5:11; 6:11). Paul's much-affirmed confidence (1:15; 2:17; 3:4-6; 4:1, 5, 13, 16; 5:6) and his declared affection and signs of friendship for the Corinthians (cf. 1:12-15) are also aspects of frank speech, because the person speaking frankly must have personal integrity and must use frankness in the context of friendship by seeking what is beneficial for the hearers.

The conventional term "painful" has been used in this commentary to refer to the letter of frank speech Paul wrote shortly before he penned what we now call 2 Corinthians 1–9 because it is Paul's own description (2 Cor 7:8-12). The Greek term λύπη (*lypē*) has a semantic range that includes "grief," "sorrow," "pain of mind or spirit," "affliction," "sadness," "distress." But the *lypē* dwelled on in 2 Cor 7:8-12 goes back to Paul's former (i.e., second) visit with the Corinthians when someone caused *lypē* not only to Paul but also, he thinks, to all the Corinthians (2:5). In 7:12 Paul refers to this unnamed person as "the one who acted unjustly/did wrong."

Paul's general use of the term *lypē* refers to the sense of pain or hurt that happens when individuals act harshly or wrongly toward each other. *Lypē* is experienced in community, in the transactions between and among individuals when one is rebuked or hurt. Paul experienced it when someone in the Corinthian community "did wrong" toward him and was not rebuked by his fellow believers (2:1-4). Since Paul's departure and subsequent harsh letter, the Corinthians have punished the man (2:5-11), and Paul expresses his concern that the man be restored lest he become overwhelmed by "overflowing *lypē*" (2:7). Paul's painful (*lypē*) letter caused the Corinthians *lypē*, and the letter itself was written in response to Paul's previous *lypē*.

For Paul, not all *lypē* is bad. There is a *lypē* that can have a positive outcome; it can lead to repentance (εἰς μετάνοιαν *eis metanoian*); it is a *lypē* that is godly (κατὰ θεόν *kata theon*); and it eventuates, without regret, in salvation (7:9-10). In what amounts almost to an aside, Paul ties the grief that the Corinthians have experienced in receiving his painful letter into a reassurance that their "repentance" in response to his letter shows that they are in fact now properly moving toward the ultimate destination of the believing life: salvation (7:10).

In the unquestioned Pauline letters, salvation is not a present reality in the life of believers. Instead, believers who are now justified and reconciled (Rom 5:9-10) look forward with confidence that what God has begun in them will ultimately result in their salvation (Phil 3:12-14).[148] Between the "already" of their having been

---

147. The mention of inner and outer person here, however, does not serve as the contrast it did in 2 Cor 4:16 but to describe Paul's distress as complete.

148. J. Paul Sampley, *Walking Between the Times: Paul's Moral Reasoning* (Minneapolis: Fortress, 1991) 20-21.

justified and reconciled and the "not yet" of their salvation, believers must do their moral reasoning and their own self-assessment to see how fully they are living the faith—that is, how well they are navigating the life of faith. Midcourse corrections are possible, Paul thinks, in the lives of believers (see the Commentary on 1 Cor 11:27-32). Titus reports to Paul that his painful letter became the occasion for the Corinthians to make such a midcourse correction, and Paul now assures them that their godly *lypē* is, therefore, placing them once again in line for salvation.[149]

As a term, "repentance" (μετάνοια *metanoia*) does not occur frequently in Paul's letters (e.g., Acts 2:38; cf. Luke–Acts, where repentance and forgiveness are the chief categories to describe restoration of right relationship with God). Here in 2 Cor 7:9-10, repentance leads to a restoration of right relationship between people: between the Corinthians and Paul. Their repentance, their turning about, their reorienting of themselves places them once again in a collegial relationship with Paul.

The other *lypē*, the one Paul describes as "worldly" (ἡ τοῦ κόσμου λύπη *hē tou kosmou lypē*) and that finds no repentance, brings about death (7:10). Once again, Paul sets up stark alternatives, as he has throughout this letter fragment. This time, according to Paul, the Corinthians have chosen the correct alternative.

Paul has to walk a fine line in his rehearsal of the events surrounding his letter of frank speech. It grieved them. He did not want to grieve them, but, with no choice but to act in their best interests even if it put him and his standing with them at risk, he wrote them a harsh letter designed to elicit repentance, a change of heart and direction. So he has to make clear that the sting or the hurt is not itself his goal and to focus instead on the results that repentance precipitated (7:8-9). Only from the perspective of successfully restored relationships can Paul say that he does not regret having stung them with frank speech—the outcome has made the pain it caused him and them worth it (7:8). "To live and to die with them," indeed (7:3).

Titus is an important player in these circumstances and times for Paul, and apparently for the Corinthians. His portrait here shows him, like Timothy, who is, along with Paul, designated a writer of the letter, *sympatico* with Paul. In all likelihood, it was Titus who delivered the painful letter. Titus's report of the letter's reception is what Paul first anxiously awaits at Troas and then seeks in Macedonia. Paul had boasted to Titus about the Corinthians (7:14). Titus, Paul's "partner and fellow worker for you" (8:23), is a "double" for Paul because God has given into Titus's heart the "same zeal for you" that Paul has (8:16; cf. the reflection about Titus made a subsequent time by Paul, 12:18).

Apparently, Titus is Paul's source of information about the Corinthians' response to his letter of frank speech. Paul seems satisfied, even overjoyed, with the "goodwill assurances" he hears from Titus.[150] In fact, however, a couple of signs suggest that Paul's response may be a bit overinflated.[151] First, Paul's concluding remark—"I rejoice that in all things I have confidence in you"—while it accords with the social conventions of the time, simply does not jibe with two features of 2 Corinthians 1–7: (1) his repeated, encoded pleading with them throughout the letter fragment to associate more fully with him and his ministry, which is described in such laudatory ways, and (2) his just-completed explicit call for more affection from them. Likewise, his statement that Titus "remembers the obedience of all of you" may be a stretch. It must have been through Titus that Paul learned of some Corinthians' dismay over his canceled visit, and it is most likely especially to them and their distress that Paul addresses his comments about vacillating in making his plans (2 Cor 1:15-22). And is it not likely Titus who informs Paul that the earlier Corinthian zeal for the collection has seriously eroded? Accordingly, we may wonder if Paul has not overstated matters when he extols the Corinthians' zeal, their readiness to clear themselves, their indignation, fear, longing, and finally their punish-

---

149. See R. F. Ward, "Pauline Voice and Presence as Strategic Communication," *Semeia* 65 (1994) 102-4, for the importance of the letter carrier, in this instance most likely Titus, in the recitation and interpretation of the contents of the letter he delivers and on the function of the reader as an arbiter of transformation.

150. See M. M. Mitchell, "New Testament Envoys in the Context of Greco-Roman Diplomatic and Epistolary Conventions: The Example of Timothy and Titus," *JBL* 111 (1992) 660-61, on the conventions of such assurances.

151. Hickling states: "Some element of distortion must be allowed for as a reasonable possibility." C. J. A. Hickling, "Is the Second Epistle to the Corinthians a Source for Early Church History?" *ZNW* 66 (1975) 285.

ment (probably of the one who had done the wrong, 7:11; cf. 2:6). But when these accolades are considered in terms of acceptable, conventional practice in Hellenistic letters of commendation such as this one,[152] one sees that Paul is quite in line with the culturally dictated expectations of placing "expressions of appreciation and confidence" at or near the close of a letter body.[153]

Several possibilities suggest themselves for this modest overinflation. It was a Cynic-Stoic convention for the moralist sage, like a choirmaster, to "pitch the note a bit high" so that the choristers might all come in on the right note. In this instance, Paul might be painting the picture as he would like it to be, hoping that his Corinthian audience would adopt the picture as their own.[154] So it may have been deliberate on Paul's part; he does think in terms of getting things completely right and working toward that. Or it may be that, in his eagerness to get beyond his troubles with the Corinthians, Paul might have glossed over what could have been Titus's more balanced report. Or it might be that Titus himself, because of his own zeal for and hopes in the Corinthians, is the source of the gloss.

Paul's alternation between singular and plural statements regarding himself in 7:5-16 is complex. Verse 2 starts with the plural so that Paul's appeal for more affection pictures himself along with the others whom he has reason to suppose the Corinthians hold in their hearts, but it quickly enough evaporates to the singular as Paul tries to clarify his relation to the Corinthians (7:3-4). Paul's travelogue and his report about hearing from Titus keep him firmly planted among a larger group via plural self-references (7:5-7). The move into his rejoicing finds him predictably in the center of the stage; he rejoices over them as he hears from Titus about their having come around in their zeal for Paul (7:7-9); indeed, the passage closes with Paul,

in the singular, rejoicing because of his great confidence in them (7:16).

His references to the painful letter and to his having written it are all in the singular—he takes full responsibility for the decision to write it, the nature of the writing, and his reason for writing (7:8-9, 12). When it comes to his comportment and to whether he has harmed the Corinthians, Paul uses the plural, just as he has regularly done throughout the letter (7:9e, 14c). When he writes about his earlier boasting to Titus about the Corinthians, he starts out in the singular, but when he broadens his scope to "everything we said to you," he reverts to his preferred plural whereby he persistently describes his own dependability and faithfulness as being consistent with the mainstream (7:14).

Most telling is his use of the plural in 7:13b: "In addition to our consolation, we rejoiced rather more over the joy of Titus." Paul's joy is doubled up with Titus's joy and so is, as it turns out, his consolation because the reference to "our consolation" in 7:13b picks up his doubled mention of Titus's consolation in 7:7. So when Paul comes to mention his comfort/consolation over the Corinthians' return to fidelity toward him, Paul joins his own consolation to that of Titus, which Paul first saw when he encountered Titus in Macedonia and initially heard Titus's report. His pairing of himself with Titus in their shared consolation (7:7, 13) previews a subsequent association of them that Paul will make in his next piece of correspondence directed to the Corinthians (12:17-18).

The reference to the Corinthians' "obedience" (ὑπακοη *hypakoē*), "of all of you" (7:15), is Paul's description of their return to agreement with his authority. Earlier, Paul, using the same term, said that he wrote them the painful letter precisely to determine "your character, whether in all things you are obedient" (2 Cor 2:9; cf. 10:6; Phlm 21).

In 7:16, Paul's laudation of his confidence in them sets the context for him to move to the next two chapters, where he treats the Corinthians' participation in the collection he has been orchestrating for delivery to the saints in Jerusalem (chaps. 8–9).

Paul has so much at risk with the Corinthians. As surely as they should have been Paul's letter of recommendation, they should also be his joy

---

152. For further studies on the rhetorical power of statements of confidence, see A. J. Malherbe, *Moral Exhortation: A Greco-Roman Sourcebook* (Philadelphia: Westminster, 1986) 125; S. K. Stowers, *"Peri men gar* and the Integrity of 2 Corinthians 8 and 9," *NovT* 32 (1990) 345, and *Letter Writing in Greco-Roman Antiquity* (Philadelphia: Westminster, 1986) 96-97, 103-4.

153. L. L. Belleville, "A Letter of Apologetic Self-recommendation: 2 Cor 1:8–7:16," *NovT* 31 (1989) 156. See the same pattern in Philemon, where, also near the climax of that argument, Paul expresses his confidence in Philemon's "obedience" and states that he expects that the slaveowner will "do even more than I say" (Phlm 21).

154. So in different terms, S. N. Olson, "Pauline Expressions of Confidence," *CBQ* 47 (1985) 295.

and his crown, as the Philippians were (Phil 4:1). Paul knows that he must answer at the judgment regarding how well he has lived out his call to be apostle to the Gentiles, and if the Corinthians turn away from him and, therefore, leave the gospel that he preaches, he will fear that he has "run in vain." He is firmly convinced that their well-being is directly tied to their adherence to his gospel and, therefore, to him; so his efforts to persuade them are critical for their destiny, as he understands matters. As their father in the faith (1 Cor 4:14-15; 9:1), he is directly responsible for them. Harsh frank speech, such as Paul has employed with the Corinthians in his painful letter, risks rejection. Paul has been willing to take that chance because he is convinced that something larger than he is at stake.

Paul's risk potentially ranges beyond the Corinthians, however, because he has learned that the Macedonians (including at least churches in Thessalonica and Philippi) are ready with their enthusiastic contribution to the collection for the saints in Jerusalem. As we shall see in 9:1-5, their projected route of delivery, surely formulated according to Paul's earlier plan (1:16), promises to bring the Macedonians through Corinth to join up with Corinthian representatives and go on to Jerusalem. If Paul's relations with the Corinthians go sour, not only will the Macedonians feel the cold Corinthian chill, but also Paul's collection for Jerusalem, a matter of utmost importance for him, may fall under a cloud.

REFLECTIONS

1. Repentance and forgiveness are complex. Some people withhold forgiveness as a means of maintaining power. Others feign forgiveness but are all too ready to recite the hurtful action later. Some make a habit out of being "sorry" but do not change their behavior. Genuine repentance, such as Paul describes, marks an end to the behavior, and real forgiveness lets the matter go. Perhaps it would be helpful to think of both repentance and forgiveness as work, as a discipline we undertake—really as a transforming of our lives. If we forgive, truly and without strings, then *we* will be different persons afterward. If we repent, we also will become different persons. Repentance and forgiveness cannot be understood as fine-tuning; they are changes from the core of our being. Our repenting and our granting of forgiveness have a better chance of being genuine if we undertake them by asking God both to help us change and to let our forgiveness be total and genuine.

2. Having confidence in another person—being able to depend on someone through thick and thin—is the most valuable asset in human relations. Restored confidence may never be as strong as it was or could have been before a violation. Often we think confidence is built up around the big issues or events—and it may be. But more realistically, confidence and dependability are actually augmented or destroyed in the littlest and most minor situations.

3. Christians care for one another because God cares for each and because God in Christ has given each of us into one another's care. Most of the time our caring for one another is relatively risk free. Sometimes, though, loving a person can lead you to risk your relationship with that person, as Paul did in writing the painful letter of frank speech to the Corinthians. If you think your friend is doing something that will prove ultimately harmful to him or to another person, should you risk the person's enmity by telling him or her the truth (see Gal 4:16)? We may decide to take that step when we realize that we value the person's well-being more than we need his or her friendship.

2 CORINTHIANS 8:1–9:15, THE MACEDONIANS AS MODELS, THE COLLECTIONS, AND THE CORINTHIANS' PARTICIPATION

OVERVIEW

Before examining details in these chapters, we must gain clarity concerning the collection for the saints at Jerusalem, the subject that dominates 2 Corinthians 8–9 and is one of the reasons for Paul's having written 2 Corinthians 1–9. Paul and the Corinthians have a history together around this collection.[155] We know that Paul has been busy—with the Corinthians as with others—setting up the collection for the saints in Jerusalem for at least a year (cf. 2 Cor 8:10). Already in 1 Cor 16:1-4 Paul has dealt with what probably was an earlier question from the Corinthians about the logistics of the collection: How should they gather it? They know Paul is given to practical suggestions, so they ask him for some. Paul provides them with the same instructions he gave to their counterpart churches in Galatia; 1 Cor 16:2-4 details his suggestions and plans as they stood at the time of that writing.

The subject matter of chaps. 8–9 is the collection that Paul variously describes as "for the saints" and "for the poor" in Jerusalem. This offering had its genesis in the conference in Jerusalem as described in Gal 2:1-10 (cf. Acts 15) and requires a rehearsal of that event for its understanding.

---

155. J. L. Martyn, *Galatians,* AB 33A (Garden City, N.Y.: Doubleday, 1997) 222-28, argues that Paul engages in two collections, one with Antioch and this one with the Corinthians and his other "essentially Gentile congregations."

❖   ❖   ❖   ❖

EXCURSUS: THE JERUSALEM CONFERENCE AND THE COLLECTION FOR THE POOR

Paul recounts to the Galatians his having gone, with Barnabas and the same Titus who figures so prominently in 2 Corinthians 1–9, to Jerusalem in response to a revelation (Gal 2:1-2). The conference had as its focus an issue generated at least in part, and perhaps completely, by Paul's mission to the Gentiles in which he did not insist on circumcision as a rite of entry into God's people. The issue can be put in the form of a question: Do Gentiles have to become Jews in order to be part of God's purpose? Paul's entire mission was a graphic no to that question. In a laconic accounting, Paul suggests that his whole mission might be "in vain" if the Gentile believers were not viewed as acceptable by their Jewish brothers and sisters in the faith (Gal 2:2). Paul reports a good outcome of the Jerusalem deliberation: Titus was not compelled to be circumcised, Paul was not subjugated to the Jerusalem leadership (James, Cephas [Paul's often-used name for Peter], and John); quite the contrary, these Jerusalem pillars "recognized the grace that had been given to" Paul (Gal 2:9 NRSV), gave Paul and Barnabas the "right hand of partnership," and collectively divided the mission among themselves in such a way that Paul and Barnabas should go to the Gentiles while the rest of them should take care of "the circumcised" (Gal 2:9). The pillars requested only that Paul (and Barnabas and Titus?) "remember the poor," which he reports himself eager to do (Gal 2:10). If we had

---

no other Pauline texts we might be baffled about who these poor people were and what remembering them might mean.

By the "right hand of fellowship" (κοινωνία *koinōnia*) the Jerusalem pillars had symbolized that Paul's mission was on equal footing with theirs, an opinion *Paul* already had before he went to the conference. So the conference ratified that Paul's previous missionizing among the Gentiles had not been in vain; the Jewish believers in Jerusalem recognized that the Gentiles whom Paul had evangelized were one with them in Christ. To put the matter differently, Paul's successful efforts at the Jerusalem conference meant that there was indeed just one people of God, not two with one being Jewish and the other Gentile.

Paul variously denominates the recipients of this offering. They are "the poor" (πτωχός *ptōchos*, Gal 2:10),[156] "the poor who are among the saints in Jerusalem" (εἰς τοὺς πτωχοὺς τῶν ἁγίων *eis tous ptōchous tōn hagiōn*, Rom 15:26), and simply "the saints" (ἅγιος *hagios*, Paul's technical term for a person set apart for, claimed by God; Rom 15:25; 1 Cor 16:1; 2 Cor 8:4; 9:1, 12).

Similarly, Paul describes the offering using a range of terms. It is a "remembering" (μνημονεύω *mnēmoneuō*, "remember/keep in mind/think of," Gal 2:10), a "collection of money" (λογεία *logeia*, 1 Cor 16:1-2), a "ministry" (διακονέω *diakoneō*; also διακονία *diakonia*, "aid/support/distribution," Rom 15:25; 2 Cor 8:4; 9:1, 12-13), and a "gift" (χάρις *charis*, 1 Cor 16:3; 2 Cor 8:6, 19).

We can develop a general picture of the way Paul's churches responded to the collection. The Macedonian churches at Thessalonica and Philippi, who seem to have had a good history with Paul, have vigorously embraced the offering and generated an astonishing collection (8:1-5). The Galatian churches are not listed in Romans, Paul's last letter, as among those who took part in the collection (Rom 15:26), so we may suppose that Paul's efforts with them (1 Cor 16:1) failed. The Corinthians started off with great enthusiasm for the collection (2 Cor 8:10); later they had some simply logistical questions and asked Paul for general guidelines about how to proceed (1 Cor 16:1-4), but there was no doubt of their readiness to take part at the time when 1 Corinthians was written.

By the time of the letter fragment 2 Corinthians 1–9, however, at least a year since the Corinthians had made a commitment to the collection (8:10), the Corinthians have lost their earlier enthusiasm for it; some (or all) may even be rebelling at taking part in it. Romans 15:26, written later than 2 Corinthians 8–9, shows that Achaia, the Roman province in which Corinth is located, *did* join with Macedonia in the collection. Whether Corinth was a part of that offering cannot be determined; perhaps Paul's inclusion of "all the saints in the whole of Achaia" among the letter recipients for 2 Corinthians 1–9 was also to increase the base from which he hoped to have participation in the collection even if the Corinthians were recalcitrant on the matter.

Paul's understanding of the collection can be pieced together from snippets of different letters. At its heart, the collection symbolizes for Paul a reciprocal partnership between Jewish and Gentile believers. Paul construes the Gentile believers as being "indebted" (ὀφείλω *opheilō*) to the Jerusalem believers who have preceded them in the faith (Rom 15:27), a picture that is in general supported by Paul's image of the olive tree in Rom 11:17-24. Paul's evangelization has been the occasion for Gentiles to be grafted onto the olive tree; now the roots of that tree nourish the engrafted Gentiles. So, shifting from botanical to business imagery, the Gentiles are indebted to their Jewish brothers and sisters in the faith who have shared spiritual matters. Paul's ready conclusion is thoroughly in line with the Greco-Roman expectations of reciprocity; therefore, the Gentile believers ought to reciprocate by being of service in physical matters (Rom 15:27). Indebtedness necessitates a response.

---

156. L. E. Keck, "The Poor Among the Saints in Jewish Christianity and Qumran" *ZNW* 57 (1966) 54-78.

When the discussion is put in terms of need and abundance, then those who have more are obligated to help those who have less or who are in need. Proportionality and fairness come into play in Paul's reckoning. How much one puts aside is supposed to be commensurate with how well one has prospered during that week (1 Cor 16:2). Those with abundance must share with those with little so that there are reciprocity and equality (ἰσότης *isotēs*, 8:13-14; 9:12). No one is to be "put upon" by this collection (8:13). At the same time, however, everyone "owes" love to others (Rom 13:8), and in this instance love calls for sharing the burden with those who have already shared what was theirs.

The "remembering of the poor"—in its being given and in its being received—becomes for Paul the supreme symbol of the unified people of God in Christ in whom truly there is "neither Jew nor Greek" (Gal 3:28 NIV). Paul construes the collection as a one-time, symbolic act in which the Gentile churches as donors and the Jerusalem believers as recipients each acknowledge that they belong to the other in Christ.[157] Paul sees in the collection a tangible confirmation that his work among the Gentiles is, indeed, recognized for what it is: an integral part of God's overall plan. Gentile believers' participation in the collection is a recognition of their indebtedness to their believing Jewish brothers and sisters (cf. Rom 1:16; 2:9-10).

157. Paul's collection is not to be identified with the famine relief of Acts 11:29 because Paul has taken at least one year to collect from the Corinthians (2 Cor 8:10; 9:2). Its symbolic significance for Paul can be seen clearly in the mutuality of Rom 15:27.

❖   ❖   ❖   ❖

Connection of 2 Corinthians 8–9 to 2 Corinthians 1–7. Several factors suggest a strong link between 2 Corinthians 8–9 and the preceding chapters.[158] First, in chaps. 1–9 Paul has made a recurring triangulation between himself, the Corinthians, and the Macedonians. For example, the first item of dispute with the Corinthians in this letter fragment concerns Paul's travel plans. He had wanted to visit Corinth first, then go to Macedonia, then return to Corinth and proceed to Judea (1:15-16). Although he does not explicitly state it—and does not need to because they surely already know—he projects a trip to Judea (an example of the rhetorical device called *synecdoche,* a generalizing locution that stands in place of Jerusalem) to deliver the collection that will be the topic of chaps. 8–9. Paul has already been explicit about that in 1 Cor 16:1-4 when he instructs the Corinthians to have the collection ready to send to Jerusalem when he returns (1 Cor 16:3). At the time of that writing, he was not clear whether he personally would go

158. F. W. Danker, "Paul's Debt to the *De Corona* of Demosthenes: A Study of Rhetorical Techniques in Second Corinthians," in *Persuasive Artistry: Studies in New Testament Rhetoric in Honor of G. A. Kennedy,* ed. D. F. Watson, JSNTSup 50 (Sheffield: Sheffield Academic, 1991) 269, argues that Paul's readers would readily have seen the way chaps. 1–7 set the stage for the discussion of the collection in chaps. 8–9.

to Jerusalem (1 Cor 16:4), but the indecision seems to have faded by the time he wrote 2 Cor 1:16.

The way matters played out in Paul's life was different from his earlier plans. The earlier, projected itinerary reflected in 1:15-16 (Corinth-Macedonia-Corinth-Judea) gave way to a journey that actually went from Corinth to Ephesus and then through Troas (2 Cor 2:12), in the Roman province of Asia, to Macedonia (2 Cor 2:13; 7:5). Paul suggests that he went from Troas to the Roman province of Macedonia because he was desperate to find Titus and get a firsthand report from him regarding the Corinthians' reception of Paul's painful letter of frank speech, a letter we may suppose Titus delivered to the Corinthians. Paul had to know that Titus was working, representing Paul, in the churches that were prominent in Macedonia, certainly Philippi and Thessalonica, and perhaps also Beroea. Not only was Titus working there, but he also was overseeing the gathering of the collection for the saints in Jerusalem, a follow-up on Titus's own presence at the Jerusalem conference, where the idea of the collection originated, as 8:16-24 demonstrates. So the collection and Titus and Macedonia and the Corinthians have all been connected to one another for Paul as a context for the entire letter reflected in 2 Corinthians 1–9. Thus, when Paul desperately wants to know how things went with Corinth, he very logically heads for Macedonia, where he knows Titus is laboring on his behalf regarding the collection.

When Paul arrives in Macedonia and receives Titus's glowing reassurances, Paul is relieved (7:13), but he also discovers another bit of information that places him once again in a curious bind: Titus has been *very* successful with the collection in Macedonia. In fact, everything there seems quite organized, and the Macedonian representatives are ready to move out on the trek that has all along been projected to go through Corinth to join with the Corinthian representatives with their offering and proceed together in a grand processional to Jerusalem to deliver it (8:1-7, 17-19).

Paul has a palpable problem. As a part of his advocacy for the collection in Macedonia, he has boasted about the Corinthians' eagerness for and commitment to the collection (8:11; 9:2-5): "Achaia [the Roman province that includes Corinth; cf. 1:1] has been ready since last year" (9:2). Paul's earlier portrait of the Corinthians appears not to have been too great a stretch; at least a year earlier, they had been quite eager about it and thoroughly committed to it (8:10-12). Spurred on by the example of the Corinthians, the Macedonians had, under Titus's tutelage, outdone themselves (8:2-6), virtually begging to be part of the enterprise.

Meanwhile, Paul's relationship with the Corinthians has been strained, at least with a significant part of that believing community, and he clearly has doubts about whether the Corinthians will be anywhere near as ready as he earlier proudly portrayed them to the Macedonians. Paul clearly imagines a scenario in which the zealous and rightly proud Macedonians arrive in Corinth with their collection and find a church not ready to take part in any collection associated with Paul because of disaffection for him. That is the burden that underlies the entire letter fragment of 2 Corinthians 1–9: If the Corinthians are not fully reconciled to Paul, then not only is his relationship to them jeopardized, but also the corrosion may spread to other churches, say in Mace-

donia, when representatives arrive at Corinth to discover a church and an apostle in disarray. The collection and the Macedonians are a major reason why 2 Corinthians 1–9 had to be written.

Paul's advocacy of one church as a model for another, of one believer as an exemplar for another, is a commonplace in his letters.[159] In fact, this feature of his paraenesis and instruction is grounded in the rhetorical and social pattern of exemplification by which his readers would have experienced most of their learning.[160] Similarly, whereas for Paul boasting about oneself is problematic and to be avoided, boasting about faith, whether it be one's own or someone else's, is positive and important as a way of signifying and affirming how the life of faith ought to be lived. Paul tells the Thessalonians, for example, that by becoming imitators of Paul and Jesus Christ they have become an example for all the believers in Macedonia and Achaia (1 Thess 1:6-7). Likewise, the Romans' faith is said to have made an impact on the whole world (Rom 1:8). Boasting about faith and real-life examples is a basic form of Pauline paraenesis that Paul has used to good effect with the Macedonians.

Now, in 2 Corinthians 1–9, the *Macedonians* become the paradigm. They have warmly and fully associated themselves with Paul's mission and, therefore, with the collection as the most recent example of cooperation. Paul's authority is obviously not challenged by them. They clearly are eager to be associated with Paul and with the collection. Even if one allows for a bit of Pauline rhetorical heightening regarding their contribution, even during difficult times and economic distress, the Macedonians remain exemplary (8:2). In short, Paul offers the Macedonians to the Corinthians as a model of how the latter should behave.[161]

159. Rhetorically this is syncrisis, or comparison. See H. D. Betz, *2 Corinthians 8 and 9* (Philadelphia: Fortress, 1985) 48 and 49n. 77, who says that it is a *topos* Paul uses again in 2 Corinthians 10–13 about himself and the opponents who have come into Corinth.

160. M. M. Mitchell, *The Rhetoric of Reconciliation: An Exegetical Investigation of the Language and Composition of 1 Corinthians* (Louisville: Westminster/John Knox, 1991) 39-46.

161. F. W. Hughes, "The Rhetoric of Reconciliation: 2 Corinthians 1.1–2.13 and 7.5–8.24," in *Persuasive Artistry: Studies in New Testament Rhetoric in Honor of G. A. Kennedy,* ed. D. F. Watson, JSNTSup 50 (Sheffield: Sheffield Academic, 1991) 259, rightly argues that Paul's depiction of the Macedonians challenges the Corinthians' sense of honor toward finishing what they had begun.

Paul's portrait of the Macedonians in 2 Corinthians 8–9 serves another important rhetorical and epistolary function: Their positive association with Paul legitimates and personifies Paul's heavy employment of the plural throughout so much of chaps. 1–9. Paul is not alone. Paul and Timothy (1:1) are not alone. Paul and "all the saints throughout Achaia" are not alone (1:1). Paul writes his entire letter to the Corinthians with the cloud of fellow witnesses that now clearly includes the Macedonian believers. The Macedonian affiliation with Paul, so solid and enthusiastic, adds considerable rhetorical weight to all he has written prior to 2 Corinthians 8–9.

So we may conclude that there are probably two reasons why chaps. 8–9 occur toward the end. First, Paul needs to confirm and enhance his own rehabilitation with the Corinthians that he thinks his painful letter and Titus's entreaties have begun to secure; only then can he make a specific appeal about the collection to them. Second, the way he handles the collection, depicting the Macedonians so positively as exemplars, adds rhetorical urgency not only to encourage the Corinthians to join in the collection but also to all that has preceded.

Second, the picture and functions of Titus show that the chapters about the collection (chaps. 8–9) are directly related to chaps. 1–7. At the time of the writing of 2 Corinthians 1–9, Titus had become of extraordinary importance for Paul. Along with his delivery of the painful letter, Titus probably facilitated the reorientation of the disgruntled Corinthians back into affiliation with Paul. It was Titus who reported to Paul the Corinthian reception of the letter and their realliance with Paul. Titus received such a welcome that he became emotionally attached to them (2 Cor 7:15); he developed a zeal for them that Paul credits with equalling his own (8:16), and he cares so much for them that he has chosen on his own accord to go to the Corinthians with the Macedonian collection and representatives (8:17).

Titus has become identified with the collection; he was in Macedonia overseeing its completion, its final stages (7:6). Because of Titus's good relations with the Corinthians, founded on his recent success in helping them return to affiliation with Paul, Paul wisely accepts his offer to return to Corinth and to make ready their participation in the collection before the Macedonians arrive.[162] A further confirmation of Titus's special role is found in a subsequent reflection about him in which Paul, having fallen into more disfavor with the Corinthians, recognizes that Titus still has their respect and links himself tightly to Titus in questions that assume affirmative answers: "I did not take advantage of you through anyone I sent you, right? . . . Titus [surely] did not take advantage of you, did he? We walked in the same spirit, right?" (2 Cor 12:17-18). Paul's stock with the Corinthians is more mercurial than Titus's, but Titus, as the one who is being sent from Macedonia to Corinth with the collection, ties chaps. 8–9 to chaps. 1–7.

Third, some scholars have questioned whether 2 Corinthians 8–9 should be considered as a fragment or fragments of other Pauline letters to the Corinthians. Chief among the arguments for such dissociation is what may seem an abruptness in the introduction of the collection as a topic of consideration; the matter is not presaged, they argue, but simply breaks awkwardly onto the scene.[163] Three considerations, however, argue for affirming that these chapters are part of the original letter fragment that begins in 2 Corinthians 1: (1) The collection must be understood to lie behind Paul's recitation of his travel plans in 2 Cor 1:16; he had projected a return to Corinth and a hope that the Corinthians would grant him help on his journey to Judea, clearly a generalizing reference to Jerusalem. Nowhere in all of Paul's letters does he relate travel plans for Jerusalem or Judea except in connection with the collection (Rom 15:25; 1 Cor 16:3-4), and Paul does not preach where others have already laid a foundation (Rom 15:20). So when he mentions in 2 Cor 1:16 his plans to go to Judea and his hopes that the Corinthians will "speed" him on, he is making an only slightly oblique indication of his hopes and concerns that will be directly addressed in 2 Corinthians 8–9—namely, the collection.

We can ponder why Paul chose the rather general reference to "Judea" at that early stage in the letter instead of more specifically and point-

162. Sometimes envoys can accomplish what the sender might not be able to do. See M. M. Mitchell, "New Testament Envoys in the Context of Greco-Roman Diplomatic and Epistolary Conventions: The Example of Timothy and Titus," *JBL* 111 (1992) 662.

163. Betz, *2 Corinthians 8 and 9*, 129-34, 139, assumes that 2 Cor 8:1 is the beginning of a new letter fragment.

edly mentioning "Jerusalem." The answer may be that, being sensitive from the start that he had to set a proper context for dealing with the collection, which had by now become a galling, problematic matter for at least some of the Corinthians, Paul simply acknowledged that he was headed for Judea and therefore did not fly the Jerusalem-collection flag quite so conspicuously. Precisely because the collection has become a ticklish, sensitive matter between Paul and the Corinthians, as chaps. 8–9 demonstrate, Paul does not turn to it directly until he has labored persistently in the preceding chapters to refurbish his ethos, to encourage a more positive Corinthian embrace of him, and to affirm his own broad affection for them. Only then is he in a position to leverage them for a recovery of their earlier zeal for participating in the collection.

If the Corinthians had been on good relations with Paul right along, then he could have addressed the collection earlier and more directly, but his own relation with them had been through a time of strain in which his moral and persuasive purchase on them was severely diminished. Clearly, Paul's first task is to recement, as much as possible, his relationship with the Corinthians; then and only then can he deal with a derivative issue, the collection.

(2) Paul did not wait until chaps. 8–9, however, to set the stage for treating this now problematic issue. While he has been reaffirming and solidifying his relation to the Corinthians in chaps. 1–7, he has also laid down the themes he uses in chaps. 8–9 to attempt to bring the Corinthians back into participation. For the present purposes, a listing with only a few comments should suffice; more detailed observations about the way the themes serve in 2 Corinthians 8–9 can be reserved for later.

Throughout the opening chapters, Paul has established that his own "ministry" (διακονία *diakonia*) has been the Corinthians' access to the gospel and that his ministry is specifically focused on reconciliation (3:7-11; 5:18-20). Now in chaps. 8–9, Paul identifies the collection as a ministry (*diakonia*) to the saints in Jerusalem (8:4; 9:1) and that it glorifies the Lord. Corinthian participation demonstrates not only their goodwill (προθυμία *prothymia*, 8:19; 9:2) but also that they identify and share in Paul's ministry of reconciliation be-

cause they as Gentiles now signal their identification with their Jewish brothers and sisters in the faith.

Again, in the earlier chapters, Paul in various ways emphasizes that the gospel characteristically overflows in "abundance" (περισσεύω *perisseuō*, 1:5; 3:9). In particular, God's "grace" (χάρις *charis*), a term that will dominate Paul's characterization of the collection and of participation in it (see below), is described as spreading to more people so that it may overflow in thanksgiving to the glory of God (4:15). A Pauline commonplace has it that persons who are the recipients of God's grace are moved to reach out to others. Paul sets up that notion in 4:15 and capitalizes on it in 8:2, 7, 14 and 9:8, 12, where he plays repeatedly on the overflow of abundance that both prompts and characterizes the collection he hopes the Corinthians will once again embrace with zeal.

In 2 Cor 7:11-12 Paul rejoices that Titus's report has reassured him about the Corinthians' reaffirmation of their σπουδη (*spoudē*), "zeal/eagerness/earnestness," for him. In 8:7 Paul characterizes the Corinthians as persons who excel in everything, including *spoudē*, and with that he builds extensively in these two chapters on their newly revitalized zeal and directs it toward their sincere and full participation in the collection (8:7-8, 16-17, 22).

Likewise, "glory" (δόξα *doxa*) is another important link Paul makes between the opening chapters and chaps. 8–9. Though modern readers might most readily remember Paul's heavy elaboration of glory in the two-covenant passage (2 Cor 3:7–4:6), the term makes significant appearance in 4:15, as noted just above, and is eschatologically mentioned in 4:17 before it resurfaces in 8:19, 23 and 9:13.

"Affliction" (θλίψις *thlipsis*), which opens the letter and is such an enduring theme within it (1:4, 8; 2:4; 4:17; 6:4; 7:4), also inaugurates the discussion of the collection with the report that the Macedonian churches are abundantly ready with their contribution to the collection despite what Paul describes as "a great test of affliction" (8:2). Their dedication to Paul and to the collection not only is exemplary for the Corinthians, but their perduring through affliction also aligns them with Paul and his ministry as reported in the opening chapters of this letter fragment. Further along in the discussion of the collection, the term "affliction" and its counterpart, "rest/relief" (ἄνεσις *anesis*), which appeared together in 7:4-5, are applied to the Corinthians (8:13; cf. 2:13).

Finally, *charis* is the single most frequently used major term in 2 Corinthians 8–9, and Paul uses it here with vast semantic range, from "grace" to "goodwill" to "favor" to "gracious deed or gift" to "thanks or gratitude" (8:1, 4, 6-7, 9, 16, 19; 9:8, 14-15). It opens 2 Cor 1:2 as it does every Pauline letter: "Grace to you." Paul's carrying out of his ministry is credited to God's grace (1:12); all believers have been affected by God's grace (4:15). Paul uses the term in his "thanks be to God" formulation as well (2:14; cf. Rom 6:17; 7:25; 1 Cor 15:57; 2 Cor 8:16; 9:15), and he warns the Corinthians to be cautious that they have not accepted God's grace in vain (6:1). Thus the term *charis* provides a profound link of 2 Corinthians 8–9 to the preceding chapters.

Paul's Understanding of Charis. Much can be learned about Paul's understanding of χαρις (*charis*) in chaps. 8–9. Too often *charis* is understood restrictively as referring to the inauguration of God's redemptive and liberating power that claims a sinner for God—and it surely is that (cf. Rom 5:2; 1 Cor 15:10)—but 2 Corinthians 8–9 will enrich that narrow understanding. In the rhetorical handbooks of Paul's time, speakers are sometimes encouraged, as a means for heightening the attention of their audience, to use the same term in a variety of ways.[164] Paul certainly would have satisfied rhetoricians with his use of *charis*, scattered as it is rather evenly throughout 2 Corinthians 8–9 with a range of semantic functions. In fact, the NIV and the NRSV shield the reader from realizing that the term appears ten times in the two chapters. For the sake of clarity and to honor the importance of this term for Paul, these translations and locations of *charis* are noted here:

	NIV	*NRSV*
8:1	"grace"	"grace"
8:4	"privilege"	"privilege"
8:6	"act of grace"	"generous undertaking"
8:7	"grace of giving"	"generous undertaking"
8:9	"grace"	"generous act"
8:16	"I am glad"	"thanks [to God]"
8:19	"the offering"	"generous undertaking"
9:8	"grace"	"blessing"
9:14	"grace"	"grace"
9:15	"thanks [to God]"	"thanks [to God]"[165]

The variety of English terms and even phrases used to translate the term *charis* is testimony to the richness of Paul's usage here. From the examples in 2 Corinthians 8–9, *charis* is understood to be given by God to people, the Macedonians, in the midst of affliction and poverty (8:1). Not only is the *charis* freely given (by God), but also it is given abundantly, beyond measure (9:14). This quality of overflowing abundance to the Corinthians—"God is able to overflow *every grace* to you" (9:8)—inexorably prompts them (or at least it should, Paul seems to suggest), since they are provided all they need anyway, to experience that same overflow of abundance into every good work. Put another way, God's grace is powerful and moves the recipients to a reflection of God's abundance so that they respond profusely by doing good works toward others. The NRSV's use of "generous undertaking" reflects the translators' efforts to express that God's grace, once received, generates grace-laden acts to others (8:6-7, 19). And to finish the circle full round, the *charis* that is received as a gift from God can and does properly flow back to God in the form of grateful thanks from the graced recipients: "*Charis* [thanks] be to God" (8:16; 9:15). So, for Paul, *charis* is all at once a gift from God, the good works that *charis* inspires, and the thanks to God for the *charis* and the abundance that it inevitably brings with it. Paul understands the collection for the saints in Jerusalem as a *charis* that represents and produces all of the just identified responses.

---

164. See *Ad Herennium* 4.14.21.

165. Curiously, the same Greek phrase (Χάρις τῷ θεῷ *charis tō Theō*) is once translated as "thanks to God" (9:15) and earlier "I am glad" (8:16) by the NIV.

2 Corinthians 8:1-7, Macedonia, Ministry, and the Corinthians

NIV

8 And now, brothers, we want you to know about the grace that God has given the Macedonian churches. [2]Out of the most severe trial, their overflowing joy and their extreme poverty welled up in rich generosity. [3]For I testify that they gave as much as they were able, and even beyond their ability. Entirely on their own, [4]they urgently pleaded with us for the privilege of sharing in this service to the saints. [5]And they did not do as we expected, but they gave themselves first to the Lord and then to us in keeping with God's will. [6]So we urged Titus, since he had earlier made a beginning, to bring also to completion this act of grace on your part. [7]But just as you excel in everything—in faith, in speech, in knowledge, in complete earnestness and in your love for us[a]—see that you also excel in this grace of giving.

[a]7 Some manuscripts *in our love for you*

NRSV

8 We want you to know, brothers and sisters,[a] about the grace of God that has been granted to the churches of Macedonia; [2]for during a severe ordeal of affliction, their abundant joy and their extreme poverty have overflowed in a wealth of generosity on their part. [3]For, as I can testify, they voluntarily gave according to their means, and even beyond their means, [4]begging us earnestly for the privilege[b] of sharing in this ministry to the saints— [5]and this, not merely as we expected; they gave themselves first to the Lord and, by the will of God, to us, [6]so that we might urge Titus that, as he had already made a beginning, so he should also complete this generous undertaking[c] among you. [7]Now as you excel in everything—in faith, in speech, in knowledge, in utmost eagerness, and in our love for you[d]—so we want you to excel also in this generous undertaking.[c]

[a] Gk *brothers* [b] Gk *grace* [c] Gk *this grace* [d] Other ancient authorities read *your love for us*

COMMENTARY

8:1-5. In his opening statements about the collection, Paul continues his preference for the plural, no doubt to emphasize the larger movement of which he is surely the leader. Once he gets into the discussion, however, he weaves together statements in the singular and in the plural (e.g., plural: 8:18-22, 24; 9:11; 10:3-7, 11-18; singular: 8:23; 9:1-5; 10:1-2, 8-10).

Paul opens his discussion of the collection with one of his formulas of disclosure (1 Cor 12:3; 15:1; Gal 1:11): He wants them to know the grace of God given to the churches of Macedonia. To be sure, all believers know the grace of God in the sense that each is dependent upon God's grace. In this instance, however, Paul wants them to know about the way God's grace has happened in the Macedonian churches. That God's grace is said to be "given" implies God as the giver and is tautologically emphatic.

Paul's description of the Macedonian churches is striking. They, like Paul, have experienced both the abundance of their joy and the depths of their poverty. Paul combines three things that would not have surprised most of his ancient auditors: The Macedonian churches have experienced at the same time an "abundance of joy," "the depths of poverty," and "a great test of affliction" (8:2).

Affliction and joy within it are a commonplace in Paul. Witness his association of the apocalyptic sufferings of the end time with the pangs of childbirth; the goal toward which the suffering moves is proleptically experienced in the context of affliction (Rom 8:18-25; cf. 1 Thess 5:3). In fact, as recently as 2 Cor 7:4 Paul has declared his own joy in the midst of all his affliction (cf. 6:10; 1 Thess 1:6). "Affliction" (θλῖψις *thlipsis*) has been a topic of considerable attention in chaps. 1–7, including his Asian crisis (1:4, 8); his anguish in writing the painful letter (2:4); human existence, with its outer nature wasting away (4:17); part of his hardship catalog (6:4); and the suffering that all believers share as they live in the world, whose structures have been marred by sin (1:4; cf. 1 Cor 7:31). Likewise, joy and rejoicing in the presence of grief and affliction lace together chaps. 1–9: Believers work to produce and are the source of joy for other believers (1:24; 2:3; 7:7, 9, 13, 16), and they share each other's joy (2:3; 7:13).

In 8:1-5 the Macedonian believers are cast as exemplars.[166] Despite their affliction (8:2), the Macedonians had responded to God's grace in kind—namely, in abundance and beyond their power. Their eagerness to be participants in the collection (8:4) sets up a distinct contrast with the yet to be noted reticence of the Corinthians (8:10-12; 9:3-5). Paul takes care to note that the Macedonians "sought" (αὐθαίρετοι *authairetoi*, "of their own free will," 8:3) partnership in the collection, a note paralleled in Paul's honoring the Corinthians' right of self-determination regarding the collection: "I say this not by command" (8:8).

The Macedonian response was beyond what Paul had hoped for (8:5; cf. a similar sentiment in Phlm 21). Paul describes this amazing reaction first with respect to the Lord and then to himself: "They gave themselves first to the Lord and, in accord with God's will, to us" (8:5). The Macedonians who "gave themselves . . . to the Lord and . . . to us" are already believers when the opportunity to participate in the collection is first presented to them. So the "giving of themselves to the Lord" is not a coming to the faith, but a zealous rededication of themselves in the light of the opportunity presented by the collection. Further, the associated "giving of themselves" to Paul is precisely what he has pleaded, obliquely and then directly, with the Corinthians to do more fully (6:12-13; 7:2-3). This little opening portrait of the Macedonians is but the first of a series that Paul employs in 2 Corinthians 8–9 as he seeks to inspire the Corinthians not only to embrace him more fully but also to return to their earlier enthusiasm over the collection, which is now coming to fruition.

8:6. The first mention of Titus in chaps. 8–9

ties up the collection's imminent conclusion with its earlier beginning in Corinth (8:6). Here we learn what the Corinthians knew all along: Titus was the one who, as Paul's agent, had also encouraged them about the collection. Now Paul is sending him back to Corinth to finish and states it in a poignant way: Titus is to complete (ἐπιτελέω *epiteleō*, "bring to its conclusion or goal"), literally, "this grace" (τὴν χάριν ταύτην *tēn charin tautēn* 8:6). "This grace," a euphemism for the collection, can be brought to its goal by people because they, as recipients of grace, must share it with others and by so doing return it to God as grace-filled "thanks" (8:16; 9:15).

8:7. Paul's concluding appeal in this opening section lays out the issue that he will pursue in the rest of this chapter and in the next—namely, why and how the Corinthians can take part in the collection—and capitalizes on his understanding of the hallmark of the Corinthians: They are dedicated to, passionately committed to, "excelling." Their zeal for "excelling" has not always been considered a positive attribute by Paul; in fact, much of 1 Corinthians is devoted to countering their tendency to use nearly every occasion to see if they can one-up each other (e.g., who is wise, who has the freedom to eat what, who has which spiritual gift). Whether positive or not, "excelling" is a characteristic of the Corinthians as Paul understands them, and in 8:7 he attempts to turn it to positive ends: "Just as you excel in all things [with a positively stated list of examples following], so we want you to excel in this grace [the collection, understood]." So the stage for further appeal is set by praise of the Macedonians and their commitment to the collection and by Paul's praise of the Corinthians themselves. Note that the last of Paul's examples of their excelling in everything is "your love for us" (8:7 NIV) or "our love for you" (8:7 NRSV). Strong Greek MSS tradition exists for each translation. Sense in context argues for the former, in which case Paul would here be, like the earlier-noted Cynic choirmaster, pitching the note just a bit high so that the choir, in this case the Corinthians, whom he wishes were more affectionate toward him (6:11-12; 7:2-3), might come in on the right note.

---

166. See H. D. Betz, *2 Corinthians 8 and 9* (Philadelphia: Fortress, 1985) 49-53, for illuminating background on the relations between the Roman provinces of Achaia and Macedonia. For the Macedonians as an example, see ibid., 48. See also S. K. Stowers, "Peri men gar and the Integrity of 2 Cor. 8 and 9," *NovT* 32 (1990) 346.

REFLECTIONS

1. Paul is onto something: Believers do and give because they have been done unto and been given to (1 Cor 4:7; 2 Cor 5:14). As 1 John puts it so succinctly: We love because God first loved us (1 John 4:19; cf. John 13:34). Believers cannot fail to love, because love received prompts love in return.

2. In Paul's world, people did most of their learning by modeling after someone, whether it was in a trade, philosophy, sport, household management, moral reasoning, or whatever. As unsettling as the thought may be today, peer pressure often pushes our children to model themselves after other youngsters whose behavioral patterns leave much to be desired. We can dilate about how terrible that is, probably to little effect. Why not instead realize that we underuse exemplification as a way to enhance moral reflection, sieze the opportunity to become better models ourselves, and make public recognition of those whose actions and comportment set a good pattern for us all?

3. Paul's notion that we, recipients of God's grace, must pass it on, that we must finish the circle by redirecting it through us to someone else, is awesome. Think about what it says about human life in its daily routine: It says that every encounter with another person is an opportunity to be a channel of God's grace. In fact, not to think of grace that way is probably to cheat God and certainly to cheat others, because it arrogates grace to us as a sort of possession whose goal and end is us as individuals and not us as community. God's grace is not to be trifled with or to be taken lightly. It comes into the world, finding expression through people. Grace achieves its goal, it becomes the grace it was intended to be, only as it reaches ever more and more people. That is why the collection for the saints was not just an option that the Macedonians or the Achaians might choose to engage in; it was a joyful obligation (as Paul expressed it in Gal 2:10).

4. Paul's description of the Macedonians' giving heartily in the midst of affliction shows his understanding that the life of faith is not an escape. Neither does it hermetically seal us off from distress and difficulty. Grace and joy in the midst of affliction, far from being a sign of God's absence, are instead a sure sign of God's power.

2 Corinthians 8:8-15, No Command but Advice: Finish What You Began

NIV

[8]I am not commanding you, but I want to test the sincerity of your love by comparing it with the earnestness of others. [9]For you know the grace of our Lord Jesus Christ, that though he was rich, yet for your sakes he became poor, so that you through his poverty might become rich.

[10]And here is my advice about what is best for you in this matter: Last year you were the first not only to give but also to have the desire to do so. [11]Now finish the work, so that your eager willingness to do it may be matched by your

NRSV

[8]I do not say this as a command, but I am testing the genuineness of your love against the earnestness of others. [9]For you know the generous act[a] of our Lord Jesus Christ, that though he was rich, yet for your sakes he became poor, so that by his poverty you might become rich. [10]And in this matter I am giving my advice: it is appropriate for you who began last year not only to do something but even to desire to do something— [11]now finish doing it, so that your eagerness may

[a] Gk the grace

NIV

completion of it, according to your means. [12]For if the willingness is there, the gift is acceptable according to what one has, not according to what he does not have.

[13]Our desire is not that others might be relieved while you are hard pressed, but that there might be equality. [14]At the present time your plenty will supply what they need, so that in turn their plenty will supply what you need. Then there will be equality, [15]as it is written: "He who gathered much did not have too much, and he who gathered little did not have too little."[a]

[a]15 Exodus 16:18

NRSV

be matched by completing it according to your means. [12]For if the eagerness is there, the gift is acceptable according to what one has—not according to what one does not have. [13]I do not mean that there should be relief for others and pressure on you, but it is a question of a fair balance between [14]your present abundance and their need, so that their abundance may be for your need, in order that there may be a fair balance. [15]As it is written,

"The one who had much did not have too much,
and the one who had little did not have too little."

COMMENTARY

8:8. Paul has to walk gingerly with the Corinthians as he tries not only to mend his relation with them but also to reinvigorate and inspire full participation in the collection, so he quickly clarifies that what he writes is not a command (8:8). The Corinthians should operate as fully out of their own free will as the Macedonians have done (8:3). But also like the Macedonians, whose abundant giving in tough times Paul described as a "test" (δοκιμη *dokimē*, 8:2), the Corinthians, through Paul's appeal to them, face a test of their own. What was only implicit in 8:1-7 becomes explicit in 8:8-15: Paul wants the Corinthians to test their own love by comparison with the zeal of the Macedonians (8:8). Paul considers himself and other believers who have been through affliction on behalf of the gospel as δόκιμος (*dokimos*, "tried and true," "approved by test," Rom 16:10; 1 Cor 11:19; cf. its opposite, ἀδόκιμος [*adokimos*, "disqualified"], 1 Cor 9:27). At the Lord's supper, believers examine (δοκιμάζω *dokimazō*), or test, themselves as to how they relate to the body of Christ (1 Cor 11:28-29). Self-assessment is an important and regular Pauline spiritual exercise.[167] Events and situations put individuals to the test as well, in Paul's view. Paul construes as a test what the Corinthians will do about the collection in the light of the Macedonian enthusiasm for it.

Paul leaves the outcome for the Corinthians to decide, but he readily gives his own opinion (γνώμη *gnōmē*), and as these Corinthians already know from one of his earlier letters, Paul thinks his *gnōmē* ought to have weight because of his trustworthiness (1 Cor 7:25).[168] Grace—and how it is responded to—like love, is best not commanded but left to the discretion of the person(s) involved (cf. Phlm 8-9). That is why Paul construes the Corinthian decision about this grace as their test.

8:9. As they face their test in this matter, Paul reminds them of the "big story" in its most cursory form, this time told in categories of wealth and poverty. In Philippians, the same story had been told in grander, probably traditional form by Paul, and there cast in terms of loftiness and humility. The Phil 2:5-11 hymn describes the exalted Christ, who humbled himself, took on the form of a slave, died, and was thereafter exalted once again by God. The story about grace in 2 Cor 8:9 is retrofitted into economic categories appropriate to the topic at hand: the collection. The Lord Jesus Christ, though rich, became poor for the sake of the Corinthians, in this telling of it, so that his poverty might be the occasion for them to become rich (cf. 6:10*b*). As the Corinthians face the test of their love and generosity toward others, Paul reminds them of the big story

167. J. Paul Sampley, *Walking Between the Times: Paul's Moral Reasoning* (Minneapolis: Fortress, 1991) 50-51.

168. See R. A. Ramsaran, *Liberating Words: Paul's Use of Rhetorical Maxims in 1 Corinthians 1–10* (Valley Forge: Trinity, 1996) 66-68.

and of the very grace in which they stand. If they understand that the Lord's abundant grace makes them what they are and gives them all that they have, then how will they possibly be able to stifle grace's overflow or rebound from them to others? Once again in this letter fragment, Paul pulls out the weighty arguments to bolster his appeal to the Corinthians.

8:10-12. The Corinthians will not be surprised that Paul has practical suggestions for them. That is in his character; they have experienced it with him throughout their relationship (cf. 1 Cor 11:22; 14:26-31; 16:2). Accordingly, he first urges them to regain their original enthusiasm for the project (8:7). Paul further argues: Finish what a year ago you started with desire; finish it out of what you have (8:10-12). The latter note, twice sounded and once restated as "not out of what you do not have," shows Paul's careful insistence that he does not now expect them to be put under unreasonable pressure to come up with more funds than is proportionally fitting.

8:13-15. Expanding on this, Paul gives modern readers a window on his sense of fairness and equity in the sharing of goods and proper care among believers. Fairness, equality (ἰσότης *isotēs*, vv. 13-14) seems to be his guideline for an individual's contributions. The principle that "those who have abundance share with those in need" is significantly developed in a reciprocating fashion: The Corinthians' current abundance should meet others' need; others' abundance will meet the Corinthians' need.[169]

In 8:13-15 the ideal seems to be cast primarily in economic categories, but when the collection is treated in Romans where once again Paul addresses his deep conviction of the propriety of reciprocity between believers, he sets it up that "material blessings" are shared by the Gentile believers in appreciation of "spiritual blessings" that the Jewish believers have shared with them (Rom 15:27). Paul finds confirmation, or perhaps the ground for his counsel, in Exod 16:18, which functions here as a maxim: "The one with much did not have too much, and the one with little did not have too little" (8:15; the NIV adds the repeated note of "gathering" in an effort to reflect the exodus story from which the quote comes).

169. F. W. Danker, "Paul's Debt to the *De Corona* of Demosthenes: A Study of Rhetorical Techniques in Second Corinthians," in *Persuasive Artistry: Studies in New Testament Rhetoric in Honor of G. A. Kennedy,* ed. D. F. Watson, JSNTSup 50 (Sheffield: Sheffield Academic, 1991) 269-70, identifies this as Paul's emphatic appropriation of the "Hellenic reciprocity structure," but sees it lying behind much of 2 Corinthians 1–7 as well—there between Paul and the Corinthians. For a reading of the collection as strictly "economic mutualism," see J. J. Meggitt, *Paul, Poverty and Survival* (Edinburgh: T. & T. Clark, 1998) 158-61.

REFLECTIONS

1. Reciprocity and care among believers are givens for Paul. Whether it has to do with possessions, as here, or with thoughtfulness about others, as in other places (cf. 1 Corinthians 8), believers are to look after one another. We might readily embrace those sentiments and think that when we have "something extra" we will share it with those less endowed. If we wait to share until we find ourselves with surplus, we may never share because we have been subtly acculturated to think we never have enough. In the process, we readily lose sight of how much is genuinely ample—and accordingly we are sometimes blind as to how much we really have to share. Furthermore, our sharing does not have to be solely or even primarily relegated to our goods or possessions; our time, though we may also feel overdrawn there, is often the dearest giving of ourselves.

2. One church's members decided that, beyond their regular annual financial pledge, they would give to the church's local and international mission budget an additional 10 percent of whatever funds serendipitously happened into their lives. If they found a dollar, they would turn over ten cents of it the next Sunday. If someone paid an old debt that the original lenders had, in effect, written off and expected never to see again, then they would give a tenth of that toward missions. Life is so full of abundance that pops up in our lives in the most unexpected ways. Why not celebrate that by sharing it with persons in need at home and around the world? If nothing else, you and your family might try keeping tabs on that kind of serendipity for a month and see what 10 percent of that figure would be.

3. Paul thinks that believers are rich simply because God, to whom everything belongs, has deigned to share all things with believers (1 Cor 3:21*b*-23). From that assumption Paul derives a powerful critique of the social and cultural values of his and our times. Paul's is a way of asking what is most important, what really counts, and what really matters. The identity of true richness is worthy of reflection. Jesus' parables touched on that issue in various ways (cf. Luke 12:13-21; 14:15-24; 16:19-31).

2 Corinthians 8:16-24, Titus and Others as Warrantors of Probity

NIV

¹⁶I thank God, who put into the heart of Titus the same concern I have for you. ¹⁷For Titus not only welcomed our appeal, but he is coming to you with much enthusiasm and on his own initiative. ¹⁸And we are sending along with him the brother who is praised by all the churches for his service to the gospel. ¹⁹What is more, he was chosen by the churches to accompany us as we carry the offering, which we administer in order to honor the Lord himself and to show our eagerness to help. ²⁰We want to avoid any criticism of the way we administer this liberal gift. ²¹For we are taking pains to do what is right, not only in the eyes of the Lord but also in the eyes of men.

²²In addition, we are sending with them our brother who has often proved to us in many ways that he is zealous, and now even more so because of his great confidence in you. ²³As for Titus, he is my partner and fellow worker among you; as for our brothers, they are representatives of the churches and an honor to Christ. ²⁴Therefore show these men the proof of your love and the reason for our pride in you, so that the churches can see it.

NRSV

16But thanks be to God who put in the heart of Titus the same eagerness for you that I myself have. ¹⁷For he not only accepted our appeal, but since he is more eager than ever, he is going to you of his own accord. ¹⁸With him we are sending the brother who is famous among all the churches for his proclaiming the good news;*ᵃ* ¹⁹and not only that, but he has also been appointed by the churches to travel with us while we are administering this generous undertaking*ᵇ* for the glory of the Lord himself*ᶜ* and to show our goodwill. ²⁰We intend that no one should blame us about this generous gift that we are administering, ²¹for we intend to do what is right not only in the Lord's sight but also in the sight of others. ²²And with them we are sending our brother whom we have often tested and found eager in many matters, but who is now more eager than ever because of his great confidence in you. ²³As for Titus, he is my partner and co-worker in your service; as for our brothers, they are messengers*ᵈ* of the churches, the glory of Christ. ²⁴Therefore openly before the churches, show them the proof of your love and of our reason for boasting about you.

*ᵃ*Or *the gospel*   *ᵇ*Gk *this grace*   *ᶜ*Other ancient authorities lack *himself*   *ᵈ*Gk *apostles*

COMMENTARY

In an echo of 8:1, Paul opens 8:16 with the claim that the same God whose grace was "given" (δεδομένην *dedomenēn*, 8:1) to the Macedonian churches is the God who "gives [διδόντι *didonti*]

the same zeal for you into Titus's heart." Thus Paul ties the Macedonian believers and Titus together with one another and with the Corinthians; and he subtly ties himself with Titus with the claim of "the same zeal," signifying that Titus's zeal for the Corinthians rises to Paul's level.

Commendatory assertions about Titus open and close 8:16-24. Titus, as we have seen, effects a strong, durative connection for Paul with the Corinthians. In fact, Paul identifies Titus as his own "partner and fellow worker to you" (8:23), a description that will come as no surprise to the Corinthians. Titus, offered as a model for the Corinthians, accepted Paul's appeal, like the Macedonians of his own free will (8:3, 17), and is going to the Corinthians. So, just as Paul has not commanded the Corinthians about the collection (8:8), so also he appeals that Titus devote himself to finishing up this offering. Like Titus, the Corinthians can now accept Paul's appeal and freely embrace participation in the collection.

In this letter fragment, Paul's earlier, repeated sensitivity to possible charges and innuendos that would challenge his integrity (1:12; 2:17; 4:2; 5:11; 6:3; 7:2) provides the background against which to read the series of steps he has taken with the collection to eliminate or at least reduce any chance of accusations of fraud. Paul sends two people for whom he uses the denominator "brother" (ἀδελφός *adelphos*), his standard way of referring to believers (8:18, 22). Their identities are or will be clear to the Corinthians, but escape modern readers. Reference to one of them, probably the second, will be made in Paul's next letter to the Corinthians (2 Cor 12:18), but nothing there resolves our question of his identity.

The first "brother" is a high-profile person whose fame in the gospel had spread "through all the churches" and who was elected by a show of hands (χειροτονέω *cheirotoneō*) to be a traveling companion of Paul and the others "in this grace which is being administered by us." This has a dual purpose: for the glory of the Lord and for our "goodwill" (προθυμία *prothymia*, 8:19). This very respected person, therefore, was handpicked to be the representative of the very churches whose collection was being sent along to Jerusalem via Corinth. Note also that honoring the glory of the Lord precedes any stated concern for securing Paul's reputation.

Between the portrait of the first "brother" and the second, Paul explicitly declares his purpose and standard of care: He seeks to avoid anyone's finding fault with his administration of this lavish gift, and, paraphrasing Prov 3:4 LXX, affirms that he has regard for, "takes into consideration" (προνοέω *pronoeō*), the good, the "honorable" (καλός *kalos*), "not only before the Lord but also before people" (8:20-21; cf. Phil 4:8). Note once again that the Lord's assessment is given pride of place over what people think.

The second "brother" is one with whom Paul apparently has quite a history because he says of him, "We have tested him in many ways and many times, finding him zealous." But he is now even more zealous "because of his great confidence in you [the Corinthians]" (8:22). So one brother has special connections with the Macedonian churches and is sent as their representative, and the other one has special connections with Paul—and apparently also with the Corinthians. Both will be traveling with Titus and are dubbed by Paul "representatives of the churches [ἀπόστολοι ἐκκλησιῶν *apostoloi ekklēsiōn*], the glory of Christ" (8:23).

The section closes (οὖν *oun*, "therefore") with Paul's challenge to the Corinthians to "give proof" (ἔνδειξις *endeixis*) before those very churches that are so positively represented in the various persons who make up this delegation, of "your love and our boast about you" (8:24).[170] Paul's "boast" about the Corinthians plays quite a role in this letter: (1) It has spurred the Macedonians to emulate the Corinthians by taking part in the collection (9:2), and (2) Paul's boast about the Corinthians has proved true when Titus sees that the Corinthians are indeed moved to a reaffirmation of Paul by his "painful" letter (7:14).

With the single exception of Paul's identification of Titus as "my partner" (8:23), Paul has used the plural throughout this passage. By using the plural so pervasively, Paul casts as completely aligned and associated with him and with his collection the Macedonian churches, their unnamed representative, Paul's unnamed representative, and Titus. All of them are equally and fully dedicated to seeing the collection through Corinth to Jerusalem. With this resounding portrait of unanimity, Paul is free to turn his attention—and theirs—to the projected arrival of this entourage in Corinth (9:1-5).

---

170. Stowers rightly says that "8:24 is the central exhortation toward which Paul's discourse moves." See S. K. Stowers, *"Peri men gar* and the Integrity of 2 Corinthians 8 and 9," *NovT* 32 (1990) 346.

REFLECTIONS

1. The term σπουδη (*spoudē*), which means "zeal/eagerness/earnestness/diligence" (8:16; "concern," NIV) has played quite a role not only here, but elsewhere in 2 Corinthians as well (e.g., 7:11-12; 8:7-8). It is a term Paul uses to describe what he considers proper commitment to something or to someone. *Spoudē* allows no mediocrity or distance, but instead betokens obligation and passion. Thus it fleshes out love so that love's ever-passionate commitment is expressed (note Paul's call for a demonstration of the Corinthians' love in 8:24). In a fashion quite alien to Paul, aloofness and distance, sometimes even a turning in to oneself and one's own interests, are viewed positively in today's culture (cf. Rev 3:15-16).

2. A transaction, a use of personal funds now collected, is viewed as an occasion to glorify the Lord (8:19). The way we allocate our funds every week and every month is a moral statement. Our budgets, whether we actually record them or not, are moral ledgers that depict where our values are. A family could have quite a discussion over where this week's or month's funds are actually going and why.

3. Our patterns of doing and spending are maps of our value systems. At a certain level we know that, because we casually talk about how we "spend" our time. We have only so much time and finite financial resources. Our lives can drift into a style where what appears most pressing at the moment determines what we do. This is to be outer-directed; what is out there (to be done) dictates the organization of our lives. We may even go on to what amounts to autopilot, not even thinking about why we are doing what we do. As with our time, so with our financial assets: Our allocation of each is a logbook of our values put into deeds. Paul's self-analysis on this count is found in 8:21, where he has regard for or takes into consideration the "good/honorable" in all that he does. What a wake-up call it might be for us if we screened our financial and temporal choices—even the smallest of them—for whether they aim for the good and the honorable!

2 Corinthians 9:1-5, Steps to Ensure That the Corinthians Are Ready

NIV

9 There is no need for me to write to you about this service to the saints. [2]For I know your eagerness to help, and I have been boasting about it to the Macedonians, telling them that since last year you in Achaia were ready to give; and your enthusiasm has stirred most of them to action. [3]But I am sending the brothers in order that our boasting about you in this matter should not prove hollow, but that you may be ready, as I said you would be. [4]For if any Macedonians come with me and find you unprepared, we—not to say anything about you—would be ashamed of having been so confident. [5]So I thought it necessary to urge the brothers to visit you in advance and finish the arrangements for the generous gift

NRSV

9 Now it is not necessary for me to write you about the ministry to the saints, [2]for I know your eagerness, which is the subject of my boasting about you to the people of Macedonia, saying that Achaia has been ready since last year; and your zeal has stirred up most of them. [3]But I am sending the brothers in order that our boasting about you may not prove to have been empty in this case, so that you may be ready, as I said you would be; [4]otherwise, if some Macedonians come with me and find that you are not ready, we would be humiliated—to say nothing of you—in this undertaking.[a] [5]So I thought it necessary to urge the brothers to go on ahead to

[a]Other ancient authorities add *of boasting*

NIV	NIV
you had promised. Then it will be ready as a generous gift, not as one grudgingly given.	you, and arrange in advance for this bountiful gift that you have promised, so that it may be ready as a voluntary gift and not as an extortion.

COMMENTARY

Moving now predominantly to the singular,[171] Paul puts his relationship to the Corinthians directly into the middle of the picture. As the text shows, he acknowledges just how much *he* has at stake in the Corinthian response. Paul has boasted to the Macedonians about the Corinthians (here the syncresis, or comparison, uses the Corinthians as the model for the Macedonians; cf. 8:1-5), saying that they have been ready since the past year, exactly the time frame he reflected in 8:10. Paul's sending the "brothers" (the two unnamed men and Titus, 8:16-24) as a sort of advance guard is his way of attempting to ensure that the so far recalcitrant Corinthians are prepared by the time Paul (later) arrives in Corinth (9:3).

Paul paints for the Corinthians a worst-case scenario: Imagine some Macedonians coming along with Paul and discovering the Corinthians not ready. Paul, resorting to the plural for just one verb, perhaps because the potential for shame is so overwhelming and pervasive, carries the scenario along: "We ourselves would be humiliated, not to mention you, in this situation" (9:4). In a culture so dominated by shame and honor as is the Roman one of which Paul and his communities are a part,[172] this public humiliation would be devastating—and Paul rightly observes that the shame would be theirs as well as his.

Reverting to the singular again, Paul dwells on his sending of these brothers to "arrange in advance" (προκαταρτίζω *prokatartizō*) what the Corinthians had "promised in advance" (προεπαγγέλλω *proepangellō*, 9:5). Paul acknowledges the range within which the Corinthian response must ultimately fall: From what he most hopes—namely, the "generous gift" produced willingly out of much bounty (εὐλογία *eulogia*)—to its opposite, and what Paul fervently hopes to avoid—namely, "as grudgingly granted" (ὡς πλεονεξίαν *hōs pleonexian*). Paul's rhetoric throughout 2 Corinthians 8–9 is designed to move the Corinthians away from the latter and toward the former.

---

171. Stowers concludes that it is "most implausible to think of chapters 8 and 9 as fragments of two letters." See ibid., 348.

172. Ibid., 347; and S. K. Stowers, *Letter Writing in Greco-Roman Antiquity* (Philadelphia: Westminster, 1986) 27-28, 77-78, 91-94.

REFLECTIONS

1. Modeling as ethical instruction and as exhortation is a rich tool that Paul regularly used and that we are far too reticent to employ. Consistent performance and dependability (also known as trustworthiness) are at the heart of any generation's most admired characteristics, but it is easy to discount their importance when it is more convenient for us to do otherwise. There is an infectious quality in failing to keep one's word; when one person defiles the currency of dependability, others also tend to lower the bar on trustworthiness. On the other side, there is a positive infectiousness of faith and zeal.

2. Giving and being responsive to others are best when they flow willingly and not grudgingly. We may wonder how we who are *obliged* to give have any room to talk about giving freely and willingly. If we start with the obligation, we will never understand the freedom. If we begin, instead, with the celebration of what and how much God has done for us and given to us, then the zeal for giving and for responding to others flows freely from it (cf. Luke 12:48; 1 John 4:19).

2 Corinthians 9:6-15, Sowing and Reaping Bountifully

NIV

⁶Remember this: Whoever sows sparingly will also reap sparingly, and whoever sows generously will also reap generously. ⁷Each man should give what he has decided in his heart to give, not reluctantly or under compulsion, for God loves a cheerful giver. ⁸And God is able to make all grace abound to you, so that in all things at all times, having all that you need, you will abound in every good work. ⁹As it is written:

"He has scattered abroad his gifts to the poor;
  his righteousness endures forever."ᵃ

¹⁰Now he who supplies seed to the sower and bread for food will also supply and increase your store of seed and will enlarge the harvest of your righteousness. ¹¹You will be made rich in every way so that you can be generous on every occasion, and through us your generosity will result in thanksgiving to God.

¹²This service that you perform is not only supplying the needs of God's people but is also overflowing in many expressions of thanks to God. ¹³Because of the service by which you have proved yourselves, men will praise God for the obedience that accompanies your confession of the gospel of Christ, and for your generosity in sharing with them and with everyone else. ¹⁴And in their prayers for you their hearts will go out to you, because of the surpassing grace God has given you. ¹⁵Thanks be to God for his indescribable gift!

ᵃ9 Psalm 112:9

NRSV

⁶The point is this: the one who sows sparingly will also reap sparingly, and the one who sows bountifully will also reap bountifully. ⁷Each of you must give as you have made up your mind, not reluctantly or under compulsion, for God loves a cheerful giver. ⁸And God is able to provide you with every blessing in abundance, so that by always having enough of everything, you may share abundantly in every good work. ⁹As it is written,

"He scatters abroad, he gives to the poor;
  his righteousnessᵃ endures forever."

¹⁰He who supplies seed to the sower and bread for food will supply and multiply your seed for sowing and increase the harvest of your righteousness.ᵃ ¹¹You will be enriched in every way for your great generosity, which will produce thanksgiving to God through us; ¹²for the rendering of this ministry not only supplies the needs of the saints but also overflows with many thanksgivings to God. ¹³Through the testing of this ministry you glorify God by your obedience to the confession of the gospel of Christ and by the generosity of your sharing with them and with all others, ¹⁴while they long for you and pray for you because of the surpassing grace of God that he has given you. ¹⁵Thanks be to God for his indescribable gift!

ᵃ Or benevolence

COMMENTARY

9:6-7. Paul, lover of metaphors, expands upon the alternatives with which 9:5 closes—"generous gift" generated out of bounty versus greed, avarice, "grudgingly granted"—and develops his thoughts around the motif of sowing and reaping. His first step is to place the responsibility directly upon each Corinthian. In so doing, he expands his earlier disclaimer that he is not commanding them what to do (8:8) and that the Corinthians need, like the Macedonians and like Titus, to take

part in the collection by their own free will (8:3). Laconically, Paul provides three guidelines: (1) "each just as he has decided in his heart," (2) "not reluctantly nor out of necessity," and (3), embracing what Prov 22:8 LXX says as true: "God loves a cheerful/gracious giver" (9:7). Because the claim about God's love is so directly interlaced with personal dispositions, we can conclude that Paul's moral reasoning does not spring simply from internal feelings, reckonings, and calculations. The decisions that are properly lodged in the heart, freely and positively embraced, are nevertheless incited, framed, and defined by God's love.

9:8. This verse has the ring of a finely hewed commonplace that captures much that is important in Paul's reckoning. The sentence has three moments. First is the declaration of a fundamental truth about God: God is able to multiply/increase in abundance (περισσεύω *perissuō*) every grace unto you (9:8*a*). The second moment describes how that divinely inspired abundance affects daily life: "so that you may have *all* sufficiency in *all* things, in *all* time" (9:8*b*, italics added). The rhetorically reinforcing wordplay on "all" in the text (ἐν παντὶ πάντοτε πᾶσαν *en panti pantote pasan*) powerfully elaborates the "abundance" grounded in God's grace as mentioned in 9:8*a* and anticipates a final "all" statement in 9:8*c*. The third moment (9:8*c*) explicitly echoes the "abundance" of the first moment (9:8*a*) and builds from the "so that" (purpose) statement of the second moment (9:8*b*): "so that you may abound in every [πᾶν *pan*, "all"] good work." Implicit in the distillation of the believer's ethical ground in 9:8 is Paul's assumption that good works are not an option for believers, but a necessity. Believers are free to determine *what* form the good works take, what shape love takes (cf. Phlm 8-14), but they are not free *not* to love; they are not free *not* to do good works. These assumptions emerged already when Paul reminded the Corinthians that "it is necessary for all of us to appear before the tribune of Christ so that each person may receive a recompense for the things done in the body, whether good or bad" (2 Cor 5:10). Believers must do good works. The good works are generated by God's grace, bountifully poured out upon believers.

9:9. Taking an image from one of the psalms and employing the image of God as sower, Paul offers confirmation for his understanding of God as the initiator of grace: God "scatters abroad, he gives to the needy" (9:9; cf. Ps 111:9 LXX). The remainder of the psalm text identifies what is scattered or sown as God's "righteousness/justice" (δικαιοσύνη *dikaiosynē*, which "remains for ever").

9:10. With echoes from Isa 55:10 and Hos 10:12 lending weight to his counsel, Paul elabo-

rates some implications of God's being the source of grace and abundance. God, the understood but unstated subject, who provides "seed to the sower and bread for food" (Isa 55:10 NRSV), "will supply and multiply your store of seed" and "will increase your 'harvest of righteousness'" (Hos 10:12 NRSV). Divinely produced abundance cascades through these rich phrases and clauses, reminding the Corinthians not only of the source of life but also of its bounty with its attendant responsibility to do the aforementioned good work (9:8), which could also be identified as the "righteousness/justice" that Paul, quoting Psalm 111, expects (9:9). Grace once received obligates the recipient to the pursuit of justice. In the instance at hand, Paul links taking part in the collection with proper pursuit of righteousness and justice just as he has earlier tied believers' reconciliation to God in Christ with the righteousness/justice that comes from God (2 Cor 5:21).

9:11-15. In the verses that remain about the collection (9:11-15), Paul adopts the plural and thus associates himself with all those who have readily committed to the collection so far, and he looks foward to the immediate future, projecting what he hopes will happen with and through the Corinthians. Because Paul is confident in his knowledge of God, he assures the Corinthians that this God of abundance will enrich them in every generosity, which will bring about "through us" thanksgiving to God (9:11). Widely in the Pauline corpus, the proper and fundamental response to God is quintessentially expressed as resulting in "thanksgiving to God" (cf. Rom 1:21; 1 Cor 14:16; Phil 4:6; Phlm 4). Already in 2 Cor 4:15 Paul has laid the grounds for understanding thanksgiving as the ultimate outcome of God's grace expressed in the lives of people. As God's grace reaches out to more and more people, more and more will respond in thanksgiving to God. Here, in 9:11, Paul recapitulates the same conviction and suggests that if the Corinthians devote their abundance to the collection, then thanksgiving will be generated "through us." Immediately, he expands the frame of reference (9:12): At stake is not merely the saints in Jerusalem and the meeting of their needs, though that is a proper goal, but who knows how many more people may be affected and join in thanksgiving to God?

Throughout these closing verses, Paul is direct

about what participation will mean *for the Corinthians.* They will "reap bountifully" if they sow accordingly (9:6 NRSV). God will give them plenty for sowing and will increase their harvest (of righteousness, 9:10). Paul assures them that they will be "enriched in every way" by God for their "generosity/liberality" (ἁπλότης *haplotēs,* 9:11). And not insignificant in Pauline communities, they will be adding to the thanksgivings to God (9:12).

Paul presents it to them as a "testing" (δοκιμη *dokimē*), returning in an inclusio to the testing that the Macedonians faced and passed by their hearty and exemplary participation in the collection (9:13; see also 8:2; cf. 2:9). In between the 8:2 and 9:13 mentions of testing, Paul has explicitly told the Corinthians: "I am testing the genuineness of your own love as compared with the zeal of the others" (8:8).

In 5:14-21 Paul developed the understanding of his ministry as one of reconciliation. There he used the plural, "our ministry." Now, as he concludes his discussion of the collection and his profound hope that the Corinthians will indeed join in it, he twice again (9:12-13) uses the term διακονία (*diakonia,* "ministry/service") to describe the collection and by so doing invites the Corinthians to make his *diakonia* their own, to identify with it as a ministry of reconciliation (echoing 5:19-20), of uniting them as God's people in Christ, whether Jews or Gentiles. That is why he can conclude his arguments for their participation with a grand portrayal: By taking part in "this ministry" they will be glorifying God (remember all the earlier reflections about glory, 3:7-18) by showing "obedience to your confession of the gospel of Christ" and by "your sharing of your liberality with" the poor in Jerusalem "and with all others" (9:13).

With the last note, Paul places their sharing in the context of the obedience ingredient to their confession, and the sharing is not just with the Jerusalem saints but, like the ministry of reconciliation, is devoted to "all others" because Christ died for all (5:14). So the collection is a special appeal for a *particular* expression of the ministry of reconciliation, but it is only one part of the sharing, caring for others, that is incumbent on persons claimed by the gospel of Jesus Christ, no matter how much or how little they have to

contribute. Once again, Paul assumes that the very ones who benefit from the Corinthian generosity will find themselves "longing for" and "praying for you" (9:14)—a hint at the same reciprocity that he expresses so clearly about the collection in Rom 15:27: "If the Gentiles have come to share in their spiritual blessings, they ought also to be of service to them in material things" (NRSV). The prayers and longings of others for the Corinthians are activated by the "surpassing grace of God," which is the groundspring of all of faithful life and certainly of faith's generosity.

It is not surprising that Paul's two-chapter appeal about the collection, which began with the defining note of "grace," rises to its conclusion by crediting God's grace as infusing all of life with generosity, with longing, and with prayers one for another. Moved by this grace and its powerful working through the lives of people everywhere, Paul closes with this theme, reworked into a sort of blessing (see the Commentary on 1:3): "Grace be to God for God's indescribable gift" (9:15). Most translations rightly put that as "Thanks be to God" (cf. 8:16 for the same Greek construction).

Grace *from* God comes as a gift. God's grace prompts grace in and among people, and that grace returns to God in the form of thanks. Second Corinthians 8–9 is a case study of all three aspects and of the power of grace. By his formulation of 9:15, Paul has almost redundantly emphasized the "giftiness" of life before God. "Grace" connotes God's free gift, freely given to those whom Paul makes clear in other places do not deserve it (cf. Rom 3:23). But Paul paints God's grace as an "indescribable gift" (ἀνεκδιηγήτῳ δωρεα *anekdiēgētō dōrea*). In doxological form, then, Paul twice highlights the gift quality of life (*charis* and *dōrea*).

With that, the text breaks off. We cannot be certain of how the letter actually concluded. Chapters 10–13 clearly have a startlingly different tone and are part of a distinct subsequent letter (see the Introduction). Subsequent to Paul's time, whoever put these letter fragments together must have edited away the concluding section of the letter that is otherwise complete in 2 Corinthians 1–9. We can only surmise that, given the sublime tone achieved at the end of chapter 9, the rest of the letter would have been collegial and warm.

REFLECTIONS

1. If we think about how hard we worked to arrive where we are, we are likely to become stingy, because there is something innately programmed into us to have us think either that by our hard work we deserve what we have or that we have been shortchanged and do not have enough. If, on the other hand, we think about how many doors have been opened to us, about how we have gotten where we are by the way things have surprisingly opened to or "broken for" us (by God's grace and by the working of the Spirit), then we are more likely to think more generously. No doubt some truth resides on both sides of those arguments. The issue is how we keep perspective. Paul may help us here. God graces. God sows. We do not deserve God's favor, but we receive it. Such beneficence, especially when we know we do not deserve it, takes away some of our control of our lives and places us in a response mode. Grace received demands a response. The grace that comes from God finds its fruition as it flows through us to others.

2. Building on the previous point, God's grace, received by us and expressed through us to another, does not stop in the other, the one to whom we show it. Curiously, that grace binds us to that other person and produces a ready-made chorus of two who should be able to sing quite a song of thanksgiving to God. God's grace cascades and overflows so powerfully that the singing duo will be heard by more—and the circle expands.

3. Giving must not be marked by the slightest degree of reluctance because then it is not freely given. Giving is a delicate transaction. If you put even the tiniest little string on the gift, then it is not truly a gift.

4. How is it that we harvest righteousness/justice (9:10) when we sow and give? We may suppose that Paul, thoroughly consonant with his Jewish heritage, considers caring for those who are in need and giving to those who have less is performing covenant righteousness/justice. In the *shalom/*peace of God, no one can be left out or left behind. To bring them along and to assist them from the abundance of what we have is to keep covenant with God.

5. Following Luther, we tend to affirm the priesthood of all believers, meaning that all of us actually share in ministry. Paul anticipates that outlook when he pictures the Corinthians as taking part in his ministry (9:13). Our giving or not giving out of our abundance, even if those pockets of abundance seem frightfully small to us at times, is a test—of our responsiveness to God's sowing and scattering among us.

2 CORINTHIANS 10:1–13:13

PAUL'S PREPARATION FOR A SHOWDOWN VISIT

OVERVIEW

The remaining chapters of 2 Corinthians (chaps. 10–13) are part of a distinct letter fragment that was written some time after 2 Corinthians 1–9 (see the Introduction). Paul's relationship to the Corinthians has suffered some recent changes, none of which have been beneficial.

First, Corinthian opposition to Paul has broken virulently into the open. As 2 Corinthians shows, subsequent to the time of his writing 1 Corinthians, Paul's relations with the Corinthians have resembled a roller-coaster ride. Before writing 2 Corinthians 1–9, Paul had been offended when the Corinthian believers did not rally to his side after one of their own had done him "wrong." Paul took that as a defection from his authority and an alienation of affection, so he canceled a promised visit and instead wrote them a painful letter of frank speech, calling them to task. As chaps. 1–9 show, Paul understands that, in response to his painful letter, the Corinthians have come about, punished the offender, and rallied to him once more.

Second, of critical importance, outsiders have now intruded into Paul's ongoing problems with the Corinthians. Already when 2 Corinthians 1–9 was written, these persons from outside, accompanied by letters of recommendation, had made contact with members of the Corinthian congregation, but Paul apparently did not then perceive them to be the substantial threat they came to be (3:1-3). We do not know much about these people because Paul follows the canons of his time by which one does not honor opponents with much delineation. Also, we cannot know who might have written the commendatory letters sponsoring the outsiders. We can know how Paul characterizes the intruders; three times he calls them "apostles" (ἀπόστολοι *apostoloi*), a term

that may describe persons who are sent as ambassadors, delegates, or messengers (cf. 8:23; Phil 2:25); but the title does not necessarily indicate that the intruders were among Jesus' earlier disciples. Twice Paul calls them "superapostles" (ὑπερλίαν ἀπόστολοι *hyperlian apostoloi*, 11:5; 12:11). Once he says such persons are "false apostles" (ψευδαπόστολοι *pseudapostoloi*, 11:13). In almost every paragraph of this letter fragment, the opponents' presence is palpable—either in some assertion they have made or in some comparison.

As Paul has indicated throughout 2 Corinthians 1–9, comportment can be a revelatory window on one's true identity. Accordingly, Paul's florid, and perhaps exaggerated, characterization of the outsiders' behavior is designed to show their true colors. Nothing in Paul's claims about them can confidently be taken as an undistorted portrait. Methodologically, we should suppose that, wherever possible, details about them are slanted to make them stand in the worst possible light.[173]

To put it most directly, the heart of the matter is that the outsiders challenge Paul's authority by wanting to be put on a par with him. Further, the outsiders, like Paul, presume that they have rights to support for their preaching of the gospel (cf. 1 Cor 9:4-12), but they, unlike Paul, apparently accept assistance (11:20; 12:13). Paul's most scathing attack centers on the outsiders' "taking advantage" of the Corinthians (11:20); they are said to enslave, devour, take on airs, and even beat the Corinthians in the face (11:20-21)—

---

173. Paul follows the conventions of his time in this regard. See J. Paul Sampley, "Paul, His Opponents in 2 Corinthians 10–13, and the Rhetorical Handbooks," in *The Social World of Formative Christianity and Judaism: Essays in Tribute to H. C. Kee,* ed. J. Neusner, P. Borgen, E. S. Frerichs, R. Horsley (Philadelphia: Fortress, 1988) 169-71.

surely rhetorical hyperbole. At every point, Paul bids to benefit by the comparison.

Third, Paul's fiscal practices, already somewhat problematic for the Corinthians, have emerged as a point of sharp contention between Paul and different groups at Corinth. Although Paul asserts that, as an apostle, he could have demanded support from the Corinthians, he assiduously and persistently avoided doing so (1 Cor 9:3-18; 2 Cor 11:9, 20-21*a*; 12:13-16). Paul has claimed to preach the gospel "free of charge" (2 Cor 11:7). Some at Corinth apparently think Paul is "robbing churches" because he accepts personal support from other churches, expressly from the Macedonians, precisely while he is in Corinth refusing assistance from the Corinthians—a surefire way to have questions raised by the locals (2 Cor 11:8-9). Some others at Corinth, the wealthy who were accustomed to use their wealth and its status as leverage inside the believing community (cf. 1 Cor 6:1-6; 11:21-22, 33-34), apparently think Paul treats the Corinthians as second-class believers when he refuses to accept their support (2 Cor 12:13). In a culture so vertically structured along patron/client lines as the Greco-Roman world, persons who offer gifts and support bid to be patrons; the recipients, by accepting the beneficence, become clients and are accordingly obliged to honor and laud the patrons.[174] Given those strictures and liabilities, Paul's refusal to accept gifts or support from the Corinthians, especially from the wealthy ones with whom he has had some special problems in the past, is understandable *from Paul's standpoint;* but from the Corinthians' perspective, sharing the culture's view as they do, Paul's refusal to accept a gift and support constitutes a shameful rebuke.[175]

The contrast with Paul's treatment of the Macedonians is palpable: Paul freely accepts support from them, while he is *at Corinth.* How can that be? On the level of interpersonal relationships, doing so has to be the utmost folly because it is virtually guaranteed to ruffle Corinthian sensibilities, though in fairness Paul appears to have no control over when and where the Philippians send him support (Phil 4:10).[176] Paul acknowledges explicitly that his relation to the Philippians, one of the Macedonian churches, is unique, though such an explanation could only fuel Corinthian fires. In his letter to the Philippians, Paul declares that, from the very beginning of his preaching of the gospel to them, he entered into a partnership with them, which he describes in terms of "giving and receiving" (Phil 1:5; 4:15).[177]

Paul's continued advocacy of the collection for the saints in Jerusalem contributes to the problem because the Corinthians flagged in their zeal for participating; yet in 2 Corinthians 8–9 Paul presses them to see it through. In order to avert any last-minute difficulties or criticisms of his handling of the funds generated for the collection by the different churches, Paul arranges for the churches to appoint a representative and adds his own proxies (8:18-23).

Fourth, Paul's relation to the Corinthians, as reflected in the letter fragment 2 Corinthians 10–13, has now clearly become one of contention. The whole document, therefore, must be read in the light of the contemporary conventions for resolving disputes. The full scope of the contention does not become apparent at first. Surely by 13:1-10, however, one can see that Paul anticipates a showdown visit, gives stern warning of his intentions, and makes one last effort to avert a direct, personal confrontation. All of the sections of this letter fragment must be read in that disputatious light. The rhetorical handbooks of Paul's time are the codification of lore and practice regarding how best to make one's case, how to put one's opponents at disadvantage, and how to put the best face on whatever the circumstance. The handbooks were the basic tools of education in antiquity, and Paul shows himself fully aware of the advice and counsel they give.[178]

In a dispute, the handbooks advise that the orator, or in this case the letter writer whose letters become speech when read to recipients, can win goodwill for his case by referring to

---

174. See G. W. Peterman, *Paul's Gift from Philippi: Conventions of Gift-Exchange and Christian Giving* (Cambridge: Cambridge University Press, 1997) 51-89.

175. Peter Marshall, *Enmity in Corinth: Social Conventions in Paul's Relations with the Corinthians,* WUNT 44 (Tübingen: J. C. B. Mohr, 1987) 242-47.

176. Twice they sent him help in Thessalonica (Phil 4:16) and the incident of support that in part occasions the writing of the Letter to the Philippians was one that seems to have come unexpectedly (Phil 4:10).

177. J. Paul Sampley, *Pauline Partnership in Christ: Christian Community and Commitment in Light of Roman Law* (Philadelphia: Fortress, 1980) 53-55. Peterman, *Paul's Gift from Philippi,* 55-65, rightly increases the scope to include friendship and social reciprocity.

178. Sampley, "Paul, His Opponents in 2 Corinthians 10–13, and the Rhetorical Handbooks," 162-77.

himself, to his hearers, and to the facts of the case.[179] Paul's rhetorical situation is slightly different from what the handbooks suppose because the people to be persuaded are themselves involved in the case as the auditors of his letter. But the same dynamic remains: Paul needs to make his understanding of the case convincing.

Though we cannot be certain of the outcome of the showdown visit Paul projects in 2 Corinthians 10–13, we can cite several indicators that suggest he likely had success in reclaiming the Corinthians in that encounter: (1) The letter fragment 2 Corinthians 10–13 was preserved; (2) the Achaians (and therefore quite possibly the Corinthians) took part in the collection for the saints in Jerusalem (Rom 15:26); (3) Paul wrote the Letter to the Romans, a subsequent letter, from Corinth, where Gaius, one of Paul's first converts there (see 1 Cor 1:14), is host to Paul "and to the whole church" (Rom 16:23); (4) he sends the Romans greetings from Erastus, Corinth's treasurer (Rom 16:23); and (5) Clement, the second century bishop of Rome, continues to identify the Corinthian church with Paul.[180]

For Paul to have overcome his latest struggle with the Corinthians (as reflected in 2 Corinthians 10–13), he must have had an unfaltering contingent, a dependable and loyal core of believers who stood by him in the hard times at Corinth. We may guess that among those are persons in positions of leadership, such as Gaius (Rom 16:23; 1 Cor 1:14), Stephanas, Fortunatus, and Achaicus (1 Cor 16:15-17). Also possibly instrumental in encouraging fidelity to Paul could be Chloe and her people (1 Cor 1:11)—whether she was a Corinthian or not, Paul's positive mention of her

179. Cicero *On Invention* 1.16.22.
180. See *1 Clem* 47.3.

without further identification indicates that she was influential at Corinth—and Phoebe. Phoebe's is perhaps the most interesting case, perhaps partly because we do not know much about her, but what we do know suggests a *much* larger picture of her association and work with Paul. She is from Cenchreae, a town near Corinth, she is a deacon in her local church (Rom 16:1), and surely she is to be counted among those to whom chaps. 1–9 are addressed ("with all the saints in the whole of Achaia," the Roman province where Corinth and Cenchreae are located; 1:1). Paul's description of her in his commendation to the Romans shows that she has been a partner, or more precisely a patron, of him and of many (we may suppose) believers. That she goes to Rome after the writing of 2 Corinthians 10–13, possibly carrying the letter to believers in the proud city of Rome and surely representing Paul, shows that she is a formidable force in her own right. Such a person cannot have played a small role in Paul's successes with the Corinthians, and, though we will never be able to know, she may have been significant in what seems to have been a positive outcome from the final struggle between Paul and the Corinthians (chaps. 10–13).

Paul had another important asset in his relations with the Corinthians: His agents who double for him. Titus and Timothy maintained good connections with the Corinthians across the years—in the commentary we see several occasions on which their relation to the Corinthians may have been stronger than Paul's—and we never see any hint that either Timothy or Titus weakened in his affection and devotion for Paul. Finally, who knows what impact the Macedonians and their fervor for Paul and his mission might have had on the Corinthians?

2 CORINTHIANS 10:1-6, PAUL'S READINESS TO DO BATTLE

NIV	NRSV
10 By the meekness and gentleness of Christ, I appeal to you—I, Paul, who am "timid" when face to face with you, but "bold" when	**10** I myself, Paul, appeal to you by the meekness and gentleness of Christ—I who am humble when face to face with you, but bold

NIV

away! ²I beg you that when I come I may not have to be as bold as I expect to be toward some people who think that we live by the standards of this world. ³For though we live in the world, we do not wage war as the world does. ⁴The weapons we fight with are not the weapons of the world. On the contrary, they have divine power to demolish strongholds. ⁵We demolish arguments and every pretension that sets itself up against the knowledge of God, and we take captive every thought to make it obedient to Christ. ⁶And we will be ready to punish every act of disobedience, once your obedience is complete.

NRSV

toward you when I am away!— ²I ask that when I am present I need not show boldness by daring to oppose those who think we are acting according to human standards.ᵃ ³Indeed, we live as human beings,ᵇ but we do not wage war according to human standards;ᵃ ⁴for the weapons of our warfare are not merely human,ᶜ but they have divine power to destroy strongholds. We destroy arguments ⁵and every proud obstacle raised up against the knowledge of God, and we take every thought captive to obey Christ. ⁶We are ready to punish every disobedience when your obedience is complete.

ᵃ Gk *according to the flesh*   ᵇ Gk *in the flesh*   ᶜ Gk *fleshly*

COMMENTARY

We cannot tell what or how much of the letter has been lost prior to 10:1. As it stands, this letter fragment opens with an appeal, a feature that sometimes occurs at the later stages in Paul's letters (Rom 12:1; Phil 4:2; 1 Thess 4:1; Phlm 9-10; cf. 1 Cor 1:10). Two factors must be kept in mind throughout chaps. 10–13: (1) Paul is distressed that (some of) the Corinthians have been seduced into fealty to rivals who have infiltrated the believing community, and (2) he is anticipating a showdown visit.

10:1-2. Paul's entreaty to the Corinthians is referenced to Christ's "gentleness/humility" (πραΰτης *prautēs*) and "clemency" (ἐπιείκεια *epieikeia*). Christ, in these characteristics, is the model Paul prefers to follow as he anticipates the showdown that will happen with the Corinthians when he makes his projected third visit (13:1, 10)—a confrontation that can be avoided if they change their ways.

Paul's two terms regarding Christ reinforce each other because their semantic fields overlap. Both suggest gentleness, with the former ranging to humility and considerateness toward others and the latter compassing graciousness, clemency, and a disposition to mercy. It is not accidental that, as he anticipates a visit to the Corinthians, Paul uses the very same term he had used earlier when he had projected a visit to the Corinthians, and there also hoped for an alteration of their dispo-

sition (1 Cor 4:21). There as here, Paul hopes that the Corinthians will change and become more as he wishes them to be. The earlier alternatives—Paul will come to them with a rod, meaning ready to punish them if they have not modified their behavior, or "in love with a spirit of clemency" (*epieikeia*, 1 Cor 4:21)—are echoed in 2 Cor 10:6. In Galatians, Paul suggests that believers, governed by the Spirit, should always be ready to respond to those who have gone astray by "restoring" them "in a spirit of gentleness" (*prautēs*, Gal 6:1). In 2 Cor 10:1, Paul practices what he preached to the Galatians.

The Corinthians have the choice of which "Paul" will come to them, whether the one who, like Christ, comes with gentleness and clemency or the one who, like the rod-bearing disciplinarian (1 Cor 4:21) or, as he puts it even more forcefully in 2 Cor 10:2-6, the bold, confident one who, with divine power, destroys all strongholds. If he does not come to them modeling Christ's gentleness and clemency, then he will come as a skilled warrior armed with God's power to wreak devastation on any resistance and obstacle that may be raised against him.

Such a detailed development of the military motif[181] as that in 10:3-6 suggests his underlying

181. A. J. Malherbe, "Antisthenes and Odysseus, and Paul at War," *HTR* 76 (1983) 143-73.

assumption that matters with the Corinthians have degenerated so far that a showdown is not likely to be averted. Nevertheless, he "appeals" (παρακαλω *parakalō*, 10:1) and "begs" (δέομαι *deomai*, 10:2; effectively doubled for emphasis) them to alter their behavior so that he will not have to use against *them* the arsenal at his disposal (2 Cor 10:1-2). To make certain that the Corinthians are not misled by any mistaken estimates of him, Paul urges them not to gamble on his being "timid/humble/pliant" (ταπεινός *tapeinos*)—as some may well have been suggesting about him (10:1)—when he comes to them.[182]

Paul's behavior surfaced as an abiding topic in 2 Corinthians 1–9, though most of those references functioned as certifications that he is, indeed, a person of high moral character who regularly seeks the advantage of those around him. Now in 2 Corinthians 10–13, however, the references to behavior, though about as frequent, function somewhat differently. Here, the comments about comportment demarcate between Paul and the outsiders, with the latter suggesting that they work on the same terms as Paul and with Paul taking umbrage at any such comparison (cf. 11:12-15).

10:3-6. Verse 3 is crucial for Paul's making certain that the Corinthians understand him. He distinguishes between his comporting himself "in the flesh"—that is, in the world—from the way he is now prepared to wage war: "not according to the flesh"—that is, not in a worldly fashion. Paul's opponents, whether inside the community or outside or both, should understand that "we comport ourselves [περιπατέω *peripateō*, figuratively "walk/behave"] in the flesh" (ἐν σαρκι *en sarki*; NIV, "in the world"; NRSV, "as human beings"; cf. 2 Cor 4:11). The life of faith has no other venue than fleshly, bodily life (cf. 1 Cor 5:10; 2 Cor 5:10). God has seen fit to fill these earthenware vessels with God's own glory (2 Cor 4:7); there is no life that is not in the body (2 Cor 5:6); believers experience life clothed in an earthly tent (2 Cor 5:1). Just so, Paul does walk—that is, comport himself—in the flesh. In that way he is indistinguishable from any other believer.

The function of 10:3*a,* however, is to set the stage for a stark contrast in 10:3*b:* "But we do not wage war according to human standards" (κατὰ σάρκα *kata sarka*; lit., "according to the flesh"), a technical phrase for Paul that often means something to the effect of "as people usually do." By employing paranomasia, a play on words hidden by the NIV and the NRSV, Paul contrasts his walking or behaving *en sarki,* "in the flesh," and therefore appearing just as every other believer, with his not making battle *kata sarka*—that is, like everybody else. A warning is implied, as suggested in this paraphrase: "Sure, we look just like everybody else who is a believer in that we carry out our responsibilities in the fleshliness of life; but do not be deceived, when we (are forced to) engage in battle, we are not like anyone else, but operate with the full panoply of God's power at our beck and call."

To buttress his forewarning, Paul draws upon a range of military images, all of which serve to position him as one of God's primary agents. Note that Paul has shifted to the plural as he places the Corinthians on notice with this militaristic self-depiction. The plural claims suggest once again that he is not alone; therefore, any opponents must reckon that they engage not just Paul but all those associated with him—and not only that, but the real warning is that they engage, through Paul, the full might of God.

Paul's powerful military imagery (to be examined in detail) sets the dominant tone for the rest of the letter fragment with a *leitmotiv* of weakness associated with Paul and the way the martial power gains expression through him. The militaristic terms are not confined to 10:3-6 because contention and dissension characterize the entire document. Paul's own mission and *modus operandi* are sometimes cast in military terms. The support Paul receives from other churches is described as "pay," "wages," "rations" (money) paid to a soldier (ὀψώνιον *opsōnion,* 11:8), his "robbing" churches uses a term that can describe plundering the spoils of battle (συλάω *sylaō*),[183] and when he describes the refurbishment he received from the Macedonians, he uses a term

---

182. Malherbe, ibid., 168-69, argues that the link between ταπεινός (*tapeinos*) in 10:1 and Paul's boldness/confidence is to be understood "in light of the Cynic descriptions of the philosopher's dress as the armament of the gods."

183. For more on Paul's employment of military imagery, see E. M. Krentz, "Military Language and Metaphors in Philippians," in *Origins and Method: Towards a New Understanding of Judaism and Christianity: Essays in Honour of J. C. Hurd,* ed. B. H. McLean, JSNTSup 86 (Sheffield: Sheffield Academic, 1993) 105-27.

common in military literature to describe the replenishing of supplies to troops at the battle front (προσαναπληρόω *prosanapleroō*, 11:9).[184] Worldly power, no matter how great, arrayed against Paul as God's agent avails nothing. Even the governor under as formidable a king as Aretas, when the former held the city of Damascus under guard in an effort to take Paul into custody, was thwarted by a through-the-wall, basket escape (11:32-33).

In 2 Cor 10:3-6, Paul describes himself as doing military service, as serving in an army (στρατεύω *strateuō*) whose "weaponry" (ὅπλα *hopla*) is not of a "fleshly, worldly" sort (σαρκικά *sarkika*, employing paranomasia by playing off of *kata sarka* from 10:2-3). Rather, his weapons are from God and are of such power as to destroy strongholds, fortresses (10:4). Analogizing from "destroying strongholds," Paul describes his own work as a most effective and thorough military action.

Every aspect of an awesomely efficient military siege is depicted, but now transferred over onto Paul's advocacy of the gospel; not by his own efforts, but by the "knowledge of God," (counter-) arguments are demolished, as is every "rampart offering resistance" (10:5).[185] Every mind is taken captive to obey Christ, and Paul promises to be ready to punish every disobedience whenever their obedience is complete (10:5-6). Paul's picture of military action is modeled from Roman peacekeeping and enforcing operations, which, with vastly superior power, sweep away obstacles, crush resistance, and establish complete compliance.[186] Tacitus, born about the time Paul wrote 2 Corinthians 10–13, captures the Roman sense of making peace that Paul here brandishes toward the Corinthians who might dare to stand against him: "Make a wilderness and call it peace."[187]

184. See Herodotus 5.36; 6.101, 118.
185. Malherbe, "Antisthenes and Odysseus, and Paul at War," 171-72, shows that Paul construes his opponents as "self-sufficient, self-confident," like some Stoics of the time who, as Seneca put it, "feel secure in their elevated citadel," not realizing that Paul has the connections and the power (with and from God) to overwhelm every obstacle.
186. See *As the Romans Did: A Sourcebook in Roman Social History*, ed. Jo-Ann Shelton, 2nd ed. (New York: Oxford, 1998) 243.
187. Tacitus *Agricola* 30.5.

Paul's primary message is this: By his association with divine power, he is not just another warrior for the gospel; on the contrary, he personifies the totality of God's force. Obedience to Christ entails association with Paul, and no disobedience will be left unchallenged. His secondary message is: Do not be misled that his being "in the flesh" along with everyone else means that he will battle as others normally do. This last point is yet another time when Paul warns against judging by externals, not internals (4:16), by face, not by heart (5:12).

Paul's self-portrait here is not unlike his wider picture of the life of faith as described in other letters. All believers live in the world, whose structures are under the power of sin; or as he puts it otherwise, they live in the old aeon even though the new creation has broken into the world in Christ's death and resurrection (1 Cor 7:31). Accordingly, believers live in the world as if they are having no dealings with it, as if their values do not come from it, and as if the norms of their behavior are not dictated by it (cf. 1 Cor 7:29-31). In the case at hand, Paul pictures believers as those whose thoughts are held captive (10:5). In other places, Paul has written about this radical shift as having been effected by a change of lordship, of slaves being bought and brought under the ownership of their new Lord Jesus Christ (1 Cor 6:20; 7:23).

Paul allies himself with all others who forcefully overcome barriers and obstacles to "the knowledge of God," probably a euphemism for the gospel—that is, for "knowledge about God" (2 Cor 10:5). This interpretation is reinforced by Paul's use of the same expression in another military metaphor earlier in his correspondence with these same Corinthians: Through Paul and his associates, God has spread the fragrance of the knowledge of God everywhere (2 Cor 2:14).

REFLECTIONS

1. Gentleness and clemency, when understood in the context of God's power and purposes, are not signs of weakness or wimpiness. We sometimes think that gentleness, compassion, kindheartedness, and a readiness to forgive are symptoms of weakness. In actuality it takes a strong person not to respond in kind to an affront or to a wrong. And it takes a strong person to forgive and to be kind when someone else is not.

2. If God is so powerful and strong that nothing can withstand or prevail against God, we might wonder what place there is for self-determination. We may reflect on two answers. First, if we oppose God and God's plan, then we can expect to be overwhelmed and overcome. God's purposes will be realized whether there is antagonism toward them or not. It is God's kingdom, God's reign, and God is bringing it whether we decide to go along with the plan or not. Second, if we do go along with God's plan, then self-determination comes into play in not only how we steward the resources and gifts God has given us but also in the way we work together with God (cf. 2 Cor 6:1).

3. Paul likes to describe God as the God of order and peace (Rom 15:33; 16:20; 1 Cor 14:33; 2 Cor 13:11; Phil 4:9); yet, in 2 Cor 10:4-6 we have a most martial picture of God and of God's awesome military power at work. How can the two fit together? Should not the God of peace be the one who repudiates such militaristic power? Paul seems to take his cues about peacekeeping from the Romans, who had sufficient military power simply to crush opposition. To maintain peace was to annihilate opposition—by utter and overwhelming force. Paul thinks of God's working the same way: "The God of peace shall soon shatter/smash/crush Satan under your feet" (Rom 16:20). Perhaps we have domesticated "peace" more than Paul has.

4. Show clemency toward others because you have received clemency—that is Paul's current casting of the rule we should adhere to with others as God or Christ has done for us (cf. Rom 15:7 for another form of it). This is a guideline that is represented in the Johannine literature as well: "I give you a new commandment, that you love one another. Just as I have loved you, you also should love one another" (John 13:34; 15:12 NRSV). At the heart of the gospel is the assumption that God's grace has not given us what our rebelliousness deserves, but has given us love instead.

5. Paul's point about walking "in the flesh" but not "according to the flesh" is a fine one. The first expression recognizes that human life is always fleshly, is inescapably part and parcel of life in the world. The second expression relates to taking our cues, our values from the world; this Paul soundly rejects. The Fourth Gospel has its own way of depicting this same phenomenon, with slightly different terminology: We are to be "in the world" but not "of the world" (see John 17:15-18).

2 CORINTHIANS 10:7-11, CONSIDER WHAT YOU KNOW

NIV	NRSV
[7]You are looking only on the surface of things.[a] If anyone is confident that he belongs to Christ, he should consider again that we belong to Christ just as much as he. [8]For even if I boast somewhat freely about the authority the Lord gave us for	7Look at what is before your eyes. If you are confident that you belong to Christ, remind yourself of this, that just as you belong to Christ, so also do we. [8]Now, even if I boast a little too much of our authority, which the Lord gave for building you up and not for tearing you down, I will not

a7 Or *Look at the obvious facts*

NIV

building you up rather than pulling you down, I will not be ashamed of it. ⁹I do not want to seem to be trying to frighten you with my letters. ¹⁰For some say, "His letters are weighty and forceful, but in person he is unimpressive and his speaking amounts to nothing." ¹¹Such people should realize that what we are in our letters when we are absent, we will be in our actions when we are present.

NRSV

be ashamed of it. ⁹I do not want to seem as though I am trying to frighten you with my letters. ¹⁰For they say, "His letters are weighty and strong, but his bodily presence is weak, and his speech contemptible." ¹¹Let such people understand that what we say by letter when absent, we will also do when present.

COMMENTARY

From what the Corinthians know and have seen about Paul, they should not be confused about him or about his purposes with them. Paul's opponents appear in this passage (φησίν *phēsin*, "they say," 10:10), and they have made three claims that surface here: They belong to Christ, perhaps in some special way or to some special degree; they have critiqued Paul's letters as "frightening" the Corinthians and as being βαρύς (*barys*, "weighty") and ἰσχυρός (*ischyros*, "strong"); and Paul's bodily presence is "weak" or "without influence" (ἀσθενής *asthenēs*), and his speech "amounts to nothing" (ἐξουθενέω *exoutheneō*).

Could anything possibly offend Paul more than someone's claiming to belong to Christ in any special way or degree? All believers belong to Christ; Christ is their new Lord. "Belonging to Christ" is so basic to Paul's view of faith that he can use it as a rebuke of the Corinthians' divisiveness (1 Cor 1:12). The genitive construction in question (Χριστοῦ εἶναι *Christou einai,* "to be of Christ") could be taken as a genitive of origin or relationship and, therefore, could have reflected their claim that they, more than Paul, are the ones who genuinely represent Christ. That, too, would be an affront to Paul, but it could play to one of his perpetual vulnerabilities: He did not associate with the historical Jesus, but depends on an appearance of the risen Lord for his call and, therefore, for his authority (1 Cor 9:1; 15:8). He was not one of the original disciples or apostles, but became an apostle only through his specific call (Rom 1:1; Gal 1:15-16).

Some criticisms bear on Paul's letters: They are frightening, weighty, and strong (10:9-10). We

know of no other Pauline community that has been treated to so many letters from him as the Corinthians, who by the time of 2 Corinthians 10–13 have received (at least) four earlier letters from Paul. Further, not all the letters have been pleasant. By Paul's own account, one of them was painful and written in tears (2 Cor 2:4); that letter was harsh frank speech. To characterize even a letter of harsh frankness as "frightening," however, possibly reflects Paul's opponents' purposeful misconstrual, because frank speech always supposes a context of friendship and caring.

The other two descriptions of his letters have a wider semantic range and require effort to discern how Paul takes them. The surest point of contact can be made with the contrast between Paul's letters' being weighty and strong compared to Paul's bodily presence ("weak") and his speech ("of no account"). The letters, though they may sometimes frighten, fare relatively well when compared with Paul in person, but only because the personal estimate is so devastatingly negative; note that the backhanded compliment, or at least recognition, that his letters are formidable is eclipsed by the utter weightlessness of the implied personal estimate of Paul. Accordingly, *barys*, whose semantic range is from "heavy/weighty/important" to "burdensome/difficult to fulfill/severe," could by the first three possible translations suggest that Paul's letters are viewed as substantial and significant, claims that have an obvious appropriateness. The last three plausible translations, however, leave room for the opponents to complain that Paul either raises the bar too high or has employed reprimand too often.

The other term applied to Paul's letters, *ischyros* ("strong/mighty/powerful/weighty/effective"), indicates, in contrast to his performance in person, that his letters have substance and command attention. Such a depiction of his letters, especially if one takes the "heavy, weighty, important" range of *barys* in view, would fit 2 Corinthians 1–9 very well. No Pauline letter, with the possible exception of Romans, has more heavyweight theological assertions and constructions per square chapter than 2 Corinthians 1–9. Part of Paul's rhetorical strategy in these chapters surely was to show himself magisterial by his capacity to depict himself and his ministry in compellingly rich conceptions. Paul does write strong letters, as his opponents charged and as the letters themselves have shown by their survival and impact on history until the present time. The point, however, by the opponents, lies in the contrast between the Paul on the page and the Paul encountered in person.

The charge of a fundamental discrepancy between Paul's impressive letters and his unimpressive presence draws a sharp warning from Paul, saying, in effect, "When I am with you next you will see the same sort of power you credit to my letters" (10:11). Earlier in the passage, Paul makes a concession that perhaps he does boast too much—a signal of what is to come. But he defiantly declares, "I shall not be shamed" (10:8). He will not leave his opponents unanswered, as the remainder of the letter fragment amply demonstrates.

The dissonance between his strong, effective letters and his personal and rhetorical performance has, in its incarnation in Corinth at least, raised questions of his status and, therefore, of his authority. In the culture of that time, honor, and with it authority, was granted when a person's performance and standing reinforced each other. To be considered "weak" was a matter of shame. Paul's opponents have found in him a discordance, a lack of continuity between his comportment, his status, and his powerful letters. Also, Paul's insistence on his own self-support at Corinth can be construed as further evidence of his lack of status, allowing opponents to argue that his authority is clearly overblown.

Paul's double-edged answer: He has a special authority (ἐξουσία *exousia*), granted to him by his Lord, for edification (οἰκοδομη *oikodomē*) of the Corinthians, not for destruction (καθαίρεσις *kathairesis*) of them (10:8). Significantly, the term translated "destruction" (*kathairesis*) is the same root of Paul's claim earlier that he destroys strongholds and arguments (10:4-5); so the Corinthians, and their outsiders, should realize that Paul genuinely brandishes such authority toward them. Edification is at the heart of community care for Paul. It is the fruit of love (1 Cor 8:1); it is every action that encourages growth and improvement in others; nowhere is it the sharing of what might be called devout thoughts. All things among believers should be done in love—that is, for edification (1 Cor 14:26; 16:14). Overall, Paul's care for his communities is probably aptly understood as encapsulated in edification. So Paul's claim that he has the authority to build up and not to destroy covers the full possible range of his exercise of his divinely given power. Finally, the declaration that the Lord has given Paul the authority to edify and not to destroy reappears verbatim as the conclusion of the body of this letter (2 Cor 13:10), thus forming an inclusio, or ring formation, that frames not only the full range of Paul's authority with the Corinthians but also all that Paul writes them in this letter.[188] Paul's stated purpose in his letters is surely not to frighten his recipients (10:9), and not simply to bring them back into solidarity with him, but to edify. Destruction is brandished as a cudgel that he certainly must hope not to use.

188. W. L. Lane, "The Key to Paul's Conflict with Corinth, *TynBul* 33 (1982) 9-10, argued that Paul's authority expressed in "building up" and "tearing down" is prophetic imagery based on passages like Jer 1:10.

REFLECTIONS

1. "Love builds up" (1 Cor 8:1); that is its nature. As Paul's relations with the Corinthians show, however, not everything that one thinks is done in love is perceived by the recipients as such. People can and do harm and destroy one another, and that not always with big or obvious actions. Sometimes people are destroyed bit by bit. Love requires that we oppose harm and destruction in its every instance. Love also requires that we be thoughtfully sensitive when what we intend as a loving action is not perceived as such.

2. Believers belong to Christ (10:7). Nothing is more basic to understand. And all believers belong equally. There is no ranking among believers when it comes to our relation to Christ. Some people create a hierarchy among believers regarding who has some special spiritual gift, such as glossolalia, speaking in tongues; those who have that gift are understood to have arrived at the apex of relations to God; the ones who do not (yet) speak in tongues are thought to be on a lesser plateau. Paul does not share such a distinction. All believers are equally "in Christ," and any gifts they have are granted by the Spirit as the Spirit has chosen for the common good (see the Commentary on 1 Cor 12:4-11).

2 CORINTHIANS 10:12-18, BOASTING WITHIN LIMIT

NIV

12We do not dare to classify or compare ourselves with some who commend themselves. When they measure themselves by themselves and compare themselves with themselves, they are not wise. [13]We, however, will not boast beyond proper limits, but will confine our boasting to the field God has assigned to us, a field that reaches even to you. [14]We are not going too far in our boasting, as would be the case if we had not come to you, for we did get as far as you with the gospel of Christ. [15]Neither do we go beyond our limits by boasting of work done by others.[a] Our hope is that, as your faith continues to grow, our area of activity among you will greatly expand, [16]so that we can preach the gospel in the regions beyond you. For we do not want to boast about work already done in another man's territory. [17]But, "Let him who boasts boast in the Lord."[b] [18]For it is not the one who commends himself who is approved, but the one whom the Lord commends.

a13-15 Or 13We, however, will not boast about things that cannot be measured, but we will boast according to the standard of measurement that the God of measure has assigned us—a measurement that relates even to you.14. . . . 15Neither do we boast about things that cannot be measured in regard to the work done by others.   b17 Jer. 9:24

NRSV

12We do not dare to classify or compare ourselves with some of those who commend themselves. But when they measure themselves by one another, and compare themselves with one another, they do not show good sense. [13]We, however, will not boast beyond limits, but will keep within the field that God has assigned to us, to reach out even as far as you. [14]For we were not overstepping our limits when we reached you; we were the first to come all the way to you with the good news[a] of Christ. [15]We do not boast beyond limits, that is, in the labors of others; but our hope is that, as your faith increases, our sphere of action among you may be greatly enlarged, [16]so that we may proclaim the good news[a] in lands beyond you, without boasting of work already done in someone else's sphere of action. [17]"Let the one who boasts, boast in the Lord." [18]For it is not those who commend themselves that are approved, but those whom the Lord commends.

a Or the gospel

COMMENTARY

The paragraph opens with comments about comparison (*syncresis*), the rhetorical trope of distinguishing oneself by association and correlation with others. In the vertically arranged Greco-Roman world, *syncresis* sometimes likens oneself to another and at other times uses the comparison to claim advantage over the analogous person. In the paragraphs that follow, Paul uses it both ways, and we will be able to observe that his opponents have employed the same rhetorical device—to Paul's displeasure. The same trope surfaces, not always favorably, as an issue several times in this letter fragment. In 10:12, Paul simply states that he presumes neither to "class" (ἐγκρῖναι *egkrinai*) nor to "compare" (συγκρῖναι *sygkrinai*) himself with others. In fact, he takes it a step further: Those who compare themselves with others show themselves "without understanding" (οὐ συνίημι *ou syniēmi*, 10:12). Paul's is a statement made by a person who gains nothing for himself by association.

Paul views *syncresis* in two very different ways. A positive use of *syncresis* was noted in the discussion of the previous letter fragment where Paul, tapping the culturally driven Corinthian inclination to excel, urges them to participate in the collection (2 Cor 8:7) by modeling themselves after the Macedonians. Likewise, he had previously employed *syncresis* when he had portrayed to the Macedonians the Corinthian enthusiasm for the collection (2 Cor 9:2). Paul readily embraces such instances of *syncresis* because they serve to encourage or spur on others. Paul takes a negative view of it, however, when the comparison is used to denigrate someone or when the comparison is self-serving. It is the latter that we find in 2 Cor 10:12-13.

Parts of this letter fragment reveal that the outsiders readily classed themselves with Paul and made comparisons with him that were favorable to themselves (11:12-15; 12:11). Paul's disparagement of comparison when it is used to gain advantage is not, however, just a strategy employed to aid him in combating his opponents; it is a deep-seated conviction that gains expression at other points in his letters. In his treatment of "spiritual gifts" (χαρίσματα *charismata*) in 1

Corinthians 12, Paul argued that, for the common good, believers should make the most of whatever gift or gifts the Spirit had given, that they should not look covetously at the gifts of others, and that each should realize that the well-being of the body is secured by each member's being different from the others (1 Cor 12:4-11, 14-26).

Any talk of comparison quickly leads Paul to its usual result: boasting, a topic he had already introduced in 10:8. Boast or not, Paul's relation to the Corinthians is special. In a wordplay on limits, divine apportionments, and spheres of influence, Paul reminds the Corinthians of his unique relation to them. His boast is constrained to the measure (μέτρον *metron*) of the sphere of influence (κανών *kanōn*) that God measured out (μερίζω *merizō*) to him: "to reach all the way to you" (10:13).[189] Paul seeks to garner goodwill by reminding the Corinthians that he is their apostle, their father in the faith; he brought the gospel to them. Paul has not been hesitant to remind them of his paternity (1 Cor 4:14-15; 9:1-2; 2 Cor 1:19, 21; 3:3).

God set the borders. God sent Paul. Paul went. Twice in as many verses Paul declares that he was first to go all the way (ἄχρι *achri*, 10:13 14) to the Corinthians, a clear bid for goodwill, especially as it asks the hearers to reach back to their memories of times when things between themselves and Paul were positive. It also claims Paul's priority over any subsequent intruders.[190] Still remembering the good times, Paul declares that in his coming to them, *he* did not extend beyond the boundaries God had set out for him, as some now have done by coming into his own, God-apportioned field (10:14).

Paul's notion of the proper boast versus the improper boast is important for understanding his

---

189. J. F. Strange, "2 Corinthians 10:13-16: Illuminated By a Recently Published Inscription," *BA* 46 (1983) 168, shows that Paul writes in terms known in the second decade CE when an authority (here God) allocates a κανών (*kanōn*), an apportioned area (here including Corinth). In the light of this interpretation, Paul understands that God has allocated the Roman province of Achaia (among others) to him and that outsiders have no right to enter into what becomes a sort of competition. Paul's self-protrait, then, is that he has exercised proper responsiveness to God's allocation, because he has brought the gospel to Corinth and its environs—and Paul suggests that the Corinthians should recognize this.

190. A. J. Dewey, "A Matter of Honor: A Social-Historical Analysis of 2 Corinthians 10," *HTR* 78 (1985) 215, says the opponents are thus open to the charge of poaching.

claims.[191] Boasting per se is not necessarily bad. Boasting about one another in Christ is absolutely appropriate (2 Cor 1:14; 7:14) because in so doing one does not brag about one's own efforts, but about the efficacy and power of God's grace at work; therefore, ultimately believers' boasting in one another is a way of giving praise and glory to God. Boasting is also viewed positively by Paul when it points to his work in the gospel, and for the same reason—namely, that it is shorthand for boasting about God's work through Paul in the gospel (Rom 15:17-18; 1 Cor 1:31; 2 Cor 1:12). Thus for Paul it is absolutely appropriate for him to boast about the Corinthians: They are the result of God's work in his labors (10:15).

In a play on the notion of limits, Paul declares that he does not "boast beyond limits in the labors of others" as do some—namely, the intruders who have gained some standing among *his* Corinthian followers (10:15). As one can readily see from Romans, Paul is very aware of the borders of his *kanōn*, his "sphere of influence" or his "field." He can boast of his work for God among the Gentiles "from Jerusalem and as far around as Illyricum" (Rom 15:17-20 NRSV), and he can project a mission to Spain (Rom 15:28). But he is very clear that he only hopes for a stopover in Rome and for their support for his mission because he proudly has a policy of not building on another's foundation, but preaching where Christ has not already been named (Rom 15:20; cf. Gal 2:9). Accordingly, he has trouble understanding how others can invade a territory and a people given by God to him for his care.

As if to demonstrate his appropriate caring, Paul expresses his hope for the Corinthians: that their faith may increase, allowing him and his coworkers an increased sphere of influence (*kanōn* again, from 10:13) among them (10:15). In a refinement, Paul has moved from outsiders poaching onto his God-appointed field (*kanōn*, 10:13-14) to his hope for an enlargement of his *kanōn* ("sphere of influence") among the Corinthians. That is an echo of what he wrote to them earlier: They are the ones who have restricted him and constricted themselves in their responsiveness to him (2 Cor

6:12). He implored them then and he appeals to them now to let him once again have fuller sway among them.

In what follows there is the slightest hint that their dalliance with these outsiders is responsible for distracting Paul from what they surely know to be his divinely prompted call to preach the gospel "in other places beyond you" (10:16). With a final mention of *kanōn*, "apportioned territory," Paul indirectly ridicules the intruders by renouncing once more for himself any boasting in "work already done in someone else's sphere of action" (*kanōn*, 10:16; cf. Rom 15:20). So Paul presents himself as the model of boasting and indirectly invites an unfavorable comparison of the Corinthian intruders with himself.

Grounding his reflections in the Jeremiah quote—"The one who boasts, let him boast in the Lord," that he used once before in 1 Cor 1:31—Paul returns to the theme that opened this paragraph: those who commend themselves (10:12, 18). In a cleverly crafted, maxim-like declaration laid down as if beyond dispute, Paul affirms that it is the Lord who commends and, therefore, who determines who is δόκιμος (*dokimos*, "tried and true, "one who has met the test," "approved," NRSV and NIV, 10:18; 1 Cor 11:19; 2 Cor 13:7; cf. ἀδόκιμος [*adokimos*] in 1 Cor 9:27; 2 Cor 13:5-7). At the center of the sentence lies the emphatic declaration "that person is tried and true." On the front is a denial ("Not the one . . ."), and on the end is the claim that functions emphatically as a *correctio* (form: not A but B) with regard to the first, so that the sentence reads, literally: "For not the one commending himself, that one is tried and true, but the one whom the Lord commends" (10:18). Commending oneself, the opening portrait of Paul's opponents in 10:12, is explicitly rejected in 10:18. In its place is the Lord's commendation, which appropriately comes to those who, like Paul, prove themselves through thick and thin as "tried and true" (*dokimos*). The notion of being *dokimos* will return as another inclusio in the peroration that concludes the letter fragment (13:3-10).

Almost hidden in this passage is a genuine Pauline gem: He hopes that their faith will increase (10:15). Nothing more is made of it here, and it does not need explanation because Paul's followers would have recognized that such a hope

191. See the treatment of boasting as self-commendation in J. Lambrecht, "Dangerous Boasting: Paul's Self-Commendation in 2 Cor 10–13," in *The Corinthian Correspondence*, ed. R. Bieringer (Leuven: University of Leuven Press, 1966) 339-46.

is fundamental to his view of the life of faith (see the Introduction). Believers start as babies in the faith (cf. 1 Cor 4:15; Gal 4:19; Phlm 10). Earlier, Paul had charged these very Corinthians with being babies too long in regard to faith (1 Cor 3:1). At the other extreme of the life of faith, believers can be mature, can be grown-ups; Paul himself models that growth (Phil 3:12, 15; cf. Abraham, the exemplary faithful person, in Rom 4:19-20). Paul advises the Romans that they have faith measured out to them (by God's grace, understood) and that they should think of themselves appropriately with regard to their measure of faith (Rom 12:3). Finally in this regard, Paul pledges to be with the Philippians for their "progress and joy in the faith" (1:25). So when Paul writes 2 Cor 10:15 he is still hoping that his Corinthian followers will experience growth in faith. Just as their earlier fractiousness among themselves convinced him that they were retarded in their growth in faith (1 Cor 3:1-3), so also now he finds that their being attracted to outsiders who have intruded into the believing community at Corinth is a sign of the still-present need for growth in faith (2 Cor 10:15).

Growth in faith is progress *in* the faith. It is not a matter of believing more today than one did last year; it is not believing something more ardently or fervently. For the Corinthians, immediately, it is being increasingly inured to the attractions and traps that the culture offers, such as status and the worldly signs of prestige; it is distinguishing self-serving apostles from other-serving ones. In the broader picture, progress in the faith means that one's self-estimate of the measure of faith is more accurate (Rom 12:3-8); that one can carry more of another's burden more fully or readily (Gal 6:2-5); that one can aim for and hope to do the higher good (1 Corinthians 7); that one can understand more fully the ramifications of believing that there is only one God and act accordingly (1 Corinthians 8); that, as one's faith grows, one can realize an ever-increasing range of freedom within which one may act faithfully before God (Rom 14:13-23); and that one can freely forgo the exercise of that freedom if doing so might harm another for whom Christ died (1 Cor 10:23–11:1).

REFLECTIONS

1. Self-promotion has become a feature of our culture, and many are attracted to it. But some are repulsed by it, and many Christians think any positive statement about oneself is excessive, dangerous, and wrong, and they cringe at the thought of saying anything positive about their "measure of faith." Perhaps a way to start thinking about the issue is to make a distinction between bragging—where the attention focuses on us—and giving thanks to God—where the recognition rests with God. What are the hazards and limits of self-promotion? Nothing is socially more painful than listening to someone who does nothing but talk about himself.

2. Perhaps we could recover boasting about God's work in our private and collective lives. If we fail to bring to the level of consciousness the ways and places God is working, we risk becoming less observant. Think how much joy we might miss, personally and collectively. The Spirit sometimes nudges or prompts us ever so slightly regarding something. If we fall out of the pattern of openly taking note of such noodlings, then those quiet movements of the Spirit may be unnoticed and that instance of God's grace lies fallow.

3. Where do you find your own value? Paul pictures that some people try to "sell" themselves to others; they push themselves and try to inflate their own personal stock. Paul and most of the world in his time (and in ours, too) think that is a dead end. Although he does not develop it, Paul differentiates those whom the Lord commends and says that they are the ones who are really "tried and true" or "approved" (10:18).

4. Comparing ourselves with others; measuring ourselves by others—it may be possible to imagine some good coming out of doing this, but it is so much more likely to be detrimental to everyone and derogatory to some. You can always find someone who is better at something or who is worse at it, but what have you truly learned about yourself in the process? If you make a series of comparisons with persons who are much better at something than you, you may begin to feel quite inadequate. If the comparisons are with persons who are much worse at something than you, then your chances of self-deception are dangerously high. Paul, building on a strong Corinthian tendency to compete among themselves, encourages the Corinthians to turn that energy toward a positive end: Outdo one another in edifying one another (1 Cor 14:12). A sweet irony attends the notion of people's trying to outdo one another in loving each other (cf. "love builds up," 1 Cor 8:1).

5. Paul believes that faith increases (10:15). What does that mean, and how does it happen? It means that one's relation to God grows, that you do not have the same "measure of faith" (Rom 12:3) today that you had when you first came to faith. Just as our love for another surely can grow, so also our trust in God can grow. An analogy with physical fitness is not awry. If you do not use your muscles, they will atrophy. If your faith is not employed on a regular basis in the decisions you make and in your choices, then it is likely to diminish rather than grow. Faith's increase is only possible through its regular employment in more and more of the decisions of life. Particularly on matters where you wonder which of two choices you should make, ask yourself what course of action would most fully express your relation to God.

6. The boasting we hear in some circles today goes like this: "I just did it for Jesus" or "The glory goes to God (or Jesus)." Such a boast may be genuine and heartfelt. Only the speaker knows that. But this practice can become a religiously sanctioned way of calling positive attention to oneself and, therefore, to one's virtue—and insofar as it does, it has its own dangers. Compare Jesus' critique of public shows of piety and righteousness (Matthew 6).

2 CORINTHIANS 11:1-15, BETROTHAL AND BETRAYAL: PAUL AND THE OPPONENTS

NIV

11 I hope you will put up with a little of my foolishness; but you are already doing that. ²I am jealous for you with a godly jealousy. I promised you to one husband, to Christ, so that I might present you as a pure virgin to him. ³But I am afraid that just as Eve was deceived by the serpent's cunning, your minds may somehow be led astray from your sincere and pure devotion to Christ. ⁴For if someone comes to you and preaches a Jesus other than the Jesus we preached, or if you receive a different spirit from the one you received, or a different gospel from the one you accepted, you put up with it easily enough. ⁵But I do not think I am in the least

NRSV

11 I wish you would bear with me in a little foolishness. Do bear with me! ²I feel a divine jealousy for you, for I promised you in marriage to one husband, to present you as a chaste virgin to Christ. ³But I am afraid that as the serpent deceived Eve by its cunning, your thoughts will be led astray from a sincere and pure*a* devotion to Christ. ⁴For if someone comes and proclaims another Jesus than the one we proclaimed, or if you receive a different spirit from the one you received, or a different gospel from the one you accepted, you submit to it readily enough. ⁵I think that I am not in the least inferior

a Other ancient authorities lack *and pure*

NIV

inferior to those "super-apostles." ⁶I may not be a trained speaker, but I do have knowledge. We have made this perfectly clear to you in every way.

⁷Was it a sin for me to lower myself in order to elevate you by preaching the gospel of God to you free of charge? ⁸I robbed other churches by receiving support from them so as to serve you. ⁹And when I was with you and needed something, I was not a burden to anyone, for the brothers who came from Macedonia supplied what I needed. I have kept myself from being a burden to you in any way, and will continue to do so. ¹⁰As surely as the truth of Christ is in me, nobody in the regions of Achaia will stop this boasting of mine. ¹¹Why? Because I do not love you? God knows I do! ¹²And I will keep on doing what I am doing in order to cut the ground from under those who want an opportunity to be considered equal with us in the things they boast about.

¹³For such men are false apostles, deceitful workmen, masquerading as apostles of Christ. ¹⁴And no wonder, for Satan himself masquerades as an angel of light. ¹⁵It is not surprising, then, if his servants masquerade as servants of righteousness. Their end will be what their actions deserve.

NRSV

to these super-apostles. ⁶I may be untrained in speech, but not in knowledge; certainly in every way and in all things we have made this evident to you.

7Did I commit a sin by humbling myself so that you might be exalted, because I proclaimed God's good news*a* to you free of charge? ⁸I robbed other churches by accepting support from them in order to serve you. ⁹And when I was with you and was in need, I did not burden anyone, for my needs were supplied by the friends*b* who came from Macedonia. So I refrained and will continue to refrain from burdening you in any way. ¹⁰As the truth of Christ is in me, this boast of mine will not be silenced in the regions of Achaia. ¹¹And why? Because I do not love you? God knows I do!

12And what I do I will also continue to do, in order to deny an opportunity to those who want an opportunity to be recognized as our equals in what they boast about. ¹³For such boasters are false apostles, deceitful workers, disguising themselves as apostles of Christ. ¹⁴And no wonder! Even Satan disguises himself as an angel of light. ¹⁵So it is not strange if his ministers also disguise themselves as ministers of righteousness. Their end will match their deeds.

a Gk the gospel of God   *b* Gk brothers

COMMENTARY

11:1-3. Twice in 11:1 Paul bids the Corinthians to put up with a little foolishness from him. With that he retells their foundational story from the perspective of the Jewish father of the betrothed, whose responsibility it is to see that his daughter is kept pure for the occasion of her marriage. His description, though laconic, is rich in its historical and literary reverberations and in its imagery. Paul enhances the reach into the past by going all the way to the story of the first couple and expresses his fear that, just as the serpent deceived Eve (Gen 3:1-7, 13; cf. 1 Tim 2:14) by its "readiness to do anything/cunning/craftiness/trickery" (πανουργία *panourgia*, 11:3; a mode of operation Paul has already renounced for himself,

2 Cor 4:2), so the Corinthians' thoughts—instead of being led captive to Christ (2 Cor 10:5) as they should be—will be led astray from a sincere and pure devotion to Christ.

Christ as bridegroom and the church as bride is a widespread image among the early believers (cf. Eph 5:23-27; Rev 19:7-9; 21:2, 9), as is the association of Jesus with an eschatological marriage feast (cf. Matt 9:15; 25:1-13). The image draws on a daring ancient Israelite portrait of God and Israel as lovers (Isa 49:18; 61:10; 62:5; Song of Songs), which almost always has as a part of the story that the beloved betrays the loved one and turns to adultery and harlotry, a note Paul echoes here (2 Cor 11:3; cf. Jeremiah 2–3; Ezek 16:1-22; Hosea 2).

As depicted by Paul, the marriage has not been consummated. Corinth remains the betrothed virgin daughter whose purity and devotion to Christ, her one husband, Paul fears, are in crisis. Paul, singularly responsible to deliver the daughter unblemished to her husband, worries that the Corinthians are in danger of being deceived. In order to fulfill his responsibilities, Paul must present (παρίστημι *paristēmi*) the Corinthians as a pure bride to Christ (11:2). *Paristēmi* is an eschatological technical term for Paul, describing the appearance, the presentation of the person or persons before God or Christ as judge; the term may also have overtones of a sacrifice presented in thanksgiving to God (cf. Rom 6:13; 12:1; 2 Cor 4:14). The notion of judgment was part of Paul's argument in a former letter (2 Cor 5:10) and is not alien to the bridal context.

11:4. Paul chides the Corinthians about how readily they, like ancient Israel, turn from their appointed lover, Christ. The claims about someone preaching "another Jesus" or the Corinthians receiving a spirit (or Spirit) different from the one they received or receiving another gospel have generated nearly endless commentary and debate about which of the three terms gets the major stress.[192] Some scholars think Paul's rhetoric here provides snapshots of what is going on in Corinth by which we can detail the profile of the controversy.[193] But this is highly unlikely because nowhere else in the letter is there any clue about a different picture of Jesus—in other words, a christological controversy—being disputed (cf. 2 Cor 4:5),[194] and nowhere is there any evidence that

claims about the spirit (or Spirit) are in contention (cf. the other instances of πνεῦμα [*pneuma*] in the letter fragment, 12:18; 13:13). Neither is there any clue in the simple mention of "Jesus," without any other name or title, because elsewhere in the corpus Paul shows himself comfortable in reducing any longer formation to the single name Jesus (Rom 3:26; 2 Cor 4:10-11, 14; Gal 6:17; Phil 2:10; 1 Thess 1:10; 4:14).[195]

A "different gospel" in the most general way is, of course, at issue. Paul knows there is no other gospel than his, but he sometimes mentions, as here (11:4), a reputed gospel (cf. Gal 1:6-9). That gospel is sometimes designated as Paul's (Rom 2:16; 16:25; 2 Cor 4:3). No one else in the early churches has such a complete identification of himself and the gospel he preaches. An attack on Paul's gospel can be construed by Paul as an attack on him; conversely, an attack on Paul is sometimes taken by him as an attack on his gospel. Similarly, a critique of his gospel can lead Paul to respond in defense of himself, and an attack on him can be challenged by a defense of his gospel. We may surmise at least one reason for Paul's close identification of himself and his gospel. For him, gospel is not fundamentally or even primarily about ideas; if it were, preaching (and teaching the gospel) would become a sort of dispensing of properly vetted ideas and claims. Rather, for Paul the gospel is God's power working to save (Rom 1:16) and is never disincarnated from a life lived. Put in different terms, the gospel is a way of living and being in the world and before God. Paul thought it incumbent on him, as the father of all the faithful who follow him, to model the life of faith for and with them. Gospel and life are always intricately interlaced for Paul. Thus an attack on his gospel is equivalent to an attack on his life, and vice versa.

"Another Jesus" is most likely Paul's own construction. He is given to such patterns of thought. In 1 Cor 8:5-6 he has already pondered other "gods" and "lords" (cf. 2 Thess 2:4); in other letters we find "another gospel" (Gal 1:7-9) and "have another view [than mine]" (Gal 5:10).

Most likely, these sweeping mentions of another Jesus, another S(s)pirit, and another gospel are prime examples of indirect speech in which

---

192. G. D. Fee, " 'Another Gospel Which You Did Not Embrace': 2 Corinthians 11.4 and the Theology of 1 and 2 Corinthians," in *Gospel in Paul,* ed. L. A. Jervis and P. Richardson (Sheffield: Sheffield Academic, 1994) 117-22, evaluates the traditional options.

193. J. Murphy-O'Connor, "Another Jesus (2 Cor 11:4)," *RB* 97 (1990) 248-51, following Windisch and Georgi in making no differentiation between the opponents' identity and role in 2 Corinthians 1–9 and chaps. 10–13, asserts that "the issue that continues to divide them [Paul and his opponents] is 'Jesus.' " C. K. Barrett, "Paul's Opponents in II Corinthians," *NTS* 17 (1971) 242, declares that "the intruders proclaim another Jesus . . . by the kind of behaviour described in II Cor. xi. 20," but Paul does not express it if he thinks so.

194. M. E. Thrall, *The Second Epistle to the Corinthians* (Edinburgh: T. & T. Clark, 1994) 296-97, denies that 3:1–4:6 has within it any christological controversy. As his title suggests (Fee, " 'Another Gospel Which You Did Not Embrace,' " 119), Fee sees "another gospel"—not another Jesus or another Spirit—as the key issue. T. B. Savage, *Power Through Weakness: Paul's Understanding of the Christian Ministry in 2 Corinthians* (New York: Cambridge University Press, 1996) 155-58, has a powerful reflection regarding "another Jesus," claiming, in effect, that Paul's opponents have substituted for Paul's Jesus as Lord (2 Cor 4:5) a portrait that has no shame and weakness in it.

195. Barrett, "Paul's Opponents in II Corinthians," 241.

the actual issues are supplanted by obviously different ones that none of the readers would be able to attach in a one-for-one relation to the real problems.[196] Paul has chosen to mention items known by everyone to be at the heart of his preaching—Jesus, Spirit, and gospel—and thereby given his hearers the perfect opportunity to think back to the origin of their faith—namely, to Paul's proclamation. Thus Paul has once again implicitly invited them to identify and affirm their alignment with Paul, with the *Jesus* he preached *to them* when he first brought the gospel to them, with the *Spirit* that came *to them* when his preaching was first effective, and with his *gospel* to which *they,* from their origins in the faith, have subscribed.

Note the context in which Paul presents these supposed alternative Jesuses, Spirits, and gospels: They are in a foundational narrative about his having preached the gospel to them as the point of origin of their faith. So in accord with his basic, foundational preaching, he mentions the Jesus that he preached among them at the beginning, the Spirit, which is, in Paul's letters, the hallmark of the origin of faith, and the gospel, which is his collective way of referring to all that he has proclaimed among them from the very first. This rhetoric is designed to elicit from his auditors an "of course" kind of response in which they affirm that there can be no other Jesus, Spirit, or gospel than that which came with Paul's original betrothal of them to Christ.

He opened this paragraph by asking them to "bear with" (ἀνέχω *anechō*) a little foolishness from him; in 11:4 he comes full round to say that they "bear with" (*anechō*) it readily enough when others represent a gospel different from his. Paul's criticism is not on the ones who preach (cf. Phil 1:15-18), but on the Corinthians' readiness to "bear with" anything and, by implication, without discernment.

11:5. Paul turns his attention to these "others." Paul probably coins the expression "super apostles" (ὑπερλίαν ἀπόστολοι *hyperlian apostoloi*) for them. The appellation "super apostles" is Paul's own sarcastic way of indirectly acknowl-

edging their claims to be superior to him (in whatever way). The hearers know who these people are, but we are left to surmise. Paul uses the term ἀπόστολος (*apostolos*) in a variety of ways. *He* is one, as he designated himself in 1 Cor 1:1 and 2 Cor 1:1, called by God and given a ministry to the Gentiles (Rom 15:15-16). He received his call through a revelation of Jesus Christ (1 Cor 15:8-11; Gal 1:11-12, 15-16). Paul does, however, use the same term, tapping into its basic sense, to describe a person who is sent on a mission (2 Cor 8:23; Phil 2:25) and who is in no way to be confused with what some gospel writers call "the twelve." Accordingly, we simply lack sufficient evidence to tell if these persons whom Paul dubs "super apostles" are from among the original disciples of Jesus or if, as may be more likely, they are persons who, like Paul, were not members of that group.[197]

Paul has always been vulnerable to the charge that he did not associate with Jesus as an original follower. Surely this complaint is part of his predicament with the Galatians, where we see his testiness in his description of the other apostles as "supposed to be acknowledged leaders (what they actually were makes no difference to me; God shows no partiality)" (Gal 2:6 NRSV). Also, when he reminds the Corinthians of the gospel he preached, Paul recounts his creedal form of the core narrative, and onto it he weaves his own story in a classic, but telling, understatement:

Last of all, as to one born in a miscarriage, he appeared even to me. For I myself am the least of the apostles and not worthy to be called apostle because I persecuted the church of God. But by the grace of God, I am what I am, and God's grace to me was not in vain; to the contrary, I worked more than any of them—not I but the grace of God in me. (1 Cor 15:8-10 NRSV)

Paul is zealous for, one might even say jealous of, the churches that have emerged because of his preaching. He thinks of them as his responsibility and often strikes an athletic note of hoping not to have run in vain as he tries to ready these communities for the parousia, the impending end

---

196. For the way indirect, figured speech worked, see J. Paul Sampley, "The Weak and the Strong: Paul's Careful and Crafty Rhetorical Strategy in Romans 14:1–15:13," in *The Social World of the First Christians: Studies in Honor of Wayne A. Meeks,* ed. L. M. White and O. L. Yarbrough (Minneapolis: Fortress, 1994) 43-46.

197. Following Barrett and Käsemann, R. P. Martin, noting 11:5 and 12:11, conjures up two distinct groups and takes the first to be the Jerusalem authorities and the second to be emissaries of the former. See R. P. Martin, "The Opponents of Paul in 2 Corinthians: An Old Issue Revisited," in *Tradition and Interpretation in the New Testament: Essays in Honor of E. E. Ellis,* ed. G. F. Hawthorne and O. Betz (Grand Rapids: Eerdmans, 1987) 285.

of the aeon (1 Cor 15:58; Gal 2:2; Phil 2:16; 1 Thess 3:5). In the same spirit, but in rather direct and considered speech (λογίζομαι *logizomai*, "I reckon"), Paul insists to his Corinthian readers that he is not the least bit inferior to "these super apostles" (2 Cor 11:5).

11:6. Contemporary rhetorical training counseled would-be orators to say something like, "Unaccustomed as I am to public speaking . . ." as a means of rousing some pity, and therefore goodwill, from their hearers.[198] Accordingly Paul concedes that he is not skilled in oratory, that he is an "amateur in speech" but certainly not in knowledge, as should be clear to them "in everything and in all ways" (11:6). In keeping with contemporaneous rhetorical strategies of defense, Paul not only seeks pity, but he also is ready to concede that a possible charge leveled against him is *partially* true:[199] He may not be the best orator. But the concession sets the context for a strong denial on a related front: He is not an "amateur" or "untrained" (ἰδιώτης *idiōtēs*) when it comes to what he knows—and that should be abundantly clear (cf. "Look at what is before your eyes," 2 Cor 10:7).

11:7. Paul is stung by criticism of his consistent practice of supporting himself while he is with the Corinthians. The matter has taken on increased proportions in Paul's history with the Corinthians. At first, his care not to be a burden to the Corinthians must have been commendatory, especially in the light of the widespread pattern of wandering sages who made a living from fleecing those with whom they shared their wisdom.[200] Now, however, the matter has reached new and unpleasant proportions because Paul treats it or adverts to it a total of three times in this letter fragment (2 Cor 11:7-11, 20; 12:13-17).

In the first treatment, he ratchets up his rhetoric to hyperbolic levels as he responds, in the isolation of the first person, to Corinthian criticism with highly loaded speech, which may even echo his portrait of Christ in 2 Cor 8:9. Paul humbled himself so that they might be exalted, he preached the gospel to them "at no cost" (δωρεάν *dōrean*), and in the heaviest of Pauline theological categories, he asks sardonically whether it was a "sin" (ἁμαρτία *hamartia*) to do so.

11:8-11. Next he reflects what must have been a charge against him: The support he received from the Macedonian believers was tantamount to robbery of those churches (11:8-9). Paul does not even attempt to refute that accusation directly, but turns it to a question of his using the Macedonian support "for ministry/service to you" (διακονία *diakonia*, 11:8). When Paul doubles up verbs, as he does in 11:9—"I have guarded myself and I shall guard myself"—he displays a clearly thought-out decision that is his incontrovertible policy, in this case, not to burden them in any way. He declares, in effect, "The case is closed" by vowing what he thinks is beyond dispute: "The truth of Christ is in me: This boast of mine [to resist burdening you] will not be silenced in the whole region of Achaia" (11:10). The reference to all of Achaia, in a passage consistently in the singular, once again serves to remind the Corinthians that, even though Paul is speaking in the singular, he in effect calls to witness all his supporters in the entire region. Paul openly ponders: Could the Corinthians possibly be confused that his refusal to accept their support means that he does not love them? In one of his most poignant, briefest, and therefore most powerful statements, Paul answers his own query: "*God* knows [that I do, understood]" (11:11, italics added).

11:12. As if he needed to be more emphatic, Paul once again doubles verbs, though this time the scope of his emphasis is broadened beyond resisting their support, to the way he does his ministry, to the entire profile of how he operates: "That which I do, thus shall I do" (11:12). The very succinctness of the declaration heightens the emphasis, as does the choice of verb, which very simply, but powerfully, refers to everything he does. The claim of consistency is of great importance for ethos enhancement, for the declaration of his dependable, unchangeable character that is the cornerstone of faithfulness and trustworthiness.[201] Paul pledges that the consistency of his patterns among the Corinthians will undercut the claims and pretensions of his opponents, will "cut

---

198. E. A. Judge, "Paul's Boasting in Relation to Contemporary Professional Practice," *AusBR* 16 (1968) 37.

199. Sampley, "Paul, His Opponents in 2 Corinthians 10–13, and the Rhetorical Handbooks," 166-67.

200. R. F. Hock, *The Social Context of Paul's Ministry: Tentmaking and Apostleship* (Philadelphia: Fortress, 1980) 48-49.

201. See Cicero *Of Oratory* 2.43.178-84; Quintillian *Institutes of Oratory* 6.2.18-19.

down the pretext of those wanting a pretext that in what they boast they may be found just like us" (11:12).

He thinks the Corinthians should "look at what is before their eyes" indeed (10:7). Paul has been faithfully dependable and consistent; that is the ethos his entire work with them has manifested. Now he finds himself besieged by intruders who would present themselves as working on the same terms as he.

11:13-15. Certainly, one distinguishing mark between Paul and them is that, unlike them, Paul continues to refuse to live off the Corinthians. That realization alone should prompt the Corinthians to the fuller understanding that these intruders are frauds. Paul says so directly and in rhetoric that, as it advances, increases in vitriol. He brings heavy rhetorical artillery to bear on them; refining his earlier reference to them as "super apostles" (11:5),[202] they are "false apostles, deceitful workers, masquerading/disguising [μετασχηματίζομαι *metaschēmatizomai*] themselves as apostles of Christ" (11:13).[203] Stripping off their disguise, Paul identifies them as Satan's "agents/ministers" (διάκονοι *diakonoi*) who can only pretend to be what Paul and his kind are in fact: ministers of righteousness (διάκονοι δικαιοσύνης *diakonoi dikaiosynēs*). These pretenders have followed, true to form, their leader, Satan, who disguises himself as an "angel of light" (11:14). In what amounts, by implication, to a verdict, Paul concludes his invective against the intruders: "Their end shall be according to their works" (11:15), a position his followers in general and the Corinthians in particular know Paul believes about everyone (1 Cor 3:14; 2 Cor 5:10; cf. Rom 2:6-11).

In that culture, Paul's practice of self-support is vulnerable to several criticisms, all of which may in some form and degree be present in the Corinthians' responses. First, some may think that Paul's failure to take support puts him on a lower social plane than other apostles because he stoops to menial labor for self-support. Paul is quick to point out that the intruders have "taken advan-

tage" of the Corinthians (11:20). Turn the rhetoric around, however, and we may suppose that the intruders relish the perquisites that come with status (cf. 1 Cor 9:4-6, which assumes exactly such prerogatives as appropriate) and deride Paul's refusal as reflecting poorly on him.

Second, in the patron/client culture that pervades every level of the social structures, patronage was a substantial way of wielding influence and creating a subset of persons indebted to the patron. Some of the Corinthians are wealthy (cf. 1 Cor 1:26). It is difficult to imagine that they were not aware that Paul accepted the patronage of Phoebe, a deacon of the church at Cenchreae, a town just a handful of miles from Corinth (Rom 16:1-2). Therefore, when Paul persisted in his pattern of refusing support from Corinthian believers, he rejected any efforts at patronage from them. To refuse gifts and support was unheard of in that culture and inevitably resulted in a shaming of those who would patronize him.[204] The consequences of shame reverberate through this letter fragment in passages such as 12:14-15, where Paul appears to be justifying his decision not to become a client of any of the Corinthians. Third, some of the Corinthians—possibly the same persons as in the previous point—may have thought that Paul's refusal of support from them made them, in effect, second-class citizens among Pauline communities because they knew that Paul accepted support from some others (cf. 12:13).

It is true that nowhere in the Pauline letters do we find an example of Paul accepting support from believers while he is working with them, so his refusal to do so with the Corinthians may fit that pattern. But more seems to be at stake here. For instance, Paul never tells the Corinthians, who seem eager to support him, that it is not his pattern "in all the churches," a response the Corinthians and we know he can make (cf. 1 Cor 7:17; 11:16; 14:33b). That would have been an easy argument for him to have made, and it might have been much more compelling to them than the justifications he offers in the letter fragment.

202. And not distinguishing two groups, as C. K. Barrett, "Paul's Opponents in II Corinthians," *NTS* 17 (1971) 252-53.

203. For more on the way people derided their opponents, see L. T. Johnson, "The New Testament's Anti-Jewish Slander and the Conventions of Ancient Rhetoric," *JBL* 108 (1989) 419-41.

204. Seneca *Of Benefits* 1.10.3-4 holds that no crime exceeds ingratitude. See G. W. Peterman, *Paul's Gift from Philippi: Conventions of Gift-Exchange and Christian Giving* (Cambridge: Cambridge University Press, 1997) 69.

REFLECTIONS

1. Paul's opponents disguise themselves as "apostles of Christ" (11:13). Across the biblical traditions, there is a problem: It is possible to cry, "Lord, Lord," and not be a true follower of Christ (cf. Matt 7:21-23). Similarly, prophets like Amos were distressed that people did all the religious ceremonies and rituals and failed to take care of one another (Amos 4:1-5). Neither the prophets nor Jesus nor Paul could contemplate that life could be divided into categories where parts were devoted to God and the rest left it open to do as one pleased. Put another way, what one believes and how one behaves must be intricately and fundamentally interconnected. The true life of faith reaches beyond the formulas and rituals so that every aspect of life, all of one's behavior, is seen as an expression of one's devotion to God.

2. The expression "God knows" (11:1) expresses a Pauline confidence (cf. Rom 2:16; 1 Cor 14:25). Unlike us humans, God does not confuse externals with internals, face with heart. This is both good news and (potentially) bad news. It can be bad news if we think we hide our actions or motives from God or if we stand in judgment of one another. But it can be good news when our contemporaries misunderstand us because we can know that we are perfectly understood by God (1 Cor 13:12).

3. The "bride of Christ" image, as powerful as it has been throughout history, may be troublesome to some today. It lauds virginity and extols purity. Paul's use of the image is not designed to set standards for women—or men—who want to marry today, but instead serves him as a way of arguing, from the religious and cultural norms of his time, for a certain standard of behavior from the Corinthians. On the positive side, then and now, however, the image expresses a presupposed intimacy of believers with Christ.

4. Paul accepts support from the Macedonians, but not from the Corinthians, because the latter want to have him become their client. If giving has a string attached to it, then that string mars the giving and the receiving. If you find yourself being edgy that somebody has not "recognized" some gift or act that you gave or did, then you may find that you did not give absolutely freely. Of course, when a gift or deed is appreciated and the recipient's joy overflows in return, your joy is redoubled.

5. How many different gospels are there? Paul thinks there is only one true gospel. There are many forms of the gospel. Each of the first four books of the New Testament is called a Gospel, but each one has a superscription that says, "The gospel [or good news, as the term means] according to" Matthew, Mark, Luke, or John. So the persons who put the New Testament together wanted to affirm that there was just one gospel that came in many forms. Today, we might do well to ask what gospel, what "good news" is being represented by our churches, by what is preached, and by the programs that are endorsed. In the same way, however, note how corporations and political groups try to co-opt religion as a means of advancing their causes.

2 CORINTHIANS 11:16–12:10, THE FOOL'S SPEECH: PAUL'S BOASTFUL COMPARISON

OVERVIEW

Paul's arrangement of passages that compose the fool's speech resembles a roller coaster, moving dramatically from the lows to the highs to the lows again. Or, described differently, Paul moves the reader from hardships (11:21*b*-29), through a story of deliverance from adversity (11:30-33), to the pinnacle of a heavenly journey (12:1-6), to adversity or hardship from which there is no extrication (12:7-10). These accounts, all strung together, amount to Paul's own exemplification of his statement to the Philippians: "I have learned in whatever situation I am to be content; I know how to be humbled and I know how to abound. . . . I can handle all things in the one who strengthens me" (Phil 4:11-13).

This entire section begins with Paul's appeal to be accepted as foolish (ἄφρων, *aphrōn;* 11:16, a development from 11:1). and when the next section opens, Paul confirms that, in the intervening verses, he knows that he has indeed been foolish (12:11). Key to the whole section, however, is the concept of weakness, which, once introduced in 11:21, forms an *inclusio,* or ring device, that reaches beyond the next hardship catalog (11:21*b*-29), which demonstrates that Paul, in his service of the gospel, and despite his noteworthy religious pedigree, has been buffeted by the vagaries of life. Who can compare with such a set of hardships? No one can be weaker, he argues (11:29). Weakness becomes an ironic badge of honor. In a curiously circuitous fashion, Paul has found a way to boast (11:30), but this time about who has lived the life of greater adversity and affliction. As in the earlier hardship catalogs, Paul shows himself, like a sage, able to abide the vicissitudes of life (albeit with a new note of irony to be examined later) and stay steadily focused on and faithful in his commitment to God and to the gospel.

From the lowest reaches to which experience can lead, as exemplified in the hardship list (11:21*b*-29), to the loftiest exposure for which one in that world could aspire—namely, transport into the heavens, Paul's fool's speech ranges (12:1-6). Then, immediately after the heavenly transit, Paul reverts to the first-person singular and describes a persistent impediment, his "thorn/stake in the flesh" (12:7-10). He openly boasts about his hardships and even employs the first-person singular—because it is an ironic boast and therefore has a certain buffer from offending the auditors. The transit to the third heaven, however, is another matter. No irony protects there. Accordingly, Paul takes the rhetorically viable route of casting the experience in the third person, as if it were about someone else whom Paul knows.[205]

205. H. D. Betz, *Der Apostel Paulus und die sokratische Tradition; eine exegetische Untersuchung zu seiner Apologie 2 Korinther 10–13* (Tübingen: Mohr, 1972), 91, 95. A. T. Lincoln, *Paradise Now and Not Yet: Studies in the Role of the Heavenly Dimension in Paul's Thought with Special Reference to His Eschatology* (Cambridge: Cambridge University Press, 1981) 75, finds Paul here in line with apologetic conventions in the Socratic tradition.

2 Corinthians 11:16-21*a*, Bearing with Fools

NIV	NRSV
¹⁶I repeat: Let no one take me for a fool. But if you do, then receive me just as you would a fool, so that I may do a little boasting. ¹⁷In this self-confident boasting I am not talking as the Lord would, but as a fool. ¹⁸Since many are boasting	16I repeat, let no one think that I am a fool; but if you do, then accept me as a fool, so that I too may boast a little. ¹⁷What I am saying in regard to this boastful confidence, I am saying not with the Lord's authority, but as a fool; ¹⁸since

NIV

in the way the world does, I too will boast. ¹⁹You gladly put up with fools since you are so wise! ²⁰In fact, you even put up with anyone who enslaves you or exploits you or takes advantage of you or pushes himself forward or slaps you in the face. ²¹To my shame I admit that we were too weak for that!

NRSV

many boast according to human standards,^a I will also boast. ¹⁹For you gladly put up with fools, being wise yourselves! ²⁰For you put up with it when someone makes slaves of you, or preys upon you, or takes advantage of you, or puts on airs, or gives you a slap in the face. ²¹To my shame, I must say, we were too weak for that!

^a Gk *according to the flesh*

COMMENTARY

11:16-19. Paul employs the fool's mode as a cover for some self-commendation. He realizes he is pressing beyond the limits he should honor. He cautions his auditors that he himself speaks (expressed in the singular) with no authority from the Lord, but as in foolishness (2 Cor 11:17; cf. 1 Cor 7:10, 12). Gone are the mainstream, the others who stand with him. In effect, he seems drawn onto his opponents' turf; others boast of worldly accomplishments (κατὰ σάρκα *kata sarka*), so Paul will boast as well (11:18).

Paul establishes the theme of the Corinthians' "putting up" or "bearing with" him, which amounts to a request for them to give him the benefit of the doubt. Already in 11:1, as he finds himself being drawn more and more to self-defense and self-promotion, he asks them to "bear with" him in "a little foolishness." They are ready enough to "bear with" apostles who intrude. Varying the terminology the slightest, Paul asks them to "accept" him "as foolish" (11:16). Reverting to the terminology of "bearing with," Paul ironically chides them as having already demonstrated that they, indeed, "bear with fools" because they put up with all kinds of extreme, wrongful treatment from the intruders (11:19).

11:20-21a. Just as he described the intruders in strikingly vivid and negative terms in 11:13, so also in 11:20 Paul characterizes the extremes the Corinthians are willing to bear from outsiders: "If someone reduces you to slavery, if someone exploits you, if someone takes advantage of you, if someone takes on airs, if someone strikes you in the face"—Paul thinks the Corinthians will "bear with" it (11:20). The list of abuses is itself foolish;

we cannot take the descriptions as reflecting exactly what the opponents are doing, because the "striking in the face" is probably a hyperbolic extension of the rhetoric toward an extreme "what will they do and you abide next?" Paul paints a satirical characterization of the Corinthians in 11:20 as people who will put up with almost anything from the outsiders. Now he wants his moment of forbearance from them. Irony becomes his mode, and he portrays himself as being ashamed that he was too weak to have prevailed over them in such a fashion, and he almost asks their forgiveness (11:21).

Note that he embraces "weakness" (11:21) and thereby introduces a theme that will permeate much of the remaining letter fragment (a root form of ἀσθενέω *astheneō*, 11 times).[206] At different points in the Corinthian correspondence, Paul has employed an ironic self-portrait.[207] Already in 1 Cor 4:10-13 he tied the weak and fool themes together and ironically applied them to himself (cf. 1 Cor 1:25). Human pretensions to strength fall of their own weight in the face of God's true power. So Paul ironically credits to his weakness his "failure" to enslave the Corinthians, as he suggests the intruders have done. The notion of weakness, once introduced here, is featured in the fool's speech and is a *leitmotiv* in all that follows.

206. J. L. Sumney, "Paul's 'Weakness': An Integral Part of His Conception of Apostleship," *JSNT* 52 (1993) 89-90, traces Paul's self-identification as apostle of weakness back to 1 Thessalonians.
207. K. A. Plank, *Paul and the Irony of Affliction* (Atlanta: Scholars Press, 1987); A. B. Spencer, "The Wise Fool (and the Foolish Wise): A Study of Irony in Paul," *NovT* 23 (1981) 349-60.

REFLECTIONS

Our bearing with others and they with us is the currency of any relationship. Try as we may to be consistently loving and thoughtful, we inevitably fall short of our ideals. So bearing with us is a necessity that we ask of our friends and loved ones. But putting up with us must have its limits. Abuse, whether physical or emotional, simply must not be borne because the damage is too severe and protracted. It is no longer Christian love that bears with abuse.

2 Corinthians 11:21*b*-29, So to Boast

NIV	NRSV
What anyone else dares to boast about—I am speaking as a fool—I also dare to boast about. [22]Are they Hebrews? So am I. Are they Israelites? So am I. Are they Abraham's descendants? So am I. [23]Are they servants of Christ? (I am out of my mind to talk like this.) I am more. I have worked much harder, been in prison more frequently, been flogged more severely, and been exposed to death again and again. [24]Five times I received from the Jews the forty lashes minus one. [25]Three times I was beaten with rods, once I was stoned, three times I was shipwrecked, I spent a night and a day in the open sea, [26]I have been constantly on the move. I have been in danger from rivers, in danger from bandits, in danger from my own countrymen, in danger from Gentiles; in danger in the city, in danger in the country, in danger at sea; and in danger from false brothers. [27]I have labored and toiled and have often gone without sleep; I have known hunger and thirst and have often gone without food; I have been cold and naked. [28]Besides everything else, I face daily the pressure of my concern for all the churches. [29]Who is weak, and I do not feel weak? Who is led into sin, and I do not inwardly burn?	But whatever anyone dares to boast of—I am speaking as a fool—I also dare to boast of that. [22]Are they Hebrews? So am I. Are they Israelites? So am I. Are they descendants of Abraham? So am I. [23]Are they ministers of Christ? I am talking like a madman—I am a better one: with far greater labors, far more imprisonments, with countless floggings, and often near death. [24]Five times I have received from the Jews the forty lashes minus one. [25]Three times I was beaten with rods. Once I received a stoning. Three times I was shipwrecked; for a night and a day I was adrift at sea; [26]on frequent journeys, in danger from rivers, danger from bandits, danger from my own people, danger from Gentiles, danger in the city, danger in the wilderness, danger at sea, danger from false brothers and sisters;[a] [27]in toil and hardship, through many a sleepless night, hungry and thirsty, often without food, cold and naked. [28]And, besides other things, I am under daily pressure because of my anxiety for all the churches. [29]Who is weak, and I am not weak? Who is made to stumble, and I am not indignant?
	[a] Gk *brothers*

COMMENTARY

Paul's distraction with the intruders leads him into the very comparison that he so much derided just a while earlier as he wrote: "When these people measure themselves by one another and compare themselves with one another, they do not understand" (10:12). Paul's is the classical and eternal problem that when setting oneself over against one's opponents, one can be drawn onto the adversaries' grounds. Strangely, one becomes like one's enemies. Here, Paul is drawn into the very *syncresis* that he so opposes.

Lest we be too harsh, we note that Paul is in a predicament. Remember that outsiders have encroached on what Paul considers to be his own territory and that some Corinthians who really owe their coming into the faith to Paul now seem drawn to this alien leadership. Paul thinks that the Corinthians should have honored their long-standing filiation to him. What is more, they should have defended him from the intruders' charges and innuendos and sent them packing. Then Paul would not have perceived the need to defend himself.

When the most evident avenue—namely, Corinthian defense of Paul—fails, what alternatives are left to him? Rhetorical handbooks and practice advise that he must aim for goodwill (*benevolentia*) by making reference (a) to himself and to his service toward the state or the community, (b) to his opponents, (c) to the jury (in the case of a letter, the recipient for whom the letter is intended), and (d) to the case or situation itself.[208] The first three are primary, according to Cicero, but (c), the jury (in this case, the Corinthians), is not very responsive to Paul, and (d), the case itself, is not directly or fully discernible in the way Paul treats it in 2 Corinthians 10–13. So Paul, for whatever reasons, has not availed himself of (d). Therefore, Paul is really left with two avenues of approach toward recovery of goodwill in chaps. 10–13: references to himself and to his opponents (a and b).

With regard to oneself, one recites, as Paul does, one's own previous efforts for the "Corinthians,"[209] from bringing the gospel to them through to the present; one references one's own credentials and generally enhances one's own ethos, or character. Regarding the opponents, one questions their motives, exposes their ethos and comportment as inappropriate or inconsiderate, and suggests their selfishness and luxurious idleness. Paul's attacks on his adversaries have been peppered across chaps. 10–11, and they will continue. But in 11:21b–12:10, the heart of the fool's speech, Paul works (sometimes ironically) to enhance his own ethos and thereby attempts to win goodwill.

To the modern ear, Paul's heavy focus on himself may grate, but in his own culture it was in the very nature of what was expected. In his letters, Paul is a good cultural example of a person who knows the importance of an enhanced ethos for his leadership role and style, and he accordingly makes certain that his letters cultivate and enrich his ethos regularly. Usually, however, Paul is not so blatant in using syncrisis, comparison, as he is in the text at hand. *Paul's opponents* have apparently used syncrisis by claiming to be different from him in certain details (e.g., readily taking support, 11:20; 12:13) and by declaring themselves like Paul in certain particulars (apostleship, authority, and having a διακονία [*diakonia*], "ministry," like his, 11:12-15). Paul is convinced of how different the intruders are, and in 11:21b-29. he undertakes syncrisis to demonstrate the difference.[210]

We have seen that it is difficult, and perhaps even doubtful, to be sure whether every detail in a given passage of 2 Corinthians is a one-for-one counter to something the opponents are saying or doing (cf. 11:4 and the Introduction).[211] So it is here in the opening part of Paul's comparison—presented in a barrage of rhetorical questions sounding like an interrogation of a witness—when he boasts, somewhat redundantly, that if the intruders are Hebrews, Israelites, and offspring of Abraham, so is he, emphatically (κἀγώ *kagō*, "I too!" 11:22). This triple insistence supports the interpretation that the outsiders are, like Paul, Jewish and lends some general support to speculation whether they may have connections with Jerusalem.

Paul's query whether the intruders are "ministers/servants of Christ" (διάκονοι Χριστοῦ *diakonoi Christou*, 11:23; cf. 11:15 and Paul's own self-depiction as διάκονος [*diakonos*] in 3:1–4:6) moves Paul from comparison ("So am I," 11:22) to superlative, framed by the iterative disclaimers that he is speaking "in foolishness" (11:21b) and "irrationally" (11:23b). He and they may be Jews, but when it comes to being ministers of Christ, Paul goes over the edge: "I am more" (ὑπὲρ ἐγώ *hyper egō*, 11:23).

---

208. See Cicero *De inv.* 1.16.22.

209. Encomiastic tradition expected a recounting or cataloging of one's deeds (*res gestae*) that benefit others. See L. L. Belleville, "A Letter of Apologetic Self-recommendation: 2 Cor 1:8–7:16," *NovT* 31 (1989) 154-55; S. H. Travis, "Paul's Boasting in 2 Cor 10–12," *Studia Evangelica*, ed. F. L. Cross (Berlin: Akademie, 1973) 6:529-30.

210. Plutarch (*On Praising Oneself Inoffensively* 540C-D, 541C) repeatedly acknowledges that self-praise will be viewed as appropriate when "defending your good name or answering a charge."

211. See G. Lyons, *Pauline Autobiography: Toward a New Understanding* (Atlanta: Scholars Press, 1985) 78, for his rather devastating critique of "mirror reading," in which every detail in a passage is read as a cue to the opponents' real position.

His evidence for being a better minister of Christ begins with his labors ("with regard to labors, far more") and immediately merges into a hardship list of great proportions (11:23-28). Once again, Paul's ministry is ironically best measured by the difficulties, adversities, afflictions, and setbacks he has encountered and surmounted in his representation of the gospel (see also 1:3-11; 4:7-10; 6:4-10). Once again, hardships endured in the service of the gospel are Paul's best evidence and confirmation of his faithfulness and dependability with regard to the gospel and to the call to service. *Nothing* deters Paul. The longer and more detailed the list—and this is the longest in all of Paul's letters—the more attestation that Paul has placed the gospel first and has pursued its propagation with a singleness of purpose that cannot be thwarted and that should not be underestimated.

This hardship catalog is impressive on several counts. First is its structure. The list opens with four parallel prepositional phrases, each beginning with the preposition "in/with" (ἐν *en*): "in labors," "in imprisonments," "in floggings," and "in [that is, near] death." Each of these phrases ends with some modifier that suggests inordinate numbers. Next in the list are events defined and linked by numbers of times or length of duration: "five times," "three times," "once," "three times," "a night and day," and "many" (11:24-26*a*). Next is a litany of troubles introduced by eight "in danger from" constructions (11:26*b* to the end of the verse) and is followed by a little summarizing phrase of rhetorical doubling, "in toil and in hardship" (11:27*a*), before the list concludes, as it began, with (four) prepositional phrases, each beginning with *en:* "with sleepless nights," "in hunger and cold," "with much fasting," and "in the cold and destitute" (11:27*b* to the end of the verse).

Second, this hardship catalog confirms some details already known about Paul and gives new information not otherwise known. Paul's imprisonments are numerous (Rom 16:7; 2 Cor 6:5; Phil 1:12-14; Phlm 1, 9-10, 13, 23; cf. Acts 16:23-40; 24:27; 28:16; Eph 3:1; 4:1; Col 4:10), though the location of them remains problematic. His having been shipwrecked we know from Acts 27:9-44. Journeys are certainly troublesome issues with the Corinthians (cf. 2 Cor 1:15-18, 23–2:3;

7:5; 9:3-4; 10:2; 12:20–13:1, 10). Danger experienced by Paul was the subject of much attention in 2 Cor 1:3-11.

The beatings mentioned in 11:24-25 (cf. 6:5) provide new information, unavailable elsewhere in his letters. The first type of beating, Paul acknowledges, is a synagogue-based Jewish punishment[212] via lashes and is grounded in Deut 25:3, which provides for a maximum of forty lashes. Contemporary Judaism, scrupulous to make certain that punishments not exceed the biblical limit, practiced a flogging that was described as "forty less one." Though it would be interesting to know what Paul did on each occasion to be judged worthy of these punishments, we are at a loss to know.[213] The other mentioned punishment, the beating with rods, is Roman (Acts 16:22-23; cf. 1 Thess 2:2) and is inappropriate treatment of Roman citizens (Acts 16:37-39), though Josephus reports that on occasion Roman citizens were subjected to such discipline.[214] Thus Paul's having received the Roman flogging with rods cannot be used with confidence to comment on the veracity of Acts regarding Paul's Roman citizenship, but Paul's reference to having been beaten with rods three times does suggest that he may have had run-ins with Roman authorities about which we otherwise know nothing.

Third, the list embraces shameful circumstances. Here is Paul as fool, "boasting" about having been in jails, punished by Jews and Romans, in danger from more and varied circumstances than one is likely to imagine, and deprived of food, clothing, and comfort. If the irony were not already apparent in the list, Paul's tag line—"If anyone is weak, am I not also weak?"—makes it clear. Neither the Corinthians nor apparently the intruders are reflected as casting any doubt that Paul has been a very successful advocate for the gospel around much of the eastern Mediterranean basin. And what does he here choose to boast about? His weakness. Despite his perils and

---

212. This beating is not to be confused with persecution. See E. P. Sanders, "Paul on the Law, His Opponents, and the Jewish People in Philippians 3 and 2 Corinthians 11," in *Anti-Judaism in Early Christianity,* ed. P. Richardson and D. Granskou (Waterloo: Wilfrid Laurier University, 1986) 1:88; A. J. Hultgren, "Paul's Pre-Christian Persecutions of the Church: Their Purpose, Locale, and Nature," *JBL* 95 (1976) 104.

213. Sanders, "Paul on the Law, His Opponents, and the Jewish People in Philippians 3 and 2 Corinthians 11," 89, sees evidence here that Paul continued synagogue attendance and submitted to its discipline.

214. Josephus *The Jewish War* 2.308.

predicaments, the gospel is powerfully present through his weakness. The only conclusion he can imagine is that it is God's doing. The gist: How can anyone deny Paul is a genuine apostle when, despite the way his life looks through the prism of his problems, the gospel he preached is powerfully present in the lives of people like the Corinthians? With this extended hardship list, Paul has documented that his life has been one long demonstration of weakness. And this weakness and his problems show unmistakably that the undeniable success of his missionizing rests solely and powerfully in God (cf. the same point made already in 1 Cor 2:5).

The Corinthians will not know at this point what we modern readers can know by reading ahead, but they will learn when Paul's folly narrative finally discloses the key to understanding it all: the Lord's own statement, "My grace is sufficient; my power is made perfect in weakness" (12:9). Before the recipients of this letter hear the just-noted key, though, they will hear Paul cap off the hardship list (11:28-29), exemplify his weakness with a description of an escape from Damascus (11:30-33), and, completing his fool's speech, tell of his transit to paradise and his thorn/spike in the flesh (12:1-8).

Though formally the list may be said to conclude with 11:27, Paul extends it with a statement that functions as a sort of "et cetera": "apart from the unmentioned things" (11:28a). Suggesting he could go on, that the list as supplied only scratches the surface, Paul finally focuses instead on the "daily pressure" he finds in his "anxiety for all the churches" (11:28), a pressure of which the recipients of the Corinthian letter are clearly part.

Paul concludes the first part of his fool's speech, most of which is composed of the hardship catalog, with an affirmation of the underlying message of the entire hardship list—namely, his theme of weakness (11:29, reprised from 11:21a) as the key to understanding not only Paul and his ministry, but also the gospel and what it reports God is doing. Through rhetorical questions designed to draw the hearers into his deliberation, Paul suggests that if anyone is weak, so is he (11:29a); *that* is what the list of hardships and difficulties has had as its subtext.

The genius of fools has always been in their freedom from convention, in their holding a lens through which we see what is not otherwise clear. In a subversion of the culture's value system—and perhaps also that of at least some Corinthians—weakness becomes Paul's badge of honor, for reasons that will become clearer at the end of the fool's speech (12:7-10). The Corinthians, and perhaps even more their intruding new leaders, ought not to be confused by this "weakness," though, because it is not powerlessness; neither does it lead to Paul's withdrawal, as the second rhetorical question in 11:29 shows: "Who is caused to stumble, and I am not burned up?" By such a comment Paul signals to one and all that any causing to stumble or sin (σκανδαλίζω *skandalizō*) will bring Paul's ire. That puts the Corinthians on notice with regard to their proper concern for one another and surely warns them that they need to scrutinize the impact the outsiders—indeed, any filiation the Corinthians may have with them—may have on each of their brothers and sisters in the faith.

If we return to the first question of 11:29a—"Who is weak and I am not weak?"—we can now see its function. There Paul models the way in which believers, whether weak or strong, ought to identify with one another and with their well-being. Paul's last rhetorical question (11:29b) is, therefore, a call to vigilance and responsibility on the part of all believers and certainly neither a Pauline pledge always to be for the ones who are harmed nor some little personal detail about himself that Paul now (of all times!) decides to share with his followers. Rather, it is Paul applying to himself and modeling what he passionately holds: No believer can stand by with impunity when another believer is made to stumble or sin, that is, go wrong.

REFLECTIONS

1. What should a believer make of hardships and afflictions? As is popularly asked, Why do bad things happen to good people? Perhaps we should declare outright that bizarre and apparently absurd things do happen, that not all things make sense. Sometimes immune systems fail, hearts give out, and other organs fail. We are finite creatures with a limited life span. But the word of faith says, with Paul, that God works *in* and *through* all things to bring about good for those who love God (Rom 8:28). Often the good that God works through something is visible only later and in retrospect. The affirmation of God working good through an occasion is not to say that the event was itself good (the death of a loved one, for example, is unabashedly an awesome loss); nor is it to be confused with saying that God "caused" it. An important function of hardships, as Paul understands them, is to help distinguish what is truly important or powerful from those things that are not.

2. What should we say about Paul's being carried away a bit? He acknowledges it; so should we. No doubt his opponents will have noticed it. Paul is indeed drawn onto his opponents' ground and, even though it fits the social conventions of the time, is boasting like a foolish person. Paul's inversion of his boast so that it focuses on his weakness goes to the heart of his gospel—namely, that the power belongs to God. Nevertheless, in his foolish boasting, Paul's frailty and humanity show through. As much as he understood and as much as he accomplished, he is still frail in some ways—like us. Biblical characters from Adam and Eve forward have always had their foibles and problems; yet, God stays committed to them—and to us. Perfection of performance is not a prerequisite to God's love, fortunately.

3. Pretentions to power often have a puffiness about them. People who are weak or who have low self-esteem sometimes bluster about, pretending to be powerful persons, apparently hoping that others may be (more) convinced by their posturing. Real power can genuinely express itself in gentleness and even in weakness. The biblical story throughout history affirms this. The Hebrews, weak and servile, were delivered from powerful Egypt. Jericho's walls were no match for Joshua. Little David bested Goliath. Jesus had a manger for a crib.

4. It is not just because Paul was an apostle that he said, "When anyone falls, I burn" (11:29). It is the duty of every believer to be troubled by failed love, by injustice, to "burn" when anyone falls, and to stand against anyone who has led to another's distress or downfall.

2 Corinthians 11:30-33, Boasting and Deliverance Through the Damascus Wall

NIV

30If I must boast, I will boast of the things that show my weakness. 31The God and Father of the Lord Jesus, who is to be praised forever, knows that I am not lying. 32In Damascus the governor under King Aretas had the city of the Damascenes guarded in order to arrest me. 33But I was lowered in a basket from a window in the wall and slipped through his hands.

NRSV

30If I must boast, I will boast of the things that show my weakness. 31The God and Father of the Lord Jesus (blessed be he forever!) knows that I do not lie. 32In Damascus, the governor*a* under King Aretas guarded the city of Damascus in order to*b* seize me, 33but I was let down in a basket through a window in the wall,*c* and escaped from his hands.

a Gk *ethnarch*   *b* Other ancient authorities read *and wanted to*
c Gk *through the wall*

COMMENTARY

Still aware of its folly, Paul refines his boasting, saying that if forced to it, as he feels he is, he will focus on his weakness (11:30), a weakness already delineated in the preceding hardship catalog (11:23-29). Paul seals that determination with an oath as to his truthfulness (11:31); the particular form of the oath certifies, as it did when Paul employed it in 1:3, the faithfulness of God to deliver.[215] Paul swears on God's faithfulness that he does not lie; when Paul boasts of his weakness, it is the same as boasting about God's power to deliver and is an affirmation that Paul, knowingly weak in many ways, represents the God of power whose forces against opposition and wrong have been described as overwhelming in 10:3-6.

Paul's resort to boasting in his weakness is not simply a strategical move in his struggle with the Corinthians; it is also and more profoundly his tapping of a fundamental truth of his life—indeed, of the life of faith everywhere and in all time. When Paul is in difficulty, beset by affliction or even by a threat to his life (1:3-11)—and, in this context, we may add, opposition—Paul trusts in God's faithfulness and mercy and expects God to deliver. That is the story of Paul's life and of the life of faith.

In 11:30-33, Paul makes exactly the same connections that he does in the opening of 2 Corinthians 1–9. There Paul began with the "blessed be God" formulation, went on to describe the endangerment of his life in Asia, and acknowledged God's faithful deliverance of him (see the

Commentary on 1:3-11). In 11:30-33, it is the work of God "who is blessed forever" (NIV, "praised") that prevents Aretas IV (the Nabatean king [9 BCE–c. 40 CE] who ruled over Damascus) from capturing Paul, even though Aretas held the city under guard because he wanted to take Paul into custody (cf. Acts 9:24-25). Such power was arrayed—ineffectively—against Paul, who is weak in and of himself to prevail. In Israel's traditions, God is blessed because God keeps promises and preserves, guards, the faithful. So here also, Paul blesses God for his own deliverance because he was let down from a wall window in a rope basket and fled Aretas's hand. Strikingly absent from the story is a single detail of anything Paul did or had to do in order to be delivered. There is no word of any plan or of specific co-conspirators, just the simple, powerful detail: "Through a window, in a rope basket, I was let down and fled his hand" (11:33).

Paul's weakness, as reflected in the Damascus basket story, is the occasion for God's power, though that point is not explicitly made in the account. Paul depicts himself as the one who trusts God and God's power to deliver him; the blessed-be formula shows that. So his boasting in this instance is covertly a boasting about God, as the "blessed be God" (11:31) formulation indicates. So Paul's weakness is an occasion for God's power. Encoded for the Corinthian audience and their intruders is the suggestion that they ought to reckon carefully before they take Paul and his boasted weakness lightly. Harking back to 11:29, the Corinthians are once again placed on warning, much as they were when Paul reminded them that he is burned up when anyone is made to fall.

215. Danker calls it "strongest reinforcement . . . an oath." See F. W. Danker, "Paul's Debt to the *De Corona* of Demosthenes: A Study of Rhetorical Techniques in Second Corinthians," in *Persuasive Artistry: Studies in New Testament Rhetoric in Honor of G. A. Kennedy,* ed. D. F. Watson, JSNTSup 50 (Sheffield: Sheffield Academic, 1991) 279-80.

REFLECTIONS

1. It may be difficult to affirm in every challenging or problematic situation, but the God we believe in is the God of the exodus, the God who delivers. It is God's character to do so, as Paul knows and expresses in 1 Cor 10:13. God will always provide an exodus, a way out. Memory and hope position us with regard to understanding the situations that bid to overwhelm us—memory, because we recite our history of God's having delivered us in the past; and hope, because we look forward confidently to the future, to a time and situation that we may not yet be able to envisage, when "the God who delivers" will do so once again (2 Cor 1:10).

2. Paul's encoded assumption should be ours: There is no circumstance, no matter how apparently stacked against us, in which God is not there with us and for us. If God is for us, Paul declaimed, then nothing can separate us from the love of God in Christ Jesus our Lord (Rom 8:38-39). Such an affirmation is no guarantee that the city governors of life will not pursue us; rather, it is a declaration that even then and there God will be for us and will ultimately deliver us. In such situations we, too, can affirm: "Blessed be God."

3. Paul's story contains within it an implicit critique of the political structures of his time and thereby raises the question of when believers should relate positively and when they should relate critically (and perhaps even subversively) to the political, social, and economic structures of their own times. Christianity is not owned by any political system or by any given social or economic framework. The Christian faith can be lived within any situation. Often religion in general and Christianity in particular have been used to lend moral authority to governing and social structures, occasionally even when the structures were oppressive to some of its citizens.

4. Paul fled from Damascus. He fled from Thessalonica when a threat to his life arose (1 Thess 2:2, 17-20; see also Acts 16:19-40). Why not stay and be flogged or killed? When should one flee? When should one stand and be counted, even at one's peril? It is clear, from Paul's recounted hardships, that he certainly was caught at times, whether inadvertently or not. Every day we face small versions of those grand challenges; discerning when to stand and when to go away to await another day is part of the daily moral calculus that is required of us. Christians have found that collective assessment, where believers communally reflect on past performance, can be a positive encouragement to improvement, to what Paul calls "edification."

2 Corinthians 12:1-10, The Man in Paradise with a Thorn/Stake in His Flesh

NIV

12 I must go on boasting. Although there is nothing to be gained, I will go on to visions and revelations from the Lord. [2]I know a man in Christ who fourteen years ago was caught up to the third heaven. Whether it was in the body or out of the body I do not know—God knows. [3]And I know that this man—whether in the body or apart from the body I do not know, but God knows— [4]was caught up to paradise. He heard inexpressible things, things that man is not permitted to tell. [5]I will boast about a man like that, but I will not boast about myself, except about my weaknesses. [6]Even if I should choose to boast, I would not be a fool, because I would be speaking the truth. But I refrain, so no one will think more of me than is warranted by what I do or say.

[7]To keep me from becoming conceited because of these surpassingly great revelations, there was given me a thorn in my flesh, a messenger of

NRSV

12 It is necessary to boast; nothing is to be gained by it, but I will go on to visions and revelations of the Lord. [2]I know a person in Christ who fourteen years ago was caught up to the third heaven—whether in the body or out of the body I do not know; God knows. [3]And I know that such a person—whether in the body or out of the body I do not know; God knows— [4]was caught up into Paradise and heard things that are not to be told, that no mortal is permitted to repeat. [5]On behalf of such a one I will boast, but on my own behalf I will not boast, except of my weaknesses. [6]But if I wish to boast, I will not be a fool, for I will be speaking the truth. But I refrain from it, so that no one may think better of me than what is seen in me or heard from me, [7]even considering the exceptional character of the revelations. Therefore, to keep[a] me from being too elated, a thorn was given me in the flesh, a

[a]Other ancient authorities read *To keep*

NIV

Satan, to torment me. [8]Three times I pleaded with the Lord to take it away from me. [9]But he said to me, "My grace is sufficient for you, for my power is made perfect in weakness." Therefore I will boast all the more gladly about my weaknesses, so that Christ's power may rest on me. [10]That is why, for Christ's sake, I delight in weaknesses, in insults, in hardships, in persecutions, in difficulties. For when I am weak, then I am strong.

NRSV

messenger of Satan to torment me, to keep me from being too elated.[a] [8]Three times I appealed to the Lord about this, that it would leave me, [9]but he said to me, "My grace is sufficient for you, for power[b] is made perfect in weakness." So, I will boast all the more gladly of my weaknesses, so that the power of Christ may dwell in me. [10]Therefore I am content with weaknesses, insults, hardships, persecutions, and calamities for the sake of Christ; for whenever I am weak, then I am strong.

[a]Other ancient authorities lack *to keep me from being too elated*
[b]Other ancient authorities read *my power*

COMMENTARY

This double-faceted passage concludes the fool's speech, combining the loftiest of experiences, a transport into the third heaven, with the lowliest, a persistent, unavoidable "thorn/stake in the flesh." The two stories belong to and interpret each other as demonstrating the extremes a person may experience in life.

12:1-7a. The first story, that of a man transported to paradise,[216] is set in the ongoing context of the fool's boast, which has been under way since 11:16. In 11:30, Paul had written, "If it is necessary to boast . . ."; in 12:1 he declares, "It is necessary to boast." But quickly acknowledging that there is no advantage in doing so, he declares his intent to proceed to "visions and revelations of the Lord." We may wonder whether the intruders have boasted of their own visions; if so, Paul answers with a considerable "one-up" here. If the Corinthians have embraced the notion that visions and revelations are important indices of genuine apostolic standing, then Paul signs in impressively. Paul suffered in comparison with the original disciples in that he never saw Jesus in the flesh, but depended on visions, on the call of Christ for his authority. In any case, Paul here enhances his ethos.

Paul chooses to cast the story of his own translation into heaven[217] in the third person and

to describe it as having happend to "a man," but there can be no doubt that the man is Paul. Rhetorical conventions of the time suggested that there might be occasions when a speaker could advantageously tell a personal story as if it were about someone else.[218] One such time would be when the telling of a story so self-aggrandizing might cause the auditors to cringe with resentment over the vainglorying. Paul has already pushed beyond modesty in his boasting; now he wants to tell the Corinthians about an event so grand as to sound too self-commending, even in the categories of Paul's time.

The story is structured around what Paul knows in contrast to what God knows. Paul knows "a man in Christ" who fourteen years earlier was snatched up into the third heaven (12:2). Paul does not know whether the transit was "in the body or out of the body," but "God knows" (12:2; we cannot determine, or rule out, whether Paul's disavowal of knowledge is sarcasm directed at some position taken by the opponents). Two verses later, Paul repeats that he knows a certain man who was snatched up into paradise and heard "unspeakable words which it is not permitted for the man to speak" (12:3-4). Repeat-

---

216. Third heaven (12:2) and paradise (12:4) are not two distinct destinations but probably rhetorical variations for effect. See Lincoln, *Paradise,* 79.

217. P. Schäfer, "New Testament and Hekhalot Literature: The Journey into Heaven in Paul and in Merkavah Mysticism," trans. P. Vermes, *JJS* 35 (1984) 33-34, rejects the assertions that 2 Cor 12:2-4 can be understood in the light of Merkavah mysticism.

218. See Plutarch, *On Praising Oneself Inoffensively* 542C, on praising another; 539A-547F, on safe self-praise. See also Quintilian 11.1.21. In intertestamental literature, the heavenly ascent accounts are, with the exception of *T. Abraham,* in the first person. See M. Dean-Otting, *Heavenly Journeys: A Study of the Motif in Hellenistic Jewish Literature* (Frankfurt: Peter Lang, 1984). M. Goulder, "Vision and Knowledge," *JSNT* 56 (1994) 53-71, argues that, given Paul's disparagement of visions, the man in 12:2 cannot be Paul.

ing for emphasis, God knows (in the Greek the reader is left to imply the related "Paul does not know") whether the journey to paradise was "in the body or apart from the body" (12:3). That is the whole of the story.

Allusive in the extreme, the account fairly begs for the audience to clamor for more details, but the story carries its own antidote to that with its built-in reference to "unspeakable words" and to the prohibition on speaking. Paul has crafted the story in such a way as to attract and to hold off the audience at the same time.

Fourteen years earlier, at the time of this transit, what was happening in Paul's life? If a date of 54–56 CE is accepted for the parts of 2 Corinthians (see the Introduction), then the vision took place sometime around 40–42, some seven years after Paul had been called or converted near Damascus (Gal 1:17c). If we take the Galatians framework of Paul's chronology, then seven years after his call Paul would have been some three years into the time when he was in the "regions of Syria and Cilicia," the areas around Antioch and his hometown, Tarsus (Gal 1:18-21; cf. Acts 15:23, 41). That would be after his Jerusalem visit of a fortnight with Cephas and James (Gal 1:18-19). Therefore, this heavenly voyage is not to be confused with any revelation or vision that occurred in conjunction with his call or conversion. Paul, however, is given to visions and revelations (12:1; 1 Cor 9:1; 15:8; Gal 1:12; 2:1-2), so a later time presents no problem.

In Paul's culture, heavenly journeys often functioned to confirm divine approval and authentication.[219] This story counts as a boast on that basis. By telling it, Paul obliquely claims special status for himself, a status so grand that his opponents might not be able to compete.

"Paradise" (παράδεισος *paradeisos*), in times before Paul, referred to an enclosure like a formal garden or a park.[220] In some Jewish literature of Paul's time, paradise was understood to refer to the Garden of Eden.[221] It was also understood as an irenic place above the earth.[222] Elsewhere in the NT the term

refers to the place where God presides and cares for those who are chosen (cf. Luke 23:43; Rev 2:7).

The notion of heaven's having layers or levels or of there being more than one heaven is well attested in other NT writings (Luke 21:26; Eph 4:10; Col 1:16, 20; 2 Pet 3:5, 7, 10, 12-13).[223] The plural is lacking in Philo and Josephus.[224] The idea of a third heaven is known from other literature.[225] The combination of third heaven and paradise, as found here in 12:2-3, is also found in other ancient literature.[226]

It is curious that, throughout his ministry with them, Paul has not said a word to the Corinthians about this event. Along with his use of the third person, his well-maintained silence to this point may further mitigate against any Corinthian aversion to his boast. His breaking of his long-standing silence on the matter does, however, indicate the degree to which the Corinthian defection distresses him; his long silence shows how little public value he credits to visions, revelations, and transports. Further, that it is a transport of some time ago reduces the chance that some critic could claim that Paul conveniently came up with a vision when he needed one.

Paul also uses the heavenly transport story to secure a comfort zone on boasting. The third-heaven man allows Paul to continue his own boast in his weakness, a theme that now stretches back through 11:29-30 to 11:21, and to add to it his boasting "in behalf of such a one" (12:5). Paul's claim in 12:6 is revealing: Such a vision and transit, he suggests, would be a solid basis for boasting, and it is the truth, as difficult as it might be to believe the recounted details. Paul could boast about "such a one"; he would not be a fool in doing so, and he would be speaking the truth if he did. But he expressly refrains from boasting about that event. He can have it both ways. By telling the story, he indirectly vaunts himself; by not boasting about it (telling it in the third person and now explicitly refusing to structure a boast

219. Andrew T. Lincoln, *Paradise Now and Not Yet: Studies in the Role of the Heavenly Dimension of Paul's Thought with Special Reference to His Eschatology* (Cambridge: Cambridge University Press, 1981) 83-84.
220. On heaven, heavenly ascents, and paradise as reflected in Jewish and Hellenistic traditions, see Lincoln, *Paradise Now and Not Yet*, 77-85.
221. See Josephus *Antiquities of the Jews* 1.37; *Sib. Or.* 1.24, 26, 30; *Pss. Sol.* 14:3; Diognetus 12:3.
222. See En 32:3; 20:7; *T. Levi* 18:10; *Sib. Or.* frag. 3, 48.

223. Dean-Otting, *Heavenly Journeys*, 275. For other Jewish treatments of heavenly ascent, see C. R. A. Morray-Jones, "Paradise Revisited (2 Cor 12:1-12): The Jewish Mystical Background of Paul's Apostolate (the Jewish Sources and Paul's Heavenly Ascent and Its Siginificance)," *HTR* 86 (1993) 177-217, 265-92.
224. *BAGD* 598.
225. Philopatris 12; *T. Levi* 3:3.
226. See *Apoc. Mos.* 37:5; *2 Enoch 8:1* (B) and *2 Enoch* 31:1-2 (A). See also Lincoln, *Paradise*, 79.

on it), he subtly renounces power and authority built on claims of visions. In fact, he can have it the way he wants them to relate to him—namely, on the basis of his consistent performance and behavior among them: "lest someone think of me more than they see in me or hear from me" (12:6).

Paul is content to let the record of his relation to them stand on its own; as he wrote near the start of this letter fragment, "Look at what is before your eyes" (10:7). Paul will not use any vision or revelation, no matter how grand, to trump his own day-to-day performance—that is, what they see in him or hear from him. If the intruders are boasting of their visions and revelations, Paul one-ups them with this extraordinary heavenly journey and then, irony of ironies, refuses to build a case for his authority upon that, choosing instead to let the matter be decided by what they have seen and heard in him. What they have encountered in him all along is the gospel lived in their midst, with the power clearly being God's and with Paul being the menial earthenware vessel through which God has made this treasure present (4:7). Once again, Paul argues that his having been "tried and true" with them should be his strongest commendation; he has a history with them that shows him trustworthy through good times and bad—and the following verses (12:7*b*-10) illustrate a persistent adverse situation for Paul that, in contrast to the heavenly transport story, is no doubt well known to them.

Paul's treatment of his heavenly transport has implications for the grounding of religious authority. As Paul has set up the issue, it may be characterized as authority based on visions and revelations versus authority based on performance. The former invites allegiance for persons who themselves alone can vouch for what they report. They have the visions or revelations; they report them; and the hearers can credit them with as much authority as they see fit. That relationship makes the audience dependent on the visionaries. By nature, visions cannot be subjected to scrutiny; they happen in a given moment and can be shared only in the telling, and they rest on the experience of the individual who has received them. Sheer reception of the vision vests the recipient with some status.

On the other side, Paul in effect renounces authority built on "visions and revelations," though he is quick to make clear that his renun-

ciation is not a cover for his lack of them. On the contrary. In contrast, Paul prefers to rest the case for his own authority with the Corinthians, and with anyone else, on his performance day in and day out. His work with them has not been a "flash in the pan" but has constituted a consistent, dependable, "tried and true" history. Such conduct holds up under scrutiny and evaluation. Furthermore, the Corinthians have been the beneficiaries of Paul's performance throughout the years. They can judge from what they have seen in him and heard from him (12:6).

12:7b-10. Forming the ultimate contrast, Paul moves from heavenly transport to a discussion of his σκόλοψ (*skolops*, "thorn/stake") in the flesh, which he says was given to him to keep him from being too elated by "an abundance of revelations" (2 Cor 12:7). He needs no explanation for the Corinthians about this *skolops*, on two counts: He expects the Corinthians to know the term as he uses it, and he seems to expect that they know well what it refers to in his life. For Paul, his *skolops* in the flesh is a perspective keeper; the passive "given me" is usually a way for Paul to designate God, and it may be so here, even though Paul identifies the *skolops* as a "messenger/agent/angel of Satan" (ἄγγελος σατανᾶ *angelos satana*, 12:7). Could he be using the passive to suggest that Satan is the one who has given him the *skolops*? In any case, Paul describes his handling by the satanic agent as a "beating or rough treatment" (κολαφίζω *kolaphizō*, "torment," the NIV and NRSV choice, regrettably encourages modern readers to make a psychological interpretation) that obviously was of such duration for Paul to appeal at three distinct times for its removal (12:8).

The *skolops* "in the flesh" (τῇ σαρκι *tē sarki*) has inspired all sorts of speculation that Paul refers to some illness or physical problem that plagued him for some time, though anyone like Paul who can have survived all the hardships he reports (Rom 8:35-39; 1 Cor 4:11-12; 2 Cor 1:8-10; 4:7-10; 6:4-10; 11:21*b*-29) and traveled so widely around and across the Mediterranean would not have had overwhelming physical problems or weakness.[227] The candidates for identification of

---

227. L. Woods, "Opposition to a Man and His Message: Paul's 'Thorn in the Flesh' (2 Cor 12:7)," *AusBR* 39 (1991) 52, argues persuasively that the hardship catalog in 2 Cor 11:23-29 suggests that any physical limitation of Paul must have been minimal.

his *skolops* in the flesh have been of two sorts: either his opponents or a physical problem such as epilepsy, hysteria, depression, headaches, or eye problems—even leprosy and malaria have had their advocates, as have stuttering, spiritual temptations (from opponents or generated from his own conscience).[228] Of identifications there is no end.[229] Truth be told, we do not have a clue. Nor can we. Nor need we. *What* the problem is—that is not a concern for Paul.

The term *skolops* refers to a pointed stake or to a thorn and is most often used in English translations to mean the latter. According to certain texts,[230] the term refers to sharpened wooden stakes (1) that form a palisade for defensive purposes, (2) that are placed in a pit or depression on the hopes that opposing soldiers might fall upon them to their great distress, or (3) that are used to impale an enemy as a means of torture.[231] Paul, who thinks of God's grand purposes as a battle (cf. 2:14; 10:3-6) and of Satan as having plans (2:11), strategies, and agents (11:14-15), ties this "stake" to Satan as one of his messengers or agents (ἄγγελος *angelos*, can also be "angel," for "angel of Satan").[232] Whatever this stake actually was, Paul here interprets it as a trap, a palisade, a torture prepared by a clever enemy to take him out of the battle plan. But it has only partial effect, and that unintended: It simply keeps him from being overly elated by his many revelations, some of which are obviously grand, as can be seen in the instance of the heavenly transit just reported.

Paul's appeal to the Lord, three times, that the stake "should leave him" (12:8; not, as the NIV would have it, that the Lord should "take it away from me"), once again could suggest that the stake is something planted by Satan as a "messenger" and Paul wishes it removed. Paul does not address why the stake was not removed. Clearly it was not (cf. Mark 14:36).

The problematic description that the thorn/stake is in some sense from Satan has traditionally been resolved by claiming that there is a sort of teamwork between God and Satan such that God "allows" Satan (cf. Rev 13:5, 7, 15) to impose this impediment on Paul or that Satan unwittingly carries out God's will.[233] Surely, Paul trusts that he can seek redress by petitioning the Lord (12:8), and that God's grace can be said to work in the thorn/stake supports the same notion (12:9).

If as a "messenger of Satan" the stake is not something that *God* has given Paul, but that Satan has in some sense given him, then provocative considerations emerge. Given Paul's statements elsewhere about Satan, and given the understandings of warfare in Paul's time, we may make the following observations:[234] Paul believes that Satan is on the prowl (in at least one instance even depicted in military terms, Rom 16:20), has his own ministers (just as Paul is a minister of God, 2 Cor 11:13 15), and has a scheme that obviously is designed to thwart God's plan.

Paul thinks believers are cued in to Satan's plans and modus operandi (2:11), which is to foil matters for believers whenever possible (1 Cor 7:5). How natural for Paul, considering God's plan to be a battle against cosmic powers, to think of the military trap of his time whereby a pit is dug and filled with pointed stakes as a surprise to the enemy, who would fall unwittingly into it, or as more nearly fits Paul, would have the stake driven into the enemy's flesh as an excruciating torture. Given such a context, God has not given the *skolops* to him; Satan's agent has.

Paul's biblical sources inform him, on a "model of affliction" patterned on Job,[235] that Satan zeros in on exemplary righteous people in hopes of leading them astray so that they will fall in status before God. In his self-depiction in 12:7-9, Paul embraces this picture. He, as the apostle of unequaled probity and standing with God, has been identified by Satan as a prime enemy. As in a military move designed to trap Paul, Satan has employed a messenger, an ἄγγελος (*angelos*,

---

228. *BAGD,* 441.

229. See C. K. Barrett, *A Commentary on the Second Epistle to the Corinthians* (London: Black, 1973) 314-16.

230. D. M. Park, "Paul's *skolops tē sarki:* Thorn or Stake (2 Cor 12:7)" *NovT* 22 (1980) 180n. 6, details a series of pertinent texts.

231. Ibid., 181.

232. Paul holds that Satan disguises himself as an "angel" (2 Cor 11:14). Later Judaism tied Satan to an angel of death. See W. Foerster, "Σατανᾶς," *TDNT* 7:162.

233. Cf. J. C. Thomas, " 'An Angel from Satan': Paul's Thorn in the Flesh," *Journal of Pentecostal Theology* 9 (1996) 44-45.

234. See S. R. Garrett, "The God of This World and the Affliction of Paul: 2 Cor 4:1-12," in *Greeks, Romans and Christians: Essays in Honor of A. J. Malherbe,* ed. D. Balch, W. A. Meeks, and E. Ferguson (Minneapolis: Fortress, 1990) 104-7, who gives "Paul's view of Satan."

235. In what follows I am indebted to S. R. Garrett, "Paul's Thorn and Cultural Models of Affliction," in *The Social World of the First Christians: Essays in Honor of W. A. Meeks,* ed. L. M. White and O. L. Yarbrough (Minneapolis: Fortress, 1995) esp. 97: "an oblique but positive assertion about himself."

"angel") of Satan. To the Corinthians, then, Paul subtly portrays himself as the one who, more effectively than others, understands and opposes Satan's plan.

Paul nowhere says that God *causes* all things to happen, though he does say elsewhere what would fit very well here: Though God does not cause all things, God does *work in* all things for good unto those who love God (Rom 8:28). So, with the stake, though God did not cause it, God can work through it to keep Paul from being too elated regarding his extraordinary revelations (12:7; cf. Rom 9:17 for God's power shown through Pharaoh). Then in this case, God has co-opted Satan's stake as a means of helping Paul keep perspective and, incidentally, showing that God is ultimately in control. It follows that Paul's prayers to the Lord that it be removed credit God with the power to remove it, but the answers to his requests show God's refusal and give Paul the occasion to understand once again the paradoxical relationship of power and weakness that he now interprets for the Corinthians.

Rhetorically, the mention of Paul's "stake in the flesh" is most assuredly not a confession of a less than exemplary life. Such a self-disclosure would not fit his needs or purposes here. Neither is it an admission that Satan or sin has insinuated itself into Paul's life. Nowhere in the Pauline corpus has Satan or sin affected Paul's life of faith.[236] Paul is clearly in a defensive mode in 2 Corinthians 10–13 because relations between him and the Corinthians have eroded to dangerous levels. Nothing would be served by an admission of failure or inadequacy. On the contrary, his "stake" must be interpreted in the light of all the hardships that have been detailed in this letter fragment; they show that he is so properly dedicated to the work of the gospel that *nothing* can distract him—not even his well-known "stake in the flesh." Accordingly, the stake must be inter-

preted the same as any of the hardships or difficulties: as an *impediment*—granted, one of unavoidable proportion—but not as a moral flaw.

What Paul got in the Lord's response to his appeal, though not a removal of the stake as he had requested, was instead a twofold assurance: that the Lord's grace is sufficient and that the Lord's power is perfected in weakness (12:9). The sufficiency of God's grace is a basic conviction for Paul. Romans may state it most directly: As much as sin may abound, God's grace abounds even more (Rom 5:20). It is a part of the grand contention that ultimately eventuates in God's victory, that grace, not sin, that righteousness, not death, will have the last word (Rom 5:21). Recycling the story of the exodus from Egypt in his earlier writing to the Corinthians, Paul made the same point about God's grace without using the term: Nothing, no matter how severe, can happen for which God does not also provide a way out, a new exodus (1 Cor 10:13). No simpler formulation of the good news is possible: God's grace is sufficient. Period.

God's power and human weakness also have a strong association in Paul's thought. Already in an earlier letter to the Corinthians, Paul took the related antinomy of wisdom and folly and allied it with power/weakness (1 Cor 1:26-30; 4:10). Indeed, human redemption is available only through God's grace and power; humans, weak and helpless because of sin, are unable to extricate themselves from sin's power without divine help (Rom 5:6; 8:26). More immediately, in 2 Corinthians 10–13 Paul has been focused on his own weakness as an avenue of God's power, and now in 12:8-10 that thought reaches its apex.

The notion of God's power being perfected or brought to its fullness ($\tau\epsilon\lambda\acute{\epsilon}\omega$ *teleō*) in weakness is also a fundamental Pauline conviction, though nowhere else said so poignantly or forcefully. Faith's beginning is precisely an exercise of God's power in weakness (Rom 5:6); what people cannot achieve is given to them freely as a gift—in other words, as grace. The gospel is defined as "God's power" to those who believe (Rom 1:16; cf. 1 Cor 1:18). Without using the term "weakness," Paul's depiction of human beings as earthenware vessels into which God has poured such treasure is "in order to show that the overwhelm-

---

236. For Paul, faith and sin are mutually exclusive (Rom 14:23). One cannot serve two masters, the Lord and sin (Rom 6:1-14; 1 Cor 6:20; 7:23). Even Romans 7, which used to be regularly interpreted along the lines of faith and sin mixed into Paul's life, despite the evidence to the contrary in Romans, has in modern times been powerfully argued not to be autobiographical, but exemplary. P. W. Meyer, "The Worm at the Core of the Apple," in *The Conversation Continues: Studies in Paul and John in Honor of J. Louis Martyn*, ed. R. T. Fortna and B. R. Gaventa (Nashville: Abingdon, 1990) 64-65. On the specific rhetoric of Romans 7, see S. K. Stowers, "Romans 7.7-25 as a Speech-in-Character ($\pi\rho\sigma\sigma\omega\pi\sigma\pi\sigma\iota\acute{\alpha}$)," in *Paul in His Hellenistic Context*, ed. T. Engberg-Pedersen (Minneapolis: Fortress, 1995) 180-202.

ing power is from God and not from us" (2 Cor 4:7).

The paradoxical (God's) power through (human) weakness frees, even compels, Paul to boast of his weaknesses. Now, to boast of his weakness gives the glory to God, whose power after all is the only and effective power in his life—indeed, in the world. Paul focuses on "the power of *Christ*" (12:9), probably because it is Christ, in Paul's gospel, who suffers the ultimate helplessness in his crucifixion and is himself the hallmark of God's power, effective in his being raised from the dead. The Greek phrase ἡ δύναμις τοῦ Χριστοῦ (*hē dynamis tou Christou*, "the power of Christ") probably refers to power that comes from Christ, that is granted by and through Christ. In wishing, therefore, for the power of Christ to "take up residence" in him, Paul in effect prays that he may be a locus of God's power being perfected in weakness. The notion of "taking up residence" (ἐπισκηνόω *episkēnoō*, 12:9) has a slight echo back to the passage where Paul was describing

human nature as like an "earthly tent" (οἰκία τοῦ σκήνους *oikia tou skēnous*, 5:1); now he wants the "power of Christ" to tent itself upon him.

In two beautifully crafted statements (12:10), Paul brings his fool's speech to a conclusion (διό *dio*, "therefore"). The first suspends a mini-hardship list between the opening verb (εὐδοκέω *eudokeō*, "I delight in/approve of") and the concluding phrase "for the sake of Christ," in last place for dramatic emphasis. The mini-list leads, of course, with weakness, the featured topic at hand, and moves in an ever more severe gradation through insults (a reference to claims against him), to hardships, to the Pauline combination of persecutions and calamities (cf. Rom 8:35)—all "for the sake of Christ," affirming Paul's solidarity with and focus upon Christ as the model of the life of faith (12:10). The second statement is the most sweeping: "For whenever I am weak, then strong I am" (this translation honors Paul's ending with the emphatic εἰμι [*eimi*, "I am"], 12:10).

REFLECTIONS

1. Christians, following Paul, have chosen the cross as the central symbol of faith because it, better than any other, seizes upon the proclamation that the power, indeed, resides with God. The story did not end with the death of Jesus, but the cross stands empty by God's power, by God's grace, by God's goodwill toward all humankind. Christ, as the perfect representation of true power, the power of God, embodies a certain ambiguity about life. On the one hand, he is crucified in weakness, subject as we are to the power of oppression and death. If the story ended there we would be most pitiable (1 Cor 15:19) and there would be no basis for hope. As the resurrected one, on the other hand, Christ becomes the epitome of power, because God, the all-powerful one, raised him from the dead and promises the same to us.

2. Believers cannot expect to be like Paul in every respect; he really was extraordinary—and that not just in his own time. The grandeur of his religious life, with its spectacular visions and numerous revelations, need not be the litmus test of our own faith. We are more likely to identify with Paul in his weakness, but if we see in that weakness, as he did, the way for God's power to be vigorously at work, then we, like Paul, can be God's agents.

3. We should reflect about what "boasting of weakness" does not mean. It should not become, as it easily could, an occasion for a cop-out, for doing very little or even nothing. In the same fashion, it could become a justification of the status quo, for not making an effort to change things, because we are so weak.

4. Paul's fool's speech, with its highs and its lows, might serve as a help in our daily perspective keeping. When we weigh out our life at the end of each day, we might use Paul's roller-coaster fool's speech as a framework for thinking that allows us to acknowledge our accomplishments without getting carried away and thinking too highly of ourselves and to admit our failures, insults, and difficulties without losing perspective and falling into despair.

2 CORINTHIANS 12:11-13, APOSTOLIC COMMENDATION AND CONFIRMATION

NIV	NRSV
[11]I have made a fool of myself, but you drove me to it. I ought to have been commended by you, for I am not in the least inferior to the "super-apostles," even though I am nothing. [12]The things that mark an apostle—signs, wonders and miracles—were done among you with great perseverance. [13]How were you inferior to the other churches, except that I was never a burden to you? Forgive me this wrong!	[11]I have been a fool! You forced me to it. Indeed you should have been the ones commending me, for I am not at all inferior to these super-apostles, even though I am nothing. [12]The signs of a true apostle were performed among you with utmost patience, signs and wonders and mighty works. [13]How have you been worse off than the other churches, except that I myself did not burden you? Forgive me this wrong!

COMMENTARY

Paul admits to being the fool, but places the responsibility for that on the Corinthians, who should have been commending him, an echo of 3:1-3. He knows—and believes they should realize also, if they merely "looked at what is before their eyes" (2 Cor 10:7)—that he is not inferior to these superlative apostles, "even if nothing I am" (12:11), playing *ad absurdum* off of his "then powerful I am," which closed the fool's speech in 12:10. Even if he is *nothing,* he is not inferior to them. He offers evidence that provides a window on what he thought were the credentials of apostles: All the distinguishing marks of an apostle have been produced among the Corinthians—and that with "all patience."

The three terms in Paul's list all interpret one reality: the working of wondrous deeds. The first two, "signs" (σημεῖον *sēmeion,* "sign," "distinguishing mark") and "wonders" (τέρας *teras,* "prodigy/portent/omen"), are often, as here, linked together in Scripture (Matt 24:24; John 4:48; Acts 2:22; Heb 2:4). The third, "mighty works" (δύναμις *dynamis*), is a common term used to describe miracles or other demonstrations of power (Mark 6:5; Acts 2:22). Paul as wonderworker is a figure not depicted in his letters, but the way he writes about himself in 12:12 leaves no doubt that he expects the Corinthians to know him in this way. Perhaps 1 Cor 2:4 alludes to such performance.

As Paul surveys his completed work for the gospel when he writes to the Romans, he offers a self-portrait that confirms the 2 Cor 12:12 picture. The parallels are striking. In Rom 15:18, Paul declines to boast except in the work that God or Christ has done through him. Christ worked through Paul "by word and deed, by the power of signs and wonders, by the power of the Spirit of God" (Rom 15:18-19 NRSV).

It is worth pondering why we do not see Paul the worker of mighty deeds in his letters. Several reasons probably account for it. Foremost is that in Paul's letters we have his wrestling with particular problems or issues that have arisen in his absence, and in every case except Romans his readers know the kinds of works he has done; so repetition of them would be pointless or perhaps even self-serving. Acts is a good comparison; it was written by someone else and depicts Paul as an apostle doing mighty works and preaching. In Acts we have no clue that Paul ever wrote a letter;

in the letters we have no depiction of Paul as a miracle worker.

The evidence is before the Corinthians both in Paul's history with them and in his representation of it in the declaration of 12:12. The Corinthians have in no way been deprived, Paul claims, by his ministry among them. In a loaded question that probably touches on sensitive matters between Paul and the Corinthians, he asks: "In what way have you been treated less well than the other churches, except that *I myself* did not burden you?" (12:13, italics added).

Once again, the persistent problem of Paul's refusal of Corinthian support is manifest. Already in this letter fragment, the issue has surfaced in 11:7-12 and again in 11:20; it will continue to be a controversy through much of the remaining verses of 12:14-18. Paul's refusal to accept support from the Corinthians for his work among them has gone from being a positive badge of honor, as it was in his early days with them, to a sign of his treating them as second-class citizens among all the churches ("How have you been treated less well?"). Paul's opponents have probably seized on this issue as a powerful critique of him and have found a sensitive hearing for it at Corinth. The argument by Paul's intruding opponents probably went something like this:

As Paul knows and earlier even wrote to you, apostles, like soldiers and even shepherds (1 Cor 9:4-7), have the right to support for their work in behalf of the gospel. They should put their time and energies into the gospel and its proclamation; besides, it is beneath them to work in self-support (as Paul so stubbornly does). If Paul is truly an apostle, he should gladly welcome your offers of support; he clearly does from the Macedonians. Paul's refusal of support by you Corinthians shows that he does not honor you. In fact, it is worse than that: His rejection of your efforts to help him is a shameful slap in your faces; it is, as everybody knows, an act of enmity, not of friendship. We, on the other hand. . . .

Paul's response, in a nutshell, is that the Corinthians have not been deprived of any of the signs and wonders that apostles do and that they have not missed out on anything with Paul, except that he doggedly insists on continuing not to accept support from them. The tone of this letter fragment suggests that Paul has gotten himself into deep water, in part because of this practice, and his determined perdurance in it does not bode well for the future of a very troubled relationship. But persist he does. In fact, he resorts to burning irony and escalated rhetoric about his not having been willing to "burden" them: "Forgive me this injustice!" (12:13).

REFLECTIONS

1. One ought to weigh the wisdom of stubborn persistence in an action that is clearly offensive to others, even when the act may be defended on the highest moral grounds. Input from others is an important consideration in our moral reflection. When we receive signals from others that our actions are not appreciated, it is an occasion for us to review those actions. Is continuing that action worth the concern, distress, or even pain caused to others? Ordinarily, not. The given action must be very important in order to justify its continuance. At some point, however, one may have to decide what is right and proper, not guided solely by what others think, and take a stand for what is deemed crucial. The two extremes outlined here are the moral range within which we often find ourselves: faithfulness to our own consciences and genuine respect for others.

2. Though Paul clearly made the decision to boast, he places responsibility for his boasting on the Corinthians. All of us have been let down by our friends sometimes. When we thought they should have come through for us, they did not. How to deal with that disappointment can be a problem. Should it be mentioned? Only if it can be done in a loving, nonjudgmental way. Should we simply ignore it? Only if we can let it forever be a bygone; if it will haunt us, then it probably is better to bring it up for discussion, but only if we can do it in a constructive way.

2 CORINTHIANS 12:14-18, PAUL'S FINAL SELF-DEFENSE

NIV

14Now I am ready to visit you for the third time, and I will not be a burden to you, because what I want is not your possessions but you. After all, children should not have to save up for their parents, but parents for their children. 15So I will very gladly spend for you everything I have and expend myself as well. If I love you more, will you love me less? 16Be that as it may, I have not been a burden to you. Yet, crafty fellow that I am, I caught you by trickery! 17Did I exploit you through any of the men I sent you? 18I urged Titus to go to you and I sent our brother with him. Titus did not exploit you, did he? Did we not act in the same spirit and follow the same course?

NRSV

14Here I am, ready to come to you this third time. And I will not be a burden, because I do not want what is yours but you; for children ought not to lay up for their parents, but parents for their children. 15I will most gladly spend and be spent for you. If I love you more, am I to be loved less? 16Let it be assumed that I did not burden you. Nevertheless (you say) since I was crafty, I took you in by deceit. 17Did I take advantage of you through any of those whom I sent to you? 18I urged Titus to go, and sent the brother with him. Titus did not take advantage of you, did he? Did we not conduct ourselves with the same spirit? Did we not take the same steps?

COMMENTARY

Stung by Corinthian disaffection, Paul projects a third visit to Corinth and alerts them that when he gets there he will not be moved on the matter of self-support. He will do then as he has always done ("I shall not burden you," 12:14); Paul's consistency has been a subtle theme of this letter fragment (cf. 2 Cor 10:11; 11:6c, 12; 12:12). Availing himself, and indirectly reminding them, of his paternal relationship to them, Paul resorts to a commonplace of that world: Parents should not take their offsprings' possessions but should store up treasures for their children; that is the way it is supposed to be, and that is all Paul is trying to do.[237]

Three poignant claims gain expression in this paragraph. Paul does not want their goods; he wants the Corinthians: "For I don't seek your things but *you*" (12:14, emphasis added to honor the rhetorical force of last position in the Greek).[238] Then, using the terminology of commerce and transferring it over into the realm of friendship, he emphatically affirms, "But I myself

would gladly spend [δαπανάω *dapanaō*] and be spent [ἐκδαπάνομαικ *dapanaomai*] for the good of your souls" (12:15). The second verb intensifies the first and extends it to the very giving of oneself in sacrifice for another, a dramatic and not unfamiliar notion in Paul's thinking about love (cf. Rom 9:3; 1 Cor 13:3; Phil 2:17).

Paul presents himself as baffled. How can it be that, when he loves them more, they might love him less (12:15)? Already in 2 Cor 6:11-13 and 7:2 Paul has noted with some sadness the asymmetry of his affection for them, which excels over theirs for him. That problem continues in chaps. 10–13.

Paul pursues the argument about his "burdening" them because he has been accused not only of treating them as second-class citizens (12:13), but also of craftily wheedling money out of them—of feathering his own nest—under the ruse of the collection for the saints in Jerusalem (cf. chaps. 8–9). In effect, Paul is charged with being duplicitous and craftily deceptive.

Paul's defense is a rehearsal of his recent history with the Corinthians and focuses on whether he or any representative of him has "taken advantage" (πλεονεκτέω *pleonekteō*, also

---

237. O. L. Yarbrough, "Parents and Children in the Letters of Paul," in *The Social World of Formative Christianity and Judaism,* ed. J. Neusner, P. Borgen, E. S. Frerichs, R. Horsley (Philadelphia: Fortress, 1988) 131, 136-38.
238. See Demetrius *On Style* 5.249.

"defraud/cheat/outwit," 12:17-18) of the Corinthians. Already in an earlier statement of affection, Paul declared that he has not taken advantage of anyone (7:2). By the time of chaps. 10–13, his claim of not having defrauded the Corinthians is not readily granted, so he extends the defense to include his emissary Titus, a person whom the Corinthians continue to love and respect. Paul rehearses his having sent Titus and the unnamed "brother" to pursue the finishing of the collection (8:16-23); Paul chose and sent just such persons of sound character and standing so that there would be no confusion about his handling of the collection.

In a series of three rhetorical questions, each of which is structured in the Greek to lead the hearers toward the answer Paul thinks they must necessarily grant, he grills the Corinthians regarding their specious suspicions that he has defrauded them in the collection. The last two questions adopt Paul's preferred image for living the life of faith—namely, walking—and affirm, via questions expecting yes answers, that he and Titus walked "in the same spirit" and "in the same footsteps" (12:18; cf. Rom 13:13; 14:15; Gal 5:16; Phil 3:17). Paul bargains from their appreciation of Titus and claims that there is not a hair's breadth of difference between Titus and himself; accordingly, the implication is that the Corinthians should be just as ready to embrace Paul.

REFLECTIONS

1. Paul makes an important distinction between possessions and having the love and affection—indeed, the very self—of another. For him, compared with personal relationships, possessions are distinctly secondary. How many families get lost in this one? Family feuds sometimes begin over the slightest amount of money or over some thing. Once under way such squabbles take on a life of their own that is totally disproportionate to the thing or money in question. In that context, we have lost the truth that relationships between people are paramount. Lamentably, money and possessions often are the cement in relationships, as wills and their being contested often painfully demonstrate.

2. It is painful to love more and be loved less. Ideally, the love you express would be met in equal return, but, as Paul knew with the Corinthians, life does not always work that way. An important issue is how you respond when the love you feel you give is not reciprocated in measure. Do you (always, sometimes, never) withdraw or cut back your loving commensurately? Realism would suggest that you surely must alter your expectations, though you may continue to show love without a price tag attached. To be sure, when your loving efforts are met with physical or emotional abuse, proper self-love requires extrication of yourself from the situation.

2 CORINTHIANS 12:19-21, PRELIMINARY ASSESSMENT AND DIFFERING EXPECTATIONS

NIV	NRSV
[19]Have you been thinking all along that we have been defending ourselves to you? We have been speaking in the sight of God as those in Christ; and everything we do, dear friends, is for your strengthening. [20]For I am afraid that when I come I may not find you as I want you to be,	19Have you been thinking all along that we have been defending ourselves before you? We are speaking in Christ before God. Everything we do, beloved, is for the sake of building you up. [20]For I fear that when I come, I may find you not as I wish, and that you may find me not as you

NIV

and you may not find me as you want me to be. I fear that there may be quarreling, jealousy, outbursts of anger, factions, slander, gossip, arrogance and disorder. ²¹I am afraid that when I come again my God will humble me before you, and I will be grieved over many who have sinned earlier and have not repented of the impurity, sexual sin and debauchery in which they have indulged.

NRSV

wish; I fear that there may perhaps be quarreling, jealousy, anger, selfishness, slander, gossip, conceit, and disorder. ²¹I fear that when I come again, my God may humble me before you, and that I may have to mourn over many who previously sinned and have not repented of the impurity, sexual immorality, and licentiousness that they have practiced.

COMMENTARY

12:19. Paul is now focused on his impending visit with the Corinthians, and he thinks back over not only this letter, but also his long-term relationship with them. As to this letter, Paul once again addresses his posture in writing this time. He imagines them considering this letter that he now is writing, and he wonders if they will take his letter simply as a self-defense, as if the *big* issue might be what they think of what he has done in this letter, for better or for worse. With apodeictic confidence, Paul describes his speaking that constitutes this letter on two levels: (1) He implies that what he has written is not tailored to fit the audience and does not take its cues from them, but (2) what he speaks, he declares "before God, in Christ" (12:19). Succinctly, Paul affirms that his speaking (and surely his writing because his letters are simply written speech) takes its cues from God and is spoken from Paul's secure standing in Christ (cf. the identical formulation in 2:17 and the Commentary there).

With the only explicitly expressed affection in the entire letter fragment, Paul addresses the Corinthians as "beloved" and declares sweepingly that all he has said and done (significantly there is no verb in the sentence, so the hearers are left to supply verbs as we have done here, taking the clue from τὰ δὲ πάντα [*ta de panta*, "everything"]) is for their "building up" (12:19). Remember that this letter fragment is framed by Paul's affirmation of his authority from the Lord to "build up, not destroy" the Corinthians (10:8; 13:10; cf. 10:4). Paul claims that he is using that authority for its intended purpose: for the edification of the

Corinthians—and he has always worked toward that goal, "in everything" (12:19).

12:20-21. This section of the letter closes with Paul's imagining his estimate of the Corinthians and their assessment of him when he and they are finally together again in the impending visit. In an ABA'B'A pattern, Paul expresses a series of fears: (A) that when he comes to them, he will find them not as he wishes; (B) that he will be found by them to be what they do not wish; (A') that a vice list will characterize them; (B') that, on his coming, "my God may humiliate me before you"; and (A) that "I may have to mourn over many" who sinned and have not repented.

In these fears, Paul recognizes that his projected appearance in Corinth will not necessarily terminate his problems with the Corinthians. Relations between him and the Corinthians have come to sorry straits. He may well recall that one such earlier visit ended in failure (2:1; 7:12) and may now wonder whether his projected visit will be any better. He has good reason to be concerned also whether the Corinthians will now finally have got over their long-standing tendencies toward quarreling, jealousy, selfishness, and disorder, to mention just a few of the vices listed in 12:20. The Corinthians have been quarrelsome and disputatious since the second letter Paul wrote them (1 Cor 1:10-12; 3:1-3; 4:6; 14:23-25, 40). And πορνεία (*porneia*, "immorality"), with its related challenge of impurity (12:21), has been a problem for them since the very first letter Paul wrote to them (1 Cor 5:9-11). With his vice list, Paul dares to dig up old bones of contention with them and seems to suggest that his much-vaunted consistency in working for their edification is matched, admittedly in reverse, by their consistent tendency to stray into the vices about which he has warned them vigorously many times (1 Cor 5:9-11; 6:9-10).

Vice lists were a commonplace in Jewish and Roman circles in Paul's time, and he employs them freely and often in his letters as part of his basic moral instruction (Rom 1:29-31; 1 Cor 5:10-11; 6:9-10; Gal 5:19-21). Vice lists function for Paul to describe behavior that is beyond the pale, that believers simply cannot do. He uses them like a fence around the life of faith and treats vices as actions that must be avoided.[239] The lists vary and seem somewhat tailored to each special situation to which they are addressed. So here the first part of the list (12:20) reflects the fractiousness that Paul believes characterizes the Corinthians. Incidentally, Clement, the second-century bishop of Rome, agreed, saying in effect that Paul really got them right when he noted they were contentious and resistant to authority.[240]

The second part of the vice list (12:21) is a less certain window onto what is happening at Corinth at the time of Paul's writing 2 Corinthians 10–13. Paul's dramatics, depicting himself as needing to go into mourning over the Corinthians, suggests that he is reaching a bit, as do his challenge to their purity and his accusations of *porneia* and debauchery. These latter dredge up long-standing complaints of Paul against the Corinthians and are a way for him once again to assert his authority as the one responsible for the purity of the bride that he as father has betrothed to Christ (11:2). Just how descriptive these images are to the situation at the time of this writing only the original hearers could assess.

Paul cashes in a cultural chip of considerable prevalence and power when he tells the Corinthians that their wandering into the nonviable territory of vice may expose him to shame. The Mediterranean culture of Paul's time was governed by the central dyad of shame and honor.[241] One always did whatever one could to enhance the latter and minimize the former. Although Paul recognized that ultimately praise and honor come only from God (Rom 2:29; 1 Cor 4:5), he also clearly realized that commendation and honor were a normal and proper part of the life of faith (6:8). The Corinthians should have commended Paul (3:1-3); the brother praised by the churches is sent along with the collection to assure the donors that their gifts are being handled properly (8:18); Paul assumes that there are people and things worthy of praise (Phil 4:8).

Paul's projected peril of Corinthian-induced shame and its associated mourning must also be understood in the context of Paul's end-time judgment convictions. As noted in 5:5 (see the Commentary), Paul thinks that all believers, himself included, must appear before the tribunal of Christ or God (cf. Rom 14:10) and give accounting for their lives. Paul expects to be held accountable at the last judgment for the way he has lived his call to be apostle to the Gentiles. Those churches that respond well and live appropriately to the gospel are Paul's "joy and crown" (Phil 4:1; 1 Thess 2:19).

239. J. Paul Sampley, "Faith and Its Moral Life: A Study of Individuation in the Thought World of the Apostle Paul," in *Faith and History: Essays in Honor of P. W. Meyer,* ed. J. T. Carroll, C. H. Cosgrove, E. E. Johnson (Atlanta: Scholars Press, 1990) 230-31.

240. See *1 Clem* 47.3.

241. A. J. Dewey, "A Matter of Honor: a Social-historical Analysis of 2 Corinthians 10," *HTR* 78 (1985) 210-16, sets up the cultural force of honor as a context for understanding Paul's argument.

REFLECTIONS

1. Paul assumes that we do assess one another, that friendship involves an occasional reckoning. The dissonance of finding a friend not as we wish can become a crisis in the relationship. How does one deal with the difference between the reality and what one yearns for in the other person? In courtship and marriage, psychologists suggest, we should love the other person for who he or she is, not for what we imagine that person can become. People, and therefore their relationships, do change, and sometimes at different paces; so the matter is of continuing importance in all relationships.

2. Paul pictures himself as always working for the Corinthians' edification. In Paul's categories, therefore, he thinks of himself as consistently loving them. Being consistently loving toward others is an awesome performance measure. While most of us may think Paul's level of performance is beyond us, his example could inspire us to aim higher.

2 CORINTHIANS 13:1-10, GROUND RULES AND CHALLENGE

NIV

13 This will be my third visit to you. "Every matter must be established by the testimony of two or three witnesses."[a] [2]I already gave you a warning when I was with you the second time. I now repeat it while absent: On my return I will not spare those who sinned earlier or any of the others, [3]since you are demanding proof that Christ is speaking through me. He is not weak in dealing with you, but is powerful among you. [4]For to be sure, he was crucified in weakness, yet he lives by God's power. Likewise, we are weak in him, yet by God's power we will live with him to serve you.

[5]Examine yourselves to see whether you are in the faith; test yourselves. Do you not realize that Christ Jesus is in you—unless, of course, you fail the test? [6]And I trust that you will discover that we have not failed the test. [7]Now we pray to God that you will not do anything wrong. Not that people will see that we have stood the test but that you will do what is right even though we may seem to have failed. [8]For we cannot do anything against the truth, but only for the truth. [9]We are glad whenever we are weak but you are strong; and our prayer is for your perfection. [10]This is why I write these things when I am absent, that when I come I may not have to be harsh in my use of authority—the authority the Lord gave me for building you up, not for tearing you down.

[a]1 Deut. 19:15

NRSV

13 This is the third time I am coming to you. "Any charge must be sustained by the evidence of two or three witnesses." [2]I warned those who sinned previously and all the others, and I warn them now while absent, as I did when present on my second visit, that if I come again, I will not be lenient— [3]since you desire proof that Christ is speaking in me. He is not weak in dealing with you, but is powerful in you. [4]For he was crucified in weakness, but lives by the power of God. For we are weak in him,[a] but in dealing with you we will live with him by the power of God.

[5]Examine yourselves to see whether you are living in the faith. Test yourselves. Do you not realize that Jesus Christ is in you?—unless, indeed, you fail to meet the test! [6]I hope you will find out that we have not failed. [7]But we pray to God that you may not do anything wrong—not that we may appear to have met the test, but that you may do what is right, though we may seem to have failed. [8]For we cannot do anything against the truth, but only for the truth. [9]For we rejoice when we are weak and you are strong. This is what we pray for, that you may become perfect. [10]So I write these things while I am away from you, so that when I come, I may not have to be severe in using the authority that the Lord has given me for building up and not for tearing down.

[a]Other ancient authorities read *with him*

COMMENTARY

13:1. Echoing 12:14, Paul announces once again his impending third visit. Paul's trips to Corinth can be logged as follows: When he wrote 1 Corinthians, from Ephesus (1 Cor 16:8), he projected a visit to Corinth (1 Cor 4:18-21; 11:34; 16:3-9); in 2 Cor 2:1-3 he mentions his second visit to them and describes it as a "painful" one where, as we have seen, he was wronged by a certain unnamed Corinthian and the rest of the believers did not come to his aid; he planned another visit to them but did not go and wrote them a letter instead (2 Cor 1:17, 23; 2:1); he plans a visit to Corinth with those Macedonians who have gathered their contribution to the collection for the saints in Jerusalem (2 Cor 9:1-5) but does not get to go before turmoil prompts his writing of 2 Corinthians 10–13. Now, finally, he plans his third visit to them.

He knows that his relationship with the Corinthians is at an all-time low and anticipates that the impending visit will be fraught with controversy and confrontation. Accordingly, he details ground rules for the way he expects them to resolve their disputes—they with him and he with them—when he arrives. Not surprisingly, he resorts to tried-and-true practices predicated on Israel's Scriptures: Two or three witnesses must corroborate any charge (Deut 19:15; cf. Matt 18:16; 1 Tim 5:19). Through the practice of multiple attestation to a charge, Paul reduces the chances of a recurrence of any single individual's wronging him (2 Cor 2:5-11; 7:12).

13:2. By careful choice of tough-sounding words, Paul labors to depict his imminent arrival in Corinth as worthy of dread. Perhaps he needs to counter the image that some at Corinth have fostered of him as a relative wimp in personal presence (10:10). First, he doubles strong verbs: "I said beforehand in warning and I tell before it happens" (προείρηκα καὶ προλέγω *proeirēka kai prolegō*). Second, he paints a picture of consistency by reminding them that when he was with them in his second visit, he told them that if he ever paid them another visit he would not "spare" (φείσομαι *pheisomai*) any of them. Third, he specifies those whom he is prepared to withstand: They are the ones who have sinned previously (an echo of 12:21), including, no doubt, the one who did the previous wrong (2:5; 7:12), but extending in the most sweeping fashion: "and all the others," whoever they may be.

Now we are in a position to understand why Paul introduced a vice list and wrote about people sinning in 12:20-21. He has taken the stringent step of identifying those who might oppose him as persons who by their opposition demonstrate

that they no longer belong to the (true, understood) community of believers (cf. 4:3-4). Their rejection of Paul is tantamount to their crossing the forbidden border into vice-list territory, into a status of sin. That is heavy language. Paul effectively ties any current opposition to the "ones who sinned before," to those whom the community has since reproved and reinstated (2:5-11). His rhetoric is designed to disadvantage those at Corinth who would deign to mount opposition to him when he arrives.

13:3. Understandably, he expects challengers because he already has word that some Corinthians "seek a demonstration [δοκιμη *dokimē*, "test/ordeal/proof"] that Christ is speaking" in him. Paul is up against some clever people who in this charge have taken what they know is a fundamental Pauline concept and turned it against him. Paul believes and has taught the Corinthians that self-testing and self-assessment are part of the discipline of the life of faith.[242] The primary and repeated locus of that self-testing is in the Lord's supper (1 Cor 11:27-32) but is in no way restricted to that occasion. The same *dokim*-root term shows up in Paul's descriptions of persons who have demonstrated character through trials and the vagaries of life (1 Cor 16:3; 2 Cor 8:8, 22) and in his wanting to know the character of the Corinthians (2 Cor 2:9; 9:13). Now they turn it against him and challenge whether there is any proof (*dokimē*) that Christ is speaking in him. He turns the notion of self-testing back on them, beginning in 13:5, and uses forms of the term *dokim* five times in three verses (13:5-7).

The very notion of Christ's being in a person is foundational for Paul; it is unthinkable that a believer would not have Christ resident (Rom 8:10; Gal 2:20; cf. Col 1:27). No wonder Paul has evoked boundary talk about sinners and vice lists (12:20-21; 13:2); he is responding in kind to their questioning of whether Christ is in him and speaking through him. Not only do some at Corinth question Paul's authority to speak, but they also express doubts about his standing in Christ.

Paul takes the question of his status in Christ and deftly attempts to move the controversy to *Christ's* power. Rather than defend himself, Paul

---

242. J. Paul Sampley, *Walking Between the Times: Paul's Moral Reasoning* (Minneapolis: Fortress, 1991) 50-51.

brings the already developed paradox of strength and weakness to bear on *Christ's* relationship to the Corinthians. What Paul packs into the next couple of verses is compressed and laconic. His premise is stated first: Whatever anyone may say about Christ in Paul, they cannot deny that Christ is powerful in and among themselves. They have experienced that power of Christ, no matter their judgment about Paul. Stated negatively and then positively for emphasis: "Christ is not weak to you but powerful in/among you" (13:3*b*).

13:4. Two crucial affirmations follow from the Corinthians' incontrovertible experience (note the two occurrences of γάρ [*gar*] that open and correlate v. 4*a* and v. 4*b*). First is a christological elaboration of the Pauline connection between weakness and power, with Christ's crucifixion on the one side and Christ's resurrection on the other. In 13:4*b* Paul identifies his own weakness with Christ's crucifixion, with which, in the Pauline tradition, *every* believer must identify. That allows Paul to elevate his own weakness, which some at Corinth seem determined to accentuate, by identifying it with Christ's crucifixion "in weakness." So, second, Paul is weak in Christ, granted, but that shared weakness unambiguously attests to Paul's own status in Christ and gives Paul the grounds to warn any opponents at Corinth that he, and those who stand with him, currently share proleptically in "*God's power,*" which has already been expressed authoritatively in Christ's resurrection. Paul announces himself ready to express that power authoritatively on his arrival in Corinth. Christ's resurrection thus becomes a warrant for Paul's authority (really for God's power expressed in Paul).

Paul's return to the plural in 13:4*b* serves him well because it portrays him as enjoying the collegiality of all those who have shared weakness in Christ's death and been adorned with God's power in the new life that has resulted (cf. Rom 6:4). From death to life, from weakness to power—those are the matrixes in which Paul's own special calling, authority, and power must be understood. With this christological and even theological identification, Paul attempts to convert a charge of weakness into a badge of honor.

13:5. From this position of reaffirmed authority, Paul turns the tables on the auditors. Those who would demand proof or a test of Paul are

called by him, through a powerful doubling of verbs with considerable semantic overlap, to "test" (πειράζω *peirazō*) and to "examine" (δοκιμάζω *dokimazō*) *themselves* (13:5*a*) whether they "are in the faith" (13:5*b*), whether Christ is indeed "in/among them" (13:5*c*, the very charge they had lodged against Paul in 13:3*a*). Clearly, the test Paul proposes employs boundary language, echoing again the same concerns that have come to dominate the letter fragment since 12:20. Paul could not resort to more basic criteria for identity: Are you still in the faith, and is Christ really in/among you?

Paul presses them with a question formed in the Greek to expect a positive answer, and no doubt evoking a curious irony because it employs a verb of recognition intensified with a prefixed preposition: "You are certain, aren't you, that Christ is in/among you?" (ἐπιγινώσκω *epiginōskō*). The intentionality of the irony is confirmed by his immediately providing an extreme alternative: "unless perhaps you are disqualified" (ἀδόκιμος *adokimos*, "not standing the test, worthless"). Once again, Paul takes their indictment of him, that they want proof (δοκιμή *dokimē*) that Christ is speaking in him (13:3), turns the notion against them by urging that they test or show proof (*dokimazō*) regarding themselves (13:5), and with yet one more turn insinuates that they may fail the test (the same root term [*adokimos*] but with the alpha-privative negating it).

To understand how the term *adokimos* functions in Paul's lexicon, consider his athletic self-portrait presented in 1 Cor 9:24-27, where he earlier wrote to the Corinthians that he—and they in emulation of him—must run in such a way as to win the prize and *so as not to be* disqualified (*adokimos*). In 2 Cor 13:5 he uses the same term to suggest that those Corinthians who would test him may themselves ironically "fail the test" or "be disqualified" from the life of faith, which, as is apparent throughout 2 Corinthians 10–13, Paul considers as analogous with a contest or a battle (cf. 10:3-6).

13:6. In keeping with his recognition (12:20) that his arrival in Corinth will occasion his assessment of them ("I fear . . . I may find you not as I wish") and their assessment of him ("you may find me not as you wish"), Paul now turns to *their* assessment of *him*: "And I hope that you know that we ourselves are not disqualified" (*adokimos*).

13:7-8. Lest the Corinthians think that he is out to win them over at any cost, Paul openly reflects about their and his final destinies. Ultimately Paul hopes that the Corinthians will do "the good" (τὸ καλόν *to kalon*) rather than "anything bad" (κακόν *kakon*, 13:7), because without restating it (see 5:10; cf. Rom 2:6-10), Paul confidently expects and has taught the Corinthians that God repays people according to what they have done in the body. So if the Corinthians do "the good/right," Paul knows their outcome with God will also be good. If he could secure their doing the right, then he could imagine and even countenance his being found "disqualified" (*adokimos*, 13:7; cf. 12:15).

Without the explicit terminology here, Paul thinks sacrificially and presents himself as being prepared to give himself up for their well-being, a notion found between Paul and other groups of persons as well (cf. Rom 9:3; 1 Cor 13:3; Phil 2:17), a profound Pauline affirmation of continuing friendship with the Corinthians. Paul depicts himself as weighing their prosperity ahead of his own; for them to meet the test is more important than for him to do so. Paul's prayer is *for them*, not that he may have some Pyhrric victory of appearing to be qualified, to have passed the test and yet find them lost (13:7). Just as he earlier said that he could not take advantage of the Corinthians (11:20-21), so now he declares that he cannot push matters to his own benefit because, as he puts it, he and those associated with him, can do "nothing against the truth but [only] in behalf of the truth" (13:8). Resorting once again to his identification with weakness over against

strength, Paul joyfully embraces weakness if it means that the Corinthians can be strong (and therefore not fall away from the faith; 13:9).

13:9. Paul concludes this section with another prayer, this one so succinct as to be the more powerful, for their κατάρτισις (*katartisis*, "being made complete/completion"), a term that appears again as his second appeal in his closing petitions (καταρτίζω *katartizō*, 13:11). What he prays (to God) for here he appeals (to the Corinthians) for in 13:11: their restoration to their former, proper condition, their being made complete, for them to mend their ways. Very simply put, Paul wishes and prays that the Corinthians would return to the way they used to be.

13:10. Paul is not spoiling for a fight. He closes by saying that he has written in this harsh frankness from a distance because he would prefer, when he does come to them, not to have to deal sharply (ἀποτόμως *apotomōs*) with them, though he readily reminds them of the Lord-given power he mentioned to them at the beginning of this letter fragment (10:8), an authority for building them up rather than destroying them. Edification is what love at work does; the Corinthians learned that from Paul long ago in his teaching (1 Cor 8:1) and in his comportment toward them. Paul calls them "beloved" and declares that "everything we do . . . is for the sake of building you up" (12:19). Edification and love are Paul's choices for the Corinthians, and his adherence to them is the ultimate sign of his honoring of his Lord-given authority. Destruction or tearing down (καθαίρεσις *kathairesis*), though mentioned, is the farthest thing from his wishes for the Corinthians.

REFLECTIONS

1. Self-sacrifice, the giving of oneself for another, is a deep-seated Christian notion. Love considers the other person and seeks the good for that person. When love for another causes self-harm, however, then love threatens to become self-hatred and, therefore, not the love that truly loves the neighbor *as oneself* (Rom 13:9; Gal 5:14). Discernment must be employed to realize when proper giving way to others drifts over the line and becomes improper treatment of oneself.

2. Differences of opinion, different notions of what ought to be done, and even disputes may be inevitable. It is not wrong in church or among friends to have differences of opinion and to find ways to adjudicate them. The critical issue becomes *how* you live with those with whom you differ, and *how* you adjudicate differences. Though arrogance and disregard for others may lead us to think otherwise, virtue and truth seldom reside on one side alone.

3. Calling on one another to make a self-test is important, even basic, to the life of faith because self-testing can become the occasion not only for repentance, for a change of one's ways, but also for improvement or growth. Worship services are a prime, regular time for such self-assessment, but nothing should prevent anyone from taking stock of oneself at any time. Believers have a responsibility to care for and about one another. The call for self-testing is not to be confused with sitting in judgment on someone else; that would be inappropriate poaching on God's turf. A good rule of thumb might be to require self-scrutiny before you ask someone else to examine his or her own life. It is always *self*testing that is to be done; the most you can do regarding another person is to request a self-test.

2 CORINTHIANS 13:11-13, CONCLUDING ADMONITIONS AND GRACE

COMMENTARY

Regularly, Paul closes his letters with pithy admonitions that very often give a real insight into his sense of what is most needed in the community. For example, 1 Corinthians closes with a string of admonitions, the last of which is, "Let everything you do be done in love" (1 Cor 16:14). Nothing could have been more apt there.

In 2 Corinthians 13, Paul concludes with a series of very pointed exhortations addressed to the Corinthians as "brothers and sisters" (ἀδελφοι *adelphoi*). The first, χαίρετε (*chairete*), could be translated "rejoice," but as a closing greeting such as this, it can readily be translated "farewell" (NRSV) or "good-bye" (NIV). Beyond that first

greeting, we find a series of trenchant commands. Heading the list is the καταρτίζεσθε (*katartizesthe*) that was mentioned in connection with the related notion in 13:9: "Restore things to the proper condition/order." Next, παρακαλεῖσθε (*parakaleisthe*): "Be comforted through a favorable change in the situation."[243] Τὸ αὐτὸ φρονεῖτε (*to auto phroneite*) is a phrase that functions, as here, in Paul's letters to urge unity or an end to dissension, or both (Phil 2:2; 4:2).[244]

243. *BAGD,* 623.
244. J. Paul Sampley, *Pauline Partnership in Christ: Christian Community and Commitment in Light of Roman Law* (Philadelphia: Fortress, 1980) 62-68; G. W. Peterman, *Paul's Gift from Philippi: Conventions of Gift-Exchange and Christian Giving* (Cambridge: Cambridge University Press, 1997) 131-32.

The last in the series, εἰρηνεύετε (*eirēneuete*), calls upon the Corinthians to "be at peace" and extends with a related promise: "and the God of love and peace will be with you" (13:11). God is regularly associated with peace and reconciliation in Paul's letters (peace: Rom 1:7 and par.; Rom 5:1; 15:33; 16:20; 1 Cor 7:15; 14:33; 2 Cor 1:2; Phil 4:7, 9; 1 Thess 5:23; reconciliation: Rom 5:10; 2 Cor 5:18-20). Paul's appeal for the Corinthians to be at peace with one another (and with Paul when he arrives on his projected visit?) is sanctioned by its identification with God as the one who champions love and peace.

The Corinthians can enact their being God's people of peace and love by greeting one another with a "holy kiss" (13:12a). This kiss is obviously a known social convention that Paul has inculcated as a practice in his churches (1 Thess 5:26; cf. Rom 16:16), and the Corinthians clearly know of it (1 Cor 16:20). Calling this kiss "holy" suggests that it is a social convention taken over from the larger culture and made acceptable for believers as an intimate greeting, one person of another.[245] Paul urges them to address one another with the "holy kiss" and from this we may suppose that he wants the love and peace to be affirmed first among the Corinthians, on the receipt of his letter, and ahead of his arrival there. We may suppose that, even though there are obviously critics of Paul among the believers, there are surely also persons still devoted to him. Thus it is possible to imagine that the troubles with Paul that we see reflected in 2 Corinthians 10–13 have riven the community of believers at Corinth once again. So Paul here urges the start of reconciliation that he may have faint hopes will prepare a better reception than he has heretofore had reason to expect.

Paul's letters generally feature greetings, from Paul and often from those with him, just in advance of the closing grace. Typically, Paul names some people or churches who join in the greeting (1 Cor 16:19; Phil 4:21; Phlm 23-24), but he also sometimes includes, as here, a sweeping reference to "all the saints" (1 Cor 16:20; Phil 4:22). The mention of "all the saints" as greeting the Corinthians bids to have a special meaning in 2 Corinthians 10–13, though, because Paul's frequent resort to the plural as a self-reference has surely been used to show that, despite opposition at Corinth, he has vast support from other Mediterranean-basin believers about whom the Corinthians surely know.

Grace opens and closes every undisputed Pauline letter, just as grace encompasses every moment of the life of faith for all believers. The life of faith is totally dependent from beginning to end on God's unmerited, freely bestowed gift. Sometimes Paul associates grace directly with God; other times, as here, he associates it with Christ. The letters typically close by affirming the grace of Christ—that is, grace from Christ, which is understood to be present for each believer who is addressed in the letter. The love of God is a reprise of that characteristic just sounded two verses before (13:11, 13). The κοινωνία (*koinonia*), "association," "communion," "fellowship," of the Holy Spirit is powerfully ambiguous here, and both aspects fit Paul's convictions very well. The term can refer to a close personal relationship of each auditor with the Holy Spirit; or it can refer to the fellowship *among* believers that is fostered by the Holy Spirit that produces, for example, all the spiritual gifts to enrich the common good of the community (1 Cor 12:7; cf. Gal 5:22). The two interpretations are not mutually exclusive. Given Paul's struggle with the Corinthians, it is easy to imagine that both aspects are possible but that the latter is surely important for Paul's rhetorical purposes. Paul often uses the term *koinōnia* to refer to the association of believers (cf. 1 Cor 1:9; Phil 1:5) that in other places is called the ἐκκλησία (*ekklēsia*), "church." The Spirit, by its joining with the human spirit, brings people into relation to God in Christ (Rom 8:16). What people came to call a trinitarian formulation is appropriate to Paul, who, though he clearly does not have a well-formulated trinitarianism, nevertheless uses references to all three—God, Christ, and Holy Spirit—to express the complex and rich divine engagement of people that Paul calls grace.

Paul's extension "be with all of you" once again affirms that all the Corinthians stand on the same ground and belong to one another because of God's love, the grace in and from Christ, and the fellowship generated by the Holy Spirit.

---

245. W. Klassen, "The Sacred Kiss in the New Testament: An Example of Social Boundary Lines," *NTS* 39 (1993) 130-33, reasonably claims it is "a public declaration of the affirmation of faith" expressed in Gal 3:28 (ibid., 135).

REFLECTIONS

It is worth pondering how those admonitions, although directed to cantankerous Corinthians, might bear on our lives today. For example, how can we "live in peace" when there is so much strife and suffering in the world today? Surely God's love and peace have always been depicted as being present even in the midst of violence. Consider the Matthean form of the birth and infancy accounts of Jesus (Matt 1:18–2:23), and notice how much violence permeates those stories; precisely in that context God's Son is born as the hope of the world. Surely, also, that is why the cross, that emblem of shame and violence, has become for us the sign of God's being "for us" (Rom 8:38-39).

THE LETTER TO THE GALATIANS

INTRODUCTION, COMMENTARY, AND REFLECTIONS

BY

RICHARD B. HAYS

THE LETTER TO THE
GALATIANS

INTRODUCTION

Paul's angry, passionate letter to the churches of Galatia provides a glimpse of the controversy that surrounded the expansion of the Christian movement into Gentile communities in the ancient Mediterranean world. The identity of the newly established mission churches was up for grabs: Were they to be understood as branches on the tree of Judaism, or were they to be understood as belonging to a new and distinctive community, neither Jewish nor pagan? Were Gentile converts bound to accept Jewish practices and values? In what ways were they free to maintain their former ways of life? By the middle of the first century CE the struggle over such questions had burst into open conflict. Paul visualizes the struggle for identity formation of the Galatian churches in a vivid image: As the apostle whose preaching had brought these communities into being, he is like a mother in the throes of labor until they are fully formed according to the image of Christ (Gal 4:19).

The Letter to the Galatians is important not only as a primary source document for reconstructing formative Christianity but also for its theological message. Paul responded to the Galatian crisis with a trenchant theological analysis of the issues at stake. This analysis, and the proclamation of the gospel that follows from it, have exercised a powerful influence on subsequent Christian theology and preaching. Both Augustine and Martin Luther, for example, took their bearings from Paul's message of radical grace, apart from works of the Law. Thus the Letter to the Galatians is the fountainhead for all subsequent Christian theological reflection about justification by faith, the cross, the power of the

Spirit, and the meaning of Christian freedom. The letter was preserved and cherished in the church because it offers a compelling model for how to think theologically about challenges faced in the community's life.

As we read this letter, we find that we have entered an argument already under way. Galatians is not a general theological treatise; it is an urgent pastoral letter written to a specific cluster of churches at a moment of crisis. Consequently, it is full of allusions to persons, events, and issues known well to the original readers and, therefore, not fully explained. To interpret the letter, then, we must do a certain amount of reconstructive guesswork about the circumstances Paul was addressing.

WHY DID PAUL WRITE THE LETTER?

Paul had founded the churches of Galatia during his missionary travels in Asia Minor, sometime after the Jerusalem meeting described in 2:1-10. Everything in this letter indicates that Paul's Galatian converts were formerly Gentile pagans (4:8-9). Paul came to them unexpectedly as a result of some sort of personal affliction (4:13-14) and preached to them the message of "Jesus Christ crucified" (3:1) as God's transformative deed to deliver humankind from "the present evil age" (1:4). The Galatians accepted the message joyfully (4:14-15), were baptized (3:26-28), and experienced dramatic manifestations of the Holy Spirit (3:2-5; 4:6). We do not know how long Paul spent in Galatia, but he left his fledgling churches there confident that they were "running well" (5:7).

At the time of the composition of the letter, however, Paul had received word that his apostolic work in Galatia was being undermined by Jewish-Christian missionaries who had arrived on the scene preaching "a different gospel" (1:6) and seeking to persuade the Gentile Galatians to be circumcised (5:2-4; 6:12-13). It is important to recognize that these missionaries were not non-Christian Jews trying to induce the Galatians to abandon their newfound Christian faith; rather, the conflict portrayed in Paul's letter is an *intra-Christian* dispute. The newly arrived missionaries in Galatia were arguing that Gentiles who had believed in Jesus should take the next step into full covenant membership by being circumcised. Apparently these Jewish-Christian preachers, telling the Galatians that Paul had failed to instruct them properly in God's Law, were finding a receptive audience among the Galatians (1:6; 3:1; 4:21; 5:4; 5:7), who were already adopting at least some aspects of Jewish Law observance (4:10-11). Outraged by this development, Paul fired off his letter to dissuade the Galatian churches from accepting this revision—Paul calls it a perversion (1:7)—of the gospel.

The identity of the rival missionaries is unknown. Paul does not identify them by name (this is perhaps a studied rhetorical tactic on his part), and we have no other sources of information about their activities or teachings. Thus we are forced to reconstruct their message from the evidence provided by Paul's polemical rebuttal. A few New Testament scholars have speculatively identified these Pauline opponents as Gnostics or as Gentile leaders indigenous to the Galatian churches, but such theories have not proved persuasive. The evidence indicates overwhelmingly that the rival missionaries were Jewish Christians, and all recent scholarly commentators have viewed them as such.

The term "Judaizers," once widely used to describe these missionaries, has recently fallen into disfavor for two reasons. First, it wrongly implies that the conflict in Galatia was between Jewish and anti-Jewish factions. In fact, Paul himself was a Jewish-Christian apostle, and the argument in this letter is between two different Jewish-Christian interpretations of the gospel. Second, the verb "to Judaize" ($\iota o \upsilon \delta \alpha \dot{\iota} \zeta \omega$ *ioudaizō*), which appears in 2:14, does not mean "to make someone else into a Jew"; rather, it means "to adopt Jewish practices." Thus the label "Judaizers" would aptly be applied to Gentiles who accepted the circumcision gospel, but it will not do to describe the rival missionaries themselves. Consequently, recent interpreters have sought other terms. The term "agitators," based on Paul's pejorative characterization of his opponents (1:7; 5:10, 12), has been widely adopted, but it, too, quickly skews our perception toward an unsympathetic interpretation of their motives. Certainly, they did not think of themselves as agitators, nor would they have defined themselves primarily as Paul's opponents. They saw themselves as preachers of the gospel and advocates of the Law. We will arrive at a deeper and more sympathetic reading of the situation if we choose a designation that does not prematurely dismiss them as troublemakers. J. Louis Martyn has dubbed them "the Teachers,"[1] and J. D. G. Dunn refers to them in his commentary as "missionaries."[2] The latter term seems most clearly to describe their activity, and it will be employed throughout this commentary (capitalized to indicate that Paul is referring to a specific group of adversaries).

The basic elements of the Missionaries' message are reasonably clear: They believed Jesus to be the Messiah of Israel and saw themselves as summoning Gentiles in the name of Jesus to come under obedience to the Law revealed to Moses at Mount Sinai. They probably regarded Jesus as the authoritative interpreter of the Law. (Throughout this commentary the word *Law* is capitalized whenever it refers to the Torah, the holy Law of Israel.) From the way that Paul constructs his counterargument against them (3:1–5:1), we may draw the following inferences with some confidence:

(1) The Missionaries preached the necessity of circumcision as a means of entering covenant relationship with the God of Israel.

(2) They called for observance of Jewish sabbaths and feast days (4:8-11) and presumably advocated obedience to everything written in the Law (3:10), promising that those who kept the commandments would find life (3:12).

(3) They taught that the Law of Moses was divinely ordained to provide moral order and restrain human fleshly impulses (5:16, 24).

---

1. J. L. Martyn, *Galatians,* AB 33A (New York: Doubleday, 1997) 117-26. Martyn's reconstruction of their teachings provides the basis for the description given below.

2. J. D. G. Dunn, *The Epistle to the Galatians,* Black's NT Commentary (Peabody, Mass.: Hendrickson, 1993) 11.

(4) They claimed to represent more faithfully than Paul the teachings of the "mother" church in Jerusalem.

(5) They based their message on Scripture, particularly on the story of Abraham and God's institution of the covenant of circumcision (Genesis 17). In accordance with Jewish tradition, they regarded Abraham as the father of proselytes, and they urged the Galatians to follow his example by being circumcised. We may infer that Deut 27:26 and Lev 18:5 also featured prominently in their preaching (see the Commentary on 3:10-14).

In short, they represented a form of traditional Jewish teaching that called for Law observance, and they sought, in the name of Jesus, to extend the good news about the Law of God to the Gentiles.

Why did Paul object so fiercely to this message? Why did he not view the Missionaries' preaching as a variant of the gospel that could be tolerated within a pluralistic early Christian movement?[3] The answer to this question must be provided through a careful reading of the letter, but we may summarize, by way of preview, some of the main lines of Paul's argument.

According to Paul's diagnosis, the Missionaries were preaching a false gospel despite their use of Christian language. We may identify four interlocking motifs in Paul's radical critique of their message.

(1) The Missionaries' emphasis on circumcision and Law observance as the *conditional* grounds for covenant membership negates the sufficiency of God's grace, which was shown through the death of Jesus for our sake (2:20-21). The cross, not the Law, is the basis of our relationship to God. In short, the Missionaries have a deficient christology.

(2) The Missionaries underestimate the power of the Spirit to animate and guide the life of the faithful community. Where God's Spirit has been poured out on the church, Paul claims, there is no more need for a written code of Law to direct and restrain the community. We need only to follow the life-giving Spirit to resist the desires of the flesh (5:16-26). In short, the Missionaries have a deficient pneumatology.

(3) The Missionaries deny "the truth of the gospel" (2:5, 14) by undermining the unity of Jews and Gentiles in Christ. The reconciling power of God is to be demonstrated not by forcing Gentiles to become Jews but by bringing circumcised and uncircumcised believers together at one common table. Thus the spread of the gospel requires a Law-free mission to the Gentiles. In short, the Missionaries have a deficient ecclesiology.

(4) The Missionaries act as though the death of God's Son on the cross had not changed the world irrevocably. They think that things can go on just as before, with the Law providing the fundamental structure for the identity of the people of God. But, in fact, the gospel is the revelation of God's apocalyptic action that has undone and transformed the world (6:14-15). In short, the Missionaries have a deficient eschatology.

Taken together, these four deficiencies constitute, in Paul's eyes, a fundamental betrayal of the gospel, a reversion to life under the Law before Christ came to set us free. That is

3. Cf. his appeal for tolerance of differences in Rom 14:1–15:13.

why Paul so vehemently seeks to persuade the Galatians to reject the overtures of the Missionaries.

THEOLOGICAL THEMES

As the constructive alternative to the Missionaries' message, Paul reproclaims his gospel of grace. The central themes of that gospel may be summarized briefly.

1. Human beings are "rectified" (set in right relation to God) not through obeying the Law but through the faithfulness of Jesus Christ (see the Commentary on 2:16), who gave himself for us (2:20). Using a different metaphor, Paul proclaims that we are adopted as God's children solely as a result of Christ's redemptive death (4:4-7), not because of anything we have done or could do. As these examples show, Paul uses various images to describe God's saving action, but the message is consistent: We are included in God's covenant people ("the Israel of God," 6:16) solely by God's gracious action in Christ for our sake.

2. Paul's proclamation focuses on the cross as a liberating event (2:20-21; 3:1, 13-14; 6:14-15). In Galatians, the cross is interpreted not primarily as an atoning sacrifice for forgiveness of sins but as a cataclysmic event that has broken the power of forces that held humanity captive, brought the old world to an end, and inaugurated a new creation. Throughout the letter Paul is reflecting upon the story of Jesus' loving self-donation to rescue us from enslavement (1:3-4).

3. As a result of Christ's death on a cross, the Spirit is given to all who are in Christ (3:13-14). The Spirit gives us life (5:25), confirms our status as God's children (4:6-7), and transforms the character of our community life so that we produce fruit pleasing to God (5:22-25). Because of the transformative power of the Spirit, there can be no artificial division between the gospel and "ethics." God's redemptive work necessarily includes the reshaping of the community's life together.

4. In the new community created by the Spirit, the markers that once separated Jews from Gentiles have been invalidated—or, speaking more precisely, annihilated (3:28; 5:6; 6:15). God's purpose is to create a single new people who are "one in Christ Jesus," bound together in faith and love.

5. Those who recognize the saving work of God in Christ and live in the power of the Spirit experience *freedom*. They are no longer constrained, enslaved, or separated from one another. The climactic exhortation of the letter, therefore, urges the Galatians to stand firm in the freedom won for them by Christ (5:1).

EPISTOLARY, RHETORICAL, AND HOMILETICAL STRUCTURE

1. Galatians as a Letter. Galatians is a real letter, not a treatise or an essay composed in the fictive literary form of an epistle. Formally, the letter contains many features characteristic of Hellenistic letters of its time.[4] Most of these formal stylistic features have

---

4. For an extensive list of such elements, see Richard N. Longenecker, *Galatians,* WBC 41 (Dallas: Word, 1990) cv-cix.

relatively little importance for our interpretation of the text. More significant is a comparison of the structure of Galatians to the structure of Paul's other letters. These usually contain the following components: opening salutation, thanksgiving or blessing, body, moral exhortation, closing (greetings, doxology, benediction). The letter to the Galatians noticeably lacks two of these characteristic elements: the thanksgiving and the closing greetings to individuals in the churches to whom the letter is addressed. These striking omissions are an indicator of the strained relationship between Paul and the Galatian churches.

The letter was composed to be read aloud to each of the assembled Galatian congregations. There is no indication in the letter itself of the identity of the person authorized to deliver and read it. The letter serves as a substitute for Paul's personal presence—a substitute recognized by Paul as frustratingly inadequate (4:20)—and seeks to reestablish his authority in the community.

2. Galatians as Deliberative Rhetoric. Because the letter was composed for public hearing, it has many structural and stylistic characteristics in common with the forms of rhetoric that were taught and practiced in the Hellenistic world. Any educated person in Hellenistic antiquity would have received training in how to structure a speech and influence an audience, and Paul's letter shows that he was well versed in such matters.

In 1979, Hans Dieter Betz made an important contribution to our understanding of Galatians by publishing a learned critical commentary arguing the thesis that Galatians was an "apologetic letter" structured in accordance with the conventions of ancient judicial rhetoric.[5] That is, Paul writes as though he were on trial before a jury, speaking in his own defense and in defense of the Spirit. The present commentary will highlight some places where Betz's proposals prove particularly illuminating. Subsequent reviewers and commentators have observed that Galatians does not fit the apologetic letter genre as neatly as Betz argued;[6] nonetheless, Betz's work catalyzed numerous other studies of the rhetorical strategies embodied in Paul's letters.[7] Out of these studies, there is an emergent consensus that the rhetorical genre of Galatians is not primarily judicial but rather *deliberative*; it belongs to a category of rhetoric whose aim is to persuade the audience to follow a certain course of action.[8] In the case of Galatians, the persuasion is primarily negative in character: Paul is trying to persuade his Galatian readers not to be circumcised and not to become Law observers. (One can also discern in the letter positive statements of the action Paul urges; the Galatians should imitate him in abandoning Torah observance [4:12], drive out the Missionaries [4:30], and stand firm in their freedom [5:1].)

5. H. D. Betz, *Galatians: A Commentary on Paul's Letter to the Churches in Galatia,* Hermeneia (Philadelphia: Fortress, 1979).

6. Particularly telling is the fact that 5:1–6:10, which Betz calls the *exhortatio,* has no parallel in actual apologetic speeches or in the instructions in rhetorical handbooks about how such speeches should be composed.

7. Among more recent Galatians commentaries, see especially Longenecker, *Galatians;* and Ben Witherington III, *Grace in Galatia: A Commentary on St. Paul's Letter to the Galatians* (Grand Rapids: Eerdmans, 1998).

8. G. A. Kennedy, *New Testament Interpretation Through Rhetorical Criticism* (Chapel Hill: University of North Carolina Press, 1984) 144-52; Witherington, *Grace in Galatia,* 25-36. Longenecker's analysis is more complicated; he sees Galatians as a mixed type, showing both forensic and deliberative characteristics. Martyn dissents from the consensus; see below on "Galatians as a Sermon."

Paul was not slavishly following a rhetorical handbook on how to write a deliberative speech, but he was employing rhetorical strategies that were simply in the air in his culture. A knowledge of how such strategies worked may occasionally help us to see how the argument is put together. For example, the rhetoricians taught that a good persuasive speech should employ arguments appealing to *ethos* (the trustworthiness of the speaker), to *pathos* (emotive impact on the audience), and to *logos* (reasoned argumentation).[9] We see Paul deploying his argument in a way that honors this recommendation. For example, the account of his own apostolic credentials in chapters 1 and 2 functions as an *ethos* argument, the lengthy exegetical discussion in 3:6-29 is clearly a *logos* argument, and his otherwise puzzling shift to a relational appeal in 4:12-20 is a classic illustration of a *pathos* argument.[10]

Perhaps the most important function of rhetorical analysis is to remind us that Paul's original readers and hearers were shaped by a culture in which rhetorical performance was cultivated and prized. Their ways of listening and judging were shaped by the prevailing conventions of oratory—a fact that became a problem for Paul at Corinth, where his opponents and some of his own converts judged him deficient in the rhetorical arts (2 Cor 10:10; cf. 1 Cor 1:18–2:5).[11] Consequently, when we hear Paul pulling out all the rhetorical stops in Galatians, we should recognize that he is arguing in a manner conventional for his time and necessary if he was to persuade his hearers to hold fast to the gospel he had preached to them.

3. Galatians as a Sermon. Without excluding either the epistolary or the rhetorical mode of analysis, Martyn has highlighted one other important way of viewing the Letter to the Galatians: It is above all "an argumentative sermon" composed to be delivered "in the context of a service of worship—and thus in the acknowledged presence of God—not a speech made by a rhetorician in a courtroom."[12] As Martyn insists, the purpose of the letter is "reproclamation of the gospel," and for that reason it is not so much an argument as an *announcement.*[13] Paul is not merely trying to persuade the Galatians to agree with his opinions; rather, he is seeking to unleash the power of the gospel once again in their midst. The effectiveness of the letter will ultimately depend not on Paul's literary or rhetorical skill but on the activity of God's Spirit when the Galatians hear the letter read.

THE INTERPRETATION OF SCRIPTURE

As has been noted, the Missionaries based their preaching partly on scriptural texts, particularly the story of Abraham. An important part of Paul's strategy is to refute their

---

9. Aristotle *Rhetoric* 1.2.
10. For further discussion of these rhetorical modes, see Longenecker, *Galatians,* cxiv-cxix.
11. See D. A. Litfin, *St. Paul's Theology of Proclamation: 1 Corinthians 1–4 and Greco-Roman Rhetoric,* SNTSMS 79 (Cambridge: Cambridge University Press, 1994).
12. Martyn, *Galatians,* 21.
13. Ibid., 22-23.

interpretations and to reclaim the biblical story (i.e., the OT) as a witness to the gospel. Paul's determination not to abandon the Bible into the hands of the Law-observant Missionaries was a crucial strategic decision that ultimately helped to preserve the OT as part of the Scripture of the Christian church. According to his reading, anyone who really listens to the Law will find that it supports his proclamation, not that of his adversaries (e.g., 4:21).[14] Indeed, he claims that Scripture "preached the gospel beforehand" to Abraham by declaring that all nations (i.e., Gentiles) would be blessed in him (3:8). This shows, among other things, that Paul saw Scripture not just as a repository of proof texts about Jesus as the Messiah but as a *story*—a story focused on God's promise to bless and redeem all nations.[15]

Paul's portrayal of Scripture as a living, speaking agent plays a significant role in his argument, not only in 3:6-9 but also in his account of how Scripture "imprisoned all things under the power of sin" (3:22) and in his argument that Scripture commands the Galatians to expel the Missionaries (4:30). Because Paul believed that Scripture was a living voice through which God spoke to the church, he dared to propose startling new readings, such as his allegorical interpretation of the Sarah/Hagar story (4:21–5:1), claiming that the Gentile believers, not the Law-observant Jewish Christians, are the true children promised to Abraham. This bold revisionary reading stands at the climax of the central argumentative section of the letter.

While the Abraham stories are the most prominent scriptural texts in Galatians, Paul's language from start to finish is salted with scriptural imagery and allusions, such as his echoing of prophetic call narratives in the account of his own call (1:15); his citations of Deuteronomy, Leviticus, and Habakkuk in 3:10-14; his artful contrapuntal evocation of Isa 54:1 in Gal 4:27; his appeal to the love commandment of Lev 19:18 (Gal 5:14); and his echoing of Isaiah's "new creation" imagery (Gal 6:15). A careful reading of the letter, then, must attend to Paul's use of Scripture throughout the argument. He produces revisionary imaginative readings of the texts in service of his preaching of the gospel. Yet, at the same time, he claims with full seriousness that only the gospel truly discloses the meaning that remained latent in these texts prior to the coming of Christ.

EARLY CHRISTIAN CONFESSIONAL TRADITIONS

In addition to scriptural quotations and allusions, Paul weaves into his argument several early Christian confessional and liturgical traditions.[16] The most widely recognized of these traditions is the baptismal affirmation of the unity of the church in Christ (3:27-28). A

---

14. Paul is able to sustain this position by ignoring the narrative about Abraham's circumcision in Genesis 17. How might Paul have responded if pressed to deal with this text? His later treatment of Abraham in Romans 4 provides some clues; see esp. Rom 4:9-12.

15. On Paul's hermeneutical strategies, see Richard B. Hays, *Echoes of Scripture in the Letters of Paul* (New Haven: Yale University Press, 1989); "The Conversion of the Imagination: Scripture and Eschatology in 1 Corinthians," *NTS* 45 (1999) 391-412.

16. For a detailed list, see H. D. Betz, *Galatians: A Commentary on Paul's Letter to the Churches in Galatia,* Hermeneia (Philadelphia: Fortress, 1979) 26-28.

number of other passages also appear to draw on early christological confessions (see, e.g., 1:3-4; 2:16, 20; 3:13-14; 4:4-5). These citations anchor Paul's arguments in a deep layer of early Christian tradition that would have been acknowledged not only by the Galatians but also by the rival Missionaries as authoritative. Paul's case will be made more persuasive if he can show how these confessional statements reinforce his gospel rather than the Law-observant anti-gospel he is combating. Here Paul stands on very solid ground, indeed, for these early confessions consistently narrate the initiative of God and/or Christ in bringing about the redemption of humankind; thus the narrative plot of the confessions supports Paul's insistence that it is Christ's grace—not the Law—that brings about rectification. Our reading of the letter will be enriched if we attend closely to Paul's deft use of these traditional materials.

Thus we see that Paul's Letter to the Galatians is a complex and rhetorically artful performance. He makes a formidable case for his gospel by linking the Galatians' experience of the Spirit with extended arguments based on Scripture and on early Christian tradition. Like a good orator, he also attempts to enlist their sympathies and to bolster their confidence in him as an authoritative interpreter of the gospel.

HISTORICAL PROBLEMS

Where were the Galatian churches located? This question is surprisingly difficult to answer. The Roman province of Galatia in Paul's time included a large area of central Asia Minor (modern Turkey). The province was named after the Galatian people, a tribe of Celtic origin that had migrated from Europe in the third century BCE and settled in the central highlands of Anatolia, the region around Ancyra (modern Ankara). In 25 BCE, Augustus created the *Provinicia Galatia,* which included not only the traditional territory of the Galatians but also a stretch of territory extending south to encompass the city of Iconium, as well as the towns of Lystra and Derbe; these places are mentioned in the Acts of the Apostles as sites of missionary activity by Paul and Barnabas (Acts 14:1-23).

Because Paul nowhere in the letter mentions any particular towns or cities, it is impossible to be sure whether "the churches of Galatia" (1:2) were located in the traditional territory of the ethnic Galatians ("North Galatia") or in the places mentioned in Acts 14, in Roman provincial Galatia ("South Galatia"). Likewise, we have no idea how many "churches of Galatia" there were.

As is so often the case in historical inquiry, scholarly argument has tended to focus on the problems for which we have the least evidence. Thus there is a massive quantity of secondary literature debating the North Galatian/South Galatian question. The debate remains inconclusive and almost entirely irrelevant for interpreting Paul's letter.

The issues that are primarily at stake in this debate are how to connect Paul's Letter to the Galatians with Luke's narrative in the Acts of the Apostles and how to date the composition of the letter. When Paul wrote to "the churches of Galatia," was he

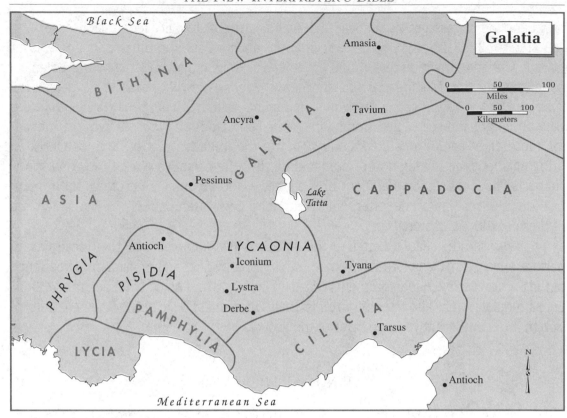

addressing churches in "South Galatia" founded during his "first missionary journey" in the Lukan schema (Acts 13-14)? Or was he writing to churches he had founded in "North Galatia" during the "second missionary journey" (Acts 16:6) and later visited once again (Acts 18:23)? Since Luke's account is highly schematized and not a comprehensive account of Paul's activity (for example, Acts never mentions the fact that Paul wrote letters to his churches), the question remains unresolvable.

In favor of the North Galatian theory is the fact that Paul addresses his readers as "Galatians" (3:1), a designation more naturally applied to ethnic Galatians than to "South Galatian" dwellers in the Roman province, who might not have referred to themselves in this way. It should also be noted that Luke never uses the designation "Galatia" for the areas mentioned in Acts 13–14; he uses it only in Acts 16:6 and 18:23. Thus, in the history of the interpretation of the letter, from the patristic era up until modern times, it was almost unanimously held that Paul was writing to churches in central Asia Minor composed of the descendants of the Celtic tribe.[17]

In favor of the South Galatian theory is the fact that it enables a reconstruction of Paul's activity that minimizes contradictions between Galatians 2 and Acts 15 (see below on the date of composition). As already noted, however, the nature of Luke's epic narrative about

17. See Richard N. Longenecker, *Galatians,* WBC 41 (Dallas: Word, 1990) lxiii-lxiv. Longenecker nonetheless subscribes to the South Galatian hypothesis.

the expansion of the early Christian mission is such that it should not be pressed for precision about matters of detail. (E.g., Acts 9:26-30 has Paul introduced by Barnabas to the church in Jerusalem shortly after his conversion experience and preaching publicly there; by contrast, in Gal 1:18-24 Paul emphatically insists that he was "unknown by sight to the churches of Judea" for at least fourteen years after his initial call.) Thus avoidance of contradiction between Acts and Galatians 2 should not be a decisive factor in determining the addressees and date of Paul's letter.

If Acts does not provide a precise chronology of Paul's life, and if even the location of the Galatian churches cannot be determined with confidence, it becomes difficult to ascertain a precise date for the composition of the letter. It must follow by some significant length of time Paul's meeting with the Jerusalem church leaders (2:1-10), which is probably to be dated about 48 or 49 CE. After the Jerusalem meeting, we have to allow time for the following events to occur: the confrontation at Antioch and Paul's falling-out with the Antioch church (2:11-21); Paul's preaching to the Galatians and their reception of the gospel; Paul's departure; the arrival in Galatia of the rival Missionaries; and the report to Paul of the changed situation. Some commentators date Galatians as early as 49 CE, while others place the letter as late as 56 CE, in close proximity to the writing of Romans. The thematic similarities between Galatians and Romans appear to favor the later date, but several recent commentators have argued for an earlier dating of 50–51 CE.[18] One advantage of this earlier dating is that it allows more time between Galatians and Romans for the refinement of Paul's position concerning the Law and the fate of Israel.

As Moises Silva has pointed out, although proponents of the South Galatian hypothesis tend to date the letter early, there is no necessary logical connection between this theory about the geographical destination of the letter and its dating. If one assumes the historical reliability of Acts, then the North Galatian hypothesis requires a date for the letter after the Jerusalem Council of Acts 15, since only afterward did Paul go to Galatia (Acts 16:6). But if one accepts the South Galatian hypothesis, the letter could have been written at any time after Paul's initial founding of the churches in Galatia.[19] In view of the paucity of hard evidence, the best we can do is to say that Galatians was written sometime in the period of 50–56 CE.[20]

One crucial question for interpretation concerns the relationship between Galatians 2 and Acts 15. Does Acts 15 describe the same meeting to which Paul refers in Galatians 2? The similarities between the accounts make it virtually certain that they are variant narratives of the same event. In both texts, Paul and Barnabas go to Jerusalem to meet with the leaders of the church and debate whether Gentile converts must be circumcised (see the Commentary on 2:1-10). There are, however, two significant discrepancies

18. E.g., J. D. G. Dunn, *The Epistle to the Galatians,* Black's NT Commentary (Peabody, Mass.: Hendrickson, 1993) 19, argues for 50–51 CE, and J. L. Martyn, *Galatians,* AB 33A (New York: Doubleday, 1997) 19-20, for about 50 CE.

19. Moises Silva, *Explorations in Exegetical Method: Galatians as a Test Case* (Grand Rapids: Baker, 1996) 129-39. If one posits a longer interval between Paul's evangelization of the Galatians and the writing of the letter, some explanation is required for Paul's statement that the Galatians are "so quickly" deserting the gospel (1:6).

20. Betz, *Galatians,* 12, identifies the years between 50 and 55 CE as "a reasonable guess" for the date of composition.

between the accounts: (1) Luke seems to describe the council as a public assembly, including all the apostles and elders of the church, whereas Paul insists that he met privately with a handful of Jerusalem leaders (Gal 2:2); (2) according to Luke's account, the council issued a statement approving admission of Gentiles but asking them "to abstain from what has been sacrificed to idols and from blood and from what is strangled and from fornication" (Acts 15:29). This latter account seems in tension with Paul's claim that the Jerusalem leaders added nothing to his Law-free gospel for the uncircumcised, except a reminder to remember the poor (Gal 2:6-10). The first of these discrepancies does not present a major difficulty; Paul could be referring to a behind-the-scenes meeting with James and Cephas and John in the context of a larger public conference. The second discrepancy is more puzzling: If the "pillar" apostles had made a public decree that Gentile converts did not need to be circumcised, why did Paul not refer to it in support of his argument in Galatians? And why did Paul not instruct the Galatians that all the apostles had agreed that Gentiles need not observe the Law save for the restrictions of the apostolic decree (Acts 15:23-29)?[21] There are several possible explanations, but the likeliest one is that Paul knew of no such declaration of the apostolic council; his letters nowhere give evidence of the existence of such an agreement. It appears that Luke has telescoped events and read back into this meeting an agreement that emerged somewhat later in the development of early Christianity.[22] In this commentary, then, it will be assumed that Galatians 2 and Acts 15 refer to the same meeting in Jerusalem and that Paul's Letter to the Galatians, therefore, was written sometime after that meeting.

GALATIANS AS SCRIPTURE

Paul treated Scripture (by which he meant the collection of writings that Christians later came to call the Old Testament) as a living voice that had the power to speak to the church in his own time (Gal 4:30). By so doing, he set a precedent that has instructed Christians ever since about how to approach Scripture with an ear tuned expectantly to listen for the Word of God. What happens, then, when Galatians itself becomes incorporated into the canon of texts that the believing community confesses to be Scripture? Can we expect to hear in Galatians a living voice that will speak to our time, just as Genesis and Isaiah spoke to Paul's situation?

Martin Luther's reading of Galatians offers a classic illustration. He read Paul's polemic against the Torah-observant Missionaries as an attack on the abuses of the Roman church of his own day, for he believed Rome was teaching justification by works in a way just as destructive of the gospel as were the teachings of Paul's opponents. Luther knew, of course, that there was a difference between the ancient Jewish-Christian preachers of circumcision

21. These restrictions are based on the requirements imposed by the holiness code (Leviticus 18–20) not only on Israel but also on non-Israelites who are resident aliens in the land.

22. On the question of the relation between Acts 15 and Galatians 2, see esp. Craig C. Hill, *Hellenists and Hebrews: Reappraising Division in the Earliest Church* (Philadelphia: Fortress, 1991) 103-47.

and the Christian sellers of indulgences in Europe 1,500 years later, but the analogy between the situations was so strong that the text of Galatians became a medium through which Luther heard God speaking directly to the struggles that he confronted.[23]

What would it mean for us to listen to Galatians for a similar word targeted to the church today? This question will be posed in the Reflections sections throughout the commentary, but it may be useful to summarize in advance some of the key themes that emerge again and again as we seek to listen to this text speaking to our time.

1. Rectification Through the Faithfulness of Jesus Christ. Much Christian preaching, particularly in some Protestant traditions, has fallen into the trap of celebrating the subjective faith experience of individuals as though religious experience were an end in itself, or as though we could somehow secure God's acceptance by the device of our believing. Indeed, Galatians has often been exploited for proof texts defending exactly such a message. Careful reading of the text, however, shows that Paul's Letter to the Galatians is a powerful attack on such self-referential accounts of salvation. From start to finish, Paul proclaims that *God* has acted to set the world right and to rescue us from slavery to human religious programs. God did this not merely through some mysterious change of feelings in the hearts of individuals, but through the faithfulness of Jesus Christ, whose love and fidelity culminated in his giving up his life on the cross for our sake. Our trust in him is a response to this saving deed. Reading Galatians in the light of this fundamental insight will require us to rethink the meaning of "faith" and "justification." It will also require us to examine critically the individualistic sentimentality that often surrounds talk in the church about "faith."

2. The Gospel and Judaism. Galatians is not an anti-Jewish text. It is, rather, a manifesto against distortions of the gospel introduced by *Christian* preachers who subordinate Christ to the Law. Reading Galatians after the Holocaust forces us to re-think how we have twisted Paul's good news into a pretext for violence. The Christian community, gathered as "the Israel of God" (6:16), as Abraham's children, must rediscover the ways in which Paul was a profoundly Jewish thinker, despite his ambiguous assessment of the Law. In order to think through this question fully, we will find ourselves moving beyond Galatians into the issues that Paul was inexorably drawn to address in Romans 9–11. As a part of the canon of Christian Scripture, Galatians should never be read in isolation from Paul's further reflections on the ultimate salvation of Israel.

3. A Church United at One Table. Paul holds forth the vision of a community of faith in which all are one in Christ (2:11-21; 3:26-29). This is not merely a matter of an isolated slogan in Gal 3:28; it is a central theme of the letter as a whole. Jews and Gentiles are no longer to be divided, because Christ's death has brought us together. Therefore, all manifestations of racial and ethnic divisiveness are betrayals of "the truth of the gospel."

---

23. Martin Luther, *Lectures on Galatians (1535)*, translated by Jaroslav Pelikan in *Luther's Works*, vols. 26-27 (Saint Louis: Concordia, 1963–64).

Galatians is one of the canon's most powerful witnesses against a cultural imperialism that excludes anyone from fellowship on the basis of criteria not rooted in the gospel.

4. Freedom, Not Autonomy. We live in an age obsessed with personal freedom. In such a time, it is far too easy to hear Paul's proclamation of freedom (5:1) as a license for the indulgence of individual desires and interests. Galatians will teach us, to the contrary, that the freedom for which Christ has set us free is a freedom to serve one another in love (5:6, 13-14). The freedom of which Paul speaks is not autonomy. It is freedom for life together in community under God (6:1-10).

5. The Crucified World and the New Creation. Galatians proclaims an apocalyptic gospel. Christ came to defeat the oppressive powers that held us captive and to "rescue us from the present evil age" (1:4). As Paul develops the implications of this confession, he discloses to his readers that the entire world of orderly religious norms that he had once zealously defended has been "crucified" (6:14); it no longer has any claim upon him. The real world in which we now live is the "new creation" brought into being by Christ, in which we are given new life and are guided by the Spirit. As the church reads Galatians, then, we are constantly challenged to reject the wisdom of business as usual—including the business of religion—and to see reality as redefined by the cross. Those who live by this rule will no longer be manipulated by the popular culture's images of security and respectability. We will live, instead, manifesting the fruit of the Spirit, and our life together will be a sign of the world to come.

BIBLIOGRAPHY

Commentaries:

Betz, Hans Dieter. *Galatians: A Commentary on Paul's Letter to the Churches in Galatia.* Hermeneia. Philadelphia: Fortress, 1979. This landmark commentary analyzes the structure of the letter in terms of Greco-Roman rhetoric and offers numerous parallels from Hellenistic literary and philosophical texts.

Bruce, F. F. *The Epistle to the Galatians: A Commentary on the Greek Text.* NIGTC. Grand Rapids: Eerdmans, 1982. Careful, philologically precise interpretation of Galatians according to the traditional Protestant paradigm.

Cousar, Charles B. *Galatians.* Interpretation. Atlanta: John Knox, 1982. Expository commentary for teachers and preachers, offering discerning theological reflections on each paragraph of the text.

Dunn, James D. G. *The Epistle to the Galatians.* Black's NT Commentary. Peabody, Mass.: Hendrickson, 1993. A sustained reading of the letter in the light of Dunn's advocacy of "the new perspective on Paul"; Dunn sees Paul arguing not against Judaism but against the inappropriate use of circumcision and food laws as exclusionary boundary markers for the covenant community. Dunn offers a wealth of parallels from ancient Jewish texts.

Edwards, Mark J., ed. *Galatians, Ephesians, Philippians.* Ancient Christian Commentary on Scripture. Volume 8. Downers Grove, Ill.: InterVarsity, 1999. Anthology of brief excerpts from patristic commentaries (Jerome, John Chrysostom, Augustine, and others).

Longenecker, Richard N. *Galatians.* WBC 41. Dallas: Word, 1990. Exhaustive critical commentary on the Greek text, attending both to ancient Hellenistic rhetoric and to Jewish exegetical traditions.

Martyn, J. Louis. *Galatians*. AB 33A. New York: Doubleday, 1997. Theologically penetrating reading of the letter as Paul's reproclamation of an apocalyptic gospel. Martyn provides detailed reconstruction of the situation in Galatia and the message of the rival Jewish-Christian Missionaries. A brilliantly cohesive interpretation of Galatians, to which the present commentary is heavily indebted.

Matera, Frank J. *Galatians.* Sacra Pagina 9. Collegeville, Minn.: Liturgical, 1992. A clear and careful exposition in a Roman Catholic commentary series that seeks to combine critical analysis with sensitivity to religious meaning. Matera argues for "the faith of Jesus Christ" (Gal 2:16) and follows Dunn in interpreting "works of the Law" as symbols of Jewish identity.

Williams, Sam K. *Galatians*. ANTC. Nashville: Abingdon, 1997. In a series aimed at modeling exegesis for theological students, Williams unpacks the letter's argument in an engaging essay style that illuminates the text theologically.

Witherington, Ben III. *Grace in Galatia: A Commentary on St. Paul's Letter to the Galatians.* Grand Rapids: Eerdmans, 1998. Taking a "socio-rhetorical" approach, Witherington argues that Galatians must be read as deliberative rhetoric, seeking to persuade the readers to turn away from circumcision. Helpfully traces recent scholarly debates about the letter.

Specialized Studies:

Baker, Mark D. *Religious No More: Building Communities of Grace and Freedom.* Downers Grove, Ill.: InterVarsity, 1999. Fascinating study showing how Paul's gospel has been read and misread in evangelical Protestant communities in Honduras. Shows how careful exegesis of Galatians yields a liberating message for Christians in the barrio.

Barclay, John M. G. *Obeying the Truth: A Study of Paul's Ethics in Galatians.* Studies of the New Testament and Its World. Edinburgh: T. & T. Clark, 1988. This fine exegetical study of Galatians 5–6 demonstrates the inner logic of these chapters and their place within the overall argument of the letter.

Bassler, Jouette, ed. *Pauline Theology,* Vol. 1: *Thessalonians, Philippians, Galatians, Philemon.* Minneapolis: Fortress, 1991. Collection of essays from the Pauline Theology Group of the Society of Biblical Literature. Includes significant essays on Galatians and on the overall shape of Paul's theology.

Beker, J. Christiaan. *Paul the Apostle: The Triumph of God in Life and Thought.* Philadelphia: Fortress, 1980. Major study of Pauline theology, arguing that the apocalyptic message of the triumph of God grounds the coherence of Paul's thought amid his varied responses to contingent pastoral problems.

Boyarin, Daniel. *A Radical Jew: Paul and the Politics of Identity.* Contraversions: Critical Studies in Jewish Literature, Culture, and Society 1. Berkeley: University of California Press, 1994. Boyarin, whose primary scholarly expertise is in the field of rabbinic Judaism, offers an original and provocative reading of Paul as a Jewish cultural critic wrestling with the tension between the universal reign of the one God and the particularity of Jewish election and ethnic difference.

Cousar, Charles B. *A Theology of the Cross: The Death of Jesus in the Pauline Letters.* OBT. Minneapolis: Fortress, 1990. Well-crafted study that draws on recent advances in research to delineate Paul's interpretation of the cross.

Dahl, Nils A. *Studies in Paul: Theology for the Early Christian Mission.* Minneapolis: Augsburg, 1977. Collection of Dahl's classic essays on Paul.

Donaldson, Terence L. *Paul and the Gentiles: Remapping the Apostle's Convictional World.* Minneapolis: Fortress, 1997. Major study of Paul's understanding of the Gentile mission.

Dunn, James D. G. *The Theology of Paul's Letter to the Galatians.* New Testament Theology. Cambridge: Cambridge University Press, 1993. Concise summary of the theology of the letter; complementary to Dunn's commentary.

Hays, Richard B. *The Faith of Jesus Christ: An Investigation of the Narrative Substructure of Galatians*

3:1-4:11. SBLDS 56. Chico, Calif.: Scholars Press, 1983. Argues for "the faithfulness of Jesus Christ" as an integral element of the gospel narrative that undergirds Paul's argument in Galatians.

————. *Echoes of Scripture in the Letters of Paul.* New Haven: Yale University Press, 1989. A study of Paul's readings of, and allusions to, the OT.

Hill, Craig C. *Hellenists and Hebrews: Reappraising Division Within the Earliest Church.* Minneapolis: Fortress, 1991. Important historical study giving a nuanced account of the relations between the Jerusalem church and the emergent Gentile mission in the Hellenistic world; particularly valuable for understanding the Jerusalem council (Gal 2:1-10) and the conflict at Antioch (Gal 2:11-21).

Käsemann, Ernst. *New Testament Questions of Today.* Translated by W. J. Montague. Philadelphia: Fortress, 1969. Contains Käsemann's seminal essay "The Righteousness of God in Paul."

————. *Perspectives on Paul.* Translated by Margaret Kohl. Philadelphia: Westminster, 1971. Collected essays. Käsemann's work continues to define many of the issues debated in the study of Pauline theology.

Martyn, J. Louis. *Theological Issues in the Letters of Paul.* Nashville: Abingdon, 1997. Collection of Martyn's essays; overlaps with and complements his commentary.

Sanders, E. P. *Paul and Palestinian Judaism: A Comparison of Patterns of Religion.* Philadelphia: Fortress, 1977. Watershed study that exposed and discredited widely held Christian caricatures of ancient Judaism, giving well-developed readings of Jewish "covenantal nomism" and of Paul's belief in salvation through participation in Christ.

————. *Paul, the Law, and the Jewish People.* Philadelphia: Fortress, 1983. Extends and nuances the account of Paul's thought given in *Paul and Palestinian Judaism.*

Segal, Alan F. *Paul the Convert: The Apostolate and Apostasy of Saul the Pharisee.* New Haven: Yale University Press, 1990. Partly in reaction against Stendahl (see below), Segal examines the way in which Paul's abandonment of Torah observance constituted a break with his Jewish heritage. Helpful on the exegesis of Paul's statements about law.

Silva, Moises. *Explorations in Exegetical Method: Galatians as a Test Case.* Grand Rapids: Baker, 1996. A series of thoughtful exegetical probes into Galatians, designed to introduce students to proper exegetical methodology. Contains good discussion of date and addressees of the letter.

Stendahl, Krister. *Paul Among Jews and Gentiles and Other Essays.* Philadelphia: Fortress, 1976. Contains Stendahl's famous essay "The Apostle Paul and the Introspective Conscience of the West" and other essays challenging the traditional "Lutheran" reading of Paul, refocusing attention on the acceptance of Gentiles as the key issue driving Paul's arguments about justification.

Tamez, Elsa. *The Amnesty of Grace: Justification by Faith from a Latin American Perspective.* Nashville: Abingdon, 1993. Develops a liberationist reading of Paul's teaching on justification.

Westerholm, Stephen. *Israel's Law and the Church's Faith.* Grand Rapids: Eerdmans, 1988. The most articulate recent defense (against Stendahl, Sanders, and Dunn) of the traditional Protestant reading of Paul's teaching on justification. Also contains useful summaries of major developments in Pauline studies in the twentieth century.

Witherington, Ben III. *Paul's Narrative Thought World: The Tapesty of Tragedy and Triumph.* Louisville: Westminster/John Knox, 1994. A wide-ranging account of the large dramatic themes of Paul's gospel.

Wright, N. T. *The Climax of the Covenant: Christ and the Law in Pauline Theology.* Edinburgh: T. & T. Clark, 1991. Collection of exegetical essays, especially valuable for interpretation of the "curse" theme in Galatians 3.

OUTLINE OF GALATIANS

I. Galatians 1:1-10, The Letter Opening

    A. 1:1-5, Salutation
    B. 1:6-10, Rebuke and Curse

II. Galatians 1:11–2:21, A Narrative Defense of Paul's Gospel

    A. 1:11-12, Thesis Statement: The Divine Origin of Paul's Gospel
    B. 1:13-24, Paul's Apostolic Call and Independence from Jerusalem
    C. 2:1-10, Paul's Meeting with the Jerusalem Leaders
    D. 2:11-21, Two Tables or One? Confrontation at Antioch
        2:11-14, Paul's Rebuke of Cephas
        2:15-21, Jews and Gentiles Alike Are Rectified Through Christ's Death

III. Galatians 3:1–5:1, Counterarguments Against the Rival Missionaries

    A. 3:1-5, The Experience of the Spirit
    B. 3:6-29, The Promise to Abraham
        3:6-9, The Blessing of Abraham Included the Gentiles
        3:10-14, Christ's Death Liberates Israel from the Law's Curse
        3:15-18, The Covenant Promise Predated the Law
        3:19-25, The Law as Temporary Custodian
        3:26-29, In Christ We Are Abraham's Seed
    C. 4:1-11, The Fullness of Time Has Come
        4:1-7, We Are Heirs and Children of God
        4:8-11, No Turning Back
    D. 4:12-20, An Appeal to Restore a Ruptured Relationship
    E. 4:21–5:1, An Allegory of Slavery and Freedom

IV. Galatians 5:2–6:10, Pastoral Counsel to the Galatians

    A. 5:2-12, A Call to Reject Circumcision
    B. 5:13-15, Freedom for Love
    C. 5:16-26, The Works of the Flesh and the Fruit of the Spirit
    D. 6:1-10, Life Together in the Church

V. Galatians 6:11-18, Postscript: The Cross and New Creation

GALATIANS 1:1-5, SALUTATION

NIV

1 Paul, an apostle—sent not from men nor by man, but by Jesus Christ and God the Father, who raised him from the dead— ²and all the brothers with me,

To the churches in Galatia:

³Grace and peace to you from God our Father and the Lord Jesus Christ, ⁴who gave himself for our sins to rescue us from the present evil age, according to the will of our God and Father, ⁵to whom be glory for ever and ever. Amen.

NRSV

1 Paul an apostle—sent neither by human commission nor from human authorities, but through Jesus Christ and God the Father, who raised him from the dead— ²and all the members of God's family[a] who are with me,

To the churches of Galatia:

3Grace to you and peace from God our Father and the Lord Jesus Christ, ⁴who gave himself for our sins to set us free from the present evil age, according to the will of our God and Father, ⁵to whom be the glory forever and ever. Amen.

[a] Gk all the brothers

COMMENTARY

1:1. The strong claim made by the opening words of his letter to the Galatians is that God has authorized Paul's mission and his message. He identifies himself as an "apostle" (ἀπόστολος *apostolos*), one who is sent, and he emphatically asserts that the sender is not any human person or institution, but "Jesus Christ and God the Father, who raised him from the dead" (v. 1*b*). Thus, from its very first line, the letter asserts Paul's authority to proclaim the gospel and to speak for God.

Paul's greetings always follow the standard pattern of epistolary salutations in Greco-Roman letters: sender to receiver, greetings.[24] Paul characteristically expands the greeting format by adding a paragraph of thanksgiving (e.g., Rom 1:8-15; 1 Cor 1:4-9; Phil 1:3-11; Col 1:3-14; 1 Thess

1:2-10; 2 Thess 1:3-12; Phlm 4-7; cf. 2 Tim 1:3-5) or a prayer of blessing (2 Cor 1:3-7; cf. Eph 1:3-14).[25] These greeting and thanksgiving sections often foreshadow concerns that Paul will develop in the body of the letter. (For example, the opening of 1 Corinthians emphasizes that the Corinthians are "sanctified in Christ Jesus," gives thanks for their rich gifts of speech and knowledge, and reminds them that they are called into the fellowship [κοινωνία *koinōnia*] of Jesus Christ [1 Cor 1:1-9]. As the letter unfolds, we discover that these themes are prominent among the matters that Paul wants to discuss with the Corinthians: the call to sanctification, the proper use of knowledge and spiritual gifts, and the importance of love within the community.)[26] Precisely be-

24. On the formal structure of letters in Paul's time, see S. K. Stowers, *Letter Writing in Greco-Roman Antiquity* (Philadelphia: Westminster, 1986).

25. Cross-references in this commentary will treat Colossians as an authentic Pauline letter, while assuming that Ephesians and the Pastoral Epistles are products of a subsequent Pauline school.

26. See Richard B. Hays, *First Corinthians,* Interpretation (Louisville: John Knox, 1997) 15-21.

cause the standard letter structure provides a framework for comparison, the distinctive features of Paul's salutation in Galatians stand out clearly.

Elsewhere Paul begins his letters by describing himself as an apostle (Rom 1:1; 1 Cor 1:1; 2 Cor 1:1; Col 1:1; cf. Eph 1:1; 1 Tim 1:1; 2 Tim 1:1; Titus 1:1), but nowhere else is that self-description set in opposition, as it is in Galatians, to a false conception about the source of his authority: "sent not from men nor by man" (NIV; the NRSV's rendering, "sent neither by human commission nor from human authorities," is a paraphrase). This suggests immediately that in the Letter to the Galatians Paul is defending his apostleship against questions or accusations (see the Commentary on 1:11-12). Paul insists that his apostleship is not an office conferred by human agency; rather, it is a divine commission, resting upon no lesser authority than the power of God, the power that raised Jesus from the dead. This is, incidentally, the only explicit reference to the resurrection of Jesus in Galatians.

1:2. While other Pauline letters explicitly name co-senders (e.g., Sosthenes in 1 Cor 1:1; Timothy in 2 Cor 1:1; Phil 1:1; and Col 1:1; Silvanus and Timothy in 1 Thess 1:1 and 2 Thess 1:1), Galatians is said to be sent by Paul and certain unnamed associates: "all the brothers with me" (NIV). The NRSV again paraphrases, in the interest of inclusive language, by rendering ἀδελφοι (*adelphoi*, "brothers") as "members of God's family"; certainly Paul's practice of calling members of the church *adelphoi* was intended to include both male and female members of the community (cf. Gal 3:28). The phrase as used here probably does not refer to all the Christians in the (unknown) location where Paul composed the letter, but specifically to Paul's missionary coworkers (cf. Phil 4:21), some of whom were women (Rom 16:1-7; Phil 4:2-3). Presumably, these colleagues were not known personally to the Galatians; if they had been, Paul would certainly have named them, since their names would lend additional weight of authority to Paul's argument. The rhetorical effect of mentioning a group of co-senders is to suggest that Paul is not an isolated preacher but that his work enjoys the support of others.

Each of Paul's other letters is addressed to a church in a specific city (e.g., Rome, Corinth, Philippi, Thessalonica; Philemon is addressed to

an individual family and the church that meets in their house). Galatians is distinctive in being directed to "the churches" of a wider geographical area or province (but see also 2 Cor 1:1; on the interpretation of "Galatia" and the location of these churches, see the Introduction). Apparently, it was written as a circular letter to be read in several churches. This may explain the surprising absence of specific greetings to individuals at the end of the letter. We do not know the name of a single Galatian Christian. Also noteworthy—in contrast to other letters that address the readers as "saints"—is the fact that Paul omits any laudatory description of the Galatians.

1:3. Paul characteristically replaces the standard greeting of Hellenistic letters ("greetings," χαίρειν *chairein*) with a grace-and-peace wish: "Grace [χάρις *charis*] and peace [εἰρήνη *eirēnē*; cf. Hebrew שלום *šālôm*] from God our Father and the Lord Jesus Christ." This may be understood either as a prayer for the readers or as a performative utterance that actually conveys the blessing of God's grace to them. Either way, it highlights a truth fundamental to Paul's gospel: God has graciously taken the initiative to bring peace and reconciliation. The grace-and-peace formula stands as a reminder of this truth, even at the beginning of a letter as severe as this one.

1:4. Only in Galatians, however, is the formula expanded by the addition of a confessional tradition that explicates the meaning of "grace and peace" through a compact narrative summary of the gospel Paul proclaimed: The Lord Jesus Christ "gave himself for our sins to rescue us from the present evil age" (v. 4; J. Louis Martyn vividly translates, "so that he might snatch us out of the grasp of the present evil age").[27] Why does Paul add this elaboration of the grace-and-peace formula? We may be sure that he was not wasting words. In the very beginning of the letter, Paul wants to underscore two themes of fundamental importance: The gospel is about *Jesus Christ's gracious self-giving* (i.e., his death) for our sake (cf. 2:20), and that self-giving must be understood as *an apocalyptic rescue operation.* Paul's gospel declares God's gracious invasion of the world, not merely a new human "religious" possibility. The expression "the present evil age" signals the

27. J. L. Martyn, *Galatians,* AB 33A (New York: Doubleday, 1997) 90.

apocalyptic frame of reference in which Paul thinks. In Jewish apocalyptic traditions, the history of the world is divided into two ages: the present age of corruption and the age to come, when God's justice will finally be established (see, e.g., Isaiah 60; 65:17-25; 2 Esdr 7:50, 113; *1 Enoch* 91:15-17, *2 Apoc. Bar.* 15:8; 44:8-15). As a result of Christ's death, Paul proclaims, we have been liberated from the destructive power of the world as we have known it. These convictions provide the foundation for Paul's response to the problem in Galatia.

Jesus carried out his rescue operation "according to the will of our God and Father." In the opening verses of this letter, Paul places heavy emphasis on the description of God as "Father" (vv. 1, 3-4). Why so? We see here a foreshadowing of a theme that will be of crucial importance for Paul's argument later: Those who are rescued by Jesus are given the Spirit and thereby made God's children, so that they can cry to God, "Abba, Father" (4:4-7). Paul wants to convince the Galatians that in Christ they are already God's children; for that reason they do not need to undergo circumcision in order to become children of Abraham (on the issue of addressing God as "Father," see the Reflections at 4:4-7). The threefold naming of God as Father in the salutation reinforces this truth about the readers' relation to God.

In v. 4 Paul is probably quoting an early Jewish-Christian christological confession, perhaps based on Isa 53:12 LXX: "And he bore the sins of many, and on account of their sins he was handed over." The allusion in v. 4 to Jesus' death as an expiatory sacrifice for *sins* (plural) is often taken as a sign of the pre-Pauline origin of the formula, because Paul, rather than focusing on discrete transgressions of Torah, characteristically thinks of *sin* in the singular as an oppressing power (see, e.g., Rom 3:9; 6:12-14; Rom 3:25-26, which likewise treats the death of Jesus as an atoning sacrifice for "sins previously committed," is also generally regarded as Paul's citation of a similar tradition; see also Rom 4:25; 5:8; 8:3; 2 Cor 5:21). If the reference to Jesus' death "for our sins" (v. 4*a*) is traditional, then Paul's account of the results of this death in v. 4*b* represents his own further interpretation of this tradition; the death of Jesus marks the end of the power of the old age (cf. 6:14-15). It would be wrong to regard this interpretation as a rejection of the Jewish-Christian atonement tradition; here, as in Rom 3:21-26, Paul adopts and endorses the view of Jesus' death as an atoning sacrifice, but he insists at the same time on defining the meaning of this event so that it is shown to be the turning point of the ages. Jesus' death does not simply procure the forgiveness of sins; rather, it transposes us into an entirely new reality by liberating us from the power of "the present evil age."

1:5. Alone among Paul's letters, Galatians concludes its salutation with a doxology (v. 5). Martyn has suggested that the purpose of this doxology is to evoke the setting of worship and to draw the Galatian hearers of the letter into affirming Paul's reproclamation of the gospel by saying the "Amen" along with him.[28] Thus, by the end of v. 5, Paul has completed his salutation and laid the theological groundwork for his response to the Galatians. If the Galatians did, indeed, join with Paul in the "Amen," they were in for a rude shock when they heard his next words.

28. Ibid., 87.

GALATIANS 1:6-10, REBUKE AND CURSE

NIV

⁶I am astonished that you are so quickly deserting the one who called you by the grace of Christ and are turning to a different gospel— ⁷which is really no gospel at all. Evidently some people are throwing you into confusion and are trying to

NRSV

6I am astonished that you are so quickly deserting the one who called you in the grace of Christ and are turning to a different gospel— ⁷not that there is another gospel, but there are some who are confusing you and want to pervert the

NIV

pervert the gospel of Christ. [8]But even if we or an angel from heaven should preach a gospel other than the one we preached to you, let him be eternally condemned! [9]As we have already said, so now I say again: If anybody is preaching to you a gospel other than what you accepted, let him be eternally condemned!

[10]Am I now trying to win the approval of men, or of God? Or am I trying to please men? If I were still trying to please men, I would not be a servant of Christ.

NRSV

gospel of Christ. [8]But even if we or an angel[a] from heaven should proclaim to you a gospel contrary to what we proclaimed to you, let that one be accursed! [9]As we have said before, so now I repeat, if anyone proclaims to you a gospel contrary to what you received, let that one be accursed!

10Am I now seeking human approval, or God's approval? Or am I trying to please people? If I were still pleasing people, I would not be a servant[b] of Christ.

[a] Or a messenger   [b] Gk slave

COMMENTARY

1:6. Immediately following the salutation, we expect to find a thanksgiving section, as in most of Paul's other letters, in which he gives God thanks for the church to which he is writing and expresses his confidence that God is at work in their midst. In this letter, however, Paul is far too upset with the Galatians to give thanks.[29] Instead, he confronts them abruptly with a strong rebuke, charging them with abandoning God: "I am astonished that you are so quickly deserting the one who called you in the grace of Christ and are turning to a different gospel" (v. 6). "The one who called you" refers not to Paul, but to God. Elsewhere in Paul's writings, including 1:15 and 5:8, it is consistently God who "calls"; the verb καλέω (*kaleō*) describes God's gracious action of summoning people into special covenantal relation (see, e.g., Rom 8:30; 9:11-12; 1 Cor 1:9; 1 Thess 2:12; 5:24). Thus Paul is rebuking the Galatians for defection not merely from the Pauline mission movement but also, more fundamentally, from God's grace (cf. 5:4: "You who want to be justified by the law have cut yourselves off *from Christ:* you have fallen away *from grace*" [NRSV, italics added]). The "grace of Christ" is closely linked with Christ's death (2:20-21).[30] "Grace," therefore, is not to be understood merely as God's

kindly disposition; rather, grace is embodied in God's powerful and costly action for the salvation of the world through Christ's self-giving on the cross. God's calling of the Galatians took place through the event of Christ's death and through Paul's proclamation of that death to them (3:1). Insofar as they have now turned their backs on that proclamation, they have turned themselves against God.

The verb "you are deserting" (μετατίθεσθε *metatithesthe*) is sometimes used in Greek literature to describe the conversion of a person from one philosophical school to another. The same verb is used in 2 Maccabees to describe defection from Torah observance: "Antiochus not only appealed to him in words but promised with oaths that he would make him rich and enviable if he would turn [μεταθέμενον *metathemenon*] from the ways of his ancestors" (2 Macc 7:24 NRSV). Ironically, Paul sees the Galatians' act of turning *toward* law observance as a similar act of defection.[31] Their defection is said to have occurred quickly, but we do not know whether this means soon after Paul's departure or in a relatively short time after the coming of the rival Missionaries to Galatia. Either way, Paul is upset with them for failing to stay the course by holding fast to what he had taught them.

The Galatians have turned "to another gospel"

29. The absence of an explicit thanksgiving section in 2 Corinthians may be similarly explained. The opening of the letter reflects a strained moment in Paul's relationship with the Corinthian church.

30. The point stands even if the reading of some ancient MSS that lack "of Christ" in this verse is the original one.

31. J. D. G. Dunn, *The Epistle to the Galatians,* Black's NT Commentary (Peabody, Mass.: Hendrickson, 1993) 39-40.

(cf. 2 Cor 11:4). This is one important piece of evidence showing that the rival Missionaries were Jewish *Christians*; they were not urging Paul's Galatian converts to renounce their newfound Christian faith. Instead, they were preaching a version of the gospel that invited Gentiles to be circumcised as a sign of their membership in the people of God (see 5:2-12; 6:12). In all likelihood, they understood this as a completion of the gospel that Paul had preached, which was in their view partial and defective. Paul's formulation in vv. 6-7*a* acknowledges that the Missionaries represent their message as a "gospel" but then immediately revokes the legitimacy of that designation. It is a so-called gospel, but not really the gospel, because there can be only one true gospel—and that is the gospel already preached to the Galatians by Paul, which did not require Gentiles to become Jews.

What does the term "gospel" (εὐαγγέλιον *euangelion*) mean? It certainly does not refer to a text that tells the story of Jesus; at the time Paul wrote this letter, there were no written texts called "gospels." The use of the term to describe such stories was a later development in early Christianity. In the ancient Roman world, the plural form of this term was often used in the propaganda of the imperial cult to describe proclamations of military victories or honors accorded to the emperor. An excellent example of this use of the term has been preserved in an inscription from Priene, in Asia Minor, dating from 9 BCE. The inscription extolls the emperor Augustus as a god and proclaims that his birthday should mark the beginning of the calendar year, because "the birthday of the god [Augustus] was for the world the beginning of the glad tidings [εὐαγγέλια *euangelia*] which have gone forth because of him."[32] The early Christian use of the term "gospel" or "glad tiding" (always in the singular)[33] may have been formulated in conscious contrast to the use of this noun in the imperial cult as a way of declaring that Jesus, not Caesar, is Lord.

At the same time, Paul's usage is certainly influenced by the OT's use of the cognate verb, which appears twice in the Greek text of Isa 52:7:

> . . . as the feet of the one who *proclaims*
> [εὐαγγελιζομένου *euangelizomenou*] a
> message of peace,
> as one who *proclaims*
> [εὐαγγελιζόμενος *euangelizomenos*]
> good things,
> for I shall announce your
> salvation,
> saying "O Zion, your God
> will reign." (author's trans.)

(For Paul's explicit citation of this passage, with minor differences, see Rom 10:15; for other passages in Isaiah using the same verb, see Isa 40:9; 60:6; 61:1; cf. Joel 2:32 LXX.) The message announced by the bearer of good news in Isaiah is the joyous news of the end of Israel's exile and oppression, the news of the reign of God.

1:7. Against this background, we should understand that the gospel is the triumphantly proclaimed message that God has at last taken control and begun to reign. That helps to explain why Paul regards the Missionaries' message as a non-gospel; in his view, it merely extends the status quo that pertained under the Law prior to the coming of Jesus. Their "gospel" does not reflect the world-transforming effect of his death and resurrection.

Paul speaks of the Missionaries as those who "confuse" (οἱ ταράσσοντες *hoi tarassontes*, better translated as "disturb") the Galatians. This description, taken in conjunction with Acts 15, provides further evidence that the newly arrived Missionaries were pressing the Galatians to be circumcised. According to Acts, some individuals came to Antioch from Jerusalem, teaching that "unless you are circumcised according to the custom of Moses, you cannot be saved" (Acts 15:1*b*). Luke then summarizes the response of the leaders of the Jerusalem church in terms very similar to the language Paul uses in Galatians. They write to the church at Antioch, saying, "We have heard that certain persons who have gone out from us, though with no instructions from us, have said things to disturb [ἐτάραξαν *etaraxan*] you and have unsettled your minds" (Acts 15:24). The verb "disturb" here is precisely the same one Paul uses in Gal 1:7. Perhaps Luke's description of the Judean agitators is influenced by the language of Paul's Letter to the Galatians. Be that as it may, the "disturbers" in Galatia are certainly preaching a message very much like the one summarized in Acts 15:1.

Paul sees such a non-gospel as a reversion to

---

32. For the Greek text and secondary literature, see G. Friedrich, "εὐαγγελίζομαι," *TDNT*, 2:724.

33. Martyn, *Galatians*, 128-32. See also B. R. Gaventa, "The Singularity of the Gospel: A Reading of Galatians," in J. M. Bassler, ed., *Pauline Theology* (Minneapolis: Fortress, 1991) 1:147-59.

"the present evil age" from which Jesus' death has rescued us (v. 4); therefore, he is adamant that it cannot be accepted as a legitimate form of the Christian message. The Missionaries are trying to "pervert [μεταστρέψαι *metastrepsai*] the gospel of Christ" (the verb carries connotations of turning the message upside down).[34] Therefore, there can be no compromise or dialogue with them. They are to be excluded and cursed.

1:8-9. Paul twice pronounces the curse: "Let them be accursed [ἀνάθεμα *anathema*]." The term refers to something or someone delivered over (sometimes as an offering) for divine destruction. Significantly, these curses are conditional; that is, they are not pronounced on specified individuals but are left open, applicable to anyone who might proclaim a false gospel. The Greek language allows Paul to make a subtle but important distinction between the two conditions in these verses. The first conditional sentence (v. 8), constructed with ἐάν (*ean*, "if") and a verb in the subjunctive mood, points to a hypothetical future possibility: "Even if it ever should happen that we or an angel from heaven should proclaim to you a gospel contrary to what we proclaimed to you, let that one be accursed." The second conditional sentence (v. 9), however, is constructed with εἰ (*ei*, "if") and a present indicative verb, pointing to a situation that is, in fact, likely to exist in the present: "If anyone is preaching to you a gospel contrary to what you received [as it seems *is* indeed happening], let that one be accursed."

Paul certainly does not anticipate proclaiming a different gospel, but by including himself hypothetically under the threat of curse, he makes an important point. He is not asking for the Galatians' personal allegiance to him; rather, what matters is their allegiance to the gospel message. Even if Paul should ever stray and begin preaching something different, the Galatians should reject him and cling to the gospel. The reference here to "an angel from heaven" has sparked speculation that the rival Missionaries were claiming that their own message was based on an angelic revelation, especially since later in the letter Paul refers to the Mosaic Law as "ordained through angels" (3:19). This is a possible inference, for Jewish apocalyptic literature of this period frequently fea-

tures an angelic figure who interprets revelatory visions.[35] On the other hand, the reference to an angel may be rhetorical hyperbole, suggesting that if the Galatians should ignore even a celestial messenger with a false gospel, they should all the more ignore the Missionaries' purely human urgings. After v. 8 provides the theoretical frame of reference (*anybody* who distorts the gospel is under a curse), v. 9 zeroes in precisely on the actual situation that Paul has heard about in the Galatian churches. (He gives no explanation of how he received this information; the letter makes no reference either to a letter from the Galatians or to messengers bearing reports about them.) Paul does not name the perverters of the gospel—if indeed he knows their names—but the artful rhetoric of vv. 6-9 will leave the readers with little doubt whom he has in mind. Paul has scored a direct hit on the rival Missionaries.

1:10. The forcefulness of Paul's language causes him to pause and reflect ruefully on a charge that was leveled against him. The Missionaries have accused him of being a sophist who tells people just what they want to hear. That, they say, is why he did not tell the Galatians about God's inconvenient and painful requirement of circumcision. In their view, Paul was offering his gentile converts a cheap, watered-down facsimile of God's truth, rather than explaining the full and salutary discipline offered in the Law of Moses.[36] In short, they charged that Paul was a "people pleaser," playing to the crowd. But now, having made the stern, uncompromising curse of v. 9 at his rivals, in v. 10 he asks the Galatians, in effect, "So does that sound like I'm a waffler seeking human approval? Am I seeking to please human beings or God?" Some commentators have argued that "trying to win the approval" of God is a bad thing, related to magic or sorcery that seeks to manipulate God.[37] In the light, however, of the strong antitheses between human and divine in the opening verses of this letter (vv. 1, 11-12), it makes better sense to understand "seeking God's approval" as the positive opposite of "seeking human approval." The latter charge is the one Paul is concerned to refute, as shown by his

---

34. H. D. Betz, *Galatians*, Hermeneia (Philadelphia: Fortress, 1979) 50.

35. Dunn, *The Epistle to the Galatians*, 45.
36. Ibid., 49-50.
37. E.g., Betz, *Galatians*, 55.

restatement of the question: "Or am I trying to please people?" The bitterly ironic tone of the questions in v. 10 shows that this is still a part of the rebuke section. Paul is chiding the Galatians for giving credence to the Missionaries' unflattering characterization of his motives.

Against such charges, Paul has a convincing rebuttal: "If I were still pleasing people, I would not be a servant of Christ." The word translated "servant" here is δοῦλος (*doulos*), which really means "slave." To be Christ's slave entails persecution, suffering, and conformity to the way of the cross. Paul can describe the scars that he bears (see 2 Cor 6:4-5; 11:23-25) as "the marks of Jesus branded on my body" (6:17)—that is, the identifying brand showing that he is a slave owned by Christ. He has hardly chosen an easy or popular life. Under such circumstances, it is patently ridiculous for his adversaries to accuse him of flattery and preaching a mini-gospel to solicit human approval.

Almost hidden away in this rejoinder is the key word "still." By inserting this word, Paul implies that he formerly was a people pleaser; his days of people pleasing were his time as a zealous Torah-observer (see 1:13-14). Thus he turns the charge around and points it back at his critics. Since he will later accuse the Missionaries of promoting circumcision in order to avoid persecution (6:12), the inference lies at hand that it is actually they, not he, who are seeking human approval (cf. 4:17).

REFLECTIONS

Sometimes we are called upon to draw the line and to pronounce anathema upon distortions of the gospel. For many comfortable, educated Christians in Western culture, this is a distinctly uncomfortable truth; we are wary of dogmatic certainty. Mindful of the harm done by overzealous "true believers," some of them Christians, we tend to prefer tolerance, dialogue, and compromise. We value a plurality of perspectives, and we believe that we can be enriched by the witness of others whose experience of God seems different from our own. Elsewhere in his letters, Paul works hard to build Christian community across boundaries formed by different understandings of God's will (Rom 14:1–15:13). Yet Paul's Letter to the Galatians stands in the New Testament canon as an urgent reminder that some versions of the gospel are perversions. The opening verses of the letter throw down the gauntlet and call the readers to reaffirm their allegiance to the singular gospel of Jesus Christ and to reject counterfeit "gospels."

A few historical examples can illustrate the point. When Martin Luther nailed his ninety-five theses to the door of the castle church in Wittenberg in 1517, protesting the sale of indulgences, he was confronting the distortion of the truth by Christian leaders who had lost sight of the gospel of God's free, unmerited grace. (It is no coincidence that Luther found in Galatians the clearest articulation of Christian freedom.) When Karl Barth and members of the Confessing Church in Germany drafted the Barmen Declaration in 1934, they said no to the Nazis' usurpation of the church. In this way, they defined the truth of the gospel against a false gospel of nationalism and ethnicity. Likewise, when in 1982 the World Alliance of Reformed Churches denounced the acceptance of racial apartheid by the Dutch Reformed Church of South Africa as a heresy, they were following Paul's example of pronouncing a curse on a dangerous perversion of the gospel. If the church is to bear witness to the gospel with integrity in "the present evil age," it must have the courage to make such discernments and to speak prophetically against destructive teachings that deny the grace of God.

These examples are instructive because each one involves a discernment about perversions of the gospel through specific social practices within the church. Paul was not cursing pagan outsiders for their unbelief; rather, he was warning Christian believers against a danger presented by preachers who spoke the language of Christian faith. Just as the Missionaries in Galatia did not understand themselves to be opposing God, so also the Roman Catholic hierarchy in the sixteenth century, the German Christians of the 1930s, and the Dutch Reformed Afrikaaners in South Africa believed themselves to be theologically justified in their actions and interpretations of the Christian message. With the wisdom of hindsight, these cases—especially the last two—look like clear instances of perversion of the gospel. (And these racial/ethnic definitions of the gospel in Germany and South Africa are closely analogous to the abuse against which Paul was fighting in his day.) One of the urgent tasks of Christian preaching, however, is to make such discernments *prospectively,* to identify ways in which the church is *now* in danger of being misled by persuasive disturbers who have repackaged the gospel and assimilated it wrongly to cultural norms of the present age. Thus the preacher working from the opening verses of Paul's letter will want to look with a critical eye at popular contemporary forms of Christian teaching and practice and weigh them against the gospel of the grace of Christ.

At the same time, we must be sure that it is really the *gospel* that provides the standards for critical evaluation. For some Christians, Paul's curse against false teaching may appear to justify harsh judgments against any ideas of which they happen to disapprove. But this is to misappropriate Paul; elsewhere, we see that he champions tolerance of diversity within the Christian community on nonessential matters (e.g., Romans 14–15; 1 Cor 8:1–11:1). It is crucial to recognize that Paul curses the rival Missionaries for promulgating a teaching that compromises the heart of the gospel. Consequently, in order to apply Gal 1:6-9 analogically to our contemporary setting, we must first delineate carefully the character of the gospel. Although Paul's opening salvo does not yet offer a specific diagnosis of the problem with the "different gospel" (1:6) that was tempting the Galatians, it does offer some crucial definitions of the standard against which all formulations of the gospel must be measured:

(1) The gospel is not a human construction; it comes from God, who has taken the initiative to rescue us (1:1, 3-4). This divine initiative can be understood only as "grace" (1:3, 6), the freely given love of God.

(2) The grace of God is embodied and made effective in the self-giving of Jesus on the cross (1:4; cf. 2:20-21; 3:1, 13; 6:14). Jesus' death somehow atones for our sins and releases us from the oppressive power of "the present evil age." (Paul's compact formulation in 1:4 does not yet explain how the death of Jesus achieves these effects.)

(3) The self-giving of Jesus is in accordance with the will of God (1:4); indeed, the fact that "grace and peace" come from "God our Father and the Lord Jesus Christ" (1:3) suggests that the death of Jesus is in some mysterious sense the act of God (cf. Rom 5:8: "God proves his love for us in that while we still were sinners Christ died for us," NRSV).

(4) The gracious God who has thus acted to liberate us is known as "God our Father" (1:1, 3-4). This implies that we are God's children, members of God's family.

(5) God raised Jesus from the dead (1:1). The resurrection shows God's power over death. Thus, as Christ delivers us from the grip of the present age, he also sets us free from the power of death.

(6) Implied in all of this is an apocalyptic analysis of the human plight and its solution. God's grace has broken into an otherwise hopeless situation and changed everything. Later in the letter, Paul will describe this apocalyptic transformation as "new creation" (6:15). The provocative choice of the word εὐαγγέλιον (*euangelion,* 1:6-9) to encapsulate the message suggests that God's invasive grace stands in opposition to the political powers of this world.

Of course, Paul develops none of these points at any length in Gal 1:1-10, but when we reread these opening sentences in the light of the rest of the letter, we can see how clearly Paul has sketched out the convictions that undergird his challenge to the Galatians. Any representation of the gospel that denies any of the six points listed above must be judged as a corrupt counterfeit.

Paul's apostolic authority is grounded in the truth of these affirmations. He is accountable to proclaim this message and no other. Because he is a slave of Christ (1:10), he is accountable to one master only, and he is no longer concerned about human approval (cf. 1 Cor 4:1-5). This text provides a stimulus to consider how our own actions may be driven by the need for human approval. In subtle and pervasive ways, our character is formed—or malformed—by our desire for applause. The congregation that wrestles with Galatians will find itself summoned to a life in which the only approval that matters is God's.

GALATIANS 1:11–2:21

A NARRATIVE DEFENSE OF PAUL'S GOSPEL

GALATIANS 1:11-12, THESIS STATEMENT: THE DIVINE ORIGIN OF PAUL'S GOSPEL

COMMENTARY

Having opened the letter with a sharp rebuke of the Galatians for their defection from the gospel he had preached to them, Paul now forcefully asserts the thesis that he will defend in the first major section of the letter (1:11–2:21): His gospel is of divine origin, and his apostleship, therefore, is not dependent on any human authority. As we have seen, this theme was already introduced in 1:1, but Paul now sets it forth emphatically in two negations and one positive assertion (note the structural similarity to 1:1):

(1) The gospel that Paul preaches is not of human origin.

(2) Paul did not receive it from a human source, nor was he taught it.

(3) It came through (God's) revelation of Jesus Christ.

Why does Paul begin with two denials rather than with the positive thesis? As the argument unfolds, it becomes clear that he is responding to charges made by the rival Mission-

aries.[38] Presumably, they have told the Galatians something like this: "Paul was originally taught the gospel by the apostles in Jerusalem. But now he has deviated from the Jerusalem-authorized version of the gospel by preaching a watered-down gospel of merely human devising, a gospel that disregards the divinely given commandments of the Law."

Paul indignantly declares that this is a complete misrepresentation of the true situation. The Law-free gospel for the Gentiles was given to him—against all his natural human training and inclination—by God. The initiative belonged entirely to God, as does the content of his message. Paul was never discipled by the Jerusalem authorities, nor has he ever been under their jurisdiction.

In v. 11, Paul addresses the Galatians for the

---

38. A historical memory of anti-Pauline polemic by some Jewish Christians is preserved in the third-century Pseudo-Clementine literature. For full texts and discussion, see J. Irmscher and G. Strecker, "The Pseudo-Clementines," *New Testament Apocrypha,* ed. W. Schneemelcher, English trans. ed. R. McL. Wilson (Louisville: Westminster/John Knox, 1992) 2:483-541. Relevant excerpts are given by H. D. Betz in an appendix to his commentary. See Betz *Galatians,* Hermeneia (Philadelphia: Fortress, 1979) 331-33.

first time as "brothers [and sisters]" (ἀδελφοι *adelphoi*; cf. 3:15; 4:12, 28; 5:11, 13; 6:1, 18). This manner of address shows that Paul still regards them as members of God's family; rather than denouncing and excommunicating them, he is appealing to them to recognize their true identity in Christ.

The somewhat unwieldy expression in v. 11, το ευαγγελιον το ευαγγελισθεν υπ εμου (*to euangelion to euangelisthen hyp' emou*), is impossible to render exactly into idiomatic English; literally, it means "the gospel that was gospeled by me." This slightly cumbersome locution suggests that Paul himself is an instrument of the gospel's power rather than an agent responsible for its content. This gospel is "not something that man made up" (the NIV's helpful paraphrase of the phrase κατὰ ἄνθρωπον [*kata anthrōpon*, "according to a human being"]). The warrant for this claim is given in v. 12. Paul did not receive the gospel message secondhand as something passed along by other firsthand witnesses (cf. Luke 1:1-2); rather, he received it directly through "a revelation of Jesus Christ." This formulation stands in sharp contrast to conceptions of the authoritative transmission of religious tradition in the Judaism of Paul's time. Consider, for purposes of comparison, the opening of the tractate *'Abot* in the Mishnah:

Moses received the Law from Sinai and committed it to Joshua, and Joshua to the elders, and the elders to the Prophets, and the Prophets committed it to the men of the Great Synagogue.[39]

While the rabbis found religious confidence in such a conception of an authoritative chain of tradition (closely analogous to what Christian theologians, such as Irenaeus, would later claim for apostolic tradition), Paul, by contrast, claims *unmediated* access to God's revelation.

Paul can also speak elsewhere—using precisely the same vocabulary of "handing down" and "receiving"—of the gospel as mediated through a process of tradition (notably in 1 Cor 11:23-25 and 15:3-7, but see also Gal 1:8-9). Does Paul contradict himself? It is important to remember that his point in Gal 1:11-12 is that his own commission as an apostle is not dependent on any

such process of tradition. Even though he can pass on traditional kerygmatic and liturgical formulas to his churches as authoritative summaries of the gospel, these formulas must be understood as particular "performances" of an underlying story that Paul has learned directly from God. When the matter is understood in this way, there is no contradiction between Gal 1:11-12 and 1 Cor 15:3-7. These two statements serve very different rhetorical functions within the arguments in which they appear. The first, rebutting an accusation that Paul has invented his own gospel, asserts that his apostolic message has a divine origin; the second recalls for the Corinthians the specific terms in which that message was presented to them originally.

The phrase "a revelation of Jesus Christ" is grammatically ambiguous. Does it mean that Jesus Christ is the one who gives the revelation (subjective genitive) or that he is the one who is revealed by God (objective genitive)? Paul's usage elsewhere settles the question clearly in favor of the latter interpretation; for example, just a few sentences later in Galatians, Paul writes that God was pleased "to reveal his Son" (v. 16; for discussion of the specific form and content of the revelation, see the Commentary on 1:16).

The last clause of v. 12 is elliptical, lacking a verb. The NRSV and the NIV both supply "I received it," repeating the main verb from v. 12*a*, resulting in the following reading of the sentence:

For I did not receive it from a human source, nor was I taught it, but [I received it] through a revelation of Jesus Christ.

This is certainly a possible interpretation, but we could equally well complete the sentence by supplying the words "it came." This would be entirely in keeping with Paul's understanding of the gospel as a dynamic power that has broken into the present time. The gospel is "the power of God for salvation" (Rom 1:16 NRSV), and Paul can speak of it as something that "comes" to those who hear it, as in 1 Thess 1:5: "Our message of the gospel came to you not in word only, but also in power and in the Holy Spirit" (NRSV; see also Gal 3:23-25, in which Paul speaks of "faith"—a virtual synonym for "the gospel"—as something that "came" into the sphere of human history). In line with this understanding, we could translate as follows:

---

39. See *m. Abot* 1:1. This comparison is noted by J. L. Martyn, *Galatians*, AB 33A (New York: Doubleday, 1997) 143.

For I did not receive it from a human source, nor was I taught it, but [it came] through a revelation of Jesus Christ.

This picture of the gospel as a powerful, in-breaking word is consonant with the meaning of "revelation" (ἀποκάλυψις *apokalypsis*). Revelation is God's activity, an act of disclosure initiated from the divine side that reorients all human perception and knowledge (see Rom 1:17, where Paul declares that in the gospel "the righteousness of God is being revealed [ἀποκαλύπτεται *apoka-*

lyptetai]"). Paul characteristically speaks of the revealing of Jesus Christ as an eschatological event connected with final judgment and the consummation of God's purposes for all creation (Rom 8:19; 1 Cor 1:7; 2 Thess 1:7). Paul's bold claim, then, is that he has been given, in advance of the last day, a privileged preview of the glory of Christ and that this revelation has determined the shape and content of the gospel that he preaches. This claim sets the agenda for Gal 1:13–2:21. (See Reflections at 1:13-24.)

GALATIANS 1:13-24, PAUL'S APOSTOLIC CALL AND INDEPENDENCE FROM JERUSALEM

NIV

13For you have heard of my previous way of life in Judaism, how intensely I persecuted the church of God and tried to destroy it. 14I was advancing in Judaism beyond many Jews of my own age and was extremely zealous for the traditions of my fathers. 15But when God, who set me apart from birth[a] and called me by his grace, was pleased 16to reveal his Son in me so that I might preach him among the Gentiles, I did not consult any man, 17nor did I go up to Jerusalem to see those who were apostles before I was, but I went immediately into Arabia and later returned to Damascus.

18Then after three years, I went up to Jerusalem to get acquainted with Peter[b] and stayed with him fifteen days. 19I saw none of the other apostles—only James, the Lord's brother. 20I assure you before God that what I am writing you is no lie. 21Later I went to Syria and Cilicia. 22I was personally unknown to the churches of Judea that are in Christ. 23They only heard the report: "The man who formerly persecuted us is now preaching the faith he once tried to destroy." 24And they praised God because of me.

a15 Or *from my mother's womb*   b18 Greek *Cephas*

NRSV

13You have heard, no doubt, of my earlier life in Judaism. I was violently persecuting the church of God and was trying to destroy it. 14I advanced in Judaism beyond many among my people of the same age, for I was far more zealous for the traditions of my ancestors. 15But when God, who had set me apart before I was born and called me through his grace, was pleased 16to reveal his Son to me,[a] so that I might proclaim him among the Gentiles, I did not confer with any human being, 17nor did I go up to Jerusalem to those who were already apostles before me, but I went away at once into Arabia, and afterwards I returned to Damascus.

18Then after three years I did go up to Jerusalem to visit Cephas and stayed with him fifteen days; 19but I did not see any other apostle except James the Lord's brother. 20In what I am writing to you, before God, I do not lie! 21Then I went into the regions of Syria and Cilicia, 22and I was still unknown by sight to the churches of Judea that are in Christ; 23they only heard it said, "The one who formerly was persecuting us is now proclaiming the faith he once tried to destroy." 24And they glorified God because of me.

a Gk *in me*

COMMENTARY

Paul begins a lengthy defense of his thesis by retelling his own history, some of which he had told the Galatians previously. The narrative here is certainly not a comprehensive autobiography; it is tailored to emphasize a few key facts that support Paul's present case. Two themes run through the narrative: (1) the divine origin of Paul's call to preach the gospel and (2) Paul's independence from the Jerusalem church. On both points, he is defending himself against misrepresentations by the Missionaries.

At the same time, if we read this narrative solely as a defense speech, we will miss one of its important functions. Paul is also offering himself as a model, an authoritative pattern for the Galatians as they seek to understand how to live faithfully before God (see the Commentary on 4:12).[40] Paul was once a zealous observer of the Law of Moses, but now he has been seized by God for a new mission and redirected into a new life. He has, in fact, "died to the Law" (2:19). Thus the Galatians, who are being urged to become subject to the Law, should instead emulate Paul's example of freedom from it. Paul's own life story shows that life in Christ is life in a sphere of freedom beyond the Law; thus, to come under the Law is not to advance—as the Missionaries are trying to persuade the Galatians—but to go backward into bondage. None of these points are yet explicit in the letter, but Paul is laying the groundwork for them by retelling his story in chapters 1 and 2.

1:13-14. "For you have heard,"[41] he reminds the Galatians, "of my earlier life in Judaism." Surprisingly, the word "Judaism" (Ἰουδαϊσμός *Ioudaismos*) appears in the NT only in these verses. (For earlier occurrences, see 2 Macc 2:21; 8:1; 14:38; 4 Macc 4:26; the term appears also in the letters of Ignatius of Antioch early in the second century CE.) Its usage here, as also in the Maccabean literature, strongly suggests that it designates a body of practices that distinguish Jews from Gentiles, particularly with reference to circumcision,

dietary laws, sabbath observance, and the system of sacrifices and feasts.[42] That is to say, "Judaism" refers not so much to a set of beliefs or doctrines as to a culture; it designates a network of habitual observances that characterize the Jewish people as members of a distinctive society set apart for God in the midst of the pagan world. Within that cultural network of practices, Paul used to live; indeed, he "advanced" in it beyond his contemporaries among his own people (v. 14). The verb "advanced" (προέκοπτον *proekopton*) was a word widely used by Greco-Roman moral philosophers, particularly Stoics, to describe their progress in the disciplines of living a wise life. Paul's use of this term here sheds light on his retrospective understanding of his former life; "Judaism" was for him a kind of moral culture in which one could seek to excel. Indeed, it was possible to compare one's own attained level of excellence to the level attained by others pursuing the same set of practices.

One of the ways in which Paul excelled in the practice of Judaism was—as he now ruefully observes—by "violently persecuting the church of God and trying to destroy it." Why would such hostile action be cited as evidence of excellence in the practice of Judaism? The key to understanding Paul's point here lies in a term he uses in the last clause of v. 14: "I was exceedingly zealous [ζηλωτὴς *zēlōtēs*] for the traditions of my ancestors." As Martin Hengel has argued, the terms "zealous" and "zeal" had assumed in Second Temple Judaism a very specific meaning related to the preservation of Jewish religious and ethnic purity by whatever means necessary, including violence.[43] The great OT exemplar of such zeal was Phinehas, who had averted a plague afflicting Israel through an act of vigilante violence by killing an Israelite man and his foreign Midianite wife, impaling both of them (apparently during the act of sexual intercourse) with a single spear (Num 25:6-18). According to the story in

---

40. See B. R. Gaventa, "Galatians 1 and 2: Autobiography as Paradigm," *NovT* 28 (1986) 309-26.

41. The word "for" (γάρ *gar*), oddly translated in the NRSV as "no doubt," shows that Paul will now begin the task of producing evidence for the thesis of 1:11-12.

42. J. D. G. Dunn, *The Epistle to the Galatians,* Black's NT Commentary (Peabody, Mass.: Hendrickson, 1993) 56.

43. M. Hengel, *The Zealots: Investigations into the Jewish Freedom Movement in the Period from Herod I Until 70* A.D. (Edinburgh: T. & T. Clark, 1961).

Numbers, the reaction of the Lord to this deed was one of glowing approbation:

The LORD spoke to Moses, saying, "Phinehas son of Eleazar, son of Aaron the priest, has turned back my wrath from the Israelites by manifesting such *zeal* among them on my behalf that in my jealousy I did not consume the Israelites. Therefore say, 'I grant him my covenant of peace. It shall be for him and for his descendants after him a covenant of perpetual priesthood, because he was *zealous* for his God, and made atonement for the Israelites.' " (Num 25:10-13 NRSV, italics added)

The story is remembered and celebrated in Sir 45:23-24; 1 Macc 2:54; and 4 Macc 18:12, each time repeating the key word "zeal."

The story of Phinehas is evoked explicitly in the account of the beginning of the Maccabean revolt in 1 Macc 2:15-28. Seeing a fellow Jew preparing to offer pagan sacrifice in accordance with the command of Antiochus IV Epiphanes, Mattathias kills him on the altar. The narrator of 1 Maccabees then comments, "Thus he burned with *zeal* for the Law, just as Phinehas did against Zimri son of Salu" (1 Macc 2:26 NRSV, italics added). Following this pivotal event, Mattathias issues a general call to resistance: "Let everyone who is *zealous* for the Law and supports the covenant come out with me" (1 Macc 2:27 NRSV, italics added).

The prophet Elijah is also remembered as a hero exemplifying "zeal" (Sir 48:2; 1 Macc 2:58) because he took the sword and slaughtered the prophets of Baal (1 Kgs 18:40), in accordance with the commandment of Deut 13:1-5 that the prophets of false gods are to be put to death. Later, giving God an account of his actions, Elijah declares, "I have been very *zealous* for the LORD, the God of hosts" (1 Kgs 19:10).

With such precedents as Phinehas, Elijah, and the Maccabean heroes, it is not surprising that Saul the zealous Pharisee was willing to employ violence against the early Jewish Christians. He saw himself as the defender of the faith of Israel, even making atonement for Israel by persecuting these apostates who were, in his view, speaking treason against the one God (Deut 13:5). The linkage between "zeal" and persecution of the church is made once more in Paul's Letter to the Philippians, where he affirms that he was "circumcised on the eighth day, a member of the people of Israel, of the tribe of Benjamin, a He-

brew born of Hebrews; as to the law, a Pharisee; *as to zeal, a persecutor of the church;* as to righteousness under the law, blameless" (Phil 3:5-6 NRSV, italics added).

Thus, when Paul speaks of his "zeal for the traditions of my ancestors" (v. 14), he is not merely speaking of a punctilious personal piety; he put his zeal into action by using force against those whom he considered enemies of the Law. (This does not mean that Paul was a member of an organized Zealot party engaged in armed resistance against Roman authority; as the examples of Phinehas and Mattathias suggest, zealot reprisals were usually targeted internally at members of the Jewish community who were perceived to be traitors.)[44]

Paul does not say where his persecuting activity occurred. Acts 8:1-3 gives an account of his "ravaging the church" in Jerusalem, but Paul's own statements in Gal 1:17 and 22 seem to imply that his activity was based in Damascus rather than Jerusalem. Nor does he narrate exactly how he persecuted the church. Despite the story of the stoning of Stephen in Acts 7, early Jewish Christians were not ordinarily subject to capital punishment in the synagogues; more likely, we should imagine that Paul was administering the penalty of disciplinary flogging of offenders, a penalty that Paul himself later suffered from synagogue authorities (2 Cor 11:24).[45]

1:15-17. In any case, Paul relates this unhappy history of persecution in order to emphasize that God brought it to an end. Paul's zeal for the Law led him to seek to destroy "the church of God," the eschatological community that God was raising up in the world. But God had other plans for Paul. And so, in a long temporal clause stretching through vv. 15-16*b*, Paul alludes to his experience of apostolic calling. Most interpreters have read these words as a reference to the "Damascus Road experience," narrated three times by Luke in Acts (9:1-19; 22:1-21, and 26:2-23). In interpreting Galatians, however, it is necessary to attend carefully to what Paul says and does not say here, for

44. For further discussion of ζηλωτής (*zēlōtēs*) and its importance for interpreting Paul's persecuting activity, see Dunn, *The Epistle to the Galatians,* 60-62; N. T. Wright, "Paul, Arabia, and Galatians," *JBL* 115 (1996) 683-92.

45. Paula Fredriksen, "Judaism, the Circumcision of Gentiles, and Apocalyptic Hope: Another Look at Galatians 1 and 2," *JTS* NS 42 (1991) 549, 556.

his Galatian addressees certainly had no access to the Lukan narrative. Paul says nothing about being on the road to Damascus or about a blinding light or a voice from heaven. He is interested neither in telling a vivid conversion story nor in talking about his own experience; instead, he wants to describe what God did. God, he says—the one who had "set me apart from my mother's womb"[46] and "called me through his grace"—was pleased "to reveal his Son in me so that I might proclaim him among the Gentiles." This densely formulated description of his calling demands close scrutiny.

Paul describes his call by using language and imagery taken from Jeremiah and Isaiah. Consequently, Paul's call must be understood on the pattern of the OT prophetic call narratives. In other words, Paul saw this event not as a conversion from one religion to another, but as a summons by the God of Israel to undertake a special prophetic mission.[47] Both of the texts that Paul echoes here foreshadow a ministry of proclamation to the Gentiles:

Now the word of the LORD came to me saying:
"Before I formed you in the womb I knew you,
and before you were born I consecrated you;
I appointed you a prophet to the nations
[LXX: ἔθνη *ethnē*, "Gentiles"]."
(Jer 1:4-5 NRSV, italics added)

Listen to me, O coastlands,
pay attention, you peoples from far away!
The LORD called me before I was born,
while I was in my mother's womb he named me.
.   .   .   .
And now the LORD says,
who formed me in the womb to be his servant,
to bring Jacob back to him,
and that Israel might be gathered to him,
.   .   .   .
he says,
"It is too light a thing that you should be my servant
to raise up the tribes of Jacob
and to restore the survivors of Israel;
I will give you as a light to the nations
[LXX: ἐθνῶν *ethnōn*, "Gentiles"],
that my salvation may reach to the end of the earth."
(Isa 49:1, 5-6 NRSV, italics added)

46. It is unclear why the NRSV and the NIV both replace the vivid image of the Greek text with a pallid paraphrase (NRSV, "before I was born"; NIV, "from birth"). The NIV places the more literal translation in a footnote as an alternative rendering.
47. See K. Stendahl, *Paul Among Jews and Gentiles* (Philadelphia: Fortress, 1976) 7-23.

We may be sure that Paul did not randomly allude to these particular texts; he finds in the figures of Jeremiah and Isaiah a prefiguration of his own apostolic calling to proclaim the gospel to the nations/Gentiles.

This is the purpose for which Paul was "set apart" by God (cf. Rom 1:1) before he was born, though he did not come to realize that until much later, when he was "called through [God's] grace" (v. 15; on God's "calling," see the Commentary on 1:6). As was noted in the discussion of 1:3-4, God's "grace" is God's powerful unmerited love that reaches out to rescue those who are trapped in the destructive grip of the present evil age. Paul recognizes that only by grace can he, the former persecutor of the church, be called and embraced by God and entrusted with a crucial apostolic mission to the Gentiles (cf. 1 Cor 15:8-10a).

That mission is the major emphasis of v. 16. Two interpretations of v. 16a are possible, one emphasizing Paul's *reception* of revelation and the other emphasizing his *proclamation* of it. Reading this passage through the lens of the Acts narrative, many interpreters have translated the passage as in the NRSV: God chose "to reveal his Son *to* me." Paul would thus be referring to some experience like the Damascus Road story in which he encountered a revelation of the Son of God. That is a possible reading, and it is consistent with v. 12 (see also 1 Cor 9:1; 15:8). The Greek text here, however, reads ἐν ἐμοί (*en emoi*), which would more naturally yield the translation given by the NIV as well as in the NRSV footnote: God chose "to reveal his Son *in* me." The prepositional phrase would then be instrumental in function: Paul is saying that it was God's purpose to reveal his Son in and through Paul's own person. (The phrase "in me" does not refer to "the inward reality of Christian experience,"[48] as though Paul were locating the event of revelation within his own heart. This sort of introspective individualism is foreign to Paul's thought world; he is describing the dynamic outreach of the gospel to the Gentiles through him.) That may sound like an extravagant claim, but it is consistent with Paul's conception of his identity and ministry. He can say, "It is no longer I who live, but it is Christ who lives in me" (2:20 NRSV). He can urge his Corinthian readers

48. R. N. Longenecker, *Galatians*, WBC 41 (Dallas: Word, 1990) 32.

to imitate him as he imitates Christ (1 Cor 11:1). He can even say that all who see the glory of the Lord are transformed into the divine image (2 Cor 3:18). In view of these convictions, it is not surprising to find Paul in v. 16 affirming that it was God's purpose to make Christ manifest *in* him in order that he might effectively proclaim Christ to the Gentiles.

On either interpretation, the disclosure of God's Son[49] is a transformative apocalyptic event. The verb "to reveal" (ἀποκαλύπτω *apokalyptō*) signals a manifestation of Christ that has transformed Paul's life from a life of zeal for the ancestral traditions to a life of "gospeling" Christ (the same verb as in vv. 8-9, 11) among the Gentiles. We should not draw a distinction between Paul's first experience of coming to believe in Christ and a later experience of commissioning for apostleship; rather, the two are one and the same. The gracious call of God was, according to Paul's account, precisely the call to become an apostle to the Gentile world. This is not merely a significant event in Paul's own spiritual journey; he presents it as a decisive moment in the unfolding of God's cosmic plan for spreading the gospel.

All of the theologically important material in vv. 15-16*b*, however, belongs to a subordinate clause in this sentence. Paul's main affirmations are contained in the independent clauses of vv. 16*c*-17: "[After my call], I did not confer with any human being, nor did I go up to Jerusalem to those who were already apostles before me, but I went away at once into Arabia, and afterwards I returned to Damascus." We see here that Paul is still producing evidence in support of the thesis stated in vv. 11-12: His gospel is dependent on no human source. This is proved by the fact that he did not take counsel with anyone—especially the Jerusalem apostles—after receiving his apostolic call. Instead, he "immediately" went away to Arabia. The verb in v. 16*c* (προσανεθέμην *prosanethemēn*) is rightly translated by the NIV as "consult"; J. D. G. Dunn has suggested that its meaning may be specified as "consult in order to be given a skilled or authoritative interpretation."[50] That is precisely what Paul insists he did *not* do; he did not consult with "flesh and blood"

(both the NRSV and the NIV use paraphrases here rather than reproducing Paul's concrete language). Paul does not dispute that the Jerusalem apostles are, in fact, legitimate apostles; indeed, he concedes that they preceded him on the scene as preachers of the gospel (cf. 1 Cor 15:5-9). His point is, however, that he did not seek them out to receive instruction in the faith; having received a commission directly from God, he went his own way. He portrays himself, as J. L. Martyn puts it, as a "lone-wolf apostle."[51]

Why did Paul go to Arabia, and what did he do there? The sketchy narrative of v. 17 gives us no answers to these questions. Most commentators suppose that he went to the cities of the kingdom of Nabatea, to the south and east of Damascus,[52] in order to preach the gospel there. This supposition is supported by Paul's passing reminiscence in 2 Cor 11:32-33 of an unpleasant brush with the authority of the Nabatean king Aretas IV (8 BCE–40 CE) in Damascus. Certainly, going to preach the gospel would be a natural sequel to the call described in vv. 15-16. The difficulty, however, is that there is no extant tradition of a Pauline mission in Nabatea. A different proposal, offered by N. T. Wright, builds on the fact that Paul's only other reference to Arabia (Gal 4:25) identifies it as the site of Mt. Sinai. Wright speculates that Paul, who had previously identified with the zealous Elijah, followed Elijah's footsteps by going off into the wilderness to Mt. Horeb (= Sinai; see 1 Kgs 19:1-18), there to seek God and to come to grips with his new prophetic commission.[53] This interesting suggestion is reinforced not only by the fact that Paul elsewhere explicitly links his own ministry with that of Elijah (Rom 11:1-6) but also by the fact that he ended his mysterious sojourn in Arabia by returning to Damascus, just as Elijah had done (1 Kgs 19:15). None of this, however, is pertinent to Paul's immediate argument, and so he says nothing more about it in v. 17.

1:18-20. Only after three years (probably after his call rather than after his return to Damascus) did Paul go to Jerusalem. The cautious discussion

---

49. This is the first reference in Galatians to Christ as God's Son. For further discussion of this title, see the Commentary on 2:20 and 4:4-7.

50. Dunn, *The Epistle to the Galatians,* 67.

51. J. L. Martyn, *Galatians,* AB 33A (New York: Doubleday, 1997) 170.

52. See H. D. Betz, *Galatians: A Commentary on Paul's Letter to the Churches in Galatia,* Hermeneia (Philadelphia: Fortress, 1979) 73-74, and literature cited there.

53. N. T. Wright, "Paul, Arabia, and Galatians," *JBL* 115 (1996).

in vv. 18-24 looks very much like an exercise in damage control. Paul cannot deny—however much he might like to—that he spent time in Jerusalem, but he is concerned to emphasize the brevity of his stay and his limited contact with members of the Jerusalem church. He spent two weeks staying with Cephas (= Peter; see 2:7-8; John 1:42) and saw none of the other apostles except James, the brother of the Lord.

This James, the brother of Jesus (Mark 6:3), is to be distinguished from James the son of Zebedee and James the son of Alphaeus, both of whom appear in the lists of Jesus' twelve disciples (e.g., Mark 3:17-18). Although there is no evidence that he was a follower of his brother prior to the crucifixion, James became a witness of the resurrection of Jesus (1 Cor 15:7) and ultimately assumed a role of authority in the early Jerusalem church (Acts 15:13-21; 21:18; cf. Gal 2:9, 12).

Paul's tantalizing narrative frustrates our curiosity to know what he discussed with Peter and James. It is sometimes suggested that Peter must have instructed Paul specifically about Jesus, so that this visit provides the basis for Paul's knowledge of Jesus' life and teachings. In fact, however, Paul seems eager to deny any such inference, and the scarcity of specific references to such traditions in Paul's letters would seem to corroborate his denial.[54] Paul tells us nothing about the content of his conversations with Peter, but he presents the visit as a matter of casual contact and emphasizes that (in contrast to the account given by Acts 9:26-30) he had no public contact with the gathered Christian community. This seems so improbable that Paul feels compelled to back up his statements with an emphatic oath that he is not lying (v. 20). This is one of the clearest signs that Paul is responding to allegations, and not merely telling his own story. The rival Missionaries in Galatia must have claimed that Paul had been taught and commissioned by the Jerusalem church. Paul emphatically denies this report.

1:21-24. After his two-week visit, Paul went away to "the regions of Syria and Cilicia." These are, respectively, the territories of Antioch (his base of mission for a time, Acts 13–14) and Tarsus (his hometown, Acts 9:11; 21:39). He mentions his area of operations once again to stress his distance from Jerusalem, as shown by vv. 22-24. The churches of Judea, including Jerusalem, had still not laid eyes upon him. This establishes once again the independence of his apostolic mission from their authority.

Of special interest here is Paul's account of what the Judean churches said about him during this period. He reports that they enthusiastically approved of his preaching, for he was "proclaiming [εὐαγγελίζεται *euangelizetai*] the faith he once tried to destroy." Indeed, they praised God for his work (v. 24). Paul thus looks back to an earlier period of independence and harmony between his mission and the Jerusalem community. At this stage, there was no dispute about the Law and no suggestion that Paul's gospel was in any sense deficient. The Judean churches understood him to be preaching the same "faith" that they shared. All of this is important because it implies that all the recent trouble and conflict had been caused not by a change in Paul's preaching, as the Missionaries alleged, but by a change of mind in the churches of Judea and Jerusalem that has created new pressure for circumcision and Law observance among the Gentiles (cf. 2:12).[55]

The expression "proclaiming the faith" in v. 23 also shows that "the faith" can function for Paul as a synonym for "the gospel." "The faith" is not just a matter of inward attitudes of the heart; it alludes to the substantive content of Christian preaching, as summarized in kerygmatic formulas such as Gal 1:3-4 and 1 Cor 15:3-5. This observation will prove important in interpreting other references to "faith" (πίστις *pistis*) later in the letter.

---

54. For his few direct references to Jesus tradition, see 1 Cor 7:10-11; 11:23-26; and perhaps 1 Thess 4:15-17. On the whole question, see V. P. Furnish, *Jesus According to Paul* (Cambridge: Cambridge University Press, 1993).

55. On this whole problem, see Paula Fredriksen, "Judaism, the Circumcision of Gentiles, and Apocalyptic Hope: Another Look at Galatians 1 and 2," *JTS* NS 42 (1991); R. Jewett, "The Agitators and the Galatian Congregation," *NTS* 17 (1970–71) 198-212.

REFLECTIONS

1. Galatians 1:11-24 raises the pressing issue of the relationship between tradition and revelation. Paul juxtaposes his gospel against all religious tradition handed on by human authorities. This poses two urgent problems for those who preach the gospel in our time. First, can the Christian message be formulated as a tradition, or is there something about the gospel that resists fixed traditional formulation? If the latter, is it possible for a community to build its life on the basis of the gospel? Second, should preachers of the Word continue to claim the same sort of unmediated authority that Paul asserted for himself? If so, are they in danger of grounding their message in an appeal to their own private experience?

The Christian church has historically accepted Paul's claim to be a witness to the risen Jesus in a way that set him apart from other Christians who have subsequently experienced the presence of Christ. Accordingly, Paul's claim to be a special apostle to the Gentiles has been acknowledged in the church, and his few extant writings have been collected and canonized as authoritative guides to Christian faith and practice. Yet, there is a certain irony about this development: Paul the lone-wolf apostle, whose message was neither conveyed nor authorized by any church, becomes the source of a body of binding ecclesiastical tradition! Paul, of course, encouraged this development; he commended his churches for keeping the traditions he had taught them (1 Cor 11:2) and scolded them when they failed to do so. In the Pastoral Epistles, we see a later and fuller development of this conception of tradition in the Pauline churches. Even in Galatians, Paul emphatically expects his readers to hold fast to the form of the gospel that they had received from him (Gal 1:8-9). Thus Paul's letters give ample evidence that the gospel can be expressed in fixed formulations that command the confessional assent of the community.

It should be clear, then, that Paul is no advocate of a free-form spirituality in which each person listens individualistically for messages from God and in effect invents his or her private religion. Paul would have been appalled by the story of Sheila Larson, who told interviewers that her religion was "Sheilaism."[56] He certainly did not think of his own message as "Paulinism." On the contrary, his ministry makes sense if and only if it really is true that his message was given him by the God who created the universe and chose to rescue fallen humanity through the death and resurrection of Jesus Christ. That is the singular, apocalyptic message that Paul was entrusted with at the time of his call, a message so clear and compelling that it required no corroboration from those who had been apostles before him.

It is, therefore, an abuse of this passage to treat it as a proof text for the sanctity of individual conscience, or private religious experience, in opposition to entrenched tradition. The bumper sticker that reads "Question Authority" does not express a Pauline perspective. The dichotomy posed in Gal 1:11-24 is not between the individual and tradition but between *God's* gospel and *human* tradition. True authority resides in preaching that gives expression to the apocalyptic gospel message.

Of course, Paul believed that this message has a way of unsettling the stable structures of the present age, because it constantly calls the community to measure its life against the eschatological truth of the gospel. Every practice, every institution, must be measured in relation to the eschatological vision of freedom and unity in Christ (see, e.g., Gal 3:28). It is not easy to build stable community structures in the church. One of the reasons why the Galatians found the message of the Missionaries tempting is that it offered the apparent security of fixed rules and structures. These issues will be addressed more specifically later in the letter, but it is important to recognize from the beginning that Paul resists the teaching of the Missionaries

---

56. R. N. Bellah et al., *Habits of the Heart: Individualism and Commitment in American Life* (Berkeley: University of California Press, 1985) 220-21, 235.

---

precisely because he sees it as turning the gospel into a domesticated human tradition and thereby making the church into another cultural community in which we might "advance" zealously if we play by the rules. He insists that the gospel is something wholly different: a message from God that breaks in on us from outside our religious culture and transforms everything.

But what, then, of the second question? What should we make of people who claim direct access to God's revelation, unmediated by any tradition? Can Christian preachers claim privileged access to revelation? The answer is both no and yes. No, we cannot say that we are among the original roster of witnesses to the resurrection, as Paul was (1 Cor 15:3-8; note that Paul describes the appearance of the risen Christ to him as "last of all"). Paul, standing close to the apocalyptic event of Christ's death and resurrection, was given a special commission to take the extraordinary news to the Gentiles, proclaiming that Israel's God had now acted for the salvation of the whole world. In that sense, Paul's position is unique, and our calling to proclaim the gospel is only analogous to his, not identical. But, on the other hand, the analogies are real; we continue to believe and proclaim that God has broken the power of the present evil age (Gal 1:4) and that the story of God's Son, Jesus Christ, is the revelation of God's purpose for creation. So we do not replicate Paul's experience of revelation, but we do continue to see the world in the light of the same revelation that he announced. The distinction is crucial: Those who lust after experiences of continuing revelation easily fall into fantasy and delusion, but those who attend steadily to the singular once-for-all revelation of Jesus Christ are given a truthful vision of reality as it is in God's new creation (Gal 6:15).

2. The connection between zeal and persecution is another theme worth pondering in this passage. Religious conviction and passion can have an ugly side. Paul sadly recognizes in his own past that his zeal for the traditions of his ancestors led him to sanction and commit acts of violence (see 1 Cor 15:9; Phil 3:6; 1 Tim 1:12-16; cf. Rom 10:1-3). The preacher who takes up this matter will want to keep two points clearly in focus.

First of all, the link between zeal and violence is not distinctive to Judaism. From time to time one encounters claims that Judaism is inherently a religion of violence and that Christianity is inherently immune to this problem.[57] The bare facts of history disconfirm this caricature: Christians have a tragic, bloody history of inquisition and persecution against dissenters, including preeminently the Jewish people. Thus we must take care not to point the finger at "Judaism" as the cause of Paul's persecuting impulse. All three of the great monotheistic religions (Judaism, Christianity, Islam) have shown the tendency to engender persecution and violence. The reasons for this are not hard to understand; those who take seriously the holiness of the one God find it difficult to tolerate people who blasphemously deny that God or transgress God's revealed law. Of course, each of these great traditions also contains its own theological checks and balances to constrain the persecuting impulse and to enjoin humility and mercy. The urgent tasks of the preacher are to warn that the laudable desire to defend the truth can contain the seeds of violence and to show how that desire must be disciplined by the deeper wisdom of the tradition.

In the case of the Christian gospel, the cross is the central symbol that short-circuits justifications of violence: God's way of dealing with dissenters and adversaries was not to destroy them but to give his Son to die *for* them. Thus when Paul received his call, he did not turn around and start persecuting Jews who failed to believe the gospel; rather, in conformity with the example of Jesus, Paul became the persecuted (Gal 5:11; 6:17) rather than the persecutor. The second point to be kept in focus, then, is that Paul's own life history provides an example that should cause Christians to turn away from zealous persecution. Paul's

---

57. See, e.g., R. Hamerton-Kelly, *Sacred Violence: Paul's Hermeneutic of the Cross* (Minneapolis: Fortress, 1992). For a critique of Hamerton-Kelly, see D. Boyarin, *A Radical Jew: Paul and the Politics of Identity* (Berkeley: University of California Press, 1994) 214-19.

story models the way in which the gospel calls us to renounce violence as an instrument of God's righteousness. Our responsibility is not to eradicate the enemies of God but to announce God's reconciling power in the world (see 2 Cor 5:17-20).

3. This leads to the final major theme that emerges from reflection on this text: the transforming power of God's surprising call. Paul was transformed from persecutor to apostle, leaving the churches in Judea marveling and giving glory to God. Paul does not tell this story as a testimony of "what Jesus did for me," as though the important thing were how Paul's sins were forgiven or his needs met. Rather, this passage is a testimony about how the *apokalypsis* of Jesus Christ turned Paul's world upside down and made him into an instrument of God's reconciling grace, reaching out to those who had previously been "strangers to the covenants of promise, having no hope and without God in the world" (Eph 2:12 NRSV). If we are to do justice to Paul's testimony, our preaching on this passage must not dwell on the inner, personal experience of conversion; we should dwell, instead, on God's act of seizing us and empowering us for tasks we never could have imagined.

GALATIANS 2:1-10, PAUL'S MEETING WITH THE JERUSALEM LEADERS

NIV

2 Fourteen years later I went up again to Jerusalem, this time with Barnabas. I took Titus along also. [2]I went in response to a revelation and set before them the gospel that I preach among the Gentiles. But I did this privately to those who seemed to be leaders, for fear that I was running or had run my race in vain. [3]Yet not even Titus, who was with me, was compelled to be circumcised, even though he was a Greek. [4]This matter arose because some false brothers had infiltrated our ranks to spy on the freedom we have in Christ Jesus and to make us slaves. [5]We did not give in to them for a moment, so that the truth of the gospel might remain with you.

[6]As for those who seemed to be important— whatever they were makes no difference to me; God does not judge by external appearance— those men added nothing to my message. [7]On the contrary, they saw that I had been entrusted with the task of preaching the gospel to the Gentiles,[a] just as Peter had been to the Jews.[b] [8]For God, who was at work in the ministry of Peter as an apostle to the Jews, was also at work in my ministry as an apostle to the Gentiles. [9]James,

a7 Greek uncircumcised   *b7 Greek* circumcised; *also in verses 8 and 9*

NRSV

2 Then after fourteen years I went up again to Jerusalem with Barnabas, taking Titus along with me. [2]I went up in response to a revelation. Then I laid before them (though only in a private meeting with the acknowledged leaders) the gospel that I proclaim among the Gentiles, in order to make sure that I was not running, or had not run, in vain. [3]But even Titus, who was with me, was not compelled to be circumcised, though he was a Greek. [4]But because of false believers[a] secretly brought in, who slipped in to spy on the freedom we have in Christ Jesus, so that they might enslave us— [5]we did not submit to them even for a moment, so that the truth of the gospel might always remain with you. [6]And from those who were supposed to be acknowledged leaders (what they actually were makes no difference to me; God shows no partiality)—those leaders contributed nothing to me. [7]On the contrary, when they saw that I had been entrusted with the gospel for the uncircumcised, just as Peter had been entrusted with the gospel for the circumcised [8](for he who worked through Peter making him an apostle to the circumcised also worked through me in sending me to the Gen-

a Gk false brothers

NIV

Peter[a] and John, those reputed to be pillars, gave me and Barnabas the right hand of fellowship when they recognized the grace given to me. They agreed that we should go to the Gentiles, and they to the Jews. [10]All they asked was that we should continue to remember the poor, the very thing I was eager to do.

[a]9 Greek *Cephas*; also in verses 11 and 14

NRSV

tiles), [9]and when James and Cephas and John, who were acknowledged pillars, recognized the grace that had been given to me, they gave to Barnabas and me the right hand of fellowship, agreeing that we should go to the Gentiles and they to the circumcised. [10]They asked only one thing, that we remember the poor, which was actually what I was[a] eager to do.

[a] Or *had been*

COMMENTARY

Paul next gives a brief account of his summit meeting with the leaders of the Jerusalem church. This account continues his defense of the thesis stated in 1:11-12: Paul received his gospel by revelation, not from any human source. Thus, even in telling the story of his concord with the Jerusalem leaders, he is careful to maintain independence from their direction. This is a delicate rhetorical and political balancing act; Paul wants to claim the endorsement of the Jerusalem apostles (who had, in fact, recognized the validity of his mission to the Gentiles) without conceding undue authority to them. This double political agenda makes Gal 2:1-10 a complex passage whose nuances must be considered carefully.

In order to follow the strategy of Paul's argument, we must keep two points clearly in mind:

(1) There are not two but three parties involved in the dispute described here: Paul and Barnabas as representatives of the Antioch church, the "pillar" apostles of the Jerusalem church, and the "false brothers" (i.e., the party within the Jerusalem church demanding circumcision of Gentile converts).[58] Paul depicts the last group as the source of the conflict, and he conspicuously does not describe them as endorsing the agreement between the first two groups.

(2) The whole narrative prefigures the conflict currently being played out in Galatia, and Paul's recounting of the matter is shaped by the debate over circumcision in the Galatian churches. It is possible that there is some direct link between the "false brothers" and the rival Missionaries who have come to Galatia; whether that is so or not, Paul tells the story in a way that makes the parallels obvious.

This much is clear. Nonetheless, 2:1-10 leaves us with many unanswered questions. Parts of the passage are difficult to follow, for Paul is so agitated that he has written convoluted and incomplete sentences. We can virtually hear him spluttering with anger as he writes; his butchered syntax reflects the strong passions that still swirl around the controversy. Any interpretation of the passage requires some filling of syntactical gaps and some hypotheses about the uncertain chronology of events briefly alluded to here.

More difficult still is the question of how Paul's account of this Jerusalem meeting is to be coordinated with the narrative of the Acts of the Apostles. Because Paul solemnly swears that this meeting took place during his second visit to Jerusalem after his call, some critics have attempted to link Gal 2:1-10 with the "famine relief visit" of Acts 11:27-30, thereby preserving the historical accuracy of the Lukan narrative.[59] The more natural reading of the evidence, however, identifies Gal 2:1-10 with Luke's story of the apostolic council in Acts 15.[60] This commentary assumes that the meeting described in Gal 2:1-10 is the same meeting described in Acts 15. There are, of course, discrepancies between the two

58. H. D. Betz, *Galatians,* Hermeneia (Philadelphia: Fortress, 1979) 81-83.

59. This view is defended by R. N. Longenecker, *Galatians,* WBC 41 (Dallas: Word, 1990) lxxiii-lxxxiii.

60. For defenses of this view, see C. C. Hill, *Hellenists and Hebrews: Reappraising Division in the Earliest Church* (Philadelphia: Fortress, 1991) 103-47; M. Silva, *Explorations in Exegetical Method: Galatians as a Test Case* (Grand Rapids: Eerdmans, 1996) 129-39.

accounts. This is not surprising, for Luke is piecing together traditional sources from an earlier period, whereas Paul is giving a firsthand account—which also, to be sure, has an apologetic agenda. Readers interested in a full explanation of the problem may refer to the standard critical commentaries and NT introductions.

2:1-2. The continuation of Paul's retrospective narrative is marked by the third occurrence of the adverb ἔπειτα (*epeita*, "then," v. 1; also in 1:18, 21). It is impossible to be sure whether the fourteen-year interval mentioned in v. 1 includes or follows the three years between Paul's call and his first visit to Jerusalem (1:18). The important point for Paul's argument is that during this lengthy period he had no direct dealings with Jerusalem; presumably he was engaged in preaching to Gentiles in Syria and Cilicia (1:21) and perhaps elsewhere in Asia Minor, working from a base in the Antioch church (cf. Acts 13–14).

This Gentile mission work, however, provoked controversy among Jewish Christians (see Acts 15:1-5), and a decision was made that Paul and Barnabas should go to Jerusalem to discuss the matter with the church there. Paul, in distinction from Acts, does not say explicitly that he and Barnabas went as representatives of the Antioch church; it is possible that Paul avoids mentioning this fact because of his subsequent falling out with that community (2:11-14). The present narrative is crafted to create the impression that Paul was operating as a freelance apostle under the guidance of revelation (v. 2), and the role of Barnabas in the Jerusalem meeting is minimized in Paul's account. Nonetheless, there are good reasons to think that Paul and Barnabas were, in fact, sent by the church at Antioch. Verse 1 corresponds closely to Acts 15:1-2, and Luke's report of opposition by Pharisaic Jewish Christians tallies well with Paul's references to the "false brothers"; they were saying, "It is necessary for [Gentile converts] to be circumcised and ordered to keep the law of Moses" (Acts 15:5 NRSV).

The composition of the delegation from Antioch to Jerusalem was significant. Barnabas, a prominent Jewish Christian, had worked closely with Paul in the Gentile mission (see Acts 13–14; 1 Cor 9:6; Col 4:10). According to Luke's account, he was "a Levite, a native of Cyprus," who became a leading member of the earliest Jerusa-

lem church (Acts 4:36-37). Luke also portrays him as Paul's early supporter and mentor who interceded for him and introduced him to the fearful and skeptical members of the Jerusalem church shortly after his call experience (Acts 9:26-27). Since Paul vehemently denies having been anywhere near Jerusalem during this period of his life (Gal 1:17-24), the accuracy of this biographical detail about Barnabas is doubtful. According to Acts 11:19-26, Barnabas was also sent by the Jerusalem church as an emissary to Antioch, where he witnessed and warmly approved the beginnings of the Gentile mission and even recruited Paul to come from Tarsus to Antioch to participate in this work. Thus Barnabas was a natural choice to represent the Antiochene church in its negotiations with Jerusalem; he was a Jew of impeccable hereditary credentials who had strong personal ties to the Jerusalem church. He also had a reputation for living up to his name ("son of encouragement") by acting as a conciliator (unlike Paul, who was a more abrasive character).

Titus, on the other hand, was an uncircumcised Greek (v. 3), presumably a convert of Paul (cf. Titus 1:4). Although he is never mentioned in Acts, he plays a large role in 2 Corinthians as Paul's emissary to Corinth (see 2 Cor 2:13; 7:6-7, 13-15; 8:6, 16-24; 12:18). The decision to take him to Jerusalem (a decision for which Paul implicitly claims responsibility) was a deliberately provocative move. The presence of the uncircumcised Titus would place the Jerusalem authorities face-to-face with a test case: Their decision about the validity of a Law-free mission to the Gentiles could not be treated as a theoretical halakhic problem, for it would have immediate impact on a particular Gentile who stood before them as evidence of the fruits of Paul's preaching.

The effect of this multicultural delegation to Jerusalem was described aptly by Martin Luther:

> By presenting himself with both of them [sc. Barnabas and Titus] he [Paul] intended to make it clear that he was at liberty to be a Gentile with Titus and a Jew with Barnabas. Thus he would prove the freedom of the gospel in each case, namely that is is permissible to be circumcised and yet that circumcision is not necessary, and that this is the way one should think of the entire law.[61]

---

61. Martin Luther, cited in Betz, *Galatians*, 84n. 252.

In other words, the very composition of the delegation bore witness to the gospel, as encapsulated in Gal 5:6 and 6:15. The gospel creates a new community in which circumcision no longer erects social barriers.

Paul declares that he made this trip to Jerusalem "according to revelation" (κατὰ ἀποκάλυψιν *kata apokalypsin*; translated by both the NRSV and the NIV as "in response to a revelation"). This statement is sometimes thought to contradict Acts 15:2, in which Paul and Barnabas are "appointed" by the Antioch church to go to Jerusalem. In fact, however, there is no real tension between these statements. The story told in Acts 13:2-3 provides an instructive parallel. Paul and Barnabas received a missionary commissioning from Antioch through a prophetic word from the Holy Spirit that came to the community during worship. This revelation was then confirmed by the community's action of sending them out after fasting, prayer, and the laying on of hands. When Paul says that he went to Jerusalem "according to revelation," he probably has something similar in mind: a prophetic word received in the worshiping assembly at Antioch and acted upon by the church (note esp. Acts 15:3: "So they were sent on their way by the church"). In 1 Cor 14:26, 30, for example, Paul speaks of prophets in the church as receiving "a revelation" from God.[62] Thus the reference to "revelation" in Gal 2:2 should merely remind us that Paul and the other early Christians believed that the Holy Spirit was powerfully at work in the church, continuing to act and speak through revelatory prophetic gifts.

Upon his arrival in Jerusalem, Paul expounded his gospel. His language describing this event is carefully chosen. He "set before them" (ἀναθέμην *anethemēn*) the gospel that he was proclaiming among the Gentiles. This verb in no way implies that he submitted his gospel to the Jerusalem leaders hoping meekly for their approval; instead, it simply means that he placed his gospel on the table before them. As the opening chapter of the letter has emphatically stated, Paul was in no doubt about the truth or divine origin of his message.

Why, then, does he say he did this "to make sure that I was not running, or had not run, in vain"? The answer to this question lies in the theology of election that Paul expounds fully in Romans 11. He sees the Gentile mission as an unexpected initiative of God to make Israel jealous and ultimately to bring them to recognize the truth of the gospel (Rom 11:11-12). His own preaching to Gentiles was a necessary part of that plan (Rom 11:13-14). God's ultimate purpose was to raise up a new eschatological people composed of Jews and Gentiles together praising the one God through Jesus Christ (Rom 15:7-13; cf. the expression "Israel of God" in Gal 6:16). God's plan requires, then, that the Jerusalem community hear Paul's account of the Gentile mission and its fruits. If they reject the legitimacy of this mission, it will indeed make Paul's work futile in one sense, for their rejection will thwart God's intent to bring Jew and Gentile together as one in Christ.[63] In fact, however, Paul did not anticipate any such failure; he believed that the gospel was the power of God at work in the world and that it would efficaciously bring the Jerusalem leaders to recognize the validity of his work. As he tells the story, that is precisely what did happen.

Paul is careful to emphasize, however, that not everyone in the Jerusalem church participated in this meeting.[64] He set forth his gospel "privately to those who seemed to be leaders" (v. 2). This is the first appearance of an expression that occurs four times in this passage: "those who seem [to be something]" (οἱ δοκοῦντες *hoi dokountes*; also twice in v. 6 and again in v. 9). The term expresses some degree of ironic distance from claims being made for the authority of the Jerusalem leaders; in Plato's *Apology,* Socrates uses the same expression to speak with withering disdain of those who "seem to be wise." In the context of Galatians, Paul's reference to the "seeming" or "reputed" leaders allows him "to recognize the *de facto* role which 'the men of reputation' play, without compromising his theological stance that God and Christ are the only authority behind his gospel."[65]

62. These comments are in agreement with F. J. Matera, *Galatians,* Sacra Pagina 9 (Collegeville, Minn.: Liturgical Press) 72.

63. Here I am in agreement with C. B. Cousar, *Galatians,* Interpretation (Atlanta: John Knox, 1982) 39; J. D. G. Dunn, *The Epistle to the Galatians,* Black's NT Commentary (Peabody, Mass.: Hendrickson, 1993) 94; J. L. Martyn, *Galatians,* AB 33A (New York: Doubleday, 1997) 193.

64. This is one of the differences from Acts 15, which describes a public consultation. Again, the difference is not difficult to understand. No doubt the really important conversation, from Paul's point of view, may have occurred in private negotiating sessions with the Jerusalem leaders.

65. H. D. Betz, *Galatians: A Commentary on Paul's Letter to the Churches in Galatia,* Hermeneia (Philadelphia: Fortress, 1979) 87.

2:3-5. In any case, Paul presented his case only to these eminent persons in the Jerusalem church. Despite pressure from the circumcision group, Titus was not compelled by these leaders to be circumcised. (This certainly does not mean that he freely chose to be circumcised; that would undercut Paul's whole argument. The point is that he remained uncircumcised.)[66] This simple fact was a great victory for Paul's position, for it symbolized Jersualem's acceptance of Antioch's Gentile mission, with its practice of receiving uncircumcised Gentiles into the church.

This decision by the Jerusalem leaders, however, was reached in the face of heavy pressure from those whom Paul calls the "false brothers" (v. 4). Who were these people? It is important to observe that they were Jewish Christians (i.e., not non-Christian Jewish undercover agents seeking to sow dissension in the church). Luke's narrative describes them as "believers who belonged to the sect of the Pharisees" (Acts 15:5), as did Paul himself (Acts 23:6; Phil 3:5). Paul, however, labels them as "false brothers" because they hold to a gospel that he regards as false (see Gal 1:6-9); the implication is that they, therefore, do not have a rightful claim to be members of Christ's family.

Despite Paul's scorn, the position of the "false brothers" is understandable. Given the clear teaching of the Law of Moses about circumcision—a teaching that Jesus had certainly never challenged or revoked—they believed that circumcision was the divinely appointed sign of covenant membership in the people of God. J. D. G. Dunn suggests that their arguments may have been similar to those attributed by Josephus to the Jew Eleazar, who sought to persuade Izates, king of Adiabene, to be circumcised after he had become an adherent of Judaism:

In your ignorance, O king, you are guilty of the greatest offence against the law and thereby against God. For you ought not merely to read the law but also, and even more, to do what is commanded in it. How long will you continue to be uncircumcised? If you have not yet read the law concerning this matter, read it now,

so that you may know what an impiety it is that you commit.[67]

Interestingly, this same passage in Josephus shows that Eleazar's opinion was not necessarily held by all Jews in the same way. Ananias, the merchant who had instructed Izates in the practices of Judaism, thought it politically dangerous for the king to accept circumcision and actually advised against it.[68] A good case can be made that Jewish thinkers of Paul's day did not necessarily pressure Gentiles to be circumcised; we know that Hellenistic synagogues attracted circles of "god-fearers," Gentiles who followed Jewish worship practices without undergoing circumcision. The prevailing Jewish eschatological hope was that Gentiles would abandon their idolatry and worship the living God of Israel, but this did not necessarily entail their converting to Judaism and being circumcised. Paula Fredriksen explains this line of thinking: "When God establishes his Kingdom . . . these two groups will together constitute 'his people': Israel, redeemed from exile, and the Gentiles, redeemed from idolatry. Gentiles are saved as Gentiles: they do not, eschatologically, become Jews."[69]

The disagreement between Paul and the "false brothers," then, may have turned on the issue of eschatology. What time was it? Was the Gentile mission a sign of the new eschatological age, in which Gentiles were granted a full place in God's kingdom? Or, alternatively, were the rules of the old age still in force, so that full participation in God's people was possible only for those who were marked by circumcision as members of the covenant?

When Paul testifies that Titus was not "compelled" to be circumcised, he uses the same verb (ἀναγκάζω *anagkazō*) that appears in 2:14 ("How can you *compel* the Gentiles to live like Jews?") and again in 6:12 ("It is those who want to make a good showing in the flesh that try to *compel* you to be circumcised"). This threefold occurrence of the verb links together three different historical settings: the meeting in Jerusalem (2:1-10), the controversy at Antioch (2:11-21), and the

---

66. The circumcision of Timothy (Acts 16:1-3) was a different matter, for his mother was Jewish. Under Jewish law, that made him a Jew rather than a Gentile. Therefore, according to Acts at least, Paul decided that Timothy should be circumcised. This report obviously stands in tension with the policy that Paul elsewhere describes as "my rule in all the churches," that all should remain in the condition in which they were called, whether circumcised or uncircumcised (1 Cor 7:17-20).

67. Josephus *Antiquities of the Jews* 20.44-45. Cited by Dunn, *The Epistle to the Galatians,* 99-100.

68. Josephus *Antiquities of the Jews* 20.40-41.

69. Paula Fredriksen, "Judaism, The Circumcision of Gentiles, and Apocalyptic Hope: Another Look at Galatians 1 and 2," *JTS* NS 42 (1991) 547.

situation in Galatia (6:12-13). In all three cases, the "compulsion" in view is not some sort of violent coercion (circumcision at knifepoint, as it were), but rather a matter of argument and social pressure, as the example of Cephas at Antioch shows (vv. 11-14). Paul projects these three situations simultaneously on the same screen, as manifestations of a single underlying conflict.

This conflict is a serious struggle, as Paul's use of military metaphors in vv. 4-5 shows. He portrays the "false brothers" as spies who have "infiltrated our ranks" in order to "enslave" the free citizens. When Paul speaks of infiltration, he must be thinking not of their spying on his meeting with the Jerusalem leaders but of their previous stealthy surveillance of the mixed church of Jews and Gentiles in Antioch. This would explain what he means by saying that they "slipped in to spy on the freedom we have in Christ Jesus"; they were suspiciously observing the freedom with which Jews and Gentiles associated and worshiped together, including the celebration of the Lord's supper. The military imagery is not accidental; Paul really does see a war in progress (see Rom 6:12-14; 2 Cor 10:3-6; Phil 1:27-30; cf. Eph 6:12-20). These "false brothers" are enemy agents, partisans of the power of the "present evil age" (Gal 1:4). That is why Paul refuses any compromise or negotiation with them. Using battlefield imagery, he insists that he and Barnabas "did not give in to them for a moment" (lit., "did not yield in submission to them for one hour").

For the first time in the letter to the Galatians, Paul introduces in vv. 4-5 the antithetically paired categories of freedom and slavery. These terms will reappear as a major theme of the epistle in 3:28; 4:1-11; 4:21–5:1; and 5:13. It is of more than passing interest, then, that in the first appearance of these words, "freedom" refers to the unqualified association of Jewish and Gentile Christians, while "enslavement" refers to the attempted imposition of circumcision on Gentile believers. Of course, the circumcision advocates did not think of themselves as trying to enslave Gentile Christians; to the contrary, circumcision was understood among Jews as a sign of freedom from the passions of the flesh, a freedom created by the secure order of the divine law.

When Paul says that he and Barnabas took this stand against circumcision of Gentiles "so that the truth of the gospel might remain with you" (thus the NIV; "always" in the NRSV has no basis in the Greek text), he does not mean that they were thinking specifically of the Galatians at that time; indeed, the Galatian churches almost surely were not even founded at the time of the meeting in Jerusalem. He means that this stand was necessary to preserve the gospel for the Gentiles as a whole, both present and future, among whom the Galatians constitute a subset. Here again we see Paul weaving his narrative about the past together with the present controversy in Galatia. "The truth of the gospel" is closely tied here (as also in v. 14) to Paul's insistence on preaching a gospel free from legal and cultural prerequisites, a gospel that focuses on God's liberating initiative.

2:6-10. In these verses, the false brothers disappear from view, and Paul focuses now on the responses of James, Cephas, and John—apparently the key leaders in the Jerusalem Christian community—to his private presentation of the gospel he proclaimed. Paul hints even more broadly about his misgivings concerning their authority, or at least concerning the reverence in which they were held by some others. He cites the OT maxim that "God shows no partiality" (lit., "God does not take the face"; see, e.g., Deut 10:17; 2 Chr 19:7; Sir 35:13)[70] in order to indicate once again that he was not overawed by these reputed pillars of the church. Having been authorized directly by God's call, Paul looked them in the eyes as their equal. Nonetheless, for the purposes of his present argument, it is useful for him to be able to state that they added nothing to his articulation of the gospel. In other words, they did not instruct Paul to add something about circumcision and law observance to his preaching.

How is Paul's report related to the outcome of the apostolic council as recounted in Acts 15? In Acts, Luke says that the conference reached a formal decision—under the guidance of James—that Gentile converts were not required to be circumcised, but that they should "abstain from what has been sacrificed to idols and from blood and from what is strangled and from fornication" (Acts 15:28-29 NRSV). In other words, they were required to observe those prohibitions of the holiness code that apply to aliens residing in Israel

---

70. See J. M. Bassler, *Divine Impartiality: Paul and a Theological Axiom,* SBLDS 59 (Chico, Calif.: Scholars Press, 1982) 171-74.

(Leviticus 17–18). This certainly would constitute an addendum to Paul's gospel. If Paul knew anything about this "apostolic decree" described in Acts 15, he offers no hint of it in precisely the places where we would expect it—in Romans 14–15 and 1 Corinthians 8–10. The likeliest hypothesis is that Luke, writing a generation later, has retrojected a later church agreement back into the period of Paul's lifetime. Paul's emphatic denial in Gal 2:6 suggests that no such understanding was reached at the Jerusalem meeting.

The theological basis for the concord that was, in fact, reached between Paul and the Jerusalem apostles is explained in vv. 7-8: It is the same God who has worked in both Peter and Paul, the same God who has "entrusted" the gospel to each. Thus, despite the fact that they are called to work in different cultural spheres, each recognizes the grace of God at work in the other's ministry. Does the formulation of v. 7 mean that there actually are two different gospels, a "gospel of the uncircumcision" and a "gospel of the circumcision"? This would seem to contradict Paul's emphatic assertion that there can be only one gospel (1:6-9). Thus Paul's formulation in v. 7 should be understood to mean that Peter and Paul are complementary instruments of the one gospel (cf. 1 Cor 3:5-9), commissioned to speak primarily to different ethnic constituencies. Thus there are "two missions in which the one gospel is making its way into the whole of the cosmos."[71]

New Testament scholars have sometimes speculated that vv. 7-8 actually contain the wording of a formal agreement reached in the Jerusalem meeting, because only in these two verses does Paul use the Greek name "Peter" rather than the Aramaic "Cephas" and because the reference to the two gospels in v. 7 is not precisely paralleled elsewhere in Paul's letters. A corollary of this theory is that the wording of v. 8 (as reflected more precisely in the NRSV) may imply a subtle status distinction between Peter, who is recognized as an apostle, and Paul, to whom this title is not explicitly applied. Despite the ingenuity of such speculations, they are finally unpersuasive. Paul gives no indication that he is quoting the text of a formal agreement; he is merely summarizing in his own words (as he does again in v.

9) what the Jerusalem apostles recognized about his ministry. And we should not make too much of the omission of the term "apostleship" (ἀποστολή apostolē) with reference to Paul's mission in v. 8. As Frank Matera has pointed out, in the Greek both v. 7 and v. 8 are elliptical: "Paul entrusted with *the gospel to the uncircumcised,* Peter *to the circumcised;* Peter entrusted with *apostleship to the circumcised,* Paul *to the uncircumcised.*"[72] The non-repetition of "apostleship" in v. 8 is no more significant than the non-repetition of "gospel" in v. 7.

Far more important exegetically is the fact that v. 8 describes the ministries of both apostles as the work of God's power. The verb "to work in" (ἐνεργέω energeō), used twice here, is a characteristic Pauline word that appears in other contexts where God's effective power through human instruments is described (e.g., Gal 3:5; 5:6; Phil 2:13; Col 1:29; 1 Thess 2:13; cf. Eph 3:20). The best parallel to v. 8 is found in Paul's discussion of the complementarity of different gifts within the one body of Christ in 1 Corinthians 12:

There are varieties of activities [ἐνεργημάτων *energēmatōn*] but it is the same God who activates [ἐνεργῶν *energōn*] all of them in everyone. . . . All these are activated [ἐνεργεῖ *energei*] by one and the same Spirit, who allots to each one individually just as the Spirit chooses. (1 Cor 12:6, 11 NRSV)

Paul's use of the same verb in v. 8 suggests that the complementarity of the two missions to the Jews and to the Gentiles is grounded in this same truth: Both missions are the work of God's Spirit. This language is not a compromise agreement worked out in a negotiation between power brokers; rather, it reflects their common recognition of a power bigger than any of the human agents involved.

Recognizing this, James and Cephas and John gave to Paul and Barnabas "the right hand of fellowship [κοινωνία *koinōnia*]," signifying that they were engaged in a common venture. (On James and Cephas, see the Commentary on 1:18-19.) John is probably the son of Zebedee, one of the Twelve who, along with Peter and his brother James (not the same James mentioned in v. 9), had been part of an inner circle of Jesus' followers;

---

71. J. L. Martyn, *Galatians,* AB 33A (New York: Doubleday, 1997) 202.

72. F. J. Matera, *Galatians,* Sacra Pagina 9 (Collegeville, Minn.: Liturgical Press, 1992) 77.

for example, the tradition says John was present with Jesus at the transfiguration (Mark 9:1 par.) and in the Garden of Gethsemane (Mark 14:33 par.). He appears in the early chapters of Acts as a preaching companion of Peter (e.g., Acts 3–4), and he is later identified by the tradition as the Beloved Disciple who stands behind the tradition of the Fourth Gospel. Paul mentions him only here. The mention of this threesome indicates that they were recognized as the leading authority figures in the early Christian community in Jerusalem. The metaphorical reference to them as "pillars" is reminiscent of the Jewish tradition of calling Abraham, Isaac, and Jacob the "pillars" of Israel.[73] Paul is clearly dubious about this title, for he once again employs the distancing locution, "those *reputed* to be pillars."[74]

The important point for the purpose of Paul's argument is that these three pillar apostles "recognized the grace that had been given to me" (see Rom 1:5; 12:3; 15:15; 1 Cor 3:10; cf. Eph 3:2, 7). Paul represents this not merely as their acknowledgment of Antioch's Gentile mission but as a special confirmation of his own particular graced calling.[75] This is a critical move in Paul's argument. It enables him to claim that the Jerusalem leaders had once given their blessing to his Law-free preaching of the gospel. If now the Missionaries in Galatia were appealing to the authority of Jerusalem to overrule Paul, this could only mean one of two things: Either the Missionaries were perpetrating a lie or—as vv. 11-14 suggest—there had been a failure of nerve on the part of the Jerusalem leaders, a turning back from what God had revealed. Once upon a time, there had been a clear understanding, and they had shaken hands on it: Paul and Barnabas would preach to the Gentiles, and the Jerusalem apostles would preach to "the circumcision" (v. 9). As sad experience would soon prove, however, this formulation was neither unambiguous nor sufficient to clarify the relations between Jews and Gentiles in mixed worshiping communities.

At the time of the Jerusalem meeting, the only stipulation added by the Jerusalem leaders was that Paul and Barnabas should "remember the poor" (v. 10), meaning that they should provide financial support for those in need. The obligation of supporting the poor and the oppressed was a deeply ingrained element of Jewish piety, a fundamental element of Israel's covenant obligations (see, e.g., Deut 15:7-11),[76] and Paul readily affirmed his eagerness to be responsive to this concern. This exhortation by the Jerusalem pillars was a primary impetus for Paul's decision to raise money from his Gentile mission congregations for "the poor among the saints at Jerusalem" (Rom 15:26). Several references in Paul's letters show that this collection became a major project of his ministry (Rom 15:25-27; 1 Cor 16:1-4; 2 Corinthians 8–9)—a project in which the Galatians themselves participated at some point (1 Cor 16:1).[77] Paul understood the collection as a gesture of solidarity between the Gentile congregations and the Jerusalem church (Rom 15:26-27); perhaps he even saw it as symbolizing the eschatological tribute of the nations to Israel's God on Mt. Zion (Isa 2:2-3; 60:1-16). As the time drew near for him to take the collected offering to Jerusalem, however, Paul was worried that it would not be accepted by the Jerusalem community (Rom 15:30-32) because of his deteriorating relations with the representatives of the church there.

When Paul wrote Galatians, however, he could point to the Jerusalem leaders' request, confident that he had kept his end of the bargain. As the Galatians knew, he was collecting money for the poor in Jerusalem.[78] It was the others, particularly Cephas, who had in Paul's judgment reneged on the agreement. Thus Paul's meeting with the Jerusalem leaders marked a high-water point of unity in the early Christian mission (though we must remember that the circumcision party was not included in the fragile unity achieved at the Jerusalem meeting). After this, as we shall see, the understanding that the Antioch and Jerusalem representatives had reached started to unravel.

---

73. R. D. Aus, "Three Pillars and Three Patriarchs: A Proposal Concerning Gal 2:9," *ZNW* 70 (1979) 252-61.

74. Interestingly, by the end of the first century, *1 Clement* applies this same title to Peter and to Paul. See *1 Clem* 5:2-7.

75. Dunn observes that "at this point 'grace' (*charis*) approaches the sense of 'charism' (*charisma*)—charism as the expression and embodiment of grace in word and action." See J. D. G. Dunn, *The Epistle to the Galatians,* Black's NT Commentary (Peabody, Mass.: Hendrickson, 1993) 108.

76. For an extended discussion with references, see Dunn, *The Epistle to the Galatians,* 112-13.

77. The absence of any reference to the churches of Galatia in Rom 15:26 is striking. Had the Galatians withdrawn their support for the collection?

78. Martyn, *Galatians,* 225, challenges this view, suggesting that Paul began organizing his collection later, after the writing of Galatians.

REFLECTIONS

For many Christian congregations, the early church's debate over circumcision may seem like a strange matter belonging to another time and place. Today, the only debates about circumcision have to do not with Christian identity, but with the health benefits or disadvantages of this surgical procedure for male infants. Why did the issue of circumcision matter so much to Paul and to the "false brothers"? Why did it pose a stern challenge to the unity of the church in the first generation of Christians?

The answer is that circumcision symbolized Jewish identity in a pagan world; consequently, it became a symbolic hot-button issue for early Christian communities struggling with the problem of how to define their identity. Were the emergent Gentile churches an extension of Judaism into pagan culture? Or did they represent a new phenomenon that could not be fully accommodated to the categories and cultural forms of Jewish tradition? When we understand Paul's meeting with the Jerusalem leaders within its historical context, we see that it defines a number of problems that remain with us today.

1. The meeting of Paul, Barnabas, and Titus with the pillar apostles of the Jerusalem church was a crucial event in the process of clarifying the identity of the church. The event should not be interpreted anachronistically, as though it were the first ecumenical council of the church catholic; it was, after all, simply a conference involving representatives of two key churches. Nonetheless, its historical significance was weighty, because it marked Jerusalem's acceptance in principle of the validity of a Gentile mission that did not require converts to become proselytes to Judaism in order to be recognized as followers of Jesus. This meant that the participants in this meeting were defining the church not as a sectarian variant of Judaism, but as a wholly new eschatological community in which Jews and Gentiles together acknowledged a common Lord.

Although this development, viewed in retrospect, might look inevitable, the outcome of the debate was by no means self-evident in the first Christian generation. The circumcision party among the Jewish Christians clearly saw adherence to Torah as the entryway and primary identity marker for the early Jesus movement: "Unless you are circumcised according to the custom of Moses, you cannot be saved" (Acts 15:1 NRSV). They may have seen Jesus as the new and definitive interpreter of the Law, but they still understood themselves—not surprisingly—as living and moving within the symbolic world of the cultural reality that Paul calls *Ioudaismos* ("Judaism"). Paul and Barnabas, on the other hand, were pressing for a radical innovation, a community whose identity was grounded solely in the story of Christ's death and resurrection.

It is not clear whether James, Cephas, and John understood the full implications of what they were agreeing to in the way that Paul did. (Indeed, subsequent developments suggest that they did not.) They may have thought they were merely acknowledging that uncircumcised Gentiles could participate in the life of the Christian community in precisely the same way that Gentile "godfearers" had previously participated in the life of the synagogue—as adherents on the periphery of the community who were not required to adopt full Torah observance, but who were also in some sense not yet full members of the people of God.

How does all this inform our reflection about Christian identity in our time? The crucial point of analogy is this: Whenever we allow the identity of our community to be fundamentally defined by any sort of national or cultural or even religious marker other than the gospel, we are repeating the error of the "false brothers." Paul insists that we must not allow the dominant culture to set the boundaries of "religion" or to define the character of our community. Instead, Paul's vision for the identity of the Christian community demands that we define ourselves exclusively in the light of the cross and resurrection (see Gal 6:14-15; cf. 1 Cor 1:18–2:5).

The dominant symbolic world in relation to which the church in Western culture must define its identity is no longer Jewish culture; rather, it is the culture of public secular rationality.[79] Wherever we find that people have begun to think of themselves as Americans first and Christians second or to meld these identities uncritically together, we are in the presence of a false gospel. Wherever we encounter pressure to allow our identity to be shaped fundamentally by market forces or by allegiance to racial or ethnic identity, we should remember the examples of Paul and Barnabas, who refused to yield even for a moment to the pressure to conform to prevailing expectations about what normal "religious" behavior looks like.

2. A minor theme of the passage is Paul's indifference to authority and reputation. He refused to regard his meeting with the "pillars" as an awe-inspiring occasion (Gal 2:6); he did not go to Jerusalem to ask for their autographs. This text, therefore, might provoke reflection on the ways we become intimidated by or inappropriately deferential to authority figures, even within the church. The gospel calls us to stand up, as Paul and Barnabas did, and bear witness clearly to what God is doing in the world. We may hope that those who are reputedly leaders in the church will listen; but whether they listen or not, our witness-bearing task is the same.

3. The central message of Gal 2:1-10 is that the progress of the gospel in the world is God's activity. That is especially clear in 2:7-8, where we are told that the conference participants recognized that God was working in both Peter and Paul and that both of them had been entrusted with a message. The same is true today: All who serve in the church's various ministries are the vehicles of God's Word. (This passage can fruitfully be linked with Paul's portrayal in 1 Corinthians 12 of the Holy Spirit working through the distribution of diverse gifts to different members of the body of Christ.) We are instruments, not entrepreneurs. The implications of this truth are wide-ranging. On the one hand, it means that we are accountable to exercise faithfully the trust we have been given; on the other hand, it means that we need not be anxious, because we can trust that God's purposes will be accomplished. Our decision is whether to cooperate with those purposes (as the participants in the Jerusalem meeting did) or to stand in the way (as the "false brothers" did).

4. The military metaphors of 2:4-5 suggest that God's activity will often encounter opposition and conflict. When that happens, we should not be surprised. As long as we live in the "present evil age" on this side of the day of the Lord, the proclamation of the gospel will call forth the opposition of enemy powers. (See the Commentary and Reflections at 1:6-10.)

5. The mutual recognition of two distinct gospel missions to Jews and Gentiles raises fascinating questions about the church's mission strategy. Should we promote particular ethnic missionary initiatives aimed at separate cultural-linguistic communities? Should the church sponsor one mission for Hispanics, one for African Americans, one for persons of Korean ancestry, and another for Anglo-Americans? Common sense would appear to commend this strategy, and the Jerusalem agreement of Gal 2:1-10 might be taken as a precedent for it. Yet, as the sequel in 2:11-21 shows, this strategy is not without its problems. The danger is that these communities will define themselves primarily in relation to ethnicity rather than in relation to the gospel and that the church will become splintered into cultural factions. In order to prevent this unhappy outcome, if there are to be special ethnically defined ministries, frequent face-to-face meetings like the Jerusalem conference are essential, so that the circumcised will have to encounter the uncircumcised face-to-face, so that we can bear witness to the diverse works being done through us by the one Spirit, and so that we can extend to one another "the right hand of fellowship" (2:9).

6. Finally, 2:10 should not be neglected as a mere throwaway line. Authentic fellowship

79. See D. S. Yeago, "Messiah's People: The Culture of the Church in the Midst of the Nations," *Pro Ecclesia* 6 (1997) 146-71.

across cultural lines in the church requires us to take seriously the covenant obligation of concern for the poor. Where such concern is not put into action, the solidarity sealed by the handshake of 2:9 will be in serious jeopardy. One could imagine a sermon on Gal 2:1-10 that would treat v. 10 as the climax of the passage, challenging members of the congregation to demonstrate their commitment to "the truth of the gospel" (v. 4) through their eagerness to fulfill the mandate to "remember the poor."

GALATIANS 2:11-21, TWO TABLES OR ONE? CONFRONTATION AT ANTIOCH

OVERVIEW

Up through 2:10, it looks as though all is well. Paul has emphatically claimed the authority of divine revelation as the source of his preaching, and he has recounted a major triumph in the Jerusalem meeting: The "false brothers" were defeated, and the leaders of the Jerusalem church affirmed their approval of Paul's mission to the Gentiles. In the next section of the letter, however, the plot of Paul's narrative takes a sharp turn; the unity achieved at Jerusalem was shattered by a subsequent conflict at Antioch. The account of this conflict (vv. 11-21) is the climax toward which Paul's story has been building.

Paul highlights his confrontation with Cephas (Peter) because it provides the background against which he views the present controversy in Galatia. The issues in the two situations are not identical, but they are closely parallel. Thus Paul can frame his account of his speech to Peter on the former occasion (vv. 14b-21) as a programmatic statement that speaks indirectly to the Galatians as well. Indeed, this speech can be seen as a concise summary of the themes of the letter as a whole.[80]

Translations and commentaries often place the termination of Paul's address to Peter at the end of v. 14 (as in the NRSV) and treat vv. 15-21 as a separate unit. It must be remembered that ancient Greek manuscripts did not employ the convention of placing quotation marks around quoted direct discourse; therefore, the question of where Paul's speech ends is a matter of interpretive judgment. This commentary will argue that the speech extends through v. 21 (as in the NIV; cf. NRSV footnote). There is no indication in the text of a change of addressee until 3:1, and the first-person plural pronouns in vv. 15-17 show that Paul is continuing to address a Jewish audience (i.e., the Jewish Christians at Antioch), not the Gentile Galatians. Consequently, vv. 11-21 should be treated as a single coherent unit. Indeed, several obscurities in Paul's highly compressed language in vv. 15-21 can be clarified if they are understood in relation to the dispute over table fellowship in Antioch.

At the same time, Paul artfully narrates this story in such a way that it serves as a transition into his direct address to the Galatians in 3:1. A movie director making a film of this text might reproduce the effect in the following way: The scene opens in a public meeting of the church at Antioch with Paul confronting Peter; as Paul speaks (vv. 14b-21), the camera pans in on his face so that the members of the Antiochene church gradually disappear from view after v. 18. Then, at 3:1, as Paul says, "O foolish Galatians," the camera pans back again to reveal Paul in an entirely different setting, pacing the floor and dictating the letter to his secretary. The desired effect is that the Galatians will hear the speech to Peter as being addressed to their situation as well.[81]

---

80. H. D. Betz, *Galatians: A Commentary on Paul's Letter to the Churches in Galatia,* Hermeneia (Philadelphia: Fortress, 1979) 113-27, followed by R. N. Longenecker, *Galatians,* WBC 41 (Dallas: Word, 1990) 80-96, describes Gal 2:15-21 as the *propositio* of the letter, the statement of the case to be defended.

81. Martyn suggests that Paul's speech becomes "a speech addressed to the Teachers [Missionaries] in Galatia," rather than to the Galatians themselves. While this suggestion may be correct, there is no direct indication of it in the text, and it underestimates the partial rhetorical parallel between Cephas and the Galatians; both parties are being swayed by outside emissaries to adopt Jewish practices. See J. L. Martyn, *Galatians,* AB 33A (New York: Doubleday, 1997) 230.

One result of this rhetorical technique is that Paul never finishes the story of the Antioch controversy; we do not find out how Peter responded to Paul's challenge, and we do not hear how the Antiochene church decided to resolve the dispute. Almost certainly this means that Paul lost. If he had, in fact, convinced Peter and the other Jewish Christians to accept his arguments, he surely would have said so in this letter, just as he did in the preceding narrative of the Jerusalem meeting (vv. 1-10). Regardless of the outcome, however, the telling of this story allows Paul to articulate the theological principles that undergird his present response to the Galatians.

The major theme of the unit is that the gospel mandates the formation of a new community in which there is no division between Jew and Gentile, a community in which Jews and Gentiles eat at one table together, not two separate tables.[82] The speech of vv. 14b-21 supports this claim by arguing that right relation to God depends fundamentally on "the grace of God" (2:21), and not on observance of the ethnically particular signs of covenant membership (circumcision and food laws). This grace has been made effective through the death of Jesus Christ, which avails for Jew and Gentile without distinction (cf. Rom 3:21-31). Consequently, Peter's withdrawal from table fellowship with Gentile believers at Antioch was, as Paul sees it, a symbolic rejection of God's reconciling grace.

82. For the image of two tables, see M. Baker, *Religious No More: Building Communities of Grace and Freedom* (Downers Grove, Ill.: InterVarsity, 1999) 79-84, 96.

Galatians 2:11-14, Paul's Rebuke of Cephas

NIV	NRSV
[11]When Peter came to Antioch, I opposed him to his face, because he was clearly in the wrong. [12]Before certain men came from James, he used to eat with the Gentiles. But when they arrived, he began to draw back and separate himself from the Gentiles because he was afraid of those who belonged to the circumcision group. [13]The other Jews joined him in his hypocrisy, so that by their hypocrisy even Barnabas was led astray.	11But when Cephas came to Antioch, I opposed him to his face, because he stood self-condemned; [12]for until certain people came from James, he used to eat with the Gentiles. But after they came, he drew back and kept himself separate for fear of the circumcision faction. [13]And the other Jews joined him in this hypocrisy, so that even Barnabas was led astray by their hypocrisy.
[14]When I saw that they were not acting in line with the truth of the gospel, I said to Peter in front of them all, "You are a Jew, yet you live like a Gentile and not like a Jew. How is it, then, that you force Gentiles to follow Jewish customs?	[14]But when I saw that they were not acting consistently with the truth of the gospel, I said to Cephas before them all, "If you, though a Jew, live like a Gentile and not like a Jew, how can you compel the Gentiles to live like Jews?"[a]
	[a] Some interpreters hold that the quotation extends into the following paragraph

COMMENTARY

2:11-13. The coming of Cephas to Antioch (v. 11) marks a major complication in the story. Antioch was a great and prosperous city in northern Syria, the third largest city in the Roman Empire (after Rome and Alexandria).[83] According to Josephus, its large Jewish population mixed freely with the Gentiles there.

The Jewish race, densely interspersed among the native populations of every portion of the world, is particularly numerous in Syria, where intermingling is due to the proximity of the two countries. But it was at Antioch that they especially congregated. . . . Moreover, they were constantly attracting to their religious ceremonies

83. Richard N. Longenecker, *Galatians*, WBC 41 (Dallas: Word, 1990) 65. For more information on the city, see W. A. Meeks and R. L. Wilken, *Jews and Christians in Antioch in the First Four Centuries of the Common Era*, SBLSBS 13 (Missoula, Mont.: Scholars Press, 1978).

multitudes of Greeks, and these they had in some measure incorporated with themselves.[84]

Even allowing for Josephus's penchant for hyperbole, we may safely conclude that Antioch was home to a substantial Jewish community that had attracted a large number of "godfearers," Gentiles who were drawn to the worship of the one God in the synagogue. Thus it is not surprising that as the early Jewish Christians began to spread the gospel message, it was at Antioch that they first began to preach extensively to Gentiles. Indeed, Antioch became a major base of operations for the mission to the Gentiles (see Acts 11:19-26; 13:1-3).

The multicultural Antiochene Christian community presented new challenges that had been neither anticipated nor resolved by the agreement at the Jerusalem meeting, which had dealt only with the issue of circumcision (vv. 6-10).[85] Paul understood the agreement to imply a comprehensive recognition of the equality and fellowship of Jews and Gentiles in Christ (cf. 3:28), but some of the strictly Torah-observant Jewish Christians at Jerusalem interpreted the agreement less liberally. In effect, the Jerusalem agreement had acknowledged a separate-but-equal Gentile mission, but it had not addressed the problem of social relations and table fellowship between Jewish and Gentile Christians. The Christians at Antioch, recognizing the grace of God in their midst (Acts 11:21-24), made a practice of eating together, Jews at table with Gentiles (v. 12a). Some Jewish Christians from Jerusalem, however, found this practice objectionable. Why?

The Law of Moses contains no prohibition of eating with Gentiles. The people of Israel were commanded to abstain from unclean foods and from meat or wine tainted by association with idolatry; but as long as certain fundamental dietary precautions were observed, there was no reason why even strictly Torah-observant Jews could not share table fellowship with Gentiles.[86]

What, then, was the nature of the issue at Antioch, and why did the "men from James" pressure Peter to stop eating with Gentile believers? Paul gives no explanation of their reasoning; therefore, we can only make guesses. It is possible that the food at the common meals was not kosher, that Peter and other Jewish Christians were disregarding basic Jewish dietary laws by eating meat with blood in it, or pork and shellfish. If so, this would explain Paul's remark that Peter had been living "like a Gentile" (v. 14). On the other hand, it seems unlikely that such flagrant violations of Jewish norms would have been practiced at Antioch, particularly if the Gentile converts were drawn primarily from the ranks of the "godfearers," who presumably would have already assimilated to Jewish dietary practices. It is more probable that the "men from James" were objecting to the practice of associating with Gentiles at table. This seems to be the implication of Paul's language in v. 12, which says nothing about the food as such but speaks of eating "with the Gentiles." Such association was not forbidden by Jewish Law, but it would have been perceived, in certain circles, as risky and impolitic: "Close association might lead to contact with idolatry or transgression of one of the biblical food laws. . . . James worried that too much fraternization with Gentiles would have bad results, and that Peter's mission [to the circumcised, 2:8] would be discredited if he were known to engage in it himself."[87]

It is possible that the pressure to shun such associations may have come from a faction in the Jerusalem church that wanted to make the emergent Christian movement look good in the eyes of their fervent Jewish countrymen. Robert Jewett has proposed that both the Antioch incident and the controversy in Galatia should be understood against the historical background of a rising Zealot movement in Palestine that advocated radical separation from Gentiles; in such an atmosphere, Gentile sympathizers among the Jewish people might have been targeted for reprisals. The early church was a movement within Judaism, but the Gentile-friendly form it took in Antioch posed difficulties for Judean Jewish Christians who wanted "to avert the suspicion that they were in

84. Josephus *The Jewish War* 7.43, 45.

85. As already noted in the Commentary on 2:6-10, Luke's narrative of the "apostolic decree" in Acts 15:22-29 is almost surely an anachronistic account. There is no evidence in Paul's letters for the existence of such an agreement on food laws.

86. E. P. Sanders, "Jewish Association with Gentiles and Galatians 2:11-14," in *The Conversation Continues: Studies in Paul and John in Honor of J. Louis Martyn*, ed. R. T. Fortna and B. R. Gaventa (Nashville: Abingdon, 1990) 170-88.

87. Ibid., 186.

communion with lawless Gentiles."[88] Consequently, the response of this faction at Jerusalem was to urge Peter, with the blessing of James, to avoid contact with Gentiles, perhaps in hopes of pressuring the Gentile converts into accepting circumcision and full Torah-observance. Jewett argues that similar motives lay behind the pressure for circumcision of the Galatian Christians: "If they could succeed in circumcising the Gentile Christians, this might effectively thwart any Zealot purification campaign against the Judean church."[89] (Note how well this hypothesis explains Paul's otherwise puzzling statements in Gal 6:12-13.)

In any case, whatever political pressures may have been exerted on Peter, Paul had no tolerance for his waffling actions. Paul "opposed him to his face" (v. 12) in a public showdown ("before them all," v. 14) at Antioch. In Paul's view, God's verdict was already pronounced upon Peter's behavior: "he stood condemned." The renderings of the NIV ("in the wrong") and the NRSV ("self-condemned") both soften the severity of Paul's judgment; because Peter's action was a betrayal of the gospel, Paul saw him as standing under *God's* condemnation.

Who were the "people from James"? Paul does not identify them, but he indicates that they were a delegation from Jerusalem seeking, with the approval of James, to urge Peter to eschew fraternization with Gentiles. We do not know why Peter was in Antioch or how long he had been there, but the imperfect tense of the verb "used to eat" (συνήσθιεν *synēsthien*) implies that his sharing table fellowship with Gentiles had been a habitual practice over some period of time, not merely an isolated incident. When confronted by the messengers from Jerusalem, however, Peter "drew back and kept himself separate." The verb "draw back" (ὑποστέλλω *hypostellō*) suggests a tactical retreat, like an army pulling back from an exposed position.[90]

By "separating himself," Peter was accommodating his actions to a well-established Jewish belief that the people of God should keep themselves free from defiling contact with the evil and

idolatrous Gentile world. As already noted, eating with Gentiles was not a technical violation of Torah, but many Jews may have preferred to separate themselves from Gentiles as much as possible, out of a general sense that Gentiles were unclean and distasteful. The *Letter of Aristeas,* a Jewish apologetic work of the second century BCE, articulates the reason for such separation:

> To prevent our being perverted by contact with others or by mixing with bad influences, [Moses] hedged us in on all sides with strict observances connected with meat and drink and touch and hearing and sight, after the manner of the Law.[91]

Such an interpretation of the purpose of the Torah could readily lead, in some circles, to a generalized attitude of wariness toward Gentiles, as we see in *Jub.* 22:16: "Eat not with them . . . for their works are unclean."[92] A similar indication of Jewish aversion for Gentiles is found in the Acts of the Apostles, in the story of Peter's vision and commission to preach to the household of the Gentile centurion Cornelius. Peter begins his conversation with them by saying, "You yourselves know how unlawful it is for a Jew to associate with or to visit any one of another nation" (Acts 10:28 RSV).[93] The Roman historian Tacitus confirms the stereotypical impression of Jews as a misanthropic people who "eat separately" from others.[94] Even if such statements are exaggerated, they offer a broad sketch of a general perception that relations between Jews and Gentiles were fraught with tension, a tension focused particularly on eating practices.

Nothing in Paul's language suggests that the dispute focused specifically on eucharistic fellow-

---

88. Robert Jewett, "The Agitators and the Galatian Congregation," *NTS* 17 (1970-71) 205. Jewett's argument is followed by Longenecker, *Galatians,* xciii-xcvi.

89. Jewett, "The Agitators and the Galatian Congregation," 206.

90. H. D. Betz, *Galatians: A Commentary on Paul's Letter to the Churches in Galatia,* Hermeneia (Philadelphia: Fortress, 1979) 108.

91. *Letter of Aristeas,* 142.

92. Philip F. Esler, *Galatians* (London: Routledge, 1998) 93-116, argues, based on passages such as the ones cited here, that Jews during the late Second Temple period universally eschewed table fellowship with Gentiles. For a more nuanced account of the evidence on this question, see Sanders, "Jewish Association with Gentiles and Galatians 2:11-14."

93. Of course, Peter follows this statement by declaring that God has summoned him to observe a different policy toward Gentiles: "But God has shown me that I should not call anyone profane or unclean" (Acts 10:28 *b*). If Peter had indeed held such views at an earlier stage, as his eating with Gentiles at Antioch would suggest (Gal 2:12*a*), his subsequent withdrawal from association with Gentile Christians would be all the more reprehensible.

94. Tacitus *Histories* 5.5.1-2. Dunn also calls attention to the recurrent motif, in Jewish literature from the Maccabean period to the first century CE, of the glorification of heroes and heroines whose fidelity to the law is demonstrated by refusal to eat "the food of Gentiles" (Dan 1:8-16; Tob 1:10-13; Jdt 10:5; 12:1-20; Additions to Esther 14:17; *Joseph and Aseneth* 7:1; 8:5). See J. D. G. Dunn, *The Epistle to the Galatians,* Black's NT Commentary (Peabody, Mass.: Hendrickson, 1993) 118.

ship between Jewish and Gentile believers; the issue seems to have been whether they could eat together under any circumstance. If, however, Peter and the other Jewish Christians were avoiding all table fellowship, this would have included the Lord's supper, which at this early time seems ordinarily to have been celebrated in the context of a communal meal (see 1 Cor 11:17-34). In 1 Corinthians, Paul insists on interpreting the Lord's supper as a powerful symbol of communal unity, but he makes no such argument in Galatians. This suggests that the manner of celebrating the Lord's supper was not a central issue at Antioch. At the same time, it also suggests that Paul could not assume the experience of sharing the eucharist as a basis for his broader argument about table fellowship. It would have been a powerful argument for Paul to say, "If you share the bread and wine with Gentiles at the table of the Lord, how can you refuse to eat ordinary meals together?" Paul's silence on this point suggests that Peter, Barnabas, and other Jewish Christians were not celebrating the Lord's supper with the Gentile Christians in Antioch.

Paul charges that Peter separated himself from the common table because he feared "the circumcision faction" (οἱ ἐκ περιτομῆς *hoi ek peritomēs*). It is not precisely clear what group Paul has in mind here. Does he mean Jewish people in general, or does the term refer to a specific group of Jewish Christians? In view of Paul's use of this expression elsewhere (Rom 4:12; cf. Acts 10:45), it seems that he is referring not to Jews in general but to members of the early Christian movement who have Jewish ancestry. Furthermore, Luke's use of the same terminology in Acts 11:2 suggests that it could sometimes designate members of a particular party or faction within the Jerusalem church that focused on maintaining clear Jewish group boundaries.[95] Thus it appears that Paul is accusing Peter of fearing other Jewish *Christians;* the problem is intra-ecclesial.

Even though the messengers from James may have focused their suasion on Peter alone, his withdrawal from the common table predictably influenced others, so that the other Jewish Christians, including even Paul's close associate Barnabas, followed his lead (v. 13). From Paul's perspective,

this was a disaster. The previously unified Antioch community was now split into two different ethnic communities, with Torah observance as the dividing wall between them. In place of one common table, there were now two separate tables.

Paul describes this mass withdrawal from the one table as "hypocrisy" (ὑπόκρισις *hypokrisis,* v. 13). The Greek word does not have quite the same connotation of malicious duplicity that is present in the English. In Greek, the ὑποκριτής (*hypokritēs*) is an actor, someone who wears a mask and plays a role. Thus *hypokrisis* is the act of playing out a scripted role. Paul's point is that Peter and the other Jewish Christians at Antioch are caught up in playing a part that does not represent their own considered convictions; they are caving in to external pressure, carrying out someone else's agenda. This is another way of expressing the charge of people pleasing (see the Commentary on 1:10).

The fact that Barnabas joined in this role playing must have been especially galling to Paul.[96] It was Barnabas who had stood with him at Jerusalem in resisting the "false brothers" (vv. 1-5). According to Luke's account in Acts, Barnabas had originally rejoiced when he came to Antioch and found Gentile believers experiencing the grace of God along with Jewish believers (Acts 11:19-26). Now, however, as Paul saw it, Barnabas had been "carried away" (v. 13) by group pressure, and Paul was left to stand alone as an advocate for God's new creation of a community in which Jews and Gentiles could eat at one table.

2:14. Paul's sharp public rebuke of Peter may seem excessive, particularly if Peter was acting out of a concern to protect Jewish Christians in Jerusalem from persecution by fervent Jewish nationalists. Paul seems to give him no credit for good motives or to make any attempt to talk the matter out privately (cf. Matt 18:15-17) or even to correct Peter "in a spirit of gentleness" (Gal 6:1). What accounts for Paul's vehement response? The answer can only be that he saw in Peter's action "the effective preaching of an anti-gospel in the midst of the Antioch church."[97] Consequently, Paul did not hesitate to take an

---

95. For this interpretation of οἱ ἐκ περιτομῆς (*hoi ek peritomēs*), see Martyn, *Galatians,* 236-40.

96. Was the Antioch incident the fundamental cause of the split between Paul and Barnabas, attributed to other causes in Acts 15:36-41?

97. Martyn, *Galatians,* 235.

uncompromising stand, because "the truth of the gospel" was at stake (v. 14; cf. 1:6-9). Paul had used the same phrase in 2:5 to describe what was at issue in the controversy over circumcision in Jerusalem. In both cases, "the truth of the gospel" is linked directly with the fellowship of Gentile and Jewish believers on equal terms: Neither circumcision nor observance of dietary laws should divide the church. "The truth of the gospel," therefore, is not merely a doctrine but a social reality, a truth that must be embodied in the practices of a community. This truth was being violated by the exclusionary social practices of Peter and those who joined him in a policy of separate tables. Paul saw in their withdrawal a failure to "walk straight" (ὀρθοποδέω *orthopodeō*) toward the truth of the gospel. (The NRSV's "not acting consistently" is a pallid paraphrase; better is the NIV's "not acting in line with the truth of the gospel.") Thus he addressed to Peter a passionate speech seeking to re-call him and the other Jewish Christians to the one table with the Gentiles.

Paul opens fire with an ad hominem argument charging Peter personally with bad faith and gross inconsistency: "If you, though a Jew, live like a Gentile and not like a Jew, how can you compel the Gentiles to live like Jews?" (v. 14*b*). To "live like a Jew" means, in this case, to observe Jewish dietary restrictions. The question presupposes that Peter does not ordinarily live a strictly Torah-observant life—and that he would make no pretense of doing so. This would be consistent with his custom of eating with Gentiles at Antioch before the arrival of the delegation from James. Paul charges that by caving in to the pressure from the Jerusalem delegation, Peter is in effect requiring the Gentile converts at Antioch to adopt a higher standard of Torah observance than he himself would normally follow.

As noted earlier, the "compulsion" in view here is not a matter of violent coercion but of manipulative group pressure; Peter and the other Jewish Christians at Antioch were in effect "compelling" Gentiles to adopt Jewish observances by boycotting the common table. There is no indication here that the delegation from James was pressing for Gentiles to be circumcised; that issue had already been clearly settled—with the approval of James—by the meeting in Jerusalem (vv. 1-10). The verb ἰουδαΐζειν (*ioudaizein*), translated here as "live like Jews" (v. 14), does not necessarily denote converting to Judaism;[98] rather, it means to adopt Jewish practices.[99] Presumably, the Gentile Christians could have overcome any objection to table fellowship by conforming their diets to the dictates of Jewish Law. This might appear harmless enough, but in this outside pressure for Gentile Christians to conform to Jewish dietary standards, Paul sees a betrayal of the gospel. (See Reflections at 2:15-21.)

98. It does apparently have this meaning in Josephus *Jewish War* 2.454. Martyn, *Galatians,* 236, however, suggests that this example, like Esth 8:17 LXX, carries connotations of superficiality and insincerity in the adoption of the Jewish way of life.
99. See, e.g., Ign. *Magn.* 10.3: "It is monstrous to talk of Jesus Christ and to practice Judaism [ἰουδαΐζειν *ioudaizein*]."

Galatians 2:15-21, Jews and Gentiles Alike Are Rectified Through Christ's Death

NIV	NRSV
[15]"We who are Jews by birth and not 'Gentile sinners' [16]know that a man is not justified by observing the law, but by faith in Jesus Christ. So we, too, have put our faith in Christ Jesus that we may be justified by faith in Christ and not by observing the law, because by observing the law no one will be justified.	[15]We ourselves are Jews by birth and not Gentile sinners; [16]yet we know that a person is justified[a] not by the works of the law but through faith in Jesus Christ.[b] And we have come to believe in Christ Jesus, so that we might be justified by faith in Christ,[c] and not by doing the works of the law, because no one will be justified by the works of the law. [17]But if, in our effort to
[17]"If, while we seek to be justified in Christ, it becomes evident that we ourselves are sinners, does that mean that Christ promotes sin? Abso-	
	[a] Or *reckoned as righteous;* and so elsewhere [b] Or *the faith of Jesus Christ* [c] Or *the faith of Christ*

NIV

lutely not! [18]If I rebuild what I destroyed, I prove that I am a lawbreaker. [19]For through the law I died to the law so that I might live for God. [20]I have been crucified with Christ and I no longer live, but Christ lives in me. The life I live in the body, I live by faith in the Son of God, who loved me and gave himself for me. [21]I do not set aside the grace of God, for if righteousness could be gained through the law, Christ died for nothing!"[a]

[a]21 Some interpreters end the quotation after verse 14.

NRSV

be justified in Christ, we ourselves have been found to be sinners, is Christ then a servant of sin? Certainly not! [18]But if I build up again the very things that I once tore down, then I demonstrate that I am a transgressor. [19]For through the law I died to the law, so that I might live to God. I have been crucified with Christ; [20]and it is no longer I who live, but it is Christ who lives in me. And the life I now live in the flesh I live by faith in the Son of God,[a] who loved me and gave himself for me. [21]I do not nullify the grace of God; for if justification[b] comes through the law, then Christ died for nothing.

[a] Or by the faith of the Son of God   [b] Or righteousness

COMMENTARY

The reasons for this judgment follow in the highly compressed argument of vv. 15-21, which serves as a *précis* of the argument of the entire letter. As noted, Paul has composed his account of this speech with the Galatians in view. Thus the theological argument of vv. 15-21 applies equally to the conflict at Antioch and to the Galatians' present quandary over circumcision. The interpreter's task is to see how the argument functions at each of these levels.

2:15-16. Still addressing Peter, Paul affirms (v. 15) his own participation in the hereditary Jewish tradition that defines its identity sharply against Gentile outsiders: "We ourselves are Jews by birth [lit., "by nature"] and not Gentile sinners." In this traditional Jewish frame of reference, the Gentiles are categorized as "sinners" (ἁμαρτωλοι *hamartōloi*) simply by virtue of their being outsiders to the covenant people. Given the more receptive attitude toward Gentiles that Paul has come to hold as the apostle to the Gentiles, we may assume that he employs this categorical label with some degree of irony. Nonetheless, the point is a serious one: He, along with Peter and the delegation from Jerusalem—and, it must be noted, along with the rival Missionaries in Galatia—is a Jew, a sharer in the heritage of Israel (see Phil 3:4-6). His purpose for emphasizing this common ethnic identity emerges as the rest of the sentence unfolds; even those Jewish Christians who are

most conscious of their ethnic identity share a common confession about justification through Christ. Paul points to this shared confessional tradition in order to use it as the foundation of his argument that Torah observance is not necessary for Gentiles in the new situation that God has brought into being.

The confession articulated in v. 16—which Paul presents as the common belief of Jewish Christians—is the heart of the message of Galatians, the gospel in a nutshell. This confession is so concisely formulated, however, that it presents numerous exegetical problems. Paul writes here in a theological shorthand, and each phrase must be unpacked carefully.[100] Consequently, we must make several crucial interpretive decisions here that will determine our reading of the letter as a whole.

The issues that demand attention are (a) the structure of the sentence in vv. 15-16; (b) the meaning of the verb "to justify"; (c) the meaning of the phrase "by works of the Law"; (d) the meaning of the expression "through the faith of [or in] Jesus Christ" (διὰ πίστεως Ἰησοῦ Χριστου *dia pisteōs Iēsou Christou*); (e) the allusion to Psalm 143 in the last clause of v. 16.

100. Betz describes this unit as consisting of "dogmatic abbreviations, i.e., very short formulaic summaries of doctrines." See H. D. Betz, *Galatians: A Commentary on Paul's Letter to the Churches in Galatia,* Hermeneia (Philadelphia: Fortress, 1979) 114.

(a) The Structure of the Sentence. The NRSV produces a simpler and more readable English text of vv. 15-16 by turning the participial phrase at the beginning of v. 16 into an independent clause and starting a new sentence in the middle of the verse:

We ourselves are Jews by birth and not Gentile sinners; yet we know that a person is justified not by the works of the law but through faith in Jesus Christ. And we have come to believe in Christ Jesus.

Unfortunately, this translation loses some important nuances of the Greek syntax. The verb "know" in v. 16*a* is actually a participle (εἰδότες *eidotes*); thus a more literal translation would read as follows:

We ourselves are Jews by birth and not Gentile sinners; yet, knowing that a person is justified not by the works of the law but[101] through the faith of Jesus Christ, even we have trusted in Christ Jesus.

The emphasis here falls on the words "even we" (καὶ ἡμεῖς *kai hēmeis*), with the *kai* understood as explicative (not a conjunction introducing an independent clause, as in the NRSV), reminding the reader that the "we" of v. 16 is precisely the same Jewish constituency signaled in v. 15. Paul's point is that "even we Jews by birth" (i.e., not just Gentiles) have placed trust in Christ *instead of* in works of the law as the ground of justification.

(b) The Meaning of the Verb "to Justify." The crucial verb "to justify" (δικαιόω *dikaioō*), which occurs three times in this verse, appears here for the first time in Galatians. To be "justified" is to be declared in the right or placed in right relationship to God.[102] The term has its origins in the language of the law court, but in Israel's prophetic literature and psalms the term takes on a distinct eschatological connotation: Even though the present may be a time of suffering and oppression, the prophets and the psalmists look to God as the source of future vindication. God will ultimately act to "justify" the covenant people by rescuing them and overthrowing their enemies and oppressors. In many OT contexts, the best English translation of the verb is "to vindicate." For example, in Isa 50:7-8*a* the mysterious "Servant" figure declares:

The LORD God helps me;
    therefore, I have not been disgraced;
therefore I have set my face like flint,
    and I know that I shall not be put to shame;
he who *vindicates* me [ὁ δικαιώσας με
    ho dikaiōsas me] is near. (NRSV, italics added)

Thus the verb "justify" points not merely to a forensic declaration of acquittal from guilt but also to God's ultimate action of powerfully setting right all that has gone wrong.

Consequently, when Paul speaks here of "being justified," he repeatedly uses the passive voice. The implied agent of "justification" is God; it is God alone who has the power to set things right. That is why—virtually by definition—no human being can be justified by works of the Law; such works, even if undertaken in obedience to God, remain limited human acts. "Justification," however, is the eschatological act of God. Thus, when he refers in v. 16 to being "justified," Paul is speaking of God's world-transforming eschatological verdict as it pertains to individual human beings. Because this verdict effectively sets right all that had gone wrong, the best English translation of the verb *dikaioō* is "to rectify" (see the excursus: "The Language of Righteousness," 238).

---

101. The Greek here is ἐὰν μή (*ean mē*), which would usually be translated as "except." Dunn (*The Epistle to the Galatians,* 137-38) finds here an ambiguity deliberately calculated by Paul to win Peter's assent to the formulation; the hearer or reader could understand the sentence to mean, "A person is not justified by the works of the Law *except* through faith in Jesus Christ." On this reading, the formula would not exclude works of the Law but promote faith in Christ as the one way through which one could attain justification by (also?) doing what the Law requires. Virtually all other commentators, however, interpret *ean mē* here as adversative ("but rather") or, if read as exceptive, as applying only to the verb rather than to the appended prepositional phrase "by works of the Law." This would yield the translation "A person is not justified by works of the Law; (a person is not justified) except through faith in/of Jesus Christ." This is a more cumbersome rendering that is essentially equivalent to the adversative sense. For discussion of the translation issue, see Richard N. Longenecker, *Galatians,* WBC 41 (Dallas: Word, 1990) 83-84; J. L. Martyn, *Galatians,* AB 33A (New York: Doubleday, 1997) 251.

102. For a full discussion, see R. B. Hays, "Justification," *ABD* 3.1129-33. See also S. K. Williams, *Galatians,* ANTC (Nashville: Abingdon, 1997) 62-65.

❖   ❖   ❖   ❖

EXCURSUS: THE LANGUAGE OF RIGHTEOUSNESS

The verb δικαιόω *dikaioō* bears a very close relation to the adjective δίκαιος (*dikaios*) and the noun δικαιοσύνη (*dikaiosynē*). These words are often translated into English as "righteous" (as in 3:11 NRSV) and "righteousness" (as in 3:6, 21; 5:5 NRSV; 2:21 NIV), while *dikaioō* is usually translated as "justify." Such translations run the risk of obscuring for the English reader many of the inner connections in Paul's thought. The following chart illustrates the relationships between these terms:

Greek	English (Latin root)	English (Anglo-Saxon root)
δικαιόω	justify	rectify
δίκαιος	just	righteous
δικαιοσύνη	justice	righteousness *or* rectification

The coherence of Paul's argument becomes clearer if the English translation consistently employs one or the other of these systems of related terms.[103] Accordingly, subsequent discussion in this commentary will ordinarily employ the terms "rectify," "righteous," and "righteousness/rectification."

103. J. L. Martyn, *Galatians*, AB 33A (New York: Doubleday, 1997), which consistently translates δικαιόω (*dikaioō*) as "rectify" and δικαιοσύνη (*dikaiosynē*) as "rectification," represents a constructive solution to this linguistic difficulty.

❖   ❖   ❖   ❖

Although "rectification" is an important motif in Paul's theology, there is nothing about his use of the verb that is unusual in the context of first-century Judaism. (To be sure, his understanding of *how* God acts to bring about rectification is sharply distinctive; see the section "The Faith of Jesus Christ," below.) His usage is thoroughly consonant with the OT examples noted above, and it is closely paralleled by the language of grateful thanksgiving found in the Dead Sea Scrolls:

As for me, my judgment is with God.
In his hand are the perfection of my way
and the uprightness of my heart.
He will wipe out my transgression through his
    righteousness. . . .
As for me, if I stumble, the mercies of God shall be
my eternal salvation.
If I stagger because of the sin of my flesh,
my judgment shall be
by the *righteousness* of God which endures forever.
(1QS 11:2-3, 12)

Thus, when Paul asserts that Peter and other Jewish Christians share his fundamental under-standing of "rectification" as God's action made effective through Christ, there is no reason to doubt his claim. The controversy arises only when we seek further clarification about the roles of "works of Law" and "the faith of Jesus Christ" in relation to the process of rectification.

(c) Works of the Law. Martin Luther found in Paul's dichotomy between "faith" and "works of the law" a hermeneutical principle that provided the theological impetus for the Reformation. Luther interpreted "works of the law" as a metaphor for all human striving for God's approval. Thus, he saw in Gal 2:16 a contrast between earning salvation through meritorious perform-ance of good deeds and receiving salvation through faith alone (*sola fide*).[104] This doctrine provided him with a powerful polemical weapon against the practices and teachings of the six-teenth-century Roman Catholic Church. Luther's reading of Paul exercised widespread influence on subsequent Christian interpreters, who associated

104. Martin Luther, *Lectures on Galatians (1535)*, *Luther's Works*, vol. 26, trans. Jaroslav Pelikan (St. Louis: Concordia, 1963) 122-41.

the attempt to earn salvation through good works with Pharisaic Judaism and, therefore, saw Paul as announcing a radical break with the Jewish understanding of God and salvation.

The difficulty with this account of the matter is that it rests upon a caricature of Judaism, as E. P. Sanders has demonstrated in his watershed study *Paul and Palestinian Judaism*.[105] Judaism has never taught that individuals must earn God's favor by performing meritorious works; members of the covenant people are already embraced by God's gracious election and mercy. Obedience to the Law is not a condition for getting in; rather, it is a means of staying in the covenant community. Sanders describes this Jewish pattern of religion as "covenantal nomism." Nearly all scholars who study early Judaism and Christianity now acknowledge that Sanders's description of Palestinian Judaism is basically correct.

How, then, are we to understand the contrast that Paul draws in 2:16 between being rectified by faith and being rectified by works of the Law? Is Paul setting up an artificial foil, a false depiction of his own Jewish heritage? A solution to this problem has been offered by J. D. G. Dunn, who has proposed that the expression "works of Law" (ἔργα νόμου *erga nomou*) refers not to meritorious deeds in general but specifically to those practices that stand as outward symbols of Jewish ethnic distinctiveness: circumcision, dietary observances, and sabbath keeping.[106] If that is right, we could paraphrase Paul as follows:

We ourselves are Jews by birth and not Gentile sinners; yet, knowing that a person is rectified not by wearing the badges of ethnic identity but through the faith of Jesus Christ, even we have trusted in Christ Jesus.

Thus Paul's critique would be targeted not at "Pelagianism" (seeking to earn salvation through good works) but at ethnic exclusivity (claiming soteriological privilege on the basis of racial or sociocultural distinctiveness). One advantage of this interpretation of "works of the Law" is that

it so clearly fits the situation Paul is addressing at Antioch.[107] By withdrawing from table fellowship with Gentiles, Peter was not seeking to earn salvation through good deeds; rather, he was seeking to maintain the boundary between the ethnic Jewish-Christian community and its Gentile neighbors. For this reason alone, Dunn's explanation is to be strongly preferred to the traditional "Lutheran" reading of the passage.

To be sure, the phrase *erga nomou* does not refer only to markers of ethnic identity; in principle, it refers—as Dunn has acknowledged—to the comprehensive range of actions required by the Torah.[108] (Martyn translates it as "observance of the Law.")[109] Still, the immediate context in Galatians suggests that the expression "works of Law" points especially to the few litmus-test practices where Jewish identity was symbolically at stake. (Indeed, it is probable that the phrase *erga nomou* was being used by the rival Missionaries in Galatia to characterize the obedience they sought to impose upon Paul's Gentile converts.)

(d) The Faith of Jesus Christ. If, then, Paul's confessional formula declares that no one is rectified through Law observance or adherence to the identity-marking practices of Judaism, what is the positive alternative? Here once again we must consider whether Luther and the Reformers were informed by an adequate exegesis of Paul. The Western Christian tradition has generally understood the phrase διὰ πίστεως Ἰησου Χριστοῦ (*dia pisteōs Iēsou Christou*) to mean "through believing in Jesus Christ." This suited Luther's theology well: In place of human striving for acceptance, salvation is conditioned solely upon believing the proclaimed gospel message. But is this what Paul meant to say? There are reasons to think that he had something different in mind; the phrase *dia pisteōs Iēsou Christou* points not primarily to our cognitive response to the preached gospel but to Jesus Christ's act of fidelity in undergoing death for our sake.

Paul's prepositional phrase is semantically ambiguous. The genitive case (*Iēsou Christou*) could be either objective or subjective—i.e., gramatically

---

105. E. P. Sanders, *Paul and Palestinian Judaism: A Comparison of Patterns of Religion* (Philadelphia: Fortress, 1977).

106. J. D. G. Dunn, *The Epistle to the Galatians*, Black's NT Commentary (Peabody, Mass: Hendrickson, 1993) 135-37. See also Dunn's essays, "The New Perspective on Paul" and "Works of the Law and the Curse of the Law (Gal. iii.10-14)," in *Jesus, Paul and the Law* (Louisville: Westminster/John Knox, 1990) 183-214, 215-41.

107. Dunn, *The Epistle to the Galatians*, 136-37, observes that the immediately preceding discussion in Galatians has focused precisely on two of these markers of ethnic identity: circumcision (2:1-10) and eating practices (2:11-14).

108. J. D. G. Dunn, "4QMMT and Galatians," *NTS* 43 (1997) 147-53.

109. Martyn, *The Epistle to the Galatians*, 250.

speaking, Jesus could be either the object or the subject of the action implied in the noun πίστις (*pistis*, "faith"). It is impossible to reproduce the ambiguity exactly in an English translation of the phrase, but we can illustrate the point by constructing a parallel expression: "We are rectified by the love of Jesus." Does that mean that we are rectified because we love Jesus (objective genitive) or because Jesus loves us (subjective genitive)?[110] The ambiguity can be resolved only by situating the sentence in a larger discourse or structure of thought.

Furthermore, the noun *pistis* offers a range of semantic possibilities for English translators. It can be rendered as "faith," "faithfulness," "fidelity," or "trust." It probably does not, however, mean "belief" in the sense of cognitive assent to a doctrine; rather it refers to placing trust or confidence in a person. The cognate verb πιστεύω (*pisteuō*) can be translated as "believe" or "trust." English, regrettably, lacks a verb form from the same root as the noun "faith." All of this contributes to the uncertainty over how to interpret Paul's statements in v. 16.

Paul uses similar expressions about the faith of/in Jesus Christ in Gal 2:20 and 3:22 and again in Rom 3:22, 26, as well as in Phil 3:9.[111] The interpretation of all these passages has been extensively debated in recent critical literature,[112] and recent English-language commentators on Galatians have lined up rather evenly divided on both sides of the question.[113] While acknowledging the lack of scholarly consensus, the commentary that follows here will develop a reading of Galatians that understands *pistis Iēsou Christou* to mean "the faithfulness of Jesus Christ" as manifested in his self-sacrificial death.[114] As v. 16 suggests, this formulation does not originate with Paul; it is the common property of early Jewish Christianity. But what does it mean? The phrase "the faithfulness of Jesus Christ" makes sense only if we read it as an allusion to a *story* about Jesus, "who gave himself for our sins to set us free from the present evil age, according to the will of our God and Father" (1:4). His self-giving was interpreted by early Christians as an act of *pistis*, faithfulness. When all humanity had fallen away into unfaithfulness, he alone was faithful to God. At the same time, his death was an act that showed forth *God's* faithfulness (cf. Rom 3:3), God's determination not to abandon his people to slavery and death. Thus, when Paul writes that a person is rectified only *dia pisteōs Iēsou Christou*, he is thinking of Christ's faithfulness as embodied in his death on a cross, which was the event through which God acted to rescue us (cf. Rom 5:8: "God proves his love for us in that while we were still sinners Christ died for us").

In the light of this understanding, we can paraphrase vv. 15-16*a* once again to clarify their sense:

We ourselves are Jews by birth and not Gentile sinners; yet, knowing that a person is rectified not by observance of the Law but through Jesus Christ's faithful death for our sake, even we have trusted in Christ Jesus in order that we might be rectified through the faithfulness of Christ and not through observance of the Law.

This interpretation is confirmed by Paul's last sentence in this paragraph (v. 21), where he sums up his argument by insisting that rectification comes not "through the Law" but through "Christ's death."[115]

(e) Paul's Allusion to Psalm 143. The last clause of v. 16 ("because no one will be rectified by works of the Law") appears redundant, but it is actually Paul's appeal to a scriptural proof to clinch his point.[116] His language here echoes Ps 143:2: "Do not enter into judgment with your servant, for no one living is righteous before you"

---

110. A third possibility is that the sentence means that we are rectified by having Jesus-like love, a quality of love that has its origin in Jesus (genitive of author). Williams opts for understanding "faith of Jesus Christ" along these lines. See S. K. Williams, *Galatians,* ANTC (Nashville: Abingdon, 1997) 67-70.

111. Relevant for purposes of comparison are also Col 3:5 and Eph 3:12. See also Rom 4:16, where τῷ ἐκ πίστεως Ἀβραάμ (*to ek pisteōs Abraam*) certainly does *not* mean "to the one who has faith *in* Abraham"; it means "to the one who shares the faith *of* Abraham."

112. For a full discussion of the options, see R. B. Hays, "ΠΙΣΤΙΣ and Pauline Christology: What Is at Stake?"; J. D. G. Dunn, "Once More, ΠΙΣΤΙΣ ΧΡΙΣΤΟΥ"; and P. J. Achtemeier, "Apropos the Faith of/in Christ: A Response to Hays and Dunn," in *Pauline Theology, Vol. 4: Looking Back, Pressing On,* ed. E. E. Johnson and D. M. Hay (Atlanta: Scholars Press, 1997) 35-92.

113. In support of "faith in Jesus Christ": Betz, Dunn. In support of "the faithfulness of Jesus Christ": Longenecker, Matera, Martyn. Williams adopts the "authorial genitive" solution and translates the phrase as "Christ-faith."

114. In addition to the arguments set forth in Hays, "ΠΙΣΤΙΣ and Pauline Christology," see Martyn, *The Epistle to the Galatians,* 270-71.

115. Martyn, *The Epistle to the Galatians,* 271.

116. For a more detailed exposition, see R. B. Hays, "Psalm 143 and the Logic of Romans 3," *JBL* 99 (1980) 107-15.

(NRSV). The parallel is more clearly evident in the Greek texts than in most English translations:

Ps 142:2 LXX (= Ps 143:2 MT	Gal 2:16d
And do not enter into judgment with your slave	
Because before you	Because by works of the Law
no living being will be justified (δικαιωθήσεται *dikaiōthēsetai*)	no flesh will be justified (δικαιωθήσεται *dikaiōthēsetai*)

The psalm does not include the phrase "by works of the Law" (Paul has added this phrase to highlight the point he is making), but the psalmist does affirm that no human being can stand before God's judgment and that all hope for deliverance rests in the power and righteousness of God. Twice in Psalm 143 the speaker invokes God's righteousness (δικαιοσύνη *dikaiosynē*):

Hear my prayer, O LORD;
Give ear to my supplication in your truthfulness;
Answer me *in your righteousness.*
. . . .
For your name's sake, O LORD, you will make me alive.
In your righteousness you will bring my soul out of tribulation.
(Ps 143:1, 11[142:1, 11] NRSV)

By alluding to this psalm Paul underscores his claim that the gospel of justification/rectification through God's act in Christ is entirely consistent with what those who are "Jews by birth" already know—or should know—through the witness of Scripture: We are set in right relationship to God only through God's own act of grace. The ground of our hope is the righteousness of God, not any human "works" or ethnic status. When Paul changes the wording of the psalm from "no one living will be justified" to "no *flesh* will be justified," he is perhaps subtly anticipating the argument he will make later in the letter against "those who want to make a good showing *in the flesh*" by compelling the Galatians to be circumcised (6:12).[117]

Thus, in vv. 15-16, Paul has set forth his grounds for challenging Peter in Antioch—grounds

that serve also as the theological basis for his challenge to the Galatians to reject the pressure to be circumcised. In the sentences that follow (vv. 17-21), Paul answers some anticipated objections and elaborates his position.

2:17-18. In v. 17, Paul dramatically articulates the objection that the emissaries from James (v. 12) had raised against the Jewish Christians at Antioch who were eating with Gentiles (and perhaps also the objection raised by the Missionaries in Galatia against Paul): Those who eat with Gentiles thereby become "sinners" (the same word as in v. 15) just like the Gentiles and thereby drag the name of Christ through the mud, making him an accomplice in sinful actions—and therefore, in effect, the table-waiter[118] of sin! The conditional sentence in v. 17 is formulated not as a contrary-to-fact condition but as a real condition: Paul and others who join him at table with Gentiles *are* "seeking to be rectified in Christ" (v. 16), and they *are* in fact being perceived as sinners by those who disapprove of their actions. The protasis of the sentence reflects the evaluative perspective of those who condemn the practice of the common table. For the sake of argument, Paul momentarily grants their point of view, saying, in effect, "All right, then, so eating with Gentiles means that we (Jewish Christians) ourselves are sinners." If that is the consequence of solidarity with the Gentiles, so be it! But then Paul asks whether it follows that Christ, by bringing together Jews and Gentiles, is thereby aiding and abetting sinful behavior: "Is Christ then a servant [διάκονος *diakonos*] of Sin? Certainly not!" Paul conjures up and then emphatically rejects an absurd image of Christ waiting upon Sin as a personified power; the term *diakonos* ("servant," often used of table servants) links the objection vividly to the scene of Jews and Gentiles eating at one table. It is impossible to say whether this image was already suggested by Paul's detractors or whether Paul has formulated it as a rhetorical stratagem to show the absurdity of the objection.

Paul next explains why he regards it as a mistake for Peter and Barnabas and other Jewish Christians to withdraw and separate themselves

---

117. Martyn, *The Epistle to the Galatians,* 253.

118. J. D. G. Dunn, *The Epistle to the Galatians,* Black's NT Commentary (Peabody, Mass.: Hendrickson, 1993) 141. Dunn suggests that Paul here may be alluding ironically to traditions of Jesus' table fellowship with sinners and his self-description as a *diakonos* (Mark 10:42-45).

(v. 12) from eating with Gentiles: "For if I build up again the very things that I once tore down, then I demonstrate that I am a transgressor" (v. 18). Paul shifts here from the first-person plural pronouns and verbs that he employed in vv. 15-17 to the first-person singular, which he uses throughout vv. 18-21. It is sometimes suggested that he does this for reasons of rhetorical tact. By using himself as an example, he makes the point more gently than if he directly confronted Peter with the accusation of transgression. In view of the confrontational tone of vv. 11-14, however, this explanation is not very satisfying. A better explanation is that Paul is already beginning the mental transition from the situation at Antioch to the situation in Galatia, no longer addressing Peter directly but beginning to address the issues raised against him personally by the Missionaries in another setting. (In terms of the cinematic analogy suggested above, in v. 18 the camera now pans in for the close-up shot of Paul's face.)

The language of tearing down and rebuilding something suggests the image of the Torah as a wall that separates Israel from the Gentiles.[119] Paul's gospel declares that Jesus Christ has torn down this wall. The image is powerfully developed in Eph 2:14-16:

For he is our peace; in his flesh he has made both groups into one and has broken down the dividing wall, that is the hostility between us. He has abolished the Law with its commandments and ordinances, that he might create in himself one new humanity in place of the two, thus making peace, and might reconcile both groups to God in one body through the cross, thus putting to death that hostility through it. (NRSV)

This passage, probably the work of one of Paul's immediate followers, expresses well Paul's understanding of his apostolic commission as the outworking of God's design to bring Jews and Gentiles together into one new people. By pressuring Paul to separate himself from eating with Gentiles, Peter and the emissaries from Jerusalem are asking him to build up again the wall of separation that he had previously torn down not just at Antioch but throughout his mission to the Gentiles.

If he does rebuild that wall, Paul insists, he will establish that he is a transgressor. There are two possible readings of this statement. Paul could mean that the very act of rebuilding the wall of commandments and ordinances would itself be an act of transgression against God's will. This would be a radical and ironic inversion of what the term "transgression" had meant in Paul's "former life in Judaism" (1:13), in which transgression referred to violations of the Law's boundaries, not to reestablishing them.[120] On the other hand, Paul could mean that rebuilding the wall of separation would show that his entire apostolic labor of preaching the Law-free gospel to Gentiles had not been a fulfillment of the will of God but a flagrant violation of God's holiness; to follow Peter in leaving the common table would show that Paul's whole apostleship had been in vain (cf. 2:2), an extended defiance of God. His practice of disregarding dietary restrictions and bringing Jews and Gentiles together in the church would have been, from this point of view, nothing but transgression against God.[121] This latter interpretation is the one that Paul's original hearers would have been more likely to grasp.

2:19-21. The issue is not left long in doubt, however. Paul moves quickly to declare that the old frame of reference, in which the Law must separate Jews and Gentiles, no longer applies. It has been abolished by the crucifixion of Jesus. Paul understands this crucifixion as a cosmic event in which he participates, with the result that he has "died to the Law" (v. 19). Because he has died to the Law, going back to it is impossible; rebuilding the wall is impossible for Paul, because, having been crucified with Christ, he has come into an entirely new life animated by Christ.

One puzzling feature of v. 19 is Paul's statement that "*through the Law*" he died to the Law. If he had written, "through the *cross* I died to the Law," his line of argument would be clear. But why does he say instead, "through the *Law*"? Nothing in the immediate context offers an explanation of what Paul means by this opaque formulation. Certainly Paul is not thinking of

---

119. For the use of this image within Hellenistic Judaism, see the *Letter of Aristeas* 139: "In his wisdom the legislator [Moses] . . . surrounded us with unbroken palisades and iron walls to prevent our mixing with any of the other peoples in any matter, being thus kept pure in body and soul, preserved from false beliefs, and worshiping the only God omnipotent over all creation."

120. This interpretation is favored by J. L. Martyn, *Galatians*, AB 33A (New York: Doubleday, 1997) 256.

121. For this reading of 2:18, see A. F. Segal, *Paul the Convert: The Apostolate and Apostasy of Saul the Pharisee* (New Haven: Yale University Press, 1990) 202-3.

"dying to the Law" through discovering the futility of his own attempts to observe it; according to his own self-description, he was "as to righteousness under the Law, blameless" (Phil 3:6). (The inappropriateness of the popular picture of Paul prior to his conversion as laboring under the burden of a guilt-ridden conscience was eloquently demonstrated by Krister Stendahl in his classic essay, "The Apostle Paul and the Introspective Conscience of the West.")[122] Commentators sometimes refer to Rom 7:11, which says that Sin working "in the commandment, deceived me and through it killed me" (NRSV). In fact, however, this passage sheds no light on Gal 2:19; in Romans, it is clear that one dies to the Law not "through the Law" but "through the body of Christ" (Rom 7:4 NRSV)—i.e., through union with his death in baptism (Rom 6:1-11). Dunn proposes that when Paul says "through the Law" he is referring to his activity as a persecutor of the church, motivated by zeal for the Law.[123] This interpretation leaves unexplained how this activity caused Paul to die to the Law; apart from God's intervention and call, he could have gone right on persecuting the church. The explanation that finds the greatest support within the text of Galatians itself is that the Law played an active role in the death of Jesus and pronounced a curse upon him (Gal 3:13). Thus, since Paul's death to the Law came about through his being "crucified with Christ" (v. 19; cf. 6:14), the Law played an instrumental role in this process. In fact, however, Paul does not offer any explicit explanation of this point, and we may be well advised to concede that we do not know exactly what Paul meant by the aphoristic statement "through the Law I died to the Law."

The point that matters for Paul is that he *has* passed through this death, leaving the Law behind, "so that I might live to God." This extraordinary assertion—driving a wedge between the Law and God—would be scandalous to the ears of Jews zealous for the Law.[124] The more usual Jewish perspective on the relation between the Law and life before God is illustrated by two passages in 4 Maccabees (4 Macc 7:19; 16:25) that apply the expression "to live to God" to those who undergo martyrdom precisely for the sake of the Law. The latter passage states the matter concisely:

By these words the mother of the seven encouraged and persuaded each of her sons to die *rather than violate God's commandment.* They knew also that those who die for the sake of God *live to God,* as do Abraham and Isaac and Jacob and all the patriarchs. (4 Macc 16:24-25 NRSV, italics added)

Unlike the Maccabean martyrs, Paul has died not *for* the Law but *to* it, and he claims thereby to have found life before God. This new life includes, of course, the fellowship of Jews and Gentiles together in a single worshiping congregation gathered in the name of Jesus. Those who are calling for a retreat from this radical new form of community are simply, in Paul's view, living on the wrong side of the cross, in the old age.

When Paul says that he has been "crucified with Christ," he is not referring merely to some sort of private mystical experience. (The "I" throughout vv. 18-21 is a paradigmatic "I," rhetorically inviting readers of the letter to join with Paul in these confessional statements.) Union with Christ's death is the common experience of all who are "in Christ." This is articulated most clearly in Rom 6:3-6 (see also Rom 7:6; 2 Cor 4:10; Phil 3:10; Col 2:20; 3:3):

Do you not know that all of us who have been baptized into Christ Jesus were baptized into his death? Therefore we have been buried with him by baptism into death, so that, just as Christ was raised from the dead by the glory of the Father, so we too might walk in newness of life. For if we have been united with him in a death like his, we will certainly be united with him in a resurrection like his. We know that our old self *was crucified with him* so that the body of sin might be destroyed, and we might no longer be enslaved to sin. (NRSV, italics added)

The cross is a transformative event that has changed the world and incorporated Paul—along with all who receive the gospel—into a new sphere of power. It is noteworthy that the verb "crucified with" ($\sigma\upsilon\nu\epsilon\sigma\tau\alpha\acute{\upsilon}\rho\omega\mu\alpha\iota$ *synestaurōmai*) is in the perfect tense, signifying a completed past action whose effects continue into the present;

---

122. See Krister Stendahl, "The Apostle Paul and the Introspective Conscience of the West," *HTR* 56 (1963) 199-215; reprinted in *Paul Among Jews and Gentiles* (Philadelphia: Fortress, 1976) 78-96.

123. Dunn, *The Epistle to the Galatians,* 143.

124. Martyn, *The Epistle to the Galatians,* 257, comments: "It is not an exercise in mere fantasy to imagine that, as Paul's messenger finished reading v. 19, the Teachers jumped to their feet, loudly charging Paul with blasphemy."

Paul's union with Christ's crucifixion is not merely a once-upon-a-time event but a reality that continues to determine his present existence.

That is why he goes on to say, "It is no longer I who live but Christ who lives in me."[125] Having died to his old identity, and to the Law that shaped that identity, Paul lives in the mysterious power of the risen Christ. This means that all his values and practices are reshaped in accordance with the identity of the crucified one. The character of that identity is sketched by the latter part of v. 20: "The life I now live in the flesh I live by faith—that is, by the faith of the Son of God who loved me and gave himself for me."[126] The hallmarks of this new identity are love and self-giving, rather than circumcision and Law observance. All of this has obvious implications for the debate over table fellowship with Gentiles.

The two participles in v. 20*b* that are translated "loved" (ἀγαπήσαντος *agapēsantos*) and "gave" (παραδόντος *paradontos*) are both aorist participles, pointing to the singular past event of the cross as the locus of Jesus' love and self-donation. In other words, the love of which Paul speaks here is not Jesus' warm feeling of affection toward humanity; rather, it is an *enacted* love, a love that was made manifest in action and in suffering. Precisely that action gives content to the expression "the faith of the Son of God." Here, once again as in v. 16, we face the question of whether to translate *pistis*, followed by the genitive case, as "faith in" or "faith of." Here in v. 20, the balance of probability tips strongly toward the latter. Paul is not claiming that he lives now by "believing in" the Son of God; he has, in fact, just (rhetorically) denied any continuing personal agency at all. Instead, it is now the *pistis* of the Son of God, Jesus Christ's own self-giving faithfulness, that moves in and through him.[127] The life that he now lives "in the flesh" (i.e., in embodied historical existence) is both animated and determined by Jesus Christ's faithfulness. As J. Louis Martyn articulates it, "Christ's faith con-stitutes the space in which the one crucified with Christ can live and does live."[128] Here the function of *pistis* parallels the role of "grace" (χάρις *charis*) in Paul's story of salvation, as a comparison to Rom 5:15 shows:[129]

Rom 5:15	**Gal 2:20**
. . . the free gift	. . . I live
in grace,	in faith,
namely the grace	namely the faith
of the one man	of the Son of God
Jesus Christ	

It is, therefore, no coincidence that Paul's next sentence (v. 21) refers to the theme of grace: Grace is embodied in Christ's faithful death for our sake.

With 2:21, Paul summarizes what he has been saying in the whole of this compact but powerful speech in vv. 15-21: Righteousness/rectification comes *not* through the Law but through Christ's death on a cross. The implication of this is that those who continue to insist on Law observance as a necessary condition for Gentiles' full participation in the people of God are in effect declaring Christ's death null and void and returning to social and religious norms that defined the status quo *before* Christ's death. They may be accusing Paul of nullifying the grace of God by ignoring the requirements of God's graciously given Law, but Paul turns the tables on this accusation. "I do not nullify the grace of God," he says. Unspoken but strongly implied is the counteraccusation: "It is *you* who nullify the grace of God by acting as though Christ's death was of no importance."

We may put Paul's point in the form of a question: If righteousness were available through the Law, why was it necessary for Jesus to die? Here we see how Paul's pattern of confessional logic begins with the kerygma and then works toward resolution of disputed points. The foundational truth is that Jesus Christ died "to set us free from the present evil age" (1:4). It follows that the Law was powerless to achieve that end. Thus rectification cannot be achieved through the Law. Verse 21 illustrates the truth of Sanders's dictum that Paul's thought moves "from solution

---

125. Paul often refers to being "in Christ"; for other references to the less common idea of Christ dwelling in the believer, see Rom 8:10; 2 Cor 13:5; Col 1:27; Eph 3:17.

126. In the expression "gave himself for me," Paul may be echoing the language of Isa 53:12. See also Gal 1:4; Rom 5:7-8; Mark 10:42-45; John 15:12-13.

127. Here we may well identify the grammatical construction as an "authorial genitive," pointing to Jesus Christ as the source or origin of the *pistis* that now animates Paul's life.

128. Martyn, *The Epistle to the Galatians,* 259.

129. For an analysis of the syntactical parallelism of these texts, see R. B. Hays, *The Faith of Jesus Christ: An Investigation of the Narrative Substructure of Galatians 3:1-4:11,* SBLDS 56 (Chico, Calif.: Scholars Press, 1983) 168.

to plight."[130] That is, Paul does not begin with an analysis of the human predicament under the Law and then offer the gospel as a solution; instead, he begins with the confession that Christ died for us and then works out the implications of that confession for diagnosing the human plight and determining the role of the Law.

Paul's formulation in v. 21 contains a deft wordplay that is difficult to translate. The word translated by the NRSV as "for nothing" is δωρεάν (*dōrean*), an adverb formed from the accusative case of the noun δωρεά (*dōrea*), which means "gift," as in Rom 5:15. We can come close to capturing the ambiguity of Paul's sentence by translating, "If rectification comes through the Law, then Christ died *gratuitously*." The Son of God did in fact "give himself" as a gift, but those who think rectification comes through Law have turned this gracious gift into a gratuitous superfluity.

That is the bottom line of Paul's charge against Peter at Antioch (and by implication against the rival Missionaries in Galatia). As Paul sees it, by caving in to the pressure of the emissaries from James, Peter has "set aside the grace of God." Their insistence on Law observance as the necessary hallmark of the identity of the people of God turns out to nullify the grace of God and render Christ's death meaningless. Paul proclaims that God has chosen to set things right in the world through the cross and through bringing into being a new people in which the old barrier between Jew and Gentile is broken down and made irrelevant. The cross cuts away all the systems of distinction by which we set ourselves apart from others, including the distinction between Jew and Gentile. Thus, when Peter refuses to eat with Gentiles, he is living as though the cross were of no effect. Those who have been crucified with Christ will no longer separate themselves from one another but will gather around one table.

130. E. P. Sanders, *Paul and Palestinian Judaism: A Comparison of Patterns of Religion* (Philadelphia: Fortress, 1977) 443.

REFLECTIONS

At the end of the day, was there to be one church or two "separate but equal" churches? That is the issue brought sharply into focus by Paul's confrontation with Peter at Antioch. Was there to be one table where Jews and Gentiles could eat together as brothers and sisters in Christ, or was it necessary to maintain two separate tables, symbolizing the separate cultural identity of the Jewish Christians? The issue was a difficult one, because the Jewish Christians who separated themselves from the common table believed that they were acting in obedience to the revealed Law of God. It was one thing to accept—as the "pillar" apostles had done at the conference in Jerusalem (2:1-10)—that Paul had a legitimate mission to preach the gospel to Gentiles; however, it was quite another thing for Jewish Christians to share table fellowship with the Gentiles who became believers. Would this not lead inevitably to compromising the distinctive identity of God's people? The actions of Peter—and the other Jewish Christians such as Barnabas who followed him in withdrawing from table fellowship with Gentiles—pointed toward the formation of two permanently separated churches, divided along ethnic lines. (And inevitably such a division implied the superiority and greater purity of the Jewish-Christian church.) This concrete social and political setting must always be kept in mind by the interpreter of Gal 2:11-21.

Preaching on this passage can be difficult because Paul's account of his passionate response to Peter (2:14-21) is compressed into an unusually dense discourse, prefiguring the major themes of the remainder of Galatians. The themes are weighty, and Paul sketches them so concisely that the congregation may struggle to grasp what he is saying. In order to keep the major issues in focus, the interpreter of Gal 2:11-21 will find it helpful to bear in mind four questions:

1. Who sets things right?
2. What role has Jesus played in setting things right?

3. What is the character of the new life that the death and resurrection of Jesus have inaugurated?

4. How is the truth of the gospel embodied in social practices?

The following reflections are keyed to these four central questions.

1. *Rectification as God's Doing.* Who sets things right? As the exegetical discussion above has emphasized, "rectification" refers to *God's* action of setting things right. God "rectifies" his people by coming to their rescue and instituting right order in a world gone wrong. The noun δικαιοσύνη (*dikaiosynē*), usually translated as "righteousness," is closely linked to the idea of God's covenant faithfulness: Those who are "rectified" are claimed by God's grace as belonging to the people of God; thus "righteousness" (the status of being rectified) is virtually equivalent to covenant membership. Paul's gospel shakes the world by disconnecting this status of belonging to the people of God from observance of the Law and attributing it instead solely to the gracious action of God, through the faithfulness of Jesus Christ. Thus rectification is God's doing from start to finish. Only God can set things right, and God has chosen to do that through the death of Jesus rather than through the Law. One of the world-transforming implications of this message is that the Law no longer defines or limits the boundaries of God's grace.

The full implications of this paradigm shift in understanding "righteousness" are difficult to grasp. Paul protests that most of his Jewish-Christian contemporaries failed to understand the logic of their own confession (2:15-16) about rectification through Christ and, therefore, inappropriately sought to police the boundaries of the covenant community. Once we understand that rectification is *God's* doing, not ours, important consequences follow. First of all, this truth sets us free from fear and anxiety. As Paul writes elsewhere, "It is God who justifies. Who is to condemn?" (Rom 8:33*b*-34*a* NRSV). Realizing that rectification cannot be a human attainment sets us free to rely fully on the boundless grace of God, disclosed in Christ's death for us. We can let go of our anxious need to make things come out right, our anxious need to ensure the "purity" of the church.

Another important consequence of this teaching is that "righteousness"—understood as "rectification"—is never a present possession, because God's final verdict lies in the future. God has not yet set all things right. That is why Paul speaks in Gal 5:5 of *awaiting* "the hope of righteousness." When we recognize that rectification is God's doing, we will find ourselves looking to the future for God to fulfill that hope, rather than supposing that we can forcibly set everything right in the present. Thus learning who sets things right is the great antidote to violence and intolerance.

2. *The Faithfulness of Jesus Christ.* What role has Jesus played in setting things right? Consistent with the message that rectification is God's doing, not ours, is Paul's proclamation that we are rectified only "through the faithfulness of Jesus Christ." We are not rectified by the strength or purity of our own believing. If Paul had meant that, then "faith" would be a new kind of "work," a human achievement by which we place ourselves into right relation with God. As was pointed out in the Commentary, when Paul says that "a person is rectified not through Law-observance but through the faithfulness of Jesus Christ," he is pointing to Jesus' act of loving self-giving on the cross. The shorthand expression "the faithfulness of Jesus Christ" refers to Jesus' death for our sake. The phrase interprets Jesus' death both as his act of radical trust in the God who gives life to the dead (cf. Rom 4:17) and, at the same time, as God's act of faithfulness toward a humanity that needed to be rescued from the grasp of sin and death. As Paul declares in Rom 5:8, "God proves his love for us in that while we still were sinners Christ died for us" (NRSV). That is why Paul can proclaim that "the righteousness of God" (i.e., God's faithful covenant love) is disclosed "through the faithfulness of Jesus Christ" (Rom 3:21-22).[131]

---

131. This passage shows conclusively the correctness of the translation "faithfulness of Jesus Christ." What sense would it make to claim that God's righteousness is disclosed through *our believing* in Jesus Christ?

This interpretation does not deny that Paul saw Jesus as the object of faith; Gal 2:16 goes on to say explicitly that "we placed our trust in Christ Jesus." But the whole emphasis of Paul's message shifts, on this reading, from the subjective state of the believer to the proclamation of what God has done for us in the event of the cross. The difference is subtle but important. Those who preach on Galatians need to drive the point home forcefully: The gospel that Paul preaches is the story of Jesus Christ, "who gave himself to deliver us from the present evil age" (1:4); it is the story of "the faithfulness of the Son of God who loved me and gave himself for me" (2:20). This means that preaching on this text should invite us not to introspective assessment of our own believing but rather to grateful acknowledgment of what Jesus Christ has done for us.

What he has done for us is not merely to enable us to believe and thereby find individual forgiveness of sins. Instead, his faithful death has created a whole new world and liberated us from bondage to powers that once held us captive. Preaching that attends to this aspect of the message of Galatians will have a narrative character, and the narrative will not be just the story of our journey from unbelief to belief; rather, such preaching will recount the story of Jesus' death as the destruction of the old regime and the inauguration of the new creation. It is unintelligible to preach Gal 2:11-21 apart from the passion and resurrection narratives.

3. *Crucified with Christ/Christ Lives in Me.* What is the character of the new life that the death and resurrection of Jesus have inaugurated? Despite the previous observations, the gospel narrative will also address the individual hearer. In 2:19-21, Paul does speak of his own experience in this new creation. What he reports, however, is nothing less than the annihilation of his old identity through the cross. He has entered into union with Christ's death in such a way that he can make the remarkable statement, "It is no longer I who live, but Christ who lives in me." What are we to make of this decentering of the personality, this replacement of the ego by the presence of the living, risen Christ? Sam K. Williams wisely remarks, "Here (vv. 19-20), as so often elsewhere, Paul is at least as much poet as theologian as he searches for language and reaches for images appropriate to his experience of Christ."[132] Paul is describing the experience of having his former life-world terminated and entering a new sphere of reality where he is no longer in charge. This is not merely a matter of having his sins forgiven (indeed, Paul never mentions "forgiveness" in this letter); instead, it is a matter of being transformed for service. Paul finds himself—to his own great surprise—the instrument of Christ's reconciling love, the agent of Christ's mission to a world of Gentiles whom he previously regarded as unclean "dogs."

Over time, Christians have found in Paul's words an apt description of the mystery of being caught up into God's transformation of the world in such a way that the very core of the self is claimed and transmuted by the power of the living God. Paul is not speaking of some sort of momentary mystical "high"; rather, he is describing the ongoing experience of living "in the flesh" as the embodiment of "the faithfulness of the Son of God who loved me and gave himself for me." By the power of that faithfulness he finds himself living a new high-risk existence, leaving behind the securities of Law and ethnic affiliation, proclaiming the message of God's love and embodying that message by sitting at one table with those whose way of life he once counted unclean. This involves concrete and costly political choices; it may mean initiating contacts with the poor in Third World countries or serving the homeless in our own cities. Christians who find themselves crossing cultural boundaries to do the work of God in ways that they never could have imagined will often find themselves explaining what has happened by echoing Paul's words: "It is no longer I who live, but it is Christ who lives in me."

132. S. K. Williams, *Galatians,* ANTC (Nashville: Abingdon, 1997) 81-82.

4. *The Truth of the Gospel: One Table.* How is the gospel embodied in social practices? Paul insists that "the truth of the gospel" (2:14) is a social reality: The gospel must be embodied in the practices of a community that shares a common life. One can betray the truth of the gospel not only by preaching false doctrine but also by engaging in false practices—particularly practices that fracture the unity of the church. The foundation of Paul's opposition to Peter is his conviction that, through the death and resurrection of Jesus, God has brought into being a new community that embraces Jews and Gentiles together as God's people. This is not merely an implication of the gospel or an inference from the gospel; rather, it is an integral part of the gospel itself. Wherever we see Christians trying to rebuild walls of separation in the church, walls that separate people along ethnic or cultural lines, we can be sure that the integrity of the gospel is being violated, and, like Paul, we should feel compelled to speak out against such practices.

As noted in the Reflections on 1:1-10, systems of apartheid or racial segregation offer particularly clear contemporary analogies to the abuses that Paul opposed in Antioch and Galatia. But it may be far too easy to pronounce condemnations on apartheid-era South Africa, while ignoring equally insidious abuses closer to home. The Jewish Christians at Antioch were not passing legislation to restrict the activity of Gentiles; they were merely withdrawing into private, privileged enclaves for their meals and worship. When the problem is stated that way, we are forced to ask whether in fact many of our churches practice a de facto ethnic and cultural exclusivity, reflecting the ethnic and socioeconomic exclusivity of our residential neighborhoods. When that happens, our assemblies deny in fact, if not in principle, the truth of the gospel.

On the other hand, the history of the church provides numerous impressive testimonies of the power of the gospel to break down the wall of separation between different races and cultures. One of the most remarkable stories of this kind from recent history emerged from the bloody conflict in Rwanda, where in 1994 members of the Hutu tribe carried out mass murders of the Tutsi tribe. At the town of Ruhanga, fifteen kilometers outside Kigali, a group of 13,500 Christians had gathered for refuge. They were of various denominations: Anglicans, Roman Catholics, Pentecostals, Baptists, and others. According to the account of a witness to the scene, "When the militias came, they ordered the Hutus and Tutsis to separate themselves by tribe. The people refused and declared that they were all one in Christ, and for that they were all killed," gunned down en masse and dumped into mass graves.[133] It is a disturbing story, but it is also a compelling witness to the power of the gospel to overcome ethnic division. Paul would have regarded these Rwandan martyrs as faithful witnesses to the truth of the gospel. Having been "crucified with Christ," they preferred to die rather than to deny the grace of God that had made them one in Christ.

133. E. Thomas, "Can These Bones Live?" *SOMA (Sharing of Ministries Abroad) Newsletter* (October 15, 1996) 1-15.

GALATIANS 3:1–5:1

COUNTERARGUMENTS AGAINST THE RIVAL MISSIONARIES

OVERVIEW

Paul has amply defended the integrity of his own proclamation. He now turns abruptly to confront his readers, addressing the specific situation in Galatia that provoked him to write the letter. After rebuking the Galatians once again for their fickle susceptibility to the preaching of the rival Missionaries (3:1), he launches a series of arguments against their teachings. The Missionaries are urging the Gentile Galatians to accept circumcision and to observe at least some of the distinctive practices of the Jewish Law. They have pressed their agenda by appealing to scriptural texts that teach the importance of circumcision—particularly the story of Abraham, who was regarded in Jewish tradition as "the father of proselytes." Paul sets forth a string of counterarguments that constitute the central section of the letter (3:1–5:1).

The line of argument in these chapters is complex, dense, and sometimes difficult to follow. The following brief summary provides a preview and overview of the discussion.

Paul begins with an appeal to the Galatians' experience of the Spirit (3:1-5) and then turns to a complicated exegetical argument (3:6-29), seeking to show that Scripture defines "Abraham's offspring" in a way very different from what the Missionaries have claimed. In 4:1-11, Paul returns to the experiential argument, asserting that the experience of the Spirit confirms his interpretation of Scripture: The "fullness of time" has come, and the Galatians are God's children apart from any observance of the Torah. Their failure to recognize this is leading them to consider turning back the eschatological clock and returning to a state of slavery (4:8-11). The next section (4:12-20) is a brief interlude in which Paul reminds the Galatians of their past affection for him and urges them not to be swayed into infidelity by the blandishments of the Missionaries. Finally, Paul concludes his counterarguments by returning to the Abraham story and proposing a provocative interpretation of the figures of Hagar and Sarah as symbols for two different ecclesial communities characterized by slavery and freedom (4:21-31). The argument builds to a climax in 5:1 with Paul's urgent appeal to the Galatians: "Stand firm, therefore, and do not submit again to a yoke of slavery."

Underlying this battery of arguments is Paul's conviction that Christ's death and resurrection have inaugurated a new age in which the old laws and norms no longer apply. "Christ has set us free" (5:1), and that has changed everything, including the markers of covenant membership that formerly distinguished Jews from Gentiles. Those who are children of God in Christ Jesus now participate in a new creation, signified by baptism (3:27-28). In this new creation, circumcision is no longer relevant.

GALATIANS 3:1-5, THE EXPERIENCE OF THE SPIRIT

NIV

3 You foolish Galatians! Who has bewitched you? Before your very eyes Jesus Christ was clearly portrayed as crucified. ²I would like to learn just one thing from you: Did you receive the Spirit by observing the law, or by believing what you heard? ³Are you so foolish? After beginning with the Spirit, are you now trying to attain your goal by human effort? ⁴Have you suffered so much for nothing—if it really was for nothing? ⁵Does God give you his Spirit and work miracles among you because you observe the law, or because you believe what you heard?

NRSV

3 You foolish Galatians! Who has bewitched you? It was before your eyes that Jesus Christ was publicly exhibited as crucified! ²The only thing I want to learn from you is this: Did you receive the Spirit by doing the works of the law or by believing what you heard? ³Are you so foolish? Having started with the Spirit, are you now ending with the flesh? ⁴Did you experience so much for nothing?—if it really was for nothing. ⁵Well then, does God*ᵃ* supply you with the Spirit and work miracles among you by your doing the works of the law, or by your believing what you heard?

ᵃ Gk he

COMMENTARY

3:1. Paul's reference to his experience of Christ's transforming grace (2:20-21) leads him to remind the Galatians of their own initial experience of hearing the gospel. Paul is astonished (cf. 1:6) that they have been led astray by the Missionaries. Indeed, he finds this so remarkable that he attributes it metaphorically to witchcraft. The verb "bewitch" (βασκαίνω *baskainō*), which occurs only here in the NT, is often used to refer to spells cast by "the evil eye." By using this term Paul characterizes the preachers of the anti-gospel as malevolent sorcerors and the Galatians as their dupes or victims. The Galatians, who had seen Paul's vivid portrayal of Jesus Christ before their own eyes, now have their eyes glazed over as if by magic. Paul tries to break the spell by forcefully scolding them to snap them out of it: "O foolish Galatians!"

What does Paul mean when he says that "Jesus Christ was clearly portrayed as crucified" before the eyes of the Galatians? Certainly he is not referring to the actual event of Jesus' crucifixion, which the Galatians did not literally witness. Most commentators have concluded that Paul is speaking of his vivid narration of the passion story in his preaching; he told the story of Jesus' death so compellingly that it was as though the Galatians had seen it with their own eyes.[134] This interpretation could also be related to Paul's claim to "carry the marks of Jesus branded on my body" (6:17). Paul's scars, incurred in his mission, are signs of his suffering with Christ in a way that makes the crucifixion palpably present to all with eyes to see. (Cf. his reference in 2 Cor 4:10-11 to "carrying in the body the death of Jesus, so that the life of Jesus may also be made visible in our bodies," NRSV). In that case, Paul's own physical scars would serve as a powerful visual aid for his preaching of the cross.

One other possibility, however, deserves attention. The verb προγράφω (*prographō*, translated as "clearly portrayed" by the NIV and as "publicly exhibited" by NRSV) is used elsewhere by Paul to mean "written beforehand" in Scripture (Rom 15:4). Is it possible that by selecting this verb Paul implies that his story of Christ crucified was told through interpretation of scriptural texts? If so, the reference would be not to the gospel passion

134. Hans Dieter Betz, *Galatians* (Hermeneia; Philadelphia: Fortress, 1979) 131.

narratives—which had not yet been written at this time—but to the lament psalms, interpreted as prefigurations of Christ's crucifixion.[135]

In any case, Paul's point is that the Galatians have had firsthand experience of Jesus Christ as the crucified one. The perfect participle "crucified" (ἐσταυρωμένος *estaurōmenos*) refers to a past action whose effects continue into the present. Paul portrayed Jesus as one whose identity was marked definitively and permanently by his death on a cross (cf. 1 Cor 2:1-2). Because the Galatians first heard the gospel in this way, Paul implies, they ought to have been immune to the message of the Missionaries, which plays down the world-changing character of Christ's death.

3:2. Following this reminder of his earlier cross-centered preaching, Paul brings the issue to a head. He poses a loaded rhetorical question that he regards as decisive for the whole dispute: "The only thing I want to learn from you is this: Did you receive the Spirit by observing the Torah [ἐξ ἔργων νόμου *ex ergōn nomou*] or from the message that elicits faith [ἐξ ἀκοῆς πίστεως *ex akoēs pisteōs*]?" (On the interpretation of the former Greek phrase, see the Commentary on 2:16; on the latter, see below.) In Paul's view, if the Galatians give a truthful answer to this question, the debate is over. They already have received the Spirit of God entirely apart from circumcision, apart from any observances of the Jewish Law.

This is Paul's first reference to the Spirit, which now will become a major theme of the letter, often in dichotomous opposition to "flesh" (4:29; 5:16-26; 6:8). As Paul will go on to argue (4:6-7), the Spirit is the single sufficient sign that the Galatians already have been adopted into God's family; therefore, the Missionaries' demand for circumcision is superfluous.

The logic of Paul's argument here closely parallels the story of the conversion of Cornelius and his household in Acts 10–11: Gentiles hear the gospel preached, and the Spirit falls upon them.

The only appropriate response to this act of God is articulated in Peter's question, "Can anyone withhold the water for baptizing these people who have received the Holy Spirit just as we have?" (Acts 10:47). Through baptism, those who have received the Spirit are received into the community of God's people. Both in Acts and in Gal 3:2, it is presupposed that receiving the Spirit is a palpable experience, a datum so vivid as to be undeniable. Paul does not seek to convince the Galatians that they really have received the Spirit; the argument works the other way around. He argues from the indisputable empirical fact that they have received the Spirit in order to convince them that no further validating action is required to ensure their status as God's children.

We have already seen in the discussion of 2:16 that *ex ergōn nomou* refers to the practice of keeping the commandments of Torah, particularly those commandments that were seen as "litmus-test" indicators of Jewish ethnic identity: circumcision, food laws, and sabbath observance. Paul has argued emphatically that no one is rectified (set in right relation to God) by such practices. Now he asks rhetorically whether the Galatians received the Spirit through such actions (knowing perfectly well that they did not).[136]

What, then, is the positive alternative? In Paul's forced-choice multiple-choice quiz, the right answer is that the Galatians received the Spirit *ex akoēs pisteōs*. What does this phrase mean? The NIV and the NRSV agree in translating the phrase as "by believing what you heard." This is, however, only one possible interpretation of an ambiguous expression. Indeed, it is an improbable interpretation because it takes the genitive noun *akoēs* as the object of the verbal noun *pisteōs*. Since the cognate verb *pisteuō* takes objects in the dative or accusative case, this is not a likely reading of the text. It is more likely that *akoēs*, not *pisteōs*, is the object of the preposition *ex*. The resulting translation possibilities are summarized in *Fig. 3*:

---

135. In Rom 15:4 the reference to things "written beforehand" points to Ps 69:9, quoted by Paul in the previous verse. On Paul's christological interpretation of the psalms, see R. B. Hays, "Christ Prays the Psalms," in *The Future of Christology: Essays in Honor of Leander E. Keck,* ed. A. J. Malherbe and W. A. Meeks (Minneapolis: Fortress, 1993) 122-36.

136. The question, which links the Galatian situation directly to the Antioch controversy through the catchphrase "by observing the Law," also suggests that there is a close link between being justified/rectified (2:16) and receiving the Spirit (3:2).

Figure 3: The Meaning of ἐξ ἀκοῆς πίστεως (*ex akoēs pisteōs*)[*]

If *akoē* means "hearing":
   (a) *pistis* = "believing": "by hearing with faith"
   (b) *pistis* = "the faith": "by hearing the faith" (i.e., "by hearing the gospel").
If *akoē* means "message":
   (c) *pistis* = "believing": "from the message that elicits faith"
   (d) *pistis* = "the faith": "from the message of the faith" (i.e., "from the gospel message").

*For discussion of these options, see R. B. Hays, *The Faith of Jesus Christ,* SBLDS 56 (Chico, Calif.: Scholars Press, 1983) 143-49.

The noun ἀκοη (*akoē*) can sometimes mean "hearing," but Paul's use of it in a similar context in Rom 10:16-17 suggests that he understands it to mean "what is heard"—in other words, the proclaimed message. Thus Martyn translates the phrase as "the proclamation that has the power to elicit faith" (i.e., option c).[137] On the other hand, Dunn argues that "the phrase is more obviously to be taken as describing an action of the Galatians (in antithesis to 'works of the law'): the hearing which stimulated and expressed itself in the faith by which . . . they received the Spirit" (i.e., option a).[138] Here the interpreter of the letter is faced with a crucial fork in the road. Does Paul attribute the receiving of the Spirit to a human action ("hearing with faith") or to divine initiative ("the message that elicits faith")? Paul's consistent emphasis elsewhere on the gospel as a word of divine power that transforms human beings (e.g., 1 Thess 2:13) strongly suggests the latter interpretation. This is confirmed by Paul's reprise of the question in v. 5, where he speaks of God as the one who supplies the Spirit and works miracles *ex akoēs pisteōs.*

3:3. Paul's next question implies that the Missionaries are telling the Galatians that they must undergo circumcision in order to be "completed." This idea may well have derived from their interpretation of the story of Abraham. Later rabbinic teaching in the Mishnah links circumcision explicitly to perfection in the light of Genesis 17: "Great is circumcision, for in spite of all the virtues that Abraham our father fulfilled, he was not called perfect, until he was circumcised, as it is said, 'Walk before me, and be thou perfect' " (Gen 17:1).[139] Paul, however, scoffs at the idea that, having begun with the Spirit (through the proclaimed message), the Galatians would now seek to be perfected "in the flesh" (i.e., by cutting off their foreskins). (The NIV's paraphrase, "by human effort," catches one implication of Paul's question but loses the ironic double entendre of his reference to "the flesh.") The very idea, he insists, is "foolish."

3:4. Paul asks another question that contains an ambiguity, reflected in the differing translations of the NIV ("Have you *suffered* so much for nothing?") and the NRSV ("Did you *experience* so much for nothing?"). The verb πάσχω (*paschō*) is capable of carrying either meaning. Because the immediate context speaks only of apparently positive experiences of the Spirit and miracles, most modern commentators have settled on the latter interpretation, reflected in the NRSV. On the other hand, the letter does contain a number of references to persecution and suffering as the lot of those who are in Christ (4:29; 5:11; 6:12, 17), and Paul elsewhere links the joyful experience of the Spirit directly with the experience of suffering (e.g., Rom 8:14-30; 1 Thess 1:6). It is possible, therefore, that he is alluding to some experience of the Galatians, unknown to us, in which they suffered for the gospel (cf. Rom 8:35-36; 1 Thess 2:14). Most patristic interpreters understood the passage as a reference to the Galatians' suffering.[140] Either way, Paul's point is that the Galatians' own experience will have been "in vain" if they now discount their own earlier reception of the Spirit by accepting the requirement of circumcision (cf. 4:11; 1 Cor 15:2). Paul qualifies his

---

137. J. L. Martyn, *Galatians,* AB 33A (New York: Doubleday, 1997) 281, 286-89.
138. J. D. G. Dunn, *The Epistle to the Galatians,* Black's NT Commentary (Peabody, Mass.: Hendrickson, 1993) 154.

139. See *m. Ned.* 3:11.
140. For citations from the commentaries of Marius Victorinus (BT 1972:31 [1167D-1168A]) and Ambrosiaster (CSEL 81.3:32), see M. J. Edwards, ed., *Galatians, Ephesians, Philippians,* Ancient Christian Commentary on Scripture, vol. 8 (Downers Grove, Ill.: InterVarsity, 1999) 37.

own question by adding "if it really was for nothing"; this clause has the rhetorical effect of holding open the possibility that the Galatians will, after all, heed Paul's appeal and reject the influence of the rival Missionaries.

3:5. The question in this verse repeats the initial question of v. 2, this time adding a reminder of the powerful manifestations of God's Spirit that the Galatians had witnessed in their midst. Indeed, Paul's wording suggests that they continue to experience these signs of the Spirit (note the present tense of the participles "supplies" and "works" in describing God's action). English translations unavoidably expand and paraphrase the highly elliptical Greek sentence, which reads literally, "Therefore, the one who supplies the Spirit to you and works miracles in your midst—from works of Law or from the message of faith?" Once again, Paul's emphasis lies on *God's* agency and initiative: It is God who gives the Spirit freely. The idea that God's action must be somehow prompted by Torah observance is presented as self-evidently ridiculous, since the Galatians had already experienced these evidences of God's working long before the rival Missionaries arrived on the scene with their gospel of circumcision.

The reference to "miracles" (δυνάμεις *dynameis;* more lit., "works of power") reminds us that Paul lived and moved in a symbolic world like the one that we see in the Gospels and the Acts of the Apostles, a world in which God was powerfully at work to perform healings and signs. For example, in reasserting his authority over the Corinthian church, Paul declares that when he was present with them, "The signs of a true apostle were performed among you with utmost patience, signs and wonders and mighty works [δυνάμεσιν *dynamesin*]" (2 Cor 12:12 NRSV). In the Corinthian correspondence, Paul seeks to counterbalance the Corinthians' excessive enthusiasm for such manifestations of power. Here in Galatians, however, Paul gives these manifestations full weight as evidence of the working of God's Spirit, prior to and apart from the practices of Torah observance.

The force, then, of Gal 3:1-5 is to call the Galatians to reflect back on their own initial experience of coming to faith and on their continuing experience of living in the power of the Spirit. Such experiences, Paul contends, should prove beyond all question that they need no fleshly marker to certify the authenticity of their conversion.

REFLECTIONS

1. Galatians 3:1-5 highlights the experience of the Holy Spirit as the sign and proof of the new life in Christ. As we shall see in the rest of chapter 3, Paul is concerned to show that this experience is confirmed by the testimony of Scripture. Nonetheless, the rhetoric of 3:1-5 suggests that the experience ought to be independently self-validating. The formerly pagan Galatians have been caught up by the power of the proclaimed gospel into a new life in which they continually experience the outpouring of God's Spirit and see the Spirit's mighty works in their community (3:5). In the face of this experience, the arguments for requiring circumcision simply lose their force.

Paul's line of argument here should be startling to Christians who insist on going strictly "by the book" of traditional teaching—as startling as it was to conscientious Jewish Christians of Paul's day. Where the Spirit breaks in and brings new life, we should acknowledge it gratefully as God's doing and not worry too much about whether all the proper rules and ecclesiastical proprieties are being observed. The preacher who follows the message of this passage will call the congregation to remember and reclaim their identity as God's people solely on the basis of their living experience of God's grace and power; no one should "bewitch" them into thinking of themselves as second-class Christians or as spiritually deficient because they have not undergone some discipline or ritual (all elitist "second blessing" theologies must stumble over this passage) or because they have not obtained the approval of some ecclesiastical bureaucracy.

2. The difficulty, however, is that this argument presupposes that the experience of the Holy Spirit is a concrete and powerful life-transforming experience that leaves no room for doubt. Paul assumes that such an experience of the Spirit characterized the members of his churches (cf. 1 Cor 12:1-13). The Acts of the Apostles, using the same language Paul employs in Gal 3:2, offers several narratives of individuals who "receive the Spirit." In virtually every case, there are clear signs of transformation: They speak in tongues and prophesy, they offer up enthusiastic praise to God, or they find themselves caught up into a new life of sharing and service (e.g., Acts 2:38; 8:17; 10:44-48). For many Christians today, the same claim could be made; for them, Gal 3:1-5 is a powerful reminder that their life depends on the Spirit and not on any "fleshly" standards. But what of churches in which most members would not claim such direct experience of the Spirit in their lives? The unavoidable conclusion is that for such communities Paul's argument from experience will fall on deaf ears. Unless they have a living experience of the power of the Spirit, they are likely to be acutely susceptible to various non-gospels that seek to define their identity on the basis of race or nation or gender or economic class or some other marker of social status. For such communities, the text of Gal 3:1-5 can only stand as a tantalizing glimpse of a living spiritual experience to which the gospel beckons them.

3. Once again in this passage, as in 2:16-21, Paul places strong emphasis on the priority of God's gracious action. The gospel message (ἀκοή πίστεως *akoē pisteōs*) is the instrument through which God supplies the Spirit and does mighty works. "Observing the Law" as a human action is set in opposition to "the message that elicits faith" (3:2, 5). The latter, which is God's doing, not ours, is alone responsible for the outpouring of the Spirit. The preacher who deals with this text will have to take great care to correct or qualify English translations, such as the NIV and the NRSV, that interpret *akoē pisteōs* as an action of the Galatians, something that *they* did instead of doing "works of the Law" in order to receive the Spirit. This interpretation, as argued in the Commentary, misreads the passage and, in fact, repeats the error of the rival Missionaries by failing to acknowledge the priority and sufficiency of God's action.

GALATIANS 3:6-29, THE PROMISE TO ABRAHAM

OVERVIEW

Although the argument from experience (3:1-5) might seem decisive on its own terms, Paul moves next into a much lengthier engagement with the interpretation of Scripture (3:6-29). His aim is to show (1) that the Galatians' spiritual experience is consonant with Scripture, rather than contradictory, and (2) that the rival Missionaries' interpretation of Scripture is incorrect—or, more precisely, inapplicable to the new eschatological situation created by Jesus' crucifixion. The unit is bracketed by references to God's promise to Abraham (vv. 6-9, 29). The overall purpose of this

complex argument is to demonstrate—against the urging of the Missionaries, who teach that Gentiles must be circumcised in order to be children of Abraham—that God's original blessing of Abraham included Gentile believers (vv. 6-9) and that the Galatians, who are "in Christ" via their baptism, are already Abraham's rightful heirs (vv. 26-29). Since the Missionaries were extolling the glories of the Law, the question inevitably arises, Where does the Law fit into Paul's narration of the Gospel? Therefore, in order to make his case, Paul must develop an account of the relation between Law and faith (vv. 10-14), between Law and promise (vv. 15-18), and the role of the Law within God's design to bring rectification only through Christ (vv. 19-25).

Galatians 3:6-9, The Blessing of Abraham Included the Gentiles

NIV

⁶Consider Abraham: "He believed God, and it was credited to him as righteousness."ᵃ ⁷Understand, then, that those who believe are children of Abraham. ⁸The Scripture foresaw that God would justify the Gentiles by faith, and announced the gospel in advance to Abraham: "All nations will be blessed through you."ᵇ ⁹So those who have faith are blessed along with Abraham, the man of faith.

ᵃ6 Gen. 15:6   ᵇ8 Gen. 12:3; 18:18; 22:18

NRSV

6Just as Abraham "believed God, and it was reckoned to him as righteousness," ⁷so, you see, those who believe are the descendants of Abraham. ⁸And the scripture, foreseeing that God would justify the Gentiles by faith, declared the gospel beforehand to Abraham, saying, "All the Gentiles shall be blessed in you." ⁹For this reason, those who believe are blessed with Abraham who believed.

COMMENTARY

3:6-7. The NRSV of these verses stays closer to the Greek syntax than does the NIV. The conjunction "just as" (καθώς *kathōs*) creates a link between the Galatians' experience of the Spirit and the retelling of the Abraham story that Paul will now undertake.[141] He wants them to see their experience prefigured in the story of Abraham; in both cases the blessing of God comes as sheer grace.

Paul begins his treatment of Abraham with a quotation of Gen 15:6, a thematic keynote for all that will follow (cf. Rom 4:3, where Paul introduces an even lengthier exposition of the significance of Abraham with the same quotation). The passage is crucial for Paul, not only because it links the verb "believed" and the noun "righteousness" but also because it focuses attention on a point in the story of Abraham *prior to his circumcision* where he is said to be accounted[142] righteous—i.e., in right covenant relationship with God (cf. Rom 4:9-12).

For that reason, Gen 15:6 provides Paul with

---

141. Martyn, *Galatians,* 294, translates, "Things were the same with Abraham."

142. The NIV's "credited" is a good translation of ἐλογίσθη (*elogisthē*), a verb whose semantic field is primarily that of commerce and finance.

crucial hermeneutical leverage against the Missionaries, who have almost certainly drawn the attention of the Galatians to Genesis 17, in which Abraham receives and obeys the commandment to circumcise himself and all the males of his household. By zeroing in instead on Gen 15:6, Paul, in effect, says, "No, the story of Abraham is not fundamentally about circumcision and obeying the Law; it is about trusting God's promise."

In v. 7, Paul offers a striking commentary on the passage he has just quoted. Genesis 15:6, of course, says nothing about Abraham's children or how their identity is to be determined (but see Gen 15:5). The inference lies readily at hand, therefore, that Paul is countering something the Missionaries have told the Galatians: that only those who are circumcised can be Abraham's true children. That is why Paul's rejoinder places particular emphasis on the demonstrative pronoun "these" (οὗτοι *houtoi*), which is unfortunately left untranslated by most English versions. It is as though Paul is saying, "No, it is not the circumcised who are Abraham's children; rather, those whose identity is derived from faith, *these* are Abraham's children."

These comments have followed Martyn's translation of οἱ ἐκ πίστεως (*hoi ek pisteōs*) as "those whose identity is derived from faith."[143] This is a helpful paraphrase of Paul's compact expression "the ones from faith." It is not entirely satisfactory to translate this odd expression as "those who believe" (NIV, NRSV). Paul has probably formulated the term in conscious opposition to "the ones from circumcision" (οἱ ἐκ περιτομῆς *hoi ek peritomēs*), his description of the emissaries from James who precipitated the Antioch incident (2:12). In both cases, the preposition *ek* serves to suggest that the object of the preposition ("faith" or "circumcision") is the source of being—or key identity marker—for the people in question. They are "faith people"[144] or "circumcision people."

3:8-9. Paul is not content, however, merely to argue for an analogy between Abraham's faith and the faith of those who now have placed their trust in Christ; instead, he goes on to quote another text from Genesis (actually a conflation of Gen 12:3 with Gen 18:18/22:18) that portrays Abraham as the conduit of blessing for the Gentile world: "All the Gentiles [ἔθνη *ethnē*] will be blessed in you." Remarkably, Paul treats this statement as something that Scripture *said to* Abraham. Scripture (ἡ γραφη *hē graphē*), personified here as a speaking character in Paul's retelling of the story, is said to have spoken prophetically, actually "foreseeing" long ago that God "is [now] justifying the Gentiles on the basis of faith" and therefore pre-preaching the gospel (προευηγγελίσατο *proeuēngelisato*) to Abraham! Strikingly, the "gospel" that Scripture announced beforehand is focused on the promise that Gentiles will be blessed in Abraham. Paul says nothing yet about Jesus;

instead, the meaning of "gospel" is articulated in terms of a blessing to Gentiles in or through Abraham. The blessing pronounced on Abraham filters down, or out, to the whole world.

The implication of all this is explained clearly in another exegetical comment by Paul in v. 9: "So, faith people [*hoi ek pisteōs*] are blessed with the faithful [πιστῷ *pistō*] Abraham." It is noteworthy that Paul describes Abraham with the simple adjective "faithful." Many English translations paraphrase to make the sentence conform more closely to preconceived notions about Pauline theology, as in the NRSV: "Abraham who believed." Dunn rightly sees that Paul "saw no danger in speaking of Abraham's faithfulness," but this accurate assessment undercuts his earlier claim that Paul is seeking to "drive a wedge between the two senses of πίστις (*pistis;* faith, faithfulness)."[145] In fact, the Greek language will not permit such a wedge to be driven. The single noun *pistis* includes in its semantic range the meanings "trust," "faithfulness," "fidelity," "faith." Therefore, Paul can read the scriptural statement "Abraham believed [ἐπίστευσεν *episteusen*] God" and conclude that Abraham is rightly to be called faithful (πιστός *pistos*). The root idea in both expressions is that Abraham placed his trust in God; that, for Paul, is the meaning of faithfulness. Thus Paul's summary remark in v. 9 links together the conclusions he has drawn from his citations of Genesis: The blessing of Abraham is ultimately intended for the whole world (not just for Jews), and Abraham's true children are those whose identity is rooted in trusting God's promise. (See Reflections at 3:26-29.)

143. Martyn, *Galatians*, 299.
144. S. K. Williams, *Galatians*, ANTC (Nashville: Abingdon, 1997) 86-87.

145. J. D. G. Dunn, *The Epistle to the Galatians,* Black's NT Commentary (Peabody, Mass.: Hendrickson, 1993) 163, 167.

Galatians 3:10-14, Christ's Death Liberates Israel from the Law's Curse

NIV	NRSV
[10]All who rely on observing the law are under a curse, for it is written: "Cursed is everyone who does not continue to do everything written in the Book of the Law."[a] [11]Clearly no one is justified [a]10 Deut. 27:26	10For all who rely on the works of the law are under a curse; for it is written, "Cursed is everyone who does not observe and obey all the things written in the book of the law." [11]Now it is evident that no one is justified before God by the

NIV

before God by the law, because, "The righteous will live by faith."[a] [12]The law is not based on faith; on the contrary, "The man who does these things will live by them."[b] [13]Christ redeemed us from the curse of the law by becoming a curse for us, for it is written: "Cursed is everyone who is hung on a tree."[c] [14]He redeemed us in order that the blessing given to Abraham might come to the Gentiles through Christ Jesus, so that by faith we might receive the promise of the Spirit.

[a]11 Hab. 2:4   [b]12 Lev. 18:5   [c]13 Deut. 21:23

NRSV

law; for "The one who is righteous will live by faith."[a] [12]But the law does not rest on faith; on the contrary, "Whoever does the works of the law[b] will live by them." [13]Christ redeemed us from the curse of the law by becoming a curse for us—for it is written, "Cursed is everyone who hangs on a tree"— [14]in order that in Christ Jesus the blessing of Abraham might come to the Gentiles, so that we might receive the promise of the Spirit through faith.

[a] Or *The one who is righteous through faith will live*   [b] Gk *does them*

COMMENTARY

Although Paul's line of argument in vv. 6-9 is clear, the next section (vv. 10-14) is one of the most difficult passages anywhere in his letters. Paul seems to be reading the OT texts he cites in strange ways. He makes the astonishing claim that Scripture itself pronounces a curse on "those who rely on the Law" (v. 10). He also seems to set Scripture against Scripture (vv. 11-12). Furthermore, he quotes Deuteronomy in support of the startling assertion that the crucified Christ became a curse (v. 13). What is going on in this confusing paragraph?

Some interpreters think that Paul is asserting the unfulfillability of the Law; those who try to keep the Law are under a curse because they are bound to fall short of perfect obedience and, therefore, incur God's wrath. This is such a ridiculous caricature of Judaism, however, that it could hardly have been taken seriously as a persuasive argument in Paul's time. If Paul had made such claims, the rival Missionaries could easily have refuted him by pointing out that the Law makes ample provision for forgiveness of transgressions through repentance, through the sacrificial system, and through the solemn annual celebration of the Day of Atonement. In fact, however, Paul does *not* say that it is impossible to obey the Law, although this supposition has been read into the text by many generations of Christian interpreters. Paul, reflecting on his own former life as a Pharisee, can say that he was, "as to righteousness under the Law, blameless" (Phil 3:6 NRSV).

This certainly does not mean that he never sinned; it simply indicates that his transgressions were dealt with according to the Law's provisions and that he, therefore, was in no way wracked by a guilty introspective conscience.[146] If Paul did not regard the Law as unfulfillable, then, how are we to understand the logic of his exposition?

It is important to bear in mind that Paul's argument drives toward the confessional affirmation of vv. 13-14: Christ's redemptive work removed the curse from Israel so that the blessing of Abraham (v. 8) can come to Gentiles and so that "we" (= all God's people, Jews and Gentiles together) can receive the promise of the Spirit. The reference to the blessing of Abraham in v. 14 links vv. 10-14 firmly to vv. 6-9; Paul is still answering the question of how Gentiles can now receive the blessing first promised to Abraham. With this in mind, we must read vv. 10-14 carefully to see how they fit into Paul's argument.

3:10. Paul coins a compressed expression, "those who are from works of Law" (ὅσοι ἐξ ἔργων νόμου *hosoi ex ergōn nomou*), which stands in antithetical contrast to οἱ ἐκ πίστεως (*hoi ek pisteōs;* v. 7). If, as we have seen, that expression means "those whose identity is derived from faith," then the phrase in this verse must mean "those whose identity is derived from works of Law." (The paraphrases of the NIV and the

146. K. Stendahl, "The Apostle Paul and the Introspective Conscience of the West," *Paul Among Jews and Gentiles* (Philadelphia: Fortress, 1976) 78-96.

NRSV offer a similar interpretation.) This description of the Torah-observant faction is already, from Paul's point of view, a decisive indictment, since he insists that those who are in Christ derive their identity from Christ and Christ alone (2:20; 3:26-28). By framing the discussion in these terms, Paul already implies that "faith" and "works of Law" are opposite and incompatible sources of identity.

These people whose identity is derived from keeping the commandments of Torah are, Paul now claims, "under a curse." The polarity between curse and blessing has already been subliminally suggested by Paul's citation of Gen 12:3 in v. 8: "I will bless those who bless you, and the one who curses you I will curse; and in you all the families of the earth shall be blessed." In v. 8, Paul quoted only the last part of the verse, but now he picks up the latent "curse" theme and turns the claim of his adversaries upside down. They were contending that the blessing of Abraham is for those who are circumcised, but Paul now provocatively assigns the blessing to uncircumcised Gentiles and the curse to the circumcised advocates of Torah observance.

He supports this scandalous claim by quoting Deut 27:26, though his wording differs slightly from both the MT and the LXX.

Deut 27:26 MT: Cursed be anyone
    who does not uphold
    the words of this law
    by observing them. (NRSV)
Deut 27:26 LXX: Cursed is anyone
    who does not remain in
    all the words of this law,
    to do them.
Gal 3:10: Cursed is anyone
    who does not remain in
    all the things that are written in the book of
      the Law,
    to do them.

Paul's citation follows the LXX closely, except that he has replaced the phrase "all the words of *this law*" (i.e., the specific covenant law of Deuteronomy 26–28) with a phrase imported from Deut 28:58 or 30:10: "all the things *that are written in the book of the Law*." The change in wording

has the effect of expanding the reference to the canonical Law of Moses as a whole.

Many readers have found Paul's appeal to this text surprising, because it seems to say exactly the opposite of what Paul claims. In Deuteronomy the curse is pronounced on those who do *not* do what the Law requires, but v. 10*a* seems to say—so many interpreters have thought—that those who conscientiously *do* what the Law requires are cursed.

To understand Paul's point, we must recognize two things. First, those who are said to be under a curse are not "those who do the Law," but rather "those whose identity is derived from works of Law." It is those who still live within the sphere of the deuteronomic covenant who are said to be subject to the curse, living under the jurisdiction of the threatening words of Deuteronomy 27.[147] Thus Paul is simply informing the Galatians of a point repeatedly emphasized in Deuteronomy: Those who enter the covenant are subject to its sanctions and curses. Paul's citation of Deut 27:26 reminds the reader of the whole structure of Israel's covenant obligations, including the solemn curses and blessings that attend the covenant in Deuteronomy 27–28.[148] Thus to be "under a curse" (v. 10) is to live under Deuteronomy's dispensation of *conditional* curses and blessings, to be subject to strict judgment contingent upon obedience.

Second, these curses apply to Israel as a whole, not merely to individual Jews living under the Law. The book of Deuteronomy is emphatic in its warning that the punishment for disobedience will be inflicted upon the nation as a whole and that the whole people will be carried away into exile before God finally intervenes to rescue and restore them. In Deut 31:29, Moses explicitly predicts that after his death the people will turn aside from God's commandments and that God's anger will fall upon them. This prediction is then given a hymnic elaboration in the Song of Moses (Deuteronomy 32), a passage of great importance for Paul's interpretation of Scripture.[149] Thus, when

147. C. D. Stanley, " 'Under a Curse': A Fresh Reading of Galatians 3.10-14," *NTS* 36 (1990) 481-511.

148. For this point and for much of what follows, see N. T. Wright, *The Climax of the Covenant: Christ and the Law in Pauline Theology* (Edinburgh: T. & T. Clark, 1991) 137-56.

149. See R. H. Bell, *Provoked to Jealousy: The Origin and Purpose of the Jealousy Motif in Romans 9–11,* WUNT (Tübingen: Mohr, 1994).

Paul warns the Galatians that those whose identity is grounded in the Law are under a curse, he is in effect saying to them, "If you affiliate yourself with those who place their hope in obeying the Law (i.e., the Missionaries), you are joining a losing team"—not because obedience is theoretically impossible, but because Israel historically has failed and has in fact incurred the judgment of which Deuteronomy solemnly warns. That is, Israel was sent away into exile, and, despite the return from exile, has never recovered the blessings promised in Deut 28:1-14.

3:11-12. In these verses, the logic of the argument becomes clearer if we make a minor change in punctuation of the Greek text (the oldest Greek MSS have no punctuation), yielding the translation, "Now because no one is rectified by the Law, it is clear that 'The righteous one will live by faith.' " The first clause provides the warrant for the second, not (as in the NRSV and the NIV) the other way around.[150] Paul takes it as a given—as he had done earlier in 2:16—that the Law does not have the power to set people in right relation to God. From that fact—confirmed by Israel's historical experience of disobedience and exile—Paul concludes that there must be some other way to be rectified. Therefore, he finds another scriptural text that bears witness to the way in which "the righteous" will at last encounter God's rectifying power.

The text to which Paul points is Hab 2:4, the same text that he later employs as the keynote of his Letter to the Romans (Rom 1:17). This passage is the source of the catchphrase *ek pisteōs* ("from/by faith"), which Paul has already used in 2:16 and 3:7-9, and which he will use again in 3:12, 22, 24 and 5:5 (see also Rom 1:17; 3:26, 30; 4:16; 5:1; 9:30, 32; 10:6; 14:23). This unusual turn of phrase appears nowhere else in the OT, and Paul uses it only in Galatians and Romans—the two letters where he quotes Hab 2:4.[151] Thus the phrase *ek pisteōs* becomes in these two letters a slogan alluding to Hab 2:4 as the revelatory hermeneutical lens through which Scripture must be read.

Habakkuk 2:2-4 is God's answer to the prophet's anguished complaint that God has allowed injustice to prevail in the world by allowing foreign rulers to oppress Israel. This passage was seen by many ancient Jewish interpreters, including the Qumran community, as an important eschatological prophecy;[152] the LXX translators read the passage as a messianic text, as did the author of the Letter to the Hebrews (Heb 10:37-38). The title "The Righteous One" (ὁ δίκαιος *ho dikaios*) appears elsewhere in the NT as an honorific title for Jesus (Acts 3:14; 7:52; 22:14; 1 Pet 3:18; 1 John 2:1) and elsewhere in Jewish sources (e.g., *1 Enoch* 38:2; 58:6) as a title for the long-awaited eschatological deliverer.[153] It is probable, therefore, that Paul is playing subtly on this background of messianic expectation. At this stage of the argument, however, Paul does not explicitly refer to Jesus; his argument can be understood non-messianically, as an assertion that Hab 2:4 provides the key to understanding how God has chosen to bring about rectification and life: through faith, not through the Law. The link created in v. 11 between the verbs "to be rectified" and "to live," which he seems to use synonymously, reflects Paul's conviction that true "life," eschatological life, is accessible only for those who are restored by faith (*ek pisteōs*) to right covenant relationship with God.

But what then of those portions of the Law of Moses that do not speak of faith and seem to make life and blessing contingent upon doing what the Law requires? Paul cannot avoid this problem, because the Missionaries who held up Abraham to the Galatians as a model for undergoing circumcision no doubt also pointed out passages such as Lev 18:5, which promises that "the one who does these things [ὁ ποιήσας αὐτά *ho poiēsas auta;* exactly the same language found in Deut 27:26] will live by them." Paul faces the issue head-on. He cites Lev 18:5 in stark juxtaposition to Hab 2:4 and declares that "the Law is not *ek pisteōs*." The conclusion is compelling that Paul portrays Lev 18:5 as an empty promise, a

---

150. Wright, *The Climax of the Covenant,* 149n. 42, crediting his student Christopher Palmer. For further defense of this reading, see A. Wakefield, "The Hermeneutical Significance of Paul's Use of Citations in Galatians 3:6-14" (Ph.D. diss., Duke University, 2000).

151. D. A. Campbell, "Romans 1:17—A Crux Interpretum for the *Pistis Christou* Debate," *JBL* 113 (1994) 265-85.

152. A. Strobel, *Untersuchungen zum eschatologischen Verzögerungsproblem auf Grund der spätjudisch-urchristlichen Geschichte von Habakkuk 2,2 ff.,* NovTSup 2 (Leiden: Brill, 1961).

153. For discussion of this motif, see R. B. Hays, " 'The Righteous One' as Eschatological Deliverer: A Case Study in Paul's Apocalyptic Hermeneutics," in *Apocalyptic and the New Testament: Essays in Honor of J. Louis Martyn,* ed. J. Marcus and M. L. Soards, JSNTSup 24 (Sheffield: JSOT, 1989) 191-215.

part of the ineffectual scheme of salvation centered on works of Torah, a scheme now rendered inoperative by the death of Jesus.[154] To live within the Law's sphere of power is to live in the world narrated by Leviticus and Deuteronomy, a world in which the Law promises life but cannot deliver it, a world in which a curse hangs over Israel (see also Lev 18:24-30, which threatens that "the land will vomit you out" if the Law is violated). In that world, no one can be justified before God (v. 11), because Israel has tragically gone the way that Deuteronomy prophesied, into infidelity and bondage (see, e.g., Deut 28:45-51). But, according to Paul's proclamation, that world no longer exists.

3:13-14. The curse pronounced by the Law has been broken by Christ's death. Paul's verb "redeemed" (ἐξηγόρασεν *exēgorasen*) is the word used to describe the emancipation of a slave. This language introduces a metaphor to which Paul will return repeatedly: Life under the Law is a form of slavery (4:1-11, 21–5:1). The result of Jesus' crucifixion, however, is to set the enslaved people of Israel free at last from the curse pronounced by Deuteronomy. Given the ugly history of Christian attitudes toward Judaism, it is important to recognize that the expression "the curse of the Law" does not mean that the Torah is a curse; rather, it refers specifically to the curse *pronounced by* the Law, as Paul has just quoted it in v. 10. It is this curse that Jesus has now nullified by his self-sacrificial death.

Paul says that "Christ redeemed us from the curse of the Law *by becoming a curse* for us." Paul's language here is deliberately paradoxical and provocative. Jesus entered so fully into Israel's enslaved condition that he absorbed and exhausted the curse fully in his own innocent death. The thought is exactly paralleled in a similarly pregnant confessional statement in 2 Cor 5:21: "For our sake [God] made him to be sin who knew no sin, so that in him we might become the righteousness of God" (NRSV). In Jesus' death a mysterious pattern of exchange was enacted, so that for our sake he took upon himself all the consequences of the world's sin. Such an awesome mystery can only be proclaimed, not explained. This mystery stands at the heart of Paul's gospel: The Son of God died an ignominious death for our sake. Jesus' death on a cross not only defines the meaning of love but also transforms everything, ending the old world under the Law and opening up a new world of grace, freedom, and blessing. That is why Paul regards a return to life under the Law as an absurd denial of God's grace.

The shocking claim that Jesus became a curse is supported by another quotation from Deuteronomy: "cursed [ἐπικατάρατος *epikataratos*] is everyone who is hung on a tree" (Deut 21:23). Paul has slightly modified the LXX, which reads, "cursed [κεκατηραμένος *kekatēramenos*] by God is everyone who is hung on a tree." Paul omits "by God," leaving the source of the curse unspecified, and uses the same word for "cursed" that appears in Deut 27:26, ensuring that the reader will link the passages together; the curse that Jesus took upon himself is precisely the curse already mentioned in v. 10. In its original context, Deut 21:23 provides the rationale for the deuteronomic law prohibiting Israel from leaving the dead body of a hanged criminal dangling on a tree overnight, for the dead body would "defile the land." By provocatively applying this saying to the crucified Jesus, Paul has given the text a twist, rereading it in the light of the story of Jesus' crucifixion (cf. v. 1). As Dunn notes, by Paul's time the passage had also been read by some other Jewish interpreters as a reference to the Roman punishment of crucifixion.[155]

It has sometimes been suggested that in Paul's earlier days as a persecutor of the church (1:13, 23) he would have brandished this very verse, Deut 21:23, against his Christian opponents to prove that the crucified Jesus had died under God's curse and, therefore, could not possibly have been the Messiah. If so, then when he experienced his transforming call to apostleship and became convinced that God had vindicated Jesus by raising him from the dead, he would have recognized that the Law that cursed Jesus must have been utterly wrong. This in turn would explain how Paul came to hold the view that the

---

154. In Rom 10:6, Paul interprets Lev 18:5 in a different and far more positive way. See R. B. Hays, *Echoes of Scripture in the Letters of Paul* (New Haven: Yale University Press, 1989) 73-83; Wright, *The Climax of the Covenant,* 149.

155. 4QpNah 1:7-8; 11QTemple 64:6-13. See also J. D. G. Dunn, *The Epistle to the Galatians,* Black's NT Commentary (Peabody, Mass.: Hendrickson, 1993) 178.

Law was abrogated by Christ's death. All this is, however, highly speculative, for Paul never hints at any such process in the development of his thought. It is far likelier that v. 13 reflects an early Jewish-Christian confessional tradition that explained the saving effects of Jesus' death by interpreting the crucifixion as Jesus' vicarious sacrifice, in which he took the effects of the deuteronomic curse upon himself. Whether Paul is the author of that tradition or whether vv. 13-14 are his citation of a tradition is impossible to determine with confidence.

In any case, the purpose of Jesus' taking the curse upon himself is explained in v. 14; the blessing of Abraham, long ago promised to the Gentiles (cf. vv. 8-9), can at last flow to them (cf. Rom 15:8-12), and the Spirit can be received by all God's people, through faith. Here again we find an ambiguity: Does Paul mean through their own faith or through the faith(fulness) of Jesus? The flow of logic in vv. 13-14 would suggest the latter: Christ redeemed Israel from the consequences of its unfaithfulness through his faithful death in order that we might receive the Spirit through Christ's faithfulness.[156] Paul, however, lets the ambiguity stand, perhaps for deliberate rhetorical purposes. The sentence could also be understood to mean that we receive the Spirit "through the faith that is elicited by Christ's faithful death in our behalf."[157]

In the previous paragraph (vv. 6-9), Paul has explicitly linked the blessing of Abraham with the rectification of the Gentiles—i.e., their acceptance into right covenant relationship with God. How is this outcome dependent on Christ's redemption of *Israel* from Deuteronomy's curse? Paul does not explain the connection (this is one reason for supposing that vv. 13-14 might be a pre-existing confessional formula), but we can make some guesses. The prophetic text that most powerfully shapes Paul's vision of the eschatological inclusion of the Gentiles is the book of Isaiah.[158] Isaiah holds

forth the vision of God's final redemption and restoration of Israel as a prelude to the gathering of the Gentiles to worship the one true God on Mt. Zion (e.g., Isa 2:2-4; 60:1-22). So long as the people of Israel remain in bondage under the curse, this eschatological scenario cannot come to pass. The confessional formula of vv. 13-14 appears to assume that at last through Christ's death the curse has been lifted, Israel has been set free, the exile has ended, so that the ingathering of the Gentiles can now begin.

This interpretation also explains how Paul can equate the "promise" with the reception of the Spirit. This is a somewhat puzzling move, because the passages in Genesis that speak of the blessing of Abraham make no reference at all to the Spirit. Thus it appears that Paul has creatively expanded the actual content of the promise; whereas Genesis speaks of God's gift of land and numerous descendants, Paul regards the promise to Abraham as being fulfilled in the church's experience of the Holy Spirit. The explanation for this inferential leap lies once again in the prophetic texts that promise Israel's ultimate restoration from exile. In Isaiah and Ezekiel, God's promise of restoration is repeatedly depicted through the image of the outpouring of God's Spirit (Isa 32:15-17; 44:1-5; 59:21; Ezek 11:14-21; 36:22-27; 37:1-14). Particularly noteworthy is Isa 44:3, in which the terms "spirit" and "blessing" are used in synonymous parallelism:

For I will pour water on the thirsty land,
  and streams on the dry ground;
I will pour my *spirit* upon your descendants [LXX:
  σπέρμα *sperma*],
  and my *blessing* upon your offspring. (NRSV)

Although Paul does not cite this passage, it probably underlies and surely illuminates Gal 3:1-14. Indeed, it helps us to see how Paul's argument from Scripture is constructively linked with his earlier argument from experience (vv 1-5); the experience of the Spirit in the church is a sign that God's eschatological restoration of Israel has begun. The fact that Gentiles such as the Galatians have also experienced this outpouring of the Spirit is consistent with the prophetic vision, which in turn was already "pre-proclaimed" in the promise to Abraham (vv. 6-9).

Dunn goes so far as to describe vv. 10-14 as

---

156. F. J. Matera, *Galatians,* Sacra Pagina 9 (Collegeville, Minn.: Liturgical Press, 1992) 121, 124-25. Paul's use of the definite article in the phrase διὰ τῆς πίστεως (*dia tēs pisteōs*) might lend support to this interpretation.

157. J. L. Martyn, *Galatians,* AB 33A (New York: Doubleday, 1997) 323.

158. F. Wilk, *Die Bedeutung des Jesajabuches für Paulus,* FRLANT 179 (Göttingen: Vandenhoeck & Ruprecht, 1998); J. R. Wagner, *Heralds of the Good News: Paul and Isaiah 'In Concert' in the Letter to the Romans,* NovTSup (Leiden: Brill, 2001).

"a midrash on Deuteronomy's three-stage schema of salvation-history": covenant, exile, and restoration.[159] That is a fundamentally correct observation, but we must also reckon with the radically revisionary character of this "midrash"; it is an interpretation that leads to the conclusion that the Torah's promise of life for those who remain within its structure of commandments is a false promise. Indeed, those who persist in trying to live under the Law after Christ has done away with its curse are, in fact, reverting to life under the curse. Hence, the urgency of Paul's argument against the Missionaries. Abraham is to be read not as a model of circumcision and Torah observance but as a prefiguration of the gospel: He simply trusts God and receives God's promise. Paul sees this same story being re-enacted in his Gentile churches.

This interpretation helps us to resolve two long-debated exegetical problems in vv. 13-14: (1) To whom do the pronouns "us" and "we" refer? (2) How are the two purpose clauses in v. 14 related to each other? According to the reading given here, "us" in v. 13 refers specifically to the Jewish people (including Jewish Christians, like Paul), who had incurred the curse of the Law through disobedience. On the other hand, the

159. Dunn, *The Epistle to the Galatians*, 180.

"we" in v. 14*b* must refer to the whole new community of God's people, transcending the Jew/Gentile distinction, on whom God is now pouring the Spirit. This means that both of the purpose clauses in v. 14 follow directly as consequences of Christ's redemptive death (v. 13). The logic of the clauses is as follows:

(a) Christ's death redeemed "us" [*Jews*] from the curse pronounced by the Law.

This has two effects:

(b_1) in Christ Jesus, the blessing of Abraham comes to the *Gentiles,*

(b_2) and "we" [*Jews and Gentiles together*] receive the Spirit.

Whether this is a traditional formula or Paul's own fresh coinage, it reflects a fundamental shift of perspective that underscores the socially inclusive gospel for which Paul is battling. The speaker of such a confession moves from an initial identification with ethnic Israel (a), through an acknowledgment of God's blessing of the Gentiles (b_1), to a final declaration that through Christ's death Jews and Gentiles alike are united in receiving the Spirit (b_2). Thus the experience of the Spirit is interpreted as the fulfillment of what Scripture has promised: the blessing of all nations. (See Reflections at 3:26-29.)

Galatians 3:15-18, The Covenant Promise Predated the Law

NIV	NRSV
[15]Brothers, let me take an example from everyday life. Just as no one can set aside or add to a human covenant that has been duly established, so it is in this case. [16]The promises were spoken to Abraham and to his seed. The Scripture does not say "and to seeds," meaning many people, but "and to your seed,"[a] meaning one person, who is Christ. [17]What I mean is this: The law, introduced 430 years later, does not set aside the covenant previously established by God and thus do away with the promise. [18]For if the inheritance depends on the law, then it no longer depends on a promise; but God in his grace gave it to Abraham through a promise.	15Brothers and sisters,[a] I give an example from daily life: once a person's will[b] has been ratified, no one adds to it or annuls it. [16]Now the promises were made to Abraham and to his offspring;[c] it does not say, "And to offsprings,"[d] as of many; but it says, "And to your offspring,"[c] that is, to one person, who is Christ. [17]My point is this: the law, which came four hundred thirty years later, does not annul a covenant previously ratified by God, so as to nullify the promise. [18]For if the inheritance comes from the law, it no longer comes from the promise; but God granted it to Abraham through the promise.
*a*16 Gen. 12:7; 13:15; 24:7	*a* Gk *Brothers* *b* Or *covenant* (as in verse 17) *c* Gk *seed* *d* Gk *seeds*

COMMENTARY

Paul now takes another tack. In vv. 15-18 he compares God's covenantal promise, spoken to Abraham, to a human last will and testament, which cannot be annulled by the subsequent action of a third party. This last will promised an inheritance to Abraham and to his "seed," which Paul identifies exclusively with Christ. The analogy has serious risks and limitations, because it compares God's promise to a human legal instrument that would become effective only upon the death of the testator, and because it seems to imply (wrongly) that the Law was instituted not by God but by some other party. These are scandalous implications; nonetheless, for the sake of argument, Paul is willing to press this analogy a long way, because it allows him to highlight two points: The Law came much later than the promise to Abraham and is, therefore, secondary, and the blessing of Abraham must be understood as an *inheritance* that rightly belongs to Gentiles as well as to Jews. From this point of view, the Missionaries' insistence that only Torah observers are Abraham's heirs appears to be a legal ploy to steal the inheritance from the Gentiles to whom God had promised it.

This line of argument, however, raises fundamental questions about the Law. If it had no saving efficacy and cannot be understood as a further specification of the covenant with Abraham, why did it come into existence? Is it to be understood as an evil entity set in opposition to God's promises? In vv. 19-24, Paul addresses these issues and contends that the Law had a limited, temporary purpose in God's design to save the world ultimately through Christ's faithfulness. Now that Christ, the Seed who is the true inheritor of the promise, has come, the Law no longer has any constructive purpose in God's economy.

In the final paragraph of this unit (vv. 25-29), Paul explains that the Galatians and all who are "in Christ" through baptism have entered a whole new world where all the old human divisions— including the distinction between Jew and Gentile symbolized by circumcision—no longer have the power to separate us from one another. All who are incorporated into Christ are thereby given an identity as "Abraham's seed"; therefore, they are all legitimate heirs whether they are circumcised or not.

The unity of the argument is sometimes obscured when this section is broken down into short, discrete paragraphs (e.g., vv. 15-18, 19-22, 23-25, and 26-29). The key to the overall logic of the section is found in the link between v. 16 and v. 29: The promise is given to Abraham and his seed, who is Christ (v. 16), and all who are in Christ are therefore Abraham's seed (v. 29).

3:15. Paul realizes that he is about to undertake a high-risk argument fraught with the possibility of misinterpretation; therefore, he prefaces this section with a disclaimer. The Greek text of v. 15*a* says, literally, "Brothers, I speak in a human way," indicating that he is aware of the limitations of the figurative analogy he is about to propose: God's dealing with humanity can be only indirectly grasped by means of such illustrations.[160] (The NRSV and the NIV give a paraphrase rather than a translation at this point.) By addressing the Galatians as "brothers" (for the first time since 1:11), Paul signals a transition, modulating his voice into a warmer tone after the scolding address of 3:1.

The term "will" (διαθήκη *diathēkē*) is semantically ambiguous, and Paul makes the ambiguity serve his daring analogy. *Diathēkē* is the ordinary term in Greek for a last will and testament, but the LXX translators also employed it to translate the Hebrew word for "covenant" (ברית *běrît*). Thus Paul fancifully reads the references in Genesis to God's establishment of a *diathēkē* with Abraham as though this "covenant" were a human "will." Once the will has been ratified by the testator, no one else can add a codicil to it or annul it. The language here is technical legal terminology,[161] but Paul has selected his words carefully to echo and prefigure other language in his argument. The term "annul" (ἀθετέω *atheteō*) is the same verb used in 2:21 ("I do not *nullify* the grace of God"); thus he subtly suggests that to

---

160. See the parallels in Rom 3:5; 6:19; and 1 Cor 9:8. Rom 6:19 is especially helpful in illuminating the sense of Gal 3:15*a*: "I am speaking in human terms because of your natural limitations" (NRSV).

161. See references in H. D. Betz, *Galatians* (Hermeneia; Philadelphia: Fortress, 1979) 155-56.

annul God's *diathēkē* by superimposing the Law upon it is a way of negating God's grace. Also, the verb "adds to" (ἐπιδιατάσσεται *epidiatas-setai*) subtly prepares the way for the etymologically related participle "ordained/put into effect" (διαταγείς *diatageis*) in v. 19. This verbal connection between v. 15 and v. 19 implies that the angelic administration of the Law (v. 19) was an addition that cannot supersede the promise made by God to Abraham.

3:16. Having set up the analogy between God's covenant and a human will, Paul now takes the role of probate judge, interpreting the language of the original *diathēkē* as precisely as possible. He observes that the promises (Gen 12:1-3, 7; 13:14-17; 15:5; 17:4-8; 22:16-18; 26:2-5) were addressed to Abraham "*and to his seed.*" (Probably the reference is particularly to Gen 17:8, in view of the repeated use of the term *diathēkē* in that context.) Paul drives home the point that the noun "seed" (σπέρμα *sperma*) is singular, not plural, and then offers a startling interpretation: The singular seed is Christ. Thus he reads the promises in Genesis as direct prophetic figurations of Christ, who is the ultimate heir designated by God's promissory testament.

This remarkable reading of Genesis has often been regarded as an instance of Paul's exegetical sleight of hand, lifting a proof text completely out of context and disregarding the obvious fact that "seed" is a collective noun that refers to Abraham's numerous descendants, more numerous than the stars of heaven (Gen 15:5). We must not, however, hastily dismiss Paul's interpretative strategy. He is certainly aware that Abraham has many children, not just one (Gal 3:7), and—most important—his exposition drives toward the climactic affirmation in v. 29: "If you [pl.] belong to Christ then you [pl.] are Abraham's seed [*sperma*], heirs according to promise." This shows that Paul knows perfectly well that *sperma* is a collective noun and that the Genesis texts point toward multiple progeny for Abraham. In v. 16, however, he plays on the grammatically singular form of the word, in a style formally reminiscent of rabbinic exegesis, to register the claim that it is only in and through Christ that the promises find fulfillment. Christ is the one true heir of the inheritance promised to Abraham, and Christ's people share

in this inheritance only by becoming incorporated into his life (cf. 2:20; 3:26-28).

Paul's exegesis looks strange by modern critical canons, but he is building upon a Jewish tradition that the messianic "seed" (*sperma*) of David will inherit a kingdom established forever, in accordance with God's covenant promise (2 Sam 7:12-14; Ps 89:3-4). Thus, in v. 16, Paul implicitly links the promise to Abraham with the promises to a "seed" that will come forth from David, the Messiah (Χριστός *Christos*). This sort of catchword linkage, known as *gezerah shawah*, was commonly employed by Jewish interpreters in Paul's day. Whether this technique would have made Paul's argument persuasive to the Missionaries, however, is doubtful. Paul's exposition of the *diathēkē* ignores the salient fact that God's covenant with Abraham expressly mandates circumcision: "This is my covenant, which you shall keep, between me and you and your seed after you: every male among you shall be circumcised" (Gen 17:10; cf. the whole context in Gen 17:9-14, 23-27). The Missionaries might well protest that Paul's adjudication of the "will" has omitted one of its central stipulations and that it is he, not they, who should be accused of trying to alter the terms of the *diathēkē*. How Paul would have answered this objection we do not know, for in the present passage he simply ignores the commandment of circumcision in Genesis 17. At this point, we have come up against one of the limitations of Paul's analogy; perhaps this explains why, when he reformulates his exegesis of the Abraham story in Romans 4, he no longer employs this particular line of argument.

3:17. Paul now drives home the point of his analogy: The Law came 430 years after the promise to Abraham (the figure is based on Exod 12:40-41) and, therefore, cannot possibly render the promise to Abraham void. The *diathēkē* was ratified directly by God, long before the Law came into being. Thus the Law must be regarded as a secondary and inferior arrangement. (It should be kept in mind that to people in the ancient world, novelty was not a virtue; the new was suspect, whereas old ideas and customs were accorded dignity and authority.) Anyone who tries to use this late and secondary codicil to invalidate the covenant with Abraham or to prevent his rightful heirs from receiving what was promised to them should, therefore, be ruled out of court.

It is probably significant that Paul attributes the establishment of the covenant/will directly to God's action but uses a much vaguer expression for the advent of the Law: The Law "came into being" somehow.[162] Paul avoids saying that God gave the Law (cf. vv. 19-20, which distance God from the Law by emphasizing the intermediary roles of Moses and the angels). This omission is necessary for the extended metaphor of vv. 15-18 to work. The covenant with Abraham trumps the Law both because of its temporal priority and because of God's direct initiative in establishing it.

3:18. Paul concludes his development of the "testament" analogy by invoking for the first time the word "inheritance" (κληρονομία *klēronomia*), which will become a key theme in several later passages (3:29; 4:1-7, 30). Using a contrary-to-fact condition, he demonstrates the absurdity of claiming that Abraham's inheritance could possibly come through the Law. The structure of v. 18*a* parallels a pattern already encountered in 2:21*b*:

Gal 2:21*b:* For if rectification were through the Law, then Christ died for nothing.

Gal 3:18*a:* For if the inheritance were from the Law, it is no longer from the promise.

162. J. L. Martyn, *Galatians,* AB 33A (New York: Doubleday, 1997) 341-42.

This parallelism highlights the virtual synonymity of "rectification/righteousness" and "inheritance" in Paul's symbolic world; both terms refer to the status of sharing in the blessing of Abraham, in right covenant relation to God, as symbolized and confirmed by the gift of the Holy Spirit. Could anyone claim that such benefits were available through the Law? Paul dismisses such a notion as contrary to everything he has said about the story of God's promise to Abraham.

In vv. 11-12, Paul set "Law" and πίστις (*pistis,* "faith[fulness]") in opposition to one another; here in v. 18, the latter term of the polarity is replaced by "promise," emphasizing yet again that *God* is the active agent who gives the promised inheritance to Abraham and his heirs. Lest there be any remaining doubt on this point, Paul hammers home his point in v. 18*b:* "But God graced Abraham through promise." The perfect tense verb "graced" (κεχάρισται *kecharistai*) indicates an action anchored in the past (the Genesis story) with effects flowing into the present. The statement may be taken as a summary of everything Paul has said so far about Abraham, pointing back not only to v. 16, but to vv. 6-9 and 14 as well. God acts freely to give grace and blessing through promise, not through Law. The interposition of the Law, therefore, can only be a hindrance to this freely promised grace. (See Reflections at 3:26-29.)

Galatians 3:19-25, The Law as Temporary Custodian

NIV

[19]What, then, was the purpose of the law? It was added because of transgressions until the Seed to whom the promise referred had come. The law was put into effect through angels by a mediator. [20]A mediator, however, does not represent just one party; but God is one.

[21]Is the law, therefore, opposed to the promises of God? Absolutely not! For if a law had been given that could impart life, then righteousness would certainly have come by the law. [22]But the Scripture declares that the whole world is a prisoner of sin, so that what was promised, being

NRSV

[19]Why then the law? It was added because of transgressions, until the offspring[a] would come to whom the promise had been made; and it was ordained through angels by a mediator. [20]Now a mediator involves more than one party; but God is one.

[21]Is the law then opposed to the promises of God? Certainly not! For if a law had been given that could make alive, then righteousness would indeed come through the law. [22]But the scripture has imprisoned all things under the power of sin, so that what was promised through faith in Jesus Christ[b] might be given to those who believe.

[a] Gk *seed*   [b] Or *through the faith of Jesus Christ*

NIV

given through faith in Jesus Christ, might be given to those who believe.

²³Before this faith came, we were held prisoners by the law, locked up until faith should be revealed. ²⁴So the law was put in charge to lead us to Christ[a] that we might be justified by faith. ²⁵Now that faith has come, we are no longer under the supervision of the law.

a24 Or *charge until Christ came*

NRSV

23Now before faith came, we were imprisoned and guarded under the law until faith would be revealed. ²⁴Therefore the law was our disciplinarian until Christ came, so that we might be justified by faith. ²⁵But now that faith has come, we are no longer subject to a disciplinarian,

COMMENTARY

3:19. This whole train of thought, however, leads inescapably to a crucial question, which Paul at last voices in this verse. If the Law of Moses cannot confer the Spirit (vv. 2-5), pronounces a curse on its adherents (v. 10), cannot bring rectification and makes empty promises of life (vv. 11-12), and cannot add anything valid to the Abrahamic covenant (vv. 15-18), "Why then the Law?" Why has God permitted the Law to come into being? What possible purpose can it serve?

Paul gives a direct answer, but unfortunately the answer is notoriously obscure. The Law, he says, "was added because of [χάριν *charin*] transgressions [παραβάσεων *parabaseōn*]." This statement has been interpreted in widely varying ways. At least five options should be considered:

(1) The Law was added to *produce* or provoke transgressions.[163] This interpretation reads v. 19 in the light of Rom 5:20: "But Law came in, with the result that the trespass multiplied; but where sin increased, grace abounded all the more" (NRSV).

(2) The Law was added to *identify* humanity's inchoate sinfulness as conscious transgression, explicit violation of the revealed divine will.[164] Compare Rom 4:15: "For the Law brings wrath; but where there is no Law, neither is there transgression [*parabasis*]."

(3) The Law was added to *restrain* transgressions, to pose a constraint on human sin. This reading points forward to Paul's image of the Law as "disciplinarian" in vv. 23-25.

(4) The Law was added to *provide a remedy* for transgressions in the interim before the coming of Christ.[165]

(5) The Law was added by God because of the transgressions of Israel in worshiping the golden calf (Exodus 32). Jerome comments: "It was after the offense of the people in the wilderness, after the adoration of the calf and their murmurings against God, that the Law came to forbid transgressions."[166] On this reading, Paul is still commenting, in line with v. 17, on the OT story of how the Law came into existence. As the citation from Jerome indicates, this explanation may be combined with number 3.

Of these explanations, the first and fourth are almost certainly to be rejected, because they do not fit intelligibly into Paul's argument here. Nothing else that Paul says in Galatians offers any hint that he has either the provocation of transgressions or the merciful remediation of transgressions in mind. The fifth option is possible, because Paul clearly is thinking in vv. 19-20 about the Exodus narrative of the giving of the Law; however, if Paul intends to allude to the golden calf incident, he has given his readers no clues to that effect.

The best options are the second and third, because each fits understandably into the line of argument in Galatians 3. Given the brevity of Paul's statement, it is impossible to decide between these two interpretations; indeed, he may

---

163. Betz, *Galatians*, 165; Martyn, *Galatians*, 354-55.
164. F. J. Matera, *Galatians*, Sacra Pagina 9 (Collegeville, Minn.: Liturgical Press, 1992) 128; R. N. Longenecker, *Galatians*, WBC 41 (Dallas: Word, 1990) 138-39 (with some qualification).

165. J. D. G. Dunn, *The Epistle to the Galatians*, Black's NT Commentary (Peabody, Mass.: Hendrickson, 1993) 189-90.
166. Jerome, *Epistle to the Galatians* 2.3.19-20 (PL 26:391C [440]), cited incorrectly as 26:366A [440] in M. J. Edwards, ed., *Galatians, Ephesians, Philippians*, Ancient Christian Commentary on Scripture, vol. 8 (Downers Grove, Ill.: InterVarsity, 1999) 45.

have had both things in mind, as his unpacking of the Law's function in the succeeding verses (vv. 21-25) indicates. The idea that Paul is pointing to the Law's disclosive function of identifying sin as transgression against God's will is supported by v. 22*a,* which highlights Scripture's revelatory function of disclosing the universality of human sin (cf. Rom 3:9-20). Furthermore, the parallel in Rom 4:15 occurs in a passage very similar to Galatians 3, dealing with the promise to Abraham, and the key term παράβασις (*parabasis*) appears in both passages. At the same time, there is also a good case to be made for the third interpretation (the Law as a restraint on sin), because Paul goes on in vv. 23-25 to explicate the Law's function as one of restrictive but protective custody, using the metaphor of the παιδαγωγός *paidagōgos* (see the Commentary on 3:24-25). It is probably best, then, to read these successive depictions of the Law's identifying and restraining functions as a twofold explanation of what Paul means by saying that the Law was "added because of transgressions."

In any case, the Law was designed as a temporary expedient, "until the Seed should come to whom the promise had been made." The NIV's capitalization of the word "Seed" correctly links this statement back to v. 16, which declared that the "seed" is to be identified as Christ. The Law, whatever its purpose, was designed to be in effect only until Christ's coming (see also vv. 24-25). Once the inheritance has been given and received, the Law becomes superfluous.

Who was responsible for adding the Law? The preceding discussion assumes that the Law was instituted by God and that the passive verb (προσετέθη *prosetethē,* "was added") points to the action of God. It has occasionally been suggested, however, that Paul is implying that the Law was introduced by angelic powers acting apart from God.[167] Such an assertion would be virtually blasphemous in the eyes of Paul's Jewish contemporaries, including the rival Missionaries in Galatia. Paul avoids making any such explicit statement; nonetheless, the wording of v. 19 is curiously indirect. Paul says, literally, that the Law was "ordained through angels by the hand of a mediator." As has been already noted, the participle διαταγείς *diatageis* ("ordained," from the verb διατάσσω *diatassō*) might be understood to echo the verb ἐπιδιατάσσεται (*epidiatassetai*) in v. 15, which referred to the illicit attempt by someone to add a codicil to a duly ratified will. This echo would cast a shadow of doubt on the motives of the angels in v. 19. The prepositional phrase "through angels" suggests, however, that the angels are God's instruments rather than the initiators of the giving of the Law. In the OT, only Deut 33:2 speaks directly of the presence of angels in the giving of the Law at Sinai (see also Ps 68:17); in this passage, they serve to enhance the glorious manifestation of God's power. Similarly, in Acts 7:53 (whose phrasing is very close to Gal 3:19) and Heb 2:2 we find depictions of the angels as agents of God's revelation to Israel, and the tradition that angels were present at Sinai was common in Second Temple Jewish texts.[168]

Paul takes this pious midrashic elaboration of the exodus story and gives it a different twist. Rather than enhancing the awesome revelatory character of the Law, the presence of angels shows that God was not acting directly at Sinai, as when God spoke to Abraham. Rather, the Law was administered through intermediary figures, thus distancing God from the Law.

3:20. The phrase "by the hand of a mediator" refers to the role of Moses in receiving the Law and transmitting it to the people (for the expression "by the hand of Moses," see Lev 26:46; Num 36:13). Philo's *Life of Moses* explicitly gives Moses the title of "mediator and reconciler."[169] This much is clear, but Paul's further statement about the mediator in this verse is another maddeningly opaque sentence. The confession that "God is one" evokes the *Shema* (Deut 6:4), the fundamental confession of Israel's faith. This confession is itself part of the very Law that Paul is now paradoxically distancing from God! The oneness of God in v. 20*b* is to be linked with the singularity of the "seed" in v. 16 and the oneness of the people of God in v. 28. The deficiency of

---

167. H. Hübner, *Law in Paul's Thought* (Edinburgh: T. & T. Clark, 1984) 24-36; Martyn, *Galatians,* 356-57.

168. For a list of references, see Longenecker, *Galatians,* 139-40.

169. Philo *Life of Moses* 2.166; see also *Assumption of Moses* 1.14. The reference to Jesus Christ as the "one mediator between God and humankind" in 1 Tim 2:5 led many patristic interpreters to see in Gal 3:19 a reference to Christ's mediatorial work. Because Paul is speaking here of the giving of the Law at Sinai, this interpretation is certainly incorrect. In Heb 8:6; 9:15; 12:24, Jesus is described as the mediator of a new covenant; here there is an explicit contrast to Moses as mediator of the old covenant, which the author of Hebrews regards as superseded by the new.

the Law, therefore, may be related to its divisive character, its inability to bring Jews and Gentiles together into a single new people. The oneness of God can be rightly reflected only in a community unified by the fulfillment of God's promise in Christ.[170] Notwithstanding these observations, there is no scholarly consensus about the meaning of v. 20. Its general sense seems to be that because the Law was delivered through an intermediary figure, it does not convey God's grace directly, as did the promise to Abraham (v. 18).

3:21. In light of these remarks about the Law, Paul raises rhetorically the scandalous inference that might be drawn from everything he has said in vv. 1-20: "Is the Law then opposed to the promises of God?" Paul's detractors would accuse him of having constructed a position that leads exactly to this horrifying conclusion (cf. Rom 7:7, 13). Elsewhere he writes, in a more measured discussion of the role of the Law, that the Law is "holy and righteous and good" (Rom 7:12). In Galatians, however, he has made no such laudatory remarks about the Law; so far, he has portrayed it only as a source of the curse. His opponents might understandably portray Paul as a renegade Jew in rebellion against God's Law—a proto-Marcionite theologian who paints the Law as an evil power working against God. But he spits out a forceful denial: "Certainly not!" (μὴ γένοιτο *mē genoito*). Paul frequently employs this rhetorical device of formulating a false inference, and then emphatically denying it, to head off misinterpretations of his thought, particularly with reference to the sensitive topic of the Law. The closest parallel is Rom 3:31: "Do we then abolish the Law by this faith? By no means! On the contrary, we uphold the Law."

In this verse, Paul declares the inference—that the Law is opposed to the promise—to be false. Why? Because the Law would be in opposition to the promise only if it had been intended by God to be the agent of life and righteousness. Paul, however, denies that premise. The Law, he argues, was given for a very different reason, which he will explain in vv. 22-24. Here we encounter another contrary-to-fact condition: "If a Law had been given which had the power to give life, then rectification/righteousness would indeed

have been from the Law" (cf. 2:21; 3:18). In that case, the Law would offer a rival system of salvation as an alternative to the promise. Paul insists, however, that the Law had no such power (cf. Rom 8:3) and was never intended for such a purpose. He has already argued emphatically that righteousness is ἐκ πίστεως (*ek pisteōs*), not ἐν νόμῳ (*en nomō*, vv. 11-12). Consequently—and this is the point of v. 21—the Law, understood rightly, is not in a relation of competition or opposition to the promise. Thus, by denying the life-giving power of the Law, Paul is not opposing the Law but affirming its true purpose.

What, then, is that true purpose? In vv. 22-24 Paul gives a twofold answer: The purpose of the Law was to "imprison all things under the power of sin" and to keep Israel in protective custody until the coming of Christ into the world.

3:22. Paul continues to use metaphors. Here he personifies the Law (actually "Scripture" in this formulation) as a jailkeeper that locks "all things" up together under the power of sin. The fact that Paul can use "Scripture" in this way as a virtual synonym for "Law" (see the parallel statement about being imprisoned under Law in v. 23) shows that he maintains a significant role for the Law as an actor in the divine redemptive drama. (Note the positive proclamatory role assigned to Scripture in v. 8.) In its role as jailer, the Scripture performs exactly the same role assigned to the Law in Rom 3:9-20: It declares all human beings, Jew and Greek alike, to be "under the power of sin" (Rom 3:9; Gal 3:23; the NIV's broad paraphrase accurately conveys the sense: "the Scripture declares that the whole world is a prisoner of sin"). In Romans, Paul explains that the Law performs this function "so that every mouth may be silenced, and the whole world may be held accountable to God." How does the Law achieve this end? "Through the Law comes the knowledge of sin" (Rom 3:19-20). In other words, the Law discloses the truth about our human condition: We are alienated from God and stand under God's righteous judgment. That is the meaning of Paul's jailkeeper metaphor in v. 22a. Paul attributes this "locking up" function to God's intentional design, as demonstrated by the close parallel in Rom 11:32, where Paul uses exactly the same verb, this time with God as the subject: "God has locked up all in disobedience so that he may be

170. N. T. Wright, *The Climax of the Covenant: Christ and the Law in Pauline Theology* (Edinburgh: T. & T. Clark, 1991) 168-72.

merciful to all." In the light of Rom 11:32, we can see more clearly what Paul is saying in Gal 3:19-22. The Law is not an adversary of God's redemptive purpose; rather, God has used the Law to illuminate Israel's condition—and there-fore, *a fortiori,* the universal human condition—of bondage to the power of Sin (cf. Rom 7:7). Thus the Law forecloses all human attempts at saving ourselves. The reason for this confinement under the power of Sin is explained in vv. 22b-24: It was a necessary step in God's design to rectify the world through Jesus Christ.

Thus in this verse as in Romans, the function of the Law in disclosing human sinfulness is part of a larger divine purpose. The reason why God used the Law to lock all things up under sin was "so that what was promised might be given through the faithfulness of Jesus Christ to those who believe" (see the reading in the NRSV foot-note). The thought here is closely parallel to 2:16, but Paul has now substituted the "promise" lan-guage of 3:14-18 for the "rectification" terminol-ogy found in the earlier passage. This suggests that the two semantic fields are generally synonymous in Paul's mind; both "promise" and "rectification" point to our inclusion in the eschatological people of God, who share in the blessing promised to Abraham.

In both passages, this blessing is made effective "through the faithfulness of Jesus Christ" (see the Commentary on 2:16). The NIV and the NRSV both reflect the awkwardness of attempting to interpret ἐκ πίστεως ᾽Ιησοῦ Χριστοῦ (*ek pisteōs Iēsou Christou*) to mean "through faith in Jesus Christ." The NRSV reads the phrase as a modifier of the noun "promise" (ἐπαγγελία *epangelia*), producing the peculiar rendering, "what was promised through faith in Jesus Christ." This makes no sense, since neither the Genesis text nor Paul's exposition of it has referred to anything being promised through faith in Jesus Christ. The NIV, on the other hand, recognizing that the prepo-sitional phrase *ek pisteōs Iēsou Christou* is prop-erly to be read as modifying the verb "given" (δοθῇ *dothē*), is forced to insert a redundant passive participle "being given," which does not appear in the Greek text. These problems are avoided if we adopt the straightforward translation given above: "so that what was promised might be given through the faithfulness of Jesus Christ

to those who believe." The long-awaited promise is brought to fulfillment through "Christ's trustful obedience to God in the giving up of his own life for us."[171]

Paul's point is that the Law teaches us to discern the depth of human sin and need, thereby locking up even God's elect people Israel in the same bondage to sin that was shared by the pagan world. In such a desperate situation, the only hope is for God to act. That was precisely God's design, and God did act through Christ's faithful death to liberate us from the power of sin and the present evil age (cf. 1:4; 2:20; 3:13).

3:23-25. Paul repeats and elaborates what he has just said, but now he develops a different metaphor that suggests the Law's functions of restraint and protection: The law was our παι-δαγωγός (*paidagōgos*) until Christ came. The noun, despite the English cognate "pedagogue," does not mean "teacher." The *paidagōgos* (lit., "child-leader") was a slave in the Greco-Roman household who supervised and guarded children. His responsibility was to walk them to and from school, to see that they behaved properly and stayed out of harm's way.[172] The *paidagōgos,* however, was not a member of the family, and when the child grew to a certain age, his services were no longer required. The Law was like that for Israel, Paul proposes. It had a certain necessary role in confining, guarding, and disciplining God's people during the interval between Moses and Christ,[173] but that interval has now come to an end (v. 25). This metaphor allows Paul to affirm that the Law once had a constructive role to play in God's overall plan, while at the same time insisting that its role is now at an end.

In sketching out this analogy, Paul uses the language of "faith" again in a way that calls for com-ment. The period of confinement was "until [εἰς *eis*] the faith [τὴν πίστιν *tēn pistin*] would be re-vealed [ἀποκαλυφθῆναι *apokalyphthēnai*]." Here, "the faith" cannot possibly refer to human subjec-

---

171. J. L. Martyn, *Galatians,* AB 33A (New York: Doubleday, 1997) 361.

172. For a helpful summary of the functions of the pedagogue, see S. K. Williams, *Galatians,* ANTC (Nashville: Abingdon, 1997) 102-3. For fuller accounts, see D. J. Lull, " 'The Law Was Our Pedagogue': A Study of Gal 3:19-25," *JBL* 105 (1986) 481-98; N. H. Young, "*Paidagogos:* The Social Setting of a Pauline Metaphor," *NovT* 29 (1987) 150-76.

173. This view of the Law as providing a protective confinement is closely parallel to explanations of the role of the Law in Josephus, *Ap.* 3.173-74 and the *Letter of Aristeas* 142. See the helpful discussion in Matera, *Galatians,* 139-40.

tive believing, because it is something that comes by revelation, and Paul has insisted from the beginning of the letter that revelation is not a matter of human possibility; rather, it is a matter of divine action and divine disclosure (see, e.g., 1:11-12). Taken by itself, "the faith" could mean "that which is believed," but in the present context, the best interpretation is that the definite article refers the reader back to the faith mentioned in the previous sentence: the faith of Jesus Christ. The correctness of this reading is confirmed by v. 24, in which Paul formulates a synonymous idea: We were under the *paidagōgos* "until Christ came" (taking *eis* again as temporal, as in v. 23). In other words, Paul sets the revelation of "the faith" in v. 23 in synonymous parallelism with the coming of Christ in v. 24. The coming of Christ "reveals" faith because "he loved me and gave himself for me" (2:20); God's faithfulness (cf. Rom 3:3) is disclosed to the world through the cross, which is God's saving action for our sake.

In the light of this exegesis, the NIV's translation of v. 24 must be judged seriously misleading. It paraphrases *paidagōgos*, ignores the parallelism with v. 23, and therefore takes *eis* in a spatial, rather than temporal, sense ("to," rather than "until"). As a result, it attributes to Paul the claim that the purpose of the Law was "to lead us to Christ." This is completely incongruous with the way Paul has developed the *paidagōgos* metaphor. Nowhere in Galatians, or in any of his other letters, does Paul argue for a progressive educative

function of the Law; its purpose, according to these verses, is protective custody. The point is critical: According to Paul, we did not make our way, under the tutelage of the Law, progressively to Christ; instead, Christ came to us. In no other way could we have been released from our confinement.

The purpose of Christ's coming was "in order that we might be rectified *ek pisteōs*" (v. 24*b*). In view of the way Paul has used πίστις (*pistis*) in vv. 22-23, the most natural interpretation is that v. 24*b* refers again to Christ's faithful death for our sake (as also in 2:16). The Law kept us locked up until that event, which was God's intended means of setting us free. Now that this liberating event has broken into our world, Paul proclaims, "we are no longer subject to a *paidagōgos*" (v. 25).

With that, Paul brings his discussion of the purpose of the Law to a decisive conclusion. Living on this side of Christ's death, he tells the Galatians, we are in a new eschatological age. Thus we need not entertain the idea of coming under the supervision of the Law. The Law has served its purpose, and its commission is at an end. Its confining role was ordained by God during the period before Christ; consequently, it was neither evil nor in opposition to God. Neither, however, should it be understood as a means to rectification and life. Least of all should it be allowed to restrict the access of Gentile Christians to receiving the inheritance that God promised to Abraham. (See Reflections at 3:26-29.)

Galatians 3:26-29, In Christ We Are Abraham's Seed

NIV

²⁶You are all sons of God through faith in Christ Jesus, ²⁷for all of you who were baptized into Christ have clothed yourselves with Christ. ²⁸There is neither Jew nor Greek, slave nor free, male nor female, for you are all one in Christ Jesus. ²⁹If you belong to Christ, then you are Abraham's seed, and heirs according to the promise.

NRSV

²⁶for in Christ Jesus you are all children of God through faith. ²⁷As many of you as were baptized into Christ have clothed yourselves with Christ. ²⁸There is no longer Jew or Greek, there is no longer slave or free, there is no longer male and female; for all of you are one in Christ Jesus. ²⁹And if you belong to Christ, then you are Abraham's offspring,ᵃ heirs according to the promise.

ᵃ Gk *seed*

COMMENTARY

3:26. Paul now begins to draw the conclusions that follow from his lengthy discussion of the promise to Abraham. The conjunction "for" (γάρ *gar*) forges a close logical connection between this verse and the foregoing context; this connection is more clearly represented by the NRSV than by the NIV. The reason why we are no longer subject to the disciplinary constraint of the Law (v. 25) is provided here. The NRSV also more accurately represents the sense of the sentence by placing "in Christ Jesus" at the beginning as an adverbial modifier of the main verb, rather than connecting it with the noun "faith," as in the NIV. This is the characteristic Pauline "in Christ" formula (see, e.g., 1:22; 2:4, 17; 3:14; 5:6), which he uses repeatedly to characterize Christian existence as a state of corporate unity with Christ.

The emphasis here falls heavily on the word "all" (πάντες *pantes*), the first word in the sentence in the Greek text. *All* the Galatian believers, without distinction, are already children (lit., "sons") of God in Christ Jesus via "the faith." No further action of circumcision or religious observance is required to secure this status. The noun πίστις (*pistis*), again used here with the definite article, carries forward the line of thought from vv. 22-25, referring to the faith(fulness) of Christ. It is through his gracious act of faithful self-giving that the Galatians have been brought into God's family as children. At the same time, since the noun is not limited by any pronoun or genitive phrase, it is slightly ambiguous; it can be understood as referring either to Christ's faith or to ours (cf. the similar ambiguity in vv. 11, 14, 24).

Paul's main point, however, is that all who are in Christ are now God's "sons." In order to see what Paul is claiming here, it is crucial to recognize that the epithet "sons of God" was employed in the OT and in Jewish tradition as a designation for Israel as God's elect people.

You are sons of the LORD your God. . . . For you are a people holy to the LORD your God; it is you the Lord has chosen out of all the peoples on earth to be his people, his treasured possession. (Deut 14:1-2 NRSV)

And the LORD said to Moses, "I know their contrariness and their thoughts and their stubbornness. And they will not obey until they acknowledge their sin and the sins of their fathers. But after this they will return to me in all uprightness and with all of (their) heart and soul. And I shall cut off the foreskin of their heart and the foreskin of the heart of their descendants. And I shall create for them a holy spirit, and I shall purify them so that they will not turn away from following me from that day and forever. And their souls will cleave to me and to all my commandments. And they will do my commandments. *And I shall be a father to them, and they will be sons to me. And they will all be called 'sons of the living God.'* And every angel and spirit will know and acknowledge that they are my sons and I am their father in uprightness and righteousness. And I shall love them." (*Jub* 1:23-25)[174]

Against this background, we see that Paul is telling the Gentile Galatians that, in Christ, they are now given the honorific name "sons of God" that was once reserved for the Jewish people alone. (This is a theme that he will develop further in 4:4-7; cf. Rom 8:14-16.) Thus this verse closely parallels Paul's earlier affirmation (v. 7) that all who are ἐκ πίστεως *ek pisteōs* are "Abraham's children." In both cases, he has taken a title that originally asserted Israel's special privilege and extended it to include Gentile believers.

3:27. Paul offers a further warrant for this claim by pointing to the practice of baptism. Presumably all the members of the Galatian churches had undergone baptism as adult believers, since all were converts from paganism. Paul now reminds them of this experience of initiation, a marker of their passage into a new life. They had been baptized "into Christ." The wording here is probably not a direct quotation of a liturgical formula, since early Christian baptism was performed "in the name of Jesus Christ" or some variant thereof (cf. Matt 28:19; Acts 2:38; 1 Cor 6:11). Rather than a quotation, Paul's wording here represents an interpretation of the significance of baptism. As in Rom 6:3-11, Paul interprets baptism as signifying union with Christ (highlighted by the NIV), which entails death to one's old life and entry into a new world. The

---

174. In addition to these examples, see also Exod 4:22-23; Hos 1:10; 11:1; Sir 36:17; 3 Macc 6:28; 4 Ezra 6:55-59; *Pss Sol* 17:26-27. For discussion of this motif, see B. Byrne, *"Sons of God"—"Seed of Abraham": A Study of the Idea of the Sonship of God of all Christians in Paul Against the Jewish Background*, AnBib 83 (Rome: Pontifical Biblical Institute, 1979).

character of this new world will be spelled out further in v. 28.

The reference to being "clothed with Christ" is probably an allusion to a feature of early Christian baptismal liturgies. Persons being baptized removed their garments, were baptized naked, and then put on a new white garment, signifying the new life they were entering.[175] Other allusions to this practice may be found in Rom 13:14; Eph 4:22-24; and Col 3:9-10. As Williams has pointed out, the language of being "clothed with" some attribute is pervasive in the OT. To take a single example, the psalmist prays that Israel's priests might be "clothed with righteousness," and later in the same psalm God declares, "Its priests I will clothe with salvation" (Ps 132:9, 16 NRSV). To be "clothed" with some quality or attribute is to take on the characteristics of that in which one is clothed.[176] None of the many OT examples adduced by Williams, however, refer to being "clothed in" a *person*. Paul's language of "putting on Christ" is another figurative way of describing the mysterious personal union with Christ to which he referred in 2:20. In such a union, those who are "in Christ" share in his divine sonship and take on his character. The baptismal imagery here, then, points to the transformation of identity that the Galatians have undergone.

3:28. The full implications of that transformation are spelled out with reference to the abolition of social distinctions. At this point, in contrast to v. 27, Paul is probably quoting an early Christian baptismal formula (cf. 1 Cor 12:13; Col 3:11). If so, he is calling to mind the words that had been pronounced over each of the Galatian believers at the time of their baptism, words that declared unmistakably the obsolescence of the Jew/Greek boundary that the Missionaries were trying to reestablish through their advocacy of circumcision. The radical vision set forth in this formula reflects the new creation that God has brought into being (cf. 6:15). In this new world in Christ, three binary oppositions that characterized all human existence in the old age have been dissolved.[177] Each of these oppositions should be examined carefully.

(1) There Is No Longer Jew or Greek. This is the element of the formula that Paul particularly wants to emphasize in the present context. In the old age, the Law protected the religious and cultural separateness of the Jewish people, setting them apart from all other peoples (collectively categorized as "the nations" [= Gentiles]). In Christ, however, this separateness is abolished, because Jews and Gentiles are constituted together as one new people of God (see 6:16; Rom 3:29-30; 15:7-13; cf. Eph 2:11-20). In the light of this new reality, ethnic distinctions no longer matter. The implication of this is, of course, that circumcision as a marker separating Jews from Gentiles no longer matters (5:6).

(2) There Is No Longer Slave or Free. Distinctions of social class are negated in the new creation. The identity of Christians as "children of God" (v. 26) is given to them by their participation in Christ; consequently, they are now related to one another as brothers and sisters, no longer in a social hierarchy that distinguishes slave and free (cf. Phlm 15-16). The baptismal formula declares that social class and power have been delegitimated in Christ.

Admittedly, the "already/not yet" tension in Paul's thought leaves room for uncertainty about the extent to which this eschatological vision of equality is to be embodied in social practice. The key to understanding Paul's thought on this question is to recognize that he sees the church as an alternative community that prefigures the new creation in the midst of a world that continues to resist God's justice. Thus Paul is not calling for a revolution in which slaves rise up and demand freedom; rather, in this verse he is declaring that God *has* created a new community, the church, in which the baptized *already* share equality. To the extent that vv. 26-29 have hortatory force, they call the Galatians to "get in line with the Spirit" (5:25) and manifest in their common life the κοινωνία (*koinōnia*) of the new creation, in which these binary social distinctions no longer count for anything. Yet, because the present sociopolitical realities of this world are soon to pass away, Paul elsewhere counsels members of his churches to remain in the social station in which they found themselves at the time of their conversion (1 Cor 7:17-24, 29-31). (The rule of thumb that believers should "remain in the con-

---

175. W. A. Meeks, *The First Urban Christians: The Social World of the Apostle Paul* (New Haven: Yale University Press, 1983) 151.

176. S. K. Williams, *Galatians*, ANTC (Nashville: Abingdon, 1997) 105.

177. For an extensive discussion of parallels to the formula in ancient religion, philosophy, and political thought, see H. D. Betz, *Galatians*, Hermeneia (Philadelphia: Fortress, 1979) 189-201.

dition in which you were called," applied to the circumcision controversy, suggests that uncircumcised Gentiles should remain uncircumcised; see 1 Cor 7:18-20.) This is not a matter of social conservatism; rather, it is a matter of eschatological patience while eagerly awaiting God's coming new order. In chap. 4, Paul will take up the slavery/freedom opposition and develop its implications by urging the Galatians to stand firm in their new freedom in Christ. This demonstrates once again that Paul expects the church to move toward the practical realization of the baptismal formula's vision.

(3) There Is No Longer Male and Female. Paul makes no use of this opposition in the argument of Galatians; this is one piece of evidence that suggests he is quoting a formula. Attentive readers of the NRSV will note that this third element breaks the formal pattern of the previous oppositions: there is no longer a *or* b; there is no longer c *or* d; there is no longer male *and* female. (The NIV misses this crucial shift.) What is the reason for this change? Paul is echoing the language of Gen 1:27: "*male and female* he created them." To say that this created distinction is no longer in force is to declare that the new creation has come upon us, a new creation in which even gender roles no longer pertain. (Paul omits this third element when he alludes to the formula in 1 Cor 12:13, perhaps because of the difficulties and controversies in Corinth over issues of sexual conduct and marriage; see 1 Cor 5:1-13; 6:12-20; 7:1-40.)

The fact that the Letter to the Galatians is not concerned with gender roles does not diminish the force or importance of this element of Paul's vision for the church as a transformed community. If the church is to be a sign and foretaste of the new creation, it must be a community in which gender distinctions—like the ethnic and social distinctions noted in the first two parts of the formula—have lost their power to divide and oppress. This does not mean that those who are in Christ cease to be men or women, any more than the male members of the community cease to be circumcised or uncircumcised. Rather, it means that these distinctions are no longer the

determinative identity markers, no longer a ground for status or exclusion. It should be noted that circumcision is an identity marker applicable only to males; therefore, a community that singles out circumcision as its key sign of covenant membership will inevitably privilege male identity as normative. There is no evidence in Paul's letters that he ever consciously considered this point, but the ritual of baptism, identical for both sexes, is distinctly appropriate as the sign of inclusion within a community in which the old distinction between "male and female" has ceased to separate those who are in Christ.

The implications of Paul's extraordinary baptismal declaration of the new creation are summed up in the final clause of v. 28: "for you are all one in Christ Jesus." The new world into which the Galatians have been initiated through baptism is a world in which the most salient feature of their identity is their unity in Christ. Because all participate in this unity, they should firmly reject invidious appeals from the Missionaries to reinstantiate the ethnic and status distinctions that characterized the world before the faith of Christ invaded the world and changed everything.

3:29. The concluding sentence of the paragraph wraps up the entire argument of vv. 6-29, particularly recalling the language of vv. 15-18. Those who are Christ's people are de facto "Abraham's seed." With this affirmation, Paul has laid all his cards on the table. In v. 16, he had asserted that only Christ was the Seed, the single true heir of the promise made to Abraham. But this was only the first move in a more complex argument. Because the baptized have entered into union with Christ, they are one new person in him and with him; therefore, they all participate equally in the same privileged status as joint "heirs according to the promise" (cf. Rom 8:14-17). The last phrase picks up again the language of v. 18, thus emphasizing that the inheritance now given to Gentile believers comes through God's free, gracious promise to Abraham, not through the Law. This is also the fulfillment of the gospel that Scripture had proclaimed to Abraham, that all the Gentiles would be blessed in him (v. 8).

REFLECTIONS

Galatians 3:6-29 must be read as a continuous block of argument in order to grasp its overall import. When it is subdivided—as it usually is for liturgical or homiletical purposes—it tends to fall apart into enigmatic fragments. When we read Paul's argument whole, however, its themes come powerfully into focus. Paul is urging the Galatians to understand themselves as heirs of God's promise to Abraham, by virtue of their union with Christ. If they stand firm in a clear-eyed recognition of the blessing they have already received, they will not be seduced into pursuing circumcision as though it were necessary to secure their place among the people of God. In the course of his richly textured argument, Paul develops a number of themes that can stimulate fundamental theological reflection.

1. *The Source of Our Identity.* Our identity is given to us fundamentally through our union with Christ. Paul saw this union as figured forth and enacted in baptism. In baptism we "put on" Christ; we enter into union with him in such a way that all other markers of status and identity fall away into insignificance (3:27-29). Centuries of the practice of infant baptism in the culture of christendom have obscured the dramatic symbolism that the early Christians saw in baptismal initiation. In baptism, the person being baptized confessed the lordship of Jesus Christ over all creation, disrobed to signify the putting off of an entire way of life, was immersed below the water as if undergoing burial (Rom 6:3-5), was raised to a new life, and was clothed in new garments symbolizing the transformation that had occurred. Baptism was a symbolic participation in Christ's death and resurrection, and no one could undergo it without realizing that one life had ended and a new one had begun.

Paul saved his appeal to baptism for the climactic place in the argument of Gal 3:6-29 because it so powerfully embodied what he wanted to say to the Galatians: They were to find their identity in Jesus Christ alone. For one who has been "clothed" with Christ, no further religious observances (such as circumcision or food laws) are necessary in order to be in right standing with God. Our human religious impulse tirelessly seeks new signs and ceremonies that we can use to set ourselves apart from others or to court God's favor. Paul insists that all of that has been put to an end in Christ.

Paul saw the rival Missionaries as pursuing a policy of cultural imperialism—that is, as he saw it, they were trying to impose specifically Jewish identity markers on Gentiles who had already been given a decisive new identity as God's people in Christ. He disapprovingly called the circumcision faction "those whose identity is derived from works of Law" (see the Commentary on 3:10).

Paul's passionate rejection of this kind of ethnic/religious "identity politics" should lead us to reflect carefully on the ground of our own identity. To what extent is our sense of who we are grounded in the gospel of Christ, and to what extent is it determined by other factors? Such questions may lead us to uncomfortable conclusions. In our time there are many movements, even within the church, that seek to define an identity based on race, on national origin, on gender, or on sexual orientation. Such movements are the contemporary analogues of the "circumcision party" within the early church, against which Paul so passionately fought. Against all such determinations of identity, Paul reminds us that we are one with Christ through baptism.

Someone might object that baptism is simply one more religious ritual and that to elevate this one above all other identity-defining practices is just one more manifestation of religious imperialism. Of course, human sinfulness can distort even baptism into a new basis for perverse pride and division, as Paul learned all too well in his dealings with the church at Corinth (1 Cor 1:10-17). The point is, however, that Paul sees baptism not as an end in itself, but as a signifier of our union with Christ, through faith. Galatians 3:26-29 should not be read apart from 3:6-9, in which Paul declares that those whose identity is rooted in faith are Abraham's children. To be rooted in faith and to be "in Christ" are, in Paul's theological vision, synonymous (3:26).

Identity derived from faith is different from all others if and only if the death and resurrection of Jesus really are—as Paul proclaimed—the singular event through which God has chosen to redeem the world. Otherwise, the gospel is merely one more religious system that will serve human pride and ambition. The character of our faith is determined by that decisive event to which it looks.

2. *The Meaning of Faith.* Galatians was Martin Luther's favorite epistle, because he saw in it a compelling expression of the doctrine of justification by faith alone. When we speak of "faith" as a central theme of this letter, however, we must observe carefully how Paul actually uses this concept. The root meaning of πίστις (*pistis*) is "trust" (see the Commentary on 2:16). Abraham is the paradigm of faith because he *trusted* in God's promise. Abraham's faith was not a matter of believing a list of propositions or a system of doctrines about God; rather, it was a matter of primal trust in the bare, direct promise of God to bless him and to give him many descendants. Paul develops this interpretation of Abraham's faith at greater length in Romans 4:

> Hoping against hope, he believed that he would become "the father of many nations." . . . No distrust made him waver concerning the promise of God, but he grew strong in his faith as he gave glory to God, being fully convinced that God was able to do what he had promised. Therefore his faith "was reckoned to him as righteousness." (Rom 4:18, 20-22)

Abraham heard God's word and trusted it. That is the picture of faith that Paul evokes in Gal 3:6-9. This sort of trust is the model for the trust that the Galatians also demonstrated when they believed Paul's proclamation of the good news of the gospel, God's blessing upon them as Gentiles outside the Law, by sheer grace. That is the faith that receives rectification and life, a kind of life that the Law was unable to give (3:11-12). Faith is not a matter of mustering a heroic capacity to believe the odd or the miraculous; it is simply a matter of receiving gratefully a gift that God has chosen to give us, completely without regard to our deserving. It is a matter of reliance on the Word of God as the one truth upon which we stake our lives.

We must beware of becoming infatuated with faith as an aspect of our own subjectivity or religious experience. Protestant preaching has often fallen into the trap of treating faith as a new kind of "work," a human achievement that somehow merits God's approval. On such a distortion, the judgment of William Law is apt: "Suppose one man to rely on his own faith and another to rely on his own works, then the faith of the one and the works of the other are equally the same worthless filthy rags."[178] A careful reading of Gal 3:6-29 provides the corrective for this error. Paul is not interested here in a phenomenological description of faith as a human disposition. Instead, he is interested in telling the story of how faith "came," breaking into the prison of human experience to set us free (3:23-25). Faith is something "revealed" to us as God's deed; it is not merely the illumination of a new human possibility. Karl Barth comments:

> The fact that I live in the faith of the Son of God, in my faith in him, has its basis in the fact that He Himself, the Son of God, first believed for me. . . . the great work of faith has already been done by the One whom I follow in my faith, even before I believe, even if I no longer believe, in such a way that He is always, as Heb 12:2 puts it, the originator and completer (ἀρχηγὸς καὶτελειωτής *archēgos kai teleiotēs*) of our faith. . . . His faith is the victory which has overcome the world.[179]

178. William Law, cited in A. G. Hebert, " 'Faithfulness' and 'Faith,' " *Theology* 58 (1955) 379.
179. K. Barth, *Church Dogmatics* II/2 (Edinburgh: T. & T. Clark, 1957) 559.

In Gal 3:22-26, *pistis* ("faith") is used by metonymy to refer to the faith(fulness) of Jesus Christ. It refers not primarily to Jesus' own subjective trust in God but rather to the act by which his fidelity to God was embodied: his self-giving death on the cross (2:20), which was the fulfillment of his mission to set humanity free from bondage (3:13, 23-25). Until this revelation of faith through Christ's death, we were imprisoned under the power of sin. Christ's act for our sake has broken that power, so that God's promised blessing has now been given to us "through the faith(fulness) of Jesus Christ" (3:22; cf. 3:14). To be sure, we who receive that blessing can and should be described as "those who believe" (3:22) or "those whose identity is derived from faith" (3:7, 9) because we look to Christ's crucifixion with the same grateful trust that Abraham displayed toward God's covenant promise. All our talk and preaching about "faith," therefore, must take care to respect the focus of Paul's proclamation on what Jesus has done. Otherwise, faith-talk will turn into one more subtle attempt at human self-affirmation.

3. *Christ Has Liberated Us from Captivity.* It is noteworthy that Paul says nothing at all in Galatians 3 about "forgiveness of sins." The effect of Christ's death is described not in terms of forgiveness but in terms of liberation from captivity. Paul uses two different metaphors to describe the bondage from which Christ has liberated us: Israel's condition of being in exile under the curse pronounced by Deuteronomy (Gal 3:10, 13) and the more general human condition of being imprisoned under the power of Sin (3:22-23). Through his death on a cross, Jesus has set both Jews and Gentiles free from these states of bondage.

For Israel, the exile is ended and the time of God's deliverance has arrived, as shown by the outpouring of the Spirit that God had promised (see the Commentary on 3:14). But Paul has dramatically reworked the meaning of this prophetic vision. In standard Jewish expectation, the time of eschatological deliverance was expected to create an Israel in which the authority of the Law would be restored and honored; indeed, something like this may have been exactly what the rival Missionaries were teaching the Galatians. In Paul's vision, however, there is no question of a return to Torah observance. With the lifting of the Law's curse, the Law's whole system of conditional blessings and curses is consigned to the past. The freedom that Christ gives is the freedom for a community that lives under the Spirit (5:16-26), no longer under the threat of the Law's curse.

For the Gentiles, the power of Sin—pictured in 3:22 as a hostile cosmic power (cf. Rom 6:12-23; 7:13-25)—is broken. Rather than living as captives in a state of ignorance and alienation from God, the Gentiles are now released to a state of freedom and are taken into God's family as children (3:26) who are rectified—that is, received as God's own people, Abraham's children (3:6-9, 26-29).

Paul will develop the implications of this liberation image more fully in chapters 4–5. With regard to the present passage, however, the implication is that our preaching should stress Christ's victory that sets us free. Christians are constantly tempted to slip into new legalisms, rigid systems of law or morality that define—and thus confine—us. Whether the confining system is first-century Pharisaic Judaism, Roman imperial ideology, pre-Reformation Catholic hierarchy, Victorian codes of propriety, capitalist consumerism, patriarchal privilege, or late modern "political correctness," the liberating message of Galatians is the same. Christ's victory is not merely a substitutionary atonement for the forgiveness of sins; rather, Christ's apocalyptic victory breaks the old systems of confinement.

4. *The Spirit as God's Promised Blessing.* Closely related to the previous point is the fact that the promised blessing given to the new community in Christ is "the promise of the Spirit" (3:14; cf. 3:2-5; 4:6-7). In place of the expectation of a promised land (Gen 17:8), Paul speaks of the Spirit as the fulfillment of God's promise to Abraham. (This fact shows that Paul is using the story of Israel's exile and restoration metaphorically.) The "inheritance" now given to the new community of Jews and Gentiles in Christ (3:18, 29) is redefined in terms of the presence of the Spirit that makes them one and assures their status as God's children. In a similar way, our proclamation of the gospel should continue to point to the ways in which we see the Spirit of God at work in our churches as a sign of the inheritance that God has graciously given us. Although claims about the Spirit's presence are necessarily elusive, Paul's example should embolden us to recognize and celebrate the Spirit's work in our midst.

5. *The Law's Place in the Christian Story.* Paul has developed an argument about the Law that sounds like sheer heresy, if not blasphemy, to devout Jewish ears. In Jewish tradition, the Law was viewed as God's gracious gift, a source of wisdom and life. The interpreter of Galatians should always remember to read this chapter against the backdrop of Ps 19:7-11, which declares that "the law of the LORD is perfect, reviving the soul" and cherishes God's ordinances as "more to be desired . . . than gold, even much fine gold" (NRSV). By contrast, Paul speaks of the Law only as a source of curse or, at best, as a temporary jailkeeper until the coming of Christ. He explicitly denies the lifegiving power of the Law (3:11-12), which the psalmist had extolled. Of all the texts in the New Testament canon, Galatians appears to be the most relentlessly negative in its evaluation of Old Testament Law. Thus this letter can easily give rise to Marcionite teachings that caricature Judaism as a harsh religion of legalism and, therefore, radically reject the Law and the Old Testament.

It is important, therefore, to realize that Paul goes right to the brink of rejecting the Law, but then pulls back decisively (3:21). The Law is not seen as a direct manifestation of God's grace, like the promise to Abraham, but it is assigned an important role in the unfolding of the story of God's redemption of the world through Christ. Even in this most anti-Law letter, Paul is not denying that God gave the Law; rather, he is resisting the demand that Gentile converts be forced to come under the Law's requirement of circumcision. Everything that Paul says must be interpreted within the framework of this specific situation. In Romans, he seeks to give a more diplomatic and balanced account of his understanding of the Law—perhaps in response to some of the criticism and controversy that this earlier polemical letter evoked. Because Christianity has a long and tragic history of violence against Jews and ignorant disparagement of Judaism, the interpreter of Galatians should take care to set Paul's statements about the Law within their proper historical setting as an *intra-Christian* argument about the ways in which the Law should or should not continue to provide direct norms for the life of the church.

We have seen that Paul identifies two purposes for which the Law was given: identifying sin as transgression and restraining sinful behavior in the era prior to the coming of Christ. To what extent do these functions remain valid now that we are no longer subject to the power of the Law? A good case can be made that the Law's diagnostic function remains valuable for the church; the Law continues to teach us that we are in rebellion against a loving God who desires our wholeness. Our sinful behavior, therefore, is to be understood not merely as destructive to human communities but also as transgression against a holy God. Without the Law, we would not have known that. On the other hand, the Law's role as disciplinarian is now decisively revoked by the coming of Christ. We are in a new situation where, according to Paul, we are to live under the guidance of the Spirit, apart from Law (5:13-26). The specific "do's" and "don'ts" of the Torah are no longer regulative for the Christian community. This claim, of course, raises its own problems, which Paul will discuss later in the letter.

Finally, Galatians 3 emphatically excludes two roles that have sometimes been assigned to the Law. First, the Law cannot confer life and righteousness. It was never designed by God for that purpose (3:10-12, 21). It can point toward these ends, but it lacks the power to confer the goals to which it bears witness (cf. Rom 8:1-4). Second, the Law does not "lead us to Christ" (see the Commentary on 3:23-25). There is a venerable history of Christian teaching on the Law as an educative preparation for the gospel, but that teaching is entirely contrary to what Paul says here. The Law does not lead us to Christ; rather, Christ came to us in our imprisonment. The difference is crucial for Christian preaching.

6. *New Creation: Unity in Christ Transforms Social Divisions.* The baptismal formula of Gal 3:28 has been widely cited as a charter for movements seeking social justice and equality. Yet, the use of Paul's words to support egalitarian social programs has been challenged by many interpreters because of evidence elsewhere in Paul's writings that he countenanced the institution of slavery within the church (1 Cor 7:17-24; Col 4:1; and the ambiguous case of the Letter to Philemon) and the subordination of women (1 Cor 11:3-16; 14:34-35; cf. Eph 5:21-33; 1 Tim 2:8-15).[180] Rarely has it been sufficiently appreciated, however, that Paul passionately argues for putting into social practice the abolition of the distinction between Jew and Gentile (see the Commentary on 2:11-21). This suggests that he did not understand the baptismal formula to prescribe merely a spiritual equality before God in a way that had no social implications. Furthermore, the evidence on the other two issues (slavery and male/female relations) is sufficiently ambiguous to suggest that Paul's vision did, in fact, destabilize traditional assumptions about power in a way that had practical implications in his communities. For example, he counseled mutuality in marital sexual relations (1 Cor 7:3-4), and women did prophesy (1 Cor 11:5) and exercise roles of leadership in the mission (Rom 16:1-7; Phil 4:2-3).[181] Whatever we may think in retrospect about the adequacy of Paul's implementation of the vision articulated in the formula, it is hard to deny that he believed the church to be a new community brought into being by the power of God's grace in which old social inequalities were being overturned and transformed (see also 1 Cor 1:18-31).[182]

In interpreting Gal 3:28, we should bear in mind its place within the argument of the letter. Paul is passionately insisting that uncircumcised Gentile Christians are not second-class citizens in the kingdom of God and that they should recognize themselves, just as they are, as "children of God" on an equal footing with Jewish Christians who equally owe their status as rectified children of God to the faithfulness of Jesus Christ. As Paul puts the case in Rom 10:12, "There is no distinction between Jew and Greek; the same Lord is Lord of all and is generous to all who call on him" (NRSV). In support of this argument, Paul appeals to the baptismal formula as the basis on which the Galatians should be acknowledged to share full equality with Jewish Christians as Abraham's heirs. Thus we see clearly that Paul regards the formula as having practical social implications for the life of the church.

In our time, then, our task is analogous to the one that Paul faced. Most of our churches do not face pressure for Gentiles to be circumcised, but we do confront numerous divisions and hostilities between different racial and ethnic groups. Our preaching and our practices must encourage the same reconciliation between (say) black and white Christians that Paul envisioned between "Jew and Greek."

Likewise, we confront continuing controversies about the full participation of women in the "inheritance" and in the life of the church. As we deal with this issue, we may take our cues from Paul and look back also to the formula of Gal 3:28 as an important starting point for our theological reflection. If we do that, it is not hard to see where our reflection will lead. Those who resist the ordination and leadership of women in the church's ministry stand in a role analogous to the rival Missionaries, who sought to reinstitute the distinctions and requirements of the old age before Christ's coming. In the community of the new creation,

---

180. For the history of the debates over the use of Paul's letters to address these issues, see W. M. Swartley, *Slavery, Sabbath, War, and Women: Case Issues in Biblical Interpretation* (Scottdale, Pa.: Herald, 1983).

181. For discussion of the evidence, see V. P. Furnish, *The Moral Teaching of Paul: Selected Issues,* rev. ed. (Nashville: Abingdon, 1985) 83-114; E. Schüssler Fiorenza, *In Memory of Her: A Feminist Theological Reconstruction of Christian Origins* (New York: Crossroad, 1983) 205-41; B. Witherington III, *Women in the Earliest Churches,* SNTSMS 59 (Cambridge: Cambridge University Press, 1980); R. B. Hays, *The Moral Vision of the New Testament: Community, Cross, New Creation* (San Francisco: HarperSanFrancisco, 1996) 46-56.

182. Betz comments: "There can be no doubt that Paul's statements have social and political implications of even a revolutionary dimension. The claim is made that very old and decisive ideals and hopes of the ancient world have come true in the Christian community." See H. D. Betz, *Galatians: A Commentary on Paul's Letter to the Churches in Galatia,* Hermeneia (Philadelphia: Fortress, 1979) 190.

our oneness in Christ overcomes and delegitimates the distinctions of race, social class, and gender that divided us when we were prisoners under the power of Sin. Of course, the practical outworking of this vision of the new creation remains the ongoing task of the church in history as we "eagerly wait for the hope of righteousness" (5:5).

7. *Hearing the Voice of Scripture.* The conviction that the Law's role as a temporary guardian has now ended does not lead Paul to a rejection of the authority of Scripture in the community of faith. Instead, he rereads Scripture with new eyes in the light of God's revelation in Christ and produces fresh and startling interpretations. This is not merely a pragmatic debate strategy, as though he were compelled to answer the Missionaries' arguments by debating them on their own turf. As we see from Paul's other letters, the ongoing dialogue with Scripture is a regular feature of his theological reflection.[183]

In Gal 3:6-29, Paul uses seven explicit quotations from Scripture, and, as we have seen, there are several other important allusions in the background of his argument (an obvious example is Deut 6:4 in Gal 3:20). Some of these passages may have been originally injected into the debate by the Missionaries (Gen 17:8; Lev 18:5; Deut 27:26), but others are surely Paul's own contribution (Gen 12:3; 15:6; Hab 2:4). Two features of Paul's use of Scripture in this section of the letter are particularly noteworthy.

First, Paul reads Scripture as a narrative with a plotline. It is not simply a respository of rules and wise sayings; rather, it tells a story of what God was doing in his dealings with Israel. The promise to Abraham anticipated God's future intention to bless all nations; this promise predated the Law by 430 years; the giving of the Law through the mediation of Moses had the effect of imprisoning everyone under Sin, setting the stage for the advent of Christ; now that Christ has come we have received the inheritance, and it makes no sense to go backward by reinstating the Law. *In order to understand our proper identity and calling, we have to understand this plotline and where we fit into it.* These observations may seem fairly elementary, but in Paul's time it was by no means a foregone conclusion that Scripture should be read in this narrative fashion. Other Jewish interpreters, such as Philo, for example, read these stories as timeless allegories of the soul's quest for transcendence.[184] Paul, by contrast, exemplifies a concern for reading Scripture as a story rooted in history, a story in which we are to find our place. In the church today, we have too often lost this larger view of Scripture's narrative coherence. We read it as a fragmented collection of pericopes or as snippets that turn up in the lectionary, or we open it at random, looking for moral rules or ad hoc spiritual illumination. Paul's example encourages us to see the larger narrative framework.

The second striking feature of Paul's reading of Scripture is that he treats it as a living voice, an agent that speaks and acts. Scripture pre-preached the gospel to Abraham (3:8), Scripture curses (3:10, 13) and blesses (3:8-9), Scripture speaks promises (3:11, 16), and Scripture locked up all things under the power of Sin (3:22). In short, Scripture for Paul is living and active. It has played a key role in God's plan, and its voice continues to be heard in the community of faith. Of course, such descriptions of Scripture's speech and action are metaphorical, but that does not mean that they are not to be taken seriously. For Paul, Scripture forms the matrix within which theological debate and reflection must be conducted, and the crucial task for the community is to hear Scripture's voice rightly. That remains true for the church today, no less than in Paul's time.

---

183. See R. B. Hays, *Echoes of Scripture in the Letters of Paul* (New Haven: Yale University Press, 1989); "The Conversion of the Imagination: Scripture and Eschatology in 1 Corinthians," *NTS* 45 (1999) 391-412.

184. See, for example, Philo, *On the Migration of Abraham* and *Who Is the Heir of Divine Things?* LCL, trans. F. H. Colson and G. H. Whitaker (Cambridge, Mass.: Harvard University Press, 1932); see also *On Abraham,* LCL, trans. F. H. Colson (Cambridge, Mass.: Harvard University Press, 1935).

GALATIANS 4:1-11, THE FULLNESS OF TIME HAS COME

OVERVIEW

As we have seen, Paul opened his counter-arguments in 3:1-5 with a direct appeal to the Galatians' own experience of receiving the Spirit in response to his proclamation of the gospel. He then turned to an argument from Scripture in 3:6-29, demonstrating that by virtue of their participation in Christ the Galatians are already "Abraham's seed" and, therefore, legitimate heirs of God's promise (which is also identified with the Spirit in 3:14, the only reference to the Spirit in that section of the letter). Now in 4:1-7 he refers again to their experience of the Spirit as proof that they are children, not just of Abraham, but of God. The Spirit is the sign that they have been adopted into God's family. Paul contrasts this experience of familial relation to God to the Galatians' former state as slaves of cosmic powers and makes the astonishing assertion that, should they place themselves under the Jewish Law, they would be returning to the same state of slavery they had previously known as pagans (4:8-11).

Galatians 4:1-7, We Are Heirs and Children of God

NIV

4 What I am saying is that as long as the heir is a child, he is no different from a slave, although he owns the whole estate. [2]He is subject to guardians and trustees until the time set by his father. [3]So also, when we were children, we were in slavery under the basic principles of the world. [4]But when the time had fully come, God sent his Son, born of a woman, born under law, [5]to redeem those under law, that we might receive the full rights of sons. [6]Because you are sons, God sent the Spirit of his Son into our hearts, the Spirit who calls out, *"Abba,[a]* Father."* [7]So you are no longer a slave, but a son; and since you are a son, God has made you also an heir.

[a]6 Aramaic for *Father*

NRSV

4 My point is this: heirs, as long as they are minors, are no better than slaves, though they are the owners of all the property; [2]but they remain under guardians and trustees until the date set by the father. [3]So with us; while we were minors, we were enslaved to the elemental spirits[a] of the world. [4]But when the fullness of time had come, God sent his Son, born of a woman, born under the law, [5]in order to redeem those who were under the law, so that we might receive adoption as children. [6]And because you are children, God has sent the Spirit of his Son into our[b] hearts, crying, "Abba![c] Father!" [7]So you are no longer a slave but a child, and if a child then also an heir, through God.[d]

[a] Or *the rudiments*   [b] Other ancient authorities read *your*   [c] Aramaic for *Father*   [d] Other ancient authorities read *an heir of God through Christ*

COMMENTARY

Using the image of the Galatians as "heirs" in 3:29 as a point of departure, Paul picks up this imagery again and develops it with specific application to the present situation of the Galatians—and all believers, Jewish and Gentile alike—now that Christ has come. In some ways, 4:1-7 can be read as a recapitulation of 3:23-29, as Dunn demonstrates:[185]

185. J. D. G. Dunn, *The Epistle to the Galatians,* Black's NT Commentary (Peabody, Mass.: Hendrickson, 1993) 210. His table is reproduced here with minor changes.

Figure 4: Parallels Between Gal 3:23-29 and 4:1-7*

3:23-29

(23) Before the coming of faith
    we were held in custody under the Law
    confined until the coming faith should be revealed
(24) The Law was our custodian until Christ came . . .

(25) But now that faith has come

    we are no longer under a custodian.
(26) For all of you are sons of God . . .
(27) You all were baptized into Christ . . .
(29) So then you are Abraham's seed,
    heirs in accordance with promise.

4:1-7

(1) As long as the heir is a child . . .
(2) he is under guardians and stewards
    until the time set by the father.
(3) As children we were enslaved
    under the elemental forces
(4) But when the fullness of time came,
    God sent his Son . . .
(5) in order to redeem those under the Law.
    in order that we might receive adoption.
(6) God sent the Spirit of his Son . . .
(7) So that you are no longer a slave but a son,
    and if a son, then an heir through God.

*Adapted from J. D. G. Dunn, The Epistle to the Galatians, Black's NT Commentary (Peabody, Mass.: Hendrickson, 1993). Used by permission of A & C Black.

Paul is not merely repeating himself. He introduces several new elements that apply the inheritance analogy directly to the situation the Galatians now face, and he more explicitly describes the sending of God's Son as a cosmic rescue operation.

4:1-2. Paul continues to set forth a picture based on the metaphor of inheritance. In these verses he describes the situation of a minor (male) heir whose father's will has made provision for his estate to be managed by "guardians and trustees" during the period of the heir's minority. In vv. 3-5, Paul will explain how this picture applies to the situation of the Galatians. The term "heir" (κληρονόμος *klēronomos*) in v. 1 is singular, as in the NIV; the NRSV has made it plural in the interest of inclusive language. These comments will follow the NIV's usage, in order to stay closer to the imagery Paul actually employs.[186]

When Paul says that the minor heir is "no different from a slave," he is employing rhetorical exaggeration, with a view to the application he will develop in vv. 3-5. The heir is, of course, in a very different position from a slave because he is the rightful owner of the property, and he will eventually take charge of it. During the period of his minority, however, he does not have authority over the management of the property, which is in the hands of "guardians and trustees." There has been much scholarly discussion of the precise legal background for Paul's terminology.[187] The former term refers to a legally appointed guardian or tutor, whereas the latter is a general term for "steward" or "administrator." This word, which appears, for example, in a number of Jesus' parables (e.g., Luke 16:1-9), regularly designates a slave charged with oversight and management of a household's affairs. Paul applies the same word metaphorically to himself, as a steward charged by God with responsibility for the church, in 1 Cor 4:1-2. Paul is speaking in general terms here for the purpose of illustration, and there is no point in seeking to pin down precise legal details presupposed by the analogy, which works only loosely in any case. The salient point is that the young heir is "under" (ὑπο *hypo*) the authority of these guardians; this is the same preposition used in 3:22-25 and in 4:3-5 to refer to being under Sin, under the Law, under the(*paidagōgos*), and under the "elements of the world" (see the Commentary on 4:3, 9).

In Paul's illustration, as in these other cases, the heir's subjection is only temporary. He is subject to the guardians and trustees only "until the time set by the father." The "time set" is a fixed day on which the heir's minority ends and he receives control of the estate. In Roman law, this date was not determined at the discretion of the individual testator. It was fixed by law; the minor was under a tutor until the age of fourteen and then under a "curator" until age twenty-five. Again, however, whether this detail corresponds precisely to the provisions of inheritance law in Paul's culture is beside the point; he is already looking ahead to his application in v. 4, thinking of the fact that it is God who appoints the time for the state of subjection to come to an end. The crucial word here is the preposition "until," which

---

186. Paul's extended metaphor presupposes the inheritance customs of his day, in which property would ordinarily be inherited by male offspring.

187. See H. D. Betz, *Galatians: A Commentary on Paul's Letter to the Churches in Galatia*, Hermeneia (Philadelphia: Fortress, 1979) 203-4; R. N. Longenecker, *Galatians*, WBC 41 (Dallas: Word, 1990) 162-64.

recalls 3:19, 23 and anticipates 4:4. Paul is highlighting the temporary character of the heir's subjection.

4:3. Now Paul applies his illustration. The little parable of the enslaved heir is a figurative depiction of the experience of Paul and his readers. Immediately, we face a crucial question: To whom do the first-person plural pronouns here and in v. 5 refer? Is Paul referring to "we Jews" (as in 2:15-16; 3:13a, and probably 3:23-25), or is he now speaking from a perspective that includes his Gentile converts (as in 3:14)? The parallel between v. 3 and vv. 8-9 requires the latter: All humanity was "enslaved" prior to the coming of the Son of God. Paul's inclusion of himself in the class of persons enslaved under the elements may in the first instance be understood as an example of his identification with his Gentile addressees, as in 1 Cor 9:21a; however, as we shall see in vv. 8-11, Paul has in mind a more radical analysis of the human plight. The Law itself is among the enslaving "elements"; thus he as Jew shared with the pagan Galatians a condition of slavery from which he needed to be liberated (see the Commentary on 4:8-11).

But this analysis leads to the second crucial problem in v. 3: the meaning of Paul's expression τὰ στοιχεῖα τοῦ κόσμου (*ta stoicheia tou kosmou*). The NRSV's "the elemental spirits of the world" and the NIV's "the basic principles of the world" represent two different interpretations of this much-contested expression.[188]

The term *stoicheia* can mean "the basics" or "rudimentary principles" of any field of knowledge (see Heb 5:12). If Paul has this meaning in mind here, he is saying, "We were enslaved to basic principles of religion (whether pagan religion or Jewish Law) that we have now outgrown or transcended." On this reading, Paul is saying that the human problem is one of ignorance, and its solution would be a revelation that brings higher knowledge, enabling us to move to maturity. This interpretation, represented by the NIV, has received the support of several recent commentators.[189] There are, however, two serious objections

to this reading. First, none of the ancient parallels in which *stoicheia* has the meaning "basic principles" speak of "the basic principles *of the world*." Second, and most telling, Paul does not speak in Gal 4:1-7 of a gradual growth or progression beyond an elementary stage of religion to a more advanced one. He speaks, rather, of an invasion of the world by God's Son to rescue us from a state of slavery to the *stoicheia*.

By far the most common meaning of *stoicheia* in the first century was "the elemental substances from which everything in the natural world is composed"—that is, according to the traditional view, earth, air, fire, and water (e.g., 2 Pet 3:10, 12). Indeed, this is the only meaning attested outside the Pauline letters in this period for the expression *ta stoicheia tou kosmou*.[190] It is not immediately evident how this meaning would be pertinent in Gal 4:3, 9 (but see Martyn's proposal, below).

Later texts, from the second century CE onward, begin to use the expression to refer to "elemental spirits" associated with these four elements. Developing out of this meaning was a tendency to associate these elemental spirits with the heavenly bodies (sun, moon, and stars), whose movements were thought to exercise determinative—and sometimes hostile—control over human life. This is the interpretation represented by the NRSV and supported by some important commentaries.[191] Thus, on this reading, the *stoicheia* can be closely linked with "the cosmic powers of this present darkness . . . the spiritual forces of evil in the heavenly places" (Eph 6:4 NRSV). It is not hard to see how Paul could associate the worship of pagan deities, in the Galatians' former life, with slavery to such celestial powers. The difficulty for this reading, however, emerges in vv. 9-10, when Paul describes the Galatians' turning to observance of Jewish Law as a return to slavery under the *stoicheia*. How could Law-observant worship of the God of Israel possibly be categorized as slavery to the principalities and powers?

In the light of the evidence, Martyn has argued persuasively that the rival Missionaries in Galatia may have sought to convince the Galatians

188. The definitive discussion of the term is now that of J. L. Martyn, *Galatians*, AB 33A (New York: Doubleday, 1997) 393-406, on which much of the following interpretation is based.

189. Richard N. Longenecker, *Galatians*, WBC 41 (Dallas: Word, 1990) 165-66; F. J. Matera, *Galatians*, Sacra Pagina 9 (Collegeville, Minn.: Liturgical Press) 149-50; S. K. Williams, *Galatians*, ANTC (Nashville: Abingdon, 1997) 109-11.

190. See also Col 2:8, 20. The use of the expression there would fit nicely into Martyn's analysis, though Martyn does not treat Colossians in his discussion. See Martyn, *Galatians*, 400-406.

191. E.g., Betz, *Galatians*, 205.

that their worship of pagan divinities was an ill-informed worship of the natural elements (the second meaning of *stoicheia*) that ought to point them to a truer form of religion, exemplified by Abraham, who moved through the contemplation of the heavenly bodies to discern the God who made and ordered them. In support of this suggestion, Martyn cites several impressive parallels from Hellenistic Jewish texts.[192] The point of the Missionaries' evangelistic strategy, then, would be to persuade the Galatians that the Law provided the true understanding of the natural world and the heavenly bodies and, therefore, regulated the calendar of human religious observance in a manner that enabled correct celebration of holy feasts at the proper times; hence, Paul's disparaging reference to observing "special days and months and seasons and years" (v. 10). This would explain why Paul could make the otherwise puzzling claim that coming under the Law would constitute a resubjection to the *stoicheia* (see the Commentary on 4:8-10).

In any case, Paul portrays all humanity as existing in a condition of slavery prior to God's dramatic intervention. That intervention is the theme of vv. 4-7.

4:4-5. The expression "when the fullness of time had come" indicates the apocalyptic frame of reference for Paul's thought. God is conceived as having a cosmic timetable and an appointed day (cf. v. 2) to break into humanity's history of misery to bring the promised redemption. (For other such apocalyptic conceptions of the appointed fulfillment of time, see Dan 8:19; 11:35; 1 QpHab 7:2; Mark 1:15; Luke 21:24; Acts 1:7; 3:21; Eph 1:10.) The decision to intervene is God's alone, and the timing is God's alone (cf. Mark 13:32, where it is only the Father who knows the time of appointed deliverance).

This passage shares with Rom 8:3-4 the motif of God's sending the Son to redeem humanity from a state of powerlessness; furthermore, both passages move to a climactic affirmation of the Spirit as a transforming power in the community of those whom the Son has redeemed (see also Rom 8:15-17). The similarity of these passages to John 3:16-17 and 1 John 4:9-10 has encouraged the hypothesis that in Gal 4:4-5 Paul is quoting

a confessional "sending formula" that was current in early Christian communities.[193] Several commentators have questioned whether this formula presupposes the heavenly pre-existence of the Son.[194] It is true that the idea of "sending" by itself can be used with reference to God's commissioning of prophets or apostles (e.g., Jer 7:25; Acts 22:21) and need not imply pre-existence. Nonetheless, regardless of the hypothetical origins of the formula, in the light of Phil 2:5-11 (also much debated) and other Pauline expressions of exalted christology (e.g., 1 Cor 8:6), it seems likely that Paul did think of the Son as pre-existent, sent forth from heaven on a rescue mission.

At the same time, two participial phrases give expression to the full humanity of the Son, who is the protagonist in this narrative of redemption. He was "born of a woman, born under Law." The expression "born of a woman" indicates simply that he was human (cf. Job 14:1; Matt 11:11). There is no indication here, or anywhere else, that Paul knew the name of Jesus' mother or that he knew a tradition of Jesus' virgin birth. The fact that Jesus was "born under Law" means that he was a Jew. Further, it means that he found himself under the same confining custody of the Law that Paul has already described in 3:23—just as the heir in 4:2 was under guardians and trustees.

It is tempting to read Paul's narrative in counterpoint with the parable of the wicked tenants (Mark 12:1-12), in which the vineyard owner sends a beloved son to reclaim an inheritance that is being badly managed by abusive administrators, who say of the son, "This is the heir; come, let us kill him" (NRSV). Almost certainly Paul is not referring to this parable, but—if he is quoting a confessional tradition in vv. 4-5—the motif of God's sending the Son may have its roots in Jesus' parable, as remembered and interpreted by the community after his death and resurrection. Whatever one might make of these parallels, however, it is clear that Paul does not have a christological allegory in mind in vv. 1-2, as v. 3 makes clear; the heir in his analogy stands not for Christ (despite

192. See esp. Wis 13:1-5; Philo *On Abraham* 69-70; Josephus *Antiquities of the Jews* 1.155-56.

193. H. D. Betz, *Galatians: A Commentary on Paul's Letter to the Churches in Galatia,* Hermeneia (Philadelphia: Fortress, 1979) 205-9, with other literature cited there.

194. E.g., J. D. G. Dunn, *The Epistle to the Galatians,* Black's NT Commentary (Peabody, Mass.: Hendrickson, 1993) 215; see also Dunn's *Christology in the Making: A New Testament Inquiry into the Origins of the Doctrine of the Incarnation* (Philadelphia: Westminster, 1980) 38-44.

3:16) but for humanity enslaved under the *stoicheia.*

The fact that God's Son was born under subjection to the Law is crucial to his mission, which was to "redeem [ἐξαγοράσῃ *exagorasē*] those under Law." The verb refers to emancipation from slavery, with overtones of paying the price to purchase the slave's freedom (cf. 1 Cor 6:19*b*-20). This is the same verb that Paul used in 3:13, the only other place in his letters that the word occurs. The link makes it clear that the Son achieved his rescue mission by taking the Law's curse on himself in his death on the cross; in order for him to do that, it was necessary that he be born as one of the people of Israel, under the Law. Although the cross is not explicitly mentioned in v. 5, it would be misleading to suppose that Paul here thinks of a redemption achieved solely through the incarnation of the Son as opposed to through his death.[195] Paul did not compartmentalize confessional statements in that fashion. Galatians 3:13 and 4:4-5 are two summarizations of the same story, and the action of "redemption" alluded to in 4:5 has already been more fully narrated in the earlier passage.

If v. 5*a* refers to Christ's redemption of Israel from the Law's curse, then the second clause of the verse refers to the rectification of Gentiles, made possible by Christ's redemptive death.[196] They are now adopted into God's family. (This is the simple meaning of the noun υἱοθεσία [*huiothesia*], rightly translated as "adoption" by the NRSV but given a needlessly complicated paraphrase in the NIV; for other uses of the term, see Rom 8:15, 23; 9:4; Eph 1:5.) This clause is closely parallel to 3:14*a*, "in order that in Christ Jesus the blessing of Abraham might come to the Gentiles." The fact that Paul now speaks of "adoption" shows that he has moved beyond the framework of his analogy in vv. 1-2, where he spoke of one who stands to receive an inheritance by birth. The Gentiles, by contrast, are embraced within God's grace as adopted children. The idea is similar to the point Paul makes in Rom 11:17-24, using the metaphor of the Gentiles as wild olive branches grafted onto a cultivated olive tree.

God's mercy has called a people "not from the Jews only but also from the Gentiles" (Rom 9:24 NRSV). The vision of the Gentiles as adopted into God's family through the death of Christ is elegantly articulated in a passage in Ephesians that can be read as a commentary on Gal 4:5*b*:

So then, remember that at one time you Gentiles by birth, called "the uncircumcision" by those who are called "the circumcision"—a physical circumcision made in the flesh by human hands—remember that you were at that time without Christ, being aliens from the commonwealth of Israel, and strangers to the covenants of promise, having no hope and without God in the world. But now in Christ Jesus you who once were far off have been brought near by the blood of Christ. . . . So then you are no longer strangers and aliens, but you are citizens with the saints and also members of the household of God. (Eph 2:11-13, 19 NRSV)

At the same time, Paul's adoption metaphor may have another nuance as well. In contrast to God's own Son, all other human beings, including Jewish believers, enter God's family only by adoption. Augustine saw this point clearly in commenting on this passage: "He says *adoption* so that we may clearly understand that the Son of God is unique. For we are sons of God through his generosity and the condescension of his mercy, whereas he is Son by nature, sharing the same divinity with the Father."[197] Thus, even if the adoption metaphor initially envisions God's acceptance of Gentiles, it must be expanded to include God's adoption of Jewish believers as well, as suggested by the parallel with 3:26: "in Christ Jesus, you are *all* children of God *through faith,*" i.e., not through the Law.

Thus by the end of v. 5 Paul has completed the first phase of his explanation of the inheritance analogy: God has liberated us from slavery to the *stoicheia* by sending the Son to invade our prison and set us free, thus bringing Jews and Gentiles alike into God's family.

4:6. But Paul is not quite finished developing his theme. He points again to the Galatians' experience of receiving the Spirit, just as he had done at the beginning of his counterargument in 3:1-5. This time, however, he does not just point

---

195. Betz, *Galatians,* 207-8.
196. If Paul is quoting a confessional formula, was it originally coined in a Gentile congregation? This would explain the shift from "those under the Law" to "we" in this verse.

197. Augustine *Epistle to the Galatians* 30 [1B.4.4-5], PL 35:2126. Cited in M. J. Edwards, ed., *Galatians, Ephesians, Philippians,* Ancient Christian Commentary on Scripture, vol. 8 (Downers Grove, Ill.: InterVarsity, 1999) 56.

to the experience; he gives it a fuller theological interpretation within the story of God's mission of rescue and adoption. The adoption was in one sense "legally" accomplished in Jesus' death and resurrection, but that is not the end of the story. God has provided experiential confirmation of our adoption by pouring out the Spirit (see the Commentary on 3:14). God not only sent the Son into the world, but also "because you are sons, God sent the Spirit of his Son into our hearts." This is the sign and pledge of our new status as God's children. (The NRSV, by opting for the inclusive-language translation "children" in v. 6a, loses the connection in the Greek text between "sons" and "Spirit of his Son"; the sense of the sentence is better conveyed in the NIV, so long as we understand, in the light of 3:28, that "sons" is a metaphor that includes both men and women in God's family.) The shift from second to first person ("*you* are sons . . . into *our* hearts") in this verse is awkward, and it has predictably created problems in the manuscript tradition (see the NRSV footnote). Williams is probably right that by shifting momentarily into the second person Paul "pointedly singles out the recipients of the letter, the Gentiles of Galatia,"[198] since it is their status as "sons" that is under dispute.

Christian interpreters have long struggled over the narrative sequence implied in this verse, which seems to make the sending of the Spirit a second action subsequent to adoption as children. It is important to realize that Paul is not describing here the life history of the individual believer; instead, he is narrating God's redemptive invasion of an enslaved world. Within the narrative, the sending of the Son must come first; once he has completed his mission through his death on the cross, then the Spirit can be sent to those who are adopted by virtue of this liberating death that demolished the prison walls. In terms, however, of the experience of individual believers, the sending of the Spirit into our hearts is a fundamental aspect of conversion/initiation, as the parallel to 3:26-29 shows (see *Fig.* 4, 281). In other words, Paul is in no way describing a "second blessing" experience for those who earlier had experienced justification. The sending of the Spirit is God's action that both effects and confirms our entrance into God's family.

The motif of God's sending forth the Spirit is reminiscent of some Jewish traditions about the sending of divine wisdom from the throne of God. For instance, in Wis 9:17, Solomon inquires of God, "Who has learned your counsel, unless you have given wisdom and sent your holy spirit from on high?" (NRSV; see also Wis 9:10). In this verse, however, Paul is speaking of the Spirit not as a source for understanding God's will and wisdom but as an intensely experienced confimation of God's gracious embrace. When the Spirit is sent into our hearts, Paul says, it cries out, "Abba, Father." We should not understand this as a reference to recitation of the Lord's prayer; rather, this is the language of ecstasy, as we can see from Paul's use of the vivid participle "crying out" (κρᾶζον *krazon*). It is sometimes suggested that the Aramaic word "Abba" was uttered by "baptizands as they rise from the water,"[199] as a grateful acknowledgment of their new status as God's children. On the other hand, it is also suggested that the use of "Abba" in spirit-inspired prayer was concisly modeled after the prayer language of Jesus, "an echo of Jesus' own prayer style" (cf. Mark 14:36).[200] Either way, Paul's point is that the Spirit is a powerful presence in the hearts of the Galatians, enabling or impelling them to cry out to the Father of Jesus Christ as their own Father.

---

198. S. K. Williams, *Galatians,* ANTC (Nashville: Abingdon, 1997) 111.

199. Martyn, *Galatians,* 391-92.
200. Dunn, *The Epistle to the Galatians,* 221.

Figure 5: Parallels Between Gal 4:4-6 and 3:13-14*

Gal 4:3-6

(4) God sent forth his Son,
   born of a woman,
   born under Law,
(5) in order that he might redeem
   those under Law,

   in order that we might receive adoption.

(6) God sent forth the Spirit of his Son
   into our hearts. . . .

Gal 3:13-14

(13) Christ redeemed
   us from the curse of the Law
   by becoming a curse for us . . .
(14) in order that the blessing of Abraham
   might come to the
   Gentiles through Christ Jesus,
   in order that we might receive the promise
   of the Spirit through the faith.

*Adapted from R. B. Hays, *The Faith of Jesus Christ,* SBLDS 56 (Chico, Calif.: Scholars Press, 1983) 118.

4:7. Paul draws this narrative of inheritance to a climactic and triumphant conclusion, assuring the Galatians of their new status in Christ. By sending the Son into the world, God has liberated them and transformed them from slaves into sons. Since they are now sons of God (cf. 3:26), they are surely now heirs (cf. 3:29). Of this truth, the presence of the Spirit in their midst is the decisive confirmation. The expression "an heir, through God" (NRSV, translating literally) is odd, because God is elsewhere described as the source, not the medium, of the inheritance (the NIV again tries to avoid the awkwardness by paraphrasing). Some copyists, feeling the difficulty here, produced vari-

ous theological corrections, including the reading "an heir of God through Christ" (NRSV note).

The sequence of thought in vv. 6-7 is exactly paralleled by Rom 8:15-17: Starting from slavery (and fear), we have received the Spirit that enables us to cry, "Abba, Father!" This Spirit bears witness of our new status as children of God and heirs. The fact that Paul repeats this argument in Romans shows that it is not merely a contingent response to the situation in Galatia—or, more precisely, that if it was a contingent response to that situation, he retained it as a central element in his account of the gospel. (See Reflections at 4:8-11.)

Galatians 4:8-11, No Turning Back

NIV	NRSV
[8]Formerly, when you did not know God, you were slaves to those who by nature are not gods. [9]But now that you know God—or rather are known by God—how is it that you are turning back to those weak and miserable principles? Do you wish to be enslaved by them all over again? [10]You are observing special days and months and seasons and years! [11]I fear for you, that somehow I have wasted my efforts on you.	[8]Formerly, when you did not know God, you were enslaved to beings that by nature are not gods. [9]Now, however, that you have come to know God, or rather to be known by God, how can you turn back again to the weak and beggarly elemental spirits?[a] How can you want to be enslaved to them again? [10]You are observing special days, and months, and seasons, and years. [11]I am afraid that my work for you may have been wasted.
	[a] Or *beggarly rudiments*

COMMENTARY

4:8. After the jubilant rhetorical climax of v. 7, Paul adopts a more sober tone again as he broods over the present peril of the Galatians. During their years of living as pagans, they "did not know God"—a typical Jewish judgment of Gentiles (see Ps 79:6). Paul repeats the reminder that during this period of ignorance they were enslaved to "beings that by nature are not gods" (cf. v. 3). This expression shows that Paul does not think of the στοιχεῖα (*stoicheia*) merely as rudimentary religious principles that have now been superseded. Instead, they are personified forces that once exercised hostile dominion over the lives of his readers. Paul elsewhere acknowledges the reality and presence of spiritual powers in the world, called by various names, such as "gods," "lords," "demons," and "rulers of this age" (1 Cor 2:8; 8:5-6; 10:20-21). Such powers are no threat to the sovereignty of the one God; indeed, through Christ, God will ultimately destroy or subdue them (1 Cor 15:23-28; Phil 2:10-11; cf. Col 1:15-20; 2:15). But, because we live in the time between the times, when all things are not yet made subject to God, these not-gods continue to exercise power and to oppress and enslave those who will serve them. Gentiles who worship idols, therefore, are under the domain of these enslaving powers.

4:9. Consequently, Paul poses an incredulous question designed to expose the absurdity of the Galatians' present infatuation with the Law, by linking the Law-observant life to their former state of slavery. The artful wording of v. 9*a* illuminates the deep theological syntax of Paul's gospel: "Now, however, that you have come to know God—or rather to be known by God. . . ." The self-correction is an artful way of calling attention to the theological "ungrammaticality" of any claim that we as finite creatures can save ourselves by attaining a higher knowledge of God. (Perhaps the Missionaries were offering the Galatians a non-gospel along these lines; cf. 1:6-7.) The Galatians have entered a new world not because of some epistemological advance of their own, but because God, in elective love, has now "known" them (see the close parallel in 1 Cor 8:2-3; cf. 1 Cor 13:12). For the OT background of God's "know-

ing" of Israel, see, e.g., Amos 3:2: "You only have I known of all the families of the earth."

Having been known by God, Paul asks them, "How can you turn back again to the weak and beggarly *stoicheia*?" Their turning to observe the Law would be a conversion, to be sure, but a wrongheaded one. The verb "turn" (ἐπιστρέφω *epistrephō*) is the same word characteristically used to describe a repentant person turning back to God or the conversion of Gentiles to serve the one true God of Israel. Paul uses this verb, for instance, of the pagan Thessalonians' response to his preaching of the gospel: "You turned [ἐπεστρέψατε *epestrepsate*] to God from idols to serve a living and true God" (1 Thess 1:9). Thus the action that the Galatians are contemplating would be a conversion in reverse—a reversion to their former state of slavery.

This is perhaps the most stunning sentence in this entire confrontational letter. Paul is suggesting that Judaism's holy observances are, in effect, no different from paganism's worship of earthly elements. He could hardly have said anything more calculated to arouse the outrage of the Missionaries, but the rhetorical shock value of his question is surely calculated. He is trying to jolt the Galatians out of the hypnotic spell of the Law-gospel.

Paul refers to the *stoicheia* as "weak and beggarly." This is a paradox, for he also attributes to them the power to enslave their adherents. Why, then, does he also call them weak? It is a stock theme of Jewish polemic against idolatry that idols are lifeless and impotent (e.g., Isa 46:3-5). Martyn cites the satirical depiction of the idolator in Wis 13:18-19:[201]

For health he appeals to a thing that is weak;
for life he prays to a thing that is dead;

.   .   .   .   .   .

he asks strength of a thing whose
    hands have no strength. (NRSV)

This passage may be particularly significant if, indeed, Wis 13:1-5 supplies the link in Paul's mind between pagan worship and "the elements." This may be part of the explanation for Paul's

---

201. Martyn, *Galatians,* 411.

disparaging reference to the weakness of the *stoicheia*. Insofar as they have any power at all, it is the power of illusion. They have already been defeated by the Son of God's victorious incursion. But Paul may also be thinking of the Law in particular as "weak." He has already noted that the Law does not have the power to give life (3:21). This is a consistent motif in Paul's critique of the Law. Particularly pertinent is Rom 8:3, in which he describes the Law as powerless because "it was weak through the flesh," and then goes on to say that God, by sending the Son, has solved the problem that the weak Law failed to solve. The connection of ideas here is very close to Gal 4:4-9.

4:10. Paul goes on with a descriptive statement about practices that the Galatians have adopted in his absence; this description provides the key to understanding the apparently outrageous implications of Paul's equating of Law with the *stoicheia*. The Galatians show themselves to be coming back under the sway of the *stoicheia* by adopting a pattern of life governed by fixed calendrical observances. The observances of the Jewish liturgical calendar were calibrated to the motions of the sun and moon (sabbath, new-moon festivals, the Day of Atonement, Passover, and other festivals). Jewish sources from the Second Temple period show that there was heated controversy between advocates of lunar and solar calendrical systems over the proper way of keeping times and seasons. For example, *Jubilees,* a text championing the solar calendar, insists that "the Lord set the sun as a great sign upon the earth for days, sabbaths, months, feast (days), years, sabbaths of years, jubilees, and for all the (appointed) times of the years" (*Jub.* 2:9). Equally interesting as background to this verse is a passage from *1 Enoch:*

True is the matter of the exact computation of that which has been recorded ... concerning the luminaries, the months, the festivals, the years and the days. ... He has the power in the heaven both day and night so that he may cause the light to shine over the people—sun, moon, and stars, and all the principalities of heaven which revolve in their (respective) circuits. These are the orders of the stars which set in their (respective) places seasons, festivals and months. (*1 Enoch* 82:7-9)[202]

---

202. These passages are cited by Dunn, whose entire discussion of Gal 4:10 is to be consulted for much helpful information. See J. D. G. Dunn, *The Epistle to the Galatians,* Black's NT Commentary (Peabody, Mass.: Hendrickson, 1993) 227-29. Cf. J. L. Martyn, *Galatians,* AB 33A (New York: Doubleday, 1997) 412-18.

Thus it is quite likely that the Missionaries would have impressed on the Galatians the importance not only of being circumcised but also of keeping the sabbaths and feasts at the proper astronomically determined times. If so, it would make sense for Paul to assert that the Galatians' newfound interest in observing Jewish festivals was leading them back into bondage under the power of the astral elements.

If that is the case, why does Paul not refer explicitly to "festivals, new moons, or sabbaths" as in Col 2:16? Why, instead of these specific references to Jewish observances, does he use the generic description, "days and months and seasons and years"? He may be alluding to the biblical creation story, which says that the lights were placed in the dome of the sky on the fourth day of creation "for signs and for seasons and for days and years" (Gen 1:14 NRSV). If this text no longer provides a warrant, as it did in Judaism, for observing special times and seasons, it can only be for the same reason that there is no longer "male and female" in Christ: The new creation has broken in. By using these generic terms, however, rather than the specific terminology of the Jewish liturgical calendar, Paul facilitates his provocative linking of the Law with the *stoicheia*. When one strips away the specific terminology of the Jewish festivals, Paul suggests, one sees that they are in essence just another kind of nature religion! He is saying, in effect, "You used to be in slavery to the cosmic elements; if you come under the Law, you will be back under the control of these same cosmic forces." Here again we see Paul using skillful, explosive, high-risk rhetoric.

4:11. Finally, after expressing his puzzlement that the Galatians could want to return to enslavement, Paul throws up his hands in anxious exasperation. He is afraid that all his work of preaching and teaching in their midst will, in fact, be subverted and come to nothing. A literal translation of his words here reads, "I am afraid for you, lest somehow I have labored in vain for you." The verb "labored" (κοπιάω *kopiaō*) is a term that Paul often uses to describe his work in spreading the gospel (1 Cor 4:12; 15:10; Col 1:29; cf. 1 Tim 4:10). For an especially close parallel, see Phil 2:16: "It is by your holding fast to the word of life that I can boast on the day of Christ that I did not run in vain or labor in vain" (NRSV). The word "in vain" (εἰκη *eikē*) also reminds us of Gal 3:4. Paul contemplates the distressing prospect that the churches he founded in Galatia might abandon the gospel and that his work will be wasted. The reference to his work among the

Galatians provides a transition to the next section (4:12-20), in which he recalls his earlier time with them and appeals to them to remember their special relationship with him.

REFLECTIONS

1. Enslavement as the fundamental human condition: Is it true? Paul characterizes life outside the sphere of Christ's power as a condition of bondage to powers that hold us captive. For many readers of Galatians, the description will seem apt: Those who suffer from addiction to drugs, alcohol, or compulsive behaviors often confess that they are in the clutches of a destructive force that overpowers them. Those who live in poverty or under political oppression know all too well that they are pawns of a system that is too powerful to fight. For all who live in such circumstances, Paul's proclamation comes as joyous good news: God has sent Jesus to share our plight and to loose our chains. Likewise, many who have lived under the grip of empty secular philosophies have found in the gospel a release from the enslaving power of materialism and hedonism—the usual forms that paganism takes in our time. For those who have experienced a transformation from darkness into light, Paul's metaphor of being redeemed from slavery will seem apt, indeed.

But what of those who live ordinary, respectable lives in conditions of prosperity in a free democratic political order? They have never knowingly worshiped false gods, nor have they known overt oppression. Will they find Paul's talk of enslavement to be either exaggerated or irrelevant? Like Jesus' interlocutors in the Fourth Gospel, they may say, "We are descendants of Abraham and have never been slaves to anyone" (John 8:33 NRSV). How does Paul's message speak to such hearers? The interpreter of this text may find an important clue in Paul's identification with the previously pagan Galatians. He insists that he—along with his Jewish compatriots—was enslaved under the στοιχεῖα (*stoicheia*) just as they were. All humanity, apart from Christ, is bound together in a solidarity of servitude. Even the most religiously devout—indeed, perhaps especially they—are entangled in subtle forms of bondage. One sees this only in retrospect, only in the light of the cross. This is a sweeping proclamation that levels all the distinctions we love to make between ourselves and others.

Thus the single message that we were all slaves and that all are now equally redeemed through Christ's death will come to different hearers with quite different impacts. For those who know their need, it is a word of hope and comfort; for those who fancy themselves free and autonomous, it is an offense and a challenge to reevaluate their true condition. Just as the Missionaries were no doubt riled by Paul's words, so also the contemporary religious reader may find a stumbling block in Paul's apocalyptic picture of redemption.

2. An apocalyptic picture it is, for according to this passage—which aptly summarizes the overall message of the letter—we are rescued from bondage by a divine act of intervention. In the fullness of time, God sent the Son into the world to redeem us. Everything, therefore, depends on God's timing, God's initiative, and God's powerful act of deliverance. The Son did not come to give us better information about God and thereby to lead us progressively to a knowledge of the truth; rather, the Son came to die for us and set us free (cf. 3:13-14). Consequently, any preaching that trumpets "humanity come of age" or implies an evolutionary view of Christianity as a more advanced form of religion has totally misconstrued Paul's message. The misunderstanding is perhaps encouraged by Paul's figurative illustration about a minor heir who eventually receives an inheritance. As we have seen, however, the illustration is being used to make two points: The Galatians used to be in slavery, and that slavery was only a temporary state, abolished by God's act of deliverance at a time appointed by God. There is actually some tension between the figurative story and Paul's application of it; therefore, the emphasis in preaching on the text should be on Paul's application (4:3-7) rather than on the illustration (4:1-2). Anyone who starts with 4:1-2 and interprets the passage to speak of a human development toward higher knowledge or faith has twisted the text.

3. The rhetorical climax of the passage comes in 4:6-7, as Paul describes the experience of the Spirit in the hearts of the Galatians. The Spirit-inspired utterance acclaiming God as "Abba" is the sign confirming that they now enjoy an intimacy with God that comes only through being part of God's family. They have been adopted by God and, therefore, enjoy all that rightfully belongs to God's children.

Once again, as in 3:1-5, we see that Paul does not try to convince the Galatians that they possess the Spirit; rather, the Spirit is the datum from which Paul argues. The Spirit is palpably, audibly present in their midst, and it serves as proof of their identity as "sons of God." Since this designation was reserved in the Old Testament for Israel (see the Commentary on 3:26), Paul is affirming that the Gentile Galatians have now entered covenant relation with God as members of God's family. (Here as throughout 3:1–5:1 he is arguing that they need not undergo circumcision to secure this status.) At the same time, in view of Paul's radical analysis of universal human bondage, it should be clearly understood that 4:6-7 does not suggest any privileged status for Jewish believers. They, like the Gentile Galatians, are adopted children. Augustine perceptively suggests that it is precisely for this reason that Paul has reported the spirit-inspired cry "Abba, Father" in both Aramaic and Greek: "Now we see that he has elegantly, and not without reason, put together words from two languages signifying the same thing because of the whole people, which has been called from Jews and Gentiles into the unity of faith."[203] If we are right in seeing this cry to God the Father as a baptismal experience, then it is the common ground for all believers; their identity as God's children and their unity in Christ are both confirmed by the Spirit in their hearts.

4. In our time, it is necessary to reflect carefully on the image of God as "Father" in this passage,[204] for some theologians have argued that this image reinforces oppressive patriarchal social structures. Furthermore, it is sometimes suggested that Paul's "Father" language excludes or alienates those whose own human fathers have been cruel or absent. In response to these concerns, three points should be kept clearly in mind by the interpreter of Gal 4:6.

First, the Jewish and Christian theological traditions, interpreted rightly, have not understood God as gendered: God, who dwells in unapproachable light, transcends such anthropomorphic categories. One consequence of Israel's prohibition of making idols and artistic depictions of God is that God cannot be crudely rendered as male or female. The New Testament's "Father" imagery must be interpreted with deference to this fundamental rule of theological grammar. God—contrary to the theories of Freud and Feuerbach—is not merely a projection of our human fathers, real or fantasized. Instead, human fatherhood is a distant and broken approximation of the true fatherhood that we learn about in Scripture's story of God's creative and loving care for us. Thus the image of God as Father provides the norm by which all human conceptions of fatherhood may be judged and healed.

Second, the consistent function of Paul's use of the image of God as Father is to emphasize that God is the giver of a promised inheritance. Thus the "Father" language highlights God's generous and loving provision for a beloved people. As Marianne Meye Thompson writes,

---

203. Augustine *Galatians* 31 [IB.4.6], cited in Mark J. Edwards, ed., *Galatians, Ephesians, Philippians,* Ancient Christian Commentary on Scripture, vol. 8 (Downers Grover, Ill.: InterVarsity, 1999) 57.

204. For a full, theologically perceptive discussion of the issues, see Marianne Meye Thompson, *The Promise of the Father: Jesus and God in the New Testament* (Louisville: Westminster/John Knox, 2000).

"Father will become a dysfunctional metaphor if we insist on the form of the term without lodging it in the biblical narrative of God's faithfulness, care and provision and if we abstract it from the particular promises made to and through Jesus, the Son, in whom and through whom the faithful have their inheritance."[205]

Third, because the promised inheritance provided by God the Father has now been graciously extended to Gentiles in Christ, the "fatherhood" of God serves as a basis for Paul to assert our common belonging to God's family. Jews and Gentiles alike have been "adopted" by God's elective grace and, therefore, can now address the one God as Father. In Gal 4:6, the cry, "Abba, Father," serves to confirm our status as God's children and thereby to bring reassurance of the freedom and blessings that we enjoy. Thus there is no distinction within God's adoptive family, and we should receive one another as brothers and sisters.

These are the central themes that should be developed in any homiletical reflection on the Father image in this passage. Paul is not reinforcing some authoritarian claim about God or about church hierarchy. Rather, he is assuring the Galatians that they can resist the authoritarian claims of the Missionaries precisely because their status as God's children is already confirmed by the Spirit.

All of this suggests that interpretation of the passage should celebrate a joyous confidence in our relation with God and with one another. This is not a relation grounded merely in our common humanity; it is a relationship created by the Spirit of Christ (4:6) in the community of baptized believers who have now been "known by God" (4:9). Within that community, to address God as "Father" is not to claim sentimental intimacy, but rather to acknowledge God as the giver of blessings and the ground of our unity.

5. The trouble is that even those who have received the Spirit can—perplexingly—fall back into slavery. We can make choices that turn us away from the grace of God to embrace once again our former state of bondage. We may forget that we are living in the fullness of time and relapse into living as though God had not sent the Son to set us free. Therefore, Paul ends this section of the letter with a rebuke (4:8-11). Interpreters who seek to hear the text's message will not fail to hear a word of warning for the church in our time also.

The full force of Paul's message comes through when we realize that the Galatians were not relapsing into paganism as such. They were considering a step that was presented to them as a higher and more spiritual form of the gospel that they had already accepted through Paul's preaching. They were not rejecting the gospel but seeking to improve upon it. But Paul diagnoses the circumcision gospel as a step back into human religiosity. There is no way, he insists, to add more deluxe or advanced features to the gospel of the cross. In 4:10, therefore, he links Judaism to pagan religion by positing a phenomenological parallelism between Judaism's observance of a calendar of holy feasts and the pagan veneration of the natural and celestial worlds. (This is Paul in his most "radical Protestant" mode. Elsewhere he is less unremitting on the question of feasts; see Rom 14:5-6 and the reference to Pentecost in 1 Cor 16:8.)

In our time, few Christians will be inclined to regard Christian faith as a preliminary step toward the keeping of Jewish Law and festivals, but there are many other forms of "spirituality" being marketed as more refined understandings of religion that somehow go beyond the primitive particularity of Paul's gospel. Some of these spiritualities claim to be Christian, and others do not. Many books on "New Age" religion now flooding popular bookstores exemplify this tendency. From the prophetic Pauline point of view, these "New Age" approaches to spirituality are "weak and beggarly" attempts to manipulate God or to find God within oneself; therefore, all of them would simply lead back into slavery to the elements of the natural world. That world is God's good creation, but when human beings worship the creation—including the human self—rather than the Creator, they fall into blindness (Rom 1:18-25) and slavery.

205. Ibid., xxx.

Most of all, such false worship leads into pathetic fixation on our own spirituality rather than on what God has done once and for all through Jesus Christ.

Paul looks at the Galatians with incredulity. They have been rescued from slavery to the elements of nature by Jesus Christ, and now they are "turning back" to slavery again (4:9). It is as though he is watching a bizarre and tragic film in which an abused adolescent, having been rescued from the clutches of the villain, spurns the rescuer and falls into another abusive relationship. Paul implores the Galatians to recognize what time it is: The fullness of time for redemption has come. Therefore, they must not run the film backward, not retrogress to an earlier sequence; instead, they should accept the freedom God has given them.

The task of the preacher working with this text is to reflect deeply on the ways in which our congregations today unaccountably reject God's gift of adoption and liberation, choosing instead familiar destructive patterns of life and religiosity. Then, after identifying such analogies and patterns, our next task is to reproclaim the good news of 4:3-7: God has sent the Son to set us free and has given us the Spirit as a sign that we are children and heirs of God.

GALATIANS 4:12-20, AN APPEAL TO RESTORE A RUPTURED RELATIONSHIP

NIV

[12]I plead with you, brothers, become like me, for I became like you. You have done me no wrong. [13]As you know, it was because of an illness that I first preached the gospel to you. [14]Even though my illness was a trial to you, you did not treat me with contempt or scorn. Instead, you welcomed me as if I were an angel of God, as if I were Christ Jesus himself. [15]What has happened to all your joy? I can testify that, if you could have done so, you would have torn out your eyes and given them to me. [16]Have I now become your enemy by telling you the truth?

[17]Those people are zealous to win you over, but for no good. What they want is to alienate you ⌊from us⌋, so that you may be zealous for them. [18]It is fine to be zealous, provided the purpose is good, and to be so always and not just when I am with you. [19]My dear children, for whom I am again in the pains of childbirth until Christ is formed in you, [20]how I wish I could be with you now and change my tone, because I am perplexed about you!

NRSV

12Friends,[a] I beg you, become as I am, for I also have become as you are. You have done me no wrong. [13]You know that it was because of a physical infirmity that I first announced the gospel to you; [14]though my condition put you to the test, you did not scorn or despise me, but welcomed me as an angel of God, as Christ Jesus. [15]What has become of the goodwill you felt? For I testify that, had it been possible, you would have torn out your eyes and given them to me. [16]Have I now become your enemy by telling you the truth? [17]They make much of you, but for no good purpose; they want to exclude you, so that you may make much of them. [18]It is good to be made much of for a good purpose at all times, and not only when I am present with you. [19]My little children, for whom I am again in the pain of childbirth until Christ is formed in you, [20]I wish I were present with you now and could change my tone, for I am perplexed about you.

[a] Gk Brothers

COMMENTARY

Paul now makes an appeal of a different kind by reminding the Galatians of their earlier warm relationship with him. He passionately urges them not to forsake the bond that they once shared. In the course of this argument, he unfavorably characterizes the motives of the rival Missionaries and employs a striking metaphor, comparing himself to a mother in childbirth. He concludes the section with a wish that he could be present with the Galatians in person, not merely through the medium of a letter.

This unit is notoriously difficult to interpret. There are three reasons for its difficulty: (1) Paul is emotionally agitated as he writes, and the discussion is somewhat disjointed; (2) he alludes briefly to events well known to the Galatians but unknown to us; (3) he employs rhetorical *topoi* and conventional expressions that are unfamiliar to us. Taken together, these factors—especially the second—require us to do some guesswork in order to read the passage. Some questions here can never be resolved with certainty. Still, the overall point is clear: Paul, like an aggrieved mother, sees his children going astray and implores them to remember their birth and early upbringing.

4:12. For the first time in the letter, Paul addresses the Galatians with a direct imperative. This imperative is, however, enigmatic. In what way does Paul want the Galatians to be like him? Paul has deliberately formulated his directive as a paradox: Because he has previously become like the Galatians, they should now become like him.

Elsewhere, Paul frequently presents himself as an example to be imitated (1 Cor 4:16; 11:1; Phil 3:17; 1 Thess 1:6; 2:14; 2 Thess 3:7, 9). This may strike some readers today as strangely immodest, but in the ancient world it was commonplace. The philosopher or moral teacher was expected to provide a model for followers to emulate, because wisdom was embodied in a way of life. In most of Paul's imitation passages, he urges his readers to be conformed to Christ's example of self-sacrificial suffering for the sake of others, as reflected in the apostle's own conduct.

In 4:12, though, Paul gives the imitation motif a different twist. When he says, "I have become as you are," he is referring to his own decision to reject the practices of Torah observance and live like a Gentile. His reason for this decision is explained in 1 Cor 9:21: "To those outside the Law I became as one outside the Law . . . so that I might win those outside the Law" (NRSV). For the sake of his mission as apostle to the Gentiles,

he "tore down" the barriers between Jew and Gentile (2:18) and adopted, in effect, a Gentile way of life. Earlier in the letter he has narrated the outworking of this decision in his account of the controversy at Antioch; he ate with Gentiles and took a stand against other Jewish Christians who refused to do so (2:11-14).

Ironically, the Galatians—the Gentiles whose non-Law-observant way of life Paul had adopted—were now starting to take on Jewish Law observance. Paul, therefore, appeals to them passionately ("I beg you") to halt this course of action and to imitate him in living a life that is not subject to the Law.

If the Galatians persist in coming under the Law, not only will they be returning to slavery, but also they will inflict a wrong on Paul by undoing his apostolic work (v. 11). In the past, the Galatians never inflicted injury on him, as he reminds them in v. 12b. This reminder belongs, as Betz has suggested, to a cluster of motifs in the passage that echo common Hellenistic ideas about friendship.[206] It was a commonplace maxim of Hellenistic philosophy that friends can have confidence that they will do no harm to one another.

4:13-14. In fact, when Paul first came to the Galatians' communities, they had received him gladly, even though he was enduring physical suffering. Far from wronging him, they took him in and accepted the gospel that he brought them.

The events to which Paul alludes in this verse remain concealed in the mists of history. He says that it was because of "weakness of the flesh" that he first proclaimed the gospel to them. This has usually been interpreted (as in the NIV) as a reference to some sort of illness, but the NRSV's more general translation is closer to the meaning of the Greek text. A good case can be made that Paul is referring to the scars and injuries that he sustained through persecution (cf. 6:17; Acts 14:19; 2 Cor 6:4-5; 11:23-25).[207] This hypothesis fits well with the suggestion that the visible portrayal of the crucifixion to which Paul refers in 3:1 may have been in fact a display of his own

206. H. D. Betz, *Galatians: A Commentary on Paul's Letter to the Churches in Galatia,* Hermeneia (Philadelphia: Fortress, 1979) 220-37.

207. A. J. Goddard and S. A. Cummins, "Ill or Ill-Treated? Conflict and Persecution as the Context of Paul's Original Ministry in Galatia (Galatians 4.12-20)," *JSNT* 52 (1993) 93-126. In support of this interpretation they cite a number of the Church Fathers, such as Chrysostom, Theodore of Mopsuestia, Theodoret of Cyrus, and Augustine, as well as Thomas Aquinas and Martin Luther (ibid., 95n. 7).

wounds, which he later calls "the marks of Jesus" (6:17). Verse 13 may be correlated in some way with Paul's reference in 2 Cor 12:7 to a "thorn in the flesh," through which he came to learn that God's power is "made perfect in *weakness*" (ἀσθένεια *astheneia*, 2 Cor 12:9)—the same word that appears here. Contrary to popular supposition, this "thorn in the flesh," rather than referring to some sort of chronic illness, may also be directly linked to the effects of persecution, as 2 Cor 12:10 suggests.

Whatever the reason, Paul's physical condition required him to travel to Galatia (to recuperate from being flogged, beaten, or stoned?), with the result that he brought the gospel to the Galatians for the first time. Others may have beaten him up, but the Galatians received him graciously. Indeed, despite the repugnance of his physical condition—whatever it was—they received him as though he were a heavenly messenger (cf. 1:8), as though he were Jesus Christ himself. This last detail may suggest once again that the apostle's wounds marked him as Christ's messenger, "carrying in the body the death of Jesus, so that the life of Jesus may also be made visible in our bodies" (2 Cor 4:10 NRSV). The Galatians could easily have been repelled by Paul's fleshly affliction (it was a "trial" to them), but they did not "scorn or despise" him. The first of these verbs (ἐξουθενέω *exoutheneō*) is, interestingly, used several times in the NT to refer to the contemptuous treatment Jesus received during his passion (Mark 9:12; Luke 23:11; Acts 4:11; cf. 1 Cor 1:28). Perhaps more significantly, the same verb is also used in Paul's account of what his detractors at Corinth said about him: "his bodily presence is *weak* and his speech *contemptible* [ἐξουθενημένος *exouthenēmenos*]" (2 Cor 10:10 NRSV, italics added). The second verb in v. 14*a*, ἐκπτύω (*ekptyō*), refers literally to the act of spitting at someone. It can be understood metaphorically to mean "to despise," or it could have its literal sense here. In antiquity, it was commonly thought that one could ward off the effects of the "evil eye" or of demonic influence by spitting three times.[208] It is impossible to tell from Paul's brief reference whether he intends the verb literally or metaphorically. In either case, he

is describing something that the Galatians did *not* do; rather than despising Paul, they saw through the outward affliction and received him with joy.

4:15. In the light of this memory of his former warm reception in Galatia, Paul now asks them a pointed question, literally, "Where then is your blessing?" (not, as in the NIV, "joy"). Despite the opinion of many commentators to the contrary, the term μακαρισμός (*makarismos*) does not refer to a state of blessedness, but to a concretely pronounced blessing, as it does in Rom 4:6, 9, the only other place where Paul uses the word. Paul is not asking the Galatians what happened to the feeling of blessedness they used to have; rather, he is asking what happened to the word of blessing they once pronounced on him. Why are they now speaking criticism of him rather than blessing him? (The NRSV's paraphrase gets closer to this sense.) This is completely in line with the thought of the passage, which focuses on how the Galatians' attitudes toward Paul have changed.

Once they held Paul in such high esteem that they would have torn out their own eyes for his sake. This gruesome image has given rise to speculation that Paul's "weakness of the flesh" was some sort of eye disease. Betz has argued persuasively, however, that Paul "alludes to a literary motif which must have been almost proverbial in his time." He cites a story from Lucian's *Toxaris* in which Dandamis negotiates the release of his friend Amizoces from captivity by sacrificing his own eyes.[209] The point is not that Paul is alluding specifically to this story but that he is employing a proverbial motif. It is as though he had said—to employ an idiom more familiar in our culture—"You would have given your right arm for me." This would not, of course, necessarily indicate that there was anything wrong with the speaker's arm; it is simply a figurative way of describing a deep and committed friendship.

4:16. All of that has now changed, however. As a result of the teaching of the Missionaries, the Galatians have begun to see Paul not as a friend but as an "enemy."[210] Whether this is really what they thought or whether this is what Paul expects them to think after reading this confron-

208. J. D. G. Dunn, *The Epistle to the Galatians*, Black's NT Commentary (Peabody, Mass.: Hendrickson, 1993) 234.

209. H. D. Betz, *Galatians: A Commentary on Paul's Letter to the Churches in Galatia*, Hermeneia (Philadelphia: Fortress, 1979) 228, referring to Lucian *Toxaris* 40-41.

210. The term "enemy" is explicitly applied to Paul in the later Pseudo-Clementine literature. See *Ep. Petr.* 2.3.

tational letter is impossible to say. Most significant is the last phrase of his sentence: "by telling you the truth." Paul portrays himself as a straight-shooting truth teller. He has insisted that his Law-free gospel is God's truth. It came by revelation (1:11-12), and Paul will not compromise the truth for any reason (2:5). The "truth of the gospel" is inextricably bound up with the vision of one table where Jews and Gentiles sit together in Christ without being divided by the barriers of the Law (2:14). Perhaps the Missionaries, on the other hand, have persuaded the Galatians that Paul has betrayed them by preaching a watered-down gospel that lacked the full benefit of circumcision and Torah observance. If so, Paul now challenges the Missionaries' motives for alienating the affections of the Galatians away from him. He, Paul, tells the truth, whereas they are manipulators and flatterers who are preventing the Galatians from living in the truth (5:7).

4:17-18. That v. 16 reflects a direct accusation of the Missionaries is suggested by the way Paul moves seamlessly into v. 17 without even naming his adversaries. It was clear enough to the Galatians whom he meant. The verb ζηλόω (zēloō), which appears three times in these verses, is ambiguous. It can mean "to desire earnestly"; therefore, it can be used with connotations of eagerly courting someone's favor, as in a romantic relationship.[211] Alternatively, it can have a religious sense, "to be zealous for God" (cf. 1:14). Finally, it can have a pejorative sense, "to be jealous or envious." The last of these meanings makes no sense in the present context, but it is likely that Paul is making a clever play on the first two. The primary meaning is the first sense: The Missionaries are "courting" the Galatians to win them over (the NIV supplies this idea). At the same time, Paul's choice of the verb zēloō is ironically appropriate, because the Missionaries pride themselves on their zeal for the Law, as Paul did also during his former life in Judaism (1:13-14). They would probably describe their courtship of the Galatians as an expression of their religious zeal.

Paul asserts, however, that this courting is a form of flattery and a devious exercise of power. Their ulterior motive, as Paul sees it, is to shut the Galatians out in order that the Galatians in turn might court them. This seems like a puzzling claim on the surface. Some commentators, followed by the NIV, suppose that the motive ascribed to the Missionaries is to lock the Galatians away from Paul, so as to have all the attention for themselves. This interpretation, however, requires an odd translation of the verb "to shut out" (ἐκκλείω ekkleiō; rendered "alienate" by the NIV), and it also requires the insertion of the words "from us," which are not in the Greek text. A better explanation is provided by the scenario Paul has already described at Antioch: The Jewish Christians withdraw from fellowship with Gentile Christians, shutting them out in order to put pressure on them to "Judaize" (2:11-14). As already suggested, Paul saw in that situation an analogy to the present crisis in Galatia (see the Commentary on 2:11-21). Paul looks at the Galatian situation with psychological realism and sees that the exclusivity of the Jewish-Christian Missionaries makes their religious "club" seem highly desirable to those who are on the outside. If the Galatians want to join the in group, they must come under the Missionaries' sphere of influence by accepting circumcision.[212]

Thus the Missionaries' "zeal" for the Galatians is "for no good purpose." In principle, Paul has no objection to other teachers coming on the scene for a good cause (v. 18; cf. the case of Apollos in Corinth, 1 Cor 3:5-9); he need not monitor everything that happens in his absence. As Betz notes, it is one of the conventions of the friendship *topos* that "true friendship does not change even when the friends are separated."[213] In this case, however, Paul thinks that the Galatians are falling for a false courtship by seducers who will lead them away not only from their relationship with him, but also from the gospel altogether.

4:19. This line of thought leads to Paul's anguished outcry. He addresses the Galatians fondly as his "children." In other letters, Paul speaks of his relation to his communities as being like that of a father to his children (e.g., 1 Cor 4:14-15; 1 Thess 2:11-12). But here he gives the

---

211. Betz, *Galatians,* 229, suggests that the term can also be used "to describe the sincere and deep concern one friend has for another."

212. For a helpful discussion, see J. D. G. Dunn, *The Epistle to the Galatians,* Black's NT Commentary (Peabody, Mass.: Hendrickson, 1993) 238.

213. Betz, *Galatians,* 232.

parental metaphor a surprising spin. As he sees the Galatians turning back into their former state of slavery, he fears that he will have to start all over with them. It is as though they had never been born into their new life in Christ, or as though the birth process was somehow incomplete. Thus Paul pictures himself as a mother again in labor pains, struggling to give birth to the Galatians once again.[214] The image suggests both the futility of the Galatians' reversion to life under the στοιχεῖα (stoicheia) and the pain that Paul experiences as he tries to wrest them back into the sphere of Christ's lordship.

Beverly Gaventa, observing that "birth pangs" is a stock image in Jewish and Christian apocalyptic texts for the suffering that accompanies God's eschatological action of bringing the new age into being (e.g., *1 Enoch* 62:4; *2 Apoc Bar* 56:6; 4 Ezra 4:2; 1QH 3.7-10; Mark 13:8; Rom 8:22; 1 Thess 5:3; Rev 12:2), has proposed that Paul sees his "birthing" of the Galatians as a part of the cosmic travail at the turn of the ages: "Paul's anguish . . . reflects the anguish of the whole created order as it awaits the fulfillment of God's action in Jesus Christ."[215] The apostolic "labor" is part of the eschatological conflict whereby God is claiming and redeeming the world. The Galatians find themselves in the push and pull of this cosmic struggle.

In v. 19*b*, however, as Gaventa also shows, Paul mutates the metaphor into something else: "until Christ is formed in you." If he had wanted to carry the birthing image through consistently, he would have had to say something like "until you are born anew in Christ." The fact that Paul transmutes his own metaphor in midsentence suggests that he has something else in view here. He is not merely concerned about the rebirth of the Galatians as individuals; rather, his vision is for the community as a whole to take on the character of Christ. The pronoun "you" is plural, and the phrase ἐν ὑμῖν (*en hymin*) is best translated not as "in (each one of) you" but rather as "among you, in your midst."[216] The apostle's

apocalyptic birth pangs are bringing forth a new community formed in the image of Jesus Christ; Christ will live in the community just as he lives in Paul (2:20; cf. the idea of conformity to Christ in Rom 8:29). Elsewhere, Paul will express this idea by using the image of the "body of Christ" (Rom 12:4-5; 1 Cor 12:12, 27). The dynamic equation between Christ and community has already anchored the exegetical argument that Paul makes in 3:16, 29: The christologically defined "seed" turns out to include all who belong to Christ. In 4:19, however, Paul runs the equation the other way: As the eschatological community is birthed into the world, it takes the form of Christ. These metaphors are bold and fantastic, but Paul finds no other way to make his radical claim with its full force.

4:20. For the present, however, Paul feels powerless, at such a distance, to help the Galatians in the midst of this struggle. He longs to be with them, but he cannot be. (In contrast to other letters, he makes no mention of a planned future visit; the comparison to 1 Cor 4:14-21 is particularly striking.) The expression translated "change my tone" is literally "change my voice." This might refer to Paul's wish to modulate his tone of voice into a gentler sound in contrast to the harsh rebuke of the present letter (1:6-9; 3:1-5; 4:8-11; cf. 5:12). Another possible interpretation is that he wishes to exchange the merely written language of the letter for a live personal conversation with the Galatians, preferring oral encounter to written text.

Paul brings the unit to an end on a note of helpless puzzlement, recapitulating the attitude of v. 11. The Galatians' rejection of the previously warm relationship with their apostle has left him stunned and perplexed. "Paul acts as if he has run out of arguments."[217] Of course, that is not the case. This is a rhetorical device to convey Paul's shock at the Galatians' abandonment of the relationship with the apostle who had previously given them birth.

The central idea of vv. 12-20, then, is that the Galatians have ruptured their relationship with Paul. They have been led astray by the false and deceptive tactics of the Missionaries, and they have abandoned their first loyalty. Paul appeals to

214. On this metaphor and the implications that follow from it, see B. R. Gaventa, "The Maternity of Paul: An Exegetical Study of Galatians 4:19," in *The Conversation Continues: Studies in Paul and John in Honor of J. Louis Martyn,* ed. R. T. Fortna and B. R. Gaventa (Nashville: Abingdon, 1990) 189-201.

215. Ibid., 194. Martyn suggests that Isa 45:7-11 is the source behind Paul's use of the childbirth imagery. See J. L. Martyn, *Galatians,* AB 33A (New York: Doubleday, 1997) 427-29.

216. Gaventa, "The Maternity of Paul," 196. Martyn, *Galatians,* 424, translates it, for emphasis, "until Christ is formed in your congregations."

217. Betz, *Galatians,* 237. This rhetorical device is known as *dubitatio.*

them to reaffirm their original bond with him by becoming as he is: free from the Law. In the course of making this argument, he employs both traditional friendship motifs and the familial metaphor of a mother giving birth to children. This appeal is designed to renew their personal adherence to the relationship with him. If Paul's personal appeal succeeds, then the other arguments in the letter—based on experience (3:1-5; 4:1-11) and Scripture (3:6-29; 4:21–5:1)—can do their work in due course.

REFLECTIONS

1. The most striking feature of this passage is its personal pathos. After lengthy rational argumentation, Paul plays the card of an appeal to emotion. In addition to all the reasons he has given the Galatians for rejecting circumcision, Paul now makes a heartfelt appeal to personal loyalty. If they have any decency, Paul implies—if they are not fickle friends—they will stand with Paul in this controversy.

What are we to make of this sort of argument? The first reaction of many readers will be to see it as shameless manipulation, a kind of emotional blackmail. Could a preacher today legitimately confront a polarizing issue in the church by appealing in a similar way to the personal loyalty of his or her congregation? Would this not be seen as desperate special pleading?

Probably so. We must recognize first of all that the sort of argument Paul makes in 4:12-20, an argument from pathos, was a familiar type of rhetoric in the ancient Mediterranean world. Audiences and readers expected this sort of appeal, and it would not have grated on their sensibilities in the same way it would on the sensibilities of a congregation in our time. Paul was artfully employing conventions of discourse in his culture. We must do the same thing in ours. We should not slavishly imitate Paul's rhetoric; rather, we must find ways of making our appeal for the gospel within genres that are rhetorically persuasive for our culture.

Second, we should note that this appeal to pathos is only a brief interlude embedded within an extended theological argument. It is not the whole argument; rather, it provides an affective appeal for the readers to weigh seriously what Paul is saying in the rest of the letter.

Finally, with these due cautions, it is worth observing that Paul did believe passionately that the gospel created deep personal relationships between believers. The Galatians, to whom Paul writes, are not merely an audience to be manipulated, not a "market" for a commodity he is selling. Rather, they are his brothers and sisters. Their earlier gratitude to him for bringing them the gospel forged a bond of love between them. Paul is genuinely distraught over the prospect of seeing that bond broken, and he cares urgently about the fate of his "children." All of this provides us with an appealing model for relationships in Christ. Are we a people whose common joy in the gospel would lead us to tear out our eyes for one another—or, if we prefer, give our right arms for one another? Or have we been courted and seduced, for no good purpose, by missionaries of a consumerism that would prefer to keep us apart and aloof?

2. Paul's appeal to the Galatians to imitate his example (4:12) should provoke sustained reflection. The ancient Mediterranean world took role modeling very seriously. To assess the meaning or truth of any philosophy, it was necessary to examine the lives of its exponents. This cultural assumption was carried over into the early church; the meaning of the gospel was to be embodied in the lives of the community's leaders. For that reason, Paul's self-depiction in the first two chapters of Galatians provides the crucial background to the exhortation of 4:12; Paul has modeled a life set free from the Law, a life willing to sacrifice all claims of racial or ethnic privilege for the truth of a gospel that calls Jews and Gentiles together at one table. That is the example he holds before the Galatians' eyes.

All of this poses an acute question for us: To whom do we look for role models who exemplify the truth of the gospel? To be sure, the canonical New Testament narrates the stories of apostles and saints who stand as permanent models for us. But we also need living embodiments of the gospel in our own time, real people in our communities to whom we can point and say, "*There* is what a life lived faithfully in Christ looks like." It will not do simply to point to faraway saints like Mother Teresa; one task of the church's ministry is to identify and acknowledge those women and men in our midst who embody the gospel. This may appear disturbingly antidemocratic, because it necessarily implies that some people among us know better than others how to practice the faith. Christian fidelity is not just a matter of untutored intuition so that everybody's opinion about it is of equal worth; rather, discipleship is a craft that must be learned from others with superior knowledge and experience. Like the Galatians, who were faced with a choice between Paul's example and the teaching of the Missionaries, we must learn to choose our role models wisely.

3. The need for such discernment leads us into reflection about the criteria we employ to identify role models who embody the gospel. The question was posed sharply in a famous essay by Plutarch: How do we tell a flatterer from a friend?[218] Paul's assertion that he tells the truth (4:16) is of no help, since both parties would make similar claims. The present passage, being an emotional appeal, does not explicitly address this problem, but it does contain a couple of hints.

First, if it is true that Paul's "weakness of the flesh" is an allusion to injuries inflicted upon him as a result of his preaching the gospel, then there is a correspondence between suffering and truth (see the Commentary on 4:13-14). The one who comes as an authentic messenger of Jesus Christ is likely to share in Christ's suffering. This is not an explicit theme of Gal 4:12-20, but it is characteristic of Paul's thought (see, e.g., Rom 8:17, 22-23; 1 Cor 4:9-13; 2 Cor 4:7-12; 6:1-12; 11:16–12:10; Phil 1:27-30). This is a paradox, but it is grounded in the proclamation of a crucified messiah.

Second, one attribute of false friends is described in 4:17: The Missionaries simultaneously court the Galatians and exclude them from the circle of the Torah-observant in group. Thus they appeal to the upwardly mobile vanity that is satirized by Groucho Marx's well-known quip: "I wouldn't join any club that would have me as a member." True friends and true messengers of the gospel do not play such exclusive games. The good news of Jesus Christ comes to us as we are, without entrance requirements and strings attached, without playing on our vanity.

4. Finally, Paul's use of the apocalyptic metaphor of "birth pangs" (4:19) suggests that something more than a ruptured friendship is at stake here. The "birthing" of the Galatian congregations was a part of God's plan to bring a new world into being, a "new creation" in which neither circumcision nor uncircumcision matters (3:28; 6:15). This puts the personal appeal of this passage in its proper cosmic context. Whatever we may feel about personal ties and loyalties, we must see the birth and life of our congregations within God's eschatological design for the redemption of the world. The aim of Paul's missionary labors was to see Christ formed in human communities of love that transcended old cultural boundaries. Wherever the church acts in ways that reinstate such cultural and ethnic boundaries, the new creation is blocked and denied, but God will continue to find ways to bring it to birth, perhaps painfully, in our midst.

218. Plutarch, *How to Tell a Flatterer from a Friend,* in *Plutarch's Moralia I,* trans. F. C. Babbitt, LCL (Cambridge, Mass.: Harvard University Press, 1927).

GALATIANS 4:21–5:1, AN ALLEGORY OF SLAVERY AND FREEDOM

NIV

21Tell me, you who want to be under the law, are you not aware of what the law says? 22For it is written that Abraham had two sons, one by the slave woman and the other by the free woman. 23His son by the slave woman was born in the ordinary way; but his son by the free woman was born as the result of a promise.

24These things may be taken figuratively, for the women represent two covenants. One covenant is from Mount Sinai and bears children who are to be slaves: This is Hagar. 25Now Hagar stands for Mount Sinai in Arabia and corresponds to the present city of Jerusalem, because she is in slavery with her children. 26But the Jerusalem that is above is free, and she is our mother. 27For it is written:

"Be glad, O barren woman,
　who bears no children;
break forth and cry aloud,
　you who have no labor pains;
because more are the children of the desolate
　　woman
　than of her who has a husband."*a*

28Now you, brothers, like Isaac, are children of promise. 29At that time the son born in the ordinary way persecuted the son born by the power of the Spirit. It is the same now. 30But what does the Scripture say? "Get rid of the slave woman and her son, for the slave woman's son will never share in the inheritance with the free woman's son."*b* 31Therefore, brothers, we are not children of the slave woman, but of the free woman.

5 It is for freedom that Christ has set us free. Stand firm, then, and do not let yourselves be burdened again by a yoke of slavery.

a27 Isaiah 54:1　　*b30* Gen. 21:10

NRSV

21Tell me, you who desire to be subject to the law, will you not listen to the law? 22For it is written that Abraham had two sons, one by a slave woman and the other by a free woman. 23One, the child of the slave, was born according to the flesh; the other, the child of the free woman, was born through the promise. 24Now this is an allegory: these women are two covenants. One woman, in fact, is Hagar, from Mount Sinai, bearing children for slavery. 25Now Hagar is Mount Sinai in Arabia*a* and corresponds to the present Jerusalem, for she is in slavery with her children. 26But the other woman corresponds to the Jerusalem above; she is free, and she is our mother. 27For it is written,

"Rejoice, you childless one, you who bear
　　no children,
　burst into song and shout, you who
　　endure no birthpangs;
for the children of the desolate woman are
　　more numerous
　than the children of the one who is
　　married."

28Now you,*b* my friends,*c* are children of the promise, like Isaac. 29But just as at that time the child who was born according to the flesh persecuted the child who was born according to the Spirit, so it is now also. 30But what does the scripture say? "Drive out the slave and her child; for the child of the slave will not share the inheritance with the child of the free woman." 31So then, friends,*c* we are children, not of the slave but of the free woman.

5 1For freedom Christ has set us free. Stand firm, therefore, and do not submit again to a yoke of slavery.

a Other ancient authorities read *For Sinai is a mountain in Arabia*
b Other ancient authorities read *we*　　*c* Gk *brothers*

COMMENTARY

Paul now brings his counterarguments against the rival Missionaries to a rhetorical climax. As we have seen, the central section of Galatians (3:1–5:1) consists of a series of arguments designed to negate the influence of these interlopers and to recall the Galatians to the Law-free gospel Paul had orginally preached to them. The personal appeal of 4:12-20 creates an emotional change of pace and invites the Galatians to reaffirm their intimate tie with Paul. The final argument of this section (4:21–5:1), then, is the *pièce de résistance,* designed to win the readers over decisively by demonstrating that the Law-free mission to the Gentiles is in fact prefigured in the Torah itself— indeed, prefigured by the very narrative on which the Missionaries have based their teaching. In the light of this demonstration, Paul concludes with a rallying cry, summoning the Galatians to stand fast in the freedom that Christ has given them (5:1).

In reading 4:21–5:1, it is of utmost importance to recognize that Paul's polemic is not directed against Jews or Judaism as such. Rather, the targets are the Jewish-*Christian* Missionaries who are disrupting his Gentile churches. This has important implications for the interpretation of the "two covenants" in this passage.

4:21. Paul goes on the offensive, taking the battle to the Missionaries' home turf. "All right," he says, "you Galatians want to be under the Law? I can play that game. Listen to what the Law says." The expression "under the Law" has appeared earlier in the argument with decidedly negative connotations. To be "under the Law" is to be in a state of confinement (3:23) from which one needs to be liberated (4:5; cf. 5:18). Thus Paul's choice of words here is laden with sarcasm. The Galatians are showing, by their susceptibility to the Missionaries' message, that they find the Law attractive and want to come under its control (4:8-11). Paul, therefore, announces his intention to show them that even the Law supports his gospel rather than the one offered by the Missionaries.

In the Greek, v. 21*b* says, literally, "Do you not hear the Law?" (thus the NRSV is closer than the NIV to the original sense of the verse: It is a matter of attentive listening). There may be an ironic echo here of the Shema (Deut 6:4): "*Hear,* O Israel. . . ." In the OT, hearing and obedience are closely linked. In the present passage, Paul wants to force the Galatians to hear the story afresh; if they do, they will receive direction about what to do. His opening question

(v. 21) points toward the climactic Scripture quotation in v. 30, which is introduced by the formula, "What does the Scripture say?" If the Galatians listen to what the Law actually says, they will hear it speaking the words "Throw out the slave woman and her child." The purpose of this paragraph is to prepare them to interpret this directive properly.

The fact that Paul can refer to the story of Abraham's two sons (Genesis 16–21) as "the Law" shows that he uses the term broadly; it includes OT narrative as well as the commandments of the Sinaitic covenant (cf. 1 Cor 14:21, where Paul introduces a quotation from Isaiah as something written in the Law). In vv. 21 and 30, the terms "Law" and "Scripture" appear to be used synonymously.

4:22. Rather than actually quoting the text of Genesis at this point, Paul gives a concise summary of the narrative. The allusive manner in which he does so suggests that the Galatians must be familiar with the story already. He names neither Ishmael nor Isaac, and he does not explain anything about the plot of the tale. Paul's use of the definite article in this verse is rightly represented by the NIV: "one by the slave woman and the other by the free woman." Again, this suggests that he is referring to characters already known to the readers, Hagar and Sarah, though he does not give their names here. C. K. Barrett has argued persuasively that the stories of Genesis 16 and 21 were being used by Paul's opponents as a primary basis for their teaching.[219] According to their telling of the story, the true descendants of Abraham, through Isaac, should be circumcised; Gentiles converted by Paul who remain uncircumcised would be in the position of Ishmael, illegitimate sons who would eventually be sent away without inheriting what was promised to Abraham. The Missionaries' interpretation of the story must have been similar to that found in *Jubilees,* giving a place of special privilege to Abraham's physical descendants through Isaac—i.e., the Jewish people:

And through Isaac a name and a seed would be named for [Abraham]. And all of the seed of his sons would become nations. And they would be counted with the

---

219. C. K. Barrett, "The Allegory of Abraham, Sarah, and Hagar in the Argument of Galatians," in J. Friedrich et al., eds., *Rechfertigung: Festschrift für Ernst Käsemann zum 70. Geburtstag* (Tübingen: Mohr, 1976) 1-16.

nations. But from the sons of Isaac one would become a holy seed and he would not be counted among the nations because he would become the portion of the Most High . . . so that he might become a people (belonging) to the Lord, a (special) possession from all people, and so that he might become a kingdom of priests and a holy people. (*Jub.* 16:17-18)[220]

If that is what the Galatians had been told about the story, then Paul is executing a bold counter-reading, reversing the polarity of the story by claiming that it is the uncircumcised Gentile converts who correspond to Isaac, the child of promise (v. 28).

It is also noteworthy that Paul refers to Sarah not by name but as "the free woman." In fact, in Genesis, while Hagar is repeatedly called "the slave woman," Sarah is never explicitly called "the free woman." Paul's use of this epithet subliminally sets up the interpretation that he wants to give, by highlighting the opposition between "slave" and "free."

4:23. Paul's initial summary of the story about Abraham's two sons[221] in v. 22 is uncontroversial. In this verse, however, Paul begins to introduce his own reading of the story; that is probably why the adversative conjunction "but" (ἀλλά *alla*, untranslated by the NIV and the NRSV) introduces this verse.[222] Abraham's fathering of one son was performed "according to the flesh," whereas the fathering of the other was performed "through promise." (This does not mean that Isaac was conceived without sexual intercourse; it refers to the fact that he was born through the power of God's promise after Sarah was past the normal age of childbearing; Gen 18:11.) Ishmael, on the other hand, was conceived apart from God's promise through the "fleshly" stratagem of having Abraham impregnate Hagar, Sarah's Egyptian slave woman (Gen 16:1-16). (The NIV omits the word "flesh" and thereby loses the key word that allows Paul to link Ishmael with the fleshly rite of circumcision.)

The opposition between "flesh" and "promise" is at first surprising; we expect the juxtaposition of "flesh" and "spirit," as in v. 29. Presumably,

in v. 23 Paul is keeping his initial narration as close as possible to the Genesis story, where there is no reference to the Spirit. The mention of "promise" also reminds the reader of Paul's earlier insistence that God granted the inheritance to Abraham "through promise" (3:18, exactly the same phrase found in 4:23) and that the Gentile Galatians are "heirs according to the promise" (3:29). Thus Paul sets the stage for his claim (v. 28) that Isaac, who was begotten "through promise," prefigures the Galatians themselves.

4:24. Having quickly sketched the story of Abraham's two sons in terms implicitly favorable to his own theological reading, Paul now starts to lead the Galatians through an explicit interpretation of the story's details. He announces his program in v. 24*a:* "These things are to be interpreted allegorically." The passive participle "interpreted allegorically" (ἀλληγορούμενα *allēgoroumena*) refers not to the symbolic character of the text but to the character of the interpretation given by the reader. Allegory was a well-known method for interpreting ancient stories of gods and heroes—such as Homer's epic tales—as containers of higher philosophical truths. Paul's contemporary, Philo of Alexandria, was a highly educated Jewish philosopher who applied allegorical methods to the interpretation of Israel's Scripture. For example, Philo read the story of Abraham's two sons as a symbolic portrayal of how the soul (Abraham) must transcend the realm of sense perception and sophistry (Hagar/Ishmael) and ascend to a higher knowledge of wisdom and virtue (Sarah/Isaac).[223]

Many modern interpreters, uncomfortable with the allegorical method of interpretation, have contended that Paul's interpretative strategy is actually typological rather than allegorical. Insofar as this distinction differentiates Paul's reading from the Alexandrian propensity to interpret narratives as coded vehicles of timeless philosophical truths, the distinction may be useful.[224] The verb "to interpret allegorically," however, simply suggests that the narrative is to be read as having a latent sense, a figurative meaning that is to be distinguished from its overt literal sense. By this defi-

220. For an extensive survey of the history of interpretation of the story of Hagar and Sarah in Jewish sources, see R. N. Longenecker, *Galatians,* WBC 41 (Dallas: Word, 1990) 200-206.

221. The fact that Abraham later had more sons by Keturah (Gen 25:1-6) is irrelevant to Paul's allegory.

222. J. L. Martyn, *Galatians,* AB 33A (New York: Doubleday, 1997) 434.

223. Philo, *Cher.* 8-9; *Sob.* 7-9.

224. In fact, it is more helpful to recognize that typology is nothing other than a particular type of allegory, in which the latent sense of a narrative is to be found in later events rather than in "higher" spiritual concepts. On this question, see R. B. Hays, *Echoes of Scripture in the Letters of Paul* (New Haven: Yale University Press, 1989) 115-16, 160-64.

nition, Paul's reading is certainly allegorical. Accordingly, the NIV translation ("These things may be taken figuratively") conveys the proper meaning. Paul is not worried about a technical method of allegory; he is merely saying that the story has a hidden significance, which he will now explain.

The two women are "two covenants." Here is a potential pitfall for Christian interpreters, who are likely to leap to the conclusion that Paul means the old covenant (Law) and the new covenant (gospel). We must remember, however, that Paul has emphatically insisted that the covenant of promise is God's covenant with Abraham, which is much older than the Sinaitic covenant (3:15-18). This means—and the point is crucial—that the two covenants do *not* represent "Judaism" and "Christianity." Rather, Paul claims that the covenant of promise and freedom is what the Law itself, rightly understood, teaches (see the Reflections). It is a matter of two rival interpretations of Israel's heritage—and both interpretations are being promulgated by Jewish *Christians* (Paul and the Missionaries). The salient difference between the two covenants in the present context is not their respective ages but their results: One bears children for slavery, the other for freedom.

The NIV's rendering of v. 24c is clearer than the NRSV's: "one *covenant* [not "one woman"] is from Mount Sinai." That covenant, the Law of Moses, is "bearing children for slavery." The connection of the Law with slavery has already been strongly implied in vv. 1-11; now Paul asserts it overtly. Furthermore, he asserts that Hagar, the slave woman, represents the Law. This is such an astounding claim that he must digress in vv. 25-27 to explain it. Regrettably, the digression leads him away from his exposition of the two covenants, and he never completes the comparison, although it is not too difficult to fill in the blanks in the light of the interpretive clues he has provided (see *Fig. 6*).

J. Louis Martyn has suggested that "bearing children" is a metaphor for gaining converts through missionary preaching.[225] This suggestion

has considerable pertinence in view of Paul's use of the childbearing metaphor in v. 19 to describe his own "birthing" of the Galatian churches. The metaphor of "birth pangs" in v. 19 leads smoothly into the allegorical treatment of childbearing in vv. 22-31. If Martyn is right, then Hagar represents the covenant proclaimed by the Jewish-Christian missionaries, whose work has provoked Paul to write the letter. They are "bearing children for slavery" through their evangelistic work of preaching a Law-observant gospel, which Paul regards as a formula for bondage to the στοιχεῖα (*stoicheia*, vv. 9-10). This proposal helps us to see how 4:21–5:1 powerfully advances the argument of the letter as a whole.

4:25. Paul elaborates on his allegorical interpretation of the figure of Hagar, but his elaboration has baffled generations of interpreters. Some ancient scribes, puzzled by the sentence, deleted the name "Hagar," leaving the clear (but pointless) statement, "For Sinai is a mountain in Arabia" (NRSV textual note). Some modern interpreters have proposed that Paul's identification of Hagar with Mt. Sinai rests on a far-fetched pun exploiting the similarity between her name and the Arabic word for "rock." It is impossible here to recount all the proposals that have been advanced to emend or interpret v. 25a.[226] The following explanation tries to make sense out of the text before us with a minimum of conjecture, bearing in mind that Paul must have intended his sentence to be intelligible to the Galatians.

One important clue does not come through in translation: Paul uses the neuter definite article (τὸ *to*) before Hagar's name. This shows that he is referring to "Hagar" as a word appearing in a text, an item in a field of elements to be allegorically interpreted. This would be best represented in English translation by putting the word in quotation marks: "Now 'Hagar' is Mount Sinai in Arabia." There is no explicit basis in the text of Genesis for this assertion. It is impossible to know with certainty why Paul posits this symbolic equation, though it may have something to do with the fact that Hagar is the mother of Ishmael, regarded in Jewish lore as the progenitor of the Arab people. An equally good explanation, how-

---

225. J. L. Martyn, *Galatians,* AB 33A (New York: Doubleday, 1997) 451-54. This interpretation is supported by the observation that, whereas the LXX consistently uses the verb "to bear" (τίκτω *tiktō*) to describe the childbearing activity of Hagar and Sarah, Paul substitutes in 4:23-24, and 29 the verb γεννάω (*gennaō*), which can mean either "beget" or "bear." Note Paul's use of the latter verb to speak of his own generative apostolic work in 1 Cor 4:15.

226. See H. D. Betz, *Galatians: A Commentary on Paul's Letter to the Churches in Galatia,* Hermeneia (Philadelphia: Fortress, 1979) 244-45; Richard N. Longenecker, *Galatians,* WBC 41 (Dallas: Word, 1990) 211-12.

ever, is that the equation is simply required by the allegory that Paul is propounding. Hagar has already been identified in v. 24 with the covenant from Mt. Sinai; what Paul is doing in v. 25 is justifying a further symbolic linkage between Mt. Sinai and Jerusalem.

The verb "corresponds" (συστοιχέω *systoicheo*) in v. 25*b* is a key to reading the whole passage. It does not mean "represents." Its root meaning is "to stand in line with" something. As many commentators have recognized, this term recalls the Pythagorean tables of opposites, which order pairs of elemental categories into opposing columns (male vs. female, hot vs. cold, etc.).[227] In an analogous way, Paul's allegory lines up the symbolic elements of the Genesis story in two oppositional columns. All of the elements in a single column are closely associated with one another.

227. See the discussion in Aristotle *Metaphysics* I.v.6-17 [986a-987a].

Figure 6: Oppositional Columns in Paul's Allegory

slave	free
Hagar	Sarah
Ishmael	Isaac
flesh	promise/spirit
Mt. Sinai	
the present Jerusalem	the Jerusalem above

In the light of this pattern, Paul's statement in v. 25*b* makes more sense. He is saying that, within his allegory, "Mt. Sinai" stands in the same column with "the present Jerusalem." This enables him to link the Sinai covenant with the empirical city of Jerusalem; both are associated with rigorous adherence to the Law. In the light of these observations, we may now offer a fresh translation of vv. 24-26:

(24) These things are to be interpreted allegorically, for these two women are two covenants. One covenant is from Mt. Sinai, bearing children into slavery: This is Hagar.
(25) Now "Hagar" is Mt. Sinai in Arabia, but she/it stands in the same column with the present Jerusalem, for (Jerusalem) is in slavery with her children.
(26) But the Jerusalem above is the free woman (Sarah); this is our mother.

On this reading, the function of v. 25*a* is to smooth the transition between the assertions made in vv. 24*b* and 25*b*. Despite the apparent geographical incongruity, Paul is explaining how "Hagar" can symbolize both the Sinai covenant (associated with a mountain in Arabia) and the present Jerusalem. The link works, he claims, because Hagar, Sinai, and Jerusalem are all in the "slavery" column.

This still leaves the question of why Paul says the present Jerusalem is in slavery with her children (v. 25*b*). On one level, this is merely a more vivid repetition of the picture already sketched in 3:23; 4:4-5; and 4:8-10: Living under obedience to the Law is in itself a state of slavery, Paul asserts, in contrast to the freedom won for us by Christ. This picture would have particular force if we understand "the present Jerusalem" as a veiled reference to the Jerusalem church, which has been the source of many conflicts and troubles for Paul (cf. 2:12).[228] The Jerusalem church, along with the children begotten through its Law-observant mission to Gentiles, remains in bondage to the Law.

A second level of meaning is possible, however, in the light of 3:10-14 (see the Commentary on 3:10-14). We should not be surprised to find multiple levels of meaning in an allegorical interpretation. The city of Jerusalem symbolizes Israel, which is, empirically speaking, in slavery under the dominion of Rome. The curse pronounced by the Law has brought "a nation from far away, from the end of the earth, to swoop down on you like an eagle" (Deut 28:49 NRSV), so that Jerusalem is

228. Martyn, *Galatians*, 439, 457-66.

under the heel of Caesar. Was the present Jerusalem in slavery? A contemporary observer would have needed to look no further for confirmation than the Antonia Fortress, where Roman troops were stationed immediately adjacent to the Temple Mount (see "Temple Mount of Herod the Great," *NIB* 8:662). This is not Paul's primary point in Gal 4:25, but the political captivity of Jerusalem provides the immediate real-world background for Paul's symbolic identification of Jerusalem with the slave Hagar. To speak of the present Jerusalem as living under slavery was hardly a far-fetched fantasy. By contrast, Paul believes, those who are in Christ are now free citizens of a heavenly commonwealth (v. 26; cf. Phil 3:20), are no longer under the curse, and, therefore, are no longer in bondage to the worldly authorities. That such a vision might underlie Paul's words is suggested also by the fact that he quotes Isa 54:1—a prophecy of the liberation and restoration of Jerusalem—in v. 27.

4:26. In contrast to the present Jerusalem in slavery, Paul links himself and the Galatians to "the Jerusalem above," which is identified with "the free woman," Sarah. (Here the NIV gives an accurate translation, the NRSV a paraphrase.) The term "free woman" (ἐλευθέρα *eleuthera*) refers, of course, to vv. 22-23, where Sarah was introduced, in opposition to Hagar, as "the free woman." Paul is still explicating his allegorical reading of the Genesis story. The image of an eschatological "Jerusalem above" is suggested in OT texts such as Isaiah 54 and Ezekiel 40–48 and more fully elaborated in later Jewish apocalyptic texts (e.g., 2 Esdr 7:26; 10:25-28; 13:36; *1 Enoch* 90:28-29; *2 Apoc. Bar.* 4:2-6). The same image appears also in Heb 12:22; 13:14; Rev 3:12; and in particularly clear form in Revelation 21.[229] The metaphor of Jerusalem as "mother" is found, e.g., in Ps 86:5 LXX and 2 Esdr 10:7, and it is pervasively presupposed by the recurrent motif of Jerusalem as a barren woman ultimately to be restored and blessed by God with many children.[230] All of this suggests that Paul is drawing on a well-established apocalyptic theme: The

people of God, despite suffering and adversity in the present, are children of a heavenly Jerusalem that will be eschatologically revealed. The novelty is that he now includes his Gentile readers among the children of this heavenly Jerusalem.

4:27. In support of this assertion, Paul cites a scriptural text, Isa 54:1. On the surface, it is not immediately apparent how the quotation functions in the argument. Close examination, however, shows that Paul has selected this quotation carefully. The reference to a "barren woman" recalls the story of Sarah's barrenness before the birth of Isaac. In the context of Isaiah 54, this traditional motif of Sarah the barren woman has been metaphorically juxtaposed with the condition of Jerusalem during the exile. The prophet uses the metaphor of God's miraculous blessing of Sarah (cf. Isa 51:1-3, the only reference to Sarah in the OT outside of Genesis) to proclaim God's miraculous restoration of the fortunes of Zion. Where the city had previously lain empty and desolate, there will now be numerous children, numerous inhabitants. (Thus the author of Isaiah 54 is already reading the Genesis narrative typologically to point to the hope of Jerusalem's restoration.) Important for Paul's use of the text, Deutero-Isaiah associates the miraculous increase of Zion's children with the gathering of the Gentiles to acknowledge the justice of the God of Israel (e.g., Isa 49:6; 51:4-5; 52:10; 54:2-3; 55:5). Thus Sarah, the free woman—the allegorical figure for the heavenly city—will cry out joyfully at the "birth" of many children, including Gentile converts. This, as Paul reads it, is the ultimate fulfillment of God's promise to Abraham and Sarah (cf. 3:8-9, 14, 29). Paul's major purpose for citing Isa 54:1 is to evoke Deutero-Isaiah's central theme of God's gracious eschatological restoration of Israel and a universal embrace of the nations.

The final line of the quotation is a little confusing, because, in the context of vv. 21-31, it appears to identify "the one who has a husband" with Hagar. This detail does not fit easily with the narrative of Genesis 16–21, but Paul probably does intend precisely this comparison. His own Gentile mission, symbolized by the figure of Sarah, has been blessed by God with remarkable fruitfulness in contrast to the Law-observant Jewish mission to Gentiles, symbolized here by Hagar,

---

229. For further references, see Richard N. Longenecker, *Galatians,* WBC 41 (Dallas: Word, 1990) 214.

230. On the history of this motif, see M. Callaway, *Sing, O Barren One: A Study in Comparative Midrash,* SBLDS 91 (Atlanta: Scholars Press, 1986); K. Blessing, "The Background of the Barren Woman Motif in Galatians 4:27" (Ph.D. diss., Duke University, 1996).

which (despite her fleshly union with Abraham) has not met with the same success.

4:28. Paul has now completed his exposition of the allegory, and he spells out its specific application to his readers. From this crucial turn, the discourse moves toward the imperative of v. 30. The direct address to the Galatians ("Now *you,* brothers") recalls earlier points in the argument where Paul shifts into the mode of second-person address to drive home the implications of his argument:

3:26: In Christ Jesus *you* are all sons of God through faith.

4:6: And because *you* are sons, God has sent the Spirit . . .

4:28: Now *you,* brothers and sisters, are children of promise. . . .

In this case, their status as children and heirs of the promise is bound up with their relation to Isaac. The Greek κατὰ Ἰσαάκ (*kata Isaak*) does not merely mean "like Isaac" (NRSV, NIV) but "in the line of Isaac"[231] or "in the pattern of Isaac."[232] Their correspondence to Isaac rests not merely on analogy; it is more substantial than that. They are the heirs for whom the promise was destined from the first (cf. 3:8). Paul spells out this crucial concept more fully in Rom 9:7*b*-8, quoting Gen 21:12: " 'It is through Isaac that σπέρμα *sperma* [seed] shall be called for you.' This means that it is not the children of the flesh who are the children of God, but the children of the promise are counted as *sperma* [seed]" (author's trans.). Note here the same antithesis between "flesh" and "promise" that appears in Gal 4:23.

The crucial identity claim in Paul's reading of the allegory is this: "You Gentile believers are the children that God promised to Abraham." He annexes the "Isaac" role for his Gentile converts and thereby confiscates it from the Missionaries, who claim circumcision as a prerequisite for this status. Once Paul has made this hermeneutical shift, the consequences follow quickly in vv. 29-30.

4:29. Paul draws a parallel between Ishmael's persecution of Isaac and the present time, in which he sees the representatives of the Law-observant covenant persecuting Law-free believers. Both sides of the comparison require some clarification.

The text of Genesis says nothing about Ishmael's persecution of Isaac. If anything, in Genesis 21 it is the other way around: Sarah's jealousy on behalf of Isaac leads her to persecute the innocent victims Hagar and Ishmael. Where does Paul get the idea of Ishmael as persecutor? Paul is interpreting Gen 21:9 in the light of a Jewish exegetical tradition that interpreted Ishmael's "playing with" Isaac as some sort of malicious activity, such as mocking, idolatry, or child molestation.[233] This tradition allows Paul to cast Ishmael, the child begotten according to the flesh, as the persecutor of Isaac—here described for the first time as begotten "according to the Spirit." Isaac thus becomes an allegorical figure for believers who receive the Spirit and cry "Abba, Father" (4:6-7).

But how does the allegory work for Paul's own time? Who is persecuting whom? We know from Paul's own testimony that, prior to his apostolic call, he persecuted the church and tried to destroy it (1:13, 23). This might suggest that this verse alludes to Jewish persecution of Christians. If, however, we have been right to read the allegory of vv. 21-31 as a figurative contrast between two different early Christian evangelistic missions, a slightly different interpretation of v. 29 is required. For Paul's analogy to work, the Torah-observant Jewish Christians must be characterized as persecutors of Paul and his Gentile converts. Would such a claim make any sense to Paul's readers? Perhaps it would. Certainly, Paul suffered considerable opposition from Jewish Christians; in 5:11 he implies that he is "still being persecuted" because he refuses to preach circumcision. Furthermore, the Missionaries are excluding uncircumcised Gentiles from fellowship (2:11-14; 4:17); the exclusion may have been accompanied by solemn threats of God's curse and judgment on those who remained uncircumcised. This sort of "harrassment and pressure tactics" could readily be characterized as persecution.[234] (Note the ref-

231. F. J. Matera, *Galatians,* Sacra Pagina 9 (Collegeville, Minn.: Liturgical Press, 1992) 171.

232. J. L. Martyn, *Galatians,* AB 33A (New York: Doubleday, 1997) 432.

233. The rabbinic evidence is gathered by W. A. Meeks, " 'And Rose Up to Play': Midrash and Paraenesis in 1 Cor 10:1-22," *JSNT* 16 (1982) 64-78, see 69-70.

234. S. K. Williams, *Galatians,* ANTC (Nashville: Abingdon, 1997) 131.

erence in 5:12 to "those who unsettle you.")
Finally, we should not dismiss lightly Paul's cryptic reference to the Galatians' having "suffered so
much" (3:4 NIV). Whatever that may mean, v.
29 assumes that the Galatians will be able to fill
in the blanks; their own knowledge of contemporary persecution of Law-free believers by the advocates of the Law-observant mission will allow
them to make sense of Paul's charge.

4:30. The stage is now set for the dramatic
climax of this passage. Paul has reversed the
traditional polarities of the Genesis narrative so
that now the Law-observant Missionaries are,
shockingly, placed in the same "column" with
Hagar and Ishmael, while the Gentile Galatians
are identified as Sarah's free children. Paul had
begun the passage by asking provocatively, "Do
you not hear the Law?" In fact, however, except
for the quotation of Isa 54:1 in v. 27, we have
not yet heard the voice of the Law in this passage.
Paul has given summaries but not quotations.
Now at last he gives the cue for Scripture to speak
directly to the Galatians (cf. the active role assigned to Scripture in 3:8, 22). The words he
quotes from Gen 21:10 are actually Sarah's demand to Abraham, but Paul lifts them out of that
context and treats them as a command spoken by
Scripture directly to the hearers of this letter:
"Throw out the slave woman and her son, for the
slave woman's son will never share in the inheritance with the son of the free woman."[235] It is a
stunning rhetorical moment. Paul has saved his
ace, his most dramatic argument, for the end. If
the Galatians have followed Paul's exposition of
the allegory, they will not miss the import of this
command: *Scripture* is speaking directly to them,
telling them to throw out the rival Missionaries
and their converts. The inheritance belongs rightly
to the children of the free woman, and they
should not tolerate the presence of troublemakers
who are trying to lure them into slavery (cf.
1:8-9). They should expel the Missionaries from
their churches.

4:31. This summarizing sentence recapitulates
what Paul has already said in vv. 26 and 28. This
time, however, he reverts to a first-person plural

formulation, gathering the Galatians to his side of
the argument.

5:1. This sentence stands as the hortatory conclusion to the whole train of argument thus far,
particularly the counterarguments of 3:1–4:31. The
NIV and some other translations and commentaries
treat this verse as the beginning of a new unit; this
division of the text obscures the role of this verse
as the culmination of the freedom/slavery antithesis
that has dominated chap. 4.

Galatians 5:1 encapsulates the message of the
letter in a single powerful slogan. It is a standard
around which Paul hopes to rally the readers.
Here, as throughout the central section of the
letter, the primary emphasis falls on the indicative
declaration of what Christ has done. Christ has
set us free (cf. 3:13; 4:4-5). Christ has liberated
us into the realm of freedom.[236] The indicative
declaration is immediately followed by a corollary
summons: Because Christ has set us free, we are
to take a firm stand in the freedom we have been
given. Paul has already narrated his action in
Jerusalem as a model of standing firm in freedom
(2:4-5), and he urges the Galatians to take their
stand also. In the situation at hand, this would
mean that they would stand firm against the
teaching of the Missionaries. The verb "stand"
(στήκω *stēkō*)—particularly when taken in combination with the last clause ("and do not submit
again to a yoke of slavery")—almost surely invokes a military image, with apocalyptic overtones
(as in 1 Cor 16:13; Phil 1:27; 4:1; 2 Thess 2:15).
In a time of cosmic struggle and opposition, the
Galatians are exhorted to hold their ground without being frightened away by the enemy.

The image of the "yoke" is often used elsewhere in a positive sense to describe the discipline
provided by teaching, particularly the teaching of
Torah.[237] In this sense, the yoke provides stability
and guidance, rather than being something to
chafe against (cf. the Matthean adaptation of this
theme to the teaching of Jesus, Matt 11:29-30).
The Missionaries may have spoken of the Law as
a yoke in these terms, as a gracious divine gift. If
so, Paul once more reverses the valence of their
language. By shifting the metaphor from the con-

---

235. In order to achieve this effect, he has to modify the wording of
the quotation just slightly, most notably by replacing "my son Isaac" (Gen
21:10) with "the son of the freewoman." This change is necessary if
Scripture, rather than Sarah, is to be heard as the speaker.

236. This interpretation follows Martyn, *Galatians*, 447, in reading the
dative case of the noun "freedom" as having a locative function: Freedom
is figuratively conceptualized as a space into which Christ has placed us.
237. See *m. Abot* 3.5.

text of benign instruction to the field of military conflict, he depicts the yoke as a symbol of enslavement. Here the Missionaries are implicitly portrayed not as kindly instructors, but as insidious slavemasters, seeking to bring the Galatians under the constraint of a new religio-cultural system of domination (cf. Acts 15:10).[238] Because

Christ has delivered the Galatian churches from slavery, they should never, under any circumstances, tolerate being subjected to it again (cf. 4:8-9). With that ringing cry, the central section of Paul's letter comes to a close.

238. See J. D. G. Dunn, *The Epistle to the Galatians,* Black's NT Commentary (Peabody, Mass.: Hendrickson, 1993) 263.

REFLECTIONS

1. *Claiming the Law as a Witness to the Gospel.* It is easy to imagine that in mounting his argument against the Missionaries, Paul could have rejected the Law altogether. Angered by the efforts of these Jewish-Christian evangelists, he might have declared a moratorium on Bible reading and announced a new covenant, under the guidance of the Spirit, that had no use any longer for Israel's sacred texts. He might have conceded that the Missionaries were right about the Law's requirements, including circumcision, and concluded that Israel's Scripture therefore had no place in shaping the thought and practice of the church. In short, he might have taken the position adopted by the twentieth-century New Testament scholar Rudolf Bultmann:

> To the Christian faith the Old Testament is no longer revelation as it has been, and still is, for the Jews. . . . The events which meant something for Israel, which were God's Word, mean nothing more to us. . . . To the Christian faith the Old Testament is not in the true sense God's Word.[239]

In Gal 4:21–5:1, however, Paul takes a very different line. He is not content to abandon Israel's Torah into the hands of his adversaries. Instead he argues passionately that the story of Abraham's two sons speaks directly to his Gentile readers. Israel's Law is not somebody else's book, for the Galatians themselves are Abraham's children, children of the promise in the pattern of Isaac. In order to receive guidance about what to do in their present time of controversy, they should listen to what Scripture says (4:1, 30). The whole passage claims that Scripture, rightly read, bears witness to the Law-free gospel for Gentiles.

Paul's strategy of argument is all the more striking if, as seems likely, the Missionaries were using the story of Isaac and Ishmael as a key text in support of their preaching of circumcision. By challenging them on the ground of their interpretation of the text, Paul set a crucial precedent for all subsequent Christian theology, preaching, and pastoral care: Scripture is foundational for the faith of the church. Normative proposals about Christian practices must be adjudicated through debating the interpretation of Scripture. As the Letter to the Galatians shows, the appeal to Scripture does not settle issues in a simple, straightforward way. The right reading of Scripture may be bitterly contested, as it was in Galatia. Still, Scripture defines the arena in which the contest must take place.

When Paul asks of the Galatians, "Do you not hear the Law?" we might well ask what he expects them to hear. On the basis of his entire argument in 3:1–5:1, we are able to give some answers. He expects them to hear in the "Law" the encompassing narrative of the Old Testament, not just rules about ritual and behavior. He expects them to hear a word of gracious promise from God, a word that predates all human striving for righteousness. He expects them

239. R. Bultmann, "The Significance of the Old Testament for Christian Faith," in *The Old Testament and Christian Faith,* ed. B. W. Anderson (New York: Harper and Bros., 1963) 31-32.

to hear a call to rejoice in the unimaginable superabundance of God's grace toward those who were formerly enslaved and deprived (4:27). Most of all, he expects them to hear themselves named as God's children, heirs of the promise.

After they have heard all that in the Law, there is one more thing Paul wants them to hear: an uncompromising command to "drive out" those who would enslave them by reading the Law as a package of rules or as a charter of ethnic privilege. This will sound harsh to many readers—as no doubt it did to the Galatians when they first read the letter. But on this point, Paul insists, there can be no compromise, for compromise will lead back to slavery.

All of this provides an important model for the church's continuing relation to Scripture. The text of the Old Testament cannot be dismissed as irrelevant or antiquated, nor can it be labeled as somebody else's book. The Old Testament is the Scripture of the Christian church. In the death and resurrection of Jesus Christ, the righteousness of God is disclosed apart from Law, but it is also attested by the Law and the prophets (Rom 3:21). We must learn to read the Old Testament as Paul read it, as a narrative of promise and grace.

To put the matter this way, however, raises at least two thorny issues. First, by claiming the Old Testament as Scripture, does Paul set the church on a path of supersessionism that leads to anti-Jewish attitudes? Second, are the methods Paul uses to reclaim the Old Testament narrative (allegory, in this case) legitimate methods? Let us address each of these issues in turn.

2. *The Problem of Supersessionism.* In the history of interpretation, Paul's allegory of the two covenants has often been read as an argument for the superiority of Christianity over Judaism. On this reading, Paul is trying to take the Bible away from the Jewish people and claim it for the Christian church. As we have seen in the Commentary section, however, this is a misreading of the passage. Paul is not rejecting Judaism as such; rather, writing as a Jewish Christian, he is contesting the interpretation of Israel's heritage offered by a rival group of Jewish-Christian missionaries who are disrupting his congregations in Galatia by seeking to impose their interpretation on a group of Gentiles. The bitter conflict played out in the Letter to the Galatians, then, is an argument between rival Jewish-Christian interpreters, all of whom share the conviction that the right interpretation of Scripture is a matter of great urgency.

Paul believed that the death of Jesus had initiated a "new covenant" (1 Cor 11:25) and that his own task as a missionary was to proclaim that new covenant to Jews and Gentiles alike (2 Cor 3:6). But we should bear in mind the way in which the "new covenant" image functions in Jer 31:31-34, a passage to which Paul alludes several times in his letters (e.g., Rom 2:15; 2 Cor 3:3). The new covenant does not overturn and renounce the old; rather, in the new covenant God writes the Law on the hearts of the people and restores them to a relationship with him that they had broken through their unfaithfulness. It constitutes an internalizing and renewal of the old covenant.

Paul's view of the matter is complex, because in his judgment the Sinaitic covenant had severe limitations. It did not have the power to give life, only the power to curse and imprison its adherents. Yet, when facing the prospect of declaring the Law antithetical to God's purposes, Paul backs away emphatically (3:21). The Law is not superseded so much as it is assigned a temporary role in God's larger purposes. Furthermore, in addition to the Law's confining function, it also has a witness-bearing function, which continues unabated. That is why Paul repeatedly cites Scripture as an authoritative point of reference for his congregations. At the same time, however, his reading of Scripture as in the present passage—is daringly revisionary and transformative. He reads Israel's holy texts in previously unforeseen ways, always through the lens of the gospel.

Where does all this leave the Jewish people who remain faithful adherents of the Law and reject the gospel that Paul preaches? The question does not arise in the Letter to the Galatians, which is concerned primarily with the issue of whether Gentile converts must come under the Law. When Paul does finally address the issue of the fate of the Jewish people in relation to the gospel, he gives a lengthy dialectical response, insisting that God has not abandoned Israel and that they will be saved eschatologically (Romans 9–11).

Thus it would be wrong to characterize Paul as a supersessionist.[240] The interpreter of Gal 4:21–5:1 should take care not to use this text as a launching platform for hostile generalizations about Judaism. The best reading of the text will insist on seeing it as an intra-Christian argument championing the freedom of Gentile converts from Law observance.

3. *The Validity of Allegory.* Paul achieves his triumphant hermeneutical transformation of the Sarah and Hagar story by employing allegorical interpretation. This method enjoyed great popularity among patristic and medieval theologians, was sharply challenged by the Reformers, and fell into serious disrepute among critical scholars in the modern era, because it seemed to disregard the original literal sense of the texts it purported to interpret. How, then, are we to evaluate Paul's practice of allegorical reading? Should we repudiate it or emulate it?

Paul's figurative reading strategy depends from start to finish on delineating correspondences between the scriptural story and the events of his own time. The *dramatis personae* of Genesis 21 become correlated with the players on the stage of the Galatian churches. The Galatians are to envision themselves in the role of Isaac, the child of promise, and they are to see the Missionaries and their converts in the roles of Hagar and Ishmael. This sort of imaginative discernment of parallels between past narrative and present situation is very different from Philo's allegories that demythologize the biblical narrative into abstract spiritual truths. In fact, Paul's method of discerning parallels between the biblical narrative and the crisis facing his readers is invariably employed whenever preachers see the circumstances of their own day illumined or prefigured by the stories of Scripture. Thus all Christian preaching is inescapably allegorical, in the Pauline sense. The function of preaching is not to give factual historical reports; rather, it is to make metaphors, linking the ancient text with the present life of the congregation in fresh imaginative ways so that the text reshapes the congregation's vision of its life before God.

By that criterion, Paul's allegory in Gal 4:21–5:1 is a brilliantly successful piece of preaching, enabling his readers to envision themselves as free children of Abraham and as children of an eschatologically restored Jerusalem caught up in joyous songs of praise to God. It moves them from fearful uncertainty about their identity to celebratory determination to stand fast in the graciously given gift of freedom. When allegory functions like that, in service of proclaiming the gospel, who can withhold the water for baptizing it? The key question is whether the allegorical reading is governed by the larger shape of the biblical story—as it is here in Galatians—or whether the method is drafted into the service of other conceptualities. Any interpretative method can be abused, including historical criticism. The tests of validity are finally theological rather than methodological.

Of course, whenever we read the text with metaphorical freedom, we must do so with a certain ironic distance from our own interpretation. Allegory is a playful method; its best practitioners, like Paul, know perfectly well that their allegorical interpretations are not identical with the literal sense of the text. Nonetheless, they dare to believe that their fresh interpretative performances are done through the lens of the gospel story with the guidance of the Holy Spirit. If so, such interpretations will disclose meanings previously hidden but now brought forth as the community needs them. Allegorical interpretation of this sort is a species of prophecy. Paul "hears" the text of Gen 21:10 speaking directly to the churches of Galatia, and his figurative reading helps them to hear the word also.

4. *The Meaning of Freedom.* Above all, Gal 4:21–5:1—the rhetorical climax of the

---

240. For a fuller discussion of the problem, see R. B. Hays, *The Moral Vision of the New Testament: Community, Cross, New Creation* (San Francisco: HarperSanFrancisco, 1996) 411-17.

letter—is a clarion call to stand fast in the freedom won by Christ. Any and all preaching on this text must highlight its summons to freedom. Interpreters of the text must beware of confusing the freedom of which Paul speaks with nationalistic discourses about freedom; this is not Fourth of July oratory. On the other hand, neither is Paul speaking merely about rugged individualism or an inner liberty of the conscience or the will. The crucial indicator of that fact is that freedom in Christ manifests itself through the formation of concrete communities where the old barriers of nation, race, class, and gender are overcome in communion at the one table (cf. 3:26-29; 5:13-15). In short, the freedom Paul proclaims is an *ecclesial* freedom; it is to be embodied in the corporate life of the church, as Gal 5:13–6:10 will make clear.

This freedom is to be sharply distinguished from "autonomy," a word that means literally "self-law." To be autonomous is to be, paradoxically, at the mercy of ourselves. By contrast, the freedom of which Paul speaks is freedom in Christ, a freedom that says, "It is no longer I who live, but it is Christ who lives in me" (2:20). It is not a freedom that chants, as did the Corinthians, "All things are lawful for me" (1 Cor 6:12; 10:23). Rather, it is a freedom for life in community, a freedom for mutual service in love.

What would it mean to "stand firm" in this place of freedom? It would mean, minimally, to form communities in which we resist the pressure to conform to standards imposed by the Law for covenant membership—or other analogous standards. We know ourselves to be free solely because of Christ's liberating invasion of the slave camp in which we all were confined prior to his coming. Thus, freedom is a gift, not an achievement. Where freedom is so understood, it leaves room for genuine diversity. We need not be bound by anxiety about pleasing others (1:10) or meeting expectations imposed on us by those who fancy themselves the guardians of order. We are accountable only to God, "in whose service is perfect freedom."

By standing firm, a community of true freedom gives the creation—which now groans in bondage—a glimpse of "the freedom of the glory of the children of God" (Rom 8:21). The freedom that we know now in Christ is a future-oriented sign, a foretaste, a pointer to the new creation.

GALATIANS 5:2–6:10

PASTORAL COUNSEL TO THE GALATIANS

OVERVIEW

In chaps. 5–6, Paul at last addresses the issue of circumcision explicitly, warning the Galatians of the dire consequences of following the Missionaries' teaching (5:2-12). He then offers them an alternative vision for a community that lives in love (5:13-15) under the guidance of the Spirit. Implied, but not stated, is a comparison between the Spirit and the Law, which the Missionaries have presented as a necessary antidote to the flesh. Paul, by contrast, commends the Spirit as the one power able to counteract the desires of the flesh (5:16-26). Finally, he instructs the Galatians on how to relate to one another as a community, including practices of mutual correction, sharing, and doing good to one another (6:1-10). Throughout this section we see Paul's pastoral concern for the Galatian churches, which have been disrupted by the incursion of the Missionaries, apparently with the result that they are experiencing dissension and conflict (5:15, 26; 6:1-4).

GALATIANS 5:2-12, A CALL TO REJECT CIRCUMCISION

NIV

[2] Mark my words! I, Paul, tell you that if you let yourselves be circumcised, Christ will be of no value to you at all. [3] Again I declare to every man who lets himself be circumcised that he is obligated to obey the whole law. [4] You who are trying to be justified by law have been alienated from Christ; you have fallen away from grace. [5] But by faith we eagerly await through the Spirit the righteousness for which we hope. [6] For in Christ Jesus neither circumcision nor uncircumcision has any value. The only thing that counts is faith expressing itself through love.

[7] You were running a good race. Who cut in on you and kept you from obeying the truth? [8] That kind of persuasion does not come from the one who calls you. [9] "A little yeast works through the whole batch of dough." [10] I am confident in the Lord that you will take no other view. The

NRSV

[2] Listen! I, Paul, am telling you that if you let yourselves be circumcised, Christ will be of no benefit to you. [3] Once again I testify to every man who lets himself be circumcised that he is obliged to obey the entire law. [4] You who want to be justified by the law have cut yourselves off from Christ; you have fallen away from grace. [5] For through the Spirit, by faith, we eagerly wait for the hope of righteousness. [6] For in Christ Jesus neither circumcision nor uncircumcision counts for anything; the only thing that counts is faith working[a] through love.

[7] You were running well; who prevented you from obeying the truth? [8] Such persuasion does not come from the one who calls you. [9] A little yeast leavens the whole batch of dough. [10] I am confident about you in the Lord that you will not think

[a] Or made effective

311

one who is throwing you into confusion will pay the penalty, whoever he may be. [11]Brothers, if I am still preaching circumcision, why am I still being persecuted? In that case the offense of the cross has been abolished. [12]As for those agitators, I wish they would go the whole way and emasculate themselves!

otherwise. But whoever it is that is confusing you will pay the penalty. [11]But my friends,[a] why am I still being persecuted if I am still preaching circumcision? In that case the offense of the cross has been removed. [12]I wish those who unsettle you would castrate themselves!

[a] Gk brothers

COMMENTARY

5:2-4. For the first time in the letter, Paul names the specific issue that has evoked his impassioned response: circumcision. (This was foreshadowed by his earlier reference to resisting pressure to circumcise Titus [2:3], but now for the first time we learn that circumcision is the primary issue confronting the Galatian churches.) The Galatians are considering being circumcised, and Paul regards the prospect as a disaster. Paul's words give us no clue about why pressure for circumcision is now being brought upon the Galatian churches despite the agreement that he had earlier worked out with the "pillars" in the Jerusalem church (2:1-10). It is likely, in the light of the subsequent controversy at Antioch (2:11-14), that at least some factions within the Jerusalem church no longer regarded that agreement as binding. We must also remember that the faction Paul calls the "false brothers" (2:4) had never been party to the agreement in the first place.

The opening of a new section is punctuated by Paul's emphatic interjection of his own authoritative persona into the discourse: "Look! I, Paul, am telling you. . . ." He has laid out a lengthy theological argument to support his position (3:1–5:1); now he arrives at the practical application of all he has said so far, and he throws the full weight of his personal authority behind his blunt declaration that circumcision will negate any benefit the Galatians might have received from Christ.

This is an extraordinarily strong claim. Does Paul mean that Jews cannot be believers, cannot receive Christ's benefits? Clearly he cannot mean that; Paul himself, as a Jew, was circumcised (Phil 3:5). What he is saying is that Gentile converts to the Christian faith must not allow themselves

to be circumcised. Why? Some of the reasons are to be found in the arguments of chaps. 3 and 4: Circumcision, as an entry to living under the Law, is a backward step to an earlier stage of the story, a step that leads into slavery. But in 5:2-4, he articulates his position in even stronger terms. He posits a fundamental incompatibility between Law and Christ; they represent separate spheres of power, such that anyone who chooses to enter the Law's sphere of power has been cut off from access to Christ. One's allegiance must rest in one sphere or the other; no compromise is possible. To choose circumcision voluntarily is to deem Christ insufficient and thereby to abandon his sphere of influence.

That, perhaps, explains Paul's reminder in v. 3 that circumcision creates an obligation to obey the whole Law. As we saw in the discussion of 3:10-14, his point cannot be that the Law requires sinless perfection, for the Law contains extensive provisions to provide atonement and forgiveness of sins. Rather, he is telling the Galatians that if they choose to be circumcised, they are crossing a guarded border into an occupied territory where the Law rules. The Law is a total way of life, a religious system that makes a total demand on one's life. To come under the Law (3:23; 4:4-5, 21) is to enter a sphere where the Law is sovereign. One cannot then pick and choose which commandments to follow; it is a total package. One must either get in or get out. (Here we no doubt hear an echo of Paul the rigorous Pharisee, who well understood the comprehensive demand of the Law during his earlier period of surpassing zeal for the traditions of his ancestors; see 1:13-14.)

Scholars have sometimes speculated on the

basis of v. 3 that the Missionaries in Galatia were urging circumcision merely as a token identity marker, without actually calling for total Law observance. In view of Paul's overall argument, however, that seems improbable. The Galatians, Paul says, "desire to be subject to the Law" (4:21), and they are already adopting the observance of sabbaths and Jewish festivals (4:10). Furthermore, as part of their case for circumcision, the Missionaries were ominously quoting Deuteronomy: "Cursed is everyone who does not observe and obey all the things written in the book of the Law" (3:10). Thus, when Paul writes that circumcision creates an obligation to do the whole Law, he cannot be telling the Galatians something they do not already know. The warning takes its force from the way Paul poses Christ and Law as mutually exclusive options, in stark contrast to the Missionaries' desire to blend them together.

The consequence of this exclusivity is spelled out in v. 4: Those who seek to be rectified through the Law have made Christ of no effect and have fallen out of grace. "Grace" is conceived here (like "freedom" in v. 1) as a location, a sphere from which the Galatians will exile themselves if they go forward with the action they are contemplating. The thought is a more pointed restatement of the conclusion of Paul's sharp challenge to Peter: "I do not nullify the grace of God; for if rectification comes through the Law, then Christ died for nothing" (2:21). Nullifying the grace of God is precisely what the Galatians will do, Paul warns, if they undergo circumcision. (The NRSV rendering of v. 4, "cut yourselves off from Christ," conveys the right idea but suggests a pun on "cutting" the flesh that is not present in the Greek text; the NIV is preferable.)

Paul's formulation of the warning carries a note of irony. He writes, literally, "You who are being rectified by the Law...." Since he has already unconditionally asserted that no one *can* be rectified by the Law (2:16; 3:11), Paul is ironically suggesting that the attempt to seek rectification through circumcision is not only futile but also illusory. His use of the verb "justify/rectify" (δικαιόω *dikaioō*) in this sentence reinforces our finding that "rectification" refers in the first instance to inclusion within the covenant people of God (see the Commentary on 2:16). That is the end the Galatians would seek through circumci-

sion. As the apostle has affirmed repeatedly, however, the Galatians have already been embraced into God's people through the faithfulness of Jesus Christ, entirely apart from any action on their part. Thus their seeking covenant membership in some other way constitutes a tragic rejection of God's grace in Christ.

5:5-6. In contrast to those who seek rectification/righteousness (δικαιοσύνη *dikaiosynē*) through the Law, "*We* [the position of the pronoun is emphatic] by the Spirit eagerly await, through faith, the [eschatological] hope of righteousness." The contrast between v. 4 and v. 5 is to be noted: Those who seek righteousness through the Law claim covenant membership as a present possession, whereas Paul and those who share his vision look to a future eschatological verdict of God. While Paul can sometimes speak of rectification as having occurred already through the death and resurrection of Jesus (e.g., Rom 5:1), his dialectical eschatology continues to insist that *dikaiosynē* is a future state of affairs. Insofar as "rectification" refers to being included within God's people, Paul's congregations have already experienced it, and they bear witness to it through fellowship between Jews and Gentiles at one table; nevertheless, insofar as "rectification" refers to God's final establishment of justice, it remains a future hope.[241]

The futurity of rectification is not a prominent theme of Galatians, but it is a deep and consistent emphasis of Paul's theology. The language of v. 5 prefigures the much fuller development of the same ideas in Rom 8:18-25: Those who have the Spirit groan along with a creation still in bondage while eagerly awaiting the fulfillment of our hope. Important here is not only the noun "hope" (ἐλπίς *elpis*), but also the verb "await eagerly" (ἀπεκδέχομαι *apekdechomai*, v. 5; Rom 8:19, 23, 25), which depicts the joyous longing with which believers expect the ultimate disclosure of God's glory and grace. The same verb appears in 1 Cor 1:7 and Phil 3:20; in both cases, it refers to the expectation of Christ's glorious coming again to transform us into his glory and to rule over creation. These passages help us to see more

---

241. The phrase "hope of righteousness" is ambiguous. Does it mean "that for which righteousness hopes" (subjective genitive) or "the hope which consists in righteousness" (epexegetical genitive)? The latter interpretation is to be preferred. See J. L. Martyn, *Galatians,* AB 33A (New York: Doubleday, 1997) 472.

fully what Paul means by "the hope of righteousness."

The capacity to wait in eager expectation is sustained, Paul says, by the Spirit and by faith. These terms carry with them in v. 5 the full weight they have acquired through his earlier exposition (2:16; 3:1-14, 22-26; 4:6-7). The Spirit is the promised blessing given to Jew and Gentile alike through Christ's faithful death; it cries out and testifies, even in this time of waiting, that we are God's children. Paul's use of the phrase "by faith" (ἐκ πίστεως *ek pisteōs*) takes on special pertinence here. It is derived from Hab 2:4 (cited in Gal 3:11), where it supplies the answer to the prophet's complaint about the suffering endured by God's people. God's answer to Habakkuk— which becomes a keynote for Paul's preaching of the gospel—is that the righteous one will live ἐκ πίστεως *ek pisteōs*. In other words, the righteous will live in a posture of trustful expectation, waiting for God to bring the promised deliverance. That is precisely the stance Paul describes in v. 5.

The apocalyptic character of the hope to which Paul refers is highlighted in v. 6, which strongly recalls the "new creation" theme hinted at in 3:28 and made fully explicit in 6:15. Those who are "in Christ Jesus" have entered a sphere that anticipates the eschatological redemption, a sphere in which the very categories of "circumcision" and "uncircumcision" have become utterly null and void. Paul says (literally) that they no longer "have strength." In this situation, the Missionaries' urging the Galatians to be circumcised appears ridiculous; it is a retrogression to a world of categories that have been abolished by the cross.

In place of these old categories now vitiated, there appears one new reality that does have strength and validity: "faith working through love." The expression "faith *working*" might have struck the first-time readers of this letter as an oxymoron. Has not Paul set "faith" and "works" in absolute opposition to each other (3:10-12)? Verse 6*b* forces us to reexamine what Paul means by both terms. His polemic against "works" is not meant to disparage the doing of good deeds (see also 6:9-10). Rather, he is targeting "works of the *Law*," the specific acts of obedience that define membership in the Jewish people as determined under the Law of Moses. This was the issue faced by the Galatians, not the issue of whether they could earn their salvation by good works (see the Commentary on 3:10). At the same time, "faith" is not merely a subjective mental attitude or an inventory of doctrinal beliefs; it refers—as it did in the case of Abraham—to trust lived out in practice. This is nowhere clearer than in v. 6. Faith is not a state of passive quiescence. In Christ, faith becomes effectively enacted through love.[242]

The word "love" (ἀγάπη *agapē*) is a favorite Pauline theme that makes its first appearance within the letter here in v. 6. More precisely, this is the first appearance of the noun. Paul used the verb once previously in the letter, in a context that defines its meaning with considerable precision. Paul now lives "by the *faith* of the Son of God, who *loved* me and gave himself for me" (2:20). The love of the Son of God is shown by his action of self-giving for our sake; this self-giving in turn is understood as the enactment of his faith. Thus Gal 2:20 provides a paradigmatic picture of "faith working through love." What does it look like? It looks like Jesus on the cross. That, Paul says, is the only thing that matters in the new creation. The church is called to embody this faith working through love in a way that corresponds to the story of the cross. The demand for circumcision is completely irrelevant to this calling.

5:7-10. In vv. 5-6 Paul portrays his positive vision of the community of faith, awaiting rectification through Christ and animated by faith working through love. In v. 7, however, his thoughts turn sadly once again to the Galatians, who have stumbled and are in danger of losing the vision. He employs the athletic metaphor of running a race (cf. 1 Cor 9:24-27; Phil 3:12-14; 2 Tim 4:7). The Galatians "were running well"; the verb is in the imperfect tense, indicating that for some time after Paul's departure they had continued to make progress, like a runner striding forward smoothly. But now something has happened to trip them up. The NIV ("Who cut in on you?") represents the Greek text precisely, while the NRSV loses the metaphor. The Galatians are now like runners thrown off stride by another runner cutting into their path and shoving them off balance. At the

---

242. Dunn comments: "Here Paul comes as close as he ever does to James (James ii.18)." J. D. G. Dunn, *The Epistle to the Galatians,* Black's NT Commentary (Peabody, Mass.: Hendrickson, 1993) 272.

same time, Paul's choice of verb almost certainly carries a witty double entendre: The Missionaries have "cut in" on them by demanding to cut the flesh of their foreskins.

The effect of the Missionaries' interference has been to divert the Galatians from "obeying the truth."[243] Again, as in 2:5, 14, we see that "the truth" entails certain behaviors, or perhaps better, certain forms of community life. The truth is not merely an idea to be acknowledged; it is a body of practices to be followed. The truth demands not just intellectual assent but practical obedience. The verb translated as "obeying" also carries the sense of "being persuaded." The Missionaries have knocked the Galatians off balance by undercutting their confidence about the gospel Paul had preached to them, so that they are no longer fully persuaded of the truth they had been taught before.

Rhetorical persuasion has played a major role in the Missionaries' strategy. But Paul asserts that this persuasion—however superficially appealing—does not come from God ("the one who called you"; cf. 1:6). The Galatians have been diverted from their original calling by someone who is not an agent of God, someone employing manipulative rhetoric. The sequence of thought recalls 1:6-9, where Paul pronounces anathema on anyone who promotes confusion by preaching a message that does not come from God. Commentators sometimes suggest that v. 8 implies that Satan is the source of the Missionaries' false persuasive power (cf. 2 Cor 12:7; 1 Thess 2:18), but that inference goes beyond what Paul says here. His main point is to deny any divine authorization for his rivals' persuasive rhetoric. The question, "Who cut in on you?" does not require an answer; Paul and his Galatian readers know perfectly well whom he is talking about.

The transition of thought in vv. 9-10 seems abrupt and puzzling, but there is more coherence here than meets the eye initially. The key to understanding the flow of thought is to recognize that, just as in 4:30–5:1, Paul is calling for the Galatian churches to expel the Missionaries from their communities.[244] That is why he quotes the proverb, "A little leaven leavens the whole batch of dough" (v. 10). This is a word of warning about the subtle corrupting power of false teaching and behavior. In 1 Cor 5:6, Paul quotes precisely the same proverb to support his order that the Corinthians expel a flagrant sexual offender from the church. Here in vv. 9-10 the issue is different, but the point is the same: The church should take action to preserve its integrity by excising the cancer before it can spread. The Missionaries' teaching is not from God (v. 8), and it must be rooted out before it corrupts the community. Paul does not repeat the directive of 4:30, but the point is clear: The proverb of v. 9 is a warrant for them to take strong exclusionary action.

Verse 10 follows logically from this reading of v. 9. Paul is confident that the Galatians will take his view of the matter and act accordingly—i.e., that they will throw out the rival Missionaries. Of course, this expression of confidence is itself an exaggeration, a rhetorical ploy designed to enlist their support; for a less sanguine view of the situation, see 4:11, 20. Nevertheless, Paul is confident "in the Lord" (v. 10) that the Galatians will see the truth; he cannot believe that God will allow his work to be destroyed.

The latter part of v. 10 also fits with this train of thought. He writes, literally, "The one who is confusing you will bear the judgment." In the last analysis, the judgment of which Paul speaks is surely God's judgment, but, in a more proximate sense, he may be speaking also of the community's act of exclusionary judgment on the troublemaker. In the light of this interpretation, we can paraphrase vv. 7-10 as follows, with explanatory expansions in italics:

You were running well. Who cut in on you *and knocked you off balance,* to keep you from obeying the truth? Their elaborate rhetoric does not come from God who calls you; *if you listen to them they will lead you astray. Therefore, you must drive them out of your community,* because a little leaven leavens the whole lump of dough. *If you let them stay in your midst, they will corrupt the entire church.* I am confident in the Lord that you will not think otherwise, *and that you will do as I say. Even if this sounds harsh, it is a matter of God's judgment.* Anyone who tries to confuse you will bear the judgment, whoever he may be.

---

243. On this whole topic, see J. M. G. Barclay, *Obeying the Truth: A Study of Paul's Ethics in Galatians,* Studies of the NT and Its World (Edinburgh: T. & T. Clark, 1988).

244. S. K. Williams, *Galatians,* ANTC (Nashville: Abingdon, 1997) 140-41.

Why does Paul formulate the word of warning in v. 10*b* in the singular, in contrast to the plural depiction of the opponents in 1:7 and 5:12? Three explanations are possible: (1) Paul is thinking of a single person, the leader of the Missionaries' efforts; (2) since there are multiple Galatian churches, perhaps there is only a single rival Missionary at work in each one;[245] (3) the warning is formulated in general terms to apply to any individual who may trouble the Galatian churches. The simplest explanation, and therefore probably the best, is the third. If Paul had in mind a single adversary, there is no reason to think that he would shrink from naming him, as he named Cephas in 2:11-14. At the same time, the indefinite expression "whoever he may be" communicates a studied disregard for the authority the Missionaries claimed, just as Paul's ironic reference to "those who were reputed to be pillars" in 2:6, 9 suggests that he was not impressed by their reputation. (The NIV captures this nuance better than does the NRSV.)

5:11. Abruptly Paul—perhaps provoked by his reference in v. 10*b* to his rivals' work of sowing confusion in the Galatian churches—responds to an ad hominem accusation. His response is so brief and cryptic that it is difficult to be sure what he is responding to. For some reason, the Missionaries were claiming that Paul sometimes preached circumcision. In the light of our knowledge of Paul's letters, the claim seems bizarre. What could Paul's rivals have meant? There have been numerous conjectures,[246] but the likeliest construction is that the troublemakers were telling the Galatians that Paul did, in fact, advocate circumcision on other occasions in other communities, but that he had kept this crucial knowledge of God's covenant seal back from the Galatians, perhaps because he was a "people pleaser," afraid to risk incurring their disfavor (cf. 1:10). The story reported in Acts 16:1-3 would provide grist for this rumor mill: Paul had, in fact, supported the circumcision of Timothy, who was well known to the believers in Lystra and Iconium (i.e., "South Galatia").[247] In short, the Missionaries alleged, Paul had waffled and failed to tell the Galatians

the whole truth about God's requirements, although he showed by his actions elsewhere that he really did recognize the importance of circumcision.

To refute this accusation, Paul points to his own experience of persecution at the hands of Jewish believers. "If I were preaching circumcision," he says in effect, "these zealous Jews would not be giving me trouble all the time." But in fact, since Paul is regularly persecuted by the circumcision faction, that proves he is not a supporter of their position. If he had given up preaching his Law-free gospel for Gentiles, there would be no point of conflict. (For references to the persecution of Christians, and of Paul in particular, see 1:13, 23; 4:29; 6:12, 17; perhaps also 4:13-14.) It may be debated whether the persecution Paul refers to originates specifically from Jewish-Christian authorities (as 4:29 would suggest) or from non-Christian synagogues (1:13-14; Acts 14:19; 17:5-14).

Paul also gives a theological reason for his refusal to "preach circumcision" (the phrase is probably his own capsule summary of the Missionaries' Law-observant gospel): If he preached circumcision, then "the offense [lit., "stumbling block" (σκάνδαλον *skandalon*)] of the cross has been abolished." The logic of the sentence requires that the *skandalon* be understood as a good thing. Paul throws this phrase out as though he expects his Galatian readers to understand what he means. Perhaps in his earlier preaching to them he had used this terminology, but there is no prior explanation for it in this letter. Presupposed is the line of thought that Paul develops in 1 Cor 1:18–2:5: The proclamation of the cross is "a *skandalon* to Jews and foolishness to Gentiles, but to those who are the called, both Jews and Greeks, Christ the power of God and the wisdom of God" (1 Cor 1:23-24 NRSV). The cross confounds all human religion and philosophy, all human wisdom. It is the strange instrument by which God has shattered the old world and brought a new one into being (cf. 2:19-21; 3:13-14; 6:14-15). Thus, in the compressed formula of v. 11*b*, Paul is saying that he could not go back to preaching circumcision (as he did in his former life, 1:13-14), because to do so would be to negate the world-transforming power of the gospel that had been divinely revealed to him. It would be to go back to business as usual in a world where

---

245. J. D. G. Dunn, *The Epistle to the Galatians,* Black's NT Commentary (Peabody, Mass.: Hendrickson, 1993) 278.

246. For a helpful list of six options, see ibid., 278-80.

247. Luke is careful to point out that Timothy's mother was Jewish (Acts 16:1). Under Jewish tradition, this made him a Jew rather than a Gentile.

circumcision served to mark the Jewish people off from the rest of the world. For the religious worldview of that former life, the cross is a stumbling block because it delegitimates the distinctions between Jew and Gentile, between sacred and profane, that structure the whole meaning of that world.

Thus, in v. 11 Paul rebuts the insinuation that he has advocated circumcision in other churches with a brief two-pronged response. The empirical evidence of his continued harassment from the circumcision party shows that the accusation is false, and, in any case, if he started advocating circumcision, it would constitute nothing less than a repudiation of the gospel—just as the Galatians will now be repudiating the gospel if they allow themselves to undergo circumcision.

5:12. The thought of the Missionaries' outrageous misrepresentation of his true position causes Paul to boil over with anger. He fires a ferocious gibe at his adversaries. It is a crude joke: "If they are so eager to start cutting on the male sexual organ, I wish they would just castrate themselves." One imagines that when the letter was read in the Galatian churches, this bold swipe would have elicited a few gasps from the congregation, followed by laughter from Paul's partisans and outrage from his detractors. We may feel that this sort of coarse humor hardly commends Paul's argument, but here, as elsewhere in the letter, Paul is exploiting the rhetorical techniques available to him to persuade his readers to take his side of the argument.[248]

The fact that Paul goes to such a rhetorical extreme to attack his opponents demonstrates how strongly he felt about the issues under debate and how furious he was about the Missionaries' misleading account of his own convictions and about their "unsettling" of his congregations. On the other hand, Paul's sarcastic linkage of circumcision with castration might justly be regarded by the Missionaries as a scurrilous libel. The argument has, by any measure, turned ugly.

248. Betz notes that "the ridiculing of eunuchs was a standby of the diatribe preacher." That is hardly what Paul is doing here, but the analogy may be relevant. Commentators have long observed that the pagan cult of Cybele, which had a prominent temple in the "North Galatian" city of Pessinus, was well-known for its castrated priests. See H. D. Betz, *Galatians: A Commentary on Paul's Letter to the Churches in Galatia*, Hermeneia (Philadelphia: Fortress, 1979) 270. Paul's vicious joke may be intended to link the Missionaries' emphasis on circumcision with this sort of pagan ritual, in which case 5:12 would provide another example of Paul's provocative portrayal of Judaism as just one more variant of pagan religion under the *stoicheia*. See 4:8-11; Martyn, *Galatians*, 478. Within Jewish tradition, however, practices of sexual mutilation were regarded with horror. As Paul well knew, the Law that the Missionaries championed lays down a stern rule: "No one whose testicles are crushed or whose penis is cut off shall be admitted to the assembly of the Lord" (Deut 23:1 NRSV). If Paul's gruesome wish were granted, then, the circumcision advocates would thereby be cut off from their own people.

REFLECTIONS

1. *No Packages of Membership Requirements.* It takes no great leap of imagination to see how Paul's comments on the issue of circumcision might be applied to other issues that arise from time to time in the life of the church. We face an analogous challenge whenever the preaching of the gospel is accompanied by some further proviso that says, "Of course you must trust in God's grace through Jesus Christ, *but* if you really want to belong to God's people, you must do one more thing. . . ." It is the "but" clause that is fatal, no matter what the "one more thing" may be. The analogy to the Galatian situation is particularly strong when the "but" clause includes some stipulation about national or ethnic identity. Paul is the eternal enemy of all efforts to bundle the gospel as part of a package deal that includes additional membership requirements. All such attempts at bundling turn out to be rejections of the grace of God.

2. A corollary of the previous point is that Christ makes a comprehensive claim on our lives. There can be no divided loyalties, no compromises, no areas where we remain autonomous agents. Karl Barth expresses the point powerfully:

> For by this covenant we are not only embraced by the fact of the death and resurrection of Jesus Christ. . . . We are also embraced (and closely so, without any empty or neutral zones) by His

living command through which He wills to sanctify us, attract us to Himself, and therefore awaken us to obedience, as partners in His covenant.[249]

Our life is totally embraced by Christ without any "neutral zones." The Law constitutes a rival symbolic universe, and precisely for that reason it must be categorically rejected. There can be no other symbolic universe, for we are encompassed by the sphere of Christ's power and grace. If we recognize that and live accordingly, we will—paradoxically—learn the meaning of freedom.

3. *The Hope of Righteousness.* Galatians 5:5 is the clearest statement in the letter that the rectification in which we trust remains a future hope. We look to the future, trusting that God will set all things right in the end. The apocalyptic language of "eager expectation" characterizes our longing for God's new world, a world that we hope for but do not yet see (cf. Rom 8:24-25). And yet, at the same time, we already find ourselves living into that new world, for in Christ circumcision and uncircumcision have ceased to be valid categories (5:6). The tension between 5:5 and 5:6 is the dialectical tension between the "not yet" and the "already." This tension is a fundamental truth about life in Christ, as we live in the strange time between his resurrection and his coming again in glory, the anomalous time that T. S. Eliot called "the time of tension between dying and birth."[250] One of the problems with the Missionaries' message was that it sought to dissolve this tension by making rectification immediately available in life under the Law, symbolized by the concrete act of circumcision. Paul's gospel resists such closure and calls us to live in a world destabilized by the cross, while looking to the future with hope.

4. *Faith Working Through Love.* In place of the fixed categories of circumcision and uncircumcision, categories that divide Jew and Gentile, the new life in Christ is characterized by the dynamic reality of "faith working through love." Faith that is kindled by God will necessarily issue forth in action. The character of faith's action is defined by "the faith of the Son of God who loved me and gave himself for me" (2:20). Thus love-empowered faith will manifest itself in sacrificial service for others (cf. 5:13-14). The participle Paul uses in the expression "faith *working* through love" comes from the verb ἐνεργέω (*energeō;* cf. the English cognate "energy"), which Paul almost always uses to describe an external power working in and through human beings. Sometimes the external power is evil—such as passions (Rom 7:5) or death (2 Cor 4:12) or "the mystery of lawlessness" (2 Thess 2:7)—but more often it is the power of God through the Holy Spirit (1 Cor 12:6, 11; Gal 2:8; 3:5; Col 1:29; 1 Thess 2:13; cf. Eph 1:11, 20; 3:20). Emblematic of this latter cluster of passages is Phil 2:13: "For it is God who is at work [ἐνεργῶν *energōn*] in you, enabling you both to will and to work [ἐνεργεῖν *energein*] for his good pleasure" (NRSV). The "faith working through love" that human beings experience, then, is nothing less than the power of God working, through us, effectually in the world. Those who experience God's power in their lives will say with Paul that "it is no longer I who live but Christ who lives in me." The faith we experience is "the faith of Jesus Christ" not only because he is its exemplar, but also because he is its active source. Thus the faith of Christ will always manifest itself in love (see 1 Cor 12:31*b*–13:13). Doctrinal orthodoxy without the active manifestation of love is not the faith of which Paul speaks.

5. *Paul's Polemic.* Paul's passionate resistance to the rival Missionaries leads him to utter, in the heat of debate, a violent wish that they would castrate themselves (5:12). Does this text provide a model for discourse in the church today, in a time when we have our own bitter controversies? In one sense, the answer is, "Of course not." Mudslinging and obscene jokes are not likely to promote peaceful resolution of disputes; Paul's outburst sits oddly

---

249. K. Barth, *Church Dogmatics* II/2 (Edinburgh: T. & T. Clark, 1957) 708.
250. T. S. Eliot, "Ash Wednesday," in *The Complete Poems and Plays, 1909–1950* (New York: Harcourt, Brace & World, n.d.) 66.

alongside his call for "faith working through love" in 5:6. One doubts that Paul would defend, in retrospect, his choice of words. Yet it is important to see the larger context in which this hostile remark is made. Paul is unequivocally calling for the Galatians to expel from their churches a group of outside agitators who are, in his view, subverting the gospel and leading people away from Christ. They are causing the Galatians to fall away from grace. This is serious business.

Paul's invective is reminiscent of the psalms that pray for harm to befall the enemies of God and of God's people (Ps 137:8-9 is the most notorious example). Discernment is called for here.

On the one hand, the presence of such texts in the canon of Scripture does not necessarily commend the hostility of the speakers' voices; the Bible is full of texts that show human beings, even God's beloved elect human beings, in the light of sober reality. Paul, like Abraham and Jacob and David, had his rough side. In that sense, he is no better than the rest of us, and Gal 5:12 offers a glimpse of Paul's unsanctified pique. In a strange way, we may find such displays of fallibility comforting, knowing that even apostles can have lapses of judgment.

On the other hand, Paul's anger has a deep and serious cause, and we should not too quickly pass over this point. The underlying anger is not isolated to this one verse; from 1:6-9 onward, controlled anger sets the tone of the whole letter. And, if one grants Paul's conviction that the Missionaries are in fact leading his churches to fall away from the grace of God, the anger would be fully justified, like Jesus' anger at the Temple money changers or like God's anger toward hard-hearted and unfaithful Israel (e.g., Deut 32:15-22). If we believe that there are times when lines must be drawn and evil named as evil (see the Commentary and Reflections on 1:6-9), then there is a time for anger (cf. Eccl 3:8). Christian faith does not mandate bland tolerance of destructive powers. Indeed, Gal 5:12 may cause us to pause to reflect on whether we have failed to be as angry as we should be toward those who corrupt and disrupt the church's faith in the gospel.

6. Finally, Paul's reference to "the stumbling block of the cross" (v. 11) reminds us of the fundamental message of the gospel, the story of the crucified Jesus Christ (3:1, 13). Invariably we encounter subtle temptations to repackage the message in ways that obscure or minimize the cross. We would dearly love to move the cross out of the center of the story, because then we could work out some sort of accommodation and coordination with other religious and philosophical worldviews; we could preach circumcision and Jesus, too—perhaps a Jesus who was an enlightened teacher of wisdom. But that would be unfaithful. There is no gospel without the offense of the cross, for the cross puts an end to all our human projects of self-justification. Paul will return to the point in his postscript (6:12-14). Our preaching, like his, must return to it again and again.

GALATIANS 5:13-15, FREEDOM FOR LOVE

[13]You, my brothers, were called to be free. But do not use your freedom to indulge the sinful nature[a]; rather, serve one another in love. [14]The entire law is summed up in a single command: "Love your neighbor as yourself."[b] [15]If you keep

[a]13 Or *the flesh*; also in verses 16, 17, 19 and 24   [b]14 Lev. 19:18

13For you were called to freedom, brothers and sisters;[a] only do not use your freedom as an opportunity for self-indulgence,[b] but through love become slaves to one another. [14]For the whole law is summed up in a single commandment,

[a] Gk *brothers*   [b] Gk *the flesh*

NIV	NRSV
on biting and devouring each other, watch out or you will be destroyed by each other.	"You shall love your neighbor as yourself." [15]If, however, you bite and devour one another, take care that you are not consumed by one another.

COMMENTARY

5:13. Many commentators consider this verse to be the beginning of the final major section of the letter, taking vv. 2-11 as the conclusion of the letter's central argument (3:1–5:11) and treating 5:13–6:10 as a unit of paraenesis (moral exhortation) appended to the main body of the discussion. There are some good reasons for this analysis; the most important factor is that only in 5:13–6:10 do we find a concentration of verbs in the imperative and hortatory subjunctive moods. By contrast, vv. 2-12 consist of warnings and reproaches. Nevertheless, the structural markers in the Greek text suggest a different division, which is followed in this commentary. The clear break point comes in v. 2 with Paul's emphatic interjection, "Look, I, Paul, am telling you. . . ." There is no such clear new beginning at this verse, which is introduced simply with the conjunction "for" (γάρ *gar*), implying that the content of v. 13*a* supplies the logical warrant for the preceding statements. (The NRSV translates the conjunction, while the NIV does not.) Verses 11-12 are a slight digression, as Paul rebuts a false accusation, and the *gar* of v. 13 should be understood to resume and support the argument of vv. 2-10, with vv. 7-10 interpreted as an implicit call for the Galatians to expel the rival Missionaries (see the Commentary on 5:7-10). The line of thought leading from v. 2 into v. 13 can be paraphrased, then, as follows:

If you let yourself be circumcised, you will be separated from Christ (vv. 2-4). Circumcision is irrelevant in the new creation brought by Christ (vv. 5-6). Therefore, you should reject circumcision and drive out the Missionaries who demand it; I am confident that you will do as I say (vv. 7-10). The reason that you should take this action is that you were called to freedom (v. 13*a*).

Thus it makes better sense to treat 5:2–6:10 as the final major unit of the letter. This section is unified by Paul's pastoral concern to show the Galatians how to conduct their lives together as a community.

Despite the fact that, structurally speaking, v. 13 does not mark the beginning of a new unit, it does serve an important transitional function. The first part of the sentence sums up the central thesis of the letter ("For you were called to freedom"), reminding the readers of the climactic manifesto of 5:1. It is God who has done the calling (1:6; 5:8), and the freedom has been won by Christ (1:4; 2:20; 3:13; 4:4-5; 5:1). Having summarized the gospel proclamation, however, Paul now confronts a new challenge: Does the freedom given by Christ leave us without moral guidance? That is the problem introduced and addressed by v. 13*bc:* "Only do not use your freedom as an opportunity for the flesh, but through love become slaves to one another."

If the Law was a temporary custodian that has now been dismissed from service by Christ, and if the Law no longer functions to regulate human life, then are we adrift on a sea of moral confusion? No doubt this was one of the major arguments put forward by the Missionaries. They sought to convince the Galatians that Paul had irresponsibly baptized them without giving them the appropriate instruction in the Law, which, they asserted, was necessary to hold humanity's sinful impulses ("the flesh") in check. The Law provides guidance (cf. the metaphor of the "yoke" in 5:1) to keep us from going astray into sin and error. This was one of the glorious benefits of the Law in standard Jewish teaching.[251] In the light

251. J. M. G. Barclay, *Obeying the Truth: A Study of Paul's Ethics in Galatians,* Studies of the NT and Its World (Edinburgh: T. & T. Clark, 1988) 107, gives numerous references. A single example will suffice: "[Moses] did not leave practical training in morals inarticulate; nor did he permit the letter of the law to remain inoperative. . . . He left nothing, however insignificant, to the discretion and caprice of the individual. What meats a man should abstain from, and what he may enjoy; with what persons he should associate; what period should be devoted respectively to strenuous labor and to rest—for all this our leader made the law the standard and rule, that we might live under it as under a father and master, and be guilty of no sin through wilfulness or ignorance" (Josephus *Against Apion* 2.174).

of this challenge, Paul must provide an alternative account of how his gospel provides sufficient moral direction for the daily life of the community of faith. Betz explains the logic behind the transition to moral exhortation that occurs in v. 13:

Paul realizes that mere polemic against circumcision and law (5:2-12 . . .) does not do justice to the Galatian trouble. There has to be a positive and viable proposal as to how to deal effectively with misconduct and failure, that is, with the "flesh."[252]

The entire unit of 5:13–6:10, then, provides Paul's positive proposal about how the community is to deal with the problem of "the flesh": They are called to live in love, under the guidance of God's Spirit, not of the Law.

The precise language that Paul uses in v. 13 should be noted carefully. The verb "use" is supplied by the NRSV and the NIV to complete an elliptical sentence that lacks a verb; Martyn's suggestion is an equally viable way of filling out the thought: "only do not *allow* freedom *to be turned into.* . . ."[253] (The Greek does not say "*your* freedom"; this possessive pronoun, too, has been supplied by the translations.) The thing that freedom must not be turned into is an ἀφορμὴν τῇ σαρκι (*aphormēn tē sarki*). The difference between the NIV ("to indulge the sinful nature") and the NRSV ("as an opportunity for self-indulgence") at this point is an indicator of the challenge of translating this phrase properly. The noun ἀφορμη (*aphormē*) means literally a staging area or base of operations for a military campaign.[254] It came to be used metaphorically in Hellenistic Greek to mean "opportunity" (NRSV), but Paul may very well be using it here with some conscious resonance of its original literal sense. The Galatians have been caught up in a cosmic conflict, and they must take care not to let the territory won for them by Christ become a staging ground for a counterattack by the hostile power of the flesh.

"Flesh" (σάρξ *sarx*) is the other key word in the expression. The paraphrases of the NIV and the NRSV convey only part of its range of connotations. It can be used in a neutral sense to mean the physical body or the stuff of which it is made (2:20; 6:13), usually with the nuance of mortality or mortal limitation (1:16; 4:13-14; cf. Rom 8:3). On the other hand, it can be used, as it is throughout 5:13-26, to refer to a sinful power resident in human existence that opposes God. In Galatians, Paul sometimes plays artfully on this ambiguity, as in 3:3 and 4:23, 29. In some contexts it is difficult to tell whether Paul is using the term metonymically to describe the fallen human creature in the state of alienation from God, or whether he is thinking of "Flesh" as a hostile power (like "Sin" and "Death"), external to the individual human self. Indeed, this ambiguity is particularly acute throughout 5:13-26. Paul's use of military metaphors throughout the passage (vv. 13, 17, 25) suggests that—at least for the dramatic imagery of his exhortation—he is employing the image of Flesh as a quasi-personified hostile power. The message of v. 13*b*, then, is, "Do not allow freedom to become a base of operations for the hostile power of the Flesh."

The positive recommendation that Paul offers as an antidote to allowing Flesh to take control comes as a surprise. We might expect him to say, "Do not allow freedom to become a base of operations for the hostile power of the Flesh, but resist sinful desires with all your might," or some such. Instead, he writes: "Through love become slaves to one another." After his forceful repudiation of slavery (4:8-9, 25-26; 5:1), this formulation comes as a shocking paradox. The Galatians are to use their freedom to become slaves! (By translating the verb δουλεύω [*douleuō*] as "serve," the NIV minimizes the paradox and loses the clear link to the foregoing imagery of slavery.) Paul does not speak of becoming slaves to God or Christ, or even of "righteousness" (cf. Rom 6:15-23). Instead, he says, they are to serve *one another* as slaves. If the way to keep Flesh from gaining a base of operations is through loving, mutual service, this suggests that the power of Flesh will try to manifest itself through pride, rivalry, and autonomy. Thus Paul's prescription has shifted the conversation into the realm of relationships within the community, as the rest of the hortatory section (5:13–6:10) will confirm.

Paul's paradoxical prescription for mutual slavery would have sounded strange and offensive to Greek ears; the ideal of Hellenistic philosophy,

252. H. D. Betz, *Galatians: A Commentary on Paul's Letter to the Churches in Galatia,* Hermeneia (Philadelphia: Fortress, 1979) 273.

253. J. L. Martyn, *Galatians,* AB 33A (New York: Doubleday, 1997) 479.

254. BAGD, 127.

particularly Stoicism, was to attain a position of autonomous detachment. A classic definition of freedom is given by Epictetus:

He is free who lives as he wills, who is subject neither to compulsion, nor hindrance, nor force, whose choices are unhampered, whose desires attain their end, whose aversions do not fall into what they would avoid.[255]

In the context of such a prevailing ideology, Paul's call for the Galatians to enslave themselves would have seemed bizarre. His counterintuitive advice, however, oddly transforms the meaning and context of slavery. Becoming "slaves to one another," where the acts of service are conceived as mutual, redefines the concept of slavery, which is necessarily hierarchical in character.[256]

The other major element in Paul's prescription for resisting the Flesh is "love." This clearly links v. 13 back to "faith working through love" (v. 6), which is the one effective power that has replaced the Law's emphasis on circumcision. Paul will next show how his counsel of love as the antidote to Flesh is related to the rival Missionaries' favored solution.

5:14. Another rhetorical shock follows hard upon the first. If we were shocked to find Paul speaking in a paradoxically positive way about slavery, we will be equally surprised to discover in this verse that the Law suddenly assumes a positive valence. Up to this point in the letter, the Law has been depicted primarily as the instrument of curse, confinement, and slavery. But now, suddenly, Paul declares that the Law finds its central meaning in a single verse from Leviticus: "You shall love your neighbor as yourself" (Lev 19:18). This remarkable reversal of field requires careful examination. How can Paul say that "the whole law" is fulfilled in loving the neighbor?

First, we should remember that in 4:21–5:1 Paul had refused to leave the Law in the possession of the circumcision party. He argued that if the Galatians will, in fact, "hear the Law," they will hear it proclaiming them to be children of the promise. Indeed, they will hear it calling for the expulsion of those who demand circumcision! This suggests that Paul has already staked a claim on a new and different reading of the Law, a

dramatic hermeneutical revision in the light of the gospel. Reading the Law through the lens provided by the cross and the resurrection of Jesus— as well as through the experience of the Holy Spirit in communities of Gentile believers—Paul now sees in it a meaning very different from anything he could have grasped during his former life as a zealous Pharisee. The Law has undergone a hermeneutical transformation, so that it now becomes a witness to the gospel (cf. Rom 1:2; 3:21; 10:5-13; 15:4; 1 Cor 10:11; 2 Cor 3:12-18).

Second, the verb translated by both the NIV and the NRSV as "summed up" (πεπλήρωται *peplērōtai*) requires careful attention. The usual meaning of πληρόω (*pleroō*) is to "fill up" or "fulfill." This term must be distinguished from the common Jewish expressions "doing the Law" (cf. 3:12) and "keeping the commandments," both of which refer to concrete obedience to the Law's specific requirements.[257] By contrast, the expression "fulfill the Law" never occurs in Jewish texts; it is, so far as we can tell from surviving sources, a distinctively Christian locution. When Paul employs this terminology, he is "using vocabulary unprecedented in Jewish tradition."[258] The NIV and the NRSV translators may have chosen "summed up" in order to avoid the impression that Paul is speaking here of "fulfilling" the Law's requirements in the sense of "doing" them all. As Martyn points out, however, the translators are reading v. 14 in the light of the close parallel in Rom 13:9, where Paul uses a different verb that does mean "summed up."[259]

Furthermore, Paul has placed this verb in Gal 5:14 in the perfect tense. Most commentators treat the perfect tense here as an instance of the rare "gnomic perfect," expressing a general maxim.[260] The possibility must be at least considered, however, that Paul is using the perfect tense in the more usual way: to narrate a past action whose effects continue into the present. The most

255. Epictetus *Diss.* 4.1.1.
256. Barclay, *Obeying the Truth,* 109.

257. Betz, *Galatians,* 275; S. Westerholm, "On Fulfilling the Whole Law (Gal 5.14)," *SEÅ* 51-52 (1986-87) 229-37.
258. J. M. G. Barclay, *Obeying the Truth: A Study of Paul's Ethics in Galatians,* Studies of the NT and Its World (Edinburgh: T. & T. Clark, 1988) 138.
259. J. L. Martyn, *Galatians,* AB 33A (New York: Doubleday, 1997) 519-23.
260. BDF #344 (p. 177) remarks that the perfect is "rarely used" in this sense. In fact, the only two examples given of the "gnomic" use of the perfect tense (Matt 13:46 and Jas 1:24) are explained as mistakes of usage: "There is a strong suspicion that the aor. . . . and the perf. are incorrectly mixed." Gal. 5:14 is not cited here.

straightforward translation of the verse, then, would yield the reading, "For the whole Law *has been brought to fulfillment* in one saying [λόγῳ *logō;* not "commandment"]."

Finally, we should observe that the scriptural text in which Paul says that the Law has been brought to fulfillment is Lev 19:18, a passage cited in Mark and Matthew, in combination with Deut 6:4-5, as *Jesus'* summary of the meaning of the Law (Matt 22:34-40; Mark 12:28-34; cf. Matt 19:19; Luke 10:25-28; Jas 2:8). Paul's citation formula implies that the quotation is already familiar to the Galatians (lit., "For the whole Law has been brought to fulfillment in one word, in the [saying]: 'You shall love your neighbor as yourself'"). It seems probable that Paul knew the widely circulated early Christian tradition of Jesus' teaching on this point and had passed it along to the Galatian churches during his founding of these communities.[261]

Later rabbinic sources reflect various debates among the rabbis about how to sum up or organize the Law under a small number of commandments or fundamental principles,[262] but these texts differ from Gal 5:14 in one crucial way: The rabbis never entertain the idea that their summarizing categories could replace the specific commandments of the Law or make it unnecessary to obey commandments such as circumcision, food laws, or the sabbath.[263] Thus these texts, even if the traditions they preserve could be traced back to the first century, would be of little use for understanding what Paul means in this verse.

In the light of all this evidence, how should we understand what Paul is claiming in Gal 5:14? The Missionaries were urging the Galatians to be circumcised and to do what the Law required in order to bring order and moral security to their lives. Paul proclaims, however, that a new reality has come on the scene "in Christ Jesus" (cf. 5:6): The Law has been brought to fulfillment. By

whom? For Paul there can be only one answer: by Jesus, "the Son of God who loved me and gave himself for me" (2:20). Paul believes that the full meaning of the Law, which was previously hidden from Israel (2 Cor 3:14-15), has now been eschatologically disclosed and brought to completion by Jesus. How did Jesus bring the Law to fulfillment? The question can be answered on two levels. First, in his teaching, he disclosed that the Law's deepest sense is brought to expression in Lev 19:18. Second, through his loving death for the sake of others, he embodied the meaning of that teaching, as Gal 2:20 indicates. By the combination of his teaching and his sacrificial death, Jesus reshaped the Law and thus brought it to fulfillment. That explains why Paul uses the perfect tense in v. 14*a.*

Does this interpretation mean that v. 14 is not, after all, a behavioral directive for the Galatians? By no means. Verse 14 provides the warrant (note γάρ *gar* again) for the imperative of v. 13. To paraphrase: "Through love become slaves to one another. Why? Because Jesus has brought the Law to fulfillment by teaching and embodying neighbor-love, thus spotlighting Lev 19:18 as the Law's true aim." The Galatians are exhorted to participate in this fulfilling of the Law through their own loving service (v. 13), which corresponds to and mirrors the love of Jesus. The logic of this exhortation runs parallel to 3:16, 29, in which, because Christ is first of all Abraham's seed, all who belong to Christ turn out to be Abraham's seed. Or again, in 3:22, the promise is given on the basis of Jesus Christ's faithfulness to all who believe. In each of these parallel cases, believers participate in Christ's faith and inheritance and love and, therefore, manifest the correlate of these blessings in their own lives and character. They are "conformed to the image of [God's] Son, in order that he might be the firstborn within a large family" (Rom 8:29).

The theological logic underlying vv. 13-14 is spelled out more fully in Rom 8:3-4:

For God has done what the Law, weakened by the flesh, could not do: by sending his own Son in the likeness of sinful flesh, and as a sin offering,[264] he condemned sin in the flesh so that the just requirement of the Law might be fulfilled [πληρωθῇ *plērōthē*] in us, who walk not according to the flesh but according to the Spirit.

---

261. J. D. G. Dunn, *The Epistle to the Galatians,* Black's NT Commentary (Peabody, Mass.: Hendrickson, 1993) 291-92.

262. See especially *b.Sabb.* 31a: "On another occasion it happened that a certain Gentile came before Shammai and said to him, 'Make me a proselyte, on condition that you teach me the whole Torah while I stand on one foot.' Thereupon he [Shammai] repulsed him with the builder's cubit which was in his hand. When he went before Hillel he [Hillel] said to him, 'What is hateful to you do not to your neighbor; that is the whole Torah, while the rest is commentary thereof. Go and learn it.' " For further references, see R. N. Longenecker, *Galatians,* WBC 41 (Dallas: Word, 1990) 243-44.

263. Martyn, *Galatians,* 515-18.

264. Here following the NRSV alternate translation.

Thus, insofar as the Galatians walk according to the Spirit, they will not allow the Flesh to pervert Christ's gift of freedom. They will instead be conformed to Christ in becoming slaves to one another, just as he became a slave for our sake (cf. Phil 2:3-8). In this way they will embody the meaning of love.

This interpretation leads us to make one more tentative exegetical suggestion. Is it possible that Paul read Lev 19:18 not as a commandment, but as a word of prophetic promise? We must recall, first of all, that Paul does not use the word "commandment" or "command" in Gal v. 14. These terms are supplied by the translators to interpret the simple word λόγος (*logos*), meaning "word," "sentence," "saying." Furthermore, the verb "love" in the Greek quotation of Lev 19:18 follows the LXX in using the future indicative form ἀγαπήσεις (*agapēseis*), rather than the imperative. This is a regular feature of the LXX's idiom; Hebrew imperatives are often rendered by Greek future indicatives. Paul was no doubt well aware of this idiosyncrasy of LXX style. That would not stop him, however, from hearing in this text an inspired prediction of a reality that would be newly brought into being by the Spirit in the community of the new creation: "The whole Law has been brought to fulfillment [by Jesus Christ] in a single [prophetic] word: 'You *will* love your neighbor as yourself.'" That is what the Greek text appears to say. Just as he saw the rectification of the Gentiles prefigured in Scripture's blessing of Abraham (3:8-9), so also Paul sees Christ's community of loving mutual service prefigured in the Law.

5:15. From this eschatological vision of neighbor-love, Paul turns his gaze back to the depressing present reality of the Galatian churches. This verse is our first clear indication that these churches were struggling with internal problems of rivalry and dissension. There is no reason to suppose that Paul is speaking here of a purely theoretical possibility. The fact that he returns in v. 26 to a similar warning against competitiveness and envy suggests that he is addressing a real situation "on the ground" in Galatia. It is impossible to tell for certain from these references whether the dissension was already brewing before the arrival of the Missionaries—in which case they might have presented the Law as a solution to the Galatians' internal struggles—or whether the infighting had actually been provoked by the Missionaries' message, with some of the Galatians opting for circumcision and law observance and claiming spiritual superiority over others who did not follow their lead. Paul's comment in v. 7 might favor the latter hypothesis; the Galatians were "running well" before the Missionaries came on the scene, but now they were facing conflict within their churches. This scenario would precisely parallel Paul's narrative about what happened in the church at Antioch (2:11-14).

The image in this verse is that of a vicious dogfight, in which the Galatians are depicted as snapping at one another with bared fangs. The verbs portray an escalating conflict, ending with their destruction of one another. The contrast to v. 13 could hardly be more stark. Paul fears that the Flesh will gain the upper hand in Galatia. (See Reflections at 5:16-26.)

GALATIANS 5:16-26, THE WORKS OF THE FLESH AND THE FRUIT OF THE SPIRIT

NIV	NRSV
[16]So I say, live by the Spirit, and you will not gratify the desires of the sinful nature. [17]For the sinful nature desires what is contrary to the Spirit, and the Spirit what is contrary to the sinful nature. They are in conflict with each other, so that you	16Live by the Spirit, I say, and do not gratify the desires of the flesh. [17]For what the flesh desires is opposed to the Spirit, and what the Spirit desires is opposed to the flesh; for these are opposed to each other, to prevent you from doing what you want. [18]But if you are led by the Spirit,

NIV

do not do what you want. ¹⁸But if you are led by the Spirit, you are not under law.

¹⁹The acts of the sinful nature are obvious: sexual immorality, impurity and debauchery; ²⁰idolatry and witchcraft; hatred, discord, jealousy, fits of rage, selfish ambition, dissensions, factions ²¹and envy; drunkenness, orgies, and the like. I warn you, as I did before, that those who live like this will not inherit the kingdom of God.

²²But the fruit of the Spirit is love, joy, peace, patience, kindness, goodness, faithfulness, ²³gentleness and self-control. Against such things there is no law. ²⁴Those who belong to Christ Jesus have crucified the sinful nature with its passions and desires. ²⁵Since we live by the Spirit, let us keep in step with the Spirit. ²⁶Let us not become conceited, provoking and envying each other.

NRSV

you are not subject to the law. ¹⁹Now the works of the flesh are obvious: fornication, impurity, licentiousness, ²⁰idolatry, sorcery, enmities, strife, jealousy, anger, quarrels, dissensions, factions, ²¹envy,[a] drunkenness, carousing, and things like these. I am warning you, as I warned you before: those who do such things will not inherit the kingdom of God.

²²By contrast, the fruit of the Spirit is love, joy, peace, patience, kindness, generosity, faithfulness, ²³gentleness, and self-control. There is no law against such things. ²⁴And those who belong to Christ Jesus have crucified the flesh with its passions and desires. ²⁵If we live by the Spirit, let us also be guided by the Spirit. ²⁶Let us not become conceited, competing against one another, envying one another.

[a] Other ancient authorities add *murder*

COMMENTARY

5:16-18. Paul now addresses the question of how the community can receive moral guidance in the absence of the Law. As we have seen, the Missionaries have argued that only the Law can curb and discipline the unruly human impulses that lead to moral chaos. In v. 16, Paul sets forth his own opposing view in the form of a thesis: "But *I* say [in distinction to what the Missionaries are saying] walk by the Spirit and you will never carry out the desire of the flesh."

The first verb in the thesis is an imperative directing the Galatians to "walk" (περιπατεῖτε *peripateite*) by the guidance of the Spirit. (Both the NIV and the NRSV translate this metaphorical verb by the more colorless "live.") Paul's metaphor of "walking"—a figure for conducting one's life in a certain manner—is based on a common Hebrew idiom; the verb הלך (*hālak*, "walk") is regularly used in this sense in the OT. This verb is the root of the noun הלכה (*hălākâ*), the body of Jewish didactic tradition about how to comply with the Law in one's daily life.

The more crucial point of translation concerns the verb in the second clause, "gratify" (τελέω *teleō*; more lit., "carry out," "bring to completion"). The NRSV has interpreted it as though it

were an imperative, coordinate with the first verb in the sentence: "Live by the Spirit and do not gratify . . ." while the NIV has read it, correctly, as an aorist subjunctive, spelling out the consequences that will follow from obeying the imperative of the first clause: "Live by the Spirit, and you *will not* gratify. . . ." These are two significantly different interpretations: the first a command, the second a promise. On grounds both grammatical and theological, the NIV is to be strongly preferred. The double negative οὐ μη (*ou mē*), which regularly occurs with the aorist subjunctive, expresses emphatic negation of a future possibility. On this reading, the sentence is a conditional promise: "If you walk by the Spirit, you will never carry out the desire of the flesh."

The expression "the desire of the flesh" ("desire" [ἐπιθυμία *epithymia*] is singular, not plural, in the Greek text) is probably a Greek rendering of an underlying Hebrew expression יצר בשר (*yēṣer bāśār*), which describes the fleshly evil impulse that underlies and empowers human sin.[265] It is important to recognize that "desire of

265. J. Marcus, "The Evil Inclination in the Letters of Paul," *IBS* 8 (1986) 8-21.

the flesh" does not refer only to sexual passions. Indeed, the list of "works of the flesh" in vv. 19-21, though it begins with three terms designating sexual misconduct, gives far more emphasis to other offenses. "The flesh" is a comprehensive term for the sphere of autonomous fallen humanity, conceived as standing in opposition to God. "Flesh" asserts itself anywhere that self-seeking human desire opposes itself to the divine will and the wholeness of the community. It is likely that the Missionaries had waxed eloquent about the fearsome power of this evil impulse and about the necessity of obeying the Law to overcome it. In contrast to their claims, Paul reassures the Galatians that they do not need the Law to resist this impulse. (Indeed, as he argues more extensively in Romans 7, the Law is actually ineffectual against the problem of fleshly desire.) The Spirit of God is the only agent powerful enough to overcome the desire of the flesh.

Why is walking by the Spirit the effective way to hold the desire of the flesh in check? Paul goes on to explain that the Spirit and the flesh are fundamentally opposed. The singular desire of the Flesh (here still, as in v. 13, imagined as a malevolent power) is to oppose the Spirit of God, while the Spirit is fundamentally set against the Flesh. The two are, as Paul explains, set in opposition to each other, like soldiers lined up in opposing ranks on a battlefield. Given this opposition, there is no doubt in Paul's mind about the eventual victor: God will finally overcome all enemies (cf. 1 Cor 15:20-28). Those who walk by the power of God's Spirit will receive the empowerment necessary to subdue the Flesh. That is why Paul can express such confidence about the outcome of the struggle.

The whole passage will be badly misinterpreted if one understands Spirit and Flesh as anthropological terms for a perennial duality within the individual human personality. "Flesh" may be in some sense an anthropological term, though it should be noted that the human self remains intact as a moral agent after the "flesh" has been crucifed (v. 24). The Spirit, on the other hand, is not the human spirit; it is God's Spirit, sent into the human sphere only after Christ's death and resurrection (3:13-14; 4:6). This means that the opposition between Flesh and Spirit came into being only through Christ; the war between them,

described in v. 17, is part of the eschatological rescue mission through which God is bringing redemption to an enslaved world.[266]

The last clause of v. 17 is difficult to interpret, because it seems to undercut what Paul has just asserted in v. 16. If Flesh can frustrate the aims of the Spirit, or if Flesh and Spirit are locked in a standoff, then how can Paul make the confident claim that walking by the Spirit will overcome the desire of the flesh? John Barclay has convincingly argued that the metaphor of warfare provides the crucial clue to interpreting the conclusion of v. 17:

Warfare excludes some options and necessitates others. If they walk in the Spirit they are caught up into this conflict, which means that they are not free to do whatever they want—ἵνα μὴ ἅ ἐὰν θέλητε ταῦτα ποιῆτε (5:17). Such conflict ensures that their freedom is not absolute, for their walk in the Spirit will set them against the flesh and thus define the moral choices they must make.[267]

This interpretation would yield a slightly different translation, as follows: "for these are opposed to each other, so that you might not [just] do whatever you want." The advantage of this interpretation is that it shows how v. 17 advances Paul's argument. He is rebutting the charge that he has left the Galatians with no moral guidance. He responds by insisting that those who walk by the Spirit will in no way carry out the desire of the Flesh (v. 16), because Flesh and Spirit are at war, so that the Spirit "provides a counteracting force which motivates and directs them to *exclude* the flesh."[268] Consequently they are not, as the Missionaries charge, left in a position where they are simply free to follow their own whims and do whatever they want. They are, in fact, given very clear marching orders.

That affirmation leads nicely into v. 18. As they walk, even though they are not under the Law, they nonetheless have clarity of purpose, because they are led by the Spirit. The expression "under Law" (see 3:23-25; 4:4-5; cf. Rom 6:14) refers to the state of slavery from which Christ has set his

---

266. J. L. Martyn, *Galatians*, AB 33A (New York: Doubleday, 1997) 494.

267. J. M. G. Barclay, *Obeying the Truth: A Study of Paul's Ethics in Galatians*, Studies of the NT and Its World (Edinburgh: T. & T. Clark, 1988) 112.

268. Ibid., 115.

people free. The concept of being led by the Spirit of God also appears in Rom 8:14, where it is part of a much longer discussion (Rom 8:1-17) about living according to the Spirit rather than according to the flesh. That whole passage may be taken as an expansion of ideas developed more briefly here.

The central point of vv. 16-18, then, is that the Spirit provides strong leadership and direction in a world that is described as an eschatological war zone. Those who say the Law is sufficient to overcome the Flesh do not recognize the time of crisis in which the church walks; those who charge that without the Law the Galatians will be left undisciplined and confused do not know the power of the Spirit.

5:19-21. Indeed, Paul continues, there is no reason at all for anyone to be confused about what is going on in the world, because "the works of the flesh are obvious." In other words, we do not need the Law to identify them. He then gives a list of fifteen such works. The list, of course, is not comprehensive; it is merely an illustrative catalog of the human behaviors that result when the flesh is given a base of operation (for similar vice lists, see Mark 7:21-22; Rom 1:29-31; 1 Cor 6:9-10; 2 Cor 12:20). The list is in some respects conventional. It begins with three terms identifying sexual offenses, continues with two words for idolatry and occult magical practices, and concludes with two terms for self-indulgent partying. The most interesting feature, however, occurs in the middle of the list: a lengthy catalog of eight words that highlight dissension and offenses against the unity of the community—enmities, strife, jealousy, anger, quarrels, dissensions, factions, and envy. Paul's concentration on these community-destroying behaviors shows that his primary concern is for the unity and peace of the Galatian churches (cf. vv. 15, 26). It also reinforces the point that "works of the flesh" are not just sensual vices. The meaning of walking according to the flesh is articulated by Paul's question to the divided Christians at Corinth: "As long as there is jealousy and quarreling among you, are you not of the flesh and behaving [lit., "walking"] according to human inclinations?" (1 Cor 3:3 NRSV).

The NIV's translation in v. 21, "those who live like this," is an attempt to render the linear aspect of the present participle πράσσοντες (*prasson-*

tes); it refers to continuing action over time, not to a single violation. Paul is not saying, for example, that a single outburst of anger will result in exclusion from the kingdom of God.

This is not the first time, Paul indicates, that he has warned the Galatians about these nasty competitive behaviors. Presumably he warned them already during the time that he was present with them, for the reference cannot be to anything he has written earlier in this letter.

Unlike the vice lists in popular Hellenistic philosophical texts, Paul's list does not simply serve the purpose of advising the readers about how to develop a virtuous character and avoid bad habits.[269] Instead, the list functions as an eschatological warning: Those who practice the works of the flesh "will not inherit the kingdom of God."[270] Paul only occasionally refers to the "kingdom of God" (Rom 14:17; 1 Cor 4:20; 15:24; Col 4:11; 2 Thess 1:5; cf. Eph 5:5; Col 1:13; 1 Thess 2:12; 2 Tim 4:1, 18), which was a major theme of Jesus' teaching. To "inherit" the kingdom means to receive the eschatological blessings promised to those who are God's children (see Matt 5:5; 25:34; 1 Cor 6:9-10; 15:50; Rev 21:7). In the context of Galatians, where the metaphor of inheritance has played a central role in the argument of chaps. 3–4 (esp. 3:15-18; 3:29–4:7), Paul's choice of language is highly significant. The Missionaries have taught that circumcision is necessary to inherit the kingdom. Paul, by contrast, indicates that one is excluded from the inheritance by these flesh-driven, community-splitting behaviors—precisely the outcomes produced, in his view, by the politics of the circumcision faction (2:11-14; 4:17; 5:15, 26; 6:13).

5:22-23. In contrast to the multiple and various "works" of the flesh, the Spirit produces the singular "fruit" of a community characterized by the gracious qualities listed in these verses. We should not interpret this fruit as referring only to character qualities of the individual; Paul is primarily concerned with the way in which the Spirit's work is made manifest in community. This catalog, like the foregoing list of fleshly works, should be understood as illustrative rather than

269. F. J. Matera, *Galatians,* Sacra Pagina 9 (Collegeville, Minn.: Liturgical Press) 207-10.
270. Matera, ibid., 208-9, notes several parallels between Gal 5:19-23 and the exposition of "the Two Ways" in 1QS 3:13–4:26.

comprehensive. Paul offers different lists of gifts and workings of the Spirit in Rom 12:6-8 and 1 Cor 12:7-11. Here in Galatians, his emphasis is on the peaceful and community-building character of the Spirit's work.

We should observe that Paul is not directly exhorting the Galatians to cultivate these qualities. Rather, he is speaking descriptively, painting a picture of the harvest the Spirit produces. The metaphor of fruit suggests one of Paul's primary points. Fruit cannot be humanly manufactured; it can grow only organically, as God gives the growth—in this case, through the life-giving energy of the Spirit (cf. Rom 8:9-11).

Not every item in Paul's catalog of fruit requires comment, but it is noteworthy that the list begins with "love" and ends with "self-control." Love, produced by the Spirit, should set the tone for all that occurs in the community's life together (cf. 5:6, 13; 1 Corinthians 13). "Self-control" (ἐγκράτεια egkrateia), a term that appears only here in Paul's letters, is set in deliberate contrast to the drunken revelry that concludes the list of works of the flesh. Paul concludes the list of fruit of the Spirit by asserting that the Spirit produces peaceful and orderly self-discipline. This is particularly significant as a response to the Missionaries' claim that only the Law could provide a means of controlling the fleshly evil impulse.[271]

Finally, we should note that amid the fruit of the Spirit, we find "faithfulness" (πίστις pistis). This is the same word translated elsewhere in the letter as "faith." By rendering it in v. 22 as "faithfulness," the translators of the NIV and the NRSV recognize its proper semantic range. This faithfulness granted to the church as a fruit of the Spirit is no different from the pistis by which the Gentiles are rectified (3:8), no different from the pistis of Jesus Christ (2:16, 20; 3:22). Faith(fulness) is a sign of the Spirit's presence and work.

Paul concludes his list of the Spirit's fruit with the slightly acerbic remark that "there is no Law against such things." The force of this comment may best be understood against the background of the common Jewish characterization of Gentiles as "lawless" sinners. The Galatians may have been warned by the Missionaries that unless they are

circumcised they will fall into moral confusion, doing things contrary to God's Law. In response, Paul describes the gracious behavior that flows from the Spirit even among uncircumcised Gentile believers, and then comments, with gentle irony, that there is no Law against this kind of conduct. The effect is comparable to the argument that Paul makes in Rom 2:25-29, where he comments that "those who are physically uncircumcised but keep the Law will condemn you that have the written code and circumcision but break the Law" (Rom 2:27).

5:24-26. In the summarizing sentences of this unit, Paul returns explicitly to the problem raised in vv. 13 and 16. "Those who belong to Christ" (cf. 3:29) will not, despite the Missionaries' warnings, be overwhelmed by the impulses of the Flesh, because they have "*crucified* the Flesh with its passions and desires." This strange formulation seems to violate the usual syntax of Paul's theology. Ordinarily, Paul speaks of Jesus Christ as the primary agent who overcomes God's adversaries, and he speaks of other human beings as the recipients of Christ's grace-giving actions. They participate mysteriously with Christ in his crucifixion and death (2:19; 6:14; Rom 6:6) and thereby are set free from sin, whose power is destroyed in Christ's crucifixion. Here, however, it is Christ's people who are said to be the agents that do the crucifying of the flesh (cf. Rom 8:13). What does Paul mean by this? The likeliest interpretation is that v. 24 is a reference to baptism; by choosing to undergo baptism, believers willingly put to death their old fleshly identity. They actively identify with Christ's crucifixion and death. In this way they "crucify" the Flesh, putting its divisive desires behind them.

This baptismal interpretation is supported by the next turn in Paul's argument in v. 25, where he refers to the Spirit's life-giving role, also strongly associated with baptism. The verse is closely parallel to v. 16, but unlike v. 16 it is clearly hortatory. The NIV rendering in this verse is helpful. Paul takes it as a given that he and his readers share together in the experience of new life brought by the Spirit (3:2; 4:6-7). If that is so—if the Spirit is the power that gives life—Paul exhorts the Galatians to "keep in step with the Spirit." The verb here is στοιχέω (stoicheō), perhaps used here in playful counterpoint to

---

271. On the importance of self-mastery in Greco-Roman thought, see S. K. Stowers, *A Rereading of Romans: Justice, Jews, and Gentiles* (New Haven: Yale University Press, 1994) 42-82.

the earlier references to the oppressive στοιχεῖα (*stoicheia*, 4:3, 9). Rather than being regimented under the confining *stoicheia*, those who belong to Christ now "walk in line" with the Spirit. The Spirit gives freedom without aimlessness and order without repression.

In v. 26, Paul once again urges the Galatians to abandon their infighting. In v. 15, he made the appeal by comparing them to snarling wild animals; here in v. 26 he speaks literally, exhorting them to forswear arrogant, envious, and competitive behavior. As noted in v. 15, this warning may have become particularly necessary because of the activities of the Missionaries, whose message and

modus operandi resulted in sharply defined group barriers, separating Law-observant Christians from those who did not keep the Law. Their strategy, as Paul sees it, is to foster envy (4:17). Paul's vision for his churches, by contrast, is that they should embody the love of Christ in ways characterized by the fruit of the Spirit. The dissension in Galatia, brought on the scene by Missionaries who championed a flesh-marked covenant, was a palpable sign that the power of the Flesh was at work to disrupt the church. Paul urgently calls them, therefore, to recover their humility and unity under the guidance of the Spirit.

REFLECTIONS

1. Galatians 5:13-26 is the most impassioned defense anywhere in Scripture of the sufficiency of the Spirit to guide the community of faith. The Missionaries' message that the Law must provide ordered governance for the community was powerfully appealing to the Galatians because it tapped into a deep and persistent human need for rules and structure. We fear that without firm guidelines we will fall into chaos. The Missionaries brought a gospel that answered this felt need. They could offer an entirely persuasive interpretation of Scripture, and they offered clear guidance about how the Galatians should conduct their lives. Their Law-observant version of the gospel could claim to be rooted in an ancient and holy tradition. It is no wonder that their message found a hearing among a group of recent converts struggling to work out how to reorder their lives in response to the gospel.

Paul insists, however, that the security offered by the Law is false security and that the gospel summons those who belong to Christ to live in freedom. (*The Revised Common Lectionary* helpfully attaches 5:1 to the reading of 5:13-25; however, it also omits 5:26, thus ending the lection on the upbeat hortatory note of 5:25 and deleting Paul's specific warnings against rivalry and envy.) Paul's counsel is a daring summons, urging the church to trust that it can live without being subject to the Law of Moses as long as the Spirit guides and shapes the community, for the community will organically produce fruit formed by the Spirit. A church guided by Paul's hopeful word would cultivate a community of flexibility and freedom, living with openness toward the unpredictable liberating movement of God's Spirit. It is a radical and inspiring vision. The church at its best has been willing to take the gamble that Paul recommends, wagering its future on the guidance of the Spirit, trusting God and performing without a safety net. One thinks of the stories of the earliest church in the Acts of the Apostles, of John Wesley going into the fields to preach to coal miners, or of the Spirit-led African American church during the civil rights movement.

But is Paul right? Can we really trust the Spirit to guide the community, or is Paul's vision of the church an ideal that cannot stand up to the pragmatic tests of human experience? Is it, therefore—as Paul's adversaries charged—a prescription for disaster? Everyone knows that there are dangers, as Paul himself saw in the Corinthian church, in communities that throw away rules and traditions and seek to live in pure spiritual spontaneity. It is all too easy for talk about the Spirit to grow careless and to serve as a cover for sexual misconduct, financial irresponsibility, and manipulative abuses by the community's leaders. In the absence of Israel's Torah as a guide to life, then, must the Spirit-led church inevitably settle into a new law of some sort, a system of rule-governed institutions? (This tendency is already exemplified within the New Testament canon by the Pastoral Epistles.) Is "the institutionalization of charisma" a necessary and unavoidable development?

Our answer to these questions will depend upon whether we believe in the real presence and activity of the Spirit in our midst. Paul is not making a theoretical appeal for human moral intuition and spontaneity over written law codes. When Paul counsels the Galatians to keep in step with the Spirit (5:25), he is not thinking of the Spirit as a theological abstraction or as an inference from human subjectivity; rather, he is thinking of the Spirit as the active presence of God that does mighty deeds in the community (3:5) and cries out audibly in the church's worship (4:6). Only a church that knows the presence of the Spirit in this way can regard Paul's counsel as credible. At the same time, Paul affirms clearly that the guidance of the Spirit will have a recognizable character (5:22-23) that distinguishes it from the works inspired by the flesh. All things considered, the dangers of seeking to follow the guidance of the Spirit are fewer than the dangers of living under the stifling and divisive regulation of the Law.

2. The opposition between Spirit and Flesh (5:17) is not an anthropological dualism, not a conflict in the human individual between the sinful lower nature and the higher, better self. Rather, the opposition is a cosmic conflict between the redemptive power of God and the rebellious fallen creation. This conflict may play itself out partly in the arena of the divided self (Rom 7:14-15), but the warfare of which Gal 5:13-26 speaks cannot be reduced to a battle within the human psyche. The arena that draws Paul's special interest is the corporate life of the church, in which the Flesh seeks to produce factions and strife (5:20), while the Spirit brings peace (5:22). But we need not limit our field of vision to ecclesiological concerns. Wherever there is violence in the world, the Flesh is rampant. Those who belong to Christ will oppose violence not by counterviolence—that would be to succumb to the deception of the Flesh—but by manifesting the fruit of the Spirit even in the face of murderous opposition, keeping in step with the Spirit of Christ.

3. A corollary of the preceding point is that sex is not the only problem. The power of the Flesh is not confined to sexual misconduct. The problem with the Flesh is much bigger, and sexual misbehavior is only one of its manifestations. It is noteworthy that in the Letter to the Galatians Paul mentions sexual offenses only in passing in his conventional vice list (5:19*b*), but devotes no further discussion to them. His warning against the Flesh's works focuses instead on envy, backbiting, and competitiveness (5:15, 20, 26). Many hearers of this letter—especially in our sexually overstimulated culture—will hear the term "flesh" and think immediately of sexual scandal. An important part of the interpreter's task, then, is to recover the fuller meaning of Paul's theological vocabulary. "Flesh" is the realm of autonomous fallen humanity, living at odds with God.

4. In addition to the call to walk by the Spirit, the other major imperative sounded in these verses is found in 5:13. The way we avoid giving the Flesh a base of operations is by becoming slaves of one another, through love. That is what Paul calls his readers to do. The freedom won by Christ must be employed as Christ employed his freedom in the act of winning ours. The antidote to fleshly rivalry is self-emptying love. According to Paul, it is through such love that Christ brought the Law to fulfillment, and it is such love that should govern our relations to one another.

GALATIANS 6:1-10, LIFE TOGETHER IN THE CHURCH

NIV

6 Brothers, if someone is caught in a sin, you who are spiritual should restore him gently. But watch yourself, or you also may be tempted. ²Carry each other's burdens, and in this way you will fulfill the law of Christ. ³If anyone thinks he is something when he is nothing, he deceives himself. ⁴Each one should test his own actions. Then he can take pride in himself, without comparing himself to somebody else, ⁵for each one should carry his own load.

⁶Anyone who receives instruction in the word must share all good things with his instructor.

⁷Do not be deceived: God cannot be mocked. A man reaps what he sows. ⁸The one who sows to please his sinful nature, from that nature*a* will reap destruction; the one who sows to please the Spirit, from the Spirit will reap eternal life. ⁹Let us not become weary in doing good, for at the proper time we will reap a harvest if we do not give up. ¹⁰Therefore, as we have opportunity, let us do good to all people, especially to those who belong to the family of believers.

a8 Or his flesh, from the flesh

NRSV

6 My friends,*a* if anyone is detected in a transgression, you who have received the Spirit should restore such a one in a spirit of gentleness. Take care that you yourselves are not tempted. ²Bear one another's burdens, and in this way you will fulfill*b* the law of Christ. ³For if those who are nothing think they are something, they deceive themselves. ⁴All must test their own work; then that work, rather than their neighbor's work, will become a cause for pride. ⁵For all must carry their own loads.

6Those who are taught the word must share in all good things with their teacher.

7Do not be deceived; God is not mocked, for you reap whatever you sow. ⁸If you sow to your own flesh, you will reap corruption from the flesh; but if you sow to the Spirit, you will reap eternal life from the Spirit. ⁹So let us not grow weary in doing what is right, for we will reap at harvest time, if we do not give up. ¹⁰So then, whenever we have an opportunity, let us work for the good of all, and especially for those of the family of faith.

a Gk Brothers   b Other ancient authorities read in this way fulfill

COMMENTARY

In the final section of Paul's pastoral counsel to the Galatian churches (6:1-10), he offers them a few brief directives about what it might mean for a community to walk by the Spirit. The specific practices he commends to them are mutual correction of one another (v. 1-2), self-examination (vv. 3-5), and financial support of the community's teachers (v. 6). In vv. 7-8, Paul places this advice in the context of God's eschatological judgment and recapitulates the contrast between Flesh and Spirit. Finally, he concludes the hortatory material with a general admonition to do good, both to everyone and specifically to others within the community (vv. 9-10).

6:1-2. Paul thinks of the church as an ex-

tended family (v. 10), in which members should take responsibility for one another. He wants the members of the Galatian churches to see themselves not as rivals competing to see who can be the most devout (5:26), but rather as brothers and sisters (ἀδελφοί *adelphoi*, v. 1) supporting one another as they walk through perilous times of spiritual warfare. Because they bear responsibility for one another, they cannot casually allow other members of the family to go astray; they have an obligation to hold one another accountable to live as faithful followers of Jesus. At the same time, the responsibility for correcting erring members must be exercised with great gentleness and humility, so that the community's discipline will reflect the character of the Lord that the community serves.

The situation envisioned in v. 1 is hypothetical and general in character. If any member of the church is "caught" (NIV) in a transgression (rightly NRSV, not "sin" as in the NIV), other members should take action. This directive shows that Paul has a realistic assessment of the human fallibility of his congregations. Despite the assurance of 5:16, he knows that believers will in fact fall into misconduct. The church must therefore have guidelines for how to respond to such situations. They must cultivate the practice of mutual correction.

The phrase "you who are spiritual" (NIV) refers to all members of the community, not to a select group of spiritual leaders. (NRSV tries to clarify this point by offering the paraphrase "you who have received the Spirit.") By addressing the Galatians in this way, Paul gently challenges them to accept and live up to the description: They are to be people whose identity is shaped by the Spirit. In this case, to be "spiritual" means to act for the mending of the community, the recovery of order and peace; it is precisely the opposite of being "fleshly," which leads to conflict. The verb translated "restore" (καταρτίζω, *katartizō*) is used, e.g., in Mark 1:19 to describe the mending of fishing nets, and Paul uses it to speak of the restoration of unity within the community (1 Cor 1:10).

While there are many passages in contemporary Greco-Roman literature that speak of the philosopher's responsibility to rebuke and correct others,[272] the closest extracanonical parallel to v. 1 is to be found in the Dead Sea Scrolls, in the Rule of the Community:

They shall rebuke one another in truth, humility, and charity. Let no man address his companion with anger, or ill-temper, or obduracy, or with envy prompted by the spirit of wickedness [cf. Gal 5:26]. . . . but let him rebuke him on the very same day lest he incur guilt because of him. And furthermore, let no man accuse his companion before the congregation without having first admonished him in the presence of witnesses. (1QS 5:24–6:1)

Because this passage envisions rebuke and correction within the common life of a community devoted to the worship and service of the God of Israel, it is strikingly close to the picture presented by Gal 6:1.[273] That Paul generally advocated such practices within his churches is suggested by 2 Cor 2:5-11. Passages such as Matt 18:15-18; Luke 17:3-4; and Jas 5:19-20 bear witness to similar disciplinary procedures in other early Christian communities. Underlying all of these texts is Lev 19:17: "You shall not hate in your heart anyone of your kin; you shall reprove your neighbor, or you will incur guilt yourself" (NRSV). It is hardly coincidental that this admonition immediately precedes the command to "love your neighbor as yourself" (Lev 19:18), which Paul takes as the epitome of the Law. The rebuke of the neighbor is an expression of loving the neighbor.

Paul is concerned not only *that* the word of correction be spoken; he is equally concerned about *how* it is spoken. The rebuke must be offered "in a spirit of gentleness"—i.e., in accordance with the fruit produced by the Spirit ("gentleness," 5:23). Furthermore, Paul issues a warning to the one who speaks the word of admonition—and here he sharpens the point by shifting from the second-person plural to the second-person singular: "watch yourself, lest you also be tempted." The possible temptation could take either of two forms: Either the admonisher could be tempted to fall into the same sin as the erring member, or the admonisher could be tempted to an attitude of pride and condescension. Paul does not specify which of these possible problems he has in view. There is no need for us to decide between them; it is sufficient to recognize that the practice of mutual correction is fraught with dangers of prideful abuse, and, at the same time, that all of us share in a common human frailty. Indeed, Paul's warning here implies an astute psychological insight: We may be most harshly condemning of those failings to which we ourselves are the most susceptible.

Verse 2 should be taken specifically in conjunction with v. 1: If the Galatians take on the responsibility for correcting one another in this way, they will in fact be "bearing one another's burdens." (Paul uses the verb "bear" [βαστάζω *bastazō*] in a similar way in Rom 15:1-2: "We,

272. For references, see H. D. Betz, *Galatians: A Commentary on Paul's Letter to the Churches in Galatia,* Hermeneia (Philadelphia: Fortress, 1979) 297.

273. J. M. G. Barclay, *Obeying the Truth: A Study of Paul's Ethics in Galatians,* Studies of the NT and Its World (Edinburgh: T. & T. Clark, 1988) 174.

the powerful, ought *to bear* the weaknesses of the powerless and not to please ourselves. Let each of us please the neighbor for the good, for the purpose of building up [the church].") To live under the guidance of the Spirit is to live in a relationship of interdependence. This can be a costly matter, because our common sinfulness gives us the capacity to inflict pain upon one another and place heavy loads upon each other. It would be far easier to live as autonomous individuals without having to worry about responsibility for the conduct of others. But that would not be life in Christ. Of course, burden-bearing entails far more than the practice of mutual admonition; it also entails the sharing of stresses and sorrows, the practice of economic sharing, and all kinds of imaginative ways of becoming slaves to one another (5:13).

What is the source of the daunting mandate to bear one another's burdens?[274] Paul leaves no doubt about the answer to that important question. If the Galatians bear the burdens of their brothers and sisters, they will "fulfill the Law of Christ." That Law is the source of the obligation to carry the weight imposed by the sin of others.

But what can Paul possibly mean by speaking of "the Law of Christ"?[275] Like "faith working" in 5:6, this expression appears at first to be an oxymoron. Through most of the letter, Paul has set "Law" and "Christ" in sharp opposition to one another (2:16, 21; 3:13; 5:4). The Law is portrayed as the confining power from which Christ has liberated us. How can Paul now suddenly speak of a "Law of Christ"?

An important clue is given by the verb "fulfill" (ἀναπληρόω *anapleroō*), which echoes the verb employed in 5:14, where Christ is said to have brought the Law to fulfillment in the one word (Lev 19:18) that foretells love of neighbor as the Law's central message. Christ "fulfilled" the Law through his self-sacrificial death (1:4; 2:20), which definitively embodied the meaning of love—and therefore also the Law's true meaning (cf. Rom 13:8-10; 15:1-4; see the Commentary on 5:13-

14). In this way, Christ took possession of the Law and transformed it hermeneutically. From the point of his death onward, the Law can be understood anew as the Law of Christ, the Law defined by and belonging to him.[276]

The Galatians, then, are being summoned to re-enact the event by which Christ brought the Law to fulfillment. The idea of repetition may be conveyed by the prefix *ana* in the verb *anapleroō*. Martyn paraphrases: "Bear one another's burdens, and in this way you yourselves will repeat Christ's deed, bringing to completion in your communities the Law that Christ has already brought to completion in the sentence about loving the neighbor."[277] To fulfill the Law of Christ, then, is to play out over and over again in the life of the community the pattern of self-sacrificial love that he revealed in his death.

The syntax of 6:2 is parallel to 5:16: The sentence begins with a present imperative verb (prescribing the community's continuing action) and ends with a clause whose verb is in the future indicative (describing the results that will follow if the imperative is heeded).[278] Fulfilling the Law of Christ will follow as a consequence of the church's simple daily acts of assuming responsibility for one another.

To be sure, Paul's startling phrase "the Law of Christ" may have an ironic polemical edge. The rival Missionaries—whether or not they used precisely this expression—linked Christ with the Law and perhaps even preached about Jesus as the authoritative interpreter of the Mosaic Torah.[279] In 6:2, then—just as in 4:21 and 5:14—Paul initiatiates a counteroffensive by claiming that his gospel articulates the true positive relation between Christ and the Law. The force of 6:2 can then be explained in the following paraphrase:

The rival Missionaries are telling you that in order to be Christ's people, authentic children of Abraham, you must be circumcised and obey the

---

274. Betz, *Galatians,* 299, has argued that Paul derives this mandate from conventional maxims of "the Hellenistic philsophical tradition" (e.g., Xenophon *Memorabilia* 2.7.1-14; Aristotle *Nicomachean Ethics* 9.11.1-6). For an alternative view that the logic of Paul's mandate is ultimately grounded in the example of Christ, see R. B. Hays, "Christology and Ethics in Galatians: The Law of Christ," *CBQ* 49 (1987) 268-90.

275. For a summary of various scholarly proposals, see F. J. Matera, *Galatians,* Sacra Pagina 9 (Collegeville, Minn.: Liturgical Press) 219-21.

276. Barclay, *Obeying the Truth,* 132-35; J. L. Martyn, *Galatians,* AB 33A (New York: Doubleday, 1997) 554-58. This interpretation represents a modification of my position in Hays, "Christology and Ethics," which contended that "the law of Christ" refers not at all to the Torah, but rather to a principle or pattern exemplified by Christ's gracious self-giving.

277. Martyn, *Galatians,* 547-48.

278. As the NRSV footnote indicates, some Greek manuscripts have a reading in which the verb of the second clause is also an imperative: "Bear one another's burdens and, in this way, fulfill the Law of Christ." The future indicative, represented in both the NRSV and the NIV, is to be preferred.

279. Betz, *Galatians,* 300-301.

commandments of the Sinaitic Law. But I say to you, by contrast, that if you bear one another's burdens, becoming slaves of one another through love—correcting one another gently instead of competing viciously as the Missionaries have led you to do—you will fulfill the Law as Christ has redefined it.

This is analogous to the ironic rhetorical inversion that Paul employs in 1 Cor 9:21: "To those outside the Law I became as one outside the Law (though I am not free from God's Law but am under Christ's Law) so that I might win those outside the Law" (NRSV).[280] In both cases, Christ dramatically redefines the meaning of "Law" so that it is precisely those outside the Law, as traditionally interpreted, who turn out to exemplify the Law's meaning.

6:3-5. The connection of these verses to the foregoing context is not immediately evident. Paul's advice here is best understood as a continuation of the warnings expressed in 5:26 and 6:1*b*. The Galatians had found themselves drawn into serious conflict with one another over the question of the necessity of observing the Jewish Law. Perhaps some individuals who had started to observe the Law fancied themselves better or more spiritually advanced than the other members of the Galatian churches, and they were tempted to adopt censorious attitudes toward the others (cf. 6:13*b*). In 5:26, Paul directly exhorts them to abandon this attitude. In 6:1-2, he offers a different model, based on the pattern of Christ, in which mutual correction would be done in a Spirit of gentleness. Then, in vv. 3-5, he addresses individuals in the community and warns them against boasting; rather than comparing themselves with each other and boasting to each other, they should conduct a sober self-assessment and keep their boasting to themselves.

The advice that each person should test his own "work" [singular] seems surprising in a letter that has disparaged "works [plural] of Law" in opposition to "faith." But this challenge to self-examination is a common Pauline theme. A close parallel in 2 Corinthians is especially illuminating: "Examine yourselves to see whether you are living in the faith. Test yourselves. Do you not realize that Jesus Christ is in you?—unless, indeed, you fail to meet the test!" (2 Cor 13:5

NRSV; cf. Rom 12:3; 1 Cor 11:28). Paul is convinced that authentic faith manifests itself in action (Gal 5:6), and that Christ and the Spirit empower such faithful action (2:20; 5:22-25). Thus to test one's "work" is to examine whether it really embodies the loving character of Christ.

It is Paul's firm conviction that God will subject our actions to eschatological judgment (e.g., 1 Cor 3:10-15), and he speaks on more than one occasion about having grounds for "boasting" in his own apostolic work (Rom 15:17; 1 Cor 9:16; 2 Cor 1:12-14; Phil 2:16). Each person will receive commendation from God, as appropriate, in the end (1 Cor 4:3-5). In the present time, however, we should keep our self-evaluation to ourselves. That is the meaning of v. 4, which would be better translated, "Each one must test his own work, and then he will direct his boast to himself alone and not to his neighbor."[281] On this interpretation, vv. 3-4 fit easily together with Paul's warning against competitiveness in 5:26. This admonition would also follow logically from the cautionary note of 6:1*b:* The person who corrects another must scrutinize his or her own motivations carefully. If correcting one's brother or sister is actually a subtle device for self-aggrandizement, comparing others unfavorably to one's own high moral character, then the practice of mutual correction will become an insidious form of spiritual "one-upmanship."

This still leaves, however, the problem of how to understand v. 5, which appears to be a flat contradiction to v. 2. After telling the Galatians to bear one another's burdens, how can Paul turn around and write, "for all must carry their own loads"? Both verses employ the same verb (*bastazō*, "bear," "carry"), but the second appears to reverse what was said in the first. Is Paul simply stringing together conventional maxims linked by catchwords, so that there is no coherent line of thought in the passage? Is he just blathering in a sententious but contradictory manner, like a first-century Polonius? Or is the juxtaposition of these sentences an artful paradox, designed to provoke thought? There are two keys to understanding how vv. 2 and 5 fit together in a coherent manner.

First, we must recognize the different functions

---

280. For similar rhetorical inversions of "the Law," see Rom 3:27; 8:2.

281. Barclay, *Obeying the Truth,* 160.

of these two sentences within the discourse. Verse 2 is an imperative, calling the community as a whole to exercise mutual responsibility through loving restoration of a transgressor. Verse 5, on the other hand, functions as a warrant for the advice that each individual should examine his or her own actions; thus, it affirms a basic truth that is foundational to Paul's theology: God will judge the world and hold each person accountable (cf. Rom 2:6-10; 3:19). When the two statements are placed in context, they are complementary rather than contradictory. Paul is saying that we are all personally accountable to God, *and* that we are called to form communities in which we help one another through mutual corrective admonition.[282]

Second, the saying of v. 5 should be interpreted as an allusion to God's eschatological judgment.[283] Verse 5 belongs to the same tradition of Jewish apocalyptic thought that is more fully articulated in 4 Ezra, written a generation later than Paul's letters:

The day of judgment is decisive and displays to all the seal of truth. Just as now a father does not send his son, or a son his father, or a master his servant, or a friend his dearest friend, to be ill or sleep or eat or be healed in his place, so no one shall ever pray for another on that day, *neither shall anyone lay a burden on another; for all then shall bear their own righteousness and unrighteousness.* (4 Ezra 7:104-105, italics added)

Paul's concise expression in v. 5 points in the same direction. The "work" of each of us will be presented individually before God at the final judgment, at which time no one else can take our place or bear our load. Thus, the future tense of the verb "will bear" is a real temporal future, not the timeless gnomic future of a proverb. This conclusion is reinforced by the clear references to eschatological judgment in vv. 7-9, as well as 5:10, which uses the same verb *bastazō* to speak of incurring God's judgment.

Accordingly, the logic of Gal 6:1-5 runs as follows:

(1-2) In the present time we are called to help and support one another in the church through mutual

counsel and admonition; by bearing each other's burdens in this way we embody Christ's reconfigured Law.

(3-4) In correcting one another, we must exercise appropriate humility and scrutinize our own work,

(5) for at the final judgment each of us must bear our own load; that is, we will be called to account not just by one another, but by God.

The tension between v. 2 and v. 5, then, serves the rhetorical purpose of highlighting Paul's paired themes of mutual responsibility and individual accountability.

6:6. This commandment for the person who is taught (ὁ κατηχούμενος *ho katēchoumenos*— the source for the English cognate "catechumen") to "share in all good things with the teacher" is to be understood as a directive to provide financial support for those who carry out the ministry of teaching in the community. There is no reason to suppose that Paul is referring to an institutionalized "catechumenate" or to restrict the application of this verse to pre-baptismal instruction. Paul can use the verb in a non-technical way to refer to the instruction given through prophecy in the church (1 Cor 14:19) or to the instruction that Jews received in the Law (Rom 2:18; for other uses of the term in the NT, see Luke 1:4; Acts 18:25; 21:21, 24). It does appear, however, that Paul recognizes the presence of some persons in the churches of Galatia who are designated as teachers of "the word." This could refer to instruction either in the interpretation of Scripture or in the emergent body of early Christian tradition; in all likelihood, Paul would have made no sharp distinction. His own writings bear witness that the teaching of Scripture was a fundamental part of his apostolic work of founding churches.[284] The sort of teaching that Paul has in mind is not an academic exercise; it is a gift of the Holy Spirit, given by God for building up the body of Christ for its work of service (Rom 12:7; 1 Cor 12:28).

Martyn has hypothesized that the instructors mentioned in v. 6 were persons whom Paul had authorized to continue teaching the gospel in the Galatian churches after his departure and that the rival Missionaries were trying to discredit and

282. Ibid., 162.
283. D. Kuck, "Each Will Bear His Own Burden: Paul's Creative Use of an Apocalyptic Motif," *NTS* 40 (1994) 289-97; Matera, *Galatians,* 215. Contra Betz, *Galatians,* 304.

284. R. B. Hays, "The Conversion of the Imagination: Scripture and Eschatology in 1 Corinthians," *NTS* 45 (1999) 391-412.

displace these Pauline teachers.[285] If so, that would explain why Paul brings up this topic in his pastoral advice to the community. On the other hand, if the situation were as Martyn imagines it, it is difficult to understand why Paul would devote only one isolated, non-polemical sentence to the problem. It is perhaps more likely that Paul mentions the support of teachers simply because it belongs to his overall vision of a community walking under the guidance of the Spirit: The members admonish one another, examine themselves in humility, and share in ordered teaching and learning to grow toward greater maturity in the faith.

6:7-8. Paul now moves toward summarizing and concluding the hortatory part of his letter. The statements of v. 7 are bits of proverbial wisdom that he applies to the Galatian situation. Both proverbs point to the certainty of God's final judgment. God cannot be "mocked"—that is, scornfully disregarded—because his judgment of the world is comprehensive and just. Paul is in effect saying to the Galatians, "Remember, this is *God* you are dealing with here, not some image of your own construction. Don't think you can get away with anything, for God judges everything in the end." The proverb about sowing and reaping is a nearly universal maxim warning that actions have consequences; for example, "Whoever sows injustice will reap calamity" (Prov 22:8 NRSV; cf. Job 4:8).[286] Paul adapts the proverb here to speak of what we will "reap" on the day of God's ultimate judgment.

Why are these warnings necessary? There is no evidence in the letter that the Galatian churches were particularly plagued by libertine behavior or by careless attitudes about the will of God. If anything, they have been conscientiously concerned to do what God requires. That is why the Missionaries have made inroads in Galatia. The best explanation is that Paul sees the Galatians as standing in danger of "mocking God" by devaluing God's gracious gift in Jesus Christ and seeking justification through other means (cf. 2:21; 5:4). Paul, therefore, warns that God's grace cannot be spurned without dire consequences (cf. Heb

12:25). The agricultural imagery of the second proverb provides a transition into a specific warning about the perilous prospect faced by the Galatians if they follow the counsel of the Missionaries.

What does Paul mean by sowing "to the flesh"? (The NIV's translation of v. 8, adding the words "to please" and rendering σάρξ *sarx* as "sinful nature," implies that Paul is concerned primarily about physical or sexual lusts; however, this interpretation distorts Paul's meaning. The NRSV is a more literal translation, though the translators have converted the sentence into a conditional formulation couched in the second person in order to achieve a gender-inclusive reading.) The meaning of "flesh" has already been shaped by Paul's previous use of the term in 3:3 and 5:13-26. He has already performed the rhetorical feat of packaging circumcision together with self-indulgence under the rubric of "the flesh," and he has associated both with the envious self-asserting desire that fractures the community (see the Commentary on 5:13-26). To sow to "the flesh," then, would mean to place one's confidence and hope for the future in the mundane expedient of cutting the flesh, i.e., circumcision.

Given the fact that Paul has presented circumcision as a package deal with other connotations of "flesh," the conclusion that he draws in 6:8 comes as no surprise: Those who sow to the flesh by relying on circumcision are giving the flesh a base of operations (5:13), and they will therefore reap from the flesh only corruption—that is, only decay and death. (For similar use of the word "corruption" [φθορά *phthora*] see 1 Cor 15:42, 50, where both the NIV and the NRSV translate it as "that which is perishable.")

By way of contrast, "sowing to the Spirit" means placing one's confidence and hope in the working of God's Spirit. Because Paul has already used the image of "fruit" to characterize the product of the Spirit's activity in the community, he can easily continue the harvest metaphor. The harvest associated with the Spirit is "eternal life." Paul does not often use this terminology, but on the other occasions that he does use it, he sets it in opposition to death, and it clearly has eschatological connotations (Rom 2:7; 5:21; 6:22-23); thus we should probably understand v. 8*b* as an allusion to the resurrection of the body, as elsewhere in Jewish apocalyptic traditions (e.g., Dan

---

285. Martyn, *Galatians,* 552.
286. For other parallels, see J. D. G. Dunn, *The Epistle to the Galatians,* Black's NT Commentary (Peabody, Mass.: Hendrickson, 1993) 329-30; J. M. G. Barclay, *Obeying the Truth: A Study of Paul's Ethics in Galatians,* Studies of the NT and Its World (Edinburgh: T. & T. Clark, 1988) 164.

12:2; 2 Macc 7:9; *Pss Sol* 3:12).[287] The opposition in v. 8 between "corruption" and "eternal life" (cf. 1 Cor 15:42-58) also encourages the inference that Paul is thinking of the resurrection of the dead. We see a similar chain of ideas in Rom 8:9-13: Paul opposes the death-producing power of the flesh to the life-giving power of the Spirit, which is linked to the resurrection of the body.

Understood in this way, v. 8 encapsulates the message of the letter as a whole. It is not a moralistic warning against sensual self-indulgence; instead, it is a warning against placing confidence in anything that belongs to the realm of the merely human—particularly circumcision. Paul insists that only the Spirit of God has the power to confer life.

6:9-10. Paul now draws his exhortation to a close with a word of general encouragement to persist in doing good. In light of the promise that we will reap eternal life from the Spirit, he urges the Galatians not to grow weary or give up, even in the face of opposition, but to endure faithfully to the end (cf. Luke 18:1; 2 Cor 4:1, 16-18). The motif of being spurred on to faithful labor by the promise of eschatological reward and the hope of resurrection is a recurrent one in Paul's thought (see, e.g., Rom 8:18-39; 1 Cor 15:58; Phil 3:10-14; 3:20–4:1; 2 Thess 3:13). The reference to "the proper time" (NIV) is, again, an allusion to the day of eschatological judgment.

The emphasis on "doing good" in these concluding verses demonstrates clearly that Paul is not opposed in principle to human efforts to do the right thing; therefore, his earlier polemic against "works of the Law" must be understood as targeted particularly against the Mosaic Law and its signs of ethnically defined covenant membership (see the Commentary on 2:11-21 and 3:10-14). Of course, as shown by 5:22-25, our efforts to do good are to be understood as Spirit-empowered manifestations of God's working in us (cf. 2:20), not as autonomous performances. The doing of the good in 6:9-10, then, is synonymous with "faith working through love" (5:6).

We should hear an eschatological nuance in Paul's phrase "as we have opportunity" (lit., "as we have time" [καιρός *kairos*]). He is saying, "While the opportunity remains, let us seize the moment to do the good" (cf. Rom 13:11-14; 1 Cor 7:29; 2 Cor 6:2; Col 4:5; cf. Eph 5:16). Thus the NRSV's "whenever we have an opportunity" is misleading, because it mutes the note of eschatological urgency.

Verse 10 delineates the scope of the community's efforts in terms both general and particular. Paul exhorts his readers to do good works "for all," thus expanding the sphere of moral concern to the world at large. On this passage, Chrysostom comments: "The way of life that comes from grace takes the whole land and sea as the table of mercy."[288] At the same time, Paul recognizes the human limitation of the Galatians' efforts to do good to others, particularly in light of the eschatological qualifier posed by the opening words of v. 10; consequently, he counsels them to focus their energies particularly on doing good to those who belong to "the household of faith" (cf. Eph 2:19; 1 Tim 3:15). The "household" in Greco-Roman antiquity was not restricted to blood relatives, but the NIV and the NRSV have both chosen to replace Paul's word by the term "family," which has more connotative resonance for readers in our time. As we interpret "family," we must remember Paul's insistence that all belong to God's family only by virtue of gracious adoption (4:4-7); if we do that, the metaphor will not mislead us.

Dunn suggests that Paul's phrase "the household of faith" may be coined by Paul in conscious juxtaposition to the common OT expression "the house of Israel." That is doubtful, because Paul's wording here does not correspond precisely to the LXX's rendering of the phrase "house of Israel." If Paul had meant to evoke this echo, he could have written, "and especially to the house of faith" (τὸν οἶκον τῆς πίστεως *ton oikon tēs pisteōs*). Nonetheless, Dunn is correct to observe that in Paul's description of the church, "the bonding characteristic of this household is faith, and not membership of ethnic Israel, and not the Torah."[289] By characterizing the community in this way, Paul's final exhortation reminds the Galatians one more time that their membership in the community of God's people depends from first to

---

287. Dunn, *The Epistle to the Galatians,* 331.

288. John Chrysostom, "Homily on Galatians 6:9-10," *Interpretatio Omnium Epistularum,* ed. F. Field (Oxford: Clarendon, 1849–62) 4.97, cited in M. J. Edwards, ed., *Galatians, Ephesians, Philippians,* Ancient Christian Commentary on Scripture, vol. 8 (Downers Grove, Ill.: InterVarsity, 1999) 98.

289. Dunn, *The Epistle to the Galatians,* 333.

last on faith, and that they therefore share a common bond with one another.

Verse 10 also shows that we cannot make a facile distinction between the particularism of Judaism and the universalism of Pauline Christianity. Paul, no less than his Jewish-Christian opponents, believed that God had elected a particular community as special recipients of God's grace and messengers of God's word. The major difference between Paul and the Missionaries lay in the question of how that community was demarcated. For the Missionaries, the key identity markers were circumcision and Law-observance; for Paul, the decisive identity markers were faith and the Spirit. On Paul's view, the Spirit-powered community was given the task of doing good and offering the message of reconciliation to the whole world (cf. 2 Cor 5:18-21), but that reconciling work had to begin at home within the community of belivers. As long as rivalry and envy prevailed because of the antagonism stirred up by the circumcision advocates (5:15, 26), the work of God was being hindered. Therefore, Paul's final appeal to the Galatians to work for the good of the household of faith constitutes another plea, in a different key, to reject the divisive message of circumcision.

REFLECTIONS

If the Galatians were looking for a detailed blueprint of how to order their lives, they might have found Paul's letter considerably less satisfying than the teachings of the Missionaries, who could point to the elaborately detailed Law of Moses as a guide to life.[290] By contrast, Paul sketches only a few short strokes in his portrayal of a community guided by the Spirit. He could hardly have done otherwise: If it is the Spirit that provides the guidance, it is impossible to be narrowly prescriptive in advance. Had Paul given the sort of comprehensive instruction manual that at least some of the Galatians desired, he would have been offering a new law code and undercutting his own argument. Nonetheless, in Paul's few short strokes in 6:1-10 he has given a remarkably rich and suggestive account of themes that might characterize the common life of a Spirit-led community.

1. *The Church as an Extended Family of Mutual Responsibility.* Paul insists that the church is to be a community in which believers share responsibility for one another's lives. Life in the Spirit is not a life of lonely striving, not a life restricted to a zone of privacy; rather, it is a life lived in community. The church, like an extended family of brothers and sisters, is characterized by the interdependence of its members. This interdependence entails not only mutual support in times of need, but also the willingness to confront one another, when necessary, with a word of admonition. Within the individualistic culture of the modern West, Paul's counsel seems strange, and many Christians would find it offensive to be held accountable by their brothers and sisters in the faith. But we should recognize that mutual support and mutual accountability are two sides of the same coin; both are rooted in the conviction that we are a people with a shared calling and a shared identity. Because we are members of one body in Christ, our common welfare depends on the spiritual health of each member, and we have a stake in helping one another walk faithfully. (As Lev 19:17-18 implies, mutual reproof and love of neighbor belong together.) A church that takes Paul's pastoral guidance seriously will seek to develop patterns of life together that enable us to profit from gentle and timely corrections offered by other members of the community. Furthermore, Paul's vision of a church that practices mutual correction is by no means isolated within the New Testament; Gal 6:1 should always be read alongside Matt 18:15-22, where Jesus teaches his disciples to confront one another openly when wrongs are committed within the fellowship—and to forgive one another freely when they are acknowledged.

290. Barclay, *Obeying the Truth,* 170.

2. *The Law of Christ and the Imitation of Christ.* By urging the Galatians to bear one another's burdens, Paul calls them to conform their lives to the self-sacrificial pattern of Jesus' life. Although he does not explicitly use the language of "imitation of Christ" in Galatians, Paul is operating within the same theological paradigm that informs his counsel in passages such as 1 Cor 11:1; Phil 2:1-13; and 1 Thess 1:6-7. Jesus' self-sacrificial death provides a model that illuminates the meaning of love; therefore, those who are "in Christ" participate in a form of life that is conformed to the crucified Lord. When we look not to our own interests but to the interests of others (Phil 2:4), we are faithfully mirroring the character of the Son of God who loved us and gave himself for us (Gal 2:20). Any interpretation of Gal 6:1-10 should highlight the transformative insight of Gal 6:2; it is through loving service (cf. 5:13-14) that Christ has brought the Law to its intended fulfillment; consequently, we participate in that fulfillment by our loving service of one another. There is always an insidious temptation to turn the Law into a barrier against our neighbors or a ladder for our own self-aggrandizing aspirations. Only when the Law is read through the lens provided by the cross does it become the Law of Christ.

3. *Renouncing Rivalry and Conflict in the Church.* Paul's concentration on the problem of discord and rivalry in the community (5:15, 20-21, 26; 6:1-5) suggests that this is one of the central issues addressed by the letter. At this point, there are obvious parallels between the Galatian churches and the churches of our own time. Paul's diagnosis of the roots of conflict is therefore of considerable interest. He suggests that boasting and strife result from "sowing to the flesh." As we have seen, in its original context, this phrase referred to placing confidence in circumcision and the merely human works of the Law. In our own time, however, one of the besetting temptations for the church is to "sow to the flesh" by investing our identity in various theories and accounts of human sexuality. The result, Paul would say, is thoroughly predictable: Wherever the church grounds its identity in fleshly practices—and particularly wherever commitment to an orthodox "party line" concerning such practices becomes an exclusionary criterion for membership in the community—we can expect to reap corruption. Indeed, we will see brothers and sisters in the church biting and devouring one another (5:15). A community that sows to the Spirit will invest its hopes not in any identity defined by sexuality but in the common identity given to us in Christ by the Spirit (cf. 3:26-29; 4:6-7).

4. *Personal Accountability and Self-examination.* The admonition that each one of us should examine ourselves and keep our boasting to ourselves (6:3-4) is a sound piece of counsel too rarely heard or heeded in the church. We live in an image-conscious age that encourages us constantly to compare ourselves with others and to worry over how we appear in the eyes of others. If we truly tested our own work (6:4) only with a view to pleasing God and maintaining the integrity of our life with God, it would go a long way toward eliminating the defensive posturing that corrupts our relationships with one another.

5. *The Community Under God's Eschatological Judgment.* The standard that counts in our self-examination is not merely our self-defined values; it is God's standard, for it is to God that we are ultimately accountable (6:5, 7-9; cf. 1 Cor 4:3-5). No matter how successfully we project an image of integrity or religiousness in the world, there is no fooling God, who knows our hearts and the real quality of our work. Only work that is the fruit of the Spirit will be of value at the time of the eschatological harvest. One of the major functions of Paul's concluding exhortation is to place all our doings under the scrutiny of God's final judgment. This has two immediate consequences: It inculcates humility (6:3-5), and it sustains our vision and hope in the midst of hard labor and adversity (6:9-10). One problem with much Christian preaching—at least in mainline Protestantism—is that it has lost sight of the eschatological horizon of God's judgment. It has therefore allowed the church to lose direction and take its bearings from "the present evil age" (1:4). The interpreter of Gal 6:1-10 must seek to reclaim the conviction that God will judge us and finally vindicate us.

This way of putting the matter immediately raises a problem: How is the warning of 6:5 related to Paul's claim that we are rectified solely through participation in Christ's triumph for us? The maxim of 6:5 makes it sound as though we are to be judged solely on the basis of our own works (cf. Rom 2:6-11; 2 Cor 5:10). This complicated theological problem requires a longer response than can be given here, but we can offer some hint of the lines along which an answer might develop. The key is to recognize that our "work" (6:4) is not an independent achievement; rather, it is the fruit of the Spirit's working in and through us (5:22-23), as suggested by the paradox of Phil 2:12b-13: "Work out your own salvation with fear and trembling; for it is God who is at work in you, enabling you both to will and to work for his good pleasure" (NRSV). Because the Spirit has already given us life, the Spirit will also direct our lives in ways consonant with God's will (5:25). We are not autonomous moral agents but instruments of God's working in the world. Or, to use a different image, it is only by virtue of Christ living in us (Gal 2:20) that we can fulfill the Law of Christ and thereby stand before God's judgment not in fear, but in hope of inheriting the kingdom of God.

6. *The Importance of Teaching.* A minor, but still significant, note in the passage is the emphasis placed on teaching in 6:6. The church needs the ministry of those who do the work of instructing others in the Word, and it should share its resources in a way that makes the ministry of teaching possible. One suspects that Paul thought the Galatians' need for proper teaching was particularly acute. There is always the temptation to think that other needs are more pressing or practical, and that teaching is an optional luxury for the church. In the absence of faithful instruction, however, the church quickly goes astray—as the Galatians were doing—and loses its sense of direction. "The Word" provides the indispensable point of orientation for the community's life.

7. *"Sowing" Our Trust in the Spirit.* Finally, Paul wraps up his exhortation by posing a stark alternative. We "sow" either to the flesh or to the Spirit. For Paul, the apocalyptic thinker, there is no middle ground. The seeds that we cast will fall either on one ground or the other. This means that we are always confronted by the choice of where to commit our hopes, our energy, and our resources; in this choice, we place our lives on the line.

The Galatians were confronted by the choice between committing themselves to a gospel of circumcision ("sowing to the flesh") and trusting in a Law-free gospel ("sowing to the Spirit"). Given subsequent historical developments, few Christian preachers today will find themselves addressing congregations that are tempted to regard the Christian gospel as a deficient, stripped-down version of Judaism. Still, Paul's warning against trusting in the flesh remains relevant, if we bear in mind the scope of the term "flesh" in his theological lexicon; it refers to all self-asserting activity that seeks security in anything other than the promise of God. When "flesh" is defined in this way, we can see that our congregations face the temptation to "sow to the flesh" whenever they are tempted to define or defend themselves through ethnic exlusivity, through material possessions, or through violence. These are the insidious dangers that we face. To allow Paul's gospel to speak to our time, then, we must proclaim boldly that from ethnic exclusivity we will reap hatred; from acquisitiveness we will reap corruption; and from violence we will reap violence. Against all of these things, if we place our trust in the Spirit, we will discover a more excellent way.

POSTSCRIPT: THE CROSS AND NEW CREATION

NIV

[11]See what large letters I use as I write to you with my own hand!

[12]Those who want to make a good impression outwardly are trying to compel you to be circumcised. The only reason they do this is to avoid being persecuted for the cross of Christ. [13]Not even those who are circumcised obey the law, yet they want you to be circumcised that they may boast about your flesh. [14]May I never boast except in the cross of our Lord Jesus Christ, through which[a] the world has been crucified to me, and I to the world. [15]Neither circumcision nor uncircumcision means anything; what counts is a new creation. [16]Peace and mercy to all who follow this rule, even to the Israel of God.

[17]Finally, let no one cause me trouble, for I bear on my body the marks of Jesus.

[18]The grace of our Lord Jesus Christ be with your spirit, brothers. Amen.

[a]14 Or whom

NRSV

[11]See what large letters I make when I am writing in my own hand! [12]It is those who want to make a good showing in the flesh that try to compel you to be circumcised—only that they may not be persecuted for the cross of Christ. [13]Even the circumcised do not themselves obey the law, but they want you to be circumcised so that they may boast about your flesh. [14]May I never boast of anything except the cross of our Lord Jesus Christ, by which[a] the world has been crucified to me, and I to the world. [15]For[b] neither circumcision nor uncircumcision is anything; but a new creation is everything! [16]As for those who will follow this rule—peace be upon them, and mercy, and upon the Israel of God.

[17]From now on, let no one make trouble for me; for I carry the marks of Jesus branded on my body.

[18]May the grace of our Lord Jesus Christ be with your spirit, brothers and sisters.[c] Amen.

[a] Or through whom   [b] Other ancient authorities add in Christ Jesus
[c] Gk brothers

COMMENTARY

To conclude the letter, Paul adds a postscript written in his own hand. This was a common practice in Hellenistic letters: An amanuensis or scribe would write out the body of the text, and the sender would add a final word of greeting or summary. In the case of Galatians this concluding paragraph is far more than a perfunctory sign-off; it functions as the *peroratio* of the letter, a carefully crafted distillation of the message designed to drive home the central points one more time.[291] For this reason the postscript provides a key to understanding the central concerns of the

letter. Paul pens the final sentences with urgency and passion, offering a last glimpse of the heart of his gospel: the cross and new creation.

Usually, Paul's letter closings contain greetings and good wishes to various individuals in the community of the addressees. The absence of such friendly words in the last paragraph of Galatians corresponds to the absence of a thanksgiving in the letter's opening: Both are signs of the strained relationship between the apostle and his churches in Galatia.

6:11. The "large letters" signify that Paul has now taken the pen and begun to compose his closing word. Some have speculated that Paul

291. H. D. Betz, *Galatians: A Commentary on Paul's Letter to the Churches in Galatia,* Hermeneia (Philadelphia: Fortress, 1979) 313.

writes in large characters because of a physical disability or poor eyesight (see the Commentary on 4:13-15, above). There is, however, no indication in the text at this point that Paul is calling attention to his physical condition. It is more likely that the large letters simply serve to give special emphasis to what he will write in this paragraph. It is as though he were writing his postscript in a larger font, with boldface type, to command the special attention of his readers.

For other passages in which Paul writes a concluding personal postscript, see 1 Cor 16:21; Col 4:18; Phlm 19; cf. 2 Thess 3:17. Romans 16:22 contains a word of greeting from the scribe, Tertius.

6:12-13. Paul immediately launches an ad hominem attack on the rival Missionaries, characterizing their motives in highly derogatory terms. He alleges that they are urging the Galatians to be circumcised only in order to make themselves look good, to avoid persecution, and to have a basis for boasting. Of course, the Missionaries themselves would have given a very different account of their motives. The Galatians must decide who is to be trusted.

The focus on circumcision in vv. 12-13 is a crucial piece of evidence disclosing the issue that triggered Paul's angry letter. Paul says that the Missionaries are trying "to compel you to be circumcised." Tellingly, "compel" (ἀναγκάζω *anagkazō*) is the same verb he used of the "false brothers" in 2:4 and of Peter in 2:14; in each case Paul speaks of rigorously Law-observant Jews trying to manipulate or coerce Gentiles into coming under the Law. Their reason for this, Paul asserts, is "to make a good showing in the flesh." Paul is once again making a play on the word *flesh,* evoking its unfavorable connotation (the sphere of the merely human, as opposed to the sphere of the divine Spirit) while at the same time alluding to the physical act of circumcision. By translating the phrase as "make a good impression outwardly," the NIV loses these connotations. The good physical impression would be good only in the eyes of Jews; Greeks and Romans tended to regard circumcision as a repugnant practice of disfigurement.

Paul also alleges that the Missionaries' advocacy of circumcision is a strategy for avoiding persecution "for the cross of Christ." The persecution in question is persecution at the hands of Jews or Jewish Christians. During this historical period there was no official Roman persecution of Christians, and, in any case, the Romans would hardly have persecuted anyone for the crime of being uncircumcised![292] Earlier in the letter Paul has referred to his own activity as a persecutor of the church (1:13, 23), and he has implied that in the present time Law-observant Jewish Christians are engaged in persecuting non-Law-observant Christians (4:29; 5:11). The motive for such persecuting activity remains a matter of conjecture. Robert Jewett has proposed that the church in Jerusalem during this period was under pressure from a rising movement of Zealot-inspired nationalism that regarded the emergent Jewish-Christian groups as suspect because of their close affiliation with Gentiles. These Judean Jewish Christians, in turn, might have sought to persuade Gentile Christians to undergo circumcision in order to defuse criticism from their zealous Jewish compatriots[293] (see the Commentary on 2:11-14). This theory has the virtue of explaining the otherwise puzzling statement by Paul in 6:12: The Missionaries want to compel the *Gentile Galatians* to be circumcised in order that *they, the Jewish Christians,* might avoid persecution.

At the same time, the reference to persecution might be understood in a more general way: All who preach the cross, as Paul does, can expect to encounter opposition and persecution from a world offended by a gospel that proclaims the end of all ethnic, social, and religious privilege and distinction. The cross has put an end to all such systems (vv. 14-15). By domesticating the gospel, however, and turning it into a minor refinement of the religion of the Sinaitic Law, the Missionaries would avoid the gospel's radical implications and thereby fit more comfortably into recognized religious categories. This would enable them to escape the sort of persecution that Paul himself constantly encountered (see on v. 17, below).

---

292. It is sometimes suggested that Gentile Christians might have wanted to adopt Jewish practices because Judaism was a *religio licita,* a legally recognized religion. According to this theory, by presenting themselves to Roman authorities as Jews, Christians could be excused from pressure to participate in the cult of emperor worship, thereby escaping persecution. There is, however, no evidence of such a scenario in Galatians. Nothing is said about the imperial cult, and all the letter's references to persecution suggest that the persecution of Christians came from Jewish sources.

293. R. Jewett, "The Agitators and the Galatian Congregation," *NTS* (1970–71) 198-212.

This does not mean that they did not speak of the crucifixion of Jesus in their preaching; presumably they did, but they did not interpret the cross, in Paul's fashion, as the apocalyptic termination of the old world of religious symbolism and obligation.

The charge raised in v. 13a is puzzling for two reasons: There is a question about the meaning of the participle that is translated "those who are circumcised" (οἱ περιτεμνόμενοι *hoi peritemnomenoi*), and it is not clear what Paul means by accusing "those who are circumcised" of not keeping the Law. Because the participle is a present middle/passive form, some interpreters have suggested that it should be translated "those who are being circumcised" and understood as a reference to the Gentile Galatians who were accepting the Missionaries' call for circumcision without yet adopting comprehensive observance of the Jewish Law. Alternatively, it could simply mean "the circumcised" (NRSV) and function as a blanket term for the Jewish-Christian Missionaries who were unsettling the Galatians. The latter interpretation makes better sense in the present context, where vv. 12 and 13b certainly refer to the Jewish-Christian Missionaries.

But if that is right, why does Paul say that they do not keep the Law?[294] We should not read into the text the idea that the Law is impossible to keep (see the Commentary on 3:10-12). Nor can we accept Dunn's suggestion that they fail to keep the Law precisely by relying on "their practice as Jews" (= "works of the Law")—thereby abusing their covenantal privilege and becoming prideful. According to this reading Paul's claim is that only those who recognize that the Law teaches faith as the ground of relation to God really obey it rightly.[295] This subtle interpretation runs aground on the verb that Paul uses in v. 13: "to keep" (φυλάσσω *phylassō*); this verb characteristically refers to performing the specific commandments of the Law. Paul does not say that they do not "fulfill" the Law (cf. 5:14; 6:2), but simply that they do not do what it requires. What, then, could Paul mean by this accusation?

The best clue we have within Galatians is the similar charge that Paul levels against Peter in 2:14: If he himself is not a scrupulous observer of the Law, why is he trying to compel the Gentiles at Antioch to live like Jews? In other words, 6:13a, like 2:14, should be understood as a charge of hypocrisy. Paul is saying that the circumcision advocates are only dabblers in the Law, not really carrying out its comprehensive requirements. This accusation reflects Paul's rigoristic interpretation of the total demand of the Law (see his self-description in 1:14 as having been "more zealous" than his Jewish contemporaries). In the eyes of Paul, the former zealous Pharisee (Phil 3:6), those who merely practice circumcision and observe some of the feasts cannot claim to be living fully in accord with everything the Law requires. There can be no partial or selective observance of the Law (see the Commentary on 5:2-4).

This interpretation is supported by Paul's final comment about the Missionaries in v. 13b. They are not really interested in keeping the Law, he asserts, for their real motive for wanting to circumcise the Galatians is "so that they may boast about your flesh" (cf. the warning against boasting in 6:3-4). In effect, he is saying that his rivals want to display the foreskins of the Galatians as trophies of their own triumphant persuasive power. This accusation of self-centered vanity is consistent with Paul's earlier warning that the Missionaries want to exclude the Galatians in order to gain influence over them (4:17).

The prohibition of boasting is a recurrent theme of Paul's correspondence. In Romans he particularly identifies boasting with the Jews' presumption of their moral or religious superiority by virtue of their knowledge of God's Law (Rom 2:17-18); Paul insists that such boasting is excluded by "the Law of faith" (cf. Gal 6:2), the teaching that Jew and Gentile alike are justified only through faith (Rom 3:27-30). Something similar is in view in Paul's accusation in Gal 6:13b: He is warning that the Missionaries want to assert the superiority of Jewish religious tradition through compelling uncircumcised Gentiles to accept circumcision. The newly circumcised flesh of the Galatians would then become the ground for these Jewish-Christian Missionaries to boast about their conquest of Gentile disobedience. In short, Paul is labeling the Missionaries' push for circum-

---

294. For a list of possible interpretive options, see J. D. G. Dunn, *The Epistle to the Galatians,* Black's NT Commentary (Peabody, Mass.: Hendrickson, 1993) 338-39.

295. Ibid., 338-39.

cision as a form of chauvinistic religious self-assertion.

6:14-15. Contrasting himself to these boastful proselytizers, Paul declares that he wishes never to boast about anything—except "the cross of our Lord Jesus Christ." It is an acute paradox to speak of boasting in the cross, for the cross is precisely the place where all human effort and pride come to an end. The cross is God's deed, not ours. To "boast" in the cross, then, is to acknowledge that our efforts lead only to death and that our confidence can rest only in God's grace, which rescues us from the present evil age. Elsewhere, Paul makes the same point by quoting Jer 9:24: "Let the one who boasts, boast in the Lord" (1 Cor 1:31; 2 Cor 10:17 NRSV). That kind of boasting precludes self-aggrandizement, for it focuses exclusively on "Jesus Christ, and him crucified" (1 Cor 2:2 NRSV) and on our hope of sharing in his sufferings and glory (Rom 5:2-3, 11).

The cross, in Paul's narrative world, is the transformative event that ended the old order of things, the event through which "the world has been crucified to me, and I to the world." This startling imagery expresses God's violent and irrevocable termination of everything that Paul had previously believed and cherished. In light of the cross he has come to count all his ethnic pride and personal achievements as a complete loss (Phil 3:4-11). His previous identity has disappeared altogether, and his new identity is given him only through his participation in Christ, who animates the life he now lives (Gal 2:19-20). That is why he can also say that the flesh has been crucified for those who belong to Christ. They participate, not just symbolically but actually, in his death; therefore, they have entered the new eschatological world where his life empowers the community to "walk in newness of life" and consider themselves "dead to sin and alive to God" (Rom 6:4, 11 NRSV).

This language of the world's crucifixion should not be understood merely as an event within the psyche of the individual beliver. It is the κόσμος (*kosmos*) that has been crucified, not merely Paul's perception of the *kosmos*. The στοιχεῖα τοῦ κόσμου (*stoicheia tou kosmou*) have been overthrown and abolished by Christ's death and resurrection (cf. Col 2:13-15). A new reality has been brought into being that determines the des-

tiny of the whole creation. That is why Paul moves on in the next sentence (v. 15) to speak of "new creation." In the new creation, the old order's categories have been dissolved into nothingness. It is not merely that circumcision is of lesser importance in the new scheme of things; rather, the whole binary opposition between circumcision and uncircumcision has been literally nullified. Thus "the world that is now passé is not Judaism as such, but rather the world of *all* religious differentiation."[296]

Paul has made this point earlier in the letter with his sweeping declaration that in Christ the categories of Jew/Greek, slave/free, and male/female have ceased to have validity (3:28), and he has drawn out the pastoral implications of this truth for the circumcision question (5:6). The implications of this message for the relation of Jews and Gentiles in the church are aptly interpreted in Eph 2:15-16:

He has abolished the Law with its commandments and ordinances, that he might create in himself one new humanity in place of the two, thus making peace, and might reconcile both groups to God in one body through the cross. (NRSV)

Now, in his climactic summary of the letter's message, he divulges the fundamental reason underlying these remarkable claims: "For neither circumcision nor uncircumcision is anything, but—*new creation*!" The broken syntax of the sentence expresses the utter discontinuity between the abolished cosmos and the new world. There is no way to finish the sentence; Paul can only blurt "new creation!" (Unfortunately, both NIV and NRSV mute the literary effect by filling the gap and smoothing Paul's exclamation into a tamer complete sentence.) We see a parallel movement of thought in the one other place that Paul speaks of new creation:

So if anyone is in Christ—new creation! Everything old has passed away; see, everything has become new! (2 Cor 5:17, author's trans.)

Paul is not speaking here about "the establishment of a new religion"[297] or the spiritual rebirth of an

---

296. J. L. Martyn, *Galatians*, AB 33A (New York: Doubleday, 1997) 565, emphasis in original; see also pp. 570-74; S. K. Williams, *Galatians*, ANTC (Nashville: Abingdon, 1997) 165.
297. Betz, *Galatians*, 320.

individual. He is claiming that the God who created the world has come to reclaim and transform it.

The ground of this hope lies in Israel's Scripture, with its prophetic visions of God's ultimate transformative justice. Particularly important is Isa 65:17-25, which begins with an extraordinary promise:

For I am about to create new heavens
  and a new earth;
the former things shall not be remembered
  or come to mind. (Isa 65:17 NRSV)

This vision of God's new creation is fundamental to Paul's theology; he proclaims not just the salvation of souls, but also God's eschatological redemption of the creation (see Rom 8:19-23; cf. Rev 21:1-5).[298]

In this new creation, the Missionaries' pressure for the practice of circumcision simply makes no sense. It is a reversion to the *status quo ante,* an attempt to reenter a symbolic world that has been obliterated by the cross. Thus with Gal 6:14-15 Paul has completed his forceful recapitulation of his argument.

6:16. Having begun the letter with a curse on the perverters of the gospel (1:8-9), Paul chooses to end it with a blessing on his readers in the hope that they will have been persuaded by his arguments to renounce circumcision and live as Gentiles under the direction of the Spirit. Since he does not know the effect that his letter will achieve, however, he formulates the blessing in conditional terms. The blessing is pronounced not on the Galatian churches generally, but specifically on "those who will follow this rule" (note the future tense). The verb "will follow" (στοιχήσουσιν *stoichesousin*) is the same word used in the exhortation of 5:25: "Since we live by the Spirit, let us *keep in step* with the Spirit." These two sentences certainly interpret one another: To keep in step with the Spirit is to follow the "rule" of 6:14-15, and to follow this rule is to be guided by the Spirit to discern the new creation. Only those readers who heed this rule are the recipients of the "peace and mercy" invoked by the apostle.

The word "rule" (κανών *kanōn*) refers literally to a measuring stick. Paul employs it metaphorically here to speak of the measure of truth and conduct articulated in v. 15 (and perhaps v. 14 as well): Boast only in the cross, for the old world is abolished and we live in the presence and hope of the new creation. Paul's frequent warnings elsewhere against boasting support the interpretation that v. 14 belongs to the rule to which Paul refers.

The blessing that Paul pronounces is deeply traditional and Jewish in character (cf. Ps 125:5; 128:6; *Pss Sol* 9:11; 11:9). "Peace" and "mercy" correspond to שָׁלוֹם (*šālôm*) and חֶסֶד (*ḥesed*), deeply resonant Hebrew words for God's blessing and grace. The most striking parallel to Gal 6:16 appears in the nineteenth benediction, the "Blessing of Peace" of the *Shemoneh Esreh* (Babylonian recension), a liturgy used regularly in the synagogue: "Bestow *peace,* happiness and blessing, grace and loving-kindness and *mercy upon us and upon all Israel,* your people" (italics added).[299] It is impossible to document the use of this specific benediction in the synagogues of Paul's day, but it is likely that he did know such a prayer and that he formed his benediction to the Galatians by analogy to it. It is important to observe that in this prayer "us" refers to the congregation praying the prayer, while "all Israel" is not a separate second group; rather, "all Israel" is the larger covenant community, the people of God to which the praying community ("us") belongs.

The potentially ambiguous wording of Gal 6:16 has generated much controversy about the meaning of the distinctive expression "the Israel of God," an expression that never occurs elsewhere in Paul's letters, in the extant literature of Second Temple Judaism, or in rabbinic literature.[300] From a purely syntactical point of view, there are two ways of reading the blessing. The question is whether Paul is referring to a single group (as in the NIV) or to two different groups (as in the NRSV). The possibilities are as follows:

(a) As for those who follow this rule, peace and mercy be upon them
—that is, upon the Israel of God.
(b₁) As for those who follow this rule, peace and mercy be upon them
—and (also) upon the Israel of God.

---

298. For references to the motif of new creation in other Jewish texts, see *Jub.* 4:26; *1 Enoch* 72:1; *4 Ezra* 7:75; *2 Apoc. Bar.* 32:6; 1QS 4:25; 1QH 11:10-14; 13:11-12. See also Martyn, *Galatians,* 565n. 64.

299. Betz, *Galatians,* 321.
300. R. N. Longenecker, *Galatians,* WBC 41 (Dallas: Word, 1990) 299.

A variation on the second option is to read the peace benediction as applying to Christians who accept Paul's line of argument and the mercy benediction as a second separate word of blessing on non-Christian Jews who may still, Paul hopes, experience God's mercy. This would yield the translation:

(b₂) As for those who follow this rule, peace be upon them
—and mercy upon the Israel of God.

Those scholars who argue for b₁ or b₂ appeal for support to the argument of Romans 9–11, especially Rom 11:25-32, where the word *mercy* appears prominently in conjunction with Paul's affirmation that "all Israel will be saved."

If Paul meant to refer, however, to the ultimate salvation of the Jewish people, including those who in the present time reject the preaching of the gospel, he has provided no clues of this sort for his readers in Galatia. He had not yet written the Letter to the Romans, and Galatians nowhere touches upon the problem of God's faithfulness to Israel or the ultimate salvation of the Jewish people. The apostle is concerned with an entirely different set of problems posed by the demand that his Gentile congregations become Law observant. In the course of his argument he has asserted in the strongest possible terms that the Gentile members of his churches in Galatia are children of Abraham, heirs of God's promised blessing (3:6-9, 29), rightful heirs of the promise through Isaac (4:28, 31), Sarah's children. It is they who fulfill the Law (5:14; 6:2). In light of these claims there is only one possible way that the original readers could have understood the blessing of Gal 6:16: The Israel of God refers to all who are in Christ (i.e., translation a).[301] It is a description of the elect eschatological community of faith composed of Jews and Gentiles alike. It is equivalent in meaning to "the household of faith" (6:10). The Israel of God, then, is another name for those who follow the rule of the new creation.[302]

For Paul to use the term "Israel" in this way is a bold move indeed, but certainly no bolder than his claim that the Gentile Galatians are Abraham's seed, children of promise in Isaac's line—indeed, it is substantively identical to that claim. Thus the blessing that Paul pronounces at the end of the letter forcefully restates the letter's central thesis.

6:17. In a final rhetorical gesture Paul demonstrates dismay at having to put up with the hassle of answering the Missionaries' arguments and rebutting their charges. He gives a surprising reason for his request that no one trouble him further with these matters: Because he bears the marks (στίγματα *stigmata*) of Jesus on his body. This expression refers to the scars that he has incurred in the course of his apostolic labors. By his own testimony Paul suffered numerous floggings and beatings, and he was once stoned (2 Cor 11:23-25; cf. 2 Cor 6:4-5; Acts 14:19). Such abuse would no doubt have left his body battered and marked by scars. Experiences such as these may lie behind Paul's reference to some sort of physical affliction that occasioned his first visit to Galatia (Gal 4:13-14).

Paul interprets these bodily scars as signs of his identification with his crucified Lord. Indeed, his battered body becomes for him a visible depiction of the gospel of the cross. This is probably what he has in mind when he describes himself as "carrying in the body the putting to death (νέκρωσις *nekrōsis*) of Jesus, so that the life of Jesus may also be made visible in our bodies" (2 Cor 4:10). The wounded apostle becomes a walking exhibit of the message of "Jesus Christ, and him crucified."[303] In all likelihood this conviction explains what Paul means when he says that in his original preaching to the Galatians "Jesus Christ was publicly exhibited as crucified" (3:1 NRSV).

The point of Gal 6:17 is that Paul's battle scars demonstrate his integrity and the truth of his message. Unlike the rival Missionaries, who seek to dodge persecution (v. 12), Paul has undergone it gladly and repeatedly for the sake of the gospel. Therefore, the Galatians should listen to him and

---

301. Thus Betz, *Galatians,* 322-23; Longenecker, *Galatians,* 298-99; Martyn, *Galatians,* 574-77.

302. This inclusion of Gentile believers within "Israel" is commensurate with Paul's pastoral strategy in 1 Corinthians. In writing to a predominantly Gentile church in Corinth, he describes Israel in the wilderness as "our fathers" (1 Cor 10:1) and refers to his readers' past as the time "when you were Gentiles" (1 Cor 12:2). In short, he narrates the Gentile Corinthians into the people Israel.

303. See S. Kraftchick, "Death in Us, Life in You: The Apostolic Medium," in *Pauline Theology,* vol. 2: *1 & 2 Corinthians,* ed. D. M. Hay (Minneapolis: Fortress, 1993) 156-81.

not to a group of slick interlopers who have not paid the price of following a crucified Lord.

One additional nuance might be suggested by Paul's reference to "the marks of Jesus." In ancient Mediterranean culture slaves were characteristically branded with a mark to show to whom they belonged. Because Paul regards himself as Christ's slave (1:10), he may be suggesting that his physical scars mark him as the possession of the crucified Lord, Jesus. In that case 6:17 would imply that the Missionaries should desist from bothering him because he is working under the orders and authority of his master. Their attempt to interfere with his apostolic work is, in fact, an interference not just with him, but also with Jesus.

6:18. The final sentence of the postscript, after all the distress and anger of this letter, pronounces a simple benediction on the readers. "The grace of our Lord Jesus Christ" surrounds and embraces this entire turbulent argument (1:3; 6:18). Grace refers to the loving favor of God, made effective in the world through Christ's death. (For other mentions of grace in Galatians, see 1:6, 15; 2:9, 21; 3:18; 5:4.) After stern warnings to the Galatian churches not to fall away from grace, in the end the apostle utters a prayer that Christ's grace will remain with their spirit. Here and only here in the letter, "spirit" is used as an anthropological term rather than as a reference to the Spirit of God.

Nearly identical benedictions are found in Phil 4:23 and Phlm 25. In Gal 6:18, however, Paul adds one word that does not appear in the others: ἀδελφοι (*adelphoi*). It is the last word before the "amen," the penultimate word before the silence into which the Galatians will have to speak their response to Paul's appeal. By poignantly addressing his readers in this last breath of the postscript as brothers and sisters, Paul affirms a continuing hope that they will not turn away from the gospel, that they will remain his brothers and sisters within the family of faith.

REFLECTIONS

1. *The Problem of Cultural Imperialism.* From a historical point of view we are in no position to assess the fairness of Paul's harsh critique of the Missionaries. We have no access to their writings and no other documents to provide information on the situation of the Galatian churches. We have only Paul's account of the matter. Were they really as chauvinistic and self-interested as Paul contends? Perhaps so, but human motivations are complex. Presumably they believed themselves to be promoting the cause of obedience to God's will. In our reflection on the text, we will not make much progress through speculative psychologizing about the Missionaries and their motives. We will do better to concentrate on the effects of their actions on the Gentile believers in Galatia.

Paul's chief objection to the Missionaries' message was that it sought to superimpose their Jewish religious culture upon Gentiles who had already encountered the gospel through Paul's Law-free preaching. Their insistence on circumcision had the effect of making Gentiles jump through a Jewish hoop in order to participate fully in the new community of the people of God. This sort of cultural imperialism was anathema to Paul.

We need to think carefully about the reason why Paul found this cultural imperialism so objectionable. It was not because he believed that there was some intrinsic value to Gentile cultural practices, not because he believed that each person had a right to make private choices about religious preference, and certainly not because he believed that proselytizing was wrong *a priori*. Paul was, after all, engaged in a lifelong project of seeking to win converts for the gospel and to transform the cultures of the Gentile communities where he established churches. Paul's objection to the Missionaries' cultural imperialism was that it had the effect of nullifying the grace of God. In communities where Gentiles had already received the Spirit, they were now being told that their experience was somehow deficient and that they had to conform themselves to Jewish religious practices in order to participate fully in God's promise of life. Thus they were being led subtly to discount the redemptive work of Jesus Christ as their one ground of hope and to substitute for it a program of human religious observances. That is why Paul put his foot down in opposition to the circumcision party.

Therefore, as we reflect on Galatians as Scripture, we must ask ourselves at what points we are in danger of superimposing our religious culture—even the cultures of particular church traditions—on communities that are responding to the gospel in fresh, indigenous ways under the guidance of the Spirit. This can happen not only when Christian missionaries encounter non-Western cultures, but also when established churches frown on charismatic churches or independent churches outside the usual denominational structure. It can happen when older Christians object to the musical and artistic forms of worship among younger Christians. It most certainly happens in every case where ethnic pride or nationalism co-opts the gospel. After reading Galatians carefully we will find ourselves prompted to scrutinize our churches to see whether we may be unintentionally nullifying the grace of God through explicit or implicit membership requirements unrelated to the heart of the gospel.

2. *Boasting in the Cross.* Paul's postscript reminds us that the cross is at the heart of the Christian message. It destroys all pride, for through the cross the whole world has been crucified. This astounding metaphor requires sustained reflection. If we are tempted to boast in our wealth or intelligence or accomplishments, we are pursuing a path that leads nowhere. The most insidious temptation—the one faced in Galatia—is the temptation to boast in moral or religious superiority. The cross destroys all such boasting and focuses our eyes upon Jesus, whose loving self-donation discloses the one truth that can be trusted, the truth of God's love for us. That is why we can boast only in "the cross of our Lord Jesus Christ." To "boast" of the cross is of course not boasting at all: The paradox redefines the verb, so that boasting becomes worship and acclamation of the crucified Jesus. Furthermore, as we focus our attention on the cross, we learn that we render true honor to the crucified Lord only by becoming conformed to him so that we become servants to one another in love (5:13). Truly to boast in the cross is to put our own lives on the line in acts of service that declare in deed as well as in word that the cross is the revelation of God's love.

3. *New Creation.* Paul's gospel is not only a negative word that proclaims the demolition of our old world of religion, value, and morality. The gospel also proclaims that God is making all things new. As the marks of Jesus on Paul's body testify, the coming of the new creation is neither easy nor complete in the present time. The breaking in of God's redemptive power has triggered costly conflict with the powers that have a vested interest in the old order. The calling of the apostle—and of the church—is to bear witness steadfastly to the coming new order of God's justice. The new creation is not, however, merely a dream or a vision; it takes on empirical reality in the community of God's people, whose life together already testifies to the reconciling power of the gospel. That is one reason why Paul was so insistent that Gentiles not be circumcised. The policy of circumcision made it look as though the Gentile converts were simply being absorbed into Judaism, but Paul was insistent that "the Israel of God" was a new eschatological reality, a community in which the circumcision/uncircumcision distinction no longer functioned to divide humanity. That is the rule that Paul invokes as the identifying standard for walking under the guidance of the Spirit: no more fleshly divisions. As we have seen earlier in the letter, where the grace of Jesus Christ is at work, God's people will find themselves united around one table, not divided at separate tables. The one table where circumcised and uncircumcised sit together in love is a sign and foretaste of the new creation.

For many readers in our time, the deepest ethnic divisions will not be those between Jew and Gentile, but between different racial groups, even within the church. Sadly, it remains true, as Martin Luther King, Jr., observed a generation ago, that 11:00 A.M. Sunday is the most segregated hour of the week in the United States. If we hear Paul's letter as a message spoken not just to ancient Galatians, but also to us, we will hear it as a call to racial reconciliation. If we can read Gal 6:15 and echo it in our hearts by confessing, "Neither whiteness nor blackness is anything, but—new creation!" then peace and mercy will be upon us indeed.

THE LETTER TO THE EPHESIANS

INTRODUCTION, COMMENTARY, AND REFLECTIONS
BY
PHEME PERKINS

THE LETTER TO THE
EPHESIANS

INTRODUCTION

REMEMBERING THE APOSTLE: GENRE, CHARACTER, AND SOURCES

Although some still argue that Paul was the author of Ephesians,[1] most scholars agree that the letter is pseudonymous. For an audience accustomed to appropriating all written texts orally—that is, through hearing their contents read and perhaps even explicated by the person who actually conveyed the letter to its recipients—multiple voices in a text were a common experience. Consequently, when scholars speak of Paul as the "implied" or "fictive" author of Ephesians, they do not mean that the writer is making a fraudulent use of Pauline authority. The gap between this letter and Paul's personal correspondence is not hard to detect.[2] Ephesians lacks the personal greetings characteristic of Paul. No associates or fellow Christians are mentioned as co-senders. Those to whom Ephesians speaks do not know the apostle (1:15; 3:2). Yet, as Gentiles who have now been brought into the people of God (2:11-13), they owe a great debt to him. Paul's insight into the mystery (μυστήριον *mystērion*) of God's saving plan forms the basis of the gospel message (3:1-13). Their familiarity with the apostle has been mediated through writing rather than through his personal presence (3:2-4).

Paul's own letters contain specific details of the relationship between the apostle and those to whom he writes. Figuring out the prior history of the apostle's ministry in a

---

1. Markus Barth, *Ephesians,* 2 vols., AB 34-34A (Garden City, N.Y.: Doubleday, 1974); Peter T. O'Brien, *Letter to the Ephesians* (Grand Rapids: Eerdmans, 1999).

2. Ernest Best, "Recipients and Title of the Letter to the Ephesians: Why and When the Designation 'Ephesians'?" in *Aufstieg und Niedergang der römischen Welt* II 25/4, ed. Wolfgang Haase (Berlin: DeGruyter, 1987).

---

particular church plays a crucial part in understanding those letters. Ephesians has no such clues. Sometimes interpreters supply reasons for a particular theme in Ephesians that have been taken from the context of another of Paul's letters. For example, the assumption that the growing numbers of Gentiles in the church have begun to denigrate the Jewish heritage of Christian faith (a concern of Romans 9–11) is proposed as the reason for writing Ephesians.[3]

Attempts to construct a setting for Ephesians run up against the literary genre of the work.[4] The author has adopted ancient rhetorical forms of celebratory and hortatory discourse.[5] The first half of the epistle (1:3–3:21) invites the audience to join in praising and thanking God for the plan of salvation that has united them with Christ. It concludes with a brief doxology (3:20-21). The second half encourages readers to persevere in the social and personal dimensions of their lives as new creations in Christ (4:1–6:20). It concludes in a dramatic peroration (6:10-20). Believers stand armed and ready to vanquish evil powers (6:10-17). They will also assist the imprisoned apostle in continuing his bold witness by remembering him in prayer (6:18-20).

Despite this clear understanding of the genre of the work, Andrew T. Lincoln cannot resist assuming that the rhetorical appeals to the audience built into the genres in question provide information about the epistle's readers. This methodological difficulty is masked by assuming that such mirror reading gives access to what literary critics mean by "implied readers." Not so, if the addressees recognize the rhetorical topoi involved. Lincoln comments, "It can be inferred from the implied author's prayers for them (3.14-19) and from his appeals which introduce and conclude the parenesis (cf. 4.1-16; 6.10-20) that their main problems are powerlessness, instability and a lack of resolve, and these are related to an insufficient sense of identity."[6] In fact, these passages tell us nothing about the problems of particular readers, actual or implied.[7] They do establish powerful images of Christian identity. The consolidation of communal identity can be understood as the basic function of celebratory rhetoric. A community that hears praises of its imperial—or, in this case, divine—benefactor, of the peace and well-being that a benefactor's gracious use of power has bestowed on it, that community also comes to know itself in relationship to the benefactor.

The lack of detail even appears in the opening greeting (1:1-2). The phrase "in Ephesus" (ἐν Ἐφέσῳ *en Phesō*) does not occur in many of the earliest manuscripts. Nor would that locale be appropriate for an audience that does not know the apostle. Paul had worked extensively in Ephesus. He may even have been imprisoned there (1 Cor 15:32). Unlike

---

3. Ralph P. Martin, *Ephesians, Colossians and Philemon* (Atlanta: John Knox, 1991).

4. David G. Meade, *Pseudonymity and Canon: An Investigation into the Relationship of Authorship and Authority in the Jewish and Earliest Christian Tradition,* WUNT 39 (Tübingen: Mohr-Siebeck, 1986) 140-42.

5. See Andrew T. Lincoln, *Ephesians,* WBC 42 (Dallas: Word, 1990) xl-xlii; and " 'Stand, therefore . . .': Ephesians 6:10-20 as *Peroratio,*" *Biblical Interpretation* 3 (1995) 99-114.

6. Andrew T. Lincoln and A. J. M. Wedderburn, *The Theology of the Later Pauline Letters* (Cambridge: Cambridge University Press, 1993) 82-83.

7. For a cautious treatment of the assumptions that Ephesians makes concerning its readers, see Ernest Best, *A Critical and Exegetical Commentary on Ephesians,* ICC (Edinburgh: T. & T. Clark, 1998) 1-6.

either Colossians (Col 4:14; 5:6-7) or the Pastorals (1 Tim 1:18-20; 4:1-7), Ephesians never refers to false teachers whose doctrines must be avoided. Therefore, the epistle appears to be addressed to Christian churches in general, not to a particular situation. Some interpreters suggest that the author was concerned with the impact of the pagan religious environment in the Lycus Valley and wrote the epistle as a circular letter to churches in the environs of Laodicea and Hierapolis.[8] Nevertheless, the author does not appear to have any personal knowledge of the addressees. The discourse alternates between the second-person plural "you" and the first-person plural "we." Sometimes "we" designates Jewish Christians associated with the author, in contrast to "you" Gentile converts. Sometimes "we" refers to all Christians as a group. Ephesians never uses the common Christian designation "brothers" (ἀδελφοί adelphoi) in addressing the audience. The only use of the term occurs in the conclusion, where it is a third-person plural reference (adelphoi).

Ephesians encourages the audience to "imitate God" (Γίνεσθε οὖν μιμηταὶ τοῦ θεοῦ Ginesthe oun mimētai tou Theou, 5:1) rather than the apostle, unlike the usual practice in Paul's letters. Even the Pastoral Epistles retain the motif of imitating Paul (2 Tim 1:8; 3:10-14). Since imitation of those who possess virtues is key to ancient paraenesis, the absence of the theme in Ephesians highlights the distance between its audience and the apostle.[9] With the exception of topoi in the household code, Ephesians has no significant parallels with the Pastoral Epistles.[10] Although the author has made extensive use of Colossians, he drops Timothy as co-sender from the opening greeting (1:1; cf. Col 1:1), even though this omission lives on in an odd first-person plural at the end (6:22; cf. Col 4:8). Perhaps this detail is more significant than it appears at first. The author and recipients of Ephesians do not belong to the circle of churches in which Timothy or Paul's other closest associates had been active.

Does Ephesians represent the first introduction these Christians have had to the apostle? Attempts to treat Ephesians as a summary designed to introduce an early collection of Pauline letters (assumed as the referent of 3:3-4) founder on the genre of the work. Ephesians does not read as an epitome of the apostle's teaching either in its formal rhetorical structure or its content. Further, the passage said to refer to other writings (3:3-4) does not indicate an established canon of Pauline letters. It could refer to the reading of Ephesians as a further explanation of what was said about the mystery (mystērion) in a previous letter. Ephesians may have taken its cue from Col 2:1-6. The apostle's trials are to benefit not only Christians known to him, but also others who have never seen him. Ephesians is claiming to express the mystery (mystērion) about which Paul was speaking.[11]

Verbal comparisons of Ephesians and Colossians are found in the tables that accompany the relevant sections of the Commentary. The sum total of such evidence makes a strong

---

8. Larry J. Kreitzer, " 'Crude Language' and 'Shameful Things Done in Secret' (Eph 5, 4, 12): Allusions to the Cult of Demeter/Cybele in Hierapolis?" *JSNT* 71 (1988) 51-77; and "The Plutonium of Hierapolis and the Descent of Christ into the 'Lowermost Parts of the Earth' (Ephesians 4, 9)," *Biblica* 79 (1998) 381-93.

9. Meade, *Pseudonymity and Canon*, 153.

10. Lincoln, *Ephesians*, lvi.

11. Meade, *Pseudonymity and Canon*, 150-51.

case for the view that the author of Ephesians knew and used much of Colossians in his own epistle. But Ephesians has also recontextualized and changed the order of images and phrases taken from Colossians.[12] Even those sections that are substantially new contain some echoes of Colossians (1:3-14; 2:5-21; 4:8-16; 5:8-14, 22-33; 6:11-17).[13] Echoes of other Pauline letters are noted in the Commentary.[14] Romans is more frequently evident in parallels to Ephesians than any other Pauline letter. Consequently, it does not seem likely that Ephesians relies simply on oral traditions circulating in Pauline churches. Knowledge of some Pauline letters themselves must be presupposed. But one can only make this argument with regard to the author of Ephesians. It is impossible to tell from the epistle whether the recipients were familiar with the passages that are cited here as parallels. The Commentary will argue that the rhetorical strategies used in the letter presuppose that the audience recognizes what it hears as tradition, not new instruction. Lincoln has suggested using the phrase "actualization of an authoritative tradition" for the reuse of Pauline material in Ephesians.[15]

David Trobisch's study of letter collections has shed new light on the place of Ephesians in the Pauline corpus. Often the first collection of an author's letters was prepared by the author himself. Trobisch argues that Paul is responsible for creating a collection composed of Romans, 1–2 Corinthians, and Galatians. After an author's death other letters would be added at the end of the original group. Finally, someone might prepare a comprehensive collection from all available versions. Trobisch suggests that the first letter to break the principle that orders a collection indicates the point at which such expansion of an existing collection takes place. For the Pauline letters, the ordering principle appears to be length. However, on that criterion, Ephesians should come before Galatians. Therefore, it represents the first epistle added to the primitive collection produced by the apostle.[16] This research tells us nothing about the original addressees or how the Pauline letter canon came to be formed. It only indicates that Ephesians represented the first letter to be added to the originating collection of four major Pauline epistles.

If the more speculative side of Trobisch's argument holds—namely, that the apostle himself was responsible for Romans through Galatians—then the question of which letters other churches may have possessed looks slightly different. An early collection by the apostle himself may have been designed to be circulated. If Ephesians assumes that its audience has heard actual letters from the apostle, then this group of letters is most likely

---

12. Best highlights the shifts in language between Colossians and Ephesians to argue for a more complex relationship between the two. Rather than conclude that Ephesians is directly dependent upon Cololossians, Best concludes that Colossians and Ephesians are independent representatives of a Pauline school tradition. See Best, *A Critical and Exegetical Commentary on Ephesians*, 20-25. Such a hypothesis has as many difficulties as the assumption that Ephesians is reworking Col. For a detailed analysis that argues that Ephesians is dependent upon Colossians and other written Pauline letters see Michael Gese, *Das Vermächtnis des Apostels, Die Rezeption der paulinischen Theologie im Epheserbrief,* WUNT 2 Reihe, 99 (Tübingen: J.C.B. Mohn [Paul Siebeck], 1997) 39-54.

13. So Rudolf Schnackenburg, *The Epistle to the Ephesians,* trans. H. Heron (Edinburgh: T. & T. Clark, 1991) 30-31.

14. Also see the chart of these relationships in Gese, *Das Vermächtnis des Apostels,* 76-78.

15. Lincoln, *Ephesians,* lviii.

16. David Trobisch, *Paul's Letter Collection: Tracing the Origins* (Minneapolis: Fortress, 1994) 50-52.

---

the group that was circulated. Ephesians may not presume that Colossians was read in the churches to which the apostle writes. Instead, Colossians provided the impetus for Ephesians to formulate Paul's own account of the mystery of salvation.

The basic picture of the apostle that Ephesians leaves with its readers contains few details. He is presented as the great apostle to the Gentiles whose Spirit-endowed insight (1:17; 3:2-3) has made the hidden plan of salvation accessible to all. This "mystery" (*mystērion*) made known through the apostle is also the tradition of the apostles and prophets who are the foundation of the church (2:20-22). Finally, the apostle's imprisonment is "for the sake of you Gentiles" (3:1 NRSV) and calls for courage to continue boldly proclaiming the gospel (6:19-20). Even these Christians who have no direct connection to the apostle's own churches are assured that the apostle suffers on their behalf. One cannot be sure whether the letter's audience knows that Paul has suffered martyrdom. Unlike the letters that Paul wrote from prison earlier, Ephesians never anticipates the possibility of his release. Unlike 2 Tim 4:6-18, Ephesians never hints that his death is near. But the conclusion of Acts indicates that an author and readers who know full well that the apostle has died may celebrate his heroic witness to the gospel without recounting his death.

WHERE EPHESIANS DIFFERS: THEOLOGY, LANGUAGE, AND STYLE

Ephesians was not composed as an epitome of Paul's teaching or as the celebration of an apostle hero. It focuses on God's foreordained plan of salvation, uniting Jew and Gentile in the body of the risen Christ. This theological insight develops a number of themes found in Paul's letters in a new direction. One no longer finds the event of salvation focused on the cross, though the traditional formulae concerning the redemptive effects of Christ's death do appear. Instead of speaking of the power of sin to hold humans in bondage, Ephesians refers to sins in the plural (αμαρτιαι *hamartiai*). Bondage is associated with evil powers whose effectiveness is linked to the earthly regions. Consequently, the dominant metaphor for redemption from their influence is exaltation "in the heavenly regions" with the risen Christ.[17]

1. Shifting Language. The language of Ephesians also departs markedly from Paul's style. The author constructs extensive, periodic sentences out of dependent clauses introduced by participles and infinitive phrases. In order to provide a readable text, translations break up these long sentences. However, the tables that compare the language of Ephesians with other Pauline letters will provide as literal a rendering as possible in order to indicate similarities of wording. Readers should consult commentaries based on the Greek text for detailed information about the elaborate Greek style in Ephesians. Such commentaries also provide lists of the unusual vocabulary used in Ephesians. Many words are either unique in the New Testament or appear in Ephesians and another New Testament writing, but not elsewhere in the Pauline letters. Some expressions appear to

17. Arland J. Hultgren, *Christ and His Benefits: Christology and Redemption in the New Testament* (Philadelphia: Fortress, 1987) 92-93.

---

replace Pauline equivalents; for example, Ephesians uses "in the heavenly places" (ἐν τοῖς ἐπουρανίοις *en tois epouraniois*; 1:3, 20; 2:6; 3:10; 6:12) where Paul would speak of "in the heavens" (ἐν οὐρανοῖς *en ouranois*; 2 Cor 5:1; Phil 3:20; Col 1:5, 16, 20).[18] Instead of Paul's "Satan" (Σατανᾶς *Satanas*), one finds "devil" (διάβολος *diabolos*) in Ephesians. The formula used to introduce citations from Scripture, "therefore it says" (διὸ λέγει *dio legei*), is also not found in Pauline letters, and the expression "good works" (ἔργοις ἀγαθοῖς *ergois agathois*) in the plural (2:10) does not appear there, though it does occur in the Pastorals.[19]

Other features of Pauline letter form are missing, such as expressions of confidence, the formal opening to the body of a letter with a request or disclosure formula. The apostle typically uses a χάρις (*charis*, translated "thanks") formula as a contrast to a previously described negative situation (e.g., 2 Cor 2:12-15).[20] Ephesians does not use such contrastive formulae. Instead, *charis* (translated "grace") appears as the foundation of salvation and appears in expressions where one would expect "faith" if Paul had composed the letter (e.g., "by grace [*charis*] you have been saved through faith," 2:8). Or one would anticipate a discussion of righteousness in connection with the salvation of the Gentiles in 2:8-10. Instead, Ephesians refers to grace as the gift of God in opposition to works. The term "works" (ἔργα *erga*) also appears without Paul's normal qualifier "of the law" (νόμου *nomou*). In 2:10, the non-Pauline plural "good works" (*ergois agathois*) appears to refer to the moral conduct of those who are in Christ. The term "law" (νόμος *nomos*) only appears in 2:15, where the "law with its commandments and ordinances" has been canceled by the cross. There is no more distinction between Jew and Gentile. The whole complex of linguistic formulae that the apostle created to describe the inclusion of Gentiles in the promise of salvation has vanished with hardly a trace.[21]

This shift may be grounded in rhetoric as well as theology. Marc Schoeni's study of the "how much the more" formulae in Romans 5 discovered an important semantic distinction between using the topic "justification" and using "reconciliation." The language of justification is structured in such a way that it discriminates and divides. It acknowledges the singular differences between Jew and Gentile. Reconciliation "sublates and unites." By incorporating the differentiated singularities into a greater whole, reconciliation denies their significance.[22] Though Paul works with both reconciliation and justification, Ephesians has taken the reconciliation imagery of Rom 5:1-11 to be the Pauline understanding of salvation. Consequently, distinctions in Paul's terminology will be overridden by unity.

18. See the discussion of the phrase "in the heavenlies" in Best, *A Critical and Exegetical Commentary on Ephesians*, 115-18.

19. Schnackenburg, *The Epistle to the Ephesians*, 25-27.

20. Linda L. Belleville, *Reflections of Glory: Paul's Polemical Use of the Moses-Doxa Tradition in 2 Corinthians 3.1-18*, JSNTSup 52 (Sheffield: JSOT, 1991) 92-93.

21. Schnackenburg, *The Epistle to the Ephesians*, 26-27; Lincoln and Wedderburn, *The Theology of the Later Pauline Letters* 130-37.

22. Marc Schoeni, "The Hyperbolic Sublime as a Master Trope in Romans," in *Rhetoric and the New Testament: Essays from the 1992 Heidelberg Conference*, ed. Stanley E. Porter and Thomas H. Olbricht, JSNTSup 90 (Sheffield: JSOT, 1993) 181.

2. "Mystery" of Salvation. Several linguistic shifts are associated with the term "mystery" (μυστήριον *mystērion*). Ephesians often uses expressions that have their closest parallels in the Essene writings from Qumran, in which we find the "mystery" of the divine plan of salvation hidden in the prophets until the end time. Paul also uses "mystery" (*mystērion*) for God's preordained eschatological plan of salvation.[23] "Mystery" designates different aspects of the overall plan of salvation: (a) 1 Cor 2:1, 7, the crucifixion; (b) 1 Cor 15:51, the end-time transformation of the righteous into resurrected bodies; and (c) Rom 11:25, the present hardening of Israel as a condition for salvation of the Gentiles, to be followed by salvation for "all Israel." In 1 Cor 4:1, Paul refers to the apostles, specifically himself and Apollos, as "stewards of God's mysteries" and uses the term in a general way for revealed knowledge in 1 Cor 13:2 (also 14:2, ironically?). Its use for the salvation of the Gentiles as hidden in the prophets until the present at Rom 16:25-27 may be an addition to the letter, but it maintains the overtones of apocalyptic revelation characteristic of Paul's usage.

When Paul applies the term "mystery" to his gospel in Rom 11:25, he is not only thinking of God's plan to summon all humanity to salvation, but he is also thinking of the story of Israel. God's promises to the covenant people and their apparent inability to recognize Christ as the fulfillment of the law issue in Paul's conviction that God must still bring salvation to Israel.[24] For Ephesians, only the first side of Paul's thought remains: God intends to bring all to salvation in Christ (3:8-9). This mystery is grounded in the will of God from the beginning (1:9) and has been made known through the preaching of the apostle (6:19). It is also embodied in his writing (3:3-4). These examples are easily viewed as developments of Paul's own usage. After the apostle's death it would be natural to consider the written expression of his gospel as the way in which the mystery becomes known to others. However, a more significant shift becomes evident when Ephesians is compared with the immediate source for these expressions, Colossians (Col 1:27; 2:2; 4:3). In every one of the Colossians examples the shorthand that clarifies the term "mystery" (*mystērion*) is "Christ." For Colossians, the mystery is the fact that salvation comes to all people through faith in Christ.

Ephesians shifts the playing field. The focus of the mystery is not the cosmic Christ of Colossians but the body of Christ, the church. The problem is not how Gentiles can participate in God's salvation while remaining free from the law. Instead, Ephesians conceives the problem as one of unity. The series of "with . . ." or "co-" terms in Eph 3:6 makes this point about the church: The Gentiles are "heirs with" (συγκληρονόμα *sygklēronomai*), "body with" (σύσσωμα *syssōma*), and "sharers [συμμέτοχα *symmeto-cha*] of the promise in Christ through the gospel." This perspective makes it quite natural for Ephesians to speak of the union of Christ, the head, with his body, the church, as a "mystery" (Eph 5:32).

---

23. See the study of Markus Bockmuehl, *Revelation and Mystery in Ancient Judaism and Pauline Christianity* (Grand Rapids: Eerdmans, 1977).

24. See James D. G. Dunn, *The Theology of Paul the Apostle* (Grand Rapids: Eerdmans, 1998) 526-29.

3. Church as Body of Christ.

This use of "body of Christ" (σῶμα τοῦ Χριστου *sōma tou Christou*) goes beyond Paul's own use of the expression. Paul employed a common image from the political philosophy of his day to appeal for order and harmony in the Corinthian church. Christians should understand that the Spirit has provided diverse gifts within the community so that the whole body can function together. Strife over gifts among Christians is as absurd as parts of the body claiming that they do not belong because they are not some other part (1 Cor 12:12-31). The image is repeated in the same sense in Rom 12:3-8. He can also extend the metaphor of Christians as members of the "body of Christ" to argue for appropriate separation from the two forms of immorality that Jews commonly associated with paganism—sexual immorality (1 Cor 6:15) and idolatrous cultic practices (1 Cor 10:17). Thus for the apostle the expression "body of Christ" (*sōma tou Christou*) involves a metaphor for how to order the concrete details of everyday Christian life. Like the term "church" (ἐκκλησία *ekklēsia*) in Paul's letters, the term "body of Christ" designates local communities of Christians.[25]

Ephesians does not address a local community. Its vision of the church is set in the largest possible framework, the cosmic body of all the faithful united with its head, the risen Christ (1:22-23; 2:6). When the image of the church as the "body of Christ" comes into the ethical exhortation, the picture is one of a "new human being" growing into the body of Christ, which serves under its head (4:13-16). Paul's reference to concrete gifts of ministry in the body are incorporated into this larger vision of the church as the agent through whom its growth takes place (4:11-12). The development toward a more cosmic image of "body of Christ" is anticipated in the hymnic tradition. Colossians 1:15-20 depicts Christ first as divine wisdom active in creation, then as redeemer. Christ the redeemer is head of the body that is the church by virtue of being "firstborn from the dead" (Col 1:18). Colossians 1:19 introduces another term that will figure in the cosmic vision of church found in Ephesians, "fullness" (πλήρωμα *plērōma*). For Colossians, "fullness" refers to divinity dwelling in Christ. For Ephesians, it will refer to the way in which Christ dwells in the cosmic body, the church (1:23; 3:19; 4:13).

Other metaphors used for the church are drawn into this picture of the church as "body of Christ." It can be described as a building or temple being built up into Christ (2:20-21). Christians are members of God's household as children of God, not as strangers or resident aliens (2:19). Because the "body of Christ" is depicted as a heavenly reality, some of the attributes that describe the church follow as natural consequences. The church must be a unity (2:14-16; 4:1-3, 10-13), holy (1:3-8; 4:17-22; 5:3-5, 25-27), universal (2:16; 3:1-6). It cannot be considered part of this world as though it were a sociopolitical institution (5:18-20).[26] If it were, the church would be subject to the powers and authorities that govern the lower regions. Because the body of Christ is the preordained vehicle by which God has chosen to unite all things with God and to subjugate the lower powers (3:10),

---

25. L. O. R. Yorke, *The Church as the Body of Christ in the Pauline Corpus: A Re-examination* (Lanham: University Press of America, 1991); Dunn, *The Theology of Paul the Apostle,* 548-64.
26. Ibid., 101-3.

the church has always belonged to the divine plan of salvation. The doxology of 3:21 insists that God is praised "in the church and in Christ Jesus."

Those who consider such a vision of the church as a dangerous precedent should attend to the metaphors used. None of them attach the reality of the cosmic body of Christ to a particular group of human authorities. No single community could embody the church. Rudolf Schnackenburg remarks:

> For the author all the congregations which lie within his field of vision do not yet, even taken together, constitute "the *ekklēsia*." This is rather an entity which has precedence over all, in which they participate and in accordance with which they should orient their lives.[27]

Similarly the "mystery" (*mystērion*) of the church united to Christ as bride thus transforms a common Jewish metaphor for Israel as the "bride of Yahweh" (Isa 65:5; Jer 2:2; Ezekiel 16; Hosea 1–3) by highlighting the realism of the unity between Christ and the church. Christ's self-offering on the cross is the foundation of its holiness (Eph 5:2, 25). Christ's loving concern for the welfare of the church extends to the realities of Christian life in this world. It is not merely a reference to the heavenly unity of the saints with their head (2:5-6). If Ephesians can use this concern to describe the conduct of husbands toward their wives in marriage, then it should also be reflected in the ways that Christian leaders go about their various ministries.

4. Ministries in the Church. The references to such ministries in Ephesians also create some difficulties. When Paul refers to himself as apostle (ἀπόστολος *apostolos*, 1:1) or servant (διάκονος *diakonos*)of the gospel chosen by God to make God's salvation known to the Gentiles (3:7-9), we are on familiar ground. The self-deprecating comment "although I am the very least of all the saints, this grace was given to me" (3:8 NRSV) sounds close to Paul's own account of his apostleship (1 Cor 15:8-10). But Ephesians appears to have slipped out of the apostolic perspective in Eph 3:5. The mystery unknown to previous generations has now been revealed to God's "holy apostles and prophets by the Spirit." Since "prophets" follows the reference to apostles, the speaker does not appear to mean the Old Testament prophets. The author appears to be looking back on a revelation transmitted by Christian apostles and prophets. When Paul refers to Christian prophets, they are not associated with the apostolic witness to the gospel. Their function involves speaking, prayer, and exhortation within the local assembly (1 Cor 11:2-16; 14:29, 32, 37). When he refers to other apostles positively, Paul highlights the unity of his message with theirs (see 1 Cor 15:11).[28]

Ephesians 2:20 puts "apostles and prophets" in the past. They are the foundation of the

---

27. Schnackenburg, *The Epistle to the Ephesians*, 295. Others see the universalism in Ephesians as a loss for the theology of local church communities. Dunn remarks, "It is also true that Paul's own transforming vision was itself soon transformed, with many of its distinctive features lost to sight. His vision of the church of God as fully manifested in the local church was displaced by the thought of the Church universal (already in Ephesians)." Dunn, *The Theology of Paul the Apostle*, 563.

28. See Dunn, *The Theology of Paul the Apostle*, 579-82.

building, the church, which is growing into Christ. By contrast, Paul describes himself as the master builder (ἀρχιτέκτων *architektōn*) who builds on the foundation, Jesus Christ (1 Cor 3:10-14). The paraenetic section of the letter treats the term "apostles" (ἀπόστολοι *apostoloi*) as first in a list of gifts to the church: apostles, prophets, evangelists, pastors, and teachers (4:11). They are to equip Christians for service in building up the body of Christ until all attain maturity, the fullness of Christ (τοῦ πληρώματος τοῦ Χριστου *tou plērōmatos tou Christou*, 4:12-13). Once again the relationship between such persons and local church communities remains undefined.[29] Only the last two, pastors (ποιμέναι *poimenai*) and teachers (διδάσκαλοι *didaskaloi*), clearly designate resident leaders of the local church. The terms may not describe any particular church order. Ephesians merely wishes to indicate in a general way that God has charged certain persons with nurturing the church by aiding others to grow in unity and knowledge of God. This concern for harmony, internal unity, and growth might represent the concerns of a church facing the death of the apostolic generation.

5. Eschatological Shift. The cosmic picture of the church already united with the risen Christ shifts attention away from the end-time coming of the Lord (as in 1 Thess 4:13–5:11). For Paul, all things are not yet subjected to Christ. When they are, when every authority and power is destroyed, then Christ will bring all under God's rule (1 Cor 15:24-28). Ephesians refers to the subjection of all authorities and powers as a present reality. The risen and exalted Christ is far above all powers, whether in this age or in the age to come (Eph 1:19-23). Similarly, believers have been freed from the powers of darkness and raised up with Christ in the heavens. This exaltation also demonstrates God's extraordinary graciousness toward the faithful in the coming ages (Eph 2:5-7). Elements of future eschatology remain part of the author's conceptual world, but they do not serve as criteria to determine one's present position in the world. Nor is a culminating event in God's saving plan anticipated in the near future. Ephesians never uses the term "mystery" (*mystērion*) to designate a future act of redemption. The mystery of bringing all things together in Christ may not be completed, but it has already become a reality in the church (1:10).

This eschatological shift is evident in another formal difference between Ephesians and other Pauline letters. The apostle typically concludes major sections with references to elements of future judgment or salvation (e.g., Rom 11:31-36; 1 Cor 1:9-10; 15:54-58; Phil 1:10-11; 3:20–4:1; 1 Thess 1:9-10; 2:19-20; 3:11-13). Such references carry a hortatory message to the audience: Take care to persevere so that God may "strengthen your hearts in holiness that you may be blameless before our God and Father at the coming of our Lord Jesus with all his saints" (1 Thess 3:13 NRSV). Ephesians retains the liturgical character of Pauline transitions by using formulaic expressions (as in 1:20-23) or doxologies (as in 3:20-21). It uses "saints" (ἅγιοι *hagioi*) as its designation for believers

---

29. Lack of concern with the local community forms a striking contrast to Paul's understanding of the local character of all church ministry, including his own office as an apostle. See ibid., 578-79.

(e.g., 1:1, 15; 2:19; 3:18; 5:3; 6:18). Concerns that the church be "holy and blameless" (ἅγιος καὶ ἄμωμος *hagios kai amōmos*) are reflected in the opening prayer (1:4) and the paraenesis (4:24; 5:27) but never appear with the reference to the Lord's coming in judgment. The conclusion to the whole letter (6:10-20) takes up the motif of divine armor, which occurs as part of the eschatological conclusion to 1 Thessalonians (1 Thess 5:8). Even here, where one would expect standing fast to be accompanied by an explicit indication that these are the "last days," there is no reference to a judgment day. All that remains are the linguistic tags "withstand on that evil day" (6:13) and "keep alert" (6:18). Ephesians never speaks of Christ's coming in judgment. Its ecclesiology short-circuits such language, since the church already exists in the unity of the saints with their exalted head.

SEARCHING FOR A SOCIORELIGIOUS CONTEXT

Scholars have mined various features of the letter to construct a background for its author or audience. Since the destination "Ephesus" was not original, those theories built on archaeological and religious descriptions of ancient Ephesus and its Artemis cult have no foundation in the text. Some advocates of an Ephesus argument claim that the pluralism of religious cults and magic practices evident there is representative of the environment of cities in Asia Minor. Since the emphasis on Christ's exaltation above the powers of the cosmos and the identification of believers with their exalted head forms the center of Ephesians, this imagery might be read as a response to pagan religion. The Artemis cult in Ephesus demonstrates the superiority of the goddess to all forces; she is queen of the cosmos, as the signs of the zodiac around her neck and the magic letters on her scepter demonstrate. Associated with her, one finds Hecate, goddess of the underworld.[30] Similar zodiac imagery is connected with other goddess figures, like Diana and Isis. Funerary reliefs at Philippi depict the deified male or female child being conducted into heavenly places.[31] Other authors compare the "seated in the heavenly places" of Ephesians with the heavenly ascent of Mithraism.[32] These parallels say little about the details of Ephesians, but they suggest religious images and prior convictions that its audience would bring with them to the letter.

Other interpreters follow the lead of classic commentaries[33] and look to ancient gnostic mythologies. The separation between the heavenly regions in which those with knowledge of God are linked with the redeemer and the lower world of darkness governed by hostile forces forms a central element in their speculation. The second- and third-century CE gnostic texts provide suggestive parallels to some of the images in Ephesians. Gnostic

---

30. Clinton E. Arnold, *Ephesians: Power and Magic: The Concept of Power in Ephesians in the Light of Its Historical Setting,* SNTSMS 63 (Cambridge: Cambridge University Press, 1989).

31. Valerie A. Abrahamsen, *Women and Worship at Philippi: Diana, Artemis, and Other Cults in the Early Christian Era* (Portland, Me.: Astarte Shell, 1995).

32. Timothy B. Cargal, " 'Seated in the Heavenlies': Cosmic Mediators in the Mysteries of Mithras and the Letter to the Ephesians," SBLSP, ed. Eugene H. Lovering (Atlanta: Scholars Press, 1994) 804-21.

33. Esp. Heinrich Schlier, *Der Brief an die Epheser* (Dusseldorf: Patmos, 1957).

writers claim Ephesians as evidence that the apostle taught a gnostic doctrine of the soul fallen from heaven and trapped by hostile powers. Once awakened and enlighted by the heavenly revealer from heaven, the soul is superior to the powers. However, peculiarly gnostic terminology or theologoumena do not appear in Ephesians, so emerging gnostic sectarianism does not provide an explanation for the theological innovations found in the epistles.

Some interpreters have tried to combine all of these motifs. A gnostic dualism between the heavenly and earthly regions is said to cause the turn toward astrology and magic in order to gain security in a dangerous, hostile universe.[34] Or they assume that since Ephesians speaks of access to God through the knowledge that comes in Christ, it must be opposed to visionaries who claim to have ascended into heaven and to have been seated in God's presence.[35] Such visionary practices linked to Jewish speculation about heavenly realities have been more easily linked to the false teaching rejected in Col 2:8–3:4.[36] Though Ephesians adopts the image of believers seeking what belongs to the risen Christ (Col 3:1-4), none of the polemic details of the Colossians text are found in Ephesians. Further, as noted above, Ephesians erases the eschatological reservation found in earlier Pauline letters. Colossians does not. It limits the believers' identification with the exalted Christ to the future coming of Christ. For Ephesians, the saints are already one with their Lord. Once again, Ephesians shows no evidence of engaging a particular religious situation.

Since Ephesians highlights the incorporation of Gentiles with Israel in the new creation that God had planned from the beginning (2:11-18; 3:6), a natural context would appear to have been relationships between Jewish and Gentile Christians. Some interpreters lift the problematic of Gentile conversion from Pauline Epistles to explain the need for ethical instruction in Ephesians. But though the center of the apostle's gospel did require that both Jew and Gentile be made righteous on the same basis, through faith (Gal 2:15-21), Ephesians never deals with those concrete details of the law that distinguish Jew and Gentile and make Paul's emphasis on righteousness through faith, not works of the law, essential. Ephesians can refer to "circumcision" and "uncircumcision" as markers of the two communities (2:11) without any indication that the distinction created a problem for relationships between Jewish and Gentile Christians in their unity. Contrast Colossians, where circumcision is spiritualized (Col 2:11) and Jewish sabbaths, holy days, and food laws are rejected (Col 2:16-17). Ephesians 2:15 refers without difficulty to the "law with its commandments and ordinances" abolished by the cross. Consequently, many scholars agree that the churches to which Ephesians was written cannot include an active Jewish Christian group.[37]

If the community envisaged by the letter consists solely of Gentiles being encouraged

---

34. Ralph P. Martin, *Ephesians, Colossians and Philemon* (Atlanta: John Knox, 1991).

35. Michael Gouldner, "Vision and Knowledge," *JSNT* 56 (1994) 53-71.

36. James D. G. Dunn, "The Colossian Philosophy: A Confident Jewish Apologetic," *Bib* 76 (1995) 153-81.

37. A. Lindemann, "Bemerkungen zu den Adressaten und zum Anlass des Epheserbriefes," *ZNW* 67 (1976) 235-51, insists not only that there were no Jewish Christians in the audience of Ephesians, but also that the author was not a Jewish Christian either. He has adopted Paul's persona to bolster faith in a church threatened by persecution.

to remember themselves as brought into a common inheritance with Jewish believers, does the reminder provide any hints about the setting of the letter? Many of our best parallels to its religious language can be found among the Essene texts from Qumran. Such comparisons, along with the exegetical forms used by the author, suggest a person with a background in first-century CE Jewish sectarianism. At the same time, the ornate Greek rhetorical style suggests a Jew with a Hellenistic education. This combination is similar to that of Paul himself. In Paul's case, the sectarian piety through which he assimilated Judaism was Pharisaism. In this case, it was some form of sectarian piety closer to that of the Essenes. The author of Ephesians not only looks to the apostle Paul as the recipient of special understanding of God's plan, but he is also a student of Paul's letters. Given the Essene interest in texts, including preserving and continuing an exegetical tradition linked to its founder, one might infer that such a person had made an effort to obtain copies of Paul's letters.

Other interpreters suggest that Ephesians attempts to ward off a crisis similar to that addressed by Paul in Rom 11:17-36. Its repeated use of "with . . ." formulae, as well as the priority given "us" into which "you," Gentiles, have been incorporated, indicates a desire to hang on to the Jewish roots of Christianity.[38] But Ephesians has surrendered the careful distinction between the church and Israel so important to Paul. Its exhortations have nothing to do with Judaism. Rather, the Gentile audience must remain committed to the new Christian way of life, to worship, to mutual love and assistance among believers, and to the moral reform that marks them as "children of God."

On the one hand, it seems more accurate to think of the early Christian movement as an "internal migration" of a sectarian group within Judaism than as a "new religion."[39] On the other hand, Ephesians clearly perceives the Jew and Gentile believers who constitute the body of the risen Christ as a "new creation," not merely the righteous remnant of Israel with some Gentiles thrown in. For its readers, the existence of any actual relationships with the Jewish communities of Asia Minor remains in doubt.[40]

Ephesians presumes that preaching the gospel involves persuading others to turn away from paganism as cultic practice and from moral laxity in conduct to become part of the Christian community. But does this orientation reflect an attitude that the Gentile Christian mission assimilated from the Hellenistic synagogue? Martin Goodman has recently assembled considerable evidence against the view that either Jews or pagans thought it would be preferable if all humans worshiped the same God.[41] Scholars find the social

---

38. David G. Meade, *Pseudonymity and Canon: An Investigation into the Relationship of Authorship and Authority in the Jewish and Earliest Christian Tradition,* WUNT 39 (Tübingen: Mohr-Siebeck, 1986) 146.

39. So Dieter Georgi, "The Early Church: Internal Jewish Migration or New Religion?" *HTR* 88 (1995) 35-68, who does not deal with Ephesians.

40. On the paucity of evidence for Jewish life in Asia Minor during the first century CE, see John M. G. Barclay, *Jews in the Mediterranean Diaspora from Alexander to Trajan (323 BCE–117 CE)* (Berkeley: University of California Press, 1996) 259-81. Lack of involvement in the Jewish revolts of the period suggests that Jews in Asia Minor maintained friendly relations with non-Jewish neighbors.

41. Martin Goodman, *Mission and Conversion: Proselytizing in the Religious History of the Roman Empire* (Oxford: Clarendon, 1994).

boundaries of those Gentile sympathizers often referred to as "god-fearers" increasingly difficult to fix clearly. Without doubt, some outsiders found their way into Judaism as proselytes (see Tob 1:8).[42] When women of the Herodian family married, they required that their husbands be converted to Judaism.[43] In some areas, though by no means everywhere, one finds Jewish communities with a range of Gentile sympathizers or benefactors. Why would outsiders act as benefactors to the Jewish community? They must have been encouraged that such acts would have a reward (cf. Rom 2:12-16). Persons within the Jewish community may have encouraged such benefactors, whose assistance they required in order to maintain the political independence of their community.[44]

Would such Gentiles have been drawn to the early Christian movement as Acts suggests (see Acts 16:11-14; 17:1-5)? Some synagogue benefactors clearly retained their pagan ties and even priesthoods within pagan cult associations.[45] If that was a normal pattern of benefaction, then the language of Ephesians that highlights the radical break of conversion might be directed toward those who thought they could retain earlier associations while belonging to the Christian group (as in 1 Cor 10:1-22). What else these Gentiles from Asia Minor might have known about Jews can only be suggested by supplementing the few hints in the letter with general evidence for the region. Ephesians itself assumes that readers are familiar with "circumcision" as the decisive criterion for belonging to Israel, with Jewish monotheism and its critique of pagan gods, with Scripture, and in a general way with Jews as separated from non-Jews by "commandments and ordinances." None of these observations go beyond what ordinary Gentiles might know about Jews. Indeed, Ephesians does not refer to the other common items of information, sabbath observance and food laws, even though they appear in Colossians. This omission may indicate that Jewish or Jewish Christian practice was not an issue for the author or his audience.

Early Christian churches appear in those cities of Asia Minor that also had Jewish communities. Louis Feldman suggests that the lack of Pharisaic influence in the inland cities of Asia Minor indicates that Judaism there was less bound to the land of Israel. Jewish inscriptions lack the pious Jewish sentiments of longing for the Temple or artistic representations of the ark or the menorah so common elsewhere. Sardis appears to have been the exception to the rule of a lower degree of Jewish identity in inland Asia Minor. Its large, wealthy, and properous community evoked sharp anti-Jewish polemic from Melito, Bishop of Sardis in the second century. Even in the fourth century, the remodeled Jewish synagogue was a larger and more impressive building than the Christian church.[46]

42. Josephus *Against Apion* 2.210. However, Roman authors are aware of the difference between persons who are Jewish sympathizers and actual proselytes. See Peter Schäfer, *Judeophobia: Attitudes Toward the Jews in the Ancient World* (Cambridge, Mass.: Harvard University Press, 1997) 80-115. Schäfer concludes that the pressure on collecting the *discus Judaicus* under Domitian was a response to increasing proselytism in Roman society (ibid., 115).
43. Josephus *Antiquities of the Jews* 20.139, 145; Goodman, *Mission and Conversion,* 63-65.
44. Goodman, *Mission and Conversion,* 87-88.
45. Paul R. Trebilco, *Jewish Communities in Asia Minor,* SNTSMS 69 (Cambridge: Cambridge University Press, 1991) 58-59.
46. Louis H. Feldman, *Jew and Gentile in the Ancient World* (Princeton, N.J.: Princeton University Press, 1993) 73.

If the relative strength and social prestige of the two communities were as Feldman suggests, such that the Jewish community far outweighed that of the Christian offshoot, then the emphasis on Jewish origins evident in Ephesians might serve to intensify communal identity among the Christian minority.

After all, Ephesians makes the extraordinary claim that God's plan for humanity is represented by this community. Some have even compared that language to claims for the peace created by the Roman Empire.[47] Though there is no clear evidence that Ephesians is concerned with imperial ideology, the suggestion points to the spiritual importance of its message. The case for creating unity through imperial expansion was evident in the architecture of the great cities of Asia Minor. The Jewish community in many Asia Minor cities owed Roman power an important debt; appeals to Roman authorities secured Jewish rights to sabbath observance, protection of money collected for the Jerusalem Temple, and the like. Ephesians envisages a different basis for human unity, a religious one. As far as one can tell, this realization was unique to the Christian mission. Not even the Romans thought that all the citizens of their empire would worship Roman gods. Jews never undertook a systematic policy of proselytism to bring pagans to the worship of God. Ephesians has set Paul's own concern for a mission that would reach the ends of the Roman Empire (Rom 15:18-23) in a global perspective. God planned to unite all things in Christ even before creation.[48]

47. Franz Mussner, *Der Brief an die Epheser* (Gütersloh: Gerd Mohn, 1982).
48. Portions of this commentary appeared originally in Pheme Perkins, *Ephesians*, ANTC (Nashville: Abingdon, 1997).

BIBLIOGRAPHY

Commentaries:

Barth, Markus. *Ephesians*. 2 vols. AB 34; 34A. New York: Doubleday, 1974. Argues that Paul wrote Ephesians during his Roman imprisonment. Use of liturgical material accounts for the differences between Ephesians and early Pauline letters. Extensive comparisons between Ephesians and the earlier epistles.

Best, Ernest. *A Critical and Exegetical Commentary on Ephesians*. ICC. Edinburgh: T. & T. Clark, 1998. The most thorough commentary on the Greek text. Sees the author of Ephesians as a member of the Pauline school, which accounts for the similarity to Colossians, whose author was writing to show Gentile Christians what their new faith requires.

Kitchen, Martin. *Ephesians*. London: Routledge, 1994. A series of essays that sees Ephesians as a summing up of the Pauline tradition after the destruction of Jerusalem in 70 CE. Includes a helpful discussion of the use of pseudepigraphy in preserving religious traditions.

Lincoln, Andrew. *Ephesians*. WBC 42. Dallas: Word, 1990. A detailed study of the Greek text that is informed by knowledge of ancient rhetorical traditions. Argues that Ephesians has made a free adaptation of material from Colossians and other Pauline letters to encourage lagging faith among Christians in the Lycus Valley.

Martin, Ralph P. *Ephesians, Colossians, and Philemon*. Atlanta: John Knox, 1991. Comments on sections of the letter for the general reader. Treats Ephesians as an encyclical letter written by a disciple of Paul to the churches in Asia Minor against gnosticizing tendencies in the area. Includes suggestions for pastors and preachers.

Mitton, C. L. *The Epistle to the Ephesians.* Oxford: Clarendon, 1951. Detailed statistics on words shared between Ephesians and Colossians that played a significant role in establishing the view that Ephesians used the latter as a source.

O'Brien, Peter T. *The Letter to the Ephesians.* Pillar NT Commentary. Grand Rapids: Eerdmans, 1999. Continues to argue for the view that Paul wrote Ephesians from his Roman imprisonment in the 60s CE, against most contemporary scholars. Seeks to show the continuity between Ephesians and Paul's earlier letters. The commentary quotes the NIV translation but analyzes the Greek text.

Schnackenburg, Rudolf. *The Epistle to the Ephesians.* Translated by H. Heron. Edinburgh: T. & T. Clark, 1991 [Ger. 1982]. Particularly helpful analysis of the logical flow of the letter. Concludes with extended discussion of the theological impact of Ephesians in classical Roman Catholic and Protestant theology of predestination, Christ and redemption, church, and Christian life.

Specialized Studies:

Adams, Edward. *Constructing the World: A Study of Paul's Cosmological Language.* Edinburgh: T. & T. Clark, 2000. Studies the use of "world," "creation," and "new creation" in the major Pauline letters (Romans; 1–2 Corinthians; Galatians).

Arnold, Clinton E. *Ephesians: Power and Magic. The Concept of Power in Ephesians in Light of Its Historical Setting.* SNTSMS 63. Cambridge: Cambridge University Press, 1989. Argues from a study of ancient religious cults and magical practices that Ephesians seeks to show the superiority of Christ's power to Christians who remained fearful of attacks by evil cosmic powers.

Best, Ernest. *Essays on Ephesians.* Edinburgh: T. & T. Clark, 1997. Reprints the author's articles on important topics in Ephesians.

Caragounis, Chrys C. *The Ephesian Mysterion: Meaning and Context.* ConB 8. Lund: Gleerup, 1977. A study of the use of the term "mystery" in Ephesians that emphasizes its use to designate God's plan of salvation history.

Dawes, Gregory W. *The Body in Question: Metaphor and Meaning in the Interpretation of Ephesians 5:21-33.* Biblical Interpretation Series 30. Leiden: Brill, 1998. Studies the comparison of marriage to the relationship between the church and Christ from the perspective of modern studies of metaphor. Emphasizes the links between this passage and the rest of the letter.

Harris, W. Hall, III. *The Descent of Christ: Ephesians 4:7-11 and Traditional Hebrew Imagery.* AGAJU 32. Leiden: Brill, 1996. Concludes that a tradition of Moses' ascending Mt. Sinai to receive Torah has been transferred to Christ in the quotation of Ps 68:19.

Klauck, Hans-Josef. *The Religious Context of Early Christianity: A Guide to Graeco-Roman Religions.* Translated by Brian McNeil. Edinburgh: T. & T. Clark, 2000. A survey of religious and philosophical movements in the non-Jewish world of early Christianity. Concludes with a discussion of Gnosticism.

Lincoln, Andrew T., and A. J. M. Wedderburn. *The Theology of the Later Pauline Letters.* Cambridge: Cambridge University Press, 1993. Contains a synthesis of the theology of Ephesians for general readers by A. T. Lincoln; concludes with an essay on the critical appropriation of the theology of Ephesians.

Meade, David G. *Pseudonymity and Canon: An Investigation into the Relationship of Authorship and Authority in the Jewish and Earliest Christian Tradition.* WUNT 39. Tübingen: J. C. B. Mohr (Paul Siebeck), 1986. A study of the role played by pseudonymous authorship in Jewish and early Christian authors; argues that the death of Paul, and hence the loss of his presence as an authority, motivated the composition of Ephesians.

Neufeld, T. Y. *Put On the Armour of God: The Divine Warrior from Isaiah to Ephesians.* Sheffield: Sheffield Academic, 1997. Studies the background to the image of divine armor in Eph 6:10-17.

Usami, Kōshi. *Somatic Comprehension of Unity: The Church in Ephesus.* AnBib 101. Rome: Pontifical

Biblical Institute, 1983. Detailed analysis of the use of bodily imagery to understand the church in Ephesians.

Wiles, G. P. *Paul's Intercessory Prayers: The Significance of the Intercessory Prayer Passages in the Letters of St. Paul.* SNTSMS 24. Cambridge: Cambridge University Press, 1974. Studies Paul's use of prayer formulae in the epistles.

OUTLINE OF EPHESIANS

I. Ephesians 1:1-2, Greeting

II. Ephesians 1:3-14, Eulogy on Salvation

III. Ephesians 1:15-23, Thanksgiving Prayer Report

IV. Ephesians 2:1–6:20, Body of the Letter

A. 2:1–3:21, Theological Reflection on Salvation in the Body of the Exalted Christ
   2:1-10, Conversion from Death to New Life
   2:11-22, Unity in Christ
   3:1-13, Paul as Prisoner for the Gospel
   3:14-21, The Apostle's Prayer

B. 4:1–6:9, Ethical Exhortations on Living as Christians
   4:1-16, Building the Body of Christ
   4:17-32, Two Ways of Life
   5:1-14, Live as Children of Light
   5:15-21, Wisdom as Thanksgiving
   5:22–6:9, Household Code

C. 6:10-20, Peroration: Be Armed with the Power of God

V. Ephesians 6:21-24, Final Greeting

EPHESIANS 1:1-2

GREETING

NIV

1 Paul, an apostle of Christ Jesus by the will of God,

To the saints in Ephesus,[a] the faithful[b] in Christ Jesus:

[2] Grace and peace to you from God our Father and the Lord Jesus Christ.

a1 Some early manuscripts do not have in Ephesus.   *b1 Or* believers who are

NRSV

1 Paul, an apostle of Christ Jesus by the will of God,

To the saints who are in Ephesus and are faithful[a] in Christ Jesus:

2Grace to you and peace from God our Father and the Lord Jesus Christ.

a Other ancient authorities lack in Ephesus, *reading* saints who are also faithful

COMMENTARY

A ncient letters begin with a greeting that identifies the sender and the recipients. Pauline letters expand the traditional formula with expressions of Christian faith or references to the divine origin of Paul's apostolic authority (1 Cor 1:1-3; Col 1:1-2). Some ancient manuscripts lack the words "in Ephesus" (ἐν Ἐφέσῳ *en Ephesō*). Without a concrete place reference, the greeting is grammatically awkward, since the designation "to the saints" is followed by the words "who are and faithful." The translation in the NRSV note, "to the saints who are also faithful," treats the "and" (καὶ *kai*) as "also" rather than as a conjunction.[49] Though there are no ancient examples, some commentators suggest that Ephesians was originally a circular letter into which the name of a particular church could be inserted. Since Ephesians reformulates sections from Colossians, one would expect the addressees to be designated "to the saints in Ephesus" (cf. Col 1:2). The "grace and peace" formula (v. 2) adds "and the Lord Jesus Christ" (see Rom 1:7) to Col 1:2. Conflation of Col 1:1-2 with Rom 1:7 may explain the dangling "who are" (τοῖς οὖσιν *tois ousin*), since Rom 1:7 has "to all those *who are* in Rome" (the NRSV changes the sentence structure).

Assuming that the author was a disciple of Paul who used Colossians and other Pauline letters to compose a letter of instruction explains the lack of precision about the addressees. Ephesians indicates that Paul was unknown to its audience (so 1:15; 3:2), but such personal distance would not be true of Ephesus, where the apostle spent considerable time (Acts 19:1-22) and from which he wrote to the Corinthians. Ephesus was probably the locus of the "mortal threat" mentioned in 2 Cor 1:8-11 (also 1 Cor 15:32), possibly the imprisonment of Philippians 1 and 2. The ties between Paul and Ephesus explain how an ancient scribe attached "in Ephesus" to this text. The mention of Tychicus as the letter carrier in Eph 6:21, combined with the assertion that he was sent to Ephesus in 2 Tim 4:12, could also generate the address.

Expressions found in the greeting are central to the letter's depiction of the author and his audience. Surprisingly, the author never again speaks of himself as "apostle" (ἀπόστολος *apostolos*). Instead, the word "apostle" appears in lists of those whose past activities provide the foundation for the church (2:20; 3:5; 4:11). The letter's "Paul" speaks of himself as the imprisoned ambassador for a gospel that revealed God's saving plan for the Gentiles (3:1-13; 4:1; 6:19-20). The reference to the "will of God" (θέλημα Θεοῦ

---

49. On the grammatical problems of this translation, see Andrew T. Lincoln, *Ephesians,* WBC 42 (Dallas: Word, 1990) 2.

thelēma Theou) introduces a theme that is echoed in the rest of the letter. The "will of God" lies behind the plan that the Gentiles would be included in salvation (1:5, 9, 11). The phrase appears in the hortatory material to highlight the orientation of Christian life (5:17; 6:6).

Of the two terms used to describe the addressees, "faithful" (πιστοι *pistoi*) and "saints" (ἅγιοι *hagioi*; lit., "holy ones"), the former never returns except in reference to Tychicus (6:21, from Col 4:7), but "saints" echoes throughout the letter. It is a standard designation for members of the Christian community (1:15, 18; 2:19; 3:8, 18; 4:12; 5:3; 6:18), but it also designates the moral purity to which Christians are called (1:4; 5:3, 27). A common self-designation among early Christians (see Acts 9:13; Rom 1:7; 1 Cor 1:2; 2 Cor 1:1), the expression was taken from OT references to Israel as a people set apart for the Lord (Lev 11:44; 19:2; 20:26). Its primary emphasis in the OT is not moral perfection but the dedication of persons, places, or objects to the service of God (Exod 28:2; Pss 2:6; 24:3). These cultic connotations emerge in Ephesians when Christians are described as "a holy temple" (Eph 2:21).

Paul regularly replaced the secular epistolary "greeting" with "grace and peace" (see Rom 1:7; 1 Cor 1:3; Gal 1:3; Phil 1:2). God is "father" (πατήρ *patēr*) both of the "Lord Jesus Christ" (Eph 1:3; see Rom 15:6; 2 Cor 1:3) and of believers, who are God's adopted children in Christ (Eph 1:5; see Rom 8:14-17; Gal 4:4-7). Their access to God as Father is possible through the Spirit (Eph 2:18; see Rom 8:16, 27; Gal 4:6). God as our common "Father" (*patēr*) is the focus of both prayer (Eph 3:14; 5:20) and the unity of the church that God's activity has brought into being (Eph 4:6). However, there is a change in how Ephesians uses the language of God as "Fa-

ther." Ephesians does not correlate it with references to either Jesus as "son" ("Son of God" appears only in 4:13) or believers as "sons." Instead, Christians attain their special relationship to God because they belong to the exalted, heavenly Christ who is head of the body, a new creation of the perfect human. References to God as "Father" occur either in set formulae of blessing, prayer, or confession (1:2-3, 17; 4:5; 6:23) or in references to prayer (2:18; 3:14; 5:20).

Another shift in imagery attaches to the theological use of the terms "grace" and "peace." "Grace" (χάρις *charis*) appears as a well-understood agent of salvation (2:5, 8); as an attribute of God that merits human praise (1:6-7; 2:7); as God's gift to Paul for the ministry he carries out (3:2-8); or as a gift to individual believers (4:7). "Peace" (εἰρήνη *eirēnē*) appears in a central image for the "mystery" (μυστήριον *mystērion*) of God's saving activity: the reconciliation of Jew and Gentile in one new human being (Eph 2:15-17). That image reshapes the exhortation to peace within the community (Eph 4:3).

Whether directed to an individual, a particular community, or—as appears to have been the case with Ephesians—to several churches, the Pauline letter was always a public event. Colossians 4:16 speaks of the reading and exchange of letters between churches in neighboring cities. The power of a whole letter, read out to an expectant community, is an important part of the event of communication. Ephesians uses the conventional greeting formulae to ready the audience for the reading that follows. Hearing the letter will remind them of how God and the Lord Jesus Christ have reshaped their lives. The ornate rhetorical style sweeps the audience up into the author's vision of membership in a cosmic church united with its exalted head.

EULOGY ON SALVATION

NIV

³Praise be to the God and Father of our Lord Jesus Christ, who has blessed us in the heavenly realms with every spiritual blessing in Christ. ⁴For he chose us in him before the creation of the world to be holy and blameless in his sight. In love ⁵he[a] predestined us to be adopted as his sons through Jesus Christ, in accordance with his pleasure and will— ⁶to the praise of his glorious grace, which he has freely given us in the One he loves. ⁷In him we have redemption through his blood, the forgiveness of sins, in accordance with the riches of God's grace ⁸that he lavished on us with all wisdom and understanding. ⁹And he[b] made known to us the mystery of his will according to his good pleasure, which he purposed in Christ, ¹⁰to be put into effect when the times will have reached their fulfillment—to bring all things in heaven and on earth together under one head, even Christ.

¹¹In him we were also chosen,[c] having been predestined according to the plan of him who works out everything in conformity with the purpose of his will, ¹²in order that we, who were the first to hope in Christ, might be for the praise of his glory. ¹³And you also were included in Christ when you heard the word of truth, the gospel of your salvation. Having believed, you were marked in him with a seal, the promised Holy Spirit, ¹⁴who is a deposit guaranteeing our inheritance until the redemption of those who are God's possession—to the praise of his glory.

a4,5 Or sight in love. 5He   b8,9 Or us. With all wisdom and understanding, 9he   c11 Or were made heirs

NRSV

3Blessed be the God and Father of our Lord Jesus Christ, who has blessed us in Christ with every spiritual blessing in the heavenly places, ⁴just as he chose us in Christ[a] before the foundation of the world to be holy and blameless before him in love. ⁵He destined us for adoption as his children through Jesus Christ, according to the good pleasure of his will, ⁶to the praise of his glorious grace that he freely bestowed on us in the Beloved. ⁷In him we have redemption through his blood, the forgiveness of our trespasses, according to the riches of his grace ⁸that he lavished on us. With all wisdom and insight ⁹he has made known to us the mystery of his will, according to his good pleasure that he set forth in Christ, ¹⁰as a plan for the fullness of time, to gather up all things in him, things in heaven and things on earth. ¹¹In Christ we have also obtained an inheritance,[b] having been destined according to the purpose of him who accomplishes all things according to his counsel and will, ¹²so that we, who were the first to set our hope on Christ, might live for the praise of his glory. ¹³In him you also, when you had heard the word of truth, the gospel of your salvation, and had believed in him, were marked with the seal of the promised Holy Spirit; ¹⁴this[c] is the pledge of our inheritance toward redemption as God's own people, to the praise of his glory.

a Gk in him   b Or been made a heritage   c Other ancient authorities read who

COMMENTARY

Greek letters usually followed the greeting with a brief thanksgiving or wish for the health of recipients. Pauline letters have transformed that feature into a longer thanksgiving for their faith, which also telegraphs themes found in the body of the letter (see Rom 1:8-9, 10-15; Phil 1:3-11; Col 1:3-8). In 2 Cor 1:3-11 the opening takes the form of a blessing (2 Cor 1:3a). Ephesians employs both the blessing (1:3-14) and the thanksgiving prayer report (1:15-23). Each consists of a single sentence, elaborately crafted from a sequence of subordinate participial and prepositional clauses. English translations break up these sentences into shorter sentences.

Unlike the undisputed Pauline letters, Ephesians does not refer in this section to the situation of its audience. Instead, the blessing period evokes the liturgical origin of the blessing formula as found in the psalms (LXX Pss 66:20; 68:35). The liturgical sense of blessing (εὐλογέω *eulogeō*) God for deeds of salvation has been combined with the rhetorical understanding of "eulogy" as eloquence or fine speaking in praise of someone. Thus Ephesians telegraphs its intention to the audience. We are about to hear a fine speech in praise of "God [the] Father of our Lord Jesus Christ." True to the rhetorical conventions of such speech, Ephesians indicates that such praise is the appropriate response to benefits conferred. In the secular sphere, speech in praise of a benefactor might elicit future benefactions by cementing the relationship between a powerful individual and those who participate in his praise.

Ephesians takes up this tradition by repeatedly underlining the fact that the blessings its audience has received come from a beneficent God who consistently intended to confer salvation. The passage is punctuated by references to election and divine will (vv. 4-5, 9, 11). Another set of phrases refers to the praise that the recipients of salvation owe their divine benefactor (vv. 6, 12, 14). The conclusion treats the present experience of salvation as the guarantee of a future inheritance and ongoing praise of God's glory. Ephesians weaves the function of Christ as heavenly mediator into the praise of God as benefactor. A series of clauses beginning with "in whom" (ἐν ᾧ *en hō*) spell out the Christian promise of salvation (vv. 7-10, 11-12, 13-14). The NRSV has created sentences that focus our attention on the benefits of salvation received in Christ: God blessed us in Christ (vv. 3-4) and destined us for adoption in Christ (vv. 5-6); redemption is through the blood of Christ (vv. 7-8*a*); knowledge of God's will unites all things in Christ (vv. 8*b*-10); we are destined to praise God in Christ (vv. 11-12), and Gentiles ("you") are included in this inheritance through preaching the gospel (vv. 13-14). Verses 9-10 have a central place in the theological understanding of Ephesians. The exaltation of Christ in the heavens

provides the foundation for bringing the entire creation into unity under Christ as head. Appropriately, the final words of v. 14 pick up the intent of the whole section, "to the praise of his [God's] glory."

The biblical tradition insists that praise is the appropriate human response to God's acts of salvation (Pss 96:1-4; 118:1). Without the appearance of Jesus, God's full plan for salvation would have remained hidden (vv. 9-10). The expression "with every spiritual blessing" (ἐν πάσῃ εὐλογίᾳ πνευματικῇ *en pasē eulogia pneumatikē*) highlights the completeness of divine salvation. Unlike human benefactors, God has not conferred a partial blessing. Jewish roots for this expression lie in the blessing of Joseph by Jacob (Gen 49:25) and in the liturgical language of the Essenes, "May [my Lord] bless you [from his holy residence]. . . . May he bestow upon you all the blessings [. . .] in the congregation of the holy ones."[50] The reference to "the holy ones" assimilates the Essene congregation to the angels who are in the heavens with God.

Ephesians has modified this Jewish form by substituting the exalted Christ for the angelic hosts and using a peculiar plural form, "the heavenlies" (ἐπουράνιοι *epouranioi*; NRSV, "the heavenly places"), to refer to heaven. That expression appears only in Ephesians, where it is used both for God's dwelling (1:3, 20; 2:6) and for a sphere in which hostile powers are active (3:10; 6:12). Descriptions of the universe in the first century CE assumed that the earth was in the center of a cosmos that stretched out to the sphere of the stars. The moon, the sun, and the planets (through Saturn) circled the earth. The region from the earth to the moon was one in which decay and death occurred. Earthy, heavy, watery, and dark substances tended toward the earth. Fire and air tended toward the heavens. In order to reach the realm of the divine, the soul would have had to ascend through all of these heavenly regions. Spiritual beings, sometimes depicted as demonic, could be associated with the planetary spheres and their power to dictate the fate of humans and nations.

This picture of the cosmos was replicated in Jewish apocalypses that described the ascent of a seer to a vision of the divine throne. By the first century CE most apocalypses assumed that the

50. 1QSb 1:3-5

journey would require passing through multiple heavens.[51] Ordinarily the fear or awe felt by the visionary is mitigated by the protection of his angelic guide. Ephesians does not develop the details of multiple heavenly regions.[52]

The explanation in v. 4 picks up the agency of Christ as the mediator of salvation and expands the description of God's plan of salvation in a temporal direction. God's plan to redeem humanity preexists the foundation of the world. The image of God's election of the righteous and condemnation of the wicked prior to creation appears in Essene texts.[53] According to these texts God ordained the course of all the cosmic powers as well as those of humankind in the act of creation.[54] Ephesians agrees with the Essene view that the elect follow the paths of holiness that God established for creatures. The formulation in v. 4 does not imply the preexistence of the individual souls of the righteous.[55] Nor does Ephesians spell out the connection between the Christ in whom the righteous are elect and God's creative activity. Its emphasis is on the experience of salvation. Those who come to believe in Christ find themselves participating in God's eternal plan.

The phrase "in love" (ἐν ἀγάπη *en agapē*) at the conclusion of v. 4 appears so awkward that some have treated it as the motive for the divine "destined" (i.e., "predestined," προορίσας *proorisas*) in v. 5.[56] However, it matches the phrase "in the Beloved" (ἐν τῷ ἠγαπημένῳ *en tō agapē-menō*), which concludes v. 6. Therefore, the expression appears to be a stylistic marker. It may be intended to refer to divine election in Christ rather than to human behavior.

Verses 5-6 develop the previous reference to divine election in Christ by introducing the Pauline motif of adoption (Rom 8:15-23; Gal 4:4-7). A striking difference between the use of pre-destination language in Ephesians and similar expressions found at Qumran is the lack of any reference to the wicked. Ephesians knows such language, as later references to "those who are disobedient" (τῆς ἀπειθείας *tēs apeitheias*; 2:2-3; 5:6) indicate. But in keeping with the author's vision of unity, God's gracious election could not be expressed as the sharp division of humankind into a righteous remnant, the holy elect, over against a majority who will never experience God's grace. Predestination also has this positive tenor in Paul's usage (see Rom 8:29-30; 1 Cor 2:7).

The description of election in Ephesians is consistently theocentric. God calls a people "for himself." Consequently, the Greek of v. 5a follows "adoption through Jesus Christ" with the prepositional phrase "in him" (εἰς αὐτόν *eis auton*), which refers to God rather than to the Son. This focus diverges from the Pauline formula in Rom 8:29, which treats the calling of the elect as necessary to provide brothers and sisters for Christ the firstborn. Verse 6 spells out the reason for the existence of the elect community: worship and praise of the one whose gracious benefits they have received through the Beloved (Jesus Christ).

Traditional Christian formulae underlie the description in vv. 7-8 of how believers receive grace through Christ: His death brings forgiveness of sins. Verse 7 adds "through his blood" and the conclusion "according to the riches of his [God's] grace" to a formula from Col 1:14. The term "redemption" (ἀπολύτρωσις *apolytrosis*; also see Rom 3:24) can be used for freeing a slave (LXX Exod 21:8; Dan 4:34). God obtained Israel as a people by liberating them from Egypt (Exod 15:16; Ps 74:2) or from captivity (Isa 51:11). Since it also came to refer to God's end-time action on Israel's behalf (Ps 130:7-8; Isa 59:29), early Christian usage points to Christ's death as effecting this salvation. The formula quoted in Rom 3:24-26 indicates that Christ's death was understood as the expiation for sin that makes redemption—God's free gift to believers—a reality.

The present tense of the verb "we have" (ἔχομεν *echomen*, v. 7) suggests that Christ continues to be the source of deliverance from sin for believers. Verse 8 specifies the expression of God's graciousness as "wisdom and insight"

---

51. Martha Himmelfarb, *Ascents into Heaven in Jewish and Christian Apocalypses* (Oxford: Oxford University Press, 1993) 32. See also *T. Levi* 2–3; 8; *2 Enoch* 3–21; *Apoc. Mos.* 35:2; 2 Cor 12:1-3.

52. For a survey of ancient traditions concerning the structure and inhabitants of the heavens, see J. Edward Wright, *The Early History of Heaven* (New York: Oxford University Press, 2000).

53. CD 2:7; 1QS 3:15-17.

54. 1QH 9[1]:10-20; 1QS 3:15-17.

55. Best observes that for Ephesians predestination is not primarily a doctrine about individual salvation but about God's purpose. See Ernest Best, *A Critical and Exegetical Commentary on Ephesians*, ICC (Edinburgh: T. & T. Clark, 1998) 119-20.

56. Ibid., 123.

(σοφία καὶ φρόνησις *sophia kai phronesis*) bestowed on believers. In the OT, insight and wisdom are characteristic of the pious who attend to God's revelation by living according to the law (Prov 1:2-7; 2:2-10; Ps 37:30-31). The Dead Sea Scrolls speak of wisdom or understanding of God's way as a special gift to the teacher(s) of the sect.[57] This revelation separates the sectaries from the rest of humanity, who lack wisdom and understanding).[58] Thus understanding forms part of the imagery of election. Characteristic of its modification of such metaphors, Ephesians bypasses the dualistic framework in the Qumran texts, which restricts knowledge to an elite minority.

The Essene examples include other virtues along with understanding: deeds of truth instead of sin, justice, loving what God loves, hatred of evil, love of God, wholehearted devotion to the quest for wisdom. The ethical section of Ephesians (4:1–6:20) takes up the concrete expression of such understanding in Christian life. Verse 9, with its reference to "mystery" (μυστήριον *mystērion*), continues to parallel the language of election found in the Essene writings. The Aramaic equivalent to "mystery" (רז *rāz*; Dan 2:18) appears in Essene interpretation of prophetic texts to refer to the secret plan of God's salvation that has been revealed to the sectaries.[59] Paul uses "mystery" (*mystērion*) in this sense to refer to God's plan for the salvation of humanity in Christ. It has a future reference, that Jews who reject Christ will be included in salvation (Rom 11:25-32). Paul designates the presence of salvation unknown to the rulers of the cosmos when they crucified the Lord of glory as "God's wisdom" (1 Cor 2:7). Like the teacher(s) of the Essene sect,[60] Paul can describe the apostles as persons who dispense these mysteries to others (1 Cor 4:1). Colossians 2:1-3 presents knowledge of the hidden mystery of God as part of the wisdom Christians attain through Paul's teaching. This mystery of salvation was hidden from prior ages but has been made manifest to the saints in Paul's preaching Christ among the Gentiles (Col 1:26-27).

The connection between revelation of the mystery and a preordained divine plan is firmly embedded in Essene writings.[61] However, Ephesians lacks the interest in the succession of times characteristic of apocalyptic speculation that anticipates the end of the present evil age by divine judgment.[62] As v. 10 suggests, the times have reached their fulfillment. The term "plan" (οἰκονομία *oikonomia*) has a range of meanings. The primary secular meanings have to do with the management of a household or city. An individual designated as οἰκονόμος (*oikonomos*) may be the treasurer of a city (Rom 16:23), the estate administrator, or the manager of a household. Often such persons were slaves with considerable power over others, but other examples indicate that freemen may have been administrators for extensive enterprises.[63] When "plan" (*oikonomia*) is associated with God, it refers to God's providential direction of all things in the cosmos.

The connection between the term "plan" (*oikonomia*) and "the fullness of time" (πλήρωμα τῶν καιρῶν *plērōma tōn kairōn*, v. 10) suggests a temporal plan rather than a providential ordering of the world. Paul used the expression "fullness of time" for the coming of Jesus as redeemer from the law and source of Christian adoption as children of God (Gal 4:4-5).[64] That expression designates a moment in the past that marked the transition from divine promise to its fulfillment. But, as we have seen when Paul uses the term "mystery" (*mystērion*) in Rom 11:25, he assumes that God's plan of salvation has not been completed. First Corinthians 15:51-57 also uses "mystery" (*mystērion*) for future stages in the unfolding story of salvation: subjection of all things to the Son, the bodily resurrection of those who belong to Christ, and finally, the return of everything to the Father. Does Ephesians assume that the exaltation of Christ in the heavenly regions marks the end of all significant times of salvation? Some argue that all the divine promises have been realized and are present now in the experience

57. 1QH 5[13]:7-9| 6[14]:8-9, 25-27.
58. 1QS 11:5-6.
59. 1QpHab 7:1-4, 13-14; 8:1-3.
60. 1QH 12[4]:27.

61. See 1QS 4:18-19, with reference to the future destruction of all evil.
62. 4 Ezra 4:37; *2 Apoc. Bar.* 40:3; 81:4.
63. See Arion's administration of Hyrcannus's wealth in Josephus *Antiquities of the Jews* 12.199-200. See also Ceslas Spicq, *Theological Lexicon of the New Testament,* 3 vols., trans. James Ernest (Peabody, Mass.: Hendrickson, 1994).
64. Best observes that unlike Gal 4:4-5, Ephesians has no reference to the incarnation. See Best, *A Critical and Exegetical Commentary on Ephesians,* 139.

of believers who participate in the heavenly exaltation of Christ.[65]

Ephesians appears to come down somewhere between anticipating a future stage of salvation and assuming that all salvation is present in Christ. On the one hand, its eschatology departs from common apocalyptic patterns in not anticipating any future critical acts of salvation from God's side. The formulaic statement in v. 10b of what the fullness of time entails suggests more a static reality than a dynamic process. On the other hand, one cannot ignore the ongoing appropriation of the gospel by human beings, which implies further unfolding of salvation.

Ephesians describes the "all things" (τὰ πάντα ta panta) gathered up in Christ in cosmic terms, all things in heaven and on earth. *How* all things are united in Christ is not specified at this point. Ephesians will develop that motif with the image of Christ as head of the cosmic body, the church.[66] The confession of Christ's present power over the cosmos can be found in the ancient Christian hymn cited in Phil 2:9-11. Colossians 1:15-20 grounds its depiction of Christ's rule over all things in the role of the preexistent son of God in creation.

Ephesians continues in vv. 11-12 with the benefits received by the elect. The expression "obtain an inheritance" (κληρονομέω klēronomeō) evokes echoes of Israel's destiny to be God's "lot" or heritage (Deut 9:29). The Essenes frequently used this expression to describe their community.[67] Ephesians makes the risen Christ the basis for Christians to obtain their inheritance. It agrees with the Essenes that the elect have been called to praise God. Compare the Essene hymn, "I shall bless him for (his) great marvels and shall meditate on his power and shall rely on his compassion."[68] The concluding phrase in this section, "we, who were the first to set our hope on Christ," has led some scholars to suggest that the author has shifted to the perspective of the Jewish Christian "we" found in 2:11–3:6.[69] In that case, the phrase

would employ the ambiguity of the Greek word Χριστός (*Christos*); it can mean both "Christ" (a specific reference to Jesus) and "Messiah" (the object of Jewish hopes). The next verse appears to contrast the "we" of this verse with the "you" of the Gentile readers. However, Ephesians has not yet introduced the Jew and Gentile distinction. Nor is such a division appropriate to the genre that draws speaker and audience together in praise of its subject.

One might treat the switch to "you" in v. 13 as a rhetorical way of drawing the audience into the act of praising God.[70] Since the audience's tacit participation is, however, presumed by the genre, another explanation would seem to be required. The verse alludes to the audience's conversion upon hearing the preaching of the gospel. This mission terminology, drawn from the earlier Pauline writings (Rom 10:14-17; Col 1:5), distinguishes the speaker from the audience.[71] Paul is the agent through whom the gospel comes to be known. The "we" of v. 12 would refer to Paul. The Essenes also combine the language of truth revealed through their teacher(s) with an initiation that includes knowledge of the mysteries of God, forgiveness of sin, and cleansing by God's Spirit.[72]

The combination of "sealing" and "down payment" (NRSV, "pledge") with reference to the Spirit appears in 2 Cor 1:21-22. Though sealing would later become part of the baptismal rite,[73] there is no evidence for those associations in 2 Cor 1:21-22 or Eph 1:13. However, the Essene example mentioned above does tie purification by "lustral waters" with the cleansing power of God's Spirit. The phrase "Holy Spirit of the promise" (NRSV, "the promised Holy Spirit") has inverted Gal 3:14, "promise of the Spirit." There the promise to Abraham has been received through faith in Christ. If the Spirit itself is understood to be the content of the promise, then OT passages that refer to the presence of God's Spirit in the last days serve as the basis for the expression (see Ezek 36:26-27; 37:14; Joel 2:28-30). Commentators who see the "you" of v. 13 as Gentiles who have been incorporated into the faith of the Jew-

65. Andreas Lindemann, *Die Aufhebung der Zeit: Geschichtsverständnis und Eschatologie im Epheserbrief* (Gütersloh: Gerd Mohn, 1975) 49-66, 95.

66. "Somatic unity." See Kōshi Usami, *Somatic Comprehension of Unity: The Church in Ephesus*, AnBib 101 (Rome: Pontifical Biblical Institute, 1983) 112-24.

67. 1QS 4:26; 11:7.

68. 1QS 10:16.

69. Gordon Fee notes a typical Pauline telegraphing of a theme in the body of the letter. See Gordon D. Fee, *God's Empowering Presence: The Holy Spirit in the Letters of Paul* (Peabody, Mass.: Hendrickson, 1994) 669.

70. So Lincoln, *Ephesians* 38.

71. See Best, *A Critical and Exegetical Commentary on Ephesians*, 148, on the mission terminology in this section.

72. 1QS 4:18-22.

73. *2 Clem.* 7:6; 8:6; *Herm. Sim.* viii 6.3; ix 16.3-6.

ish believers treat the Spirit as evidence that the promise of Jew and Gentile joined together is being fulfilled.[74] This reading reflects the theological use of Spirit and promise in Gal 3:14. If the "we"/"you" contrast between v. 12 and v. 13 is not read as referring to Jewish and then Gentile believers respectively,[75] then there is little reason to explicate this expression as a theological account for the election of the Gentiles. The language suits poetic celebrations of divine election similar to that in Essene sources.

Although Ephesians depicts the gifts of salvation as fully present in the lives of believers, the designation "pledge" suggests a future perfection to this experience. A Semitic loan word, "pledge" (ἀρραβών arrabōn) is used in commercial texts for "security," guarantee," or "deposit." The translation "pledge" would be misleading if it suggested a legal promise to fulfill a commitment that establishes a human right against God. Rather, the deposit indicates that one has already received part of what has been promised to secure future delivery. Throughout the eulogy, Ephesians emphasizes the abundance of divine graciousness (vv. 3, 6, 8). The congruence between present and future salvation is reinforced by the phrase that specifies inheritance, "toward redemption as God's own people" (lit., "toward redemption of his possession"). Verse 7 indicated that believers have "redemption" (ἀπολύτρωσις apolytrōsis) from sin through the death of Christ. The meaning of "possession" (περιποίησις peripoiēsis; NRSV, "God's own people") in v. 14 is contested. If taken as a nominal form that designates an action, it would mean "the possessing." The expression might then be a shorthand reference to believers' taking possession of their inheritance. However, the word can also be used to refer to a possession, in this case the people as God's possession (so NRSV; see LXX Mic 3:17; 1 Pet 2:9; Acts 20:28).

In keeping with the genre of praising a benefactor, the expression might refer to God's redeeming God's own (or Christ's) possession. The benefits experienced by the speakers in the present will continue to characterize their lives. Their experience of the Spirit guarantees this relationship. God is, and will continue to be, the redeemer of the people. Finally, the eulogy concludes

with the human response to divine graciousness, praise of God's glory (v. 14c).

The compressed poetic style of the opening eulogy suggests a number of theological themes without providing a conceptual development for any of them. The linguistic and metaphoric parallels from the OT, from Jewish and non-Jewish writings of the Greco-Roman period, and from the earlier Pauline letters provide hints as to what first-century Christian audiences may have brought to their understanding of each phrase. It is easy to apprehend the dynamic involvement of God with human destiny that runs through this section. Its language of election embraces all things in a divine plan that existed before anything came into being. Despite their minority status in the world of first-century CE Asia Minor, Christians found themselves the center of God's cosmic design because they belonged to the risen Lord, who is exalted over all of the heavenly powers. Benefits that humans might expect to receive from "the heavens" have been conferred by God in Christ.

We have seen that Ephesians adopted images that were suited to the cosmic picture of its age. The simpler OT imagery of a heavenly dome over the earth was replaced by a multiplicity of heavenly regions. God's power operates through all of them. The "mystery" (mystērion) of God's plan invites believers to recognize that all things in the cosmos are brought together in the risen Christ. Ancient readers would readily think of a divine force behind the observed motions of the cosmos. Ancient audiences could imagine the arduous journey of the soul beyond the regions of the earth and moon through the spheres to the divine heavens.[76]

Ephesians is making a claim about the universe as Paul's readers know it. The imagery of heavenly regions is not merely decoration for asserting the powerful sovereignty of God. Anyone who could journey like an apocalyptic visionary to the most distant regions of the universe would find God's creative and saving power at work to gather all things into Christ. Ephesians is not interested in a divine plan that was simply programmed into

---

74. Fee, *God's Empowering Presence*, 670.
75. Schnackenburg, *The Epistle to the Ephesians*, 64-65.

76. See M. R. Wright, *Cosmology in Antiquity* (New York: Routledge, 1995). J. E. Wright argues that poorly understood Hellenistic cosmology led 1st-cent. Jewish and Christian authors to shift from the traditional single heaven to multiple heavenly regions. See Wright, *The Early History of Heaven*, 139-84.

the creation of the universe as some Stoic cosmologies envisaged the multiple formations of a divine, rational spirit generating the universe. For Ephesians, the providential action of divine power is oriented forward, toward a redemption that brings all things in the cosmos together in Christ.

The dilemma of God's presence to believers in a vast universe was eloquently framed by Augustine. The God who is inside us, closer than we are to ourselves, is also "outside," quite beyond our comprehension. We cannot reach God without God's having come toward us. Citing Joel 2:28, Augustine comments on the conceptual dilemma of divine presence:

When you are "poured out" (see Joel 2:28) upon us, you are not wasted on the ground. You raise us upright. You are not scattered but reassemble us. In filling all things, you fill them all with the whole of yourself.[77]

Augustine also recognized that the distinction between God as creator and human creatures is

77. Augustine, *Confessions*, 1.4 (3), in Augustine, *Confessions*, trans. Henry Chadwick (Oxford: Oxford University Press, 1992) 4.

essential to the dynamic of praise. Ephesians indicates that the purpose of our election is to praise God's glory. We cannot engage in that praise without the ability to perceive God's redeeming power at work.

Ephesians uses the language of divine election to describe the experience of God's grace touching the lives of believers. In this context, it is important to note the difference between Ephesians and the linguistic background provided by the Essene writings. Unlike the Qumran texts, Ephesians does not depict election as the division between a few righteous and the majority of human beings who are alienated from God. Instead, Ephesians sees redemption as the purpose that God has embedded in creation as a whole. Though Ephesians recognizes the human need for redemption from sin, its imagery suggests that God would have brought all things together in Christ even if Adam had not sinned. Forgiveness enables the elect to live before God in the holiness to which they are called (1:4).

REFLECTIONS

The opening words of Ephesians, after the epistolary greeting, are, "Blessed be the God and Father of our Lord Jesus Christ" (1:3). These words are a variation of "Blessed be God" or "Blessed are you, Lord God," which are standard formulae that ring through Jewish prayers. In the Passover seder, the prayer that accompanies the lighting of the candles is, "Blessed are you, Lord, our God, who makes us holy with your commandments and commands us to light the festival lights." Every prayer for the rest of the meal will begin with the same Hebrew phrase, "Blessed are you, O Lord, our God." Even visitors have it down by the end.

This opening prayer introduces several motifs that echo through Ephesians: God's rule over the universe, the holiness of God's people, a religious life as light shining in darkness, the joy that we take in salvation. The writer Anne Lamott, apologizing for her simple religion, has said that she had only two basic prayers: "Help, help, help" and "Thank you, thank you, thank you."[78] "Blessed be God"—these words remind us that the first movements of prayer should be thanksgiving and praise directed to God. The moments of asking, lament, or reaching out in the emptiness of despair, equally necessary to the life of prayer, make no sense without this framework. God is Lord of the universe, but not a distant force unconcerned about human beings. Instead, God is our greatest benefactor. Inhabitants of Greco-Roman cities were familiar with elaborate orations in praise of wealthy benefactors. Augustine complained that as holder of the chair of rhetoric in Milan he would be expected to eulogize the emperor on state occasions. Lies were the price of the honor that he was seeking: "I was preparing to recite praises of the emperor, most of which were lies, and by so lying win favor from those who

78. Anne Lamott, *Traveling Mercies: Some Thoughts on Faith* (New York: Pantheon, 1999).

knew [that they were lies]."[79] Ephesians has combined the traditional Jewish prayer with the familiar civic rhetoric of eulogy to drive home the point that God is the true source of goodness. Praise of God is the whole truth, not a pack of lies.

We also see the sense of a powerful new expression of God's person and love reshaping traditional forms of articulation. God is not simply "ruler of the universe." God is "Father of our Lord Jesus Christ." The Gospels tell the story of the life and ministry of Jesus, but Ephesians does not reflect in the same way on the human life of Jesus. Rather, it begins with the ongoing, present life of Christ, the risen Christ exalted in heavenly glory. In traditional Jewish formulae, the commandments are seen as the sign of God's blessing; but in Ephesians, because of Jesus' death on the cross and his heavenly exaltation, the signs of God's favor are spiritual blessing, forgiveness of sin, and, most important, election or adoption as God's people. We see the importance of this shift later in the letter (2:11-22). The commandments separated Jews from non-Jews. The spiritual blessings that have been won on the cross are for all people. Even today it is easy to forget that claim.

There is more to the tale. Ephesians sees the plan of salvation as a hidden order that existed even before the universe was created. This vision takes an even more dramatic turn when we translate it into the twenty-first-century cosmos. We have stunning visual photos as well as color renderings of radiation from other spectra that map the universe further and further back in time. Rather than check our astronomy at the church door, we need to bring these pictures in. There is no reason for today's believers to keep their faith locked up in the smaller universe of the first century. Add to that vision the mathematical speculations of physicists who imagine that there are other universes.[80] Ephesians suggests that we stretch our imaginations. Before any of this even existed, God's plan encompassed the human story of faith. Various astronomical theories, equations, and observations speculate about the probable fate of the material universe, but Ephesians assures us that God's plan of salvation does not depend on these calculations and that somehow the universe is ordered so that all things return to God in Christ.

The structure for the spiritual return of all things to God is already unrolled from its hiding place in God's eternal wisdom. That is the mystery Ephesians invites us to contemplate. What is the structure? The cosmic body of Christ (1:10). Remember that this section of Ephesians is poetic rhetoric, not the theological language of dogmatic textbooks. The nuts and bolts of a theological explanation for this vision are not provided. But put its affirmation of faith into the dramatic sweep of twenty-first-century science, and the consequences are breathtaking. Cosmology will not prove the truth about the hidden faith structure of the universe, whether it is dressed up in first-century or twenty-first-century garb; but it will instruct us about imagining God. We are summoned to a vision of a God who encompasses the whole cosmos and who is active in all of creation.

There is another question that Ephesians puts to the modern imagination that concerns the path of holiness. It is a fundamental tenet of biblical theology that creation is a witness to God (see Pss 19:1-4; 104:14-23; Isa 40:25-26; Rom 1:19-22).[81] That witness calls for human response of praise and piety, walking in holiness. We are familiar with poets and artists who find God through the beauty of creation. The nineteenth-century Jesuit poet Gerard Manley Hopkins ends his poem "Pied Beauty" with, "All things . . . he fathers-forth whose beauty is past change: Praise him."[82] Ephesians points to a further movement beyond awe and praise, that of discipleship. Holiness is a way of life that corresponds to the God revealed in creation.

---

79. Augustine *Confessions* VI.6 (author's trans.).

80. See, e.g., Brian Greene, *The Elegant Universe: Superstrings, Hidden Dimensions, and the Quest for the Ultimate Theory* (New York: Norton, 1999).

81. See the discussion of this motif in Walter Brueggemann, *Theology of the Old Testament: Testimony, Dispute, Advocacy* (Minneapolis: Fortress, 1997) 528-51.

82. The poem can be found in Christopher Ricks, ed., *The Oxford Book of English Verse* (Oxford: Oxford University Press, 1999) no. 584.

Creation has not lost its power to inspire awe in the twenty-first century. Praise of the Creator, who is greater than the beauty that "he fathers-forth," should follow. But that is the step we often find missing in the modern imagination. For example, Christians might well ask what happened to faith in the science fiction movies. Perhaps you have noticed. In most "sci-fi" movies (not to mention computer games) religion has been written out of most, if not all, of "the universe"—whether we take it in spacial, galactic terms or in temporal ones. The implicit prediction is that God will not be around in 3030. Think about it. People would have said the same about the long-term chances of the emerging Christian faith in 60 CE. They would have thought that empires, gods, perhaps even Rome, would remain to 1000 CE. But this group of believers?

NIV

¹⁵For this reason, ever since I heard about your faith in the Lord Jesus and your love for all the saints, ¹⁶I have not stopped giving thanks for you, remembering you in my prayers. ¹⁷I keep asking that the God of our Lord Jesus Christ, the glorious Father, may give you the Spirit[a] of wisdom and revelation, so that you may know him better. ¹⁸I pray also that the eyes of your heart may be enlightened in order that you may know the hope to which he has called you, the riches of his glorious inheritance in the saints, ¹⁹and his incomparably great power for us who believe. That power is like the working of his mighty strength, ²⁰which he exerted in Christ when he raised him from the dead and seated him at his right hand in the heavenly realms, ²¹far above all rule and authority, power and dominion, and every title that can be given, not only in the present age but also in the one to come. ²²And God placed all things under his feet and appointed him to be head over everything for the church, ²³which is his body, the fullness of him who fills everything in every way.

a17 Or a spirit

NRSV

¹⁵I have heard of your faith in the Lord Jesus and your love[a] toward all the saints, and for this reason ¹⁶I do not cease to give thanks for you as I remember you in my prayers. ¹⁷I pray that the God of our Lord Jesus Christ, the Father of glory, may give you a spirit of wisdom and revelation as you come to know him, ¹⁸so that, with the eyes of your heart enlightened, you may know what is the hope to which he has called you, what are the riches of his glorious inheritance among the saints, ¹⁹and what is the immeasurable greatness of his power for us who believe, according to the working of his great power. ²⁰God[b] put this power to work in Christ when he raised him from the dead and seated him at his right hand in the heavenly places, ²¹far above all rule and authority and power and dominion, and above every name that is named, not only in this age but also in the age to come. ²²And he has put all things under his feet and has made him the head over all things for the church, ²³which is his body, the fullness of him who fills all in all.

a Other ancient authorities lack and your love   b Gk He

COMMENTARY

The thanksgiving of Pauline letters often signals themes taken up in what follows. The second, long periodic sentence in Ephesians serves that function. Ephesians combines phrases from Colossians (Col 1:3-4, 9, 18) with its own emphasis on knowledge of God's saving power in Christ to create its thanksgiving. Rhetorically, the thanksgiving can be a way of gaining the goodwill of one's audience. The eulogy joined author and audience in the praise of their common benefactor, God (v. 13). Now the thanksgiving assures Christians who had not known the apostle Paul that their reputation for faith and love has won them a place in his prayers. Paul used a similar strategy in addressing Christians in Rome, whom he had not yet visited (Rom 1:8-15).

The thanksgiving falls into three sections: (a) the formal thanksgiving and prayer report (vv. 15-16); (b) the content of Paul's intercession (vv. 17-19); and (c) a christological expansion on God's energizing power in the exalted Christ (vv. 20-23). The intercessory report asks for insight and wisdom (vv. 17-19). The content of that knowledge returns to phrases from the eulogy: (a) Spirit, wisdom, revelation, and one's ability to "come to know" (ἐν ἐπιγνώσει *en epignōsei*) in v. 17 echo the wisdom, insight, and making "known to us the mystery" (μυστήριον *mystērion*) of vv. 8-9; (b) hope, riches, and inheritance in v. 18 pick up the earlier "first to set our hope" (v. 12), wealth (v. 7), and inheritance (v. 14).

Many commentators detect a hymnic formula describing the exaltation of Christ in vv. 20-21, which has been expanded by a scriptural proof text (Ps 110:1) and its application to Christ and the church. Emphasis on the role of the church in God's plan (v. 22) is an addition peculiar to Ephesians.[83] The combination of Ps 110:1 and Ps 8:6 describes the eschatological triumph of the Lord independently of ecclesial imagery elsewhere in the NT (see 1 Cor 15:25-27; Heb 2:8-9).[84] The image of the risen Christ as head of the church derives from Col 1:18. The puzzling concluding clause (v. 23c), "the fullness of him who fills all in all" (τὸ πλήρωμα τοῦ τὰ πάντα ἐν πᾶσιν πληρουμένου *to plērōma tou ta panta en pasin plēroumenou*), reformulates the mystery of God's plan from v. 10.

1:15-16. The prayer report combines Col 1:3-4 and Phlm 4-5. Pauline thanksgivings make it clear that the appropriate response to evangelization is a reputation for Christian faith. The apostle's preaching would not be successful if his churches did not become known to others as places of faith and mutual love (see 1 Thess 1:3-12).

1:17-19. The thanksgiving modulates into the prayer wish for the readers in these verses. The theocentric focus of the eulogy continues. A key element in the praise of God was "glory" (δόξα *doxa*, vv. 12, 14). This emphasis leads to a reformulation of the title for God. The earlier "Father of our Lord Jesus Christ" (v. 3) becomes "God of our Lord Jesus Christ" and "Father of glory" (v. 17a). The phrase "Father of glory" (ο πατὴρ τῆς δόξης *ho patēr tēs doxes*) is not a common expression for God. Paul refers to Jesus as "the Lord of glory" in 1 Cor 2:8. The phrase "God of glory" occurs in Ps 28:3 (LXX), where "glory" (*doxa*) is associated with the storm-god theophany tradition. James 1:17 refers to the "Father of lights" as the source of every good gift, a sentiment similar to that in Eph 1:3.

The initial content of the petition also reminds readers of the earlier emphasis on wisdom and knowledge of God's plan (vv. 8-9, 17b). Given the earlier reference to believers as being "marked with the seal of the promised Holy Spirit" (v. 13), the expression "spirit of wisdom" (πνεῦμα σοφίας *pneuma sophias*) probably intends more than human perception of divine wisdom. God's Spirit is the source of all wisdom and knowledge among the elect. The author is not thinking of particular charismatic gifts that are possessed only by some members of the community, such as the special insight possessed by the apostle (3:3, 5).

Verse 18 describes the result of wisdom as "the eyes of your heart enlightened" (πεφωτισμένους τοὺς ὀφθαλμοὺς τῆς καρδιας *pephōtismenous tous ophthalmous tēs kardias*). This expression resembles the Essene language of election as in the blessing pronounced over those who enter the covenant: "May he illuminate your heart with the discernment of life and grace you with eternal knowledge."[85] By the second century, baptism was commonly described as enlightenment.[86] Ephesians 4:18 speaks of Gentiles who do not know God as "darkened in their understanding." The addressees are warned not to return to that state. Ephesians treats the darkness-to-light image as a reference to the moral conversion associated with turning to God. The fact that individuals might revert to darkness shows that illumination of the heart is not a transformation that becomes permanent as soon as someone becomes a Christian.

Although the OT regularly uses "heart" (לב *lēb*) for the seat of human understanding (Ps 10:11; Prov 2:2), the phrase "eyes of your heart" (*tous opthalmous tēs kardias*) has no biblical antecedents. However, Prov 20:27 (LXX) speaks of the breath of humans as the light of the Lord searching out hidden storerooms of the belly. Other Jewish texts refer to the darkened or clouded eye as equivalent to a depraved will.[87] These examples suggest that the expression "eyes of your heart" is associated with change in conduct. Greek moralists may have contributed to

---

83. Lincoln concludes that these verses cite traditional material but are not taken from a hymn. See Andrew T. Lincoln, *Ephesians*, WBC 42 (Dallas: Word, 1990) 51.

84. James D. G. Dunn, *Christology in the Making: A New Testament Inquiry into the Origins of the Doctrine of the Incarnation* (Philadelphia: Westminster, 1980) 108-9.

85. 1QS 2:3.

86. So Justin Martyr *1 Apol.* 61.12; 65.1; *Dialogue with Trypho* 39.2; 122.1, 2, 6.

87. *T. Iss.* 4:6; *T. Benj.* 4:2. See Ceslas Spicq, *Theological Lexicon of the New Testament*, 3 vols., trans. James Ernest (Peabody, Mass.: Hendrickson, 1994).

such expressions. Matthew 6:22-23 also refers to an "eye" (ὀφθαλμός *ophthalmos*) that is healthy and one that is evil or diseased. This saying refers to the inner light required for ethical discernment. Platonic and Stoic philosophers commonly link that light with reason. Matthew challenges the philosophic assumption that humans can rely on such inner light, since the eye can be darkened.[88]

The content of enlightenment reiterates earlier statements about Christian hope (vv. 18*b*, *c*, 14*a*). Since the passage speaks of "his [God's] glorious inheritance," some commentators presume that the meaning of "saints" (ἅγιοι *hagioi*) has shifted from saints as God's elect to saints as "the holy ones"—that is, angels (so Deut 33:2-3; Ps 89:6, 8; Dan 8:13). On this reading, Ephesians would be similar to the Essene writings in claiming that the heritage of the elect lies with the angelic hosts.[89] Against this interpretation of v. 18, v. 15 has used "saints" (*hagioi*) for those who are fellow Christians within the audience.

Verse 19 shifts from knowledge of one's place among God's elect to recognition of the power of God at work in those who believe. An echo of Col 1:11, the phrase is replete with words for power. The author does not focus on the cosmological manifestations of divine power.[90] Just as the eulogy's account of God's activity in creation (vv. 3-5) was not cosmological but soteriological, so also v. 19 describes the power of God as "for us who believe" (εἰς ἡμᾶς τοὺς πιστεύοντας *eis hēmas tous pisteuontas*). Verse 19*b* shifts from "you" (plural) to the inclusive "we" in order to set up the parallelism between God's work in the believer and what God has done in raising Christ (v. 20).[91]

The expression "working of his great power" connects v. 19*b* with v. 20*a*. Some interpreters treat it as the introduction to the next section.[92] Colossians 1:29*b* speaks of God's powerful energy at work in the struggles of Paul's ministry. Colossians 2:12 speaks of God's power ("energy") to raise the dead. Since Ephesians uses expressions associated with divine energy and power to connect God's activity within believers and the resurrection of Christ, the phrase may be derived from earlier Christian formulae.

1:20-23. The concluding section of this chapter is widely recognized as the development of a creedal formula. Attempts to isolate the specific words of a hymn have not been persuasive.[93] Verse 20 alludes to the ancient tradition of resurrection as heavenly exaltation at God's right hand (Dan 12:2-3; Acts 2:32-33; Phil 2:9-11). The audience already knows that Christ serves to mediate God's gracious blessings from the heavens (v. 3). Ephesians treats the exaltation of Jesus rather than the cross as the focus of God's saving power.[94] Paul links the resurrection of Jesus and divine power in contexts that contrast resurrection with the cross (Rom 1:4; 1 Cor 6:14; 2 Cor 13:4; Phil 3:10). Ephesians may have shifted the traditional emphasis in order to highlight the permanent victory of God's power.

Hellenistic Jewish court tales celebrated exaltation as the victory of a righteous sage over the enemy (see Daniel 1–7). Daniel 7:13-27 depicts a human figure ascending to God's throne. With his ascent comes vindication for the righteous and eternal dominion for the "holy ones of the Most High" (Dan 7:27). With the corporate interpretation of the heavenly figure as representative of the righteous, Dan 7:13-27 provides a key to the connection between heavenly exaltation of a figure to God's throne and the eventual triumph of God's elect. This apocalyptic scenario also includes two other elements that are represented in Ephesians: (a) use of the "holy ones" (Dan 7:18, 21, 25, 27) in a way that could refer to the righteous or the angelic hosts[95] and (b) exaltation as victory over powers that threaten human and divine order (Dan 7:23-25).

The exaltation christology of Ephesians requires that Christ be superior to all the heavenly powers (v. 21). The text does not indicate whether the reader should consider this catalog of powers as hostile (so Daniel) or angelic (so Heb 1:3-4). Colossians 1:16 associates a list of powers with the affirmation that the cosmos was created in Christ, "whether thrones or dominions or rulers

88. Hans Dieter Betz, *Galatians* (Philadelphia: Fortress, 1979) 84 87.
89. Rudolf Schnackenburg, *The Epistle to the Ephesians,* trans. H. Heron (Edinburgh: T. & T. Clark, 1991) 75. See 1QS 11:7-8.
90. As in, e.g., 1QS 11:18-19.
91. Joachim Gnilka, *Der Epheserbrief,* HTKNT (Freiburg: Herder & Herder, 1980) 91; Ernest Best, *A Critical and Exegetical Commentary on Ephesians,* ICC (Edinburgh: T. & T. Clark, 1998) 169.
92. Lincoln, *Ephesians,* 60.

93. Ibid., 51.
94. Markus Barth and Helmut Blanke, *Colossians,* AB 34B (New York: Doubleday, 1994) 169.
95. John Collins, *Daniel* (Minneapolis: Fortress, 1993).

or powers" (ἐξουσία *exousia*). Ephesians 1:21*a* omits "thrones" and includes δύναμις (*dynamis*; NRSV, "power"; for *exousia* the NRSV shifts to "authority"). Similar lists in apocalyptic texts can be associated with angels[96] or with Satan's cohorts.[97] Ephesians concludes the list of powers with the statement that Christ has the name above every name. This topos appears elsewhere in early christological formulae (see Phil 2:9-11, "Lord"; Heb 1:4-5, "Son"). The concluding phrase (v. 21*c*) evokes the apocalyptic picture of present and future ages. Just as the Son of Man and the holy ones in Dan 7:13-27 receive an eternal dominion, so also the exalted Christ enjoys eternal rule. This affirmation raises a theological question when this passage is compared with Paul's account in 1 Cor 15:23-28. There the Second Coming will be needed to complete the Son's domination of all the powers. At that point, Christ will hand dominion over to the Father. Though Ephesians focuses on the Father in its depiction of divine power, the author does not anticipate a "handing over" of the kingdom to God.

The scenario in Ephesians cannot be squared with the historical perspective of apocalypses like Daniel, which correlate heavenly or symbolic figures with political powers. In such historical apocalypses no claim to dethrone hostile powers could be sustained without the corresponding defeat of evil in its sociopolitical manifestations. The significance of language about Christ's exaltation over the powers in Colossians and Ephesians remains contested. Ephesians refers to an angelic leader of the hostile powers (2:2; 6:11). If the powers of this list are hostile, then Christ is a victorious conqueror.[98] Others have highlighted the reference to Christ's superior name. They suggest that Ephesians is concerned with the use of angelic names in magical texts. The Christ whose name is superior to those of any such powers has rendered the powers of magic impotent.[99] When Ephesians is read over against the ideology of the Roman emperor cult, its encomium to the exalted Christ (esp. 2:11-22) appears to copy the style of speeches in praise of the emperor.[100]

Identification of the list of powers with causes of sociopolitical or individual evil presumes that the powers in this list are the demonic powers referred to later in Ephesians. Since the eulogy and the thanksgiving both depend upon traditional formulaic phrases for divine blessing, the positive use of angelic powers and name formulae in christological acclamations and hymns seems to be more appropriate in this section. God has made all things subject to the risen and exalted Lord (1 Cor 15:25). That same power will be effective in the resurrection of the faithful (Phil 3:21).

In the earlier Pauline letters, references to the future completion of salvation indicate that the present subjection of all things remains a stage in an ongoing process: (a) Christ turns all things over to the Father (1 Cor 15:28); (b) believers are transformed into the image of the risen one (Phil 3:21). Unlike these examples, Ephesians remains focused on the present evidence of salvation. Verse 22*b* takes from Ps 110:1 the image of Christ as head over the universal church: "He has put all things under his feet." This motif picks up the earlier statement that God's preordained plan was to bring all things together in Christ (v. 10). Ephesians consistently uses "church" (ἐκκλησία *ekklēsia*) in the universal sense found in Colossians (e.g., Col 1:18, 24).

In 1 Cor 12:12-27 (and Rom 12:4-5) Paul adopts a common philosophical image for the political community as a body in which each has an assigned role. Differences in status, activity, and power are necessary for the well-being of the whole. Paul's appropriation of this image to promote concord in the Corinthian community also fits common philosophical usage.[101] Colossians 1:18 has universalized the image by alluding to philosophical traditions that transferred the communal sense of "body" (σῶμα *sōma*) to the harmonious coordination of the cosmos. The universe was considered to be a living being. Hence the move to describing it as a body was not as great

96. See *1 Enoch* 61:10; *2 Enoch* [J] 20:1; *T. Levi* 3:8.
97. *Ascen. Isa.* 2:2.
98. Rudolf Schnackenburg, *The Epistle to the Ephesians,* trans. H. Heron (Edinburgh: T. & T. Clark, 1991) 77.
99. Clinton E. Arnold, *Ephesians: Power and Magic. The Concept of Power in Ephesians in the Light of Its Historical Setting,* SNTSMS 63 (Cambridge: Cambridge University Press, 1989) 55f.

100. Eberhard Faust, *Pax Christi et Pax Caesaris. Religionsgeschichtliche, traditionsgeschichtliche und sozial geschichtliche Studien zum Epheserbrief,* NTOA 24 (Freiburg: Universitätsverlag; Göttingen: Vandenhoeck & Ruprecht, 1993) 324-80.
101. Tacitus *Annals* 1.12, 13; Plutarch *Life of Galba* 4.3; Philo *On the Special Laws* 1.210; Cicero *On Duties* 1.25.85.

as it would be for today's readers.[102] For Colossians, the image of Christ as head of the body makes a natural transition between the creation of all things in Christ and the church that comes into being through the death and resurrection of Jesus.

Ephesians has adopted the imagery of Colossians for a different purpose: to express the completeness of salvation. Christ's superiority to the powers of the cosmos makes the existence of the church possible. However, Ephesians distinguishes the subjection of the powers from the function of Christ as head of the church. Christ is not a distant potentate ruling the church.[103] The concluding description of the "body" (sōma) as "fullness" (πλήρωμα plērōma) involves several exegetical difficulties. Is "fullness" in apposition to "body" or to Christ (as in Col 1:19; 2:9)? In Ephesians, "fullness" (plērōma) makes better grammatical sense as a reference to the body.

The meaning of the term "fullness" (plērōma) is more problematic. Elaborate discussions of a divine "fullness" as the goal of salvation appear in gnostic writings from the second and third centuries CE. There "fullness" refers to the realm of divine light that is permanently separated from the darkness, chaos, and evil of this world. A primordial fall led to elements of that light being held captive in this world by the rulers of the planetary spheres (often equated with the OT God). Christ, or some other redeemer figure, must break into this world in order to provide the souls that possess light with the means to return to the "fullness."[104] Gnostic texts often suggest that when all the light has been restored the "deficiency"—that is, the lower world—vanishes.[105] However, Ephesians shows no evidence of the gnostic dualism.[106] Therefore, it is more probable that Ephesians has taken the term from a hymnic tradition like Col 1:19.[107]

The noun "fullness" (plērōma) can have an active sense ("that which fills") or a passive sense ("that which is filled"); it can also refer to the activity of filling. In the OT the noun is used in the active sense (Pss 95:11; 23:1; 49:12; Jer 8:6; Ezek 12:19; 19:7; 30:12). Ephesians 1:23 echoes OT descriptions of God or a divine attribute filling all things (Isa 6:3; Jer 23:23-24 LXX; Isa 6:3; Wis 1:7; 7:24). Later in the epistle, both Christ (4:10) and the Spirit (5:18) are agents of filling. Since Eph 4:10 refers to the ascent of Christ above the heavens in order to fill (πληρόω plēroō) the universe, the phrase "fullness of him who fills all in all" probably belongs to the same tradition. Nothing remains outside the Christ who fills all.[108] Ephesians does not indicate how the church as Christ's fullness is related to his presence to all things.

The ecclesial conclusion of the thanksgiving sounds a motif that will reappear in the letter. Christ's body, the church, experiences the divine life and power of God that fills all things. Readers sometimes assume that the equation between the church and "fullness" (plērōma) is a call to action, that the Christian mission is responsible for filling the world with Christ. Ephesians does not identify the church with the "all things" (πάντα panta) of the cosmos. Instead, without explaining how the two activities of "filling" are related, this section of Ephesians suggests a special relationship between the church and Christ by using the image of head and body.

The opening of the thanksgiving period gave a more conventional picture of the addressees as the community of the elect. They have become known to others as a community that has faith in the Lord Jesus and demonstrates that faith in love. They believe that the risen Lord has been exalted at God's right hand and have experienced God's power in their lives. When the prayer report turns to imagery of the cosmic power of Christ, Ephesians moves beyond the world as structured by human powers and communities to a world that includes the heavens and ranks of angelic (or demonic) powers. Verse 21 insists that Christ has the name greater than any other, not only in the present age but also in the future. Whether involved in magical practices or not, many persons in the first century CE would have agreed that proper knowledge of angelic or magical names

---

102. E.g., Plato Timaeus 30B-34B; 47C-48B; Cicero On the Nature of the Gods 1.35; 3.9; Seneca On Anger 2.31.7, 8.

103. Kōshi Usami, Somatic Comprehension of Unity: The Church in Ephesus, AnBib 101 (Rome: Pontifical Biblical Institute, 1983) 154-66.

104. E.g., Gos. Truth 41, 1-16; Ap. John 30, 16.

105. Craig A. Evans, "The Meaning of plērōma in Nag Hammadi," Bib 65 (1984) 259-65.

106. Karl Martin Fischer, Tendenz und Absicht des Epheserbriefes, FRLANT 111 (Göttingen: Vandenhoeck & Ruprecht, 1973) 173-200.

107. Schackenburg, The Epistle to the Ephesians, 74.

108. Andrew T. Lincoln, Ephesians, WBC 42 (Dallas: Word, 1990) 77.

was critical to one's life. Magicians could use the knowledge of such names to enlist the aid of cosmic powers. Angelic powers might be named to facilitate the soul's journey into the heavens either at death or as part of a mystical vision. For the apocalyptic visions of the rise and fall of earthly rulers, the angelic or demonic figures behind the human community were also perceived as a real threat. Consequently, the vision of Christ's exaltation found in Ephesians removes believers from the influence of all other powers.

The lists of powers in Colossians and Ephesians aim to embrace all forces that are thought to control humans and events in the cosmos. Since neither angelic nor magical names are used, the claims made for God's effective power in the risen Christ are not wedded to a particular mythological scenario. A modern list of cosmic powers could be substituted for the ancient examples.[109] Perhaps the ambiguity over whether the powers are demonic or angelic was also deliberate. Ephesians intends to fold all "powers" in the cosmos into the power of God expressed through the exalted Christ. Christians should not assume that other powers in the cosmos, or in the political order, stand between them and salvation. Nor do other powers contribute positive benefits to human life.

The "filling" (*plēroō*) already exists as a divine reality (v. 23). Christians are not subject to powers that must be overcome, as was the case for those who thought that heavenly powers stood between the soul and salvation in the heavens. If Christians recognize the presence and power of God in all things, they have a secure basis for the hope for the "riches of [God's] glorious inheritance" (v. 18). The theology of election in Ephesians reminds Christians that God is the source of their hope

and faith. Hope (ἐλπίς *elpis*) as a Christian virtue is not a psychological trait but a response to what God is.[110]

Finally, Ephesians challenges the tendency to define the church from the perspective of its existence as a sociopolitical institution. It stands the earlier Pauline usage of church on its head. The local assemblies to which the earlier letters refer have given place to the cosmic vision of church as a divine reality. The "body" image was used for both sociopolitical entities and for the universe as a whole. Consequently, Ephesians builds on the earlier tradition in order to expand the vision of church from local to cosmic community.

Since Ephesians shows no signs of the gnostic dualism between the divine realm and the material world, the "fullness" (*plērōma*) of the body is not limited to the heavenly realm where Christ is exalted. Ancient thinkers who depicted the divine spirit or wisdom pervading the universe[111] presumed that this spirit had a natural affinity with human intellectual and spiritual capacities. Ephesians rejects the view that human knowledge of God is part of creation as such. It is received as divine gift. The shift from cosmological to soteriological imagery highlights another central conviction of this letter: Redemption belonged to the divine plan prior to creation. Unlike gnostic myth, creation is not a hostile trap for light that belongs to the divine world. It is oriented toward salvation that comes in Christ. Knowledge of God comes with the conversion of human understanding through revelation (vv. 17-18).

---

109. Markus Barth and Helmut Blanke, *Colossians*, AB 34B (New York: Doubleday, 1994) 202.

110. Hans Conzelmann, "Der Brief an die Epheser," in *Die Briefe an die Galater, Epheser, Philipper, Kolosser, Thessalonicher und Philemon*, ed. Jürgen Becker, Hans Conzelmann, and Gerhard Friedrich (Göttingen/Zürich: Vandenhoeck & Ruprecht, 1985).

111. As in Philo *Allegorical Interpretation of the Laws* 3.4.

REFLECTIONS

Reputation or publicity? How do our churches become known for their faith in Jesus and loving service to others? In the ancient secular letter form, the ones sending the letters often indicated that they had heard some good news from or about the recipients and expressed pleasure about learning it. In an age before instant global communication, people could go for weeks or months without news of family, friends, or business associates, and such news was always treasured. Likewise, in the thanksgiving sections of Paul's letters, he also often expresses pleasure about some news he has heard about the recipients, but the news he mentions is always more than routine events. The news for which Paul gives thanks has to do with the fundamental Christian virtues: faith, love, and hope (1:15, 18).

All churches, it could be argued, have some measure of these virtues, but what impresses the author of Ephesians is that this congregation has a word-of-mouth reputation for them. "I have *heard* of your faith in the Lord Jesus and your love toward all the saints," Ephesians says in the thanksgiving prayer section. What is the difference between a reputation based on word of mouth and one generated through a publicity blitz? One big difference is the source. We know who is making a recommendation or telling us a bit of news when we hear something by word of mouth. Paul names sources of information about particular churches in some of his letters (e.g., 1 Cor 1:11; 1 Thess 3:6-10). Since Ephesians is a general essay in the Pauline tradition, we do not find specific details, but the opening formula suggests the intimacy of a word-of-mouth report.

We are familiar with the fact that "word of mouth" can take what filmmakers consider a small movie to big-time status. Some record companies started paying teens in tickets, posters, and CDs to talk up their favorite stars on the Internet. But for all the marketing research, focus groups, and big-budget advertising, no one has found a way to turn publicity into reputation. How does "the buzz" get going around a particular church? Not by advertising. When people come to our worship, our Bible study, our church school, our church suppers, and all the other things we do, they have to feel that special spirit. And Ephesians reminds us that the source of the energy, power, and spirit at work in the church is ultimately God (1:19-20).

Ephesians' thanksgiving prayer tells us something else about the genuinely successful church. The people in such a church have a goal, a destination. And because they know where they are going, they are people of hope.

Sometimes people find it difficult to distinguish hope from faith, but Ephesians makes the distinction very easily. Faith is "in the Lord Jesus" (1:15); that is to say, faith is entrusting our lives to Jesus today, in the present tense. Hope is about the future, about where it is that our present trust in Jesus eventually leads. Hope, therefore, requires wisdom, knowledge, or insight into the glorious heavenly inheritance that awaits believers (1:17-18).

What is it that we need to know about that destiny? Some Christians think that the way to find out is to study reports about near-death experiences. Scholars have compared these modern reports on brushes with death to medieval accounts of mystical journeys into the heavens.[112]

Ephesians shows no evidence of "traveling to the other side," of advocating a spiritual asceticism aimed at gaining visions of the enthroned Christ and his angels.[113] Instead, Ephesians relies upon a theological insight grounded in early Christian exegesis of Pss 8:6 and 110:1. The risen Christ is exalted above all the powers in the universe (Eph 1:20-22*a*). Combining that insight with the Pauline metaphor of the church as the "body of Christ," originally an image of local churches, produces the striking new image of Eph 1:22*b*-23: Christ is head of a body that fills the entire cosmos. The main purpose of this image is not to give us a secret peek into the heavenly places but to give us confidence in the power of God, "who fills all in all."

What has that to do with the Christian need to know? Many Christians still think of heaven in spatial terms as a house or a castle or a park area filled with people. They fail to adjust their imagination of heaven (or, to use the odd term favored by the writer of Ephesians, "the heavenlies") to suit this cosmic picture of God's power and glory.

---

112. Carol Zaleski, *Otherworld Journeys: Accounts of Near Death Experiences in Medieval and Modern Times* (New York: Oxford, 1987).

113. That some form of this spirituality was being promulgated among the churches of the Lycus Valley seems the best understanding of the false teaching opposed in Col 2:6-23. See James D. G. Dunn, *The Epistles to the Colossians and to Philemon,* NIGTC (Grand Rapids: Eerdmans, 1996) 145-87.

The danger in thinking of heaven in spatial terms rather than in terms of God's power was brought home to me one day when a woman timidly knocked on my office door. It was several months after her mother's funeral, and the woman, in obvious distress, said that she had to have an answer to a question because one of her siblings was in real despair over it. The problem? Given the billions and billions of people who had died since humans first emerged on earth and were likely to die before the end of the world, she feared that her mother had to be lost in so vast a crowd. Given the enormous number of people jammed into heaven, she could not see how God could restore the bond of love, the relationship between the mother and her children.

"No problem," I assured her. As far back as the Middle Ages this question has been argued. People have wondered how God could get the bits of bodies shattered by martyrdom or accident back together again. It must be by God's creative power, they concluded. Today we have an even easier way to imagine it. Think of that DNA code or the capacity of computers to store, sort, find patterns, and match data. If puny little human brains can figure out ways to do that, God can restore bodies and families. Remember, God is not an object generated by the laws of physics and biology. Neither is the reality of being transformed into God, being with the holy ones in heaven. It is that creative power of God to touch, be embedded in, or linked to every single part of the universe. A few weeks later, I ran into her in the market. "That was so helpful," she said, "but how did you know it?" "Just theology," I replied.

So even though the metaphors in this section of Ephesians seem strange, both the working of God's power (1:19-20) and the exaltation christology that has the body of Christ "filling all in all" (1:23) have an important message about Christian hope.

BODY OF THE LETTER

EPHESIANS 2:1–3:21, THEOLOGICAL REFLECTION ON SALVATION IN THE BODY OF THE EXALTED CHRIST

Ephesians 2:1-10, Conversion from Death to New Life

NIV

2 As for you, you were dead in your transgressions and sins, ²in which you used to live when you followed the ways of this world and of the ruler of the kingdom of the air, the spirit who is now at work in those who are disobedient. ³All of us also lived among them at one time, gratifying the cravings of our sinful nature[a] and following its desires and thoughts. Like the rest, we were by nature objects of wrath. ⁴But because of his great love for us, God, who is rich in mercy, ⁵made us alive with Christ even when we were dead in transgressions—it is by grace you have been saved. ⁶And God raised us up with Christ and seated us with him in the heavenly realms in Christ Jesus, ⁷in order that in the coming ages he might show the incomparable riches of his grace, expressed in his kindness to us in Christ Jesus. ⁸For it is by grace you have been saved, through faith—and this not from yourselves, it is the gift of God— ⁹not by works, so that no one can boast. ¹⁰For we are God's workmanship, created in Christ Jesus to do good works, which God prepared in advance for us to do.

a3 Or our flesh

NRSV

2 You were dead through the trespasses and sins ²in which you once lived, following the course of this world, following the ruler of the power of the air, the spirit that is now at work among those who are disobedient. ³All of us once lived among them in the passions of our flesh, following the desires of flesh and senses, and we were by nature children of wrath, like everyone else. ⁴But God, who is rich in mercy, out of the great love with which he loved us ⁵even when we were dead through our trespasses, made us alive together with Christ[a]—by grace you have been saved— ⁶and raised us up with him and seated us with him in the heavenly places in Christ Jesus, ⁷so that in the ages to come he might show the immeasurable riches of his grace in kindness toward us in Christ Jesus. ⁸For by grace you have been saved through faith, and this is not your own doing; it is the gift of God— ⁹not the result of works, so that no one may boast. ¹⁰For we are what he has made us, created in Christ Jesus for good works, which God prepared beforehand to be our way of life.

a Other ancient authorities read in Christ

COMMENTARY

The body of the letter picks up the "you" and "us" of 1:18-19 in a long Greek sentence (vv. 1-7) that the NRSV and the NIV have divided into several sentences. The section shifts from the Gentile past of the letter's audience, "you," to the experience of salvation shared by all Christians, "we." The expression "by grace you have been saved" (v. 5c) returns in the conclusion of this section, which also moves from "you" (vv. 8-9) to "we" (v. 10).

The Greek sentence in vv. 1-7 divides into two halves, each beginning with a plural pronoun and a variation of the phrase "being dead in trespasses" (vv. 1, 5). The first half begins with "you" and contains a lengthy expansion on sins that then incorporate "us" (v. 3) in the story of sin and grace (v. 4). The second half continues with the "us" from vv. 3-4 and depicts salvation as being raised to the heavens (v. 6). The "you" of the first half of the sentence reappears in a parenthetical phrase in v. 5b, "by grace you have been saved." This phrase returns in the next sentence (vv. 8-9) to anchor a Pauline "faith not works" contrast. Verse 10 returns to the "we" who are predestined to good works.

Grammatically, the "you" and "we" of vv. 1 and 3 are objects of God's action. The subject of the Greek sentence (vv. 1-7) is not mentioned until v. 4. "God, who is rich in mercy" is the agent of new life and exaltation. The adjective "rich" (πλούσιος plousios) in v. 4 and the "riches of his grace" (πλοῦτος τῆς χάριτος ploutos tēs charitos) in v. 7 provide a link to the previous sections: "riches of his grace" (1:7) and "riches of his glorious inheritance" (1:18). Thus the opening section stresses the graciousness of God's life-giving power, not the sinfulness of life without God.

Three negative statements are reversed in the event of salvation:[114] (a) dead through trespasses (vv. 1, 5), made alive in Christ (v. 5); (b) living according to passions (v. 3), risen with Christ (v. 6); (c) subject to a demonic power (v. 2; v. 3b, treating "children of wrath" as equivalent to "those who are disobedient"), seated in the heavenly regions with Christ (v. 6). Romans 6:1-14 uses a number of "with" compounds to insist that Christians no longer live under sin or the passions of the body (vv. 12-14): crucified with, died with, buried with, live with. There "raised" lacks the "with" prefix when applied to believers. For Romans, being in the risen Christ remains for the future (Rom 6:8). Colossians 2:10-13 attaches similar verbs to a concrete issue: that Christians

are free from physical circumcision through baptism—by being buried with, raised with, and made alive with Christ (Col 2:12-13). Ephesians may have derived its language of conversion from these two passages. Although Colossians combines Christ's victory over the powers with the Christian's present participation in resurrection, there is no parallel to the co-enthronement language of Eph 2:6. The exhortation to set the mind on "things that are above, where Christ is" in Col 3:1-2 avoids placing Christians "in the heavens." Ephesians removes all spatial and temporal separation between believers and the exalted Christ by including "seated us with him in the heavenly places" (v. 6) as a consequence of conversion.

2:1-3. The author turns to address his audience. The connection between sin and death (v. 1) is characteristic of the Pauline tradition (Rom 5:12-21; 1 Cor 15:56; Col 2:13). The Essenes also describe persons who join the sect as being raised from the "worms of the dead" to the "lot of your holy ones."[115]

Verse 2 introduces a familiar apocalyptic topos: All who are not among the elect belong to a sinful humanity inspired by a demonic angelic power. The designation "sons of disobedience" (τοῖς υἱοῖς τῆς ἀπειθείας tois huiois tēs apeitheias; NRSV and NIV, "those who are disobedient") exhibits a pattern familiar from the Essene writings: "sons of darkness," "sons of deceit," "sons of guilt."[116] An angelic power inspires the evil deeds that human beings do: "in the hand of the Angel of Darkness is total dominion over the sons of deceit; they walk on paths of darkness."[117]

The two "following the course of" clauses attached to "you once lived" are unclear. The expression "course of this world" combines a temporal word, αἰών (aiōn, "course"; translated "age" in 1:21; 2:7), and a spatial one, "world" (1:4; 2:12). Since gnostic sources often used the term aiōn for the spiritual beings associated with levels of the heavenly "fullness," interpreters who see gnostic influence in Ephesians treat aiōn as a spiritual being. This reading makes the two clauses variants of each other.[118] However, to fit

---

114. Chantel Bouttier, *L'Epître de Saint Paul aux Ephésiens*, Commentaire du Nouveau Testament, 2nd série Ixb (Geneva: Labor et Fides, 1991) 93.

115. 1QH 19[11]:10-14.
116. See respectively, 1QS 1:10; 1QM 1:7, 16; 1QS 3:21; 1QH 13[5]:7.
117. 1QS 3:20-21.
118. Joachim Gnilka, *Der Epheserbrief,* HTKNT (Freiburg: Herder & Herder, 1980) 66.

the gnostic examples, *aiōn* could not be used to describe this world. For example, the hostile Jewish God is described as "god, the *archōn* (ἄρχων) of the aeons and powers" or as "the *archōn* of the powers."[119] The Johannine expression "*archōn* of this world" (John 12:31; 16:11; NRSV, "ruler"; NIV, "prince") is the expression one would expect of a spiritual power responsible for evil (also see 1 Cor 2:6, 8; 2 Cor 4:4, "god of this *aiōn*"; NRSV, "god of this world"; NIV, "god of this age").

Since *aiōn* is consistently used as a temporal term in Pauline writings and elsewhere in Ephesians, it should have that meaning here.[120] The NRSV obscures the difficulties in the text by translating the phrase "course of this world." That expression is too neutral. When either an apocalyptic or a Pauline text refers to "this age," the assumption is that the evil powers that dominate the present age are under divine judgment. For the Essenes, the present time involves conflict between those who follow paths of truth and those who do deeds of injustice. God's plan will bring that situation to an end: "There exists a violent conflict in respect of all his decrees since they do not walk together. God, in the mysteries of his knowledge and the wisdom of his glory, has determined an end to injustice and on the occasion of his visitation he will obliterate it forever."[121]

Ephesians has not developed the dualism found in such apocalyptic writings, but the imagery in this section echoes apocalyptic language. Therefore *aiōn* must refer to the temporal span of this world as limited by God's judgment. The second "following" clause clearly refers to a demonic figure responsible for evil. Unlike the Essene writings that depict a dualistic struggle in the hearts of humans between the Angel of Darkness and the Prince of Lights,[122] Ephesians highlights the overwhelming power of God. Since Christ is above every "authority" (ἐξουσία *exousia*,1:21), the ruler of such powers has no authority over believers.

Gnostic mythology embedded the triumph over the powers in a mythological reading of the Genesis story. The evil *archōn* whose power is shat-

tered by the coming of the revealer is the God of Genesis. When awakened to their divine nature, the gnostic descendants of the spiritual Adam and Eve can laugh at the vain attempts of the *archōn* and his powers to govern the elect. For example, *Hypostasis of the Archons* has the gnostic ancestress Norea confront the chief *archōn* with the defiant words: "It is you who are the rulers of darkness who are accursed. . . . For I am not your descendant; rather it is from the world above that I am come."[123] The introduction to this tractate in the fourth-century codex tells the recipient that it has been copied because of an inquiry about the reality of the powers described by the apostle in phrases taken from Col 1:13 and Eph 6:12. Even in antiquity, gnostic myths were used to provide clues to the cosmological soteriology of Ephesians.

However, this same text shows what is not gnosticizing about Ephesians. The key lies in the description of the ruler as governing the "power of the air" (ἐξουσία τοῦ ἀέρος *exousia tou aeros*). The region of the "air" continues the engagement with popular Hellenistic cosmology evident in the expression "heavenly regions."[124] "Air" is the murky, polluted region between the planet earth and the moon in which the four elements (earth, water, air, and fire) are mixed.[125] In some accounts, the visible universe is divided into three regions connected to each of the four elements: (a) the stars and the sun are linked with fire; (b) the moon with air; and (c) the earth with water.[126] Ancient writers regularly argued that "demons," in the neutral sense of spiritual beings, must occupy the air. Philo treats the δαιμόνια (*daimonia*) as both beneficent agents of God and as evil angels.[127] Plutarch's teacher Ammonius, whose views also appear in Philo, developed Plato's demiurge into a lower power that rules the sublunary world. This power was also designated Hades or Pluto.[128]

To a first-century reader familiar with such cosmology, Eph 2:2 attributes human sinfulness to the rulers of the sublunary region. Read in astrological terms, the connection between phases

---

119. *Apoc. Adam* 64, 20-26; *Hypostasis of the Archons* 92, 8-10.
120. Andrew T. Lincoln, *Ephesians*, WBC 42 (Dallas: Word, 1990) 95.
121. 1QS 4:17-19.
122. 1QS 3:20-21.
123. *Hypostasis of the Archons* 92, 22-26.
124. Bouttier, *L'Epître de Saint Paul aux Ephésiens*, 99.
125. Tamsyn Barton, *Ancient Astrology* (London: Routledge, 1994).
126. Plutarch *On the Face in the Moon* 943F, citing Xenocrates.
127. Philo *The Giants* 8-18.
128. See Philo *Questions and Solutions on Genesis* 4.8. See also John Dillon, *The Middle Platonists* (London: Duckworth, 1977) 169-70.

of the moon and the passions would provide an explanation for the action of the lower powers. Firmicus says that horoscopes that have the waning moon in relation to mercury indicate a particularly malicious character: "They willingly associate themselves with all kind of wickedness, defend evil men and evil deeds, and their depravity increases from day to day; they are even hostile to men of their own kind."[129] The parallel formulation in Eph 2:3 refers to those trapped in sin as following "the desires or urgings of flesh and thoughts" (τὰ θελήματα τῆς σαρκὸς καὶ τῶν διανοιῶν *ta thelēmata tēs sarkos kai tōn dianoiōn*; NRSV, "senses"). As the astrological example demonstrates, planetary forces work on both the physical body and the ideas in an individual's mind. The term "spirit" (πνευμα *pneuma*) in v. 2 has no connection with references to God's "spirit" elsewhere in Ephesians. Popular Stoic defenses of astrology used the all-pervading "spirit" as an explanation of how astrological influences are transmitted.[130]

Some interpreters see the combination of Hellenistic cosmology and Jewish apocalyptic imagery of vv. 1-3 as a demonizing of the "neutral" (though not always beneficent) powers that would imply that a personal power of evil is at work in leading people into sin.[131] Ephesians assumes that disobedience means not walking in the paths established by God but does not require a cosmic being opposed to God in order to make that point. The letter derives its language about the universality of sin from Paul. The "we" links the sender with the audience in a past of alienation from God. God's wrath (Eph 5:6; Col 3:5, 6) belongs to the demonstration of divine righteousness in Paul (Rom 1:18, 25; 3:5; 4:15; 5:9; 9:22; 12:19; 13:4-5). The comments on grace and works in vv. 8-9 recall Paul's discussion of the law, but unlike Paul, Ephesians uses "righteousness" (δικαιοσυνη *dikaiosynē*) only in a conventional, moral sense as the opposite of "sin." This letter sees no need to defend the possibility of righteousness apart from the law, a central problem of Paul's theology.[132]

Verse 3c asserts that "we . . . like everyone else" are subject to God's wrath "by nature" (φύσει *physei*). Sometimes Paul uses "nature" (φύσις *physis*) for the natural or created order (Rom 1:26; 1 Cor 11:14). In Gal 2:15, those who are Jewish "by nature" (*physei*)—that is, by birth—are not sinners like Gentiles (and in a similar sense of Gentiles, Rom 2:27). Thus, though Paul can speak of all humans as being implicated in sin from the beginning (Rom 5:12-21), he would hardly describe the Jew as "child of wrath" by nature (*physei*). Wisdom 13:1 exhibits the Jewish patterns of speech employed by the apostle. Without the law, human beings are by nature idolaters. The expression "by nature, children of wrath" fits the depiction of Gentile ignorance of God in Rom 1:18-32.

Romans 2:14-16 indicates that Gentiles who do not have the law but perform its requirements "by nature" (*physei*) will be appropriately rewarded by God. Consequently, Paul does not use "nature" (*physis*) to describe a principle that separates humans from God. Use of Eph 2:3 as evidence for the doctrine of original sin belongs to later theological development. The formula in this passage must be based on the general Jewish tradition of Gentile sinfulness, even though the "we" includes Paul as a Jewish Christian.[133]

2:4-7. The subject of this section finally emerges in v. 4: God's graciousness toward those lost in sin. "Rich in mercy" (πλούσιος ἐν ἐλέει *plousios en eleei*) and "love" (ἀγάπη *agapē*) were introduced as characteristics of God's actions toward us in the eulogy (1:5, 7-8) and thanksgiving (1:18). Elsewhere the expression "make alive with Christ" is embedded in Pauline descriptions of baptism (Rom 6:1-14; Col 2:11-13). Some interpreters think that readers would naturally understand a reference to baptism here.[134] However, Ephesians moves in a different direction. Its emphasis lies on the power of God evident in heavenly exaltation. The gift of life in vv. 5-6 develops the christological vision of 1:19-23. The earlier passage described God's power; here it depicts God's love. In both instances, exaltation above the heavens with the risen Christ is the key to the Ephesians' understanding of salvation.

The three "with" expressions—"made alive

129. Firmicus *Mathēsis* 5.6.10.
130. Barton, *Ancient Astrology,* 104.
131. Andrew T. Lincoln, *Ephesians,* WBC 42 (Dallas: Word, 1990) 95.
132. On Paul's argument, see James D. G. Dunn, *The Theology of Paul the Apostle* (Grand Rapids: Eerdmans, 1998) 354-85.

133. Rudolf Schnackenburg, *The Epistle to the Ephesians,* trans. H. Heron (Edinburgh: T. & T. Clark, 1991) 92.
134. Karl Martin Fischer, *Tendenz und Absicht des Epheserbriefes,* FRLANT 111 (Göttingen: Vandenhoeck & Ruprecht, 1973) 121-22.

with" (συζωοποιέω *syzōopoieō*), "raised up with" (συνεγείρω *synegeirō*), and "seated with" (συγκαθίζω *sygkathizō*)—are interrupted by a parenthetical comment, "by grace you have been saved" (v. 5*c*). The same expression opens the next sentence (v. 8). Ephesians 1:7 attached the grace of God to a formulaic description of the cross as sin offering. Since vv. 1-3 described the past life of sin as "being dead," the parenthetical comment in v. 5 may be intended to remind readers of the fact that forgiveness of sin is central to "being made alive." It also suggests that the traditional Pauline juxtaposition of cross (dying with Christ) and resurrection (Rom 6:1-4) has not been completely erased by the emphasis on heavenly exaltation.

An Essene parallel to the exaltation of the righteous has been found in a scroll fragment that links exaltation and suffering.[135] The text speaks of God's saving activity toward the righteous: "and upon the poor he will place his spirit, and the faithful he will renew with strength. For he will honor *the devout upon the throne of eternal royalty* . . . and the Lord will perform marvellous acts such as have not existed, just as he sa[id] for he will heal the badly wounded and will *make the dead live.*"[136] Ephesians makes the exaltation of the faithful a function of their identification with the exalted Christ (1:20-22). This relationship erases the temporal gap between the present in which the righteous live and their future glory.

Verse 7 provides an apparent reason for the heavenly exaltation of the righteous: to prove a point and show "the immeasurable riches of his grace." The Greek expression ἐν τοῖς αἰῶσιν τοῖς ἐπερχομένοις (*en tois aiōsin tois eperchomenois*), translated "in the ages to come" by the NRSV, could have a very different reading. Should the word αἰών (*aiōn*, "age") be taken as a temporal term or as a reference to the powers that dominate human life? Ephesians 3:10 speaks of the manifestation of God's wisdom to the rulers and authorities in the heavenly places. If *aiōn* referred to powers, then this phrase would be a variant of 3:9-10.[137]

This understanding requires the participle (*eperchomenois*) to mean "attack" rather than the more usual meaning of "coming on" or "approaching." But several grammatical problems make this reading difficult.

The Greek verb ἐνδείκνυμαι (*endeiknymai*; NRSV and NIV, "show") uses the preposition εἰς (*eis*) or the dative case for those to whom something is shown. However, this phrase begins with ἐν (*en*, "in").[138] A temporal sense of *aiōn*, combined with the usual meaning of "approaching" for the participle (*eperchomenois*), provides a grammatically acceptable reading, "in coming ages" (as in the NIV). Verse 7 extends the manifestation of salvation that has taken place in the exaltation of Christ (1:6-10), in the inheritance given the faithful (1:18-20), and in their exaltation with Christ (2:6) into the indefinite future.

2:8-10. The parenthetical reference from v. 5 to salvation by grace returns in vv. 8-9 with a number of familiar Pauline expressions: grace (Rom 3:24; 11:6), faith (Gal 2:16), gift (Rom 3:24), boasting excluded by faith (Rom 3:27). The speaker shifts from "you" to addressing the audience as "we." Verse 8*b* underlines the fact that salvation is entirely God's gift, not the result of human effort. Verse 9 highlights that point by rejecting works. Though these expressions are easily expanded in the light of Paul's theological controversies over the role of the law, it is less clear why they are introduced at this point in Ephesians. Certainly, the Essene parallels to the language of election in the epistle would have assumed that obedience to the law is required for salvation. The shorthand "works" (ἔργα *erga*) in v. 9 alludes to the Pauline "works of the law" (Rom 3:27-28; 4:2-5; 9:32; Gal 2:16; 3:2-5, 9-10; Rom 11:6 contrasts works and grace). However, the parallel phrase in v. 8, "your own doing" (ἐξ ὑμῶν *ex hymōn*), allows a more general reading. An audience familiar with the conversion language of popular philosophical teachers might conclude that turning away from sin, the powers of the cosmos, can be accomplished by human efforts or human teaching.

This passage also departs from its Pauline antecedents in substituting "being saved" for Paul's

---

135. 4Q521.
136. 4Q521 frag. 2 col. 2:6-7, 12, italics added.
137. See Heinrich Schlier, *Der Brief an die Epheser* (Dusseldorf: Patmos, 1957) 112-14; Martin Dibelius and D. Heinrich Greeven, *An die Kolosser, Epheser, an Philemon,* HNT 12 (Tübingen: Mohr-Siebeck, 1953); Hans Conzelmann, "Der Brief an die Epheser," in *Die Briefe an die Galater, Epheser, Philipper, Kolosser, Thessalonicher und Philemon,* ed. Jürgen Becker, Hans Conzelmann, and Gerhard Friedrich (Göttingen/Zürich: Vandenhoeck & Ruprecht, 1985); Andreas Lindemann, *Die Aufhebung der Zeit: Geschichtsverständnis und Eschatologie im Epheserbrief* (Gütersloh: Gerd Mohn, 1975) 129-30.

138. Lincoln, *Ephesians,* 109-10.

term "justification." Grace prohibits boasting rather than the cross or justification through faith (as in Rom 3:27; 1 Cor 1:28-31). The "for" (γάρ *gar*) that attaches v. 10 to the preceding indicates a further explanation of why boasting is excluded. This sentence shifts back to the generalized "we" of vv. 4-7. It also qualifies the apparent rejection of works in v. 9 by suggesting that the righteous have been elected to perform certain good works. The last phrase, "be our way of life," provides an inclusion with the "you once lived" in v. 2.

Essene writings would agree that divine election is expressed in the "good works" of the righteous, walking according to God's decrees. But this view generally takes the form of predestination. The good works of the sons of light are contrasted with the works of those dominated by the spirit of injustice, "in agreement with man's birthright in justice and in truth, so he abhors injustice; and according to his share in the lot of injustice he acts irreverently in it and so abhors the truth."[139] Though Paul rejects the idea that good works create the righteousness that will stand up in God's judgment, he can describe the moral conduct that God expects as "good work" (Rom 2:7; 13:3; 2 Cor 9:8; Col 1:9-10). The ethical exhortation that concludes Ephesians requires holy and blameless conduct. The thanksgiving opened with a reminder that the faith for which the Ephesians were known included love of one another. With its emphasis on the present reality of salvation, some readers might infer that ritual identification with the risen Christ and particular convictions about the powers of the cosmos form the core of Christian experience. Verse 10*b* points to the purpose of divine election, the good works that have also been preordained by God.

Verse 10*a* introduces the image of Christians as God's special creation. The Greek word for "what he has made us" (ποίημα *poiēma*) is used in the LXX for creation as God's work (Pss 9:14; 14:25). It has the same sense in Rom 1:20. By itself the affirmation that "we are [God's] creation" could refer to God's original creation. Ephesians 1:4 described election to "holy and blameless" conduct as established before the creation. The next clause contains the phrase "created in Christ" (κτισθέντες ἐν Χριστω *ktisthentes en*

Christō), though most interpreters assume that Ephesians is not referring to the divine plan in creation, but to the Pauline "new creation" (Gal 6:15; 2 Cor 5:17). Galatians 6:15 uses "new creation" as the replacement for the divisive categories of Jew or Gentile. Ephesians may have introduced this expression as a link to the theme of the next section.

The opening of the body of the letter continues the tone set by the eulogy and thanksgiving concerning God's salvation. The initial description of sin raises a question: What does it mean to speak of humans as trapped in sin or subject to a malevolent power? Traditional Christian theology understands all humans as subject to original sin. Taking "by nature" (*physei*, v. 3) in the common sense of "by birth," humans are alienated from God and implicated in the sinfulness that began with Adam. A variant understanding appears in the Essene accounts of predestination. Though God is not directly responsible for the deeds of the wicked, God does permit the existence of the two conflicting powers and foreknows the existence of two "lots" of human beings. This predestination does not vitiate the need for God's grace among the righteous. They recognize that God's spirit enlightens, cleanses from sin, and sustains the life of holiness.

We have seen that Ephesians' use of "ruler of the power of air" to describe the force that governs the lives of sinners enabled its author to connect with first-century cosmological speculation. Augustine refers to Rom 7:7-25 as evidence that the irrational divisions of human willing are punishment for the sinful condition of humans in Adam. He rejects the dualistic view of the Manichees that attributes such divisions to the conflict between good and evil powers.[140] This caveat indicates the dangers of personifying the dualistic powers of apocalyptic. Individuals may conclude that they are not implicated in the works to which they have been predestined. Does Ephesians imply that human psychic and intellectual life is inherently distorted? Ephesians 2:3 treats the entire human person, bodily desires and mental life, as alienated from God. The dark side of this perspective hints that humans are not able to devise the needed "good works" on their own.

---

139. 1QS 4:24.

140. Augustine *Confessions* viii 9.21–10.22, 24.

Yet the dualism implied by such a reading conflicts with another motif in Ephesians: the close connection between the world that God created and salvation. As we have seen, v. 10 speaks of "us" as God's creation in a way that encompasses both God's initial creation and redemption.[141]

Ephesians has placed its description of sin in subordinate clauses. The focus of the opening period is God's grace and love experienced by the redeemed. That experience of God is not inher-

141. Gnilka suggests reference sto the combination of the two in Col 1:15-20. See Joachim Gnilka, *Der Epheserbrief*, HTKNT (Freiburg: Herder & Herder, 1980) 112-22.

ently known to human beings. Conversion implies turning away from a life in which God was absent. Ephesians uses the religious metaphors of its age in speaking of the past as "dead in sins" or as following the powers that govern the age and the lower world. By depicting believers alive, risen, and exalted in the heavens with Christ, Ephesians breaks the sense that humans are constrained by a complex web of powers that are not under their control. When the question of evil arises, no Christian can claim that he or she had no choice but to participate. God did not predestine God's creatures to works of injustice but to good works.

REFLECTIONS

There is a puzzle about evil that often escapes our attention. People can be trapped, or as Ephesians calls it "dead in your sins" (2:1), and not know it. Part of the reason why such effects of sin are not obvious can be found in the mythological-sounding phrases in the next verse: People are "following the course of this world, following the ruler of the power of the air, that spirit that is now at work among those who are disobedient" (2:2). In first-century mythology, an audience would have no trouble imagining a demonic ruler. The practices of magic were directed at harnessing or warding off the influences of such powers. Some scholars think that Ephesians drew up its picture of the body of Christ filling the cosmos to prove to believers that such forces had no way to enter their lives. In the industrialized world of the twenty-first century, we do not typically describe the force that drives people to destructive behavior as independent powers. But we do know that people are subject to many formative influences that mask the reality of "being dead in sins." Our most obvious examples come from persons in programs to aid in their recovery from addictions to drugs, alcohol, or gambling. They know the experience of being ruled by "powers."

On the one hand, in addressing sin Ephesians seems to fit the addiction-recovery model very well. First, according to Ephesians, before we can see our former lives as darkness, we must first experience self-recognition and conversion. Second, no one can make the journey from a way of life that is marked by death to a new life single-handedly. Not only does it take the shared power of other persons, but it also takes the power of God to break the deadly patterns of the old life. It takes the power of God to sustain the new life. Ephesians speaks of this process using the familiar language of grace, "for by grace you have been saved through faith, and this is not your own doing; it is the gift of God" (2:8a).

On the other hand, however, Ephesians looks at conversion from a point of view unlike the personal, psychological focus of modern recovery movements. Just as Paul understood that his conversion from persecuting the church to Christian apostle had been God's preordained plan (Gal 1:11-17), so also the writer of Ephesians sees every Christian life as preordained by God. Each life has a purpose, "good works, which God prepared beforehand to be our way of life" (2:10).

We often assume that speaking of a divine plan for a person's life only makes sense when we are speaking about the great heroes of faith, such as Martin Luther King, Jr., Nelson Mandela, Gandhi, Billy Graham, and Pope John Paul II. They are the modern successors to the apostles, since their lives changed the world. Ephesians makes the transition from heroes of the faith, like Paul, to every Christian. Every Christian has some "good works" that are his or her divine calling. These works are not burdensome commandments but an appropriate response to the extraordinary salvation already extended to us by God. How do we decide what good works are God's plan for us? They cannot be simple variants of the passions that motivate the actions of all human beings. Ignatius of Loyola (d. 1556) composed a process of spiritual discernment for Christians who are seeking to find out what God intends for them. The most important rule is, "The love which moves me and makes me choose something has to descend from above, from the love of God."[142]

The quotation from Ignatius indicates the significance of spatial imagery, which plays an important role in Ephesians as well. Christians need to order their way of life around God first. The passions and concerns of daily life remain part of Christian experience, but they now belong to something greater. Ephesians goes so far as to instruct Christians that they are "seated in the heavenly places" (2:6). Of course, that image cannot describe the actual experience of Christians in this life. However, it establishes a perspective. Suppose we could look down on our lives from above, from God's presence. What would the script for that life be? Surprisingly, perhaps, there is more freedom in that world than in the old life controlled by sin and death.

---

142. Ignatius of Loyola *Spiritual Exercises* 184. See Ignatius of Loyola, *Personal Writings,* trans. Joseph A. Munitiz and Philip Endean (London: Penguin, 1996) 319.

Ephesians 2:11-22, Unity in Christ

NIV

[11]Therefore, remember that formerly you who are Gentiles by birth and called "uncircumcised" by those who call themselves "the circumcision" (that done in the body by the hands of men)— [12]remember that at that time you were separate from Christ, excluded from citizenship in Israel and foreigners to the covenants of the promise, without hope and without God in the world. [13]But now in Christ Jesus you who once were far away have been brought near through the blood of Christ.

[14]For he himself is our peace, who has made the two one and has destroyed the barrier, the dividing wall of hostility, [15]by abolishing in his flesh the law with its commandments and regulations. His purpose was to create in himself one new man out of the two, thus making peace, [16]and in this one body to reconcile both of them to God through the cross, by which he put to death their hostility. [17]He came and preached peace to you who were far away and peace to those who were near. [18]For through him we both have access to the Father by one Spirit.

[19]Consequently, you are no longer foreigners and aliens, but fellow citizens with God's people and members of God's household, [20]built on the foundation of the apostles and prophets, with

NRSV

11So then, remember that at one time you Gentiles by birth,[a] called "the uncircumcision" by those who are called "the circumcision"—a physical circumcision made in the flesh by human hands— [12]remember that you were at that time without Christ, being aliens from the commonwealth of Israel, and strangers to the covenants of promise, having no hope and without God in the world. [13]But now in Christ Jesus you who once were far off have been brought near by the blood of Christ. [14]For he is our peace; in his flesh he has made both groups into one and has broken down the dividing wall, that is, the hostility between us. [15]He has abolished the law with its commandments and ordinances, that he might create in himself one new humanity in place of the two, thus making peace, [16]and might reconcile both groups to God in one body[b] through the cross, thus putting to death that hostility through it.[c] [17]So he came and proclaimed peace to you who were far off and peace to those who were near; [18]for through him both of us have access in one Spirit to the Father. [19]So then you are no longer strangers and aliens, but you are citizens with the saints and also members of the house-

[a] Gk *in the flesh*   [b] Or *reconcile both of us in one body for God*
[c] Or *in him,* or *in himself*

Christ Jesus himself as the chief cornerstone. [21]In him the whole building is joined together and rises to become a holy temple in the Lord. [22]And in him you too are being built together to become a dwelling in which God lives by his Spirit.

hold of God, [20]built upon the foundation of the apostles and prophets, with Christ Jesus himself as the cornerstone.[a] [21]In him the whole structure is joined together and grows into a holy temple in the Lord; [22]in whom you also are built together spiritually[b] into a dwelling place for God.

[a] Or *keystone* [b] Gk *in the Spirit*

COMMENTARY

The "you" are now identified specifically as Gentiles, while the "we" belong to the "commonwealth of Israel." The "once but now" pattern applies to the prior division of the two groups, now brought together as one. Since the next section (3:1-21) depicts the apostle as the one who proclaimed this mystery, some interpreters treat 2:11–3:21 as a single section. However, 3:1 marks a strong rhetorical transition by introducing the apostle's character. Therefore, it introduces a new section in the epistle.

Alterations between "you," "us both," and "you" divide this section into three parts: vv. 11-13; vv. 14-18; and vv. 19-22. The middle section contains a number of formulaic phrases that have been described as fragments of an early Christian hymn (vv. 14-16).[143] This liturgical-sounding piece has been combined with an echo of Isa 57:19 and applied to the argument (vv. 17-18). The catchword "peace" (εἰρήνη *eirēnē*) ties the two parts of this section together. A reference to the cross in v. 16*b* ties the midsection to the conclusion of the first "you" section (v. 13).

The final "you" section (vv. 19-22) introduces a new image for the community: the household of God. It highlights the results of becoming part of Christ by describing the dwelling of God as being built up. Antithetical parallels with the first "you" section make the second "you" section a response to the first.[144] Verse 11 speaks of the Jew/Gentile distinction as "in the flesh by human hands." The new dwelling is "in the Spirit" (ἐν πνεύματι *en pneumati*, v. 22; NRSV, "spiritually"), a temple

that has not been made by humans (v. 21). Verse 12 reminds the audience that they were once "without Christ." Now they are built on the cornerstone that is Jesus Christ (v. 20). Finally, v. 12 speaks of Gentiles as being alienated from the polity of Israel, as strangers and "without God in the world." Now they can count themselves as fellow citizens and members of God's household (v. 19).

Phrases from Col 1:19-22 inform Eph 2:14-16. Colossians describes "peace" (*eirēnē*) as the reconciliation with God brought about through Christ's death on the cross. However, Colossians does not provide the image of a dividing wall of hostility that is central to Ephesians (vv. 14, 16*c*). Ephesians departs from the cosmological perspective of Colossians, which referred to reconciling heaven and earth, to focus on the human dimension. Salvation has brought Jew and Gentile together in a single body.

2:11-13. "Remember" (vv. 11-12) calls the audience's attention back to their former state just as "you were dead" did at the beginning of v. 1. They were once called "the uncircumcision" by the "circumcision." What is the significance of such an observation? The description of circumcision as "in the flesh by human hands" plays down its crucial significance as a sign of the covenant with God (Gen 17:11-14). Echoes of earlier Pauline conflicts seem to be at work (Gal 2:1-14; Phil 3:2-3; Col 2:11). The fact that Jews required circumcision was well known.[145]

143. Gerhard Wilhelmi, "Der Versöhner-Hymnus in Eph 2,14ff," *ZNW* 78 (1987) 145-52.

144. Chantel Bouttier, *L'Epître de Saint Paul aux Ephésiens*, Commentaire du Nouveau Testament, 2nd série Ixb (Geneva: Labor et Fides, 1991).

145. Josephus *Antiquities of the Jews* 1.192; Tacitus *Histories* 5.5, 2. Given the practice of circumcision by other peoples, its use as the sole identifying criterion to class a person as "Jew" can be debated. Shaye J. D. Cohen, *The Beginnings of Jewishness: Boundaries, Varieties, Uncertainties* (Berkeley: University of California Press, 1999) 39-49, finds no evidence that first-century Jews used circumcision as a mark to identify fellow Jews.

Colossians 2:11 speaks of believers receiving a circumcision "not of human hands" (see 2:13). Within first-century Judaism, references to "spiritual circumcision" or circumcision of the heart distinguish members of sects that claim true devotion to God from other Jews (Deut 10:16; Jer 4:4).[146] By speaking of the "circumcision made in the flesh by human hands" (also Rom 2:25-29), the speaker in Ephesians dissociates himself from those Jews who used the derogatory term "uncircumcised" for the Gentiles. The expression "in the flesh" (ἐν σαρκί *en sarki*) was used for those born Gentiles in v. 11*a* (NRSV, "by birth") and then for the external circumcision of Jews in v. 11*b*. Whatever exists merely "in the flesh" cannot express God's new creation (v. 10).

Lest the audience shrug off this bit of ethnic backbiting, v. 12 details the privileges enjoyed by those who belong to Israel. The formulation echoes Rom 9:4-5, but has converted positive statements in Romans to negative expressions describing what the Gentiles lack. The list begins where Rom 9:4-5 ends, with Christ. Romans 9:5 treats the fact that the Christ (Messiah) was Jewish as the culmination of Israel's privileges. The opening "without Christ" in Eph 2:12 forms a counterpart to the beginning of v. 13, "but now in Christ Jesus," and stands in parallel to the concluding phrase "without God in the world."

The middle two phrases of v. 12 situate the deficiencies—being without the Christ, hope, and God—in the fact that the audience did not belong to the Jewish people. Ordinarily the term "alienated" (ἀπηλλοτριωμένοι *appēllotriōmenoi*; NRSV, "being aliens") refers to separation from someone or something to which one was formerly attached. This meaning hardly fits the case of Gentiles and Israel, since the Gentiles were excluded from the prior covenant (Exod 19:6; Pss 80:8-9; 105). The term "commonwealth" (or "body politic," πολιτεία *politeia*) can be used of those who possess citizenship rights.[147] Ephesians

may be referring to the OT depiction of Israel as God's people (Deut 5:1-3; Isa 65:9) rather than the particular ethnic or citizenship status of Jews and Gentiles. The phrase "covenants of promise" serves as a generalizing reference to the OT covenants.

The emphasis on uniting Jew and Gentile suggests a context that includes actual experiences of Jew and Gentile separation in the first century CE. Jewish exclusiveness frequently led to charges of misanthropy.[148] There is considerable debate over the extent to which first-century Jews encouraged sympathetic Gentiles to join the commonwealth of Israel.[149] When the initiative came from the Gentile convert, Jews did accept proselytes.[150] Relationships between Jews and Gentiles in the cities of Asia Minor seem to have been more complex than a simple division suggests. For example, inscriptions and other documents show that Jews and Gentiles exchanged benefactions.[151]

Evidence for relationships between followers of Jesus and the Jewish communities of Asia Minor remains scant.[152] Paul's sufferings there (2 Cor 1:8-9) appear to have been at the hands of civil authorities. Matthew's polemic against the Pharisees reflects the situation in Syria (Matt 23:34-36). Expulsion of Johannine believers from the synagogue cannot be securely located (John 9:22). The "synagogue of Satan" sayings in Revelation do refer to cities in Asia Minor (Rev 2:9; 3:9). Josephus preserves evidence from the first century BCE that Jews in Asia Minor asked Roman authorities or local city councils to confirm their rights to follow ancestral customs.[153] By the beginning of the second century CE, there were fledgling Christian churches in all the cities of Asia Minor where we know of Jewish communities. This convergence suggests that these Christian groups began among the Jews of the synagogues.[154]

---

146. *Jub.* 1.23; Philo *On the Special Laws* 1.205; 1QpHab 11:13; 1QS 5:5.

147. In his apologetic reply to calumnies against the Jewish people, Josephus speaks of their ancient constitution (*politeia; Against Apion* 2.188, 222, 226, 287) derived from the virtuous lawgiver and prophet, Moses (*Against Apion* 2.154-63). See the discussion in Paul Spilsbury, *The Image of the Jew in Flavius Josephus' Paraphrase of the Bible*, TSAJ 69 (Tübingen: J. C. B. Mohr [Paul Siebeck], 1988) 100-102. The peculiarity of using *politeia* in Ephesians arises because the characteristic of a constitution, its laws and ordinances, has been abolished.

148. Josephus *Against Apion* 2.258; Tacitus *Histories* 5.5.1.

149. See Martin Goodman, *Mission and Conversion: Proselytizing in the Religious History of the Roman Empire* (Oxford: Clarendon, 1994).

150. Josephus *Against Apion* 2.210.

151. Paul R. Trebilco, *Jewish Communities in Asia Minor*, SNTSMS 69 (Cambridge: Cambridge University Press, 1991).

152. Jack T. Sanders, *Schismatics, Sectarians, Dissidents, Deviants: The First One Hundred Years of Jewish-Christian Relations* (Valley Forge: Trinity Press International, 1993).

153. Josephus *Antiquities of the Jews* 14.259-61; 16.163. See Louis H. Feldman, *Jew and Gentile in the Ancient World* (Princeton, N.J.: Princeton University Press, 1993).

154. Feldman, *Jew and Gentile in the Ancient World*, 73.

The description of what Gentiles lack may have been common in Jewish communities. The related expression in Col 1:21 lacks the details about belonging to the community of Israel and sharing its covenant promises. The expression "without God" (ἄθεοι *atheoi*) in Eph 2:12 refers to a frequent motif in the Bible—that is, the Gentiles are ignorant of God (LXX Jer 10:25; 1 Thess 1:9; 4:5; Gal 4:8). The expression can be used for someone considered to be godless in the sense of impious. That usage makes it parallel to the expression "those who are disobedient" in v. 2.[155] In that case, the meaning of Eph 2:12 would be close to Gal 4:8, "not know[ing] God . . . enslaved to beings that by nature are not gods." However, the expression "without God" might reflect local polemics. Josephus reports the slander against Jews that they were "atheists [*atheoi*, "without God"] and haters of humankind."[156]

Despite the Jewish cast to its depiction of Gentiles, the "now" (νυνι *nyni*) does not speak of Gentiles joining the commonwealth of Israel. Instead, Ephesians uses the expression "brought near by the blood of Christ" (v. 13). Ephesians 1:7 spoke of redemption in Christ's blood as forgiveness. More immediately, readers have been reminded that they are exalted in the heavenly places with Christ (2:6). This set of spatial terms would lead the audience to conclude that they have been brought near to God rather than to the commonwealth of Israel as such.

The OT refers to Gentiles as "far off" (see Deut 28:49; 29:22; 1 Kgs 8:41; Isa 5:26; Jer 5:15). The term "come near" or "approach" (ἐγενήθητε ἐγγύς *egenēthēte engys*) also appears in Essene writings for joining the sect[157] or for the knowledge of the law, which comes through God's Spirit. Persons who "approach" in this sense are separated from others who disregard the law: "To the degree that I approach my fervour against all those who act wickedly . . . increases; for everyone who approaches you, does not defy your orders."[158] Thus for the Essenes, to "come near" could mean increasing distance from other Jews whose observance of the law did not meet the standards of the sect.[159]

2:14-18. Attempts to isolate a continuous hymnic piece in vv. 14-16 have resulted in very different solutions, though most agree that the phrases "dividing wall" and "in his flesh" (v. 14), "the law with its commandments and ordinances" and "in himself" (v. 15), and "through the cross" (v. 16) are likely to be expansions by the author of Ephesians. Rudolf Schnackenburg prefers to read vv. 14-16 as an elaborate periodic sentence similar to those found earlier in Ephesians. Its phrases alternate between references to the negative things that must be destroyed and to the positive result of Christ's coming, making peace. References to Christ are threaded throughout: (a) "himself . . . in his own flesh" (v. 14); (b) "in himself" (v. 15); (c) "in one body . . . in himself" (v. 16).

The negative phrases all refer to what must be destroyed: (a) a barrier (v. 14*b*); (b) law of commandments and decrees (v. 15*a*); (c) enmity (vv. 14*c*, 16*b*). Unity is not merely the end of human enmity. It also involves reconciliation with God through the cross. Verse 16 is the only explicit reference to "the cross" in Ephesians. This reference is connected with images in this section taken from Col 1:20-22: "making peace," God's willingness to "reconcile," the "blood of his cross," and being "estranged." Ephesians has used the hymnic phrases from Colossians to depict the new unity of Jew and Gentile.[160]

Verse 14 shifts from the "you" form of the previous verse to "we." "Christ is our . . ." formulae appear elsewhere in the Pauline Epistles, with Christ being called wisdom, righteousness, sanctification, redemption (1 Cor 1:30), life (Col 3:4), and hope (1 Tim 1:2). Making peace between estranged parties does not always imply that they become "one." The body metaphor requires harmonious concord, but such peace could embrace differentiated parts. However,

---

155. So Joachim Gnilka, *Der Epheserbrief,* HTKNT (Freiburg: Herder & Herder, 1980).

156. Josephus *Against Apion* 2.148.

157. 1QS 9:15-16.

158. 1QH 14[6]:13-15.

159. Ephesians uses "come near" for Gentile converts in a way that masks the break with family and associates required of proselytes. See Philo, *Virt.* 20.102-21.108; *Spec. Law* 1,9.51-55). Cohen, *The Beginning of Jewishness,* 156-62, finds that classification of proselytes was asymmetrical. Non-Jews considered proselytes to have become Jews. However, treatment of proselytes within the Jewish community indicates that they were not considered to be Jews. Ephesians can only be speaking as an outsider to the Jewish community in formulating this account of the unity of Jew and Gentile.

160. Rudolf Schnackenburg, *The Epistle to the Ephesians,* trans. H. Heron (Edinburgh: T. & T. Clark, 1991) 107.

readers know that God planned to bring all things together in Christ (1:10). If the Gentile deficiencies result from being separated from Israel, one might have thought Ephesians would argue that "brought near" (*egenēthēte engys*) meant incorporation into Israel. Since that is not what occurs, some interpreters assume that Ephesians has the reconciliation of Gentile and Jewish believers in mind (as Rom 15:7-13).[161]

Spacial and sociopolitical estrangement become enmity in v. 14*c*. Evidence for severe or sustained hostility between Jews and Gentiles in Asia Minor is weak. If we look to the Essene usage of "come near" for joining the sect, enmity would imply intrasectarian polemic. The pious Essene becomes the enemy of all Jews who are not observant. Ephesians appears to view the law as a source of enmity, since Christ has made peace by abolishing its various precepts (v. 14*b*).

Jews often faced the accusation that their law made them "haters of humanity." Josephus replies that any fair observer would find that the law has quite a different result. His account of the Jewish constitution should show any reader of goodwill that "we possess laws best designed to produce piety, fellowship with one another and sympathy toward humanity at large, as well as justice, strength in hardships and contempt for death."[162]

The law as a "dividing wall" that protects the holiness of the people appears in an apologetic context in the *Letter of Aristeas*: "The legislator . . . being endowed by God for the knowledge of universal truths, surrounded us with unbroken palisades and iron walls to prevent our mixing with any of the other peoples . . . thus being kept pure in body and soul . . . and worshiping the only God omnipotent over creation."[163] The overloaded Greek phrase in Eph 2:14*b*, τὸ μεσότοιχον τοῦ φραγμοῦ (*to mesotoichon tou phragmou*, "the dividing wall of the hedge," or "fence," encircling a vineyard) may be a reflection of a phrase like the "palisades and walls" of *Aristeas*. By itself, *to mesotoichon* might suggest the dividing wall in the temple area that prohibited Gentiles from entering on pain of death (Acts 21:27-31). The parallel phrase in v. 15*a* makes it clear that what the author has in mind as the barrier between Jew and Gentile is the law with its various ordinances.[164]

The sectarian polemic in Essene legal texts connects building a "wall"—that is, sectarian legal interpretation—and separation. Echoing Mic 7:1, the *Damascus Document* has "the wall is built, the boundary far removed."[165] The same text also speaks of those who have removed the boundary, "builders of the wall" who go astray after false teaching, "in the age of devastation of the land there arose those who shifted the boundary and made Israel stray."[166] Such apostate "builders of the wall," and those who follow their interpretations of the law, will be subject to God's wrath.[167] Concluding a letter that contains a number of halakhic rules concerning temple offerings and purity regulations, the Essene author comments, "We have segregated ourselves from the rest of the people and we avoid . . . associating with them in these things." Since the letter is addressed to an outsider whose group its author encourages to adopt similar halakhic rulings,[168] one must assume that such action would lead to reconciliation between the two groups. From a sectarian point of view, destroying the "dividing wall" could only mean destroying the separation created by divergent legal rulings.

The expression τὸν νόμον τῶν ἐντολῶν ἐν δόγμασιν (*ton nomon tōn entolōn en dogmasin*, "the law of commands in decrees"; NRSV, "the law with its commandments and ordinances"; NIV, "commandments and regulations") has sometimes been understood to imply that only part of the law is abolished: the ceremonial or other statutes that divide Jews from Gentiles, or those elements that are "in decrees" made by those who interpret the law, what the NT elsewhere refers to as "traditions of the elders" (Matt 23:1-4, 15-24; Mark 7:5-8).[169] The assumption that the law is divisible has little support in Jewish texts. Both apologetic writers like Josephus and the writer of *Letter of Aristeas* and intrasectarian texts like the CD and 4QMMT assume that

161. Chantel Bouttier, *L'Epître de Saint Paul aux Ephésiens*, Commentaire du Nouveau Testament, 2nd série Ixb (Geneva: Labor et Fides, 1991) 115-20.

162. Josephus *Against Apion* 2.146.

163. *Letter of Aristeas* 139.

164. Ernest Best, *A Critical and Exegetical Commentary on Ephesians*, ICC (Edinburgh: T. & T. Clark, 1998) 259-61.

165. CD 4:12.

166. CD 4:19; CD 5:20.

167. CD-B 19:21-32.

168. 4QMMTa 92-93. 4QMMTa 113-114.

169. Markus Barth, *Ephesians*, 2 vols., AB 34-34A (Garden City, N.Y.: Doubleday, 1974) 287-91.

Moses' legislation, including the peculiarly Jewish rites and customs and proper halakhic interpretation, belong together. As the Essenes would say, interpretation enables individuals to "turn away from the path of the people on account of God's love."[170] Therefore, Ephesians refers to the whole law. The additional nouns, "commandments and ordinances," exclude understanding what is abolished as a sectarian reading of the law. Though Paul carefully avoids speaking of the law as "abolished" (Rom 3:31), Ephesians has no concern to affirm the divine character of the law (cf. Rom 7:12).

Verse 15*b* fills out the positive hints in v. 14, completing the rhetorical structure of the section by matching the final "making peace" with the earlier "he is our peace." The expression "made both groups into one" is elaborated as "he might create in himself one new humanity in place of the two." Creation of the new humanity is the result of abolishing the law. Galatians 3:26-28 links being "in Christ" with abolition of the fundamental categories that divide persons. Paul used the formula to support his contention that righteousness that comes through faith has no place for inheriting God's promises by being under the law (Gal 3:23-25, 29). Since the expression "no male and female" in the Galatians formula alludes to Gen 1:27, the connection between baptism and "new creation," or restoration of the state of humankind prior to its alienation from God, probably belonged to the original formula.[171]

A gnostic reading of Eph 2:14-15 would draw upon speculation about the division of Adam and Eve from their original unity. In this myth the creator god gained control over beings who were spiritually superior to him. For example, Adam tells his son Seth:

And we resembled the great eternal angels, for we were higher than the god who had created us and the powers with him. . . . The god, the ruler of the aeons and the powers, divided us in wrath. Then we became two aeons. And the glory in our hearts left us, along with the first knowledge that breathed within us.[172]

Though some gnostic texts treat baptism as renewing the androgynous, divine image, *The Apocalypse of Adam* concludes with what appears to be polemic against the angelic guardians of baptism for permitting its waters to be defiled.[173] Any who would receive those rites become subject to the rule of the powers.

Unlike either Galatians or later gnostic readers, Ephesians does not connect its new humanity with baptism. Some commentators spontaneously assume that all conversion language in Ephesians has a baptismal *Sitz im Leben*.[174] The expression "new creation" or "new creature" rather than "new humanity" appears in Paul's writings (2 Cor 5:17; Gal 6:15). Ephesians is probably dependent upon Col 3:10 for the idea. However, Ephesians departs from both Colossians and the later Gnostics by not speaking of the image of God when referring to new creation.

The connection between "new creation" and a humanity reconciled with God through the death of Christ appears in 2 Cor 5:17-21. The connection between v. 15 and reconciliation in v. 16 suggests that Ephesians has that imagery in view.[175] Verse 16 employs traditional formulae about the effectiveness of the death of Christ (see v. 13; Rom 5:10; 2 Cor 5:18). The traditional formulation might have used "body" as a reference to Christ's body. Since Ephesians uses "one body" (ἐνὶ σώματι *eni sōmati*) for the unity created in Christ, described earlier as exalted head of the body (1:23), the expression here must refer to the new entity of Jew and Gentile, the church. "Through the cross" indicates that the death of Christ is understood as the sacrifice that brings reconciliation (also 5:2).

Although Ephesians does not use a citation formula, v. 17 alludes to Isa 57:19 (and possibly Isa 52:7), in which the peace is preached (εὐαγγελίζω *euangelizō*) to both those near and far off.[176] Verse 18 employs a Pauline theme: All Christians have access to God in the Spirit (Rom 5:1-2; Gal 3:18). The following points of v. 18 parallel v. 16: (a) reconcile to God; access to the Father; (b) both groups; (c) in one body; in one

---

170. CD-A 19:29.

171. So Hans Dieter Betz, *Galatians* (Philadelphia: Fortress, 1979) 181-85; Dennis R. MacDonald, *There Is No Male and Female: The Fate of a Dominical Saying in Paul and Gnosticism,* HDR 20 (Philadelpha: Fortress, 1987).

172. *Apoc. Adam* V 64, 14-28.

173. *Apoc. Adam* 84, 5-22.

174. Rudolf Schnackenburg, *The Epistle to the Ephesians,* trans. H. Heron (Edinburgh: T. & T. Clark, 1991) 94, 121.

175. Andrew T. Lincoln, *Ephesians,* WBC 42 (Dallas: Word, 1990) 193-94.

176. Best, *A Critical and Exegetical Commentary on Ephesians,* 270.

Figure 7: Coin Depicting the Deified Emperor Augustus

Assarion (Matt 10:29; Luke 12:6) is the designation of various copper coins struck outside of Palestine. In NT times, sixteen assaria equaled one *denarius,* a typical day's wage. The obverse of the coin pictured here shows the Emperor Augustus and reads "Deified Augustus, Father"; the reverse shows an altar between the letters S(ENATVS) C(ONSVLTO), meaning "By the Consent of the Senate," and reads "Providence."

Photographs and text by Dr. E. Jerry Vardaman; coin as pictured is 2 times actual size.

Spirit; (d) through the cross; through him. It is impossible to tell whether ἐν (*en,* "in") designates the spirit as locus of access to God or as its instrument.[177] The phrase "in one Spirit" (ἐν ἑνὶ πνεύματι *en heni pneumati*) is framed by "access to the Father" (τὴν προσαγὴν . . . πρὸς τὸν πατέρα *tēn prosagēn . . . pros ton patera*). It recalls the earlier description of the Gentiles as "without God in the world" (v. 12). The term "access" (προσαγωγή *prosagōgē*) also brings the audience back to the eulogy in which God was depicted as a powerful benefactor. In a secular context the expression "we gain access" (ἔχομεν τὴν προσαγωγήν *echomen tēn prosagōgēn*) might be used of persons who are fortunate enough to be admitted to the presence of the emperor. Whether ambassadors or individuals, the purpose of such an audience was to press a request for benefits. Readers in the cities of Asia Minor would be familiar with efforts to gain access to the governor as he made his rounds of the province. Verse 18 makes a striking point

about abolishing hostility in Christ: Access for one group does not mean exclusion for others.

2:19-22. The next shift in imagery can be linked to the imperial example in v. 18. Access to a powerful person often implied entry into an impressive building. Slaves who served powerful men could assert authority over freedmen of higher status by granting or denying physical access to their master and his household. Cities in Asia Minor vied with one another to secure imperial favor by building a temple to Augustus.[178] In religious contexts the issue becomes access to God associated with a temple.[179] Ephesians combines both images by calling Christians "members of the household of God" and "holy temple in the Lord." Referring to concrete examples of temple construction, Ephesians depicts the temple as in the process of being built up (vv. 21-22).

177. Fee opts for the locative sense. See Gordon D. Fee, *God's Empowering Presence: The Holy Spirit in the Letters of Paul* (Peabody, Mass.: Hendrickson, 1994) 683.

178. Eberhard Faust, *Pax Christi et Pax Caesaris. Religionsgeschichtliche, traditionsgeschichtliche und sozial geschichtliche Studien zum Epheserbrief,* NTOA 24 (Freiburg: Universitätsverlag; Göttingen: Vandenhoeck & Ruprecht, 1993).

179. Access to the throne room of the powerful, whether monarch or deity, required passing through gates, pillared antechambers and the like. The architecture of palace and temple was seen to reflect that of the heavenly throne room. See J. Edward Wright, *The Early History of Heaven* (New York: Oxford University Press, 2000) 75-78.

Verse 19a returns to the description of the Gentiles as strangers. The term "aliens" (ξένοι xenoi) refers to persons who dwell in a place that is not their homeland. Since the LXX does not make a sharp distinction between the Greek words translated "strangers" (xenoi) and "aliens" (πάροικοι paroikoi), the second may be a rhetorical variant of "stranger." It corresponds to "aliens from the commonwealth of Israel" (v. 12) since aliens do not enjoy citizenship rights. First Peter 2:11 uses "aliens" (paroikoi) when speaking of Christians in an exhortation to watch their conduct among "Gentiles" (non-Christians). The designation "citizens with" (συμπολῖται sympolitai) reverses their previous exclusion from citizenship. However, the phrase "with the saints" is ambiguous. If v. 19 were strictly parallel with v. 12, "the saints" (οἱ ἅγιοι hoi hagioi) should be used as in Jewish texts to refer to the righteous of Israel. Since Ephesians has announced the destruction of the law, it would make little sense to declare that Christ has made the Gentiles "fellow citizens" (sympolitai) with Israel. Without its founding legislation, Israel could not claim to be a "commonwealth." Therefore "saints" (hoi hagioi) must designate those who are Christian believers regardless of their origins. The shift from the civic metaphor to the familial, "members of the household" (οἰκεῖοι oikeioi; cf. Gal 6:10), has been prepared by the earlier indication that Christians were preordained to be God's children (1:5).

Verse 20 shifts from household members to the building itself. Paul used a building image in 1 Cor 3:9-11, where the foundation is the Lord, the apostle is the master builder, and others build upon his work. Ephesians has shifted the imagery. Christ is portrayed as either a capstone or a cornerstone (see below). Apostles and prophets are the foundation. This comment places "apostles" (ἀπόστολοι apostoloi) in the past relative to the epistle and its audience. Ephesians 3:5 explains how the apostles serve as foundation, and how they are the ones to whom the mystery of God's plan has been revealed. The Essene writings show a similar regard for their founder: God's revelation to him provided the insight necessary to found the new community. Since Ephesians uses "prophets" (προφῆται prophētai) after the term "apostles," it appears to have Christian prophets in mind (e.g., Matt 7:15; 1 Cor 12:10, 28).

Old Testament texts about the cornerstone in Zion were applied to Jesus (Isa 8:14; see also Luke 2:34; Rom 9:32; 1 Pet 2:8). However, the capstone held the building together. Its location at the top of an arch also fits Ephesians' consistent references to the exaltation of Christ (4:16). The unity of the initially separate "you" and "us" gains the organic form of a building whose diverse materials must be properly fitted together and held in place by the capstone.

Designation of the building as "temple" retrieves the access to God image from v. 18, along with its reference to the Spirit. Though the term "grow" (αὔξω auxō) has been seen as discordant with Christ as capstone of a building, it anticipates the later description of the body growing together in the unity of the Spirit (4:3, 11-16). The presence of God's Spirit in the community described as temple was well-established in Paul's writings (1 Cor 3:16; 6:19-20). By shifting to the temple in which the Spirit dwells, Ephesians suggests that the community will be the locus of God's presence in the world.[180]

Every comment about Jew and Gentile in this section belongs to well-established motifs in Jewish apologetic or sectarian writings except the extraordinary claim that God abolished the law in order to unify the two. This concern extends Paul's own polemic against those who thought Christians ought to be incorporated into Israel by adopting peculiarly Jewish observances. However, attempts to find a particular Jewish or Jewish Christian problem behind this section of Ephesians have failed. Although v. 12 might suggest that the Gentiles are to be brought into Israel, Ephesians avoids claiming that the church has replaced Israel. In the present reality of the church as a single community built up together in Christ, there is no distinction between Christian and Jew. Even the concern for harmony between Jewish and Gentile believers evident in Rom 15:1-13 is moderated. Nothing in Ephesians suggests that tensions between the two groups were creating difficulties (cf. Rom 14:1-23).

It is also impossible to use Ephesians to support theories of an ongoing covenant with Israel that

180. Fee, *God's Empowering Presence*, 684-85.

will bring it to salvation outside of Christ. Ephesians consistently insists that God's plan from the beginning has been a "new creation" that requires abandoning the barriers that distinguished Jew from Gentile.[181] At the same time, Ephesians does not presume that all of the covenants, images, and promises of Israel belong to Gentile Christians by virtue of their Jewish heritage. The church is not separated from the God revealed in the story of Israel, but only exists through God's new act of creation. To recognize Christ's exaltation as head of the body of Christian believers requires an insight into the mystery of God's plan that is not available to nonbelievers.

Indeed, Ephesians leaves no opening for the continuing observance of the law by Jewish Christians.[182] Despite the differences in their origins, both Jewish and Gentile believers are reconciled to God through Christ. Both are brought into the body of Christ and have the same Spirit. They have a common foundation and belong to a build-

181. See the extended argument in Andrew T. Lincoln, "The Church and Israel in Ephesians 2," *CBQ* 49 (1987) 605-24.

182. Jack T. Sanders, *Schismatics, Sectarians, Dissidents, Deviants: The First One Hundred Years of Jewish-Christian Relations* (Valley Forge: Trinity Press International, 1993) 196-98.

ing designed to be held together by one capstone. While diversity of origins is no barrier to coming into the church, it is not an excuse for a building of clashing architectural styles! Thus the emphasis on unity in Ephesians rejects the possibility of God's people being divided into multiple sects.

Since all legal ordinances are abolished, the church cannot be a sect within Judaism like the Essenes—a group grounded on claims not only to the Spirit, but also to a founder with inspired insight into God's will and to identification as "the holy ones" of God's promise. Though Ephesians shares many religious images with Essene writings, it does not understand the church as a religious group centered on interpreting the teachings and halakhic ordinances of a human founder. Instead, Ephesians insists that the reality of the church is in its head, the exalted Christ made present through the Spirit. Whatever the particular arrangements in local communities, they should reflect the symbolic truth about the church. Its unity is based in incorporation of different groups into a new humanity that no longer preserves the socioreligious boundaries established by the law.

REFLECTIONS

1. *Baptismal Unity.* After describing conversion as the transition from death to new life, a jarring shift introduces a gap between the Jewish Christian speaker and his Gentile audience, "So remember that you were once gentiles in the flesh" (2:11; the NRSV has "by birth," which weakens the metaphor). It goes on to list everything that those who are not part of God's covenant people lack, ending with the dramatic *atheoi in tou kosmou,* "without God in the world." When the Greek term *atheos* was applied to someone, it did not simply mean that this person did not believe in the God of the Jews (as the NRSV suggests by capitalizing the word). Instead, it was a term of cultural insult, a form of what we might call "hate speech," since it was often used derisively of someone who disdained or denied the gods and their laws—in short the structure and glue of civil society. In essence, to call someone *atheos* was to say that he or she was "uncivilized." Pagans could sling the term back at Jews (and later at Christians) because they would not participate in the religious practices of everyone else. The most wonderful example of this expression as a "fight song" occurs in the martyrdom of Polycarp (d. 167). The Roman proconsul, not wishing to execute the aged bishop, tried to persuade Polycarp to renounce his faith by swearing an oath by the "good fortune" of Caesar and shouting, "Away with the atheists." Polycarp refused, but in a dramatic tour de force looked at the multitude gathered in the arena, waved his hand toward them, and looking up to heaven said, "Away with the atheists!"[183]

183. *Martyrdom of Polycarp* chap. 9. See *ANF* 1:41.

Given this background, it is a shocking turn for Ephesians to refer to the readers, even in passing, as *atheoi,* surprising for the preacher to suddenly stir up the ethnic and religious tensions that separated Jews from the larger society of the Greco-Roman cities in which they lived. Ephesians hangs a lot of weight on the past tense, "you once were," but now in Christ that gulf has been bridged (2:13-14). Of course, this passage recalls one of Paul's most important theological insights. As he argued that his Gentile converts should not be required to adopt Jewish customs, Paul formulated the insight that God had a different plan. God intended to bring all humanity together in a single people. Paul reached back behind the idea of covenants with Moses and David, which emphasized the separateness of Israel, to the covenants with Abraham (Rom 4:1-25; Gal 3:15-20).[184] Paul used the baptismal formula to insist that God did not intend for the church to be split along socioeconomic, ethnic, or gender lines (Gal 3:26-28). When the Corinthians were divided over various spiritual gifts, Paul referred to that formula again in combination with the metaphor of the church as the body of Christ (1 Cor 12:13). Baptism confers one Spirit, which works toward unity in building up the body of Christ.

Ephesians 2:11-22 incorporates these familiar Pauline themes. Yet the author's voice sounds the note of Israel, privileged to be the original recipient of God's promises, speaking to the "other," the Gentiles who have now been incorporated into God's people (2:18-19). The closest Paul comes to addressing Gentile Christians from the perspective of Jewish Christians is the famous metaphor of Gentile Christians as wild olive branches grafted onto God's carefully cultivated tree in Rom 11:11-36. However, the tone is quite different. Paul struggles to explain the weak Jewish response to the gospel in contrast to that of non-Jews. He warns Gentile Christians against overbearing pride. Reading Ephesians, we would never infer that such difficulties existed. One would infer, rather, that the entire heritage of Israel had passed into the church, which then extended God's summons to the rest of the world. Christians learned from the horrors of the Holocaust and its legacy that a religious vision that can no longer affirm a positive ongoing relationship between God and the Jewish people in the end fails the gospel.

How does Ephesians 2 contribute to Christian/Jewish relations today? We need to remember Paul's anguish over the fate of fellow Jews who did not accept Jesus as Messiah in Romans 9–11. Paul concluded that Jewish disbelief had opened the way for non-Jews. God's plan of salvation had to include a place for Israel (Rom 11:11-32). God's love for Israel did not end when the church came into being. Ephesians provides a sharp reminder to the Gentile converts that they owe their knowledge of God to the Jewish people. There is a special bond between Christians and Jews because of this inheritance. The other religions from which non-Jewish converts come to faith in Jesus cannot replace Judaism. Only the Scriptures written and preserved by the Jewish people provide authentic revelation about God. Jesus was not the incarnation of a global divine force, a Hindu avatar, or a Bodhisattva. He is the Son of the God who called Abraham, who appeared to Moses on Sinai, who made a covenant with David, and who inspired the prophets. So Christians recognize that we owe the Jewish community an enormous debt for our faith in God. We should come to dialogue with our Jewish friends as grateful learners, not as people who have all the answers.

Ephesians also posits a challenge to both Jews and Christians by insisting that cultural and religious divisions are contrary to God's vision of human salvation. Circumcision or lack of circumcision is "in the flesh," ethnic divisions (2:11) that divide people into opposing camps. So Christians and Jews should not just talk about shared beliefs and then go their separate ways. They should find ways to witness to faith in the God who unites us. Social projects that embody a shared concern for justice are one way of recognizing common values grounded in Scripture. Christian and Jewish leaders also have to speak out against anti-Semitic and racist

---

184. For a description of the theological significance of the three types of covenant, see Bernard Anderson, *Contours of Old Testament Theology* (Minneapolis: Fortress, 1999) 32-35.

incidents. When swastikas are spray painted on the local high school or a synagogue and its Torah scrolls are defaced, Christians have to show that they are as outraged as their Jewish neighbors. After all, God did not bring us non-Jews into the household of faith to trash the place. God brought us in to build a glorious new creation: the body of the Messiah.

2. *Architecture, Empire, and Peace.* The architectural images in this passage further develop the theme of reconciling traditional enemies. In 2:14-15 the law and the commandments are pictured as a wall that kept Jew and Gentile apart. That wall is now destroyed because the cross marked the end of the law. Was a physical wall intended? Some interpreters have seen behind this image the actual barrier in the Temple that prohibited Gentiles from going further on pain of death. By the time Ephesians was written, the Temple had been destroyed when Titus looted and burned the city to end the Jewish revolt in 70 CE. The late twentieth century witnessed the power of tearing down a wall when the wall that had separated communist East Berlin from West Berlin was destroyed. But the "wall" can also be spiritual, the separation between Jew and non-Jew that is built into the commandments that govern Jewish life. In that case, the wall only came down within the Christian community. That, too, can be a familiar experience. We may form close, personal relationships with people of very different racial, ethnic, socioeconomic, or educational backgrounds in the church community. But do such experiences translate into what happens at work, on the street, in school? Not always. When it does not, can we honestly say that Christ bridges the gap of our hostilities and differences?

The section concludes with another architectural image already familiar from Paul's letters: the church as a building or a temple (2:21). Combined with the claim that Christ has brought hostile factions together, this image poses a challenge to the erection of temples and other buildings dedicated to the glory of Rome and its emperor. Safety from pirates on the seas, growing prosperity and trade passing along the roads and through the harbors of the Roman East were all claimed as benefits bestowed by the emperor. New buildings told the story. Ephesians hints that Christians have a different story to tell. Empires may spread a dominant culture or language that forces former enemies to live together in peace. But that is not the new creation in which people are genuinely sisters and brothers in Christ. Take the power away, and the old tribal hatreds flare up with horrible costs in suffering for civilian populations. The former Soviet Union, the Balkans, Africa, the Philippines, Sri Lanka—all stories in a single day's paper. How to create peace? Unfortunately, the only quick solutions have been to put up various walls, a U.N. peace-keeping force, or a massive separation of the warring populations, creating hundreds of refugees. The peace of empires is not true peace. Religious voices that call for conversion, justice, mutual hospitality, and community as foundations for peace are often the first to die when hostility breaks out.

3. *Sign of the Cross.* Since Ephesians highlights the triumph of the risen Christ, readers might be tempted to minimize the cross. That would undercut a central conviction of Pauline theology. The cross has achieved what no human ever could: reconciliation of a sinful humanity with God. Does that mean that God is a stern, capricious ruler who needs to be appeased or "bought off"? Not for the writer of Ephesians. God is a loving benefactor, offering all people a stake in salvation. By dying on the cross, God breaks down a wall that separated humanity from God. Humans are too trapped in the deadly effects of sin to return to God on their own—or to even notice the wall that is keeping God out. Why is the cross important to Christians today? People still need to be convinced of God's unconditional love for them. "Lift high the cross, the love of Christ proclaim," the hymn announces. It is always a favorite. A very wise spiritual director once remarked, "People have to be loved into forgiveness." He liked to ask students to make two lists: (1) people you need to forgive and (2) people you would like to thank. The first list is the hard one to deal with, but if you start with the second list, forgiving starts to become a possibility, too.

Ephesians 3:1-13, Paul as Prisoner for the Gospel

NIV

3 For this reason I, Paul, the prisoner of Christ Jesus for the sake of you Gentiles— ²Surely you have heard about the administration of God's grace that was given to me for you, ³that is, the mystery made known to me by revelation, as I have already written briefly. ⁴In reading this, then, you will be able to understand my insight into the mystery of Christ, ⁵which was not made known to men in other generations as it has now been revealed by the Spirit to God's holy apostles and prophets. ⁶This mystery is that through the gospel the Gentiles are heirs together with Israel, members together of one body, and sharers together in the promise in Christ Jesus.

⁷I became a servant of this gospel by the gift of God's grace given me through the working of his power. ⁸Although I am less than the least of all God's people, this grace was given me: to preach to the Gentiles the unsearchable riches of Christ, ⁹and to make plain to everyone the administration of this mystery, which for ages past was kept hidden in God, who created all things. ¹⁰His intent was that now, through the church, the manifold wisdom of God should be made known to the rulers and authorities in the heavenly realms, ¹¹according to his eternal purpose which he accomplished in Christ Jesus our Lord. ¹²In him and through faith in him we may approach God with freedom and confidence. ¹³I ask you, therefore, not to be discouraged because of my sufferings for you, which are your glory.

NRSV

3 This is the reason that I Paul am a prisoner for[a] Christ Jesus for the sake of you Gentiles— ²for surely you have already heard of the commission of God's grace that was given me for you, ³and how the mystery was made known to me by revelation, as I wrote above in a few words, ⁴a reading of which will enable you to perceive my understanding of the mystery of Christ. ⁵In former generations this mystery[b] was not made known to humankind, as it has now been revealed to his holy apostles and prophets by the Spirit: ⁶that is, the Gentiles have become fellow heirs, members of the same body, and sharers in the promise in Christ Jesus through the gospel.

7Of this gospel I have become a servant according to the gift of God's grace that was given me by the working of his power. ⁸Although I am the very least of all the saints, this grace was given to me to bring to the Gentiles the news of the boundless riches of Christ, ⁹and to make everyone see[c] what is the plan of the mystery hidden for ages in[d] God who created all things; ¹⁰so that through the church the wisdom of God in its rich variety might now be made known to the rulers and authorities in the heavenly places. ¹¹This was in accordance with the eternal purpose that he has carried out in Christ Jesus our Lord, ¹²in whom we have access to God in boldness and confidence through faith in him.[e] ¹³I pray therefore that you[f] may not lose heart over my sufferings for you; they are your glory.

[a]Or of   [b]Gk it   [c]Other ancient authorities read to bring to light
[d]Or by   [e]Or the faith of him   [f]Or I

COMMENTARY

Paul now becomes "prisoner for Christ," a phrase used in Philemon 1.[185] Verses 2-13 read as a long digression until the prayer report introduced in v. 14. The pattern of alternating pronouns continues: "you" (vv. 2-6); "I" to "we" (vv. 7-12); and "you" (v. 13).

Verse 1 is an anacoluthon (an abrupt mid-sentence shift to a different grammatical construction), which identifies the subject but lacks a verb. Verse 2 begins with a "for surely" that assumes that the audience has heard of the mission entrusted to Paul. Verses 3-7 spell out the origins

---

185. The phrase desmios tou Christou ("prisoner of Christ") should not be spiritualized as though it indicated Paul's attachment to Christ. It implies that preaching the gospel is the reason for his imprisonment. See the discussion of the conditions of ancient imprisonment and the rhetoric of imprisonment in Paul's own letters by Craig S. Wansink, Chained in Christ: The Experience and Rhetoric of Paul's Imprisonments, JSNTSup 130 (Sheffield: Sheffield Academic, 1996).

and content of Paul's service. Verse 13 finally states the consequence that is to follow from recognizing what Paul's ministry is: Do not be discouraged by his imprisonment (cf. Phil 1:12-13; 2:17-18). The intervening sentences (vv. 8-12) expand the account of Paul's ministry by describ-

ing the content of the mystery being revealed. Reference to his boldness (v. 12) anticipates the exhortation to the audience in v. 13, so that they do not "lose heart over my sufferings."

This section forms a key piece of evidence for the hypothesis that Ephesians has drawn on the

---

Figure 8: Eph 3:1-13 and Col 1:23-28

Theme	Ephesians	Colossians
Introduce Apostle	[3:1] I Paul the prisoner for you	[1:23c] I Paul a servant (Eph 3:7)
		[1:24a] . . . for you
Sufferings of the Apostle	[3:1] prisoner [3:13] in my trials for you	[1:24b] the deficiency of the trials of Christ in my flesh for his body
Office of the Apostle	[3:7] of which I have become a servant	[1:25] of which I have become a servant
	[3:2] the administration of the grace of God given to me for you	[1:25] according to the administration of God given to me for you
Revelation of the Mystery	[3:4-5a] the mystery of Christ that was not known to other generations	[1:26] the mystery that was hidden from the aeons and the generations
	[3:9] the mystery hidden from the aeons	
	[3:5] has now been revealed to his holy apostles and prophets	[1:26] but now has been manifested to his holy ones
Content of the Mystery	[3:6] that the Gentiles would be an inheritance with, body with, and sharers with the promise in Christ Jesus through the gospel	[1:27] the wealth of the glory . . . in the Gentiles, which is Christ in you, the hope of glory
Mystery Preached	[3:8] to preach to the Gentiles the incomprehensible wealth of Christ	[1:27-28a] to make known what the wealth of the glory of this mystery in the Gentiles, which is Christ in you . . . whom we announce
God's Power in the	[3:7c] according to the activity of his power	[1:29b] according to apostle the activity that is working in me in power

---

text of Colossians. It combines the sequence of topics in Col 1:23-28 with echoes of earlier parts of Ephesians, especially the previous section (2:11-22). *Figure* 8 sets out the parallels between the two letters; a more literal translation has been provided to make the verbal parallels clearer.

Ephesians has taken the basic structure of Paul's self-presentation from Colossians. In v. 3, "as I wrote" suggests that the audience would be familiar with the existence of other Pauline epistles. References to Eph 2:11-22 demonstrate how carefully this section has been integrated into the epistle: (a) you Gentiles (v. 1; 2:11); (b) "holy apostles and prophets" (v. 5; 2:20); (c) "with" expressions to designate incorporation of Gentiles (v. 6; 2:19); (d) share a promise (v. 6; excluded from promise, 2:12); (e) in the body of Christ (v. 6; 2:16); (f) access to God (v. 12; 2:18). Other expressions point to earlier sections of Ephesians: (a) "commission" (οἰκονομία *oikonomia*, "administration," vv. 2, 9; 1:10); (b) grace of God (vv. 2, 7-8; 1:6-7; 2:5, 7-8); (c) mystery revealed (vv. 3-4, 9; 1:9); (d) rulers and powers (v. 10; 1:21); (e) heavenly places (v. 10; 1:3, 20; 2:6).

Rhetorically, the account of Paul's ministry serves to establish the character of the speaker. Such descriptions often appear as digressions in ancient rhetoric. A key requirement is establishing the reliability of the speaker. Since the audience has no personal knowledge of Paul on which to judge his character, Ephesians asserts that they can discern the truth of his claim to special insight from what he has written (vv. 3-4). Ephesians also establishes a relationship between the apostle and his audience by reminding them that the apostle's suffering benefits the Gentiles (from Col 1:24-25; also see Phil 1:5-7). The exhortation not to lose heart over his sufferings (v. 13) adds an element of pathos to the relationship between Paul and the audience.

3:1. "This is the reason" connects this section with the previous reference to the Gentiles' being incorporated into the temple of God (2:22-23). The addition of "for the sake of you Gentiles" integrates the biographical notice into the theme of bringing Gentiles into the body of Christ. Verse 13 does not spell out how suffering is integral to the apostle's mission. Readers

may be familiar with Paul's view that suffering confirms the connection between the apostle and the crucified (1 Cor 4:1-13; 2 Cor 6:3-11). Just as the cross is not a major theme in Ephesians, so also apostolic hardships are not a topic of discussion. The letter contains only two other references to the sufferings of the apostle (v. 13; 6:20). Both connect his imprisonment with bold speech. Neither passage uses the reference as evidence for the heroism of the apostle (cf. 2 Tim 2:8-10;[186] which equates Ephesians and 2 Timothy). Nor does Ephesians develop the soteriological picture of apostolic suffering in Col 1:24.[187]

3:2-7. The first half (vv. 2-4) of the lengthy digression in vv. 2-7 recalls what the audience may already know about Paul. Description of Paul's mission as "commission" (*oikonomia*) is taken from Col 1:25. Ephesians also uses *oikonomia* as God's plan of salvation (1:10; 3:9; NRSV, "plan"; NIV, "administration"). In those cases, "plan" connects the saving activity of God with the order established in creation. Consequently, the "commission" entrusted to Paul is part of the process by which God's plan to unite all things in Christ is effected. The experience of God's grace involves understanding the divine purpose in Christ (1:9-10).

Paul used the phrase "stewards [οἰκονόμοι *oikonomoi*] of God's mysteries" in 1 Cor 4:1. There the term "mystery" (μυστήριον *mystērion*) reminds readers of the cross as the mystery unknown to the powers (1 Cor 2:7). For Ephesians, "mystery" (*mystērion*) refers to bringing together all things in the exalted Christ. Verse 3 attributes the apostle's knowledge of the mystery to revelation.

The Essenes also attributed the insight of their founder to divine revelation. Revelation to the elect is essential to their salvation.[188] We have seen that Ephesians does not treat its revelation as the key to a sectarian version of inherited Jewish tradition. Nor does Ephesians argue that Paul's preaching represents what was already re-

---

186. Contra Ralph P. Martin, *Ephesians, Colossians and Philemon* (Atlanta: John Knox, 1991) 41; O'Brien, *Ephesians* 252.

187. Contra Chantel Bouttier, *L'Epître de Saint Paul aux Ephésiens,* Commentaire du Nouveau Testament, 2nd série Ixb (Geneva: Labor et Fides, 1991) 138.

188. 1QS 11.6-7, 15-19.

vealed in Scripture (cf. Rom 4:1-25; Gal 3:6-22; 4:21-31).

The phrase "as I wrote before briefly" (καθὼς προέγραψα *kathōs proegrapsa*) is enigmatic. In ordinary correspondence, it would imply previous communication between the author and the recipients. Or in some instances it would refer to attached correspondence.[189] However, Ephesians is not a letter between parties who have business or friendship with each other. Although its author is familiar with Paul's letters, and particularly Colossians, a reference to "wrote briefly" hardly suggests a collection of Paul's epistles. The NRSV translation ("as I wrote above in a few words") follows exegetes who conclude that the expression refers to an earlier passage in Ephesians (1:9-10; 2:11-22). But Ephesians could be assuming prior reading of individual Pauline letters or extracts from them in the churches.[190] Verse 4 makes the reading of the letter itself evidence of the apostle's insight.

In describing that mystery (vv. 5-7), the epistle returns to motifs already presented, especially in 2:11-22. The "with" verbs in v. 6 pick up use of such expressions in 2:19-22. The foundation stone of the building to which the Gentiles are joined in 2:20, the "apostles and prophets" are now the privileged recipients of insight into the mystery of Christ.

By insisting that the mystery was unknown in past ages, Ephesians appears to assert that not even the righteous persons or prophets of the OT had knowledge of the blessings to come to the Gentiles.[191] However, the phrase should not be pressed to yield a theology of prior revelation. In apocalyptic writings such revelation formulae indicate that readers now have insight into divine mysteries that have been concealed from the rest of humanity (e.g., Matt 13:17). In a historical apocalypse, the seer receives both a vision and its interpretation. Since the vision refers to future events, only divine inspiration could provide the required understanding (Dan 10:1). Or the apocalypse may reveal hidden wisdom given to an ancient seer but sealed until the time of fulfillment (Dan 12:9; 2 Esdr 14:5-10). Thus "not made known . . . now revealed" is a way of indicating that the time of fulfillment has come. The reference to "apostles and prophets" (v. 5; 2:20) indicates that the author of Ephesians does not consider Paul the sole recipient of insight into God's plan of salvation.

The expression *"his* holy apostles and prophets" supports the claim that Ephesians was not composed by Paul. He would have used the expression "us apostles" (as in 1 Cor 4:9). Verse 7 uses the self-designation "servant of the gospel" from Col 1:23. Paul uses the Greek term διάκονος (*diakonos*, "servant") in a variety of senses: (a) political rulers, who need not be aware of a place in God's order (Rom 13:4); (b) individuals in local churches (Rom 16:1; Phil 1:1); and (c) himself (and Apollos) as missionaries who established churches (1 Cor 3:5-7; 2 Cor 3:6; 6:4). Since the false teachers who had come to Corinth take on a false appearance as "servants [NRSV, "ministers"] of righteousness" (2 Cor 11:15), "servant" plus a genitive expression was probably a common term for traveling missionaries.

Ephesians takes over the depiction of God's power (δύναμις *dynamis*) from Col 1:29. However, it drops the reference to apostleship as weakness and struggle found in Col 1:29*a*. Stylistically Ephesians needs a shorter phrase. Thematically, the sufferings of the apostle are not the topic of discussion. Ephesians repeatedly stresses the extraordinary manifestation of God's gracious power in the salvation of the Gentiles. See the use of "power" (*dynamis*) in 1:19. The power of God demonstrated in the resurrection and exaltation of Christ may have been taken from Col 2:12.[192]

3:8-13. Ephesians breaks off the previous sentence only to begin describing the apostle's mission again (v. 8; contrary to the NRSV and the NIV, v. 7 belongs to the digression that began in v. 2). The passage opens with a striking description of the apostle as "least [ἐλαχιστοτέρω *elachistoterō*] of all the saints." Readers familiar with Paul's letters immediately think of his self-designation "least of the apostles" (1 Cor 15:9). The apostle uses his late call and efforts in found-

189. See John L. White, *Light from Ancient Letters* (Philadelphia: Fortress, 1986) nos. 4 and 7.

190. David G. Meade, *Pseudonymity and Canon: An Investigation into the Relationship of Authorship and Authority in the Jewish and Earliest Christian Tradition,* WUNT 39 (Tübingen: Mohr-Siebeck, 1986) 149.

191. Lincoln, "The Church and Israel in Ephesians 2," *CBQ* 49 (1987) 619-22

192. So Markus Barth and Helmut Blanke, *Colossians,* AB 34B (New York: Doubleday, 1994) 270.

ing churches as evidence for the power of God's grace working in his mission (1 Cor 15:10). Since Ephesians has consistently used "saints" (ἅγιοι *hagioi*) for believers, referring to Paul as "least of all the saints" is somewhat puzzling. Earlier Ephesians described the Gentiles as being added to the "saints" ("us"), fellow "citizens with the saints" (2:19). The apostle whose knowledge of the mystery of God makes this incorporation possible can hardly be described as "least" among Christians. The expression may be dictated by the rhetorical requirements of self-praise. By having Paul deprecate his own achievement, Ephesians has him magnify the graciousness of the divine benefactor who has given him the task of preaching the gospel.[193]

The summary of his message intensifies earlier formulations of the mystery embedded in God's creative plan. The Greek text of v. 9a is uncertain. The twenty-seventh edition of the Nestle-Aland Greek text brackets the "all" (πάντας *pantas*; NRSV and NIV, "everyone") following the infinitive "to enlighten" (NRSV, "to make see"; NIV, "to make plain"). The problem is finding the referent of "all" (*pantas*). It does not agree grammatically with "Gentiles" in v. 8. "Saints" is too far away from the adjective, and such an assertion would in any case contradict the expression "least of the saints." Therefore some interpreters prefer to follow the manuscript tradition that lacks *pantas* (NRSV note, "to bring to light"). On that reading, the apostle illuminates the mystery itself, not individuals about the mystery.[194]

However, Eph 1:18 asks God to enlighten (φωτίζω *phōtizō*) the addressees. To "enlighten the heart" occurs in apocalyptic language as God's activity. Paul claims such enlightenment for his preaching in 2 Cor 4:6 with reference to God's creation of light in Gen 1:3. The "I" of the Essene teacher is described as mediating the divine illumination he received from God to the community through his teaching, "like perfect dawn you have revealed yourself to me with your light";[195] "you exhibit your power in me and reveal yourself in me with your strength to enlighten them";[196] "through me you have enlightened the face of the

Many . . . for you have shown me your wondrous mysteries."[197] Comparison with Essene language indicates that "all" stands in place of its designation for those illuminated through the Teacher, "the many." Despite the grammatical difficulties, it would have to refer back to "the saints." The NRSV translation "make everyone see" does not capture the appropriate nuances of transmitting what is essentially God's illumination of the hearts of the elect. It suggests that the apostle fulfills a routine teaching task to provide cognitive information about God's design.

As the Essene example indicates, divine illumination operates within the community of those chosen by God. Readers of Ephesians know that community is the church. The cosmic images that Ephesians uses for the church also have some roots in this type of apocalyptic terminology. The church identifies with the exalted Christ, just as the Essenes spoke of their sect as joining the heavenly community of the "holy ones" (angels), "He [God] unites their assembly to the sons of the heavens."[198] From that perspective, it is not difficult to see how Ephesians can conclude that the church, which belongs in the heavenly regions with Christ, would make God's hidden plan of salvation apparent to the various powers of the universe (vv. 10-11). As we have already seen, the terminology of divine predestination "in accordance with the eternal purpose" belongs to this revelation pattern (v. 11; 1:11). Therefore, there is no reason to treat the "aeons" and "powers" in v. 10 (NRSV and NIV, "rulers and authorities") as mythological, hostile powers actively seeking to prevent souls from reaching heavenly regions as in gnostic accounts of salvation.[199] Ephesians does recognize the existence of evil forces in the cosmos that are defeated by God (2:2; 6:12). The existence of the church serves as evidence of God's power over evil. The teaching of individuals in the church is not a contest against mythological powers.[200]

Nevertheless, scholars continue to link the cos-

193. Rudolf Schnackenburg, *The Epistle to the Ephesians*, trans. H. Heron (Edinburgh: T. & T. Clark, 1991) 136.

194. See ibid, 138n. 28.

195. 1QH 12[4]:6.

196. 1QH 12:23.

197. 1QH 12:27.

198. 1QS 11:8.

199. Contra Heinrich Schlier, *Der Brief an die Epheser* (Dusseldorf: Patmos, 1957).

200. Contra Hans Conzelmann, "Der Brief an die Epheser," in *Die Briefe an die Galater, Epheser, Philipper, Kolosser, Thessalonicher und Philemon*, ed. Jürgen Becker, Hans Conzelmann, and Gerhard Friedrich (Göttingen/Zürich: Vandenhoeck & Ruprecht, 1985). See Andrew T. Lincoln, *Ephesians*, WBC 42 (Dallas: Word, 1990) 186.

mological terms in Ephesians with religious cults that personified the soul's ascent into the heavens as a defeat for planetary powers. The claim that its author was opposed to the cosmic speculation in the Mithras cult depends upon reading αἰώνων (*aiōnōn*) as a reference to the god Aion rather than as a temporal term designating "ages."[201] Readers familiar with the zodiacal grades and astronomical speculation attached to the Mithras initiation rites could understand Ephesians to mean that such mystery cults have no power to liberate the soul. However, the apocalyptic terminology used throughout the letter suggests that the temporal reading of αἰων (*aiōn*) is intended in Eph 3:9-11.

Verse 12 returns to the apostle's character. Boldness (παρρησία *parrēsia*) in speech was widely regarded as an attribute of the wise or of those, like Moses, favored with special access to God. Both meanings are evident in Ephesians. Paul's boldness is demonstrated in apostolic preaching despite imprisonment (6:19-20). He does not teach for human rewards, or he would speak in a way that flatters the audience (1 Thess 2:2; 2 Cor 3:12; Phil 1:20; Philo *On the Speecial Laws* 1.321). In the religious context, "boldness" belongs with access to God in prayer, a motif already mentioned in 2:18 (Job 27:10; Philo *Who Is the Heir of Divine Things?* 5-7; Josephus *Antiquities of the Jews* 2.4.4; 5.1.3). Both uses connect with what follows. Bold speech in defense of the gospel belongs to the image of the imprisoned apostle (v. 13); direct access to God in prayer, to the prayer formula of vv. 14-21.

The final sentence in this section returns to the personal relationship between the author and the addressees that opened the long digression (vv. 1-2). Although their only connection with the apostle is through reading, the audience should have such appreciation for Paul's role in bringing salvation to the Gentiles that they despair at his suffering. Ephesians leaves the connection between Paul's suffering and the "glory" (δόξα *doxa*) that accrues to the Gentiles undefined. "Glory" is always associated with praising God or God's gift of salvation in Ephesians (1:6, 12, 14, 17-18; 3:16, 21).

Accustomed to the catalogs of apostolic suffer-

ing in other Pauline letters, the dramatic pictures of Paul in prison and on trial in Acts, and later martyrdom stories, readers might expect to hear about the imprisoned apostle in Ephesians. Commentators often bring in details from 2 Timothy in referring to this section of Ephesians as the portrayal of a heroic martyr. Yet Ephesians has less to say about the apostle's sufferings than any other Pauline letter. The reference to bold speech and the willingness to suffer for such speech serve as proof of character. They indicate that the message has not been crafted to flatter or suit the prejudices of an audience and that the speaker does not seek some personal gain or advantage. This section of Ephesians concerns the message that God entrusted to the apostle, not the personal details of his life.

The description of the mystery of God in vv. 5-11 follows the same pattern of rhetorical celebration evident in the earlier sections of Ephesians. Its claims are repeated using established patterns of language for divine revelation, election, and salvation. Throughout this section of Ephesians the activity of God's gracious power forms the basis for many statements about human activity. Neither the apostle as one who brings enlightenment about the divine mystery nor the church as manifestation of the many-sided divine wisdom (v. 10) possesses what they convey. Depiction of the church as heavenly reality, not as a human institution, should not be taken as triumphalism, since its truth is a mystery of God's plan known to the elect, not an expansionist sociopolitical program.

From that perspective, Ephesians considers the church as the culmination of God's plan for the entire universe. Therefore, anyone who does not respond to the gospel and become one with Christ has no hope of salvation. Ephesians does mean to say that God intends all peoples to become one in Christ. It presents the church as the new humanity that results. But it is also important to note the perspective from which Ephesians makes such claims—a position of sociopolitical powerlessness. Christian communities emerged at the margins of Jewish communities, which were themselves minorities in the urban centers of Asia Minor.

The dramatic opening, "I Paul am a prisoner for Christ," evokes the fragile character of the early Christian movement. Its Jewish heritage, especially the apocalyptic images of divine elec-

---

201. Timothy B. Cargal, " 'Seated in the Heavenlies': Cosmic Mediators in the Mysteries of Mithras and the Letter to the Ephesians," SBLSP, ed. Eugene H. Lovering (Atlanta: Scholars Press, 1994) 814-16.

tion, provided an extraordinary self-understanding as the church was being transformed from a sect of Jewish believers into a Gentile church of Jewish heritage. Ephesians reminds readers of two essen-tial factors in this surprising development: the sure grasp of God's mysterious plan by particular indi-viduals (especially Paul) and the power of God working to extend salvation to all.

REFLECTIONS

Even though the first readers of Ephesians did not know Paul personally, they benefited from his missionary activity. Paul understood his own conversion as a calling to make Christ known among the Gentiles (Gal 1:15-16). He also understood that the considerable sufferings he endured in service to the gospel were a necessary part of the process. The apostle must show in his own life the "life out of death" pattern of the crucified and risen Jesus: "Always carrying in the body the death of Jesus, so that the life of Jesus may be made visible in our mortal flesh. So death is at work in us but life in you" (2 Cor 4:11-12 NRSV).

The writer of Ephesians uses the dramatic opening "I Paul am a prisoner of Christ Jesus for the sake of you Gentiles" (3:1 NRSV) to shock the audience into attention. The author then inserts a summary of the message that Gentiles are to be God's people (3:2-6). He reminds them that God gave Paul the mission to make this plan of salvation known (3:7-12). With a characteristic twist, the author of Ephesians finds a cosmic significance in the gospel. As the message of salvation is made known among human beings, it becomes known to the powers that control the world as well (3:10). We have such ready access to all forms of media that we *expect* religious leaders to attract the attention of world leaders. When one of the television networks recently ran a mini-series called "Jesus," it managed to bump the most popular show on television out of the top spot. It is hard to remember a time when the church was made up of small groups of people meeting in houses. It had no buildings at all. In an age without media, having no buildings, statues, or inscriptions means very little presence in the public sphere. How could Christians ever think that their existence was God's plan for the world? How could they go even further and imagine that it was revealing God's wisdom to the forces that control the universe?

Yet, that is exactly the kind of vision, courage, and faith that changes the world. Once a movement has succeeded in changing how we live or eradicating some injustice, it is easy to forget what it took to get there. It is easy to forget that some of our greatest human benefactors, people like Gandhi and Martin Luther King, Jr., went to jail for their efforts. Like Paul, they eventually paid with their lives for insisting that God intended us all to be merciful, just, equal. In short, it is to come closer to the vision of all humanity united as God's new creation that Ephesians emphasizes. These leaders had talents and education that would have enabled them to live comfortable and productive lives without getting involved in transforming humanity.

Letters from jail also play a significant role in encouraging the movement. We have several from Paul himself and from close associates writing in Paul's name. Martin Luther King, Jr.'s famous "Letter from a Birmingham Jail" explains that he could not stay comfortably in Atlanta. He had to go where injustice was, even though fellow ministers criticized his decision as foolish. Dr. King could appeal to precedent, of course, and he was not shy about reminding his readers of Paul's missionary journeys and of the great Hebrew prophets who left home to take God's Word elsewhere. He also insisted that ultimately all communities are related:

> Injustice anywhere is a threat to justice everywhere. We are caught in an inescapable network of mutuality, tied in a single garment of destiny. Whatever affects one directly, affects all indirectly.
> . . . Anyone who lives inside the United States can never be considered an outsider anywhere within its bounds.[202]

---

202. Martin Luther King, Jr., "Letter from a Birmingham Jail," in *Norton Anthology of African American Literature,* ed. H. L. Gates, Jr., and N. Y. McKay (New York: Norton, 1997) 1854.

This quotation captures for a particular situation the significance of Paul's insight that in the end human beings cannot be considered separately. We need to see ourselves as interconnected members of the one body of Christ just as much as we need to see ourselves as united in a single political body. "No one can ever be considered an outsider"—that is what we hear Paul announcing to the Gentiles. And we might agree with him that his is, indeed, a revelation of God's plan, the full truth of which is still being revealed to the world.

Ephesians 3:14-21, The Apostle's Prayer

NIV

[14] For this reason I kneel before the Father, [15] from whom his whole family[a] in heaven and on earth derives its name. [16] I pray that out of his glorious riches he may strengthen you with power through his Spirit in your inner being, [17] so that Christ may dwell in your hearts through faith. And I pray that you, being rooted and established in love, [18] may have power, together with all the saints, to grasp how wide and long and high and deep is the love of Christ, [19] and to know this love that surpasses knowledge—that you may be filled to the measure of all the fullness of God.

[20] Now to him who is able to do immeasurably more than all we ask or imagine, according to his power that is at work within us, [21] to him be glory in the church and in Christ Jesus throughout all generations, for ever and ever! Amen.

[a]15 Or whom all fatherhood

NRSV

14 For this reason I bow my knees before the Father,[a] 15 from whom every family[b] in heaven and on earth takes its name. [16] I pray that, according to the riches of his glory, he may grant that you may be strengthened in your inner being with power through his Spirit, [17] and that Christ may dwell in your hearts through faith, as you are being rooted and grounded in love. [18] I pray that you may have the power to comprehend, with all the saints, what is the breadth and length and height and depth, [19] and to know the love of Christ that surpasses knowledge, so that you may be filled with all the fullness of God.

20 Now to him who by the power at work within us is able to accomplish abundantly far more than all we can ask or imagine, [21] to him be glory in the church and in Christ Jesus to all generations, forever and ever. Amen.

[a] Other ancient authorities add of our Lord Jesus Christ   [b] Gk fatherhood

COMMENTARY

"For this reason" picks up 3:1. The section continues with a prayer report (vv. 14-19) and a concluding doxology (vv. 20-21). The petitions (vv. 16-19) ask that the process of salvation be completed in the hearts and minds of the letter's recipients. The doxology returns to the theme of God's power at work within the community of faith.

This prayer report exemplifies boldness and access to God (v. 12). Since the apostle entrusted with the "commission of God's grace" (v. 2) prays for them, readers can be certain that God will grant his request. There is no reason to treat the petitions as evidence of difficulties in the churches.[203] Because the prayer asks for the love of Christ and fullness of God (v. 19), it forms an appropriate rhetorical conclusion to the speech in praise of God's powerful grace.[204] The letter next turns to a different type of speech: ethical exhortation (4:1–6:20). That section of the letter is framed by references to Paul's imprisonment (4:1; 6:20). The prayer report facilitates the transition between the two halves of the epistle by disposing the audience to a Christian way of life.

203. Contra Andrew T. Lincoln, *Ephesians,* WBC 42 (Dallas: Word, 1990) 197-98.

204. Gordon D. Fee, *God's Empowering Presence: The Holy Spirit in the Letters of Paul* (Peabody, Mass.: Hendrickson, 1994) 695f.

The prayer report reintroduces the theme of love. The addressees are known for their love (1:15). God's love for us (2:4) has been demonstrated in the election to holiness, "to be holy and blameless before him in love" (1:4). The prayer report speaks of the community with its *roots* and *foundation* in love (3:17), an echo of the earlier image of the church in which Gentiles *grow together* with Jews into the temple *founded on* apostles and prophets (2:20-21).

3:14-15. The apostle's kneeling position departs from the usual custom of standing to pray (as in Mark 11:25; Luke 18:11, 13). Luke has Jesus kneel in Gethsemane (Luke 22:41) rather than lie prostrate on the ground, as in Mark (Mark 14:35). Luke also refers to kneeling at prayer in Acts (Acts 7:60; 9:40; 20:36; 21:5). With the exception of Acts 9:40, all of these scenes are associated with death. Jesus and Stephen are about to die. Paul is departing on the journey to Jerusalem that will lead to his imprisonment and death. Kneeling is often the gesture of suppliants begging for a favor from a powerful or important person (as in Matt 17:14; Mark 1:40; 10:17). In these scenes, kneeling expresses the deep emotions of those involved; here it adds pathos to the image of the imprisoned apostle.

The prayer includes a play on words that cannot be easily reproduced in English. He prays to the Father (πατήρ *patēr*) from whom every πατριά (*patria*; "clan," "group derived from a single ancestor," "race") is named (the NRSV's "family" must be understood as a reference to the extended family). Ephesians follows the common Christian tradition of referring to God as "father" ("and the Lord Jesus," 5:20, also 6:23; "our Father," 1:3, also 2:18; 4:6; "of Jesus," 1:4; "Father of glory," 1:17). But what is meant by the assertion that every clan "in heaven and on earth" is named from the Father? Some interpreters suggest that the phrase implies that God is superior to all the powers because God created them. Persons tempted to use the names of heavenly powers for magical purposes fail to recognize the origin of all those names in God.[205] Others suggest some form of Hellenistic cosmological specula-

tion.[206] Stoic cosmology proposed a biological image of the origins of all things out of the divine spiritual substance, "God, mind, fate and Zeus are all one, and many other names are applied to him. In the beginning all by himself he turned the entire substance through air into water."[207] God appears as father in Platonist cosmologies as well.[208] In gnostic cosmologies, the "first" Father generates all of the subsequent aeons of the heavenly pleroma.[209]

Though Ephesians uses images characteristic of the cosmology of its time, the letter shows no evidence of debate on the subject. Its emphasis on God as creator (also 4:6) provides the general context for this play on words. Everything belongs to the one clan because everything has been created by the one Father-creator.

3:16-19. The first petition (vv. 16-17) returns to God's power (1:17-23). It also contains variations of phrases from Colossians ("riches of glory," Col 1:27; "hearts held together in love," Col 2:2; and "rooted and built up in him," Col 2:7). Two parallel expressions ask for inner strengthening of the faithful. The first depicts God as the agent of inner strengthening (v. 16). The power through which God raised Christ operates through believers (1:19; 3:6). Unlike Rom 7:22, Ephesians does not use the expression "inner being" (εἰς τὸν ἔσω ἄνθρωπον *eis ton esō anthrōpon*) as the antithesis to outer, bodily passions that overwhelm reason. Nor does the expression refer to the "new humanity" (τὸν καικὸν ἄνθρωπον *ton kainon anthrōpon*; NRSV and NIV, "new self") of 4:24.[210] The parallel phrase in v. 17, "in your hearts" (ἐν ταῖς καρδίαις ὑμῶν *en tais kardiais hymōn*), indicates that "inner being" refers to the basic intelligence and will of human persons.

The second formulation of the petition (v. 17) specifies what is meant by the first. Strengthening by God's Spirit is not a prior condition for the indwelling of Christ. The phrase "rooted and

---

205. Clinton E. Arnold, *Ephesians: Power and Magic: The Concept of Power in Ephesians in the Light of Its Historical Setting*, SNTSMS 63 (Cambridge: Cambridge University Press, 1989) 58-59; Cargal, " 'Seated in the Heavenlies,' " 155.

206. Chantel Bouttier, *L'Epître de Saint Paul aux Ephésiens*, Commentaire du Nouveau Testament, 2nd série Ixb (Geneva: Labor et Fides, 1991).

207. A. A. Long and D. N. Sedley, *The Hellenistic Philosophers*, vol. 1, *Translations* (Cambridge: Cambridge University Press, 1987) 46B.

208. Plato *Timaeus* 28C; 37C; 41A; Philo *On the Special Laws* 2.165; 3.189.

209. E.g., *Ap. John* II 2,27-5,11.

210. Contra Heinrich Schlier, *Der Brief an die Epheser* (Dusseldorf: Patmos, 1957) 168.

grounded" is a variation on the "rooted and built up" of Col 2:7. Since it also designates God's mercy and goodness toward the elect (v. 19; 2:4), "love" (ἀγάπη *agapē*) means both God's love in the faithful and their love for others (1:15).

The second petition (vv. 18-19*a*) indicates the other fruits of the Spirit. It also consists of two parallel expressions: Understanding and knowing are the objects of stengthening (1:9, 17; 3:4-5). The first object of understanding is not clearly specified. "Breadth and length and height and depth" (v. 18) are not dimensions of a particular object. The cosmological images in Ephesians might lead one to anticipate that they refer to God's presence to all parts of the cosmos (as in Ps 139:7-12). Only God's wisdom can comprehend the cosmos (Job 11:7-9). Sirach 1:1-10 personifies God's incomprehensible wisdom. At the same time, Wisdom is a gift that the Lord bestows on the righteous: "It is he who created her; he saw her and took her measure; he poured her out upon all his works, upon all the living according to his gift; he lavished her upon those who love him" (Sir 1:9-10 NRSV). Ephesians 3:10 presented God's multisided wisdom (σοφία *sophia*) as manifest to the powers through the church. These petitions ask that God endow believers with the wisdom needed to hold fast to the gift of salvation.

Others suggest that the expression indicates expansion of the human mind or spirit. An apocalyptic reading would treat "the saints" (οἱ ἅγιοι *hoi hagioi*) as a reference to the angelic hosts. The object whose dimensions are comprehended would be a heavenly object, such as the new Jerusalem (Ezek 48:16-17; Rev 3:18; 21:6) or the temple of God (Ezek 40:1–43:12). An extremely fragmentary wisdom text from Qumran that is introduced as instructions from a sage to the righteous contained a section involving something with roots from the heavens to the abyss being measured by God.[211] In another fragment, astronomical measurements had special significance as the hidden wisdom conveyed in a vision of the heavens ordered from God's throne by the movements of the sun and the moon.[212] Members of the sect needed this knowledge in order to follow a liturgical calendar that is in accord with the divine order. Participation in divine wisdom is also

a presupposition of these texts. Although the apocalyptic timetable is foreign to Ephesians, Essene language is not. Exaltation to the heavens, where Christ is seated on the divine throne, would certainly endow the saints with such knowledge. It also sets them among the angels. Since Ephesians is using figurative language, not discursive description, a Jewish liturgical fragment may have been the basis for this prayer formula.

More distant possibilities include philosophical reflection on the ability of the human mind to encompass the vast expanses of the cosmos. In interpreting Exod 33:23, Philo distinguishes the mind's ability to know all things that exist below God from its inability to grasp the divine: "It is an ample gift for the best sort of mortals, knowledge of things bodily and immaterial below the Existent."[213] He also repeats an argument for natural knowledge of God as creator based on a survey of the order and harmony of the universe from the region of fixed stars down to the earth. Such knowledge is contrasted with direct apprehension of God apart from created things given to Moses.[214] Though Ephesians might concur with these views, nothing in the letter suggests a philosophical interest in the modes of knowing God.

Since "fullness" (πλήρωμα *plērōma*) occurs in the final petition (v. 19*b*), the dimensions of the heavenly pleroma in gnostic speculation have also been seen as the referent of this phrase in v. 18*b*. Only those whose origins lie in the heavenly church can conceive the dimensions and properties of the aeons that have come forth from the Father.[215] Reading Ephesians as a response to magical practices leads to comparison with prayers and spells designed to gain divine power for individuals.[216] The four dimensions are named in a prayer that the magician is to say in order to draw down and retain divine light.[217]

The parallel expression in v. 19*a* indicates that Ephesians is not concerned with knowledge in terms of human minds stretched to their limits in apprehending the creator or with cosmological

---

211. 4Q298.
212. 4Q286 frag. 1.

213. Philo *On the Change of Names* 8-9.
214. Philo *Allegorical Interpretation of the Laws* 3.99, 100-101.
215. So *Tripartite Tractate* 58, 29-60.1
216. Clinton E. Arnold, *Ephesians: Power and Magic: The Concept of Power in Ephesians in the Light of Its Historical Setting*, SNTSMS 63 (Cambridge: Cambridge University Press, 1989) 89-96.
217. PGM IV 970-85. See Hans Dieter Betz, ed., *The Greek Magical Papyri in Translation*, vol. 1, *Texts* (Chicago: University of Chicago Press, 1986) 57

speculation but with the experience of the love of Christ (cf. Rom 8:38-39). Ephesians characteristically uses "the exceeding" (τὸ ὑπερβάλλον *to hyperballon*) with expressions for salvation ("immeasurable greatness of his power," 1:19; "immeasurable riches of his grace," 2:7). The shift from knowledge to "faith and love" in v. 17 indicates that Ephesians is not a speculative tract. There is no polemic in Ephesians against knowledge (unlike Col 2:2-3). The strengthening to which the prayer refers points to earlier images of the community, not to individual knowledge of God or the cosmos.

The final petition (v. 19*b*) reinforces this orientation. The community must become what the church in its heavenly reality already is, "filled with all the fullness [*plērōma*] of God." The phrase echoes Colossians, which speaks of the "fullness of deity in Christ" (see Col 1:19; 2:9) and of believers "filled in him" (see Col 2:10). Ephesians 1:23 has already established the immediate context for this phrase. The church is the "fullness of Christ," who in turn fills the entire cosmos. The expression "fullness of God" (πλήρωμα τοῦ Θεου *plērōma tou Theou*) in this petition highlights the theocentric element in the epistle. God's preordained plan, which culminates in Christ, is the object of praise. The shift to divine fullness also indicates that no future revelations or acts in the drama of salvation remain to be achieved.[218]

3:20-21. The concluding doxology cannot be entirely divided from the earlier prayer, since this is the only doxology in the NT to mention Christ and the church as the locus of praise. The reference to both "all the saints" and Christ in vv. 18-19 makes this focus appropriate. The doxology also fits the pattern of alternating pronouns so evident in the epistle. The "you" of the earlier prayer formula is once again joined to the author's "we." In addition, the reflection on God's power working within the believing community picks up the references to being strengthened in power (v. 16) and to being filled with God (v. 19). Therefore, the doxology should be seen to flow from the intercessory prayer formula.[219]

218. Andrew T. Lincoln, *Ephesians,* WBC 42 (Dallas: Word, 1990) 215.
219. Gordon D. Fee, *God's Empowering Presence: The Holy Spirit in the Letters of Paul* (Peabody, Mass.: Hendrickson, 1994) 696.

Doxologies refer to the person being praised, contain a praise formula—usually with the word "glory" (δόξα *doxa*), an eternity formula—and often a concluding amen. The doxology typically occurs at or near the end of a letter ("to our God and Father be glory forever and ever. Amen" [Phil 4:20]; see also Rom 16:25-27; 2 Tim 4:18; Heb 13:21; 1 Pet 5:11). The doxology in Rom 11:36 concludes the theological section of that letter, as is the case here. Though doxologies are not ordinarily attached to a previous intercession, Phil 4:19 belongs to an expression of thanks that comes close to a prayer formula. The gifts that the Philippians have sent Paul in prison are to be repaid by Paul's "master God." Paul assures readers that their gift is a pleasing sacrifice (Phil 4:18) and that "God will repay every need of yours according to his riches in glory in Christ." Many of the terms in this sentence ("fill," "wealth," "glory," "in Christ") appear in Eph 3:14-19.

Ephesians begins by celebrating the power of God to deliver even more than humans might ask or think. It retrieves the description of the great power of God that raised Jesus and is at work in believers from 1:19-20. The doxology also models the praise of God's glory for which the elect were predestined (1:6, 12).

This ringing affirmation of God's extraordinary power picks up a note that is already evident in the intercessory prayer report: Believers have received the grace and Spirit of God long before they come to ask God for them. Such confidence is part of the access to God that Christians enjoy. The extraordinary character of such expressions becomes evident when one considers the usual mode of making a request of a powerful person or benefactor. Not only should the request be enveloped in extensive praise of the patron's goodness, but it should also be hedged with "if it would not be too much trouble . . . ," "if you could . . . ," and other similar expressions. If the person from whom one seeks a favor is considerably more powerful, intermediaries or a prior note of introduction will be produced. It is possible to see all of Ephesians 1–3 as an exposition of God's saving power. The intercessory prayer report and doxology merely confirm what the letter has already stated. God has gathered the elect into the heavenly regions with Christ. In Ephesians, the apostle does not intercede with God to do things.

Instead, the prayer asks God to bring to perfection the work of salvation that has already begun among the elect. What that will mean in the concrete terms of Christian life remains to be spelled out in the second half of the epistle.

REFLECTIONS

The previous section ended with Paul's concern that his sufferings might cause his audience to lose heart. Since Ephesians was written after Paul's martyrdom, its author could not express confidence that God could return the apostle to the mission field, which Paul himself used in earlier letters (see Phil 1:21-26; Phlm 22). Instead, Ephesians returns to two themes already sounded loud and clear in the opening chapter: glory (3:13) and prayer (3:14). This prayer concludes with a doxology praising God's power to go beyond anything we can imagine (3:20-21). Rhetorically, this prayer makes a dramatic statement of faith. Indirectly it answers the question that must have tugged at the hearts of second-generation Christians. As they saw the apostles arrested and martyred, they must have wondered whether the church could survive. Notice the slight twist that appears in the doxology, "to him be all glory *in the church* and in Jesus Christ" (3:21 NRSV, italics added). For us, "glory in the church" does not turn up in doxologies, but it certainly does in our imagination. We have TV shots of the worship at general conventions, at St. Peter's in Rome, at the Church of the Nativity in Bethlehem, and even at great stadium crusades. Those of us who regularly participate in such worship services may forget the extraordinary impact such experiences make on Christians from small churches who experience it for the first time. All those phrases about "glory in the heavenly realms" take on physical reality as the music of the choir echoes off the stone vaulting of Westminster Abbey or Chartres Cathedral.

Step back for a moment into the house-church world of the first century. The Temple in Jerusalem, which had been a marvel, lies in ruins. Even Jews have no physical site in which they could experience such dramatic worship of God. So who had the buildings, the sacred processions and sacrifices, the dramatic public events that could take your breath away? Neither Jews nor Christians. Those *atheoi* ("godless people") did. And the Roman imperial administration did. When Christians imagined Christ returning in glory or Christ enthroned in glory, they undoubtedly had such images in mind. They only had to look at their coins to see the imperial version: temples dedicated to Roman glory and deified emperors. We should not take the phrases about strengthening the hearts and inner being of Christians lightly. It must have required extraordinary inner confidence to remain a faithful Christian with no external signs of the truth of our faith. "That Christ may dwell in your hearts through faith, as you are being rooted and grounded in love" (3:17 NRSV) is an extraordinary prayer. Accomplish that, and you have the whole Christian life.

The Lutheran theologian Dietrich Bonhoeffer, who was jailed and executed for joining a plot to assassinate Hitler, left a prison correspondence that is one of the classics of twentieth-century theology. In one letter, he advises his friend to take in the Holy Week services in St. Peter's and St. John Lateran at Rome, mentions a service of some twenty years earlier in a Greek Orthodox church, and then mentions a small convent church outside Rome where the nuns' singing made an impression.[220] This letter shows what a powerful support such memories of the larger church at prayer can be in the life of faith. Like Paul, Bonhoeffer had put his life at risk for his suffering sisters and brothers. He had returned to Germany despite the urging of colleagues to remain in the United States, where he had been lecturing. He felt compelled to take the risk of direct attack against an evil that he could see was destroying his own country.

---

220. Dietrich Bonhoeffer, "3 February 1944," in *Letters and Papers from Prison,* ed. Eberhard Bethge (New York: Macmillan, 1972) 218.

Yet prison does strange things to the mind. In the same letter, he muses on the lives of his generation in contrast to the great theologians and artists of the previous centuries. People no longer seemed to want to achieve what is great. "Where is there today the combination of fine *abandon* and large-scale planning that goes with such a life?" he remarked. That could issue in a bit of cynicism. There is nothing great to accomplish, so devote your life to chasing personal wealth. But Bonhoeffer has a different answer: Perhaps our lives can be fragments that God can sort out, consigning some to the dustbin and completing others: "The important thing today is that we should be able to discern from the fragment of our life who the whole was arranged . . . their completion can only be a matter for God and so they are fragments that must be fragments." Set this observation alongside the prayer report in Eph 3:14-21. Paul is not proclaiming a triumphalist Christianity that has conquered the world, as many people imagine when they read this prayer. He is providing prayers for the witnesses, prisoners, martyrs for the gospel and their friends—everyone whose life is somehow fragments in need of sorting. The Christian virtues of faith, hope, and love can latch on to the fullness of God and find completion in that experience.

EPHESIANS 4:1–6:9, ETHICAL EXHORTATIONS ON LIVING AS CHRISTIANS

Ephesians 4:1-16, Building the Body of Christ

NIV

4 As a prisoner for the Lord, then, I urge you to live a life worthy of the calling you have received. ²Be completely humble and gentle; be patient, bearing with one another in love. ³Make every effort to keep the unity of the Spirit through the bond of peace. ⁴There is one body and one Spirit— just as you were called to one hope when you were called— ⁵one Lord, one faith, one baptism; ⁶one God and Father of all, who is over all and through all and in all.

⁷But to each one of us grace has been given as Christ apportioned it. ⁸This is why it*ᵃ* says:

"When he ascended on high,
  he led captives in his train
  and gave gifts to men."*ᵇ*

⁹(What does "he ascended" mean except that he also descended to the lower, earthly regions*ᶜ*? ¹⁰He who descended is the very one who ascended higher than all the heavens, in order to fill the whole universe.) ¹¹It was he who gave some to be apostles, some to be prophets, some to be evangelists, and some to be pastors and teachers, ¹²to prepare God's people for works of

a8 Or *God*   *b8* Psalm 68:18   *c9* Or *the depths of the earth*

NRSV

4 I therefore, the prisoner in the Lord, beg you to lead a life worthy of the calling to which you have been called, ²with all humility and gentleness, with patience, bearing with one another in love, ³making every effort to maintain the unity of the Spirit in the bond of peace. ⁴There is one body and one Spirit, just as you were called to the one hope of your calling, ⁵one Lord, one faith, one baptism, ⁶one God and Father of all, who is above all and through all and in all.

⁷But each of us was given grace according to the measure of Christ's gift. ⁸Therefore it is said,

"When he ascended on high he made
    captivity itself a captive;
  he gave gifts to his people."

⁹(When it says, "He ascended," what does it mean but that he had also descended*ᵃ* into the lower parts of the earth? ¹⁰He who descended is the same one who ascended far above all the heavens, so that he might fill all things.) ¹¹The gifts he gave were that some would be apostles, some prophets, some evangelists, some pastors and teachers, ¹²to equip the saints for the work of ministry, for

*ᵃ*Other ancient authorities add *first*

NIV

service, so that the body of Christ may be built up [13]until we all reach unity in the faith and in the knowledge of the Son of God and become mature, attaining to the whole measure of the fullness of Christ.

[14]Then we will no longer be infants, tossed back and forth by the waves, and blown here and there by every wind of teaching and by the cunning and craftiness of men in their deceitful scheming. [15]Instead, speaking the truth in love, we will in all things grow up into him who is the Head, that is, Christ. [16]From him the whole body, joined and held together by every supporting ligament, grows and builds itself up in love, as each part does its work.

NRSV

building up the body of Christ, [13]until all of us come to the unity of the faith and of the knowledge of the Son of God, to maturity, to the measure of the full stature of Christ. [14]We must no longer be children, tossed to and fro and blown about by every wind of doctrine, by people's trickery, by their craftiness in deceitful scheming. [15]But speaking the truth in love, we must grow up in every way into him who is the head, into Christ, [16]from whom the whole body, joined and knit together by every ligament with which it is equipped, as each part is working properly, promotes the body's growth in building itself up in love.

COMMENTARY

Ephesians presumes that conversion leads to moral renewal. The new moral life is indicated by the self-designation "saints" ("holy ones," ἅγιοι *hagioi*), praise for mutual love (1:15), and indications that the elect are "holy and blameless" (1:4) before God and are created for good works (2:10). Paul's letters frequently include sections of paraenesis (moral advice or admonition). Pauline paraenesis has stronger ties to the forms and content of Hellenistic philosophers than other sections of his epistles.[221] Ancient moralists held that people should be reminded of what they know so that they will act accordingly.[222] Therefore, the epistle's paraenesis need not reflect actual vices among the addressees. These moralists also held that a teacher's life was to provide a visible example of his teaching.

This section returns to the image of the imprisoned apostle (4:1) and establishes friendship between author and audience that was also considered fundamental to hortatory discourse. Paul's paraenesis often opens with the verb παρακαλέω (*parakaleō*, "I beg" or "I appeal"; Rom 12:1; 2 Cor 10:1; 1 Thess 4:1) and a brief list of virtues (v. 2). The beginning then shifts

from convention to a theme of the letter: unity in the body of Christ (vv. 3-6). Verses 2-4 draw on Col 3:12-15. Verse 7 makes the transition from exhortation to the heavenly exaltation of Christ (vv. 8-10). His status is the basis for the gifts of salvation. The conclusion (vv. 11-16) describes unity as working together in the body of Christ. This concern refers back to the growth image (2:21).

4:1-6. The exhortation to "lead a life worthy of [your] calling" echoes Jewish understanding of divine election. God's calling is to create a people who are devoted to God's law. God works:

to enlighten the heart of man, straighten out in front of him all the paths of justice and truth, establish in his heart respect for the precepts of God; it is a spirit of meekness, of patience, generous compassion, eternal goodness . . . potent wisdom which trusts in all the deeds of God and depends upon his abundant mercy . . . of generous compassion with all the sons of truth.[223]

Though Pauline churches no longer follow the law, the conviction that election leads to a new life remains (1 Thess 2:12).

An exhortation to holiness could be expanded by a list of virtues (vv. 2-3). For the Essenes, the virtues distinguish the community of the "sons of

---

221. Abraham J. Malherbe, "Hellenistic Moralists and the New Testament," in *Aufstieg und Niedergang der römischen Welt* II 26/1, ed. Wolfgang Haase (Berlin: DeGruyter, 1992).

222. Dio Chrysostom *Orations* 17,2.

223. 1QS 4:2-5.

light" from the "sons of darkness," whose vices that text goes on to describe.[224] The list in v. 2—humility (ταπεινοφροσύνη *tapeinophrosynē*), gentleness (πραΰτη *prautē*), patience (μακαροθυμία *makrothymia*)—adopts the final three of the list in Col 3:12. These virtues are found in the Essene example also. "Humility" (*tapeinophrosynē*) does not appear outside Jewish and Christian lists. To the non-Jew, "humility" suggests demeaning lowliness.[225] "Gentleness" (*prautē*), on the other hand, does have positive connotations in Hellenistic ethics. It is opposed to wrath, disposed to forgiveness and to moderate punishment, and lives without jealousy or spite.[226] Those who have this trait can bear hardship or loss with tranquility. "Patience" (*makrothymia*) also belongs to both traditions. In Jewish and Christian sources, it appears as an attribute of God (Jer 15:15; Rom 2:4; 9:22; 1 Tim 1:16; 1 Pet 3:20) or of human beings (Prov 25:15; 2 Cor 6:6; Gal 5:22).

The exhortation "bearing with one another in love" appears in Col 3:13 and in the Essene description of the "sons of light." "Love" (ἀγάπη *agapē*) can be the foundation of all Christian virtues (1 Cor 13; Gal 5:14). Galatians 5:15 uses negative examples to highlight the communal implications of the love command. It dictates how persons relate to, and speak about, one another.

Verse 3 shifts to the specific focus of this section: unity. Two clauses, "unity of the Spirit" and "in the bond of peace," indicate that the fruit of the Spirit is peace (Rom 8:6; 14:17; 15:13; Gal 5:22). "Peace" (εἰρήνη *eirēnē*) as gift of the Spirit goes beyond social interest in communal concord. It refers to the fullness of salvation that comes from God (Rom 14:17; 15:13). The term "bond" (σύνδεσμος *syndesmos*) derives from Col 3:14-15, in which love is described as the "bond of perfection" (NRSV, "love, which binds everything together in perfect harmony"). It also creates a verbal echo with the apostle's self-designation "prisoner" (δέσμος *desmos*).

The reference to election from Col 3:15 introduces a list of "one" (ἕν *hen*) expressions (vv. 4-6). It ends with the one God who governs and fills the entire cosmos (v. 6). Some interpreters treat vv. 4-6 as an independent liturgical fragment.[227] However, the section appears to be an ad hoc creation from standard Pauline expressions. First Corinthians 12:12-13 (one body, Christ, one Spirit, baptized into one body) provides an initial framework for vv. 4-5, while 1 Cor 8:6 provides a formula for God's creative activity. Gordon Fee proposes an essentially trinitarian structure in the series that he calls "one of the more certain and specific Trinitarian passages in the corpus."[228] The first term in each verse provides its key image: one body (v. 4), one Lord (v. 5), and one God (v. 6). The first two verses indicate how persons have become part of the body that is God's elect. Verse 6 has taken over a philosophical formulation for the creative activity of God.[229]

Conversion included coming to know the one God, creator of all (2:12*b*, 18). The creation formula that indicates the transcendence of God, God's activity, and God's omnipresence undergirds the letter's insistence that other forces in the cosmos have no effective power.

4:7-10. Verse 7 incorporates exhortation by referring to "grace" (χάρις *charis*). The expression "each of us was given grace" resembles Rom 12:6, where diversity of gifts is associated with the particular grace given to each person in the community. Ephesians substitutes "according to the measure of Christ's gift" for "grace given." This usage conflates Rom 12:6 with the reference to "measure" in Rom 12:3. There Paul warns against false estimation of one's own gifts. If Ephesians has this section of Romans in view, then one would anticipate what follows in vv. 11-13, a discussion of gifts that require proper understanding of one's place in the community.

A digression interrupts the development that v. 7 anticipates. Ephesians has depicted the creative activity of God as equivalent to the plan that culminates in the body of Christ (1:9-10, 20-23; 2:5-7; 3:9-11). Verses 8-10 contain another description of the soteriological activity of Christ. It uses a form of biblical exegesis familiar from the

224. 1QS 4:9-11.

225. Ceslas Spicq, *Theological Lexicon of the New Testament,* 3 vols., trans. James Ernest (Peabody, Mass.: Hendrickson, 1994).

226. Aristotle *Nichomachean Ethics* 4.11, 1125[b]; Plato *Republic* 3.387.

227. Markus Barth, *Ephesians,* 2 vols., AB 34-34A (Garden City, N.Y.: Doubleday, 1974) 429.

228. Gordon D. Fee, *God's Empowering Presence: The Holy Spirit in the Letters of Paul* (Peabody, Mass.: Hendrickson, 1994) 702.

229. See Pseudo-Aristotle *On the Origin of the World* 6.397b, 11.14-15; Philo *The Cherubim* 125-126.

Qumran scrolls, the *pesher.*[230] Citation of a section of biblical text is followed by its application, often introduced by the formula, "its interpretation is that. . . ."[231] Interpretation involves demonstrating that the biblical text refers to events connected with the past, the present, or the future (end of all things) history of the sect. The Qumran text 1QpHab 7:4-5 treats the pesherim as revelations of divine mysteries: "Its interpretation (Hab 2:2) concerns the Teacher of Righteousness, to whom God has disclosed all the mysteries of the words of his servants, the prophets."

Ephesians 4:8-10 is a pesher on Ps 68:19 [67:19]. Fragments of a pesher on this psalm have been found at Qumran. That commentary connects with Ps 68:12-13, 26-27, 30-31, but the remains are too slight to permit any reconstruction of the sect's understanding. Ephesians may have taken its citation from a comparable text.

This type of interpretation begins with the theme and continues with as many details as fit the subject. Subunits of a text may be picked up, cited with an introduction ("as for when it says"), and followed by additional identifications. Applied to Eph 4:8-10, it is clear that the only phrase from the psalm citation on which the pesher comments is "he ascended." Nothing is said about either the "captivity taken captive" or the gifts bestowed on humankind. It is easy to link both of these themes to the overall imagery of Ephesians by understanding "captivity" (αἰχμαλωσία *aichmalōsia*) as the powers to whom Christ's ascent reveals God's plan. The author has "he gave," found in the psalm, in both v. 7 and v. 11. But the connection is not made in the exegetical style of a pesher. Therefore, the psalm interpretation was not originally formulated to fit the paraenesis in vv. 7 and 11-16.

Taken as a fragment of early Christian exegesis, the opening argument of the pesher is strikingly similar to John 3:13: "No one has ascended into heaven except the one who descended from heaven, the Son of Man" (NRSV).[232] A related piece of exegesis is connected with the use of Ps 110:1 in Acts 2:32-35 as David's prediction that the risen Jesus would be exalted to God's right hand. That psalm was incorporated into Eph 1:20-23. The argument in Acts 2:34 seeks to show that David was speaking prophetically of the Christ and not of himself. All of these examples use the ascent and descent imagery to advance Christian claims for Jesus as the one who has been exalted to God's right hand.

Both the form and the content of the pesher suggest that the regions to which Christ descends refers to the earth, not to some region below the earth (unlike Rom 10:7; 1 Pet 3:18-21; Rev 1:18). The objection that "lower regions of the earth" (τὰ κατώτερα μέρα τῆς γῆς *ta katōtera mera tēs gēs*) cannot mean simply earth and must mean hades ignores the fact that the regions of the air are also connected with earth in ancient cosmology.[233] Since Ephesians does not interpret the phrase about captives, one cannot treat it as the key to the passage as Arnold does in proposing that Eph 4:9 refers to initiation rites that involved descent to hades.[234] "The lower parts of the earth" (NRSV) and "the lower, earthly regions" (NIV) are suitably ambiguous translations. Though Eph 2:2 distinguishes the heavenly regions from the "air" (the area below the moon that has malevolent powers responsible for evil), it never refers to regions below the earth (cf. Phil 2:11).[235]

The final clause, "that he might fill [πληρόω *plēroō*] all things" (v. 10), fits the cosmological perspective of Ephesians. The phrase "filling the universe" was used earlier in connection with God's power and with the exalted Christ in his body (1:23; 3:19). Ephesians 4:13 speaks of the Christian community maturing in the "full stature of Christ." Cosmological images always serve the soteriological framework of the epistle. Here, the omnipresence of God (Eph 4:6; as in Philo *Allegorical Interpretation of the Laws* 3.4; *Life of Moses* 2.238) grounds the image of Christ as universal savior. God's preordained plan becomes known only when Christ is exalted in the heavens.

---

230. See Devorah Dimant, "Pesharim, Qumran," *ABD* 5:244-51.
231. E.g., Isa 40:3 in 1QS 8:13-16; Isa 24:17 in CD 4:13-15.
232. See Chantel Bouttier, *L'Epître de Saint Paul aux Ephésiens,* Commentaire du Nouveau Testament, 2nd série Ixb (Geneva: Labor et Fides, 1991), 183-185, who makes too much of the Moses typology.

233. Timothy B. Cargal, " 'Seated in the Heavenlies': Cosmic Mediators in the Mysteries of Mithras and the Letter to the Ephesians," SBLSP, ed. Eugene H. Lovering (Atlanta: Scholars Press, 1994) 819.
234. Clinton E. Arnold, *Ephesians: Power and Magic: The Concept of Power in Ephesians in the Light of Its Historical Setting,* SNTSMS 63 (Cambridge: Cambridge University Press, 1989) 57; Larry Kreitzer, "The Plutonium of Hierapolis and the Descent of Christ into the 'Lowermost Parts of the Earth' (Ephesians 4, 9)," *Biblica* 79 (1998) 381-93.
235. Rudolf Schnackenburg, *The Epistle to the Ephesians,* trans. H. Heron (Edinburgh: T. & T. Clark, 1991).

4:11-16. Verse 11 picks up the gifts mentioned in v. 7. A single Greek sentence (vv. 11-16) links a list of teaching functions in the community (vv. 11-12) with the need for the church to grow to perfection (vv. 13-16). Romans 12:3-8 orders those gifts that might cause division in the community: prophecy, ministry, teaching, exhorting, contributing to charity (ὁ μεταδιδούς *ho metadidous*; NRSV, "the giver"; for this meaning of the verb, see Job 31:17; Prov 11:26; Luke 3:11), serving as a leader (προιστάμενος *proistamenos*, "standing at the head"; with this meaning, cf. 1 Thess 5:12; 1 Tim 5:17),[236] and performing acts of mercy (ὁ ἐλεῶν *ho eleōn*; NRSV, "the compassionate"). Romans associates each task with a requisite virtue. These virtues provide the "measure" by which the performance of members of the community can be evaluated.

Ephesians 4:11-12 begins with a list of such functions, but unlike Rom 12:7-8, the list extends beyond the local church. "Apostle, prophet, evangelist" are clearly external to local churches. Ephesians has twice used "apostles and prophets" in a way that suggests an activity that has already been completed (2:20; 3:5). The term "evangelist" (εὐαγγελιστής *euangelistēs*) appears in only two other places in the NT (Acts 21:8, Philip; 2 Tim 4:5, Timothy). In both cases, the evangelist has been commissioned by the apostles to preach the gospel. Though the term "pastor" (ποιμήν *poimēn*) appears to be a particular designation for Peter (John 21:15-17), 1 Pet 5:1-5 indicates that the term applied to those who served as elders in the local communities of Asia Minor (also Acts 20:28). A pre-Christian example that uses the term "shepherd" for the community's supervisor also appears in an Essene text.[237] Teachers (διδάσκαλοι *didaskaloi*) appear in all the Pauline lists of church offices (Rom 12:7; 1 Cor 12:28). Teaching may refer to basic instruction or to ongoing exhortation (Gal 6:6). Paul can refer to himself as "teacher" (1 Cor 4:17; Col 1:28; 3:16), though "teacher" comes third after apostles and prophets in 1 Cor 12:28. Thus Ephesians begins with those functions connected with the founding of the community and moves on to those of local leaders.[238]

Ephesians treats these activities as service to the body of Christ (as in Rom 12:4-8; 1 Cor 12:12, 27-30). Diverse manifestations of the Spirit in the community are forms of service (so 1 Cor 12:5). Verses 12b-16 describe the purpose of service as equipping and building up the body. Paul used the verb "build up" in arguing that love should govern relationships among members of the church (1 Cor 8:1; 10:23; 14:3-5). Ephesians 2:21 used the noun "structure" (οἰκοδομη *oikodomē*) for the church as a temple being built for the Lord. That building is also spoken of as "growing" (αὔξω *auxō*), an image that this section will connect with both "body" (σῶμα *sōma*) and "love" (ἀγαπη *agapē*) in v. 16.

Although the particular offices refer to those who are in charge of guiding churches after the apostle's death, Ephesians assumes that all Christians are part of the building process (cf. Gal 6:1-6). Maturity involves the community as a whole, and not merely particular individuals. A series of short phrases describes the goal of ministry: unity of faith, knowledge of the Son of God, "perfect man" (εἰς ἄνδρα τέλιον *eis andra telion*; NIV, "mature"; NRSV, "maturity"), measure of the full stature of Christ (v. 13). All of these phrases appear to be equivalent to the "new humanity" created in Christ (Eph 2:15). That expression described unity in concrete terms, Jews and Gentiles joined in a single community. But if the Jewish believer gives up those elements of the law that make him or her Jewish, then the "Jewish" side of the equation loses its significance.[239] Ephesians 4:4-5 included with "one Spirit, one Lord, one God" the terms "one body, one faith" and "one baptism." Presumably the "unity of faith" and "knowledge" depicted as future goals in v. 13 represent the same faith and knowledge that Christians already experience.

If the "unity of knowledge" is both present experience and future goal, then Ephesians is not dependent upon gnostic images of the church as a heavenly aeon. For Gnostics, the gathering of the scattered light from the world of darkness into the heavenly pleroma could be said to complete the deficiency in the heavenly church.[240]

236. Josephus *Antiquities of the Jews* 8.123, sec. 300; Fitzmyer 1993.
237. CD 13:7-11.
238. Schnackenburg, *The Epistle to the Ephesians*, 182.

239. Jack T. Sanders, *Schismatics, Sectarians, Dissidents, Deviants: The First One Hundred Years of Jewish-Christian Relations* (Valley Forge: Trinity Press International, 1993) 200-201.
240. E.g., *Tripartite Tractate* 23, 3-23.

The contrast between maturity and childishness (vv. 14-16) is commonplace in ethical exhortation. Paul uses it to castigate the Corinthians for their divisions (1 Cor 3:1-4). Philo uses "tossed around on the sea" for idolaters whose souls lack the necessary anchor in knowledge of the true God.[241] The problem of "trickery" and "deceitful scheming" that can lead the elect astray adds elements from Jewish apocalyptic to the philosophical picture of those who are morally immature. Essenes had to be on guard against the spirit of deceit.[242] Early Christians also anticipated the emergence of false prophets within their communities. The expression "deceit" for false teachers appears in later writings of the NT (2 Pet 2:18; 3:17; 1 John 4:6; Jude 11; also Acts 20:29-30; 1 Tim 4:1; 2 Tim 3:13). Since the author of Ephesians has read Colossians, he knows that Paul had warned against specific forms of false teaching (Col 2:2-4, 8). Since the word "scheming" (μεθοδεία *methodeia*; NIV, "schemes"; NRSV, "wiles") appears in 6:11 for the devil, the phrase "deceitful scheming" may suggest a demonic source for false teaching.

The concluding phrases in this long sentence shift back to the positive conditions for building up the body of Christ, speech as "the truth in love." Paul used "love" (*agapē*) as the key to communal solidarity (Rom 12:9-10). Love for fellow members was characteristic of the Essene sect.[243] Since Ephesians refers to "speaking truth in love" in contrast to deceit, its concern appears to be speech rather than solidarity. Jealousy and divisive speech show that the Corinthians remain "people of the flesh, as infants in Christ" (1 Cor 3:1 NRSV). Paul's open presentation of the gospel contrasts with the cunning of false teachers (2 Cor 4:2; 6:7). Truth opposes the error of false teaching, and love opposes its deceit.[244]

Verse 16 echoes the exhortation in Col 2:19 to resist false teaching. Ephesians shifts its focus from the head's holding parts of the body together to the body's growth into Christ (as in Eph 1:22-23). All of the parts need to work properly for the body to grow. The verb "knit together" (συμβιβάζω *symbibazō*) appeared in the architectural image of Eph 2:21. The phrase "every ligament . . . as each part is working properly" draws on terms used earlier in the letter: "according to the power [ἐνέργεια *energeia*, 1:19-20; 3:7] in measure [μέτρον *metron*, 4:7, 13] of each part." Though Ephesians has specified the functions of other parts of the body, the term "measure" implies God's gift to each one. Ephesians also uses *energeia* ("power") for God's active power present in the exalted Christ and working through the apostle. Though Ephesians does not make such associations, some interpreters assume that the ligaments are the teachers and "each part" the other members. Consequently, Rudolf Schnackenburg concludes that Ephesians seeks to strengthen the power of the teachers in the community. Their office binds others to Christ.

Paraenesis played an important role in early Christian churches. Both teachers and individuals were expected to engage in such hortatory speech. Concern for the unity of religious and civic communities was also a common topic of deliberative rhetoric. Unlike the use of the "body" metaphor in 1 Corinthians and Romans, Ephesians does not point to a crisis of disunity. Exhortation serves the function of reminding the audience of what has already been true of its experience. Election requires that Christians live a style of life appropriate to that calling. Most of the concrete virtues listed (vv. 2, 14-15) support social cohesion, since they moderate competitive, divisive behavior.

The formula "one faith, one Lord, one baptism, one God" underscores the dilemma of religious pluralism. The phrases indicate that for Ephesians there can be only one true people of God. Those who are not part of the "body of Christ," whether Jews or Gentiles, are not included in salvation. The generalities of such formulae make a surface unity possible. The problems arise when people ask what the practical consequences ought to be. Ephesians does not grapple with situations of communal discord as Paul does in 1 Corinthians or Rom 14:1–15:13. The comments in vv. 11-16 suggest general emphasis on building up the church so that all grow to maturity in faith through sound teaching, speech that reflects love, mutual concern, and support of others. Ephesians does not explain how such activities are parceled out. Who are the shepherds and teachers? How do they relate to those founding figures in the

241. Philo *On the Decalogue* 67.
242. 1QS 3:21-22.
243. 1QS 1:9.
244. Lincoln, *Ephesians*, 276.

common tradition, the apostles, the prophets, and the evangelists? How do the gifts that each member of the community receives serve the common task of building up the body of Christ?

The catalogs of charismata in Rom 12:6-8 and 1 Cor 12:8-11 that have influenced this section of Ephesians provide one possibility for filling out the picture of individual activities within the body of Christ. Other interpreters reach back to the earlier section on the unity of Jew and Gentile (2:14-22). The "one" formula refers to bringing together in a single community, body, and temple building those who were formerly divided. Following medical discussions of the time in which the operation of the body was explained by its being articulated and joined together with the head through nerves, Ephesians can attribute all of the growth in the body to Christ. The special feature of this body for Ephesians is bringing into one the foreign peoples to whom the gospel has been preached.[245]

245. Kōshi Usami, *Somatic Comprehension of Unity: The Church in Ephesus*, AnBib 101 (Rome: Pontifical Biblical Institute, 1983).

REFLECTIONS

Ephesians 4:1 adds to what is otherwise a standard opening for a section of moral exhortation the note that Paul is imprisoned. This reminder directs our attention back to a similar phrase in 3:1 and the reference to Paul's afflictions in 3:13. Perhaps we are even to think that he continues in the unusual kneeling posture of 3:14, as the NRSV's translation "beg" for the Greek *parakal* suggests. However, the verb can have a more positive meaning of encouraging someone; hence the NIV's "urge." We all know the difference between begging or pleading with someone whom we doubt will follow our advice and encouraging someone to continue an effort already well begun. The tone we imagine Paul using makes all the difference to our interpretation of this advice. Since Ephesians shows no evidence of seeking to correct the failures to live out the gospel of a particular community—unlike 1 Corinthians, for instance—let us assume that the author is encouraging Christians in a way of life already well begun. Even the list of basic Christian virtues in 4:2 could reflect habits that the audience is seeking to cultivate.

These virtues have a communal orientation, since they enhance the unity that is the defining characteristic of the Christian community. Ephesians 4:3 makes the transition from the general, other-centered virtues of humility, gentleness, generosity of spirit, and love to unity with a metaphorical prison image. What holds them all in place? Not the bands that hold a bundle together or the fetters that bind Paul, the prisoner. What holds them all together is a bond or fetter of peace.

It is easy to see chains as a reminder of slavery and prison cruelty. But we also live in a society in which any kind of permanent tie to others is treated as optional. Coaches tell kids that they cannot be on teams unless they will show up for practice and games on Sunday morning. People think nothing of ditching a community or church meeting or even a social event if something they would rather do comes along. Hardly evidence of persons who are "making every effort to maintain the unity of the Spirit" (4:3). Ephesians 4:4-6 picks up Paul's image of the church as a single body with one Spirit and adds a string of "one" clauses, concluding with the most important unity of all, that of God operating through all things. Our bond of unity with the church community and its presence to the larger human community should be more important than any of those alternatives that drag us away.

Ephesians 4:7 begins to specify how we are obligated to the church community by speaking of God as benefactor once again. God has distributed gifts to all members of the church so that it can be built up. At our college, the most popular spring break activity is not getting drunk on Florida beaches. It is the volunteer option, spending the week in some poor area of the East Coast, from Maine to North Carolina, building housing, cleaning out old houses, painting houses for the poor, fixing parks for children, and the like. Even students faced with twenty-hour bus rides, rusty cold showers, rats, bats, and garbage come back encouraging their friends to sign up. What did they discover that made such an impact? A spirit binding people together in a common effort to build up the human and church community. Those who have never used tools before discover some gifts they never knew they had. Ephesians 4:11 lists the experts charged with spreading the gospel and caring for the church. The danger is thinking that professionals create the church. Paul originally used the image in 1 Cor 12:14-31 to undercut those who thought their spiritual gifts of speaking in tongues made them superior to others. He insisted on the diversity of gifts required for the one body to function well. Ephesians 4:11-16 is less concrete, but it also moves from church leaders to the body composed of all believers, which has to grow up in love (4:16).

Ephesians adds another note to this practical training in love, concord, humility, generosity, and the like: a concern for the truth. Children are easily tricked, since they lack the knowledge or experience necessary to protect themselves against deceitful persons or false information. Even respected journalists have been conned by what appeared to be reliable information from knowledgeable sources. Scientists say that at least 50 percent of such public information is wrong. People who make some effort to avoid being taken in by false or misleading information seem to lose all critical sense where religion is concerned. They presume that anything someone asserts about his or her religious tradition with sincerity and conviction is religious truth. In that respect, we may be worse off than the post-apostolic generation of Christians whom Ephesians urges toward maturity in understanding of their faith (4:14).[246]

246. P. Berthoud, "Vérité et foi," *La revue réformée* 48 (1997) 49-54.

Ephesians 4:17-32, Two Ways of Life

NIV	NRSV
[17]So I tell you this, and insist on it in the Lord, that you must no longer live as the Gentiles do, in the futility of their thinking. [18]They are darkened in their understanding and separated from the life of God because of the ignorance that is in them due to the hardening of their hearts. [19]Having lost all sensitivity, they have given themselves over to sensuality so as to indulge in every kind of impurity, with a continual lust for more.	17Now this I affirm and insist on in the Lord: you must no longer live as the Gentiles live, in the futility of their minds. [18]They are darkened in their understanding, alienated from the life of God because of their ignorance and hardness of heart. [19]They have lost all sensitivity and have abandoned themselves to licentiousness, greedy to practice every kind of impurity. [20]That is not the way you learned Christ! [21]For surely you have heard about him and were taught in him, as truth is in Jesus. [22]You were taught to put away your former way of life, your old self, corrupt and deluded by its lusts, [23]and to be renewed in the spirit of your minds, [24]and to clothe yourselves with the new self, created according to the likeness of God in true righteousness and holiness.
[20]You, however, did not come to know Christ that way. [21]Surely you heard of him and were taught in him in accordance with the truth that is in Jesus. [22]You were taught, with regard to your former way of life, to put off your old self, which is being corrupted by its deceitful desires; [23]to be made new in the attitude of your minds; [24]and to put on the new self, created to be like God in true righteousness and holiness.	25So then, putting away falsehood, let all of us speak the truth to our neighbors, for we are members of one another. [26]Be angry but do not sin; do not let the sun go down on your anger, [27]and do not make room for the devil. [28]Thieves must give up stealing; rather let them labor and
[25]Therefore each of you must put off falsehood and speak truthfully to his neighbor, for we are all members of one body. [26]"In your anger do not	

NIV

sin"ª: Do not let the sun go down while you are still angry, ²⁷and do not give the devil a foothold. ²⁸He who has been stealing must steal no longer, but must work, doing something useful with his own hands, that he may have something to share with those in need.

²⁹Do not let any unwholesome talk come out of your mouths, but only what is helpful for building others up according to their needs, that it may benefit those who listen. ³⁰And do not grieve the Holy Spirit of God, with whom you were sealed for the day of redemption. ³¹Get rid of all bitterness, rage and anger, brawling and slander, along with every form of malice. ³²Be kind and compassionate to one another, forgiving each other, just as in Christ God forgave you.

ª26 Psalm 4:4

NRSV

work honestly with their own hands, so as to have something to share with the needy. ²⁹Let no evil talk come out of your mouths, but only what is useful for building up,ª as there is need, so that your words may give grace to those who hear. ³⁰And do not grieve the Holy Spirit of God, with which you were marked with a seal for the day of redemption. ³¹Put away from you all bitterness and wrath and anger and wrangling and slander, together with all malice, ³²and be kind to one another, tenderhearted, forgiving one another, as God in Christ has forgiven you.ᵇ

ªOther ancient authorities read *building up faith*   ᵇOther ancient authorities read *us*

COMMENTARY

The call to turn aside from a past way of life occurs in Hellenistic moralists as well as in Christian catechesis. Those who were addressed as "you Gentiles" (2:11) are now encouraged to separate themselves from the immorality of the Gentiles (4:17; cf. 1 Pet 2:12). Rhetorically, this introduction creates a boundary between the readers and the larger world.[247] The section divides into two parts: (a) the vices typical of the outsiders (vv. 17-24) and (b) a catalog of virtues (vv. 25-32) that characterize the "new self" (v. 24). This division reflects a common theme in paraenesis: description of the "two ways," virtue and vice. In Essene writings, the ways of the sons of light (members of the sect) are contrasted with those of the sons of darkness.[248]

Ephesians continues to use "we" for the author and the audience. Address to the audience as "you" returns when the list of injunctions is expanded in vv. 29-32. The genre of hortatory discourse (instruction by someone who exemplifies the teaching given) makes the "you" address more appropriate than the inclusive "we." Verses 17-24 establish the two groups, "alienated from the life of God" and "renewed in . . . your minds." Verses 25-32 contain a series of imperatives, or moral *sententiae*. Verse 25 is the topic sentence that refers to one negative action, "putting away," and one positive one, "speak truth." Verses 26-31 describe what is to be put away, while v. 32 turns to positive relationships among Christians. This section has close relationships to Rom 1:21, 24 and Col 3:5-10 as *Figs.* 9 and 10 indicate.

247. Andrew T. Lincoln, *Ephesians*, WBC 42 (Dallas: Word, 1990).
248. 1QS 4:2-17.

Figure 9: Eph 4:17-19 and Rom 1:21, 24

Item	Ephesians	Romans
non-Jews lack effective knowledge of God: mind	**4:17c** in emptiness (ματαιότης *mataiotēs*) of their minds	**1:21** they have been given over to worthlessness (ἐματαιώθησαν *emataiōthēsan*) in their thoughts
non-Jews lack effective knowledge of God: darkened intelligence	**4:18a** being darkened in understanding	**1:21** their foolish heart was darkened
consequences of idolatry: impurity	4:19 they handed themselves over to the practice of every impurity	**1:24** God handed them over to impurity

Ephesians uses a graphic description of the Gentile way of life to encourage readers to remain separated from their former conduct. Colossians provides images for both the old way of life and the new human beings that Christians have become:

Figure 10: Eph 4:17-24 and Col 3:5-10

Item	Ephesians	Colossians
not like the Gentiles	**4:17** you no longer walk as the Gentiles walk	**3:7** in which you also once walked
vices: impurity, greediness	**4:19** in practice of every impurity in greediness	**3:5** sexual immorality, impurity, passion, evil desire, and greediness (which is idolatry)
put off old human being	**422a** put off from yourselves the old human being according to the former way of life	**3:8** now you put off . . . **3:9** having taken off the old human being with the deeds . . .
reject passions of old human being	**4:22b** corrupted according to the passions of error	See vices in **3:5**
renew the intellect	**4:23** be renewed in the spirit of your mind	**3:10** renewed in knowledge
put on the new human being	**4:24** and put on the new human being	**3:10** and having put on the new
the new creation	**4:24** created according to God	**3:10** according to the image of the one who created him

Ephesians has not followed the order in Colossians and has introduced stylistic variants in phrasing. Verses 20-21 are a rhetorical appeal to the audience. They follow an established practice in paraenesis, invoking prior instruction. The variations in describing the new creation may have a theological motivation. Since v. 24 ends with a reference to the moral categories of righteousness and holiness, Ephesians is not thinking of the elect as created in God's image but as predestined to a way of life.

The second section (vv. 25-32) continues to echo Col 3:8-12. Both are employing a standard form of ethical teaching—lists of vices to be avoided and virtues to be practiced. This form of teaching is so common in antiquity that the vices in such a list should not be culled for evidence about the community. A number of the items in this section will reappear in what follows: (a) not conducting oneself like the Gentiles (4:25–5:2; 5:3-14, 15-20); (b) darkness (v. 18; 5:8, 11; 6:12); (c) error (v. 18; 5:6); (d) impurity and greed (v. 19; 5:3, 5); and (e) righteousness (v. 24; 5:9; 6:14).

4:17-24. Ephesians reminds the audience to reject the Gentile way of life. The word "Gentiles" (τὰ ἔθνη ta ethnē) was previously used for Christians of Gentile origins in contrast to Jewish Christians (2:11; 3:1). Now it designates "pagans," non-Christian Gentiles. Other phrases suggest baptismal conversion: "testify in the Lord" (v. 17a), being "unclothed" and "clothed" (vv. 22, 24).[249] The rest of the sentence uses characteristic terms for Gentile ignorance of God (e.g., Wis 12-15; 18:10-19).[250] Romans 1:19-21 employs similar language. Having abandoned knowledge of the creator, the Gentiles are locked in immorality and worship of false gods. Ephesians uses two expressions that refer to the mind: "futility of mind" and "darkened understanding." The LXX uses "understanding" interchangeably with "heart." In the OT the "heart" (לֵב lēb) is the seat of understanding. Ephesians has drawn its terminology from Rom 1:21, "they became futile in their thinking" and "their senseless minds [καρδία kardia "hearts"] were darkened." Ephesians has expanded the series to involve two forms of mental darkness followed by "hardness of heart" (v. 18). The OT frequently refers to disobedient Israel as hard hearted (Ps 95:8; Isa 6:10; 63:17; Jer 7:26; 17:23).

These phrases fill out the earlier reference to

non-Christians as "those who are disobedient" (2:2). Such language seeks to gain an emotional response, not to provide information. All three descriptions are consequences of being separated from the "life of God" (4:18). This expression does not answer the question of whether any trace of God's life remains with those who do not know the creator. Rather, being alienated from the "life of God" describes those who are not participants in the covenant (Eph 2:12). Unfaithful Israelites can also be described with such language as Essene examples indicate, "for futile are all those who do not know the covenant. And all those who scorn his [God's] word he shall cause to vanish from the world."[251]

The concluding clause presents typical examples of pagan vice (v. 19; cf. Rom 1:24). The cover term "impurity" (ἀκαθαρσία akatharsia) appears in Essene material as the contrary to the holiness that comes from joining the new covenant community.[252] Unlike Rom 1:24, in which God hands the Gentiles over to immorality, Ephesians makes the Gentiles responsible for handing themselves over to vice. The Greek word that describes their having become callous (ἀπηλγηκότες apēlgēkotes) occurs only here in the New Testament and is not widely used elsewhere. Ephesians employs a few standard vices as illustrations—disordered sexual passions, greed, and uncleanness. Their only purpose is to awaken revulsion for the life that believers have left behind.

Verses 20-21 repeat the appeal to follow prior instruction with the unusual phrase "you learned Christ" (ἐμάθετε τὸν Χριστόν emathete ton Christon). For some interpreters, the continuation "as truth is in Jesus" suggests an audience familiar with traditions about the teaching of Jesus.[253] Others think Ephesians is combating speculation that separated the heavenly revealer from the earthly Jesus.[254] The text does not explain what is meant by the cryptic expression, though prior catechesis must be implied.[255]

Verses 22-24 are based on Col 3:8-10. They combine two motifs used for conversion: changing

---

249. Chantel Bouttier, *L'Epître de Saint Paul aux Ephésiens,* Commentaire du Nouveau Testament, 2nd série Ixb (Geneva: Labor et Fides, 1991); Schnackenburg, *The Epistle to the Ephesians.*
250. *Letter of Aristeas* 140; 277; *Sib. Or.* 3.220-235.

251. 1QS 5:19-20.
252. 1QS 5:20-21.
253. So Schnackenburg, *The Epistle to the Ephesians* 199.
254. So Heinrich Schlier, *Der Brief an die Epheser* (Dusseldorf: Patmos, 1957) 213.
255. Joachim Gnilka, *Der Epheserbrief,* HTKNT (Freiburg: Herder & Herder, 1980) 228.

clothing (putting off vice, putting on Christ, Rom 13:12, 14; 1 Thess 5:8) and transformation from the old human being (Rom 6:6) into the new (Gal 3:27; Col 3:10). Putting off vices and putting on virtues are commonplace in ethical exhortation.[256] The difficulty with reading the old and the new "man" as Adam and Christ (Rom 5:12-21)[257] is that Paul always defers the believer's conformity to the image of Christ as spiritual Adam to the future resurrection (1 Cor 15:22-23, 53-54; Phil 3:21).

The general exhortation to "be renewed in the spirit of your minds" (v. 23) indicates the end of the intellectual deficiencies of pagan reasoning. The paraenesis in Romans begins with a similar expression: "Be transformed by the renewing of your minds" (Rom 12:2 NRSV). Ephesians has radicalized the inherited images by describing the believer as completely re-created "according to God" (see v. 24).[258] Ephesians omits the term "image" (εἰκών *eikōn*) from Col 3:10. Most interpreters assume that the Greek "according to God" (κατὰ θεόν *kata Theon*) means "according to the likeness of God" (so NRSV). However, Ephesians has shown little interest in the creation speculation of Colossians. The phrase "according to God" is complemented by the virtues that describe God's elect, "righteousness and holiness."[259] It anticipates the phrase in 5:1, "be imitators of God," and is oriented toward the present behavior of believers.[260] The Essene writings also employ the contrast between "deceit" and "truth" to distinguish those who belong to the community from outsiders.[261]

4:25-32. Ephesians shifts to a series of short exhortations, *sententiae*, that describe vices to be avoided and virtues to be cultivated. Colossians 3:8-9, 12-13 provides the core for these verses. Each exhortation describes what is to be done and provides a reason for such conduct. Truthful speech is to replace lying because of the corporate character of Christian life, since all are "members of one another" (v. 25; 4:12, 16; Rom 12:4-5). Verse 15 treated "speaking the truth in love" as key to building up the body of Christ. The connection between anger and work of the devil (v. 27) echoes Gen 4:7 (and 6:11).[262] The topic of anger occurs in Greco-Roman moralists, in the Sermon on the Mount (Matt 5:21-22), and in Essene writings.[263] *Testament of Dan* 5:1-2 provides the virtue of truth-telling with a motive clause that includes God's presence to the community and driving Beliar away.

The reference to the reformed thief (v. 28) has no parallel in Colossians but is also traditional (see 1 Cor 6:10; 1 Pet 4:15). The alternative in the second clause, laboring with one's hands, was established by Paul's own example (1 Thess 4:11; 2:9; as part of the apostolic hardship list, see 1 Cor 4:12; against the disorderly who take advantage of communal charity, see 2 Thess 3:6-11). Ephesians has generalized the advice. The motive clause points toward a communal concern, sharing what is gained by such labor with those in need. Exhortations to share appear elsewhere without the reference to earning one's own living (see Rom 12:13; 2 Cor 9:6-12). Such examples might suggest that the apostle merely requires those Christians who are wealthy enough to include fellow Christians among those who receive their benefactions (see 1 Tim 6:17-19).

The need to engage in manual work (v. 28), indicated in the catalogs of Paul's hardships by the phrases "in toil and hardship" (2 Cor 11:27) or "the work of our own hands" (1 Cor 4:12); "working for a living" (1 Cor 9:6); and "worked night and day" (1 Thess 2:9), describes the situation of the majority of believers (1 Cor 1:26). They are to provide for themselves and others rather than seek to live off the largess of wealthy patrons (1 Thess 4:11-12; 2 Thess 3:6-13). Some interpreters suggest that the original warning against stealing also spoke to particular social issues.[264] Slaves or other servants were commonly accused of theft (e.g., Titus 2:10; Phlm 18). Thus this advice ensures the respectable behavior of Christians who are not among the elite and whose affiliation with the new religious movement might render them suspect.

256. On putting off vices, see *Letter of Aristeas* 122; Lucian *Dialogues on Death* 10.8.9. On putting on virtues, see Philo *On the Confusion of Tongues* 31.

257. So Markus Barth, *Ephesians*, 2 vols., AB 34-34A (Garden City, N.Y.: Doubleday, 1974).

258. Bouttier, *L'Epître de Saint Paul aux Ephésiens*, 211; Gnilka, *Der Epheserbrief*, 229.

259. Rudolf Schnackenburg, *The Epistle to the Ephesians*, trans. H. Heron (Edinburgh: T. & T. Clark, 1991) 201.

260. Andrew T. Lincoln, *Ephesians*, WBC 42 (Dallas: Word, 1990). 287

261. 1QS 4:2–5:10.

262. Bouttier, *L'Epître de Saint Paul aux Ephésiens*.

263. Plutarch *On Controlling Anger* 452E-464D. See CD 7:2-3.

264. Joachim Gnilka, *Der Epheserbrief*, HTKNT (Freiburg: Herder & Herder, 1980) 271.

Verse 29 returns to the opening theme. Concern for what one says, here expressed by the semitism "come out of your mouths," is commonplace in Wisdom literature (see Prov 10:31-32; 12:17-19; Sir 5:10-14; 18:15-19). The Essenes required their members to control speech. After warnings against angry speech and lying, the *Rule of the Community* turns to misuse of communal property, retaliation, and then negligent speech.[265] Penalties are attached to trivial speech and interrupting one's fellows. The context for this speech among the Essenes is a communal assembly for instruction. Ephesians will refer to assemblies for worship later (5:19). The concern for speech aimed at the religious edification of the hearer suggests conversation among fellow believers, not interaction with outsiders.

The reference to the Holy Spirit (v. 30) interrupts the series of concrete examples. Some commentators treat "and do not grieve the Holy Spirit of God" as a motive clause parallel to "do not make room for the devil" (v. 27) and "as God in Christ has forgiven you" (v. 32).[266] As such, it reinforces the exhortation in v. 29. The phrase "grieve the Holy Spirit" is unusual, though 1 Thess 5:18 speaks of quenching the Holy Spirit in the context of communal prophecy. Essene texts refer to "defiling" the Holy Spirit that one has received from God.[267] Neglecting the legal and moral precepts of the sect would be the occasion for such defilement. The phrase itself resembles the prophetic word in Isa 63:10, "They rebelled and grieved his holy spirit" (NRSV).

Ephesians indicates that the Spirit was conveyed in a ritual of "sealing." Since Eph 4:5 referred to "one baptism," the rite in question was probably baptism. The final phrase of v. 30, "for the day of redemption," may also be traditional. It introduces a rare note of future salvation into the letter. This passage highlights the effect of the Spirit in the community. Believers are to feel a particular concern for their behavior because it affects the holiness of the community.[268]

Another effect of incorporation into the Christian community, forgiveness (χαρίζομαι *charizomai*, v. 32), serves as the final motivating clause

in this section. Verse 31 opens with a list of vices that Christians will avoid (bitterness, wrath, anger, wrangling, slander; see Col 3:5, 8). These vices all refer back to anger (ὀργίζομαι *orgizomai*, v. 26) and the behavior it causes. Concern to rise above anger and its manifestations forms a common element in both Greco-Roman and Jewish exhortation. The section concludes with communal love and harmony, virtues that are the opposite of the divisions caused by anger (v. 32; cf. Gal 5:22; Col 3:12-13). God's forgiveness as the motive for Christian forgiveness appears in Col 3:13 (as well as the Lord's prayer; see Matt 6:14).

Though composed of shorter exhortations, this section can be seen as the continuation of the last section. That section concluded with the metaphor of the body of Christ joined together and growing to maturity through love (vv. 15-16). The primary focus of both the virtues and the vices developed in this section can be said to be communal harmony. The audience must remain committed to a way of life that is unlike their previous life as "pagans," a life that accepted greed, sexual immorality, and other evils. Of course, the writer of Ephesians and its readers know that there were philosopher-preachers who sought to turn people away from their irrational accommodation to passions that swamp rational human behavior. True to its Jewish heritage, however, Ephesians assumes that those who are ignorant of the true God will not be capable of any consistent moral insight or activity.

Ephesians expresses an understanding of Christian life that runs throughout the Pauline tradition. Christians have been transformed in Christ. The Spirit of God works in the community of believers to effect a new way of life. At the same time, Christians must be actively engaged in strengthening what they already are. Conversion, baptism, putting off the old and putting on the new human being, and being sealed with the Spirit and freed from sin are not past events whose effects remain, as though the temple of God were a monumental piece of architecture. Rather, they have introduced believers into a new reality, the body of Christ, which is still in the process of growing into its head. Like the body, the development of the whole depends upon, and contributes to, the well-being of individual members.

The reference to the "day of redemption" re-

---

265. 1QS 7:2-11.
266. Gordon D. Fee, *God's Empowering Presence: The Holy Spirit in the Letters of Paul* (Peabody, Mass.: Hendrickson, 1994) 713f.
267. CD 5:11-12.
268. Schnackenburg, *The Epistle to the Ephesians*, 209.

minds the audience that human conduct will be subject to divine judgment. However, the primary emphasis of the epistle remains the present life of the community. Relations with others are central to the concrete examples of the new Christian way of life. False speech, anger, theft, bitterness, slander, and the like destroy relationships among human beings. The many faces of anger indicate that ethical maturity is fairly rare. Believers would insist that only God's Spirit can transform us from the old way of life to the new.

Ephesians also recognizes that believers must constantly turn away from sinful behavior. They do not claim to be completely free of passions like the Stoic sage. When anger occurs, it must be put away and not harbored (v. 26). Hanging on to anger or other resentments provides opportunity for the devil. As we have seen from the Essene writings, "the devil" actively leads believers away from God. Though it is easy to think that many of the virtues listed in this section of Ephesians are "for saints only," this section does not support such an approach. All Christians are striving to-ward the holiness and perfection that are given by the Spirit.

The communal emphasis in Ephesians distinguishes its Jewish heritage from treatment of the same themes by pagan moralists. Virtues are not the result of individual reason and its ability to order human life. Rather, God calls together a community of persons to live in holiness and justice. The earlier section of the letter spoke of the Christian community in which Christians—both Jews and Gentiles—become one as the new human being (2:15). This creation was also predestined to walk in good works (2:10). The ethical section of the letter depicts those works. Their focus on the needs of others, as well as on harmonious relationships, indicates how the communal body grows into Christ. Christian community requires face-to-face involvement with others. The forms of speech being recommended are essential to the maturing of the body of Christ, words to support faith, expressions of love, and forgiveness.

REFLECTIONS

Most of the ethical exhortation in this section is standard fare, as the exegesis demonstrates. The author opens with a characteristically Jewish view of Gentile immorality. Earlier in the letter the Gentile otherness of the addressees formed a central element in the rhetorical affirmations of unity in Christ (2:11). Now those baptized into Christ are encouraged to separate themselves from the immorality of that Gentile past. What does the dualism of ethical conversion mean to contemporary Christians? For some, getting rid of a deluded way of thinking and a life-style marred by lust and greed describes their experience of coming to Christ. We all know that whenever we decide to make a major life change, perhaps to adopt new habits of diet and exercise or emotional and spiritual health, the transition takes time and discipline. Reminders or partners in improvement do not hurt either. Some people become so panicked about their exercise routine that they do not dare take a day or two off even when they need to rest a minor injury. Such compulsion usually spells trouble. Other people make changes that are not enough to make a difference and then announce, "It isn't working." Nutritionists find that many people consume more calories in low fat foods than they did before.

A pre-school teacher tells the story of the four year old who was sent to apologize to a child he had hit on the playground. Several minutes later, he struck again. When the teacher called him over, the boy explained, "That's okay. I'll apologize to him later." A major misunderstanding! It took the teacher quite a while to persuade him that hitting another child was never okay. That was not the point of apologizing.

When a pre-school child comes up with a skewed view of the moral universe, teachers and care-takers wonder what the child sees going on at home. We have all overheard the pre-school set solemnly imitating something we say or do, or recognized that the presence of the car-seat witness means a major change in driving habits. The difficulty with the dualism of old and new self is not that we lack old-self vices, bad habits, or lack of charity to get rid of. It is the separation between ourselves and others that the author seems to call for. We have friends and even family members who belong to different religious traditions or who reject all religion. We consider some of them good persons and others "bad apples," but the list does not fall along neat religious lines.

How do we deal with persons whose moral views and conduct we consider wrong? Ephesians 4:20-23 reminds us that we have not been taught to approve everything in the name of charity. When the kids start school, after-school debriefing about who said and did what becomes a major necessity—how to handle another child's misbehavior; when to run to the teacher and when to handle it themselves. In some inner-city classrooms where children go home to violent or disordered situations, debriefing in a morning circle helps the kids clear the emotional air so they can learn. Ephesians does not solve all the dilemmas that arise even on the school playground, but the collection of moral precepts focuses our attention on a key element: truthful speech.

Most of the items in the collection deal with aspects of speech and its impact on human relationships. We struggle constantly over definitions of "free speech," "hate speech" and the like. What is Christian speech? This passage gives us a list of things that it is not. No anger, quarreling, bitterness, ruining the reputation of another, lying, deceit. Christian speech is truthful, helpful, positive, builds up, is kind, has words of forgiveness—a much bigger order than avoiding language about other drivers that one does not wish to hear echoed from the car seat. We have begun to gain public agreement that women and minorities are not required to put up with verbal attacks or harassment in the workplace. Perhaps Christians could contribute to cleaning the verbal air. Christian speech does not mean verbally assaulting others with our religion at every turn. It does mean a higher standard of verbal interaction with others than many of us practice. And perhaps along with that focus on speech should go listening. A wise pastor with a reputation as a great listener once shared his secret. "After the initial greeting," he said, "I never make any statement until I have asked at least three questions and heard the answers."

Tucked into the sayings on anger and speech, we find an exhortation concerning work (4:28). Paul frequently encouraged congregations to follow his example of working at a trade. The alternatives for people who did not belong to the wealthy aristocracy were either criminal activity or living off wealthy patrons. The disdain for the worker in antiquity was such that those philosophers and intellectuals who were not aristocrats generally lived off such benefactors. Paul himself had to defend his way of life against criticism from wealthy Corinthian Christians who thought manual labor degrading to the apostle (1 Cor 9:3-27; 2 Cor 11:7-11). We live in a society where work has been undergoing global changes, not all of them beneficial to us as individuals or as a human community. We live in a culture in which what we do is more likely to define what people think of us as persons than what our family roots are.

Christian theology needs to catch up in the area of work. Ephesians provides two bits of advice that remain significant because they are so general: (a) Do not steal, and (b) the paycheck is not all yours; some has to be given away. Those who say, "I never steal," need to look around their workplace. We may not engage in it, but all sorts of theft goes on. Public officials steal from all of us by abusing privileges meant to help them serve others; workers, both blue and white collar, make off with materials that belong to the company; others—including teachers and ministers—steal by not giving the time and attention to their jobs that they should. We all know the demoralizing effect that working in such an environment has on us. The metaphor of our being connected to one another as though we were all parts of one body applies to that community as well.

Pope John Paul II's encyclical *Laborem exercens* (1981) called upon Roman Catholics to engage in serious Christian reflection about the nature of work. On the one hand, work is a spiritual necessity. Our identity as persons is bound up with what we create in working. On the other hand, social and economic systems can generate structures of injustice and inhuman working conditions that destroy human persons.[269] As Christians we need to continually examine the intersection between work and our ethical values.

269. For a discussion of the encyclical and its impact, see Gregory Baum, "Laborem Exercens," in *New Dictionary of Catholic Social Thought,* ed. Judith A. Dwyer (Collegeville, Minn.: Liturgical Press, 1994) 527-35.

Ephesians 5:1-14, Live as Children of Light

NIV

5 Be imitators of God, therefore, as dearly loved children [2]and live a life of love, just as Christ loved us and gave himself up for us as a fragrant offering and sacrifice to God.

[3]But among you there must not be even a hint of sexual immorality, or of any kind of impurity, or of greed, because these are improper for God's holy people. [4]Nor should there be obscenity, foolish talk or coarse joking, which are out of place, but rather thanksgiving. [5]For of this you can be sure: No immoral, impure or greedy person—such a man is an idolater—has any inheritance in the kingdom of Christ and of God.[a] [6]Let no one deceive you with empty words, for because of such things God's wrath comes on those who are disobedient. [7]Therefore do not be partners with them.

[8]For you were once darkness, but now you are light in the Lord. Live as children of light [9](for the fruit of the light consists in all goodness, righteousness and truth) [10]and find out what pleases the Lord. [11]Have nothing to do with the fruitless deeds of darkness, but rather expose them. [12]For it is shameful even to mention what the disobedient do in secret. [13]But everything exposed by the light becomes visible, [14]for it is light that makes everything visible. This is why it is said:

"Wake up, O sleeper,
  rise from the dead,
and Christ will shine on you."

a5 Or *kingdom of the Christ and God*

NRSV

5 [1]Therefore be imitators of God, as beloved children, [2]and live in love, as Christ loved us[a] and gave himself up for us, a fragrant offering and sacrifice to God.

[3]But fornication and impurity of any kind, or greed, must not even be mentioned among you, as is proper among saints. [4]Entirely out of place is obscene, silly, and vulgar talk; but instead, let there be thanksgiving. [5]Be sure of this, that no fornicator or impure person, or one who is greedy (that is, an idolater), has any inheritance in the kingdom of Christ and of God.

[6]Let no one deceive you with empty words, for because of these things the wrath of God comes on those who are disobedient. [7]Therefore do not be associated with them. [8]For once you were darkness, but now in the Lord you are light. Live as children of light— [9]for the fruit of the light is found in all that is good and right and true. [10]Try to find out what is pleasing to the Lord. [11]Take no part in the unfruitful works of darkness, but instead expose them. [12]For it is shameful even to mention what such people do secretly; [13]but everything exposed by the light becomes visible, [14]for everything that becomes visible is light. Therefore it says,

"Sleeper, awake!
  Rise from the dead,
  and Christ will shine on you."

a Other ancient authorities read *you*

COMMENTARY

References to God and Christ link 5:1-2 with 4:32. A list of vices follows (vv. 3-5). The warning against being deceived contrasts "those who are disobedient" (v. 6) with "children of light" (v. 8).

The section ends with a liturgical fragment celebrating Christ as light (v. 14). Some interpreters treat vv. 1-2 as the conclusion of the previous section. Others treat all of vv. 1-5 as part of the previous section, beginning a major section with "let no one deceive you" (v. 6) and continuing through v. 21. Lists of vices, however, do not typically open sections of paraenesis. Therefore, 5:1-2 must introduce the list.[270] The *UBSGNT* avoids that difficulty by treating 5:1-5 as the conclusion to a section that begins at 4:25. Their second division picks up the parallelism between v. 6, "let no one deceive you," and v. 15, "be careful then how you live." Since vv. 15-21 introduce a new image, the wise and the foolish, it is preferable to treat them separately as the transition between the general exhortation and the household code of 5:22–6:9.

Ephesians 5:3-8 draws on Col 3:5-8, as the following chart indicates:

270. Gnilka, *Der Epheserbrief,* 242.

Figure 11: Eph 5:3-8 and Col 3:5-8

Item	Ephesians	Colossians
vices not even named among Christians	**5:3** sexual immorality and all impurity or greed	**3:5** sexual immorality, impurity . . . and greed
vices of speech to be replaced with thanksgiving	**5:4** indecency and foolish talk or vulgar talk	**3:8** indecent speech
those who have no inheritance in the kingdom	**5:5** every evil or impure or greedy person who is an idolater	**3:5** and the greed (which is idolatry)
God's judgment falls on the wicked	**5:6** for because of these things the wrath of God comes	**3:6** through which the wrath of God comes
contrast past with present	**5:8** once . . . but now	**3:7-8** once . . . and now

---

The vices are arranged in groups of three. They pick up themes from the previous section: impurity and greed (4:19); immorality as a consequence of idolatry (4:18); unguarded, degenerate speech (4:29); and divine judgment (4:30).

Verses 6-14 urge separation from the ways of darkness. These verses echo some of the dualistic language found in the Essene texts and conclude with a liturgical fragment (v. 14) that provides a christological basis for the light imagery.[271]

5:1-5. The graciousness of God (4:32) serves as the motivation for an appeal to be "imitators of God" (μιμηταὶ τοῦ θεου *mimētai tou Theou*). Encouragement to find and imitate a model was a prominent feature of ancient paraenesis, "Nay, if you will but recall also your father's principles, you will have from your own house a noble illustration of what I am telling you . . . after

271. So Lincoln, *Ephesians.*

whom you should pattern your life . . . regarding his conduct as your law, and striving to imitate and emulate your father's virtue."[272] Since the model indicates both what sort of person the young should aspire to be and what they should avoid, advice is typically given in an antithetical form, "not . . . but. . . ."

Paul uses this imitation pattern regularly. Christians may be encouraged to imitate other churches (1 Thess 2:14) or Christ (1 Thess 1:6). However, his most common usage follows the philosophic example of the child imitating a parent. Thus Paul underlines the "father in Christ"/"child" relationship between himself and those churches he founded (1 Cor 4:14; 11:1; Phil 3:17; 1 Thess 1:6). The phrase "as beloved children" in v. 1*b*

272. See Abraham J. Malherbe, "Hellenistic Moralists and the New Testament," in *Aufstieg und Niedergang der römischen Welt* II 26/1, ed. Wolfgang Haase (Berlin: DeGruyter, 1992) 282-83. For Jewish examples, see *T.Benj.* 3.1; 4.1.

recalls this pattern. Christians routinely refer to themselves as children of God (Rom 5:5; Gal 4:5-6; 8:15; Phil 2:15; "destined for adoption," Eph 1:5). However, the injunction to imitate God does not appear elsewhere in the NT. Philo does, however, speak of imitating God in the context of those who have power to rule others. They ought to copy God's beneficence: "The best is to use all their energies to assist people and not to injure them; for this is to act in imitation of God, since he also has the power to do either good or evil, but his inclination causes him only to do good. And the creation and arrangement of the world shows this."[273]

Ephesians is not concerned with exercising power over others. Ephesians 4:24 referred to the new human being as "created according to the likeness of God in true righteousness and holiness." This expression develops the motif of the Christian as a new creation in God's image. Therefore, one would expect some account of the virtues that characterize God to follow. The expression "live in love" (περιπατεῖτε ἐν ἀγάπη *peripateite en agapē*, v. 2a) meets that requirement. God's love was introduced in the opening eulogy as the cause of election to holiness (1:4). "Love toward all the saints" described the audience in the epistolary thanksgiving (1:15; 4:2, 15-16). God's love is expressed in extending salvation to those separated from God by sin (2:4). The Christian's grounding in love is formed by knowledge of the love of Christ (3:17-19). The general exhortation to love in 5:2 continues with an illustrative clause, "as Christ loved us" (v. 2b). Christ's death as an acceptable self-offering to God provides the concrete example of that love (v. 2c). Ephesians 1:7 uses Christ's death as sin-offering to illustrate the extraordinary graciousness of God in bringing about salvation. The blood of the cross abolished the wall of separation between Jew and Gentile (2:13). This passage uses established formulae to highlight the self-offering in Christ's death (Gal 1:4; 2:20). A more concrete application of the exemplary love of Christ for the community of the faithful occurs when Ephesians applies the image to the traditional motif of the relationship between husbands and wives in 5:25-27.

There is a difference in orientation between the Ephesians vice list (vv. 3-5) and that in Col 3:5-8. Colossians describes the vices as being put to death by conversion. In Ephesians, the vice list describes pagan outsiders (4:17). This passage calls Christians to separate themselves from others in their environment. The term "fornication" (πορ-νεία *porneia*) includes a variety of illicit activities, including adultery and prostitution (Sir 23:16, 27; Philo *On Joseph* 43-44; *T. Reub.* 1.6; 2.1; 3.3; *T. Iss.* 7.2; 1 Thess 4:3; 1 Cor 6:12-20). Fornication and impurity (ἀκαθαρσία *akatharsia*) often appear together in vice lists (Gal 5:19; 2 Cor 12:21; Col 3:5; 1QS 4:10). Since the other two sins in the list refer to sexual activities, some scholars suggest that "greed" should be understood as unrestrained sexual greed, such as the violation of the command against coveting the neighbor's wife.[274] Ephesians is not merely warning against such behavior (cf. 1 Thess 4:3-8). Rather, Christians are not even to speak of such vices. The conclusion, "as is proper among saints," might be trading on the semantic ambiguity of the term "saints" (ἅγιοι *hagioi*). If translated "holy ones," the expression can refer to "the angels." This dual meaning provides the logical force behind the phrase. Such vices would not belong to speech among the angels.

The second triad includes two clear examples of censured speech: foolish talk and vulgar talk.[275] The Greek word εὐτραπελία (*eutrapelia*, "vulgar talk") has a more positive meaning in common usage than it does in this triad. Usually it refers to "witty" or clever speech.[276] The context in Ephesians indicates that the author has one of the Aristotelian excesses in mind: vulgar or obscene speech. This use of the word may reflect a cultural sense that the proper bearing of a wise person requires seriousness in speech. Persons who are facile with words are less appropriate models than those whose lives exemplify the words they utter: "Let us choose . . . not men who pour forth their words with the greatest glibness, turning out commonplaces . . . but men who teach us by their

---

273. Philo *On the Special Laws* 4.34, 186-187.

274. *T. Levi* 14.5-6; *T. Jud.* 18.2; 1QS 4:9-10.

275. Some scholars assume that "vulgar talk" does not refer to speech in general but to ritualized vulgarity that is connected with celebration of mystery cults in antiquity. See Heinrich Schlier, *Der Brief an die Epheser* (Dusseldorf: Patmos, 1957) 239; Larry J. Kreitzer, " 'Crude Language' and 'Shameful Things Done in Secret' (Ephesians 5:4, 12): Allusions to the Cult of Demeter/Cybele in Hierapolis?" *JSNT* 71 (1998) 51-77. Against such proposals see Lincoln, *Ephesians*, 330.

276. See Aristotle *Nichomachean Ethics* 4.8, 1128a.

lives, men who tell us what we ought to do and then prove it by their practice."[277] Or the term may reflect the sectarian emphasis on disciplined speech that one observes in the Essene documents, "and whoever giggles inanely causing his voice to be heard shall be sentenced."[278] The speech of the Essene sectary avoids all vices, "From my mouth no vulgarity shall be heard or wicked deceptions. . . . I shall remove from my lips worthless words."[279]

Prohibited forms of speech are to be replaced by exhortation or thanksgiving. The philosopher exhorts others to virtue. The Essene turns speech to piety and the saving deeds of God: "With hymns shall I open my mouth and my tongue will ever number the just acts of God."[280] The thanksgiving proposed in Eph 5:4*b* fits this pattern. Ephesians 1:3-14 provided a concrete example of the type of speech the author has in mind. Ephesians 5:18-20 returns to the topic of communal speech in prayer and praise of God. Thanksgiving is central to the Christian life and prayer elsewhere in Paul's writings (2 Cor 4:15; Phil 4:6; 1 Thess 5:18).

The conclusion also has parallels in the Essene writings. Though the phrase "kingdom of God" is peculiarly Christian (on exclusion from the kingdom, see 1 Cor 6:9-10; 15:50; Gal 5:21), the "inheritance" terminology belongs to the language of Jewish piety. The wicked do not belong to God's covenant, "all those not numbered in his covenant will be segregated, they and all that belongs to them . . . all those who scorn his word, he shall cause to vanish from the world."[281] The righteous receive an inheritance that unites them with the angelic hosts ("sons of the heavens"), "to those whom God has selected he has given them [= righteousness, knowledge of God, and so forth] as an everlasting possession; until they inherit them in the lot of the holy ones. He unites their assembly to the sons of the heavens."[282]

The vices listed are typical examples of wickedness, sexual immorality, impurity, greed, and idolatry (see Wis 14:12; *T. Jud.* 19.1; 23.1; Philo

On the Special Laws 1.23.25). Paul uses these vices in a longer list of those who *will not inherit* the kingdom (1 Cor 6:9-10). Ephesians employs the present tense "has any inheritance in" instead of the future. The Essene examples show that Jews could speak of both present and future participation in the inheritance of the elect.

The vice triad in v. 5 parallels the list in v. 3.[283] The unusual dual genitive in "kingdom of Christ and of God" recalls the references to God and then Christ in vv. 1-2. Verse 5 opens with a peculiar phrase, the second-person plural of the verb "to know" (ἴστε *iste*), followed by the participle γινώσκοντες (*ginōskontes*). The form *iste* may be either indicative or imperative. Most translations opt for the imperative and suggest that the additional participle reflects a semiticizing Hebrew infinitive absolute, hence the translation "be sure of this" (NRSV). However, some scholars treat the finite verb as an indicative that refers back to vv. 3-4, "for this you know." In this case, the participle would refer to what follows in v. 5, and could be translated "recognizing that." This reading makes the general orientation of the paraenesis in this section clearer. The author is not correcting believers who lack holiness that they ought to have but is reinforcing an established Christian way of life.

5:6-14. Ephesians insists on separation between "children of light" and "those who are disobedient." This dualism is characteristic of the Essene writings that have provided parallels for much of the imagery in Ephesians. The Essene texts also show a concern to avoid being deceived. They describe the agent of deceit in mythological terms as the "angel of darkness." The Prince of Lights guides the sectaries, "In the hand of the Prince of Lights is dominion over all the sons of justice; they walk on paths of light. And in the hand of the Angel of Darkness is total dominion over the sons of deceit."[284] Ephesians has not mythologized those who may lead its audience astray. There is no evidence that particular false teachers are in view. The unbelieving Gentile world is a sufficient source of "deception" (2:2-3; 4:17-18). Outsiders may seek to counter a Chris-

---

277. Seneca *Epistles* 52,8. See Malherbe, "Hellenistic Moralists and the New Testament," 285.
   278. 1QS 7:16.
   279. 1QS 10:21-24.
   280. 1QS 10:23.
   281. 1QS 5:18-19.
   282. 1QS 10:7-8.

283. On the chiastic structure of Eph 5:3-5, see Stanely E. Porter, "*iste ginōskontes* in Ephesians 5,5: Does Chiasm Solve a Problem?" *ZNW* 81 (1990) 270-76.
   284. 1QS 3:20-22.

tian's new life by justifying their vices[285] or by the sort of ridicule and abuse described in 1 Pet 4:3-5.

The image of the wicked as persons who justify their actions by claiming that God does not judge was common in Jewish writing (see Exod 5:9 LXX; Deut 32:47; Wisdom 2; *T. Naph.* 3.1). In Eph 3:6 the author spoke of salvation as making the Gentile converts "sharers [συμμέτοχοι *symmetochoi*] in the promise." Here the same word is translated "be associated with" (v. 7) and warns against sharing in the deeds of those who remain outside Christ (cf. 2 Cor 6:14–7:1). In the Essene case, the call for separation from the "sons of darkness" has a clear sociological meaning. Persons become members of a new community, with its own interpretation of the Mosaic law, ritual calendar, worship, and detailed instructions governing the lives of members. Contacts with outsiders are limited. It would be natural to read Ephesians as requiring a similar withdrawal, except that the letter nowhere hints at the kind of social structures required to sustain such a move. Therefore the dissociation required in this passage seems to apply primarily to the activities that characterized the life-style of non-Christians. The emphasis on "fruit of the light" and "pleasing to the Lord" in vv. 9-10 suggests that a Christian's general conduct is in view.

Ephesians may also anticipate that Christians will be active moral agents in their world. They are to "try to find out" (δοκιμάζω *dokimazo*, "discern" or "test") what is pleasing to the Lord (v. 10). This expression implies that believers must determine what is suitable behavior in concrete circumstances. For the philosopher, such moral discernment is the activity of reason.[286] Earlier, Ephesians spoke of the renewal of mind that comes with conversion (4:23). Romans 12:2 treats that renewal as the basis of the ability to discern God's will. Elsewhere Paul also uses the verb *dokimazo* in the sense of taking responsibility before the Lord, who is to come in judgment (Phil 1:10-11). Failure to "discern" what is required will lead to divine punishment (1 Cor 11:28-32).

Christian responsibility is not limited to one's own conduct. Verse 11 moves beyond refusal to participate in evil. Christians should also "expose" (ἐλέγχω *elegcho*) evil deeds. The verb can refer to divine condemnation (Wis 4:20; 2 Esdr 12:32-33). Or sinners can be "convicted" by persons who hold up their sin before their eyes (Lev 19:17 LXX; Sir 19:13-17; 1 Cor 14:24-25). The philosopher moralist also sought to upbraid hearers for their vices in order to effect reform. The philosopher as a good physician of the soul will vary his speech from stinging rebuke to gentle encouragement as suits the condition of his audience.[287]

Who is the audience of the rebuke envisaged by Ephesians? Some say it is fellow Christians in danger of falling back into their former life-style (as in Matt 18:15-17; Gal 6:1).[288] This policy can be found among the Essenes, who have nothing to do with outsiders, "He should not reproach or argue with the men of the pit but instead hide the counsel of the law in the midst of the men of sin. He should reproach with truthful knowledge and with just judgment those who choose the path, each one according to his spirit."[289] Or does Ephesians intend believers to confront outsiders with the evil of their actions? The description that follows in vv. 12-13 suggests that the latter interpretation should be preferred. Although the evils that such people do are not to be spoken of among believers (vv. 3, 12), they can be exposed. (See John 3:19-21 for a similar image.) Ephesians does not indicate what form such a confrontation might take. The epistle presumes that its readers are familiar with the process of conversion in their own experience of moving from darkness to light, from death to life (2:1-2; 4:17-18).[290]

The liturgical fragment that concludes this section (v. 14) clearly marks the transition back to the experience of conversion. The connection between the cryptic phrase "everything that becomes visible is light" and the citation said to illustrate the point is unclear. Ephesians spoke of "eyes of your heart enlightened" to recognize God's offer of salvation (1:18). Essene hymns

---

285. Rudolf Schnackenburg, *The Epistle to the Ephesians,* trans. H. Heron (Edinburgh: T. & T. Clark, 1991) 222.

286. Epictetus *Discourses* 1.20,7; 2.23,6.

287. Dio Chrysostom *Orations* 77/78, 38, 42. See Abraham J. Malherbe, "Hellenistic Moralists and the New Testament," in *Aufstieg und Niedergang der römischen Welt* II 26/1, ed. Wolfgang Haase (Berlin: DeGruyter, 1992).

288. So Joachim Gnilka, *Der Epheserbrief,* HTKNT (Freiburg: Herder & Herder, 1980) 255f.

289. 1QS 9:16-18a. See also 1QS 5:24-25.

290. Andrew T. Lincoln, *Ephesians,* WBC 42 (Dallas: Word, 1990) 335.

speak of God "brightening the face" of the righteous or of their teacher: "I give you thanks Lord because you have brightened my face with your covenant. . . . Like perfect dawn you have revealed yourself to me with your light."[291] This passage contrasts the teacher illuminated by God with deceivers who would lead people astray. The hymnic fragment in Eph 5:14b identifies Christ as the source of illumination for the righteous.

The origin of the citation is unclear. Within the epistle, "death" consistently refers to the preconversion situation. Consequently, the fragment seems to be associated with the baptismal imagery of arising from death (Rom 6:4, 13). The Christian remains awake and vigilant in anticipation of the day of the Lord, while others are in darkness or drunken sleep (Rom 13:11-14). Its form is similar to the short fragment in 1 Tim 3:16. Some commentators agree with those patristic authors who saw here images of Jerusalem from Isa 60:1 (also Isa 51:9; 52:1).[292] The Lord has summoned the captive city to awake, be clothed in festal garments, arisen and shine because the light of the Lord's glory has dawned. This imagery recurs in descriptions of the coming messiah.[293] Clement of Alexandria, in his exhortation to the pagans treats this passage as a word of the Lord.[294]

Other commentators have turned to gnostic texts that picture humanity lost in drunken sleep until the revealer comes from the divine world of light to awaken them.[295] Ephesians was popular among second- and third-century Gnostics. This passage may have inspired the final section of a gnostic hymn that describes the descents of the revealer:

And I filled my face with the light of the completion of their aeon. And I entered the midst of their prison which is the prison of the body. . . . And I said, "I am the Pronoia of pure light; . . . Arise and remember that it is you who hearkened, and follow your root, which is I, the merciful one, and guard yourself against the angels of poverty . . . and beware of the deep sleep and the enclosure of the inside of Hades." And I raised him up and sealed him in the light of the water with the

five seals in order that death may not have power over him.[296]

This gnostic example also suggests a ritual context that included baptism and sealing against the powers of the lower world. It shares the cosmology of Ephesians in treating salvation as exaltation to a realm above the powers of this world. However, Ephesians does not exhibit the sharp dualism of the gnostic author. It does not equate the body with the imprisonment of the soul by passions. Nor does Ephesians show characteristic gnostic tendencies to either ascetic denial of bodily reality or its libertine overcoming. Therefore, gnostic parallels should be treated as dependent upon Ephesians rather than as its source.

This passage illustrates a feature that characterizes much of the ethical exhortation in the New Testament. On the one hand, lists of fairly specific vices indicate conduct that is unacceptable. On the other hand, the virtues to be cultivated are phrased in a more general way, such as love or imitation of Christ or discernment of what is pleasing to God. Unlike groups within Judaism—Pharisees or Essenes, for example—Christians did not attempt to specify the positive obligations of Christian life by interpreting the Law. Consequently, they had constantly to ask what conduct pleases God in every particular situation. Hans Dieter Betz has suggested that uneasiness about Christian freedom in the face of human sinfulness led the Judaizers in Galatia to advocate adopting Jewish customs.[297] Ephesians has learned from the apostle Paul that the law created a separation among people that Christ has abolished.

Because Ephesians is not addressed to a particular crisis, its exhortation only expresses the guiding images of the Christian life. However, this section indicates that Christians take moral renewal seriously. They strive for a perfection that does not even need to speak of the evils that typify life without Christ. This injunction does not imply withdrawing from the world. The exhortation to name evils that are being hidden by others shows that Christians must act as a form of moral conscience for fellow believers. Though the two positions—not speaking of evils and exposing

291. 1QH 12[4]:5-6.
292. Chantel Bouttier, *L'Epître de Saint Paul aux Ephésiens*, Commentaire du Nouveau Testament, 2nd série Ixb (Geneva: Labor et Fides, 1991) 230.
293. *T.Levi* 18.3-4; *T.Jud.* 4.1.
294. Clement of Alexandria *Exhortation to the Greeks* 9.84.
295. Heinrich Schlier, *Der Brief an die Epheser* (Dusseldorf: Patmos, 1957) 239-40.
296. *Ap. John* II 31,2-25.
297. Hans Dieter Betz, *Galatians* (Philadelphia: Fortress, 1979) 5-8.

them—might appear contradictory at first glance, the philosophical moralists indicate how the two can work together. Vices do not have to be named or spoken of in a community where they do not occur. Anyone who has mastered a subject no longer thinks of the lessons that were required in order to do so. For the ancient moralists the ethical life is best learned by imitation rather than verbal instruction. Nonetheless, verbal exhortation is needed. Such exhortation may take the mild form of reminder and encouragement as in Ephesians. Or it may take the harsh form of reprimand (as in 1 Cor 5:1-13, for example). The "wise" who serve as models for imitation do not need either type of parenesis. But they do have an obligation to instruct others. Ephesians has applied this model to the Christian life.

REFLECTIONS

The last section of Ephesians ended with a call to forgive "one another as God in Christ has forgiven you"—in other words, to imitate Christ in the act of forgiveness. This theme is continued in this section of the letter by the command to be "imitators of God" (5:1).

How do we "imitate" God? Most Christians look to the Gospels, to the actions and teachings of Jesus for a pattern. The command to love enemies (Matt 5:43-48), the petition "to forgive us . . . as we have been forgiven" in the Lord's prayer (Matt 6:12), and the parable of the unforgiving servant (Matt 18:21-35) are examples of how to shape the Christian life of love and forgiveness in imitation of the divine example. Moreover, Jesus' death appears as a motive for Christian love in the Johannine tradition (John 13:34; 15:11-17; 1 John 4:7-11).

So when Ephesians calls on Christians to imitate the sacrificial love of Christ, we are on familiar ground (even though Paul's letters ordinarily speak of God's love on the cross independently of the command to love others; see Gal 2:20; 5:14). How do we put life into such familiar Christian slogans? Mere repetition induces amnesia. The gospels turn to narrative to make their point. First John takes another tack. It asks readers to reflect on the love that is the very nature of God. The parable of the unforgiving servant contains a pointed lesson. Not all forgiveness transforms a person's behavior. It should do so, but it does not.

So we need to feed the imagination with powerful stories of the transforming effects of forgiveness and love. June Sprigg tells a delightful tale of three months spent living with the remaining elderly Shaker ladies at Canterbury Shaker Village in New Hampshire between her sophomore and junior years of college. She had been permitted to play their piano and small organ. When she was refused permission to play the grand organ, she went to her room and threw a toddler-sized fit—with a few added curse words that toddlers do not know. To her horror she realized that the elderly sister Bertha in the office was on her way over: "The glint stayed in her eye, and I thought, God help anyone who really does hurt someone she loves. . . . I didn't know then . . . what she heard in my blubbering explanations that sometimes I just lost it. . . . The main point was, everything was all right. The thing I had dreaded most had happened, and it was still all right. Bertha had seen the worst side of me, and she loved me just the same. . . . God was in Heaven, all was right with the world."[298] The world is all right when people like sister Bertha imitate God by seeing the worst side and loving all the same. Those who have never been on the receiving end of such love will have a difficult time extending it to others.

This human example is an analogy for what Ephesians invites us to meditate on: God's love exhibited in the death of Jesus. Many people today will admit that they would prefer not to meditate on the cross. They are not alone. Paul knew some Christians in Corinth with a similar mental block (1 Cor 1:18-31). For twenty-first-century Americans the culture of pleasure has made the language of sacrifice dysfunctional. Yet it is impossible to speak about Jesus as God's

298. June Sprigg, *Simple Gifts: Lessons from Living in a Shaker Village* (New York: Random House, 1998) 208-10.

love for us without it. God's Son gave up being God to die on a cross, to paraphrase the famous hymn in Phil 2:6-11. Ignatius of Loyola concludes the *Spiritual Exercises* with directions for meditation to gain a sense of God's love. He suggests beginning much as this letter did, by recalling all the benefits received from God. He also points out that love only works when it is expressed in deeds more than in words. So contemplating benefits received should lead to consideration of what we can give back to the source of the general blessings of creation and salvation as well as the source of our individual talents.[299]

Ephesians moves to this second dimension, that love returns to God, by drawing upon the traditional patterns of moral exhortation. For an ancient reader, the language of sacrifice in 5:2 would evoke the idea of a sphere of sacred holiness that had to be kept pure because it belonged to God. Animals who were to be sacrificed had to be without blemish (Lev 1:3; 4:32). Persons entering the sanctuary might be required to wash or to wear special garments. Sometimes those seeking to consult a god or goddess at one of the oracle shrines also had to refrain from sex or food or other activities for several days beforehand. Moses had to warn the people of Israel away from Mount Sinai. He also told them to engage in purifying themselves by putting on clean clothing and abstaining from sex (Exod 19:12-15). People thought of God's holiness as a powerful force that had to be respected. An unholy offering would provoke God to destroy the person who made it (Lev 10:1-3). Both Jews and non-Jews would recognize that only special words could be spoken or sung in the context of a sacred offering. Ephesians combines that image with the idea that, as children of God, Christians belong to the heavenly regions, to light and not darkness. Once again the moral universe is described in dualistic categories that many modern Christians consider unrealistic. Communities, like that of the Shakers, that attempt to create zones of light independent of the world and its ways, are dead or dying. Of course, there is no evidence that Ephesians expected Christian "children of light" to move out of the world to separate community groups as the Jewish Essene sect had done. But Sprigg discovered a spirit among the Shakers that was not unrealistic at all: "They were human beings, not impossibly perfect saints. . . . Doing unto others as I would have them do unto me didn't mean that I had to be perfect or a Goody Two-shoes, or a Holy Roller, thank God. I could be my own real self. In fact God wanted me to be my own real self. All I needed was to keep in mind that kindness is never a mistake, that we all make mistakes, and that forgiveness is the key."[300] This summary may serve as a key for modern Christians wondering what it means to live in the light of Christ.

299. Ignatius of Loyola, *Spiritual Exercises,* secs. 230-237, in *Personal Writings,* 329-30.
300. Sprigg, *Simple Gifts,* 11.

Ephesians 5:15-21, Wisdom as Thanksgiving

NIV	NRSV
[15]Be very careful, then, how you live—not as unwise but as wise, [16]making the most of every opportunity, because the days are evil. [17]Therefore do not be foolish, but understand what the Lord's will is. [18]Do not get drunk on wine, which leads to debauchery. Instead, be filled with the Spirit. [19]Speak to one another with psalms, hymns and spiritual songs. Sing and make music in your heart to the Lord, [20]always giving thanks to God the	15Be careful then how you live, not as unwise people but as wise, [16]making the most of the time, because the days are evil. [17]So do not be foolish, but understand what the will of the Lord is. [18]Do not get drunk with wine, for that is debauchery; but be filled with the Spirit, [19]as you sing psalms and hymns and spiritual songs among yourselves, singing and making melody to the Lord in your hearts, [20]giving thanks to God the Father at all

NIV	NRSV
Father for everything, in the name of our Lord Jesus Christ. ²¹Submit to one another out of reverence for Christ.	times and for everything in the name of our Lord Jesus Christ. 21Be subject to one another out of reverence for Christ.

COMMENTARY

This section opens as though it would conclude the paraenesis. It combines a summons to conduct oneself wisely (vv. 15-18a) with a quasi-doxology (vv. 18b-20). An additional hortatory phrase (v. 21) permits the author to insert the household code (5:22–6:9) before the peroration (6:10-20). Ephesians 5:15-20 consists of a series of "not . . . but" clauses derived from material found in Colossians, as the following table indicates:

Figure 12: Eph 5:15-20 and Col 3:16-17; 4:5

Item	Ephesians	Colossians
not like the unwise	**5:15** how you walk, not like the unwise but the wise	**4:5** walk in wisdom toward those outside
the times are evil	**5:16** employing the opportunity because the days are evil	**4:5** employing the opportunity
forms of worship	**5:19a** speaking to one another in psalms and hymns and spiritual songs	**3:16b** instructing one another in all wisdom, singing psalms, hymns, spiritual songs
sing to God from the heart	**5:19b** singing and praising the Lord with your hearts	**3:16c** singing with thanks in your hearts to God
giving thanks to God	**5:20** giving thanks always for all things in the name of our Lord Jesus Christ to God the Father	**3:17** and everything whatever you do . . . all things in the name of the Lord Jesus, giving thanks to God the Father through him

Ephesians draws on other traditional material in verses 17b-18a (see Prov 23:31; *T. Jud.* 14.1; Rom 12:2). The two sections highlight the purposes for which the new community exists: praise of God's graciousness (1:6, 11) and walking in good works (2:10). "Filled with the Spirit" forms a transition between the sapiential "not . . . but" clauses and the worship section. On the one hand, "filled with the Spirit" serves as the antithesis to being drunken. On the other hand, the Spirit inspires worship and thanksgiving. Groups of three structure the material: (a) three "not . . .

but" phrases (vv. 15b, 17-18); (b) three types of music (v. 19a); and (c) three participial phrases in the worship section: speaking to one another (v. 19a), singing and praising (v. 19b), and giving thanks (v. 20).

The contrast between the wise and the foolish person (vv. 15-16) is common in wisdom material (see Prov 4:10-14). The Essenes internalized the feud between the spirits of light and darkness as the contest between Wisdom and Folly: "Until now the spirits of truth and injustice feud in the heart of man and they walk in wisdom or in folly."[301] Though Ephesians does not speak of a contest between spiritual beings, it does reflect elements in the apocalyptic scheme. The warning "be careful how you live" highlights the constant danger that the righteous might be deceived in the present evil age. Essenes separate from "men of sin" by careful observance of the law, "to convert from all evil and to keep themselves steadfast in all he prescribes in compliance with his will . . . those who persevere steadfastly in the covenant."[302]

The Essene covenant community protects its members in an age ruled by Belial, "all those who enter in the Rule of the Community shall establish a covenant before God in order to carry out all that he commands and in order not to stray from following him for any fear, dread or grief that might occur during the dominion of Belial."[303] Ephesians makes a similar point in 5:16. The verb ἐξαγοράζω (exagorazō; NRSV and NIV, "make the most of") means to purchase or to "buy back"—that is, "redeem"—something (as in Gal 3:13; 4:5). The meaning of the verb with the noun "time" is not clear. The Greek καιρος (kairos, "time") can refer to a particular time, a favorable time, or even the time of crisis in an eschatological sense (as in Rom 13:11). Ephesians picks up the eschatological overtones of kairos by adding the clause "because the days are evil" (v. 16b). The expression suggests that the times themselves require one to be cautious.[304]

The need for wisdom is intensified by the end-time perspective (vv. 17-18). While "being drunk" (μεθύσκομαι methyskomai) and its resulting folly is a common item in vice lists (see Prov 23:29-35), the blindness or unconsciousness of a drunken humanity also appears as a metaphor in eschatological contexts (see Rom 13:11-13; 1 Thess 5:1-10). The antithesis, "being drunk" or "being filled with the Spirit," has antecedents in the story of Hannah (1 Sam 1:12-18). Similarly, the crowd suspects the apostles of drunkenness on Pentecost (Acts 2:13).[305] There is no reason to assume that Ephesians speaks of abuses in the church (as was the case in 1 Cor 11:21-22)[306] or attraction to cultic orgies attached to a pagan god like Dionysus.[307] The positive injunction "be filled with the Spirit" (πληροῦσθε ἐν πνεύματι plērousthe en pneumati) supports a chain of participles used as examples of Spirit-filled behavior.

Entry into the Essene covenant involved being cleansed of sin by the Spirit: "He will sprinkle over him the Spirit of Truth like lustral water (in order to cleanse him) from all the abhorrences of deceit and from the defilement of the unclean spirit."[308] Humans were divided according to which spirit ruled their hearts: "For God has sorted them into equal parts until the appointed end and the new creation . . . so they decide the lot of every living being in compliance with the spirit there is in him [at the time of] the visitation."[309] Likewise, Christians received the Holy Spirit upon joining the church as the guarantee of their inheritance (1:12-14). The Spirit provides believers access to God (2:18) and dwells within them (3:16; 4:4).

Praise and thanksgiving (vv. 19-20) are the proper responses to what God has done in the believer (1:14; 3:20). Essene writers would agree that praising God is essential to the life of the righteous: "He shall bless his Creator in all that transpires . . . [and with the offering] of his lips he shall bless him."[310] It is not possible to distinguish the various types of song referred to. Hymns and liturgical fragments are often cited in didactic contexts by NT authors (e.g., Phil 2:5-11; 1 Tim 3:16).

Since v. 21 introduces the household code material, some commentators treat it as the beginning of that section. However, the participle belongs in the chain begun earlier. The phrase "reverence for Christ" reflects the OT "fear of God" (Ps 36:2 in Rom 3:18). Paul uses the verb ὑποτάσσω (hypotassō, "be subject") for obedience to rulers in Rom 13:5 (also 1 Pet 2:13; Titus 3:1). Some interpreters assume that Ephesians created v. 21 from the opening of the household code in Col 3:18. Others suggest that it represents

301. 1QS 4:23-24.
302. 1QS 5:1, 4.
303. 1QS 1:16-18.
304. So Rudolf Schnackenburg, *The Epistle to the Ephesians,* trans. H. Heron (Edinburgh: T. & T. Clark, 1991) 233.
305. Against this connection, see Lincoln, *Ephesians,* 343

306. Contra Heinrich Schlier, *Der Brief an die Epheser* (Dusseldorf: Patmos, 1957) 246; Joachim Gnilka, *Der Epheserbrief,* HTKNT (Freiburg: Herder & Herder, 1980) 269.
307. Contra Franz Mussner, *Der Brief an die Epheser* (Gütersloh: Gerd Mohn, 1982) 148.
308. 1QS 4:21-22.
309. 1QS 4:25-26.
310. 1QS 9:26.

a variant of NT exhortations to humility within the community (e.g., Rom 12:3, 10; Gal 6:2-3; Eph 4:2; Phil 2:3-4).

Essene writings provide another context in which the expression "submit" or "be subordinate" applies. Unity is a function of the ranks that members occupy: "No one shall move down . . . nor move up from the place of his lot. For all shall be in a single Community of truth, of proper meekness, of compassionate love and upright purpose, towards each other."[311] Order determined by the individual's insight and holiness governs relationships between members of the community, "each one obeys his fellow, junior under senior. And their spirit and their deeds must be tested year after year in order to upgrade one according to the extent of his insight and the perfection of his path. . . . Each should reproach his fellow in truth, in meekness and in compassionate love."[312] There is no such ranking in Ephesians. However, the Essene example also shows that "be subject to one another" is connected with virtues of humility and mutual correction as well as rank. Therefore, the expression

in Ephesians indicates how exhortation is to be conducted within the church.

Both praise of God and conduct pleasing to the Lord require the assistance and participation of others. "Be subject to one another" as shorthand for the practice of mutual instruction and encouragement requires lives open to the observation and participation of others. Ephesians never forgets that believers are a single body in Christ. Its growth depends upon the well-being of all members. Mutual responsibility is particularly striking in churches like those addressed by Ephesians. The death of the apostles left others to carry on without the strong presence of an apostle-founder.

Believers must attend to their own conduct. Ephesians never suggests that such attention requires detailed moralism and legal observance. It does require consistent turning away from the old way of life. At the same time, this community exists as a worshiping community. Members must gather to offer praise and thanksgiving to God through Jesus Christ. Like their Jewish contemporaries, these Christians recognize that worshiping God and the blessing of God's presence in the Spirit are the keys to wisdom.

311. 1QS 2:24-25.
312. 1QS 5:23-25.

REFLECTIONS

The conclusion to chapter 5 injects an eschatological note. Evils were thought to increase as the world came to an end (e.g., Mark 13:3-23). But like the conclusion to the Lord's prayer, "do not bring us to the time of trial, and rescue us from the evil one" (Matt 6:13 NRSV), the reference to "evil days" (5:16) could be generalized to apply to any time or culture in which Christians find faith under pressure. Ephesians speaks of "wise" and "foolish" instead of the more apocalyptic "children of light" and "children of darkness," thus drawing upon the wisdom tradition. In this tradition, fools are ignorant of God (Psalm 14), and wisdom is life's greatest asset: "For the protection of wisdom is like the protection of money, and the advantage of knowledge is that wisdom gives life to the one who possesses it" (Eccl 7:12 NRSV). For the Jewish tradition, the wisdom that orders the world and calls the wise to banquet at her table (Prov 8:1–9:12) is embodied not only in the collections of general maxims, but also in the Torah. Sirach reflects the convergence of these two traditions in the second century BCE: "If you desire wisdom, keep the commandments and the Lord will lavish her upon you" (Sir 1:26 NRSV).[313] When Eph 5:17 exhorts the audience to avoid folly by seeking the will of the Lord, does the writer assume that they will go to Scripture, even though Christ has ended the binding force of the commandments (2:15)? Does he include, as the earlier wisdom writings do, the broad sweep of human experience and maxims from the general wisdom of the ancient Near East? Appeals to Scripture in the moral exhortation of both the Pauline and deutero-

313. Brueggemann, *Theology of the Old Testament,* 689-90.

Pauline letters are so rare that one cannot be certain of the first. Use of maxims and ethical arguments that are common currency in the Greco-Roman studies suggests a positive reply to the second question.

So Christians today must incorporate the wisdom about human nature, society, and moral imperatives of their time into ethical deliberation. Modern medicine has revolutionized much of our understanding of life and death. We no longer think that women who find themselves unable to conceive a child are cursed by God. Instead, we face the question of how to choose appropriate medical intervention. We are on the threshold of a revolution in genetic testing that will require Christians to think long and hard about what knowledge is worth having. In other cases, medicine has given us clearer answers. We know that addicts need specialized help to break the physiological and psychological chains of addiction. They are not able to completely control their actions. We know that persons with depression or bi-polar disorder may commit suicide. But their families are no longer run out of the church. Nor do we conclude that the suicide is in rebellion against God. We understand that human actions have an impact on the environment, so we recognize that God's command to "fill the earth and subdue it" (Gen 1:28) cannot be a license to wipe out the diversity of God's creation. Our faith tells us to seek "all that is good and right and true" (Eph 5:5). Even when we disagree about the right thing to do in a particular situation, we should be trying to promote what is good.

The section concludes with public Christian speech, the language of worship. Psalms are included in the mix. What other hymns and songs are envisaged, we do not know. Though we are accustomed to think of music in the context of liturgical prayer, we do not always think singing necessary to forming a Christian character. Music was central to the Shaker experience. The famous dancing that brought believers closest to angels ended so long ago that in 1972 Sprigg met only one sister who had witnessed that tradition. "She said that dancing Believers looked like 'angels,' and she spoke with respect and awe of the effect of the dance on the faithful Believers, who found blessed unity in their efforts to move as one."[314] Shaker hymns remain. Some, like "Simple Gifts," have become secular hits, causing some consternation to Believers. Worldly fame does not regard the religious message of the hymn that the "right place" is living out Mother Ann's gospel.[315] These Shaker examples remind us that the songs of Christian worship are not individuals singing to themselves or performances by the choir. They are another way of drawing the community together in its common faith.

314. Sprigg, *Simple Gifts*, 85.
315. See the liner notes to the hymn in Joel Cohen with the Shakers of Sabbathday Lake, the Schola Cantorum, and The Boston Camerata, *Simple Gifts: Shaker Chants and Spirituals,* Erato Disques, 1995. No. 4509-98491-2.

Ephesians 5:22–6:9, Household Code

NIV	NRSV
22Wives, submit to your husbands as to the Lord. 23For the husband is the head of the wife as Christ is the head of the church, his body, of which he is the Savior. 24Now as the church submits to Christ, so also wives should submit to their husbands in everything. 25Husbands, love your wives, just as Christ loved the church and gave himself up for her 26to	22Wives, be subject to your husbands as you are to the Lord. 23For the husband is the head of the wife just as Christ is the head of the church, the body of which he is the Savior. 24Just as the church is subject to Christ, so also wives ought to be, in everything, to their husbands. 25Husbands, love your wives, just as Christ loved the church and gave himself up for her, 26in

NIV

make her holy, cleansing[a] her by the washing with water through the word, [27]and to present her to himself as a radiant church, without stain or wrinkle or any other blemish, but holy and blameless. [28]In this same way, husbands ought to love their wives as their own bodies. He who loves his wife loves himself. [29]After all, no one ever hated his own body, but he feeds and cares for it, just as Christ does the church— [30]for we are members of his body. [31]"For this reason a man will leave his father and mother and be united to his wife, and the two will become one flesh."[b] [32]This is a profound mystery—but I am talking about Christ and the church. [33]However, each one of you also must love his wife as he loves himself, and the wife must respect her husband.

6 Children, obey your parents in the Lord, for this is right. [2]"Honor your father and mother"—which is the first commandment with a promise— [3]"that it may go well with you and that you may enjoy long life on the earth."[c]

[4]Fathers, do not exasperate your children; instead, bring them up in the training and instruction of the Lord.

[5]Slaves, obey your earthly masters with respect and fear, and with sincerity of heart, just as you would obey Christ. [6]Obey them not only to win their favor when their eye is on you, but like slaves of Christ, doing the will of God from your heart. [7]Serve wholeheartedly, as if you were serving the Lord, not men, [8]because you know that the Lord will reward everyone for whatever good he does, whether he is slave or free.

[9]And masters, treat your slaves in the same way. Do not threaten them, since you know that he who is both their Master and yours is in heaven, and there is no favoritism with him.

[a]26 Or *having cleansed*   [b]31 Gen. 2:24   [c]3 Deut. 5:16

NRSV

order to make her holy by cleansing her with the washing of water by the word, [27]so as to present the church to himself in splendor, without a spot or wrinkle or anything of the kind—yes, so that she may be holy and without blemish. [28]In the same way, husbands should love their wives as they do their own bodies. He who loves his wife loves himself. [29]For no one ever hates his own body, but he nourishes and tenderly cares for it, just as Christ does for the church, [30]because we are members of his body.[a] [31]"For this reason a man will leave his father and mother and be joined to his wife, and the two will become one flesh." [32]This is a great mystery, and I am applying it to Christ and the church. [33]Each of you, however, should love his wife as himself, and a wife should respect her husband.

6 Children, obey your parents in the Lord,[b] for this is right. [2]"Honor your father and mother"—this is the first commandment with a promise: [3]"so that it may be well with you and you may live long on the earth."

[4]And, fathers, do not provoke your children to anger, but bring them up in the discipline and instruction of the Lord.

[5]Slaves, obey your earthly masters with fear and trembling, in singleness of heart, as you obey Christ; [6]not only while being watched, and in order to please them, but as slaves of Christ, doing the will of God from the heart. [7]Render service with enthusiasm, as to the Lord and not to men and women, [8]knowing that whatever good we do, we will receive the same again from the Lord, whether we are slaves or free.

[9]And, masters, do the same to them. Stop threatening them, for you know that both of you have the same Master in heaven, and with him there is no partiality.

[a]Other ancient authorities add *of his flesh and of his bones*
[b]Other ancient authorities lack *in the Lord*

COMMENTARY

This section adopts a pattern of instruction on duties of household members from Col 3:18–4:1 (also see 1 Pet 2:18–3:7; Titus 2:1-10). The Stoic philosopher Hierocles detailed duties to gods, city, and household.[316] Other such descriptions occur in both Greco-Roman and Hellenistic Jewish writers.[317] Seneca wrote: "How a husband should conduct himself towards his wife, or how a father should bring up his children, or how a master should rule his slaves, this department of philosophy is accepted by some as the only significant part."[318] Comparative material extends back to Greek authors on household management and forward to neo-Pythagorean schools as well.[319]

Most scholars agree that the household code came to NT writers from Hellenistic Jewish sources. Some exegetes detect an apologetic accommodation to larger social mores in the household codes. Conversion by inferior members of a household could be viewed as dangerous insubordination. The attention paid to women and slaves in 1 Peter suggests that such exemplary behavior is being recommended in order to ameliorate tensions that adherence to the new sect is causing.[320]

A wisdom text from Qumran includes instruction for husbands and wives after comments on the appropriate honor due one's parents.[321] The addressee is a poor person who might think that true piety is beyond his grasp. Unfortunately, the text is too fragmentary to determine what the sociological dynamics behind this reference to the addressee as poor might have been. The NT examples are atypical in addressing subordinate parties in the household first. In 1 Peter, a subsequent word to slave masters is lacking. That omission may reflect the socioeconomic situation of its community.

Colossians 3:18–4:1 provides single sentence instructions for each group except slaves, where the advice is expanded to include obedience to the heavenly Lord. In taking over the material from Colossians, Ephesians reformulates it to indicate that all parties are Christian. The most striking interruption of the parallel clause form comes in the address to husbands (vv. 25-32). That digression concludes with a statement that addresses both husbands and wives (v. 33).

Since the other Christian household codes invoke Christ either as the Lord to whom obedience is paid (Col 3:23) or as the model in suffering unjust treatment (1 Pet 2:18-25), the Christ and church application here probably originated as an example of subordination (Eph 5:23-24). Most conventional discourse on the topic of household management was addressed to males, for whom harmonious governing of the household and ability to rule were closely related.[322]

---

316. See Abraham J. Malherbe, *Moral Exhortation: A Greco-Roman Sourcebook* (Philadelphia: Westminster, 1986) 85-104.

317. E.g., Greco-Roman writers: Cicero *On Duties* 1.17, 58; Dio Chrysostom *Orations* 4.91. Hellenistic Jewish writers: Pseudo-Phochylides 175-230; Philo *On the Posterity and Exile of Cain* 181.

318. Seneca *Epistles* 94.1; see Malherbe, *Moral Exhortation,* 127.

319. See Aristotle *Politics* 1235^b 1-14; Xenophon *Household Management.* See also Martin Dibelius and D. Heinrich Greeven, *An die Kolosser, Epheser, an Philemon,* HNT 12 (Tübingen: Mohr-Siebeck, 1953) 48-50; Abraham J. Malherbe, "Hellenistic Moralists and the New Testament," in *Aufstieg und Niedergang der römischen Welt* II 26/1, ed. Wolfgang Haase (Berlin: DeGruyter, 1992) 204-13; David L. Balch, "Neopythagorean Moralists and the New Testament Household Codes," in *Aufstieg und Niedergang der römischen Welt* II 26/1, ed. Wolfgang Haase (Berlin: DeGruyter, 1992) 380-411.

320. So David L. Balch, *Let Wives Be Submissive: The Domestic Code in 1 Peter,* SBLMS 26 (Atlanta: Scholars Press, 1981) 63-80.

321. 4Q416 3:15-19, parents; 4:2, wife.

322. See Balch, *Let Wives Be Submissive,* 36-40.

Figure 13: Eph 5:22–6:9 as Household Code

Item	Ephesians	Colossians and other parallels
to wives	**5:22** wives [be subject, from v. 21] to your own husbands as to the Lord	**Col 3:18** wives, be subject to your husbands as is proper in the Lord
	5:33*b* let the wife respect her husband	**1 Pet 3:1** likewise, wives be subject to your own husbands
		Titus 2:4-5 train young women to be loving of their husbands, loving of children . . . subject to their own husbands
reason for conduct	**5:23-24** husband head of wife as Christ is head of church [his body, Christ its savior]; church subject to Christ, wife subject to husband in everything	[**1 Cor 11:3** head of every man is Christ; head of a woman, her husband; head of Christ, God]
		Titus 2:5 that the word of God might not be slandered
		1 Pet 3:1*b***-2** unbelieving husbands may be won over without a word by reverent and chaste behavior
		[**1 Pet 3:3-6** expansion: inner virtue to replace outward adornment; follow example of holy women such as Sarah; do right and have nothing to fear]
to husbands	**5:25-27** husbands, love your wives, as Christ loved the church and gave himself up for her	**Col 3:19** husbands, love your wives and do not be harsh with them
		1 Pet 3:7*a* likewise, husbands live considerately (with your wives) as the weaker vessel, bestowing honor on the woman
	[**vv. 26-27** expansion: Christ cleanses church, presents her holy and unstained]	[cf. **1 Pet 3:2-6,** holiness of the virtuous wife]
	5:33*a* let each one love his wife as himself	

Figure 13: Eph 5:22–6:19 as Household Code, *cont.*

reason for conduct	**5:28-32** therefore husbands ought to love their wives as their own bodies; the one who loves his wife loves himself, no one hates his own flesh, but nourishes and cherishes it as Christ does the church, because we are members of his body [cites Gen 2:24 exegical comment, vv. 31-32]	**1 Pet 3:7***b* because you are fellow heirs of the grace of life, so that your prayers may not be hindered
to children	**6:1** children, obey your parents in the Lord, for it is just	**Col 3:20** children, obey your parents in everything for this is pleasing to the Lord
reason for conduct	**6:2-3** cites Exod 20:12 + comment, "this is the first commandment with a promise"	
to fathers	**6:4** fathers, do not provoke your children to rage but nourish them with education and knowledge of the Lord	**Col 3:21** fathers, do not provoke your children
reason for conduct		lest they become discouraged
to slaves	**6:5-7** slaves obey your lords according to the flesh with fear and trembling, in your single heartedness, as to Christ, not with eye-service as pleasing people, but as slaves of Christ, doing the will of God from the heart, serving with zeal, as to the Lord and not human beings	**Col 3:22-23** slaves, obey in all things your lords according to the flesh, not with eye-service as pleasing people but in single-heartedness, fearing the Lord. Whatever you do, work from the heart as for the Lord and not for human beings
		1 Pet 2:18 household slaves, be subject in all fear to your masters, not only to the good and gentle but also to the harsh
		Titus 2:9-10*a* slaves to be subject (ὑποτάσσεσθαι *hypotassesthai*) to their own masters in all things, to be pleasing, not to be obstinate, not thieving, but showing

Fig. 13: Eph 5:22–6:9 as Household Code, *cont.*

		complete, good faithfulness
reason for conduct	**6:8** knowing that each, whatever good he does, this he will get back from the Lord, whether slave or freeman	**Col 3:24-25** knowing that from the Lord, you will receive back the reward of the inheritance; you serve the Lord Christ. For the wicked will get back the wrong he has done, and there is no partiality
		1 Pet 2:19 for this is as reason for gracious favor if in consciousness of God someone bears pains, suffering unjustly
		[**2:20** explanation: no merit in enduring deserved punishment; God bestows favor on (χάρις παρὰ θεῳ *charis para Theō*) those who do good and endure suffering]
		[**2:21-25** example for imitation: Christ as suffering servant brought salvation from sin and healing]
		Titus 2:10*b* so that in everything they may adorn the teaching of God our savior
to masters	**6:9***a* and lords, do the same things toward them, giving up the threat	**Col 4:1** lords, treat your slaves justly and equitably
reason for conduct	**6:9***b* knowing that their Lord and yours is in the heavens and there is no partiality with him	**Col 4:1***b* knowing that you also have a Lord in heaven
		[see **Col 3:25***b*]

Though attached to the exhortation of slaves, Col 3:25 constitutes an independent judgment saying, which may have been intended to refer to the unjust masters.[323] Ephesians 6:9 read Col 3:25 in that sense and relocated the warning about divine impartiality to the end of the saying addressed to the masters. Two levels of development are evident in the rest of the household

code: first, OT citations and comments to husbands (5:30-31) and children (6:2-3); second, the ecclesial imagery of Christ as head of the body (5:28-32; see also 1:22-23; 2:16; 3:6; 4:15-16, 25). The addition of OT citations is independent of the "body of Christ" ecclesiology. First Peter uses OT examples in its address to slaves and women. In the former case, OT allusions are associated with Christ as suffering servant. In the latter, Sarah is the exemplary holy woman. Such developments suggest that the household code

323. So Markus Barth and Helmut Blanke, *Colossians,* AB 34B (New York: Doubleday, 1994) 445-47.

material was used in catechesis. The audience of Ephesians would recognize this section of paraenesis as part of its own tradition.

5:22-24. Verse 22 lacks a verb. The participle "being subject" (ὑποτασσόμενοι *hypotassomenoi*) can be supplied from v. 21. The same verb can be used for subjection to authorities and masters or for voluntary subordination on the part of those who might otherwise command respect (1 Pet 5:5).[324] The household codes presuppose that Christians will subordinate themselves to others, as do the exhortations to obey civil authorities (Rom 13:1; Titus 3:1; 1 Pet 2:13). Of course, Christian women, slaves, or children cannot be subject to the religious opinions of husbands, masters, or parents if the latter oppose Christian faith.

Two parallel statements about the wife's subordination to her husband (vv. 23*a*, 24*b*) frame the two statements about the church (vv. 23*b*, 24*a*). The opening metaphor, "husband is the head of the wife," echoes Paul's use of "head" for an order of hierarchical subordination in 1 Cor 11:3. Ephesians 5:23*b* refers Christ's position as "head" (κεφαλη *kephalē*) to his role as savior. The depiction of Christ's exaltation as head (*kephalē*) of the church in 1:20-23 highlighted the cosmic dimensions of salvation. The question of how far to push the metaphor is raised by the juxtaposition of husband as head (*kephalē*) of his wife with Christ as head (*kephalē*) of the church. Some interpreters point to 1:20-23 as evidence that the image should be referred to the power that Christ exercises on behalf of those who are members of his body. Others attempt to push the effect of the metaphor further. Insofar as the husband's authority is compared to that of Christ, the phrase "in everything" (ἐν παντι *en panti*) does not require wives to accept degrading or unworthy (i.e., unchristlike) forms of subjection.

Some commentators have seen this passage as evidence that gnostic images of the spiritual marriage between the soul and the savior influenced Ephesians.[325] Valentinian Gnostics enacted this mythological motif in a rite referred to as the "bridal chamber." That rite reversed the loss of humanity's original androgyny that occurred when

Adam was divided from Eve. "His separation became the beginning of death. Because of this Christ came to repair the separation which was from the beginning and again unite the two, and to give life to those who died as a result. . . . But the woman is united to her husband in the bridal chamber."[326]

Another gnostic text refers to this section of Ephesians: "For they were originally joined to one another when they were with the father before the woman led astray the man, who is her brother. This marriage has brought them back together again and the soul has been joined to her true love, her real master, as it is written, 'For the master of the woman is her husband.' "[327] Other gnostic texts speak of the church as a preexistent entity in the divine world (πλήρωμα *plērōma*). "Those which exist have come forth from the Son and the Father like kisses . . . the kiss being a unity, although it involves many kisses. That is to say, it is the church consisting of many men that existed before the aeons, which is called in the proper sense "the aeon of aeons."[328] The Savior's function is to restore the preexistent church to its original unity. Though it is easy to understand why these later gnostic writers would read Ephesians as evidence for their views, the epistle itself never suggests that the church as body of Christ pre-exists except in God's foreordained plan of salvation. Nor does Ephesians use the gnostic imagery of the soul's reunion with its true spouse, returning instead to the traditional theology of the cross. Christ's death on the cross is the source of both the unity (2:14) and holiness (2:1-10; 5:2) of the church.

5:25-33. Ephesians begins the exhortation to husbands with "love your wives," but omits the conventional "never treat them harshly" found in Col 3:19. Instead, Ephesians develops the body of Christ motif. Christ's self-sacrifice is a model to be imitated (Eph 5:2). Paul spoke of the local church as the pure bride of Christ (2 Cor 11:2). Ephesians assumes that Christ's death brought into being a church that is holy and unblemished. Some interpreters also find references to the bride of the Song of Songs (Cant 5:1).[329] "Washing of

324. See *Letter of Aristeas* 257; Barth and Blanke, *Colossians,* 433.

325. Heinrich Schlier, *Der Brief an die Epheser* (Dusseldorf: Patmos, 1957) 264-76; Karl Martin Fischer, *Tendenz und Absicht des Epheserbriefes,* FRLANT 111 (Göttingen: Vandenhoeck & Ruprecht, 1973) 181-200.

326. *Gos. Phil.* 70,10-19.

327. *Exegesis on the Soul* 133,4-10.

328. *Tripartite Tractate* 58, 22-33.

329. Chantel Bouttier, *L'Epître de Saint Paul aux Ephésiens,* Commentaire du Nouveau Testament, 2nd série Ixb (Geneva: Labor et Fides, 1991) 245; J. Paul Sampley, *"And the Two Shall Become One Flesh": A Study of Traditions in Eph 5:21-33,* SNTSMS 16 (Cambridge: Cambridge University Press, 1971) 45-51.

water by the word" refers to baptism (1 Cor 6:11; Titus 2:14; 3:5). The "word" was probably the name of Christ used during the ritual. Old Testament images might also be involved. Ezekiel 16:8-14 describes God's bathing the battered nation, anointing and clothing her so that she can enter into a covenant with God, whose glory she now shares. For Ephesians, the church now exists in holiness and glory. The church as "bride" does not depict the eschatological future as a wedding in the manner of Rev 19:5-10.[330]

This extended description of the church as a bride prepared for the wedding highlights what has been accomplished by Christ's self-giving love. Husbands should love their wives with similar devotion. Ephesians does not imply that husbands are agents of holiness for their wives. Holiness comes to individual Christians through their incorporation into the body of Christ.[331] However, the audience might assume that husbands are responsible for instructing their wives in holiness (cf. 1 Cor 14:34-35).[332]

Ephesians resumes with another development of the metaphor (vv. 28-30). The wife is like her husband's own body. A similar sentiment appears in Plutarch, who insists that the husband should not rule his wife in the way in which a master rules property but in the same way that the soul directs the body.[333] When Ephesians speaks of "nourishing" (ἐκτρέφω *ektrephō*) one's own flesh, the letter uses terms that would have been familiar to its audience. Ancient marriage contracts often included the husband's obligation to provide his wife with clothing and nourishment.[334] The conclusion returns to the activity of Christ. Conventional images continue to be transposed into the larger picture of the church's relationship to Christ. The author interrupts his presentation with another insertion of the "we" perspective (v. 30) so that the entire community is designated "body of Christ."

Ephesians uses the term "mystery" (μψστήριον *mystērion*) here, as elsewhere, for the hidden purposes of God (v. 32; cf. 1:9; 3:3; 4:9; 6:19).

The Essenes also speak of patient study of the law as learning to perceive the mysteries.[335] The quotation from Gen 2:24 appears in other contexts to bolster the prohibition of divorce (e.g., Mark 10:7-8). Essene legal codes use the related passage from Gen 1:27 in formulating their prohibition against divorce.[336] Ephesians may be familiar with the use of Gen 2:24 in such legal material. However, its exhortation to husbands gives no indication of addressing such issues.

Gnostic speculation regarded the division of Adam and Eve in Gen 2:23-24 as the source of death and human subjugation to the powers of the lower world. The savior comes to reveal that their true home lies above this world. The lost unity is restored when the soul is reunited with a heavenly counterpart. Consequently, gnostic exegetes interpreted Gen 2:24 as Adam's recognition of the heavenly wisdom figure:

> And Adam saw the woman beside him. In that moment the luminous Epinoia appeared, and she lifted the veil which lay over his mind. And he became sober from the drunkenness of darkness. And he recognized his counter-image, and he said, "This is indeed bone of my bones and flesh of my flesh." Therefore a man will leave his father and mother and cleave to his wife and they will both be one flesh. For they will send him his consort.[337]

For the gnostic interpreter the "mystery" (*mystērion*) involves liberation from the domination of the lower powers, including the god of the Genesis story. For some, this freedom implied ascetic renunciation of all passions and desires, since passions were widely regarded as the means by which the demonic powers controlled human behavior. Other Gnostics of the Valentinian school assimilated human marriage to the "bridal chamber" reunification of the soul with its counterpart. This section of Ephesians appears in references to that ritual.[338] The term "mystery" (*mystērion*) refers to the gnostic sacrament, "Indeed marriage in the world is a mystery for those who have taken a wife. If there is a hidden quality to the marriage of defilement, how much more is the undefiled marriage a true mystery!"[339]

330. Contra Markus Barth, *Ephesians*, AB 34-34A (Garden City, N.Y.: Doubleday, 1974) 669.

331. Contra Franz Mussner, *Der Brief an die Epheser* (Gütersloh: Gerd Mohn, 1982) 158.

332. 4Q416 frag. 2 1:6-9.

333. Plutarch *Advice to the Bride and Groom* 142E.

334. Joachim Gnilka, *Der Epheserbrief*, HTKNT (Freiburg: Herder & Herder, 1980) 285.

335. 4Q416 frag. 2 4:1.

336. CD 4:21.

337. *Ap. John* II 23, 4-15.

338. See *Gos. Phil.* 64, 31-32.

339. *Gos. Phil.* 82, 2-6.

These gnostic texts exhibit a widespread concern over the passions that are involved in marriage. Paul's exchange with those in Corinth who viewed all sexuality as an obstacle to perfection provides an earlier example (1 Cor 7:1-31) of concern over these passions. When faced with Christians who resorted to prostitutes, Paul used the dual images of belonging to the body of Christ and becoming "one flesh" with a sexual partner to argue the immorality of that behavior (1 Cor 6:12-20). He argued that marriage is an appropriate vehicle to "glorify God in your body" (6:20) against the radical ascetic view. Ephesians may have taken the "one flesh" language from earlier Pauline instruction, but it shows no concern with the practical issues that Paul was addressing in that earlier context. Nor does Ephesians move in the Valentinian direction of explaining Christian marriage as an image of the heavenly union that restores the soul to freedom from passions and death. Translation of the term "mystery" *mystērion* by the Latin *sacramentum* in some versions of the Old Latin and Vulgate traditions gave rise to use of this text in support of marriage as a Christian sacrament.[340]

Ephesians does not mythologize human marriage. Instead the text limits application of the "mystery" (*mystērion*) to the relationship between Christ and the church (v. 32). The earlier description of the growth of the body into its head through the activity of nerves, tendons, and joints (4:15-16) had established an organic relationship between Christ and the church. This "mystery" (*mystērion*) is another aspect of that saving reality.

The final verse brings the long digression back to the essential point of the exhortation: the relationship between husband and wife. It reaffirms the hierarchical view of marriage and the household in ancient times. Modern translations prefer the more neutral term "respect" for the "fear" or "reverence" (φοβέομαι *phobeomai*) required of the wife. The ancient author and his readers would presume that she, like all other members of the household, is subject to the authority of its male head. The term "fear" (*phobeomai*) can be used of all social relationships in which subordination is involved. On the other hand, the relationship between husband and

wife is different from that between the husband/ master and his slaves. The relationship between husband and wife modeled upon Christ's self-sacrificing love indicates a constant concern on the husband's part for her well-being that is not part of other hierarchical relationships in the household.

6:1-4. Ephesians returns in these verses to the traditional shorter exhortation. The Essene example indicates that "children" (τέκνα *tekna*) refers to adults obligated to care for and respect aging parents, "Honour your father in your poverty and your mother in your steps, for like grass for a man, so is his father, and like a pedestal for a man, so is his mother. For they are the oven of your origin, and just as they have dominion over you and form the spirit, so you must serve them."[341] Paul used the obligations of adult children toward their parents to describe relationships between himself and his converts. Paul refuses material support despite his needs. Rather, he insists that the Corinthians show him the love due a father (2 Cor 11:9).[342] As a solicitous father, Paul seeks to present the community to Christ as a pure bride (2 Cor 11:2).

The OT citation (vv. 2*a*, 3) is closer to LXX Exod 20:12 than to Deut 5:16. The conviction that the law teaches its followers "what is right" appears in Jewish apologetic. Attacks on paganism described the evil of disobedient children as the result of idolatry (Rom 1:29-31). This section affirms a conventional understanding of the appropriate relationship between children and parents. Some philosophers admit that children should disobey a father who tries to prohibit the study of philosophy.[343]

Ephesians focuses on the requirement that parents educate their children (v. 4). The Essene example used the education received from parents as the basis for the obligation of adult children toward their parents. A treatise attributed to Plutarch argues that training one's children in philosophy will guarantee the social conformity that is the object of the household code paraenesis.

---

340. Rudolf Schnackenburg, *The Epistle to the Ephesians*, trans. H. Heron (Edinburgh: T. & T. Clark, 1991) 256.

341. 4Q416 frag. 2, col. 3:16-17.

342. O. Larry Yarbrough, "Parents and Children in the Letters of Paul," in *The Social World of the First Christians: Essays in Honor of Wayne A. Meeks*, ed. L. Michael White and Larry Yarbough (Minneapolis: Fortress, 1995).

343. Markus Barth and Helmut Blanke, *Colossians*, AB 34B (New York: Doubleday, 1994) 441.

The author writes: "Through philosophy . . . it is possible to attain knowledge of what is just and unjust . . . that one ought to reverence the gods, to honor one's parents . . . to be obedient to the laws, to yield to those in authority, to love one's friends, to be chaste with women, to be affectionate with children, and not to be overbearing with slaves."[344] Parental affection toward, and education of, children appears in Paul's use of parent/child imagery to describe his relationship to the churches he founded (1 Cor 4:14-21; 1 Thess 2:7-12.[345]

Sirach 30:1-13 recommends strict discipline, constant correction, and beating so that the son will become like his father. However, warnings against excessive harshness can also be found. The Pseudo-Plutarch treatise, for example, contrasts the education of freeborn children to that of slaves. Beating is for slaves. Exhortation, reasoning, and encouragement should be used for children.[346]

Ephesians is less interested in the negative aspects of discipline than in the positive responsibility for instruction. The term "discipline" (παιδεία *paideia*) spans the range between appropriate discipline for young children to the philosophical instruction of the older adolescent (Sir 1:27 connects "fear of the Lord," *paideia*, and wisdom"). The second term, "instruction" (νουθεσία *nouthesia*), refers to verbal correction or education. Thus Ephesians indicates that Christian fathers will be devoted to training their children in virtuous behavior.

6:5-9. The instruction to slaves (vv. 5-8) is more lengthy than that given the other subordinate groups. As *Fig.* 13 indicates, this material is an adaptation of Col 3:22-25. The conventional Christian modification (slaves serve the Lord, not just human masters) remains. Discussion of how slaves are to be treated appears in all ancient codes.[347] The NT codes are distinctive in addressing slaves directly rather than merely providing rules to the master. Slaves were members of early

Christian communities (1 Cor 7:20-24; Gal 3:28; Philemon). Ancient authors often depicted slaves as unreliable, groveling and fawning on masters whom they secretly despise. If the master relaxes his stern discipline or turns his back, slaves become disobedient, steal from the household, and deserve punishment (cf. Luke 12:41-48). The virtuous slave depicted in the Christian household code is not to be lumped with such cultural stereotypes. His or her dignity lies in service to the Lord.[348] An owner might free, in his will, those slaves whom he considered zealous and affectionate.[349] Ephesians shifts that possibility of human reward for devoted service to the Lord, who governs the behavior of all Christians regardless of their status (v. 8).

Judgment brings the slave and the master under the same Lord. The warning that Col 3:25 addressed to wicked slaves has been reformulated in v. 8, which speaks of the Lord's rewarding each person, slave or free, for any good he or she does. The reminder that God is an impartial judge appears at the end, reinforcing this admonition to masters. The partiality that power and position gave individuals in human courts does not apply in front of the heavenly judge (cf. Rom 2:10-11; 2 Cor 5:10). Though the warning addressed to masters appears stronger than that in Col 4:1, the imperatives are weaker. Instead of the positive characteristics—just and equitable treatment—required of masters in Colossians, v. 9*a* has an unclear admonition to "do the same" (τὰ αὐτὰ ποιεῖτε *ta auta poieite*) and avoid threatening behavior. The latter reflects a common theme in master/slave relationships: the injuries that result from a master's rage. Consequently, philosophers exhort masters to avoid anger in dealing with slaves.[350] A female Pythagorean philosopher, Theano, directs similar advice on treatment of household slaves to young wives. They must avoid mistreating slaves through excessive toil and must restrain the cruel temper that some people exhibit in punishing

344. Pseudo-Plutarch *Education of Children* 7DE; see Abraham J. Malherbe, *Moral Exhortation: A Greco-Roman Sourcebook* (Philadelphia: Westminster, 1986) 30-31.

345. Yarbrough, "Parents and Children in the Letters of Paul."

346. Pseudo-Plutarch *Education of Children* 8F; see also Pseudo-Phocylides 207.

347. David L. Balch, "Neopythagorean Moralists and the New Testament Household Codes," in *Aufstieg und Niedergang der römischen Welt* II 26/1, ed. Wolfgang Haase (Berlin: DeGruyter, 1992) 380-411.

348. Barth and Blanke, *Colossians*, 446

349. *POxy* 494.6; see Andrew T. Lincoln, *Ephesians*, WBC 42 (Dallas: Word, 1990) 419. Ancient slave names preserve the paternalism of this ideology with commonplaces such as *philodespotos* ("master loving") and *philokyrios* ("lord loving"). See Dale C. Martin, *Slavery as Salvation: The Metaphor of Slavery in Pauline Christianity* (New Haven: Yale University Press, 1990) 28-29.

350. Seneca *On Anger* 3.24.2; 32.1.

slaves.[351] Thus the behavior required of Christian slaveowners does not differ appreciably from that enjoined by Hellenistic moralists. The difference appears in the motive clauses. The eschatological understanding that the Lord in the heavens treats all alike undermines a fundamental assumption in the hierarchy of power, that those in power enjoy their position through divine favor.[352]

Christians today often find the household code ethic an awkward accommodation to cultural patterns that would be considered unjust or, in the case of slavery, immoral. First-century readers of Ephesians would find its concern for proper roles and subordination quite natural. Women were expected to defer to their husbands. Adult children continued to be subject to the authority of their parents. In that context, Ephesians directs those in authority to moderate common forms of abusive power. The father's authority over wife and children requires self-sacrifice for their welfare. It does not permit subjecting them to dehumanizing labor or harsh punishments. Ephesians 5:22-33 contains a unique development of the traditional ethic in the extended description of the husband's love and concern for his wife.

Ephesians presumes households in which both dominant and subordinate parties share a common faith, unlike the situation in 1 Peter where wives and slaves are subject to non-Christians. Since the household was considered the fundamental unit of the larger society, the relationship of Christians to the larger social structures is also at stake. Both Rom 13:1-7 and 1 Pet 2:13-17 incorporate the piece on civic hierarchy and concord that pertains to Greco-Roman treatments of household management.

Most exegetical attempts to detect some radical modification of the ethical injunctions based on special Christian insight or compassion fail to prove their case. Guiding images and motivational statements have been shaped by Christian language and views of the world. But the content and social implications of this paraenesis are not peculiar to the Christian variants. What is the significance of the early Christian appropriation of such ethical commonplaces? Does it lend the authority of Scripture to a particular sociocultural understanding of order or of family? Does the fact that the initial impetus for use of such material may have been apologetic or used to lessen the tensions between converts and those on whom they depended make the material irrelevant in another setting? Ephesians, which gives no evidence of the problems addressed in 1 Peter, would seem to counter that view. For Ephesians, this ethic describes a well-ordered Christian household independent of the views or actions of outsiders.

---

351. Balch, "Neopythagorean Moralists and the New Testament Household Codes," 405.

352. Balch, "Chantel Bouttier, *L'Epître de Saint Paul aux Ephésiens,* Commentaire du Nouveau Testament, 2nd série Ixb (Geneva: Labor et Fides, 1991) 255.

REFLECTIONS

1. When Eph 5:21 advises Christians to "be subject" to one another, no one bats an eye, but when the same verb is addressed to wives with regard to husbands in 5:22, protest erupts. Someone inevitably asks whether the verb has a different meaning. Popular substitutions, such as "defer to" or "respect," fail to capture the point of the verb. It does imply a hierarchy of command, though the obedience offered may be the voluntary submission of mutual Christian love, as in 5:21 (or 1 Cor 16:16), rather than military style obedience to the command of a superior officer or government authorities (Rom 13:1). Of course, we do use "respect" to mean "do what they say" when we have police officers involved in schools and youth recreational programs to teach kids to respect law enforcement officers. We also intend that they come away from such experiences with the disposition to obey a command from the police immediately. Why? Because the orders are given in a context where the child's safety or that of a whole group of people is at stake. In an emergency, such as a building fire, the ability to follow orders quietly and quickly can mean the difference between life and death.

There is no inherent problem about the meaning of the verb in Scripture. Nor is it difficult to find social situations in which we expect the same sort of obedience. Without it, lives would be at risk. Couple the verb with the metaphor of the body, which dominates the development of the image in 5:23-24, and the command/response element of the verb becomes evident in another way. What happens when disease or accident cuts the link between the brain and the rest of the nervous system? We all know the answer: paralysis, various bodily movements or words and sounds unintended by the person. We can see the frustration of victims with a body out of control. What generates the hue and cry is not that the metaphor is dead, but that it no longer reflects either the experience or the ideal of respect in marriage for many Christians.[353] Conservatives reply that there would be less divorce and social disorder if the view of husband as head of the family were more widely accepted. Liberals retort that this text has been used to exonerate abuse against women and children. Moderates try to thread the needle by agreeing that families need respect for authority and that it is an abuse of Scripture to require wives and children to suffer violence. They propose a more contemporary view of headship in which husbands and wives share the responsibility according to their particular gifts and expertise. Even children have a role to play when it comes to computers or other modern electronics. The person who understands what needs to be done and has the expertise can direct and help the others. Such arrangements seem an obvious application of Eph 5:21, "be subject to one another."

Insofar as Ephesians employs the conventional wisdom of its time in adapting the household code to Christian use, Christians certainly must consider the social structures and wisdom of their own time in formulating an ethic for marriage. At the same time, we should be conscious of the fairly recent cultural origins of modern family relationships.[354] Merely replacing a patriarchal hierarchy determined by gender with an economic one determined by the size of one's paycheck is no improvement. If authority and responsibility are shared, then consensus and communication are critical virtues. Listening to others is an essential habit. The atomized American family is not a school for such virtues. Early in his freshman year, a Chinese American student commented on a visit to his roommate's house, "I couldn't get used to it. Everyone had their own TV, music system, computer, phone line. They thought I was poor because in our family we share these things." Equating individual liberty with the isolation of personal pleasures hardly represents an advance in ethical insight.

Ephesians has expanded the traditional household code with an elaborate metaphorical argument addressed to husbands (5:25-32). The terms "head" and "body" link the author's vision of Christ as head of a body, the church, with another tradition that applied Gen 2:24 in legal debates over divorce. This passage spawned elaborate mythological developments in later gnostic circles, but seems more rhetorical decoration to today's readers. The basic point that husbands should love and care for their wives with the same concern they show for their own bodies (5:28-29) is the take-home message for most congregations. The sacrificial and sanctifying actions of Christ in regard to the church (5:25-27) make sense as ecclesiology but translated usually emerge in commonplaces about marriage as a path of holiness. Lots of rhetoric to support moral commonplaces. Lincoln addresses this issue by pointing out that the readers of Ephesians were intensely involved in their new relationship with Christ, as is indicated in these verses. They experience themselves as being cleansed, beautified, made holy, and as obligated to respond with an appropriate life-style and thanksgiving. This involvement gives the metaphor its power. He comments, "Since they were participating in the reality of this relationship, the writer's appeal to them to model their marriages on it, so that those marriages would be an equally real reflection of its dynamic, would have had a powerful effect."[355] In short, if the metaphor limps, it may say as much about our experience of the realities of salvation as it does about our view of marriage.

353. For a detailed survey of the theological and exegetical debate with concern for modern theories of metaphor, see Gregory W. Dawes, *The Body in Question: Metaphor and Meaning in Ephesians 5:21-33* (Leiden: Brill, 1998).
354. See E. J. Graff, *What Is Marriage For? The Strange Social History of Our Most Intimate Institution* (Boston: Beacon, 1999).
355. Lincoln, *Ephesians*, 390.

2. Ephesians 6:1-3 takes the generalized command to obey parents (Col 3:20) as an introduction to the specific commandment from the Decalogue (Exod 20:12; Deut 5:16). This citation indicates that the freedom from rules and regulations, which separated Israel as God's covenant people from Gentiles (2:15), did not apply to the Decalogue. Verse 2*b* attaches a particular significance to this commandment, the promise of a prosperous life in the land. Both Jews and Gentiles were accustomed to the legal conventions that gave the father of a family authority over the lives of all offspring regardless of their age, even though married children lived in separate households.[356] Such advice could be addressed to adult children in their relationships with parents as well as to those still in the household. Ephesians 6:4 indicates that the author has the latter in view. Anyone who deals with a group of school-aged children quickly finds a wide divergence in their willingness to obey parents or other adults.

Fear of punishment only compels short-term obedience. Parents and other adults sometimes try to discipline children with fear, but as soon as the adults are not looking, such kids are often out of control again. To name how a child's behavior might make parents or others feel is a much more reliable way to discipline. Older adolescents who avoid being drawn into serious trouble by their friends sometimes say that what kept them from going astray was their awareness of what it would have meant to a parent or some other family member if they had been injured or arrested. So Ephesians may have a point in shifting attention from the idea of a covenant curse, found in the earlier commandments, to the idea of promise, appended to this one. However, push the observable benefits of the promise too far into the future, and most young people lose motivation. The best coaches know that even a small taste of success does more to motivate compliance with a tough practice routine than threats or general promises.

Ephesians also modifies the instruction to fathers by dropping the motive clause from Col 3:21*b* and adding an injunction to provide children with an upbringing that includes knowledge of the Lord. What would such an education entail? If Deut 6:4-7 is the model envisaged, it makes concrete demands on Christian parents. Children have to see that their parents love God with their whole heart, that they know God's Word, and that they are anxious to share it with their children. "Keep these words that I am commanding you today in your heart. Recite them to your children and talk about them when you are at home and when you are away, when you lie down and when you rise" (Deut 6:6-7 NRSV).[357] Many churches, when an infant or an older child is baptized, ask parents to participate in some kind of faith-reflection experience, even if a parent is not a church member. Sometimes, as a result, an unbaptized parent comes to be baptized along with his or her son or daughter. The baptismal rituals in the various churches ask both the parents and the church community if they are willing to assume the responsibility for helping this child to grow up knowing the Lord. A Christian education is not information to be taught. It is a way of life to be lived. What is taught are the Scriptures, the songs, the prayers, and the faith stories that help us do that. But even more important, the parents and the larger community teach by example.

3. Despite acknowledging slaves as fellow members of the body of Christ, early Christians only condemn the more unpleasant aspects of the slave/master relationship: fawning, deceitful, and lazy behavior on the slave's part and harsh, threatening behavior on the master's. Christ is master of both slave and free Christian. Like the benevolent master, he will reward each according to the good service rendered. Scholars have pointed out that household and managerial slaves could anticipate advancement in the local pecking order; could benefit from an owner's patronage, and even possess names or epithets such as "master-loving" that support

---

356. O. Larry Yarbrough, "Parents and Children in the Letters of Paul," in *The Social World of the First Christians; Essays in Honor of Wayne A. Meeks,* ed. L. Michael White and O. Larry Yarbrough (Minneapolis: Fortress, 1995) 128n. 9.

357. Also see Deut 6:20-25; Prov 22:6. For a general discussion of education in ancient Israel, see James L. Crenshaw, *Education in Ancient Israel: Across the Deadening Silence* (New York: Doubleday, 1998).

the patronal ideology of master/slave relations.[358] Introducing Christ as the master who owns both slave and master reinforces the institution as it was being lived. It does not pose a challenge to it. By affirming Christians on the wrong side of the abolition debate in the nineteenth-century United States, the exhortations to slaves in the New Testament have come to enjoy a prominence in twentieth- and twenty-first-century arguments over the authority of Scripture. Its support for other sociocultural institutions comes into question by analogy with the debate over slavery.

That an expansion of equal rights had to progress to challenge all barriers of race, class, gender, and ethnic group was evident to those involved in the women's movement after the Civil War. The country could not get over that division without a new vision of humanity. Frances Ellen Watkins Harper sounded the call at the 11th National Women's Rights Convention in 1866: "We are all bound up together in one great bundle of humanity, and society cannot trample on the weakest and feeblest of its members without receiving the curse in its own soul."[359] Injustice is fostered if the weakest and feeblest buy into the ideology of the power elite. W. E. B. Du Bois noted the fracture in the souls of black churches between those seeking assimilation to a white-dominated culture of power, education, and business success and those with the recognition that freedom does not yet exist: "Back of this still broods silently the deep religious feeling of the real Negro heart, the stirring, unguided might of powerful human souls who have lost the guiding star of the past and are seeking in the great night a new religious ideal."[360] Ephesians 6:5-9 poses a troubling question for the Christian conscience: Do we stifle the new movements of the Spirit by clothing assimilation to a cultural ideology as service to Christ?

358. Dale B. Martin, *Slavery as Salvation: The Metaphor of Slavery in Pauline Christianity* (New Haven: Yale University Press, 1990) 28-34.

359. Quoted in Gates and McKay, *African American Literature*, 462.

360. W. E. B. Du Bois, "The Souls of Black Folk," in ibid., 711.

EPHESIANS 6:10-20, PERORATION: BE ARMED WITH THE POWER OF GOD

NIV	NRSV
[10]Finally, be strong in the Lord and in his mighty power. [11]Put on the full armor of God so that you can take your stand against the devil's schemes. [12]For our struggle is not against flesh and blood, but against the rulers, against the authorities, against the powers of this dark world and against the spiritual forces of evil in the heavenly realms. [13]Therefore put on the full armor of God, so that when the day of evil comes, you may be able to stand your ground, and after you have done everything, to stand. [14]Stand firm then, with the belt of truth buckled around your waist, with the breastplate of righteousness in place, [15]and with your feet fitted with the readiness that comes from the gospel of peace. [16]In addition to all this, take up the shield of faith, with which	10Finally, be strong in the Lord and in the strength of his power. [11]Put on the whole armor of God, so that you may be able to stand against the wiles of the devil. [12]For our[a] struggle is not against enemies of blood and flesh, but against the rulers, against the authorities, against the cosmic powers of this present darkness, against the spiritual forces of evil in the heavenly places. [13]Therefore take up the whole armor of God, so that you may be able to withstand on that evil day, and having done everything, to stand firm. [14]Stand therefore, and fasten the belt of truth around your waist, and put on the breastplate of righteousness. [15]As shoes for your feet put on whatever will make you ready to proclaim the *a*Other ancient authorities read *your*

NIV

you can extinguish all the flaming arrows of the evil one. [17]Take the helmet of salvation and the sword of the Spirit, which is the word of God. [18]And pray in the Spirit on all occasions with all kinds of prayers and requests. With this in mind, be alert and always keep on praying for all the saints.

[19]Pray also for me, that whenever I open my mouth, words may be given me so that I will fearlessly make known the mystery of the gospel, [20]for which I am an ambassador in chains. Pray that I may declare it fearlessly, as I should.

NRSV

gospel of peace. [16]With all of these,[a] take the shield of faith, with which you will be able to quench all the flaming arrows of the evil one. [17]Take the helmet of salvation, and the sword of the Spirit, which is the word of God.

18Pray in the Spirit at all times in every prayer and supplication. To that end keep alert and always persevere in supplication for all the saints. [19]Pray also for me, so that when I speak, a message may be given to me to make known with boldness the mystery of the gospel,[b] [20]for which I am an ambassador in chains. Pray that I may declare it boldly, as I must speak.

[a]Or In all circumstances   [b]Other ancient authorities lack of the gospel

COMMENTARY

The final section of the letter returns to the theme of divine power, introduced in its opening section (1:19-21). Christ has triumphed over powers at work in the present age (1:21; 2:2; 3:10). His exaltation provides the energy at work in believers and in the ministry of the imprisoned apostle (3:7). Ephesians 6:10-20 is the peroration that brings the letter to a rhetorical conclusion.[361]

The unit falls into three sections. Verses 10-13 contain an opening statement and the command to take up God's weaponry against the hostile spiritual powers (see 2:2; 4:27). Verses 14-17 link items of divine armor with virtues or gifts of salvation. Finally, vv. 18-20 return to the theme of prayer. This prayer asks that the imprisoned apostle continue his bold witness to the mystery of salvation (vv. 19-20; cf. 3:1-13). Readers know the content of the "mystery of the gospel" (μυστήριον τοῦ εὐαγγελίου *mystērion tou euangeliou*, v. 19; from 1:9; 3:3-4, 9; 5:32). By enlisting their prayers on behalf of the apostle, Eph 6:18-20 indicates that the discourse has brought its audience to maturity as members of the body of Christ.

The call to battle marks a striking departure from the realized eschatology of exaltation above the heavenly powers, which suggested that the

victory was already won. Lincoln detects an emotional appeal similar to those calls to battle that were composed for famous generals in the histories of the time.[362] If vv. 10-17 are the general's call to battle, what is the rhetorical impact of the shift in vv. 18-20? The general-orator is already in chains (v. 20)! Suddenly the image has shifted from armed soldier to the bold martyr able to disregard the threats of soldiers arrayed against him (cf. 2 Maccabees 7).

Both the image of the conquering general and that of the bold prisoner have antecedents in the Pauline letters. As prisoner, Paul testifies to imperial guards (Phil 1:12-14) and even fights with the beasts (1 Cor 15:32; a metaphorical expression for the hardships endured while preaching in Ephesus). As general, the apostle lays siege to those who resist knowledge of Christ with powers provided by God (2 Cor 10:3-6).[363] One may compare how first-century Cynic and Stoic philosophers spoke of the invulnerability of a wise man's soul when fortified by reason and secure virtue: "full of virtues human and divine, [the wise man] can lose nothing. . . . The walls which guard

---

361. So Andrew T. Lincoln, " 'Stand, therefore . . .': Ephesians 6:10-20 as *Peroratio*," *Biblical Interpretation* 3 (1995) 99-114.

362. E.g., Cyrus in Xenophon *The Education of Cyrus* 1.4; Hannibal and Scipio in Polybius 3.63; Anthony and Augustus in Dio Cassius *History* 1.16-30. See Lincoln, " 'Stand, therefore . . .': Ephesians 6:10-20 as *Peroratio*."

363. Abraham J. Malherbe, "Antisthenes and Odysseus, and Paul at War," *HTR* 76 (1983) 143-73.

the wise man are safe from both flame and assault, they provide no means of entrance, are lofty, impregnable, godlike."[364] Cynics referred to their rough garb as armor in the war against the temptations of a soft life, lovers, false opinions, or other forms of cultural imprisonment.[365] Dio argued that the philosopher's true weapons are words, not beggarly forms of dress.[366] Paul, however, does not give any description of the weapons that he uses, saying only that his weapons "have divine power to destroy" (2 Cor 10:4). The weapons appear to be the lowly form of life that his opponents have used as evidence against him (2 Cor 10:7-10.[367]

Second Corinthians 10:1-10 provides an indication that the general's call to arms and the bold prisoner image could be combined in describing the apostle. The apparent humiliation of imprisonment may even form part of the attack. The combination speaks eloquently to the rhetorical situation of the audience. Ephesians hints that imprisonment (and perhaps already death) has removed the apostle from the field. However, its readers are ready to take up the arms provided by God.

Details of divine armor do not occur in the earlier letters. First Thessalonians 5:8 picks two pieces of armor as metaphors: for the virtues of faith and love, the breastplate; and for hope of salvation, the helmet. Ephesians 6:14-17 must have created its picture of the armor from other sources. The closest parallels appear in descriptions from Isaiah, as *Fig.* 14 indicates.

A blessing of the "prince of the congregation" at Qumran also uses battle imagery to establish the new covenant: "He will renew the covenant . . . to establish the kingdom of his people forever [to judge the poor with justice]." This individual will be a fortress: "May the Lord raise you to an everlasting height, like a fortified tower upon the raised rampart." The word of his mouth is a sharp weapon: "May [you strike the peoples] with the power of your mouth. . . . With the breath of your lips may you kill the wicked." And he will be clad in armor: "May your justice be the belt [of

---

364. Seneca *On the Constancy of the Wise Man* 6.8. See Abraham J. Malherbe, *Moral Exhortation: A Greco-Roman Sourcebook* (Philadelphia: Westminster, 1986) 160.
365. Pseudo-Diogenes *Epistles* 34.
366. Dio Chrysostom *Orations* 19.10-12.
367. Malherbe, "Antisthenes and Odysseus, and Paul at War."

Figure 14: Eph 6:14-17 and the Armor of the Lord

Item	Ephesians	Isaiah and other parallels
belt ("having girded your loins")	**6:14** truth	**Isa 11:5** (LXX) righteousness
breastplate	**6:14** righteousness	**Isa 59:17** (LXX) righteousness (also **Wis 5:18**)
military sandals ("having shod your feet")	**6:15** equipment of the gospel of peace	[**Isa 52:7** (LXX) "the feet of those who preach the tidings of peace"]
shield	**6:16** faith	**Wis 5:19** holiness
helmet	**6:17** salvation	**Isa 59:17** (LXX) salvation
		Wis 5:18 impartial judgment
sword	**6:17** the Spirit, which is the word of God	[**Isa 49:2** (LXX) placed in the mouth of the servant "a sharp sword"]
		Wis 5:20 "wrath as a large sword"

---

your loins, and loyalty] the belt of your hips. May he place upon you horns of iron and horseshoes of bronze."[368]

Use of the Isaiah material in the book of Wisdom and in 1Q28b shows that the metaphor did not include a fixed set of correlations between armor and virtues. The blessing of the Prince of the Congregation from Qumran also indicates that the armor of the Lord can be transferred from God to human agents. Both Qumran and Ephesians refer to this armor without any citation formulae. Both assume that the audience will recognize the biblical cast of the imagery. Such recognition plays an important part in the linguistic code of each document. In the Essene text, God's blessing on the leader of the renewed covenant people equips him to be the agent of divine justice and judgment among the peoples. In Ephesians, the enemies to be resisted are no longer human but spiritual, quasi-demonic powers that govern the lower world. God's armor expresses the superior power of the creator already evident in the exaltation of Christ into the heavens. The philosophical tradition of the sage armed against the passions and false reasonings of humankind would not be sufficient in either context.

6:10-13. The introduction in verse 10 echoes Col 1:11. A call to be vigilant frequently appears in apocalyptic conclusions. Readers know God's power in the salvation that they have already experienced (1:19; 3:16, 30). Wearing the soldier's armor (v. 11; from Wis 5:17) presents a more striking metaphor for divine protection than do the earlier references to divine power. Though the concrete details of the armor are biblical, not Roman, the audience probably envisaged the fully armed Roman soldier when they heard these words (Jdt 14:3).[369]

The idea that Satan has designs on the righteous is familiar (2:2). The paraenesis warned against permitting anger to provide opportunities for the devil (4:27), but the catalog of powers in v. 12 has been a source of controversy since antiquity. Gnostic authors used this verse as evidence that the soul is trapped in a world created by the evil creator and his subordinate powers. One account of this mythology is introduced as

the revelation of the meaning of the apostle's words: "On account of the reality of the authorities inspired by the spirit of the father of truth, the great apostle referring to the 'authorities of darkness' [Col 1:13] told us that 'our contest is not against flesh and [blood]; rather, the authorities of the universe and the spirits of wickedness [Eph 6:12]."[370] Gnostic mythology gave more explicit expression to the hints in Ephesians that God has already given victory to the elect.[371]

Other exegetes have taken the peculiar term "cosmic powers" (κοσμοκράτορες *kosmokratores*) as evidence that Ephesians refers to the powers behind astrology and magic.[372] In inscriptions "cosmic power" implies that the deity invoked is omnipotent and universal. Use of the term in the plural is unusual, and Clinton Arnold contends that Ephesians wishes to demote Artemis and other deities in doing so. They are not universal rulers but members of the lower class of powers referred to as demons. Paul agrees that the pagan gods can be described as demons (1 Cor 10:20).

While the terms "ruler" (ἀρχη *archē*) and "authority" (ἐξουσία *exousia*) are frequently found in the New Testament (Eph 1:21; 3:10), the expressions "cosmic powers" and "spiritual forces of evil in the heavenly places" seem to have been coined by the author of Ephesians. They are equivalent to other descriptions of evil powers in Jewish apocalyptic (*Jub.* 10:3-13; *1 Enoch* 15:8-12; *T. Sim.* 4:9). By expanding the double expression "rulers and authorities" with these new terms, Ephesians has conveyed a sense that powers of evil pervade the cosmos. However, God's power is superior to any such forces. The expression found in v. 10 ("in the strength of his power") could be an allusion to Isa 40:26 LXX, "in the strength of might." Isaiah refers to the creative power of God in bringing forth the universe and its heavenly bodies.[373]

Verse 13 picks up the exhortation of v. 11. Given the strength of the forces arrayed against

---

368. 1Q28b 5:21-26.

369. Polybius 6.23. See Andrew T. Lincoln, *Ephesians,* WBC 42 (Dallas: Word, 1990) 435; Best, *Ephesians,* 591.

370. *Hypostasis of the Archons* 86,20-25.

371. Andreas Lindemann, *Die Aufhebung der Zeit: Geschichtsverständnis und Eschatologie im Epheserbrief* (Gütersloh: Gerd Mohn, 1975), 655.

372. Clinton E. Arnold, "The 'Exorcism' of Ephesians 6.12 in Recent Research: A Critique of Wesley Carr's View of the Rule of Evil Powers in First-Century AD Belief," *JSNT* (1987) 113-21.

373. Robert A. Wild, "The Warrior and the Prisoner: Some Reflections on Ephesians 6:10-20," *CBQ* 46 (1984) 287.

them, Christians must be well armed to withstand the day of battle. What does Ephesians mean by the expression "that evil day" (ἐν τῇ ἡμέρᾳ τῇ πονηρᾷ *en tē hēmera tē ponēra*)? Possibilities range from the evils of the time just before the end, particular instances of temptation, or simply everyday life in the present age. The apocalyptic background of much of the imagery makes a reference to end-time evil seem the most natural (cf. 1 Cor 7:26; 1 Thess 5:2-4). Elsewhere in Ephesians, however, apocalyptic expressions are usually converted to descriptions of present reality (see 1:21; 2:3, 7; 1:14, 18; 4:30; 5:5).[374] The vagueness of the concluding clause, "having done everything, to stand firm," suggests that the author has an indefinite future in mind. The structures of the present age will continue for an unknown period. The phrase does not specify what is meant by "having done everything." It could refer to having put on the armor or to having resisted the enemy when under attack.

6:14-17. Verse 14 picks up the verb "stand" (ἵστημι *histēmi*) from the end of the previous sentence. A series of participles describes being those standing as properly equipped with each piece of armor (vv. 14-17). As *Fig.* 14 indicates, the equipment and characteristics associated with the various items of armor have been taken from traditions concerning the armor of the Lord. Although the previous verses suggested that the combat was primarily defensive, most of the virtues in this section speak of positive actions. Such offensive acts bring the image closer to that of the Lord arming to come in judgment or to the Essene Prince of the Congregation ready to establish the new people of God. When Eph 4:24 uses the verb "clothe" (ἐνδύω *endyō*) for the new human being created in God's image, that new being is created in righteousness and holiness of truth. Righteousness, goodness, and truth are fruits of light (5:9). Thus virtues that Christians have "put on" when they were converted provide the desired armor. Military-style hobnailed sandals or short boots used as equipment for the gospel of peace suggest readiness for a long march, if readers associate the image with Isa 52:7. Romans 10:15 uses the same passage from Isaiah for messengers of the gospel. For Ephesians, the peace that comes through

preaching the gospel is constituted by the unity of Jew and Gentile in the body of Christ (2:14, 17).

Since v. 16 refers to withstanding an attack, some commentators reject the possibility that preaching the gospel is being referred to in v. 15.[375] Others suggest that the expression "whatever will make you ready to proclaim the gospel of peace" refers to the soldier as being armed to do battle in order to preserve a peace that has already been established, not to create that peace.[376] Ephesians speaks of peace as given by God's plan of salvation, harmoniously uniting all things in heaven and on earth in Christ (1:10). This plan has already been made known to the "rulers and authorities" in the heavens (3:10).

Unlike the small round shield (ἀσπίς *aspis*), the θυρεός (*thyreos*) was a full-length shield of leather-covered wood that protected the whole body.[377] Burning arrows have been used in attacks on besieged cities since Assyrian times. A soldier who became terrified by flaming arrows caught in his shield might throw it down and become vulnerable to enemy spears.[378] For the audience, these familiar images must also be linked to the use of "shield" for God (Gen 15:1; Pss 5:12; 18:30; 28:7) and to the arrows and sword God has readied for the wicked (Ps 7:12-13; Isa 50:11).

Arrows appear as metaphors for sins of speech (Prov 26:18). The blasphemous words that the wicked speak against God are fiery arrows that eventually ignite divine wrath.[379] The closest parallel to the image in Ephesians can be found in one of the Essene hymns. The righteous person, the speaker in this hymn, trusts in the Lord despite the attacks being mounted against him: "They—they attack my life on your account, so that you will be honored by the judgment of the wicked . . . heroes have set up camp against me surrounded by all their weapons of war; they loose off arrows without any cure; the tip of the spear, like fire which consumes trees."[380] It is the speaker's testimony to the truth about God that excites the attack of the wicked: "You have set

---

374. So Rudolf Schnackenburg, *The Epistle to the Ephesians,* trans. H. Heron (Edinburgh: T. & T. Clark, 1991) 275.

375. So Andrew T. Lincoln, *Ephesians,* WBC 42 (Dallas: Word, 1990) 449.

376. Schnackenburg, *The Epistle to the Ephesians* 278.

377. Polybius 6.23. See Lincoln, *Ephesians.*

378. Thucydides *The Peloponnesian War* 2.75,5.

379. CD 5:12-16; 1QH 11[3]:16; 27.

380. 1QH 10:23-26.

---

me as a reproach and a mockery of traitors, foundation of truth and of knowledge for those on the straight path."[381] Ephesians has already indicated that "the ruler of the power of the air" is the spirit working in "those who are disobedient" (2:2). Therefore the fiery arrows of the evil one might represent the speech of the wicked. If Ephesians makes the same associations with fiery darts that the Essene hymnist does, then the earlier reference to the "gospel of peace" should be taken in an active sense. The message conveyed by the faithful about God's salvation provokes the assaults that they suffer.

The active imagery returns in v. 17, which highlights offensive weapons. Along with the helmet, the faithful are encouraged to take up the sword that is the word of God. "Sword" refers to the short sword used in close combat. Ordinarily, the metaphor refers to the sword that comes from God's mouth to strike down God's enemies (Rev 1:16; 2:12, 16; 19:13, 15). In this context, "word" (ῥῆμα *rēma*) must refer to the Christian message, the gospel (as in Rom 10:8; 1 Pet 1:25).

6:18-20. Ephesians concludes the peroration by returning to the theme of prayer that opened the letter. The formula has been appropriated from Col 4:2-4. By turning the reader's attention back to the imprisoned apostle, the writer softens the dramatic emotional impact of the call to arms. The author now appeals to the audience's emotions. They should be eager to follow the example of the heroic apostle that has been set before them. Ephesians has already indicated that prayer is necessary for those who would receive divine power (1:15-23; 3:14-21). Exhortations and references to continual prayer are a regular feature of Pauline letters (Rom 1:9-10; Col 1:3; 4:12; Phil 1:4; 4:6; 1 Thess 5:17). The phrase "for all the saints" reminds the audience of its ties to all believers (1:15; 3:18). Prayer is regularly described as the activity of the Spirit in the believer (Rom 8:15-16, 26-27; Gal 4:6).

Philippians speaks of the effects of Paul's imprisonment. It has made others confident in preaching the gospel (Phil 1:14-16). The prayers offered on his behalf by the Philippians can be credited with delivering the apostle from prison— along with the agency of the Spirit (Phil 1:19-20).

The prayer formula at the conclusion to Ephesians has generalized this pattern. One can no longer anticipate that the apostle will be freed from prison.[382] Ephesians even omits the reference to an "open door" for proclaiming the gospel from Col 4:3. However, the addressees can share Paul's courageous testimony to the gospel through praying for him.

The self-description of the apostle as "ambassador in chains" (v. 20) has taken the term "serve as ambassador" from 2 Cor 5:20. Philemon 9 combines the terms "ambassador" and "prisoner." The reference to chains appears elsewhere in Acts 28:20 and 2 Tim 1:16. Both the weight and the manner of chaining prisoners made chains extremely painful. Coupled with lack of nourishment, such imprisonment could result in permanent damage to the prisoner's limbs. Because of the physical torture involved in being chained, later legislation referred to slavery and low social rank as "the punishment of bonds."[383] When the realities of prison are grasped clearly, the suggestion that the apostle would continue to boldly proclaim the gospel is more evidently heroic than is the case for readers who think only of modern prisons. The prison context also indicates that to speak of an ambassador in chains would be considered an oxymoron.[384] A wretched, dirty creature in chains could hardly make the rhetorical show necessary to accomplish the task of ambassador. Nevertheless, both Philippians and Philemon indicate that Paul did manage to use imprisonment as an opportunity to spread the gospel. This section indicates that he will continue to do so.

Much of the drama of this peroration depends upon the range of emotional associations that an audience attaches to the rich imagery that makes up the passage. Life as a combat with astral powers located in the lower regions of the air has been coupled with believers, putting on the armor of the divine warrior. Swords and arrows will not be effective against such weapons. But the tone of victory may be swept away when Ephesians

---

381. 1QH 10[2]:10.

382. On the uncertain fate of anyone sent to prison, the resulting depression and suicide, and the importance of that language for Paul's choice of life in Phil 1:19-26, see Wansink, *Chained*, 41-60; 96-125.

383. Brian Rapske, *The Book of Acts in Its First Century Setting*, vol. 3, *The Book of Acts and Paul in Roman Custody* (Grand Rapids: Eerdmans, 1994).

384. Lincoln, *Ephesians*, 454

shifts to the imprisoned apostle. Though the harsh conditions of imprisonment would seem to make witness to the gospel impossible, Philemon demonstrates that Paul might even convert fellow prisoners.

Ephesians does not suggest that its readers are about to be imprisoned as Paul is. But the world in which they live is not going to be transformed. Hostile powers still govern the present age. They may attack the saints through the fiery arrows of verbal polemic. At one level, the armor appears to be equivalent to the new clothing that Christians put on when they are converted. At another, as the parenetic section of the letter indicates, preparation to withstand attack must be continu-ous. Believers must hear sermons, read scripture, talk with other Christians, engage in regular prayer, sing the praises of God, and so on.

Ancient philosophers highlight the connection between open or bold speech and freedom. Someone who has a secure grasp on his or her identity as a believer cannot be forced to surrender that truth. The armed soldier of this section provides an image of the secure believer. Such persons cannot be found shifting from one opinion to another, "tossed to and fro and blown about by every wind . . . by their craftiness in deceitful scheming" (4:14); their position should instead be "speaking the truth in love" (4:15).

REFLECTIONS

This section creates a striking visual image: the Christian standing as a fully armed Roman infantry soldier against assault, flaming arrows thrown down from above. By reminding us of armed guards at the beginning, the author also heightens the pathos of Paul, a chained prisoner speaking boldly as an ambassador for the gospel. No ambassador presented in chains has much of a chance for the success of his embassy. The initial depiction of humans armed against forces that are more than human, against spiritual powers, fits an established pattern in apocalyptic texts. Ordinarily, the conflicts of the evil times at the end of the world are described as demonic in inspiration. Angelic figures like Michael do battle against the spiritual forces that the faithful righteous ones struggle against on earth. This scenario understands the sufferings of the righteous as part of the testing that belongs to the last days.[385] Though its images suggest such a scenario, Ephesians departs from the apocalyptic vision in two ways: timetable and victory. There is no reference to the impending divine judgment that closes the time of struggle (cf. 1 Thess 5:1-11). Nor does Ephesians foresee a future victory over the powers, as in 1 Cor 15:24-28. The heavenly exaltation of Christ has already defeated them (Eph 1:20-23).

Consequently, the image of Christian life as a struggle between the soul, which belongs to the heavenly kingdom of Christ, and evil powers, which operate in this world from the heavens, provided a prime text for Gnostic and Manichaean salvation myths.[386] The spiritual practice of monks in the Egyptian desert saw the ascetic engaged in a direct struggle with the demons. Their appearance revealed the impurity of the monk's own heart. Recitation of phrases from Scripture had the power to drive demons away, even if the monk did not understand the meaning of those words.[387] Contemporary readers are less likely to see the demons as external beings than internal forces that infect the psyche. The quest for holiness forces a confrontation with the tangled web of confusion, sin, and ignorance in the human heart. Nor should the injunction to take up the armor of God and stand firm be limited to individuals. Groups are also subject to a dynamic that works for evil that no one individual would engage in separately. Psychologists note that group discussion can lead persons to extreme statements they would

---

385. For discussion of this scenario as it appears in the Dead Sea Scrolls, see John J. Collins, *Apocalypticism in the Dead Sea Scrolls* (London: Routledge, 1997) 57, 93-104.

386. Robert A. Wild, S.J., "The Warrior and the Prisoner: Some Reflections on Ephesians 6:10-20," *CBQ* 46 (1984) 294-95.

387. Douglas Burton-Christie, *The Word in the Desert: Scripture and the Quest for Holiness in Early Christian Monasticism* (New York: Oxford, 1993) 123-24.

never make on their own. Combine that dynamic with religious ritual, and people who are ordinarily tolerant of others become capable of violence toward deviant members of the group or outsiders.[388] The concern Ephesians shows for the way Christians speak, pray, and sing indicates that the ethical consequences of language were already well known.

Remember the emphasis on bold preaching of the gospel in 6:19. That may be the key to the whole drama in this section. By the time Ephesians was written, the apostle Paul had died. Christ may have defeated the powers in the heavens, but the gospel still must be proclaimed on earth (6:15). Anyone who does so can expect to enter the arena against all the personal and social forces that resist transformation by the Word of God.[389] Father Wild suggests that we see this passage as an ideal image to encourage Christians in all the tasks required of them: "The cosmic and demonic powers still seek to exercise a tyranny over the Christian, and in that sense the Christian appears to be 'in bonds.' In actuality, however, the bonds are broken and the powers are defeated 'in Christ.' They have God's armor, and it is God who guarantees their freedom."[390]

---

388. Robin Dunbar, *Grooming, Gossip, and the Evolution of Language* (Cambridge, Mass.: Harvard University Press, 1996) 143.

389. Clinton E. Arnold, *Ephesians: Power and Magic. The Conception of Power in Ephesians in Light of its Historical Setting*, SNTSMS 63 (Cambridge: Cambridge University Press, 1989) 120-21.

390. Wild, "Warrior and the Prisoner," 294.

FINAL GREETING

NIV

²¹Tychicus, the dear brother and faithful servant in the Lord, will tell you everything, so that you also may know how I am and what I am doing. ²²I am sending him to you for this very purpose, that you may know how we are, and that he may encourage you.

²³Peace to the brothers, and love with faith from God the Father and the Lord Jesus Christ. ²⁴Grace to all who love our Lord Jesus Christ with an undying love.

NRSV

²¹So that you also may know how I am and what I am doing, Tychicus will tell you everything. He is a dear brother and a faithful minister in the Lord. ²²I am sending him to you for this very purpose, to let you know how we are, and to encourage your hearts.

²³Peace be to the whole community,ᵃ and love with faith, from God the Father and the Lord Jesus Christ. ²⁴Grace be with all who have an undying love for our Lord Jesus Christ.ᵇ

ᵃ Gk *to the brothers*   ᵇ Other ancient authorities add *Amen*

COMMENTARY

Ancient letters ended with information about the sender's immediate plans, additional instructions, or words to particular individuals. Since Ephesians is not addressed to an audience that knew Paul personally, such concrete details are lacking. By contrast, Colossians ends with an extended list of greetings and instructions to named individuals (Col 4:10-17). Ephesians has taken wording for the final greeting from Colossians, as *Fig.* 15 indicates.

The final words diverge from Colossians. Ephesians does not conclude in the apostle's own hand (as do Gal 6:11; Phlm 19), and the reference to Paul's imprisonment has been relocated to the peroration (v. 20).

In Colossians the double reference to how Paul is doing (4:7) and how "we are" doing (4:8) makes sense because Col 1:1 identified Timothy as co-sender of the letter. There is no cosender in Eph 1:1, but its author has retained the second plural reference anyway. Tychicus appears in Acts 20:4 as one of Paul's companions from Asia Minor. His name reappears in the pastorals as emissary to Ephesus and Crete (2 Tim 4:12; Titus 3:12). The notice that connected Tychicus and Ephesus provides a basis for the speculation—ap-

pearing in those manuscripts that add the phrase "in Ephesus" to the opening (1:1)—that this general letter was addressed to Christians in Ephesus.

The final greeting (vv. 23-24) expands the short form found in Colossians somewhat awkwardly. Its structure reflects the "grace to you and peace from God our Father and the Lord Jesus Christ" of the opening greeting (1:2). The expression "love with faith" (ἀγάπη μετὰ πίστεως *agapē meta pisteōs*) is unusual, as is the lack of a vocative or a second-person plural for those who are the object of the concluding blessing. Instead of personal greetings, Ephesians employs generalized expressions: "peace to the brothers" (NRSV, "the whole community") and "grace be with all who have an undying love for our Lord Jesus Christ." Consequently, any Christians who happen upon the letter may feel themselves included as its addressees. This form of address may indicate that Ephesians was composed as a circular letter.

The letter's final prepositional phrase, "in incorruptibility" (ἐν ἀφθαρσίᾳ *en aptharsia*, translated as the adjectival "undying" in the NRSV and NIV), is awkward. One might expect the term "incorruptibility" to describe a divine attribute (Rom 1:23; 1 Tim 1:17). If so, the phrase refers to the

---

Figure 15: Eph 6:21-24 and Col 4:7-9, 18

Item	Ephesians	Colossians
information about the sender	**6:21** and that you may know how I am and what I am doing,	**4:7** how I am doing,
person who brings the letter	**6:21*b*** Tychicus, the beloved brother, faithful minister in the Lord will make everything known to you	**4:7*b*** Tychicus, the beloved brother, faithful minister, and fellow servant in the Lord will make everything known to you
recommendation for the bearer	**6:22** whom I have sent to you for this purpose, that you may know how we are doing, and to be encouraged in your hearts	**4:8** whom I have sent to you for this purpose, that you may know how we are doing and be encouraged in your hearts
final blessing	**6:23-24** Peace to the brothers, and love with faith, from God the Father and the Lord Jesus Christ. Grace with all who love our Lord Jesus Christ in incorruptibility.	**4:18** I, Paul, write the greeting with my own hand. Remember my bonds. Grace be with you.

Lord exalted in incorruptibility. But one would expect a verbal form to connect "the Lord" with the prepositional phrase or the adjective modifying that word. Therefore, the phrase probably modifies the verb "love" (ἀγαπάω *agapaō*) as in the NRSV and the NIV. It asserts that love of Christ is not subject to decay. This reading is grammatically clearer, though it still yields an awkward expression. First Corinthians 15:42 uses the prepositional phrase to describe the risen body. A formulaic passage in 2 Tim 1:10 speaks of Christ abolishing death and bringing to light life and incorruptibility through the gospel. These examples show that if "in incorruptibility" refers to

believers, "incorruptibility" should refer to their eschatological situation, not the quality of their love of the Lord. Perhaps Ephesians is referring to those who love the Lord as the church that exists with him "in the heavenly places" (2:6-7). Its existence is the result and evidence of the richness of God's grace toward those who believe. Thus the author indirectly returns to one of the great themes of the letter. The existence of the church, united in love with its head, is the sign of God's loving providence. God wills to unite all people in the new creation. Like all divine attributes, the response to God's grace—love for the Lord Jesus—is also incorruptible.

THE LETTER TO THE PHILIPPIANS

INTRODUCTION, COMMENTARY, AND REFLECTIONS
BY
MORNA D. HOOKER

THE LETTER TO THE

PHILIPPIANS

INTRODUCTION

The characteristic note of Paul's letter to the Philippians is above all that of joy—a remarkable feature, in view of the fact that this letter was written in prison, where its author was held under a capital charge! Paul's faith triumphs over adversity and causes him to rejoice, whatever happens. The letter is written to a Christian community with whom Paul has had a long and happy relationship; though they are not yet perfect, they are nevertheless his joy and his crown, in whom he hopes to boast on the day of judgment (2:16; 4:1).

The founding of the Christian community at Philippi (probably in about 50 CE) had marked a significant development in Paul's ministry, opening up a new area for missionary work. According to Acts 16, Paul was prevented by the Holy Spirit from preaching in Asia or Bithynia, so he made his way to Troas, where he received a summons, in a dream, to go to Macedonia. This was considerably farther west than Paul had so far ventured. The Acts account is of particular interest, since it is at this precise point (Acts 16:10) that the "we" passages begin, suggesting that either Luke or his source had accompanied Paul on this mission.

Philippi was a fairly small city in the first century CE (approx. 10,000 inhabitants), situated on the Via Egnatia, which ran from east to west, taking travelers to the Adriatic coast and hence, by boat, to Italy. The port of Neapolis lay ten miles to the south and Thessalonica 100 miles to the southwest. Philippi had originally flourished because of gold mines nearby, but these had been worked out long before the first century CE, and the

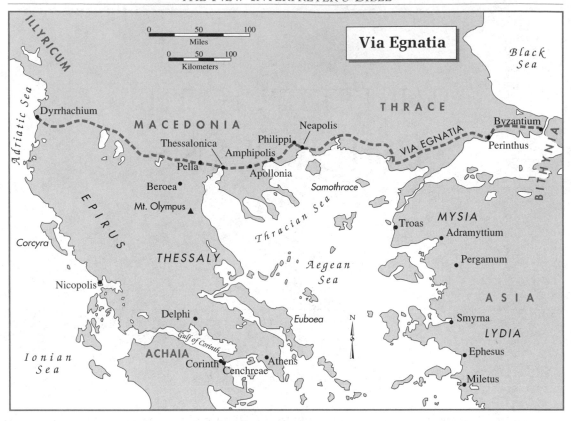

city was important mainly as an agricultural center, being situated on the edge of a fertile plain where grain and wine were produced. The original inhabitants of the area had been Thracians, but in the fourth century BCE it had been taken by Philip II of Macedon, who founded a Greek city on the site of an earlier village and gave it his own name. The city had come under Roman rule in the second century BCE, and after Antony and Octavian defeated Brutus and Cassius at the battles of Philippi in 42 BCE it had been refounded as a Roman colony, and many Italians had been brought in and settled. It was not (contra Acts 16:12) "the leading city of the district of Macedonia." Macedonia was in fact divided into four districts, and Philippi was in the first of these. (Luke may have been confused, or it is possible that he wrote "a city of the first district of Macedonia," as the NRSV margin suggests.) The fact that the city was a Roman colony gave its citizens great privileges, for they enjoyed considerable property and legal rights and were exempt from the taxes imposed on those without this status. Citizens of the colony were also citizens of Rome, and the city's administration was modeled on that of Rome.

When Paul came to Philippi, therefore, he would have found a sizable nucleus of Roman citizens, many of whom were Italian by birth and who constituted the aristocracy of the city. He would have found Roman administration and discipline as well as Roman culture. The official language was Latin (public inscriptions in the city were written in Latin), and the city was loyal to Rome, which meant, among other things, that the cult of the emperor would have been much in evidence. The men who are described in Acts 16:16-21 as dragging Paul and Silas before the magistrates are clearly understood by Luke to have been Roman citizens, but the majority of the inhabitants of the city would have been Greeks who had flocked in after the earlier conquest by Philip of Macedon. In the rural areas around Philippi in particular Paul would have found some of the original inhabitants of the land, the Thracians. No archaeological evidence has been found for a Jewish presence in the city; perhaps it was not sufficiently important commercially to attract them. It is notable that Luke makes no reference to a synagogue in Philippi; to be sure, Paul discovers "a place of prayer," but apparently the only people gathered there are women, and the one with whom Paul speaks is not herself Jewish, but a God-fearing Gentile. This account supports the belief that any Jewish presence in Philippi was minimal. Paul's converts would have been entirely, or almost entirely, Gentile. As for their previous religious beliefs, the mixed population of the city meant that various religious cults would have been practiced in the city, alongside the official cult of the emperor.

In the letter itself, there are possible reflections of these circumstances. The term Paul uses to address the Philippians in 4:15 is a Latin form of their name, rather than Greek. The name "Clement" in 4:3 is also Latin, but the names "Syntyche" and "Euodia" (4:2) are Greek. The reference to bishops and deacons in 1:1 may indicate a more developed organization (under Roman influence) than elsewhere, while the references to "citizenship" (see the Commentaries on 1:27 and 3:20) would have had a special nuance for the inhabitants of Philippi. Finally, the declaration of Jesus Christ as Lord in 2:11 may well have been intended as a deliberate challenge to the loyalty they were expected to give to the Roman emperor as Lord.

AUTHORSHIP AND INTEGRITY

The authenticity of the epistle is not seriously in dispute, though doubts have been expressed from time to time. F. C. Baur's objections were entirely subjective—the letter did not conform to what he expected from a Pauline epistle—and more recent attempts to apply objective literary tests to the letter (with a negative result) have been treated with considerable skepticism.[1]

More serious questions, however, have been raised concerning the epistle's integrity. Many commentators believe that it consists of two—or even three—letters that have been joined together. The arguments in favor of this hypothesis are as follows:

(1) There are abrupt jumps in Paul's argument, most notably at 3:1. It is suggested that these are easier to understand if they are due to an editor's piecing various letters together. In fact, however, this "solution" merely creates another problem: Why did an *editor* make such unsuitable joins? The more it is argued that it is difficult to understand why Paul should move abruptly from one topic to another, the more difficult it becomes to

---

1. See A. Q. Morton and James McLeman, *Paul, the Man and the Myth* (London: Hodder & Stoughton, 1966); their method was based on too many questionable assumptions to carry conviction.

comprehend an editor's motives in doing so. Indeed, it is easier to attribute sudden changes in subject to Paul than to an editor!

(2) Paul had recently received a gift from the Philippian church, brought to him by Epaphroditus. Thus it is frequently assumed that one of the chief reasons why he had written to them was to thank them for that gift. This he does in 4:10-20, almost at the end of the letter, whereas courtesy and literary convention alike would surely have demanded that he begin his letter by expressing his thanks. It is suggested, therefore, that 4:10-20 is part of an earlier "thank-you" letter. Since the earlier part of the letter was clearly written some time after the receipt of the gift (news about Epaphroditus's illness having reached the Philippians and information about their reaction having come to Paul, 2:26), it is possible that Paul has indeed already expressed his thanks, either by letter or by a message of some kind. If that is the case, then his apparently belated and comparatively muted reference to the Philippians' gift in 4:10-20 is understandable. This would, of course, mean that any such earlier letter has been lost. If, on the other hand, we assume that this letter has been incorporated into the existing letter, then part of it (its opening paragraph at the very least) has been lost; it would seem, moreover, that the editor who placed it here did not feel that this (to us) strange position was inappropriate.

It has been pointed out, however, that there are in 4:10-20 "echoes" of the vocabulary used in 1:3-11 and that the two passages thus form an inclusio. If this is deliberate, then not only does it suggest that one of Paul's main purposes in writing to the Philippians was to express his thanks for their gift, but it means also that the letter must have been composed as a unity.[2]

(3) In a letter written to the Philippian church by Polycarp, a second-century bishop and martyr, there is a reference to letters written by Paul to the Philippian church.[3] Unfortunately there is great debate as to whether the plural should be taken seriously and whether Polycarp was perhaps confused about the destination of some of Paul's epistles. Even if we take Polycarp's words as evidence that more than one letter to the Philippians was in existence in his time, however, this does not prove that these letters were later amalgamated. There is no textual evidence to support the view that letters that were still separate in Polycarp's day were subsequently brought together. If there was, in fact, more than one letter, the others appear to have been lost.

In spite of the various problems this theory involves, the view that what we know as the letter to the Philippians represents an amalgamation of two or three letters is popular among many commentators. Although there is considerable disagreement about precisely how to distribute the material, 1:1–3:1 is usually allocated to one letter and 4:10-20 to another; there is much debate, however, as to where the fragment of letter beginning in 3:2 might end, and this uncertainty is an indication of the fragility of the arguments. Moreover, attempts to produce a coherent series of letters leave us with a huge problem:

2. G. W. Peterman, *Paul's Gift from Philippi,* SNTS monograph 92 (Cambridge: Cambridge University Press, 1997) 90-120.
3. Polycarp *Epistle to the Philippians* 3.

Why should an editor piece Paul's letters together in this way? Had the originals been damaged, so that one or two letters existed as fragments only? If so, why did the editor make such a bad job of joining them together? The problems arising from this theory are such that it seems much easier to accept the letter as a unity. The features in Philippians that puzzle us (such as the sudden change of subject in 3:2 and the position of 4:10-20) are probably due to factors in Paul's situation that we do not fully understand.[4]

PLACE AND DATE

The place and date of writing the letter have proved equally contentious. It is clear that Paul was writing from prison (1:7, 12-18); therefore, the question at issue is where this prison was situated. The traditional answer (dating from at least the second century) was Rome, and there are strong arguments to back this up. The chief of these is that the situation reflected in the letter suits the conditions of Paul's imprisonment in Rome, insofar as these can be reconstructed from Acts. Paul had appealed to Caesar and had been taken as a prisoner to Rome. There he waited for a long time in custody (at least two years, according to Acts 28:30). Acts tells us that Paul was under house arrest during this time, but Luke does not complete the story. The tradition that Paul was martyred in Rome means that we must allow that at some stage he found himself in prison under a capital charge, which is the situation reflected in Philippians 1. Support for Rome as the place where the letter was written is found in two incidental references in Philippians. The first is the mention of the praetorium in 1:13; unfortunately the meaning of the word is uncertain, since it can refer to a building as well as to the praetorian guard, and both building and guard could be situated in cities other than Rome. However, the context of 1:13 seems to indicate that Paul had the guard in mind, and they would have been more likely to have been stationed in Rome than elsewhere. The second is the reference to Caesar's household in 4:22, a term that included a large number of officials. Again, they could be found throughout the empire, but there would certainly have been a far greater number of them in Rome than elsewhere.

Three arguments have been brought against Rome as the place of origin. The first is that Philippians is much more "like" earlier letters, such as Romans, than it is like the other letter Paul may have written from Rome—Colossians (though the authorship, as well as the place, of that letter is strongly disputed). This, however, is a subjective judgment. Philippians is "like" Romans in some ways, and unlike it in others; similarly, it has interesting parallels as well as differences with Colossians. These similarities and differences are hardly surprising, since letters reflect the particular circumstances in which and the situations for which they were written. Moreover, Romans was probably the last of Paul's letters to have been written before his Roman imprisonment.

4. Loveday Alexander has analyzed Philippians in the light of the structures of contemporary Hellenistic letters and argued that the latter are by no means inconsistent with the unity of the letter. See Alexander, "Hellenistic Letter-Forms and the Structure of Philippians," *JSNT* 37 (1989) 87-101.

A second argument has been given far more weight and relates to the distance between Rome and Philippi (approx. 800 miles), which would have made any journey between the two cities very long and tedious (approx. two months). Philippians implies several such journeys—news of Paul's imprisonment sent to Philippi, Epaphroditus sent by the Philippian church to Paul, news of Epaphroditus's illness sent to Philippi and news of their concern sent back to Paul, and now the letter itself sent to Philippi—far too many, it is suggested, to be possible if the distance was so great. The strength of this objection, too, seems to have been exaggerated. Communications in the ancient world were reasonably good, and Rome and Philippi were both strategically placed for such journeys. Travel was, of course, arduous and slow by modern standards—but this is reflected in the letter itself, in the reference to the anxiety of the Philippians as they await news of Epaphroditus. Moreover, since Paul spent at least two years in custody in Rome, there was plenty of time for numerous journeys.

The third objection to Rome as the place where this letter was written is that Paul says in 2:24 that he is hoping to visit the Philippians on his release, whereas in Rom 15:22-29 he had said that he planned to go on from Rome to Spain. If Paul is imprisoned east of Philippi, he could visit the city en route to Rome and Spain, but to visit it after Rome would be to head in the wrong direction. Romans 15:22-29 was written before his imprisonment, however, and several years in prison (both at Caesarea and at Rome) could well have caused Paul to change his mind. It would not have been the first time that Paul had altered his plans (see 2 Cor 1:15-23).

Two other suggestions as to the place of writing have been made. One is Caesarea, where Paul is said to have been imprisoned for two years (Acts 24:27) and where he was kept in a building called a praetorium (Acts 23:35). Caesarea was even farther from Philippi than was Rome, however, and the journey just as tedious. The serious objection to placing the letter's composition in Caesarea is that Paul was at no time in danger of execution while he was there, and it is difficult to relate his situation at Caesarea to what he says in Phil 1:19-26.

The other suggestion, which has gained wide support, is Ephesus, which is situated much closer to Macedonia so that the journey between the two cities would have been much shorter. There is, to be sure, nothing in Acts to indicate that Paul had been imprisoned there, but Paul says that he has been in prison many times (2 Cor 11:23). He also refers to an occasion when his life was in danger in Asia (2 Cor 1:8-10): Was this the occasion when he fought with wild beasts at Ephesus (1 Cor 15:32)? Unfortunately, we do not know what Paul was alluding to in that passage, but it can hardly have been meant literally, since he survived the experience. While it is possible that Paul was imprisoned in Ephesus, there is no evidence at all that he was incarcerated there for a considerable length of time under a capital charge. Moreover, Paul had many friends in Ephesus, whereas he appears to have been feeling extremely isolated when writing to Philippi.

If Paul wrote Philippians from Ephesus, then we would need to date it about 52–54 CE; if from Caesarea, then it would have been written about 60 CE. If, as seems most probable, we place it in Rome, then the date of composition would have been the early 60s.

PURPOSE FOR THE LETTER

Opinions differ widely as to the reason why Paul wrote the letter. Many commentators assume that his main purpose was to deal with some major problem in the Philippian church, which they deduce must have been that of disunity. Paul does not rebuke the church, however—apart from the implied mild rebuke directed to two leaders in 4:2. The gentleness with which Paul deals with that situation suggests that the problem is a minor one; when there were serious problems in a community Paul did not hesitate to deal with them vigorously.

Paul seems to have had two main reasons for writing. The first is to reassure his readers about his own situation. This he does—unusually—at the beginning of his letter (1:12-26), in order to allay their natural concern for him. The other reason is to commend Epaphroditus and to explain why he is returning to Philippi. Paul is probably anxious lest Epaphroditus be criticized for not staying with Paul.

A subsidiary reason for writing seems to have been to express his thanks (probably for a second time) for their gift to him. Although the section where he does so comes at the end of the letter (4:10-20), there are possible references earlier (1:5; 2:17, 25) that hint at his gratitude for what he regards as a response to the gospel rather than simply as a personal gift. The generosity of the church is witnessed to elsewhere (see 2 Cor 8:1-6).

It was probably Epaphroditus's return to Philippi that gave Paul the opportunity to send a letter. Paul took advantage of this journey to offer the Philippians encouragement and advice. How much of this was particularly related to the situation in Philippi we do not know, for what Paul wrote was appropriate to any Christian community. The references to suffering are particularly apt in the Philippian situation, however, since we know that the members of the church were being persecuted (1:28-29), and the stress on mutual forbearance was apposite in view of 4:2. The warning against Judaizers in 3:2 is fleeting, perhaps because Paul realized that there was no great danger from Judaizers in a city where there were almost no Jews.

These Judaizers are only one group among several who are often labeled "opponents." It is, perhaps, helpful to distinguish between them, since there appear to have been four distinct groups who are referred to in this letter: (1) Those who are personally opposed to Paul and whose motives in preaching the gospel are questionable (1:15-18). These people are nevertheless regarded as Christians, since they are acknowledged to preach the gospel. (2) The people who are described as opponents of the Philippians and who are persecuting them (1:28-29). This group consists of pagan outsiders. (3) Those attacked in 3:2 who are almost certainly Judaizers, whether Jewish or Gentile by birth. (4) The people described as "enemies of the cross of Christ" (3:18-19), who appear to be a group of libertines claiming to be Christians, but whom Paul clearly considers to be living in a manner totally at variance with the gospel.

IMPORTANCE OF PHILIPPIANS

Philippians has had a great influence on the thought of later theologians, largely because of the significant ideas expressed in the so-called hymn in 2:6-11. To a large extent, the passage was interpreted in a way never intended by Paul. Poetic langage was analyzed as though it were the language of dogma, and the passage was taken as an authoritative statement about the divine and human natures of Christ. In the nineteenth century, the "kenotic" theory of the incarnation was based upon it. If we wish to attempt to understand the passage in its historical context, we need to remember that Paul wrote what he did here, not in order to deal with the issues of Christ's divinity and humanity that so exercised the Church Fathers in the fourth and fifth centuries, but to spell out the way in which those who are in Christ ought to live. The passage is, indeed, an important christological statement—but its importance lies not only in what it says about Christ, but also in its implications for the lives of those who acknowledge Christ as Lord. It is Paul's insight into the relevance of divinity (who and what God is and does) to true humanity (who and what men and women should be and do)—of what we term "theology" to "ethics"—that makes this letter of great and lasting theological significance.

BIBLIOGRAPHY

Commentaries:

Bockmuehl, Markus. *The Epistle to the Philippians.* Black's NT Commentary. Peabody, Mass.: Hendrickson, 1998. Orig. pub. London: A & C Black, 1997. A balanced commentary, based on the author's own translation. Scholarly but readable, this is likely to appeal to a broad range of readers.

Caird, G. B. *Paul's Letters from Prison.* NCB. Oxford: Oxford University Press, 1976. A short commentary based on the RSV text. A useful guide in spite of its brevity.

Fee, Gordon D. *Paul's Letter to the Philippians.* NICNT. Grand Rapids: Eerdmans, 1995. A very thorough, but nevertheless readable, commentary, since detailed discussion is confined to the footnotes. Based on the NIV translation, though with frequent disagreements.

Lightfoot, J. B. *Saint Paul's Epistle to the Philippians.* 7th ed. London: Macmillan, 1883. A classic commentary on the Greek text. Dated, but still valuable. Contains a famous essay, "The Christian Ministry."

O'Brien, Peter T. *The Epistle to the Philippians.* NIGTC. Grand Rapids: Eerdmans, 1991. A useful modern commentary for those who wish to grapple with the Greek text.

Specialized Studies:

Bloomquist, L. Gregory. *The Function of Suffering in Philippians.* JSNTSup 78. Sheffield: Sheffield Academic Press, 1993. A technical study that applies the insights of rhetorical and epistolary analysis to Philippians to see what light they throw on the theme of suffering.

Martin, R. P. *Carmen Christi: Philippians 2:5-11 in Recent Interpretation and in the Setting of Christian Worship.* SNTSMS 4. Grand Rapids: Eerdmans, 1983. A classic survey of the history of interpretation of Phil 2:5-11, together with the author's own exegesis. Now inevitably somewhat dated.

Martin, Ralph P., and Brian J. Dodd, eds. *Where Christology Began: Essays on Philippians 2.* Lousiville: Westminster John Knox, 1998. A useful collection of essays assessing recent interpretation of Phil 2:5-11.

Peterman, G. W. *Paul's Gift from Philippi: Conventions of Gift Exchange and Christian Giving.* SNTSMS 92. Cambridge: Cambridge University Press, 1997. A technical study of Paul's response to the financial help he received from the church in Philippi, in the light of contemporary conventions regarding the exchange of gifts.

Wright, N. T. *The Climax of the Covenant: Christ and the Law in Pauline Theology.* Edinburgh: T. & T. Clark, 1991. Contains, among much else, a revised version of an essay orginally published in *JTS,* NS 37 (1986) on the meaning of ἁρπαγμός (*harpagmos*) in Phil 2:6.

OUTLINE OF PHILIPPIANS

I. Philippians 1:1-11, Letter Introduction

    A. 1:1-2, Address

    B. 1:3-8, Thanksgiving

    C. 1:9-11, Intercession

II. Philippians 1:12-26, Paul's News About Himself

    A. 1:12-18*a*, Paul's Imprisonment

    B. 1:18*b*-26, The Approaching Crisis

III. Philippians 1:27–2:18, The Christian Life, Part 1

    A. 1:27-30, Stand Fast!

    B. 2:1-4, Our Life in Christ

    C. 2:5-11, The Mind of Christ

    D. 2:12-18, Our Necessary Response

IV. Philippians 2:19-30, Future Plans

    A. 2:19-24, Timothy

    B. 2:25-30, Epaphroditus

V. Philippians 3:1–4:1, The Christian Life, Part 2

    A. 3:1-11, The True Basis for Confidence

    B. 3:12–4:1, Keep Going!

VI. Philippians 4:2-23, Letter Conclusion

    A. 4:2-9, Various Exhortations

    B. 4:10-20, A Personal Note of Thanks

    C. 4:21-23, Closing Words

PHILIPPIANS 1:1-11

LETTER INTRODUCTION

OVERVIEW

This opening section follows the typical pattern of Paul's letters: The greeting or address (vv. 1-2) is followed by a thanksgiving (vv. 3-8), which here merges into a prayer of intercession (vv. 9-11). Paul's thanksgivings frequently introduce the themes that are going to be taken up in the body of the letter.[5] We find Paul touching here on three topics to which he is going to return: (1) the Philippians' participation in the gospel, (2) the way in which God is going to continue the work begun in them until it is brought to completion on the day of Jesus Christ, and (3) Paul's own imprisonment and defense of the gospel.

It is interesting to note that there is no specific reference in these verses to the need for unity in the Philippian community, unless the frequent use of the word "all/every" ($\pi\hat{\alpha}\varsigma$ *pas*), found seven times in the first nine verses, is a hint of this. The fact that Paul does not here refer directly to the theme of unity throws doubt on the assumption of many commentators that disunity and personal ambition were serious problems in the Philippian community.

5. See Paul Schubert, *The Form and Function of the Pauline Thanksgivings*, BZNTW 20 (Berlin: A. Töpelmann, 1939) 180.

PHILIPPIANS 1:1-2, ADDRESS

NIV

1 Paul and Timothy, servants of Christ Jesus,

To all the saints in Christ Jesus at Philippi, together with the overseers[a] and deacons:

[2]Grace and peace to you from God our Father and the Lord Jesus Christ.

[a]1 Traditionally *bishops*

NRSV

1 Paul and Timothy, servants[a] of Christ Jesus,

To all the saints in Christ Jesus who are in Philippi, with the bishops[b] and deacons:[c]

2Grace to you and peace from God our Father and the Lord Jesus Christ.

[a] Gk *slaves*   [b] Or *overseers*   [c] Or *overseers and helpers*

COMMENTARY

Ancient letters usually began with the opening formula, "X to Y, Greetings." Paul adopts the formula but transforms it at every point: The writers, recipients, and greetings are all defined in Christian terms. The letter is from Paul and Timothy. The reference to Timothy does not mean that he helped to dictate the letter, which is very much Paul's own (see also 2:19-24); he is included as a matter of courtesy, since he was

known well to the Philippians (see Acts 16:1-12; subsequent visits are probably implied in Acts 19:22; 20:3-4). He is nevertheless listed with Paul as an equal, unlike 2 Corinthians, Colossians, and Philemon, where Paul describes himself as "an apostle [or prisoner] of Christ Jesus" and refers to Timothy as "our brother."

In such opening greetings, Paul typically describes himself as an "apostle" (e.g., 1 and 2

Corinthians; Galatians), but here he refers to both Timothy and himself as "servants of Christ Jesus" (see also Romans). Is this, perhaps, because he does not feel the need to emphasize his own authority as an apostle when writing to the Philippians? Or is there some particular reason for choosing the word "servants"? The Greek term is δοῦλοι (*douloi*), a word that in the ancient world was used of slaves (see the NRSV note). Has it perhaps been chosen because Paul already has in mind the theme elaborated on in chap. 2, where he speaks of Christ's taking the form of a slave (2:7)? Certainly in chap. 3 Paul describes his Christian calling in terms of being conformed to the pattern of Christ, and he urges the Philippians to imitate his example. Is Paul using the term *douloi* here, then, because he wishes to remind the Philippians that they must not think too highly of themselves (see 2:1-4)?

The parallel with Philippians 2 is not a good one, however, since δοῦλος (*doulos*) there suggests a lack of status and subjection to the powers that hold humanity enslaved. The phrase "*douloi* of Christ" on the other hand is, paradoxically, a term of honor. To be a "*doulos* of God" was an honorable calling in the OT. The psalms contain frequent references to God's people as *douloi* (e.g., Ps 19:11, 13 [18:12, 14]), and David, in particular, is described as God's *doulos* (Ps 89:3[88:4]). If the word does have a forward look here, then it must also be to 2:11, where Christ is proclaimed as κψριος (*kurios*), "Lord." Paul and Timothy proudly declare their allegiance to Christ and then send greetings in his name (v. 2).

The letter is addressed to "all the saints in Christ Jesus at Philippi." "The saints" (οἱ ἅγιοι *hoi hagioi*) is a term used of the people of God (e.g., Ps 34:9[33:10]), called to be holy because they belonged to a holy God (cf. Lev 19:2; Deut 7:6; 14:2). But these "saints" owe their status to the fact that they are "in Christ Jesus." Already in the opening verse of the epistle we find this crucial phrase "in Christ," which is so important for Paul. Those who are in Christ are those who have been baptized into him, who have metaphorically shared his death and resurrection, dying to their old lives of sin in order to live with him a new life of righteousness. In chap. 2, Paul will remind the Philippians of what it means to be in Christ Jesus, including the fact that the community should be united. Some have argued that it is in order to stress this essential unity that the letter is addressed to *all* the saints.

Somewhat surprisingly, Paul adds the phrase "with the bishops and deacons," as though they were not included among "the saints." This is the only Pauline letter in which they are specifically addressed. For some reason he appears to wish to single them out for special mention. But why? And who were they? The use of the two words ἐπίσκοποι (*episkopoi*, "bishops") and διάκονοι (*diakonoi*, "deacons") together in v. 1 suggests that particular office bearers are in mind. Nevertheless, the words are not yet technical terms; the fact that they follow the reference to Paul and Timothy as *douloi* is a clear indication that we are not yet dealing with any kind of hierarchy. (The variant reading *"fellow* bishops," properly ignored by the translators, is clearly due to a scribe who was worried on this point.) For this reason, the NIV's "overseers" is preferable to the NRSV's "bishops" (see also the NRSV note), although the more general term "superintendents" might be better. The word *episkopoi* is used in the plural, and there is no suggestion as yet of a monarchical bishop. Rather, it refers to those who have pastoral oversight of the congregation (cf. 1 Thess 5:12). Elsewhere in the NT the term appears to be used synonymously with the word πρεσβύτεροι (*presbyteroi*, "elders"; Acts 20:17, 28; Titus 1:5-7; 1 Pet 5:1-2), a word that in the Pauline corpus is found only in the Pastoral Epistles (1 Tim 5:1-2, 17, 19; Titus 1:5). Commentators writing in the early centuries of the common era agreed that the two terms were used interchangeably in the NT. Apart from the Pastorals (1 Tim 3:2; Titus 1:7), this is the only occurrence of *episkopos* in the Pauline corpus. The term διάκονος (*diakonos*) is used more frequently, usually in a way that emphasizes the service being rendered (e.g., Rom 15:8, of Christ; 1 Cor 3:5; 2 Cor 6:4). The reference to Phoebe as a *diakonos* of the church in Cenchrae (Rom 16:1) shows how the word was beginning to be used of someone called to a specific ministry, but "deacon" is an anachronistic translation, while the NRSV's "helpers" is too vague. The more general "ministers" is preferable.

Is Paul referring to two groups of people or one? *Diakonos* cannot be regarded (like πρεσβύτερος *presbyteros*) as a synonym of ἐπίσκοπος (*episkopos*), since it denotes service, not seniority; but it is possible that we should translate the whole phrase as "superintendents who are also ministers"—that is, "leaders of the community who also serve." It seems more likely, however, that Paul is referring to two groups, and this suggests that some kind of structural organization is beginning to emerge in the Philippian Christian community. It will not be long before the words he uses here have become technical terms.

Although none of Paul's other letters begin in this way, there are plenty of examples of contemporary official letters that began by greeting both the community and its leaders. As in Philippians, these leaders are not usually mentioned again in the text of the letters, but they would presumably have had a particular responsibility for dealing with the matters raised in them. Why does Paul follow this custom of naming specific leaders here? Three explanations have been suggested. The first is that the *episkopoi* and the *diakonoi* had organized the gift that had been sent to Paul from the church (4:10-19), and he therefore thought it appropriate to acknowledge this fact by sending them a special greeting. The second is that he considered them to need a special word of encouragement (or reprimand) and was indicating that he hoped they would take note of what he was about to write. Were the leaders of the Philippian community tending to regard themselves as better than others? Were they therefore in need of the warning given in 2:3? Were the two women mentioned in 4:2, Euodia and Syntyche, among these leaders? Or did Paul perhaps follow the term "overseers" with the term "ministers" in order to remind the leaders gently that they should be serving the community? The third explanation is that the Christian community in Philippi was influenced by the structures of the society in which it existed, thus reflecting the Roman genius for organization. Written late in Paul's life, the letter indicates the beginnings of a need for structural organization that would later develop throughout the church. Of these three explanations, the first seems the most probable, but they are by no means exclusive.

Paul greets his readers in his usual manner (v. 2), wishing them grace and peace. The usual secular opening, "Greetings," is replaced by the reference to divine grace; "peace" is the customary Jewish greeting. Both gifts derive from "God our Father," whose people the readers are, and from "the Lord Jesus Christ," in whom they have their existence and whose servants Paul and Timothy are (v. 1).

REFLECTIONS

1. From its very first line, Philippians reflects the transformation brought by the gospel to every part of human life. The traditional epistolary opening formula is subtly changed. Writers and recipients alike are defined by their relationship to God and to Christ, and what the writers wish for their readers consists of gifts from God the Father and the Lord Jesus Christ. More than two thousand years later, it is easy to miss this significant emphasis; phrases that would have impressed the Philippians by their innovative approach now seem to us merely part of the conventional letter opening. To their first readers, however, these opening verses would have been a reminder that the whole of life had been transformed by the proclamation of the gospel.

2. Whatever the reason for the special reference to those who held office in the Philippian church, the letter is addressed to the whole community. All are "in Christ Jesus" and so belong to the fellowship of God's people. Once again, the terms have become so familiar that we no longer appreciate their real significance. We think of "saints" as very special people and forget that we are *all* called to be saints—to be members of God's people and, therefore holy, like God. This new status belongs to those who are "in Christ," who claim their new relationship with God because of their relationship with Christ. It is because Christ is God's holy one that those who belong to him are "saints" (the Greek word ἅγιοι [*hagioi*] means "holy ones"). Our proper emphasis on individual responsibility has tended to make us think of sanctity as something personal and private, but Christianity is primarily a calling to belong to a community. The church is not simply a group of individuals who happen to have responded to the gospel; it is the community of God's people, whose corporate life is an essential expression of their divine calling. Paul would certainly have endorsed John Wesley's maxim that "Christianity is essentially a social religion; and that to turn it into a solitary religion, is indeed to destroy it."[6] Paul's emphatic "all" (1:4, 7-8) will remind us how important this idea is.

3. The terms "bishop" and "deacon" signify to us offices within the church. However, we need to remember that for Paul and his first readers, the words referred primarily to functions rather than to status. The bishops had pastoral oversight, and the deacons were those who served the community. Status was undoubtedly as important in first-century Philippi as it is in our modern world; yet, for himself and for Timothy, Paul claims the title "slaves [NRSV and NIV, "servants"] of Christ." The gospel throws all our human values on their heads: The truly great are servants, and those who are really first are those who are slaves of all (Mark 10:44). It is notable that although Paul uses the terms "slave/servant" and "servant/minister" of both Jesus and himself, he never uses the term "bishop" of either. The essence of the gospel is seen in service, not in the exercise of authority.

6. John Wesley, *Forty-four Sermons,* XIX.1.1.

PHILIPPIANS 1:3-8, THANKSGIVING

NIV

[3]I thank my God every time I remember you. [4]In all my prayers for all of you, I always pray with joy [5]because of your partnership in the gospel from the first day until now, [6]being confident of this, that he who began a good work in you will carry it on to completion until the day of Christ Jesus.

[7]It is right for me to feel this way about all of you, since I have you in my heart; for whether I am in chains or defending and confirming the gospel, all of you share in God's grace with me. [8]God can testify how I long for all of you with the affection of Christ Jesus.

NRSV

3I thank my God every time I remember you, [4]constantly praying with joy in every one of my prayers for all of you, [5]because of your sharing in the gospel from the first day until now. [6]I am confident of this, that the one who began a good work among you will bring it to completion by the day of Jesus Christ. [7]It is right for me to think this way about all of you, because you hold me in your heart,[a] for all of you share in God's grace[b] with me, both in my imprisonment and in the defense and confirmation of the gospel. [8]For God is my witness, how I long for all of you with the compassion of Christ Jesus.

[a] Or *because I hold you in my heart*   [b] Gk *in grace*

COMMENTARY

Paul's thanksgiving for the Philippian community is unqualified and intensely personal. Timothy has been forgotten, and Paul has lapsed into the first-person singular. He expresses joy (v. 4), gratitude (v. 5), confidence (v. 6), affection (v. 7), and longing for them all (v. 8). His opening words, stressing his constant prayer for them, are typical of his letters (see esp. 1 Thess 1:2-3): He thanks God every time he remembers them (v. 3). It is possible, however, that we should translate the last phrase of this sentence (lit., "at your every remembrance") somewhat differently and read it as "for your every remembrance [of me]," rather than "at [my] every remembrance of you." This suggestion is attractive because it would mean that Paul begins his letter by thanking the Philippians (or rather God!) for their gift, instead of apparently somewhat ungraciously ignoring it until the last page of his letter. This translation, however, is grammatically difficult; we would ordinarily expect the object of the remembrance (in this case "me") to be expressed. Theologically, it is even more difficult: Would the Philippians' gift have been the first thing Paul mentioned? Was he not far more grateful to God for their progress in the gospel than for any financial gift?

The reference to joy (v. 4) is typical of this epistle, in which joy is a constant theme. The noun χαρά (chara) and the cognate verbs "to rejoice" (χαίρω chairō) and "to rejoice with" (συγχαίρω sygchairō) are used fourteen times. The four occurrences of "all" (πᾶς pas) in two lines of Greek text ("every," "constantly/always," "every/all," "all") are surely indications of the measure of Paul's gratitude, rather than hints of the need for unity, as some suggest. The first particular cause of Paul's joy is the Philippians' participation ("sharing/partnership") in the gospel (v. 5). This could be a reference to the way in which the Philippians have supported Paul by their prayers, but it seems to suggest rather more. In 4:3 he describes Euodia and Syntyche as having struggled beside him in the cause of the gospel, and he speaks of others at Philippi who have been his "co-workers." It is possible, however, that what Paul has in mind particularly in v. 5 is the financial help they have given him. The word κοινωνία (koinōnia, "sharing," "partnership") is, in fact, used elsewhere in Paul's letters with reference to financial contributions (Rom 15:26; 2 Cor 8:4; 9:13), as is the cognate verb κοινωνέω (koinōneō, Rom 12:13; Gal 6:6; Phil 4:15). If Paul is thinking of their gift, then it is interesting to note the way in which he refers to it: By their giving the Philippians have become partners *in the gospel.* What they have given is not a personal gift to Paul (though it has brought him material comfort), but rather a means whereby they share in the task of spreading the good news.

If this is the meaning, then we do have a reference to the Philippians' recent gift in the opening lines of the letter. Their generosity toward him is one of the reasons why Paul remembers them constantly with joy. They have shared in the promotion of the gospel "from the first day until now" (v. 5), and we know from 4:15-16 that they had given financial aid in the early days of Paul's ministry in Macedonia. Their readiness to share in the work of the gospel is seen in v. 6 as "a good work"—not, however, a good work for which they are responsible, but one begun in them by God and one that Paul is "confident" will be brought to completion by the day of Christ Jesus. (A similar contrast and connection between beginning and completing is found in Gal 3:3.) As always, Paul's confidence about the future is grounded in what God has already done in the past (cf. Rom 5:9-10). However, we should, perhaps, see the "good work" as referring to more than the Philippians' partnership in the gospel. Paul probably has in mind God's work in saving the community, of which their eagerness to assist in spreading the gospel is evidence.

The OT expectation of the day of the Lord is here interpreted as "the day of Christ Jesus." Paul sometimes refers to this event as "the day" (Rom 13:12; 1 Cor 3:13; 1 Thess 5:4) or "that day" (2 Thess 1:10), sometimes uses the OT expression "the day of the Lord" (1 Thess 5:2; 2 Thess 2:2; probably 1 Cor 5:5), and occasionally specifies that it is "our Lord Jesus Christ" (1 Cor 1:8) or "our Lord Jesus" (2 Cor 1:14). In Philippians, however, he prefers the phrase "the day of Christ" (1:10; 2:16) or, as here, "the day of Christ Jesus." The reference to Christ would certainly remind the Philippians once again that what will happen in the future is the completion of what has already been begun: It is the Christ in whom they believe, and whose story is told in 2:5-11, whose coming is now expected. Paul gives no hint as to when he expects this day to arrive. It will be a day of judgment, bringing both salvation and condemnation; judgment will be made "through Jesus Christ" (Rom 2:16), and Christ will save his own from wrath (1 Thess 1:10). This is why Paul is confident (v. 6).

"It is right" (i.e., "only natural," REB), says Paul, for him to think/feel this way about the Philippians (v. 7). Here we have the first occurrence of the key verb φρονέω (phroneō, "to think/feel"), used ten times in Philippians. Its meaning is less cerebral than "think" but more deliberate than "feel"; we lack an appropriate English verb that combines the activity of heart and head. It refers to an attitude or mind-set; it will be used in 2:5 of the attitude of Christ himself, an attitude that should be shared by those who are "in him." Perhaps there is already something of this sense in the use of the word in v. 8, for Paul goes on to say that he longs for the Philippians "with the compassion/affection [lit., bowels] of Christ." In Hebrew thought the bowels were regarded as the seat of human emotion, but Paul claims to love the Philippians with the bowels of Christ. That is, his affection for them is no mere human affection but is rooted in the love and compassion of Christ—a love and compassion that will be spelled out in 2:6-11.

The reason why he should feel this way toward them is stated in v. 7, but the first phrase is ambiguous, as the different translations of the NRSV ("you hold me in your heart") and the NIV ("I have you in my heart"; cf. the NRSV note) indicate. The Greek construction can be understood either way, but the order of the words slightly supports the NIV. Either interpretation makes sense, since the basis of this special regard is the fact that the Philippians are all participants with Paul in the grace experienced both during his imprisonment and in the defense and confirmation of the gospel. The Greek word meaning "fellow participants" (συγκοινωνοί *sygkoinōnoi*, "share") echoes the word used in v. 5. In what sense do the Philippians "share [with Paul] in God's grace"? Is this another reference to the financial assistance they have given him in prison? Or is Paul linking their experience to his because they are involved in the same struggle as he, a struggle that inevitably brings suffering (vv. 19-30)? Whichever it is, it is notable that Paul describes it as a sharing in grace, rather than as a sharing in labor or in suffering. Equally notable is his reference to the defense and confirmation of "the gospel." We might have expected him to refer to his *own* defense, but clearly he sees his own imminent trial as part of a much greater event in which the gospel itself is on trial. In this trial, the faith and behavior of the Philippians play a significant part. It is, perhaps, the legal imagery of v. 7 that leads Paul to call on God as his "witness" to "testify" how he longs for the Philippians (v. 8). He is clearly eager to assure them of the strength of his warm feelings for them.

REFLECTIONS

Because Christians are members of a community, their commitment is expressed in Christian fellowship. Paul refers twice in these verses to the fact that the Philippians have "shared" in the gospel and in grace; clearly they have shared not only in what they have received, but also in what they have given. The Christian community is called to partnership in the gospel (1:5) by helping the work of evangelism and in mutual support of other Christians by prayer and giving.

Many of our own letters begin with a "thank you," and in view of the fact that he has received money from the Philippians, we might well expect Paul to do the same. As in all his letters (with the exception of Galatians) Paul does, indeed, begin with thanksgiving, but his thanks are directed not to the Philippians but to God. Whether or not there is a subtle allusion to the Philippians' gift in these opening verses, it is God who is thanked for the Philippians' response to the gospel, since God is the source of that gospel (1:5) and the one who not only began the good work in them but can be depended upon to complete it as well. Paul praises God rather than the Philippians for their faithfulness and support, since whatever they do is a sharing in the gospel they have received and a sharing in God's grace as well (1:7). At the same time, Paul's thankfulness for the Philippians' progress in the gospel would certainly have encouraged them.

Our own prayers turn very quickly to petition and intercession, and we frequently take for granted the gift of the gospel and God's grace. Paul, on the contrary, pours out his heart in gratitude to God for all God has done and is continuing to do. When we remember Paul's situation in prison, with a capital sentence hanging over him, we are surely rebuked by his approach. This attitude pervades the whole epistle; even when Paul refers in 1:7 to his own imprisonment, he describes the Philippians as those who "share in God's grace." We might have expected him to say that they shared in his suffering! But he regards every circumstance as an experience of grace; therefore, his first response is thanksgiving, not petition. He remembers the Philippians constantly—with joy (1:4), with confidence (1:6), and with a love that is more than human affection, because it derives from Christ himself (1:8).

Paul's constant prayers of thanksgiving for the Philippian church would undoubtedly have strengthened his own bonds with that community. In our prayers for other Christians, do we spend enough time remembering them with joy, with confidence, and with love, or do we rush straight into intercession for them? We sometimes worry about how intercession works, as though prayer is empty unless it brings about certain results. Perhaps we ought to consider this problem in relation to the whole question of Christian prayer. We would do well to remember the saying of Meister Eckehart: "If the only prayer you ever say in your life is 'thank you,' that would be sufficient." Certainly we can see how Paul's outpouring of thanks would strengthen the Philippians' own faith as well as cement the relationship between them and Paul.

PHILIPPIANS 1:9-11, INTERCESSION

NIV	NRSV
[9]And this is my prayer: that your love may abound more and more in knowledge and depth of insight, [10]so that you may be able to discern what is best and may be pure and blameless until the day of Christ, [11]filled with the fruit of righteousness that comes through Jesus Christ—to the glory and praise of God.	[9]And this is my prayer, that your love may overflow more and more with knowledge and full insight [10]to help you to determine what is best, so that in the day of Christ you may be pure and blameless, [11]having produced the harvest of righteousness that comes through Jesus Christ for the glory and praise of God.

COMMENTARY

The introduction concludes with Paul's prayer for the Philippians, a prayer that their love may increase "more and more" in "knowledge" and "insight" (v. 9). The object of this love is not specified, but it is clear from the rest of the letter that it includes the people of Philippi as well as God. Paul's emphasis elsewhere on love as the fulfillment of the law (Rom 13:8-10; Gal 5:14) is open to the charge that it is too vague. Here he specifies that the Philippians need knowledge of God and insight so that they can distinguish the things that matter (v. 10), and thus make the right moral decision. The aim is that they should be "pure and blameless" on the day of Christ—some-

thing about which Paul has just expressed confidence (v. 6). "The harvest/fruit of righteousness" (v. 11) is ambiguous. It can mean either the fruit that *is* righteousness or the fruit that *comes from* righteousness. In the first case, "righteousness" (δικαιοσύνη *dikaiosynē*) is a synonym for the moral purity and blamelessness just described; in the second, it refers to the relationship with God that comes through being in Christ and that bears fruit in the form of purity and blamelessness. The second interpretation seems more likely, since the metaphor suggests that the "fruit" is produced by something else; it is supported by Paul's reference to the righteousness from God that comes through faith (3:9). Because their purity derives from the righteousness that is theirs through Jesus Christ, it will, of course, be to the glory and praise of God. There are some remakable variants in the Greek text, and one early manuscript (P⁴⁶) reads "for the glory of God and my praise." This reading seems at first highly unlikely, but one wonders how it arose if it was not original. Moreover, the word ἔπαινος (epainos), meaning "approval," "commendation," or "praise," is ordinarily used in classical Greek and by Paul of a recognition directed to humans. Later in the epistle Paul speaks of boasting about the Philippians on the day of Christ (2:16) and describes them as his "joy and crown" (4:1), while in 1 Cor 4:5, when describing his ministry, he refers to the *epainos* everyone will receive from God when the Lord comes. It is just possible, then, that Paul was expressing this idea here; if so, then we have to remember that it is God who will do the commending/approving and that what Paul has been able to do among the Philippians has been done through the grace of God. But Jewish prayers commonly end in a doxology, and we expect this one to do the same. The text followed by both the NIV and the NRSV is almost certainly the correct one.

REFLECTIONS

1. When Paul finally turns to making requests, they are for the Philippians, and not for himself. What he asks for is a growth in Christian love—that it may overflow and that it may be enriched by knowledge and insight. Head and heart are not opposed: Our love for God grows as we learn more about God and about God's love for us. Augustine's dictum "Love and do as you like"[7] is far more profound than it might seem at first sight, for if our love is informed by knowledge and insight we will understand something of God's nature and will; therefore, what we want to do will be in accordance with God's purpose. Similarly, true Christian love for others is not a sentimental affection but a sincere desire for what is best for them. Love is often said to be blind, but such blindness can stop us from discerning the deepest needs of those we love. True love, on the other hand, requires knowledge and insight in order to help others reach their full potential.

2. The source of our love for God and for other people is God. The goal that we be "pure and blameless on the day of Christ" (1:10) will also be achieved by God, who "began a good work" in us (1:6). And what we offer to God is the "harvest/fruit of righteousness"—a righteousness, or right relationship with God, that we possess only because we are "in Christ." No wonder Paul concludes this section with the declaration that this is all to the glory of God! For Paul, this is the motive and goal for the whole of life. Is it, we may ask ourselves, also ours?

3. The introductory section of the epistle is permeated by Paul's confidence in God. He is confident that God will complete what God has begun (1:6); confident that God's grace is with him, even in prison (1:7); confident that his prayers for the Philippians will be answered and that by their lives God will be glorified. Paul's confidence is not just a vague hope; it is based firmly on what God has done in the past and on his conviction that God is consistent. God has begun a good work and will not give up; it will be completed on the day of Jesus Christ—the same Jesus who was crucified and exalted (2:6-11). Do we today base our hopes for the future on what God has done in the past? Or do we think of the future in terms of an escape from this life, rather than as a completion of what has been started here?

7. Augustine *Homilies on First Epistle of John* viii.8.

PAUL'S NEWS ABOUT HIMSELF

OVERVIEW

It is unusual for Paul to begin the main body of his letter by reporting his own news; 2 Corinthians is the only other exception. He probably does so here because he has heard that the Philippians are anxious about him. Even here, however, he tells them little about what is happening to him. His main concern is that, in spite of his imprisonment, his work as an apostle is continuing.

PHILIPPIANS 1:12-18*a*, PAUL'S IMPRISONMENT

NIV

¹²Now I want you to know, brothers, that what has happened to me has really served to advance the gospel. ¹³As a result, it has become clear throughout the whole palace guard*a* and to everyone else that I am in chains for Christ. ¹⁴Because of my chains, most of the brothers in the Lord have been encouraged to speak the word of God more courageously and fearlessly.

¹⁵It is true that some preach Christ out of envy and rivalry, but others out of goodwill. ¹⁶The latter do so in love, knowing that I am put here for the defense of the gospel. ¹⁷The former preach Christ out of selfish ambition, not sincerely, supposing that they can stir up trouble for me while I am in chains.*b* ¹⁸But what does it matter? The important thing is that in every way, whether from false motives or true, Christ is preached. And because of this I rejoice.

a13 Or whole palace   b16,17 Some late manuscripts have verses 16 and 17 in reverse order.

NRSV

12I want you to know, beloved,*a* that what has happened to me has actually helped to spread the gospel, ¹³so that it has become known throughout the whole imperial guard*b* and to everyone else that my imprisonment is for Christ; ¹⁴and most of the brothers and sisters,*c* having been made confident in the Lord by my imprisonment, dare to speak the word*d* with greater boldness and without fear.

15Some proclaim Christ from envy and rivalry, but others from goodwill. ¹⁶These proclaim Christ out of love, knowing that I have been put here for the defense of the gospel; ¹⁷the others proclaim Christ out of selfish ambition, not sincerely but intending to increase my suffering in my imprisonment. ¹⁸What does it matter? Just this, that Christ is proclaimed in every way, whether out of false motives or true; and in that I rejoice.

a Gk brothers   b Gk whole praetorium   c Gk brothers
d Other ancient authorities read word of God

COMMENTARY

Paul addresses the community as "brothers" (NIV; paraphrased as "beloved" in the NRSV; see also 4:8). The Greek term used here (ἀδελφοι *adelphoi*), though masculine in form, was understood to include women as well as men. He assures them that the setbacks he has endured have, in fact, helped the progress of the gospel (v. 12). This paradox is demonstrated, first, in the fact that the cause of his imprisonment has become widely known (v. 13) and, second, in the fact that other Christians have been emboldened by his imprisonment to preach the gospel (v. 14).

What has been made known is that Paul's imprisonment (lit., "chains") is "in Christ." The NIV and the NRSV both describe this as being "for Christ"; the phrase we might have expected Paul to use. In fact, however, he prefers his favorite expression, "in Christ" (ἐν Χριστῷ *en Christō*), which he has already used in v. 1 and which serves here to remind us that he interprets the suffering he experiences as a sharing in the suffering of Christ. Paul's imprisonment is thus not simply the *result* of his proclamation of the gospel, but a *means* of proclaiming it, since the fact that his imprisonment is "in Christ" has "become known/clear": φανερὸς γίνομαι (*phaneros ginomai*, "to make manifest/known/clear") is a phrase often used of revelation.

The cause of Paul's imprisonment has been made known "throughout the whole imperial/palace guard." The Greek word πραιτώριον (*praitōrion*) was used both of the imperial guard, whose headquarters were in Rome, and of the building that housed them there (see the alternative translations in the NRSV and the NIV margins); it was also used of the residency of a Roman governor in the provinces. Here, followed by "to everyone else," it probably refers to the guard itself, rather than to a building; since the guard could serve outside Rome, this does not settle the question of the place of Paul's imprisonment, though Rome seems the most likely option. For Paul, what is significant is that knowledge of the gospel has penetrated the Roman establishment.

Paradoxically, "most of the brothers" have been encouraged by Paul's imprisonment to speak the word with greater boldness (v. 14). Presumably, Paul's own courage and confidence in the Lord have inspired other Christians. The reference to boldness/courage and fear indicates that there is danger for them, too. The phrase "in the Lord" can be taken with the word that precedes it in Greek (NIV, "brothers in the Lord"), to which, however, it adds nothing. It should, therefore, probably be linked with the word that follows (NRSV, "confident in the Lord"), indicating the source of their encouragement. They speak "the word," a common expression for the gospel in

the NT; its meaning is clear, whether or not we follow those MSS that read "of God" (as in the NIV; cf. NRSV).

We now discover that some of those who are fearlessly proclaiming the word have been emboldened to do so because Paul is out of the way! They preach Christ "from envy and rivalry . . . out of selfish ambition, not sincerely" (vv. 15*a*, 17). Their intention is to cause Paul distress in prison. Others, however, have precisely the opposite motives. They preach Christ from "goodwill" and out of "love," since they know that Paul has been put in prison "for the defense of the gospel" (vv. 15*b*-16). Whereas their actions arise from what they *know* (v. 16), the members of the other group are motivated by what they wrongly *suppose* (v. 17 NIV). The contrast between the two groups is emphasized by the chiastic structure of vv. 15-17. Astonishingly, Paul declares in v. 18 that their motives do not matter, since both groups are preaching Christ, and he, therefore, rejoices.

Both the NIV and the NRSV describe the second group as preaching from "goodwill" (v. 15). In fact, the Greek word εὐδοκία (*eudokia*) is more often used in the sense of "divine will/good pleasure," as it is in 2:13. Possibly Paul is not referring here to the preachers' attitude toward him but to the fact that they are preaching in obedience to the divine will and out of love—a love that is not for Paul alone, though it certainly includes him. They understand that Paul has been "put here [i.e., in prison] for the defense of the gospel" (v. 16; cf. v. 7). The "here" is missing in Greek, and the verb κεῖμαι (*keimai*) means "to stand," "to lie," "to be placed," or "to be appointed." There is probably something of this last sense here: Paul's imprisonment is not an accident of fortune, but part of the commission he has received from God.

Who were the people whom Paul describes as preaching Christ out of "false motives"? They certainly cannot be the "dogs" of 3:2, who glory in circumcision and not in Christ, for there is no suggestion in chap. 1 that those whom he had in mind were preaching the wrong gospel (cf. Gal 1:6-9, where the "different gospel" preached by the Judaizers is dismissed as a false gospel, and Gal 5:4, where those who accept this "other" gospel are said to cut themselves off from Christ).

The people Paul had in mind in chap. 1 were apparently preaching the right gospel from the wrong motives, so they could not have been either Judaizers or Gnostics. Why were they envious of Paul? Was it because before his imprisonment he was winning more converts than they were? Was their rivalry the kind of rivalry reflected in 1 Cor 1:12, which gave undue honor to Christian leaders? Were these people like those whom Paul attacked in 2 Corinthians, who criticized him because they expected their leaders to be respected members of society, whereas Paul frequently experienced physical distress and humiliation—even imprisonment—for the sake of the gospel? Yet in 1 and 2 Corinthians, Paul appears to consider such attitudes to be a misunderstanding of the gospel, and it is difficult to understand how he thought Christ was being truly preached by these people if their motives were such a denial of love and Christian fellowship.

If the letter was written from Rome, there could well have been Christians living there who were suspicious of Paul and who felt that his approach was bringing the Christian community into conflict with the Roman authorities, and therefore into physical danger. They might have been relieved that Paul was out of the way, in prison, unable to cause trouble by disputing with his fellow Jews, which could so easily lead the state to intervene. Rumors of their activities would have reached Paul in prison, and he might have misunderstood their motives. He was clearly hurt, but his language here was perhaps exaggerated. Whatever the explanation, it seems that Paul did not criticize these people on the grounds of their doctrine or conduct—save only in their attitude to him. They proclaimed Christ (vv. 15, 17); therefore, he presumably regarded them as "brothers" (v. 14). In spite of their attitude, then, and in spite of his imprisonment, he rejoices! (See Reflections at 1:18*b*-26.)

PHILIPPIANS 1:18*b*-26, THE APPROACHING CRISIS

NIV

Yes, and I will continue to rejoice, [19]for I know that through your prayers and the help given by the Spirit of Jesus Christ, what has happened to me will turn out for my deliverance.*a* [20]I eagerly expect and hope that I will in no way be ashamed, but will have sufficient courage so that now as always Christ will be exalted in my body, whether by life or by death. [21]For to me, to live is Christ and to die is gain. [22]If I am to go on living in the body, this will mean fruitful labor for me. Yet what shall I choose? I do not know! [23]I am torn between the two: I desire to depart and be with Christ, which is better by far; [24]but it is more necessary for you that I remain in the body. [25]Convinced of this, I know that I will remain, and I will continue with all of you for your progress and joy in the faith, [26]so that through my being with you again your joy in Christ Jesus will overflow on account of me.

a19 Or salvation

NRSV

Yes, and I will continue to rejoice, [19]for I know that through your prayers and the help of the Spirit of Jesus Christ this will turn out for my deliverance. [20]It is my eager expectation and hope that I will not be put to shame in any way, but that by my speaking with all boldness, Christ will be exalted now as always in my body, whether by life or by death. [21]For to me, living is Christ and dying is gain. [22]If I am to live in the flesh, that means fruitful labor for me; and I do not know which I prefer. [23]I am hard pressed between the two: my desire is to depart and be with Christ, for that is far better; [24]but to remain in the flesh is more necessary for you. [25]Since I am convinced of this, I know that I will remain and continue with all of you for your progress and joy in faith, [26]so that I may share abundantly in your boasting in Christ Jesus when I come to you again.

COMMENTARY

In v. 18b, Paul introduces another reason for rejoicing: the fact that he confidently expects "deliverance" (v. 19). What kind of deliverance does he have in mind? Could it be that he expects to be spared the need to stand trial? This seems unlikely, since in v. 20 he eagerly expects to speak boldly and not be put to shame—presumably at the trial. Does he expect to be vindicated at that trial and set free? This is possible, but if so, then his confidence in v. 19 would seem to be at odds with his doubts regarding the outcome in vv. 20-24, though it is certainly echoed in v. 25. The third possibility is that Paul has a heavenly vindication in mind. What he is confidently hoping for is a favorable verdict from God; the judgment of the earthly court, whether life or death, v. 20, is immaterial. This solution is supported by the fact that the words translated "this/what has happened to me will result in/turn out for my deliverance" are an exact quotation of the LXX version of Job 13:16, where Job expresses confidence about his vindication in a heavenly court. Moreover, although both the NRSV and the NIV have translated σωτηρία (sōtēria) as "deliverance," this word is used on every other occasion of its occurrence in the Pauline corpus in the sense of "salvation," God's final saving action (see the NIV marginal note). Paul's hope for a heavenly judgment in his favor is based on expectation regarding his behavior at the forthcoming earthly trial (v. 20). It is for this that he needs the Philippians' prayers and the support of "the Spirit of Jesus Christ." This is an unusual description of the Spirit, but it is highly appropriate, since Jesus was also put on trial before an earthly court and was vindicated by a heavenly judge, as we shall be reminded in 2:6-11. Paul is thus following in Jesus' footsteps. Perhaps Paul is also thinking of the Spirit as a paraclete or legal advocate, as does John (see John 14:16, 26; 15:26; 16:7-11; cf. 1 John 2:1).

It is Paul's eager expectation and firm hope (since it is founded upon God) that he will not be put to shame at the trial but will behave in such a way that now, as always, Christ will be exalted in him (v. 20). The possible shame stands in contrast to exaltation, but whereas it is Paul who might be ashamed, it is Christ who will be exalted by Paul's bold witness to him. The idea that God will come to the defense of the people, so that they are not put to shame and so that God is exalted, is common in the psalms, and the two verbs used here, meaning "to be ashamed" (αἰσχύνω aischynō) and "to exalt" (μεγαλύνω megalynō) are found together in the LXX (see Pss 34:3-5 [33:4-6]; 35:26-27[34:26]; 40:15-17[39:16-17]; cf. 1QH 4:23-24). The "now as always" indicates that Paul has had this experience before.

Christ will be exalted in Paul, "whether by life or death." The phrase "in my body" is a literal translation of the Greek but is somewhat misleading, for the word σῶμα (sōma) means more than a body of flesh. Paul does, to be sure, sometimes use the word in this sense, but the fact that Christ will be glorified in Paul's sōma whether he lives or dies indicates that Paul is not thinking here simply of his fleshly body. Rather, he is using sōma in the sense he often gives it, of the whole person. Thus whether Paul continues to live in the flesh or not, Christ will be exalted in him.

As far as Paul is concerned, however, "living/to live is Christ" (v. 21). These words are reminiscent of Gal 2:20, but they are balanced here by the parallel statement "dying/to die is gain." The verse is a neat rhetorical summary, especially effective when read aloud in Greek because of the similarity in sound of the words Χριστός (Christos) and κέρδος (kerdos, "gain"). There are parallels in ancient Greek writers to the idea that death can be a gain, in the sense that it is a release from troubles.[8] Paul, however, is far more positive. This verse suggests a very intimate relationship with Christ, but Paul is surely thinking here of more than his own personal religious experience. The theme of the whole passage is the way in which the gospel is proclaimed, whatever Paul's own circumstances, and this verse links what is said in v. 20 with what follows in v. 22. For Paul, "to live is Christ" means not only that to live is to experience Christ, but also that to live is to magnify him; death will be gain because it will mean not only to "be with Christ," but also to find new ways to magnify him, perhaps through death itself.

8. E.g., Socrates. See Plato Apology 40c-d; Josephus Antiquities of the Jews 15:158 of death in battle.

Paul does not, in fact, spell out here the nature of the gain brought by death, though in v. 23 we learn that it means "to depart and be with Christ." Elsewhere he describes Christians who die as dying "in Christ" (1 Cor 15:18); they are "with Christ" (1 Thess 4:14); death cannot separate them from the love of God in Christ Jesus (Rom 8:38). In v. 22, however, he elaborates on what "living/to live" will mean. This, too, will involve a form of gain, since it will mean "fruitful labor," literally, "the fruit of labor." The phrase is ambiguous and could mean future fruit from past labor, but Paul is clearly thinking of the advantage of future work that will bear yet more fruit. The contrast between the gain brought by death (v. 21) and the fruit produced by life (v. 22) is once again underlined by the similarity of the words κέρδος (*kerdos*, "gain") and καρπός (*karpos*, "fruit"). The life that he is talking about is life "in the flesh" (NRSV). The NIV translates the expression as "in the body," but the Greek word used here is σάρξ (*sarx*, "flesh"). We see here the difference between *sarx*, which refers to the limitations of the life ended by death, and the *sōma*, which embraces much more.

Paul does not know whether to hope for life or for death. "Choose" (NIV) and "prefer" (NRSV) are both proper translations of the Greek αἱρέω (*aireō*), but "prefer" is more appropriate here, since Paul is in no position to choose. He is "torn/hard pressed between the two"; the NRSV's "hard pressed" is closer to the literal meaning of the Greek, but the NIV's "torn" perhaps expresses the tension better. On the one hand, he wishes "to depart and be with Christ" (v. 23), and he piles up superlatives to express his conviction that this would be "better by far." The conviction that death would be gain has sometimes been interpreted as implying a belief in an intermediate afterlife between death and resurrection—a kind of "waiting room" where Christians await the next stage. There has been considerable debate as to whether this idea is consistent with Paul's teaching about the parousia and the resurrection in his earlier epistles. There, however, he uses verbs of sleeping to express the idea of dying, a common Jewish metaphor for death (see, e.g., 1 Cor 15:18; 1 Thess 4:14; 5:10). Since the image of sleep implies a lack of consciousness, the idea behind chap. 1 is perhaps that if Paul falls asleep

in death, his next moment of awareness will be at the resurrection; hence, dying is seen as "gain." It is important to remember, however, that all these ideas are metaphors—attempts to explain something beyond our understanding. Since God is outside both time and space, questions about when and where are meaningless. Paul's conviction is simply that death will mean being with Christ and sharing his resurrection life.

To remain in the flesh (*sarx*), on the other hand, "is more necessary for you." Whatever his personal indecision, therefore, Paul is confident that for their sake he will "remain and continue" with them. There is a play on words in the Greek, which uses three different words for "remain" in vv. 24-25, all formed from the same root: ἐπιμένω (*epimenō*), μένω (*menō*), and παραμένω (*paramenō*). The last of these words can also have the meaning "to stay alive." What has persuaded Paul is not a sudden divine revelation, but his conviction that God will act for the benefit of the Philippians. The decisive factors here—as everywhere else in this epistle—are the needs of others and the progress of the gospel, and not one's personal preferences. The new lease on life he hopes for is not seen as a personal reward, but as an opportunity to be useful to his churches. It will thus serve their progress in the gospel.

The Greek word προκοπή (*prokopē*, "progress"), picks up a word used in v. 12, though this fact is disguised by both the NIV and the NRSV translations of that verse. The two occurrences form an inclusio, underlining the theme of the whole paragraph: Whatever happens to Paul is used by God to advance the gospel. Here the word should be linked with "the faith," which, unusually in Paul, is used with the definite article "only" (correctly translated in the NIV) and no further definition; it seems to have a meaning here similar to "the gospel." Paul's continuing ministry will also bring the Philippians joy (the keynote of the gospel). The result (v. 26) will be that the Philippians' boasting in Christ Jesus will overflow. The Greek word καύχημα (*kauchēma*) is properly translated "boasting" in the NRSV, in contrast to the NIV's "joy." The cause of boasting is Christ Jesus, but it is "on account of me" (the NIV translation is here preferable to that of the NRSV)—that is, "because of my coming to you again." The word for "coming" is παρουσία (*parousia*), the word used elsewhere of the coming of Christ at the end time, and in secular Greek of the triumphant entry of kings and governors into cities. It might perhaps have something of this sense of triumph here, but it is also the ordinary word for "coming" or "presence" (see, e.g., 2:12) and was probably simply the natural word for Paul to use.

REFLECTIONS

1. Once again, we find that a conventional feature of a letter has been transformed. Although Paul's opening words lead us to expect a report regarding his own situation, what he, in fact, gives us is a description of how the gospel is progressing, rather than simply how things are with him. As an apostle, this is his chief concern. He begins on a positive note ("what has happened to me has helped to advance the gospel"), and ends with a triumphant reference to future boasting in Christ. Throughout the whole section, we see how Paul confidently expects the message of the gospel (life through death) to be worked out in his own experience and in the experience of the church. He proclaims the gospel of crucifixion and resurrection not only with his lips, but also with his whole life.

Paul's own afflictions, therefore, are seen as an opportunity for the gospel: People talk about his case; therefore, they learn about the Christian faith, and other Christians are encouraged to make a similar stand. Christian churches that endure harassment and persecution today may draw comfort from Paul's words. Throughout history, persecution has often strengthened the church. In our own time, we have seen vigorous Christian communities emerge after years of oppression by state authorities. In spite of all its failures, the church bears witness to the power of the gospel, because the pattern of the gospel (life through death) is being worked out in the life of the church. The amazing fact that oppression leads to growth reflects the paradox that lies at the heart of the gospel—namely, that God's power is revealed through the weakness of the cross and that victory comes through apparent defeat (1 Cor 1:23-27).

Paul cheerfully accepts whatever circumstances he finds himself in, even imprisonment, acknowledging that he has been "put here for the defense of the gospel." Instead of chafing at the restrictions imposed upon him and pining for the time when he might preach freely again, he regards his imprisonment as an opportunity. His attitude is reflected in the searching words of the Methodist Covenant Service:

> Put me to what you will, rank me with whom you will; put me to doing, put me to suffering; let me be employed for you or laid aside for you, exalted for you or brought low for you; let me be full, let me be empty; let me have all things, let me have nothing.

Paul has been "laid aside" for God, but he sees even this as an opportunity for God to be glorified.

2. The fact that Paul elsewhere condemns those who preach false gospels (see, e.g., 3:2, 18-19) often leads us to suppose that he was totally intolerant of others' views. In this section, however, we see a remarkable tolerance of those whose motives are dubious. This is because their jealousy of him and their ill will toward him are unimportant, so long as Christ is proclaimed. When Paul believes that the gospel is under attack, he is implacable; here he thinks the opposition is merely directed to him, and he can therefore be generous. This passage reminds us that the gospel is far greater than the worthiness of its ministers: God can work through men and women in spite of their faults and failings. Clearly there comes a point, however, at which our own selfish attitudes can contradict and swamp the message of the gospel. In the next section, Paul will urge his readers to live "in a manner worthy of the gospel" (1:27), which means having the message of the gospel stamped on their lives and attitudes. "Proclaiming Christ" is a matter of living out the gospel, not just of declaring its message.

Paul's words remind us, too, of how easy it is to delude ourselves about our motives in undertaking Christian service. Truly disinterested service is rare, indeed! The preacher is perhaps particularly in danger of succumbing to selfish ambition, enjoying the plaudits of those who are impressed by fluent oratory and good storytelling. Paul rightly contrasts true and false motives, but in practice most Christians probably belong to both camps. The battle against envy, rivalry, selfish ambition, and insincerity is a constant one.

3. Paul was clearly the kind of person who easily caused controversy and provoked opposition, not just from enemies, but from fellow Christians also. Those who are passionately committed to a cause frequently embarrass others who share the same aims, but who do so more quietly. Civil rights supporters, animal rights protestors, and environmentalists are all examples of groups who have been divided as to the best method by which to campaign for their cause. German church leaders who protested about what the Nazi Party was doing in the 1930s, campaigners for racial justice in the United States and South Africa; men and women who have protested against the exploitation of native peoples in South America, Indonesia, Nigeria, and Iran have all embarrassed others who believed in the same cause but who supported it in less aggressive ways. In the same way, Paul, who was so often imprisoned, must have been a great source of embarrassment to those Christians who preferred a softer approach. Sometimes these subtler ways work better, but the church certainly needs men and women with Paul's courage, who are not afraid to suffer for that in which they believe. There is a place for both approaches, and we must aim to live out God's particular calling for us.

4. Although in this passage Paul is discussing the possibility of his execution, the dominant notes are joy and hope; even imprisonment and the threat of death cannot extinguish them. Rabbi Hugo Gryn used to tell of his experiences in Auschwitz as a boy. Food supplies were meager, and the inmates took care to preserve every scrap that came their way. When the Festival of Hanukkah arrived, Hugo's father took a lump of margarine and, to the horror of young Hugo, used it as fuel for the light to be lit at the festival. When he was asked why, his father replied, "We know that it is possible to live for three weeks without food, but without hope it is impossible to live properly for three minutes."

Paul confidently expects "deliverance," but this deliverance, as we have seen, is not from death. What he hopes for is that he will be given the courage to stand firm at his trial and so be vindicated by the heavenly court. By contrast, we are, perhaps, inclined to pray too much for deliverance from illness and sorrow, pain and death, rather than for courage to endure these things. The real danger is to succumb to their power, instead of trusting in God (as Christ did) to bring us through them. Paul is convinced that God can be glorified not only by the way the Christian lives, but also by the way he or she dies. Living (and dying) "properly" means for Paul that Christ is exalted in his "body," or person. His thought is echoed centuries later in the line from George Herbert's hymn "King of Glory": "In my heart, though not in heaven, I can raise thee."

As for the outcome of his trial, Paul is uncertain what to hope for. As always, however, the needs of his congregations take priority over his own personal desires. Paul's spirituality, though intensely personal, is never an individual matter. He is a member of a community, the body of Christ, and the well-being of that community and the progress of the gospel are all-important. Our own piety tends to be far more individualistic. Many Christians regard religion as a private concern and think of the Christian gospel as primarily an offer of personal salvation. Without minimizing the necessity for the individual to respond to the gospel, we ought perhaps to remember the gospel's wider implications.

5. Underlying Paul's prayers for himself and for his churches is his conviction that God is in control of human destiny. Clearly he believes that the verdict at the trial lies ultimately in God's hands. But if God "looks after his own," it is definitely *not* in the sense that God will see to it that Paul is released! Rather, God can be relied on for the assurance that, whatever happens, there will be an opportunity to turn the situation to good effect. One of the temptations into which Christians frequently fall is to suppose that God "looks after his own" by saving them from disasters of all kinds and by blessing them with prosperity, health, and good fortune. The constant cry, "Why should this happen to me?" implies that God has let us down. We expect God to reward us for our allegiance and to save us from all trials and tribulations. The Christian gospel offers no such hope. What it does offer is the assurance that, whatever happens, the Christian who trusts in God will not be let down by God or be put to shame. Whatever experiences we undergo, we may confidently expect to find Christ sharing them with us, and so we discover that disaster leads to new opportunity, sorrow to joy, and death to resurrection life.

Perhaps our problem is our own limited horizon, which leads us to approach the gospel with the everyday attitudes that govern our behavior elsewhere. We might ask, "What's in it for me? What does the gospel offer me?" The answer to these questions is, of course, "A great deal!" But the questions ignore the fact that the gospel is primarily about God's self-revelation in Christ and about the things that God has done. The gospel invites us to forget, as Christ did, our own concerns and desires, and to find joy and salvation in offering praise and glory to God.

THE CHRISTIAN LIFE, PART 1

OVERVIEW

Paul now turns to pastoral advice, offered to a community facing opposition and persecution. This advice may well have been shaped in response to information that had reached him regarding the Philippian church, but it will also certainly reflect his own experiences and deliberations in prison. It is difficult to know which of these influences was the more important. There is, for example, a strong emphasis on unity in these verses, and many commentators believe that this emphasis reflects a situation of division and conflict in the Philippian church. The instruction in 4:2 to Euodia and Syntyche "to be of the same mind/agree with each other in the Lord" lends some support to this view; but Paul does not rebuke the community for a lack of unity, and the absence of such rebuke suggests that division was not a serious problem there. Nevertheless, the attitude he urges the Philippians to adopt is clearly the one he later presses on the women, and he may well have their disagreement in mind here. If Paul emphasizes the need for unity, however, this may well be in part because of the divisions referred to in 1:15-18 that he has himself encountered during his imprisonment. Preachers who exhort their congregations to particular courses of action are not necessarily rebuking them for their failures. These preachers may, of course, be emphasizing something because they know of certain problems within the communities they are addressing, but they are just as likely to be sharing insights into the gospel that have been shaped by their own experiences and meditations. Paul was well aware of the dangers and temptations facing a young Christian community subject to persecution and pressure.

This section gives advice on how the Philippians should behave. Apart from the emphasis on unity, the instructions are general rather than particular. The readers are to live "in a manner worthy of the gospel" (1:27); to "look to the interests of others" (2:4); to be "blameless" (2:15). What Paul is anxious to do is to instill an attitude—the attitude of Christ himself, set out in 2:5-11. Although Paul begins a new theme here, it is firmly linked to the preceding paragraphs, since the behavior he appeals for is that appropriate to the gospel, about which he has been speaking.

PHILIPPIANS 1:27-30, STAND FAST!

NIV

NRSV

[27]Whatever happens, conduct yourselves in a manner worthy of the gospel of Christ. Then, whether I come and see you or only hear about you in my absence, I will know that you stand firm in one spirit, contending as one man for the faith of the gospel [28]without being frightened in any way by those who oppose you. This is a sign to them that they will be destroyed, but that you

27Only, live your life in a manner worthy of the gospel of Christ, so that, whether I come and see you or am absent and hear about you, I will know that you are standing firm in one spirit, striving side by side with one mind for the faith of the gospel, [28]and are in no way intimidated by your opponents. For them this is evidence of their destruction, but of your salvation. And this is

will be saved—and that by God. [29]For it has been granted to you on behalf of Christ not only to believe on him, but also to suffer for him, [30]since you are going through the same struggle you saw I had, and now hear that I still have.

God's doing. [29]For he has graciously granted you the privilege not only of believing in Christ, but of suffering for him as well— [30]since you are having the same struggle that you saw I had and now hear that I still have.

COMMENTARY

The opening word, μόνον (*monon*, "only," as in the NRSV), indicates the move to exhortation: "There is just one thing!" Although this one thing is then extensively discussed, it is in fact well summed up in the opening command, "Live your life/conduct yourselves in a manner worthy of the gospel of Christ." The verb πολιτεύομαι (*politeuomai*) is not the one Paul ordinarily employs in commands regarding behavior (indeed, he uses it nowhere else). It is derived from the noun used in 3:20, meaning "commonwealth" or "citizenship" (see the Commentary on 3:20). Its basic meaning is "to exercise the rights and duties of citizens," though it came to be used with the more general meaning of "to behave." The translations of the NRSV and the NIV: "live your life/conduct yourselves" are, therefore, accurate, but they fail to convey the idea Paul was probably trying to express in using this particular word here—namely, that the behavior required of the Philippians is a reflection of the "citizenship" they now enjoy as members of the Christian community. Those members of the church in Philippi who were citizens of that city would also have been Roman citizens; thus they would have been well aware of the privileges and obligations of citizenship. Paul has probably chosen this particular verb because he thinks of Christian behavior not simply as something undertaken by individuals, but as the expression of the life of the whole community. His meaning is, "Let your life as a community be worthy of the gospel of Christ."[9]

If they do this, then the question of whether Paul is able to come and see them will be irrelevant. The life worthy of the gospel involves "standing firm in one spirit, striving side by side with one mind" (NRSV). Paul here uses the Greek

terms for "spirit" (πνεῦμα *pneuma*) and "soul" (ψυχη *psyche*), but the NRSV aptly translates the latter word as "mind"; the community should act "as one person" (hence the NIV's "one man"). The words signify here that which unites the Philippians, not separate parts of the individual. "In one spirit" has no parallel in Greek literature and probably refers to the Holy Spirit (see 2:1). It is the Spirit that unites them and enables them to stand firmly and resist opposition. The "one mind" they share comes from the fact that they are all in Christ. Paul elaborates on what it means to be in one spirit and to have one mind in chap. 2. The verb "striving side by side" seems to be an athletic metaphor and points forward to the imagery of 3:14 (cf. 4:3); the NRSV translation here captures well the implication of "togetherness" in the Greek. "The faith," which was used in v. 25 in a sense parallel to "the gospel," appears here to be almost tautologous: "the faith which is the gospel."

We do not know who the opponents mentioned in v. 28 were. The fact that Paul speaks in vv. 29-30 of the Philippians' enduring suffering and being engaged in a struggle suggests that they were real opponents and not just potential ones. It is sometimes suggested that these opponents were Judaizers, the group of conservative Jewish Christians who gave Paul such problems in Galatia, but it seems more likely that the opposition came from outside the church. The community's enemies could be either Jews or pagans, but once again the reference to suffering and to the Philippians' sharing in "the same struggle" as Paul himself is enduring suggests that their problems may be with the civil authorities. According to Luke, Paul had met opposition in Philippi from businessmen in the city (Acts 16) who were annoyed because his mission was undermining

9. See Raymond R. Brewer, "The Meaning of *Politeuesthe* in Philippians 1:27," *JBL* 73 (1954) 76-83.

their financial interests. The opposition faced by the Philippian community could well have arisen from similar grievances, leading to unrest and charges before the civil authorities, rather than from organized persecution.

The Greek underlying "This is evidence/a sign" (v. 28) is not nearly as clear as the English translations suggest. Paul uses the relative pronoun "which," and this probably refers to the behavior he is hoping the Philippians will show, though it might refer to "the faith of the gospel." One can certainly see how "the faith of the gospel" could be said to demonstrate both salvation and destruction, but the order of the Greek does not support this interpretation. It is difficult, however, to understand how the fact that the Philippians are standing firm and are not in any way intimidated can be a "sign" or "evidence" to their opponents of their own destruction and of the Philippians' salvation. They were surely very unlikely either to observe it or to heed it! It is not surprising, then, that there are variant readings in some MSS, which have either "but to you of salvation" or "but to us of salvation" instead of "but of your salvation." These, of course, solve only part of the difficulty and are clearly attempts to do so. In fact, it is easier to understand how the Philippians' steadfastness could be a sign to their opponents of the Christians' coming salvation than it is to see how the opponents could interpret it as a sign of their own coming destruction. The Greek word ἔνδειξις (endeixis) means "indication" or "demonstration." Paul perhaps means that when the gospel is lived out in an appropriate way, that is a proclamation of its message, a living demonstration of the salvation from destruction that it offers. The Philippians' behavior is thus at one and the same time evidence of the truth of the gospel and a warning to those who oppose it.

The last clause of v. 28 is ambiguous. The NIV has taken it as a comment on what has just been said: The Philippians will be saved (and their opponents destroyed?) by God. But the preposition (ἀπό apo; lit., "from") denotes origin rather than agency, and Paul has used nouns, "destruction" and "salvation," not verbs. The ambiguity is better expressed by the NRSV's "And this is God's doing." But to what does "this" refer? Does it refer to the salvation and destruction, as the NIV supposes? Does it refer to the omen (the "sign" or "evidence") of that salvation or destruction? Or does it refer to that which was described as the "sign" or "evidence" of that salvation and destruction—namely, the Philippians' steadfastness in the face of suffering? These last two possibilities are not exclusive; if the "sign" is from God, so is the steadfastness of which it consists. Certainly the next verse seems to support the last possibility, since Paul speaks next of the Philippians' having been "granted" (the verb χαρίζομαι [charizomai] is a cognate of χάρις [charis], "grace") the privilege of suffering on Christ's behalf. Not only is their ability to resist evil a gift from God, but so also is the suffering itself, because it is ὑπὲρ Χριστοῦ (hyper Christou), "for/on behalf of Christ." This remarkable phrase, which is repeated at the end of the verse, is exactly parallel to the phrase used frequently in the NT, especially by Paul, to describe Christ's suffering and death for others.[10] Here, however, it is *Christians* who suffer *for Christ.* This reciprocal relationship is extraordinary. In what sense can the Philippians' sufferings be "for Christ"? Does Paul simply mean that they are suffering because they are Christians? The parallel between "believing in" and "suffering for" supports this, but the repetition of the phrase and the use of the verb *charizomai* suggest that there is more to it than this. We need to remember that although Paul speaks of Christ's dying *for* us, he also insists that the Christian needs to die *with* Christ (e.g., Rom 6:3-10) and is expected to suffer with him (e.g., Rom 8:17).

In 3:10, Paul speaks of his desire to know the fellowship of Christ's sufferings by being conformed to his death and so to his resurrection, but it is clear from 1:29-30 that both he and the Philippians are already experiencing that "sharing/fellowship" of suffering. Through baptism into Christ, we make his death our own, but this means that those who share Christ's sufferings and death are united to the power of his resurrection and life. This power is not something that stops short with them, however, since they become its channels, through whom grace and joy and comfort are brought to others. Suffering "for Christ" means, therefore, that the Philippians—

---

10. See, e.g., 1 Thess 5:10, "our Lord Jesus Christ died for us" (cf. Rom 5:8); 1 Cor 15:3, "Christ died for our sins" (cf. Gal 1:4); Rom 8:32, "[God] gave him up for all of us" (cf. Gal 2:20). See also John 10:15, "I lay down my life for the sheep," and Heb 2:9, where Christ is said to "taste death for everyone."

because they are "in Christ"—are granted the privilege of sharing in the redemptive work of Christ. Their sufferings are in reality his and can, therefore, be used by him. Paul and the Philippians are, indeed, as he expressed in v. 7, "partners in grace."[11] The clearest expressions of this idea are to be found in 2 Cor 1:3-7; 4:7-12; and 6:4-10, where Paul describes his own experience, and in Col 1:24. We now understand why the Philippians are a sign of both salvation and destruction: In their believing and their suffering they are an embodiment of the gospel.

It is for good reason, then, that Paul returns to the theme of his own sufferings in v. 30. The Philippians are now sharing in the same "struggle" (ἀγών agōn), another athletic image, as they know Paul to have been and still be enduring. The reference to what the Philippians have witnessed in the past is presumably to the incident mentioned in 1 Thess 2:2, where Paul again uses the word agōn for the opposition he encountered

in Philippi. He speaks there of being shamefully treated in Philippi, and this is likely to be a reference to the incident described by Luke in Acts 16:19-40. The struggle is the same, not because the Philippians are also suffering imprisonment (there is no hint of this), but because they, like Paul, are under attack from those who oppose the gospel and are engaged in a battle with the forces of evil. If the Philippians can take comfort from this, it is not simply because they are all, as it were, in the same boat, but because they have seen in Paul's case how suffering can be used "for Christ."

Many of the ideas in this paragraph are picked up by Paul in a later section of the epistle, 3:17–4:1, which suggests that the two passages mark the beginning and the end of a larger section of the epistle. The ideas taken up later include those of following Paul's example, sharing the sufferings of Christ, the future destinies of those opposed to the gospel (destruction) and of believers (salvation), the citizenship of Christians, and the exhortation to stand firm. (See Reflections at 2:12-18.)

11. See M. D. Hooker, "A Partner in the Gospel: Paul's Understanding of His Ministry," in *Theology and Ethics in Paul and His Interpreters: Festschrift for V. P. Furnish,* ed. Eugene H. Lovering and Jerry L. Sumney (Nashville: Abingdon, 1996) 83-100.

PHILIPPIANS 2:1-4, OUR LIFE IN CHRIST

NIV

2 If you have any encouragement from being united with Christ, if any comfort from his love, if any fellowship with the Spirit, if any tenderness and compassion, [2]then make my joy complete by being like-minded, having the same love, being one in spirit and purpose. [3]Do nothing out of selfish ambition or vain conceit, but in humility consider others better than yourselves. [4]Each of you should look not only to your own interests, but also to the interests of others.

NRSV

2 If then there is any encouragement in Christ, any consolation from love, any sharing in the Spirit, any compassion and sympathy, [2]make my joy complete: be of the same mind, having the same love, being in full accord and of one mind. [3]Do nothing from selfish ambition or conceit, but in humility regard others as better than yourselves. [4]Let each of you look not to your own interests, but to the interests of others.

COMMENTARY

2:1-2. This section begins with a question headed by "If," but there is no doubt about the answer: "If—as is, of course, the case!" The assurance is conveyed in Greek by the word οὖν

(*oun*), "therefore" (NRSV, "then"; unfortunately omitted by the NIV). The verb is missing and thus has to be supplied; the NRSV has chosen "there is," the NIV "you have." Paul's appeal is based on the "encouragement" the Philippians possess "in Christ." The word παράκλησις (*paraklēsis*), here translated "encouragement," can mean both "comfort" and "exhortation"; commentators are divided as to which meaning it has here, but it is perhaps unnecessary to choose. In fact, the English word "encouragement" conveys both senses, and the noun is probably used here to denote the power that enables the Philippians to do the things listed in vv. 2-4. In Christ, believers find both comfort and strength.

As in 1:27, union with Christ forms the basis of the appeal to an appropriate way of life. It is because Christians are "in Christ" that they are united to him and to one another and are able to share his mind and strength. It is this union that is the source of the "encouragement" that provides, in turn, the "consolation/comfort" of love, "sharing in/fellowship with the Spirit," "compassion/tenderness and sympathy/compassion." Paul (unlike the NIV) does not specify whose love he has in mind; no doubt Christ's love for us comes first, but he may well be thinking also of Christians' love for Christ and for one another. Similarly, although the Spirit is the origin of fellowship (the term is κοινωνία [*koinōnia*] once again; see 1:5; 3:10), Paul's phrase probably refers also to our participation in the life and work of the Spirit and the fellowship with other Christians that the Spirit creates. The word translated "compassion" in the NRSV and "tenderness" in the NIV is σπλάγχνα (*splagchna*; lit., "bowels"), which was used in 1:8 with the genitive "of Christ Jesus." It is clear from the context that Christ is the source of compassion here also.

On the basis of what they have in Christ, Paul now appeals to the Philippians to behave in such a way as will "make [his] joy complete" (v. 2). The Philippians have already brought him joy (1:4; cf. 4:1), and if their behavior reflects their common life in Christ, they will fulfill Paul's joy. The underlying exhortation is to "be what you are," to live "in a manner worthy of the gospel of Christ" (1:27). They are to "be of the same mind" (NRSV), literally, to "think the same." Here we have again the key verb φρονέω (*phroneō*), which Paul has already used in 1:7 (see the Commentary on 1:3-8). It occurs again in the last phrase of 2:2 ("being . . . of one mind," NRSV; this is obscured in the NIV's "one in . . . purpose") and in the

opening words of v. 5. As has already been noted, the verb refers to attitude, rather than to intellectual thought. The members of the Christian community must share a common attitude, and what that attitude is will be spelled out in vv. 5-11. For the moment, the command to "be of the same mind" is amplified by the next three phrases: They are to "have the same love"—which is in effect the same love as Christ, since he is the source of love (v. 1)—to be "in full accord," and to think or feel one thing.

2:3-4. The same theme is continued in these verses, expressed in a couple of contrasts. Once again, the first verb is missing. The NRSV and the NIV supply "do," but perhaps we should understand *phronein,* since actions are based on attitudes. On the one side stand selfish ambition (cf. 1:17) and empty conceit. This latter term is κενοδοξία (*kenodoxia*); the *keno* part of the stem means "empty," and the *doxia* is related to δόξα (*doxa*), meaning "glory." Those who have illusions about themselves are also "vainglorious"; there is a contrast not only with the second part of the verse, but also with the true glory that comes at the climax of v. 11. On the other side we have the attitude that in humility considers others to be better than oneself. We are accustomed to thinking of humility as a virtue, but it was not considered to be such in the Greek world, where it was regarded as servility. Paul's converts might well have been surprised to find him urging them to behave with humility, but the reason will be made clear in v. 8. The noun ταπεινοφροσύνη (*tapeinophrosynē*) is akin to the verb ταπεινόω (*tapeinoō*) used in v. 8 and also to the verb φρονέω (*phroneō*); it refers to the attitude of being humble. The background to its use here is to be found in the OT. To be sure, men and women are often humbled by others, or by God (Ps 119:67, 71, 75), but those who are brought low may hope for God to save them (Job 5:11; Ps 142:6). Humility is the proper attitude toward God (Ps 138:6; Prov 3:34; 11:2). At Qumran, humility is recognized as the appropriate attitude both toward God and toward other members of the community (1QS 2:24; 4:3; 5:23, 25). Here, Paul urges the members of the Christian community in Philippi to regard others as better than themselves; this is not meant to foster false modesty or a lack of self-esteem, but to encourage a recognition of the rights and achievements of others. His choice of the word ἡγούμενοι (*hēgoumenoi*, "considering/regarding") is significant, for the same verb will be used again in v. 6 of the attitude of Christ.

Verse 4 provides a parallel contrast between concern for one's own interests and concern for the interests of others. The NIV translation includes two words that are not in the NRSV: "only," which is not in the Greek, and "also," which represents the Greek word καὶ (*kai*) and is found in some Greek MSS but not in all. The addition weakens the contrast, and the passage seems to make better sense without it; others may have thought so, too, and so omitted it, which means that the word may well have been part of the original text. If that is the case, then Paul was perhaps more realistic than his later "corrector," and his instruction to be concerned with the interests of others *as well as* one's own is in line with the commandment to love one's neighbor *as oneself.* The shorter text, on the other hand, seems to agree with 1 Cor 10:24. But we should, perhaps, understand the *kai* as having the meaning "rather." That is, they should be looking to the interests of others *rather* than their own. What are the "interests" with which Christians are concerned? Paul does not specify. Indeed, there is no noun in the Greek, merely the definite article, followed by the words "your own" and "of others." Perhaps he is being intentionally vague; the phrases could refer to possessions, to rights, to spiritual gifts, or to points of view.

The themes of these four verses all lead into the "hymn" that follows. Christ's actions provide not simply an example for believers to copy but also the foundation of their Christian existence. (See Reflections at 2:12-18.)

PHILIPPIANS 2:5-11, THE MIND OF CHRIST

NIV

[5]Your attitude should be the same as that of Christ Jesus:
[6]Who, being in very nature[a] God,
    did not consider equality with God
        something to be grasped,
[7]but made himself nothing,
    taking the very nature[b] of a servant,
    being made in human likeness.
[8]And being found in appearance as a man,
    he humbled himself
    and became obedient to death—
        even death on a cross!
[9]Therefore God exalted him to the highest place
    and gave him the name that is above
        every name,
[10]that at the name of Jesus every knee
        should bow,
    in heaven and on earth and under
        the earth,
[11]and every tongue confess that Jesus Christ
        is Lord,
    to the glory of God the Father.

[a]6 Or *in the form of*   [b]7 Or *the form*

NRSV

[5]Let the same mind be in you that was[a] in Christ Jesus,
 [6] who, though he was in the form of God,
    did not regard equality with God
    as something to be exploited,
 [7] but emptied himself,
    taking the form of a slave,
    being born in human likeness.
    And being found in human form,
 [8] he humbled himself
    and became obedient to the point of death—
    even death on a cross.

 [9] Therefore God also highly exalted him
    and gave him the name
    that is above every name,
[10] so that at the name of Jesus
    every knee should bend,
    in heaven and on earth and under the
        earth,
[11] and every tongue should confess
    that Jesus Christ is Lord,
    to the glory of God the Father.

[a] Or *that you have*

COMMENTARY

Origins of the Christological "Hymn." Philippians 2:5 introduces one of the best known and most influential passages in the Pauline corpus. It is commonly referred to as a hymn (and for the sake of convenience it will be referred to as such here). Whether or not it was composed as a hymn is uncertain. Its style is solemn and rhythmical, and thus it has a certain poetic quality, reflected in the fact that both the NIV and the NRSV set the passage as poetry. However, its structure does not conform to the rules of Greek poetry. Its pattern of regular stresses and the use of parallelism remind us of Hebrew poetry (as in the psalms); thus it has been suggested that it was originally composed in Aramaic. Its lines can be arranged in many different ways, and the very fact that this is possible should warn us to beware of imposing our own ideas of poetic structure onto the material. In particular, it is dangerous to do what some commentators do, and excise one or more lines as "Pauline additions" to an original passage, on the grounds that they do not fit the expected pattern.

It is, nevertheless, possible that Paul is quoting an earlier composition at this point. Certainly the introductory ὅς (*hos*, "who") in v. 6 suggests that what follows is a creedal statement of some kind—though we must beware of thinking that it is any kind of formal creed. Who, then, composed the passage? One possibility is Paul himself. We know from his other letters that he was capable of using colorful language as well as the rhetorical devices of parallelism and chiasm that are employed here. With his Jewish background, he was obviously capable of writing in a "Semitic" style. Another possibility is that it was a pre-Pauline composition that he took over and used. In support of this theory, we should note that the hymn contains many unusual words, some of which are not found in Paul's other writings or even elsewhere in the NT. This, of course, may be due to its poetic style, but many commentators believe that this passage, in fact, reflects the beliefs of the Christian community before Paul. But in that case, why should Paul quote it here? Was it something that was known to the Philippians? Or was it simply particularly appropriate to his purpose here? Certainly it was

the latter, for, as we shall see, whatever its origin, Paul has used the passage in a very Pauline way, and its theology is much more Pauline than a superficial reading might suggest. A third possibility is that the "hymn" was originally not a Christian composition at all, but was "gnostic," celebrating the descent and exaltation of a redeemer figure, and that Paul took it over and adapted it. This view, at one time very popular, has almost nothing to be said for it. There is no evidence that the myth of the heavenly redeemer existed in pre-Christian times or that Paul was confronted by gnostic ideas at Philippi. Even if such a gnostic composition existed, it seems unlikely that it would be Semitic in form or that Paul would have made use of it. A final suggestion is that the "hymn" might have been composed by a member of one of Paul's churches (possibly even at Philippi), which would explain why the ideas are so similar to his, even though the language is somewhat different. Whether Paul actually composed these lines, however, he has used them, and by using them has made them his own.

Ideas. More important than the origins of the passage are the ideas it contains and their relevance to Paul's argument. But what are these ideas? And what is their background? Here again, we find widely diverging views.

The first thing to strike us is the fact that the passage falls into two main sections, the first dealing with Christ's voluntary humiliation, the second with his exaltation. This pattern is familiar from other passages in Paul's letters, though there are interesting differences. To begin with, the treatment of the theme is much more extended than usual. Second, the emphasis throughout the first section is on Christ's self-giving. Elsewhere, Paul usually speaks of God as the one who sends or gives his Son, though it is not unknown for him to refer to Christ's giving himself (cf. Gal 2:20 with Rom 8:32), and there is an interesting parallel with his reference to Christ's obedience in Rom 5:18-19. In Phil 2:6-8, the focus is on Christ's action. His exaltation in 2:9-11 is, however, the work of God, and here we have the third interesting difference from parallel Pauline expressions, for the language is of exaltation, rather than of resurrection. Where Paul speaks of exaltation elsewhere, it is something that *follows* resurrection (Rom 8:34; 1 Cor 15:27); that is, his usual contrast is between death and resurrection. Elsewhere, too, the confession of Jesus as Lord is linked with the belief in his resurrection (Rom 10:9-10; cf. Rom 1:3-4, where he is declared to be Son of God by resurrection from the dead).

Philippians 2 is the earliest passage in the Pauline literature to raise in our minds serious questions about the pre-existence of Christ. Already Paul has made statements implying a change in status on Christ's part, notably in 2 Cor 8:9, where Christ, who was rich, became poor for our sake—this is the language of incarnation. Now we find Christ, who was in the form of God, emptying himself, taking the form of a slave, and *becoming man*; his subsequent obedience to death is apparently the second stage in the process of self-emptying.

It is not surprising to find Christ being thought of here as pre-existent. In Jewish thought, to speak of something or someone in this way was to affirm that they were part of God's plan. Thus in Eph 1:4, Christians are said to have been chosen in Christ before the foundation of the world. Earlier Jewish writers, moreover, building on Genesis 1, where God speaks and the world is created, had described the role of God's Word (identified with wisdom and with the law) in creation (e.g., Prov 8:22-31; Wis 7:22-26; Sirach 24). For Paul, Christ is wisdom (1 Cor 1:24, 30) and the fulfillment of the law (Rom 8:3; 10:4); he represented God's nature and purpose from the beginning (2 Cor 4:4, 6). In 1 Cor 8:6 we find hints that Christ was being seen as the agent of creation, an idea elaborated later in Col 1:15-20. In Philippians 2, however, Paul is not concerned with Christ's activity in his pre-existent state, but with the idea, found already in 2 Cor 8:9, of his change in status. In Philippians 2 Paul spells this out more fully and goes on to describe Christ's subsequent exaltation. For the first time, therefore, we have a pattern that may be depicted in *Fig.* 16:

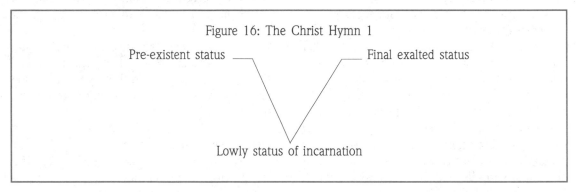

Figure 16: The Christ Hymn 1

Pre-existent status — — Final exalted status

Lowly status of incarnation

We should note that Philippians 2 does not attempt to deal with questions about what the pre-incarnate Christ was *doing;* it is not until we come to Col 1:15-20 that this kind of problem is tackled. Nevertheless, we have moved a step beyond statements that "God sent his Son" to an emphatic declaration that Christ's incarnation was a deliberate act of self-emptying.

The turning point in the pattern is marked by the emphatic διο (*dio,* "therefore") in 2:9. Be-cause Christ acted in this way, God has highly exalted him. What is meant by the expression "highly exalted" (ὑπερύψωσεν *hyperypsōsen*)? Does the ὑπέρ (*hyper*) element indicate something more exalted than the status Christ enjoyed before? If it is only now that Christ is given "the name that is above every name," does this mean that the one who "was in the form of God" did not enjoy "equality with God" in his pre-existent state? If so, we must amend the diagram as follows:

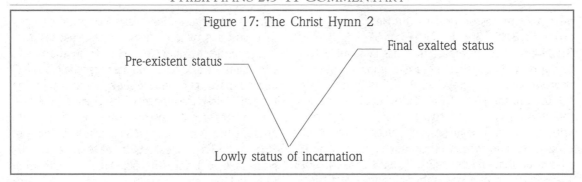

Figure 17: The Christ Hymn 2

Pre-existent status

Final exalted status

Lowly status of incarnation

To answer these questions, we must look closely at the text, but before we do so we must consider the question of background.

Background. If the roots of Paul's ideas in this passage are to be sought in Judaism (and not in Gnosticism), then where should we look to find them? Two main suggestions have been made, the first of which finds the background to Philippians 2 in the so-called Servant Song of Isaiah 53. The terminology is somewhat misleading. Isaiah 52:13–53:12 is the last of four passages that have been labeled "songs" by modern scholarship. In fact, there is nothing to isolate these passages from their context. Nor is there a distinct individual who is known as "my Servant." Rather, the phrase is used from time to time to refer to Israel or to a group within Israel, sometimes (possibly) to one individual. The parallels between Isaiah 53 and Philippians 2 have been found in the term "servant," in the idea of voluntary submission to suffering, and in the reference to death. On further investigation, however, these links prove to be illusory. The word used in the LXX of Isaiah 53 for "servant" is παις (*pais*), not δουλος (*doulos*), as in Phil 2:7. Moreover, the phrase "my servant" in Isa 52:13 is a title of honor—the very opposite of the degradation implied in the reference to a slave in Phil 2:7. It is true that the person described in Isaiah 52–53 dies a shameful death, but that is *in spite of,* and not *because of,* his status as God's servant. Moreover, it is by no means certain that the figure described in Isaiah 53 was understood to have suffered voluntarily. He suffered without protest (Isa 53:7); but that is not to say that he did so willingly, any more than a slaughtered lamb can be considered to be a willing victim. The assumption that Isaiah 53

describes voluntary sacrifice is the result of Christian interpretation of that passage, and the question at issue is whether that Christian interpretation is already reflected in Philippians 2. Finally, the phrase "he poured out himself/his life to death" in Isa 53:12 is often said to be reflected in the words ἑαυτὸν ἐκένωσεν (*heauton ekenōsen*), "he emptied himself" (v. 7), and μεχρι θανατου (*mechri thanatou*), "unto death" (v. 8). As we shall see, however, not only are these words widely separated in the Greek, but they refer to two distinct actions on Christ's part: the action of the pre-existent Christ in emptying himself and becoming man and the action of the human Jesus in being obedient even to death. There is no justification for piecing them together and seeing them as an echo of Isa 53:12 (where the LXX verb is in any case quite different).

The alternative suggestion regarding the background of the passage is that it is based on the story of the fall of Adam in Genesis 3. Links have been found in the phrase "in the form of God," which is reminiscent of Gen 1:26, and in the contrast between Adam, who grasped at equality with God, and Christ, who did not grasp at/cling to/exploit that equality. Whereas Adam was stripped of his privileges, Christ deliberately emptied himself, becoming what Adam had become—a slave, subject to death. Adam's rebellion (though Adam himself is not named in Philippians 2) is thus contrasted with Christ's obedience. In favor of this interpretation we may point to Paul's use of Adam elsewhere (most clearly in Rom 5:12-21 and 1 Cor 15:21-22, 42-50) and to the language Paul uses at the end of Philippians 3 (where the implications of the "hymn" for Christians are, as we shall see, worked out), language that echoes that which he uses elsewhere to describe our restoration to the glory Adam lost (Rom 8:18-30, 39; 1 Cor 15:35-57; cf. 2 Cor 3:12–4:6). This interpretation has been objected to not only because the phrase ἐν μορφῇ θεοῦ (*en morphē theou*), "in the form of God," in v. 6 is not used in the LXX of Gen 1:26, but also because the word μορφη (*morphē*) is not synonymous with the word εἰκών (*eikōn*), "image," which *is* used there and which is used by Paul elsewhere (see in particular Rom 8:29; 2 Cor 3:18; 4:4; Col 1:15; 3:10). Moreover, although some have tried to exclude the idea of pre-existence from Philippians 2 and have argued that it is the actions of the human Jesus that are contrasted with those of Adam,[12] it is difficult to make sense of v. 7 without acknowledging that it was the *pre-existent* Christ who became man. How, then, can we have a figure who is described in Adamic terms, who then *becomes* man and takes on Adam's likeness?

The idea that Christ became man is found elsewhere in Paul, and it is perhaps wise to begin looking for an answer to this conundrum there. Particularly interesting is Rom 8:3, since the background of this verse is the idea of the renewal of creation and the restoration of the glory lost by Adam. God, we are told, sent his Son in the likeness of sinful flesh; the result is that men and women are delivered from slavery and themselves become children (lit., "sons") of God (Rom 8:14-17). The same ideas are expressed in Gal 4:4-7. In both these passages, however, unlike Philippians 2, the initative is taken by God, who sends the one described as God's Son. A parallel to Christ's self-emptying in Phil 2:7 is found in 2 Cor 8:9, where he is said to have become poor for the Corinthians' sake, with the result that they have been made rich. All three passages describe what we may term "incarnation," and in all three, the result of Christ's becoming man is that human beings are made what he eternally is.

Elsewhere, we find this same idea that men and women are conformed to what Christ is, and so become what they were meant to be. In 2 Cor 3:18, Christians see the glory of the Lord reflected in the face of Christ and are transformed into the same image; in 2 Cor 4:4 we learn that Christ is

himself "the image." Similar ideas are developed in Colossians, where Christ is described as "the image of the invisible God" (Col 1:15) and where Christians are said to have taken off "the old man" and to have put on the new, which is being renewed after the image of its creator (Col 3:9-10). All these passages make use of Adamic language, since Adam was created after the image of God and was understood to have reflected the glory of God before the fall. Similar ideas seem to lie behind the passage at the end of Philippians 3, where we are told that the Lord Jesus Christ will transform our bodies of humiliation and conform them to his own body of glory.

There are two passages in which the comparisons between Adam and Christ are made explicit. In Rom 5:12-21, the comparison is the climax of the argument in the preceding chapters, where we are told that what happened in Christ was in many ways *not* the equivalent of what happened in Adam (Rom 5:15-17) because in Christ the grace of God was at work. The nature of this grace was spelled out in the opening verses of the chapter, where we were told that Christ died "for us" (Rom 5:8) and that we have been reconciled to God through the death of the Son (Rom 5:10). In 1 Cor 15:21-24, Christ stands over against Adam as the one who brings life instead of death and who is then identified as the Son who reigns until he hands everything over to his Father. Later in the chapter, Adam is described as the first man, who became a living soul (1 Cor 15:45, quoting Gen 2:7), whereas Christ is the second Adam, who is a life-giving Spirit. The first man is from the dust, the second man from heaven. Just as human beings have borne the image of the first man, so also they may bear the image of the second. The point of Paul's argument here is the nature of the future resurrection, when Christians will share the glorious body of Christ. In both these passages, Christ is understood to have reversed the effects of Adam's fall, and the reason why he is able to do so is because he is both man and Son of God. The relationship between Adam and Christ is not that of two successive competitors in a task, the first of whom fails while the second succeeds. Rather, Christ has to *undo* the failure of Adam, reverse his disobedience, and bring life where Adam brought death. Christ is thus greater than Adam.

The use of Adamic imagery elsewhere encourages us to suppose that it underlies Philippians

---

12. Notably J. D. G. Dunn, *Christology in the Making* (London: SCM 1980) 113-21.

2–3, where we have similar ideas of Christ's becoming human, with the result that men and women become what he is. How, then, are we to deal with the objection that Phil 2:6 cannot be intended as a contrast between Adam and Christ, since the *result* of Christ's action is that he became man and took on human form? It is precisely in this anomaly that we find the solution to the problem. As has already been noted, Paul does not regard Adam and Christ as equals, since for him Christ is always greater than Adam. Christ is the true "image of God," after whom Christians are now being re-created, while Adam is the distorted copy, whose disobedience resulted in humanity's becoming enslaved to sin and death. If we were to set out the two actions of Adam and Christ diagrammatically, the pattern would not be that found in equating Adam with Christ but in seeing Christ as greater than Adam.

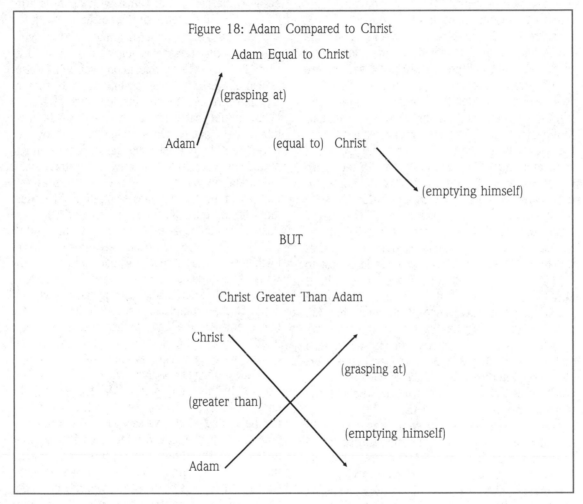

Figure 18: Adam Compared to Christ

To make sense of the parallel with Adam, therefore, we have to understand Christ to be the pattern of what humanity was meant to be: the perfect image of God and the reflection of God's glory. If Paul uses the phrase *en morphē Theou* rather than the one used of Adam in Genesis, that is with good reason, for it would make no sense at all to say that one who was created "after the image of God" (i.e., a man) became man! Christ is himself that image after whom Adam was created.

The fact that Paul does not use the word "image" here is thus no reason to reject the reference to Adam. The logic of the passage demands a contrast—between "the form of a slave," which expresses the condition into which Adam fell, and "the form of God," which expresses the condition of the one who is greater than Adam. Why, then, in Philippians 2 does Paul use the particular term *morphē*, whereas similar statements in Romans 8 and Galatians 4 refer to God's Son? The basic meaning of the word seems to be "visible form," and since children are often like their parents, it has been suggested that the phrase is comparable to the title "Son of God."[13] This visible form is perhaps to be identified with God's glory, which features in OT theophanies (e.g., Exodus 32). Or perhaps it is the expression of the inner reality that is at one and the same time concealed by and revealed by the glory. This presumably lies behind the NIV's "in very nature God," a translation that is nevertheless misleading (see below). The idea that God has a "form" that cannot be seen by humans is found in various Jewish writings.[14] Particularly interesting is the passage in the Talmud that interprets Gen 1:27 as meaning that God created Adam "in the image of the likeness of his form."[15] We do not know how early this particular interpretation came to be, but the fact that it distinguishes "the image" from "the form" is significant. A parallel idea is found in Philo (a contemporary of Paul) who uses the term "image" to describe what is closest to God. So God is the pattern of the image (who is also God's Word) and this image is in turn the pattern for humanity, since "God made the Man after the image of God."[16] In later Judaism, we find the hope of future restoration, when men and women will again be like God. Thus *Gen. Rab.* 21:7 interprets Gen 3:22 as referring to the world to come, when God will say, "Behold, the man *has become* as one of us."

Ideas such as these may well lie behind Paul's use of Adamic language. For him, Christ is the *true* "image of God" (2 Cor 4:4; Col 1:15), the one who is "in his form," whereas Adam, who was created "after" God's image, became subject to sin and death because of his disobedience (Rom 5:12-21) and is now only a distorted copy of what he was meant to be. Those who have borne the image of the first Adam may, in turn, bear the

image of the last Adam (1 Cor 15:42-49)—last, not in the sense that he came into existence last, but because he represents the eschatological goal of humanity, God's original purpose for creation.[17] He is the one through whom all things exist (1 Cor 8:6; Col 1:15-16), the embodiment of God's glory, according to whose image men and women are being restored (Rom 8:28-30; Col 3:9). If Phil 2:6 uses the phrase *en morphē Theou* rather than "the Son of God," this may well be precisely because the contrast of Christ with Adam is fundamental to the theme of the passage.[18]

2:5. The key to understanding how and why Paul uses this passage is found in v. 5, which reads literally: "Think this among you which also in Christ Jesus." Once again, we find that a missing verb has to be supplied after "which." What should that verb be? In v. 1, it made little difference whether we supplied "to be" or "to have," but here these two verbs can be interpreted in very different ways. The traditional interpretation was to understand the verb as "to be," as in the King James translation: "Let this mind be in you, which was also in Christ Jesus"; this interpretation is reflected in both the NRSV and the NIV. The Philippians are urged to have in themselves the disposition that Christ showed. It has been argued, however, that Paul's appeal in these verses (like his ethical appeals elsewhere) is not to the example of the earthly Jesus, but to the events of the saving kerygma.[19] In other words, Paul is not urging the Philippians to imitate Christ, but to be what they already are, "in him," to think among themselves what they think "in Christ." In this interpretation, the missing verb is once again φρονέω (*phroneō*), which is used at the beginning of the verse and which occurred twice in v. 2; we should understand Paul's command to mean "show among yourselves the attitude that arises from the fact that you are in Christ." In support of this view, we may note the use of Paul's customary phrase "in Christ" and

---

13. C. A. Wanamaker, "Philippians 2.6-11: Son of God or Adamic Christology?" *NTS* 33 (1987) 179-93.

14. See M. Bockmuehl, " 'The Form of God' (Phil. 2:6): Variations on a Theme of Jewish Mysticism," *JTS* NS48 (1997) 1-23.

15. *b. Ket.* 8a.

16. Philo *Allegorical Interpretation of the Law* III.96.

17. If 1 Cor 15:47 describes Christ as "the second man," that is surely because, as man, Adam preceded Christ; in terms of our own experience, also, we share in the physical body of Adam before we are transformed into the spiritual body of Christ.

18. See further Morna D. Hooker, "Adam *Redivivus:* Philippians 2 Once More," in *The Old Testament in the New Testament: Essays in Honour of J. L. North Worth,* ed. Steve Mayise, JSNTSup 189 (Sheffield: Sheffield Academic, 2000) 220-34.

19. Notably by E. Käsemann, "Kritische Analyse von Phil 2:5-11," *ZThK* 47 (1950) 313-60; English trans., "A Critical Analysis of Phil 2:5-11," *JThC* 5 (1968) 45-88.

the fact that if Paul is referring simply to the behavior of Christ as a model, then vv. 9-11 are strictly irrelevant. Syntactically, it is also much more natural to supply *phroneō* from the first part of the verse than the verb "to be" and to translate ἐν ὑμῖν (*en humin*) as "among yourselves" rather than "in yourselves."

The choice, then, is between a command to have the attitude that was in Christ Jesus and a command to have an attitude that belongs to those who are in him. This antithesis between imitation and kerygma, however, is too stark. It is true that ethical behavior is never simply a question of imitating Jesus, but it is not true that Paul does not appeal to the example of Jesus Christ when giving ethical exhortations (cf. Rom 15:1-3, 7; 2 Cor 8:9). Of course, the Philippians' behavior depends on the fact that they are in Christ, and the fact that they are "in Christ" depends on the saving events of the gospel. But the attitude that is appropriate to those who are in Christ is that shown by the historical person whom they know as "Jesus," and the very fact that they are in Christ is the result of that attitude. It is, perhaps, no accident that the phrase Paul uses in v. 5 is not "in Christ" but "in Christ *Jesus,*" as though to remind the Philippians of what the one they now call Lord was like. The best translation of this verse, therefore, is one that conveys the whole extent of Paul's appeal, which is *both* to the attitude shown by Christ Jesus *and* to the attitude that is therefore appropriate to those who are "in him."[20] The NRSV's marginal note, which suggests the translation "Let the same mind be in you that you have in Christ Jesus," though probably intended to represent the kerygmatic interpretation, in fact best represents this ambiguity.

2:6. If the basic meaning of the word μορφη (*morphē*) is "visible form," then the NRSV's "in the form of God" is preferable to the NIV's "in very nature God." There is a certain (and necessary) anomaly in the expression, since the form of God cannot be seen. Similar ideas are expressed in Col 1:15, where Christ is described as "the image of the invisible God," and in John

1:18: "No one has ever seen God: the only Son [or the only God], who is in the Father's bosom, he has made him known."

The meaning of the word ἁρπαγμός (*harpagmos*), "something to be exploited/grasped" (v. 6), has proved even more contentious than that of the word *morphē*. From the time of the church fathers, there have been many different interpretations of it. The main dispute has been about whether the word referred to something Christ already possessed, but did not cling to, or whether it referred to something he did not yet possess, but might have clutched at. These two interpretations are represented in the two diagrams in *Fig.* 18, on page 505.[21] If "equality with God" is regarded here as something the pre-existent Christ already possessed, then how are we to explain the language of the second part of the "hymn," which suggests that God has now bestowed on Christ a status that he did not enjoy before? If, on the other hand, he did not yet possess equality with God, could he truly be said to be "in the form of God"?

It now seems, however, that the most likely interpretation of *harpagmos* is that it refers to "something to be exploited."[22] In this view, equality with God was something that Christ already possessed, but which he chose not to use for his own advantage. The implication of this passage is that God bestowed on him the status and honor he had not claimed for himself. (Christ's voluntary humiliation and the bestowal of this status of honor upon him are best represented by *Fig.* 18, 505.) There is another interesting parallel with the Fourth Gospel in the phrase "equality with God," since a very similar phrase is used in John 5:18, where Jesus is accused of making himself equal to God. His opponents regard his claim to be God's Son as a usurpation of a role that does not belong to him.

Verses 6-11 are unique in the Pauline literature in telling us what Christ did *not* do, before spelling out what he did. Why do they include this negative emphasis? One suggestion is that there is a reference here to Lucifer, who is said

---

20. See M. D. Hooker, "Philippians 2:6-11," in *Jesus und Paulus, Festschrift für Werner Georg Kümmel zum 70. Geburtstag,* ed. E. Earle Ellis and Erich Grässer (Göttingen: Vandenhoeck & Ruprecht, 1975) 151-64; reprinted in M. D. Hooker, *From Adam to Christ* (Cambridge: Cambridge University Press, 1990) 88-100.

21. For a full discussion of the various possibilities, see N. T. Wright, "ἁρπαγμός and the Meaning of Philippians 2:5-11," *JTS* NS 37 (1980) 321-52; reprinted in revised form in *The Climax of the Covenant* (Edinburgh: T. & T. Clark, 1991) 62-90.

22. See R. W. Hoover, "The *Harpagmos* Enigma: A Philological Solution," *HTR* 64 (1971) 95-119.

to have rebelled against God and to have attempted to make himself like God (Isa 14:12-14). Lucifer, however, was never "in the form of God," nor was he created "in the image of God," and all the objections to a contrast with Adam (and none of the arguments in favor) apply to him. The most likely explanation of the negative is that it is intended as a deliberate contrast with Adam, who desired to be like God (cf. Gen 3:5, 22). Logically Genesis presents us with a contradiction by affirming both that Adam was created "in the image and likeness of God" (Gen 1:26) and that he was tempted to become like God (Gen 3:5). This tension between *being* like God and *desiring* to be like God is due to the fact that different sources have been combined there, but can nevertheless be seen as expressing two aspects of the truth, since men and women are both *like* God, yet distant *from* God as well. Verse 6 perhaps reflects this tension and provides a christological solution: Christ, who was "in the form of God," might well have claimed the privileges of equality with God as his right, but did not do so. What Adam desired, Christ was content to forgo.

2:7-8. Whatever precise meaning we give to the first statement concerning what Christ did *not* do, the next verb, κενόω (*kenoō*), is clearly intended to describe the very opposite: "he emptied himself/made himself nothing" (v. 7). The NIV translation avoids raising the awkward question, Of what did he empty himself? This question led, in the nineteenth century, to the so-called kenotic theory of the incarnation, which held that in becoming man, Christ emptied himself of the attributes of divinity, such as omnipotence and omniscience. Paul shows no interest in such matters, and the verb (which he uses elsewhere in the sense of "to nullify"; Rom 4:14; 1 Cor 1:17; 9:15; 2 Cor 9:3) was probably chosen to stress the contrast between the possibility Christ rejected, of claiming what was rightfully his, and his abandonment of his privileges. Once again, there may also be an intended contrast with Adam, who, as a result of the fall, was stripped of his power.

The contrast between what Christ did and did not do is seen much more clearly in Greek than in either of the English translations, for (in spite of earlier warnings about imposing a pattern on

the material!) there does seem to be a shape to vv. 6-7*a*. Literally, the passage reads as follows:

Who, being in the form of God,
    Did not consider as something-to-be-exploited
Equality with God,
    But made himself nothing,
        Taking the form of a slave!

Here we see yet another clear contrast: between being in the form of God and taking the form of a slave. The OT name for God is "LORD"—the name that Christ himself is given in vv. 9-11. Had Christ exploited his equality with God, he might have been acknowledged as such from the beginning. Instead, he took the form—and status—of a slave. These final words shock us because of their incongruity: This is not what we expect of one who is in the form of God and who could, if he had wished, have claimed equality with God. There could be no greater contrast than this. Yet we should not think of this process as some kind of exchange. Christ did not cease to be "in the form of God" when he took the form of a slave, any more than he ceased to be the "Son of God" when he was sent into the world. On the contrary, it is *in his self-emptying and his humiliation that he reveals what God is like,* and it is through his taking the form of a slave that we see "the form of God." The NRSV's "though" in v. 6 is misleading. There is no conjunction in the Greek, but if we supply one, then it should perhaps be "because." There is an interesting parallel once again in the Fourth Gospel, where the glory of Jesus—and therefore of God—is revealed in the cross.

The condition of being a slave is now identified with that of being human, which suggests that the contrast between Adam and Christ is continuing. According to Gen 1:26, 28, Adam was intended to have dominion, as God's representative, over the earth, a dominion that he lost at the fall, when he was condemned to a life of servitude (Gen 3:17-19). Elsewhere, Paul describes the condition of men and women as that of slavery to cosmic forces, from which the Son of God rescues them (Gal 4:3-7; cf. Rom 8:15). In Romans 5-7, these forces are named as sin, the law, and death, and in various passages Paul speaks of Christ as coming under the power of all three (sin, insofar as he was "in the likeness of sinful flesh," Rom 8:3; law, Gal 4:4; and death, Phil 2:8). Christ deliberately identified himself with humanity, in bondage to evil forces (a similar idea is found in Heb 2:14-15). Whether Paul is thinking of these powers here we do not know; what is clear is that to adopt the form of a slave (with all the dishonor and lack of privileges that implies) is the complete opposite of claiming the status and privileges of equality with God.

Adam was created after the image and likeness of God, but now Christ is born "in human likeness" (ἐν ὁμοιώματι ἀνθρώπων *en homoiōmati anthrōpōn*) and is found in human form. The word translated "form" or "appearance" here is not *morphē* but σχῆμα (*schēma*). None of the three terms, *morphē*, *en homoiōmati anthrōpōn*, or *schēma*, is meant to suggest that Jesus was not truly human; they indicate, rather, that he shared fully in our human existence. If we are correct in understanding Paul to be thinking of Christ as the true image of God, according to whose image and likeness Adam was created, then there is a deep irony here. The true man now identifies himself with the condition of fallen humanity, and in place of the stark contrast in the first few clauses of the "hymn" we have two clauses in parallel. And the next line, "he humbled himself" (which corresponds to Christ's action of emptying himself in v. 7), introduces, not a contrast with his humanity, but its logical outcome: death (v. 8). Christ, however, was "obedient to the point of/to death"—and with that one word, "obedient" (ὑπήκοος *hypēkoos*), contrasts with Adam leap once again to mind. Adam was disobedient to God's command, and it was his disobedience that led to death for all (Rom 5:12-19). But to whom is Christ obedient? Paul does not say. The word "to" (μέχρι *mechri*) means "as far as." He was presumably obedient to the laws to which he was now enslaved, which decreed the universal rule of death; but ultimately he was obedient to God. Whereas for Adam death was the result of his disobedience, for Christ it was the result of his obedience in identifying himself totally with the human condition. Moreover, in his case this death was by crucifixion, the punishment reserved in the Roman world for rebels and disobedient slaves, thus marking the reality of Christ's self-identification with those who are slaves.

The last phrase in v. 8 is often excised as a Pauline addition to the original "hymn," because it is said to spoil the structure, but we should not amend the structures to suit our expectations. Moreover, the logic of the passage seems to demand this nadir of humiliation that, paradoxically, was for Paul the climax to the first half of the passage. More than two thousand years of Christian piety have obscured from us the shock and horror with which these final words would have been heard by their original audience. Crucifixion was the cruelest and most shameful of deaths, and there could be no greater contrast with the opening lines of the "hymn," or with the exaltation that follows.

There is, in fact, an interesting similarity between the first five lines (see above) and the five lines just examined. It is true that the structure is different (AABBC instead of ABABC), but that is because the content is different; these later lines explore what it meant for Christ to be human, rather than what it meant for one who was in the form of God to take on the form of a slave. For that reason, they use parallelism rather than contrast. But in this second group of lines, as in the first, the punch line comes at the end, with the shock of the reference to crucifixion:

having become in human likeness,
and being found in human appearance,
he humbled himself,
becoming obedient to death,
even death on a cross! (author's trans.)

2:9-11. In the rest of the passage, we move into a totally different mood—and into a different structure again. The triumphant "Therefore" in v. 9 introduces the action of God, who now responds to Christ's self-emptying and humiliation. This final section appears to fall naturally into three shorter sections, each of three lines, coming to a climax in v. 11c:

Therefore God has highly exalted him,
and given to him the name
that is above all names,
that at the name of Jesus
every knee should bow,
in heaven and on earth and under the earth,
and every tongue confess

that Jesus Christ is Lord
to the glory of God the Father! (author's trans.)

Throughout these final lines of the passage, the emphasis is on the superlative. The name given to Jesus is "the name that is above every name." The statement that "every knee" should bow or bend is further spelled out with the description of those to whom the knees belong and who are "in heaven and on earth and under the earth." Every living creature, including spiritual and demonic powers, will acknowledge Jesus as Lord; the adjective translated "under the earth" may well include the dead as well.

The verb Ηυπερύψωσεν (*hyperypsōsen*), "highly exalted/exalted to the highest place," emphasizes the magnitude of the honor bestowed on Christ. The *hyper* element does not necessarily imply "higher than before," but since Christ made no claims for himself and is now exalted to the highest position possible, it does, in effect, mean that. He is now universally acknowledged to be "equal with God." The idea that the risen Jesus is given a status that he did not have before is implied in Rom 1:3-4 and 10:9 as well as in non-Pauline texts such as Matt 28:18 and Acts 2:36.

To give someone a name is to give him or her status and power. The name bestowed on Jesus here is "the name that is above every name," which is clearly the name of God (v. 9). Perhaps the fact that this name is not clearly specified is deliberate. By tradition, the name of God could not be spoken or written. Challenged by Moses to give a name in Exod 3:14, God replies, "I am who I am." But since the LXX commonly uses "the Lord" as a substitute for the divine name, we are not surprised to find in v. 11 the universal proclamation that "Jesus Christ is Lord." It is puzzling, then, to find the passage continuing with "that at the name of Jesus" (v. 10). In spite of what some commentators have occasionally argued,[23] the name that is given to Christ at his

exaltation cannot be the name "Jesus," for that is the name he has already borne throughout his human life. Why, then, is it mentioned here? Presumably to emphasize that it is the one who came in the likeness of men (Jesus) who is now proclaimed as Lord. When the name of Jesus is mentioned, then all creation should acknowledge that "Jesus Christ is Lord" (cf. Rom 10:9; 1 Cor 12:3). In the Roman city of Philippi, where the cult of the emperor was so important, the proclamation of *Jesus* as Lord would be seen as a challenge to political loyalties. But the pattern of behavior that Paul had placed before the Philippians would have been just as much of a challenge to the whole Roman social ethos.

There is an obvious contrast between Christ's proclamation as Lord and the earlier references to his taking the form of a slave and dying a slave's death. There are possible contrasts with Adam also: in the declaration that Christ will be acknowledged "in heaven and on earth and under the earth," since Adam was given dominion over the earth alone, and in the final line, which declares that what is now done is "to the glory of God the Father." At the fall, Adam failed to honor God and ceased to reflect God's glory—an idea that may well have influenced Rom 1:23 and 3:23. What Adam failed to do, the one who became man and is now proclaimed as Lord is able to do. The exaltation of Jesus, far from diminishing God's own position and honor, actually resounds to God's glory. The words "every knee shall bow/bend . . . and every tongue confess" are taken from Isa 45:23, where they refer to the worship of God. Here, knees are bent at the name of Jesus, and the confession made in v. 11 is of the universal lordship of Jesus Christ—but the end result of offering praise to him is the glory of God. Once again, the final phrase takes us by surprise and forms the punch line of the stanza—and of the hymn. Yet we should not be surprised, for whoever honors Jesus must also glorify God, because in Jesus we see the one who is "in the form of God" and who mirrors God's glory. (See Reflections at 2:12-18.)

23. Notably C. F. D. Moule, "Further Reflexions on Philippians 2:5-11," in *Apostolic History and the Gospel: Festschrift for F. F. Bruce*, ed. W. Ward Gasque and Ralph P. Martin (Exeter: Paternoster, 1970).

PHILIPPIANS 2:12-18, OUR NECESSARY RESPONSE

NIV

¹²Therefore, my dear friends, as you have always obeyed—not only in my presence, but now much more in my absence—continue to work out your salvation with fear and trembling, ¹³for it is God who works in you to will and to act according to his good purpose.

¹⁴Do everything without complaining or arguing, ¹⁵so that you may become blameless and pure, children of God without fault in a crooked and depraved generation, in which you shine like stars in the universe ¹⁶as you hold out[a] the word of life—in order that I may boast on the day of Christ that I did not run or labor for nothing. ¹⁷But even if I am being poured out like a drink offering on the sacrifice and service coming from your faith, I am glad and rejoice with all of you. ¹⁸So you too should be glad and rejoice with me.

[a]16 Or hold on to

NRSV

12Therefore, my beloved, just as you have always obeyed me, not only in my presence, but much more now in my absence, work out your own salvation with fear and trembling; ¹³for it is God who is at work in you, enabling you both to will and to work for his good pleasure.

14Do all things without murmuring and arguing, ¹⁵so that you may be blameless and innocent, children of God without blemish in the midst of a crooked and perverse generation, in which you shine like stars in the world. ¹⁶It is by your holding fast to the word of life that I can boast on the day of Christ that I did not run in vain or labor in vain. ¹⁷But even if I am being poured out as a libation over the sacrifice and the offering of your faith, I am glad and rejoice with all of you— ¹⁸and in the same way you also must be glad and rejoice with me.

COMMENTARY

2:12-13. Paul now continues with his appeal concerning the way in which the Philippians should behave, picking up many of the themes discussed in 1:27–2:4. As in 1:27, he urges the Philippians to live in a way that is appropriate to the gospel, whether he is present or absent. The introductory "therefore" shows us that this appeal is based firmly on what he has just said about Christ. He addresses his readers as "beloved" or "dear friends," another indication of the cordial relationship between them. There is no hint that the Philippians are not doing well. They have always been obedient, he says; so now, let them work out their own salvation with fear and trembling—not simply when he is with them, but even more when he is absent. Paul does not say to whom the Philippians were obedient; the NRSV assumes that it was to Paul himself, and there is some support for this in the references to his presence and absence. Ultimately, however, it is God to whom they owe obedience, and Paul is simply the one through whom God's commands are channeled.

The word used for "presence" (παρουσία parousia) also has the sense of "coming" and was used by Paul of his own hoped-for return to Philippi in 1:26. It is not clear whether Paul is referring to his presence with them in the past or to a possible future visit (cf. 2:24). Another possibility is that he is thinking of "presence" and "absence" in the more radical sense, discussed in 1:23-25, of remaining in this life or departing from it. If his intent is the latter, then his quotation in v. 15 from Moses' "farewell discourse" to the Israelites in Deuteronomy 32 is given added poignancy. It will certainly have occurred to Paul that this letter may well be his own farewell discourse to the Philippians. There may, indeed, already be an allusion (though not a linguistic one) to Deut 31:27, where Moses says that if the Israelites have been rebellious during his lifetime, they will surely be even more rebellious after his death.

The Philippians are to be obedient; the verb ὑπακούω (*hypakouō*) echoes the "obedient" used of Christ in v. 8. And they are to work out their own salvation "with fear and trembling." Such fear and trembling are not caused by any uncertainty regarding their salvation, but are the appropriate attitude in the presence of God, an attitude that might better be described in English as "awe." The "your" (better "your own," as in the NRSV) is slightly emphatic, and it may be intended to strengthen the point that Paul's presence or absence should be immaterial. The fact that the Philippians are urged to "work out" their own salvation does not conflict with the Pauline insistence that salvation is the work of God alone. Verses 6-11 have described the gracious action of God in Christ, but that gracious action demands a response—what Paul elsewhere describes as "the obedience of faith" (Rom 1:5). The Philippians are to complete what God has done by living it out in their own lives. But this is not simply an individual matter. Paul has already urged the Philippians to avoid selfish concern for their own interests (v. 4). The "your" is plural in Greek, and the life that is to be lived is that lived in the community of believers. Paul's words, like those of Moses, are addressed to the people of God, not to a collection of individuals.

Verse 13 reminds us of the other side of the equation. Although Paul has urged the Philippians to work out (κατεργάζομαι *katergazomai*) their own salvation, it is in fact God who is at work (ἐνεργέω *energeō*) in them. The two verbs are based on the same root, ἔργον (*ergon*), meaning "work" or "action," and the relation between the two activities is spelled out in the rest of the verse, since the purpose of God working in them is that they should will and work (the same verb, *energeō*) to God's good pleasure. What the Philippians now will and work is, in fact, the work of God within them. The NIV is ambiguous and perhaps understands all the verbs to refer to the activity of God; the NRSV, which understands the willing and the working to be done by the Philippians—as a result of God's own work in them—is preferable. The fact that God is at work is the basis for Paul's confidence that his own presence or absence makes no difference to the Philippians'

obedience. Once again, we may have an echo of Moses' farewell to Israel, when he assured the people that, though he was about to die, the Lord would still be with them (Deut 31:7-8).

2:14-16. What does this mean in practical terms? They are to do everything without murmuring/complaining or arguing (v. 14). Is this a hint that the Philippians are at present bickering among themselves? Many commentators think so, but there has been little evidence so far to support this view (but see the Commentary on 4:2). Why, then, should the Philippians be warned not to complain or argue? The answer is perhaps to be found in v. 15, where Paul says that the Philippians are "children of God without blemish/fault (ἄμωμα *amōma*, "without blame") in a crooked and perverse/depraved generation." These words are a clear echo of Deut 32:5, a verse that is confused in both Hebrew and Greek, but whose main sense is clear. The Israelites are accused of being blameworthy (μωμητά *mōmēta*), and described as no children of God, a crooked and perverse generation. Paul now turns this idea inside out: Christians have *become* God's children, and they must therefore live *without* blame in *the midst of* a crooked and perverse generation.

This contrast with the Israelites, who were denounced in the wilderness as unworthy to be called the children of God, gives us the explanation for the command to avoid complaining/murmuring and arguing, since the Israelites were frequently accused of complaining about God's provision for them. The first noun, γογγυσμός (*gongysmos*, "complaint"), and its cognate verb are used frequently in the OT of Israel's attitude toward God in the wilderness (e.g., Exod 16:1-12; Num 14:27-29). This complaining is referred to by Paul in 1 Cor 10:1-13, where he describes the behavior of the Israelites and what happened to them as a result as an "example" of what Christians must not do; in v. 10 he refers to the story in Numbers 16, where the people complained and many were destroyed. The second noun, διαλογισμός (*dialogismos*), which can mean simply "discussion," seems to be used here with the meaning "argument." Unlike *gongusmos*, it is not used in the Greek versions of the Pentateuch. Nevertheless, in view of the other echoes of the wilderness story, it is possible that Paul may have in mind the disputes between Moses and the people such as are recorded in Exod 17:1-7 and Num 16:1-11. Because of Christ's attitude and action, those who are in him are enabled to live as Israel was called (but failed) to live, as God's "blameless and innocent/pure children."

But who are the members of this new "crooked and perverse/depraved generation"? Does this phrase refer to those to whom it was once applied—namely, the Jews? If so, is that because, like Israel of old, they are rejecting what God offered them by opposing the gospel (cf. Matt 17:17)? Or does it refer to those people referred to in 1:28, whether Jews or Gentiles, whose refusal to accept the gospel was being expressed in opposition to the Philippian church? The phrase should probably be understood as a general one, referring to everyone who is not included among the children of God.

In contrast, the Philippian Christians "shine like stars." The verb could be understood as a command, but the NIV and the NRSV are probably correct in taking it to be a statement of fact. The word translated "stars" is φωστῆρες (phōstēres), which can refer to anything that gives light. There may be an echo of Dan 12:3 in this phrase, since there it is said that the wise will shine like the lights of the heaven and the implication is that they will illuminate others. But is that idea present in Philippians? Or is the emphasis in Philippians on the contrast between light and darkness? The answer to that question lies in v. 16 in the verb ἐπέχω (epechō): Does it mean "hold fast" (as in NRSV; cf. the NIV margin) or "hold out" (as in NIV)? If we follow the NIV, then the verb picks up the idea of light as showing the way, and the Christian community is seen as offering the gospel ("the word of life") to those among whom they live. If we accept the NRSV's translation, then Paul is continuing to think of the struggle in which the Philippian community is engaged (see 1:27-30). On the whole, this latter interpretation suits the context better. In contrast to those who met God's gifts with complaints and arguments, they *hold fast* to the word of life—but that means, inevitably, that they will also be an example to those around them (1:28).

Once again we find the expression "the day of Christ," which Paul has already used in 1:6 and 10. It is the Christ whose story Paul has just told who is now expected to come. Since every tongue

has not yet confessed Jesus Christ to be Lord (vv. 10-11), Paul presumably assumes that this will take place then. Paul expects to boast on that day that his work has not been in vain. For Paul, boasting in his own achievements is excluded (e.g., Rom 3:27; 1 Cor 1:29), and the only proper ground for boasting is in what God has done in Christ (e.g., Rom 5:11; 1 Cor 1:31; Phil 3:3). But he frequently speaks of boasting about his congregations (see 1 Cor 15:31; 2 Cor 1:14; 7:4, 14; 9:2-3; 1 Thess 2:19). The reason for this is spelled out in Rom 15:17: "In Christ Jesus, then, I have reason to boast of my work for God." What he boasts of is not his own achievement, but what God has done in him and what God has enabled him to will and to do (v. 13) because he is in Christ. There is thus an interesting parallel between the idea that Paul will boast on the day of Christ and the statement in vv. 9-11 that the honor accorded to Jesus Christ as Lord is "to the glory of God the Father."

The image of "running in vain" (v. 16) is used again by Paul in Gal 2:2 (cf. 1 Cor 9:27). Here he links it with the idea of toiling in vain, a phrase that echoes words in Isa 49:4. In their original context, these words refer to the attempts of someone who was called to be God's servant to bring Israel back to the Lord, attempts that have apparently met with failure but that are followed by the summons to be a light to the Gentiles. The ideas are clearly relevant to Paul's own situation, but whether the echo is a conscious one we cannot be sure.

2:17-18. The idea that his efforts are in vain seems to bring Paul back in v. 17 to his own situation and the possibility of martyrdom that looms over him. Some commentators have doubted whether Paul is, in fact, contemplating martyrdom here, because a few verses later he expresses the hope that he will be released (v. 24). That hope depends, however, on "how things go with" him (v. 23), and there is no inconsistency between his attitude in v. 24 and his recognition in v. 17 that things may not go well; "but even if" the outcome is death, he will nevertheless rejoice. The metaphor he uses is that of "being poured out as a libation/like a drink offering." Libations of wine were the regular accompaniment to both Jewish burnt offerings (e.g., Exod 29:38-41; Num 28:1-15) and pagan sacrifices. But if it is Paul's own life that may be poured out in this way, who is it that offers "the sacrifice and the offering/service" that his libation accompanies? Is it Paul himself, who offers to God the faith of those Gentiles who have responded to the gospel (cf. Rom 15:16 where a different Greek word for "offering" is used)? Or is it the Philippians who make the sacrifice? The latter would seem more appropriate at the end of a paragraph urging them to respond to the gospel. Is it then their *faith* that they offer—or what grows out of their faith? Once again, the context suggests that Paul has in mind a sacrifice that is the *result* of their faith (NIV, "coming from your faith"); compare again the phrase "obedience of faith" in Rom 1:15, which refers to the obedience that issues from faith.

But why the sacrificial imagery, if Paul is thinking simply of conduct? Is it, perhaps, because their lives are to be seen as mirroring the self-sacrificial actions of Christ? Or (the suggestions are not exclusive) is Paul alluding once again to the gifts the Philippians have sent to him and that are, in effect, an offering to God? In favor of this interpretation we may point to the fact that the word for "sacrifice" (θυσία *thysia*) is used again in 4:18 of the gifts the Philippians sent to Paul, which are "an acceptable sacrifice, pleasing to God," while the noun translated "offering" or "service" (λειτουργία *leitourgia*) is used in 2:30 of the service that they wished to render Paul but were unable to offer. And over this sacrifice, Paul is ready, if necessary, to pour out his own life, thus making their partnership in the gospel (1:5) complete.

"Even if" this happens, Paul declares that he is glad and will rejoice with the Philippians, and he urges them to be glad and to rejoice with him in turn. As in 1:18*b,* the possibility of martyrdom cannot diminish his joy, a joy in which they should share. The emphatic use of the verbs χαίρω (*chairo*) and συγχαίρω (*sygchairo*; twice each) picks up the note of joy first sounded in 1:4, where it was caused by the fact that the Philippians had shared with him in the gospel "from the first day until now." If Paul is about to lose his life, then that "now" may mark the end and the climax of that partnership in the gospel.

REFLECTIONS

1. This section of Philippians (1:27–2:18) demonstrates clearly the way in which theology and ethics are inseparably joined together. As in Judaism, so in Christianity, theological affirmation leads to ethical demand; neither can exist without the other. The link is made clear in Paul's opening words, commanding the Philippians to live "in a manner worthy of the gospel of Christ" (1:27). Nor is this link a tenuous one. The account of Christ's gracious actions and subsequent exaltation in 2:6-11 forms the core of this passage, and everything before and after it depends on it. The demand to live in a certain way is a necessary obligation laid upon all Christians, arising from the fact that they are "in Christ" only as the result of what Christ has done. Those who claim Christ as Lord cannot refuse this demand without denying that truth—the truth of the gospel itself. If we are really "in Christ," then we must share the attitude that was his and that now belongs to all who are in him.

2. The theological statement in 2:6-11 concentrates on the actions of Christ and God. Later theologians were concerned to define the "nature" of God and of Christ, and we, like them, tend to assume that if we want to know about the "nature" of Christ, we must concentrate on the opening and closing lines of this passage, on the statement that he is "in the form of God," and on the declaration that he is Lord. But it is typical of the biblical material that God is revealed through what God does, and here we find that God is revealed through what Christ does. Having been told that Christ is "in the form of God," we find our attention immediately focused on what he did. Christ reveals himself in his gracious actions—in his refusal to exploit his rights, in his self-emptying, in his self-humiliation, and in his obedience, even to the point of death. And because he is "in the form of God," his actions reveal not simply his own character or nature, but what God is like as well. The birth, ministry, and death of Jesus are a consistent whole, and in them all, we see the divine character revealed. Christ's exaltation by God is the vindication of Christ's actions, and not their undoing; it is precisely because he is humble and obedient that he also is Lord. His exaltation is God's triumphant affirmation that in Christ's actions we have the perfect revelation of the love and compassion of God. To acknowledge this Jesus as universal Lord is to accept as Lord the humble, obedient figure on the cross. And since divine "being" is revealed in divine "action," we begin to understand why theology and ethics are inseparable. The basic ethical exhortation is to "be like God" (cf. Lev 19:2), which means, in effect, to *behave* like God. These few verses thus form one of the most profound statements in the Pauline corpus about the nature of God.

Asked to describe the nature of God, most people would probably appeal to ideas regarding omnipotence and omniscience, to God's immeasurable distance from us and God's unutterable holiness. Paul, by contrast, describes what he refers to elsewhere as "grace." What resounds to God's glory (in other words, what reveals God's nature) is the proclamation of the crucified Jesus as Lord. Paul's understanding of "glory" here is remarkably similar to that of the Fourth Evangelist, although the Evangelist takes the further step of identifying crucifixion and exaltation, and so speaks of the moment of Jesus' death as his glorification (John 12:16, 23; 13:31-32; 17:1). But Paul, too, apparently sees Christ's self-emptying and death as the revelation of God's glory, and he uses similar ideas elsewhere, notably in 1 Cor 1:25, where he speaks of God's "folly" and "weakness" as demonstrations of true wisdom and strength. This revelation of God's nature confounds all our expectations and turns our preconceptions upside down.

3. The nature of God is revealed in what *we* call "the incarnation," and if we want to know what it means to be "in the form of God," then we must look at one who took "the form of a slave." Paul, of course, does not use our technical term; nor does he concern himself with the problems of how it could take place. Yet he expresses, in his own way, what later came to be referred to as the divinity and the humanity of Christ. Christ is divine because, as we have seen, he did not cease to be "in the form of God" when he adopted "the form of a slave." He is human because, as Paul stresses, Christ completely identifies with our situation. And yet there is a difference between him and us! In contrast to men and women, Christ humbled himself and was obedient. And because the one who took the form of a slave was also "in the form of God," we know that his humility and his obedience are rooted in the will of God. It is by Christ's obedience to the will of God that the relationship between God and humanity, broken by Adam, is restored, and reconciliation takes place.

Paul, the theologian, expresses here in his own way the truth that Matthew and Luke spell out in very different ways in their nativity stories. Paul shows no knowledge of those traditions, choosing instead to sum up in theological language what the evangelists prefer to express in narrative. We may well feel that the nativity stories are easier to understand! But do we *really* comprehend them? It is easy to concentrate on the details in the stories—on the angels and the star, the shepherds and the wise men—and miss the point they are trying to make: God with us! The Son of God born in weakness and humility, accepting poverty and vulnerability. The familiarity of the stories obscures their meaning. Paul's statement reminds us of their significance—that God revealed his self-giving love for men and women in the birth of his Son.

4. What are the implications of these verses for Christian living? What does it mean for Christians to acknowledge *this* Jesus as their Lord? Because this passage upsets our normal assumptions about what God is like, it has a radical effect on our understanding of what God expects from us. Instinctive human attitudes are turned on their heads. Those who confess Jesus as Lord should not be looking for status or power; nor should they be acting from "selfish ambition or conceit" (2:3). Rather, they should be humbly considering others better than themselves. And because they are concerned with the interests of others (2:4), they will be of one mind and one purpose, "having the same love" and of one accord (2:2). In stark contrast to the modern spirit of encouraging competition and giving rewards to individuals who get to the top, Paul insists on mutual concern and service.

Paul's words are a terrible indictment of the lives and attitudes of many who have called themselves "Christian." How many of us have really taken the self-giving of Christ as a model for Christian behavior? How many have been more concerned with airing our own opinions than with coming to a common mind with others? How many church leaders have seen their own role in terms of position and power, and have forgotten that true honor comes to those who "make themselves nothing"? How many have been prepared to take on the role of a slave? We can all point to notable examples of Christians who have endeavored to show the same attitude as Christ. Mother Teresa may spring at once to mind. Unfortunately, the very fact that such examples are notable proves how exceptional they are. It has to be confessed that the church as a whole has never taken to heart the true significance of this passage. We have gloried in the sublime statement in 2:5-11, and have ignored its implications for our lives—attempting to detach theology from ethics, God's gracious act from the divine demand that follows, ignoring the "therefore" that insists we "work out" salvation in our lives. Some Christians have emphasized the idea that Christ suffers *for* us to such an extent that they have assumed that Christian life consists simply of enjoying the benefits of his passion, and have conveniently ignored the persistent emphasis in the New Testament on the need to share Christ's self-giving and poverty and sufferings. We have found it all too easy to forget, in the words of Kenneth Grayston, that those who acknowledge Jesus as Lord claim for themselves "not only the exaltation, but also the renunciation, and the service, and the willing obedience."[24] Is this, perhaps, why, in Philippians, the day of judgment is referred to as the day of Christ or the day of Christ Jesus (see the Commentary on 1:6), reminding us that it is by *his* actions and example that we shall be judged?

But if, as Christians, we feel indicted for our frequent failure to follow in the footsteps of Christ, we can also take courage from the description of his final triumph. Those who confess that "Jesus is Lord"—and who live in his service—can be assured that his way is God's way and that the final victory will be his. At a time when Christians formed a tiny minority in the ancient world, Paul confidently declared that ultimately every tongue would confess Jesus to be Lord and that every knee would one day bow before him. Christians today, who in certain parts of the world feel outnumbered and isolated, may take courage from these words.

5. As so often in Paul's letters, his instructions about how we should live and show our obedience are general and imprecise. We are told to live "in a manner worthy of the gospel of Christ," but most of his hints about what that might mean refer to the attitudes that are appropriate to the Christian community. We are sometimes tempted to wish that Paul had given more precise advice on just how Christians should behave in particular circumstances. But Christian obedience does not mean living in accordance with a set of rules; rather, it means responding in the appropriate way to the self-giving love of God. The vision that Paul provides us with is, in fact, far more valuable than any set of rules. Christians in the modern world are faced with innumerable ethical dilemmas, which multiply each year with advances in science and medicine. We cannot expect to find ready-made answers to these modern-day questions in the Bible! We may be grateful that Paul, in his ethical teaching, always went back to first principles. In effect, he is saying, "This is the gospel. This is what God is like. This is what God has done for you, and this is what God expects *you* to be like. Work out what that

24. Kenneth Grayston, *The Epistles to the Galatians and to the Philippians,* Epworth Preacher's Commentary (London: Epworth, 1957) 99.

means for yourselves!" If we are to do that, then we, too, need to go back to first principles, to ask, What is the Christlike thing for us as a Christian community, for us as individual Christians, to be doing? How do we respond, in obedience, to what God has done?

The answers to these questions are not necessarily easy! In any particular ethical dilemma, we may well find Christians sincerely supporting opposite viewpoints. If someone is apparently in an irreversible coma, is it more "worthy of the gospel" to preserve life by continuing treatment or to allow the patient to die? When a tyrant like Hitler arises, is it right to resort to war in order to put a stop to his atrocities? What is the Christlike approach to using fetal tissue in medical research, in order to prevent disease? How does one balance the advantages and disadvantages to societies and environment when "development" seems to clash with "conservation"? In seeking to answer these questions, we may not always make the right choice. What is important is that we should approach all such problems in humility (not thinking we know the answers) and in love, looking to the interests of others, and not seeking to exploit what we consider to be our rights.

We see, then, that although Paul may not have given us precise guidelines about what to do in particular situations, he has, throughout this section, given us very significant hints. The basis for all our actions is our life in Christ. Unity is a "must" for those who are "one" in Christ. The humility (2:3) and obedience (2:12) expected of Christians are rooted in the humility and obedience of Christ himself. The source of all these qualities is Christ, in whom Christians also find encouragement, love, fellowship, and compassion (2:1). In both 1:27–2:4 and 2:12-18, Paul appeals not only for unity and humility, but also for courage. The courage to stand firm (1:27-28; 2:16) is a way of witnessing to opponents, and it is especially necessary in view of the possibility of sharing Christ's own experience of suffering (1:29-30; 2:17). And because our suffering, like everything else, is "in Christ," we find that this, too, becomes, in a sense, *his* suffering. So it is "for others"; in 1:29, remarkably, it is "for Christ," and in 2:17 Paul speaks of his being poured out as a libation. Like everything else, suffering is transformed "in Christ"; whereas we usually think of suffering in negative terms, Paul views it positively, since it is used by God to witness to the truth of the gospel and to bring comfort to fellow Christians.

6. Throughout this section we see plainly (1) that Christian obedience must be understood as the response to God's grace, rather than to a set of rules; (2) that the response we are called on to make is the response made by Christ himself; (3) that we are enabled to make that response because we are in him; (4) that because in him we are one community, relationships within that community—rooted in love, selflessness, and concern for others—are especially important; and (5) that the result of our obedient response will be a powerful witness to others. When a Christian community really takes this teaching seriously, then they are like light in a dark world (2:15; cf. Matt 5:14-16). Christians can never see their response to the gospel merely as a matter between themselves and God. Once again we see the truth of Wesley's description of Christianity as "a social religion." What we believe is revealed in the way we behave, and whatever we do is inevitably a proclamation to others of the gospel we believe. The basic rule, therefore, is to make sure that we believe the right gospel with heart and mind and soul and strength. Our behavior should be the expression of that belief.

PHILIPPIANS 2:19-30

FUTURE PLANS

OVERVIEW

Paul turns from exhortation to practical matters. Although he is separated from the Philippians (2:12), he plans to keep in touch with them by sending Timothy and Epaphroditus to Philippi. These two paragraphs (vv. 19-24 and vv. 25-30) both read like letters of commendation, of the kind usually sent with letter bearers. Neither of these commendations is strictly necessary, since Timothy was well known to the Philippians and since Epaphroditus came from Philippi; but Paul takes the opportunity to speak warmly of them both. It is sometimes argued that "travel plans" of this kind are more appropriate at the end of a letter (cf. Rom 15:22-29; 1 Cor 16:1-12) and that this supports the idea that 3:2 is the beginning of a second letter. But Paul was not bound by structures in this way.

PHILIPPIANS 2:19-24, TIMOTHY

NIV

[19]I hope in the Lord Jesus to send Timothy to you soon, that I also may be cheered when I receive news about you. [20]I have no one else like him, who takes a genuine interest in your welfare. [21]For everyone looks out for his own interests, not those of Jesus Christ. [22]But you know that Timothy has proved himself, because as a son with his father he has served with me in the work of the gospel. [23]I hope, therefore, to send him as soon as I see how things go with me. [24]And I am confident in the Lord that I myself will come soon.

NRSV

[19]I hope in the Lord Jesus to send Timothy to you soon, so that I may be cheered by news of you. [20]I have no one like him who will be genuinely concerned for your welfare. [21]All of them are seeking their own interests, not those of Jesus Christ. [22]But Timothy's[a] worth you know, how like a son with a father he has served with me in the work of the gospel. [23]I hope therefore to send him as soon as I see how things go with me; [24]and I trust in the Lord that I will also come soon.

[a] Gk his

COMMENTARY

What Paul hopes to do is, like all his activities and plans, "in the Lord" (v. 19). Timothy seems to have been one of Paul's most constant companions, mentioned frequently in his letters as well as in Acts 16–20. In 1:1 he was named as co-author of the letter, but it is now clear that this was a matter of courtesy and that the real author is Paul alone. Paul plans to send Timothy to them soon, not immediately and not, therefore, as the bearer of the letter. Paul looks forward to receiving news of the Philippians via Timothy, and he is confident that this news will be good, since he expects to be cheered by it. The "also" (picked up in the NIV but missing from the NRSV) indicates his assumption that they will, of course, be cheered by Timothy's visit. Paul has no one else like Timothy, who is genuinely concerned for the welfare of the Philippians (v. 20). The contrast with everyone else who is pursuing his or her own interests (v. 21) reminds us of Paul's exhortation in 2:1-4. Clearly his concern there for the Philippian community reflected his own experience of the attitudes shown by those Christians with whom he is in touch in prison. These people are failing to do what Paul has urged the Philippians to do—namely, to put the interests of other people first.

If Paul is in prison in Rome, some 800 miles from Philippi, it is, perhaps, not surprising that he cannot find anyone else who is prepared to undertake the long journey to Philippi. Even from Ephesus, such a journey might be difficult. Timothy is already well known to the Philippians

(according to Acts 16 he had accompanied Paul on his first visit to the city). Like a son learning a trade from his father, Timothy has served with Paul in the work of the gospel (v. 22). The verb "serve" (δουλεύω douleuō) picks up the δοῦλοι (douloi) of 1:1 as well as echoing the δοῦλος (doulos) of 2:7. Paul speaks of Timothy in similar terms in 1 Cor 4:17 and 16:10. And now we learn the reason for the delay in Timothy's visit: Paul plans to send him as soon as he sees "how things go" with him (v. 23)—presumably in order to bring news of the outcome of his trial to the Philippians. But since Paul has expressed confidence regarding his release, he trusts "in the Lord" that he will be able to visit them soon (v. 24). (See Reflections at 2:25-30.)

PHILIPPIANS 2:25-30, EPAPHRODITUS

NIV

25But I think it is necessary to send back to you Epaphroditus, my brother, fellow worker and fellow soldier, who is also your messenger, whom you sent to take care of my needs. 26For he longs for all of you and is distressed because you heard he was ill. 27Indeed he was ill, and almost died. But God had mercy on him, and not on him only but also on me, to spare me sorrow upon sorrow. 28Therefore I am all the more eager to send him, so that when you see him again you may be glad and I may have less anxiety. 29Welcome him in the Lord with great joy, and honor men like him, 30because he almost died for the work of Christ, risking his life to make up for the help you could not give me.

NRSV

25Still, I think it necessary to send to you Epaphroditus—my brother and co-worker and fellow soldier, your messenger[a] and minister to my need; 26for he has been longing for[b] all of you, and has been distressed because you heard that he was ill. 27He was indeed so ill that he nearly died. But God had mercy on him, and not only on him but on me also, so that I would not have one sorrow after another. 28I am the more eager to send him, therefore, in order that you may rejoice at seeing him again, and that I may be less anxious. 29Welcome him then in the Lord with all joy, and honor such people, 30because he came close to death for the work of Christ,[c] risking his life to make up for those services that you could not give me.

[a] Gk apostle [b] Other ancient authorities read longing to see
[c] Other ancient authorities read of the Lord

COMMENTARY

Paul considers it necessary to send Epaphroditus to Philippi as well—no doubt as the bearer of the letter (v. 25). Epaphroditus had been sent by the Philippian church to bring Paul their gift and to assist him in prison. Why is it now "necessary" for Paul to send him back? Apparently because the Philippians have heard that Epaphroditus has been seriously ill and are anxious as to whether he has made a full recovery (vv. 26, 28). This has made Epaphroditus long for the Philippians; the same verb (ἐπιποθέω *epipotheō*) was used of Paul's own longing for them in 1:8 (the reading in the NRSV margin, "to see," is almost certainly a later addition). Epaphroditus is described as Paul's "brother, co-worker/fellow worker and fellow soldier"; since he is mentioned only here and at 4:18, we do not know whether he and Paul had worked together in Philippi or whether this is a recognition of what Epaphroditus has done since—possibly in the fulfillment of his recent mission. He is also the Philippians' "messenger"; the word used is ἀπόστολος (*apostolos*), meaning "someone who is sent" to act on behalf of another. The NRSV note offers the transliteration "apostle," but the term is not being used here in the quasi-technical sense it has when Paul describes himself as "an apostle of Christ" (e.g., in 1 Cor 1:1). The task carried out by Epaphroditus is defined as being "minister to my need." Neither the NRSV nor the NIV's paraphrase, "to take care of my needs," conveys adequately the sense of the Greek. The noun is λειτουργός (*leitourgos*), a word that is usually used of someone who offers priestly service and is akin to the noun λειτουργία (*leitourgia*), used in 2:17 and 30. The word suggests that Paul regards Epaphroditus's ministry to his needs as a priestly offering to God, in whose service Paul is in prison. This ministry was a necessary one: As a prisoner, Paul would have been dependent on friends and relatives for the necessities of life, including food.

Epaphroditus's distress (v. 26) was caused by the difficulties of communication in the ancient world. News had reached the Philippians of his illness, and they needed to be reassured that he had fully recovered. His illness had clearly been severe—hardly an unusual event at that time. Commentators speculate about what it was and when it struck him, but we do not know these details. Paul attributes his recovery to divine mercy (v. 27): Epaphroditus had not died, and Paul had thus been spared additional sorrow. The phrase "sorrow upon sorrow/one sorrow after another" is a common one, and there is no need to ask what particular sorrow he had in mind. He had plenty! But since Epaphroditus is now better,

Paul is "eager to send him" to Philippi, so that they may rejoice and so that Paul may be the more free from sorrow. Both the NRSV and the NIV understand the Greek ἀλυπότερος (*alypoteros*) to mean "less anxious," but the word is formed from the noun λύπη (*lypē*), "sorrow," used in v. 27. The English paraphrase probably arose from the difficulty of understanding how Paul could be saved sorrow by Epaphroditus's return: Would his departure not *add* to Paul's sorrow? The answer is probably to be found in the mutuality of experience that belongs to those who are "in Christ." In vv. 17-18 Paul spoke of the Philippians and himself rejoicing together. In 2 Cor 1:3-7, he describes the way in which God consoles those who are afflicted and how this consolation is then shared by others who are in Christ. Here, the fact that the Philippians will rejoice at Epaphroditus's return perhaps means that Paul expects to share their joy and so be relieved of his sorrow.

The Philippians are urged to welcome Epaphroditus (v. 29); some commentators have supposed that this means that they have been criticizing him for failing to complete his commission. There is no justification whatever for this notion in the text; we are told only that the Philippians have heard of his illness, and he could scarcely have been blamed for that! Perhaps, though, Paul wishes to assure them that Epaphroditus has accomplished the task entrusted to him, even though he is returning early. He is to be welcomed "in the Lord" with joy and to be held in honor because of what he has done for "the work of Christ." In this context, these words refer to his ministry to Paul, described in these terms because Paul is imprisoned for the sake of the gospel. In undertaking the work of Christ, Epaphroditus came close to death (v. 30). In this last phrase we have a fascinating echo of the words used in 2:8 of Christ's obedience "to death" μέχρι θανάτου (*mechri thanatou*). Like Timothy, who considered what would benefit others, and not himself, Epaphroditus has risked his life in order to make up for the help the Philippians could not give Paul. Paul's words at the end of v. 30 are not meant as criticism of the Philippians, for they had sent generous contributions to assist him. But they were not with him in prison and, therefore, could not minister to him personally. A similar expression is used in 1 Cor 16:17, where the arrival of some members of the church makes up for the absence of the rest. Paul urges the Philippians to honor their representative, who has not only carried out the task entrusted to him but also has done it at considerable personal cost.

REFLECTIONS

Paul's practical arrangements concerning the delivery of the letter, the return of Epaphroditus, and the visit of Timothy provide us with an insight into his theology. At a down-to-earth level, we now see what it means for men and women to live "in the Lord" (2:19, 24, 29) and, therefore, to work out in their daily lives how to share the attitude of Christ, being concerned for others rather than themselves. Paul's plans to send Timothy and Epaphroditus to Philippi arise out of his concern for the Philippian community, while Timothy, Epaphroditus, and the Philippians themselves have all demonstrated a Christlike attitude by their behavior. The community of believers "in the Lord" is bonded together by love. Such a society provides mutual support, of the kind provided by the Philippians through Epaphroditus. As with all loving relationships, however, its members are inevitably vulnerable, because they share the sorrows and cares of others, as well as their joys. Hence the mutual experience of joy and sorrow is shared by Paul, Epaphroditus, and the Philippians. Paul and Epaphroditus have shared the Philippians' concern at the news of Epaphroditus's illness. Now the joy the Philippians experience at his safe return is shared by Paul and overcomes his own sorrow at being left alone.

Paul's words remind us of the support and comfort that can be experienced by Christians, even when they are on their own. The mutual concern and prayers of those who belong to Christ mean that they need never be out of touch. Even with a capital charge hanging over his head and deliberately sending home the man who had come to suppport him in prison, Paul shares the joy of Epaphroditus's friends at his recovery. He does not need Epaphroditus's physical presence and material assistance to know the comfort of belonging to a community that is as concerned for him as he is for them. The fact that Christianity is not a solitary religion means that we are able to share with one another its rewards and joys as well as its demands and sorrows!

PHILIPPIANS 3:1–4:1

THE CHRISTIAN LIFE, PART 2

OVERVIEW

The very first word of this section in both the NRSV and the NIV, "Finally," is a surprise. We are just halfway through the letter. So why should Paul be drawing to a close? In fact, as we shall discover, he has a great deal still that he wishes to say! And the first issue that he discusses, in 3:2-11, appears to be a totally new one, introduced very abruptly in v. 2. When we note, in addition, that the Greek word χαίρετε (*chairete*) is translated as "farewell" instead of as "rejoice" in the NRSV note, we can understand why many commentators argue that 3:1*a* marks the end of one letter and the beginning of another, even though they have to assume that the concluding words of one and the opening words of the other are missing (the division is made either after v. 1*a* [see the break in the NRSV text] or at the end of v. 1). Others argue that the letter breaks off at 3:1*a* and resumes again at 4:4 and that 3:1*b*–4:3 is thus an insertion from another letter. This explanation leaves us with an even more puzzling problem, however, for the more vigorously modern interpreters argue that 3:1 leads naturally into 4:4, the more one is left wondering why an ancient editor should have inserted a fragment from another letter at such an unsuitable point! If either of these explanations is right, then we have to assume that a later editor joined two letters together, either because those letters (or the copies that he had) were incomplete or because (for reasons we can only guess at) he decided to omit parts of what Paul had written. Although there is no textual evidence to suggest that two letters have been joined at 3:2, those who support this theory point to the fact that Polycarp, when himself writing to the Philippians at the beginning of the second century, referred to the letters that Paul had written to them.[25] Since he may be referring to a letter or letters that have not survived at all, however, this proves

nothing. The interpreter's decision on this matter, therefore, will depend on three things: (1) the translation of the opening words of 3:1, (2) whether or not the abrupt change of topic is probable within a single letter, and (3) whether the links between chaps. 1–2 and chaps. 3–4 are such as to suggest that they were written as a unity.

First, we should note that the Greek phrase τὸ λοιπόν (*to loipon*), translated here as "finally," is usually used with a much more general meaning. Here, it may mean "and so," in which case it is perhaps used to pick up and reiterate the command to rejoice in 2:18. Whichever way we translate the phrase, however, its use certainly does *not* indicate that the letter is near its end (cf., e.g., 1 Thess 4:1, where the word *loipon* is used to introduce what is in effect the main body of the epistle's teaching).

As in 1:12, Paul addresses the recipients of the letter as "brothers" (here, as often, paraphrased by the NRSV as "brothers and sisters"; see also 1:14; 3:17; 4:1). His command to rejoice is expressed in the same word (χαίρετε *chairete*) that he used in 2:18. In some contexts, however, the word could be employed as a term of greeting, although ordinarily on meeting rather than on parting. The infinitive χαίρειν (*chairein*) was commonly used at the beginning of a letter, as in Jas 1:1. Only in 2 Cor 13:11 is the verb used at the end of a letter, and there, as here, it is much more likely that it means "rejoice!"

Second, we have to examine whether the change of topic in 3:2 is too abrupt to be conceivable within a single letter. In a formal composition, we would not expect a writer to switch from one theme to another in this way; in a letter to people for whom Paul has pastoral responsibility, and whom he also regards as friends, it is less surprising that he jumps from one topic to an-

25. Polycarp *Epistle to the Philippians* 3.

other, as his active mind remembers other issues he felt it necessary to write about.

In fact, although Paul's outburst in 3:2 may seem an abrupt change of topic, the theme of the chapter as a whole picks up what he has said in chap. 2. Paul's warning in 3:2 quickly leads into a description of his own experience, which is clearly modeled on the example of Christ. Moreover, as we shall see, there are many echoes of the vocabulary of chap. 2. In particular, the commentary will argue that what Paul has to say in 3:20-21 not only looks back to 2:6-11, but also is the logical conclusion to that passage.

PHILIPPIANS 3:1-11, THE TRUE BASIS FOR CONFIDENCE

NIV

3 Finally, my brothers, rejoice in the Lord! It is no trouble for me to write the same things to you again, and it is a safeguard for you.

²Watch out for those dogs, those men who do evil, those mutilators of the flesh. ³For it is we who are the circumcision, we who worship by the Spirit of God, who glory in Christ Jesus, and who put no confidence in the flesh— ⁴though I myself have reasons for such confidence.

If anyone else thinks he has reasons to put confidence in the flesh, I have more: ⁵circumcised on the eighth day, of the people of Israel, of the tribe of Benjamin, a Hebrew of Hebrews; in regard to the law, a Pharisee; ⁶as for zeal, persecuting the church; as for legalistic righteousness, faultless.

⁷But whatever was to my profit I now consider loss for the sake of Christ. ⁸What is more, I consider everything a loss compared to the surpassing greatness of knowing Christ Jesus my Lord, for whose sake I have lost all things. I consider them rubbish, that I may gain Christ ⁹and be found in him, not having a righteousness of my own that comes from the law, but that which is through faith in Christ—the righteousness that comes from God and is by faith. ¹⁰I want to know Christ and the power of his resurrection and the fellowship of sharing in his sufferings, becoming like him in his death, ¹¹and so, somehow, to attain to the resurrection from the dead.

NRSV

3 Finally, my brothers and sisters,[a] rejoice[b] in the Lord.

To write the same things to you is not troublesome to me, and for you it is a safeguard.

2Beware of the dogs, beware of the evil workers, beware of those who mutilate the flesh![c] ³For it is we who are the circumcision, who worship in the Spirit of God[d] and boast in Christ Jesus and have no confidence in the flesh— ⁴even though I, too, have reason for confidence in the flesh.

If anyone else has reason to be confident in the flesh, I have more: ⁵circumcised on the eighth day, a member of the people of Israel, of the tribe of Benjamin, a Hebrew born of Hebrews; as to the law, a Pharisee; ⁶as to zeal, a persecutor of the church; as to righteousness under the law, blameless.

7Yet whatever gains I had, these I have come to regard as loss because of Christ. ⁸More than that, I regard everything as loss because of the surpassing value of knowing Christ Jesus my Lord. For his sake I have suffered the loss of all things, and I regard them as rubbish, in order that I may gain Christ ⁹and be found in him, not having a righteousness of my own that comes from the law, but one that comes through faith in Christ,[e] the righteousness from God based on faith. ¹⁰I want to know Christ[f] and the power of his resurrection and the sharing of his sufferings by becoming like him in his death, ¹¹if somehow I may attain the resurrection from the dead.

---

a Gk *my brothers*   *b* Or *farewell*   *c* Gk *the mutilation*   *d* Other ancient authorities read *worship God in spirit*   *e* Or *through the faith of Christ*   *f* Gk *him*

COMMENTARY

3:1. Paul half apologizes for writing "the same things" to the Philippians, while assuring them that he does not find it troublesome to do so. Is he referring to what he has just written: "rejoice in the Lord"? That seems unlikely, since such a command appears to be an improbable "safeguard" for the Philippians. Markus Bockmuehl argues in his commentary that joy was frequently regarded as the source of strength (so Neh 8:10); in the other passages he cites, however, strength appears to be the source of joy, which is hardly relevant.[26] The other possibility is that Paul is referring to what he is *about* to write—namely, his warning in v. 2. But since those he warns about have not been mentioned earlier in the letter, we must conclude that Paul is referring to warnings he has given in earlier letters or possibly by word of mouth (unless, of course, we decide that v. 1*b* introduces part of another letter that had already discussed these people). The fact that Paul's warnings are a safeguard suggests that he does not believe the Philippians to be in imminent danger but that he considers it wise to be issuing the warning in case the danger becomes a real one.

3:2. Since the term "safeguard" suggests that what follows is a warning, the first word of this verse, βλέπετε (*blepete*), which would ordinarily mean "pay attention to" when used, as here, with the accusative, has been translated "watch out for/beware of." The triple "beware" in the NRSV is perhaps too peremptory; but the tone is certainly emphatic, for the command is introduced abruptly and is given three times. The effect is heightened in Greek by the use of alliteration, with each warning being directed against something beginning with the letter *K:* τοὺς κύνας . . . τοὺς κακοὺς ἐργάτας . . . τὴν κατατομήν (*tous kynas . . . tous kakous ergatas . . . tēn katatomēn*). Those against whom Paul issues his warning are clearly Jews of some kind, though the terms he uses to describe them are totally unexpected. The epithet "dogs" was sometimes used by the Jews as a term of derision for Gentiles; dogs were scavengers and so were naturally associated with uncleanness.

Paul now applies the term to these people, thus indicating that the ones he has in mind are not, in fact, the people of God. "Evil workers/those who do evil" is equally unexpected. In the book of Psalms, it is those who do not obey the Torah who are repeatedly described as "evildoers" (e.g., Ps 5:5), while those who are faithful to the Torah are righteous (e.g., Pss 1:6; 5:12). Once again, the description is one that Jews would naturally apply to Gentiles and to non-observant Jews. The final warning, against "those who mutilate/mutilators of the flesh" is bizarre. The Greek word used here is κατατομη (*katatomē*), meaning "mutilation," and Paul has deliberately substituted it for the word περιτομη (*peritomē*), meaning "circumcision." The irony of his words reaches its climax here, as the Jews' proudest claim is turned on its head. Whereas circumcision was understood to be the sign of the covenant between God and Abraham, mutilation—making gashes in the flesh—was something done by pagan priests. Mutilation was specifically forbidden to the priests of Israel (Lev 21:5), for any kind of physical defect debarred men from being priests, since they must be holy to their God (Lev 21:18-23).[27] For Paul, circumcision is worth nothing unless it is "circumcision of the heart" (Rom 2:28-29).

Three times over, Paul has applied to a group of Jews terms that they would have thought appropriate only for outsiders: "dogs," "evildoers," "mutilation." Taken together, his threefold description amounts to a denial of the claim of the people he has in mind to be true Jews. The people who pride themselves on being insiders are, in fact, in the position of those whom they despise. The irony of Paul's description lies in the fact that those whom he is describing are the very people who cared desperately about keeping themselves pure, about obeying the commandments of the Torah, and about preserving circumcision as the essential mark of those who belonged to Israel.

---

26. See Markus Bockmuehl, *The Epistle to the Philippians,* Black's NT Commentary (Peabody, Mass.: Hendrickson, 1998).

27. Deut 23:1 goes further, excluding from the assembly of the Lord those men whose sexual organs have been damaged. In some circles, 2 Sam 5:8 seems to have been understood as a perpetual prohibition of those who are blind or disabled in taking any part in worship. See 1QSa 2:5-7; *m. Hag.* 1:1. Mutilation is thus understood to put one outside the company of God's people. Sacrifices offered to God had to be "without blemish," so it was natural to think that those who worshiped God must meet the same requirement.

But all this is the righteousness of the law (v. 6), which Paul now regards as worthless compared with the righteousness that comes to him in Christ (v. 9). If Paul urges the Philippians to "beware of" these people, then perhaps it is lest they, too, make the mistake of supposing that it is "the righteousness of the law" that is important.

Who *were* the people Paul is attacking here? Clearly it was some group who claimed to be Jewish. But were they Jewish by birth, or were they Gentile converts? And were they also Christians? It is sometimes suggested that Paul was referring to Jews who had rejected the gospel and were opposing the claims of Gentile Christians to belong to the people of God. Why, then, should he think it necessary to warn the Philippians against them? The answer could be that the Jewish community was persecuting the Christians in Philippi; Paul's own imprisonment had almost certainly come about because of the opposition of Jews in Jerusalem. His warning here, then, might echo the injunction in 1:27 to stand firm in the the face of opposition. But as we have already seen, there seem to have been very few Jews in Philippi! The argument in this chapter seems to suppose a more subtle danger, that of putting confidence "in the flesh." Moreover, Paul himself had once opposed the gospel and persecuted the Christian community (v. 6); yet, in describing his own life as a Jew in vv. 4-6 he does not refer to himself as a dog, as a worker of evil, or as belonging to the mutilation! On the contrary, he includes his devotion to the Torah among his former assets.

It is important to note that Paul's bitter attack here is not on Judaism per se. His argument in vv. 4-11 suggests that he probably had in mind a group of *Christian* Jews who disagreed with him about the terms on which one could belong to the people of God and were insisting that Gentile Christians become Jewish proselytes. This is supported by the reference to this group as "the mutilation," which suggests that Paul has in mind those who were actively pursuing a policy of circumcising converts.

These Judaizers might, of course, be *Gentile* Christians who, with all the enthusiasm of converts, assumed that it was necessary to accept all the practices of Judaism. It is sometimes argued that Paul's description of his own inherited privi-

leges rules this interpretation out, since he is comparing his own credentials with those of fellow Jews. Since he is insisting that he had many of these privileges by birth and race, however, his argument would have added poignancy if it were directed against Gentile Judaizers who regard as essential the very things Paul has abandoned.

The meaning of the passage is not greatly affected by our decision on this point, since the focus of Paul's argument quickly shifts to his own experience. Nothing more is said about these people (unless vv. 18-19 are a reference to the same group), which suggests that Paul's words are indeed intended as a safeguard against possible danger rather than as a warning against an imminent threat to the Philippian community such as that which confronted the Galatians.

3:3-4. In contrast to those whose claims he has ridiculed, Paul declares: "For it is *we* who are the circumcision, who worship in/by the Spirit of God" (v. 3). The belief that true circumcision is not a literal one (Rom 2:28-29) is found in Jer 4:4 and 9:26 (cf. 1QS 5:5); for Paul it is faith, not circumcision, that is essential (Rom 4:9-12). The verb "to serve" (λατρεύω *latreuō*) is usually used of priestly service in the Temple; here that service is no longer offered by the priests but by *all* God's people. There are variant readings here, one of which is given in the NRSV note, but the text is almost certainly correct. The idea of a new spiritual worship is set out in John 4:23-24. The fact that the Spirit had been poured out on those who were *not* circumcised is a key element in Paul's argument with the "Judaizers" (Gal 3:1-5, 14; cf. Acts 10:44-8; 11:15-18).

The "we" are now identified further as those who "boast/glory" in Christ Jesus, a description that encompasses all Christians, whether Jews or Gentiles. By contrast, others "put/have . . . confidence in the flesh." The two verbs used here are almost synonymous in meaning, though "boasting" (καυχάομαι *kauchaomai*) perhaps goes a little beyond "having confidence" (πείθω *peithō*). It is *because* they have confidence in Christ that believers may justly boast of what God has done for them. Jews would certainly not have regarded boasting in the law as putting confidence in the flesh. For Paul, however, the law operates in the sphere of flesh and is ineffectual because of the weakness of the flesh (see Romans 7). There is added irony, of course, in the fact that the rite of circumcision is literally carried out in the flesh.

Those who mock earthly privileges are usually people who do not themselves have any. This is not true in Paul's case, however, since he has every reason to boast in the privileges that have come to him by birth and upbringing—except his overwhelming conviction that such privileges are worthless by comparison with those that have come to him "in Christ." What he now thinks about his former boast that he was a Jew is expressed in the phrase "to have confidence in the flesh," which he uses three times in vv. 3-4. The Greek word σάρξ (*sarx*), here translated "flesh," is used of humanity in its weakness. It denotes what is physical, external, visible, and temporal, in contrast to the spiritual, internal, invisible, and eternal. Flesh is not in itself sinful, though it can easily fall prey to sin. It represents everything that we would call "human" or "worldly." The contrast Paul makes here between having confidence "in the flesh" and boasting "in Christ" is similar to that expressed in Isa 31:3: "The Egyptians are human, and not God; their horses are flesh, and not spirit." The significant point to notice is that as a Christian, Paul regards all the privileges given by God to Israel as belonging to this sphere of "flesh"; those who belong to Christ, on the other hand, worship in/by *the Spirit* of God."

In human terms, then, Paul had every reason to be confident—more so than others. By "I have more," Paul perhaps meant simply that he had the best possible credentials that any Jew could have; but it is possible that the "anyone else" refers in particular to those Gentiles who had succumbed to the teaching of Judaizers and become proselytes. Paul himself had been circumcised on the eighth day, as the law required (Lev 12:3), because he was an Israelite by race (v. 5), and not a proselyte. The translation "of the people of Israel" in the NRSV and the NIV is misleading. The Greek word γένος (*genos*) implies racial descent, and Paul means that he was Jewish *by birth*. Paul had taken pride in the fact that he belonged to the tribe of Benjamin—perhaps because Benjamin was one of Jacob's favorite sons and because the tribe had later remained faithful to the house of David. His claims are summed up in the phrase "a Hebrew of Hebrews": He is a Hebrew, born of pure Hebrew stock. It is possible that the phrase implies a knowledge of the Hebrew language, which few Jews any longer spoke.

3:5-6. In addition to these inherited privileges, Paul had excelled in everything Jewish. He had been a member of the small sect of the Pharisees, who were faithful and sincere upholders of the law. Pharisees were renowned for their strict adherence to the law, and spelled out the implications of every regulation in the law in an attempt to avoid any accidental infringement. They also believed that the levitical rules of purity for the priests should be applied to all Jews, since the whole nation should be holy to God. Paul's summary of his own credentials adds further irony to his description in v. 2 of a group of Jews as "dogs," "workers of evil," and "the mutilation": To Pharisees above all others, such people had no claim to belong to Israel. Paul's zeal for the law had been evidenced by his persecution of the church (v. 6; cf. Gal 1:13). And because he had lived in accordance with Pharisaic standards, he had been blameless in terms of what the law demanded. The NIV's "legalistic righteousness" is unfortunate. Paul is not caricaturing his previous life as a religion of legalism; on the contrary, he is listing it among the privileges he once possessed. But this was the righteousness specified in the law, not the righteousness of God (Rom 10:3), and being blameless according to its precepts was not sufficient (cf. Mark 10:20-21 and par.). The NRSV's triple "as to" in vv. 5-6 reflects well the rhythm of the Greek.

3:7-9. Paul now uses the image of a profit-and-loss account to compare the advantages he enjoyed as a Jew with those that have come to him as a result of his being in Christ. The things that he had once regarded as assets he now writes off as a loss for the sake of Christ (v. 7). After this initial contrast between the two sides of the ledger, the next few lines reiterate and amplify this idea of his overwhelming gain in Christ (the amplifications are in italics):

He regards *everything* as loss for the *surpassing value/greatness* of *knowing* Christ *Jesus his Lord;* for the sake of Jesus Christ, indeed, he *has* lost all things and regards them *as rubbish, in order that* he might gain Christ *and be found in him.*

The core statement is repeated, with slight variations, three times over: "These/all things I consider loss/I have lost for the sake of Christ [Jesus my Lord]." A similar comparison between what was once regarded as valuable and the overwhelming value of what is now on offer is found in the parable of the pearl of great price (Matt 13:45-46).

Paul's skillful use of repetition and expansion emphasizes the point he is making. The noun "gain" (κέρδος *kerdos*, v. 7) is echoed by the verb "to gain" (κερδαίνω *kerdainō*, v. 8), the verb "regard/consider" (ἡγέομαι *hēgeomai*) is used three times, as is the name "Christ"; the noun "loss" (ζημία *zēmia*) occurs twice, followed by the verb "to lose" (ζημιόω *zēmioō*); the adjective πάντα (*panta*) is used twice, a fact that is obscured by English translations that switch from "everything" to "all things." The triple statement of the same theme (clearer in the NRSV than in the NIV) builds up to a climax that leaves us in no doubt that the gain of being "in Christ" far outweighs the value of everything Paul once possessed. The fact that on the third occasion he uses a passive verb (ἐζημιώθην *ezēmiōthēn*), "I have lost/suffered the loss," may indicate that he has been forcibly stripped of his privileges by his fellow Jews, who now disown him. Nevertheless, Paul's point is that he has willingly abandoned things that he no longer values. The word he now uses to describe them, σκύβαλα (*skybala*), is in fact more contemptuous than the translation "rubbish" suggests, for it means literally "excrement" or "refuse." That Paul now regards his former privileges in this way has already been demonstrated by his language in v. 2.

The things that Paul now prizes are "knowing Christ Jesus" (v. 8), being "found in him" (v. 9), and having the righteousness that comes "from God." What does Paul understand by "knowing Christ"? Some commentators have suggested that Paul is here influenced by the language of Gnosticism, but it seems more likely that the influence (if there was any) was in the other direction. It is far more probable that his words are rooted in the OT understanding of religion as the knowledge of God. The knowledge of God is based on God's self-revelation to the people and is, therefore, both an acknowledgment of what God has done and a recognition of God's claims upon the people. To know God is thus to honor God and to obey God's will; it is not simply to have

knowledge of "facts" about God but to enter into a personal relationship. Here, however, Paul speaks about knowing *Christ Jesus his Lord*. This phrase immediately reminds us of the passage in the previous chapter in which Paul described how Christ Jesus acted in such a way that he was acknowledged as universal Lord. We have seen that this passage was an account of the unfolding of Christ's character, and hence also a revelation of the nature of God, and that it led into the demand for an appropriate response, in obedience, from the Philippians (2:12-13). The Christ whom Paul desires to know is the Christ who emptied himself and was obedient to death: To know him is to be like him. Precisely what it means to know Christ Jesus as Lord was spelled out in 2:1-15, and pointing us back to that passage is Paul's threefold use of the verb he used in 2:6 of Christ, "consider/regard" (*hēgeomai*), which he now uses of himself. Just as Christ considered the privileges that belonged to equality with God as something he should not exploit, and therefore abandoned them, so also Paul has now abandoned all the privileges that belonged to him as a Jew, because he does not consider them of value in comparison with knowing Christ. For Paul, therefore, to know Christ *as Lord* means to acknowledge his actions as the self-revelation *of God* and to recognize Christ's claims by adopting the same pattern for his own life.

These ideas are spelled out even more clearly in the third statement of Paul's theme in vv. 8-9. He has abandoned his old privileges in order to gain Christ and to be found in him. It is probably no accident that the word εὑρεθῶ (*heurethō*, "be found") echoes the participle used of Christ in 2:7: Christ was found in human form, and Paul is now found in Christ. This is an experience Paul already enjoys; there is, therefore, no need to assume, as some commentators have done, that Paul must be thinking of being found in Christ on the last day.

Paul now expresses the contrast in a new way: He has abandoned his own righteousness, a righteousness he described in vv. 5-6 as being "from the law," for that which comes "through faith in Christ" (v. 9). This new righteousness, which denotes a right relationship with Christ, is "from God" and is "based on/by faith." Paul has more to say about the righteousness he shares as a result of being in Christ than about the old righteousness he has abandoned, but it is worth noting which phrases here are balanced against each other. The obvious example is the contrast between the righteousness that is "from the law" and that which is "from God." The contrast is a familiar one in Pauline literature. In Rom 8:3, for example, he sums up his argument (set out in the preceding chapters) that the law could not bring true righteousness, by declaring that what the law could not do God has now done: God has sent the Son in the likeness of sinful flesh, with the result that men and women are declared righteous in him. The contrast in that passage between the law and God is not meant to suggest that the law is evil. Paul has spent the whole of Romans 7 arguing that the law (given by God!) is good, but that it is ineffectual because of the weakness of the flesh. We see echoes of this argument in Philippians in the description of Christ's incarnation (2:7), in the reference to the flesh (3:3-4), and in the contrast between the righteousness that comes from the law and that which comes from God.

In contrast to the righteousness Paul calls his own (cf. also Rom 10:3), based on his own endeavors, he sets that which is "through faith in Christ." The precise meaning of the phrase πίστις Χριστου (*pistis Christou*), here translated "faith in Christ," is much disputed. The noun *pistis* is broader in meaning than our English word "faith," and it can also mean the faithfulness that is the basis of faith. However, the chief problem is that in Greek we have a genitive that may be either subjective or objective; it could mean, therefore, either the faith (or faithfulness) that was Christ's or our faith in Christ. The traditional English translation is the one given in the NRSV and the NIV, but the alternative is given in the NRSV note. Which is the correct interpretation here? Opinion is sharply divided, and for an informed judgment one needs to consider all the passages where Paul uses the phrase (the other examples are found at Rom 3:22, 26; Gal 2:16 [twice], 20; 3:22; and, in some MSS, 3:26). In Philippians, we should note that at the end of the verse Paul spells out the fact that the righteousness he has in Christ comes to him through faith: Is he simply repeating himself? This final phrase— "based on/by faith"—is not balanced by any comparable phrase about the righteousness that comes

from the law, and it is difficult to explain why Paul should think it necessary to repeat the reference to faith if he has already said that the righteousness from God comes to us through *our* faith in Christ. Moreover, we expect the righteousness that is opposed to what he terms his own righteousness to be that which belongs to Christ himself—the righteousness pronounced by God on one who has faith or is faithful (cf. Paul's comment about the faith of Abraham in Rom 4:3) and now shared by those who are "found in him." This righteousness would then be understood as being *"from* God" but *through* the faithfulness of Christ (the preposition διά [*dia*, "through"], used with the genitive, has an instrumental sense). Finally, we should note that it is appropriate if Paul has Christ's own faith or faithfulness in mind here, in view of what was said in 2:6-11 about Christ's self-emptying and obedience (the result of faith!) and consequent vindication. For all these reasons, it seems likely that the genitive is subjective and that Paul is thinking here of the righteousness that is shared by those in Christ because of the faithfulness of Christ himself.[28]

3:10-11. Verse 10 introduces another purpose clause, though its precise relationship to what Paul has been saying is not clear. However we explain the grammar, this verse picks up and expands the idea of "knowing Christ," which was mentioned in v. 8. Paul's aim is "to know Christ and the power of his resurrection." We are surprised to find Paul mentioning Christ's resurrection before his sufferings and death, but he links our righteousness (v. 9) with Christ's resurrection elsewhere (Rom 4:25). The term used in Romans is δικαίωσις (*dikaiōsis*), meaning "vindication," rather than δικαιοσύνη (*dikaiosynē*), "righteousness" (as in v. 9), which suggests that there is a sense in which believers share in the vindication of Christ at his resurrection; see also Rom 5:18, where Christ's obedience (cf. Phil 2:8) leads to acquittal and to life for all. Belief in the resurrection of the body was a distinctively Jewish idea.

28. For a discussion of "the faith of Christ," see Richard B. Hays, *The Faith of Jesus Christ: An Investigation of the Narrative Substructure of Galatians 3:1–4:11,* SBLDS 56 (Chico, Calif.: Scholars Press, 1983); M. D. Hooker, "ΠΙΣΤΙΣ ΧΡΙΣΤΟΥ," *NTS* 35 (1989) 321-42, reprinted in Hooker, *From Adam to Christ* (Cambridge: Cambridge University Press, 1990) 165-86; I. G. Wallis, *The Faith of Jesus Christ in Early Christian Tradition* (Cambridge: Cambridge University Press, 1995) 118-24.

It was taken over into Christianity, but was now understood to be dependent on the resurrection of Christ.

Christ's resurrection is described elsewhere as the result of an act of divine power (Rom 1:4). Here, it is seen as itself the source of power in the lives of believers. Those who are in Christ share his faith, his righteousness, and his resurrection—but only if they are prepared to share also in "his sufferings." Paul uses once again the word κοινωνία (*koinōnia*), meaning "sharing/fellowship," which he used in 1:5 (cf. 2:1 and 4:15, and in particular 1:7 and 4:14, where compounds of the word are used with reference to suffering). This is an experience that has already begun for Paul and the Philippians! Christians must be ready to become "like [Christ] in his death" (cf. Rom 8:17). The verb meaning "becoming like" (συμμορφόω *symmorphoō*), provides another echo of 2:6-7 (μορφη *morphē*), as does θάνατος (*thanatos*), "death," as though to remind us once again that being in Christ means following his example. Being conformed to Christ's death is an ongoing process in the life of the believer (cf. 2 Cor 4:10-12), but attaining "the resurrection from the dead" clearly lies in the future—even though Christians already know the power of Christ's resurrection (worked by God) in their lives! Now we realize that Paul mentions Christ's resurrection before his death because he is describing Christian experience. It is the power of Christ's resurrection that is at work in Paul's life, even in the midst of suffering, and that provides the assurance of his own future resurrection.

The introductory "if somehow" in v. 11 seems to introduce an element of doubt, but Paul can hardly be dubious about whether those who are in Christ will share his resurrection. The phrase is intended, rather, to remind the Philippians that Christians have not yet arrived at their final destination. Christ's resurrection has already occurred, but their own lies in the future, and it is necessary to go on "being conformed" to Christ's obedience and death if they are to attain the resurrection. The fact that their righteousness is "from God" does not absolve them from moral endeavor, for the goal still lies ahead—a theme Paul elaborates on in vv. 12-16.

REFLECTIONS

1. At first sight, Paul's bitter attack on those whom he characterizes as "dogs" (3:2) does not seem very promising material for Christian exposition. We need to remember, however, that behind the sarcasm, what he is denouncing is the attitude that claims exclusive rights to divine favor and bars the great majority of men and women from fellowship with God. The language Paul uses is a parody of the terms that were used by devout Jews to distinguish between themselves and outsiders, and the terms he hurls at this group echo those that *they* would have used of those people who in their view were excluded from God's people. To them, Gentile "dogs" and those who did not observe the law—doers of evil—were outside God's covenant, the essential mark of which was circumcision. In contrast to their claim that they alone were God's holy people, Paul maintains that the true people of God consist of all who worship by the Spirit of God (3:3). It is the presence of God's Spirit, therefore, that is now the essential mark of God's people—the Spirit who was at work in Jesus and who was poured out on Jews and Gentiles alike when they believed the gospel—and through that Spirit they are now able to worship God sincerely. What Paul is offering us, therefore, is an *inclusive* model of the people of God rather than an exclusive one. No one need be kept out, for this community is open to all.

Unfortunately, the early Christians quickly succumbed to the temptation to adopt the exclusive model for themselves. They soon came to regard Jews as dogs.[29] All too quickly the conviction of a few that they alone were the elect of God infected, in turn, various sections of the Christian community, each of which claimed that *their* particular beliefs and practices

---

29. See Shylock's famous complaint, many years later, in Shakespeare's *The Merchant of Venice* I.iii.

were the essential hallmarks of the church, and that others, therefore, were not true believers. Far too often, religious people imagine that they "know" the mind of the Lord and suppose that God shares their prejudices and beliefs! The result is that they try to keep God to themselves and imagine that the privilege of belonging to God (a privilege meant for the entire human race) makes them superior to other people. In relationships with people from other denominations and of other faiths, it is very easy for Christians to suppose that their own prejudices and preferences represent God's will and that those of other people are inferior. If Paul were alive today, might he not condemn many of us for claiming exclusive understanding of the divine will and for forgetting that *all* who worship God by the Spirit belong to God's people? While the presence of the Spirit should mean unity, it does not mean uniformity, for the Spirit's gifts are many and varied (Romans 12; 1 Corinthians 12), and members of the Christian community are very different. But through the same Spirit, all may worship God.

As time passed and the Letter to the Philippians, along with Paul's other letters, was accepted as Scripture and became part of what we now know as the New Testament, the original circumstances in which Paul was writing were forgotten. Readers forgot that his purpose in this passage was to defend the rights of Gentiles to be Christians against a majority in the church who assumed that it was necessary to first become a Jew in order to be a Christian. The result was that Paul's words took on a very different meaning; taken out of their original context, they appeared to be a condemnation of all Jews. Tragically, this misunderstanding encouraged the growth of anti-Semitism in the church, and Paul's words were interpreted as anti-Jewish polemic. We need to be very careful when reading Scripture! It is so easy to misunderstand it and to assume that we can simply read it without considering what it meant to its original readers and why its authors were writing as they did. Precisely because it is so difficult to recover the original situation, many people today concentrate simply on the text as we have it. In this passage, we see clearly how, by doing that, one might assume that Paul was endorsing bigotry and exclusion, when, in fact, these were the attitudes he was attacking.

2. Privileges of birth and circumstance can easily lead to pride and boasting, and that is just as true in the modern world as it was for the first-century Jew. Perhaps it is surprising that Paul claims that Christians also boast—but this is a very different kind of boasting! Those who now belong to God's people are described as boasting/glorying *in Christ Jesus,* in contrast to those who have confidence in the flesh (3:3). Once again, Paul offers us an inclusive understanding of God's people instead of an exclusive one. Whereas the things about which Paul had once boasted (3:4-6) *separated* him from others, being in Christ *unites* all who boast in him, for they worship in the Spirit of God, relying on God alone. Thus no one can claim to be better than any other person. In the realm of what Paul calls "the flesh," some are inevitably superior to others; but in the realm of the Spirit, in which those who are "in Christ" live, these distinctions are abolished (Gal 3:28), and the different gifts given to individuals are signs of their *unity,* not of division. No one group of Christians can claim that the particular gift given to them is superior to those given to others, nor can they claim that they are superior to others (1 Corinthians 12–14). Those who are in Christ boast in him alone, and the fact that he was born in human likeness and lived a human life as it was meant to be lived has opened up to all humans the possibility of sharing that life.

3. In this passage, Paul is spelling out some of the implications of what it means to believe. To believe in the gospel is to put one's trust in God. We need at least four terms in English—"faith," "belief," "trust," "faithfulness"—to convey all the meanings of one Greek noun, πίστις (*pistis*). To trust in something or someone means to rely on them, and complete trust suggests that there is no need to rely on anything else. So if men and women come to put their trust in God, they must abandon all other props. It is easy to think of faith in very positive terms, as acceptance—acceptance of the grace of God at work in Christ—and to forget this other, more negative aspect of faith—the need for renunciation. Before Paul could accept Christ, he had to renounce those things on which, as a Jew, he had relied (3:7-11). Just as the rich young ruler had to renounce his wealth in order to become a disciple (Matt 19:16-26; Mark 10:17-27; Luke 18:18-26), so also Paul had to renounce the privileges that kept him from accepting the gifts that were now offered him in Christ. He does renounce them, not because they were wrong in themselves (both the law and circumcision had been given by God), but because they belong to the old era of the flesh and have been replaced by something far better: a new relationship with God, freely offered to all, and not confined to those who were able to claim to be righteous according to the law.

In spite of Paul's contrast between the righteousness of his own that he has abandoned and the righteousness that comes in Christ, it is all too easy for Christians to cling to what they regard as their own righteousness. We assume that our faithful attendance at church, our Christian conduct and adherence to moral principles, *deserve* some special consideration from God and constitute some special claim on God. Again and again, when disaster falls, people ask, "Why did this happen to me?" as though living an upright life ought to give them some kind of immunity from suffering. There are even some television evangelists who preach a perversion of the gospel, suggesting that God rewards believers with material goods. How seriously, then, do we take Paul's declaration that he regards his own righteousness as worthless, compared with that offered to him in Christ?

4. At his conversion, Paul renounced reliance on the law. The problem was not that the law was evil, but rather that the good could be the enemy of the best. Paul, in his zeal to keep the law of God, had persecuted Christians, a clear indication that righteousness according to the law could be opposed to the righteousness of God. Now he discovered that loving other people was more important than living according to a set of rules. Was this a lesson that had not been learned by one earnest Christian who caused his brother great pain because he thought it more important to worship in his own church on Sunday morning than to join a family lunch to celebrate his brother's eightieth birthday? It is easy to be so caught up in church activities and good works that we forget that God is worshiped and served in the ways we relate to others and in the way we live our everyday lives. It is possible to be so busy striving after what we are sure is right that we can miss more important needs. Yet we must be careful not to fall into the opposite temptation! Abandoning one's own righteousness for that of God can easily lead to the temptation to suppose that there is no need for moral endeavor or personal discipline. Paul insists that the Christian must become what he or she already is. Luther expressed the same idea somewhat differently when he said that the nature of a Christian does not lie in what he or she has become, but in what that person is becoming.

PHILIPPIANS 3:12–4:1, KEEP GOING!

NIV

¹²Not that I have already obtained all this, or have already been made perfect, but I press on to take hold of that for which Christ Jesus took hold of me. ¹³Brothers, I do not consider myself yet to have taken hold of it. But one thing I do: Forgetting what is behind and straining toward what is ahead, ¹⁴I press on toward the goal to win

NRSV

12Not that I have already obtained this or have already reached the goal;[a] but I press on to make it my own, because Christ Jesus has made me his own. ¹³Beloved,[b] I do not consider that I have made it my own;[c] but this one thing I do: forgetting what lies behind and straining forward to

[a] Or *have already been made perfect*   [b] Gk *Brothers*   [c] Other ancient authorities read *my own yet*

NIV

the prize for which God has called me heavenward in Christ Jesus.

[15]All of us who are mature should take such a view of things. And if on some point you think differently, that too God will make clear to you. [16]Only let us live up to what we have already attained.

[17]Join with others in following my example, brothers, and take note of those who live according to the pattern we gave you. [18]For, as I have often told you before and now say again even with tears, many live as enemies of the cross of Christ. [19]Their destiny is destruction, their god is their stomach, and their glory is in their shame. Their mind is on earthly things. [20]But our citizenship is in heaven. And we eagerly await a Savior from there, the Lord Jesus Christ, [21]who, by the power that enables him to bring everything under his control, will transform our lowly bodies so that they will be like his glorious body.

4 Therefore, my brothers, you whom I love and long for, my joy and crown, that is how you should stand firm in the Lord, dear friends!

NRSV

what lies ahead, [14]I press on toward the goal for the prize of the heavenly[a] call of God in Christ Jesus. [15]Let those of us then who are mature be of the same mind; and if you think differently about anything, this too God will reveal to you. [16]Only let us hold fast to what we have attained.

17Brothers and sisters,[b] join in imitating me, and observe those who live according to the example you have in us. [18]For many live as enemies of the cross of Christ; I have often told you of them, and now I tell you even with tears. [19]Their end is destruction; their god is the belly; and their glory is in their shame; their minds are set on earthly things. [20]But our citizenship[c] is in heaven, and it is from there that we are expecting a Savior, the Lord Jesus Christ. [21]He will transform the body of our humiliation[d] that it may be conformed to the body of his glory,[e] by the power that also enables him to make all things subject to himself.

4 [1]Therefore, my brothers and sisters,[f] whom I love and long for, my joy and crown, stand firm in the Lord in this way, my beloved.

[a] Gk upward   [b] Gk Brothers   [c] Or commonwealth   [d] Or our humble bodies   [e] Or his glorious body   [f] Gk my brothers

COMMENTARY

3:12. What Paul has just said might perhaps be understood as complacency, so he hastens to remind the Philippians that he has not yet "obtained" what he is aiming for. The "this" (not expressed in the Greek) that he has not yet obtained is probably specifically "the resurrection from the dead," which he has just described as something he must still attain. However, it may refer to other aspects of that great gain for which he has abandoned "everything" (vv. 7-11); this understanding is reflected in the NIV's "all." Certainly Paul knows that he has not yet "been made perfect/reached the goal." The verb τελειόω (*teleioō*) means "to complete," "to bring to perfection," "to reach a goal." It was also used in the mystery religions in the sense of "to initiate," "to consecrate," and some commentators

suggest that Paul is using it with that meaning here, and thus is possibly attacking a group of "gnostic Christians" who claimed to be perfect already.[30] Similar language is used in Judaism, however; for example, by the Qumran community, who regarded themselves as perfect because of their obedience to the law (see the Commentary on 3:15). Paul probably has in mind his previous way of life, in which he claimed to be "blameless/faultless" according to the law (v. 6). Now he realizes that he has not yet achieved his new—much greater—goal, which will be reached only at the resurrection. The NRSV translation already suggests the athletic imagery that domi-

30. This suggestion was made by Walter Schmithals in an article originally published in 1957, translated and republished in W. Schmithals, *Paul and the Gnostics* (Nashville: Abingdon, 1972) 95-104.

nates the rest of the paragraph: Paul presses forward to grasp what he has not yet obtained, which once again can mean either the resurrection in particular or the completion of the experience described in vv. 7-11. Both the NIV and the NRSV have understood the Greek phrase ἐφ ᾧ (*eph hō*) in different ways—the NRSV as indicating result ("because"), the NIV as purpose ("for which"). The latter seems more appropriate in the context, since it emphasizes the fact that Paul's endeavors now are not simply the response to what Christ has done, but the completion of God's purpose for him.

3:13-14. For a third time Paul emphasizes that he has not yet reached his goal (v. 13), this time repeating the verb "to lay hold of/make my own" (καταλαμβάνω *katalambanō*), which he has already used twice in v. 12. The NIV has followed the text that is noted in the NRSV, reading οὔπω (*oupō*, "not yet") instead of οὐ (*ou*, "not"), even though the latter is better attested. The sense seems to require the "yet," which probably explains why the change was made. The "one thing" Paul does (v. 13) is to aim for the prize (v. 14), and like an athlete running a race, he ignores what is behind him and concentrates on the goal ahead (cf. Jesus' saying about the plowman, Luke 9:62). What is it that Paul does not look back at? Possibly it is the progress he has made thus far, but more probably he is thinking of the privileges he once prized but has now discarded (vv. 7-8). "The goal" on which Paul has set his eyes (the Greek σκοπός [*skopos*] is linked to the verb σκοπέω [*skopeō*], "to look at," used in v. 17) is "the prize," which is defined by the phrase (translated literally in the NRSV note) "of the upward calling of God in Christ Jesus." The precise meaning of this phrase is uncertain. Does it mean that the prize will be the divine summons to heaven? Or does it mean that the prize will be given to those who have obeyed the call of God, which is the way the NIV has understood it? Yet a third suggestion is that Paul is thinking of the ceremony at the end of a race, when the winner was called forward to receive a prize. Perhaps we should not attempt to choose between these various interpretations. Certainly the NIV is correct to remind us that the call of God came to Paul at the beginning of the race; thus he is pressing forward in order "to take hold of that for which Christ Jesus took

hold of" him (v. 12). Nevertheless, the prize for which he is aiming will be the realization of that call.

3:15-16. Verse 15 is one of the passages in the letter that often has been seen as offering support to those who argue that Paul is writing to a divided community, since there are apparently people in Philippi who "think differently" from Paul on some matters. Moreover, the reference to those described as "mature" in the English translations has sometimes been taken as an ironic reference to a group who are claiming to be "perfect," since the Greek word τέλειος (*teleios*) can have both meanings. But the word can scarcely be ironic, since Paul includes himself among those who are "mature"! Paul's injunction in v. 15, "Let us be of the same mind/all of us should take such a view of things," picks up once again the verb φρονέω (*phroneō*), used in 2:5 of the attitude that belonged to Christ and to those who are in him, and in 2:2 (twice), where Paul urged the Philippians to "think the same." Here, it is not so much a question of having the *same* mind (as in the NRSV) as of thinking in a particular way; the lengthy English paraphrases represent a mere two words in Greek, meaning "this let us think." Paul's injunction is linked to what has just been said with the word οὖν (*oun*, "therefore"; NRSV, "then"; ignored in the NIV) and so refers to the attitude Paul has been describing, an attitude that has its origins in the attitude of Christ himself.

It is puzzling, however, to find Paul speaking of himself now as *teleios*, after using the cognate verb *teleioō* in v. 12 to deny that he had reached his goal. Nevertheless, he is certainly capable of using cognate words (or even the same word) in close proximity with slightly different meanings, and both the NIV and the NRSV are probably correct in understanding *teleios* here to mean "mature" rather than "perfect" (cf. 1 Cor 14:20, where it has this meaning). In the present context, however, *teleios* probably has a more specific meaning than is conveyed by the English word "mature." The word is sometimes used in the LXX of those who are wholeheartedly devoted to God and so blameless before God (e.g., Gen 6:9; Deut 18:13). A similar idea occurs in the Qumran literature (expressed in the Hebrew word תמים [*tamîm*]), where the members of the community were required to live "perfectly," in accordance with the law (1 QS 1:8; 2:2; 8:20). Paul has exchanged a life that was without fault according to the law (v. 6) for the purity and blamelessness that belong to Christ and to those who live in him; the new community consists of those who are *teleios* in Christ. Even though Christians will not finally be made perfect until the last day, the typical Pauline injunction to "be what you are" is reflected in the fact that they can be described already as "mature."

Those who are truly mature think about the Christian life in the way Paul has just described it, fully aware that they have *not* yet arrived at their final destination. "And if" on any point the Philippians "think differently," or otherwise than they should, God will reveal this to them also— how, Paul does not say, but this is presumably part of their growth in knowledge and insight, for which he prayed in 1:9. Paul's introductory "and" rather than "but" suggests that any different opinion that may exist in the Philippian community is not a major affair. Those whom Paul addresses are included, with himself, among the "mature," even though he recognizes that there is a possibility that some aspect of their thinking and behavior is not in line with the attitude he has been advocating. Paul's words are basically words of encouragement rather than of reprimand: Those who are truly mature are ready to recognize when they are wrong and to accept guidance. So Paul concludes this paragraph with an exhortation (again including himself) to "live up to/hold fast to" what has already been attained (v. 16). The verb στοιχέω (*stoicheō*, "to be in line with") suggests already the idea of imitation, which will be taken up in the next verse.

3:17. Paul now calls on the Philippians to "join" in imitating him. Out of context, this might sound extraordinarily conceited, but Paul is, of course, referring to the endeavors he has been describing in vv. 7-16, which are rooted in Christ's hold on him (v. 12). The apostle's task is to be a role model whose example can be imitated (cf. 1 Cor 4:16; 11:1; 1 Thess 1:6; 2 Thess 3:7, 9). But with whom are they to join? Is it with one another? This is how the NRSV has understood the command; the "others" in the NIV translation are not mentioned in the text. However, it is possible that Paul's words should be

understood as meaning "be imitators *with* me" rather than "be imitators *of* me."[31] In this case, Paul would be appealing to the Philippians to join *him* in imitating Christ. The objection to this interpretation is that there is no specific reference to Christ, and the vast majority of commentators, therefore, understand Paul to be calling on the Philippians to imitate him. It is important to remember, however, that 2:6-11 is central to all of Paul's argument. As we have seen, 3:7-16 is, in effect, a description of how Paul has followed the example of Christ set out in 2:6-11, and that passage was itself introduced as a pattern for the life of the Philippian community. Moreover, we are about to have further echoes from 2:6-11 in the final verses of this chapter. Whichever way we translate these introductory words, therefore, there is an *implicit* command to imitate Christ. Paul's logic is very similar to 1 Cor 11:1, where he urges the Corinthians: "Be imitators of me, as I am of Christ!" Although Paul himself is no longer among the Philippians, they can still observe the pattern they should be following in "those who live according to the example/pattern" given to the Philippians by Paul.

3:18-19. In these verses Paul refers once again to a very different group, whose way of life is opposed to the gospel. Whom does he have in mind now? Is it the same group described in v. 2? They seemed to be "Judaizers," Christian converts who placed great emphasis on keeping the law. The group now under attack regard their "belly/stomach" as their god and find their glory "in their shame." These words have, indeed, been interpreted by some commentators as a sarcastic attack on Jewish practices, with "belly" and "shame" understood as mocking references to the strict observance of food laws and the insistence on the rite of circumcision. Such language would be far more abusive than the irony used in v. 2, however, where Paul's words were carefully chosen to show how those who were *claiming* to be the people of God were in fact *not* members of God's people.

What Paul says in these verses seems far more appropriate if it is intended as an attack on those

---

31. In support of this interpretation, it has been pointed out that nowhere else in the NT is a compound formed with σύν (*syn-*, "with") such as we have here (συμμιμηταί *symmimētai*, "fellow imitators") used with an objective genitive denoting a person.

who really were living lives of indulgence. The existence of Christians who indulged in gluttony and shameful sexual practices is known to us from 1 Corinthians 5–6, where we find the Corinthians boasting (1 Cor 5:6) in spite of their immorality and toleration of people within their community who are "sexually immoral or greedy" (1 Cor 5:11). Some of these people seem to have been claiming that "all things are lawful" for Christians (1 Cor 6:12). Paul's teaching that Christians were not "under the law" was apparently being misunderstood as permitting self-indulgence (cf. 3 Macc 7:11, where Jews who abandoned the law are said to have transgressed the commandments for the sake of their bellies). In 1 Cor 6:13, Paul quotes what is apparently a slogan among these Christians: "Food is meant for the stomach [or belly] and the stomach [or belly] for food" (see also Paul's warning in Gal 5:13, 16-21). It would appear to be these people about whom Paul has "often told" the Philippians and now tells them again "with tears"—which suggests that, although Paul implicitly warns the Philippians against them, there is no one from this group in Philippi. In direct contrast to those who live in accordance with the pattern Paul has given them, these people "live as enemies of the cross of Christ" (v. 18); they are "enemies of the cross," because their whole manner of living is a denial of the revelation of God in Christ, whose self-emptying led to death on the cross. Paul's quarrel with these people concerns their behavior, not their teaching. They claim to be Christians, but fail completely to see the relevance of 2:6-11 for their own lives. Clearly they have not thought it necessary to "think like Christ," for (once again we have the familiar verb φρονέω [phroneō]) "their mind[s] is/are on earthly things" instead of on their heavenly call (v. 14). The "end/destiny" that awaits these people is not salvation but destruction, the fate that also lies in store for the opponents of the Philippian Christians, mentioned in 1:28.

3:20-21. In contrast to the "enemies of the cross," *our* citizenship is "in heaven" (v. 20; the word order emphasizes the "our"). The introductory "but" of the English translations stresses the contrast, but in Greek the link word is γάρ (gar), meaning "for." Paul has now returned to the theme he was pursuing in v. 17: Those who share the mind of Christ may confidently expect to share his victory, for they are already citizens of heaven. The word translated "citizenship" (πολίτευμα politeuma) echoes the verb πολιτεύομαι (politeuomai), which occurred in 3:20; it is used both of the commonwealth or state to which people belong and the citizenship (the privileges and duties) given to them. The idea that one belonged to a distant commonwealth could well have been familiar to Jews of the diaspora, but the term would have been particularly significant to the citizens of Philippi, who, because the city was a Roman colony, held citizenship in the distant city of Rome also. They may have been especially proud of their Roman citizenship. If Acts 16:12, 37-38 is to be believed, it was in Philippi that Paul declared himself to be a Roman citizen; perhaps, then, he is reminding the Philippians that they are all citizens of an even greater country. In fact, many of the Philippian Christians may well have been slaves and, therefore, without status of any kind; how much *more* meaningful it was to assure *them* that they were citizens of heaven! The idea that human beings have their citizenship in heaven is found also in Philo, a near contemporary of Paul.[32]

And from heaven, says Paul, "we are expecting/eagerly await a Savior," who is identified as the Lord Jesus Christ. The term "Savior" (σωτήρ sōtēr) is an unusual one for Paul (used nowhere else in the undisputed Pauline letters, though occurring once in Ephesians and no fewer than ten times in the Pastorals). Perhaps, again, it may have a particular nuance in this letter, since the Roman emperor was commonly given the title "Savior" in the imperial cult, where he was venerated as a god. The Philippians would have been well aware of this practice, as was Paul, who had appealed to Caesar, but who expected salvation from another source.

The idea that Christians can expect future salvation has already occurred in 1:19, 28 and 2:12. Now Paul links this specifically with the appearance of "the Lord Jesus Christ" from heaven (cf. 1 Thess 1:10; 5:2-10). Although Paul has described our citizenship as something that exists (already) "in heaven," his picture is of heaven brought to earth, rather than of our being translated to heaven. As in Rom 8:18-30 and 1

---

32. See Philo *On the Confusion of Tongues.* 77-88.

Cor 15:42-57, Paul speaks of the transformation of humanity. His expectation is part of the hoped-for restoration of a world that was plunged into chaos when Adam sinned. The imagery is thoroughly Jewish, envisaging the transformation of the body rather than the release of a soul from the body. Paul's language here echoes Rom 8:29, where Christians are destined to be conformed to the image of God's Son, and 1 Cor 15:42-44 and 52-54, where they are raised (if dead) or changed (if alive) from a mortal, perishable, physical body, characterized by weakness and dishonor, to an immortal, imperishable, spiritual body of power and glory. Here, however, Paul prefers to contrast "the body of our humiliation [ταπείνωσις *tapeinōsis*]" with "the body of his glory [δόξα *doxa*]." The NRSV's literal translation of these phrases (in contrast to the paraphrase of the NIV and the NRSV note) reminds us that Christ shared "the body of our humiliation" and that we hope to share in "the body of his glory." The language is a deliberate echo of 2:6-11, where Christ humbled himself (ἐταπείνωσεν *etapeinōsen*) and where his consequent exaltation redounded to the glory (*doxa*) of God.

Paul's vocabulary here is, in fact, full of echoes of that earlier passage. The verb "is" (ὑπάρχει *hyparchei*) in v. 20 in the phrase "is in heaven" was used of Christ ("was") in 2:6; the phrase "Lord Jesus Christ" echoes the proclamation in 2:11; the verbs "transform" and "conformed/be like" (v. 27) are both compound verbs, the first based on the word μορφη (*morphē*, "form/very nature," vv. 6-7), the second on the word σχῆμα (*schēma*, "form/appearance," v. 8); the reference to "all things/everything" echoes the triple "every" of 2:9-11. The transformation of the body of our humiliation will be the work of Christ, through "the power that enables him [also] to make all things subject to himself/bring everything under his control"—the same power that was given him when every knee bowed to him and every tongue confessed him Lord (2:10-11). This power is ultimately the power of God, who has put everything under Christ's feet (1 Cor 15:28; cf. Ps 8:6).

The echoes of the vocabulary of 2:6-11 are not accidental. There is a sense in which 3:7-11 and 20-21 are the necessary completion of that passage, which told us of Christ's incarnation, death, and exaltation but said nothing about how these affect the believer. Now we realize that he was born in human likeness and shared our human death in order that Christians might be transformed into his likeness and share his vindication. This is a familiar theme in Paul, which is usually expressed in formulaic sayings that make clear the connection between what Christ became and what Christians become by means of a linking word (ἵνα *hina,* "in order that/so that"; see, e.g., 2 Cor 5:21; 8:9; Gal 3:13-14; 4:4-5). Sometimes these sayings refer to Christ's incarnation, sometimes to his death; in Phil 2:6-11 we find that both these aspects of Christ's sharing in our humanity are expressed. The interchange that allows Christians to become what Christ is occurs only when believers are "in Christ," however;[33] when they, in turn, are willing to share in Christ's death, then they experience his resurrection and become like him (3:9-10, 21).

4:1. The command (so rightly the NRSV) to "stand firm" provides another echo of 1:27, where the same verb was used; it thus brings this long section on the Christian life (which was interrupted by 2:19-30) to an end. Therefore, because of everything Paul has been saying, they must stand firm in the manner he has described ("in this way/that is how you should"). Paul heaps up laudatory descriptions of the Philippians: They are beloved and longed-for, his joy and his crown. The word "joy" (χαρά *chara*) repeats a theme that runs through Philippians; the term "crown" (στέφανος *stephanos*) is perhaps suggested by the image of the successful athlete in 3:12-14 (cf. 1 Cor 9:25). On the day of Christ, Paul expects to "boast" about the Philippians (2:16; cf. 1:3-11) and to be rewarded. Needless to say, they are to stand firm "in the Lord."

---

33. For further discussion, see M. D. Hooker, *From Adam to Christ* (Cambridge: Cambridge University Press, 1990) 1-100.

REFLECTIONS

1. Paul's image of the Christian life as a race reminds us that we can never rest on our laurels. But this particular race is not a competition in which only one person can succeed: Like the so-called Caucus-race that is organized by the Dodo in Lewis Carroll's book *Alice's Adventures in Wonderland,* it is possible for everyone who takes part to win and for everyone to receive a prize. The end is assured, not because of what we are able to do (though we must do our best!), but by virtue of the fact that it rests ultimately on the hold Christ has on us: He has made us his own, and we belong to him (v. 13). The tension between what Christians already are and what they are called to be is neatly expressed in Paul's use of two words with the same root, first, to declare that he is not yet "perfect" (v. 12), and second, to appeal to those who, like himself, are "mature" (v. 15). John Wesley was only one person among many who have believed that Christian perfection is not only a proper aim but a real possibility—but Wesley was nevertheless skeptical about those who actually *claimed* to be perfect! It has been well said that the mark of true maturity is to know that one is *not* yet perfect. In this life, the goal always remains beyond us, demanding our continual endeavor, beckoning us forward.

2. Paul describes the goal of the Christian as "knowing Christ" or sharing his mind (3:8, 10). The pattern of the gospel must be stamped upon all who call Christ "Lord." Christ himself is the blueprint for Christian behavior, but the apostle, modeling himself on Christ, becomes in turn the pattern for the Philippians, because they know him (3:17). Now that Paul is no longer among them, there are other models to follow—those who live according to the pattern Paul gave them—and so the process continues. Individual Christians and Christian communities that embody the gospel serve to demonstrate the love of God to the world. The gospel is proclaimed in deed as much as in word. When Paul declares that "Christ Jesus has made me his own," he describes a task that is both a privilege and a responsibility. Teresa of Avila expressed this task well when she said: "Christ has no body on earth but yours. Yours are the eyes through which Christ's compassion is to look out to the world. Yours are the feet with which he is to go about doing good. Yours are the hands with which he is to bless us now." It is a privilege, indeed, to belong to him, and so to the people of God. But it is also a responsibility. And what a responsibility! Do others look at us and think, "In that person I can see something of what it means to be like Christ"? Would *we* dare to claim to be examples to others of what it means to live like Christ? Something of what can happen when that privilege and responsibility are taken seriously can be seen in the life of Lord Macleod of Iona, who worked first in the Glasgow slums and then built up the Christian community on Iona. Asked on one occasion "What makes you tick?" he promptly answered, "The fact that Christ Jesus made me his own."

3. To reject Paul's call to share Christ's mind and be like him is to live as an enemy of the cross (3:18). Two millennia later, we have forgotten the excruciating pain, the shame, and the horror that crucifixion involved; society has turned the cross into a hallowed symbol, and it is worn as a piece of jewelry or a charm. The result is that we are no longer appalled at the nature of Christ's death, and we no longer grasp the significance of what it means to share his sufferings and to become like him in death. Those who live as enemies of the cross see religion only in terms of benefit and advantage and are not prepared to share the humiliations and depravations that commitment to Christ can involve. In our modern world there are, however, men and women who have *not* been ashamed of the cross—men and women, for example, of the caliber of Dietrich Bonhoeffer, who was prepared to withstand the evil of Nazism and to accept the consequences.

4. At baptism, believers are marked with the sign of the cross, a reminder of what is involved in the confession of faith that is made, either by the person being baptized or by someone else on his or her behalf. To be marked with the sign of the cross implies an obligation to be conformed to the likeness of the crucified Lord—to love as he loved, to obey as he obeyed, and to be prepared to accept the consequences. Those who are not ashamed of the cross will not only be ready to share in Christ's sufferings and death, but they will also share in his exaltation (3:21). The Christian hope cannot be spelled out in detail, for we do not know—any more than did Paul—what lies beyond death. But Paul's conviction is that those who are like Christ in their lives and in their deaths will be like him in the life beyond. Because Christ was content to share our human life, he enables us to share his resurrection life, and he will one day make us truly like him.

LETTER CONCLUSION

PHILIPPIANS 4:2-9, VARIOUS EXHORTATIONS

NIV

²I plead with Euodia and I plead with Syntyche to agree with each other in the Lord. ³Yes, and I ask you, loyal yokefellow,[a] help these women who have contended at my side in the cause of the gospel, along with Clement and the rest of my fellow workers, whose names are in the book of life.

⁴Rejoice in the Lord always. I will say it again: Rejoice! ⁵Let your gentleness be evident to all. The Lord is near. ⁶Do not be anxious about anything, but in everything, by prayer and petition, with thanksgiving, present your requests to God. ⁷And the peace of God, which transcends all understanding, will guard your hearts and your minds in Christ Jesus.

⁸Finally, brothers, whatever is true, whatever is noble, whatever is right, whatever is pure, whatever is lovely, whatever is admirable—if anything is excellent or praiseworthy—think about such things. ⁹Whatever you have learned or received or heard from me, or seen in me—put it into practice. And the God of peace will be with you.

[a]3 Or loyal Syzygus

NRSV

²I urge Euodia and I urge Syntyche to be of the same mind in the Lord. ³Yes, and I ask you also, my loyal companion,[a] help these women, for they have struggled beside me in the work of the gospel, together with Clement and the rest of my co-workers, whose names are in the book of life.

⁴Rejoice[b] in the Lord always; again I will say, Rejoice.[b] ⁵Let your gentleness be known to everyone. The Lord is near. ⁶Do not worry about anything, but in everything by prayer and supplication with thanksgiving let your requests be made known to God. ⁷And the peace of God, which surpasses all understanding, will guard your hearts and your minds in Christ Jesus.

⁸Finally, beloved,[c] whatever is true, whatever is honorable, whatever is just, whatever is pure, whatever is pleasing, whatever is commendable, if there is any excellence and if there is anything worthy of praise, think about[d] these things. ⁹Keep on doing the things that you have learned and received and heard and seen in me, and the God of peace will be with you.

[a] Or loyal Syzygus   [b] Or Farewell   [c] Gk brothers   [d] Gk take account of

COMMENTARY

4:2-3. In this appeal to Euodia and Syntyche we find at last clear evidence of dissension in the Philippian church. Many commentators believe this to have been a serious problem in the community and thus interpret these verses as an indication of Paul's real purpose in writing.[34] He

---

34. This view is argued at length by Davorin Peterlin, in *Paul's Letter to the Philippians in the Light of Disunity in the Church*, NovTSup (Leiden: Brill, 1995).

deals with the women briefly and gently, however, speaking warmly of their work for the gospel, which suggests that, although they certainly needed to see the relevance of his teaching for their conduct, the matter was not out of hand. The fact that he addresses them by name supports this notion, since Paul frequently names his friends and fellow workers but very rarely those with whom he disagrees.

Paul addresses each woman in turn, using the same verb (the NRSV's "urge" is perhaps preferable to the NIV's "plead with" as a translation of παρακαλῶ *parakalō*), and so avoiding the taking of sides. He urges them "to be of the same mind/to agree with each other in the Lord"; the phrase is identical with that used in 2:2, although the NIV's translation disguises this fact. Paul also appeals to someone whom he addresses as "loyal companion/yokefellow" to help these two women, who have worked side by side with Paul in the cause of the gospel. In Philippi as elsewhere in the Pauline mission, women played an important role in the Christian community (for Philippi, see Acts 16:11-15; see also Rom 16:1-15). Euodia and Syntyche are described as having "struggled/contended" alongside Paul, and this verb (συναθλέω *synathleō*, used already in 1:27) continues the athletic imagery of 3:12-14. The punctuation used by the NIV and the NRSV could be thought to suggest that Paul is appealing for help to "Clement and other fellow workers," together with this loyal companion, but it is better to understand these words as belonging to the immediately preceding phrase and to assume that these people, too, have been working alongside Paul and the two women.

But who is the unnamed "loyal companion/yokefellow"? And why does Paul not name him? Many suggestions as to his identity have been made, some of which (such as that Paul is referring to his wife) can be ruled out (since the adjective is masculine in form). Some commentators have argued that the word translated "companion/yokefellow" is, in fact, a proper name, "Syzygus" (see the NIV and NRSV margins); unlike the names "Euodia" and "Syntyche," however, which are both found in Greek inscriptions of the period, there is no evidence that "Syzygus" was ever used as a name. Other suggestions have included Silas, Luke, and Timothy, but Timothy is both with Paul and remaining with him (2:19-24; unless, of course, we regard that passage as part of another letter). The best suggestion is, perhaps, the one favored by Lightfoot, that Paul is referring to Epaphroditus.[35] It is true that Epaphroditus was still with Paul when he wrote this letter (2:25-30), but he is about to set off for

35. J. B. Lightfoot, *Saint Paul's Epistle to the Philippians,* 7th ed. (London: Macmillan, 1883).

Philippi, presumably carrying the letter, and will be present when the letter is read. Had Paul been addressing anyone else, it is strange that this person is referred to in this way, rather than being named; but after the long reference to Epaphroditus earlier in the letter, it was, perhaps, not necessary to name him again. It is true that Paul could have given him the message in person—perhaps he did, which would make it even more unnecesary to name him here! The commission to him here would, however, give him extra authority to deal with what may have been a delicate situation.

Paul's reprimand of the two women is muted. He merely reminds them of the relevance of the teaching he has given earlier in the letter. He urges them to be of the same mind "in the Lord," a phrase that reminds us that the appeal for unity is based on the fact that those who are in Christ should share the attitude of Christ. Like Clement and the other leaders who are not named, these women have labored side by side with Paul for the sake of the gospel, and their "names are in the book of life." The image is a familiar one in both the OT (e.g., Exod 32:32; Ps 69:28; Dan 12:1) and the NT, especially in the book of Revelation (e.g., Rev 20:12-15). Citizens of Philippi, whose names would be recorded in the civic register, would certainly understand an image calling to mind its heavenly counterpart.

4:4-7. Paul repeats his command to rejoice, and this, too, is "in the Lord." (The alternative translation suggested in the NRSV note, "Farewell in the Lord always," makes no sense!) Christians should be known for a quality that is rendered in both the NIV and the NRSV as "gentleness." The Greek term ἐπιεικής (*epieikēs*) is more positive than that. It denotes generosity toward others and is a characteristic of Christ himself (cf. 2 Cor 10:1); the NEB's "magnanimity" and the REB's "consideration of others" catch its meaning.

This paragraph consists of a series of commands that appear to have little connection with each other. The abrupt statement that the Lord is near seems equally detached from what immediately precedes it. In what sense is he near? Is this a reference to space or to time? The words are reminiscent of Ps 145:18, "The LORD is near all who call upon him," but they could also have a sense similar to the prayer for the Lord's coming in 1 Cor 16:22. The former meaning leads naturally into the injunction not to be anxious, but the latter is also appropriate, since the statement would then echo the expectation of Phil 3:20. Perhaps Paul would have said that such questions are meaningless, for the Lord who is expected from heaven is also the Lord who is present with his people. Whether this nearness is primarily spatial or temporal, his people should rejoice.

The affirmation that the Lord is near leads naturally into the injunction not to be anxious in v. 6, a saying that is reminiscent of Jesus' teaching in Matt 6:25-34. All prayer and supplication are to be accompanied by thanksgiving, something that has characterized the whole of this letter. The result will be that the peace of God will guard their hearts and minds "in Christ Jesus." The peace promised here is far more than an absence of conflict. Rather, it is total well-being, and it comes from God—once again, to those who are in Christ Jesus and who share his attitude, so that his "heart and mind" become theirs.

4:8-9. Paul's final appeal is to "think about" various admirable qualities, all of which are appropriate to those whose minds are guarded by Christ. This time, the introductory "Finally" seems a more appropriate translation of the Greek phrase τὸ λοιπόν (*to loipon*) than it did in 3:1. Paul has reached the end of his injunctions, if not the end of his letter. The verb he employs here is not the familiar φρονέω (*phroneō*), which he has used repeatedly in this letter, but λογίζομαι (*logizomai*), "to consider," "to take into account," which he used in 3:13. The virtues listed here are often described as typical of the qualities that were admired in the pagan world, and certainly there is nothing particularly Christian about them (contrast the list at the beginning of chap. 2). The

terms "true," "just/right," and "pure" echo familiar Pauline themes, but the vocabulary as a whole is unusual in the NT, and several of the words are not used elsewhere by Paul. Has he adopted a list of virtues from popular moral philosophy? If so, why? Is he making a deliberate attempt to show that Christianity is not incompatible with pagan culture at its best? Almost all the terms he uses here can be found in Jewish literature, however, so we cannot be certain about his source. What we can be sure of is that he is claiming that anything and everything that is "excellent or praiseworthy" is divine in origin.

Although the appeal in v. 8 is not specifically Christian, that in v. 9 is. Since Christ is himself the embodiment of all the virtues listed in v. 8, there is a logical link between Paul's appeal to "think about" these things and to "put into practice/keep on doing" what they have "learned and received" from Paul; the verbs are semitechnical, and refer to the learning and receiving of tradition—in this case, of the gospel. The Philippians have also heard and seen these things in Paul. Once again, therefore, they are urged to imitate Paul, who embodies for them the gospel message. The verse reminds us yet again of the close link between the proclamation of the gospel and the moral demand to be like Christ, which rests on those who respond.

Once again, Paul assures the Philippians that they will have peace, but this time the promise refers to the God of peace, rather than to the peace of God. The phrase is a familiar one in Pauline greetings. Here it reminds us that God (and not just the blessings that come from God) is with his people. (See Reflections at 4:21-23.)

PHILIPPIANS 4:10-20, A PERSONAL NOTE OF THANKS

NIV

[10]I rejoice greatly in the Lord that at last you have renewed your concern for me. Indeed, you have been concerned, but you had no opportunity

NRSV

10I rejoice[a] in the Lord greatly that now at last you have revived your concern for me; indeed,

[a] Gk *I rejoiced*

NIV

to show it. [11]I am not saying this because I am in need, for I have learned to be content whatever the circumstances. [12]I know what it is to be in need, and I know what it is to have plenty. I have learned the secret of being content in any and every situation, whether well fed or hungry, whether living in plenty or in want. [13]I can do everything through him who gives me strength.

[14]Yet it was good of you to share in my troubles. [15]Moreover, as you Philippians know, in the early days of your acquaintance with the gospel, when I set out from Macedonia, not one church shared with me in the matter of giving and receiving, except you only; [16]for even when I was in Thessalonica, you sent me aid again and again when I was in need. [17]Not that I am looking for a gift, but I am looking for what may be credited to your account. [18]I have received full payment and even more; I am amply supplied, now that I have received from Epaphroditus the gifts you sent. They are a fragrant offering, an acceptable sacrifice, pleasing to God. [19]And my God will meet all your needs according to his glorious riches in Christ Jesus.

[20]To our God and Father be glory for ever and ever. Amen.

NRSV

you were concerned for me, but had no opportunity to show it.[a] [11]Not that I am referring to being in need; for I have learned to be content with whatever I have. [12]I know what it is to have little, and I know what it is to have plenty. In any and all circumstances I have learned the secret of being well-fed and of going hungry, of having plenty and of being in need. [13]I can do all things through him who strengthens me. [14]In any case, it was kind of you to share my distress.

[15]You Philippians indeed know that in the early days of the gospel, when I left Macedonia, no church shared with me in the matter of giving and receiving, except you alone. [16]For even when I was in Thessalonica, you sent me help for my needs more than once. [17]Not that I seek the gift, but I seek the profit that accumulates to your account. [18]I have been paid in full and have more than enough; I am fully satisfied, now that I have received from Epaphroditus the gifts you sent, a fragrant offering, a sacrifice acceptable and pleasing to God. [19]And my God will fully satisfy every need of yours according to his riches in glory in Christ Jesus. [20]To our God and Father be glory forever and ever. Amen.

[a] Gk lacks *to show it*

COMMENTARY

The fact that this "thank-you note" comes almost at the end of the letter is something of a puzzle. Some commentators believe that Paul's main purpose in writing to the Philippians was to express his thanks for their gift to him. If that is the case, he has left it until very late in the letter to do so! There are, to be sure, possible references to their gift in 1:3, 5 and 2:25, 30, but these are scarcely expressions of thanks. Even now, Paul thanks the Lord, rather than the Philippians, for their concern for him! Why is Paul seemingly so tardy, and so reticent, to express his thanks?

One possible explanation is that Paul wrote to the Philippians when Epaphroditus first arrived. Some commentators suggest that the past tense in v. 10, "I rejoiced" (see the NRSV note) rather than "I rejoice," is an indication that the gift had

arrived sometime earlier. Certainly there has been some communication between Paul (or those with him) and the Philippians, since the latter have heard of Epaphroditus's illness (2:26). If Paul wrote such a letter, then either we must conclude that it has not survived, or we must suppose that this is it and that an editor has combined two or more letters into one. An alternative suggestion is that Paul was embarrassed by the Philippians' gift, since it contravened his principle of not accepting financial assistance (see 1 Cor 9:15-18; 2 Cor 11:7-10; 1 Thess 2:9); hence his delay in mentioning it. For Paul to receive support from the Philippians when he was in prison, however, was a very different matter from receiving it from those among whom he was working. To accept money from Christians in Thessalonica and

Corinth when he was working there might have seemed like profiting from the gospel, but the Philippians had long supported his missionary endeavors outside Philippi, and could, therefore, be seen as partners in his work—something about which Paul had indeed boasted to the Corinthians (2 Cor 11:7-10). There was no need for him, then, to feel embarrassed by their gift—except, perhaps, by the generosity of an impoverished church (2 Cor 11:7-10).

Recent study of social and rhetorical conventions in the Greco-Roman world has indicated that effusive thanks might have suggested a dependency on the donor or an obligation to reciprocate.[36] If Paul did not immediately express his thanks to the Philippians with the enthusiasm that seems appropriate to our modern ways, then this was because he regarded them as his partners in the gospel, and not as his paymasters. Moreover, although 1:3-8 is certainly not a formal expression of thanks, the links in language ("joy/rejoice," 1:4; 4:10; "share," 1:5, 7; 4:14-15) and in theme (in the early days and now, 1:5; 4:10, 15) suggest that Paul had their gift very much in mind in those opening verses.

We wonder, however, whether commentators may not have exaggerated the problem. It is true that the Philippians sent Paul gifts of some kind (4:18). But their main contribution to his welfare may well have been to send Epaphroditus to look after his needs (2:25)—something that, under the circumstances, Epaphroditus was unable to do. Nevertheless, the Philippians have been partners with Paul in the gospel from the very beginning (1:5). In the early days, they shared in "giving and receiving" (4:15). Now they have again shown their concern for Paul (4:10) and shared in his troubles (4:14), not simply by their gifts but by sending Epaphroditus to him. It is clear from 2:30 how greatly Paul valued Epaphroditus's ministry, which mirrored the self-giving of Christ. Seen in this light, the fact that this section comes at the end of the letter is perhaps understandable. If there is any embarrassment on Paul's part, it is due to the fact that he has been forced by circumstance to send Epaphroditus back to Philippi, which might appear ungrateful. But it may well have been the Philippians, rather than Paul, who

36. See, e.g., G. W. Peterman, *Paul's Gift from Philippi*, SNTSMS 92 (Cambridge: Cambridge University Press, 1997).

were in danger of feeling embarrassed, since their well-intentioned plan had foundered. Paul, therefore, emphasizes what he owes to the Philippians and how they have been his partners from the beginning (1:15; 2:25; 4:10-19). This partnership has been demonstrated not only in their gifts (4:15-16, 18) but also in their concern (2:25; 4;10, 14). The Philippians need not feel that Epaphroditus's return means that they have failed to give Paul what was due to him, since he has "been paid in full" (4:18).

4:10. This section is introduced as a thanksgiving with the familiar verb χαίρω (*chairō*, "to rejoice"). This is no hollow emotion; the adverb "greatly" (μεγάλως *megalōs*) is an indication of the strength of Paul's joy, which, like the joy he urges on the Philippians (3:1; 4:4), is "in the Lord." Equally familiar is the verb φρονέω (*phroneō*, "to think"), used here twice in the sense of "to be concerned." By their concern for Paul, the Philippians are showing precisely the Christlike attitude he has been urging them to share. The "[now] at last" sounds a bit grudging, as though their concern for him was belated. Some commentators suggest that the words are a quotation from a note to Paul from the Philippians: "At long last we are able to send you a gift." There was no way of indicating such a quotation in an ancient letter, but the recipients would, of course, have recognized it; there is almost certainly an example of such a quotation in 1 Cor 7:1. But even if the words are Paul's own, there is no need to suppose that they are meant as a rebuke. The sense is not "at long last you have thought about me," but "after all this time you have once again shown your concern for me, long after I might have expected you to do so." (The verb ἀναθάλλω [*anathallō*] means "to cause to bloom again.") In other words, the statement should be read positively, not negatively. In case his words should be misunderstood, however, Paul hastens to explain that the interval has been due to the lack of opportunity, and not to a lack of concern.

4:11-13. Paul's gratitude is not due to any real need on his part (v. 11), since he has learned to be content, whatever he has. Rather, as v. 14 will make clear, it arises from this tangible evidence of the special relationship between the Philippians and himself. The adjective translated "content" (αὐτάρκης *autarkēs*) means also "self-sufficient"; the noun is used at 2 Cor 9:8. The virtue of "self-sufficiency" or "contentment" was a favorite one among Cynics and Stoics, but Paul's self-sufficiency is of a very different kind, for—paradoxically—it comes from God. It arises from Paul's decision, described in 3:7-11, to give up everything in order to gain Christ. As a result, Paul can cope with every circumstance; he knows both how "to have plenty" and how "to have little/be in need." The verb here is ταπεινόω (*tapeinoō*) and means literally "to be humbled"; it echoes 2:8, where the verb was used of the action of Christ in humbling himself and reminds us once again that Paul's experience derives from his union with Christ. The verb translated "learned" here is μανθάνω (*manthanō*), commonly used of disciples or pupils learning from a rabbi or teacher. In the next verse, however, Paul uses a different verb, μυέω (*mueō*), in a similar sense; this word was often used of being initiated into the mystery religions, which is why the NIV and the NRSV render it, "I have learned the secret." It is possible that Paul is thinking of his achievement of "self-sufficiency" as a metaphorical initiation, but the verb could also be used in a more general sense. What he has learned is to be both well fed and hungry, to have plenty and to be in need—or, rather, how to cope with these situations; the NIV repeats the word "content" to make the meaning clear. Verse 13 reveals the secret of Paul's ability to do "everything"; it is through the one who gives him the strength he needs.

4:14-16. The paragraph division of the NRSV seems more logical than that of the NIV. In spite of what he has just said, it was nevertheless good of the Philippians to share in his distress. The verb συγκοινωνέω (*sygkoinōneō*, "to share") is a compound of the verb also translated "shared" in v. 15; equivalent nouns are used in 1:5 and 7 ("partnership" [κοινωνία *koinōnia*] and, lit., "fellow participants" [συγκοινωνοι *sygkoinōnoi*]). The fellowship of those in Christ involves sharing with one another at all levels: The Philippians have shared Paul's distress, just as they shared with him "in the matter of giving and receiving" (v. 15). This does not mean that the Philippians gave and Paul received. On the contrary, the giving and receiving were mutual, since he goes on to say that he has been paid in full (i.e., for what he has given them; v. 18). It has been shown

recently that the commercial language Paul employs here echoes imagery commonly used in contemporary literature to describe the social reciprocity that should characterize relationships between equals.[37] The Philippians alone had shared with Paul in this particular way, and they alone had been true partners with him in the gospel (1:5). Paul refers to their support also in 2 Cor 11:8-9. The fact that the Philippians were the only Christians who supported Paul is significant, since it suggests that the bond between him and them was particularly strong. At least a part of the explanation as to why other churches did not contribute to his expenses seems to lie in Paul's own fierce independence and his refusal to depend on others for support (see 1 Cor 9:1-18; 1 Thess 2:9).

This financial support had been given to Paul "in the early days of the gospel" (v. 15). At first sight, this statement makes little sense. It was only *after* the early days (lit., "the beginning") of the gospel that Paul arrived in Philippi. The NIV has understood the statement from the Philippians' point of view—the early days of the gospel as far as they were concerned—and has paraphrased accordingly. Probably, however, Paul was thinking of the great expansion of missionary work following his departure from Philippi and, therefore, means the beginning of the spread of the gospel, which took place after he left Macedonia. Since Thessalonica is in Macedonia, v. 16 appears to be a bit of an afterthought: Even before he had left Macedonia, they had begun to help him.

4:17-19. Verse 17 picks up the theme of vv. 11-12. Paul does not need gifts, and he is certainly not "seeking/looking for" any. The fact that he insists that he is not asking for a gift so quickly after reminding the Philippians of their earlier assistance would seem to confirm that the Philippians may be feeling that they have not done as much for him as they would have liked. What he is looking for is not another gift, but the amount that stands to their credit, and this is more than enough. Paul has returned once again to the metaphor of the financial ledger, which he used in 3:7-8, and he hastens to assure them that the books have been balanced. "I have been paid in full," he declares; the Greek word ἀπέχω (*apechō*),

37. P. Marshall, *Enmity in Corinth*, WUNT 2:23 (Tübingen: J. C. B. Mohr [Siebeck], 1987) 157-64; Peterman, *Paul's Gift from Philippi*, 51-89.

which he uses here, is the word that would have been used on a receipt. Thus Paul has been paid more than enough. The implication seems to be that the Philippians had once been in his debt; what they owed him, of course, was the fact that he had brought them the gospel. Now Paul changes the metaphor again. The gifts brought by Epaphroditus were "a fragrant offering, an acceptable sacrifice, pleasing to God." Though the gifts were offered to Paul, they have in effect been offered to God, since they are being used for "the defense and confirmation of the gospel" (1:7). It seems, then, that the account is being held with God and that the Philippians are storing up treasure in heaven (cf. Matt 6:20; 19:21).

It will be God, therefore, who recompenses them (v. 19). The unusual phrase "my God" (see also 1:3) is not intended to imply that Paul's God is not the God of the Philippians also; indeed, in the very next verse he refers to "our God." If he speaks of "my God" here, it is because he wishes to stress that he is relying on God to do for him what he is unable to do for himself. His God will "fully satisfy/supply" all their needs, just as Paul has been "fully satisfied/supplied" by the Philippians. Not only does the verb in v. 19 echo that used in v. 18, but also the word "need/needs"

(χρεία *chreia*) is the same as that used in v. 16. Moreover, God will do this "according to his riches in glory in Christ Jesus"; since God's riches are immeasurable, God is able to meet every conceivable need. The NRSV follows the Greek more accurately than does the NIV here: These riches are "in glory," rather than "glorious." We are reminded of 3:21 and the promise that we will share Christ's body of glory. Paul is, perhaps, thinking now of what we would call "spiritual" needs rather than material ones. If the Philippians have not yet "been made perfect" (3:12), God will supply what they lack, and they will share the riches of God's glory "in Christ Jesus," whose self-emptying, death, and exaltation as Lord brought glory to God the Father (2:11).

4:20. It is hardly surprising that this section is rounded off with a doxology. The only possible response of the Christian church to this revelation of God's glory is to *give* God glory, and now, of course, this God is "*our* God and Father." The greatness and goodness of God are reflected and proclaimed by the worshiping community, and this process will continue "for ever and ever"— literally, "to the ages of ages," a thoroughly Jewish expression. The final "Amen" is the affirmation that this will be so. (See Reflections at 4:21-23.)

PHILIPPIANS 4:21-23, CLOSING WORDS

COMMENTARY

Paul's closing words follow the pattern of conventional letter-endings of his time, although this ending has, of course, been thoroughly Christianized. It may seem strange that after the doxology of v. 20 he should add greetings (vv. 21-22) and

then the grace (v. 23). However, many NT letters (including, among Paul's, 1 and 2 Thessalonians and Galatians) conclude with a fourfold pattern consisting of:

(a) personal information or instruction
(b) formal benediction or doxology
(c) brief personal counsel or greetings
(d) simple benediction.

This pattern is followed here.

The greetings are general: to "every saint/all the saints in Christ Jesus" (the last phrase is probably a reminder, once again, of their fundamental relationship with Christ [echoing 1:1], though it is possible to take it with the word "Greet") from "the brothers/friends" who are with Paul and "all the saints." The distinction between "brothers [and sisters]" and "saints" is slightly puzzling, but Paul probably means by the former those who are fellow workers in the cause of the gospel. "Those who belong to Caesar's household" would have included officials and servants of all kinds who were employed in the service of the emperor, in particular, what we would term "civil servants." Although the majority of these persons would have resided in Rome, others would have been found throughout the empire (including Philippi); so once again this reference cannot settle the issue of the place of Paul's imprisonment, though it certainly points to Rome.

The grace in v. 23 is Paul's typical ending, though certainly no formality. We can scarcely read it without remembering his account of "the grace of the Lord Jesus Christ," which he has given us in chap. 2. Paul uses here the phrase "with your spirit" (see also Gal 6:18; Phlm 25) rather than his more typical "with you," but there is no real difference in meaning. Interestingly, he uses the plural "your" but the singular "spirit," perhaps because he thinks of the Christian community as a unity in Christ.

Many MSS conclude the letter with a final "Amen" (see the NRSV note). It is difficult to decide whether the word was added at some stage or was accidentally omitted. Certainly it provides a fitting end to the epistle—but that may be precisely the reason why an ancient scribe added it! Both the NIV and the NRSV translators appear to have agreed that this was what happened, and they were probably correct.

REFLECTIONS

1. The note of joy continues to echo throughout this chapter. Paul urges the Philippians to rejoice (4:4), and he does so himself (4:10). What he refers to is not a superficial cheerfulness but a deep joy in what God has done in Christ and is continuing to do through the saints. The fact that this joy is "in the Lord" reminds us not only that it derives from the Lord, but also that it is shared by those who live in him. Paul is not thinking of something that is merely an emotional experience or that is in any sense transient but of the deep and lasting joy that comes through a deepening relationship with Christ; this joy is thus expressed in sharing his love and concern for others. If many Christians today lack such joy, is this perhaps because they see their faith to a great extent as an individual matter, and so do not see Christian life in terms of mutual respect and concern or experience the love and support of fellow Christians? Can we experience the *joy* of the gospel without *living* it?

2. Christians today can learn from the way in which Paul handled the problem of the dispute between Euodia and Syntyche. We do not know precisely what the trouble was, but it sounds all too familiar! Clearly there were rivalry and tension between them. By appealing to them "to be of the same mind," Paul reminds them of his teaching in 2:2 and his elaboration of what that meant in 2:3-4. But even more important, the appeal "to be of the same mind *in the Lord*" would remind them that this "mind" was the mind of Christ, who had emptied himself, had humbled himself, and had been obedient to death. As so often in his ethical appeals, Paul takes us back to the gospel and works things out from first principles: If Christ behaved like that, how must those who are "in Christ" behave? Put like that, it is clear what Euodia and Syntyche should do! If they do not do it, then they are in effect denying that they are "in Christ," denying that the way of Christ has been affirmed by God as God's way. Could we, perhaps, try more often to go back to first principles in attempting to sort out the problems that inevitably arise between members of the Christian community? Should we, perhaps, worry less about who is right and who is wrong and ask instead, "What does it mean for us, as a community, to have the mind of Christ?"

3. In 4:2-3, Paul is concerned with relations within the Christian community, but in 4:5 he turns to the church's dealings with those outside. Consideration of others is to be shown to *everyone,* not just to fellow Christians. Since this attitude, too, is a reflection of that seen in Christ, Paul is in effect urging the Philippians to let their lives be a proclamation of the gospel.

4. Like the concluding page of many a letter, this final chapter of the epistle is something of a hodgepodge—a collection of different ideas—as Paul mentions the various things he still wants to say, though there are unifying themes. In a series of commands, Paul has already urged the Philippians to live "in the Lord." They have been told to stand firm in the Lord (4:1), to be of the same mind in the Lord (4:2), to rejoice in the Lord (4:4), and to behave appropriately toward others (4:5). In 4:5-7, the command not to worry but to pray is sandwiched between a promise that the Lord is near and the assurance that the Philippians will be guarded by the peace of God.

Paul's declaration that "the Lord is near" in 4:5 may well cause us problems today. Two thousand years later, we wonder what this "nearness" means. For Paul, it certainly included a belief in a future coming. Ought Christians today expect an imminent parousia? Some, of course, do. But all too often this expectation leads them to opt out of everyday life and to do nothing except speculate about the date of the Second Coming and await its arrival. In contrast to this, Paul's words are intended to encourage the Philippians to behave with consideration toward others and to think positively about their present lives (4:6). Should we, then, interpret Paul's words in solely spatial terms? The Lord is certainly near in that sense, though too few of us are sufficiently aware of his presence. To know that Christ is with us in our everyday lives ought to be a great comfort to us. But we need also to remember that Paul's statement looked back to the promise in 3:21 that the Lord will come *to transform us and make us like himself.* In terms of human history, the final coming of the Lord may seem no nearer than when Paul wrote these words. But for those in Christ, the promise of 3:21 is sure. Paul's declaration that the Lord is near reminds us—paradoxically!—of a destiny that will be fulfilled *beyond* space and time.

5. Few of us find it easy to follow the advice of 4:6. We tend to worry about *everything*! Our attitude is the very opposite of the trust in God that Paul commends. It is sobering to remember that Paul was in prison, facing a capital charge, when he wrote this letter. And that was not his only problem, for his responsibility for the churches was a constant concern (2 Cor 11:28). Moreover, the people to whom he was writing were unlikely to be living comfortable lives. Most of them were poor, many were slaves, and few of them would have known the meaning of security. In marked contrast, those of us who live in comparative wealth and luxury today are frequently those who are most worried and anxious. The secret of Paul's composure is that he is relying on God, and not on material goods, as he goes on to spell out in 4:10-14. This freedom from worry and anxiety does not, of course, imply an irresponsible attitude toward life and one's obligations. It is interesting to note that the verb used in 4:6 was also used in 2:20 of the genuine concern Timothy felt for the Philippians' welfare. It is a mark of the Christian maturity spoken of in 3:15 to be able to distinguish between the anxiety that cripples and destroys the individual and the concern for others that builds up the whole community.

6. Paul directs the Philippians to pray (4:6)—with thanksgiving. Once again, we find that Paul's prayers are suffused with thanksgiving. And once again we should remember that Paul had a capital charge hanging over his head and was writing to people who had very little in material terms. All too often our own prayers are nothing but a "shopping list," *without* thanksgiving; our anxiety about the future obscures the benefits that have been showered upon us. Gratitude to God for all that we have been given will allow the peace of God to guard our hearts and minds, protecting us against all that might destroy us (4:7).

7. The virtues mentioned in 4:8 were among those that were honored in the pagan world, a fact that reminds us that we should not be afraid to take over the best in our secular world and claim it for Christ. In a sense, of course, this is but a recognition that everything that is true and pure comes from God. Christians, however, have often been afraid to acknowledge the good and true in the secular world—in art, for example, in music and drama, or in indigenous customs. We are appalled today to remember the way in which nineteenth-century missionaries refused to allow Africans to use drums and dancing in their worship, believing them to be "pagan." General William Booth, founder of the Salvation Army, was much sounder when he took over secular tunes for hymns, demanding, "Why should the devil have all the best tunes?" If God is the origin of all that is good and true and honorable, then Christians should certainly acknowledge these qualities, wherever they are found.

8. If Paul has taken over the principle of self-sufficiency (4:11) from the pagan world, then he has certainly turned it on its head. For the Stoics, the principle indicated a certain detachment from the world. This principle is still much admired today, for example, among those attracted by Buddhism. Although Paul could cope with plenty and with need, he does not cut himself loose from the concerns of the world. His gospel certainly cannot be interpreted as a message to the poor to put up with poverty. For the Stoics, again, self-sufficiency meant relying on one's inner resources. For Paul, it meant relying on God in Christ to provide the necessary resources. He has, he says, learned to be content, whatever his circumstances (4:11). Paul's language suggests that being content was not something that came easily, and this is hardly surprising, in view of the hardships and dangers in which his missionary work involved him. His contentment is no spineless resignation, but a joyful acceptance of what God provides.

And in Paul's case, God used the Philippians to provide what he needed. Their action in giving and receiving is described in sacrificial language, reminding us once again of the central theme of the gospel: Christ's gift of himself. They share in the divine giving, and the result, once again, is that God is given glory (4:20).

Paul reminds us here of something that we too often forget: The riches of God are sufficient to deal with all our needs. But unlike some propounders of popular "prosperity" gospels, he does not promise us earthly wealth. Far more valuable than that is the attitude Paul has acquired through being in Christ, an attitude that accepts riches and poverty with equal joy and thanksgiving.

9. In 4:11-20, Paul expresses his gratitude to God—and to the Philippians—for their gift. But far more important than the gift itself were the love and concern the Philippians showed toward Paul—a love and concern that led them to help him. As so often, it is the thought that counts! The most significant gifts often cost us very little—sometimes nothing, except a few moments to say a friendly word or to make a telephone call, the stamp to post a letter or a card. What matters is that someone has been remembered with affection and concern. Do we always remember to show appreciation for what others do for us in these simple ways? Do we remember to help those who, like Paul, are going through a rough patch and need our prayers and concern?

10. We can easily overlook the significance of the phrase "those of Caesar's household" in 4:22. These people are acknowledged by Paul to be "saints," members of God's people. It cannot have been easy in the ancient world for those who were in Caesar's employ to acknowledge Jesus as Lord. Not many years later, with the outbreak of persecution against Christians, it became impossible; those who continued to hold the faith lost their employment and usually their lives as well. The tension between various responsibilities and allegiances is one with which Christians have had to cope from the very earliest days. There are Christians in some countries today who still experience these tensions and whose witness to the gospel puts many of us to shame. We should remember them in our prayers. For those of us who are not in danger of active persecution, the temptations are more subtle. Are we willing to stand up for the gospel in a society that scorns its principles? If our faith comes into conflict with our career or our standard of living or our standing in society, which do we sacrifice? No doubt, Paul's answer would have been to point us back once more to Christ's own self-emptying and urge us yet again to share his mind.

THE LETTER TO THE COLOSSIANS

INTRODUCTION, COMMENTARY, AND REFLECTIONS
BY
ANDREW T. LINCOLN

THE LETTER TO THE
COLOSSIANS

INTRODUCTION

Colossians is a rich and yet enigmatic Pauline letter. It contains a magnificent hymnic passage about the cosmic scope of Christ's role, develops the notion of believers' union with Christ, and has extensive exhortations about the ethical implications of this relationship. There are also fascinating treatments of the theme of reconciliation, of the heavenly world with its cosmic powers and its relation to the earthly realm, and of the notions of growth, maturity, and fullness; and there is the first occurrence in early Christian literature of the use of the "household code," the set of instructions for various groups within the household. While claiming to have been written by Paul (and Timothy), however, Colossians has a style quite distinct from earlier Pauline letters and theological and conceptual emphases that differ somewhat from these letters. In addition, its thought is developed in opposition to a teaching or philosophy about which the letter itself gives only a few scattered clues.

Much is to be gained simply by focusing on the text, following its argument closely, and thereby appreciating the impact of its message. But other questions—about the force of particular terms in their first-century context, about the situation of the writer and the first readers, about the teaching that is being opposed—arise naturally from a close reading. Clearly, the more that can be discovered about the historical setting, the better our appreciation of the message and the writer's pastoral strategy in conveying it. This Introduction looks at four key areas for the interpretation of Colossians: its form, structure, and persuasive strategy; the "philosophy" it opposes; the main themes that characterize its presentation of the Pauline gospel; and the identity of its author and those to whom it was addressed. The results of the discussion of these issues will inform the Commentary and Reflections that follow.

FORM, STRUCTURE, AND PERSUASIVE STRATEGY

The form of Colossians follows the Pauline letter's modification of the ancient letter form. The letter opening identifies the senders and the recipients and contains an initial greeting (1:1-2). There follows a statement of thanksgiving, with its opening formula found in 1:3 ("we thank God") and its intercessory prayer report.[1]

The thanksgiving section of Colossians introduces major themes of the letter, but there has been much debate about whether it ends at 1:12, 1:14, 1:20, or 1:23. The note of thanksgiving clearly continues through 1:12-14 with the participle, "giving thanks" (εὐχαριστοῦντες *eucharistountes*) and its relative clauses that take up traditional liturgical formulations. These in turn lead into the Christ hymn of 1:15-20, which is no longer a discrete independent composition. It now serves the function of the thanksgiving section to signal significant themes, this time specifically christological ones. The closing part of the Pauline thanksgiving typically consists of liturgical material that reflects or substitutes for the Jewish *bĕrākâ*, or "blessing," and has at its conclusion an "eschatological climax" in which the present time of thanksgiving is linked with the final days of the supreme rule of God.[2] Here both its introduction and the hymnic passage itself provide the liturgical material, and an eschatological climax may be seen in the brief application of the hymn in 1:21-23, where the readers' own reconciliation with God is with a view to their being presented as "holy and blameless and irreproachable before" God (1:22*b*). The appropriation of the hymn's language of reconciliation for the change that has taken place in the readers indicates that 1:21-23 retains a close connection with what precedes it. The talk of not "shifting from the hope of the gospel that you heard, which has been proclaimed to every creature under heaven" both makes explicit the paraenetical implications of the earlier material in the thanksgiving and provides an inclusio (a literary bracketing device) with 1:5, which had mentioned the hope the readers had heard of in the gospel that was growing in the whole world. In this way 1:3-23 can be seen as a coherent unit that forms an extended thanksgiving.

The letter body then begins with 1:24. The last clause of 1:23*c* had provided a transition in which the language of the writer shifts from first-person plural to singular and focuses on Paul: "of which I, Paul, became a servant." Paul's relation to the readers becomes the subject of the next section up to 2:5, which can be seen as the body-opening. Again an inclusio confirms this as a distinct unit, since it begins and ends with an expression of rejoicing: "I am now rejoicing in my suffering for your sake" (1:24*a* NRSV) and "rejoicing to see your good order and the firmness of your faith in Christ" (2:5*b*). A disclosure formula

---

1. See P. T. O'Brien, *Introductory Thanksgivings in the Letters of Paul,* NovTSup 49 (Leiden: Brill, 1977) 100-104.
2. Cf. J. T. Sanders, "The Transition from Opening Epistolary Thanksgiving to Body in the Letters of the Pauline Corpus" *JBL* 81 (1962) 348-62.

frequently serves as evidence of the body-opening;[3] this is found in 2:1, "For I want you to know . . ." (NRSV), alerting the readers to the importance of what follows—namely, Paul's desire for their unity in love and their assured understanding of Christ.

The phrase "as therefore" in 2:6 serves as a transition, introducing the major concern of the letter in the body-middle. Scholars disagree about whether the paraenesis, or ethical exhortation, should be treated as part of the body of the Pauline letter or as a separate section following it. In the case of Colossians, this issue is made more complicated by the fact that from 2:6 through 4:6 all the material is structured by imperatives and is hortatory. A division is apparent, however, within this material. The warning of 2:8 is about being taken captive by philosophy and empty deceit and has a particular teaching in view. It is followed by an extensive warrant in 2:9-15 based on the writer's view of Christ and of believers' relationship to Christ. The exhortations of 2:16–3:4 are all directly related to elements in the teaching being opposed. What is more, if an eschatological climax indicates an occurrence of transition in thought,[4] then such a transition can be seen in the assertion of 3:4, "When Christ who is our life is revealed, then you also will be revealed with him in glory."

Although there is still some relation to the alternative teaching in what follows from 3:5, the exhortations become more general from this point and employ traditional paraenetical forms, such as the listing of vices (3:5-11) and virtues (3:12-17) and the household code (3:18–4:1). The exhortations also become more frequent in this section. Although there are six imperatives in 2:6–3:4, there are eighteen instances of a verb in the imperative mood in 3:5–4:6. If it is the case that the body of the Pauline letter has as a generally distinctive characteristic two parts to its argumentation a more tightly organized theological part and a less tightly constructed appeal for the concrete working out of the view of Christian existence advocated earlier—then the central part of Colossians can still be seen to approximate these two parts. The exhortations of 2:6–3:4, with their focus on the alternative teaching and their more extended theological warrants, correspond to the first part, and the more general exhortations of 3:5–4:6 correspond to the usual paraenesis of the second part. In this way, 2:6–4:6 as a whole can be seen to constitute the body-middle.

The twenty-four imperatives of this section clearly make its tone one of warning, admonition, and exhortation. Issues raised in the thanksgiving section and the body-opening are elaborated here. The writer's concern about the recipients' knowledge and understanding (1:9; 2:2) and his related interest in their continued faithfulness to the gospel (1:23) are amplified in the exhortations of 2:6–3:4. The implicit paraenesis about "every good work," patient endurance, and thankfulness in 1:9-12 becomes explicit in the exhortations of 3:5–4:6. Assertions from the Christ hymn of 1:15-20 are employed in the christological warrant for the warning against the philosophy in 2:9-10, 15, 19, and what

3. Ibid., 354; J. L. White, "The Introductory Formulae in the Body of the Pauline Letter" *JBL* 90 (1971) 91-97.

4. J. L. White, *The Form and Function of the Body of the Greek Letter* (Missoula, Mont.: Scholars Press, 1972) 112-13n. 13.

is involved in the reconciliation accomplished by Christ's death (1:22) is developed in 2:10-15.

The following section, 4:7-9, relates the intention to send Tychicus and Onesimus as emissaries. The sending of emissaries was one means, along with a visit of the apostle or the sending of a letter, of bringing about the benefit of Paul's presence. This mention of what has been called "the apostolic parousia" indicates the body-closing.[5]

There then comes the closing of the letter as a whole. Among the concluding elements found in the Pauline letters are hortatory remarks, requests for prayer, a wish of peace, greetings, a command to the recipients to greet one another with a holy kiss, an autographic subscription (i.e., a reference to the writer's own handwriting), and a grace benediction. With the exception of the request for prayer, made earlier in the paraenesis in 4:3-4, the wish of peace, and the mention of the greeting with the holy kiss, all these elements are found in the closing section of Colossians. Personal greetings from his companions and from Paul himself are listed in 4:10-15. The hortatory remarks are contained in 4:16-17, which urge the recipients to exchange letters with the church at Laodicea and to pass on a message to Archippus. The placing of these remarks is slightly unusual, since the only other letter closing that has an exhortation after the final greeting is 1 Thessalonians (see 1 Thess 5:27). Paul's autograph is appended in 4:18. Its call to the readers to remember his "chains" is unique to a letter-closing. The final item is the brief grace benediction in 4:18c ("grace be with you"); and, as in other Pauline letters, the parallel with the opening greeting in terms of grace can be seen to provide an epistolary inclusio.

Epistolary analysis, therefore, yields the following outline:

I. Letter Opening—Address and Greeting (1:1-2)
II. Extended Thanksgiving Section (1:3-23)
III. Letter Body (1:24–4:9)
    A. Body-Opening (1:24–2:5)
    B. Body-Middle (2:6–4:6)
        1. Exhortation Related to the Philosophy (2:6–3:4)
        2. More General Exhortation (3:5–4:6)
    C. Body-Closing (4:7-9)
IV. Letter Closing—Greetings, Hortatory Remarks, Autographic Subscription, and Grace Benediction (4:10-18)

Since the letter was a substitute for speech and since Paul's letters were meant to be read aloud to their recipients, it is also appropriate to view their contents in the light of the conventions of ancient rhetoric. Although the categories from the ancient rhetorical

5. See R. W. Funk, "The Apostolic Parousia: Form and Function," in *Christian History and Interpretation,* ed. W. R. Farmer et al. (Cambridge: Cambridge University Press, 1966) 249-68.

handbooks should not be applied rigidly or mechanically, they may be employed, where they fit, to illuminate the letter writer's persuasive strategy.

The rhetorical situation or exigency of Colossians is produced by the writer's awareness of what he considers to be a false teaching that will have harmful consequences for the readers if they are taken in by it. To dissuade them from being enticed by the proponents of this teaching, he first encourages the letter's recipients by reminding them of the gospel and its hope, which he and they have in common, of the change of status it has effected, and of the fruits of Christian behavior it has produced among them. Assuring them of his special relationship to this gospel and of his desire for their increased knowledge and understanding of it, he underlines that they must remain committed to it. He spells out what this continuing commitment will mean by exhorting them both to resist the baneful influence of the teachers of the philosophy and to exemplify distinctively Christian patterns of behavior.

Of the three main rhetorical genres—forensic, deliberative, and epideictic—the first, with its aim of persuading an audience to make a judgment about events in the past, can be dismissed in regard to Colossians. If the deliberative genre involves the author's seeking to bring about some action in the future by persuading or dissuading the audience, and if the epideictic involves the author's seeking to persuade the audience to hold or to reaffirm some present point of view by assigning praise or blame, then it is not immediately obvious which more appropriately describes Colossians. Exhortation can function in both deliberative and epideictic genres, depending on whether it is calling for a change of behavior or reiterating common values.[6] Colossians could, in fact, be viewed as a case in which the genres of epideictic and deliberative rhetoric are mixed and overlap. After all, the actions that the recipients are being persuaded to take in the future are precisely to hold on to the values of the gospel that the writer believes they at present share with him. Only 2:20-21 suggests that some of the recipients may have succumbed to the philosophy. In the main the letter simply contains warnings against the teaching and against allowing its proponents to condemn or disqualify the Colossian believers. Nevertheless, the fact that the central section of the letter has as its focus the call for the specific future action of resisting the philosophy does suggest that the deliberative genre of rhetoric predominates. To be sure, such an action is a consequence of the reaffirmation of present values, but it goes beyond mere reaffirmation.

In an analysis of Colossians as a persuasive speech, 1:3-23 constitutes the *exordium*. The *exordium* functioned as the introduction, indicating the aim of the speech and attempting to secure the hearer's goodwill.[7] Since in Colossians the author claims to have no personal acquaintance with the people being addressed, it is necessary for him to establish an initial positive relationship with them if they are to be receptive to his message. So expressing his thankfulness for their faith and love, declaring his knowledge of the fruit-

6. See D. E. Aune, *The New Testament in Its Literary Environment* (Philadelphia: Westminster, 1987) 191, 208.
7. See Aristotle *Rhetoric* 3.13-14.

fulness of the gospel in their lives, seeing them as part of the worldwide growth of the Christian movement, mentioning Epaphras as the go-between, assuring them of his constant prayers, citing the Christ hymn, and reminding them of their change of status and relationship in respect to God are all part of establishing a positive relationship that will make them conducive to accept what follows. In particular, the Christ hymn draws readers into its praise, and its application explicitly appeals to their own experience of Christ's reconciling work. The two elements combine effectively to create an initial sympathy for the writer's thoughts and concerns.

The rest of the analysis takes up and modifies the suggestions of the French commentator J.-N. Aletti. He points out that if the *propositio,* or thesis, of a discourse is not a simple one, then its component elements are set out in a *partitio,* a division of the thesis into separate headings. He sees the *exordium* as concluding with such a *partitio* in 1:21-23. It has three headings: the work of Christ to achieve the holiness of believers (1:21-22); the need for the recipients to continue in the faith of the gospel (1:23*a*); and the recognition of the role of Paul in proclaiming this gospel (1:23*c*).[8] As has been noted, the exordium anticipates either directly or indirectly the themes to be dealt with in the discourse. Here at the end of the *exordium* there is a clear move to apply the preceding material to the letter's recipients. It would be natural, therefore, for this initial application to contain the main points to be made in this primarily deliberative discourse.

The *propositio* is usually followed by a section of proof, or *probatio.* This confirmation of the thesis can be seen to run from 1:24 to 4:1 and takes up both the language and the conceptuality of each of the elements of the *partitio,* but in reverse order. It functions not so much as the proof of propositions but more as the confirmation and elaboration of themes. Paul's role in the proclamation of the gospel is treated in 1:24–2:5, the need for faithfulness to this gospel in 2:6–3:4, and the holiness of believers' lives in 3:5–4:1.

This leaves 4:2-6 as the *peroratio.* According to Aristotle, the *peroratio* aimed to recapitulate leading themes, to make the audience well disposed toward the speaker, and to produce the required kind of emotion in the hearers.[9] Here the summing up is carried out in a generalizing fashion. It picks up particularly the key motifs of thanksgiving and prayer (4:2), recalling for readers not only the mention of thanksgiving in 1:12; 2:7; and 3:15-17 but also the writer's own extended introductory thanksgiving and its intercessory prayer report in 1:3-23. Talk of declaring the mystery of Christ (4:3), and doing so in the requisite manner (4:4), takes up the earlier references to the mystery and may well have in view what the author has attempted in his own rehearsal of the gospel in the face of opposing teaching in this discourse in 2:6–3:4.

The writer had also expressed his concern for the readers' spiritual wisdom (1:9) and made clear that such wisdom is to be found in Christ (2:3). Now he calls on the Colossians to live wisely in relation to outsiders (4:5). This requirement of wise living sums up well

8. J.-N. Aletti, *St. Paul Épître aux Colossiens,* ÉB (Paris: Gabalda, 1993) 39.
9. Aristotle *Rhetoric* 3.19.

the exhortations of 3:5–4:1; the interest in outsiders points appropriately to the motivation behind the use of the household code of 3:18–4:1 in particular. Knowing how to answer everyone (4:6) can be seen as a summary of what the writer wishes his communication to achieve for his readers and would include, therefore, their being in a position to respond adequately to the proponents of the philosophy. The *peroratio*'s function of making the audience well disposed to the speaker and arousing emotion would be achieved by its request for prayer (4:3*a*), by the reminder of Paul's imprisonment for Christ (4:3*b*), and by the sense of urgency conveyed through the exhortations to be watchful (4:2*b*) and to make the most of the time (4:5*b*).

Aristotle delineated three modes of persuasion: "The first kind depends on the personal character of the speaker (*ethos*); the second on putting the audience into a certain frame of mind (*pathos*); the third on the proof, or apparent proof, provided by the words of the speech itself (*logos*)."[10] Ethos presents the speaker as having wisdom, excellent character, and goodwill. In Colossians the author's wisdom is displayed not only through the quality of the advice and instruction offered but also through the depiction of Paul's special role in his commission to make known God's Word, the previously hidden mystery (1:25-26; 4:3). Paul's character is conveyed through the unique role he has in respect to the sufferings of Christ (1:24) and by the references to Paul's imprisonment for the gospel (4:3, 18). His goodwill is manifested in his prayers for the Colossians (1:3-4, 9-12); in his relation to Epaphras as the link between him and the Colossians (1:7-8; 4:12-13); in conveying news and extending greetings (4:10-18); in the effort he expends to ensure that all believers, and especially the readers, will be mature, united in love, have assured understanding, and therefore not be deceived (1:28–2:4); and in assuring them of his spiritual presence with them and his rejoicing on their account (2:5).

A number of these features also function in the letter's pathos, putting the audience into a suitable frame of mind to receive the message by evoking their empathy and sympathy. The writer's rejoicing in the readers' faith, the mention of his prayers for them, and the references to his sufferings and imprisonment and to his struggles and efforts on their behalf are all intended to produce a positive emotional effect that will make them responsive to his exhortations. The use of the Christ hymn early in the letter evokes common feelings of praise and worship that also prepare the recipients for the message to follow.

If *logos* is the use of argument and appeal to reason to support the speaker's viewpoint and to convince the audience, then the assertions about Christ in the hymnic material can be seen as laying the groundwork for the arguments that follow and that take up its terminology in 2:9-15. The writer employs a form of deductive argument that involves a statement and a supporting reason. A number of his exhortations have warrants, and in these cases the exhortation constitutes the conclusion, and the supporting warrant constitutes

10. Ibid., 1.2.

the premise. Colossians, then, has all three modes of argumentation—*ethos, pathos,* and *logos*—in its rhetorical arsenal.

This rhetorical analysis has produced the following outline:

   I. Exordium (1:3-23)
        concluding with Partitio (1:21-23)
  II. Probatio (1:24–4:1)
        A. Paul's Role in the Proclamation of the Gospel (1:24–2:5)
        B. Exhortation to Faithfulness to the Gospel (2:6–3:4)
        C. Exhortation to Holiness of Life (3:5–4:1)
  III. Peroratio (4:2-6)

The Outline that precedes the commentary combines structural elements from both epistolary and rhetorical analyses with more topical headings.

Colossians is a letter that attempts to persuade its recipients to take certain actions in the future. Ancient letters could be classified on the basis of the purpose they were meant to achieve or the circumstances they were designed to meet. In terms of the listings found in Pseudo-Demetrius and Pseudo-Libanius, Colossians would in all probability be called by the former an "advisory type" in which "we exhort (someone to) something or dissuade (him) from something" and by the latter a "paraenetic style" in which "we exhort someone by urging him to pursue something or to avoid something."[11] As a paraenetic letter, Colossians shares numerous features with other letters of moral guidance produced in the Greco-Roman philosophical schools. Teachers in these schools would also frequently combine the three major functions of affirmation, correction of rival views, and exhortation in the attempt to shape their students' lives. Sometimes their letters would be composed in the name of a past philosopher and addressed to figures from the past while clearly having a contemporary audience in view.[12]

THE "PHILOSOPHY" OPPOSED IN THE LETTER

A Variety of Proposals. Despite, and probably because of, the somewhat meager evidence provided by the letter, the academic industry of publishing books and articles on the teaching that provoked the writer's response shows no signs of abating. This commentary is not the place for interaction with the mass of secondary literature that also shows little sign of reaching a consensus. All that can be done here is to mention some of the more recent proposals, to caution the reader about the difficulties involved in any

---

11. See A. J. Malherbe, *Ancient Epistolary Theorists* (Atlanta: Scholars Press, 1988) 37, 69.

12. For an illuminating discussion of the similarities between Colossians and the moral exhortations of the Greco-Roman philosophical schools, see W. T. Wilson, *The Hope of Glory: Education and Exhortation in the Epistle to the Colossians* (Leiden: E. J. Brill, 1997) esp. 10-131, 219-29.

reconstruction, and then to provide a brief and tentative sketch of what appears to be the most plausible view.

In the past, scholars looked to a Jewish form of Gnosticism or to Jewish mysticism or to Hellenistic mystery cults or to neo-Pythagoreanism or to a syncretistic mix of some of these as the background that provides the identity of the philosophy. Recent monographs and commentaries have offered further variations. Sappington develops the view that some form of Jewish mysticism is the distinctive ingredient of the teaching, providing a full examination of the similar pattern of ascetic and mystical piety to be found in a number of Jewish apocalypses.[13] The distinctive contribution of DeMaris is to introduce Middle Platonism into the discussion as the context in which the letter's debate about achieving knowledge was conducted. He sees the teaching being opposed, therefore, as a mix of "popular Middle Platonic, Jewish and Christian elements that cohere around the pursuit of wisdom."[14] As the title of his monograph suggests, Arnold also finds a mix.[15] He provides the fullest investigation of local inscriptional and literary evidence, particularly that which deals with the practice of magic. For him the syncretistic teaching contained Jewish (cultic observances) and pagan (mystery cult initiation) elements that cohered within the general framework of magic and folk religion. Two further contributors to the debate refrain from a syncretistic solution. Dunn, in his commentary and in an article that preceded it, holds that the teaching was purely Jewish, a diaspora "synagogue apologetic promoting itself as a credible philosophy more than capable of dealing with whatever heavenly powers might be thought to control or threaten human existence."[16] Martin, on the other hand, views it as purely Hellenistic, claiming that Cynic teachers entered the Christian assembly to observe and then delivered a critical invective against Christian practices, to which the author of Colossians responds.[17]

The very number and variety of proposed solutions to the identity of the philosophy should caution against any overly confident claims to reconstruct it. Although the writer's prescription for curing the ailment he believed to be a threat to the well-being of his readers comes across reasonably clearly, the ailment itself defies any really accurate diagnosis. The writer had no reason for defining more exactly the teaching involved. He expects his readers to know perfectly well what he was talking about, and so he merely touches on some of its features, using some of its catchwords and slogans. Since the evidence the letter provides is piecemeal, it pushes the interpreter beyond the text to find an explanatory framework for the fragmented reflection of the teaching and its practices, found in the writer's response. Determining which does greatest justice to all the elements in the letter's

13. T. J. Sappington, *Revelation and Redemption at Colossae*, JSNTSup 53 (Sheffield: JSOT, 1991).

14. R. E. DeMaris, *The Colossian Controversy: Wisdom in Dispute at Colossae*, JSNTSup 96 (Sheffield: JSOT, 1994) 17.

15. C. Arnold, *The Colossian Syncretism*, WUNT 2/77 (Tübingen: J. C. B. Mohr, 1995).

16. J. D. G. Dunn, "The Colossian Philosophy: A Confident Jewish Apologia," *Biblica* 76 (1995) 153-81; *The Epistles to the Colossians and to Philemon*, NIGTC (Grand Rapids: Eerdmans, 1996) 35.

17. T. W. Martin, *By Philosophy and Empty Deceit. Colossians as Response to a Cynic Critique*, JSNTSup 118 (Sheffield: Sheffield Academic, 1996).

polemic remains the criterion for evaluating the various proposals. Some of them fail to explain parts of the letter adequately, but in itself this criterion still allows for a number of competing hypotheses.

There are at least two further difficulties in any attempt to employ the letter to reconstruct the alternative teaching. How many of the writer's direct references to the philosophy in this polemical letter can be taken as straightforward description rather than negatively slanted caricature? And if reconstruction is based on the part of the letter that is in direct interaction with the opposing teaching, is it legitimate to see other parts of the letter as having the teaching more indirectly in view and to use their discussion to complete the reconstruction?

Despite the difficulties, and provided that one remains both self-conscious about how to proceed and tentative about one's conclusions, it is still worth the effort to take up the letter's clues, to point to similar concepts in the thought of that time, and thereby to endeavor to sketch the best picture available of the teaching in view. After all, this teaching caused the writer enough concern to provoke a response to it, and some historical reconstruction is necessary if we are to appreciate that response as fully as possible. This sketch will proceed in three stages. It will begin with the explicit terminology mentioned in 2:18, move to a more disputed issue involving 2:8, 20, and then suggest a general characterization of the teaching. Other aspects will be discussed in the course of the commentary.

Visionary Experience and Asceticism. Two major features of the philosophy, as the writer depicts it, appear to be the claim to visions (and "the worship of angels" associated with such visions) and ascetic practices (including fasting as a preparation for visionary experiences). Even this feature involves questions of interpretation, however, since 2:18, in which it is mentioned, has a number of difficulties. In it the readers are urged not to let anyone who (literally) "takes pleasure in or insists on self-abasement and the worship of angels, which he has seen when entering" disqualify them. The term ταπεινοφροσύνη (*tapeinophrosynē*), rendered here, as in the NRSV, as "self-abasement," as opposed to the NIV's "false humility," occurs three times in Colossians (2:18; 2:23; 3:12). In its third occurrence, it denotes the positive virtue of humility, but that does not appear to be in view in the first two instances where it is connected with the philosophy. Because of its close association with worship in both cases, it is likely that it stands for some cultic practice rather than a disposition of lowliness and was a quasi-technical term in the philosophy for fasting. This makes sense in a context in which practices connected with food and drink (2:16); regulations about not handling, not tasting, not touching (2:20-21); and an emphasis on severe treatment of the body (2:23) are mentioned.[18]

This interpretation gains further strong support from the use of *tapeinophrosynē* as a technical term for fasting in Tertullian[19] and in *The Shepherd of Hermas.*[20] Cognate terms

18. See F. O. Francis's influential essay "Humility and Angelic Worship in Colossae," in *Conflict at Colossae,* ed. F. O. Francis and W. A. Meeks (Missoula, Mont.: Scholars Press, 1973) 163-95.
19. Tertullian *On Fasting* 12.
20. *The Shepherd of Hermas* Vision 3.10.6; Similitude 5.3.7.

are also employed in the LXX for "fasting" in contexts where the practice is an expression of abasement before God (e.g., Lev 16:29, 31; 23:27, 29, 32; Isa 58:3, 5; Ps 34:13-14). Fasting was also frequently a preparation for visionary experience and the reception of divine revelations (Dan 10:2-9; 4 Ezra 5:13, 20; 9:23-25; 2 Bar 5:7-9; 12:5-7; 43:3). Sometimes it is the preparation specifically for entrance into the heavenly realm.[21] All this is highly relevant to Col 2:18, where the two elements associated with fasting are "the worship of angels" and visionary experience.

But what was this "worship of angels"? It was often assumed that the phrase referred straightforwardly to humans worshiping angels, either in place of or alongside Christ or God. But if that were the case, it is very strange that the writer is not more forthright in his condemnation of such a practice instead of simply mentioning it in passing. An attractive case has been made by F. O. Francis,[22] however, that the phrase should be taken as involving a subjective rather than an objective genitive construction and thus refers to the angels' worship—that is, the worship in which the angels are engaged. What has this to do with humans? Fasting would be the preparation that enabled human beings to share in heavenly worship with angels. The notion of participation in angelic worship was a common one in Second Temple Judaism. It is found in apocalypses[23] and in the Qumran literature where the community on earth is described as having liturgical fellowship with the inhabitants of heaven.[24] It is by no means foreign to the NT (cf. 1 Cor 11:10; Heb 12:22-23; Revelation 4; 5).

On the other hand, C. E. Arnold has mounted a strong case for taking the objective genitive not as actual worship of angels by humans but as the writer's way of describing the philosophy's practice of invoking angels in order to deal with the threat of hostile powers. He relies heavily on the evidence of the Greek magical papyri, believing that, although most date to the third and fourth centuries CE, they reflect ideas and practices that go back to the first century CE and earlier and that are corroborated by the lead curse tablets and magical amulets in use in this earlier period.[25] He shows convincingly that in both Jewish and pagan sources angels were invoked for protection, for revelations, for cursing other humans, for warding off evil, and for dealing with evil spirit powers. They were intermediaries who were also associated with the planets and stars and were viewed as being active in influencing the fate of humans. Moreover, the evidence for a syncretistic mixing of Jewish angelic and pagan divine names in magical practice is clear. Elements of Jewish belief about angels and actual Jewish names for angels could be combined with pagan deity cults. Frequently the setting for invoking angels is a visionary experience and the invocation is connected with stringent purity regulations.

Arnold bolsters his argument by isolating the evidence of this type of veneration of

21. See *Apoc. Abr.* 9, 12; Philo *On the Life of Moses* 1:67-70; *On Dreams* 1:33-37.

22. F. O. Francis, "Humility and Angelic Worship in Col 2:18," in *Conflict at Colossae,* ed. F. O. Francis and W. A. Meeks (Missoula, Mont.: Scholars Press, 1973) 163-95. Francis has been followed by numerous recent scholars.

23. E.g., *2 Enoch* 20:3-4; *T. Job* 48-50; *Apoc. Abr.* 17; *Asc. Isa.* 7:37; 9:28, 31, 33.

24. Cf. 1QH 3:20-22; 11:10-12; 1QSb 4:25-26.

25. C. E. Arnold, *The Colossian Syncretism* WUNT 2/77 (Tübingen: J. C. B. Mohr, 1995) esp. 8-102.

angels in popular Judaism and in paganism in Asia Minor, claiming that the invocation of angels in the context of magical practices was a major feature of Phrygian-Lydian folk belief.[26] Add to this his demonstration that the term θρησκεία (*thrēskeia*) in the sense of worship rather than religion was overwhelmingly employed with the genitive for the object of worship, and his case for treating the phrase "the worship of angels" as the writer's polemical depiction of the practice of invoking angelic help becomes a very strong one indeed.[27] He rightly distinguishes between calling on, invoking, and praying to angels and an "angel cult" in which these intermediaries were the objects of adoration and worship. Although there is evidence of the latter in some of the pagan material, he finds none in Jewish or Christian texts and inscriptions. He shows easily, however, that the author of Colossians was not the only one to dub the veneration entailed by invocation as "worship of angels."[28]

In deciding between these two interpretations, we should recall that the evidence for taking the key phrase as a subjective genitive is very weak. In the two examples of *thrēskeia* in a subjective genitive construction that are usually cited (4 Macc 5:7 and Josephus *Antiquities of the Jews* 12.253), the reference is to the religion of the Jews, not to their act of worship; and there appear to be no texts where this term is employed for angelic activity. For this reason, and in the light of the case made by Arnold, it is more likely that "worship of angels" refers to the practice of invoking angels, a practice that the writer of Colossians, in line with his unfavorable evaluation of the philosophy as a whole, deems no better than worshiping angels. The practice may well have fulfilled the same functions that it did in popular magic—namely, coping with the threat of evil powers and providing special knowledge—but there is no need to follow the rest of Arnold's analysis and connect all of the philosophy's features with the magical tradition. It is one thing to see magic as being part of the religious milieu that helps to explain the appeal of the philosophy, but it is another to make magic the key that unlocks the door to the whole philosophy.

The next part of 2:18 fills out the reconstruction of the philosophy. What is insisted on by its proponents are fasting and veneration of angels "which he has seen when entering." The syntax could be construed as "entering into what he has seen," but it is more natural to take the neuter plural relative pronoun as modifying the whole of the preceding phrase, as in the previous verse, 2:17, and later in 3:6. The mention of "seeing" is a reference to what has been observed in visions. It may appear strange that fasting was part of what was seen in visions, but again such a feature was not uncommon in apocalyptic writings where instruction in fasting for the purpose of obtaining visions could itself be the subject of visions. The most likely reference of the participle translated "when entering" (ἐμβατεύων *embateuōn*) is to the visionary entering the heavenly realm. This, after all, is where a visionary is most likely to see and invoke angels; in apocalyptic writings, visionary experience was frequently conceived of in terms of the translation of the spirit and its

26. See ibid., 61-89.
27. Ibid., 91-95.
28. Ibid., 57-59.

entry into heavenly places (see, e.g., Rev 4:1-2).[29] The evidence of Col 2:18, then, indicates an insistence on fasting as preparation for visionary experience and invocation of angels in the heavenly realm.

The "Elemental Spirits of the Universe" and Dualistic Cosmology. Fasting, purity regulations, obtaining wisdom, visions, and even invocation of angels can all be found in various traditions within Judaism. Why not then simply conclude that the teaching being opposed was a particular strand of Judaism? This does not explain enough of the writer's emphases that appear to be directed against a strong dualistic strain in the philosophy. The stress in the hymnic material on Christ's agency in both creation and redemption and his reconciliation of heaven and earth, the insistence that God's presence and saving activity were in the physical body of Christ (1:22; 2:9), the discussion of "the body of flesh" in 2:11, and the treatment of the heavenly and earthly realms in 3:1-5 all suggest that the Jewish elements in the teaching had been assimilated into a framework that treated the earthly realm and the body as inferior and evil in contrast to the heavenly realm. In other words, the strands typical of Jewish apocalyptic writings and of popular Judaism now appear to be functioning within a Hellenistic dualistic cosmology. In addition, it is a reasonable inference from the letter's language about the principalities and powers (1:16, 20; 2:10, 15) that the philosophy held such heavenly powers to be threatening and hostile and in need of appeasement.[30] While belief in evil powers in heaven is, of course, found in Jewish apocalypses, their role as intermediaries who had to be placated is much more difficult to discover and far more closely akin to the function of similar powers in Hellenistic cosmology.

A key question in this regard is how to interpret the phrase τὰ στοιχεῖα τοῦ κόσμου (*ta stoicheia tou kosmou*) in 2:8, 20. A minority of scholars take the phrase to refer to elementary principles or rudimentary teachings of the world (NIV, "the basic principles of this world"). But since the genitive is "of the world" and not "of this world," "world" in this context is most naturally taken to denote the cosmos.

The term *stoicheia* itself means first of all the component parts of a series and came to be applied to the physical components of the cosmos—earth, fire, water, and air (see 2 Pet 3:10, 12).[31] In Hellenistic thought these parts were believed to be under the control of spirit powers. Together with the stars and heavenly bodies they could be conceived of as personal forces who controlled the fate of humans. For this reason the majority of interpreters opt for a translation such as "the elemental spirits of the universe" (NRSV). This also fits well the context of thought in the letter, for elsewhere the writer emphasizes Christ's supremacy and victory over just such spiritual agencies. It is significant also that,

---

29. See also *1 Enoch* 14:8; 71:1; *2 Enoch* 3:1; 36:1-2; *T. Abr.* 7-10; *Apoc. Abr.* 12, 15-16, 30; *T. Levi* 2:5-7, 10 ; 5:1, 3; 2 Bar 6:4.

30. J. D. G. Dunn, *The Epistles to the Colossians and to Philemon,* NIGTC (Grand Rapids: Eerdmans, 1996) 184n. 35, admits that the weakest point of his hypothesis that the philosophy came from the Jewish synagogue is its failure to correlate such material satisfactorily and that this evidence provides the best support for the view that the philosophy was syncretistic.

31. See also Diogenes Laertius 7, 136-37; Philo *Who Is the Heir of Divine Things?* 134.

when the same phrase was employed by Paul in Gal 4:3, 9, it was to warn Gentile Christians that to turn to the law would be equivalent to returning to their previous enslavement to the *stoicheia*, who are linked with their pagan deities, designated by Paul as "beings that by nature are not gods" (Gal 4:8).

One difficulty for this interpretation is that explicit use of *stoicheia* to refer to personified cosmic forces outside the NT is first found later in the *Testament of Solomon* 8:1-4; 18:1-5, where they are described as the cosmic rulers of darkness (see also Col 1:13). Moreover, the date of Pseudo-Callisthenes, in which King Nectabenos of Egypt is said to control the cosmic elemental spirits by his magical arts, is uncertain.[32] Given other pointers in the direction of such a reference, there is no reason why the NT might not be the first extant source for this explicit usage. Arnold, however, claims that these references and those in the magical papyri[33] belong to traditions that predate the actual writing and originate in the first century CE or earlier.[34] In any case, the book of Wisdom could earlier speak of the elements, referring to earth, air, fire, and water (Wis 7:15), and then condemn Gentiles for treating these elements as gods: "They supposed that either fire or wind or swift air, or the circle of the stars, or turbulent water, or the luminaries of heaven were the gods that rule the world" (Wis 13:2 NRSV). Philo also speaks of the *stoicheia* as "powers"[35] and reports worship of them as named deities.[36] Jewish apocalyptic literature had also already paved the way for this development by associating angels closely with the elements and heavenly bodies.[37]

In all probability, in the philosophy against which the letter is directed these elemental spirits were classed with the angels and were seen as controlling the heavenly realm and as posing a threat both to human well-being and to access to the divine presence. It was thought that an effective means of placating such powers was the rigorous subduing of the body in order to gain visionary experience of the heavenly dimension and to invoke the assistance of good angels in dealing with the hostile spirits. Through such visions also special knowledge and access to the divine presence could be obtained. This program as a whole, claiming to be wisdom (see 2:8, 23) and incorporating elements of Jewish calendrical and dietary law observances (2:16), appears to have been offered to the readers to supplement the apostolic gospel they had heard, so that in the view of the writer it undermined the sufficiency of what God had done in Christ. It reduced Christ to just another intermediary between humans and God, to one among a number of links to the heavenly dimension, one among a number of means of dealing with the hostile powers.

One of the chief concerns of Hellenistic religious thought was how a person could escape from the lower earthly realm and reach the heavenly world and the divine. Usually the purified soul was believed to ascend after death and to remain above. It was possible,

---

32. Pseudo-Callisthenes I.12.1.
33. See PGM IV.475-829; XXXIX.18-21.
34. Arnold, *The Colossian Syncretism,* 170-73.
35. Philo *On the Eternity of the World* 107-9.
36. Philo *On the Contemplative Life* 3-4.
37. See 4 Ezra 6:3; *Jub.* 2:2; *1 Enoch* 60:11-12; *2 Enoch* 4:1; *T. Abr.* 13:11.

however, to experience this ascent of the soul during one's lifetime and to enter the heavenly sphere through various ecstatic experiences.[38] It was, of course, primarily the mystery cults that fostered this way of ascent. Often such cults demanded strict discipline, but their attraction was that by such means and through initiation into secret rites they promised freedom from the evil body, enlightenment, privileged knowledge, access to the heavenly realm, and union with the god or goddess. As people came to the view that, despite the apparent order of the heavenly regions, there were powers in them opposed to humanity, not only mystery religions but also magic flourished in order to influence the cosmic powers favorably. The philosophy being advocated in the Lycus Valley area, in which Colossae was located, would have spoken to these same needs, and, with certain features analogous to concerns of the mystery cults and magic traditions, would have seemed attractive for the same reason.

The "Philosophy" as Syncretistic. Despite the attempts of some scholars to avoid this conclusion, it seems clear from 2:18-19 that the one insisting on fasting and invocation of angels through visionary experience is viewed by the writer as a believer who is in some spiritual danger. This person is "puffed up without cause through a fleshly mind" (2:18) and is "not holding fast to the head, from whom the whole body . . . grows with a growth that is from God" (2:19 NRSV). The participle "holding" (κρατῶν *kratōn*) is singular in its Greek form and so does not refer to the readers but to the same person who was in view with the earlier singular form of the participle "insisting" (θέλων *thelōn*). It would make no sense for the writer to depict someone who made no claim to a relationship to Christ in the first place as not holding fast to Christ. This factor alone would appear to rule out viewing the philosophy simply as Judaism. Nor is there any evidence for use of the verb "to hold" meaning "to have an initial intellectual grasp," which would be required on the hypothesis that a Cynic critic of Christian worship is being described. Instead the proponent(s) of the teaching have taken a number of elements from Judaism and the Christian gospel and linked these with typical cosmological concerns from the Hellenistic world. It is quite plausible that a Hellenistic Jew who had left the synagogue to join a Pauline congregation or a Gentile convert who had had some previous contact with the synagogue would advocate such a philosophy, and the writer evidently was concerned that it might appeal to others among his preponderantly Gentile Christian readers. To label such teaching Hellenistic Jewish syncretism is not, therefore, simply an "easy both-and solution"[39] but an eminently plausible and fitting description of its components.

Obviously the Pauline gospel had a base in particular congregations in the Phrygian area, which included the Lycus Valley. It is equally clear that there was a strong Jewish presence in the area, because in 200 BCE Antiochus III had settled two thousand Jewish families in Lydia and Phrygia. It is not at all surprising, then, to find knowledge of specific features of Judaism in the syncretism that could have been picked up from the teaching

38. See especially Plutarch *The Obsolescence of Oracles* 39-40; *Corpus Hermeticum* XI.20.
39. Dunn, *The Epistles to the Colossians and to Philemon,* 31.

of local synagogues. Jewish cultic regulations and calendrical observances have a role, but it remains significant that there is no mention of the law as such, as would surely be expected if the teaching were a straightforward variety of Judaism. It is also significant in this regard that the writer dismisses such elements as simply human tradition. This does not sound like the Paul of Galatians or Romans dealing with the law and having to account in his arguments for the claim that such observances were commanded by God, nor is it like the use of the charge of human tradition in Mark 7:1-13, where it is directed against the oral tradition. In addition, circumcision is mentioned in 2:11, but it functions in the writer's argument primarily as a metaphor for dealing with the physical body as a whole. The cultic and calendrical items and the interest in visionary experience also found in Judaism appear, then, to have been put to markedly different use in the philosophy.

The concepts of heaven and earth played an important part in Jewish thought, the apocalyptic writings included an increasing emphasis on the transcendent realm, and Hellenistic Judaism evidenced some similar cosmological concerns to those suggested for the philosophy. Yet in none of these strands was there the strong cosmological dualism that Colossians appears to combat. Such spatial concepts, however, readily lent themselves to a dualistic framework, which, as we have seen, was current in Greco-Roman cosmological speculation. Still, cosmological dualism and an emphasis on special knowledge do not mean that there should be an identification of the philosophy with Gnosticism. At most what is suggested are certain "gnosticizing" tendencies. It is not until the Gnosticism attested in the Nag Hammadi documents that some of the letter's terminology is found in a clearly identifiable gnostic schema.

THE LETTER'S MAIN THEOLOGICAL THEMES

The writer does his theological reflection in response to the specific dangers he sees in the rival teaching and employs traditional materials in the process. Due attention will be given in the commentary to the way these elements shape the writer's thought, but it would be a mistake to reduce the letter's theology simply to the writer's mode of theologizing. This mode has produced the letter as we now have it, and it is the assertions of that final form that have made their impact on the development of Pauline thought and on the thinking of later Christians, however much or little we think we can know about the details of the preceding interaction with the philosophy or the writer's modifications of the traditional materials he employs to make his points. The following brief depiction of some of the letter's dominant theological emphases will concentrate primarily on the product of the writer's theologizing in the conviction that it is with these claims that contemporary readers of the letter need to engage. Although, for the sake of convenience, the depiction is divided into separate topics, it should be clear that in the theology of the letter these are inextricably interwoven and that what connects them is the assessment of the person and work of Christ. In the theology of Colossians, christology is central and everything else flows from the belief that Christ is the key to the understanding of reality.

The Apostolic Gospel. The writer addresses the situation faced by his readers with a combination of confidence in the sufficiency of the Pauline gospel and a pastoral concern that the readers should not weaken in their allegiance to this gospel. The theology of the letter consists in reflections on the implications of this apostolic gospel. It does so because the writer is convinced that the gospel is the word of truth (1:5), conveying reliable insight into God's purposes for humanity and the world through what has taken place in Christ. As such, it is also the conveyor of hope and of God's grace (1:5-6) and can be spoken of in a personified and dynamic fashion as bearing fruit and growing both among the readers and in the whole world (1:6). It is depicted as universal in its scope and spread ("proclaimed to every creature under heaven," 1:23), and its dynamic quality is again in view when the readers are exhorted to petition God to open a door for "the word" (4:3), to provide opportunities for the gospel to continue its progress. As the "word of God" (1:25), the gospel has its source in God, and, as "the word of Christ" (3:16), it has Christ as its content.

Another synonym for "gospel" is the term "mystery," with its connotation of a previously hidden purpose of God that has now been disclosed. The content of the mystery is Christ among you—that is, among the Gentiles (1:26-27)—or simply Christ (2:2; 4:3). This exclusive focus on Christ as being at the heart of the gospel message is reinforced when the notion of proclaiming the gospel can be expressed simply as proclaiming him (1:28). The gospel not only has at its center a person but it also entails received teaching about this person. In two places this is the force of the phrase "the faith" (1:23; 2:7), and in the latter context the formulation "Christ Jesus the Lord" encapsulates the tradition that has been received by the readers (2:6).

The gospel is the apostolic or, to be more precise, the Pauline gospel. The letter makes clear the intimate connection between the apostle and the gospel. The opening words provide the credentials for Paul's exposition of the gospel in response to the rival teaching. As apostle, he is the authorized representative of the one at the center of the message (1:1). But it is 1:23c–2:5 that underlines that, as Paul played his unique role in its missionary proclamation, he became the suffering servant of the gospel who participated in the same pattern of suffering experienced by Christ. Service of the gospel was also stewardship of the mystery on the part of Paul; just as the gospel has a teaching content and is universal in its scope, so also Paul's stewardship of it involves a teaching role that is universal in its reach, "teaching every human being" (1:28). His commitment to this gospel ministry entailed the strenuous effort of the athlete in a contest (1:29) and is symbolized by the chains of his imprisonment for the mystery of Christ (4:3, 18). Paul's service of the gospel is carried on by the team of his associates and coworkers. Epaphras was the initial link between the gospel the readers received and Paul (1:7), and he continues this role (4:12-13), while Tychicus and Onesimus have a similar function as further links with the apostle (4:7-9).

Christology. In responding to the rival teaching, the writer did not limit himself to criticisms of it; his positive recommendation of the Pauline gospel sets out some of the most profound reflections on the person of Christ to be found in the NT. The focus on Christ is such that there is almost no mention of the Spirit (but see 1:8-9; 3:16). Christ as the center of God's purposes and, therefore, the key to reality is what, according to the hymn, holds the cosmos together; but this notion of Christ is also, appropriately, what holds the thought of the letter together.

The most distinctive feature of the christology of Colossians is its sustained treatment of Christ in relation to both the creation and the reconciliation of the cosmos. Christ is not simply to be seen as the firstborn of all creation (1:15); rather, all things were created in, through, and for him (1:16). God is the Creator, but Christ is both an agent of creation and, more than that, its goal. The climactic "for him" in 1:16 adds to the assertions of 1 Cor 8:6 about Christ's agency that he is also the one to whom all creation is directed, the very purpose of its existence. Not only so, but all things hold together in him (1:17); their integrity and coherence depend on his role. The claim is not that it is some rational principle or even personified Wisdom that holds the key to the created universe but that it is the person believers confess as Christ who does so. The hymnic material does not explain why, although Christ has always been the agent and sustainer of creation, it is in need of reconciliation. Presupposing that need, it underlines that the one who was firstborn, agent, and goal in creation is also appropriately firstborn, agent, and goal of reconciliation in the new creation.

One major implication of this belief in the cosmic Christ is that he is sovereign over the powers of evil seen as threatening human life. In 1:15-20 such cosmic powers are depicted as being created in and for Christ, as having fallen out of harmony, and as being reconciled through Christ's death. Christ is, therefore, head over every ruler and authority (2:10). Whereas the hymnic material speaks of the powers' reintegration through Christ's death as a way of making peace and a reconciliation, in 2:15 what took place through the cross is described as stripping them of their power and triumphing over them. It looks very much, then, as if the making of peace is to be interpreted in terms of pacification. In the language of worship of 1:20 the hostile powers are depicted as already reconciled, but 1:13 has also made clear that the power of darkness is still operative and opposed to Christ's rule. The letter's thought about Christ's relation to the cosmic powers appears, then, to share the Pauline eschatological perspective with its "already" and "not yet." Through Christ the powers have already been pacified and reintegrated into God's purposes, and believers can already appropriate this achievement, but the full recognition of their new situation by the powers themselves awaits the eschaton.

A formulation about Christ in cosmic terms, echoing the thought of 1:15-20, is employed in an ecclesiological context in 3:11: "Christ is all and in all." In the first part of the verse, there is an adaptation of the baptismal formulation, found also in Gal 3:28 and 1 Cor 12:13, which states that in the new humanity there are no longer ethnic, cultural, and social distinctions. Rather, adds the second part, Christ is all and in all. If he has this status in the cosmos, then he most certainly has it in the church that is the focus for and the medium of his pervasive presence in the cosmos. Since Christ is now absolutely everything, all that matters, the old human categories of evaluation are rendered insignificant.

Colossians also characteristically describes Christ's status in terms of lordship. In line with assertions in the undisputed Pauline letters, it assumes that, by virtue of his exaltation to the right hand of God (3:1), Christ is Lord. He is now the one to whom believers are accountable (1:10) and owe absolute allegiance (2:6; 3:17). Even everyday life in the household is to reflect this relationship (3:18–4:1). Indeed, in the motivation slaves are to have, "fearing the Lord," Christ substitutes for Yahweh in Jewish scriptural terminology (3:22).

There are also other formulations used of God that are functionally equivalent to those employed of Christ. Being nourished by Christ the head is the same as receiving growth from God (2:19), and the "kingdom of his beloved Son" (1:13) is equivalent to the "kingdom of God" (4:11). Whereas the undisputed Pauline letters talk of creation as "for him" with reference to God (Rom 11:36; 1 Cor 8:6), Colossians uses this phrase of Christ (1:16); and while the undisputed letters of Paul speak of God as all in all (1 Cor 15:28), Colossians employs the same language of Christ (3:11).

Colossians depicts Christ's relationship to God in terms of oneness yet distinction. The Lord Jesus Christ still has a Father (1:3) and is the beloved Son (1:13). He is not the Creator but the agent and goal of creation. At the same time, in 1:15-20, his agency is portrayed in terms of Wisdom with the implication that all the qualities of Wisdom as God immanent in creation are now to be found in Christ (see also 2:3). The expression "image of the invisible God" (1:15) sums up the relationship well. Christ is the one who uniquely makes God's presence visible and God's purposes effective. Colossians does not call Christ "God," but the striking formulations of 1:19 and 2:9 put the two in the closest possible relationship and provide an equivalent to the Johannine notion of incarnation: All the fullness of God dwells in Christ bodily.

The letter's combination of universalism and particularism is related to its christology. On the one hand, it sets out the universal horizons of Christ's work and claims as Lord. Yet, on the other hand, it presses the necessity of faith in this particular person in whom God is uniquely revealed for entry into the new humanity.

Soteriology. The actual terminology of "salvation" is not employed in Colossians, but the language of rescue and transference is found in 1:13. Here the divine rescue act is from one dominion to another, from the power of darkness to the kingdom of the beloved Son. Both deliverance and redemption (1:14) stand for God's act of liberating humanity. Through Christ, believers are freed from the hold of the cosmic powers and their regulations (2:15-16, 20). Their liberation is experienced at present in terms of the forgiveness of sins (1:14; 2:13; 3:13), an emphasis needed because the opposing philosophy engendered a sense of guilt about life in the body that served to reinforce the hold of the powers.

The "once . . . now" contrast underlines the transference from plight to solution that God effects (1:21-22; 3:6-8). The depiction of the plight from which rescue is needed includes alienation and hostility (1:21), the old humanity and its vices (3:5-9), the wrath of God on this disobedient way of life (3:6), the flesh in its negative ethical sense (2:18, 23), and the death caused by sin (2:13). The depiction of the new situation and its benefits brought about through Christ includes reconciliation (1:22); the new humanity, both individual and corporate (3:10-11); and its virtues (3:12-14); the inheritance of God's people (1:12; 3:24); access to the heavenly realm (3:1-2); and being made alive (2:13). Among this variety of ways of portraying what God has achieved for humanity, reconciliation stands out. It appears in the hymnic material as the salvific image for God's accomplishment in Christ on a cosmic scale, where it is reinforced with the language of peacemaking (1:20), and it is this image that is then specifically applied to the readers (1:21-22). Later, too, they will be exhorted to appropriate the peace achieved by Christ in their corporate living (3:15).

The other major benefit highlighted in the letter can be termed wisdom (1:9, 28; 2:3, 23; 3:16; 4:5), knowledge (1:6, 9-10, 27; 2:2-3; 3:10), or understanding (1:9; 2:2). So God's rescue act in Christ also entails a revelation, a disclosure of God's previously hidden purposes in Christ, into which one can be given increasing insight. The mystery that was hidden has now been revealed to God's people (1:26-27), and the writer wants them to obtain "all the riches of assured understanding, the knowledge of God's mystery" (2:2).

Both the death and the resurrection of Christ play their part in the divine deliverance that produces the new humanity and the benefits it enjoys. Christ's death is spoken of as "the blood of his cross" (1:20), is seen as occurring in his body of flesh through death (1:22), and is described through the image of circumcision (2:11). Three further images describe how in Christ's death God overcame humanity's sense of condemnation: erasing the accusing record, setting it aside, and nailing it to the cross (2:14). It is not surprising that, when it comes to the reversal of death and the experience of new life, Christ's resurrection is at the fore as the means by which these are achieved for humanity. His resurrection makes him the firstborn from the dead, the first among brothers and sisters who will follow in his footsteps as they, too, are raised (1:18). Indeed, through union with Christ in his resurrection, they can already experience what it is to be made alive by God (2:12-13). Being raised with Christ also entails sharing his exaltation—thereby being given access to the heavenly realm—and participating in the future revelation in glory of Christ's life (3:1-4).

Eschatology. The letter's perspective on God's purposes for history and the cosmos provides the framework and presupposition for what it says about Christ and his agency in the rescuing of humanity. Colossians shares this basic eschatological framework with the undisputed Pauline letters in which Paul had in turn modified the Jewish eschatology he had inherited in the light of what he now believed to have taken place in Christ. Both these letters and Colossians see what God has done in Christ as having affected the whole cosmos with its two parts: heaven (in which there are also evil powers) and earth (the primary setting for humanity). They also see the time between Christ's death and resurrection and the eschaton as a period of tension between aspects of the blessings of the end times that can be experienced in the present and those that remain future. In Colossians, the stress is clearly on the present aspects. The decisive act that brings about the reintegration of the cosmos has already taken place, and believers can already appropriate its consequences so that they are no longer under the domination of the powers. Yet the powers continue to exist in their hostility to God's purposes and to pose a threat, so clearly the full realization of Christ's victory over them is not yet and is reserved for the eschaton.

Similarly, in response to the alternative teaching, Colossians emphasizes what has already taken place in believers' relationship of union with Christ. Romans 6 may well contain the notion of participation in Christ's resurrection, but it does not talk of this participation as having already taken place. Colossians does speak of believers as having been raised with Christ (2:12-13; 3:1). Indeed, it can go so far as to depict believers' lives as being linked with the life of the exalted Christ in heaven (3:2-3). Although the writer can appeal to a sense of urgency about the use of time (4:5), there is no imminent expectation of the end in this letter. Yet, as the writer moves away from thanksgiving and polemic to paraenesis or ethical exhortation, future references appear: negatively, to the coming wrath of God (3:6), and positively, to the reward of the inheritance (3:24).

Yet if Colossians can state that cosmic reconciliation has already been achieved and believers have already been raised with Christ, one might still want to ask whether anything substantial is left for the future. Crucial here is the assertion of 3:4 that Christ, who is believers' life, will be revealed, and believers will be revealed with him in glory. But will this be only the revelation of a present state of affairs, or will it involve some future change? Three considerations suggest that the latter option is in view. First, in 1:18 Christ has been described as the "firstborn from the dead" (πρωτότοκος ἐκ τῶν νεκρῶν *prōtotokos ek tōn nekrōn*). The clear implication is that, just as his resurrection was in bodily form, so also those who participate in the restored creation will experience a bodily resurrection from the dead. Second, the writer of Colossians stands in the Pauline school, and in Paul where life is found in an eschatological context it is equivalent to the resurrection or transformation of the body (Rom 8:11; 1 Cor 15:45; 2 Cor 5:4). Third, and similarly, if Colossians is interpreted as being in basic continuity with Paul, then, although it does not explicitly mention the resurrection of the body and the transformation of the cosmos, it is hard not to see these clear connotations of "glory" carrying over from Paul (Rom 8:17-23; 1 Cor 15:40-43; Phil 3:20-21).

The present and future aspects and the emphasis on eschatology in Colossians are summed up in its use of the term "hope" (ἐλπίς *elpis*). By definition hope entails some expectation about the future, and that temporal connotation is retained despite this letter's primary stress on its present content and heavenly dimension. Believers' hope is at present secured in heaven and so can be seen as foundational for their faith and love (1:4-5). Because Christ is the hope of glory (1:27), it is not surprising that this hope can be said to be located in heaven, where Christ now is until his revelation (3:1-4). Hope is closely identified with both Christ and the gospel (1:23). This is presumably because hope stands for confident assurance on the basis of what has already been achieved and is precisely what, in the writer's view, would be undermined by the philosophy.

Christian Existence in the Church and in the World. Believers' identity is dependent on their relationship with Christ. The primary way of viewing that relationship in Colossians is in terms of union with Christ, which is also the significance of the initiation rite of baptism (2:12). Believers can be said to be "in Christ" or "in the Lord" (1:2, 4, 28; 2:6-7), and the motif of incorporation into Christ is the thread running through 2:9-15. In union with Christ, readers have fullness (2:10). In him they were spiritually circumcised (2:11), and "with him" they died (2:20), were buried (2:12), were raised (2:12; 3:1), and were made alive (2:13). Since Christ is viewed as at present above, at the right hand of God, believers' union with him gives them a heavenly orientation that then is to be worked out on earth (3:1-2, 5). The relationship is such that believers' lives can be described as hidden with Christ in God (3:3); indeed, their life is Christ (3:4). Christian identity is inextricably bound up with the Christ who has died, been raised, is exalted in heaven, and is to be revealed.

Union with Christ is not a static relationship. It is seen in terms of growth (1:10; 2:19), leading to perfection or maturity (1:28; 3:14; 4:12). Those who are united to Christ have been filled (2:10), but the writer can also pray that they may be filled with the knowledge of God's will (1:9). Again there is an "already" and a "not yet" pattern to Christian existence. Believers have been given what is needed, but they must also appropriate this if they are to move toward their fullest potential. They have received Christ Jesus the Lord, but are exhorted to continue to live their lives in him (2:6-7) and are warned about the consequences of not continuing and holding fast (1:23; 2:19).

To live one's life in Christ the Lord (2:6) is to acknowledge his cosmic lordship as laying claim on all of life (3:17). The philosophy focused on specific rituals and on special days and abstinence from certain foods, but the sphere of Christ's lordship and, therefore, of obedient Christian response to that lordship is as broad as life itself. Everyday relationships in the most significant social and economic unit, the household, are singled out to illustrate what it means for the rule of the Christ who is Lord of the cosmos to be brought to bear within the structures of this world in which believers find themselves (3:18–4:1).

Believers have become new persons (3:10). This new humanity is not simply an individual but a corporate entity that transcends the divisions of the old humanity (3:11) and is an anticipation of the new creation as a whole. Reflecting its significant place in the writer's thought, in the Christ hymn the church is in fact mentioned before the reconciliation of the cosmos (1:18). Although Christ is the head over every ruler and authority, only the church, and not these powers or the cosmos as such, is designated his body (1:18,

24; 2:19; 3:15). Because of this special relationship to Christ, the church is the precursor of the reconciled cosmos. As Christ's body, it is distinctively related to its head, deriving its life and growth from him (2:19). Set in a cosmic context, Christ's body in Colossians is seen as a universal phenomenon. Similarly, Colossians employs the term ἐκκλησία (*ekklēsia*), for the assembly of the church with both a universal (1:18, 24) and a local (4:15-16) reference.

This church is a worshiping community. In implicit contrast to the veneration of angels and the ascetic regulations practiced by the philosophy, prominent in its worship are the word of Christ, the teaching of which inculcates wisdom, and thankful singing to God (3:16). The virtues that are to characterize the lives of its members are those that promote harmony and unity in the community (3:12-13). Peace, the reconciling activity of Christ that has been celebrated as affecting the cosmos (1:20), is to be appropriated particularly in the new community and allowed to rule (3:15). And what is necessary above all, if this community is to be what it is meant to be, is love (3:14; see also 1:4, 7).

A Theology of Wisdom and Grace. If setting out some of the themes of the letter reminds us that its theology transcends the setting that produced it, such a procedure may have its own dangers in obscuring this theology's essential characteristics. Perhaps what makes Colossians distinctive is its combination of a wisdom theology with a polemical theology of grace. Both elements are a result of the confrontation with the rival philosophy.

The philosophy's claims to wisdom (see 2:23) have provided the catalyst for a development of the Pauline gospel in terms of wisdom. This theme is explicit in each of the major sections of the letter's persuasive argument, occurring in the *exordium,* in each of the three sections of the *probatio,* and in the *peroratio.* In the first part of the letter, the intercessory prayer report reveals the concern that the recipients be "filled with the knowledge of God's will in all spiritual wisdom and understanding" (1:9), and the hymnic material in 1:15-20 is dominated by the application to Christ of the language and concepts associated with wisdom in the Hellenistic Jewish tradition.

In the body of the letter there is first a depiction of Paul and his gospel in terms of wisdom. Paul himself is humanity's great Christian wisdom teacher, "warning and teaching everyone in all wisdom" (1:28). The content of his gospel is "Christ himself, in whom are hidden all the treasures of wisdom and knowledge" (2:2-3). Next, in more direct interaction with the philosophy, the writer claims that its teachings may have a reputation for wisdom in its "worship of angels," fasting, and severity to the body. In fact, however, these are of no value in what he deems to be the real issue: dealing with the flesh in the negative sense of the sphere of humanity's opposition to God (2:23). Over against this otherworldly and ascetic wisdom, he then provides his own teaching on practical wisdom that is designed to deal with the sins of the old humanity. In the course of this, he makes clear that, because of their relationship to Christ, believers are to play their own role in such wise teaching of the community: "teach and admonish one another in all wisdom" (3:16). Finally, in the concluding exhortations, he can summarize the practical advice he has given, particularly in the household code, in terms of living wisely in regard to outsiders (4:5).

So wisdom features at all levels in the letter's theology. Christ embodies wisdom; Paul, supremely, but also all other believers are recipients and then teachers of wisdom; and Christian living is walking in wisdom. The wisdom christology of the hymn leads to the cosmic and univeral dimensions of the letter's theology. These in turn color the depiction of believers' relation to the exalted Christ. United to this Christ, they have a genuine heavenly orientation that works itself out in their lives on earth. James 3:13-18 contrasts two sorts of wisdom: a wisdom that is from above, displaying itself in a life of goodness and gentleness on earth, and a wisdom that is earthly, unspiritual, and devilish, characterized by envy and selfish ambition. Colossians can be seen as presenting, in contrast to what it regards as earthly wisdom, a wisdom that has its source where Christ is—above— but that then becomes firmly earthed in the everyday. The letter constitutes its writer's own wise teaching. What is more, he provides this in the typical wisdom mode of paraenesis, as he affirms, corrects, and exhorts in the attempt to produce other mature practitioners of wisdom.

This wisdom theology is universal in scope; however, its conviction that God's activity in Christ is the wisdom that provides the key to the understanding of reality is an exclusive one. At this point the polemical setting leaves a lasting mark on the theology. This version of the Pauline gospel sees itself as antithetical to other types of claims. Those espoused by the philosophy, according to the theological perspective of Colossians, should not be set alongside its own in a "both/and" relationship.

Colossians is polemical, because, like the Paul of Galatians in a different set of circumstances, it will not allow God's gracious activity in Christ to be undermined. To add new practices and regulations to the gospel is to suggest not only that believers are disqualified unless they adhere to them but also, more fundamentally, that what God has already done in Christ is deficient. Colossians is essentially Pauline in having none of this. In its defense of the apostolic gospel, Colossians does not make grace a separate theme so much as an underlying presupposition that it reinforces through both the content and the mode of its theologizing. This presupposition is made explicit in the very first mention of the gospel, where to hear the gospel and to comprehend the grace of God are equated (1:5-6). From then on, the insistence on what God has already achieved in Christ for the cosmos and for the church and the "realized eschatology," with its stress on the present experience of the benefits of end-time salvation, are in the service of this gospel of grace. This is also the force of the repetition of the motif of thanksgiving at key places throughout the letter (1:3, 11-12; 2:7; 3:15-17; 4:2). Christian thanksgiving is nothing other than the grateful recognition of the grace of God in Christ at the center of life. The mode of argumentation of Colossians is also in line with this element of its theology. Only after an extended thanksgiving section do the exhortations follow, and these are punctuated by the reminders to give thanks. For Colossians the gospel is grace, and no response to it can depart from that foundation by adding human achievements as a requirement. Instead, authentic Christian living is motivated by a response to and empowered by an appropriation of the undeserved favor of God in Christ.

Colossians is frequently referred to as having a bridging role between the undisputed and the disputed letters in the Pauline corpus. If its wisdom content and mode signal a significant development in the articulation of the Pauline gospel, its polemical theology of grace makes clear its essential continuity with that same gospel.

AUTHOR AND ADDRESSEES

Whereas there is widespread scholarly agreement that Ephesians and the Pastoral Epistles are pseudonymous, more dispute surrounds Colossians and 2 Thessalonians. Colossians is closely related to Ephesians. Although a tiny minority of scholars hold that Colossians is in some way dependent on Ephesians, for the majority it is clear that the dependency is the other way and that the author of Ephesians has used Colossians as the model on which he builds.[40] On this view, the relationship between Colossians and Ephesians plays no role in the debate about the authorship of the former.

In this debate the argument revolves around judgments on style, vocabulary, indications of what looks like a later setting than Paul's lifetime, and changes in theological perspective. In the case of Colossians, as with the other disputed letters, no one argument is decisive, although many consider that the issue of style comes very close to being so. Instead, it is a matter of a cumulative argument involving all these factors; of course, judgment will differ about the weight of any individual factor.

Colossians, however, allows a possible mediating position. Since it names both Paul and Timothy as it authors, some have suggested that the actual author could have been Timothy, writing either just before or just after Paul's death.[41] Nonetheless, the very fact that scholars opt for this solution indicates that they have accepted that the style differs so much from the undisputed Pauline letters that it cannot be attributed directly to Paul.

The introduction of the question of Paul's use of amanuenses, or secretaries, whom he may also in some instances have named as co-authors, complicates the issue of authorship still further. If secretaries are given the maximum possible role in the writing of the letters, this could mean that the only writings we actually have from Paul himself are the few brief passages he claims to have written in his own hand. If it is simply urged that we take the naming of co-authors with full seriousness, then Timothy is the co-author of 2 Corinthians, Philippians, and Philemon and, along with Silvanus, of 1 and 2 Thessalonians. Yet, with the exception of 2 Thessalonians, these are all among the undisputed letters, the comparison with which has caused the authorship of Colossians to be questioned in

40. For a detailed discussion of the relation between Colossians and Ephesians and its role in the debate about the authorship of Ephesians, see A. T. Lincoln, *Ephesians* WBC (Dallas: Word, 1990) xlvii-lxxiii.

41. See, e.g., E. Schweizer, *The Letter to the Colossians* (Minneapolis: Augsburg, 1982); Dunn, *The Epistles to the Colossians and to Philemon.*

the first place. Clearly modern notions of authorship should not simply be assumed in regard to Paul's letters; on the other hand, we have no evidence of how Paul actually used any secretaries or co-authors. It appears best, then, to proceed cautiously with the criteria listed above in order to build a cumulative case that would indicate whether or not it is likely that Colossians was written in Paul's lifetime and that he put his name to it.

In regard to style, W. Bujard has provided the most thorough analysis of the letter, concluding that its style is not Paul's.[42] What is most telling here is that the grammar and syntax of Colossians differ so much from the undisputed Pauline letters. Colossians lacks the adversative, causal, consecutive, recitative, copulative, and disjunctive conjunctions that are characteristic of Paul's style. Instead it is characterized by long sentences with relative clauses, nouns linked in genitive constructions, and the piling up of synonyms. There are some thirty cases of amassed synonyms in Colossians. It also lacks completely the articular infinitive, a construction frequently employed by Paul to represent a dependent clause. Whereas Paul uses repetition to develop his argument in a logical direction, the repetitions in Colossians mostly function to build rhetorical effect. Colossians employs "which is" (ὅ ἐστιν *ho estin*) as a special idiom five times (1:24, 27; 2:10, 17; 3:14), a feature absent in the undisputed letters. Such differences bear on a writer's personal style. It is one thing to say that in order to address a new situation writers are likely to adapt their ideas or take on new vocabulary, but it is quite another thing to assert that they would abandon their characteristic style of writing for some other. There is nothing about the setting of the Colossian letter that would demand such a major shift in style.

The argument about vocabulary is less decisive. There are thirty-four words that do not occur elsewhere in the NT (*hapax legomena*) and a further ten that would be found only in Colossians were it not for the fact that they occur in Ephesians, which is dependent on Colossians. Also significant is the absence of so many key Pauline terms, such as "sin" (in the singular), "to believe," "promise," "law," "freedom," "boasting," the "justification" and "salvation" word groups, and, despite the actual address, the absence of the vocative "brothers and sisters" that is employed liberally in the body of the undisputed letters. Quite striking is the uncharacteristic combination of characteristic Pauline terms, so that, whereas "blood" and "cross" and "body" and "flesh" appear separately in the undisputed letters, here we have the phrases "blood of the cross" (1:20) and "body of flesh" (1:22; 2:11).

The changes of theological emphasis in the letter do not appear to be as decisive for authorship as some scholars claim. A number of these different emphases could be reasonably attributed to Paul's addressing his message to a different pastoral setting. So, for instance, the notion of realized eschatology using spatial categories is far more to the fore than in the undisputed Pauline letters, with this letter spelling out explicitly that believers have already been raised with Christ (2:12; 3:1) and stressing that hope is already present in heaven (1:5). Yet, it can be argued that these notions are in basic continuity

42. W. Bujard, *Stilanalystische Untersuchungen zum Kolosserbrief als Beitrag zur Methodik von Sprachverglechen* (Göttingen: Vandenhoeck & Ruprecht, 1973). This work is summarized briefly in English in M. Kiley, *Colossians as Pseudepigraphy* (Sheffield: JSOT, 1986) 51-59.

with Paul's eschatology and are developed here because of the concern of the philosophy with cosmological questions and the need to assure believers of the security of their salvation. Similarly, the focus on a cosmic christology and the depiction of Christ's work of salvation in relation to the cosmic powers and the cosmos as a whole can be explained as the apostle's development of earlier strands in his teaching in the face of the philosophy's particular interests.

On the other hand, while Colossians does mention the future revelation of Christ in glory, there is no mention of the imminence of the parousia or the eschaton at all, and the Spirit is mentioned explicitly only once (1:8). There is no reason why the interaction with the philosophy should have caused these characteristic emphases to disappear to this extent. Their almost complete absence gives a quite different dynamic to the relation between eschatology and ethics than that found in the undisputed letters of Paul. In those letters, end-time events frequently shape ethical appeals and the Spirit and the fruit and gifts of the Spirit are seen as the present manifestation of the salvation of the end times among believers. In addition, while Paul could use the term "mystery" in a number of different ways, there is no such variety in Colossians, where its personal content in reference to the one at the heart of the gospel message, Christ, is constant (see 1:26-27; 2:2; 4:3). The notions of Christ's body and of the church now become universal entities (1:18, 24), in contrast to Paul's characteristic employment of them with reference to local groups of believers (although Colossians can also retain the reference of "church" to a local group in 4:15-16); and for the first time in the Pauline corpus the idea of Christ as the head is brought into relation with that of the church as the body (1:18; 2:19). Despite this area of theological differences not being decisive in itself, since a number of the variations may well be explicable in terms of the circumstances of the letter, the question remains whether, when the differences are taken all together, Paul would have changed his perspective on so many significant matters.

Both the stress on "the faith" as a body of teaching (1:23; 2:7) and the inclusion of the household code (3:18–4:1) may well reflect a setting after the death of the apostle. In such a setting it would be necessary to maintain continuity with his teachings and to provide more help to churches of the Pauline mission on how to live in society over a longer period than Paul had anticipated. In particular, 1:24–2:5 reads very much like an admiring portrait of Paul from a follower. What stands out here in comparison with Paul's own reflections on his apostolic office are the exclusive focus on Paul and the stress on the universality of his mission. In Colossians, Paul alone is the apostle, while the undisputed letters mention other apostles, even if sometimes somewhat disparagingly. And here his ministry is for everyone without exception (1:28). There is no recognition that James, Peter, and John had a mission to Jews, while Paul and Barnabas were to go to Gentiles (see Gal 2:9). Indeed, Paul's gospel can be said to have been preached to every creature under heaven (1:23). Furthermore, while Paul can speak of his sufferings for the benefit of others (2 Cor 1:3-7), nowhere does he speak of these tribulations as making up a deficiency in Christ's sufferings or for the sake of the universal church (1:24).

The strongest arguments for the letter's authenticity are its close links with Philemon, whose Pauline authorship is undisputed, and the less than straightforward reading of

4:7-16, with its greetings to and mention of specific people, that is required if the letter is not authentic. Those who are persuaded on grounds of style and other factors that it is improbable that Paul wrote the bulk of the letter point out that there is a reasonable alternative explanation for the last section. Its features are typical of ancient pseudepigraphical letters that strive for verisimilitude as part of the device of pseudonymity.[43] Biographical reminiscences, personalia, and details of pseudo-recipients and their setting all further the appearance of genuineness. In Colossians not only does the author speak in Paul's name but, to add verisimilitude to his taking on the persona of Paul, he has also built on the list of greetings in Philemon and added one or two names known to the recipients from the Pauline mission. In the Pastoral Epistles, held by most scholars to be pseudepigraphical, the typical devices of verisimilitude are distributed throughout the letters, but also, as in Colossians, such details are grouped together at the end of 2 Timothy (see 2 Tim 4:9-22).

In the nature of the case, there can be no overwhelming proof for one's position on authorship; on balance, however, the cumulative argument that Paul was not the author and that Colossians was written by a follower after the apostle's death appears to have the greater probability. If this is indeed so, then there are implications for the identification of the addressees, since there are grave doubts about the existence of Colossae, let alone any church there, after 61 CE. Colossae was a small town in the Lycus Valley in the region of Phrygia. By the first century it was very much in the shadow of the neighboring cities of Laodicea and Hierapolis. But there are two ancient reports of an earthquake in the Lycus Valley. Tacitus says that Laodicea was destroyed by an earthquake in 60–61 CE,[44] and Eusebius talks of Laodicea, Hierapolis, and Colossae as all being destroyed by an earthquake in 63–64 CE.[45] It is usually suggested that these are references to the same earthquake and that the more important Hierapolis and Laodicea were rebuilt more quickly, while Colossae remained uninhabited for a considerable period. There are coins from the late second and the third century referring to Colossae but no mention of it in ancient evidence for the earlier period after 61 CE. So it is likely that it was not an inhabited site for quite a long time after Paul's death. Some have suggested, therefore, that the church at Colossae was chosen as the addressee as part of the letter's attempt at verisimilitude, precisely because there was a Pauline church there during the apostle's lifetime but not afterward. This also meant that the writer was able to make use of the greetings in Philemon, a letter that was sent to Colossae. If all this is true, then an address to the Colossians is a convenient one in a pseudepigraphical letter actually intended for the former neighboring church of Laodicea and perhaps also that of Hierapolis, as the letter itself hints despite its address to pseudo-recipients (see 2:1; 4:13, 15-16).[46]

43. See L. R. Donelson, *Pseudepigraphy and Ethical Argument in the Pastoral Letters* (Tübingen: Mohr, 1986) 7-66.
44. Tacitus *Annals* 14.27.
45. Eusebius *Chronicle* 1.21-22.
46. So A. Lindemann, "Die Gemeinde von 'Kolossä.' Erwägungen zum 'Sitz im Leben' eines deuteropaulinischen Briefes," *WD* 16 (1981) 111-34; P. Pokorny, *Colossians* (Peabody, Mass.: Hendrickson, 1991) 21.

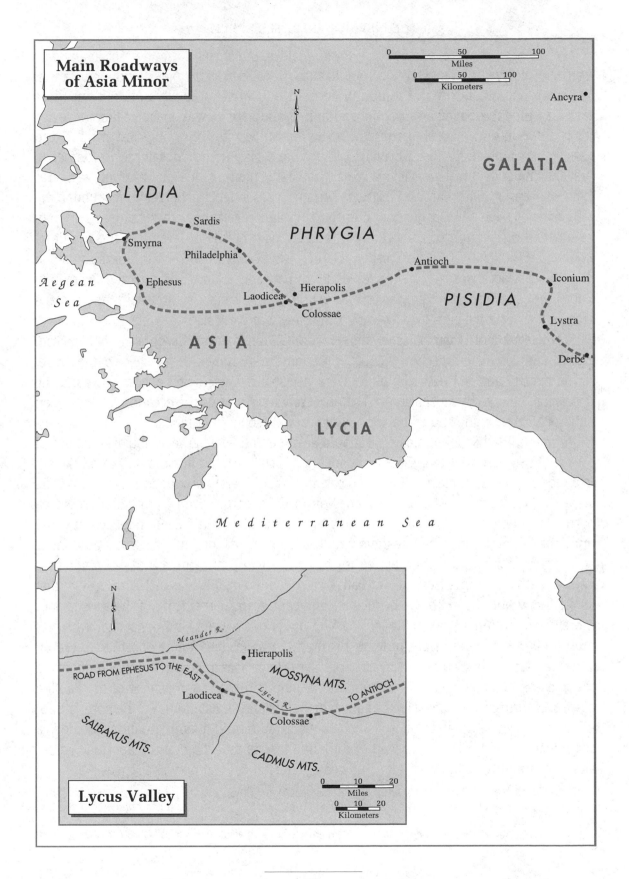

Main Roadways of Asia Minor

Miles
0   50   100

Kilometers
0   50   100

Ancyra

GALATIA

LYDIA

Sardis

Smyrna

Philadelphia

Antioch

Iconium

Ephesus

Hierapolis

PISIDIA

Laodicea

Aegean
Sea

Colossae

Lystra

ASIA

Derbe

LYCIA

Mediterranean Sea

N

Meander R.

Hierapolis

ROAD FROM EPHESUS TO THE EAST

MOSSYNA MTS.

TO ANTIOCH

Laodicea

Lycus R.

Colossae

SALBAKUS MTS.

CADMUS MTS.

0   10   20
Miles

0   10   20
Kilometers

Lycus Valley

To conclude that Colossians is pseudonymous is, of course, not to detract in any way from the validity of its message or from its authority as part of the New Testament canon. What was canonized by the church were not the complete thoughts of Paul but those texts in which it recognized apostolic tradition. Pseudonymity was, in fact, a literary device for passing on authoritative tradition. In the Jewish Scriptures writings are attributed to great personages like Moses, David, Solomon, and Isaiah, and apocalypses, testaments, prayers, and collections of sayings were written in the name of ideal or authoritative figures from the past.[47] The earliest Christian writers of pseudepigrapha remained under the influence of such Jewish notions of authorship and revelation, whereby pseudonymity involved the assertion of authoritative tradition. The Epistle of Jeremiah, the Epistle of Enoch (*1 Enoch* 92–105), the Epistle of Baruch (*2 Apoc. Bar.* 78-87), the letters contained in 1 and 2 Maccabees, and the correspondence between Solomon, Hiram, and Pharaoh in Eupolemos and Josephus[48] provide examples from Jewish literature. However, the pseudepigraphical letter form employed by early Christians was particularly a Greco-Roman literary device. The pseudonymous didactic letters of the philosophical schools, such as the Pythagorean, Cynic, and Neo-Platonist school productions, attempted to convey the presence of the sender to the readers and in doing so would invent personal references and extraneous mundane details for the sake of verisimilitude. The purpose was to provide the occasion for passing on philosophical teaching and portraying a particular philosopher as a model.[49]

In evaluating this phenomenon, it should be remembered that the notion of "intellectual property," so essential to discussion of legitimate claims to authorship and to plagiarism in a modern context, played little or no role in ancient literary production. We know little about the circumstances of the composition of Colossians. Given its direct address to a particular problem, it does not seem likely that it was slipped into a letter collection in the hope that some later general readers would take it for one of Paul's originals and find it edifying. If, instead, it was intended for a specific group of readers in Asia Minor after Paul's death and came from one of Paul's close followers, it is reasonable to believe that its readers would have known of such a significant event as the death of the apostle and, therefore, would have taken the letter as a product of a trusted Pauline teacher who was presenting his teaching not simply as his own but as in the Pauline apostolic tradition. Whether written by Paul or by a disciple of his, the letter was treated as faithfully conveying the apostolic message and has a foundational status in the canon as part of the Pauline corpus. If written by a disciple of Paul, then Colossians, in its attempt to be both faithful and creative in its interpretation of the Pauline tradition in a later situation, provides a canonical model for those engaged in the same task of reflecting on the apostolic gospel and reformulating it in the face of changed circumstances and new challenges.

47. See D. G. Meade, *Pseudonymity and Canon* (Tübingen: Mohr, 1986).

48. Eupolemos, as preserved in Eusebius *Preparation for the Gospel* 9.31.1-34.5; Josephus *Antiquities of the Jews* 8.2.6-7.

49. See Donelson, *Pseudepigraphy and Ethical Argument in the Pastoral Epistles,* 7-66; Wilson, *The Hope of Glory,* esp. 49-50.

Although the following commentary is written from the perspective that the letter is to be dated sometime after Paul's death and that the interpretation of 1:24–2:5 and 4:7-16 in particular is to be linked to the device of pseudonymity, this is a matter still under dispute. For those who disagree with such a stance on authorship, all that is necessary in most of what follows is, of course, to make the mental substitution of "Paul" or "Timothy" or both for "the writer."[50]

50. For a major commentary defending authorship of Colossians by Paul, see P. T. O'Brien, *Colossians, Philemon,* WBC 44 (Waco, Tex.: Word, 1982) esp. xli-xlix.

BIBLIOGRAPHY

Commentaries

Barth, M., and H. Blanke. *Colossians.* Translated by A. B. Beck. AB 34B. New York: Doubleday, 1994. The original German draft of this full and detailed commentary was completed in 1991. Despite its publication date, its extensive bibliographical references are to works no later than 1986.

Dunn, J. D. G. *The Epistles to the Colossians and to Philemon.* NIGTC. Grand Rapids: Eerdmans, 1996. A recent full-scale commentary on the Greek text that interacts with a wide range of secondary literature but is readable and sensitive to the theological nuances of the letter.

Harris, M. J. *Colossians and Philemon.* Grand Rapids: Eerdmans, 1991. Provides detailed analysis of the Greek syntax and brief outlines for suggested homiletical expositions.

Lohse, E. *Colossians and Philemon.* Translated by W. R. Poehlmann and R. J. Karris. Hermeneia. Philadelphia: Fortress, 1971. For many years this has served as the standard detailed critical commentary on Colossians. Contains useful excurses on key issues, including a comparison between the thought of Colossians and Pauline theology.

Martin, R. P. *Colossians and Philemon.* NCB. Greenwood, S.C.: Attic, 1974. A concise commentary, based on the RSV, with stimulating exegetical observations.

―――. *Ephesians, Colossians, and Philemon.* Interpretation. Atlanta: John Knox, 1991. A short commentary geared to the needs of teachers and preachers.

O'Brien, P. T. *Colossians, Philemon.* WBC 44. Waco, Tex.: Word, 1982. A detailed commentary on the Greek text. The format of the series in which it appears allows its author to focus on each pericope's form, structure, and setting and to provide a brief summary of its thrust.

Pokorny, P. *Colossians: A Commentary.* Translated by S. S. Schatzmann. Peabody, Mass.: Hendrickson, 1991. A worthwhile resource with suggestive discussion of the structure of the letter and its argument. The original German commentary was published in 1987.

Schweizer, E. *The Letter to the Colossians.* Translated by A. Chester. Minneapolis: Augsburg, 1982. The German edition was published in 1976, but this remains a helpful critical commentary for preachers and teachers. Its writer says that no section was written without having first been preached, and the commentary contains a forty-five-page essay on the history of interpretation of Colossians.

Studies on Colossians

Arnold, C. E. *The Colossian Syncretism.* WUNT 2/77. Tübingen: J. C. B. Mohr, 1995. A worthwhile attempt to characterize the teaching the letter opposes and the author's response, utilizing more fully than others local inscriptional and textual evidence, including the magical papyri.

Barclay, J. M. G. *Colossians and Philemon.* Sheffield: Sheffield Academic, 1997. An excellent introductory guide to the issues of the letter's authorship, purpose, and theology.

D'Angelo, M. R. "Colossians." In *Searching the Scriptures.* Volume 2: *A Feminist Commentary.* Edited by E. Schüssler Fiorenza. New York: Crossroad, 1994. A concise commentary focusing on the issues most acute for feminist interpretation and endeavoring to uncover the collaboration of its theology of submission in the history of enslavement.

DeMaris, R. E. *The Colossian Controversy.* JSNTSS 96. Sheffield: JSOT, 1994. Argues that the teaching combated in the letter combined Jewish and Christian elements with popular Middle Platonism.

Francis, F. O., and W. A. Meeks, eds. *Conflict at Colossae.* Missoula, Mont.: Scholars Press, 1973. A collection of important essays in the debate about the nature of the Colossian "philosophy."

Kiley, M. *Colossians As Pseudepigraphy.* Sheffield: JSOT, 1986. A study of some of the issues surrounding the authorship of the letter, claiming that it is pseudonymous and in the process providing a useful summary of the thoroughgoing analysis of the style of Colossians by the German scholar W. Bujard.

Lincoln, A. T., and A. J. M. Wedderburn. *The Theology of the Later Pauline Letters.* New York: Cambridge University Press, 1993. Wedderburn writes on Colossians, focusing especially on theological and hermeneutical questions raised by the christological hymn of 1:15-20 and on the themes of baptism and eschatology.

Martin, T. W. *By Philosophy and Empty Deceit: Colossians as Response to a Cynic Critique.* JSNTSS 118. Sheffield: Sheffield Academic, 1996. A recent innovative study, claiming that the opposing teaching is straightforward Cynic philosophy and that the author is responding to Cynic criticisms of the Christian gospel.

Sappington, T. J. *Revelation and Redemption at Colossae.* JSNTSS 53. Sheffield: JSOT, 1991. Argues that the ascetic-mystical piety of Jewish apocalyptic literature provides the most appropriate background for interpreting Colossians and its polemic.

Wilson, W. T. *The Hope of Glory: Education and Exhortation in the Epistle to the Colossians.* Leiden: E. J. Brill, 1997. A fine study that is particularly helpful in setting Colossians in the context of the moral exhortations of the philosophical schools and in its analysis of the worldview of Colossians.

OUTLINE OF COLOSSIANS

III. Colossians 1:24–4:9, The Letter Body

    A. 1:24–2:5, Body-Opening: Paul's Proclamation of the Gospel and Its Relation to the Readers

    B. 2:6–4:6, Body-Middle: Exhortations

        2:6–3:4, Exhortation to Faithfulness to the Gospel
          2:6-7, Live in Accordance with the Tradition About Christ
          2:8-15, Do Not Be Captured by Human Tradition
          2:16-23, Do Not Be Judged by the Codes of a Different Teaching
          3:1-4, Seek the Things That Are Above
        3:5–4:1, Exhortation to Holiness of Life
          3:5-11, Put to Death What Is Earthly
          3:12-17, Put on Love, Appropriate the Peace of Christ, and Be Thankful
          3:18–4:1, Let Christ's Lordship Shape Household Relationships
        4:2-6, Concluding Exhortation: Pray, Live Wisely, and Speak Graciously

    C. 4:7-9, Body-Closing: Passing on News

IV. Colossians 4:10-18, The Letter Closing

THE LETTER OPENING

NIV

1 Paul, an apostle of Christ Jesus by the will of God, and Timothy our brother,

²To the holy and faithful[a] brothers in Christ at Colosse:

Grace and peace to you from God our Father.[b]

a1 Or believing   b2 Some manuscripts Father and the Lord Jesus Christ

NRSV

1 Paul, an apostle of Christ Jesus by the will of God, and Timothy our brother,

2To the saints and faithful brothers and sisters[a] in Christ in Colossae:
Grace to you and peace from God our Father.

a Gk brothers

COMMENTARY

The letter begins with the usual epistolary format of an introductory address and greetings. The senders are identified as Paul and Timothy. If the letter is Pauline, the placing of Timothy alongside Paul raises the issue of the former's role in the composition of the letter. Is he meant to be considered simply as a co-sender or also as a co-author? The naming of others in an address of a letter actually written by an individual was not the ordinary occurrence in antiquity.[51] This would suggest that Timothy is named because he had a significant role in collaborating as a co-author. It is easy to see why those who wish to give Timothy the dominant role in writing this letter as a way of accounting for the differences, especially stylistic ones, from the undisputed Pauline letters might favor this view. But it is a slim basis for such an explanation, since among the undisputed letters with which the style of Colossians has to be compared, 2 Corinthians, Philippians, and Philemon include Timothy in the address with Paul, and 1 Thessalonians includes not only Timothy but also Silvanus. Those who hold the letter to be pseudonymous would simply argue that at this point its author has used 2 Corinthians, Philippians, and Philemon as models.

51. See E. R. Richards, *The Secretary in the Letters of Paul*, WUNT 2/42 (Tübingen: J. C. B. Mohr, 1991) 47n. 138.

In any case, as the letter stands, the primary authority for its message is Paul. Timothy's name comes second with the simple description "our brother" (cf. 2 Cor 1:1; Phlm 1); but Paul is named first, and only he is said to be "an apostle of Christ Jesus by the will of God" (cf. 2 Cor 1:1). Whether by Paul himself or by a follower writing in his name, an appeal is made to Paul's apostleship as the source of the letter's authority. Paul is seen, on account of his encounter with and commissioning by the risen Christ, as this Christ's authorized representative. Behind this apostolic role, it is claimed, lies the will of God; the letter will later expand on Paul's place in God's purposes in history (1:23c-29).

Whereas the Corinthian and Thessalonian correspondence and even Philemon contain an address "to the church," and Galatians is addressed "to the churches," Colossians designates its recipients as "the saints and faithful brothers and sisters in Christ." The former term signals that the readers are viewed as being set apart as God's elect people. None of the undisputed letters describes its recipients as "faithful brothers and sisters." The family metaphor for believers, found in various places in the Pauline letters, now becomes part of the address. Despite a relationship in which the writer claims not to have actually met the recipients (1:4, 9; 2:1), this gives the salutation a more intimate and personal note. Although the adjective translated as "faithful" (πιστοῖς *pistois*), could mean simply "believing," it is more likely that in view of its later usage in 1:7 and 4:7, 9 it refers to the readers' fidelity and steadfastness. The writer will later call on them to continue to exercise these qualities (1:23; 2:6-7).

The family metaphor continues into the greeting with its reference to "God our Father." The greeting begins as the usual Pauline one of grace and peace with its adaptation of Hebrew and Greek forms of greetings. But, unlike the greetings of the undisputed Pauline letters, there is no mention of "our Lord Jesus Christ" alongside "God the Father" as the source of grace and peace. The expression "grace to you and peace" is used in 1 Thess 1:1, but immediately preceding this the church is said to be "in God the Father and the Lord Jesus Christ." The omission of this phrase in Colossians might be explained by the fact that the writer has just previously designated the recipients as those "in Christ in Colossae,"

but a similar relating of the recipients to Christ in 1 Cor 1:2; Eph 1:1; and 2 Thess 1:1 does not prevent the writers of those letters from going on to mention Christ in the grace and peace greeting. The absence in Colossians of the usual reference to Christ in the actual greeting remains striking, particularly in a letter whose focus on Christ will be so strong.

What had become the typical Christian greeting in the Pauline letter in this case aptly sets the tone for what is to follow. What has been done for believers through God's undeserved favor in Christ will be the linchpin of the writer's argument; indeed, grace will stand as a synonym for the gospel in 1:6. In addition, peace will be highlighted as one of the major elements of that grace (1:20; 3:15), not simply as an inner contentment but as the experience of relationships on the cosmic and human levels being brought into conformity with the Creator's purposes for harmony.

REFLECTIONS

The double identification of the addressees as those who are "in Colossae" and "in Christ" (following the order in the Greek syntax) is suggestive both for the issues to be dealt with in Colossians and for broader questions about Christian identity. The readers are located both in their particular geographical environment, shaped by its religious, social, and political realities, and in the sphere of Christ's lordship. One of the key questions with which the letter grapples is how the latter bears on the former. The phrase "in Christ" refers to the relationship of believers' incorporation into and union with Christ. Again and again in various forms the writer will appeal to the implications of this relationship in his attempt to persuade the readers to remain true to the Pauline gospel in the way they view alternative teaching and live out their calling in the social structures of their day. Interpreters of Colossians will want to take advantage of their study of this letter's particular proposals to reflect on the same issue as it confronts contemporary Christians. The double identification of Christians can provide the lens for our self-understanding as we consider some of the dominant religious and social aspects of the culture that shapes us and what it means, in the midst of these, to be decisively reshaped by our relationship to Christ.

COLOSSIANS 1:3-23

AN EXTENDED THANKSGIVING

OVERVIEW

Colossians 1:3-23 is an extended thanksgiving section that, rhetorically speaking, can also be seen as an exordium (see Introduction). It functions to make the readers positively inclined to receive the letter's later exhortations and also introduces the main themes and concerns that inform those exhortations. The initial prayer of thanksgiving in 1:3-8 forms one sentence in the Greek text. It is followed by an even longer Greek sentence that extends to 1:17 and is further evidence of the distinctive style of Colossians in comparison to the undisputed Pauline letters. The first part of this sentence constitutes the usual intercessory prayer report of a Pauline letter in 1:9-12, which concludes on a note of thanksgiving. The thanksgiving is then extended by formulations about the salvation God has accomplished in Christ in 1:13-14, which lead into the citation of material in praise of Christ in 1:15-20. What is said in these verses about Christ's work of reconciliation is then applied to the readers in 1:21-23, where in particular the three main themes of the rest of the letter are set out before they are taken up in reverse order.

COLOSSIANS 1:3-12, OPENING THANKSGIVING AND INTERCESSORY PRAYER REPORT

Colossians 1:3-8, Opening Thanksgiving

NIV

³We always thank God, the Father of our Lord Jesus Christ, when we pray for you, ⁴because we have heard of your faith in Christ Jesus and of the love you have for all the saints— ⁵the faith and love that spring from the hope that is stored up for you in heaven and that you have already heard about in the word of truth, the gospel ⁶that has come to you. All over the world this gospel is bearing fruit and growing, just as it has been doing among you since the day you heard it and understood God's grace in all its truth. ⁷You learned it from Epaphras, our dear fellow servant, who is a faithful minister of Christ on our[a] behalf, ⁸and who also told us of your love in the Spirit.

[a]7 Some manuscripts *your*

NRSV

3In our prayers for you we always thank God, the Father of our Lord Jesus Christ, ⁴for we have heard of your faith in Christ Jesus and of the love that you have for all the saints, ⁵because of the hope laid up for you in heaven. You have heard of this hope before in the word of the truth, the gospel ⁶that has come to you. Just as it is bearing fruit and growing in the whole world, so it has been bearing fruit among yourselves from the day you heard it and truly comprehended the grace of God. ⁷This you learned from Epaphras, our beloved fellow servant.[a] He is a faithful minister of Christ on your[b] behalf, ⁸and he has made known to us your love in the Spirit.

[a] Gk *slave*   [b] Other ancient authorities read *our*

COMMENTARY

The thanksgiving section is just as much a report on the writer's prayers for his readers, rather than a direct transcript of a prayer, as is the so-called intercessory prayer report. As such, it is now addressed to the readers rather than to God. While it reflects something of the writer's prayer life, its primary function is to assure the readers of the writer's goodwill toward them and his appreciation of the qualities of their Christian faith. Such opening thanksgivings in the Pauline letters frequently set the scene for the concerns of the letter, and this one is no exception. The writer does not hesitate to signal ahead of time some of the matters on which he will elaborate. For example, he mentions in the context of thanksgiving the readers' hope, laid up for them in heaven (v. 5), but he will remind them of this hope and its significance later. He mentions that the gospel they received was the word of truth from an apostolic representative (vv. 5, 7-8), but again this is a matter that will need reinforcing. In the light of the later message, his reference to their knowledge of the grace of God (v. 6) is also significant, for an understanding of the sufficiency of that grace is essential if the teaching that threatens the community is to be resisted.

1:3-5a. Despite these verses' being a report of a thanksgiving that now has an epistolary function of assuring the readers of the writer's goodwill toward them, the readers are not directly congratulated on their Christian virtues. This would clearly be inappropriate, since such virtues derive ultimately from God. Instead, the report speaks of the writer's constantly being thankful to God, who is described in the formula characteristic of the Pauline letters as "the Father of our Lord Jesus Christ" (cf. Rom 15:6; 2 Cor 1:3; 11:31). Paul and his churches held Jesus Christ to be Lord with all the connotations of κύριος (*kyrios*) from the Greek Scriptures where it was used of Yahweh (cf. Rom 10:13; Phil 2:10). At the same time, within a Jewish monotheistic framework, they still held that this Lord had a God but that this one God was now to be characterized by the intimate relationship with Christ of Father to Son.

The writer speaks only of having heard of the readers' faith and love, since Paul did not person-

ally found the church at Colossae. The founder was Epaphras, who has provided this good report (vv. 7-8). Their faith is described as "in Christ Jesus." English translations disguise the fact that this phrase could refer either to the object of faith or to the sphere in which that faith is operative. Paul and the writer of Colossians elsewhere (cf. 2:5) do not use the preposition ἐν (*en*) for the object of faith, and so here it is likely that the reference is to Christ as the sphere in which believers live and exercise their faith. The notion of believers' status or standing "in Christ" is important for the writer (see his designation of the addressees as "faithful brothers and sisters in Christ" in v. 2), and he will later draw out some of the implications of this incorporation into and solidarity with Christ for the readers' lives (2:6-7, 10-12). The readers' love, which is also grounds for the writer's thanksgiving, is said to be "for all the saints," suggesting that they have given evidence of a practical concern for other believers that extends beyond the confines of their local group.

With the mention of "hope" in v. 5*a*, the familiar triad of Christian virtues—faith, hope, and love—is recalled (see Rom 5:1-5; 1 Cor 13:13; Gal 5:5-6; 1 Thess 1:3; 5:8). But what is distinctive about their association here is that faith and love are made dependent on hope and, as in Gal 5:5, hope is not so much a subjective Christian virtue as the content of salvation, that which is hoped for. By definition, hope, even as the content of salvation or the object of expectation, has a future dimension; but now the addition of the spatial description ("laid up for you in heaven") underlines that it exists not as a vague wish for the future but as an assured reality in the present. The language recalls other images for salvation in the NT, such as "treasures in heaven" (Matt 6:20) and "an inheritance . . . kept in heaven for you" (1 Pet 1:4). It reflects the concept found in Jewish apocalyptic literature that what will be manifested in history at the eschaton, at the consummation of salvation, is already present in heaven, a concept employed to stress the certainty of future salvation. This is also the force of such language in Colossians: The hope of believers' salvation is secured in heaven and nothing can alter that. The content of this hope is ultimately Christ, who will be called "the hope of glory" (v. 27); it is in heaven because the writer believes the exalted Christ is at present above (3:1). Later the writer will talk with equal seriousness about the possibility of the readers' shifting away from this hope (v. 23), but for now it is the security of the salvation God has provided through Christ that is underscored.

Some commentators have suggested that the stress on hope is because the rival teachers were robbing believers of this prospect by denying the future element in salvation and claiming that the resurrection was past already. But this is to misread the opposing teaching and to miss the force of the language. The threat of the rival teachers places the assured hope of salvation in jeopardy through its insistence on further means (rigorous ascetic observances, esoteric knowledge, and visionary experiences) in addition to the message about Christ as being necessary if full salvation is to be attained. Those readers exposed to such teaching need to know that there is nothing inadequate about the apostolic message they have received and to be assured, in the face of any insecurities induced by the teachers, that the gospel centered in Christ is well able to provide a certain hope.

1:5b-8. A further relative clause in the Greek text now makes explicit the link between the hope of which the writer has been speaking and the gospel that the readers have received. They have previously heard of that hope "in the word of truth, the gospel." By talking of the gospel in these terms the writer already is implicitly setting it over against the rival teaching, which he will label as "empty deceit" (2:8). Just as the psalmist could refer to God's commandments in the Torah as "the word of truth" (Ps 119:43; see also Ps 119:142, 160), so also the writer of Colossians can speak of the gospel as the word of truth and as "the word of God" (v. 25). Just as in the Jewish Scriptures God's Word can be personified, so also here the gospel takes on an almost personal quality as the writer speaks of its dynamic activity. The gospel has come to the readers and has taken a firm place in their lives. Indeed, it is "bearing fruit" (καρποφορέω *karpophoreō*), producing a crop of good deeds as a result of its reception,

and is "growing" (αὐξάνω *auxanō*), attracting an increasing number of adherents in the whole world. This note of prophetic optimism about the universal proclamation of the gospel will be sounded again in v. 23. Here it is mentioned to remind the readers that in their adherence to the gospel they are part of a larger whole, a movement that is encompassing the Roman Empire. The universal appeal of the gospel may also be intended to counter the elitism of the rival teaching, which catered to initiates who were prepared to undergo certain rituals and observances. What the gospel was achieving on a broader scale, it was also effecting in the lives of the readers, bearing fruit among them from the time they first received its message.

Their initial hearing with faith is also characterized as a coming to know "the grace of God in truth." The phrase "in truth" (ἐν ἀληθείᾳ *en alētheia*) could be taken adverbially to refer to the readers' genuine comprehension, but more likely it links the grace of God with the truth of the gospel (v. 5). The reminder that the truth they first believed focused on the gracious activity of God is significant in the light of the place of human effort in the writer's sketch of the rival teaching. The realization that the readers owe their salvation to God's grace should serve to undermine those who would make ascetic and visionary achievements requirements for a full relationship with God.

The link between the apostolic gospel of Paul and Timothy and the readers is provided by Epaphras (vv. 7-8; see also 4:12-13; Phlm 23). In relation to the readers, Epaphras was the evangelist and teacher in the Lycus Valley from whom they had learned the gospel. If hearing the gospel (v. 6) draws attention to the initial reception, learning highlights the consequent catechesis (see also "just as you were taught," 2:7). As a result of his activity among the readers, Epaphras is depicted as being able to report to Paul and Timothy about their love in the Spirit. Again love is singled out (cf. v. 4) as a major fruit produced by the gospel, and this time it is associated, in one of the few references in this letter to the Spirit (see also 1:9; 3:16), with this power of the new age, whose first and all-encompassing fruit is love (cf. Gal 5:22).

In relation to Paul and Timothy, Epaphras is "our beloved fellow servant" and "a faithful minister of Christ on our behalf" (where the reading "on our behalf," rather than "on your behalf," has the much stronger external attestation). "Servant" or "slave of Christ" (δοῦλος Χριστου *doulos Christou*) was a self-designation of Paul as an apostle (cf. Rom 1:1; Gal 1:10; Phil 1:1—including Timothy), as was "minister" (διάκονος *diakonos*; see 1 Cor 3:5; 2 Cor 11:23), which could also be used of close co-workers such as Apollos, Timothy, or Tychicus (see 1 Cor 3:5; Col 4:7; 1 Thess

3:2). Together with the indications of affection ("beloved") and commendation ("faithful"), these terms place Epaphras in the closest possible relationship to Paul and his immediate co-workers and confirm for the readers that what has been presented to them by Epaphras has the seal of approval as the apostolic gospel. (See Reflections at 1:9-12.)

Colossians 1:9-12, Intercessory Prayer Report

NIV

⁹For this reason, since the day we heard about you, we have not stopped praying for you and asking God to fill you with the knowledge of his will through all spiritual wisdom and understanding. ¹⁰And we pray this in order that you may live a life worthy of the Lord and may please him in every way: bearing fruit in every good work, growing in the knowledge of God, ¹¹being strengthened with all power according to his glorious might so that you may have great endurance and patience, and joyfully ¹²giving thanks to the Father, who has qualified you[a] to share in the inheritance of the saints in the kingdom of light.

a12 Some manuscripts us

NRSV

9For this reason, since the day we heard it, we have not ceased praying for you and asking that you may be filled with the knowledge of God's[a] will in all spiritual wisdom and understanding, ¹⁰so that you may lead lives worthy of the Lord, fully pleasing to him, as you bear fruit in every good work and as you grow in the knowledge of God. ¹¹May you be made strong with all the strength that comes from his glorious power, and may you be prepared to endure everything with patience, while joyfully ¹²giving thanks to the Father, who has enabled[b] you[c] to share in the inheritance of the saints in the light.

a Gk his   b Other ancient authorities read called   c Other ancient authorities read us

COMMENTARY

The link with v. 8 through "for this reason" suggests that "since the day we heard" has in view the reception of the news about the readers from Epaphras. Certainly the report of the intercessions made on their behalf appears to be in the light of the full situation that Epaphras is depicted as having communicated. The stress in the first part of the report is on their growth in knowledge both of God's will and of God, a knowledge that involves spiritual wisdom and understanding (vv. 9-10). Again and again the letter will emphasize the true source of wisdom and knowledge (e.g., 1:27-28; 2:2-3; 3:10, 16). Together with the labeling of the rival teaching as a "philosophy" in 2:8 and the assertion in 2:23 that for all its claims

it only has the appearance of wisdom, these emphases suggest that the prayer report has an eye on the alternative teaching being offered. The same may well be true of the language of growth and fullness it contains (see 2:9-10, 19). The writer's prayer for the readers, then, is for more, not less, than what others are offering; but he believes this will be found in an ever-increasing appropriation of what they already have in the gospel. In the OT, wisdom frequently involves practical knowledge—that is, the ability to choose right conduct—and here in Colossians the wisdom and insight produced by the Spirit have an explicitly ethical dimension. They are meant to enable the readers to "walk" (a Hebraism common in the

LXX and taken up in the Pauline letters to refer to ethical conduct or a way of living) in a manner consistent with their confession of Christ as Lord and fully pleasing to him.

The writer elaborates on such a way of life in the four participial clauses that follow in vv. 10b-12. The first two participles were previously employed in v. 6 to speak of the activity of the gospel itself both in the world and among the readers. Now the fruitbearing and growth that were marks of the gospel are the characteristics to be desired for the readers. The fruit produced is to be good works, and the growth is to be in their knowledge of God. The good works contrast with and replace the "evil works" (v. 21) of the readers' previous way of life, a juxtaposition elaborated in the vices and virtues contained in the paraenesis in 3:5-17. For the undisputed Pauline letters, too, it should be remembered, authentic faith showed itself in doing good (see Rom 13:3; 2 Cor 5:10; Gal 6:10; 1 Thess 5:15); and the expression "every good work" is found in 2 Cor 9:8 (see also 2 Thess 2:17).

The third participial clause (v. 11) focuses on the power the readers will require to enable them to live lives that are fully pleasing to their Lord. It combines two nouns and a verb referring to power or strength and adds "all" before the first noun and "of glory" after the second in order to convey an impression of something of the divine might available to the readers and to make its point as forcefully as possible. Nothing less than God's glorious power at work within them will be necessary to live worthily of their Lord. But it is worth noting that this power is not for its own sake or for displays of wonder-working; it is "for all endurance and patience." The ability to face trials, distractions, and opposition in faithfulness requires more than a survivor instinct or stoic fortitude. Divine resources are needed; it is no accident that patience or long-suffering, which will be mentioned again in the paraenesis in 3:12, is depicted as a fruit of the divine Spirit in Gal 5:22.

The fourth and final participial clause indicates that the life worthy of the Lord, which the writer has requested in his prayer for the readers, will be marked by thankfulness and joy. Joy, of course, is yet another fruit of the Spirit (Gal 5:22; see also Rom 14:17; 1 Thess 1:6). It is a natural accompaniment to the activity of giving thanks to God, who is designated as Father (cf. v. 3), preparing the way for Christ to be called "his beloved Son" in the following verse. Thankfulness to God for all that God has done for believers in Christ is clearly one of the most essential Christian qualities for this writer; he will call for it again and again in his exhortations (see 2:7; 3:15, 17; 4:2). It is possible that this emphasis is made because thankfulness and joy were in short supply in the philosophy, with its severe ascetic regulations (see 2:20-23). The writer's own extended thanksgiving, within which this explicit mention of thankfulness occurs, can be seen as his modeling of the virtue he wishes to see in others.

Three activities of the Father that provide cause for believers' thanksgiving will be specified. The most immediate, in the relative clause that completes v. 12, is that God has qualified them "to share in the inheritance of the saints in light." In the Jewish Scriptures the inheritance of God's holy people was primarily the promised land. In fact, the two terms used together here in Colossians, μερίς (meris, "share" or "portion") and κλη ρος (klēros, "inheritance"), are frequently used together in the LXX with reference to the land (e.g., Deut 10:9; 32:9; Josh 19:9). But Yahweh as the source of salvation could also be seen as the portion of the people's inheritance (Ps 15:5 LXX). Here in Colossians, too, the inheritance of God's people moves beyond the terrestrial and is rather the transcendent realm of light. Light has connotations both of transcendent splendor, the environment of the heavenly world, and of holiness, ethical purity.

In the Qumran literature, with its dualism between light and darkness, the concept of inheritance had already been developed in this direction, so that the portion of God is that of light[52] and God's people inherit or share the portion of the Holy Ones,[53] the angels in heaven. Some have suggested that ἅγιοι (hagioi, "holy ones") in v. 12 should also be taken as "angels." With an eye on the rival teaching's veneration of angels (see 2:18), the writer would then be claiming that God had already provided for communion with the angels. Elsewhere in the Pauline writings "holy ones" can include angels in its range of

---

52. 1QM 13.5.
53. 1QS 11.7-8; 1QH 11.7.

meanings when the context requires (see 1 Thess 3:13; 2 Thess 1:7, 10), but ordinarily it is employed to refer to the saints—that is, to Christian believers. Since the writer uses the term "angels" in 2:18, if he had wanted the readers to find a reference to angels here, he would more likely have used the same term, particularly when he has just previously employed "holy ones" to designate believers as God's holy people in 1:2, 4 and will take up the same term in a similar way in 1:26 (see also 3:12). The thought here, then, is that God has enabled the readers to share with all God's chosen people an inheritance in the realm of light. It is a functional equivalent to the notion that their hope is already secure in heaven (1:5). Later in the paraenesis a future aspect to the inheritance will emerge, as in 3:24 it is viewed as still to be conferred; but here in the context of the thanksgiving the emphasis is that God has already enabled believers to share in the present in this inheritance in the realm of light.

Even if this reading does not present quite as striking and direct a counterpart to the philosophy, the latter may still be in view in two ways. First, if the realm of light has a transcendent heavenly dimension, then again the readers are being reminded that they already have the access to heaven that was of such concern for the rival teachers. Second, the reminder is underlined by the emphasis that God has already qualified them for access to heaven, in which case there can be no reason at all for allowing anyone to disqualify them by insisting on fasting, "the worship of angels," and visionary experience (2:18) as necessary for such access.

REFLECTIONS

The thanksgiving (1:3-8) and intercessory prayer (1:9-12) are not actual prayers but *reports* that now serve conventional epistolary functions. They do not, therefore, provide a warrant for using public prayer to preach or to direct subtle messages to the congregation. It is, however, essential to the effectiveness of teaching and preaching that the congregation sense that the exhortations addressed to them come from someone who has identified with their needs, who is genuinely appreciative of their faith and commitment, who prays thankfully and faithfully for them, and whose prayers are directed toward growth and enrichment in their journey with God.

1. The prominence of hope in the thanksgiving is a reminder of the security of a salvation that is centered in Christ in the transcendent realm; it is not dependent on the feelings or efforts of humanity, not confined to the perspectives of this world. Later it will also be stressed that it is possible to shift away from this hope (1:23) and that what is distinctive about such salvation, as compared to the rival teaching, is that it is worked out within the structures of everyday life in this world (3:1–4:1). The tensions between assurance and the necessity of continuing in the faith and between transcendent and immanent aspects of salvation are vital parts of the preacher's theological framework. The discernment of knowing when to emphasize which pole, when to reassure or when to challenge, is an essential skill in the preacher's pastoral repertoire. Here, in the context of thanksgiving and as an antidote to any suggestion that the gospel message is inadequate, the emphasis on assurance and on the transcendent security of believers' hope in the exalted Christ is the writer's initial and appropriate pastoral stress.

2. There is a host of different ways in which contemporary believers can be tempted to feel that the basic gospel message is inadequate and that it needs to be supplemented by additional religious rites or disciplines, more sophisticated knowledge, or some compelling experience, if they are to be accepted by God or to reach their full potential as human beings. They need to hear that, although the gospel has riches that are yet to be fathomed and implications for all areas of life that are yet to be explored, there is no inadequacy about its basic message. They need to know that the hope that is at the heart of it and inseparable from the person of Christ is secure and that such hope is the potent incentive to a life of faith and love.

3. In a worthy desire to avoid abstraction and to do justice to the concreteness of their lives, perhaps too often Christians' prayers for one another remain at the level of immediate physical needs or specific direction in life or problems of relationships. Sometimes this may be because we wait to pray for others until they have a problem that requires attention or because we have a view of God in which God's primary role is to "fix" things for us. Sometimes such praying also unconsciously reveals our preoccupation with empirical reality and masks doubts about the reality of such dimensions to life as growth in the knowledge of God, spiritual wisdom, or divine empowering for patient and joyful endurance. These reports of prayers of thanksgiving and intercession teach us about holding individuals and communities before God in the whole of their relationship with God and, therefore, not being afraid to pray, both in thankfulness and in petition, in this large and more general way about their equally real spiritual well-being and progress.

4. What is striking in this initial section, even allowing for the hyperbole it contains, is the writer's confidence about the dynamic force and the progress of the gospel. Without such a perspective there can be, on the one hand, a lack of expectancy about any lives being transformed as a result of one's witness to the gospel. On the other hand, there may be an overreliance on one's own persuasive powers or on the latest communication techniques to produce results. The gospel that preachers are privileged to proclaim has its own inherent power. As Paul put it in Rom 1:16: "I am not ashamed of the gospel; it is the power of God for salvation for everyone who has faith" (NRSV). And the writer of Colossians is confident in his praying that the very dynamic of the gospel is also able to reproduce itself in and shape the lives of believers, as it bears fruit and grows (cf. 1:6 with 1:10).

5. Colossians 1:1-14 appears in Year C of the lectionary cycle paired with Old Testament readings emphasizing justice and Luke's parable of the Samaritan who acts as neighbor to the victim in the ditch. The broader theme can aid reflection on the significance of the discussion in Colossians of the spiritual wisdom and understanding that entail bearing fruit in every good work (1:9-10) and serve as a reminder that such good work will later be elaborated in terms of justice and fairness (4:1). In turn, the distinctive contribution of Colossians to the overall theme might well be seen in its stress on the hope of the gospel as the motivation for the faith and love that find their expression in the pursuit of justice.

COLOSSIANS 1:13-23, THANKSGIVING THROUGH INTRODUCTION, CITATION, AND APPLICATION OF PRAISE OF CHRIST

Colossians 1:13-14, Transitional Introduction to the Praise of Christ

NIV	NRSV
[13]For he has rescued us from the dominion of darkness and brought us into the kingdom of the Son he loves, [14]in whom we have redemption,[a] the forgiveness of sins.	[13]He has rescued us from the power of darkness and transferred us into the kingdom of his beloved Son, [14]in whom we have redemption, the forgiveness of sins.[a]
[a]14 A few late manuscripts *redemption through his blood*	[a] Other ancient authorities add *through his blood*

COMMENTARY

These verses continue the reasons for giving thanks to God that the writer had begun to spell out in v. 12. The grounds for connecting them with what follows are (1) that the terminology for those who experience salvation switches from the second-person plural of v. 12, a reference to the readers, to the first-person plural, a reference to believers in general, and (2) that in the last part of v. 13 the focus shifts to Christ, who will be the subject of the hymnic material in vv. 15-20. In their formulations these two verses may already employ traditional confessional statements to lead into the praise of Christ.

Again both scriptural and Qumran references help to illuminate the language of v. 13. "Deliverance" (ῥύεσθαι *hryesthai*) is the LXX terminology (see, e.g., Exod 6:6; 14:30) for Israel's salvation from the Egyptians prior to the possession of the land as an inheritance (see v. 12). The Qumran literature extols God as the deliverer of the faithful from their enemies[54] and talks of the dominion of Belial over the sons of darkness.[55] Now the writer emphasizes as a cause for thanksgiving that God in a new rescue act has delivered believers from the dominion of darkness (and any tyranny of its hostile cosmic powers) and has transferred them into a new sphere of rule—namely, "the kingdom of his beloved Son." The undisputed Pauline letters usually speak of the kingdom of God (e.g., Rom 14:17; 1 Cor 6:9-10; 15:50; Gal 5:21), but in one place they see the kingdom of Christ as representing the present stage of God's rule (1 Cor 15:24-28). Given the mention of light in v. 12 and the contrast here between the dominion of darkness and the kingdom of Christ, the sphere over which the Son rules is to be seen as being bathed in the splendor and holiness of the divine radiance.

It is through their relationship to God's Son that believers experience redemption. This is simply another way of talking about God's rescue act.

The term ἀπολύτρωσις (*apolutrōsis*, "redemption") was rare in nonbiblical Greek and is used only once in the LXX, but cognate verbs are employed of the divine act of deliverance or liberation from Egypt (Deut 7:8; 9:26; 13:5; 15:15; 24:18). Connotations of a ransom payment for release should be read into this term only if the context warrants it, and there are no explicit indications of such a force here. Since "the forgiveness of sins" is in apposition to redemption, this phrase depicts the primary way in which believers experience their liberation at present. They can be assured of a restored relationship with God in which they are freed from guilt and their offenses against God are no longer held against them.

Forgiveness will be mentioned again in 2:13, this time in connection with the term "trespasses" (παραπτώματα *paraptōmata*) instead of "sins" (ἁμαρτίαι *hamartiai*), in the context of the writer's interaction with the philosophy. The stress on what God has already done in releasing believers from the dominion of darkness and on their already having forgiveness may well be meant to reinforce for the readers that nothing more needs to be done to appease hostile powers of darkness, who can have no hold over them through their sinful deeds. The traditional formulations may also have baptismal associations. "Beloved Son" was the designation given Christ at his baptism (see Mark 1:11 par.), the forgiveness of sins was closely associated with baptism (e.g., Acts 2:38), and the notion of a decisive transfer from one realm to another is also a baptismal theme (see Rom 6:1-11). Baptismal motivation is clearly at work later in chaps. 2–3 with the explicit mention of baptism in 2:12 and the employment of the language of dying and rising with Christ and putting off the old person and putting on the new. An allusion to baptism is a further effective means of recalling the significant change of status that the readers continually need to appropriate. (See Reflections at 1:21-23.)

---

54. 1QH 2.35.
55. 1QS 1.18, 23-24; 1QM 14.9.

Colossians 1:15-20, Citation of Hymnic Material in Praise of Christ

NIV

¹⁵He is the image of the invisible God, the first-born over all creation. ¹⁶For by him all things were created: things in heaven and on earth, visible and invisible, whether thrones or powers or rulers or authorities; all things were created by him and for him. ¹⁷He is before all things, and in him all things hold together. ¹⁸And he is the head of the body, the church; he is the beginning and the firstborn from among the dead, so that in everything he might have the supremacy. ¹⁹For God was pleased to have all his fullness dwell in him, ²⁰and through him to reconcile to himself all things, whether things on earth or things in heaven, by making peace through his blood, shed on the cross.

NRSV

15He is the image of the invisible God, the firstborn of all creation; ¹⁶for in*a* him all things in heaven and on earth were created, things visible and invisible, whether thrones or dominions or rulers or powers—all things have been created through him and for him. ¹⁷He himself is before all things, and in*a* him all things hold together. ¹⁸He is the head of the body, the church; he is the beginning, the firstborn from the dead, so that he might come to have first place in everything. ¹⁹For in him all the fullness of God was pleased to dwell, ²⁰and through him God was pleased to reconcile to himself all things, whether on earth or in heaven, by making peace through the blood of his cross.

a Or *by*

COMMENTARY

In its present form in the thanksgiving, the citation of the original hymn with its modifications falls into two parts: 1:15-17, dealing with Christ's role in the sphere of creation, and 1:18-20, dealing with his role in the sphere of redemption.

1:15-17. Christ is the one who supremely makes the invisible God visible. As "the image of the invisible God," he is the manifestation of the divine in the world of humans. This very first assertion about Christ draws our attention to the dynamic nature of the relation between the spheres of redemption and creation that produced the formulation of the hymn as a whole. Although the first part of the hymn speaks of Christ's agency in creation, it is what was first believed about his role in redemption that enabled early believers to make claims about his role in creation. In 1 Cor 15:49 and 2 Cor 4:4 Paul had used the term "image" (εἰκών *eikōn*) for the resurrected and exalted Christ, who as the last Adam now represented humanity as God had always intended it to be. This notion was then pushed back as far as it could go. If the resurrected Christ was the supreme expression of the image of God, then he must always have been so. This creates the para-

dox that the one who can be described in Adamic language (cf. Gen 1:27) can also be held to have existed before Adam and to have been on the side of the Creator as well as on the side of the creation. The sort of language that had been employed of Wisdom in Wis 7:26 ("she is a reflection of eternal light, a spotless mirror of the working of God, and an image of his goodness," NRSV) becomes a resource for expressing this belief about the status of Christ in God's purposes.

Wisdom could be spoken of in Proverbs as the beginning of God's work—the first of God's acts—and in Philo as firstborn.[56] Here in v. 15*b* Christ is similarly seen as "the firstborn of all creation." The term πρωτότοκος (*prōtotokos*) was employed frequently in the LXX, mostly in genealogical and historical contexts, to indicate not simply temporal priority but sovereignty of rank (e.g., Ps 89:27). Of course, if the term were taken simply in its strict temporal sense, it would make Christ the first of God's creatures, as in later christological debates the Arians held. In reply, Athanasius was quick to point out that the next lines of the passage in v. 16, with their assertion

56. Prov 8:22; Philo *Questions and Answers on Genesis* 4.97.

that all things were created in and through Christ, contradict such an interpretation: "But if all the creatures were created in him, he is other than the creatures, and he is not a creature, but the creator of the creatures."[57] At this early stage of christological reflection, such issues were not in view; no problem would have been contemplated in holding that, like Wisdom as God immanent in creation, Christ was both sovereign and first within creation and the divine agent of creation.

The comprehensive scope of Christ's agency in creation is stressed in v. 16. Twice it is asserted that "all things" were created in or through him. Both parts of the cosmos, the heavenly and invisible sphere as well as the earthly and visible realm, are included in this scope. To underline the significance of such an assertion made in worship, the writer spells out that the invisible things created in Christ include the cosmic powers, to which some would give too much deference (see 2:10, 15).[58] This language about the cosmic powers can be traced to Jewish belief in angelic beings. Each of the four representative names here—thrones, dominions, rulers, powers—is mentioned in *2 Enoch* 20–22, where in the seventh heaven angels are set in rank (see also 2 Macc 3:24; *1 Enoch* 61:10; *T. Levi* 3). In the context of creation the powers are to be thought of as benign, but in v. 20 they are seen as part of the "all things" in need of reconciliation, and in the later references in the letter, as hostile and threatening to God's purposes in Christ and the well-being of believers. In v. 16 the thought is that if such powers were originally created in Christ and for him, then they are certainly in principle subject to him and should have no threatening hold over his people.

Whereas 1 Cor 8:6 could depict Christ as the medium and agent of all things and God as the goal, Col 1:16 goes further in its christological reflection so that here Christ can be said to be the goal of creation also. This addition of "to him" or "for him" also goes beyond what is said of Wisdom; thus it may reflect the hymn's understanding of Christ's role in redemption that it adds to the conceptuality of the wisdom tradition. It

asserts that the creation of all things was for Christ and to enhance his glory. Something of what is intended by portraying Christ as the goal of creation will be developed in v. 20 in terms of reconciliation. Verse 17 is itself a summing-up of the two previous verses. Because of his agency in creating all things, Christ, again like Wisdom (cf. Sir 1:4), can be said to be before all things and, like the Logos (cf. Sir 43:26), the one in whom all things cohere. The one who, because of his preexistence, helped to bring all things into being is also the one who continues to sustain the whole creation and prevent its disintegration into chaos.

1:18-20. The hymnic material moves more explicitly to the realm of redemption by the addition of the term "the church" to what may originally have been simply a statement about the relationship of Christ to the cosmos as his body. In the original, Christ, like the Logos, would have been thought of as pervading with his presence and as ruling the cosmos. Now, in its present form in the thanksgiving, the praise of Christ's supremacy over the church as his body matches the earlier praise of his supremacy over the realm of creation.

It is easy, but probably mistaken, to see head and body as two parts of one anatomical image in which the head contains the brain that directs the body's nervous system. The two terms "head" and "body" had previously been employed separately by Paul, "head" for authoritative origin and "body" for the organic interdependence of believers in the church. They now come together for the first time in the Pauline corpus, and it is probably Hellenistic views about the cosmos that have provided the catalyst for the combination. As the excursus explains, the body was used as an image for the cosmos, and in that context "head" sometimes occurred with it (see Excursus: "The Existence, Structure, and Background of a Possible Hymn," 601-5). In an Orphic fragment, Zeus is seen as head of the cosmos, pervading it with his rule as it lies in his mighty body.[59] Philo used "head" for the Logos as the ruling principle of the cosmos as the body.[60] So this background of cosmic speculation and Paul's use of "body" for the church made it natural for the two separate images to be brought together for Christ's relation

57. Athanasius *Orations Against the Arians* II.62.

58. Contra W. Wink, *Naming the Powers* (Philadelphia: Fortress, 1984) 11, 64-67, the powers are best understood not as including both things visible and things invisible but as an elaboration of the latter.

59. Fragment 168.

60. Philo *On Dreams* 1.128; See also Philo *Questions and Answers on Exodus* 2.117.

to believers. The term "head" (κεφαλή *kephalē*) denotes Christ's rule or authority over the church as his body. The LXX often employs this term to translate the Hebrew ראש (*rōʾš*)) in the sense of "ruler" or "leader" (e.g., Deut 28:13; Judg 11:11; 2 Sam 22:44), and in the use of the term connotations of authority were often connected with those of origin or beginning, since the origin was held to be determinative for what followed from it.[61] Paul had employed *kephalē* in this sense in 1 Cor 11:3, and it will be used with this force again by the writer of Colossians in 2:10.

The transfer of "body" imagery from the cosmos to the church to indicate that the church is Christ's true body was natural enough, since Paul had already used this imagery in connection with local groups of believers in Rom 12:4-5 and 1 Cor 10:16-17; 12:12-27. In this context, in v. 18, as later in v. 24, the reference is, however, to the universal church. In both passages, "body" (σῶμα *sōma*) is explained by the addition of the term "church" (ἐκκλησία *ekklēsia*). Paul had used the latter term most frequently for the actual gathering of a group of local Christians or for the local group itself, and Colossians retains that usage in 4:15-16. But in a number of places Paul appeared to indicate an entity broader than the merely local congregation (see 1 Cor 10:32; 12:28; 15:9; Gal 1:13; Phil 3:6), and here in vv. 18 and 24 it is certainly the universal church that is in view.

In v. 18*b* Christ is called "the beginning." Although this term had been used in Prov 8:22 LXX for Wisdom's position in the creation, here the following phrase "firstborn from the dead" makes clear that it is Christ's position in the new creation that is signified. Like both "head" and "firstborn," "beginning" (ἀρχή *archē*) had two linked connotations: primacy in the temporal sense and primacy with reference to authority or sovereignty. The clarifying phrase "firstborn from the dead," while providing a parallel with the earlier section through the designation "firstborn," indicates that Christ is to be ranked supreme in the new creation on account of his temporal primacy in the resurrection from the dead. As in the undisputed Pauline letters, Christ's resurrection makes him the firstborn among many brothers and sisters (Rom 8:29), the firstfruits of those

61. S. Bedale, "The Meaning of κεφαλή in the Pauline Epistles," *JTS* 5 (1954) 211-15.

who have died (1 Cor 15:20, 23). His resurrection is determinative for all those who will follow. If Christ has supremacy in the realm of new creation through his resurrection, then, the writer adds in v. 18*c* in an effort to ensure that his reason for citing this material will not be missed, God's undisputed purpose must be that Christ should have preeminence in everything.

Christ's preeminence is not simply because he happened to be one individual whom God raised ahead of time but because he is a particular individual with a unique relation to God and a unique role in God's work of reconciliation. This is made clear in the following two verses, introduced by "because." In Christ "all the fullness was pleased to dwell." Although the Greek text does not mention God in v. 19, both the NIV and the NRSV in their different ways relate the fullness to God in an interpretative gloss. Such an interpretation of the writer's meaning is surely justified by 2:9, since there he asserts that in Christ "the whole fullness of deity dwells bodily." It is also significant that the verb "was pleased" (εὐδόκησεν *eudokēsen*) would ordinarily be expected to have a personal subject. This, too, suggests that "all the fullness" stands for God in all the divine fullness. In the Jewish Scriptures God can be depicted as actively filling all things (e.g., Jer 23:24), so that outside of God nothing has existence. To say that this fullness of God dwells in Christ, then, is most likely to mean that just as there is nothing in heaven or earth that is outside the divine presence and power, so also there is nothing outside the scope of Christ's presence and power, because Christ now sums up all that God is in interaction with the cosmos.

Again speculation about Wisdom may have contributed to the language of the hymn. The writer of Wis 1:6-7 speaks of Wisdom as a kindly spirit and asserts that this spirit of the Lord has filled the world, using the verb "to fill" rather than the noun "fullness." The noun does occur in later syncretistic literature with a gnosticizing tendency, such as in *Corpus Hermeticum* 6.4; 16.3 and the *Odes of Solomon* 7.11, 13; 16.3; 17.7; 36.1-2. It also plays an important role in second-century Gnostic writings, where it denotes the totality of the emanations that come from God and represents the sphere of perfection and salvation in closest proximity to God and opposed to the lower material realm (e.g., *The Gospel of Truth*) 16.34-36, 41; *Tripartite Tractate* 70, 75, 77, 78, 80). It is possible that the writer of Colossians picks up on the term again in 2:9-10, because it played a part in the philosophy against which he warns, where it had a significance somewhere within the development between Hellenistic Jewish cosmic speculation and gnostic usage. It is not enough to dismiss this possibility by asserting that the use of the term here would have encouraged the very syncretism to which the writer is opposed.[62] The writer is quite capable of taking up the language and patterns of thought of opposing teaching and employing them in line with his own understanding of the gospel. If the philosophy was advocating ascetic techniques and special knowledge gained through visions to placate the powers and to participate in the divine fullness, then this first reference in the hymnic material would reinforce that such fullness is not to be found outside of Christ. Since the divine fullness has taken up residence in him, it is not to be conceived as inherently inimical to the physical realm.

If we ask when the divine fullness was pleased to dwell in Christ, then the context presents us with two main options. Given the use of the same verb, "to be pleased," in the account of Jesus' baptism with its descent of the Spirit (cf. Mark 1:9-11), the designation "beloved Son" in v. 13 and the background of Wis 1:6-7, with its focus on the spirit of the Lord, it could be argued that baptism is the point at which the divine fullness indwelt Christ.[63] On the other hand, this verse is most immediately a supporting statement for a previous assertion that began with a reference to Christ's status by virtue of the resurrection, and so the resurrection might well have been intended as the point at which the divine fullness became resident in Christ (see Rom 1:4).[64] But to ask the question about a particular point in time may be pushing the text for information it was not intended to give. The claim may simply be a more general one: In Christ's existence as a whole, culminating, of course, in his death and resurrec-

tion, the divine fullness can be seen to have been displayed.

The second half of the supporting statement begun in v. 19 lends credence to this more general interpretation, since it brings into view, in connection with the indwelling of the divine fullness, the death of Christ. The subject and main verb of v. 20*a* carry over from the previous verse. It is God in the divine fullness who was pleased, at the same time as taking up residence in Christ, to reconcile all things through Christ. The implication of such a statement is, of course, that at some stage the cosmos with its original harmony, as God had created it in Christ, was put out of joint, so that it became in need of being restored to harmony through Christ. The compound form of the verb ἀποκαταλλάσσω (*apokatallassō*, "to reconcile") is employed here and in v. 22; it is used elsewhere in the NT only in Eph 2:16 in dependence on this passage. The simpler καταλλάσσω (*katallassō*) is found in Rom 5:10 and 2 Cor 5:18 for the reconciliation of humanity to God. It is preferable to take "to/for him" in v. 20*a* as a reference to Christ rather than to God (in contrast to both the NIV and the NRSV). In this way, the parallel with v. 16 is maintained, so that, there as here in vv. 19-20, the activity described is "in him," "through him," and "for him." And just as Christ is the means and the goal of creation, so also he is the means and the goal of reconciliation.

The verb "to be reconciled" (*apokatallassō*) is usually followed by the dative of the person to whom one is reconciled. The use here of εἰς (*eis*, "to" or "for") with the accusative reinforces the view that there has been a deliberate attempt to parallel the syntax of the earlier part of the hymnic material and that Christ is the goal of the reconciliation of all things rather than Christ or God being the one to whom all things are reconciled. The parallel clause in v. 20*b* explains that the reconciliation through Christ was a "making of peace" (εἰρηνοποιέω *eirēnopoieō*) through him. This is the only instance in the NT of the compound verb, and the masculine form of the participle confirms that the writer intended "all the fullness" to be taken in a personal sense. The enmity that had invaded the creation, reflected in the activity of hostile cosmic powers, is seen as having been overcome through Christ and in

62. Contra J. D. G. Dunn, *The Epistles to the Colossians and to Philemon,* NIGTC (Grand Rapids: Eerdmans, 1996) 100-101.

63. P. Pokorny, *Colossians: A Commentary,* trans. S. S. Schatzmann (Peabody, Mass.: Hendrickson, 1991) 84-86.

64. A. J. M. Wedderburn, *The Theology of the Later Pauline Letters* (New York: Cambridge University Press, 1993) 32-33.

particular through the historical event of his death. The combination of images for that death in the phrase "through the blood of his cross" is not found in the undisputed Pauline letters. Paul employed the two images separately: "blood," to denote Christ's violently taken life in contexts where the sacrificial nature of his death was to the fore, and "cross," the more general image, to convey the ignominy of this death by Roman execution. The bringing together of the two in this context certainly roots Christ's cosmic reconciliation in a Pauline view of his death, but it may well indicate the work of a later disciple drawing on Paul's thought.

Just as the first part of the hymnic material underscored that the "all things" created through Christ were "in heaven and on earth, things visible and things invisible," so also the final part (v. 20c) stresses that the "all things" reconciled through him are to be understood equally comprehensively, "whether things on earth or things in heaven." Appropriately, because of its final position, the emphasis falls on the heavenly things, the cosmic powers added in explanation in v. 16c, since it is these powers in particular that the readers need to know have already been taken care of in God's purposes in Christ. Such powers do not require appeasing or reconciling by any special practices the readers may be urged to undertake themselves.

The immediate application of this passage in praise of Christ will be examined in the Commentary on 1:21-23, but it is worth noting at this point that there will be further application in the letter as a whole. It is a commonplace that the thanksgiving sections of Pauline letters frequently indicate concerns that will be dealt with later in the letter, but the distinctive hymnic material within the thanksgiving of Colossians has its own particular role in accomplishing this. Paul's ministry is treated in relation to Christ's body, the church, in v. 24 (see also v. 18). The notion that in Christ are all the treasures of wisdom (2:3) builds on the hymn's portrayal of Christ as embodying all the attributes of Wisdom. Christ's relation to the cosmic powers, his being indwelt by the fullness of deity, and his headship, all introduced in the hymn, are elaborated in 2:9-10, while 2:15 is a further interpretation of what took place between Christ and the powers on the cross (cf. 1:20). The head/body imagery of 1:18 is developed in 2:19, and the assertion that Christ is all and in all in 3:11 correlates with the cosmic conceptuality of the hymn and draws out its significance for the new creation.

In this way Col 1:15-20 functions as an effective part of the writer's rhetorical strategy in the exordium, constituted by the thanksgiving section. It establishes a positive relationship with the readers through the citation of material that they may well have in common with the writer; it encourages them to assent to its praise as they are carried along by its rhythms and flow; and it makes them conducive to accepting the subsequent message that has made the perspective of the hymn its foundation. (See Reflections at 1:21-23.)

❖　　❖　　❖　　❖

EXCURSUS: THE EXISTENCE, STRUCTURE, AND BACKGROUND OF A POSSIBLE HYMN

THE EXISTENCE OF A POSSIBLE HYMN

There is a major scholarly debate regarding these verses, and voluminous secondary literature has been written about their hymnic nature. Some of the questions raised are these: Is there a hymn to be found here at all? If so, did the writer compose it? Or was it a preformed hymn that he has used? In either case, what would be its background; from what sphere of thought does it come? What was its structure? If it was preformed, has the writer made some additions? If so, are these additions simply modifications, or are they corrections of the original? It is easy to become impatient with the intricacies and sometimes speculative nature of these discussions.

Many of the questions admit of no definite solution. Yet, since most of them do arise from the text and even tentative conclusions about them affect one's exegesis, a brief summary of the issues is in order.

Colossians 1:15-20 forms a discrete unit within the thanksgiving. In contrast to both the preceding and the following contexts, which are marked by the number of personal pronouns, it contains no references to believers or to the readers in particular. The relative pronoun ὅς (hos, "who"), which begins vv. 15, 18b, is not a natural part of the context. It has all the indications, as in 1 Tim 3:16, of being part of preformed material that may have been preceded by some such words as "We praise our Lord Jesus Christ. . . ." There is the repetition both of propositions with ἐστιν (estin, "is"), which provide a series of affirmations about Christ, and of various forms of πᾶς (pas, "all"), which emphasize the universal scope of Christ's activities. The designation "firstborn" occurs in vv. 15b and 18b. The notion of the creation of all things in relation to Christ's agency is found in both v. 16a and v. 16d. Verse 16 also contains the chiastically arranged phrases "in heaven and on earth, things visible and things invisible," while v. 20c speaks of "things on earth or things in heaven" (NIV). In vv. 17-18a there occur side by side two clauses that begin "and he is. . . ." The focused and elaborate description of Christ, the carefully constructed nature of the passage, the parallel correspondences in its parts, the recurrence of words and phrases in the same sequence, and the use of terms not found elsewhere in the Pauline corpus are all more natural in a liturgical formulation or hymn than in the free-flowing style of a letter, whose writer waxes poetical at this point. It is not a matter of conformity to an obvious Greek hymnic form. "The rhythm and pattern come, as in the Psalms which were also no doubt in the liturgical stock of Pauline churches, from verbal repetition and the reiteration of ideas in regular order."[65] Colossians 3:16 will speak about the singing of psalms, hymns, and spiritual songs, so it would not be at all strange if in the course of the letter the writer had recourse to quoting, either exactly or with some additional words of application, one such hymn that might also be known in the worship life of the addressees.

THE STRUCTURE OF AN ORIGINAL HYMN

How was the hymn structured? Were there one, two, or three strophes? Has the letter's writer made his own additions to the hymn? Scholars have developed no clear consensus about the number or content of the strophes in an original hymn, and so I shall set out here what appears to be the most plausible reconstruction, followed by some justifications for particular aspects.

Strophe I
who is the image of the invisible God
   the firstborn of all creation,
for in him were created all things
   in heaven and on earth
   things visible and invisible
   [whether thrones or dominions or rulers or powers]—addition (i)

Transitional Strophe II
   all things were created through him and for him
and he himself is before all things
   and all things hold together in him
and he himself is the head of the body [the church]—addition (ii)

65. J. L. Houlden, *Paul's Letters from Prison* (Harmondsworth: Penguin, 1970) 157.

Strophe III
who is the beginning
   the firstborn from the dead
[so that he himself might have preeminence in all things]—addition (iii)
    for in him all the fullness was pleased to dwell
    and through him to reconcile all things for him,
      making peace through him
        [through the blood of his cross]—addition (iv) after "making peace"
    whether things on earth or things in heaven

As can be seen, this reconstruction proposes that some additions have been made to an original hymn. Some have argued that if additions were made to an original, then omissions could also have been made.[66] This is possible, but it does not entail the abandonment of any reconstruction. It only serves as a reminder that all such reconstruction is hypothetical and that we are working with probabilities, not certainties.

The lines beginning "who is . . ." followed by a second line designating Christ as firstborn, first in the realm of creation and then in the realm of redemption, mark the start of two separate strophes. Some scholars are satisfied with two strophes of quite different lengths. But it appears more likely that vv. 16d-18a, with the repetition of the creation theme, the two sets of parallelisms, and the description of Christ in the last line as the head of the body, form a transitional strophe that prepares for the move to the realm of redemption in the final section of the hymnic material. Unlike Martin's proposal,[67] this reconstruction includes "things visible and things invisible" as the last line of the original first strophe because of the chiasm with the preceding line and the repetition at the end of the last line of the term "invisible" (ἀόρατος aoratos) from the end of the first line. Again, unlike Martin's reconstruction,[68] here the clause "making peace through him" is included in the hymn, since the verb is a *hapax legomenon* in the Pauline corpus and has a fitting parallel in the previous line. The phrase "whether things on earth or things in heaven" is retained rather than being treated as an interpretive gloss, since it has a parallel in the first strophe, where the order is reversed.

The writer's first addition, "whether thrones or dominions or rulers or powers," spells out that the reference to Christ's agency in the creation of all created things includes the very cosmic powers some of the readers are being induced to see as a threat to their well-being (cf. 2:10, 15). The term σῶμα (*sōma*, "body") in v. 18a could have originally been, or could have been understood as, a reference to the cosmos, which was common in Philo[69] and Hellenistic Judaism; and so in the second addition the writer specifies that he understands Christ's headship as being over the church as the body. Paul had already used body imagery for the local congregation in 1 Corinthians and in Romans, and so in this context it is deemed appropriate to extend its scope to the universal church. Verse 18c, with its final or purpose clause ("so that he himself might have preeminence in all things"), fits awkwardly in terms of style; one would have expected a simple assertion or a participial clause in conformity with the rest of the material. It appears, therefore, to be a third addition, in which the writer wishes to elaborate on the significance of Christ's resurrection for the situation of the addressees. Its force is that, since Christ has preeminence in the realm of the resurrection as well as in the realm of creation, he was meant to have preeminence in everything, including by necessary implication their own perspective on the cosmos and its powers. The fourth addition ("through the blood of his cross," v. 20b) is meant to ensure that the reconciling work of Christ, though cosmic in scope, is not thought of in a speculative way but is anchored in the historical event

66. E.g., N. T. Wright, "Poetry and Theology in Colossians 1.15-20," *NTS* 36 (1990) 444-68.
67. R. P. Martin, *Colossians and Philemon,* NCB (Greenwood, S.C.: Attic, 1974) 56.
68. Ibid., 60-61.
69. E.g., Philo *On Dreams* 1.128.

of the crucifixion. The somewhat awkward insertion of this phrase before "through him" would also account for the uncertainty about the originality of the latter in the textual tradition.[70]

THE HYMN'S BACKGROUND

Gnosticism

Käsemann held that, once the additions "of the church" and "through the blood of his cross" were removed, the original hymn no longer displayed any specifically Christian characteristics.[71] It could, in fact, be seen as a pre-Christian gnostic hymn that dealt with the metaphysical and supra-historical drama involving the gnostic redeemer. This hymn had been taken over into Christian usage in a baptismal liturgical reinterpretation and finally was cited by the writer in a refutation of what Käsemann considered to be the gnostic countermovement that provoked the letter. There is irony to this reconstruction, since the hymn had originally come from Gnosticism and was now being employed to refute it. But there is very little to be said in favor of the proposal. Apart from its being extremely doubtful whether one can speak of any clear gnostic redeemer myth in the first century CE, the hymn contains a perspective inimical to Gnosticism—namely, that creation and redemption are both related to the same source or agency. The Christian character of the phrase "the firstborn from the dead" cannot be doubted and appears to wreck any idea of a pre-Christian hymn. In addition, the repeated references to the creation of all things and the use of the verb "to be pleased," which was employed in the LXX for God's electing decree, recall the thought and language of the Jewish Scriptures.

Rabbinic Exegesis of Genesis 1:1

The influence of Jewish Scriptures is emphasized by Burney, followed by Davies and Caird, and more recently modified by Wright.[72] Burney attempts to demonstrate that the origin of the hymnic material lay in a typically Jewish interpretive exegesis of Gen 1:1 and its first Hebrew word, בראשית (*běrē'šît*, "in the beginning"), which was made possible by the use of ראשית (*rē'šît*, "beginning") in connection with Wisdom in Prov 8:22. The Hebrew of the latter text could be read as "the LORD created me at the beginning of his work" or "the LORD created me as the beginning of his work." Burney sees Col 1:15*b* ("the firstborn of all creation") as an allusion to Prov 8:22 and then claims that everything that might be said about Wisdom on the basis of Gen 1:1 is here applied to Christ. He asserts that this sort of connection would be obvious to a rabbinic scholar and that in Colossians 1 "we have an elaborate exposition of Bereshith in Gen 1.1 in the Rabbinic manner."[73] His proposal plays on the range of connotations of both the Hebrew preposition ב (*bě*) and the noun *rē'šît* and can be set out in summary form as follows:[74]

Bereshith = in *reshith*—"in him all things were created" (1:16*a*)
Bereshith = by *reshith*—"all things were created by or through him" (1:16*d*)
Bereshith = into *reshith*—"all things were created to or for him" (1:16*d*)
Reshith = beginning—"he himself is before all things" (1:17*a*)
Reshith = sum total—"all things hold together in him" (1:17*b*)

70. It is found, e.g., in P[46] א A C D[c] Ψ 048 33 181 326 syr[p,h] cop[bo] goth Chrysostom Theodoret and omitted in e.g., B D* G I 81 104 436 it[ar,c,d]vg cop[sa] arm eth Origen Ambrosiaster. The inclusion of the phrase constitutes the more difficult reading and, therefore, favors its originality.
71. E. Käsemann, "A Primitive Christian Baptismal Liturgy," in *Essays on New Testament Themes* (London: SCM, 1964) 149-68.
72. C. F. Burney, "Christ as the ΑΡΧΗ of Creation," *JTS* 27 (1926) 160-77; W. D. Davies, *Paul and Rabbinic Judaism,* 3rd ed. (Philadelphia: Fortress, 1980) 150-52; G. B. Caird, *Paul's Letters from Prison* (Oxford: Clarendon, 1976) 175; Wright, "Poetry and Theology in Colossians 1.15-20," 444-68.
73. Burney, "Christ as the ΑΡΧΗ of Creation," 174-75.
74. Ibid., 176.

Reshith = head—"he is the head of the body" (1:18*a*)

Reshith = firstfruits—"he is the beginning, the firstborn from the dead" (1:18*b*)

Conclusion— Christ fulfills every meaning that may be extracted from reshith—"so that he himself might have preeminence in everything" (1:18*c*).

Burney's proposal is ingenious, and although some have dismissed it as too ingenious, it might account for some of the process of thought that led up to the composition of part of the original hymn. It is strange that, despite its title, Burney's article actually underplays the significance of ἀρχή (*archē*, "beginning"), which would be the most natural correspondence to *rē'sît* as "beginning" in 1:15-20 and is in fact the term used to translate it in the LXX of Prov 8:22. This is a failure that Wright's modification of the proposal attempts to remedy.[75] The proposal provides, however, no explanation for the last part of the hymn, 1:19-20. And whether any of the Gentile Christians who made up the majority of the letter's addressees (3:5-7) would have caught or were meant to have caught any of these subtleties of Hebrew exegesis in a hymn composed in Greek must be extremely doubtful.

The Wisdom Tradition in Hellenistic Judaism

What cannot be doubted is that Burney was right to see the figure of Wisdom lying behind the hymn's depiction of Christ. Its language and thought resemble Jewish Hellenistic speculation not only about Wisdom but also about the Logos. Both Wisdom (Wis 7:26)[76] and the Logos[77] are spoken of as the image of God. Through Wisdom, God created all things (Prov 8:27-31; Sir 24:5-6).[78] Wisdom is depicted as firstborn,[79] as is the Logos.[80] The Logos (Sir 43:26) holds all things together,[81] and Wisdom is the beginning of God's ways (Prov 8:22). In Philo, the Logos is also head of the body, the world of souls,[82] announces God's peace,[83] and mediates between the disparate elements of the universe.[84] It looks very much, then, as if the Hellenistic Jewish composer of the hymn has taken the various attributes of Wisdom or the Logos and applied them to Christ in his relation to the cosmos. The hymn in its original form presupposes some major disruption in cosmic harmony and, therefore, sees Christ not only, like Wisdom or the Logos, as the divine agent in creation but also now as the divine agent in reconciliation, restoring harmony to the cosmos.

75. Wright, "Poetry and Theology in Colossians 1.15-20," 444-68.
76. See also Philo *Allegorical Interpretation* 1.43.
77. See Philo *On the Confusion of Tongues* 147; *The Special Laws* 1.81.
78. See also Philo *On Flight and Finding* 109.
79. Philo *Questions and Answers on Genesis* 4.97.
80. Philo *On the Confusion of Tongues* 146; *On Husbandry* 151; *On Dreams* 1.215.
81. Philo *On Flight and Finding* 112; *Who Is the Heir of Divine Things?* 23.
82. Philo *On Dreams* 1.128.
83. Philo *Who Is the Heir of Divine Things?* 206.
84. Philo *Concerning Noah's Work as a Planter* 10.

❖   ❖   ❖   ❖

Colossians 1:21-23, Application of Praise of Christ

NIV	NRSV
[21]Once you were alienated from God and were enemies in your minds because of[a] your evil behavior. [22]But now he has reconciled you by Christ's physical body through death to present	[21]And you who were once estranged and hostile in mind, doing evil deeds, [22]he has now reconciled[a] in his fleshly body[b] through death, so
[a]21 Or *minds, as shown by*	[a] Other ancient authorities read *you have now been reconciled* [b] Gk *in the body of his flesh*

NIV	NRSV
you holy in his sight, without blemish and free from accusation— [23]if you continue in your faith, established and firm, not moved from the hope held out in the gospel. This is the gospel that you heard and that has been proclaimed to every creature under heaven, and of which I, Paul, have become a servant.	as to present you holy and blameless and irreproachable before him— [23]provided that you continue securely established and steadfast in the faith, without shifting from the hope promised by the gospel that you heard, which has been proclaimed to every creature under heaven. I, Paul, became a servant of this gospel.

COMMENTARY

In one lengthy sentence the writer begins relating and applying the content of the hymn in praise of Christ to the situation of his readers and in so doing sets out the agenda for the rest of the letter. Addressing the readers directly, the writer employs the schema "once . . . now" to draw a contrast between their pre-Christian past and their Christian present (vv. 21-22*a*). This was not uncommon in the NT letters and probably originated in early Christian preaching. The people being addressed, too, have experienced the pattern of redemption depicted in the hymn, because at one time they were in a state of alienation, characterized by a hostile attitude accompanied by evil deeds, but now have been reconciled by God.[85] Such a description most appropriately fits a predominantly Gentile readership. Their reconciliation, as part of the cosmic reconciliation achieved by Christ, also took place through his death. As in the previous description of that death in v. 20, the writer again brings together two terms that appear separately in the undisputed Pauline letters, this time "body" (σῶμα *sōma*) and "flesh" (σάρξ *sarx*). While distinguishing this mention of the body from the earlier one with reference to the church, the combination stresses the physicality of Christ's death and, by making clear that the physical body of Christ was the means of reconciliation, may well have been meant to contrast this view of redemption with that of the philosophy and its denigration of the physical body (2:23).

The purpose of the reconciliation was to make those formerly alienated from God acceptable to God and to provide those previously characterized by evil actions with a new quality of life before God. "Before him" could be a reference to Christ in line with the earlier "his flesh" in this verse, but if "to be reconciled" is understood as a "divine passive" with God as the implied agent, then it makes sense to view the ultimate arbiter of believers' lives as God also. The verb "to present" (παρίστημι *paristēmi*) could be used in a cultic or legal context, and both images may be in view here, since, of the three accompanying adjectives, the first two have cultic and the third legal connotations. "Holy" (ἅγιος *hagios*) and "without blemish" (ἄμωμος *amōmos*) were employed of sacrificial animals that were consecrated to God and, therefore, had to be without defect (see Exod 29:37-38; Num 6:14; 19:2 LXX); they came to denote also ethical purity (see Pss 14:2; 17:24 LXX). Similarly the third term, ἀνέγκλητος (*anegklētos*), drawn from a judicial setting in which it meant "free from accusation," came also to have the force of "morally blameless" or "irreproachable."

For all the emphasis on the sufficiency and effectiveness of Christ's work of reconciliation, there is now an equal emphasis, no doubt provoked by the letter's occasion, on the readers' responsibility to continue in the faith. The conditional construction translated as "providing that . . ." need not express doubt that they will do so. But it does make clear that cosmic reconciliation is not some automatic process; it works itself out in history in relation to the response of faith, and that response entails not abandoning the content of faith. The definite article before "faith" suggests that it is not simply the attitude

---

85. The NIV and the NRSV translate the aorist active third-person singular form of the verb, which is most widely attested in the manuscript traditions. The aorist passive second-person plural form, however, is the more difficult reading because it does not agree with the second-person plural accusative form of "you" in 1:21*a*. The latter form also has strong external attestation (P[46] and B) and provides the best explanation for the other variants that arose as an attempt to correct the syntax.

of faith that is meant but the teaching about the apostolic gospel, which is mentioned in the next part of the verse (see also 2:7).

The implied exhortation is reiterated through three terms that all make the same point. The readers are to be established or firmly founded; they are to be securely based or steadfast, and they are not to shift away from the content of their faith, whose base or foundation is now described as "the hope promised by the gospel that you heard." This recalls the language of v. 5, where, significantly, hope as the assured reality of salvation was the foundation for faith and love. Again this certain promise of hope is emphasized as the component of the gospel the readers had first heard and to which they must hold fast in the face of any teaching that might attempt to rob them of it. Finally, in v. 23c, in an attempt to underline the validity of this original gospel message, they are reminded of its universality and apostolicity. Echoing v. 6 and its mention of "the whole world," the writer talks of the gospel's being preached to every creature under heaven, again seeing the present Gentile mission as anticipating the completion of the worldwide proclamation and perhaps contrasting this with a teaching that was more local and specialized in its appeal. There then follows the assertion, lending the authority of Paul to the message and to be developed in the following section, that it is this gospel "of which I, Paul, became a servant."

As noted in the Introduction, the three parts of the application of the praise of Christ set the agenda for the rest of the letter—but in reverse order. The role of Paul in proclaiming the gospel (v. 23c) that is announced here will be taken up in 1:24–2:5, the need to continue in the faith of the gospel the readers have heard (1:23a) will be treated in 2:6–3:4, and the holiness of believers achieved through the work of Christ (1:21-22) will be the subject of the exhortations in 3:5–4:1.

REFLECTIONS

Because this passage is so rich christologically, and yet its way of envisioning Christ may not be immediately comprehensible to contemporary Christians, these reflections will center around the cosmic role of Christ and the reconciliation accomplished in him.

1. Taking for granted the church's long tradition of worshiping Christ as God or becoming preoccupied with questions about the background of the Christ hymn can both, in their different ways, lead to overlooking the staggering claims of its content. For the writer, talk about the cosmic Christ is not about some abstract idea, not about the personified figure of Wisdom. Rather, as he has underscored through the terminology of "blood" and "cross," it is about a crucified person: Jesus. It must have taken a subsequent event of some magnitude to bring about the identification of a near contemporary, who had been ignominiously executed, with the assertions of this hymn. Early Christians held, of course, that this event was not just an inner experience of forgiveness or reconciliation on the part of Jesus' followers, which, as in 1:21-23, was seen as a consequence of what had happened to Christ, but was the raising of Christ from the dead, which led to the designation of him as "firstborn from the dead."

Today there are many, both Christians and others, who have a renewed interest in the historical Jesus of Nazareth but who are at a loss about how this is to be related to the church's confession of Christ as the second person of the Trinity. A sympathetic attempt to enter into the thought world of the Christ hymn may not only be enlightening about this early stage in the development of belief about Jesus, but it may also help in our own endeavors to understand both the humanity and the divinity of Christ. Without a belief that God raised Jesus from the dead or some experience of Christ's aliveness, there is little incentive to think of Jesus as any more than a Jewish prophet, sage, social revolutionary, or healer. But once we share that same essential starting point with early Christians, we face similar questions about the status of the resurrected Jesus.

Study of the hymn shows that early Christian thought moved from what was believed about

Christ on the basis of his resurrection and of believers' experience of salvation through him to what he must have been from all time. This is reflected in the designations "image" and "firstborn" for his role in creation. A similar thought process is found in the Jewish Scriptures, where reflection on the activity of Yahweh in rescuing Israel in the exodus led back to the depiction of Yahweh's role in creation. In the Christian belief expressed in the hymn in Colossians, the movement back from Christ's role in redemption to his role in creation is aided by the transference to Christ of what Judaism held about Wisdom as the one God active in creation and in the world and revealed to Israel in the form of Torah. Now, as the embodiment of Wisdom, Christ is held to be the agent of the one God in creation, the one through whom creation is kept going, and, through his death and resurrection, the revealer and accomplisher of God's purposes for humanity and the cosmos. Just as in Judaism Wisdom was the figure that brought together transcendence and immanence, the universal and the particular, so also in Christian belief Jesus of Nazareth is seen as the point at which the particular and the universal, the human and the divine, uniquely intersect.

2. Recognition that the language of the Christ hymn of Colossians is that of poetry and praise should lead to a hesitancy to fill in its theological gaps in the light of later doctrinal formulations, but not to an unwillingness to stop and ask what we mean when, as contemporary Christians, we repeat its assertions. It is one thing to note that the notion of the preexistence of Wisdom as a personification of God's interaction with the created world is transferred to Christ. But what is going on when we claim that Christ was pre-existent? When this notion was applied in Jewish thought to Torah, its force was not so much to make a statement about the actual existence of the law before the world was created as to see the law as the climactic manifestation of the wise purposes of God in creation and thereby to ascribe ultimacy to its revelation of those purposes. Similarly, when we apply this notion to Christ, we are ascribing ultimacy to him in God's revelatory plan. The one whom we have come to know from the gospel tradition as the crucified and risen Jesus is to be thought of as, prior to his human existence, already at one with God in summing up God's purposes for creation. In terms of the Christ hymn, the divine Wisdom has now been fully embodied as God's human image, so that to speak of Christ is also to speak of God. Because of what we believe to be the perfect fit between God's purpose and the life, death, and resurrection of Jesus, Christians speak of Jesus Christ as pre-existent, although in his role in creation he had not yet become the human being Jesus of Nazareth. By way of loose analogy, although her coronation did not take place until 1953, British subjects can still talk of the *queen's* having been born in 1925.

Christians need to be clear that their ascription of ultimacy to Jesus Christ that leads to trinitarian formulations is not an abandonment of belief in one God. Again the Christ hymn helps here. Through the use of the traditions about Wisdom, it remains within the conceptuality of Jewish monotheism but, by applying such terminology to a human being, constitutes a new departure within that monotheism:

> Christ is *both* to be identified as the divine Wisdom, i.e., none other than the one creator God active in creation and now in redemption, *and* to be distinguished from the Father, not as in a dualism whereby two gods are opposed, nor as in a paganism where two gods are distinguished and given different (and in principle parallel) tasks, but within the framework of Jewish creational monotheism itself.[86]

Some will have a more urgent and existential question about the assertions of the hymnic passage. What does it mean in a world of fragmentation, suffering, and confusion to repeat its claim that all things cohere in Christ or that they have been reconciled in him? It reflects an absolutely basic conviction that, despite the vastness of the cosmos, its determinative principle

---

86. N. T. Wright, "Poetry and Theology in Colossians 1.15-20," *NTS* 36 (1990) 463.

is not impersonal. The God who is the ground of existence bears a human face—that of Jesus Christ. This means, too, that, despite fragmenting and chaotic forces at work, we humans can trust that the pattern of Christ's death and resurrection is more fundamental and gives the power that sustains the world its distinctive character. So, although it defies present empirical verification, we confess that what holds the world together is not the survival of the fittest or an unending cycle of violence but the reconciliation and peace of Christ. To look at the underside of a tapestry reveals no intelligent pattern. The alternative vision of the hymn holds that, when the upper side is seen, design and beauty will be apparent. The pattern with Christ at the center will be there for all to see when the reconciliation that has taken place through his death and resurrection is fully realized.

At present, as Colossians itself suggests, there remains a hiddenness to the particular pattern of believers' lives (3:3). There is much that remains ambiguous, unexplained, and painful. But this is also where the writer's emphasis on hope comes into play. The hope of cosmic harmony is an assured one, even though it is not yet visible. As believers, we have been given essential pieces of the overall pattern. Christ's resurrection is determinative for what is to follow—he is the firstborn from the dead. Thus, like the first readers of this letter, we need to see our own fragmentary experiences of reconciliation in the present as the pledge and guarantee of the fuller reconciliation to come.

3. The hymnic material in Colossians tells a story of Christ's role in the cosmos from creation to consummation. In our postmodern context, we frequently encounter an aversion to overarching stories or grand metanarratives. Such narratives are seen as making absolute claims that are inevitably oppressive and violent. We need to acknowledge that various formulations of the Christian story have had such lamentable consequences. But the key question is whether the overarching christological narrative implied by the hymn in Colossians necessarily perpetuates violence toward others.

Colossians 1:11-20 features in the lectionary cycle as one of the readings for the celebration of Christ the King Sunday in Year C, and this could provide an appropriate context for reflecting on this issue. The other readings all focus on the nature of kingly power, with Luke's crucifixion story underlining how different Jesus' kingship is from usual human expectations of royal rule. This is a reminder that in Colossians, too, the cosmic reign of Christ, meant to effect not uniformity but a harmonious unity, is described as being accomplished through violent means—"through the blood of his cross." But this violence is not perpetrated *by* Christ but rather the violence is perpetrated *on* him. This cosmic narrative has at its heart not a pantocrator's tyranny or benevolent dictatorship but the brutal death of a victim. There can be no universal statements without at the same time focusing on someone bleeding and suffocating on a cross. Paradoxically, this victim is the cosmic ruler; his rule is achieved through the experience of suffering, and his peacemaking is accomplished through the absorption of violence.

The hymnic material's story is oriented toward God's purposes of *shalôm* for the whole creation, including reconciliation for the alienated and marginalized and justice for the oppressed, purposes brought about through the solidarity of Christ in his death with suffering victims. The reference to his death is now set in the context of Christ's role in creation and his cosmic rule means that it was not just one more act in a cycle of unending violence. Rather, there are grounds, through the vindication of his resurrection, for the hope that alienation and suffering throughout the creation will cease. This christological narrative actually subverts violence. It is always open to misuse, but those who profess allegiance to it can have no excuse for employing it in a narrow partisan fashion that encourages the marginalization or exclusion of those who do not share the particular christological formulations of their own tradition. After all, the hymn tells of the Christ of the cosmos, not of one who is the exclusive possession of one particular group. Attempts to impose on others this hymn's particular beliefs about Christ should have been ruled out, because there can be no rehearsing or living out the hymn in any way other than the way of peace and reconciliation demonstrated in the death of its protagonist.

4. If what happened in Christ's death and resurrection happened to the one who is God's unique and supreme agent in the cosmos, then the implication is that the readers have given their allegiance not to one intermediary among others, not to one cultic god among others, but to one who has a rightful, unparalleled claim on their lives. They simply cannot afford, therefore, to neglect their relationship with him through the gospel and the apostolic teaching of that gospel (see 1:23). "Continuing steadfast in the faith" is not a defensive attitude of clinging to old formulations come what may but an essential aspect of all creative attempts to interpret the gospel in the midst of the competing ideologies of our own times, if such attempts are to retain continuity with the apostolic gospel.

Contemplating the significance of the person and work of the Christ who is celebrated in worship will also remain an indispensable means of developing roots in the faith. If the first readers of Colossians were familiar with the hymn lying behind the passage, then the writer is in effect asking whether they understand the significance of what they sing. For us, too, the proper perspective on any confusion being sown by the variety of versions of the Christian gospel will derive from a recognition of the supremacy and sufficiency of Christ in both creation and new creation that we acknowledge in our own praise. If this status of Christ is truly appreciated, then both the dualistic tendencies and the world-denying spirituality that are always in danger of creeping into the life of the Christian church are undercut. Since Christ is the one at work in creation as well as in redemption, then the created world is immeasurably enhanced, not relegated to some inferior status by the work of reconciliation. Salvation is not rescue from a totally evil world but the claiming of the rightful possession of this world by the one who was an agent in its creation. The scope of salvation is as broad as life and as vast as the cosmos.

The effect of such a belief should be to make redeemed humans more fully human. It should enable them to appreciate the creation and to work to transform the structures of this world rather than to produce a private piety or spirituality that attempts to cut itself off from the body, ignores the natural environment, and disdains culture. If reconciliation of all things in Christ is at the center of God's purposes, then the pursuit of peace and acts of reconciliation by Christians serve those purposes. Working for a fair distribution of the world's resources, being concerned for animal welfare, and struggling to prevent the collapse of the ecosystem through the pollution of air, soil, and water have everything to do with this passage's celebration of cosmic reconciliation.

5. It has always been a pressing question for Christians whether a loving God would consign the majority of humans, who do not believe in Christ, to perdition. The hymn of Colossians has often been thought to provide a resource for responding to this concern, and some have claimed that Col 1:20 teaches a universal reconciliation in which every human being will be saved.[87] Whatever the merits of such an interpretation of the triumph of God's grace, it appears to be putting a question to Colossians that it was not designed to answer. Certainly the purpose of God's reconciliation through the work of Christ is depicted as cosmic in scope, and this gives grounds for hope. Yet when reconciliation is related to human beings in the application to the readers, it is made abundantly clear that any experience of reconciliation cannot be separated from the response of faith. Indeed, there is no guarantee even here, unless there is a continuance in faith, and later in the letter the writer can assert that the future for those who are disobedient holds an experience of the wrath of God (3:6). Contemporary discussions about

87. For a history of interpretation of this issue, see E. Schweizer, *The Letter to the Colossians,* trans. A. Chester (Minneapolis: Augsburg, 1982) 260-77.

whether a Christian approach to salvation should be pluralist, exclusivist, or inclusivist, which of necessity have a different agenda from that of the writer of this letter, may well need not only to develop the implications of cosmic reconciliation but also to ensure that in doing so they take seriously the present necessity of faith and the future judgment of God, if they are to claim continuity with Colossians. We should certainly, therefore, hope that all will be saved, but whether and how this becomes reality has to be left in the hands of God, where, of course, it belongs.

Rather than a provocation to speculation about whether every individual will be included in salvation, perhaps the real challenge of this hymnic material lies in its depiction of the church as the forerunner of a reconciliation that will be cosmic and universal in scope. This is surely a major implication of the image of the church as Christ's body. The worldwide community of believers is meant to be a microcosm in which the divine purpose in reclaiming the entire creation is anticipated and through which, as a reconciled and reconciling community, that purpose is furthered. If this is the case, then the most urgent task of Christians is to play their part in making the church a place of healing for broken relationships, where divisions caused by class, race, wealth, education, age, gender, nationality, or religious tradition are overcome, and an agent of peace and justice in situations of conflict, whether in the home or the workplace, at the national or the international level. Whatever the details of the future prepared by a loving and just God, our present focus is to say and do all we can as agitators for the values of the coming new world.

6. All the talk about the use of a hymn and its possible structure should remind us that the writer of Colossians has chosen to use the language of praise of Christ at a vital point in his message in order to reinforce the perspective he and his readers shared and to draw out its implications. It is an effective means of communication because it builds on religious experience—that of worship—and taps the religious emotions so frequently associated with songs of praise. From the perspective of Old Testament studies, Brueggemann has called attention to the power of doxology in the encounter with contemporary idolatries and ideologies. In its response to God, he claims, praise is also an assertion of an alternative world. The liturgy sings and proclaims that God reigns, disestablishing worldly powers and exposing their claims to ultimacy and control.[88]

Much the same can be said of the hymn in praise of Christ in Colossians. Its doxological language reinforces for its readers the alternative vision of the Pauline gospel in which Christ is supreme in the cosmos over all powers and has dealt with their disintegrating threat through his work of reconciliation. The language of worship still has both an educative and affective force. Theological reflection and preaching would do well, therefore, to learn to employ the resources of traditional and contemporary hymns and poetry and to include a rhetoric of devotion in its repertoire in the attempt to instruct, to move, and to motivate congregations to live out of the alternative world of gospel values, where the crucified and risen Christ is cosmic Lord.

---

88. See W. Brueggemann, *Israel's Praise: Doxology Against Idolatry and Ideology* (Philadelphia: Fortress, 1988).

THE LETTER BODY

COLOSSIANS 1:24–2:5, BODY-OPENING: PAUL'S PROCLAMATION OF THE GOSPEL AND ITS RELATION TO THE READERS

NIV

24Now I rejoice in what was suffered for you, and I fill up in my flesh what is still lacking in regard to Christ's afflictions, for the sake of his body, which is the church. 25I have become its servant by the commission God gave me to present to you the word of God in its fullness— 26the mystery that has been kept hidden for ages and generations, but is now disclosed to the saints. 27To them God has chosen to make known among the Gentiles the glorious riches of this mystery, which is Christ in you, the hope of glory.

28We proclaim him, admonishing and teaching everyone with all wisdom, so that we may present everyone perfect in Christ. 29To this end I labor, struggling with all his energy, which so powerfully works in me.

2 I want you to know how much I am struggling for you and for those at Laodicea, and for all who have not met me personally. 2My purpose is that they may be encouraged in heart and united in love, so that they may have the full riches of complete understanding, in order that they may know the mystery of God, namely, Christ, 3in whom are hidden all the treasures of wisdom and knowledge. 4I tell you this so that no one may deceive you by fine-sounding arguments. 5For though I am absent from you in body, I am present with you in spirit and delight to see how orderly you are and how firm your faith in Christ is.

NRSV

24I am now rejoicing in my sufferings for your sake, and in my flesh I am completing what is lacking in Christ's afflictions for the sake of his body, that is, the church. 25I became its servant according to God's commission that was given to me for you, to make the word of God fully known, 26the mystery that has been hidden throughout the ages and generations but has now been revealed to his saints. 27To them God chose to make known how great among the Gentiles are the riches of the glory of this mystery, which is Christ in you, the hope of glory. 28It is he whom we proclaim, warning everyone and teaching everyone in all wisdom, so that we may present everyone mature in Christ. 29For this I toil and struggle with all the energy that he powerfully inspires within me.

2 For I want you to know how much I am struggling for you, and for those in Laodicea, and for all who have not seen me face to face. 2I want their hearts to be encouraged and united in love, so that they may have all the riches of assured understanding and have the knowledge of God's mystery, that is, Christ himself,[a] 3in whom are hidden all the treasures of wisdom and knowledge. 4I am saying this so that no one may deceive you with plausible arguments. 5For though I am absent in body, yet I am with you in spirit, and I rejoice to see your morale and the firmness of your faith in Christ.

[a] Other ancient authorities read *of the mystery of God, both of the Father and of Christ*

COMMENTARY

A major function of this body opening is to establish not only Paul's unique relation to the gospel and, therefore, his special apostolic authority but also his apostolic presence with the recipients (2:5a). The picture of Paul that emerges, while just possible as an actual self-portrait, is probably better interpreted as that of a follower looking back in admiration over the apostle's career. As part of the literary device of pseudonymity, the writer, by taking on the persona of the imprisoned apostle, establishes his credentials in the Pauline tradition and strengthens his bond with the readers so that they will be ready to accept the extensive exhortations that follow. At the same time the passage is rhetorically effective. The emphasis on Paul's sufferings on behalf of the church, on the energy he expends in proclaiming Christ, and on the intensity of his pastoral concern demonstrates the excellence of his character as an apostle (ethos) and at the same time arouses in the readers admiration and sympathy (pathos).

In addition, this section continues to stress the knowledge and wisdom available to the readers through the revelation provided by Paul's gospel, and it does so as it leads up to the first explicit mention of the opposing teaching or philosophy in 2:4. The apostolic gospel involves the fulfilling or completing of the word of God (1:25), the revealing or making known of the mystery of Christ (1:26-27), and the teaching in all wisdom (1:28) so that believers might have understanding and knowledge of the mystery—that is, of Christ, in whom are hidden all the treasures of wisdom and knowledge (2:2-3).

1:24. Paul is said to be rejoicing in his sufferings for the sake of readers he has neither evangelized nor visited. Even such readers are to see themselves as intimately linked with Paul, because his sufferings have all been part of the Gentile mission that has enabled them to hear and believe the gospel. The meaning of the elaboration of this thought in the second part of the verse has been highly disputed. It is strange to move from the hymnic material (1:15-20), stressing the all-sufficiency of Christ's reconciling work on the cross,

to a statement that appears to suggest that there is something lacking in Christ's afflictions.

The claim is that in his physical body (presumably "flesh" [σάρξ *sarx*] is used because "body" [σῶμα *sōma*] will have an ecclesiological force in the last part of the clause) Paul is filling up what is lacking in Christ's afflictions and that he is doing this for the sake of Christ's body, the church. The term ὑστέρημα (*hysterēma*) occurs nine times in the NT in the sense of "need"/"want"/"deficiency," but this is the only place where it is associated with Christ. Similarly, this is the only place in which the noun θλῖψις (*thlipsis*), used elsewhere of the tribulations of the last days and of the afflictions experienced by various humans, is employed for the sufferings of Christ. The verb ἀνταναπληρόω (*antanaplēroō*, "to fill up/complete for someone else") is found nowhere else in the NT or the LXX. The combination of unusual usages may be confirmation that the formulation comes from someone other than Paul.

But what is to be made of this formulation? The interpretation that the sufferings endured by Christ for the redemption of believers were insufficient and needed to be supplemented by those of the church is highly unlikely. It is in conflict with the earlier emphasis on the sufficiency of Christ's reconciling work that the writer needs to make in the face of the implications of the Colossian philosophy. Another view looks to Paul's notion of the mystical union between Christ and believers and appeals to Phil 3:10, where Paul talks of sharing Christ's sufferings. But this provides no explanation for either how the sufferings are at the same time for other believers or how they complete what is lacking.

A more recent interpretation that has persuaded many suggests that the Jewish concept of the messianic woes makes sense of the formulation.[89] It is claimed that the idea was current in some Jewish apocalypses that there would be a period of worldwide tribulation, occasioned by the rising tide of human sin, a time that was to be both the death throes of this age and the birth pangs of

---

89. See especially R. J. Bauckham, "Colossians 1:24 Again: The Apocalyptic Motif," *EvQ* 47 (1975) 168-70.

the age to come. During this period a quota of suffering would have to be borne by the people of God before the age to come could be ushered in. Early Christians reinterpreted this concept, focusing attention on the messianic community, which, in the light of the Messiah's death and resurrection, must first share his suffering if it would share his glory (Rom 8:17). Certainly in Paul's thought and in other parts of the NT suffering is one of the major characteristics of the period of the overlap of the ages, and one of the others is the proclamation of the gospel (see also Mark 13:7-13; 2 Thess 2:3, 10-12). Within this pattern of thinking, it is claimed, the quota of suffering is no longer some arbitrary amount that has been assigned deterministically but that which the task of witness to the gospel demands (Rev 6:9-11).

Colossians 1:24 would fit such a pattern because the context here is also the worldwide proclamation of the gospel and Paul's unique vocation within it. Paul's sufferings are "for your sake" and "for the sake of his body, that is, the church" because they are part of his ministry to the Gentiles. That ministry is in turn hastening the day of glory, since, according to 1:27, Christ among the Gentiles is the hope of glory. Although *thlipsis* is used elsewhere in the NT of the final tribulation, it need not be held as part of this interpretation that "the afflictions of Christ" is a technical term meaning "the woes of the Messiah." The phrase could, in fact, be taken as an objective genitive meaning not the tribulations suffered by Christ but the tribulations suffered for Christ.

Despite its attractions, there are, however, problems with this view. The Jewish concept of the woes in fact had no place for a suffering Messiah and did not hold that the Messiah would come before the suffering of God's people took place. In addition, the assumption that there was at the time of the writing of this letter a clear-cut teaching about the "messianic woes" is dubious. There is considerable variation in the depiction of the nature, subject, and time of the woes in the writings from which the notion is said to come (e.g., 2 Bar 20; 25; *1 Enoch* 47; 4 Ezra 4:12, 33-37; 7; 13:16-19). And the thought of taking on a quota of suffering to hasten the inauguration of the new age does not fit particularly well in a

letter that elsewhere contains no mention of the imminence of the eschaton. Perhaps the most that can be said is that the writer is taking up a greatly modified version of a still-developing tradition about the woes.

In any case, it seems safe to assert that the sufferings are not the redemptive sufferings of Christ (for which, as noted, *thlipsis* is never used) but the subsequent afflictions of Paul for the church in connection with his witness to the gospel. They can be called the afflictions of Christ in the sense that Paul actively participates in the same pattern of suffering that Christ experienced by continuing his role as servant (see the Commentary on 1:25-27). They are lacking so long as the work of proclamation is incomplete—that is, until the parousia. Paul, as the suffering apostle to the Gentiles, is depicted, then, as playing a major part in making up the deficiency through his unique missionary role. In this way his share in the afflictions of Christ is not redemptive but missionary in character. He is portrayed as rejoicing in such suffering because it is for the sake of his Gentile converts and, therefore, by no means meaningless. Instead, his suffering is part of the fulfillment of God's plan in bringing in the consummation through the worldwide proclamation of the gospel.

1:25-27. In 1:23 Paul is said to have become a servant of the gospel, and now in 1:25 he is called a servant of the church. Paul's vocation thus binds him together with the readers. It is part of the same divine initiative through which the readers have experienced the benefits of reconciliation. The combination of the twofold designation as servant with the stress on Paul's sufferings in 1:24 recalls the Suffering Servant figure from Isaiah 40–55. Paul himself appears to have defined his vocation in the light of this background. His description of his call in Gal 1:15-16 echoes the language of Isa 49:1, 5-6; and he can apply Isa 49:8 to his own preaching to the Corinthians in 2 Cor 6:1-2 and Isa 49:4 to his own mission in Phil 2:16. When he says in Rom 15:8-9 that Christ became a servant of the circumcised to confirm the promises to the patriarchs and in order that the Gentiles might glorify God for God's mercy, the second part of that statement is less appropriate to the mission of the earthly Jesus and more applicable to Paul's continuation of Jesus' servant ministry in his Gentile mission. That Paul sees himself completing that role is confirmed in Rom 15:20-21, where he cites Isa 52:15 to describe his own mission strategy. It is likely, then, that this depiction of Paul's role builds on the earlier strand of thought and takes his suffering to be a distinctive part of the extension and completion of Christ's mission as suffering servant.

All this is in line with the stewardship[90] Paul received from God for the benefit of the readers. In 1 Cor 4:1-2, Paul refers to Apollos and himself as stewards of the mysteries of God, and in 1 Cor 9:17 he speaks of his ministry as a stewardship with which he has been entrusted. Here also the stewardship is of a mystery. It involves fulfilling or completing the word of God (1:25c), a synonym for the apostolic gospel, which as the word of the truth (1:4) can now also be said to convey the very Word of God.

The word of God in the gospel is further described, taking up a "revelation schema" probably used in early Christian preaching,[91] as the mystery hidden throughout the ages and generations but now revealed. The term "mystery" was common in Jewish apocalypses (e.g., Dan 2:18-19, 27-30; 4 Ezra 14:5; *1 Enoch* 51:3; 103:2) and in the Qumran writings (e.g., 1QM 3.8; 16:9; 1QS 3.21-23; 1QH 7.27; 10.4), where it denoted a secret aspect of God's purposes that needed to be disclosed. It could, however, also carry connotations of the mysterious, that which is beyond ordinary human comprehension. In the apocalypses it usually referred to an event that would only be revealed at the end of history, although, since it was already prepared in heaven, the seer could have knowledge of it at present (e.g., 4 Ezra 14:5; *1 Enoch* 9:6). In the Qumran literature, however, "mystery" could also refer to an event that has already taken place, such as the community's participation in the angelic assembly (e.g., 1QS 11.5-8).

While Paul can employ both the singular and the plural of the term "mystery" ($\mu\upsilon\sigma\tau\acute{\eta}\rho\iota\upsilon\nu$ *mystērion*) with a variety of references, it is in

Colossians that its use with reference to the heart of the gospel message, God's activity in Christ (1 Cor 2:7), becomes constant. Colossians 1:26-27; 2:2; and 4:3 all focus on the eschatological fulfillment of God's purposes of salvation in Christ. Whereas this mystery was hidden from previous ages and generations, it has "now" (the time of eschatological fulfillment) been revealed, and the privileged recipients of the revelation, via Paul's ministry, are God's "saints." All Christian believers as God's holy people (1:2), not a select few who have received special visions and knowledge (2:18), have access to the central mystery: God's plan for history and the cosmos.

The phrase "the riches of the glory" (1:27a) stresses the surpassing worth of this mystery that is now, in fact, an "open secret"; as a result of Paul's mission, it is "among the Gentiles," the means of incorporating the Gentiles into God's plan of salvation. The further summary of the mystery in 1:27b ("which is Christ among you, the hope of glory") makes the same point in a different formulation. At the center of the mystery are the person and work of Christ; the glory of the mystery derives from the Christ who embodies the gospel's assured hope of the future glory to be restored to humanity and the cosmos (see 3:4; see also Rom 8:17-25). This Christ is not just among the Gentiles but now more specifically "among you," the Gentile Christian readers. The preposition $\dot{\epsilon}\nu$ (*en*) can be translated "in" (so NIV, NRSV), but in line with the first part of the verse, of which this second part is a further explanation, it more probably has the force of "among."[92]

1:28-29. The stress on the universal scope of the proclamation of the open secret constituted by Christ is continued through the threefold repetition of "every person." It is hard to avoid the conclusion that this is in opposition to the notion of mysteries and esoteric knowledge for a select group of initiates. In Paul's vocation, proclamation is not divorced from teaching, and instructing also

---

90. By translating it as "commission," the NIV and the NRSV flatten out the force of οἰκονομία (*oikonomia*), which has in view the administration carried out by a steward.

91. See N. A. Dahl, "Form-Critical Observations on Early Christian Preaching," in *Jesus in the Memory of the Early Church* (Minneapolis: Augsburg, 1976) 32-33.

92. See E. Lohse, *Colossians and Philemon* Hermeneia (Philadelphia: Fortress, 1971) 76; P. Pokorný, *Colossians: A Commentary,* trans. S. S. Schatzmann (Peabody, Mass.: Hendrickson, 1991) 103; M. Barth and H. Blanke, *Colossians* AB 34B (New York: Doubleday, 1994) 265. It is no objection to this interpretation to say, as does J. D. G. Dunn, *The Epistles to the Colossians and to Philemon,* NIGTC (Grand Rapids: Eerdmans, 1996) 123, that it makes the phrase add hardly anything to the preceding "among the nations," since the style of Colossians contains many redundancies for effect with synonymous parallels and repetitions of thought.

involves admonishing. The activity of admonishing can take place through encouragement or reproof, but it usually implies that there is some difficulty or problem in the attitude or behavior of its recipients that needs to be overcome. The apostolic preaching and teaching about Christ "in all wisdom" can be seen, therefore, as an essential part of the answer to the writer's prayer for the readers in 1:9 that they might be filled with knowledge "in all wisdom." Paul is portrayed as a wisdom teacher whose teaching is not just for a select few but for everyone. Whatever other claims to wisdom there might be, his teaching provides the means to true wisdom, and the goal of his mission is to present every person perfect or mature in Christ (see 1:22). In this perspective, whether the language employed is that of perfection or of fullness (2:9-10), completion is available in believers' relationship to Christ and nowhere else. Because of such a conviction, Paul is depicted as pouring all his efforts into attaining this objective. The human effort and the toll it takes are immense ("I toil and struggle"), but they are matched by the equally immense divine resources for the task—literally, "in accordance with his energy that he energizes in me in power." The term "energy" (ἐνεργεια *energeia*) will be employed in connection with God's raising Christ from the dead (2:12); for the writer of Colossians, it was this power that was also operative in Paul's accomplishment of his missionary task. In this way, the proclamation of the mystery among the Gentiles can be traced back through Paul's apostleship to the power of God.

2:1-3. The readers of the letter are now drawn more specifically into the scope of Paul's mission as those on whose behalf his struggles have been carried out. The imagery of the athletic contest (ἀγών *agōn*) is continued from the preceding verse to underline the strenuous exertion demanded by Paul's missionary vocation (cf. 1 Cor 9:25-27). Yet no sooner have the recipients of Paul's task been narrowed from "every human being" (1:28) to "you" than they are broadened again to include "those in Laodicea" and "all who have not seen me face to face." This raises questions about who the intended recipients of the letter really are. If deutero-Pauline, was Colossians meant to be a general letter to all the churches of the Gentile mission in Asia Minor, with Laodicea as the immediate destination

(cf. 4:13-16; see also the section "Author and Addressees," 577-83, in the Introduction)?

In 2:2 the goal of Paul's struggles for the recipients is expressed in terms of their hearts being encouraged (a formulation found only in the disputed Pauline letters; see 4:8; Eph 6:22; 2 Thess 2:17), and this encouragement will entail and foster the readers' unity as they are held together in love (see 3:14, where love is described as "the bond of perfection"). In the style typical of this writer, alliteration and the heaping up of synonyms are combined to underscore that the goal is "all the riches of the full assurance of understanding" and is "the knowledge of God's mystery, Christ." Here the content of the mystery is simply Christ rather than "Christ among you," as in 1:27. The understanding of Christ desired by the writer for his readers goes beyond merely an intellectual grasp and entails the full assurance or deep conviction that will enable them to appropriate and live out of the richness it provides (see also 2:6-7). They will be able to do this, because in Christ are all the resources they need—"all the treasures of wisdom and knowledge." All that Wisdom stood for (1:15-20), including instruction on living wisely (2 Bar 44:14 and 54:13 use the language of "treasures of wisdom" with reference to the teaching of the law), can now be found in Christ. Anyone who is interested in secret or hidden knowledge is to be assured that true wisdom and knowledge are "hidden" in Christ and, therefore, are also paradoxically no longer hidden but revealed to all those who believe in the apostolic gospel.

2:4-5. If all this talk of understanding, knowledge, wisdom, and mystery in 1:25–2:3 (and 1:9-10) has suggested that the writer has had an eye on the opposing teaching, then 2:4 explicitly confirms this. "I am saying this . . ." is retrospective, referring to what has just been said. And the reason for having said it is to prevent anyone from deceiving the readers by persuasive speech. The writer is naturally attempting to employ persuasive speech, and so the context with its mention of deceiving means that here the term should be taken negatively as connoting plausible, but in the end specious, arguments. Such claims about special wisdom and knowledge have the effect of undermining the sufficiency of the essential mystery of what God has done in Christ.

Yet, before launching into a more detailed interaction with the offending teaching and as part of his own persuasive strategy, the writer lets the addressees know that he is not issuing his warning because only he has assured understanding and they are all gullible and easily led astray. Instead, he assures them of his solidarity with them, even though he is not physically present, and of his joy at the reports he has received that the community is basically in good shape. It is frequently observed that the two terms used to describe their condition, "morale" (τάξις *taxis*) and "firmness" (στερέωμα *stereōma*), were also used in military contexts, where they denoted military formation or order and the solid front presented by an army. But the terms could be employed more generally in other contexts, and here they should be taken to indicate the good order that the community maintains and the firmness or solidity of its faith in Christ. "I rejoice" in 2:5*b* forms an inclusio with "I rejoice" in 1:24*a*, setting the tone of this section and its attempt to cement the links between the readers and the gospel originating in Paul's unique mission. Paul's vocation has been depicted as having been designed to meet precisely the need of the readers for growth in understanding and maturity in Christ. Thus both his sufferings for them and the effectiveness of his agonizing toil in producing well-grounded congregations like theirs are a cause for joy.

REFLECTIONS

1. What is the relationship between this depiction of Paul's ministry and present-day proclamation of the gospel? It is often assumed that, for this passage to have any bearing on the present, Paul should be taken as a model for Christian ministry and existence. Yet, as we have seen, the primary thrust of the passage does not move in this direction at all. Paul is portrayed, rather, as having a unique mission, as providing the foundational apostolic link with the gospel of Christ. Even his suffering, which in 2 Cor 1:6-7, for example, is seen as an experience shared by other believers, is in Colossians uniquely his own and has the special role of "completing what is lacking in Christ's afflictions for the sake of his body." Paul's suffering is described in the first-person singular, and there is no mention of the readers or the whole church joining him in his missionary role of suffering service. Here a suffering church is not the point; rather, it is the apostle suffering for the church.

Since the passage focuses so intensely on Paul and his ministry, it would certainly be in line with its purpose to preach a sermon celebrating the person and achievement of the apostle Paul and all that Christians, and in particular Gentile Christians, owe him in inheriting a law-free gospel together with his reflections on the implications of that gospel. Such a celebration could, of course, be critically appreciative. But, given the denigrating characterization of Paul as the distorter of the simple message of Jesus that is still all too frequently heard even in churches, it would be entirely appropriate to stress the immense debt of gratitude owed to the apostle. An interpretation in this vein need not remain simply at the level of a historical sketch or eulogy of a heroic human being. Taking its lead from the portrait of Paul in Colossians, a homily or lesson on Paul's impact and our links with him can draw out and reflect on (1) the theological dimensions of Paul's significant role as suffering servant, steward of the mystery, and wisdom teacher in the working out of God's reconciling purposes for the cosmos; (2) the centrality of Christ in his proclamation; (3) Paul's pastoral objectives for his Gentile converts; and (4) his sense of being energized for his struggles through the divine power at work in the resurrection of Christ.

Reflection on Paul's ministry of the Word would be appropriate when 1:15-28 appears in the lectionary in Year C (Proper 11) alongside Amos 8:1-12 and Luke 10:38-42. Amos pronounces God's judgment on Israel, which will entail a famine of hearing the words of the Lord, so that even those seeking the Lord's Word will not find it. The Gospel reading celebrates the salvation Jesus brings to Israel as Mary takes the "better part," the role of the disciple in attentively listening to the words of Jesus in defiance of the social codes. In this context, the Colossians passage underlines the privileges of the new era of salvation in which the Word of God is made fully known (1:25). Paul's preaching and teaching make it possible for ethnic barriers to be overcome and for Gentiles now to have access to Christ's wisdom, since what is proclaimed among them is the content of the Word of God or the revealed mystery is precisely Christ. And here there is no scarcity or famine but "the riches of the glory of this mystery" (1:27); as 1:15-20 has shown, everything that could be predicated of God's Wisdom and more is now made available in Christ.

2. Some of the items listed in the discussion of the portrait of Paul raise the persistent question of whether they are totally unique to Paul's ministry or whether they should also characterize any proclamation of the gospel. One might well point to the fact that the depiction of Paul's ministry of preaching and teaching in 1:28 shifts temporarily from the use of "I" to "we," indicating perhaps that not only Timothy (1:1) but also other apostolic coworkers may be in view. Certainly some of the language of 1:28-29 is employed of Epaphras in 4:12.

The rhetorical function of the passage may also help us here. The Commentary stresses its elements of ethos and pathos. Ethos points to the character of the speaker in such a way as to lend credence to the message. The characterization of Paul can then serve as a reminder of the intimate link between the message and the messenger. Audiences do judge the message by the character of the messenger as perceived through his or her attitudes and actions. The way Christian preachers and Christians in general live their lives, therefore, affects the way their message is received. The pathos of this passage may lie in its evoking from the readers both sympathy and admiration for the apostle. The latter aspect of admiration easily shades into emulation. Admiration for Paul's sense of vocation, for his keeping Christ central in his preaching, for his goal of presenting all believers as mature in Christ, and for his labors to achieve this goal can properly lead to these aspects of his ministry being considered models.

Despite Paul's sufferings having a special role, there may well also be justification for taking them as exemplary. Paul's sufferings have a unique place in the worldwide proclamation of the gospel. The extended delay of the parousia, however, means that the task of universal proclamation is not nearly as complete as Colossians supposes. It would be difficult to maintain either from an exegesis of the text or the history of the church that an implication of the passage is that Paul has absorbed such a disproportionate amount of the afflictions of Christ that the readers or other later believers can expect a life free from suffering or need only bear some minimal amount. Instead, while the missionary task remains, the afflictions of Christ continue regardless of the amount of them borne by Paul. Paul, then, can be seen as modeling the pain and cost of missionary proclamation and the ability to rejoice in the midst of such suffering. Indeed, in the undisputed letters he envisages that suffering, including suffering that is for the benefit of others, is the lot of other ministers of the new covenant and of all believers until the eschaton (see Rom 8:17-18; 2 Cor 1:3-11; 4:7-12).

3. The dominance of the theme of wisdom and its acompanying terminology of mystery and knowledge is also worth pondering. In our day, just as much as at the time of the Letter to the Colossians, there is no lack of those offering wisdom whether in the form of a return to ancient mysteries or of new scientific cosmologies. Gurus abound to offer their wit and wisdom about how to lead our lives, to cope with life's vicissitudes, and to find fulfillment. What does it mean for us if, with Colossians, we take Paul as our wisdom teacher, pointing us to and explicating the source of wisdom in God's revelation in Christ?

Since the wisdom found in Christ is cosmic in scope, Christians will claim to have already discovered the essential clues about meaning and life; but they will also know that they can never exhaust such wisdom and that their own grasp of it remains partial and provisional. They will, therefore, always be ready to explore new perspectives from their own foundation and to learn from the best of human knowledge and wisdom. Their own particular starting point in Christ and the rich tradition of Christian theology and wisdom will provide a basic means of discrimination in the face of other claims.

At the same time, if the church believes that all the treasures of wisdom and knowledge are hidden in Christ (2:3) and that its task is to teach wisdom (1:28; 3:16), a major but too often neglected implication is that it will do everything to encourage its members, whatever their particular field of vocation or interest, consciously to relate these to their faith in Christ. Without risking such a Christian perspective on all aspects of life and a corresponding acting out of its implications, the impression will be produced that the church has reduced the cosmic dimensions of wisdom, and indeed of Christ's lordship, to private religious convictions and corporate religious rites. Nor should we forget that Colossians will measure the wisdom of any teaching not simply by its claims but by its results (2:23)—what quality of living it produces—and that it will summarize much of its own ethical teaching about living all of life under the lordship of Christ as "walking in wisdom" (cf. 4:5).

COLOSSIANS 2:6–4:6, BODY-MIDDLE: EXHORTATIONS

OVERVIEW

It has been argued that on an epistolary analysis the heart of the letter is to be found in its body-middle, extending from 2:6 to 4:6. The present section would then constitute the opening half of the body-middle. On a rhetorical analysis, it has been suggested that this section is the middle of the three divisions of the *probatio,* the proof of the main propositions of the argument. Both analyses thus confirm the central significance for Colossians of this section, in which the writer interacts with the opposing teaching or philosophy. Certainly the letter is more than a polemical confrontation with the philosophy, but the positioning of this section reminds the interpreter that the danger from the opposing teaching is at the center of the letter's rhetorical situation. The teaching has provoked the writing of the letter, but the writer then uses the opportunity provided by the perceived danger to fashion a more general message of exhortation, in which the concerns and the language of the philosophy are taken up into a new framework and thereby given new content. In line with such a view of the role of the philosophy, the section begins (2:6 15) and ends (3:1 4) with passages that appear a little more general in orientation but still remain intimately connected to the writer's concern about misleading teaching.

Colossians 2:6–3:4, Exhortation to Faithfulness to the Gospel

Colossians 2:6-7, Live in Accordance with the Tradition About Christ

NIV	NRSV
⁶So then, just as you received Christ Jesus as Lord, continue to live in him, ⁷rooted and built up in him, strengthened in the faith as you were taught, and overflowing with thankfulness.	6As you therefore have received Christ Jesus the Lord, continue to live your lives*^a* in him, ⁷rooted and built up in him and established in the faith, just as you were taught, abounding in thanksgiving. *^a Gk to walk*

COMMENTARY

In many ways these two verses sum up everything the writer has to say. They make the general point that he will spell out in more detail in interaction with the philosophy. The "therefore" points back to the assurance he has expressed about the well-groundedness of the readers' faith (2:5*b*). Given this, his basic exhortation is that they are to carry on in the fashion in which they have begun and to become even more steadfast in the faith. Christ has been the beginning point for their faith, and the cultivation of their relationship with him will be the means by which they are enabled to continue effectively. The exhortation takes the form of a variation on the indicative/imperative construction. In the indicative part ("as you received Christ Jesus the Lord") the focus is not on the readers' initial experience of receiving Christ into their lives by exercising faith. Instead, the verb employed (παραλαμβάνω *paralambanō*) denotes the receiving of tradition that has been passed on (cf. 1 Cor 15:1, 3; Gal 1:9; 1 Thess 4:1; 2 Thess 3:6). Since the gospel centers in Christ and his lordship, the title "Christ Jesus the Lord" can serve as an effective encapsulation of this tradition. As 2:8 will make clear, the writer sets the Pauline gospel and the philosophy over against each other in terms of tradition. It is not that one is seen as gospel and the other as tradition, but rather that both take the form of tradition. The difference is that whereas the gospel is regarded as the apostolic tradition about Christ, the philosophy is depicted pejoratively as merely human tradition. But the personal aspect of this formulation about the gospel tradition remains significant. The writer believes that Christ as a living person and the reality of his lordship are mediated by the traditions about him, so that receiving those traditions entails not only learning about but also being shaped by Christ Jesus the Lord as the powerful source of a new way of life.

The imperative clause "walk in him" makes precisely this point. (On the force of "walk" [περιπατέω *peripateō*] see the Commentary on 1:10, where in the intercessory prayer report a similar relationship between believers' conduct and their confession of Christ's lordship is set out.) Given the earlier stress on the cosmic scope of Christ's lordship (1:15-20), it should occasion no surprise that the writer expects his readers' behavior to reflect this reality. Yet the motivation stressed here is not so much obedience to this Lord as it is living out of the resources of a relationship of incorporation into him, which is the force of the phrase "in him."

Four participles in v. 7 indicate aspects of living in relation to the Lord. The imagery of the first two conveys that Christ the Lord is the soil in which the readers are to continue to put down their roots and to grow, the foundation on which they are to continue to be built. The notion of solidity is also conveyed through the third participle. They are to be made firm or established in the faith, just as they were taught. This echoes the language of 1:23 and reinforces the importance of the tradition they have received (cf. 2:6) as that which must be appropriated for their living. The fourth participle introduces a different topic, but one that is typical of the letter: thanksgiving (cf. 1:12; 3:16-17; 4:2). The lives of those who appropriate the tradition are to have a surplus of thankfulness. This should not be a surprising emphasis in the context, for it is precisely in drawing on the tradition that believers are reminded of all that God has done in Christ on their behalf and thereby filled to overflowing with gratitude.

REFLECTIONS

1. These two verses make absolutely clear that in Christian existence orthodoxy and orthopraxis go hand in hand; "talking the talk" cannot be separated from "walking the walk." But what is said in Colossians takes us beyond such basic assertions. The pattern of this exhortation to Christian living that involves an indicative statement followed by an imperative is sometimes referred to by the slogan "Become what you are." This is helpful in pointing out that the indicative of the new life in Christ, to which the apostolic teaching points and which it attempts to safeguard, is more than simply a possibility; it is real. At the same time, the fact that an imperative is still needed makes clear that the new situation is still in progress and that the relationship between who one is in Christ and how one lives is not an automatic one. The pattern shares, therefore, in the eschatological tension typical of Pauline thought. The indicative reflects what God has already done in Christ in inaugurating the new order, while the imperative is the exhortation to appropriate and live this out in the midst of the powers of this present age that are still at work. Here the formulation about having "received Christ Jesus the Lord" (2:6) highlights that it is the implications of that lordship for all of believers' lives that need to be lived out.

In a letter that from this point will consist of a whole series of imperatives, it is crucial for the writer to establish what he sees as the proper perspective on Christian ethical exhortations. They do not represent an impossible ideal or a crushing burden. It is not uncommon to hear people complaining that their employers are increasing their workload or expanding their jobs but not providing them with the necessary resources. Colossians underscores that the necessary resources have already been made available for the task of Christian living and that there is no need to be numbed by the sense of powerlessness that makes us spectators in life. What is more, the motivation for living the good life is not a fear of punishment or a sense of duty or a need to be needed or a hope of reward (whether in the afterlife or in this life in terms of self-fulfillment). For those of us who are prone to be driven by such motivations, the relationship symbolized by the indicative and the imperative can provide a healthy reminder that the primary dynamic that should govern Christian behavior is rather a living out of our relationship to Christ, an appropriating of what God has already accomplished in Christ. This also puts the emphasis where it belongs in Christian living—not on human willpower or effort but on God's grace—and enables such living to be characterized by thankfulness (2:7).

2. In reflecting on how the church can best resist succumbing to today's alternative lordships that compete for adherence, we would do well to consider again the way in which these verses assign particular importance to the role of tradition and catechesis in the process of appropriating the reality of Christ's lordship. Colossians assumes that, if there is to be an effective demonstration of that lordship, believers will continually avail themselves of the resources of Christian teaching about their roots and foundation in order to nourish and support their active allegiance to Christ as Lord. Only those churches that are providing consistent Christian education will be in a position to make the same assumption.

Colossians 2:8-15, Do Not Be Captured by Human Tradition

NIV	NRSV
[8]See to it that no one takes you captive through hollow and deceptive philosophy, which depends on human tradition and the basic principles of this world rather than on Christ.	[8]See to it that no one takes you captive through philosophy and empty deceit, according to human tradition, according to the elemental spirits of the universe,[a] and not according to Christ. [9]For in him the whole fullness of deity dwells bodily, [10]and you have come to fullness in him, who is the head of every ruler and authority. [11]In him also you were circumcised with a spiritual circumcision,[b] by putting off the body of the flesh in the circumcision of Christ; [12]when you were buried with him in baptism, you were also raised with
[9]For in Christ all the fullness of the Deity lives in bodily form, [10]and you have been given fullness in Christ, who is the head over every power and authority. [11]In him you were also circumcised, in the putting off of the sinful nature,[a] not with a circumcision done by the hands of men but with the circumcision done by Christ, [12]having been buried with him in baptism and raised with him	
[a] 11 Or *the flesh*	[a] Or *the rudiments of the world* [b] Gk *a circumcision made without hands*

621

NIV

through your faith in the power of God, who raised him from the dead.

[13]When you were dead in your sins and in the uncircumcision of your sinful nature,[a] God made you[b] alive with Christ. He forgave us all our sins, [14]having canceled the written code, with its regulations, that was against us and that stood opposed to us; he took it away, nailing it to the cross. [15]And having disarmed the powers and authorities, he made a public spectacle of them, triumphing over them by the cross.[c]

[a]13 Or *your flesh*   [b]13 Some manuscripts *us*   [c]15 Or *them in him*

NRSV

him through faith in the power of God, who raised him from the dead. [13]And when you were dead in trespasses and the uncircumcision of your flesh, God[a] made you[b] alive together with him, when he forgave us all our trespasses, [14]erasing the record that stood against us with its legal demands. He set this aside, nailing it to the cross. [15]He disarmed[c] the rulers and authorities and made a public example of them, triumphing over them in it.

[a] Gk *he*   [b] Other ancient authorities read *made us*; others, *made*   [c] Or *divested himself of*

COMMENTARY

This section consists of the issuing of a general warning against the opposing teaching, followed by a series of assertions about what God has done in Christ for the readers. In this context, the latter are clearly meant to function as antidotes to some basic features of the alternative teaching. It is not, however, until the next section (2:16-23), with its mention of practical aspects of the philosophy, that the philosophy's specifics come a little more clearly into view. For the present-day reader this necessitates that inferences drawn from these later, more explicit details are employed to fill out some of the positions against which the assertions of this earlier section appear to be aimed. (See the section "The 'Philosophy' Opposed in the Letter," 560-68, in the Introduction for a general treatment of this issue.)

2:8. The strong warning to "beware" or "be on your guard against" indicates that the writer sees a real danger being posed by the views circulating in his readers' location. They are to beware lest anyone capture their allegiance and thereby lead them away from the Christ of the apostolic gospel. The Greek pronoun τὶς (*tis*) is indefinite but singular, leaving open the possibility that writer and readers may be aware of a particular individual who is a key proponent of the teaching.

Three negative evaluations of the alternative teaching are given to dissuade the readers from being taken in by it. A variety of teachings and religions in the ancient world could be designated philosophies. "Philosophy" here has negative connotations simply because of the context, particularly the phrases that follow. This philosophy is seen as being in opposition to the faith, in which the readers are to be established (cf. 1:23; 2:7); the description "empty deceit" writes it off as being devoid of truth in comparison to the gospel, earlier described as "the word of truth" (1:5). It is seen as being in accordance with human tradition rather than the tradition that has Christ Jesus the Lord as its content and source (cf. 2:6). Whereas these antitheses have been implicit, the final depiction has an explicit antithesis: The alternative philosophy is according to "the elemental spirits of the universe" (NRSV) or "the basic principles of this world" (NIV) and not according to Christ. The contrasting translations represent the two main competing interpretations of a highly disputed phrase, though the NIV has inserted an extra interpretive gloss by translating τοῦ κόσμου (*tou kosmou*) as "this world" instead of "the world." (Reasons have already been given for opting for the interpretation represented by the NRSV. See the section "The 'Elemental Spirits of the Universe' and Dualistic Cosmology, 565-67, in the Introduction.) So the writer bluntly asserts that the philosophy should not be seen as presenting the readers with a both . . . and situation, in which the gospel sits comfortably with elements from other traditions. Instead, the gospel about Christ is incompatible with the teaching into which it has been amalgamated. Two different authorities lie behind the philosophy and the Pauline gospel—in the one case the cosmic spirits or powers and in the other case Christ.

2:9-15. To reinforce the point about different authorities (see the "for" at the beginning of 2:9), the writer's strategy in these verses is to remind the readers of all that they already have "in Christ." The English translations often obscure this, but the phrase "in him" occurs at the beginning of v. 9 and at the end of v. 15, and "in him" or "in whom" is found five times in these verses. It is not surprising that, where incorporation into Christ is so dominant a note, a reminder of the readers' baptism, the event that represents their union with Christ, is an important part of this argument (vv. 11-12).

2:9-10. The earlier hymnic material had asserted of Christ, "in him all the fullness was pleased to dwell" (1:19). Now this language is taken up again. It is made clear that "all the fullness" refers to the fullness of the deity, and the present tense "dwells" replaces "was pleased to dwell." But the main change is the addition of the adverb "bodily" (σωματικῶς *sōmatikōs*). The assertion of v. 9 as a whole makes two points over against the philosophy. Since the totality of deity is embodied in Christ, there can be no grounds for a person who confesses Christ to seek God or fullness elsewhere or to think that the way to this divine fullness is through cosmic intermediaries. What is more, there is no dualism between the God of the higher world and the body viewed as some prisonhouse of the soul in the lower world. The apostolic gospel holds together the two concepts the philosophy deemed incompatible, because all the fullness of the deity not only dwells in Christ but dwells in him bodily—that is, it dwells in one who became incarnate in a body of flesh (cf. 1:22).

Through their incorporation into Christ, the readers have themselves been filled. This could be taken to mean that believers have all the fullness of deity within them, just as Christ does. But such an interpretation clearly runs counter to the unique status and role the writer has been anxious to claim for Christ. Its force is probably, therefore, more general. Because of their link with the fullness of deity through Christ, by definition there can be nothing lacking about their relation with God, no deficiency that needs to be filled by

further teachings and practices offered by the philosophy.

This is also the case because the one through whom they have been filled is the head over every principality and power. Principalities and powers had already been shown to have been created and reconciled through Christ in 1:16, 20, and Christ had already been designated as head over the church in 1:18; now Christ's headship is said to be over these powers. Believers need not see themselves as subject to the powers. Instead, the cosmic powers are subject to the Christ through whom believers have been filled. To acknowledge the truth of this assertion would be to make the ascetic and cultic observances of the philosophy that were designed to appease the principalities and powers completely redundant. Everything depends, then, on the readers' appropriation by faith of God's saving actions in Christ, and it is this very thing that their baptism proclaimed.

2:11-12. Instead of talking about their union with Christ in his death, burial, and resurrection as proclaimed in baptism, as does Paul in Romans 6 and as might have been expected here, the writer speaks of their union with Christ in his circumcision, burial, and resurrection. This change in formulation produces a more complex argument, but it is highly significant. The use of the metaphor of circumcision for Christ's death is another means of taking on and undermining the viewpoint of the philosophy.

It is not that the philosophy is to be thought of as advocating physical circumcision and, therefore, as Jewish. After all, there is no clear polemic against circumcision, and it is not listed as among the philosophy's observances in vv. 16-23.[93] Nor is there any clear evidence that the philosophy employed the term "circumcision" for its own initiation rites, as some have held.[94] Rather, the use of the metaphor of circumcision enables the writer to deal once more with the philosophy's view of what has to be done with humans' body of flesh. The observance of detailed ascetic regulations was meant to enable people to divest themselves of the encumbrance of the physical

---

93. J. D. G. Dunn, *The Epistles to the Colossians and to Philemon,* NIGTC (Grand Rapids: Eerdmans, 1996) 155-56, concedes the lightness of any polemic and holds that debate with Jews about the significance of spiritual circumcision should be envisaged.
94. E.g., E. Lohse, *Colossians and Philemon,* trans. W. R. Poehlmann and R. J. Karris, Hermeneia (Philadelphia: Fortress, 1971) 102.

body and rise above it in visionary experience of the upper realm. "The stripping off of the body of flesh" is the terminology the writer picks up in v. 11, as he claims that the stripping off of the body of flesh that really matters has already taken place for the readers in their union with Christ in his circumcision.

This is to take the phrase "the circumcision of Christ" as an objective rather than subjective genitive construction. In other words, it refers to the circumcision Christ underwent rather than to the circumcision that belongs to him or is effected by him (as opposed to the NIV).[95] The circumcision he underwent is his death. It was not merely the stripping off of a token part of the flesh, the foreskin, but a cutting off of his whole body of flesh through death. When taken in this way, the phrase allows the argument to have the parallel already mentioned—that is, with the notion of union with Christ in his death, burial, and resurrection found in Romans 6.

Just as believers' dying with Christ is not a physical death but a spiritual dying to sin with clear ethical consequences, so also their being circumcised with Christ is not the cutting off of their physical existence in death but a spiritual circumcision that also has particular ethical consequences. Theirs is "a circumcision made without hands"; and "made without hands" always stands in implicit contrast to "made with hands," an expression typically employed in the LXX for idols as human constructs. The former refers to that which is the work of God and belongs to the new order inaugurated by the divine activity in Christ (see Mark 14:58; 2 Cor 5:1). What union with Christ in the stripping off of his body of flesh means ethically for believers will be spelled out later in 3:9, where the cognate verbal form "having stripped off" ($\dot{\alpha}\pi\epsilon\kappa\delta\acute{\upsilon}o\mu\alpha\iota$ *apekdyomai*) is employed with reference to having put off the old humanity and its practices. This, together with the use of the same participle in 2:15, confirms that the notion of divesting oneself of the physical

body is the key issue the writer is tackling at this point.

Union with Christ in his circumcision corresponds to union with Christ in his death, but the writer holds off actual mention of baptism until reminding the readers of their burial with Christ. The return to the more traditional formulation, taking up the language of Rom 6:4, indicates that the writer is moving away from direct engagement with the philosophy and is underscoring more generally the decisive significance of his readers' incorporation into Christ. The vivid imagery of burial, with its counterpart in immersion in the baptismal waters, stresses the reality of the death to and break with the life of the past. Neither the NRSV nor the NIV reflects the fact that the Greek syntax does not explicitly connect union with Christ in his resurrection with baptism. The Greek term $\dot{\epsilon}\nu$ $\dot{\wp}$ (*en hō*), which follows the mention of baptism in 2:12*b*, is best taken, with the majority of commentators, as "in him" rather than "in it" and as paralleling the same phrase at the beginning of 2:11.

The formulation about union with Christ in his resurrection does, however, differ from that of Romans 6. In Colossians believers are said to have already been raised with Christ, while in Rom 6:5, 8 the future tense is used of the relationship. The difference in formulation is real but should not be exaggerated. A closer examination of Romans 6 indicates that Paul could also speak there of a present as well as a future aspect of sharing Christ's resurrection life. In Rom 6:4 Paul talks of a present walk in newness of life; in Rom 6:10-11, he argues that in identification with Christ believers are to consider themselves alive to God; and in Rom 6:13 he urges them to live as those who have been brought from death to life. These expressions presuppose that in Paul's thinking about believers' union with Christ in his resurrection there was an "already" as well as a "not yet" aspect. The shift in emphasis to the "already" aspect in Colossians makes sense in this context, where the writer wants to underscore all that believers have in Christ and to minimize the uncertainty about salvation induced by the philosophy. Since this is a shift in emphasis rather than a major change of thought, it should not be made a decisive factor in the issue of authorship.

If baptism is still implicitly in view in the

---

95. Cf. R. P. Martin, *Colossians and Philemon,* NCB (Greenwood, S.C.: Attic, 1974) 82-83; P. T. O'Brien, *Colossians, Philemon,* WBC 44 (Waco, Tex.: Word, 1982) 117; J. D. G. Dunn, *The Epistles to the Colossians and to Philemon,* NIGTC (Grand Rapids: Eerdmans, 1996) 158. Contrary opinions can be found in E. Schweizer, *The Letter to the Colossians,* trans. A. Chester (Minneapolis: Augsburg, 1982) 143; M. J. Harris, *Colossians and Philemon* (Grand Rapids: Eerdmans, 1991) 103; P. Pokorny, *Colossians: A Commentary,* trans. S. S. Schatzmann (Peabody, Mass.: Hendrickson, 1991) 124-25.

mention of having been raised with Christ, then it is significant that, while baptism as the external event is one aspect, faith as the internal response is the accompanying aspect of the one complex of "conversion/initiation." The faith that links believers to Christ's resurrection is "faith in the power of God who raised him from the dead."

2:13-15. The same power of God operative in Christ's resurrection has been effective for the readers. With a slight variation on the imagery of resurrection with Christ, the writer reminds them that God has made them alive together with Christ. And if this is the case, then their pre-Christian past must, comparatively speaking, be viewed as a condition of spiritual and moral death. Already in Judaism a life in disease, sin, alienation, or captivity could be seen as a life in Sheol, or the realm of death (see Pss 13:1-3; 30:3; 31:12; 88:3-6; 1QH 3.19; 11.10-14); and Paul depicts death as a power of the old age, connecting it closely with sin (see Rom 5:12-21; 6:23; 1 Cor 15:56). In Colossians this previous state of death was brought about and characterized by the readers' "trespasses," their deliberate acts of disobedience, and by what, from the writer's Jewish Christian perspective, is described as the "uncircumcision of your flesh." This phrase indicates both that the readers are Gentiles and that previously their uncircumcised physical state also represented a state of spiritual uncircumcision, an alienation from Israel's living God that entails death. But the power of God that was effective in Christ's being brought to life and that the readers have also experienced through their faith has reversed all this. The writer asserted in v. 11 that believers have undergone a circumcision made without hands in their union with Christ; v. 13c now goes on to make clear that their trespasses have also been dealt with, since God has granted full and free forgiveness.

The problem for the interpretation of v. 14 is to identify what has been dealt with by being erased and nailed to the cross. Both the NIV's "the written code with its regulations" and the NRSV's "the record . . . with its legal demands" could suggest that the Mosaic law is in view. But the term χειρόγραφον (*cheirographon*) denotes a handwritten document or a bond of indebtedness, while δόγματα (*dogmata*) refers to regulations or

stipulations. The use of the latter term in Eph 2:15 clearly, because of the context, refers to the Mosaic law; but that cannot be determinative for this earlier usage in Colossians. The clue here is provided by the use of the cognate verb in v. 20 in connection with submitting to the ascetic regulations of the philosophy. The NIV correctly translates the twofold condemnatory function of the document. It is described as "against us" and as that which "was opposed to us." This language is just possible as a very harsh dismissal of the law, but so it is much more unguarded than even Paul in Galatians and very unlikely in a letter that nowhere else polemicizes against the law. And to argue that what is in view is not the law per se but only the law in its condemnatory function[96] is to have to read far too fine a distinction into the verse. The document itself is said to be opposed to humanity and, when one brings into play the ascetic regulations mentioned later, the clear implication is that it is condemnatory of humans because of their body of flesh.

The chirograph or document may well be best interpreted in the light of the use of this term in apocalyptic writings.[97] The motif of books in which good and evil deeds are written down with a view to the judgment is common (cf. *1 Enoch* 89:61-64, 70, 71; 108:7; *Apoc. Zeph.* 7:1-8; *T. Abr.* 12:7-18; 13:9-14; *2 Enoch* 53:2-3; Rev 20:12) and the actual term *cheirographon* is employed for such books in *Apoc. Zeph.* 3:6-9; 7:1-8 (where it is transliterated in the extant Coptic version) and *Apoc. Paul* 17 (where the Latin equivalent is found). A book of indictment held by an accusing heavenly power with regulations designed to deal with the body of flesh would fit well as the reference in this context. The writer is then claiming that God has erased[98] this indictment and has, literally, "taken it out of the middle," which was the position occupied by an accusing witness at a trial. The accusatory book has in effect been ruled out of court. It was canceled and set aside by being nailed to the cross.

96. Contra Dunn, *The Epistles to the Colossians and to Philemon*, 165-66.
97. See T. J. Sappington, *Revelation and Redemption at Colossae*, JSNTSup 53 (Sheffield: JSOT, 1991) 214-20; also Martin, *Colossians and Philemon*, 84-85; M. Barth and H. Blanke, *Colossians*, trans. A. B. Beck, AB 34B (New York: Doubleday, 1994) 369-72; Dunn, *Colossians and Philemon*, 164-66.
98. The same notion is used in *1 Enoch* 108:3 and *Apoc. Zeph.* 7:8.

The language of being nailed to the cross recalls either the *titulus,* which contained a person's indictment (see Mark 15:26), or Christ himself. Nailing the indictment to the cross would not in itself cancel it, and so it is likely that what is in view is that the indictment was nailed to the cross when the body of Christ was nailed to the cross, particularly when we remember that in both 1:22 and 2:11 the writer emphasized that it was Christ's body of flesh that underwent death on the cross. The thought may well be, then, that through the death of Christ's fleshly body any indictment of the body of flesh by the heavenly powers has already been dealt with by God. Such an interpretation is supported by the later reading of this text in *The Gospel of Truth* 20:24-25: "He put on that book; he was nailed to a tree." It need not be seen as the writer's endorsement of the philosophy's point of view about the body. Instead, he assumes its proponents' position for the sake of the argument and in order to undermine it. It is simply another way of making clear that there are no grounds for believers to feel guilty.

A quite different image for what was accomplished on the cross is employed in v. 15. It involves a further play on the "stripping off" terminology and thereby on the philosophy's view of the body of flesh. Now the writer's claim is that, instead of the readers' having to strip off the flesh to appease the powers, through Christ's death God has stripped off the principalities and powers. There is debate about whether the participle is to be taken as strictly middle in force, "having divested himself of," or as middle with an active sense, "having stripped or disarmed" the cosmic powers. Because of the difficulty of the notion of God divesting Godself of the powers and because of questions about how early the second meaning can be attested elsewhere, some have suggested that the subject of the clause has shifted to Christ. Thus Christ is pictured in his death as divesting himself of the powers like rags and thereby nullifying any influence they might have over humanity.[99] The later *Gospel of Truth* 20:30 31 interprets the passage in this way with Christ as subject: "having stripped himself of the perishable rags." But there are no grounds syntactically for arguing for a change of subject, particularly since the final "in him" is almost certainly to be taken as a reference to Christ.

Despite queries about the dating of the usage of the verb with an active force, taking the clause to mean that God has stripped the powers in the sense of divesting them of their accusing power is by far the best solution.[100] This is also supported by the context. After all, the previous image has made the point that the condemnatory record held by the powers has been dealt with, and the next clause speaks of their being exposed to public shame, which fits well with the notion of their having been stripped. What all this amounts to is that in Christ, particularly in his death, God has triumphed over the cosmic powers. The image of the triumphal procession that followed a military victory is evoked (cf. 2 Cor 2:14). Here the hostile powers are the defeated enemies who are paraded in God's train. Those who held the powers in such awe that they thought it necessary to appease them by whatever means possible are given a totally different perspective. The true attitude for Christian believers is to hold the powers in contempt as having been totally disgraced by God's redemptive activity on behalf of humanity and to celebrate and appropriate the victory and liberation God has achieved in Christ.

99. So Dunn, *Colossians and Philemon,* 167-68.

100. Cf. M. J. Harris, *Colossians and Philemon* (Grand Rapids: Eerdmans, 1991) 110; P. T. O'Brien, *Colossians, Philemon,* WBC 44 (Waco, Tex.: Word, 1982) 126-28; P. Pokorny, *Colossians: A Commentary,* trans. S. S. Schatzmann (Peabody, Mass.: Hendrickson, 1991) 141; E. Schweizer, *The Letter to the Colossians,* trans. A. Chester (Minneapolis: Augsburg, 1982) 151.

REFLECTIONS

1. With a rich variety of imagery this section has made the point that the resources to be found in what God has already done in Christ and in believers' relationship of incorporation into Christ are more than sufficient to deal with whatever plight the opposing philosophy alleges the readers to be in. Faced with the strangeness of some of the imagery, the interpreter has a delicate task. On the one hand, there is a need to resist the impulse to translate these images immediately into more straightforward theological language. They had their original impact precisely as images or metaphors, and so first we need to do our best to enter the first-century world and attempt to appreciate their likely force. They are not mere ornaments to be discarded for more literal language that gives a greater purchase on the real world. These metaphors have their own unique function in bringing to expression insights into aspects of reality that would not be appreciated without them.

The central metaphors about Jesus' death's effecting forgiveness and constituting a victory have achieved classic status in the Christian tradition. They need to be explored as continuing ways of articulating God's action in the world and of shaping the life of the Christian community. However, some of the images attached to them, such as erasing a record book of angelic indictment, do not have the same status; it is probably futile to pretend that they can or that they should retain their original force in our own culture. What may be needed in such cases is to determine the analogies that underlie the metaphors and then in an act of imagination to explore whether there might be striking contemporary images to make graphic how Christ's death deals with whatever has a hold over people's lives in our world. For those under the thrall of consumerism, to visualize it as a symbol of the credit card being cut up when Christ was cut off from life might have the desired effect. The point is helping people to grasp that when Christ died to the old order and thereby took away its power, present-day gods and principalities were included in that event.

2. That last point reveals a stance on a major issue that has exercised writers on Paul and on Colossians: How to interpret the references to the cosmic powers and elemental spirits.[101] As the Commentary has made clear, the writer holds that Colossians, in its original context, was referring to supernatural spiritual agencies. He also holds that contemporary Christians are not bound by the specific cosmologies of the New Testament writers, including the cosmic demonology of Colossians. In our time, therefore, when for a variety of good reasons, including theological ones, the majority of Christians in the West do not operate with a belief in a host of evil spirits in the heavens called thrones or dominions, the most helpful appropriation of these texts is most likely to be by way of analogy. This entails seeing an equivalent to such cosmic powers in the systems, institutions, and ideologies of our day. In relation to human life they play a similar role to that of the elemental spirits of Colossians, because they have, within and beyond them, a driving force for good or evil that is more than the sum of the effects of any individuals who may represent them or of any of their tangible manifestations.

When faced with undesirable conditions in our world, such as the status of refugees, homelessness, or renewed tribal conflicts, we and our politicians are no strangers to talk of being the victims of economic or political forces beyond our control. Forces of evil larger than individual acts of sin can include some that have a counterpart in the first-century world, such as the lure of astrology or of the occult; but they will also include unjust social, political, and economic structures. They include ideologies that hold people in bondage, frequently without their being conscious of it, such as the ideology of redemptive violence in which peace and security are thought to be obtainable only through the violent use of power.[102] Among other such ideologies are materialism, consumerism, sexism, nationalism, and the type of postmodernism that denies any reality to truth and justice and asserts that the only realities are preference and desire. And forces of evil can include nuclear and chemical armaments, ecological disaster, and other consequences of human sin that have become destructive and

---

101. For an extensive justification of the stance taken here, see A. T. Lincoln, "Liberation from the Powers: Supernatural Spirits or Societal Structures?" in *The Bible in Human Society,* ed. M. D. Carroll, D. J. A. Clines, and P. R. Davies (Sheffield: Sheffield Academic, 1995) 335-54. For a somewhat different approach, see the brilliant trilogy of W. Wink, *Naming the Powers* (Philadelphia: Fortress, 1984); *Unmasking the Powers* (Philadelphia: Fortress, 1986); and *Engaging the Powers* (Minneapolis: Fortress, 1992).

102. See Wink, *Engaging the Powers,* 13-31.

threatening. The writer of Colossians brings the gospel of Christ's death and resurrection to bear on his readers' perception of evil in a first-century context. Contemporary interpreters need to take the same gospel and bring it to bear on the powers of evil and perceptions of them that pose a threat to faith in our time and location.

3. In this section, the good news of God's having dealt with the cosmic powers in Christ is expressed in terms of both Christ's headship over the powers (2:10) and Christ's death, which removes their indictment in a public triumph (2:14-15). Clearly this latter view of the salvation accomplished through Christ's death is part of the basis of what has become known as the Christus Victor model for the atonement.[103] From its perspective, the human need to which this solution corresponds is for liberation from both the consequences of sin and the powers of evil. The imagery for Christ's victory over the powers involves disarmament and triumphant procession, but any triumphalistic use of such a model ignores the paradox at its heart. The powers of evil are defeated not by some overwhelming display of divine power but by the weakness of Christ's death. By all ordinary standards of judgment, Christ's crucifixion looks like a victory for the violence of evil powers over God's purposes in this one who was the divine image. Christ was indicted, stripped, and nailed to the cross in the public humiliation of his death. Yet, Colossians can reverse this language because, seen in the light of his resurrection, the death of the victim, who has absorbed the destructive forces of the powers, becomes precisely the point at which their domination is decisively brought to an end. Their claims, their accusations, and their oppressive and divisive influence have all been subverted by a very different power: the power of the victim on the cross.

The challenge issued to the readers of Colossians is one that remains for Christians: Is this proclamation about Christ's death a metaphor by which we are prepared to live? Do we believe that this answer to the power of evil is really sufficient? The gospel proclaims that Christ has conquered evil; yet, evil still threatens and flourishes. So are additional means needed to cope with the reality of evil in our world? Presumably some of the original readers were tempted to turn to angelic powers for help for this very reason and thought this was compatible with their Christian faith. They reasoned that their confession of Jesus' lordship needed to be supplemented by other means of coping and bargaining with the forces of evil as they affected their daily lives. How far do contemporary Christians still make their own deals with other powers, whether materialism, rationalism, pragmatism, or violence, in order to live with the impact of evil on their lives and in society? For all readers of Colossians, a major test of authentic adherence to the gospel and to the confession of Christ as Lord is whether they are convinced enough of the sufficiency of God's action in the crucified Jesus to gamble their lives on the paradoxical power of the way of the cross rather than making compromises with other powers.

4. This passage has an obvious role to play in thinking about the significance of baptism. Colossians 2:12-13 focuses on the movement from the dominion of death and sin to the sphere of new life that is expressed through baptism, with its participation in Christ's burial and resurrection. This underlines that baptism is not simply an inititation rite but has to do with issues of life and death and with appropriation of the release from the domination of the powers of this age (cf. 2:20).

Baptism reminds believers that their pre-Christian past is to be regarded as a state of spiritual death, because their sins had cut them off from a living relationship with God. We need to be convinced, with the writer of Colossians, that to live life in pursuit of our own selfish ends is to be in the cul-de-sac that leads to death. Idolatry can be related to particular vices (see 3:5). The inevitable result of making something contingent and created the center of power

---

103. This model received particular emphasis and elaboration in the patristic period. See G. Aulén, *Christus Victor: An Historical Study of the Three Main Types of the Idea of the Atonement* (New York: Macmillan, 1969).

rather than the Creator is not only a distortion of reality but also enslavement within the system of sin whose wages is death.

Bringing God into the analysis of the human plight gives it seriousness as a state of death, but it also provides the only hope. The conviction that the world is in the hands of a God who is the first and ultimate power, an actor in the drama who is more important than us, is what provides the opening to freedom. In Colossians this is formulated in terms of "faith in the power of God, who raised him from the dead" (2:12). If the plight is death, then the solution must involve a raising to life. Baptism proclaims that this is in fact what God has accomplished not only for Christ but also for believers. "God made you alive together with Christ" (2:13).

The claim involved is that the resurrection of Christ was an event through which God changed the power structures within history. Although there are many past events in which one feels no sense of personal involvement, there are others that are quite different. Most British people can still hardly think about the events of the Second World War without a sense of involvement, because they are members of a community that owes its continuity and some of its national characteristics to what happened then. Similarly, Colossians views Christ's resurrection as supremely an event that brings into being and defines a whole new situation and a new community. Baptism seals believers' involvement in that event. What God accomplished for Christ is to be seen as having been accomplished for him as representative of a new humanity that is included in him. Through faith and baptism, believers are linked with the life of this new resurrection power within history. It decisively shapes and identifies them, aligning them with a new center of power and breaking the system of sin and the hold of death over their lives.

5. Immediately after this passage has talked of believers' experience of the new order of life inaugurated through the resurrection, it moves on to assert God's forgiveness of all trespasses. To experience the forgiveness of sins is a sign that the hold of the past has been broken and that a new and liberated life has begun. Forgiveness remains really good news because it restores our relationship with the God who made us and with other human beings. It brings release from greed, from the need to exploit, from shortsighted self-interest, from the trap of believing that violence can be overcome only with violence, from all those attitudes that stand in the way of the achievement of God's purposes of love and justice for this world.

But a further issue arises from our interpretation of the philosophy and of 2:14 (see Commentary on 2:13-15). If our interpretation is correct, then from the perspective of the writer of Colossians, some of his readers are suffering from a sense of false guilt. The indictment against them is not based on God's law but on the philosophy's view that life in the body is sinful. It is out of a sense of guilt on this account that some are undergoing rigorous ascetic requirements. The writer's emphasis is that, whatever its origin, people need assurance that the sense of guilt that has a hold over them has been dealt with in Christ and that in God's eyes they are now forgiven and guilt-free people.

There is a pastoral point worth pondering here. Whether we consider people's guilt to be real or imagined, their *sense* of it is real to them. There may well be an analogy to be drawn between the sense of guilt of some of the first readers of Colossians and the condition we would diagnose today as shame. This is the unhealthy type of shame that is not attached to anything a person has done wrong but is the person's sense of being inferior, unworthy, or unacceptable as a person. When with Colossians we point to God's forgiveness in Christ, we may also need to make explicit that the grace that supplies such forgiveness is the grace that accepts us as we are. It is this dimension of forgiveness as producing acceptance in the eyes of the most significant Other that can begin to heal the sense of unhealthy shame. And the gospel of Colossians is the gospel of just such grace (see 1:6). The letter again and again stresses that, though they are undeserving, humans are considered worthy to receive all that

God gives in Christ and, in the words of this passage, to receive fullness in Christ (2:10), to be made alive together with him (2:13), and to be liberated from any accusing forces that would tell them otherwise (2:14-15).

From a broader theological perspective, we may also need to see shame, whether about the body or about the self, as indeed part of the sin that needs forgiveness. Feminist theologians, among others, have pointed out that sin is not always to be thought of in terms of acts of proud self-assertion; it can also involve shameful self-diminution.[104] Both types of sin can be seen as culpable and requiring forgiveness, because they hinder the authentic relationship with God for which human beings were intended.[105] Forgiveness is needed for complicity with shame. From this perspective, the writer of Colossians, in proclaiming God's forgiveness and depicting the effects of Christ's death in erasing and removing the specific requirements of the philosophy, can be seen as not only dealing with those requirements, but also, in so doing, offering the antidote to the complicity in shame about the body that has made them plausible.

This whole topic of forgiveness invites a more general biblical and theological treatment when Col 2:6-15 appears in the lectionary (Year C, Proper 12) alongside Old Testament readings (see Psalm 85; Hos 1:2-10), in which the theme of forgiveness is prominent, and Luke 11:1-13, with its petition, "Forgive us our sins, for we ourselves forgive everyone indebted to us" (NRSV).

104. See S. N. Dunfee, "The Sin of Hiding: A Feminist Critique of Reinhold Niebuhr's Account of the Sin of Pride," *Soundings* 65 (1982) 316-27.
105. See L. G. Jones, *Embodying Forgiveness* (Grand Rapids: Eerdmans, 1995) esp. 35-69.

Colossians 2:16-23, Do Not Be Judged by the Codes of a Different Teaching

NIV

[16]Therefore do not let anyone judge you by what you eat or drink, or with regard to a religious festival, a New Moon celebration or a Sabbath day. [17]These are a shadow of the things that were to come; the reality, however, is found in Christ. [18]Do not let anyone who delights in false humility and the worship of angels disqualify you for the prize. Such a person goes into great detail about what he has seen, and his unspiritual mind puffs him up with idle notions. [19]He has lost connection with the Head, from whom the whole body, supported and held together by its ligaments and sinews, grows as God causes it to grow.

[20]Since you died with Christ to the basic principles of this world, why, as though you still belonged to it, do you submit to its rules: [21]"Do not handle! Do not taste! Do not touch!"? [22]These are all destined to perish with use, because they are based on human commands and teachings. [23]Such regulations indeed have an appearance of wisdom, with their self-imposed worship, their false humility and their harsh treatment of the

NRSV

16Therefore do not let anyone condemn you in matters of food and drink or of observing festivals, new moons, or sabbaths. [17]These are only a shadow of what is to come, but the substance belongs to Christ. [18]Do not let anyone disqualify you, insisting on self-abasement and worship of angels, dwelling[a] on visions,[b] puffed up without cause by a human way of thinking,[c] [19]and not holding fast to the head, from whom the whole body, nourished and held together by its ligaments and sinews, grows with a growth that is from God.

20If with Christ you died to the elemental spirits of the universe,[d] why do you live as if you still belonged to the world? Why do you submit to regulations, [21]"Do not handle, Do not taste, Do not touch"? [22]All these regulations refer to things that perish with use; they are simply human commands and teachings. [23]These have indeed an

[a] Other ancient authorities read *not dwelling*   [b] Meaning of Gk uncertain   [c] Gk *by the mind of his flesh*   [d] Or *the rudiments of the world*

NIV	NRSV
body, but they lack any value in restraining sensual indulgence.	appearance of wisdom in promoting self-imposed piety, humility, and severe treatment of the body, but they are of no value in checking self-indulgence.[a] [a] Or *are of no value, serving only to indulge the flesh*

COMMENTARY

2:16-17. As a consequence (again "therefore" provides the link) of his perspective on how God in Christ has dealt with the issue of the supposed hold of cosmic powers over humanity because of humanity's existence in physical bodies, the writer can now exhort the readers not to allow anyone to judge them negatively for failing to comply with the philosophy's regulations. The regulations singled out are requirements about food and drink and calendar observance. These are clearly parts of the philosophy taken over from Judaism, but now apparently they are put to use in its proponents' program for dealing with the cosmic powers. The issue of food and drink, however, is likely to be not so much one of purity laws as of abstinence as part of a strict asceticism. In the OT there are prohibitions against certain foods, but stipulations about drink are found only in regard to the particular cases of priests ministering in the tabernacle (see Lev 10:9) and those under Nazirite vows (see Num 6:3), though Jews in the diaspora were also cautious about wine in case it had been offered to idols. But there is no indication here that the motivation for abstinence from food and drink was due to observance of Torah. Rather, the requirement of abstinence should be linked with the mention of fasting in preparation for visions in v. 18, of ascetic regulations in vv. 21-22, and of severity to the body in v. 23.

The writer describes the calendar observances required by the philosophy in terms of feasts or festivals, new moons, and sabbaths. These three calendrical features are listed together in the OT (see LXX 1 Chr 23:31; 2 Chr 2:3; 31:3; Ezek 45:17; Hos 2:13), where they were days on which special sacrifices were to be made to God.[106] Again

there is no hint here that such special days are being observed because of the desire to obey Torah as such or because keeping them was a special mark of Jewish identity. Instead, it is probable that in the philosophy they were linked to a desire to please the cosmic powers, the "elemental spirits of the universe" (vv. 8, 20), held to be associated with the heavenly bodies and, therefore, in control of the calendar. Sabbath observance would have been no exception to this. Elchasai would later teach his followers that the sabbath was to be observed because it was one of the days controlled by the course of the stars.[107] It was precisely because of such links with cosmic beings that Paul had earlier found it so easy to make the point to the Gentile Christians in Galatia that to observe "days, months, seasons and years" under the law would be just like going back to enslavement under the elemental spirits of the universe (see Gal 4:9-10).

In addition to the earlier undermining of the need for such practices in vv. 9-15, the writer adds in v. 17 a further warrant for his exhortation. The observances are dismissed as mere "shadow" in comparison with the "body," the true reality that belongs to Christ. Such a comparison, deriving from Platonic thought, was common in Hellenistic writings, including Hellenistic Jewish texts.[108] "Shadow" represented the lower world of the senses, the world of appearances, in contrast most frequently to "image" but also to "body," representing the invisible realm of true ideas or true being. It may well be, as some have suggested,[109] that the writer is using the language

---

106. See the chart "Agricultural and Civil Calendar," in *The New Interpreter's Bible,* vol. 1 (Nashville: Abingdon, 1994) 275.

107. See Hippolytus *Refutation of All Heresies* 9.16.2-3.
108. See Philo *On the Confusion of Tongues* 190; *On the Migration of Abraham* 12; Josephus *The Jewish War* 2.28.
109. See E. Lohse, *Colossians and Philemon,* trans. W. R. Poehlmann and R. J. Karris, Hermeneia (Philadelphia: Fortress, 1971) 116-17; R. P. Martin, *Colossians and Philemon,* NCB (Greenwood, S.C.: Attic, 1974) 91; Pokorny, *Colossians,* 144.

of the philosophy to his own ends. In the perspective of the philosophy, the practices advocated for those in the lower earthly realm would have been the shadow that reflected and provided access to the true reality of the divine presence in the upper realm.

By introducing an eschatological element—the practices are the shadow of what is to come—the writer treats the regulations not as a present reflection of a heavenly reality but as belonging decisively to the past; for him, as for Paul, the age to come has already been inaugurated in Christ. The other element introduced into the comparison is the connection of the true reality with Christ. By asserting that the "body" belongs to Christ, the writer claims that with the presence of the true reality in Christ, who has already been designated the "image" of the invisible God in 1:15 and the one in whom all the fullness of the deity dwells in 1:19 and 2:10, the shadow no longer has any grounds for continued existence; the practices of the philosophy are superfluous.

2:18-19. A discussion of a number of aspects of v. 18, which is a key text for analysis of the teaching the writer is opposing, has been provided in the Introduction (see the section "Visionary Experience and Asceticism," 562-65, in the Introduction), and so its results will be assumed here. Not only are the readers not to allow anyone to judge or condemn them (v. 16), but they are also not to let anyone disqualify them. The verb employed for "disqualify" (καταβραβεύω *katabrabeuō*) evokes the image of an umpire ruling against a contestant in a game and thereby depriving that person of any prize. The writer recognizes the potential of the philosophy for making the readers sense that they are missing out on the experience of the heavenly realm it offers through participation in its practices. In 3:1-3, he will claim that they can already experience this realm in Christ, but here he concentrates on providing a negative assessment of this major feature of the philosophy. It has already been argued that the phrase "the worship of angels" is to be taken as a derogatory description of the practice of invoking angelic aid and that the best translation of the most debated part of the verse (v. 18*b*) is that the proponent of the philosophy is depicted as "insisting on fasting and worship of angels, which he has seen, when entering." The "seeing" refers to

visionary experience and the "entering" to entrance into the heavenly realm through such an experience. Fasting was required as the preparation for visions and for the visionary's ability to invoke the angels in the heavenly realm.

The writer characterizes the person who would insist on these experiences in a way that disqualifies those who have not had them as "puffed up without cause by his fleshly mind" (v. 18*c*). This characterization is doubly ironic or sarcastic. In the first place, the insistence on self-abasement in the form of fasting is said to have led to a pride or conceit that has no basis in reality. Second, to attribute this conceit to a mind of flesh would again be to combine two concepts that the philosophy would have held to be incompatible. In Hellenistic thought, it was the mind or the soul (the terms could be used interchangeably) that was deemed capable of escaping the realm of the physical to achieve in this life the experience of the upper realm and the divine (see the section "The 'Elemental Spirits of the Universe' and Dualistic Cosmology," 565-67, in the Introduction). The writer denies that any such thing has happened and claims that instead the attitude of the philosophy's advocate is evidence that the mind has remained firmly bound to the whole realm of flesh; for a follower of Paul, there would remain connotations of the sinful sphere of the flesh in such an indictment (see Rom 8:5-6 for the closest correspondence to this language in the undisputed letters of Paul).

Such a person is also charged with "not holding fast to the head" (v. 19*a*). The clear implication is that the proponent of the philosophy who is in view is someone who could be expected to adhere to Christ—namely, a Christian believer. One of the reasons why this person's hold on Christ is put in question is that the attitude of superiority and condemnation he or she shows toward other believers who do not share the philosophy's views amounts to ignoring the rest of the body (v. 19*b*) and is thereby detrimental to the well-being and growth of the body of all believers, over whom Christ is head. For the writer, one's attitude to the body, the church, is indicative of one's relation to its head, since the two are intimately connected. Christ, the head, is the source of the church's growth. His headship, therefore, is understood in the sense of both rule and origin. It is significant, however, that at the end of v. 19 this growth can also be said to come from God and so reflects the emphasis throughout the letter on Christ as the agent of God's activity.

There are, however, other agents in the church's growth: the members of the body. Paul had used "body" imagery for the church in Romans 12 and 1 Corinthians 12, which describe the mutual contributions of the body's members. Here the writer's stress is on corporate growth rather than simply interdependence. Believers are depicted as the ligaments and sinews that supply and connect the body and without whose proper functioning any growth would be severely impeded. By not holding firmly to the head, the philosophy's advocate is in danger of being deprived of the essential connection with the true source of fullness (see v. 10). By implication, such a person is a loose ligament out of alignment with the rest of the body, and the philosophy fails to pass the key test of contribution to the growth of the whole body.

2:20-23. The writer now approaches the task of distancing the readers from the philosophy from yet another angle. He reminds them of their union with Christ in his death, previously discussed using the imagery of circumcision (v. 11), and points out that through union with Christ they have died with Christ to the elemental spirits of the universe. Paul could talk of believers' having died to sin and the law as personified powers of the old age. Now the writer extends the thought to dying to the cosmic powers. In fact, the preposition employed in the formulation here is not "to" but "from," so that the force is that in their death with Christ the readers have come out from under the control of these powers. Since in Christ's death any hold of the powers over humanity on account of the body of flesh has been dealt with and the powers themselves have been disarmed and vanquished (cf. vv. 11, 14-15), participation in that death in union with Christ means that believers, too, enjoy liberation from the powers.

On this basis, the writer presses home the question: "Why, as living in the world, do you submit to regulations?" The clause "as living in the world" has proved difficult for interpreters. Does the participle "living" (ζῶντες *zōntes*) stand in contrast to having died with Christ, or is it a more general reference to existing? Since the writer does not appeal to resurrection with Christ until 3:1, the latter is probably to be preferred. Does "in the world" have a neutral force or the more negative sense of "this world" or worldly existence? Connected with this, how is ὡς (*hōs*, "as") to be taken? Many take it with the not very frequently attested meaning of "as if" and understand the expression as a whole to be saying that those being addressed are living as if they are still in the world in its negative sense. It appears simpler to take *hōs* in its more frequent sense of "while" and "world" (κόσμος *kosmos*) as alluding to the use of the term in the previously mentioned "elemental spirits of the universe or world." Thus the force of the question is, If you have come out from under the control of the elemental spirits of the world, why, while living in the world over which they can no longer lay claim, are you submitting to regulations that have as their presupposition that the elemental spirits are still in control? The natural implication of the present tense in this question is that some of the readers are, indeed, beginning to succumb to the rival teaching.

Three examples of the regulations are provided in v. 21. All are ascetic prohibitions. The first and third, "do not touch" and "do not handle," appear to be saying much the same thing. Some have attempted to find a distinction, claiming that the first refers to sexual abstinence, since the verb translated as "touch" (θιγγάνω *thingavō*) can refer to sexual relations (see 1 Cor 7:1). But elsewhere the context and the object of the verb make this connotation clear. The writer does not supply an object for any of the verbs, and it is fairly clear that the issue of food and drink that was dealt with in v. 16 is again in view. The verb *thingavō* could also be used with food as the object, meaning "to eat." It may well be that the attempt to pin down the exact reference of each prohibition is misguided. The examples function more as a caricature of the negative nature of the philosophy than as descriptions of actual regulations.[110] If any distinction is to be made, the force of the three prohibitions is most likely best captured by "Do not eat"; "Do not taste"; and "Do not even handle." The absolute nature of these formulations is part of the writer's ironic exag-

110. See E. Lohse, *Colossians and Philemon,* trans. W. R. Poehlmann and R. J. Karris, Hermeneia (Philadelphia: Fortress, 1971) 123.

eration of the philosophy's stance, which would not, of course, have treated all food and drink as taboo, but would have treated certain foods and drink as taboo at particular times for the purpose of subduing the physical body and being in a state of purity in readiness for visionary experience and access to heaven.

The writer can caricature the regulations because from his perspective they deal only with foodstuffs that are destined to perish with use anyway. This perspective is similar to that from which the Jesus of Mark 7:19 and Paul in 1 Cor 6:13 dealt with those who gave issues about food too high a priority. In the case of Colossians, regulations about food and drink are being given far too high a priority because they are simply human commands and teachings (v. 22*b;* see also 2:8), a phrase that recalls the Jesus tradition in Mark 7:7, which in turn had cited Isa 29:13. In Mark 7:7, the Isaiah passage had been employed with reference to the tradition of the elders, not of the Torah itself; and again this makes improbable the view that the Jewish purity laws as such are the content of the regulations in Colossians.[111] A Pauline disciple would scarcely have dismissed what, in fact, had been commanded by God in the Torah as merely human commandments.

The writer's third attack on the regulations to which some of the readers appear to be submitting is to suggest that their claims are a facade, masking a very different reality. The details of the syntax of v. 23, however, are notoriously difficult to unravel. In all likelihood, the "and" between the term for "self-abasement" or "fasting" and the phrase "severity to the body" was not in the original text (contra the NRSV and the NIV)[112] but was added by scribes to provide a smoother reading. Without the "and" there is a clear reference back to the two practices mentioned in v. 18—worship and fasting—followed by a phrase in apposition that represents the writer's assessment of either the latter or both of these practices. The verse may well, then, be best translated: "which things [the regulations] have a reputation

for wisdom in self-chosen worship and fasting, severity to the body but of no value to anyone for dealing with the gratification of the flesh" (author's trans.).

What is clear is that the writer's earlier stress on wisdom and knowledge (1:9-10, 28; 2:2-3) has been in response to the claims of the philosophy to provide these. He regards those claims as suspect; the reputation for wisdom is undeserved. The prefix "self-chosen," added to "worship," simply underscores that the invocation and veneration of angels is an activity undertaken freely and deliberately. The reason for questioning the reputation for wisdom comes in the evaluation at the end of the verse, and the key is the comparison between "body" and "flesh." For all the philosophy's strenuous ascetic requirements, designed to deal with the problem of the body, they turn out, according to the writer, to be of no value whatsoever in dealing with the problem of gratification of the flesh.

The question remains whether "flesh" ($\sigma\acute{\alpha}\rho\xi$ *sarx*) here has the physical sense accorded it in the philosophy and in many of the writer's own earlier references or whether he is giving it a moral twist in line with both the predominant Pauline usage of the term and what is likely to be the case in 2:18. We have seen no reason to believe that the advocates of the philosophy are taking satisfaction in the flesh in the sense of their ethnic identity. It seems best, then, to see here an indictment parallel to that of 2:18, with the notion of a hollow reputation that matches being puffed up without cause and a gratification of the flesh that matches having a mind of flesh. Later in 3:5, the writer also will give the terminology of the philosophy his own ethical connotations. Here the charge is that for all the effort taken to deal with the supposed problem of the body, the philosophy's regulations, as the attitudes of its advocates indicate, are of no value in dealing with the real problem: that of the flesh in the sense of the sphere of humanity in its sinfulness and opposition to God. In fact, the regulations pander to this dimension of human existence (cf. Paul's formulations about not gratifying the desires of the flesh in Rom 13:14; Gal 5:16).

111. Contra J. D. G. Dunn, *The Epistles to the Colossians and to Philemon,* NIGTC (Grand Rapids: Eerdmans, 1996) 191-92.

112. See P[46], B. See also Dunn, *Colossians and Philemon,* 188.

REFLECTIONS

1. The polemical nature of the pastoral warnings in this passage raises questions about when it becomes necessary to issue a "health warning" against certain forms of spirituality or to expose a particular teaching's tenets as hollow wisdom and about how this is to be done. On the one hand, we need to be aware of the conventions of first-century polemics and resist imitating what may be elements of caricature in this writer's approach.[113] But, on the other hand, this should not prevent us from having the courage to be forthright, but fair, about what we deem to be the dangers of succumbing to misguided views and practices that have the potential for undermining adherence to the Christian gospel.

It is unlikely that we shall find any precise modern equivalent to the philosophy and its practices that are attacked in Colossians. Nevertheless, some of its features do tend to recur in a variety of forms and should put us on our guard when we encounter them. A list might include (1) emphasizing criteria in addition to the gospel message, whether they be visions and other special experiences or abstaining from wine or meat, as necessary for a "higher spirituality" by which other Christians are then judged defective; (2) a concern with other spiritual agencies or powers that detracts from the centrality and sufficiency of Christ; (3) teaching and practices that produce elite groups within the church to the detriment of the whole body of believers working and growing together; (4) claiming that a prime human need is to discover or rediscover some special esoteric knowledge in addition to what is found in the gospel and Christian teaching; and (5) dualistic views that treat the bodily and the material as inferior or evil and obscure the fact that humanity's plight is ethical—and by extension, views that treat any part of our humanity as inferior, asserting that the intellect or the personality needs to be transcended.

Obviously, discernment is needed in warning against suspect spiritualities. It would be foolish, for example, to discount asceticism and visions and dreams as part of spirituality and to ignore the contribution to the church's tradition from individuals and groups who value such practices and experiences. What is at issue is not these emphases themselves, which can be part of a healthy response to greed, lust, and materialism and to a reduction of human experience to the rational and empirical, but rather the motivation behind them and the attitude with which they are promoted. Fasting and other ascetic disciplines done during the season of Lent, for example, can be seen not as treating food and pleasures as evil but as a temporary suspension of the proper use of God's good gifts in order to gain perspective and to learn not to abuse them. A problem arises when particular practices or experiences are set up as requirements for others to fulfill if they are to be complete Christians, when they reflect a disparagement of ordinary physical existence, when they are accompanied by a spiritual pride that judges others, or when they are placed at the same level of importance in Christian living as the need for love and justice.

Taking our lead from Colossians, we also need to warn against the dualistic view that too frequently passes for Christianity, in which culture and sexuality are deeply suspect and in which the gospel is about being rescued from the world before it is finally destroyed and we are transported to some spiritual hereafter. This is a distortion of this letter's depiction of the Christ who has created and reconciled the cosmos and whose lordship of this world claims every area of human life, including culture and society. In line with Colossians, authentic spirituality will diagnose the real problem not as the body or the earth or any aspect of created reality but as the flesh (see 2:18, 23)—that is, the sphere of sin. True spirituality will see the solution as an appropriation of the reconciliation offered in Christ with its restoration of a

---

113. See L. T. Johnson, "The New Testament's Anti-Jewish Slander and the Conventions of Ancient Polemic," *JBL* 108 (1989) 419-41.

proper relationship to the Creator and participation in the divine purposes of harmony for the whole creation.

2. The loose network of attitudes and beliefs that is often labeled "new age" spirituality provides some analogies to the philosophy opposed by Colossians. A wide variety of interests flows into it, including an emphasis on human potential, a fascination with extraterrestrial beings and UFOs, astrology, magic, witchcraft, ecological concerns, and channeling of spirits from the beyond. However, a major aspect of the phenomenon is a syncretistic spirituality that stresses experiences of transcendence in the attempt to go beyond the limitations of everyday life in the visible world. "New age" thinking is not a coherent system of beliefs, but its dominant attitude toward the world is holistic, with the self, the earth, and the spirit world all being linked within the one universe. Yet within this perspective there are dualistic features, and the questions "new age" thinking addresses are similar to those the philosophy raised: What powers are in control of life? What forces are available to be tapped into to help us control our own destinies?

Just as the writer of Colossians attempts to address the philosophy's concerns from his own perspective, rooted in the Pauline gospel, and to critique what he viewed as erroneous in the rival teaching, so also we need to develop our own twofold response to similar movements in our time. What do the concerns of their adherents say to the churches about what the latter have neglected in the resources of their own tradition? What elements have to be seen as antithetical to or undermining of that tradition?

In its concern to view human, animal, natural, and cosmic life as part of an undivided unity and in its reaction to the dualisms of Western thinking and the perceived dualisms of Christianity, "new age" thinking assumes a pantheistic monism. In this monism, Christ, when he is given attention, is seen as one of many manifestations of the all-pervasive divine consciousness. Certainly cosmic harmony is also a concern of Colossians. It may well be time, therefore, that we paid far greater attention to Christ as Wisdom, as the one who sustains and brings to harmony the ambiguities and complexities of the cosmos and who provides integration in our lives. Yet, for Colossians, this Christ is the unique manifestation of the divine Wisdom. As cosmic Lord, he is present and active within the natural order, but, rather than being identified with it or reduced to it, he remains transcendent and sovereign over it.

In contrast to "new age" philosophy, which views our problem as an ignorance that keeps us from discovering our true selves, the god within us, Christ's death and resurrection reveal our plight to be an alienation caused by our sin. In terms of the concepts of this passage (esp. 2:18, 23), what is needed is not the pseudo-wisdom of the search for mystical experiences that will open us to an awareness of cosmic consciousness or the cultivation of techniques that will unlock the treasures of wisdom that are hidden within us. What is needed, rather, is the wisdom of the crucified and risen Christ that releases us from the destructive and binding consequences of our selfish disruption of and resistance to God's purposes for cosmic harmony. In particular, it is our identification by faith with Christ's death (2:20) that has released us from the dominion of this alienated system of the old order and from the hold of any of its powers that would take advantage of our estrangement from the Creator. We are freed to live in alignment with the divine purposes of harmony for the cosmos as we maintain allegiance to the one in whom those purposes have been embodied and through whom they are being fulfilled.

3. Colossians reminds us that holding fast to Christ the head means that believers are not on a journey of individualistic spirituality but have become members of a community in which they need to live together in love and be accountable to one another in public worship (see 2:19). In this community, spiritual growth is not a private preoccupation but a corporate matter. Amid all the talk and activity associated with "church growth," and while by no means incompatible with a desire for and strategies to achieve greater numbers, the passage also reminds us that these are not the ultimate measures of growth. Genuine growth that comes from God and that is a result of authentic adherence to Christ as head is recognized by the way in which the whole body functions healthily as its members work together to provide nourishment and support for one another.

Colossians 3:1-4, Seek the Things That Are Above

NIV	NRSV
3 Since, then, you have been raised with Christ, set your hearts on things above, where Christ is seated at the right hand of God. ²Set your minds on things above, not on earthly things. ³For you died, and your life is now hidden with Christ in God. ⁴When Christ, who is your*ᵃ* life, appears, then you also will appear with him in glory.	**3** So if you have been raised with Christ, seek the things that are above, where Christ is, seated at the right hand of God. ²Set your minds on things that are above, not on things that are on earth, ³for you have died, and your life is hidden with Christ in God. ⁴When Christ who is your*ᵃ* life is revealed, then you also will be revealed with him in glory.
ᵃ4 Some manuscripts our	*ᵃ Other authorities read* our

COMMENTARY

This unit does not mark a new section of the letter but is closely connected with what precedes. Its exhortations are still in close interaction with the philosophy. But, whereas 2:16-23 had been a primarily negative critique, 3:1-4 contains the writer's positive counterpart to the philosophy's concerns. The following section also begins in direct interaction with the rival teaching in 3:5, but from then on its exhortations become more general and less immediately controlled by such interaction.

3:1. For his more positive exhortations, the writer returns to the theme of union with Christ. The opening clause, "if then you have been raised with Christ . . . ," picks up on the assertion of 2:12*b* and parallels the opening clause of 2:20, "if you died with Christ. . . ." Both dying with Christ and being raised with Christ have a close association with baptism, and so once more it is likely that the readers are being reminded of the significance of their baptism. Not only did it entail their death with Christ to the elemental spirits of the universe but also it signified that they now participate in the new life and order of the age to come. In Paul's thought, believers' present experience of the life of the age to come could

be expressed in terms of their links with the heavenly realm (1 Cor 15:47-49; Gal 4:26; Phil 3:20). Here, too, the writer can phrase the imperative that follows from present possession of resurrection life in spatial terms: "Seek the things that are above."

"Above" (ἄνω *anō*) is synonymous with "heaven"; the writer indicates that there is, in his view, a valid and legitimate concern with the heavenly dimension in contrast to the misguided concern of the philosophy. In the face of the insistence on ascetic observances in order to participate in heavenly life, he asserts that through God's gracious initiative the readers have already been brought into such life. It is on the basis of their union with Christ in his resurrection that they are the ones—all of them, not a special group of initiates—who can be exhorted to further their relationship to the heavenly realm. Resurrection life is heavenly life, and by being united with Christ in his resurrection, the readers have access to the realm above.

The imperative here, then, is again based on an indicative. Since the readers already have access to the life of heaven, they are to pursue this access. There may no longer be any need for the rigorous activity entailed in the philosophy's achieving of visionary experiences, but there is to be the eager determination to take advantage of what has been achieved for them, to "seek" the genuine realm above. This is not an activity in addition to the salvation achieved by God's actions in Christ but a part of it, since "above," as the writer immediately points out, is where Christ is. In line with the rest of early Christian thought, he holds that by virtue of the resurrection Christ had been exalted to heaven. This stress on where Christ is helps to make explicit the presupposition of the earlier indicative clause—namely, that their union with Christ's resurrection means that the readers participate in the heavenly realm where the resurrected Christ is at present.

It is clear, then, that the writer is not recommending seeking this realm above for its own sake. The motivation for the upward direction and the heavenly orientation to which he exhorts his readers is christological. "The things above" cannot be separated from the Christ who is there, and the centrality and supremacy of Christ in this realm are conveyed by the expression "seated at the right hand of God." Here, as earlier in Paul (cf. Rom 8:34; 1 Cor 15:25), the christological interpretation of Ps 110:1 common to the early church is taken up. Its function in this context is to underscore once more the rule of Christ over any cosmic powers the readers may associate with the heavenly realm. There need no longer be any sense of threat from above. Since the upper world centers around the one with whom they have been raised, and since he is in a position of authority at God's right hand, there is nothing to prevent believers from having permanent access to this heavenly world and to God's presence.

3:2. The writer issues a similar imperative in this verse, but this time the verb is varied and the exhortation is strengthened by the contrast between "things that are above" and "things that are on earth." The imperative amounts to an injunction to be heavenly minded rather than earthly minded. To set one's mind on some object implies concentration and firm purpose and indicates that more than isolated visionary experiences are in view. But what is to be made of the contrast between the heavenly and the earthly? For the philosophy, this entailed a cosmological dualism in which the upper realm was good because it was spiritual and immaterial, while the lower realm was evil because it was physical and material. The writer, however, is not telling the readers to avoid concern with the earthly creation as such. His contrast is controlled by his eschatological perspective and has an ethical dimension. Because of Christ's exaltation, heaven highlights the superiority of the life of the new age and is the source of the rule of Christ (v. 1) and of life (v. 3). The earth, on the other hand, takes on the connotations of the arena of this present evil age. "Things on earth" refers, then, to life in bondage to the cosmic powers (2:8, 20), the sphere of the flesh (2:18, 23), and the practices of the old humanity (3:5-9).

The writer's pastoral strategy can now be seen clearly. It might appear precarious to tell his readers to concentrate on the things above, when it was the excessive concern of the proponents of the philosophy with such matters that prompted the letter in the first place. He by no means completely disparages his readers' concern with the heavenly realm. Instead, he attempts to redirect it. In the process it emerges that two antithetical positions about participation in the heavenly realm are in confrontation. The philosophy's advocates take the earthly situation as their starting point, from which by their own efforts and techniques they will move beyond the body, gain visionary experience, and ascend into the heavenly spheres. The writer moves in the reverse direction, seeing the starting point and source of the believer's life in the resurrected Christ in heaven, from where it works itself out in earthly life (see 3:5-17) and from where it will eventually be publicly revealed (v. 4). Most important, he turns the tables on the philosophy by employing spatial and cosmic concepts to point to the sufficiency of Christ. The advocates of the philosophy appear to have wanted to add to belief in Christ the notion of appeasing other intermediaries in order to gain further knowledge and experience. For the writer of Colossians, there was no going beyond the one in the supreme position at God's right hand.

3:3-4. Believers' relationship with Christ is now elaborated in terms of its present hiddenness and future glory. The clear implication of "you have died" is that this is a reference to their having died with Christ (cf. 2:20), a dying both to the elemental spirits and to what have just been designated "earthly things." Because of their union with Christ in his death and resurrection, the readers' having died to the sphere of sin is inseparably connected to their new life. "Your life," then, is not simply a reference to their biological existence but to the existence that results from incorporation into Christ. This has a hidden aspect, however. Union with Christ is a hidden reality accessible to faith, not sight—not even visionary sight—but nevertheless a reality that provides the resources for believers living out their Christian existence in the world. The choice of the term "hidden" (κρύπτω *kryptō*) may have been prompted by the philosophy's interest in the notion of hidden or secret knowledge (cf. 2:3).

It is striking that believers' lives are said to be hidden "with Christ in God." They are "in God" because they are bound up with Christ, who is himself in God. In contrast to any ascent of the soul in order to appease the powers and achieve union with God, believers already have such a relationship on the basis of their link with Christ; and, by its very nature, being in God provides a security that needs no completion.

But for this writer, as for Jewish apocalyptic writings, hiddenness is not simply a mystical concept but is linked to God's purposes for history. That which is at present hidden in heaven is yet to be revealed in history. The mystery of God's plan for salvation has been revealed in Christ (1:26-27), but part of it remains hidden, including the true nature of believers' relationship with Christ, and awaits full revelation at the consummation.

The depiction of believers' relationship with Christ in v. 4 is also distinctive. Their lives are so bound up with Christ that the one who will be revealed at the end can be called "our life."[114]

---

114. The choice between two textual variants here makes little difference to the meaning. The reading "your life" has the strongest external attestation, but, despite the NRSV and the NIV, it seems more likely that at an early stage a scribe changed an original "our" to "your" to conform to the surrounding syntax than that an awkward change was made in the other direction, because the identification of Christ with the readers' life appeared too exclusive.

This identification between Christ and believers is reminiscent of Paul's formulations in Gal 2:20 and Phil 1:21 and sums up the way in which for believers Christ embodies what is of greatest value in life. Believers' relationship with Christ will be revealed in its full glory when Christ is manifested or revealed. Although some have disputed it, this is a reference to the parousia. It is true that being made manifest, or revealed, is not necessarily the same thing as "coming," but elsewhere in the Pauline corpus Christ's being revealed from heaven is synonymous with his coming (see 2 Thess 1:7, 10). The language of being revealed rather than coming is shaped by the hidden/revealed contrast of vv. 3-4, but nevertheless constitutes the letter's only reference to the parousia. At the parousia's unveiling of Christ's glory, the readers will also experience the unveiling of the consummation of their salvation as they share the glory of Christ that God had intended for humanity.

This formulation brings together a number of Pauline themes: the glory to be revealed, which includes the revelation of the sons and daughters of God and involves the redemption of their bodies (Rom 8:18-19, 23); the transformation of believers' bodies of humiliation into conformity with Christ's glorious body (Phil 3:21); and the resurrection of believers as entailing a body of glory in the image of the heavenly Christ (1 Cor 15:43, 49). The "then" in v. 4b makes the writer's assertion emphatic. Such experience of heavenly glory will only become available to sight at the consummation. This shows the normal Pauline eschatological reserve emerging forcefully despite the writer's earlier emphasis for the sake of his readers on "realized" eschatology. Colossians 3:1-4 can now be seen to demonstrate that believers' relationship "with Christ" receives its dynamic from the history of salvation. Believers have died and been raised with Christ, their lives are at present hidden in heaven with Christ, and they will be revealed in glory with Christ.

REFLECTIONS

1. Appropriately, Col 3:1-4 serves as an alternative reading for Easter Day in Year A of the lectionary cycle. In that context, it underscores that Christ's resurrection is not to be viewed as some extraordinary, isolated event but one that inaugurated a new order in which believers have become participants.

The passage can serve, therefore, as a reminder that the real new age began with the resurrection of Jesus—not with a planetary shift from the Age of Pisces to the Age of Aquarius. In some aspects of the latter "new age" spirituality, with its concern for transcendence of the everyday material world, the claim is made that the universe is inhabited by spiritual beings who have to be placated by means of ceremonies and incantations and that ordinary people need the help of shamans, sorcerers, and mediums who, through long training, have learned to penetrate this spirit world and are equipped to show others the unity and fullness of cosmic life. Encounters with spirit guardians and "out of the body" experiences are offered through a variety of techniques, including use of drugs, meditation, and ritualized dance. Such claims do not appear too far removed from those of the philosophy. The letter writer's attempt to redirect his readers' concern with the heavenly realm and to advocate a genuine heavenly mindedness rooted in the Pauline gospel is suggestive for the contemporary church in the midst of those who are groping for transcendence. Christian proclamation will need to redirect contemporary interest in "the transcendent" to a relationship with a transcendent person, the risen and exalted Christ. The message of Colossians updated for such a situation might well be, "Since there is so much concern for experience of the transcendent, seek that transcendence in which the risen and exalted Christ is central." Contemporary readers of Colossians might do well to reflect on whether their worship, both public and private, is simply a routine exercise or an experience of transcendence shaped by encounter with the heavenly Christ and whether their lives are characterized by the sort of heavenly mindedness that transforms every part of life by seeing it in relation to the lordship of the exalted Christ.

2. Consideration of this section of Colossians in connection with what follows inevitably raises questions about the relationship of otherworldliness and this-worldliness in Christian existence. On the one hand, the extreme of this-worldliness might ask, "What can talk about spirituality and heavenly existence possibly mean to someone living on the poverty line and in squalid conditions?" On the other hand, the extreme of otherworldliness might ask, "What can the poverty line and squalid conditions matter to someone who has the hope of heaven?" For the writer of Colossians, being heavenly minded rather than earthly minded is not some compensation for life's ills but is motivated by attending to one's relation to the church's Lord, who from his position with God controls the course of human history and who will at its culmination bring the life of heaven to transform the earth. As becomes clear in the next section, heavenly mindedness is not to be understood as a form of absentmindedness about ordinary life or social and economic conditions. Having a heavenly reference point is, instead, the very thing that should drive believers on within their social situation to pursue justice and fairness (cf. 4:1).

This passage's exhortation to "seek the things above," when taken in context, provides no justification for the popular reduction of the Christian hope to the individualistic one of "going to heaven when I die." Both the notions of Christ's resurrection, participation in which opens up access to the heavenly, and of his future revelation in glory with believers at the parousia are part of the broader Pauline eschatological hope that is retained here. That hope is for believers to share Christ's resurrection life in transformed bodily form. We should not forget that the vision of the hymnic material in 1:15-20 is for a reconciled cosmos, explicitly including heaven and earth. In the meantime, believers' roles in the working out of this cosmic drama are sustained by their relationship to their Lord in heaven. This relationship is such that Christ is said to be the life of believers and their lives are depicted as being hidden with Christ in God, so that not even their physical death before the parousia will be able to affect their participation in the final act of the drama.

3. In the meantime, however, there does remain a "hiddenness" to believers' lives in Christ. Amid all the letter's emphasis on the wisdom and knowledge believers have in Christ, it is salutary to remember this. By no means everything about Christian living is apparent, not only to outsiders, for whom much of it appears foolish, but also to Christians themselves, for whom there remain mystery and much questioning until the final revelation. We will not see all that is entailed in our new identity until the eschaton, and there will be times when everything seems to tell against its reality. So while the relationship with Christ speaks of assurance, our present experience of it is partial and provisional. Its hiddenness necessitates that Christians live by faith and not by sight and, therefore, without all the answers to the meaning of many events in their lives.

Colossians 3:5–4:1, Exhortation to Holiness of Life

OVERVIEW

After the exhortations to genuine heavenly mindedness there now follows a series of ethical exhortations. The preceding exhortations and the first of the ethical exhortations are linked to the conceptuality of the philosophy and ensure that the ensuing more general paraenesis is not viewed as completely independent of the situation being addressed by the letter as a whole. Given the infrequency of exhortations about worship in paraenesis and the place of particular worship practices in the philosophy, it is probably more than a coincidence that 3:16 provides instruction about Christian worship. The paraenesis includes a collection of *sententiae,* ethical sentences, common among Hellenistic philosophers and adopted by Hellenistic Judaism, that were frequently in the form of imperatives and gave rules of conduct for daily life. From the same sources are derived the catalogs of vices and virtues in 3:5, 8, 12 and the household code taken up in 3:18–4:1. The contrast between two patterns of conduct reflected in the vices and virtues, the "Two Ways," is found both in Jewish Scriptures and in other writings (see Deut 30:15-20; Psalm 1; *T. Ash.* 1:3, 5; 1QS 3.13–4.26); it is also used frequently in Greco-Roman ethical thought, which had in turn influenced Hellenistic Judaism (see Wis 14:25-26).[115]

115. See also Philo *On the Sacrifices of Abel and Cain* 20 45.

Colossians 3:5-11, Put to Death What Is Earthly

NIV	NRSV
⁵Put to death, therefore, whatever belongs to your earthly nature: sexual immorality, impurity, lust, evil desires and greed, which is idolatry. ⁶Because of these, the wrath of God is coming.ᵃ ⁷You used to walk in these ways, in the life you once lived. ⁸But now you must rid yourselves of all such things as these: anger, rage, malice, slander, and filthy language from your lips. ⁹Do not lie to each other, since you have taken off your old self with its practices ¹⁰and have put on the new self, which is being renewed in knowl-	⁵Put to death, therefore, whatever in you is earthly: fornication, impurity, passion, evil desire, and greed (which is idolatry). ⁶On account of these the wrath of God is coming on those who are disobedient.ᵃ ⁷These are the ways you also once followed, when you were living that life.ᵇ ⁸But now you must get rid of all such things— anger, wrath, malice, slander, and abusiveᶜ language from your mouth. ⁹Do not lie to one another, seeing that you have stripped off the old
ᵃ6 Some early manuscripts *coming on those who are disobedient*	ᵃ Other ancient authorities lack *on those who are disobedient* (Gk *the children of disobedience*) ᵇ Or *living among such people* ᶜ Or *filthy*

NIV

edge in the image of its Creator. [11]Here there is no Greek or Jew, circumcised or uncircumcised, barbarian, Scythian, slave or free, but Christ is all, and is in all.

NRSV

self with its practices [10]and have clothed yourselves with the new self, which is being renewed in knowledge according to the image of its creator. [11]In that renewal[a] there is no longer Greek and Jew, circumcised and uncircumcised, barbarian, Scythian, slave and free; but Christ is all and in all!

[a] Gk *its creator*, [11]*where*

COMMENTARY

3:5-8. The ascetic regulations insisted upon by the advocates of the philosophy were designed to deal with people's "members on the earth"—that is, their physical bodies, which are dependent on the lower, material realm. In v. 5, the writer takes up this notion but gives it his own ethical twist. Both the NRSV and the NIV miss the force of this with their paraphrases of v. 5*a*. The language at first sounds as if the writer is contradicting his previous polemic against asceticism and severity to the body: "Put to death the members on the earth." But then comes the list, not of physical parts of the body, as the reader might expect, but of vices. His point is that a genuine concern for the heavenly realm arising out of believers' union with Christ will not lead to the gratification of the flesh, for which he has criticized the philosophy (cf. 2:23). In the thought of Paul there is an "already" and a "not yet" to dying with Christ, whereby those who have died to sin (Rom 6:2-4) still need to be exhorted to put to death the deeds of the body (Rom 8:13). Similarly here, those who have died with Christ (2:20; 3:3) still have to be told to put to death sinful practices.

The writer is fond of lists of five. In v. 5 he lists five vices, as also in v. 8, while in v. 12 he will catalog five virtues. The first five vices start off as explicitly sexual ones and gradually become more general. Heading the vices is "fornication" (πορνεία *porneia*), a broad term denoting general sexual immorality that is also used more particularly of adultery and intercourse with prostitutes. "Impurity" (ἀκαθαρσία *akatharsia*) is usually associated with sexual sin and is also found in combination with *porneia* in 2 Cor 12:21; Gal 5:19; and 1 Thess 4:3, 7. Because of its context

here, the third vice, "passion" or "lust" (πάθος *pathos*), also has a primary connotation of uncontrolled sexual appetite. "Evil desire" (ἐπιθυμία κακή *epithymia kakē*) takes the list in a more general direction, referring to all forms of sinful desire, to what Paul might call "the desires of the flesh" (Rom 13:14; Gal 5:16, 24). The fifth vice, "covetousness" (πλεονεξία *pleonexia*), is the insatiable greed whereby people assume that things or other people exist simply for their own gratification. Interestingly, and in line with Jewish tradition, covetousness is equated with idolatry.[116] The thought is that all idolatry involves some form of covetousness. When humanity refuses to acknowledge the various aspects of life as the gifts of the Creator, it attempts to seize these things for itself and thereby elevates some desired object to the center of life. In the language of Rom 1:25, humanity ends up worshiping and serving created things rather than the Creator. This is the opposite attitude to the thanksgiving that recognizes God at the center of life (cf. 3:17).

An eschatological motivation is provided for putting to death these practices. The vices are so serious that on account of them the wrath of God is coming, and the implication is that those who are found indulging in them will experience that holy anger of God and the judgment that results from it. The implication is clear, although the original text in all likelihood did not contain the phrase "on the children of disobedience" (so NIV).[117] The

---

116. See *T. Jud.* 19:1 and Philo *The Special Laws* 1.23, 25 for the link between covetousness and idolatry. See also Wis 14:12; *T. Reub.* 4.6; and *T. Jud.* 23.1 for the link between fornication or sexual lust and idolatry.

117. See P[46], B. The later addition appears to have been made under the influence of the parallel in Eph 5:6.

"once . . . but now" contrast of vv. 7-8 (cf. 1:21-22) recalls the decisive change that has taken place for the readers, so that, whereas their lives were once characterized by such vices and deserved the coming wrath, this is no longer the case. Instead, the present is to be characterized by a total transformation in which the readers are responsible for putting aside or discarding like old clothes all vices.

A further list of five is provided to ensure that the readers understand the extent of their responsibility to abandon the old way of life. Anger, which heads this new list of sins, is given an overwhelmingly negative evaluation in the OT (see Prov 15:1, 18; 22:24; Eccl 7:9), in Hellenistic Judaism (see Sir 1:22; 27:30; *T. Dan* 2.1–5.1), and in the NT (see Matt 5:22; Gal 5:20; Jas 1:19-20), presumably because of the estrangement from others that nearly always accompanies its expression. "Rage" or "wrath" (θυμός *thymos*) is synonymous with "anger" (ὀργή *orgē*), though Stoic writers sometimes distinguished them, with rage denoting the initial explosion of anger.[118] "Malice" (κακία *kakia*) includes any attitude or action that intends harm to another. Malice can express itself through "slander" (βλασφημία *blasphēmia*), the abuse and vilifying of others; shameful, foul, or obscene language (αἰσχρολογία *aischrologia*) can be the form such abuse often takes. The vices listed here, then, would all be destructive of harmonious relationships, and there can be no place for them in the new way of life, in which believers are related to one another in the body of Christ.

3:9-11. The emphasis on sins of speech, which comes to the fore at the end of the catalog of vices, is continued in the prohibition of lying. There can be no room for lies in the new community, because they poison communication and breed suspicion instead of mutual trust. The warrant used for the exhortation is formulated in terms of the transformation believers have undergone. The imperative is based on the indicative of having stripped off the old person and its practices and having put on the new. The language of "stripping off," instead of simply "putting off," again picks up the ascetic terminology of the philosophy (cf. 2:11, 15) and this time gives it an ethical twist. This is not the stripping off of the

physical body in acts of severity and self-abasement (cf. 2:16, 23) but a stripping off of the old sinful way of life. Paul talks of the old person's having been crucified with Christ in Rom 6:6 and about putting on Christ in Gal 3:27, where this is equivalent to being baptized into Christ; but he does not use the language of putting off the old person or putting on the new person. Some claim that this language derives from an early Christian baptismal practice of removing clothing before being baptized nude and then putting on a new garment.[119] This is possible, but the evidence for such a practice is actually from after the middle of the second century with *The Gospel of Philip* 101 and Hippolytus's *Apostolic Tradition.* The meaning of the imagery in *The Gospel of Thomas* 37, which contains no reference to baptism, is too doubtful for it to count as an allusion to the practice. In any case, the clothing imagery of putting off vices and putting on virtues was widespread among Greek and Hellenistic Jewish writers. It is far more certain that the imagery in Colossians is connected with the significance of baptism than with baptismal practice.

The translation of τὸν παλαιὸν ἄνθρωπον (*ton palaion anthrōpon*) as "old self" and τὸν νέον (*ton neon*) as "new self" (NRSV and NIV) though better than "old nature" and "new nature," tends to narrow the reference of its literal meaning, "person." The old person is the person as identified with the old humanity, living under the present evil age and its powers. The new person is the believer as identified with the new humanity, the new order of existence inaugurated by Christ's death and resurrection. Verse 10 makes clear that this new person is not yet totally new but is in process of renewal. The underlying thought is the familiar "already" and "not yet" of the new age.

The present focus of renewal is on knowledge. This is significant in the light of the letter's setting. Any search for further esoteric knowledge is to be seen as unnecessary for those who, as part of the new humanity, are continually being renewed in and growing in knowledge (cf. 1:10). The readers should expect to experience a constant development of perception that will result in their ability to live lives appropriate to the new order, a thought equivalent to Paul's formulation in Rom

---

118. E.g., Diogenes Laertius 7.114; Seneca *On Anger* 2.36.

119. E.g., W. A. Meeks, *The First Urban Christians: The Social World of the Apostle Paul* (New Haven: Yale University Press, 1983) 155.

12:2 about being "transformed by the renewing of your minds." That the renewal in knowledge of the new person is in conformity with the image of the one who created it underscores, through the allusion to Gen 1:27, that the believer is part of a new creation, a new humanity in whom the image of God is restored.

If v. 10 has focused primarily on the individual aspect of the new humanity, v. 11 highlights the corporate aspect, as it asserts that within the new humanity the barriers of the old order are abolished. This is an adaptation of the baptismal formula found in Gal 3:28. It is noticeable that here, however, as in 1 Cor 12:13, there is no mention of male and female. Given the problems Paul perceived about the conduct of women in the Corinthian church, the omission of this aspect in 1 Cor 12:13 is understandable. The omission may also be significant in Colossians, which will go on to introduce the household code, which demarcates more firmly different roles for husbands and wives. This should not, however, be overemphasized, since the code also discusses the roles of masters and slaves, and yet slave and free are mentioned in the Colossians version of the formula (v. 11). Nevertheless, women's asserting their freedom in Christ was a factor in the Pauline churches, while slaves' demanding their freedom apparently was not.

In the adaptation of the formula "Greek" is mentioned before "Jew" in the first pairing, possibly on account of the Gentile readership, although the dividing of humanity into Greek and Jew in the first place reflects the writer's Jewish perspective. The second pairing, "circumcision and uncircumcision," repeats the contrast, but this time puts greater emphasis on the religious aspects of the ethnic and cultural division. The thought of the new creation in v. 10 may have influenced this addition, since in Gal 6:15 Paul had written, "For neither circumcision nor uncircumcision is anything, but a new creation is everything!" Here

the proclamation of Christ among the Gentiles (cf. 1:27) entails that the old humanity's categorization of people into these two classes is no longer meaningful in the new humanity. If Jews divided humanity into Jews and Greeks, Greeks divided it into Greeks and barbarians, with the latter category denoting non-Greek speakers and conveying the additional overtones that such people were uncultured and uncivilized. The term "Scythian" intensifies the note of cultural contempt. The Scythian tribes around the Black Sea were considered the lowest kind of barbarian. Josephus considered them "little better than wild beasts" (see also 2 Macc 4:47 for an ironic statement indicating the low regard in which Scythians were held).[120] The terms "slave" and "free" will be discussed further under the household code. They are found in the earlier formulations in 1 Cor 12:13 and Gal 3:28; here the claim of the Pauline churches that this basic social division makes no difference in terms of believers' standing in Christ and in the new community is continued.

While the philosophy, with its condemnation of those who did not follow its rules and were still bound to the realm of the physical, introduced divisive distinctions into the body of Christ, this formulation stresses inclusiveness and does away with all distinctions based on ethnic, religious, cultural, or social criteria within the new humanity. The relation to Christ is all that matters and transcends these other categorizations. This is the force of "Christ is all and in all." He permeates and pervades the new humanity. This emphasis on Christ's centrality recalls the focus on his supremacy in both creation and redemption (1:15-20) and his paramount place in the realm above (3:1). If Christ is all in all in relation to the cosmos, then nothing less can be the case within the community of the new humanity.

120. Josephus *Against Apion* 2.269.

REFLECTIONS

1. The thrust of this passage provides another reminder that for the writer of Colossians the real issue is not learning special techniques to deal with the powerful forces at work for evil in our lives and in our society but is instead learning how to live the Christian life individually and corporately. He holds that there is no need for a diminished view of the self in which the body is deemed inferior and people are put in thrall to hostile powers that have a divisive influence. What is wrong is not an inherent flaw in the material world; it is sin, a flawed relationship with the Creator, that has produced alienation. Being restored in the image of the Creator through Christ, therefore, is what makes possible life as it was intended to be lived.

The lists of vices and virtues reflect the writer's assumption that the behavior of believers should at least match that enjoined by the conventional ethical wisdom of the day. In fact, the expectation that these standards will receive general consent adds to the persuasiveness of the appeal. In their new context, as part of the characterization of the old and new humanities, the vices and virtues selected are those that will either disrupt or enhance the life of the Christian community.

The vices, for which there is no longer any room in Christian existence, are of two main types: (1) sexual immorality and greed and (2) anger and hateful speech. That the exhortations are still needed today is indicated by the existence of some Christian groups and churches that are strongly judgmental of any failure to maintain the strictest standards of sexual conduct but are rife with malicious intrigue and spiteful gossip and of others that are so tolerant and keen to avoid any dissension that they are loath to rebuke or discipline even flagrant breaches of sexual morality.

It is easy to pass over these lists simply as conventional examples of early Christian moralism. Yet it may be worth pausing to reflect on some of the vices in a broader context. For example, it is because Christians want to celebrate the goodness of the sexual expression of human love in committed, lifelong relationships and to affirm the option of a healthy celibacy that they will be concerned, with the writer of Colossians, that the distorted practices of an uncontrolled and exploitative sexuality be rooted out or "put to death." The mention of "covetousness" invites us to broaden our reflections. It is, of course, colored by its context in a list that begins with sexual immorality, but it takes the issues in a more general direction. Greedy desire not only produces sexual exploitation but also fuels the materialism that controls the lives of individuals and societies, leading so frequently to a despising of the poor whose worship of this particular god of mammon is alleged not to be devoted enough. Anger, hatred, and malicious speech are at the roots of violence, whether that violence is domestic, leaving battered wives and children in its wake; national, producing civil wars and ethnic cleansings; or international, leading to the stockpiling of weapons through the arms trade and both the threat of their use and their actual use to wipe out human lives.

A broader perspective also compels us to ask whether anger is always a bad thing. What about the victims of violence and oppression? Should not they be allowed righteous anger? Have we not also learned that suppression of anger leads to repression and depression? A more qualified theological evaluation might well want and need to discuss how to express anger and resentment without being overcome by it, while still taking with full seriousness the destructive effects with which it is linked in Colossians. After all, anger can be evidence of the fact that evil is being taken seriously. The inability to be angry about injustice is surely a character deficiency. At the same time, anger and hatred can be a means of reestablishing a sense of self in the face of violation. Perhaps what needs to be stressed is that these appropriate human reactions are never meant to be the permanent characteristics of a life lived in the new order but a part of the costly process of moving to a love of one's enemies, not from a position of weakness but from one of appropriate strength. The listing of anger as a major vice reminds us, however, how easy it is even for victims of violence to perpetuate its cycle if they allow anger to fester and smolder into vengeance. Repressed bitterness and prolonged hatred, even as the result of acts that have wrecked our lives, have their own destructive effects.

The seriousness with which these lists of vices are to be treated emerges from the way they are evaluated theologically. In particular, the greed or covetousness that also underlies the sexual impurity the writer indicts is to be seen as idolatry. When we treat any part of the created order as ultimate, as a god, it then in fact functions like a god for us. But its control has destructive, rather than beneficial, ends. In terms of these lists of vices, sexual immorality, greed, and anger, seen as worship of the gods of Eros, Mammon, and Mars, can take over a person in a destructive way. The same is true of other objects of covetousness, such as power and prestige. But also the conduct of both lists is seen as characteristic of the old way of living, which incurs the righteous wrath of God (3:6). Two implications can be drawn from this assertion in its context. On the one hand, God's wrath, the divine judgment, is not on account of the body but on account of sin. On the other hand, the ultimate problem with sinful actions is not the harm they cause us or others, real though it is, but their affront to a holy God, with the consequence of that God's judgment.

2. Again there is benefit to be gained from seeing particularly 3:5-6 in the broader lectionary context (Year C, Proper 13). While Col 3:1-11 is the epistle reading, Hos 11:1-11 is the Old Testament reading and Luke 12:13-21 the Gospel. The parable of the rich man who fails to see his life and possessions as being on loan from God follows the warning, "Be on your guard against all kinds of greed." Hosea 11 depicts God's anguish in the face of people's propensity to idolatry. In the end, the divine anger and wrath, though merited by humans, will not be executed. They are real, but they do not have the last word, because they are in the service of God's kindness and love, which prevail. Here, too, in Colossians, despite the seriousness of the warning, it has become clear that the God of judgment is also a gracious giver, who has not only provided reconciliation instead of alienation (1:21-23) but has also made available new resources of life and power through Christ's resurrection (3:1-4) and has created the new person that is to be appropriated (3:10). Humans are required neither to save themselves from their plight nor to search for additional means to supplement the solution provided in the gospel. They are to realize that the one who knows the depth and seriousness of their plight has already provided at great cost a solution fully sufficient to match it and that all that is needed is to appropriate fully and thankfully what has been offered.

3. What are the contemporary equivalents of the categories listed in 3:11 that ought not to be obstacles to unity and reconciled relationships within the church? Certainly male and female still need to be added, and, in the light of contemporary understanding of sexual orientation, gay/lesbian and straight should be included. In a global context, the disparity between "First World" and "Two-thirds World" Christians scarcely reflects a universal community displaying the overcoming of differences in a loving and just reconciliation in Christ. Depending on our particular social location, we will also know how far there is to go in the church's being any different from our society's marginalization of particular ethnic groups, whether they be African American, Hispanic American, or Native American. The categories of "slave" and "free" in Colossians also remind us of the economic and class differences that are meant to be overcome in the church today.

As if such categories do not present enough of a challenge, since the time of Colossians the church has also experienced the barriers to unity produced by denominational and theological labeling. Is it more important to be known as evangelical or to promote a common gospel? Is it more important to be known as catholic or to focus on the one church and its sacraments? Is it more important to be thought liberal than to be concerned for a reasoned and critical articulation of the gospel in interaction with our culture? Is it more important to promote the charismatic movement than to be open to the variety of workings of the one Spirit?

Colossians 3:12-17, Put on Love, Appropriate the Peace of Christ, and Be Thankful

NIV

¹²Therefore, as God's chosen people, holy and dearly loved, clothe yourselves with compassion, kindness, humility, gentleness and patience. ¹³Bear with each other and forgive whatever grievances you may have against one another. Forgive as the Lord forgave you. ¹⁴And over all these virtues put on love, which binds them all together in perfect unity.

¹⁵Let the peace of Christ rule in your hearts, since as members of one body you were called to peace. And be thankful. ¹⁶Let the word of Christ dwell in you richly as you teach and admonish one another with all wisdom, and as you sing psalms, hymns and spiritual songs with gratitude in your hearts to God. ¹⁷And whatever you do, whether in word or deed, do it all in the name of the Lord Jesus, giving thanks to God the Father through him.

NRSV

12As God's chosen ones, holy and beloved, clothe yourselves with compassion, kindness, humility, meekness, and patience. ¹³Bear with one another and, if anyone has a complaint against another, forgive each other; just as the Lord*a* has forgiven you, so you also must forgive. ¹⁴Above all, clothe yourselves with love, which binds everything together in perfect harmony. ¹⁵And let the peace of Christ rule in your hearts, to which indeed you were called in the one body. And be thankful. ¹⁶Let the word of Christ*b* dwell in you richly; teach and admonish one another in all wisdom; and with gratitude in your hearts sing psalms, hymns, and spiritual songs to God.*c* ¹⁷And whatever you do, in word or deed, do everything in the name of the Lord Jesus, giving thanks to God the Father through him.

a Other ancient authorities read *just as Christ*   *b* Other ancient authorities read *of God*, or *of the Lord*   *c* Other ancient authorities read *to the Lord*

COMMENTARY

3:12. The writer now issues further exhortations about the qualities necessary for living in the new community. Just as believers have already stripped off the old person, but still need to discard specific vices, so now, although they have already put on the new person, they still need to clothe themselves with specific virtues. The readers are described as God's elect, holy and beloved. All three designations were used for Israel in the LXX (esp. Deut 7:6-8), and the cluster here provides a forceful reminder to the Gentile readers that through God's initiative in Christ they have now been chosen and set apart for God, who has bestowed upon them the divine love. So it is as the new people of God that they are to put on the qualities of the new humanity.

The five virtues listed in 3:12 are those required for harmonious living as a community. The new people of God need a deep and heartfelt sympathy for the situations of others and active consideration (compassion and kindness) for others' interests and needs. The term for humility (ταπεινοφροσύνη *tapeinophrosynē*) is the same word used in 2:18, 23 to refer to the self-abasement and fasting that were part of the philosophy's ascetic program. More generally in the Greco-Roman world, the term was associated with contemptible servility. Here, among the virtues, it is viewed positively as the ability to count others better than oneself (cf. Phil 2:3), which is based on a proper sense of self-worth and not simply weakness of character. Closely associated with this quality is gentleness (NIV), entailing courtesy, considerateness, and a willingness to waive one's rights rather than to be concerned for personal gain in one's relations with others. Also intimately related to these virtues is patience, the ability not to become frustrated and enraged but to make allowances for others' shortcomings and to tolerate their exasperating behavior.

3:13. The two participial clauses in this verse may well have imperatival force; they function to underline the qualities required in the previous clause by highlighting the kinds of relationships in which they will need to be displayed. They reflect a realism about problems of relationships in any community and the inevitability of complaints, clashes, and grievances. The solution offered is bearing with one another and forgiving one another. Bearing with others involves fully accepting them for who they are, with their weaknesses and faults, and allowing them worth and space. The motivation and grounds for the all-important ability to forgive others lie in the readers' own experience of forgiveness (cf. 1:14). Knowing oneself to have been forgiven by Christ should release the generosity required to forgive others.

3:14-16. A verb needs to be supplied for the beginning of v. 14, which simply reads "above all these love . . ." That verb is the main verb from v. 12, "put on" (ἐνδύω *endyō*). However, it is not entirely clear how far the imagery of clothing is to be extended and whether it is being suggested that love is the item to be put on over the the other virtues (NIV) or whether the stress on the supreme importance of love is more general (NRSV). Either way, love is described as the "bond of perfection." The thought is reminiscent of 1 Corinthians 13, where love is the greatest of the virtues (1 Cor 13:13) and its depiction (1 Cor 13:4-7) encompasses the virtues listed here in v. 12 (see also Gal 5:22-23). Love functions in this way perfectly or in a way that leads to perfection or maturity; either construction is possible. In the latter case, the perfection in view is that of the community as a whole. The broader context of relationships within the new people of God (vv. 11-12) and the one body (v. 15) reinforces the implication that love acts as a bond not only for the other virtues but also for the community in which they are to be displayed. Perfection, then, is not some individually gained state but a corporate one achieved in a relationship of love.

In 1 Corinthians 13 love is a personified power of the new age; here it is like a garment to be put on or appropriated by believers. In Colossians, it is more explicitly the peace of Christ that is personified and seen as ruling in the new order. Through Christ, God has made peace and brought about reconciliation (1:20-22), and believers have been called by God into that peace. The notion of calling points to the actualization of God's electing purposes and recalls the designation "God's chosen" in v. 12. God has brought believers into this new order of peace. Now they are to let this peace have its sway and take control both at the center of their individual lives and in the one body that their calling had in view. God's gracious initiative and believers' responsibility to respond to that initiative go hand in hand. In being called into the one unified body of the corporate new humanity, the readers have been called to live out its transcending of divisions (v. 11); they have been called to appropriate Christ's peace. So far in the letter, the term "body" (σῶμα *sōma*) has been used of the universal body of Christ (1:18, 24; 2:19). The terminology of "one body" in v. 15 has reference to the unity of that same body, though drawing on the Pauline use of body imagery for the unity of the local church in Romans 12 and 1 Corinthians 12 and with the expectation that the primary sphere of realizing that unity for the readers will be in their local house churches.

The short exhortation of v. 15*c* ("And be thankful") sets the tone for the last part of this section and introduces a threefold emphasis on thanksgiving (cf. v. 16*c*, "with gratitude," and *v. 17b*, "giving thanks"). Thankfulness is a key response to the gospel in this letter (see the earlier references in 1:11-12; 2:7 and the writer's own extended thanksgiving in 1:3-23). Its grounds are all that has been accomplished in God's gracious initiative in Christ. The readers' thanksgiving will come to natural expression in their communal worship.

One of the features of the philosophy was what the writer calls its "worship of angels." This may well be one reason why the writer reminds his readers of the kind of worship in which they should be participating. In that worship, the word of Christ, the message of the gospel that centers in Christ, is to provide the focus. They are to give space to the word of Christ and allow it to dwell richly among them (cf. 1:27). This will entail listening to, meditating on, and responding in praise and thanksgiving to that word as it is preached and taught. Then it will be an abundant resource as it permeates their lives.

As the readers teach and admonish one another, the word of Christ will have a firm place in the community and will be the source for all the wisdom they need. In contrast to the philosophy's concern for wisdom, which results only in the appearance but not the reality (2:23), in attending to the word of Christ the readers will be taken up with the one "in whom are hidden all the treasures of wisdom" (2:3). And they will not travel the route to this wisdom alone but together, as they learn from one another. The task of teaching and admonishing in all wisdom, therefore, is seen to be not only that which Paul exercised (cf. 1:28) but also that of all believers.

In the Greek syntax the mention of "psalms, hymns and spiritual songs" is in the dative case and is linked more closely to the preceding participles "teaching and admonishing" (διδάσκοντες καὶ νουθετοῦντες *didaskontes kai nouthetountes*) than to the following one, "singing" (ἄδοντες *adontes*). The use of psalms, hymns, and songs, therefore, is a primary means by which mutual teaching and admonition take place. It is significant that when the writer of Ephesians takes up this language from Colossians in Eph 5:19, he clearly gives it this force. Hymns were meant to function as vehicles not only for worship but also for instruction. Much of what is hymnic in the Pauline corpus has a didactic and paraenetic function, and this writer has employed the hymnic material in 1:15-20 in this fashion (cf. Phil 2:6-11; 1 Tim 3:16).[121]

121. See S. E. Fowl, *The Story of Jesus in the Ethics of Paul: The Function of the Hymnic Material in the Pauline Corpus* (Sheffield: JSOT, 1990).

It is difficult to draw any hard and fast distinctions among the three categories of song mentioned here. They are the three most common terms for religious songs in the LXX, where they are used interchangeably. In all probability, the adjective "spiritual" (πνευματικός *pneumatikos*), signifying "inspired or prompted by the Spirit," applies to all three words and not just the last. Inspiration by the Spirit need not necessarily be equated with spontaneity, however. And all forms of hymnody found in the early church are likely to be in view, from liturgical pieces that had already become established in worship, such as 1:15-20, to chants and songs freshly created in the assembly. But of more importance than the type of songs sung was the attitude with which they were sung. The songs should flow out of gratitude and thanksgiving, come from the heart, and be directed in praise to God.

3:17. The language of this verse makes unmistakably clear that the scope of the paraenesis is being extended from community life and worship to encompass all of life. To do everything "in the name of the Lord Jesus" is to recognize that his lordship claims every part of a believer's life. But it also becomes clear that the obedience involved is not some burdensome duty but the accompaniment and natural expression of the thanksgiving believers offer to God through Christ, as the writer returns at the end of the section to one of his dominant motifs. By stressing that there can be no discontinuity between the readers' worship and everyday life, this verse provides an appropriate transition to the household code, whose duties now give more specificity to "whatever you do."

REFLECTIONS

Colossians 3:12-17 is the lection appointed for the First Sunday After Christmas (Year C). Its theme of the life of the new humanity is appropriate to the start of a new year, and its specific exhortations can give perspective and direction to the seasonal activity of making resolutions. What better resolve than to put on and grow in the virtues that will always remain incumbent for Christians and to find specific ways of expressing these.

1. It is important to realize that the forgiveness that is in view is in the context of relationships among believers and presupposes mutuality: "Forgive each other." Forgiveness is not the overlooking or absorbing of hurt that comes from a weak sense of our own selves. Those who are exhorted are first reminded of the identity they have been given as a result of God's calling. Their election as a holy people, consecrated to God's purposes, means that they are also loved by God (3:12). Knowing oneself to be loved by God in Christ provides the proper sense of self and the source for relating in forgiving love to others (3:13). In the context of a relationship to God in Christ and to others in the new community of the church, forgiveness has as its goal not merely the healing of one's emotions from an offense or a hurt but the reconciliation with others that will display God's purposes of harmony, being realized in Christ. The realistic recognition that believers as new persons are still in the process of renewal means that forgiveness is essential for the functioning of the new humanity. Any community in which forgiveness is not an integral part will be a superficial one. And what is required for sustaining community is likely to be more than a single act of forgiveness; rather, the lives of the people in that community will be characterized by the continuing practices of forgiveness that draw their resources from the forgiveness already enacted by Christ.[122]

Of course, the requirement of practicing forgiveness is not limited to settings of mutuality; sometimes these can be lacking even within the church. But when it comes to exhorting people to forgiveness in settings beyond those in which both parties can be assumed to desire reconciliation, care is needed. For some who are victims in relationships, this could result in the perpetuation of abuse and violence and a further diminution of any sense of self-worth. Forgiveness is not a remedy for healing all relationships. Sometimes those relationships simply have to be escaped or ended. But the issue of forgiving those who have made one's life hell on earth will remain.

2. Closely related to forgiveness is love. The sacrifice of one's own interests out of concern for the welfare of others is the quality above all that is necessary in the new humanity. Most of the evils that have marred the history of the church have been due to the absence of this virtue, which is meant to be the binding agent, the superglue in church unity. Hope always remains, because in Pauline thought just as sin is a power of the old age, so also love is a power of the new age. Here, too, it is available as the supreme virtue to be put on, the power to be appropriated, the resource that enables one to allow the concerns of another to weigh more heavily than one's own desire for self-fulfillment and to reach out toward another with no expectation of reward.

3. The goal of the costly activities of both forgiveness and love comes into view with the mention of the rule of Christ's peace both within believers' hearts and in the one body. This notion of the rule of peace would no doubt have called to mind the *Pax Romana,* the militarily imposed peace that brought the absence of war through Rome's adjudication or umpiring of disputes in the empire. The rule of Christ's peace is of a quite different kind, however, entailing a reconciliation with God, cosmic in its scope, that was brought about through Christ's becoming the victim of Roman crucifixion. Believers are now called to appropriate and live out the peace of Christ that has been achieved, to let it rule in their own lives and in the church. It involves not a removal from all conflict but a centeredness that comes from knowing that in the new humanity Christ is in control and all in all. Such peace removes the need for manipulation of others or fear about others' opinions and enables reconciliation to continue to be the hallmark of the body of Christ as it shapes and controls Christian vision and actions.

4. The life of the Christian community living in the world as the bridgehead of the new humanity is to be distinguished not only by the quality of its interpersonal relationships but also by the quality of its worship. For Colossians, what is central is the word of Christ, the gospel, to which worship is the response. The focus is on its spoken proclamation, as attested

---

122. For a helpful discussion of forgiveness as "a habit that must be practised over time within the disciplines of Christian community," see L. G. Jones, *Embodying Forgiveness* (Grand Rapids: Eerdmans, 1995) esp. 163-204.

by the mention of teaching and admonition that follows. By extension, we can see the centrality of the word of Christ maintained through Scripture, of which Colossians itself is now a part, and through the sacraments, which are at least visible words.

What is particularly telling is the relationship set out between the gospel and the community, as the readers are told to "let the word of Christ dwell in you richly." This suggests that the purpose of the focus on gospel proclamation is the formation and shaping of the community to embody the word of Christ in its witness in the world. The responsibility for the gospel's being allowed its continuing, settled, and distinctive function as an inexhaustible source for formation is not simply that of preachers and teachers but of the whole assembly as it engages in mutual wise admonition and teaching (3:16). How far do we ensure that our services, or at least house groups, give the opportunity for all believers to play a role as wisdom teachers?

For those who do have specific responsibilities for preaching and teaching the word of Christ, this emphasis in Colossians provides a reminder that such responsibilities are to be exercised on behalf of the community and will have as their goal the community's formation. This may sound like a statement of the obvious, but our experience of sermons may tell us that, if this insight were really absorbed, it would have much more impact on the way preaching is carried out. Rather than aiming simply to inform or persuade, the sermon would aim to shape the identity and life of the Christian community. Rather than simply being a distillation of the preacher's own experience of or insight into the gospel, the sermon would aim to allow the listeners to enter into their own encounter with the word of Christ, which addresses us through the Scriptures.

In the community's worship, psalms, hymns, and spiritual songs have a twofold function. On the one hand, they play a part in the community's being formed by the word of Christ. If Col 1:15-20 was originally part of such hymnody, then the letter itself is the writer's attempt to allow that particular word about Christ to do its job. On the other hand, such songs are an offering of praise to God. Praise is the appropriate response to the good news of God's actions in Christ; it is an indication that grace has had its liberating effect, moving us from preoccupation with ourselves to the worship of God that constitutes what it is to be truly human. Far from leading simply to a passive acceptance of the status quo, the thankfulness that underlies such praise is also the motivation that ensures that the worshiping community brings to bear the lordship of Christ in every aspect of its life in the world (3:17).

Colossians 3:18–4:1, Let Christ's Lordship Shape Household Relationships

NIV	NRSV
[18]Wives, submit to your husbands, as is fitting in the Lord.	18Wives, be subject to your husbands, as is fitting in the Lord. [19]Husbands, love your wives and never treat them harshly.
[19]Husbands, love your wives and do not be harsh with them.	
[20]Children, obey your parents in everything, for this pleases the Lord.	20Children, obey your parents in everything, for this is your acceptable duty in the Lord. [21]Fathers, do not provoke your children, or they may lose heart. [22]Slaves, obey your earthly masters[a] in everything, not only while being watched and in order to please them, but wholeheartedly, fearing the Lord.[a] [23]Whatever your task, put yourselves into it, as done for the Lord and not for
[21]Fathers, do not embitter your children, or they will become discouraged.	
[22]Slaves, obey your earthly masters in everything; and do it, not only when their eye is on you and to win their favor, but with sincerity of heart and reverence for the Lord. [23]Whatever you	

[a] In Greek the same word is used for *master* and *Lord*

NIV

do, work at it with all your heart, as working for the Lord, not for men, [24]since you know that you will receive an inheritance from the Lord as a reward. It is the Lord Christ you are serving. [25]Anyone who does wrong will be repaid for his wrong, and there is no favoritism.

4 Masters, provide your slaves with what is right and fair, because you know that you also have a Master in heaven.

NRSV

your masters,[a] [24]since you know that from the Lord you will receive the inheritance as your reward; you serve[b] the Lord Christ. [25]For the wrongdoer will be paid back for whatever wrong has been done, and there is no partiality.

4 [1]Masters, treat your slaves justly and fairly, for you know that you also have a Master in heaven.

[a] Gk *not for men*   [b] Or *you are slaves of*, or *be slaves of*

COMMENTARY

In this section, the three basic relationships within the ancient household become the focus of the paraenesis, as the writer indicates that the heavenly mindedness to which he has exhorted his readers needs to be worked out in every aspect of daily life. In each of the three relationships, those expected to have the subordinate role in the relationship—wives, children, and slaves—are addressed first and then those who have the authoritative role—husbands, fathers, masters. In practice, of course, the address to the latter would frequently be to the same person, the male head of the household, in three different relationships. After the address of each group comes an imperative that, except in the case of husbands and fathers, is followed by a warrant giving the reason or motivation for the required conduct. The exhortation to slaves is the longest in the section, and in it the pattern of imperative followed by a warrant is repeated. The section constitutes the writer's adaptation of what has become known as "the household code" and appears to be the first instance of the use of such a schema in the NT.

❖   ❖   ❖   ❖

EXCURSUS: "THE HOUSEHOLD CODE": ITS ORIGIN AND ADAPTATION

Although some scholars had maintained that the household code was a Christian creation and others that it had been adapted from Stoic moral philosophy, the view that predominated for a considerable time was that the household code derived from the attempts of Philo and Josephus to show the links between the social duties of Judaism and Hellenistic moral philosophy. It was presumed that this type of Hellenistic Jewish ethical teaching was mediated to early Christianity via the Hellenistic synagogues.[123] More recently, however, it has been shown convincingly that such a hypothesis does not do sufficient justice to the more general discussion of household management in the ancient world and that the thought of Philo and Josephus needs to be situated within this broader stream of tradition.[124] This broader tradition, which also treats husband/wife, parent/child, and master/slave relationships and focuses on authority and subordination within these relationships, connects the topic of the household to

---

123. See J. E. Crouch, *The Origin and Intention of the Colossian Haustafel* (Göttingen: Vandenhoeck & Ruprecht, 1972) esp. 95-101, who provides the most detailed exposition of this view.
124. See D. L. Balch, *Let Wives Be Submissive: The Domestic Code in 1 Peter* (Chico, Calif.: Scholars Press, 1981), and also his review of the issues in "Household Codes," in *Greco-Roman Literature and the New Testament*, ed. D. E. Aune (Atlanta: Scholars Press, 1988) 25-50.

the larger topic of the state and derives from the classical Greek philosophers.[125] All the elements of their discussion are continued down into the later Roman period. Philo and Josephus also adapted Aristotle's outline of household subordination in their interpretation and recommendation of Mosaic law.[126] Typical of the content of all such discussions is the notion that the man is intended by nature to rule as husband, father, and master and that failure to adhere to this proper hierarchy is detrimental not only to the household but also to the life of the state.

Setting the household code within this tradition becomes significant for assessing its use within early Christianity. The tradition reveals that proper household management was regarded as a matter of crucial social and political concern. Any upsetting of the household's traditional hierarchical order could be considered a potential threat to the order of society. In Greco-Roman culture, wives, children, and slaves were expected to accept the religion of the *paterfamilias,* the male head of the household, and so religious groups that attracted women and slaves were particularly seen as likely to be subversive of societal stability. Stereotyped criticism about breeding immorality and sedition was leveled by Greco-Roman writers against the cults of Dionysus and Isis, which attracted female devotees, and also against Judaism, because Jewish slaves rejected the worship of their Roman masters' gods. Dionysius of Halicarnassus criticized foreign mystery cults and praised the virtues of Roman households with their insistence on the obedience of wives, children, and slaves.[127] And significantly, Josephus's stress on subordination within the three household relationships is a response to slander against the Jews in an attempt to show that Judaism was not subversive of the ethic demanded by Greco-Roman society.[128]

As women and slaves joined the new Christian movement in large numbers, it, too, became the object of suspicion and criticism. It may well, therefore, have been the need to respond to accusations from outsiders and to set standards in line with common notions of propriety as much as the need to respond to enthusiastic demands for freedom on the part of believers that led Christians to produce their own version of the household code. This was certainly a major factor by the time of the code's use in 1 Peter (see 1 Pet 2:12; 3:15-16).

In the first extant Christian household code here in Colossians, the reasons for its introduction are not made explicit. The primary reason for its adaptation appears to be that the writer found it appropriate in re-calling those who might have been attracted by the philosophy, with its stress on asceticism and visionary experiences, to the significance of earthly life with its domestic duties. It may well be, however, that his re-call takes this particular form precisely because of the social factors that have been noted. The philosophy had taken over some elements of Judaism in its observances, and they had become part of a package of teachings and practices that resembled those of mystery cults. What is more, by the second century CE, in popular thought asceticism, philosophy, and magic were all associated with signs of deviancy from social norms.[129] If "worship of angels" is the writer's description of the practice, frequently attested in magical traditions, of invoking angels in order to placate and ward off evil spirit powers, then the teaching being opposed in Colossians would bear all the marks of social deviance. It could be characterized as philosophy, was clearly ascetic, and advocated practices associated with popular magic. It would not be at all surprising that the writer would want to distance Pauline churches from outsiders' perception of this explosive combination. His instructions signal that, far from attempting to destabilize society, life in Christian households had its distinctive motivations but provided a model that those concerned with virtue in Greco-Roman society ought to be able to recognize not as subversive but as falling within the bounds of received wisdom about the household. The summarizing exhortation in 4:5 about living wisely in regard to outsiders lends support to this suggestion.

125. See Plato *Laws* 3.690A-D; 6.771E-7.824C; Aristotle *Politics* 1.1253b, 1259a.
126. See Philo *Hypothetica* 7.1-14; *On the Decalogue* 165-67; Josephus *Against Apion* 2.22-28.
127. Dionysius of Halicarnassus *Roman Antiquities* 2.24.3–2.27.4.
128. Josephus *Against Apion* 2.24, 27, 30.
129. See J. A. Francis, *Subversive Virtue: Asceticism and Authority in the Second Century Pagan World* (University Park: University of Pennsylvania Press, 1995) esp. 47, 49, 53.

This first use of the code in Christian literature reflects a stage in which Christians were conscious of criticisms of subverting the social order and of the need to adjust to living as Christians in the Greco-Roman world without unnecessarily disrupting the status quo. The death of the apostle Paul and the delay of the parousia are also likely to have been secondary factors contributing to this need to take a more long-term perspective on assimilating to life in society while preserving a Christian identity. This use of the code can also be seen as part of the process of stabilizing communal relations in the Pauline churches while retaining continuity with their earlier ethos. As M. Y. MacDonald observes of the code, "On the one hand, the rule-like statements reflect a more conservative attitude toward the role of subordinate members of the household; they leave much less room for ambiguity and, consequently, for exceptional activity on the part of certain members. On the other hand, the instructions are not incompatible with Paul's own teaching about women and slaves (cf. 1 Cor 11:2-16; 1 Cor 14:34-36; 1 Cor 7:20-24; Philem 10-20)."[130]

What is distinctive about Colossians' and subsequent Christian adaptation of the code is the series of exhortations to different groups within the household, all of which are treated as moral agents in their own right. What is distinctive about the content of the code in Colossians is the way in which the warrants, with their motivation, link the exhortations to believers' relationship to Christ as Lord, so that each group, including by implication husbands and fathers, is seen as equally accountable to the church's one Lord.

In its context in Colossians, the household code now forms part of the paraenesis in the writer's version of apostolic wisdom. His prayer for his readers was that they be "filled with the knowledge of God's will in all spiritual wisdom and understanding, so that you may lead lives worthy of the Lord" (1:9-10). With their roots in the wisdom found in Christ (2:2-3), the recipients are to be wisdom teachers themselves (3:16) and to live wisely in regard to outsiders (4:5). The code is situated between these last two references to wisdom and represents the writer's perspective on wise living in the household. It is not surprising that household duties would have been seen as part of wise conduct, because the Jewish wisdom tradition contained practical advice for all three household groups. All three relationships are discussed in Sir 7:19-28. Elsewhere there are frequent mentions of what is considered wise behavior for husbands and wives (see, e.g., Prov 5:18-19; 12:4; 18:22; 19:13*b*; 31:10-31; Sir 9:1; 26:1-4, 13-18), for parents and children (see, e.g., Prov 1:8; 6:20; 10:1; 13:24; 15:20; 19:13*a*, 18, 26; 23:13-14; Sir 3:1-16; 30:1-13), and for masters and slaves (see, e.g., Prov 14:35; 17:2; 19:10; 27:27; 29:19, 21; Sir 33:25-33). Not only so, but the justice and equity demanded of masters in the code is explicitly said to be the product of wisdom in Prov 2:9, and, of course, the fear of the Lord, to which slaves are exhorted, is in this tradition deemed to be either the beginning of wisdom (Prov 9:9; Sir 1:14) or wisdom itself (Sir 1:27; 19:20). The wisdom tradition offered moral guidance based on the sages' experience of and observations on human affairs and life in the world and attempted to discern in this a divine pattern and purpose. Now the wisdom teaching of Colossians takes up an early Christian version of accumulated reflection on household management from the Aristotelian and Hellenistic Jewish traditions and by this means attempts to determine the shape of believers' conduct in the light of Christ's lordship.

---

130. M. Y. MacDonald, *The Pauline Churches: A Socio-historical Study of Institutionalization in the Pauline and Deutero-Pauline Writings* (Cambridge: Cambridge University Press, 1988) 102-3.

❖   ❖   ❖   ❖

3:18-19. Within the marriage relationship wives are addressed first and are exhorted to subordinate themselves voluntarily to their husbands. The verb ὑποτάσσεσθαι (*hypotassesthai*) refers to taking a subordinate role in relation to another person. What it involves more specifically depends on the social expectations attached to the relationship to which it is applied. Elsewhere in the NT it is employed of the relationship of wives to husbands in Eph 5:22 (where this verb is implied from the previous verse); Titus 2:5; and 1 Pet 3:1. Outside the NT there are only two examples of the use of this verb for the relationship,[131] while the more usual term is "to obey."[132]

In the light of the fact that this latter verb is employed here in the case of children (v. 20) and slaves (v. 22), some have argued that a distinction is to be made between "to submit/be subordinate" and "to obey." Although there is clearly a difference between willing submission and imposed obedience, there is really no meaningful difference between voluntary subordination and voluntary obedience. "To submit" is the broader term, but in the expectation of the ancient world a wife's submitting to her husband would have entailed her being willing to obey him. Submission and obedience of wives to husbands are explicitly paralleled in 1 Pet 3:5-6. The motivation for such submission ("as is fitting in the Lord") means that subordination is being required not simply because it is the role society has allotted the wife but also because, in the writer's view, it is appropriate for members of the community that confesses Christ as Lord (cf. 2:6-7). Thereby the patriarchal marriage pattern is reinforced and given a christological warrant.

The exhortation to husbands has both positive and negative formulations, both of which would make easier their wives' willingness to be subordinate. After the exhortation to wives to submit, the readers might well have expected that husbands would then be told to rule their wives. Instead, the exhortation is for them to love their wives. Such an exhortation is found in other ancient writings but is fairly infrequent, and the verb "love" (ἀγαπάω agapaō) never occurs in Greco-Roman discussions of household management that set out the husband's duties. So in terms of contemporary instructions on marriage, this writer's requirement of husbands is by no means merely conventional.

Earlier in the chapter (v. 14), love has been seen as the culmination of the virtues listed in vv. 12-13. The exhortation to sacrifice one's own interests for the welfare of others, which was so necessary for the harmony of the community, now finds a more specific application in the husband's role in contributing to marital harmony. Husbands are asked to exercise the self-giving love that has as its goal only their wives' good and that will care for their wives without expectation of reward.

Although both the NRSV and the NIV translate the negative formulation of the exhortation to husbands as a prohibition against them acting harshly, the passive form of the verb indicates that bitterness or harshness is being experienced by its subject. A better translation would be "do not be embittered with them." The opposite of compassionate love is a hard-heartedness that harbors resentment and bitterness toward others. It is against such an attitude and the conduct it engenders that the writer warns husbands.

3:20-21. The advice to children and parents is included, because it is one of the three basic household relationships treated in the discussion of household management in the Aristotelian tradition. But the general apologetic factors that had become linked with the code also applied to this relationship. When Tacitus attacked the Jews, he could charge, "Those who converted to their ways follow the same practice, and the earliest lesson they receive is to despise the gods, to disown their country, and to regard their parents, children, and brothers as of little account."[133] Attacks on the Christian movement also spoke of their subversion of children (cf. the variant readings of Luke 23:2 where Jesus is indicted for "leading astray both women and children").

The writer exhorts children to obey their parents in everything. This endorses the unanimous view in both Greco-Roman and Hellenistic Jewish writings. In Greco-Roman society in the first century CE, the father had almost absolute legal power over his children, and Hellenistic Judaism stressed the status and authority of parents. In both cultures parents were viewed as deserving of honor and obedience in all things. Colossians upholds this authority structure, but again relates it to

---

131. See Plutarch *Advice on Marriage* 33; Ps-Callisthenes *History of Alexander the Great* 1.22.4.

132. See Philo *Hypothetica* 7.3: "Wives must be in servitude to their husbands, a servitude not imposed by violent ill-treatment but promoting obedience in all things." See also Josephus *Against Apion* 2.24: "The woman, it [the law] says, is in all things inferior to the man. Let her accordingly be obedient, not for her humiliation, but that she may be directed; for God has given authority to the man."

133. Tacitus *Histories* 5.5.

Christ's lordship by adding, "this is pleasing in the Lord." The tradition of Judaism expressed by Philo as "If you honor parents . . . you will be pleasing before God"[134] has here been Christianized. The warrant now recalls the goal the writer has for all his readers in 1:10—that is, leading lives worthy of the Lord, fully pleasing to him. It treats children as persons who in their own right have a relationship with this Lord that both transcends and includes their duty to their parents. The term τέκνον (*teknon*, "child") denotes primarily a relationship rather than age and could be used of adults as well as small children. From the context, the children in view here are old enough to be conscious of a relationship to their Lord, to which appeal could be made, but young enough still to be living with their parents.

Fathers have obligations, as do their children as well. The plural "fathers" (πατέρες *pateres*) could be employed for both parents. However, the change of wording from "parents" in the previous verse and the fact that in Greco-Roman society the authority was vested in the father and that in Judaism the father was responsible for discipline make it almost certain that it is again the male heads of households who are being addressed, this time in their role as fathers. They are urged not to provoke or irritate their children lest the children become discouraged. This is in line with other advocates of moderation who advised gentle persuasion rather than harsh threats.[135] Nevertheless, it is noticeable that the writer does not exhort fathers to exercise their authority. Instead, he presupposes that authority and then sets the bounds for its use. He also presupposes that children are not simply their fathers' legal property but are owed dignity as human beings in their own right. Fathers should not, therefore, drive their children to exasperation or resentment. This would rule out excessive discipline, unreasonably harsh demands, arbitrariness, constant nagging and condemnation, and any gross insensitivity to children's sensibilities that would break their spirit and make them listless and unresponsive.

3:22–4:1. In the longest section of the code (vv. 22-25) slaves are exhorted to obey their masters in everything, underlining the complete allegiance owed by slaves to the head of the household. In the traditional discussions of household management in both Greco-Roman and Hellenistic Jewish treatments, the ownership of slaves as property was simply axiomatic. The focus was on how a master should rule his slaves. In the first century CE a third of the population of Greece and Italy was enslaved, but the main supply of slaves was no longer through war or piracy but through birth in the house of a slaveowner. This produced a social climate in which houseborn slaves were given training for a wide variety of tasks and in which Roman legal practice had to keep pace by guaranteeing such slaves more humane treatment.[136] For this reason it should not be assumed that there was always a wide separation between the status of slave and freed person, that all slaves were badly treated, or that all who were enslaved were trying to free themselves. Clearly Pauline churches contained as equal members masters and slaves from the same household (see 3:11).

It could be that the greater proportion of paraenesis being addressed to slaves rather than masters reflects the social composition of the church or churches addressed, which would have contained more slaves than slaveowners, or that the code reflects the perspective of the leaders of the churches, which would have been more that of the masters than the slaves. Certainly the paraenesis reflects typical views of the behavior of slaves: attempting to ingratiate themselves (3:22-23), defrauding their masters and exploiting their good favor (3:25).[137]

On the other hand, it may well be that this section of the code is more extended because the writer sees the slave/master relationship as paradigmatic for the motivation of all the members of the household. Its warrants and motivations contain five references to Christ as Lord. The exhortations to slaves and masters place both in the same relation to Christ as Lord. The reference to "fearing the Lord," which recalls wisdom teaching, is found in the first exhortation to slaves (3:22c). But the last line of the code is also now

---

134. Philo *On the Change of Names* 40.

135. See, e. g., Menander in Stobaeus, *Anthology* 4.26.7, 13; Ps. Phocylides 207.

136. On the conditions for slaves, see especially S. S. Bartchy, ΜΑΛ-ΛΟΝ ΧΠΗΣΑΙ: First Century Slavery and the Interpretation of 1 Corinthians 7:21 (Missoula, Mont.: Scholars Press, 1973) and ABD 6.58-73.

137. See K. R. Bradley, *Slaves and Masters in the Roman Empire* (New York: Oxford University Press, 1987) 26-31, 35, 343.

highly significant for its reference to Christ's lordship. "Knowing that you also have a master or lord in heaven" now subjects the householder to the same binding obligation to Christ as that required of wives, children, and slaves; and since in the ancient household the masters were the same persons as the husbands and fathers, the force extends back to the earlier exhortations to those in the superior social position and places the whole household under the lordship of Christ. This notion that the masters of the household have a master over themselves is quite different from other discussions of the household in antiquity.[138] In line with this, the center of gravity in the Colossian code can now be seen to be the exhortations to slaves, "because it is precisely this group that is able to represent most adequately the relation of all Christians to Christ."[139] The writer does not say that in the slave/master relationship the master represents Christ, but the relationship within the ancient household that demonstrates both the possession of all believers by their Lord and their obligation to this Lord is that of slaves to their master. For this reason, it is the one that receives most attention as a paradigm for the motivation that should inform all members of the household and that is summed up in the command of 3:24*b:* "Serve the Lord Christ." The basic insight lying behind such a paradigm is, of course, indebted to Paul, since he had held that all humans are under some power and had used slavery as a metaphor for this perspective. Humans are either slaves to sin or slaves to God (Rom 6:15-23), and even if Christian believers are free persons in social terms they are still slaves of Christ (1 Cor 7:22).

In any case, the exhortations should not be interpreted as a reaction against unrest among Christian slaves caused by talk of Christian freedom or the baptismal formulations of Gal 3:28 and Col 3:11. There is simply no evidence that Christian slaves posed a social threat by calling for emancipation. The writer's own perspective evidently sees a distinction between the equal status of slaves and masters in the church and their roles in the Christian household, where hierarchical social structures still pertain. Never-

theless, what remains striking and unprecedented about his use of the code in comparison with traditional discussions of household management is that slaves are addressed directly and not simply as members of the household but as full members of the church.

The appeal to slaves is to obey in everything their masters "according to the flesh." This designation already introduces a Christian perspective and points to a play on the term "lord/master" (κύριος *kyrios*), which runs through the passage. In obeying their fleshly masters, slaves are to see obedience as part of their responsibility to their true Master or Lord. After the initial literal use in 3:22*a,* all the other uses of the term in 3:22*b*-24 refer to Christ, and then in 4:1 fleshly or earthly masters are reminded that they have a heavenly Master or Lord.

Despite this relativizing of the relationship, slaves' obedience to their masters is to be thoroughgoing and exhibit integrity. This is described first negatively and then positively. It will exclude the dissimulation and fawning of trying to catch their masters' eye or of currying favor (3:22*b*). Rather, obedience will be carried out "in singleness of heart" (3:22*c*), a phrase underlining purity of motivation and singleness of purpose. This sort of inner commitment is made possible by "fearing the Lord" (3:22*d*). Just as the motivation and guiding principle for conduct in the Jewish Scriptures was the fear of Yahweh, so also now slaves are to carry out their duties motivated by awe of Christ and his sovereign claim as Lord. Those who fear the Lord will, in whatever they do, work, literally, "from the soul" (3:23*a*)—that is, wholeheartedly and unreservedly, because they are doing it for the Lord and not for other human beings (3:23*b*). This last point simply underscores that obedience to the heavenly Master is ultimately determinative and provides a specific application of the earlier exhortation of 3:17, "Whatever you do, in word or deed, do everything in the name of the Lord Jesus."

The exhortation of 3:23 is grounded in the reminder in 3:24 that the reward that really counts will come from this Master. Some discussions of household management recommended motivating slaves by holding out various rewards, such as praise, more food, or better clothes and shoes.[140] The writer of Colossians attempts to

---

138. See M. Gielen, *Tradition und Theologie neustestamentlicher Haustafelsethik* (Frankfurt: Anton Hein, 1990) 118.

139. Ibid., 119.

140. See Xenophon *The Economist* 13.9-12.

motivate Christian slaves by holding before them the prospect of eschatological reward: the inheritance previously described in 1:12. A contrast with Roman law, in which a slave could not inherit anything, may also be intended. Through their relationship with Christ, slaves are treated as sons and daughters with full rights to the inheritance of the saints in light.

Both the NRSV and the NIV take the verb in 3:24*b* (δουλεύετε *douleuete*, "serve") as indicative. In the light of the preceding and following assertions about rewards and the conjunction "for" in the following clause, which acts as a warrant, it may well best be taken as an imperative: "Be slaves of the Lord Christ." This provides a forceful underlining of the whole perspective of these exhortations to slaves and, though addressed to slaves, of the motivation in the code as a whole. Slaves are to see themselves, particularly in the light of future judgment and reward, as slaves first and foremost not of their fleshly masters, but of their true Master, Christ.

Unlike even the best of earthly masters, with this Lord there will be no hint of partiality, and this means that there will not only be reward for genuine service but retribution for wrongdoing. In the OT and other Jewish writings, impartiality in judgment is attributed to God (e.g., Deut 10:17; Sir 35:14-16; *Jub.* 5:15-19), but here by implication this quality is transferred to Christ as Lord, who has been named as the one who recompenses (3:24*a*). Situated at the end of the exhortation to slaves and immediately before that to masters, the mention of retribution to wrongdoers and of impartiality may well function both as a warning to slaves and as a reassurance to them. Not only if they do wrong, but also if they are treated wrongly, they can know that there will be an impartial judgment by the one who is Master of both slaves and masters.

Indeed, in 4:1, when masters are addressed they are reminded of this very point that they, too, have a Master in heaven (cf. 3:1), to whom they are accountable. So, in the sphere of Christ's lordship, masters are on the same footing as slaves; they are slaves of a heavenly Master (see 3:26*b*). Again, for Colossians, a heavenly orientation is no escape from issues of social concern. Here it provides the motivation for the exhortation for slaveowners to treat their slaves in accordance with the fundamental principles of justice and fairness. What is required of masters, of course, is a complete reversal of the earlier view of Aristotle that the relationship between master and slave in the household was one in which it was inappropriate to talk about justice, since there can be no injustice in relating to things that are one's own, and a slave is a man's chattel.[141] More humane views of the treatment of slaves are found in the later traditions about household management. But the justice and equity required of Christian masters set a high standard. Indeed, they are to emulate the judgment of the heavenly Lord, who, according to Isa 11:3-4, "with righteousness [or justice] shall judge the poor, and decide with equity [or fairness] for the meek of the earth" (NRSV). Again this early Christian adaptation of the household code assumes the hierarchical structure of the master/slave relationship and has a view of justice that does not attempt to change the social structures (this was simply not an option for a powerless minority) but to ameliorate and transform conditions within them.

141. See Aristotle *Nicomachean Ethics* 5.1134b.

REFLECTIONS

To the question, "How would you preach on the household code?" one answer would be, "Follow the lectionary readings, and you will not have to do so!" *The Revised Common Lectionary* omits Col 3:18–4:1; Eph 5:21–6:9; Titus 2:1-10; and 1 Pet 2:13-18; 3:1-7. Whether this is the best way to handle these passages might be debated. Certainly at some point in the teaching ministry of the church their existence as part of Scripture needs to be faced, and questions need to be asked about how they are to be interpreted by contemporary Christians.

1. It is easy to dismiss Colossians' introduction of the household code as marking a greater emphasis on hierarchical than egalitarian aspects in the Pauline churches and as a retrograde step for the position of women and slaves in its accommodation to patriarchy and slavery. Certainly its painful heritage is still with us and cannot be ignored.

It is hard to know, however, whether the intention of the writer was in any way to restrict leadership in the church on the part of exceptional women and of slaves and to put power more firmly in the hands of male heads of households. Pauline churches still seem to have been able to make a distinction at this stage between what went on in the community's gatherings for worship and what went on in the everyday life of the household in closer contact with the surrounding society. It is significant that in Col 4:15 a house church in Laodicea can still be mentioned under the name of a woman, Nympha. Nevertheless, it has to be faced that there were negative implications for women and slaves as a probably unforeseen consequence of the household code's being taken over into Christian paraenesis. Later, by the time of the Pastoral Epistles, the distinction between church and household is ignored as the church itself is understood on the model of the patriarchal household. The author of those letters writes from the perspective of the male householder, forbidding women any roles that would give them authority over men and, in contrast to the reciprocity of Colossians, addresses only slaves and not masters about their duties.

2. Despite these negative consequences, the intent of the writer of Colossians in introducing the household code may still have something positive to say to us. In response to the philosophy's emphasis on visionary experiences and ascetic practices that detracted from the significance of the structures of everyday life, the introduction of the household code at this point in the letter enabled the writer to underline the value of such structures. It is part of his claim that any spirituality that does not enable believers to cope with ordinary life and live distinctively within its structures is bogus.

One concern of many contemporary Christians is the overcoming of the division between the sacred and the profane, of the separation between religion and culture. For those who agree with the assertion of Linda Sexson, "Religion is not a discrete category within human experience; it is rather a quality that pervades all experience,"[142] the code's construal of the mundane as sacred—ordinarily sacred—can be deemed an important contribution. Charles Taylor, too, has argued that central to contemporary notions of identity and crucial for any sense of the dignity of the self is the affirmation of ordinary life, the conviction that everyday living is not merely of infrastructural importance but can be "the very center of the good life."[143]

3. If it is the case that the Colossians code is part of the writer's wisdom teaching, then there is an important corollary. Everyday life is to be valued, but it is of the essence of the practical aspects of wisdom teaching that the form of such a claim needs continual reexamination. Brueggemann asserts that the sages:

> Are constantly facing new experience that must not only be integrated into the deposit of learning, but must be permitted to revise the deposit of learning in the light of new data. This means that their word of nurture and instruction is very much "on the run." . . . Wisdom teachers may encounter Yahweh with a tone of finality. It is known among such interpreters, however, that the work must all be done again, tomorrow.[144]

This knowledge, however, has often eluded interpreters of Colossians. The history of the code's interpretation shows all too clearly a reluctance to recognize that the evaluation of what wise

---

142. Linda Sexson, *Ordinarily Sacred* (New York: Crossroad, 1982) 6.
143. Charles Taylor, *Sources of the Self: The Making of the Modern Identity* (Cambridge: Cambridge University Press, 1989) 13. For Taylor's tracing of the development of this conviction, see 211-302.
144. W. Brueggemann, *Theology of the Old Testament* (Minneapolis: Fortress, 1997) 685, 691.

living in the household and in society entails must by its very nature change with changing times and circumstances.

A critical appropriation of this passage, therefore, would entail present-day Christians' attempting to do something similar in their own settings to what the writer did in his. They need to bring to bear what they hold to be the heart of the Christian message and of their relationship to Christ as Lord on contemporary conventional values in regard to the family and to social structures. Those who consider love and justice to be the central thrust of the Bible's ethical teaching will, for example, in the area of marriage want to work out a view of marriage in which both partners are held in equal regard, in which justice will require that male domination not be tolerated, and in which love will ensure that the relationship does not degenerate into a sterile battle over each partner's rights to fulfillment. Instead of assigning love to the husband and submission to the wife, a contemporary appropriation of Colossians will be aware that the letter earlier required humility, forgiveness, and love from all. It will urge mutual expression of such qualities that challenge both assumptions about love as a romantic feeling or ecstatic experience and assumptions about freedom and rights that result in self-centered competition for control.

In the case of children and parents, respect for parents and the honoring of children's dignity and worth can still be seen as expressions of Christian love and justice that speak to a society in which, on the one hand, parental power can frequently be abused, including even sexual abuse, and, on the other hand, attempts to exercise parental responsibility can be denounced in the name of children's rights or autonomy. In the case of slaves and masters, there is no really analogous pairing in most households in Western society. There is a significant difference between their situation in the ancient world and that of employees and employers, labor and management, in more democratic societies. Exceptions remain. Some Western businesses employ foreign workers for cheap labor under conditions that amount to slavery; and some families take on immigrants, often illegally, as little more than household slaves. This part of the code can still serve as a reminder that Christians will always have the responsibility of bringing the lordship of Christ to bear on their everyday work and its conditions of employment, even though specific applications of this lordship will become obsolete and new forms of social and economic obedience will need to be found to meet changing structures. Certainly two tasks will remain encumbent on believers whose concern is not human approval but serving the Lord Christ: ensuring that relationships within the church embody Christ's ultimate disregard for any distinctions based on social status and pursuing justice and fairness in their spheres of employment.

Colossians 4:2-6, Concluding Exhortation: Pray, Live Wisely, and Speak Graciously

NIV

[2]Devote yourselves to prayer, being watchful and thankful. [3]And pray for us, too, that God may open a door for our message, so that we may proclaim the mystery of Christ, for which I am in chains. [4]Pray that I may proclaim it clearly, as I should. [5]Be wise in the way you act toward outsiders; make the most of every opportunity. [6]Let your conversation be always full of grace, seasoned with salt, so that you may know how to answer everyone.

NRSV

[2]Devote yourselves to prayer, keeping alert in it with thanksgiving. [3]At the same time pray for us as well that God will open to us a door for the word, that we may declare the mystery of Christ, for which I am in prison, [4]so that I may reveal it clearly, as I should.

[5]Conduct yourselves wisely toward outsiders, making the most of the time.[a] [6]Let your speech

[a] Or opportunity

always be gracious, seasoned with salt, so that you may know how you ought to answer everyone.

COMMENTARY

On an epistolary analysis, this section constitutes the closing part of the body-middle, which runs from 2:6 to 4:6, rounding off the letter's main exhortations, while a rhetorical analysis has suggested that it can be read as the peroratio, the summing up of the letter's message. Either way, to treat its contents only as further general exhortations would be to miss the way in which they provide an important summarizing conclusion and recall earlier parts of the letter, not least its programmatic statement in 1:22-23. The stress on prayer and thanksgiving (4:2) not only reminds readers of the writer's own extended thanksgiving with its intercessory prayer report in 1:3-23, but also rounds off the motif of thanksgiving that has featured throughout (cf. 1:12; 2:7; 3:15-17). The reminder of Paul's imprisonment (4:3c) points back to the depiction of Paul and his suffering for the gospel in 1:24–2:5, which had been announced in 1:23c. The notion of declaring the mystery of Christ in the requisite manner summarizes what the writer has attempted to do in the face of the philosophy in 2:6–3:4 and which had been announced in 1:23ab. The need to walk wisely (4:5a) sums up the paraenesis of 3:5–4:1, and the need to have outsiders in view when doing so is an appropriate description of the motivation for the last part of such paraenesis in the household code of 3:18–4:1. Again the need for holiness of living had been announced ahead of time in 1:21-22. Finally, 4:6 can be seen as expressing what the writer hopes his message will achieve for the readers, putting them in a position to have the appropriate answer for people.

The peroratio was also expected to make an appeal to the readers in the process of its summing up. Features that would make the readers well disposed to the speaker (pathos) include the request for prayer for his ministry (4:3a) and the mention of Paul's chains (4:3c). The latter, together with the stress again on Paul's commission to declare the mystery of Christ (4:3b), would also strengthen the focus on the speaker's character (ethos). In addition, the section appeals to the readers' emotions by conveying a sense of urgency with its call to alertness (4:2b) and to make the most of the time (4:5b).

4:2. The readers are urged to pursue a life characterized by prayer. The writer's own earlier prayer report indicates the importance he attaches to prayer (cf. esp. 1:3, 9). Prayer will reflect the readers' dependence on God, and for prayer they will need the perseverance that overcomes fatigue and discouragement (see Rom 12:12). They will also need the alertness that keeps at bay spiritual complacency. Staying alert and awake involves renouncing the sleep associated with absorption in the old way of life and its "dominion of darkness" (cf. 1:13). Such alertness will be motivated and accompanied not by anxiety but by thanksgiving, one of the letter's dominant themes. Thanksgiving is the proper response of those who are awake to all the blessings of God mediated in Christ. It was demonstrated earlier by the writer in his own prayer, in which he not only asked that the readers might give joyful thanks (1:12) but also offered such thanks to God (1:3-8, 15-20).

4:3-4. In their prayers the readers are to include intercession for the writer, who has taken on the persona of Paul (and Timothy) as part of the device of pseudonymity. In particular, prayer is asked for the apostolic ministry of proclaiming the mystery of Christ. In the earlier depiction of Paul's role in declaring it, the mystery was equated first with Christ among you (1:27) and then simply with Christ himself (2:2). In proclaiming this mystery, the apostle was dependent not only on his own strenuous efforts but on God's work within him as well (1:29). It is not surprising, then, that prayer for the apostolic ministry should take the form of asking that God open a door for the Word (cf. 1 Cor 16:9; 2 Cor 2:12)—that is, prepare the way by providing "windows of opportunity" for the gospel. This gospel is not only identified with Christ as its content but is also associated with Paul and his imprisonment (4:3c). Being bound was the mark of the suffering apostle (cf. 1:24), the appropriate insignia of the proclamation of the gospel among the Gentiles.

The prayer to be offered is not just for opportunities for proclamation but also that the proclamation be made in the requisite way: "that I may reveal it, in the way that it is necessary for me to speak" (v. 4). Both the NRSV and the NIV add the notion of clarity, but the verb φανερόω (phaneroō) is simply part of the terminology of disclosing or unveiling the mystery (cf. 1:26). The last clause could refer to the divine necessity or compulsion upon the apostle (cf. 1 Cor 9:16) to disclose the mystery or, more probably, to the necessity of expressing the disclosure in the appropriate way. Significantly, the writer of Ephesians takes this clause to be about the manner of proclamation and makes this clear by adding the idea of boldness (see Eph 6:20). Here, since the writer considers himself a representative of Paul, the exhortation can be understood as a request for prayer that he might proclaim the Pauline gospel in the appropriate manner. Presumably that is a manner that does justice to its truth, hope, dynamic, and scope (cf. 1:5-6).

4:5-6. The writer had earlier declared that all wisdom is to be found in Christ (2:3), and the hymn he had cited, in which Christ takes on the attributes of Wisdom, had given eloquent expression to this notion (1:15-20). Now he appeals to his readers to walk in wisdom, to live wisely. In the Jewish tradition, wisdom involved not simply right knowledge but skill in living—ethical insight into God's will as revealed in the Torah. For this writer, spiritual wisdom also involves living rightly, but now in displaying conduct worthy of or pleasing to Christ as Lord (cf. 1:9-10). This has been the burden of the ethical exhortations in 3:5–4:1 and particularly of 3:17 and the household code that follows in 3:18–4:1. This is particularly significant, since it is wise living in regard to outsiders that the writer has in view here. As we have seen, a prime reason for the introduction of the code was that it enabled the writer to address issues in the community's life that were of vital importance in outsiders' perception of whether Pauline churches were a threat to the stability of society.

Wise behavior entails having the right attitude to time. The imagery used is the commercial language of the marketplace and indicates that the readers are to buy up time eagerly, capitalizing on the opportunities it offers for living out what is pleasing to their Lord. Those who are awake and alert (4:2) as they wait for the revelation of Christ in glory (3:4) will not allow present opportunities for obedience to Christ as Lord to slip past unseized. Instead, they will be ready with the right word spoken in the right way. Only now does the focus change from the earlier proclamation of the word of the gospel in the apostolic ministry to the readers' regular conversation with others, in which answers to anyone's queries about their distinctive beliefs and conduct can be given (v. 6). The writer adapts a current idiom about attractive speech. Plutarch, for example, could talk of conveying "a certain grace by means of words as with salt."[145] So the readers' speech should always be gracious—that is, attractive, persuasive, and beneficial. It is not to be insipid or bland but salted with wit and wisdom.

By cultivating such speech Christians will know how to give appropriate and persuasive responses—they will, as 1 Pet 3:15 has it, always be prepared to give an answer to everyone who asks them to give the reason for the hope that they have. In many ways this has been precisely the model of the writer's own exposition of the gospel in answer to the claims of the philosophy: striving not only to be persuasive and attractive to those who might succumb to the rival claims but also to be forceful and ironic in attempting to expose those claims. What the writer has tried to accomplish in the letter is indeed to put his readers on a firmer footing in their understanding and appropriation of the Pauline gospel. From this basis they will be able to give an answer to advocates of the philosophy and to any other questioners of the validity and sufficiency of the gospel in which they believe.

145. Plutarch *On Talkativeness* 654F. See also Plutarch *Table-Talk* 685A.

REFLECTIONS

If these short concluding exhortations can be seen to serve a summarizing function, then any reflections on their content will appropriately draw on the overall message of the letter and its impact.

1. A life characterized by prayer is a recognition of our creaturely dependence on the Creator God and a sign that this relationship has been restored through reconciliation. Three elements of prayer are featured in this section: the necessity of alertness, its characterization by thanksgiving, and its participation in the mission of the proclamation of the gospel.

Alert prayer enables us to shake off and see through the deceptive values and shadows of the old order. It heightens our perception of and keeps us in touch with reality. And, since for Colossians at the heart of reality is the grace of God in Christ, such prayer will also entail a watchfulness that this grace is not jeopardized.

Prayer is to be accompanied by the thankfulness that is also an indispensable characteristic of the new community (see 1:12; 2:6-7; 3:15-17). Its presence or absence functions as a test of whether a person has truly understood that the gospel is one of grace, of undeserved gift. It is the mark not of striving to attain the fullness of knowledge and experience of God's presence, as in the philosophy, but of having received these freely in Christ. It is also the opposite of self-centered acquisitiveness and unproductive envy with their accompanying angry resentfulness or bitterness (see 3:5, 8). Thankfulness, then, is an essential aspect of the faith that acknowledges God as the Creator, Sustainer, and Redeemer of life, that recognizes, despite everything, that God's grace in Christ is at the center of life. Prayer characterized by such thankfulness is not a technique for ignoring life's problems and pain, but its practice enables these to be faced by placing them in their true context.

Prayer is also a major means of participating in the cosmic drama of reconciliation. For the writer of Colossians, Paul and his apostolic team, including his successors, have the primary responsibility for the proclamation of the gospel throughout the world. The role of members of the Pauline churches is to be in solidarity with that wider mission through prayer. Not surprisingly, at the heart of the mission is the gospel, designated as "the mystery of Christ," and the suffering, imprisoned apostle remains the model for missionary proclamation (see 1:24–2:5). Prayer, then, will focus on both the missionaries and their message. As in the depiction of the church's mission in the book of Acts, where prayer precedes major breakthroughs in the spread of the gospel, here it is expected that the provision of opportunities for proclamation will be in response to the church's praying.

2. The final exhortations to wise living in the world and appropriate verbal witness to the source for such living can be seen as major goals of the letter. What its message has aimed to produce is not withdrawal from the world but a reclaiming of that world for the one who is its Lord. The earlier grounding of the readers in the rich resources of wisdom in Christ has been meant to enable them to be not only wise teachers of one another, not only discriminating evaluators of counterfeit claims, but also practitioners of wisdom before a watching world and wise witnesses in the face of inquiries from outsiders. So in addition to their prayerful support for global mission, local communities of believers have the responsibility for working out and implementing the implications of Christ's lordship for family life, for the work sphere, for social structures, for economic matters—for all the areas of life in which onlookers will be able to catch a glimpse of the practical wisdom of gospel values. In the biblical tradition, the wise person discerns the times and seasons (see Eccl 3:1-8). Here the discerning use of time by believers entails buying up the opportunities to display Christ's lordship. Their lives are no longer determined by the times and seasons of the astral powers (see 2:16); rather, they have been released from their burdensome past through God's forgiveness (2:13-14), and so they are now free to make time serve the ends of the one who is Lord not only of space but also of time and to seize the moment for service.

3. Again it is worth noting that Colossians does not put a heavy burden on believers in regard to evangelism. The emphasis is not on marches for Jesus, preaching on street corners, or handing out tracts. There are those with special responsibilities for missionary proclamation and evangelism, but most of us are expected to use our time in wise living in the world. It is in that context, as outsiders observe transformed lives and different values, that questions will be asked and that we then have a responsibility for witness that provides answers. This will not be the sort of witness that provokes the taunt, "Christ is the answer, but what is the question?" because it will be a response to actual questions raised by the way we live. The answers this letter expects believers to cultivate will not trample on the sensibilities of their conversation partners or subject them to a harangue in the name of the gospel but will aim to be appropriate to each questioner and his or her specific queries, and, with the use of good humor and intelligence, to be a persuasive witness.

COLOSSIANS 4:7-9, BODY-CLOSING: PASSING ON NEWS

NIV	NRSV
[7]Tychicus will tell you all the news about me. He is a dear brother, a faithful minister and fellow servant in the Lord. [8]I am sending him to you for the express purpose that you may know about our[a] circumstances and that he may encourage your hearts. [9]He is coming with Onesimus, our faithful and dear brother, who is one of you. They will tell you everything that is happening here.	7Tychicus will tell you all the news about me; he is a beloved brother, a faithful minister, and a fellow servant[a] in the Lord. [8]I have sent him to you for this very purpose, so that you may know how we are[b] and that he may encourage your hearts; [9]he is coming with Onesimus, the faithful and beloved brother, who is one of you. They will tell you about everything here.
[a]8 Some manuscripts *that he may know about your*	[a] Gk *slave* [b] Other authorities read *that I may know how you are*

COMMENTARY

Some of the issues surrounding how both this and the following section of the letter are to be read, if one has come to the conclusion that what precedes was not written by Paul, have been raised in the Introduction (see the section "Author and Addressees," 577-83). One of the attractions of the mediating view that Timothy composed the letter in the names of both Paul and himself is that it enables these sections to be taken in a relatively straightforward way. It is not, however, as will become clear in the next section, without its own difficulties if, as nearly all who hold that Colossians was by Paul and/or Timothy argue, the letter was written at the same time as

Philemon. Other letters in which Timothy is named as co-author have a quite different style. If Timothy was able to get Paul to write the closing greeting himself (4:18), it requires considerable speculation to explain why Paul would not have been able to dictate the rest of the letter and why he was able to write the companion letter to Philemon.

As has been noted, if the letter is pseudonymous, then 4:7-18 is its attempt at verisimilitude. Similar features can be found in other ancient pseudepigraphical letters, not least the Pastoral Epistles within the NT (see, e.g., the details about individuals and the greetings in 2 Tim 4:9-22).

Since the author describes Onesimus as "one of you" (4:9), it is not surprising that all the names found in this section, with the exception of Tychicus and Nympha (and probably Jesus Justus), would be drawn by the writer from the letter of Paul that had been sent to Onesimus's owner—namely, Philemon.

In the final section of paraenesis the readers had been asked to pray for Paul's proclamation of the mystery of Christ and had been reminded of his imprisonment. It forms a natural progression for the writer to mention now that Tychicus is being sent to provide his readers with further information about Paul's welfare and circumstances. The commendation of an emissary is also found toward the end of some of Paul's letters (see Rom 16:1; 1 Cor 16:10). Its use here enables the writer to avoid having to say anything more specific about Paul's situation. He can instead simply point the readers to Tychicus. Tychicus features elsewhere in the NT as one of Paul's coworkers and is particularly associated with Asia Minor (see Acts 20:4; 2 Tim 4:12). He is likely to have been known to the letter's recipients as one of the leading representatives of the Pauline mission. The threefold description of him as "a beloved brother and faithful servant and fellow slave in the Lord" reinforces his close relationship with Paul and his proven record of reliable ministry and allegiance to Christ.

Two reasons are given for Tychicus's being sent (v. 8). The first repeats the explanation already supplied in v. 7: It is so that the readers "may know how we are." The second reason is so that Tychicus might encourage the hearts of the recipients, a task presumably to be accomplished not only by conveying the news about Paul but also by providing his own ministry to the readers in line with the concerns of the letter. The writer then adds that Tychicus will be accompanied in his mission by Onesimus, recommended as a Pauline coworker through the designation "the faithful and beloved brother." His links with Colossae are underlined by the additional clause, "who is one of you."

At the end of the recommendation (v. 9c), the readers are surprisingly told for the third time that the visit of the two is to let them know about "everything here." Clearly the writer wants to emphasize their role as links between Paul and the churches of the Lycus Valley, as links in the chain of Pauline tradition. Tychicus and Onesimus may well be seen, then, as representing the apostolic heritage in this region in succession to Epaphras, who had originally brought the gospel there (see 1:7; 4:12-13).

THE LETTER CLOSING

[10]My fellow prisoner Aristarchus sends you his greetings, as does Mark, the cousin of Barnabas. (You have received instructions about him; if he comes to you, welcome him.) [11]Jesus, who is called Justus, also sends greetings. These are the only Jews among my fellow workers for the kingdom of God, and they have proved a comfort to me. [12]Epaphras, who is one of you and a servant of Christ Jesus, sends greetings. He is always wrestling in prayer for you, that you may stand firm in all the will of God, mature and fully assured. [13]I vouch for him that he is working hard for you and for those at Laodicea and Hierapolis. [14]Our dear friend Luke, the doctor, and Demas send greetings. [15]Give my greetings to the brothers at Laodicea, and to Nympha and the church in her house.

[16]After this letter has been read to you, see that it is also read in the church of the Laodiceans and that you in turn read the letter from Laodicea.

[17]Tell Archippus: "See to it that you complete the work you have received in the Lord."

[18]I, Paul, write this greeting in my own hand. Remember my chains. Grace be with you.

10Aristarchus my fellow prisoner greets you, as does Mark the cousin of Barnabas, concerning whom you have received instructions—if he comes to you, welcome him. [11]And Jesus who is called Justus greets you. These are the only ones of the circumcision among my co-workers for the kingdom of God, and they have been a comfort to me. [12]Epaphras, who is one of you, a servant[a] of Christ Jesus, greets you. He is always wrestling in his prayers on your behalf, so that you may stand mature and fully assured in everything that God wills. [13]For I testify for him that he has worked hard for you and for those in Laodicea and in Hierapolis. [14]Luke, the beloved physician, and Demas greet you. [15]Give my greetings to the brothers and sisters[b] in Laodicea, and to Nympha and the church in her house. [16]And when this letter has been read among you, have it read also in the church of the Laodiceans; and see that you read also the letter from Laodicea. [17]And say to Archippus, "See that you complete the task that you have received in the Lord."

18I, Paul, write this greeting with my own hand. Remember my chains. Grace be with you.[c]

[a] Gk slave   [b] Gk brothers   [c] Other ancient authorities add Amen

COMMENTARY

The letter closing consists of a series of greetings from those said to be with Paul and from Paul himself (4:10-15), instructions about an exchange of letters with the church at Laodicea (4:16), a message to Archippus (4:17), Paul's autograph (4:18a), a final exhortation to remember his imprisonment (4:18b), and a very brief grace benediction (4:18c).

4:10-11. Greetings come first from the trio of those who are said to be the only Jewish Christian

coworkers of Paul and who are commended as having been a comfort to him. Whereas in 1:12 he talked of "the kingdom of his beloved Son," the writer here employs the more traditional terminology in depicting these men as coworkers for "the kingdom of God." Aristarchus, who had been described in Philemon 24 as a fellow worker of Paul, is now said to be a fellow prisoner. It is unlikely that this designation is simply figurative, referring to a relationship to Christ. The readers are meant to assume that Aristarchus shared Paul's physical imprisonment. This is a difficulty for the view that Colossians was written by Paul or Timothy at about the same time as Philemon, since in that letter Aristarchus is not a prisoner and Epaphras is (Phlm 23), while in Colossians the status of the two is reversed.[146]

Next to be named in v. 10*b* is Mark (cf. Phlm 24), whose mention is elaborated. It is made clear that he is the cousin of Barnabas so that the readers are able to associate him with the tradition of the early missionary activity of Paul and Barnabas. The Acts account gives Paul's negative assessment of John Mark's earlier desertion as the cause of the split with Barnabas (Acts 15:38), but if Phlm 24 is set alongside the Acts tradition, then Mark's rift with Paul was temporary and he later rejoined Paul's mission. There is a further cryptic addition to the mention of Mark. The readers are told that they have already received instructions about him and that if he comes to them, they are to welcome him (v. 10*c*). This may play on the Acts tradition, suggesting that Pauline churches may have had reservations about Mark but that these are now to be put aside. Alternatively, it has been suggested that this may have been a way of referring to Mark's being known to have had a role in the region after Tychicus and Onesimus, so that at the time of the letter's composition, of all those listed as sending greetings, Mark may have been the only one still in contact with the letter's recipients.[147]

The third Jewish companion of Paul to send greetings is "Jesus, who is called Justus" (v. 11*a*). He has two names, since "Jesus" is the Greek form of his Hebrew name and "Justus" would have been the name he used in the Greco-Roman environment. Nothing further is known of him, although a number of scholars have supported the conjecture first made by Theodor Zahn that at the end of Phlm 23 the name "Jesus" in Greek should have a final sigma and, therefore, be associated not with the preceding Christ, but be seen as a separate name that leads off the list of those then mentioned in Phlm 24 as sending greetings.[148] It is possible that an early scribe was confused by the mention of another Jesus immediately after a reference to Christ, but there is no manuscript evidence to support this interesting conjecture.

4:12-13. Epaphras, also described, like Onesimus, as "one of you," is next listed as sending greetings. Having named Epaphras earlier as the initial link between the Pauline mission and Colossae (1:7-8), it would be natural for the writer to mention him again here. Earlier he was called a fellow slave and a servant of Christ; now he is simply a slave of Christ Jesus. A twofold commendation follows. First, Epaphras is depicted as being in constant prayer for the readers. This matches what has been said about Paul in 1:9; the rest of 4:11 also corresponds to the earlier depiction of the apostle. In his prayers, Epaphras struggles (cf. 1:29; 2:1), and the goal of those prayers is that the readers might stand as "perfect" or "mature" (cf. 1:28) and that they might be fully assured in all the will of God (cf. 1:9; 2:2). This first part of the commendation serves, then, to recall the purpose of the letter as a whole. The second part is the writer's witness to how much hard toil Epaphras is expending (the NIV, in contrast to the NRSV, rightly translates ἔχει πολὺν πόνον [*echei polyn ponon*] in the present tense) on behalf of the readers and of those in Laodicea, situated some ten miles from Colossae, and in Hierapolis, some fifteen miles away. Epaphras, then, is presented as the original representative of the Pauline mission in the whole Lycus Valley area, which has already been seen to be the object of the writer's concern (2:1).

4:14-15. The final pair of Paul's companions to extend greetings are Luke and Demas, also listed in Phlm 24. Later in the Pastoral Epistles, Demas will be mentioned negatively (2 Tim 4:10). Here only Luke has a further description added, the mention of his medical profession. That he is called "the beloved doctor" may suggest that the readers are expected to know of a tradition of his having been of help to Paul and his coworkers in times of sickness. Later traditions associate this same Luke with the author of Luke–Acts.

In v. 15 the readers are instructed to convey

---

146. Dunn appeals to the hypothesis "that Paul's imprisonment was such as to permit certain of his associates to take turns sharing his confinement." See J. D. G. Dunn, *The Epistles to the Colossians and to Philemon*, NIGTC (Grand Rapids: Eerdmans, 1996) 275-76.

147. See P. Pokorny, *Colossians: A Commentary*, trans. S. S. Schatzmann (Peabody, Mass.: Hendrickson, 1991) 192.

148. See, e.g., E. Lohse, *Colossians and Philemon*, trans. W. R. Poehlmann and R. J. Karris, Hermeneia (Philadelphia: Fortress, 1971) 172n. 26, 207n. 16.

greetings from the writer to the brothers and sisters in Laodicea and to Nympha and the church in her house. If the letter were really from Paul to the church in Colossae, there are two difficulties at this point: There is no greeting to the church in Philemon's house, and the recipients are not told to greet one another, which was Paul's usual custom (cf. Rom 16:16; 1 Cor 16:20*b*; 2 Cor 13:12*a*; Phil 4:21*a*; 1 Thess 5:26), but instead are told to greet believers elsewhere, an instruction found nowhere else in the Pauline letters. And why would Paul want greetings extended to Laodicea via the Colossians when he says in the next verse that he has written a separate letter to the Laodiceans and that this letter to Colossae is in any case to be read to them? On the supposition of pseudonymity this feature is seen as providing a clue to the real recipients—namely, the Laodiceans (see 2:1). It could also be that Nympha, whose name is not drawn from elsewhere and who at least gave hospitality to a house church as a patroness to the Pauline movement and may possibly have been its leader, lived among the Laodicean recipients at the time the letter was written and was known by name to its writer.

4:16. The instruction that this letter be read to the church at Laodicea and that the addressees read the letter from Laodicea adds further support to the view that the device of pseudonymity allows the real recipients to become transparent at this point. If that is the case, the attempt to identify the Laodicean letter (whether as written from Laodicea by Epaphras or as Philemon or Ephesians or simply as a lost letter) was futile from the start. However, that the writer can draw on the practice of exchanging letters as part of the attempt to attain verisimilitude suggests that this was occurring in Pauline churches at the time of writing. The process of recognizing the more than occasional significance of the apostle's letters that later led to their achieving canonical status was apparently under way.

4:17. Though there are no greetings to any individuals associated with Colossae, the letter's recipients are told to pass on a message to Archippus. Again the formulation is slightly strange, because in Philippians, the only Pauline letter in which individuals are singled out for instruction, Euodia and Syntyche are addressed directly (Phil

4:2). Archippus had been mentioned in Phlm 2 as a member of Philemon's household and called a "fellow soldier." Here the message to be communicated to him is that he should pay attention to the service or ministry he has received in the Lord in order to complete it. Perhaps the best guess at the significance of this enigmatic message is that Archippus, who had been one of Paul's co-workers, is the only one of the addressees of Philemon still living in the Lycus Valley among the recipients of Colossians at the time of its writing. It may be that he needs to be re-called by them to the fulfilling of a role in keeping the Pauline tradition distinct from the views of the rival philosophy.[149]

4:18. The introduction of a greeting from Paul in his own hand takes up a feature of the closing sections of the undisputed letters (see 1 Cor 16:21; Gal 6:11; Phlm 19). The wording is, in fact, exactly the same as that of 1 Cor 16:21. On the supposition of pseudonymity, the writer of Colossians employs this feature to authenticate his letter as being in the Pauline tradition. It can also be seen as functioning to underscore the instruction to Archippus that has immediately preceded it and to evoke reminiscences of the apostle, as does the following exhortation.

The call to remember Paul's chains in v. 18*b* is unique for the closing section of a Pauline letter. It is a dramatic and rhetorical flourish. Paul himself used a similar technique effectively in Gal 6:17 with the more general mention of carrying the marks of Jesus branded on his body. Elsewhere in the undisputed letters Paul can call himself a "prisoner of Christ Jesus" (see Phlm 1, 9), but other references to his imprisonment arise naturally from the context and are not used for self-conscious effect (see Phil 1:7, 13-14, 17; Phlm 13). The appeal to others to remember "my chains" may be part of this writer's use of the device of pseudonymity designed to evoke sympathy and admiration for the persona of the imprisoned apostle whose identity he has taken on.

The final grace-benediction of v. 18*c* is shorter than that of any of the undisputed letters. The brief "grace be with you," however, not only recalls the opening greeting in 1:2*b* but also can be seen as an effective evocation of the central

149. See Pokorný, *Colossians*, 195.

message of the letter with its stress on the sufficiency of all that God has provided for the readers in Christ. These benefits of salvation, which are already theirs, have come from the same grace of God that the writer now calls on to remain with them.

REFLECTIONS

In a letter that has treated the church as the body of Christ and has dealt with the cosmic scope of Christ's work and its implications for the lives of believers, the ending provides a further appropriate reminder that this same church is made up of particular individuals and local groups on earth and is dependent on social networks. The body of Christ fulfills its cosmic role in the midst of concrete, everyday relationships. Even if some of the features of the ending arise from the verisimilitude of a pseudepigraphical letter, they still reflect the need for the human structures of church life to be given constant attention. Team work, loyalty, praying for one another, and sheer hard work are indispensable. People need the reassurance of being greeted and made welcome. They need words of approval and recommendation for what they have done and reminders about tasks that still need to be done. Links between local groups need to be strengthened as introductions are made and communications are exchanged. In this way the apparently mundane contents of the letter's closure reinforce one of the main themes of its message: A right relationship to the exalted Christ manifests itself not in a spurious otherworldliness but in and through the real human relationships and structures of life in this world. It is here that believers are most in need of experiencing the reality of the letter's final benediction: grace in the ordinary.

THE FIRST LETTER TO THE THESSALONIANS

INTRODUCTION, COMMENTARY, AND REFLECTIONS
BY
ABRAHAM SMITH

THE FIRST LETTER TO THE
THESSALONIANS

INTRODUCTION

B oth 1 and 2 Thessalonians are powerful witnesses to the early church's struggles with the suffering of its members. The Thessalonian letters make it clear that separation from leaders, alienation from former friends, and perennial threats of persecution and even death were not solely the concerns of the fledgling communities behind the Synoptic Gospels (Matthew, Mark, and Luke), the virtually introverted Johannine believers, and the persecuted minority group addressed by John's apocalypse.

These struggles and the constraints through which the early churches were pressed to view them resound on every page of 1 and 2 Thessalonians. In consequence, the two letters offer remarkable challenges to contemporary churches. Understanding these challenges, however, does not come easily. Since all letters (past or present) are occasional documents, they imply more than they state explicitly. The circumstances that the first-century letter writers and their audiences took for granted must be reconstructed before we can even begin to interpret their letters as responses to those circumstances. Moreover, certain thought patterns shared by Paul and the church at Thessalonica (but not directly obvious to us) also must be reconstructed because the letters assume these patterns without directly drawing attention to them.

Reconstruction of the letters' circumstances and some of the writer's thought patterns is enhanced by examining the general nature and functions of most ancient letters—that is, the various formulae expected in a typical first-century letter and the basic strategies letter writers used to make their letters effective. Over the years of biblical scholarship, proven methods of careful analysis have developed that highlight these aspects of first-century letters. These methods will be used in this commentary to place 1 and 2 Thessalonians in the historical and literary milieu of the first century CE. It is important as well to place them more directly in the environs of early Christianity, particularly Pauline Christianity, to the extent that we can reconstruct it from the surviving literary and historical evidence. Accordingly, this introduction will begin with an examination of several general historical contexts related to Paul and the city of Thessalonica, and then move to a more specific reconstruction of the specific occasions and purposes of each letter. Next, the Introduction will focus on the literary character of the letters. With these matters in place, it will then be possible for readers to move on to the in-depth analysis in the commentary with sufficient grounding for understanding each letter's challenges and reflecting on their meaning for today.

THE GENERAL HISTORICAL CONTEXTS OF 1 AND 2 THESSALONIANS

Three general historical contexts are essential for understanding 1 and 2 Thessalonians. Obviously, one critical historical context is Paul's work among the Gentiles. Equally important is the context of the city of Thessalonica itself, especially the city's ongoing dependence upon Roman patronage and the role that dependence likely played in the relations between Paul's church and the larger Thessalonian society. Yet another critical context is Paul's apocalyptic gospel—both the distinctive features of its thought pattern and its appeal to the church Paul founded in Thessalonica.

The Context of Paul's Work Among the Gentiles. Through the revelation of the risen Jesus to him (1 Cor 9:1; 15:8; 2 Cor 12:1-3; Acts 9:22, 26; Gal 1:12), Paul was called to preach the gospel among the Gentiles (Gal 1:16). He carried that gospel over considerable territory in the cities of the eastern Mediterranean. According to Wayne Meeks, the Pauline house-church movement took root in at least four provinces of the Roman Empire: Galatia (modern-day Turkey, e.g., the churches of Galatia), Asia (e.g., Colossae and Ephesus; see 1 Cor 16:19), Macedonia (e.g., the churches at Philippi and Thessalonica), and Achaia (the church at Corinth).[1]

In his Letter to the Romans (among whom he did not establish a church), Paul noted that his plan was to preach the gospel from Jerusalem to Illyricum (modern-day Dalmatia just to the east of the Adriatic Sea), to go on from there to Rome, and from there to Spain (Rom 15:19, 24). His goal, then, was a westward mission that would take him about ten thousand miles during the course of his career.[2] While it is possible to see Paul's travel to Thessalonica only as a reaction to difficulties he met at Philippi (1 Thess 2:1-2), the move was likely a strategic one, a part of the effort to move westward with his gospel to the Gentiles. Paul's letters and the book of Acts attest to his travel and to that of his coworkers, including Timothy, Titus, and Epaphroditus.

Just how Paul supported his house-church movement and extensive travel among the

1. Wayne Meeks, *The First Urban Christians: The Social World of the Apostle Paul* (New Haven: Yale University Press, 1983) 41.
2. Ronald F. Hock, *The Social Context of Paul's Ministry: Tentmaking and Apostleship* (Philadelphia: Fortress, 1980) 27.

Gentiles is not altogether certain. On the basis of 1 Cor 4:12 (where Paul indicates that he "worked with his own hands") and Acts 18:3 (which identifies a trade for Paul), some scholars suggest that Paul's vocation involved some kind of leatherworking, whether that of making tents or other leather products.[3] If leatherworking was indeed Paul's vocation, we can imagine him traveling, like other artisans, with tools in hand, setting up a workshop wherever the local leather-workers' guild of a city met. Even if we cannot identify Paul's exact occupation, however, we can still imagine him plying some trade to support himself (1 Thess 2:9), though he certainly received help from others, and from some of them repeatedly (e.g., the Macedonians, who included at least the Philippians; 2 Cor 11:8-9; Phil 4:15-16). For his intended work in Spain, moreover, Paul even desired help from the Roman churches, though he had not established those churches (Rom 1:13; 15:28–16:2).

More certain than his vocation is the pastoral care Paul extended to his churches in the course of his career.[4] Not only did he establish churches, but also his letters witness to his profound love for and anxiety about these assemblies as he shaped them and nurtured their growth (2 Cor 11:28). His letters also testify to his use of the hortatory tradition—that is, the well-known tradition of exhortation. Examination of the letters of Plato, Epicurus, and Seneca, among others, reveals the evolution of a tradition in which philosophers placed "exhortations to the philosophical life into the form of letters."[5] Such letters were designed to help the recipients internalize the values of a particular philosophy, to help them "avoid feelings of isolation and the demoralizing effects they might have," and to affect their "habits and disposition."[6] Thus, in line with his call to take the gospel to the Gentiles, Paul seems to have planted house churches in strategic locations and to have sent them letters and emissaries in his absence in order to strengthen the solidarity of the assemblies and to correct any problems occurring in the wake of his departure. The church at Thessalonica was one of these assemblies that Paul established, molded, and nurtured.

The Context of the City of Thessalonica. In Paul's time Thessalonica was a part of the vast Roman Empire. When the city, named for Alexander's half-sister Thessaloniki, was founded in 316 BCE, one of Alexander's generals (Cassander) was its first benefactor. Due to the squabbles of Alexander's successors, however, Thessalonica eventually received Rome as its new patron in 167 BCE.[7]

The city was a commercial and cultic center. It did not stand toe to toe with Athens, the great intellectual capital. Nor did its size match that of Alexandria, the great international city of the day. Yet it was no mean place. With the construction of the Via Egnatia (Rome's gateway to its eastern colonies) in 130 BCE, Thessalonica benefited from the traffic of travelers and became a key trading center in the region.[8] Archaeological

3. Ibid., 21.
4. Abraham J. Malherbe, *Paul and the Thessalonians: The Philosophic Tradition of Pastoral Care* (Philadelphia: Fortress, 1987).
5. Stanley Stowers, *Letter Writing in Greco-Roman Antiquity* (Philadelphia: Westminster, 1986) 37.
6. Walter T. Wilson, *The Hope of Glory: Education and Exhortation in the Epistle to the Colossians* (Leiden: Brill, 1997) 47, 48.
7. R. Malcolm Errington, *A History of Macedonia,* trans. Catherine Errington (Berkeley: University of California Press, 1990) 133.
8. Meeks, *The First Urban Christians,* 17-18.

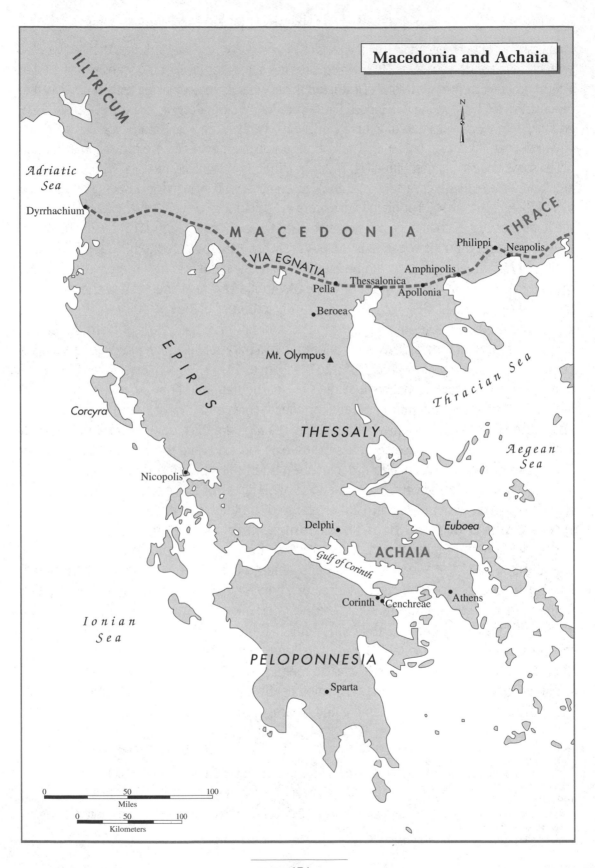

Macedonia and Achaia

ILLYRICUM

Adriatic
Sea

Dyrrhachium

MACEDONIA

THRACE

VIA EGNATIA

Philippi
Neapolis

Amphipolis

Thessalonica

Pella
Apollonia

Beroea

EPIRUS

Mt. Olympus ▲

Thracian Sea

Corcyra

THESSALY

Aegean
Sea

Nicopolis

Delphi

Euboea

ACHAIA

Gulf of Corinth

Ionian
Sea

Corinth
Cenchreae
Athens

PELOPONNESIA

Sparta

| 0 | 50 | 100 |
Miles

| 0 | 50 | 100 |
Kilometers

evidence suggests that the city enjoyed a rich cultic life—one that included indigenous Macedonian cults like those of Cabirus and Dionysus, foreign cults like those of Isis and Serapis, and the Roman imperial cult.[9]

The inhabitants of Thessalonica actively cultivated the beneficence of the Romans. The city's loyalty to the emperor Augustus (Octavian) and his successors favored it with the status of a free city (having an independent government) and with beneficence from both local and foreign Roman patrons. By the time Paul visited Thessalonica, sometime during the imperial reign of Claudius (41–54 CE), the Thessalonians had already erected a statue of Augustus as one of several honors to the Romans. Moreover, all of the Macedonians (in Thessalonica and beyond) had honored Augustus "by inaugurating an 'Augustan era.' "[10]

These data about the city in Paul's day are crucial to the interpretation of the Thessalonian epistles because the letters presuppose conflict between those in the church and other Thessalonians. It is likely that the Christians' glorification of Christ precipitated the conflict with the communities favorably disposed to the Roman government. If so, terms found in 1 Thessalonians, such as παρουσία (*parousia*, "coming" or "presence," 1 Thess 2:19; 3:13; 4:15; 5:23); ἀπάντησις (*apantēsis*, "meeting," 1 Thess 4:17) and ἀσφάλεια (*asphaleia*, "security," 1 Thess 5:3) are not politically innocuous. Rather, as Helmut Koester asserts, these terms present Paul's view of Jesus' "coming" or "return" as that of a king being greeted by a delegation that has come out to meet him.[11] Koester notes, moreover, that Paul's view of "peace and security" "points to the coming of the Lord as an event that will shatter the false peace and security of the Roman establishment."[12] Other terms in 1 and 2 Thessalonians could also be reread in the light of this possible political conflict. The attribution of the appellation "Father" to God may have been used in opposition to the imperial establishment, for the term figured in the ideology of Augustus Caesar as he sought to construe his empire as one large family.[13] Even such terms as "gospel" (εὐαγγέλιον *euangelion*) and "savior" (σωτήρ *sotēr*) in 1 and 2 Thessalonians or any of the other letters attributed to Paul could well have suggested "opposition to the imperial religion of the *pax Romana* [Roman peace]."[14]

If these terms carried the political weight that has been suggested, it is not difficult to understand why some Thessalonians (those not accepting Paul's teachings) would castigate Paul's salvific assembly, which viewed Jesus (not Augustus) as the benefactor and inaugurator of a new age.[15] In the eyes of these Thessalonians, support for Jesus weakened support for the Romans, who had brought tangible benefits to the city.

9. Craig Steven de Vos, *Church and Community Conflicts: The Relationships of the Thessalonian, Corinthian, and Philippian Churches with Their Wider Civic Communities* (Atlanta: Scholars Press, 1997).

10. M. B. Sakellariou, *Macedonia: 4000 Years of Greek History and Civilization* (Athens: Ekdotike Athenon S.A., 1983) 196.

11. Helmut Koester, "From Paul's Eschatology to the Apocalyptic Schemata of 2 Thessalonians," in *The Thessalonian Correspondence,* ed. Raymond F. Collins (Leuven: University of Leuven Press, 1990) 446.

12. Ibid., 447.

13. Mary Rose D'Angelo, " 'Abba' and 'Father': Imperial Theology and the Jesus Traditions," *JBL* 111 (1992) 623.

14. Richard Horsley, "Innovation in Search of Reorientation: New Testament Studies Rediscovering Its Subject Matter," *JAAR* 62 (1994) 1157.

15. On Roman imperial propaganda and its celebration of Augustus as the inaugurator of the new age, see Helmut Koester, "Jesus the Victim," *JBL* 111 (1992) 13.

It is important to note, moreover, that criticism of the Pauline believers would have been severely hostile because most Gentiles vehemently opposed Christianity's exclusivistic claims on its adherents' lives. According to Segal, "Like the Jews and unlike the many clubs and associations that were a part of the civic life of the Hellenistic world, the Christians were exclusive in the sense that no *truly committed* gentile Christian could maintain cult membership. Thus, Christianity was subversive to the basic religious institutions of gentile society."[16] This shift in loyalty from various cult memberships to exclusive ties with the Christian assembly also meant that Christian believers lost the prestige they could have assumed through the commitments to their former networks.

Given this potential for conflict, why did any of the Thessalonians join this assembly? Why did they remain? What would they find valuable in Paul's gospel that could shape and nurture their lives? Answers to these questions are found in an exploration of Paul's apocalyptic gospel.

The Context of Paul's Apocalyptic Gospel. When Paul preached to the people of Thessalonica, some believed his gospel, even in the face of the hostile response of other Thessalonians (1 Thess 1:6; 2:13-16). But what exactly was Paul's gospel?

Beyond the hortatory tradition that seems to have shaped all of Paul's letters, both 1 and 2 Thessalonians are shaped by apocalyptic thought.[17] Proponents of this type of worldview hold that there is a fundamental distinction between the forces of good and the forces of evil. They envision an old age ruled by the forces of evil and a new one ruled by God, and they believe in an imminent judgment, at which time God will bring an end to the evil forces. Studies of Paul's letters reveal that all of Paul's churches and letter recipients struggled (healthily or unhealthily) with the delicate tension between the "already" and the "not-yet" aspects of his apocalyptic thought. The "already" refers to the things God accomplished through Jesus' death and resurrection; the "not yet" refers to those things yet to be accomplished at the parousia. Hence a reckoning of this tension—its distinctiveness and consequences—may give some insight into what Paul's hearers (and the followers of his tradition) took for granted about Paul's thought.

The *distinctiveness* of the delicate tension between the already and the not-yet lies in Paul's modification of Jewish apocalyptic thought. For many Jews, there were two sequential ages (or aeons)—one old and one new. For Paul, however, the power of the old age was already dealt a severe blow with the death and resurrection of Jesus (Gal 6:14-15), an event that also marked the dawning of the new age (Gal 1:4).[18] Moreover, for Paul, the manifestations of the old age—while doomed (1 Cor 2:6; 7:31)—are not yet

16. Alan Segal, *Paul the Convert: The Apostolate and the Apostasy of Saul the Pharisee* (New Haven: Yale University Press, 1990) 164. Wayne Meeks, "Social Function of Apocalyptic Language in Pauline Christianity," in *Apocalypticism in the Mediterranean World and the Near East: Proceedings of the International Colloquium on Apocalypticism,* ed. David Hellholm (Tübingen: Mohr, 1983) 691. Charles Wanamaker, *The Epistles to the Thessalonians,* NIGTC (Grand Rapids: Eerdmans, 1990) 276.

17. According to Wilson, *The Hope of Glory,* 49, "The history of the early church evidences a tradition, established, it seems, primarily by the apostle Paul, of letter-writing as an instrument of moral instruction."

18. J. Paul Sampley, *Walking Between the Times: Paul's Moral Reasoning* (Minneapolis: Fortress, 1991) 10.

at an end. They still affect believers, who await Jesus' parousia as the climactic event that will mark the consummation of the new age already begun (1 Cor 15:51-57). Therefore, believers live "between the times"—that is, between the already of what God has done through Jesus' death and resurrection and the not yet that awaits as the object of hope: resurrection (Phil 3:11), full adoption (and its consequence, heirship; Rom 8:15-17; Gal 4:4-7), and full conformity to Christ (Phil 3:21).[19]

Given the delicate tension of these aspects, what are the *consequences* of Paul's apocalyptic thought pattern? One consequence is that God's redemption or salvation of believers from sin's enslaving powers and death's corruption is a process that begins with God's free offering of grace (Rom 5:15), the creation of a new sphere of existence (2 Cor 5:17; Gal 6:15) not dependent on any previous entitlement (such as one's class status) or human performance (such as the keeping of the law), and the declaration of justification by God through the believer's faith (or reorientation, Rom 5:1). That process—lived between the times—is one of sanctification, in which the Spirit both dwells in believers as God's pledge (or down payment, 2 Cor 1:22; 5:5) of the final consummation and acts as God's agency of transformation, conforming their lives to the image of God found in Jesus Christ (2 Cor 3:18). A second consequence is that believers struggle to live according to the spirit of the new age even while they still are plagued by manifestations of the old age—sin, trials, and death.

A third consequence of this tension is that believers—who have already conformed to Christ's death—presently conform to Christ's suffering and live expectantly in the hope that they will conform to his resurrection and glorification (Rom 5:2; Phil 3:10-11). Thus throughout the tenure of their lives "in Christ," from baptism to the other side of the parousia, the life of Jesus is the theme of their existence.

Finally, a fourth consequence of this tension is that the new sphere of existence entails products of transformation. These fruits show God at work in the edification of God's people, in the strengthening of the individual believer against the old age's manifestations, and in the persuasion of others through the proclamation of the gospel and the believer's conformity to Christ. The fruits of the Spirit (Gal 5:22) stand in opposition to the works of the flesh (or of the natural [and self-seeking] person; Gal 5:16,17).

While we cannot be sure of the full content of Paul's preaching in Thessalonica, it is known that he spoke strongly about the relationship that believers have with God. Paul's repeated references to God as "Father" only make sense if he shared with the community their incorporation into the family of God, a family in which Jesus is God's special son (1 Thess 1:10), but one in which all believers can be the children of God as well (1 Thess 1:1, 3; 3:11). It is also known that he preached about the death and resurrection of Jesus and how these events were the basis for rescue from the coming wrath of God (1 Thess 1:10). Accordingly, he likely spoke to the assembly about one of the ultimate benefits of the new age: God's deliverance of believers from death.

Paul's repeated emphasis on the role of the Holy Spirit and sanctification suggests that

19. Ibid. On Paul's thought world and the lives of believers between the death and resurrection of Jesus and his parousia, see ibid. See also W. Trilling, *Conversations with Paul* (New York: Crossroad, 1987).

his message also covered the more immediate and ongoing benefits of the new age. In the course of his description of the foundational events, Paul repeatedly mentions the Holy Spirit as proof of God's choosing of believers for salvation (1 Thess 1:4-5) and as a source of inspiration in the face of opposition (1:6). Even his later comments on the Holy Spirit as a gift from God (4:8) that helps believers to do God's bidding (4:3-8) and as a presence that should not be quenched (5:19) are offered in the context of what the Thessalonians are already doing and what they should continue doing (4:11; 5:11). It is in the course of reiterating some of his previous instructions that Paul describes sanctification, or the ongoing maturation of believers, as the will of God (4:3).

Because Paul writes of continuing opposition as something that he warned them of when he was with the church (1 Thess 3:3-5; cf. 2:1-2), he likely spoke to the Thessalonian believers about the continuing manifestations of the old age as well. The hostilities they were suffering, in fact, were a sign of the old age; and Paul could assume that they would understand him when he spoke of his inability to get back to the church as due to opposition from Satan (2:18).

It appears, then, that the Thessalonian church would have known at least the rudimentary form of Paul's mature gospel: the initiative of God in incorporating believers into God's family, the overlapping of the two ages, and some of the benefits and costs accruing to believers because of the tensions between these two ages. Exactly what had appealed to the Thessalonian believers about this gospel is not clear, and we should resist unfounded assumptions. In earlier studies of this church, some scholars too quickly suggested that the appeal was based on the relative deprivation of the Thessalonians in general (the belief that the Thessalonian Christians before their conversion were among the lower classes, even though they lived at a time when the economic life of Thessalonica in general was on the upswing). Other scholars presumed that the appeal was based on status inconsistency, the belief that the achieved status of the Thessalonian Christians before conversion was radically different from their inherited status and thus a source of tension for which they found some ease in early Christianity. However, we simply do not have enough material evidence to determine the status levels of the Thessalonian believers. And in the judgment of the most recent careful assessment of the little evidence we have available, these descriptions are examples of "ethnocentric anachronisms."[20]

If we look to Paul, a possible appeal may be that his gospel came with "power" (1 Thess 1:5). Indeed, much of 1 Thessalonians seems to be directed toward reminding the church of the power of this gospel both over the Thessalonians who believed it (1:6-10; 2:13-16) and over the apostles who proclaimed it (2:1-12). It is also likely that the gospel's power brought a level of prestige to this community for which they were even willing to accept hostility of and alienation from their former networks of support and honor. As we shall see, the issue of the gospel's power and prestige will be crucial to both letters. Furthermore, we must not forget that both 1 and 2 Thessalonians, to the extent that they expose Paul's gospel, demonstrate the extraordinary hope of that gospel. Little wonder then that Jürgen Moltmann

20. De Vos, *Church and Community Conflicts,* 169.

---

has advocated so forcefully that modern persons shun resignation and despair and embrace the hopefulness of Paul and other early Christians.[21] While many today might find difficulty in seeing the value of Paul's apocalyptic gospel, it was both an all-embracing statement about God's plan for the world and a "critique of this age and its values."[22] Many of those who heard Paul's preaching (including the Thessalonians) would have found in it a powerful challenge to the existing order. As we shall see as well, both Thessalonian letters also imply this challenge.

SPECIFIC OCCASIONS AND PURPOSES OF 1 AND 2 THESSALONIANS

Paul's gospel not only brought the church at Thessalonica into being, but also became the basis upon which Paul molded its character and sustained its growth. Thus one could expect his apocalyptic gospel to be tightly woven into the hortatory tradition that he adopted—a tradition noted for shaping the distinctiveness of communities and for providing them with nurturing resources.[23] Because history has afforded us with two exhortative letters addressed to the Thessalonians, we have the opportunity to explore the distinctive appropriations of Paul's gospel in two related, but different, hortatory documents.[24] It is necessary, therefore, to clarify as much as possible the circumstances that gave rise to each letter. An appreciation of the similar yet distinct occasions and purposes of each letter will help us to see their respective appropriations of Paul's gospel in stark relief.

Specific Occasion and Purposes of 1 Thessalonians. Drawing exclusively on Paul's writings, we can say little with certainty about the specific occasion of his earliest extant letter. Paul formed the church that received this letter shortly after he left Philippi, where he and others were "shamefully mistreated" (1 Thess 2:2). His stay at Thessalonica must have been long enough for him to receive support from the church at Philippi on more than one occasion (Phil 4:16). Still, the tenure in Thessalonica also met with difficulty (2:2) and, most unfortunately for both parties, with a painful separation (2:17). When efforts to return to the Thessalonian church proved futile (2:18), Paul dispatched Timothy from Athens (3:1-2) with instructions to strengthen the community. As a set of follow-up instructions, in line with his desire to form, mold, and nurture communities, Paul wrote the letter we now know as 1 Thessalonians.

If we rely somewhat on the material from Acts, a few more details about the circumstances are evident. From Athens, Paul moved on presumably to Corinth (Acts 18:11-17), the place from which he likely wrote the first Thessalonian letter. Acts also suggests that Paul arrived in Corinth before Gallio became proconsul (Acts 18:11-17). If,

---

21. Jürgen Moltmann, *Theology of Hope: On the Grounds and Implications of a Christian Eschatology* (New York: Harper & Row, 1967).

22. Sampley, *Walking Between the Times,* 108.

23. For more on the connections between apocalyptic language and the hortatory tradition, see Malherbe, *Paul and the Thessalonians,* 80.

24. This is the case even if Paul did not write both of the letters and even if we have no way of determining whether the same community actually received both letters. This commentary assumes that Paul wrote only 1 Thessalonians and that the dating of 2 Thessalonians and concrete details about its audience are difficult to determine. Still, it is justifiable to assume that the audience of 2 Thessalonians knew and respected 1 Thessalonians because 2 Thessalonians often adopts and adapts the language and style of 1 Thessalonians.

indeed, Paul wrote to the Thessalonians from Corinth, we may deduce that the letter was likely written around 50 or 51 CE because the famous Delphi inscription dates Gallio's arrival in Corinth to sometime between January and August of 51 CE.

Some details about the specific historical circumstances, however, differ between Paul's letter and the Acts account. While both suggest that the trip to Philippi preceded the trip to Thessalonica (Acts 17:1; cf. 16:11-40; 1 Thess 2:2), which was about 90 miles southwest of Philippi on the Via Egnatia, Acts gives the impression that the Thessalonian converts included both Jews and Gentiles (Acts 17:4), while Paul implies that there were Gentile converts only (as can be inferred from 1 Thess 1:9, 10). If one accepts 1 Thess 2:14-16 to be from Paul's hand and not an interpolation (see the Commentary), these verses also support an ethnic constituency of Gentiles.

Acts 17 also mentions Paul's going to a Jewish synagogue, which is not mentioned in 1 Thessalonians. To the extent of our archaeological data today, there is no evidence for a synagogue in Thessalonica at this early period. What must be remembered, however, is that Acts has a stereotyped pattern similar to ancient novelistic literature of the period. For example, in Chariton's *Chaereas and Callirhoe,* one of the ancient Greek novels, virtually everywhere the two protagonists, Chaereas and Callirhoe, go they find a shrine to Aphrodite, the goddess of love, where they offer her worship and thanks. Likewise, virtually everywhere Paul travels in Acts 13–28, he finds Jews and a Jewish synagogue. The function of the stereotyped narration of shrines in both cases is that the universal significance and power of an adherent's deity is highlighted if the writer can demonstrate that that the deity is worshiped all over the Mediterranean world.

If the Thessalonian Christians were a Gentile congregation, it is possible to posit some basic factors about the occasion of 1 Thessalonians. First, as has been noted, opposition from Gentile neighbors was likely a critical ingredient in the occasion of 1 Thessalonians. Their hostility was likely aroused by the Christian believers' countercultural glorification of Christ. A second factor in the letter's occasion was a concern for stability. Given the hostility from unbelievers, the congregation is encouraged to remain steady on its course. In 1 Thessalonians, Paul speaks of his leadership team (Paul, Silvanus, and Timothy) "living" if the community "stands firm" (3:8), and he implores God to "strengthen" the hearts of his congregation against external social alienation (3:13). Therefore, 1 Thessalonians seems written to encourage a beleaguered church to persist in its new way of life, in accordance with the apocalyptic gospel it has received, despite the fact that it might have been difficult for the members to see the power of God—and the prestige pertaining to that power—at work in their lives.

Specific Occasion and Purposes of 2 Thessalonians. Since some scholars are reticent to assign 2 Thessalonians to Pauline authorship, the determination of the specific occasion and purposes of the letter can only follow after a brief discussion of the evidence. Both 1 and 2 Thessalonians have simple letter openings (1 Thess 1:1; 2 Thess 1:2) and more than one thanksgiving notice (1 Thess 1:2; 2:13; 3:9; 2 Thess 1:3; 2:13). In addition, in both letters one of the thanksgiving notices (1 Thess 3:9; 2 Thess 2:13) is followed by a wish-prayer (1 Thess 3:11; 2 Thess 2:16) that itself is subsequently followed by the transitional marker "finally" (λοιπόν *loipon*, 1 Thess 4:1; 2 Thess 3:1).

These similarities could suggest that Paul wrote both letters. However, many scholars think the similarities simply indicate that the author of 2 Thessalonians (not Paul) mimicked a copy of 1 Thessalonians to give his work authority at a time when other followers of Paul were also composing works in the apostle's name (2:1-2; cf. 3:17). Furthermore, because scholars respect Paul's creative abilities, they suggest that the similarities are signs pointing to the pseudonymous character of 2 Thessalonians. Bonnie Thurston's lament is typical: "The question this evidence [of literary similarity] raises is why Paul would so slavishly follow his own precedent. Why would Paul use his own work so unimaginatively?"[25]

Arguments for or against Pauline authorship of 2 Thessalonians usually have to reckon with stylistic differences (e.g., the relatively limited diction of 2 Thessalonians), the different tones of the letters (e.g., the apparently "cooler" tone of 2 Thessalonians), and different uses of eschatology (e.g., the use of futuristic eschatology to create a distinction between believers and outsiders in 1 Thessalonians and its use to critique an overrealized eschatology within the Christian community in 2 Thessalonians).

While judgments can vary on each of these points, perhaps the most salient argument against Paul's authorship is that the letter seeks to authenticate itself from other apparently spurious letters (cf. 3:17). But it is difficult to understand how anyone could write a forgery while an author was still alive.

Any individual piece of evidence against Pauline authorship of 2 Thessalonians is not sufficient; however, the cumulative effect of these pieces of evidence leans more against it. Whatever one's conclusions about the debate, the force of this commentary's examination suggests that the more crucial matters are the difference in what occasioned the two letters and their common testament to the continuing influence of Paul's apocalyptic gospel.

As for the occasion of 2 Thessalonians, two issues appear to be prominent. On the one hand, the writer (as with Paul in 1 Thessalonians) has a general concern for stability in the face of continuing hostility from the congregation's neighbors. The writer of 2 Thessalonians assumes that the earlier opposition and loss of prestige faced by the Thessalonians at its foundation and shortly thereafter (see the section "Specific Occasion and Purposes of 1 Thessalonians," 681-82) have not abated. In 2 Thessalonians the congregation is enjoined to "stand firm and hold fast to the traditions" (2:15), and the writer implores God to strengthen "the hearts" of the congregation (2:17) because of the mounting afflictions they are suffering from unbelievers. In this respect 2 Thessalonians is generally similar to 1 Thessalonians, and it is not surprising that the second letter mimics the first in form and diction.

On the other hand, a new issue emerges in 2 Thessalonians—namely, the introduction of an enthusiastic brand of apocalypticism, a view that compensates for the letter recipients' loss of power through an overrealized eschatology. Koester persuasively argues that the origin of the enthusiastic message—even if its proponents justified it on the basis of 1 Thessalonians—actually lies in "the apocalyptic fervor of the second half of the first

25. Bonnie Thurston, *Reading Colossians, Ephesians, and 2 Thessalonians: A Literary and Theological Commentary* (New York: Crossroad, 1995) 160.

century."[26] It is not surprising that the writer uses several examples of apocalyptic material (assuming that the material will be convincing to his hearers) not to *support* the enthusiasm, but to *counter* it. Moreover, the writer's use of 1 Thessalonians is both plentiful (to show adequate acquaintance with it) and non-enthusiastic (to highlight the importance of not abandoning the everyday world as the enthusiasts would likely advocate).[27]

It is not necessary, then, to see 2 Thessalonians as Paul's correction of his own earlier writing, as some scholars purport. Nor need one postulate 2 Thessalonians as an argument advanced to dispute the claims of Colossians and Ephesians (though 2 Thessalonians does critique a realized eschatology on the order of the ones found in those letters). Rather, Earl Richard's hypothesis about 2 Thessalonians seems to be on target. The work was composed "to discredit the claims, made in Paul's name, of apocalyptic preachers which were causing alarm within the community (2:2) and social unrest within its ranks (3:6-12)."[28] It is critical to note, moreover, that Paul's apocalyptic thought (whether or not he wrote 2 Thessalonians) influenced the church that read 2 Thessalonians. Thus both 1 and 2 Thessalonians are apocalyptic documents, but the latter works against an enthusiastic brand of apocalypticism.

With these brief remarks about the letters' occasions and purposes, we are closer to understanding the circumstances and thought patterns of 1 and 2 Thessalonians. Another necessary step, however, is to consider some of the literary conventions of the day, to see how letters were read and heard in Paul's time in terms both of the various parts of ancient letters and of the special acoustical features that shaped the flow and argument of ancient letters.

LITERARY CHARACTER OF 1 AND 2 THESSALONIANS

In determining the basic literary character of the two letters, Pauline scholarship profits from a variety of widely acknowledged perspectives and methods. This commentary assumes an audience-oriented perspective in which contemporary readers seek to understand the audience that each author had in mind when composing the respective letters. Generally, the audience-oriented approach used here draws on two methods, epistolary analysis and rhetorical criticism, not to restrict Paul and other early Christians to the handbooks of their age, but to make contemporary readers aware of the basic textual markers by which the audiences for the two letters would have read or heard them. It is generally accepted that early Christian letters offered nuanced variations on Hellenistic epistolary formulae as well as on the rhetorical practices of (to the gods or to the addressees) and prayer reports, and perhaps one or more parts of the conventional epistolary body (i.e., the main part of a letter).

As well, it is generally accepted that early Christian letters reflect rhetorical (or persuasive speech) conventions, as if the letters were all influenced by the rules that ancient Greeks and Romans applied to speeches. Accordingly, some scholars find in the letters the basic speech design indexed in handbooks on speech preparation—namely, an exordium (or opening of an argument), a *pistis* (or proof section, i.e., the central part of an argument)

26. Koester, "From Paul's Eschatology to the Apocalyptic Schemata of 2 Thessalonians," 455.
27. Ibid., 456.
28. Earl J. Richard, *First and Second Thessalonians* (Collegeville, Minn.: Liturgical, 1995) 299.

and the peroration (or closing of an argument). Others even characterize particular Christian letters in one of the three broad modal forms of argumentation: the deliberative mode (with the goal of persuading or dissuading), the epideictic mode (with the goal of praising and blaming), or the defensive mode (with the goal of accusing or defending).

Whether Paul learned the epistolary and rhetorical conventions in school or assimilated them from the larger culture is not known. What is generally believed, however, is that Paul (like anyone else of his time) was not straitjacketed by the rules and need not be held to exaction on the basis of either the set of practices in the handbooks of the period or those in the scholarly reckonings of our own age.

THEOLOGICAL CHALLENGES

Anticipating the results of the epistolary and rhetorical analyses of the two letters, the outlines that follow the bibliography are plausible reconstructions of the audience's apprehension of the textual markers for the two letters. Before turning to the bibliography and the outlines, however, contemporary readers can immediately appreciate some of the everyday theological challenges that these two texts present to modern audiences in the light of the historical and literary environments previously mentioned. In the course of the Commentary, the following challenges will be explored more fully.

Appreciating the signs of God's power already evident in a community lies at the heart of 1 Thessalonians (1:5; 2:13). Discovering that the effectiveness of the gospel extends beyond the limited parameters of one's own environs is a critical lesson as well (1 Thess 1:8; 2:14-16). Drawing on the past to discover models of perseverance in the face of present suffering is also a repeated challenge (1 Thess 1:6-7; 2:1-11; 3:1-11). Remaining firm in one's convictions without being beguiled by enticing words or false hopes is paramount for 2 Thessalonians (2:1-3). Knowing both how to wait on God and yet move toward practical pursuits is equally important (2 Thess 3:6-13). And discerning how to reach out in love to disorderly persons in the church without demonizing them is key to the spirit of 2 Thessalonians (3:14-15). These insights from 1 and 2 Thessalonians offer remarkable challenges for contemporary churches. But when fathomed sufficiently, 1 and 2 Thessalonians offer much deeper reservoirs of assistance to our world.

BIBLIOGRAPHY

Best, E. *A Commentary on the First and Second Epistles to the Thessalonians.* London: Black, 1972. A monumental work that critiques earlier German scholarship on interpolation and authenticity theories.

Collins, Raymond. *The Birth of the New Testament: The Origin and Development of the First Generation.* New York: Crossroad, 1993. An in-depth study with a variety of perspectives to show the value of 1 Thessalonians as the first work of the NT.

Gaventa, Beverly. *First and Second Thessalonians.* Interpretation. Louisville: John Knox, 1998. An exegetical work on 1 and 2 Thessalonians with interpretive insights for liturgy, Bible study, and preaching.

Hughes, F. W. *Early Christian Rhetoric and 2 Thessalonians.* Sheffield: JSOT, 1989. A rhetorical analysis of 2 Thessalonians that assumes it to be a pseudonymous work written against the realized eschatology found in Colossians and Ephesians.

Jewett, Robert. *The Thessalonian Correspondence: Pauline Rhetoric and Millenarian Piety.* Foundations and Facets. Philadelphia: Fortress, 1986. An audience-oriented rhetorical analysis that reads the two letters against the background of a radical form of millenarianism.

Malherbe, Abraham J. *Paul and the Thessalonians: The Philosophic Tradition of Pastoral Care.* Philadelphia: Fortress, 1987. An often-cited monograph on Paul's nurturing techniques of pastoral care.

Marshall, I. H. *1 and 2 Thessalonians.* Grand Rapids: Eerdmans, 1983. Traditional study with a careful and sustained critique of interpolation theories, letter-sequence hypotheses, and arguments on the pseudonymous character of 2 Thessalonians.

Menken, Maarten J. *2 Thessalonians.* London: Routledge, 1994. A literary analysis that situates 2 Thessalonians in several settings: its literary environment, Jewish apocalypticism, and the world of pseudonymity.

Richard, Earl J. *First and Second Thessalonians.* Sacra Pagina. Collegeville, Minn.: Liturgical, 1995. Assumes 1 Thess 2:14-16 to be an interpolation and 2 Thessalonians to be pseudonymous.

Smith, Abraham. *Comfort One Another: Reconstructing the Rhetoric and Audience of 1 Thessalonians.* Louisville: Westminster, 1995. An exploration of the ancient consolatory conventions in 1 Thessalonians.

Thurston, Bonnie. *Reading Colossians, Ephesians and 2 Thessalonians: A Literary and Theological Commentary.* New York: Crossroad, 1995. A commentary on 2 Thessalonians, Colossians, and Ephesians that reads 2 Thessalonians against the distinctive religious culture at Thessalonica.

Wanamaker, Charles. *The Epistles to the Thessalonians: A Commentary on the Greek Text.* NIGTC. Grand Rapids: Eerdmans, 1990. Combines rhetorical and social critical scholarship in an argument for both Pauline authorship of the two letters and a reverse sequence in the letters' composition.

OUTLINE OF 1 THESSALONIANS

I. 1 Thessalonians 1:1-5, The Exordium

II. 1 Thessalonians 1:6–5:22, Maintaining an Apocalyptic Way of Life

A. 1:6–2:16, A Gospel of Consistent Power
1:6-10, An Unstoppable Word
2:1-12, Continuing with the Gospel
2:13-16, The Word's Relentless Power

B. 2:17–3:13, Concern for the Church's Survival and Moral Training
2:17-20, Aborted Trips and the Parousia
3:1-8, A Visit of Consolation in Hostile Times
3:9-13, An Expected Trip and the Parousia

C. 4:1–5:22, Commending Persistence in the Distinctive Life
4:1-12, Walking a Distinctive Life
4:13–5:11, Maintaining the Apocalyptic Hope
5:12-22, Nurturing Resources for the Distinctive Life

III. 1 Thessalonians 5:23-28, The Peroration

THE EXORDIUM

NIV

1 Paul, Silas[a] and Timothy,

To the church of the Thessalonians in God the Father and the Lord Jesus Christ:

Grace and peace to you.[b]

[2]We always thank God for all of you, mentioning you in our prayers. [3]We continually remember before our God and Father your work produced by faith, your labor prompted by love, and your endurance inspired by hope in our Lord Jesus Christ.

[4]For we know, brothers loved by God, that he has chosen you, [5]because our gospel came to you not simply with words, but also with power, with the Holy Spirit and with deep conviction. You know how we lived among you for your sake.

[a]1 Greek *Silvanus*, a variant of *Silas*   [b]1 Some early manuscripts *you from God our Father and the Lord Jesus Christ*

NRSV

1 Paul, Silvanus, and Timothy,
    To the church of the Thessalonians in God the Father and the Lord Jesus Christ:
    Grace to you and peace.

[2]We always give thanks to God for all of you and mention you in our prayers, constantly [3]remembering before our God and Father your work of faith and labor of love and steadfastness of hope in our Lord Jesus Christ. [4]For we know, brothers and sisters[a] beloved by God, that he has chosen you, [5]because our message of the gospel came to you not in word only, but also in power and in the Holy Spirit and with full conviction; just as you know what kind of persons we proved to be among you for your sake.

[a]Gk *brothers*

COMMENTARY

In epistolary analysis terms, 1 Thess 1:1-5 includes a prescript (1:1) and the first of three thanksgiving reports (1:2-5; see also 2:13; 3:9-10). In the epistolary patterns of his day, Paul opens the letter with a typical tripartite prescript (letter writer, letter recipient, and salutation; 1:1). Following the prescript, a thanksgiving report (1:2-5) presents three participial phrases that stress Paul and his coworkers (or his "pastoral care" team) praying for the community (1:2), remembering the Thessalonians' laudable resourcefulness (1:3), and acknowledging the community's election (1:4-5), respectively.[29] However, some scholars think the initial thanksgiving, as an introduction to the letter, continues—after an interruption at 2:1-12—from 2:13 to 2:16. Others even suggest that the thanksgiving extends to 3:13, with yet another interlude at 2:17–3:8.

In rhetorical terms, however, it seems best to limit the letter's initial introduction to 1:1-5 for two reasons. First, in Greek the first thanksgiving proceeds with a gradual increase in length for each of its three participial phrases as if to reach a resolution only in the last one (1:4-5). Second, with an initial prescript and a thanksgiving report ending in 1:5, the opening would conclude symmetrically with an acknowledgment both of what Paul's leadership team "knows" (εἰδότες *eidotes*) about the church (1:4-5) and what the church "knows" (οἴδατε *oidate*) about his leadership team (1:5).

One can argue that the first five verses of 1 Thessalonians alone sufficiently execute the twin goals of an ancient exordium—namely, to gain an

29. Paul's coworkers in his ministry among the Thessalonians include Silvanus and Timothy. Of course, Paul's plural verbal and nominal forms are not epistolary. That is, Paul bears sole authorship, as three later passages (2:18; 3:5; 5:27) using the first-person singular attest.

audience's goodwill and to intimate a work's basic issues.[30] To gain the audience's goodwill, Paul presents an unadorned yet emotionally evocative prescript; a typical, yet important, thanksgiving report; and an acknowledgment of the powerful forces already and continuously unleashed in the church's life. The opening or prescript here (1:1), unlike those in the other undisputed Pauline letters (cf. 1 Cor 1:1-3; Phil 1:1-3), appears in an unelaborated form. No extended self-descriptions characterize the letter senders ("Paul, Silvanus, and Timothy"). Nothing but the basics are given in the depiction of the recipients ("To the church of the Thessalonians in God the Father and the Lord Jesus Christ"). Even the salutation ("Grace to you and peace"), likely Paul's variation of the Jewish "mercy and peace" greetings, is stated without embellishment. What the opening lacks in elaboration, however, it captures in its list of *dramatis personae* and in the powerful Jewish images it evokes.

Besides the recipients, other critical players include God, Jesus, and the founding figures: Paul, Silvanus (cf. Acts 17:9; 18:5), and Timothy (2 Cor 1:1; Phil 1:1; 2:19-34; Phlm 1). Timothy is a vivid part of the community's memory, moreover, because of the recent consolation and strength (3:2) he brought to the church. (Perhaps, though we cannot be sure, he also transported the letter to the church.)

The prescript also evokes at least two powerful Jewish images. Although the word ἐκκλησία (*ekklēsia*, "church," 1:1) could denote simply an "assembly" in profane Greek, it possibly evokes here a holy community called into being by God, as with the Hebrew expression קְהַל יהוה (*qĕhal YHWH*) from the Old Testament. Hearing the expression Χριστός (*Christos*), the Greek term for the English expression "Christ," moreover, auditors would likely register the concept of the Jews' long-expected deliverer—only now, Paul's Gentile auditors can claim this deliverance as well. The critical players in place and some poignant Jewish images noted, Paul's prescript already pro-vides a moving and comforting context for a church assaulted by the painful ordeal of aliena-tion.

Like the prescript, the thanksgiving report cap-tures the audience's goodwill. Its inclusion alone could have effected a *captatio benevolentiae* ("captivation of goodwill"), for the praise of the gods in any form was standard fare for securing the favorable disposition of ancient Greco-Roman audiences.[31] The specifics of the thanksgiving re-port could have had an endearing effect as well, for the three participial clauses depict the persist-ence of the foundational leaders' concern, the visible demonstration of the church's apocalyptic life, and the verities of the church members' status as believers. With a rhythmic and comforting diction, then, Paul announces the persistence with which his team makes their prayers (1:2; cf. Rom 1:9; Phlm 4; *Phaedrus* 254a; *Protagoras* 317e), continues with a recollection of discrete stages in the church's active life (i.e., the church's "work of faith," "labor of love" and "steadfastness of hope," 1:3; cf. Rom 5:2-5; 1 Cor 13:12; Gal 5:5-5), and finally indicates the church's hearty guarantees, including God's initiative and the gos-pel's powerful effect (1:4-5).

The thanksgiving's rhythmic flair is matched in rhetorical force only by its choice of diction, as if Paul brushed his epistolary canvas in colors drawn from the rich palette of the Septuagint or from other Jewish literature. Often deemed a signal of "group identity or a close sense of group kinship" (e.g., Deut 15:3),[32] the expression ἀδελφοι (*adel-phoi*, "brothers and sisters") here connotes a fic-tive kinship group, all of whose members can claim God as their Father (cf. 1:1). Similarly, the expressions "beloved by God" (Deut 33:12) and "chosen" (Deut 4:37; 7:6-8; 10:14-15; 14:2) are election terms drawn from the OT, leading one scholar to aver: "It is clear by this early stage in his thinking Paul has already developed the con-cept of the church as the Israel of God."[33]

In sum, Paul's opening remarks touched the heart of the church because of the inclusion of

30. Robert Jewett, *The Thessalonian Correspondence: Pauline Rheto-ric and Millenarian Piety*, Foundations and Facets (Philadelphia: Fortress, 1986) 76. On the *captatio benevolentiae* ("captivation of goodwill") in an exordium, see Quintilian 3.8.6; Cicero *De Inventione* 1.15.20; and Aristotle *Rhetoric* 3.14.7. On the exordium's forecasting function, see Cicero *De Part. Or.* 27.97; Quintilian 3.8.10; cf. Aristotle *Rhetoric* 3.13-14.

31. See Quintillian 3.7.7.
32. Charles Wanamaker, *The Epistles to the Thessalonians*, NIGTC (Grand Rapids: Eerdmans, 1990) 77. See also Philo *On the Special Laws* 2.79; Josephus *Antiquities of the Jews* 10.20.
33. I. H. Marshall, "Election and Calling to Salvation in 1 and 2 Thessalonians," in *The Thessalonian Correspondence*, ed. R. F. Collins (Leuven: University of Leuven Press, 1990) 262.

an encomium to God, the persistence of his team's prayerful actions, the noting of the church's active life as believers, the consoling depiction of the church as secure in God's initiating work, and the characterization of the gospel as a powerful force.

The first five verses of the letter also announce three of the basic themes treated in Paul's missive. First, the verses announce the effectiveness of his leadership team's initial word (or gospel) and its subsequent practices. Besides its function in foreshadowing the letter's "knowledge" diction, the repetition of knowledge terms ("knowing" and "you know") also stresses *what* Paul and his coworkers know and *what* the church knows (1:4-5). Paul and his coworkers know the status of the church because of the effectiveness of the powerful gospel (1:4-5*a*). The church knows the effectiveness of Paul and his coworkers, whose subsequent actions and practices were effected for the sake of the church (1:5*b*). Accordingly, Paul will note repeatedly the knowledge (2:1-2, 5, 11; 3:3-4; 4:2; 5:2) or, with the related diction of remembrance (2:9-10; 3:6), the memory of the church. Furthermore, the rest of the letter will echo the effectiveness of the team's gospel (or word) and its pastoral care practices in providing a sufficient basis for the church's survival. For a young church beset by local hostility, reminders of these certainties were absolutely necessary.

Second, Paul's opening verses announce the theme of persistence—both that of Paul's leadership team and that of the church. Paul's emphasis on continually giving thanks to God (conveyed with the temporal adverb "always" [πάντοτε *pantote*], 1:2) and on the team's constant memory of the church (conveyed with the temporal adverb "constantly" [ἀδιαλείπτως *adialeiptōs*], 1:2) is complemented by the church's continuous signs of success, with the expression "steadfastness of hope" (1:3) vividly attesting to the church's endurance despite continuing alienation from the larger society. Moreover, because Paul prefaces his remarks about the church's continuing activity with the comprehensive category "all" [πάντων *pantōn*] of you" (1:2), Paul not only thanks God for all of the church, but he also speaks laudably about the continuing activity of all in the church. For a church plagued by the hostile actions of unbelievers, the persistence demanded (and for

which Paul gives thanks) needs to be the goal of everyone in the assembly.

The focus on persistence—illustrated in the lives of Paul's leadership team and of all the church—is not surprising in a letter peppered with thanksgivings (2:13; 3:9-10), wish-prayers (3:11-13; 5:23), and a benediction (5:28). Nor is this focus surprising in a letter that commends the perennial life of joy, prayer, and thanksgiving (5:16-18) and exhorts the church to continue to do what it was taught to do (4:1-2), whether by God (4:9) or by Paul's leadership team (4:11). It is also not surprising that the persistence demanded has specific force for all of the church in a letter that charges individual members to be constant in their responsible behavior to each other (4:4-6; 5:11).

The emphasis on persistence was likely a needed message for Paul's church, for the fierceness of the hostility (read in the light of 2:14-16) suggests circumstances that could have precipitated a falling away. Paul apparently had that fear, as 3:5 makes clear. The letter, then, is certainly a paraenetic letter (one that encourages persistence in a certain way of life), as Malherbe has frequently noted, even if there are other factors at work as well.[34]

A third theme of the letter is the distinctiveness of the church from the rest of the Thessalonians. Perhaps Paul reveals this theme with the expression "in [ἐν *en*] God the Father and the Lord Jesus Christ" (1:1) in the salutation. Whether the term characterizes the present existence of the church or, more instrumentally, implies that the church of the Thessalonians "lies in what God accomplished by Christ's life, death and resurrection,"[35] the expression distinguishes Paul's *ekklēsia,* or church, from any other. The acknowledgment of the gospel's coming with the Holy Spirit (1:5), moreover, sets the church apart, especially if the auditors here understood the Holy Spirit—as some of Paul's later auditors and interpreters would discern—to be a pledge (or first installment) of the new age's final consummation (2 Cor 1:22; cf. Eph 1:14).

It is little wonder, then, that in the rest of the

34. See, e.g., Abraham Malherbe, *Paul and the Thessalonians: The Philosophic Tradition of Pastoral Care* (Philadelphia: Fortress, 1987) 70.
35. Ernest Best, *A Commentary on the First and Second Epistles to the Thessalonians* (London: Black, 1972) 62.

letter Paul makes distinctions between this community of believers and the larger society. As a part of a new and radically distinctive φιλία (*philia*), or friendship network, Paul's alternative community faces the temptation to return to its former networks for financial, social, and emotional support (3:5). Paul's highly dualistic diction, however, virtually places a wedge between the community and its fictive kin (Jesus, Paul, the churches of Judea and of Macedonia and Achaia), on the one hand, and the non-Christian Thessalonians, on the other hand (2:14). The church, while composed of Gentiles, is told not to act as the Gentiles do (4:5) and is commended to "behave properly toward outsiders" (4:12), as if the church's members are insiders (4:12). Indeed, the first instance of the "insiders/outsiders" typology beyond the first five verses occurs as early as 1:10 when Paul breaks into solemn—if not formulaic—diction with a declaration of Jesus' deliverance of "us" (ἡμᾶς *hēmas*), as if to separate all the believers from all the unbelievers.[36] "Others" or "outsiders" may grieve without hope, but for Paul's church, the coming of Jesus, or the parousia, neutralizes death and all other forms of separation (4:13-18). While others speak about "peace and security" as children of the darkness,

Paul describes the Thessalonian believers as "children of the day" (5:1-11).

Even the support mechanisms the church once had in its *philia*, or friendship networks, in Thessalonica are now replaced within the circle of the new fellowship. For comfort and support in the wake of its leaders' absence, the members of the community are urged to look to one another (4:18; 5:11) and to demonstrate love toward each other and to all (3:12), especially through individuated aid to those requiring special attention (5:14). For its sense of prestige, usually gained through traditional kin and clan networks, the community is exhorted to share in the kingdom and glory of God (2:12), a glory marked by the moral excellence of one's walk before God (cf. 2:12; 4:1). The church's life now is distinguished by its holiness (4:1-8).

So, with a powerful *captatio benevolentiae* achieved in the first five verses, Paul begins to write his letter. And given the themes of effectiveness, persistence, and distinctiveness announced in these verses, the specific goal of Paul's proposition for the entire letter seems clear. Paul writes to encourage a beleaguered church to use the words and practices of their foundational leaders as resources for persisting in the church's distinctive, apocalyptic life.

36. On the arguments for and against the formulaic character of 1:9-10, see Wanamaker, *The Epistles to the Thessalonians*, 84-89.

REFLECTIONS

Paul's thanksgiving notices often reveal his thanks to God for evidences of faith and fruitfulness in the lives of believers. What counts as a reason for thanksgiving in our churches? Is it numerical growth? Is it property lists? Is it the size of the office staff or figures in the annual budget? Or are these matters that only scratch the surface of church life?

The measuring stick by which we assess church life is too often influenced by our consumer-oriented and profit-driven culture. So profit driven is the larger culture that Jeffrey Goldfarb has commented that we now believe that "if something is profitable it is true, real, and good; if it is not, it is without true meaning."[37] Tragically, the identity of all too many churches is formed on the wheelbase of economics.

Paul's powerful thanksgiving (1:1-5), however, speaks appreciatively to God about a richness and a productiveness in the lives of the Thessalonian believers. To borrow the descriptive comparison of Peter Gomes, Paul's goal for those believers was not the "good life" (if that means getting all the material goods one can get) but the "life that is good" (i.e., the life that

37. Jeffrey C. Goldfarb, *The Cynical Society: The Culture of Politics and the Politics of Culture in American Life* (Chicago: University of Chicago Press, 1991) 16.

truly provides meaning).[38] Paul's thanksgiving highlights three indications of productivity in the life of the Thessalonian believers, three evidences of "the life that is good."

First, those believers had responded positively to the loving initiative of God. Although Paul dearly loved this community of believers, his words about his own love for them (2:8; 3:12) come only after he has spoken about God's effective love for the church (1:4). Paul was not content to describe the church's laudable attributes (1:3) without peering further back to call attention to God's active role in their history (1:4). To paraphrase the words of Abraham Heschel, "Long before we searched for God, God was already searching for us."[39]

Second, the believers at Thessalonica had welcomed and accepted caring leaders, leaders who not only brought to them the good news of the gospel, but who also cared enough to persistently monitor their growth as believers. Paul's constant prayers for and memories of that church reflect his consistent concern about the group's spiritual growth. The revolving door syndrome that plagues many churches today is often a woeful testament to ministries that spend too much time monitoring church building projects and not enough time building the lives of members. The quality of our witness to the larger world, however, depends not so much on our numbers as on our nurturing, not on our statistics but on our stability as people of God. As with Paul and his leadership team, our greatest concern ought to be that of inculcating convictions, aiding spiritual growth, and helping people to develop endurance to deal with life under pressure.

Third, Paul was thankful to God for the qualitative distinction in the lives of these believers. Paul's commendation is not just about their work, but their work of faith; not just their labor, but their labor of love; not just their steadfastness, but their steadfastness of hope in the Lord Jesus Christ (1:3). Their routines of life were now all transformed, supported by the decisive event of the coming of Jesus into the world and governed by a purposefulness that transcended yet included them.

A God who initiates salvation, caring leaders who nurture believers, and believers who eagerly follow a new orientation marked out by the gospel—these are the three realities that make for truly productive lives as believers. Without these, church members may merely have "the good life," but not "the life that is good."

---

38. Peter Gomes, *The Good Book: Reading the Bible with Mind and Heart* (New York: Morrow, 1996) 180.
39. Cf. Abraham J. Heschel, *God in Search of Man: A Philosophy of Judaism* (New York: Farrar, Straus & Cudahy, 1955) 136.

1 THESSALONIANS 1:6–5:22

MAINTAINING AN APOCALYPTIC WAY OF LIFE

OVERVIEW

With its concerns for persistence in an apocalyptic way of life and self-sufficient survival apart from former networks of support, the letter shifts from its exordium to its proof (i.e., the larger portion of a document conveying its main argument). Here, Paul labors first to prepare a way (1:6–3:13) for his later challenge to the Thessalonians to continue walking in the ways of his apocalyptic gospel and its ethical imperatives (4:1–5:22). A sequential analysis of 1:6–5:22 supports this understanding, but two preliminary steps are in order. Given the audience-oriented nature of this commentary, first, it is important to observe the benefits of epistolary analysis in illuminating possible aural textual markers of the letter's epistolary structure in 1:6–5:22. Second, it is necessary to use any other critical tools to justify in broad strokes the larger rhetorical units of 1:6–5:22. Then the commentary can move forward with its sequential rhetorical analysis and examine more carefully the means Paul uses in persuading the church to maintain its distinctive life.

For our purposes, the benefits of epistolary analysis lie not with scholarly discussions about the ending of the epistolary thanksgiving or the beginning of its epistolary body. In fact, the repeated instances of thanksgiving notices in 1 Thessalonians, as we have seen, render hopeless a consensus on the beginning of the body of the letter. Furthermore (as noted in the Introduction), we need not think that Paul was straitjacketed by the theoretical epistolary patterns of his day. In fact, the presence of several thanksgiving notices should signal the greater importance for Paul of continuously giving thanks, just as he later directly exhorts the church to do (5:18).

Two important conclusions made by epistolary analysis, however, are fruitful for our discussion. First, although the largely autobiographical nature of the first three chapters and the abundance of imperatives in the last two could lead some interpreters to see a radical divide between these two sets of chapters, epistolary analysis suggests that the end of chapter 3 (3:9-13) functions like a hinge. That is, the final thanksgiving (3:9) and prayer formula (a petition, 3:10; and a concluding wish-prayer, 3:11-13)[40] together echo not only the earlier issues of Paul's desired visit (3:10; cf. 2:17-18) or the church's need for strength (3:13; cf. 3:2-3), but also the later issues about the life of holiness (3:13; cf. 4:3-8) and love (3:12; cf. 4:9-12) and about the parousia (3:13; cf. 4:13–5:11).[41] So it is not the case that only chapters 4 and 5 are exhortative. As with other letters of exhortation, additional features of exhortation—not just the inclusion of imperatives—are also prominent. First Thessalonians' focus on the imitation of models (1:6; 2:14), its use of prayer forms (1:2-5; 2:13; 3:9-13; 5:23), and the recalling of a teacher's previous instructions and deeds (2:1-12; 3:4; 4:2, 6) also bespeak its exhortative interest. Thus the entire letter is exhortative.

Second, if Jeffrey Weima is correct in his assertion that the Pauline letter closings, or postscripts, usually begin with a peace formula, that found in 5:23 ("May the God of peace . . . ") marks a separate, final section in the letter (5:23-28).[42]

If we accept these results of epistolary analysis along with other distinctive markers, it is possible to support the division of the proof section into three discrete, yet interrelated, parts (1:6–2:16; 2:17–3:13; 4:1–5:22). Two additional pieces of

---

40. E.g., Peter T. O'Brien, *Introductory Thanksgivings in the Letters of Paul* (Leiden: Brill, 1977) 156.

41. Ibid., 160.

42. Jeffrey Weima, *Neglected Endings: The Significance of the Pauline Letter Closing* (Sheffield: JSOT, 1994) 187.

evidence justify this partition. First, an obvious transitional marker between the material in the first three chapters and the last two is the adverb "finally" (λοιπόν *loipon*) in 4:1. In the undisputed Pauline letters, this same transitional expression marks a letter's final unit (cf. 2 Cor 13:11) or the last subsection of a unit (cf. Phil 3:1). Therefore, the presence of "finally" (*loipon*) suggests that 1 Thess 4:1 begins a new and final unit of the proof, though not one totally distinct from the previous material. Second, relative changes in the temporal perspectives of discrete units of 1 Thessalonians separate some parts of the letter from others. Accordingly, from 1:6 to 2:16, Paul remarks for the most part on events occurring in the more distant past. In 2:17–3:13, he turns to the more recent past to accentuate the struggles and joys of his leadership team and the church up to the time of the letter's composition. In 4:1–5:22, Paul shifts to a mostly imperatival form to signal the behavior he desires in the believers' future, though to some extent he acknowledges that they are already doing what he wants them to continue to do. Thus the transitional nature of 3:9-13, the delineation of 5:23-28 as a separate part of the letter, the transitional marker "finally" in 4:1, and the letter's relative temporal changes all render the document into three separate units for the proof section.

1 THESSALONIANS 1:6–2:16, A GOSPEL OF CONSISTENT POWER

OVERVIEW

It is possible to demonstrate on rhetorical grounds that Paul's audience would have heard all of 1:6–2:16 as a string of three subunits (1:6-10; 2:1-12; 2:13-16). In accordance with one of the themes of the exordium (1:1-5), these three subunits together depict the effectiveness of the word of God (or gospel) and the pastoral care of Paul's leadership team.

Two of the subunits (1:6-10; 2:13-16) are parallel in their sequential development and in their effect. In their sequential development, these subunits practically begin with an emphasis on the church's commendable "reception" (δεξάμενοι *dexamenoi*, 1:6; ἐδέξασθε *edexasthe*, 2:13) of the word of God. Each subunit then continues its commendation of the church with illustrations of the believers' moral growth beyond their reception of the word even in the face of local opposition. So, in 1:6-10, Paul notes not only the church's initial reception of the word in affliction (1:6), but he also notes the church's continuing exemplary status as evinced by other believers (whose reports validated the Thessalonian believers' fundamental break with an old way of life and their continuing movement along the trajectory of their new lives, 1:9-10). And in 2:13-16, again Paul notes both the initial reception of the word (2:13*a*) and its ongoing work among the believers (2:13*b*) as revealed in their survival despite separation from their leaders (in a manner similar to the survival of the churches of Judea, 2:14-15). Finally, each subunit concludes with a note about God's wrath (1:10; 2:16; cf. Rom 1:2-8, 32; 2:8-9).

In their effect, both 1:6-10 and 2:13-16 have three goals. For one, they signal the importance of the word of God to the church in the foundational moments. "Word" here does not refer to the OT or the LXX but to an inspired word about God's actions in Christ that the foundational leaders preached to the church at Thessalonica. Second, these subunits widen the angle of Paul's scope to remind the church of other believers with whom they have solidarity, either because the church has become a model of endurance itself (1:7) or because the church has imitated the endurance of others (1:6; 2:14). Third, these subunits encourage constancy or forbearance, another theme of the exordium (1:1-5), simply by amplifying that theme. In 1:6-10, the two infinitives "to serve" (δουλεύειν *douleuein*, 1:9) and "to wait" (ἀναμένειν *anamenein*, 1:10) signal both the community's constant devotion to a new way of life and their ongoing confidence in the return of Jesus. And in 2:13-16, the church's ability to survive beyond the initial foundational visit attests to its continuing forbearance. Thus the two subunits are parallel and direct their focus to the effectiveness of the word of God and of the leaders in shaping the Thessalonian believers into emulators and models of endurance.

With the second subunit (2:1-12), a virtual explanation of 1:6-10, Paul shifts to an emphasis on his leadership team. Yet the emphasis is not on the team's defense, as if it must exonerate itself against claims of financial exploitation or alterations in its theology, as some scholars have argued. Rather, it is on the team's ability to continue in its goals of the proclamation of the gospel and of the shaping and nurturing of the Thessalonian church despite the repeated instances of hostility the believers faced.

1 Thessalonians 1:6-10, An Unstoppable Word

NIV

⁶You became imitators of us and of the Lord; in spite of severe suffering, you welcomed the message with the joy given by the Holy Spirit. ⁷And so you became a model to all the believers in Macedonia and Achaia. ⁸The Lord's message rang out from you not only in Macedonia and Achaia—your faith in God has become known everywhere. Therefore we do not need to say anything about it, ⁹for they themselves report what kind of reception you gave us. They tell how you turned to God from idols to serve the living and true God, ¹⁰and to wait for his Son from heaven, whom he raised from the dead—Jesus, who rescues us from the coming wrath.

NRSV

⁶And you became imitators of us and of the Lord, for in spite of persecution you received the word with joy inspired by the Holy Spirit, ⁷so that you became an example to all the believers in Macedonia and in Achaia. ⁸For the word of the Lord has sounded forth from you not only in Macedonia and Achaia, but in every place your faith in God has become known, so that we have no need to speak about it. ⁹For the people of those regions[a] report about us what kind of welcome we had among you, and how you turned to God from idols, to serve a living and true God, ¹⁰and to wait for his Son from heaven, whom he raised from the dead—Jesus, who rescues us from the wrath that is coming.

[a] Gk *For they*

COMMENTARY

As Paul begins to describe events in the more distant past, he commences in 1:6-10 with the foundational moments as he recalls them and as others have reported them to him. A critical element in the church's foundation is the role of the word of God. It is the "word" (of God) that the Thessalonians received in spite of "persecution" (1:6).[43] The result of that reception in the midst of persecution was not a weakening of his

team's efforts. Rather, as indicated in a result clause (1:7), the Thessalonians became an "example" (τύπος *typos*) to other believers. Furthermore, the continuing power of the gospel has been demonstrated beyond the confines of Thessalonica, for Paul describes the "echoing" (ἐξηχέομαι *exēcheomai*) of the word of God in other parts of Macedonia and also in Achaia (1:8).

Thus Paul's earlier declaration of the gospel's power on the church (cf. 1:5) now receives elaboration with a striking description of the gospel's continuing power (1:6-10). With hyperbole, an apocalyptic orientation, and stirring images drawn

43. "Persecution" here and elsewhere in the commentary does not imply a widescale assault on Christianity. Rather, it refers to the experience of some kind of undefined and localized harassment by Paul and those who would have read 1 or 2 Thessalonians.

from the currencies of his day, moreover, Paul lauds the Thessalonian believers for their imitation of their foundational leaders and the Lord, their own model behavior, and the persistence of their faith as acknowledged by others. Surely, his description of the church's exemplary behavior is exaggerated (1:8). In contrast to persons dwelling in the two Roman provinces of Macedonia and Achaia, could persons in every place (1:8) have known about the church's "faith in God"? Or does Paul here speak as one who wants to demonstrate his church's vitality by speaking about its renown in increasingly wider regions?

Notwithstanding Paul's exaggeration, the apocalyptic time in which the church's formation occurs is depicted in a straightforward manner. Two expressions, "persecution" (θλῖψις *thlipsis*, 1:6) and "wrath" (ὀργή *orgē*, 1:10), frame 1:6-10 and capture Paul's apocalyptic orientation. The first is a general category for affliction (cf. 3:3-4, 7) and probably refers to the Jewish apocalyptic belief that certain woes would precede the consummation of the new age (Dan 12:1; Matt 24:9-14; Mark 13:19, 24). The second is an expression connoting God's coming vengeance, from which the Thessalonians, in Paul's apocalyptic framework, are rescued. The church is praised, then, not only because it faced apocalyptic persecution from the very beginning of its existence, but also because its zeal, as given in the reports of others, has not flagged. Thus the power of the gospel is not a singular, one-time force on the church at the moment of the church's incorporation into the family of God. Even now its power continues to make an impact on the church as the believers await Jesus' return.

To describe the extraordinary change in the lives of believers, Paul depends on three well-known images from his day: imitation, "turning," and slavery. The language of imitation was prevalent in Paul's time. Teachers often noted exemplary figures for their students.[44] Philosophers held up models from the past or present for emulation. Paul himself frequently uses the diction of imitation to talk about his relationship with the members of his churches (1 Cor 4:6; 11:1; Phil 3:17; 1 Thess 1:16; cf. 1 Cor 4:6; Gal 4:12). Notable in this case, however, is the church's impressive

move from imitation (1:6) to example (1:7). That is, the church has so well grasped the conviction of those it imitated that it is now itself a model for other believers.

"Turning" language was equally prevalent in Paul's time. The word "to turn" (ἐπιστρέφω *epistrephō*, 1:9) was used in philosophical circles as one of the key words describing conversion to a philosophy.[45] Elsewhere, Paul uses the expression to speak about entrance into a new way of life (2 Cor 3:16; Gal 4:9). Others in Macedonia and Achaia were reporting the fundamental break, or turning, of the Thessalonian believers from their former cultic memberships to a new way of life (1:9).

The parlance of slavery was also commonplace in Paul's time, to describe both physical slavery and the powers over one's life in a metaphorical way. In his other letters Paul uses the diction of slavery repeatedly to depict the status of Jesus or of believers. In Philippians Paul calls himself and Timothy "slaves [δοῦλοι *douloi*] of Christ Jesus" (1:1) and later speaks of Jesus as one who took on the form of a "slave" (δοῦλος *doulos*, 2:7). Beyond its opening, where Paul both calls himself a "slave of Jesus Christ" (Rom 1:1) and speaks of the Romans as a part of the nations brought to "obedience" (ὑπακοη *hypakoē*, 1:5), the letter to the Romans redounds with the language of slavery. On the one hand, Paul writes about slavery to sin (6:6, 17, 20) and to decay (8:19-21), about a spirit of slavery (8:15), of obedient slaves to sin (6:16), and of "obedience to passions" (ὑπακούειν ταῖς ἐπιθυμίαις αὐτου *hypakouein tais epithymiais autou,* 6:12). On the other hand, he writes about a slavery to righteousness (6:17) and to God (6:22), about service (i.e., slavery) to God (12:11) and to the law of God (7:25), and about the "obedience" (*hypakoē*) that leads to righteousness (6:16).[46] In Galatians Paul combines the language of turning with that of slavery:

Formerly, when you did not know God, you were enslaved [ἐδουλεύσατε *edouleusate*] to beings that by nature are not gods. Now, however, that you have

---

44. Boykin Sanders, "Imitating Paul: I Cor. 4:16," *HTR* 74 (1981) 358.

45. Abraham J. Malherbe, *Paul and the Thessalonians: The Philosophic Tradition of Pastoral Care* (Philadelphia: Fortress, 1987) 26n. 89. On *epistrephō*, see (from Malherbe's list) Epictetus *Discourses* 3:16-15; 22:39; 23:16, 37; 4:4, 7.

46. For a careful look at Paul's slave terminology in Romans 8, see Wayne Rollins, "Greco-Roman Slave Terminology," *1987 SBL Papers,* ed. Kent H. Richards (Atlanta: Scholars Press, 1987).

come to know God, or rather to be known by God, how can you turn [ἐπιστρέφετε *epistrephete*] back again to the weak and beggarly elemental spirits? How can you want to be enslaved [δουλεῦσαι *douleusai*] to them again? (Gal 4:8-9 NRSV)

Paul evidently found little problem employing the category of slavery in his arguments. Thus in the case of 1 Thessalonians, Paul uses the infinitive "to serve" (δουλεύειν *douleuein*, 1:9) to characterize the church's new allegiance.

Although some scholars think the phrases and themes of 1:9-10 are so unlike the rest of Paul that this material is temporally pre-Pauline, others suggest that the unusual wording is to be expected because Paul indicates that he is only reporting what others have said. Thus the verses, they assume, are contemporary to Paul's time, and they likely reflect a view of Christian beliefs espoused by other Jewish Christian preachers—a view that Paul edited for his purposes.[47]

In the case of the former opinion, some scholars hold that the expression "turned to God from idols," along with the description of God as "living and true," was a typical message preached to Gentiles before Paul's time. Some even locate the setting of the messages in the diaspora synagogue, where it is assumed that Gentiles would have first heard the Christian gospel.

In the case of the latter opinion, some scholars argue that 1:9-10 seems to combine a message about the role of Jesus as an eschatological deliverer (in line with the Son of Man christology one finds in Q, the common source found in Matthew and Luke) to Paul's own interest in Jesus as the Son of God and as a resurrected figure.[48] Thus they insist that Paul simply revised a message that was probably preached elsewhere by others during the tenure of his ministry.

While either position may well be true, the debate need not consume us because we have no evidence that Paul's readers (or auditors) would have been able to make the distinctions assumed about Paul's redaction and the kinds of sources he used. More critical to Paul's young church was that these verses were written to inspire the believers to see that they were no longer subject to the presumed powers of the false gods (cf. 1 Cor 8:5) in whom they had originally believed. And against the possible temptation to return to the cult memberships of their non-Christian neighbors, the members of the church would now hear reminders of their new, distinctive, and ongoing life as believers.

Thus in the opening subunit of the proof, Paul's laudation describes the extraordinary change wrought on the lives of the Thessalonians. This laudation, however, actually commends the unstoppable character of the word of God. Neither difficulties nor distance can overcome it.

47. Earl J. Richard, *First and Second Thessalonians,* Sacra Pagina (Collegeville, Minn.: Liturgical, 1995) 75.

48. Ibid., 56, 75.

REFLECTIONS

In the aftermath of WWI, the English poet W. B. Yeats penned "The Second Coming," a prophetic poem of approaching anarchy. He wrote "things fall apart; the centre cannot hold," and he spoke of the crumbling of certainties on which people had grounded their lives. In like manner, Chinua Achebe's novel *Things Fall Apart* tells the story of an Igbo (Nigerian) farmer who commits suicide rather than face another day of his culture's disintegration. The center did not hold.

A meaningful life requires reliable resources—not a round of fads and fashions or words that fail to hold up under the heat of struggle. It is unfortunate that many people rest their fortunes and their lives on things that cannot hold: on beauty that fades, on perishable pharaohs who know Joseph, on antiquated perceptions, on supposed truths that last for but a season. When our lives are built on things that fall apart, consistency is difficult to maintain, and the end result may be disillusionment and the death of the spirit.

What helped the believers in Paul's young church at Thessalonica to remain stable? What helped them move from being imitators to being examples? What buoyed their lives so that despite affliction they served God and waited on their deliverance through Christ? It was their full reception of God's unstoppable word to them, the word that remained a reliable resource in their lives.

For us today, the unfailing truth of God's promises still provides us with a center that holds. When wells dry up, when famine comes, when disaster ruins all that is around us, the word of God remains a ready and reliable resource. It is both a ballast and a buffer—a ballast bringing security to otherwise insecure lives—and a buffer to shield us from self-destruction. R. Kelso Carter was right to sing:

> Standing on the promises that cannot fail,
> When the howling winds of doubt and fear assail,
> By the living Word of God I shall prevail,
> Standing on the promises of God.

1 Thessalonians 2:1-12, Continuing with the Gospel

NIV

2 You know, brothers, that our visit to you was not a failure. ²We had previously suffered and been insulted in Philippi, as you know, but with the help of our God we dared to tell you his gospel in spite of strong opposition. ³For the appeal we make does not spring from error or impure motives, nor are we trying to trick you. ⁴On the contrary, we speak as men approved by God to be entrusted with the gospel. We are not trying to please men but God, who tests our hearts. ⁵You know we never used flattery, nor did we put on a mask to cover up greed—God is our witness. ⁶We were not looking for praise from men, not from you or anyone else.

As apostles of Christ we could have been a burden to you, ⁷but we were gentle among you, like a mother caring for her little children. ⁸We loved you so much that we were delighted to share with you not only the gospel of God but our lives as well, because you had become so dear to us. ⁹Surely you remember, brothers, our toil and hardship; we worked night and day in order not to be a burden to anyone while we preached the gospel of God to you.

¹⁰You are witnesses, and so is God, of how holy, righteous and blameless we were among you who believed. ¹¹For you know that we dealt with each of you as a father deals with his own children, ¹²encouraging, comforting and urging you to live lives worthy of God, who calls you into his kingdom and glory.

NRSV

2 You yourselves know, brothers and sisters,ᵃ that our coming to you was not in vain, ²but though we had already suffered and been shamefully mistreated at Philippi, as you know, we had courage in our God to declare to you the gospel of God in spite of great opposition. ³For our appeal does not spring from deceit or impure motives or trickery, ⁴but just as we have been approved by God to be entrusted with the message of the gospel, even so we speak, not to please mortals, but to please God who tests our hearts. ⁵As you know and as God is our witness, we never came with words of flattery or with a pretext for greed; ⁶nor did we seek praise from mortals, whether from you or from others, ⁷though we might have made demands as apostles of Christ. But we were gentleᵇ among you, like a nurse tenderly caring for her own children. ⁸So deeply do we care for you that we are determined to share with you not only the gospel of God but also our own selves, because you have become very dear to us.

9You remember our labor and toil, brothers and sisters;ᵃ we worked night and day, so that we might not burden any of you while we proclaimed to you the gospel of God. ¹⁰You are witnesses, and God also, how pure, upright, and blameless our conduct was toward you believers. ¹¹As you know, we dealt with each one of you like a father with his children, ¹²urging and encouraging you

ᵃ Gk brothers   ᵇ Other ancient authorities read *infants*

and pleading that you lead a life worthy of God,
who calls you into his own kingdom and glory.

COMMENTARY

Paul's introduction of the word "welcome" or "entrance" (εἴσοδος *eisodos*, 1:9) was likely a preparation for his use of the same word later when he describes the foundational "visit" (*eisodos*, 2:1) of his leadership team. In Greek, 2:1-12 is divisible into four discrete sections (vv. 1-2; vv. 3-4; vv. 5-8; vv. 9-12) by the repetition of a single transitional marker: "for" (γάρ *gar*). Still, the repetition of the word "gospel" (vv. 2, 4, 8, 9) in all four sections suggests that the common theme of the sections is the foundational leaders' continuous use of the gospel. Thus with a shift in focus from the church to the foundational leaders, Paul now continues his elaboration of the gospel's power (cf. 1:5) as it was used by his leadership team. As we shall see, the team never parted from the use of the gospel and maintained impeccable character despite repeated difficulties.

2:1-2. The first section, cast in the vocabulary of an athletic metaphor, presents the basic theme of the entire subunit—commitment to the noblest declaration and inculcation of the gospel's teaching despite continuing insults. With the expression "great opposition" (πολλῷ ἀγῶνι *pollō agōni,* v. 2), literally a "great contest," Paul speaks of the foundational leaders' difficulties in athletic terms, a commonplace among the Cynic and Stoic philosophers of his day.[49] Moreover, Paul's description of the difficulties in Philippi ("we had already suffered and been shamefully mistreated [προπαθόντες καὶ ὑβρισθέντες *propathontes kai hybristhentes*]") and of the foundational team's "courage" (ἐπαρρησιασάμεθα *eparrēsiasametha*) draws on the coinage of the Cynic philosophers' tradition of suffering.[50] Unlike the Cynics and the Stoics, however, the source of Paul's courage lies in God (v. 2), not in the individual. As readers would recall, although Paul mentions the foundational leaders' experience

of "great opposition" (πολλῷ ἀγῶνι *pollō agōni*, v. 2) and he notes his church's reception of the word "in spite of persecution" (or better, "in great persecution" [ἐν θλίψει πολλῃ *en thlypsei pollē*], 1:6), he also notes in his exordium that the gospel came to the church not only in word, but also "with full conviction" (ἐν πληροφορίᾳ πολλῃ *en plērophoria pollē*, 1:5). Thus, unlike the Cynics and Stoics of Paul's day, the sufficiency of the foundational leaders and of the church was not in themselves, but in God—in the one who had brought about a conviction that was sufficient to meet every opposition that the believers would face. Furthermore, the struggle in which Paul is engaged is also different from that of the Cynics and the Stoics. For Paul, the contest is in the arena of proclaiming the gospel, not in all of life.[51]

The rich texture of antitheses in the second and third sections has suggested to many scholars that Paul seeks here to distinguish the foundational leaders from the hucksters who abused the otherwise noble philosophical practices of Paul's day. The distinction here from sham philosophers, however, should be viewed more as self-description than self-defense. Paul never says that he has been accused of improper motives, goals, methods, or actions. Furthermore, Abraham Malherbe has shown that some ancient philosophers[52] within the hortatory tradition used the antithetical style and even some of the same diction as 2:1-12 not in response to an actual accusation, but as a way of distinguishing what they did from other philosophers.[53]

2:3-4. In the second section Paul highlights his team's endurance and the distinctiveness of their motives and goals vis-à-vis the sham philosophers of the day. The vices listed in v. 3 (deceit, impure motives, trickery) were typical of charla-

49. See Epictetus *Diss.* 1.24.1-2.
50. Abraham J. Malherbe, "Exhortation in First Thessalonians," *NovT* 25 (1983) 249.

51. Richard, *First and Second Thessalonians,* 93.
52. E.g., the Stoic Dio Chrysostom in *Discourses* 32.
53. Abraham J. Malherbe, *Paul and the Thessalonians: The Philosophic Tradition of Pastoral Care* (Philadelphia: Fortress, 1987) 3-4.

tans.[54] By contrast, Paul's team has "been approved," literally tested through trial. And with language reminiscent of Jer 11:20 and 12:3, Paul speaks of God's continuous, ongoing testing of the foundational team's hearts (cf. Gal 1:10; Prov 17:3).

2:5-8. In the third section Paul shifts from a focus on the source of the foundational leaders' courage and the nature of their motivations to their pedagogical style. With an appeal to the auditors' knowledge and to God as a witness (whether read simply as an oath or also as an allusion to Job 16:19 or Ps 89:37),[55] Paul lauds the foundational team for neither demanding glory (as did charlatans) nor treating their novices harshly (as did some austere philosophers). Thus, on the one hand, Paul and his coworkers avoided using flattery to gain goodwill[56] and even refused to exercise their rights or "demands" (βάρος *baros*; lit., using their "weight"). On the other hand, these leaders (like some of the Cynics) also avoided the method of severe criticism, seeking rather to exercise compassionate persuasion.

It should be noted that interpretations of v. 7 vary because the manuscript evidence is divided. A single Greek letter, ν (*n*), is added to the Greek word ἤπιοι (*ēpioi*, "gentle") in some manuscripts of 1 Thessalonians but not in others. So scholars wonder if Paul actually wrote "we were gentle" or "we were infants [νήπιοι *nēpioi*]" (see the NRSV note to v. 7). In the latter case, Paul would be saying that "the apostles were not 'heavies,' making much of themselves through various demands (v. 7*a*), but were as unassuming among the Thessalonians as infants."[57]

This commentary, however, agrees with those scholars who consider "gentle" (ἤπιοι *ēpioi*) to be the original formulation because Paul does not usually use νήπιοι (*nēpioi*, "infants") positively (cf. Rom 2:20; 1 Cor 3:1; 13:11; Gal 4:1, 3). Furthermore, if Paul draws on language found within the philosophical hortatory tradition throughout 2:1-12, it would not be uncommon for him to combine "gentleness" and nurse im-

agery. In his work *How to Tell a Flatterer from a Friend* (69 BCE), for example, Plutarch, in an attempt to critique the severe type of philosopher, writes:

> The very circumstances in which the unfortunate find themselves leave them no room for frank speaking and sententious saws, but they do require gentle usage and help. When children fall down, the nurses do not rush up to them to berate them, but they take them, wash them up, and straighten their clothes, and, after all this is done, they then rebuke and punish them.[58]

Perhaps anticipating his use of the father/children metaphor to describe the foundational leaders' relationship to this church (v. 11; cf. 1 Cor 4:14-17; 2 Cor 6:11-13; Phlm 10), Paul initially writes about the nurse/children relationship. Nurses in that society were cherished for the affection they showed to children, and the idea of a nurse caring for her own children intensifies that affection.[59] Given the context of Paul's self-description of the foundational leaders' pedagogical style, moreover, Paul's use of the metaphor focuses on the role of nurses in the maturation of children or, in this case, the maturation of the Thessalonian believers (cf. Gal 4:19). In accordance with his mission of forming, shaping, and nurturing communities, Paul and his coworkers reached out to their own children during the foundational moments to shape them without severe chastisement. Ever noting the consistency of the foundational team's effort in those moments, Paul shifts metaphors from nurse to father as an oblique suggestion that the maturation process did not stop. From the earliest foundational moments to later ones, Paul and his coworkers continued to shape the development of the Thessalonian church.

2:9-12. Continuing the basic self-description of the foundational leaders' commitment, a fourth section commends the leadership team's self-sufficiency, evinces the effectiveness of the team's continuing pedagogical style, and orients the auditors toward God's rule and glory (not that of others). Paul's foundational team worked "night and day" (v. 9)—that is, constantly—to sustain themselves as they preached the gospel and not

---

54. Abraham J. Malherbe, "Gentle as a Nurse: The Cynic Background to 1 Thess 2," *NovT* 12 (1970) 203-17.

55. On the witness diction, see Charles Wanamaker, *The Epistles to the Thessalonians,* NIGTC (Grand Rapids: Eerdmans, 1990) 97.

56. As did philosophers like Dio Chrysostom (*Discourses* 32) and Plutarch (*Ad Apollonium* 117F) as well.

57. Beverly R. Gaventa, *First and Second Thessalonians,* Interpretation (Louisville: John Knox, 1998) 27.

58. Malherbe, *Paul and the Thessalonians,* 55.

59. Earl J. Richard, *First and Second Thessalonians,* Sacra Pagina (Collegeville, Minn.: Liturgical, 1995) 100.

"to burden" (ἐπιβαρεω *epibareō*) financially or literally "to weigh in on" (cf. "demands," βάρος *baros,* in v. 7) anyone in the church (cf. 2 Cor 11:9*b*). Exactly what type of work they did in Thessalonica is unknown, although some scholars infer manual labor through a reading of 1 Cor 4:12. What is clearer, however, is that Paul continued a pattern that he used elsewhere of never receiving funds from a church while he worked among the believers to establish and shape that church (2 Cor 11:7-9; Phil 4:15-16), even though Paul acknowledged that he had a right to be sustained financially for his work in proclaiming the gospel (1 Cor 9:14-18). What is also clear is that Paul's reference to the foundational team's self-sufficiency not only shows the great affection the team had for the Thessalonian believers, but it also serves as a model for them. Later Paul will charge the Thessalonians to "work with your hands" with the goal of not being dependent on outsiders (4:11).

Indeed, Paul's reference to the character and care of the foundational team's pedagogical activity throughout these verses is intended to be paradigmatic. Paul's description of the team as "holy," "righteous," and "blameless" (ἀμέμπτως *amemptōs,* v. 10) at the foundational moments describes the type of character he desires among the Thessalonians, as revealed in his later wish-prayers (3:13 and 5:23). These wish-prayers show Paul's concern for the believers' sanctification or ongoing maturation, for he prays that their hearts might be established "unblamable in holiness" (ἀμέμπτους ἐν ἁγιωσύνη *amemptous en hagiōsynē,* 3:13) and that God will "sanctify" (ἁγιάζω *hagiazo*) them and make them "blameless" (ἀμέμπτως *amemptōs,* 5:23).

Likewise, the individuated care of Paul and his coworkers for members of the church is paradigmatic. That is, the foundational team was like fathers with their children, exhorting "each one of you" (v. 11). Like many philosophers in his day, Paul offered individuated pastoral care, and he seems to commend the same in his later advice when he urges the church to offer aid for different types of needs among the believers (5:14).

All of Paul's hortatory expressions in vv. 11-12 ("urging," παρακαλου ντες *parakalountes*; "encouraging," παραμυθούμενοι *paramythoumenoi*; and "pleading," μαρτυρόμενοι *martyromenoi*)

are paradigmatic as well. Paul uses παρακαλέω (*parakaleō*)—a word for which he displayed a considerable fondness throughout his writings (cf. Rom 12:8; 1 Cor 1:10; 14:3; 2 Cor 8:17; 9:5; Phlm 9-10)—repeatedly in this letter to indicate general exhortation or consolation (a specific type of exhortation, 3:2, 7; 4:1, 10, 18; 5:11, 14; cf. 2:3). The second of these hortatory terms, while not as common in Paul's letters as the first one (cf. Phil 2:1), appears again in 5:14 when Paul commends care for the fainthearted: "encourage the fainthearted." While the third term is rare in Paul (cf. Gal 5:3) and appears later in 1 Thessalonians in a different form ("solemnly warned," διαμαρτύρομαι *diamartyromai,* 4:6), Paul's exhortation with all three expressions had the goal of helping the church "to conduct [περιπατέω *peripateō*] . . . a life [or "to walk" or "live"] worthy of God" (v. 12). Thus all three terms, like those that described the special character of the foundational leaders among the believers (v. 10), were related to the development of the community's distinctive ethos.

As readers will recall, the church's distinctiveness was a key theme noted in the exordium. Its importance here for Paul, however, is made clearer when one notes this letter's repeated use of language related to walking. Paul's foundational concern that the church "walk" or (so NRSV) "lead" (περιπατεῖν *peripatein,* v. 12) a life worthy of God is the first instance of a refrain sounded again in the latter part of the letter (*peripatein,* "to walk" or "to live," 4:1; περιπατῆτε *peripatēte,* "to live," "to walk," or "to behave," 4:12).

Paul's imagery of "walking" could have emanated from Greco-Roman moral philosophy. Epictetus speaks of life as a walk or way.[60] Perhaps, however, the "walking" metaphor actually had its roots in the LXX (e.g., 1 Kgs 2:4; 36:6; Isa 38:3; Jer 3:17; 9:14; 11:8; Ezek 36:26-27). As a translation of the Hebrew word הלך (*hālak*), *peripateō,* or "walk," in the LXX usually connoted one's actions as "an expression of one's commitments and devotion."[61] According to James D. G.

---

60. Wilson includes the following ancient witnesses to the idea of "walking" as a way of life: Epictetus *Diatribae* 2.12.3; Plutarch *De Profectibus in Virtute* 76C; Maximus of Tyre Orations 16.2. See Walter T. Wilson, *The Hope of Glory: Education and Exhortation in the Epistle to the Colossians* (Leiden: Brill, 1997) 41.

61. For the previous list and the citation, see Joseph O. Holloway, "*Peripateo* as a Thematic Marker for Pauline Ethics" (Ph.D. diss., Southwestern Baptist Theological Seminary, 1990) 7.

Dunn, "the characteristic Jewish use [of *hālak*] was in commendation of a 'walk in the law/statutes/ordinances/ways of God' (hence 'halakah')."[62] Also since Paul had been a Pharisee (Phil 3:5), he would have been familiar with halakah, the oral laws that were transmitted in the Pharisaic schools.

In a letter concerned with the consistency and the commitment of the church's life before God, *peripateō* was an apt expression. The "walk" toward which Paul charged the church was one grounded in God's continuous call, as suggested by the present-tense participle "is calling" (καλοῦντος *kalountos*, v. 12). Moreover, in the light of the present opposition and Paul's assertion that the worthy walk is that of a God who "calls you into his kingdom" (i.e., a sphere of eschatological inheritance in which some of the benefits of the end time were already available; 1 Cor 6:9,10; cf. Rom 14:17; 1 Cor 4:20; 15:24; Gal 5:21), that walk was also apocalyptic. It was an ethical imperative that demanded of believers an unbroken commitment to holiness (cf. 4:1) or the life of the new age despite the fact that they lived among people who believed in neither the dawn of the new age nor its imminent consummation (see the Introduction).[63] Thus the ethos Paul commends is one in which the members of his church would seek to live worthy lives—lives that would reflect their persistence or sanctification and God's continuous call.

Altogether, then, the individual sections of vv. 1-12 laud the foundational leaders' persistence in their roles of proclaiming the gospel and nurturing the Thessalonian believers despite the hostility they encountered and in the light of the worthy walk to which their lives and that of the church were oriented. Just as the foundational leaders established the church with the gospel of God (v. 2), their shaping of the community throughout their tenure after the initial foundational preaching also was grounded in that gospel (v. 9). At no point did the severity and persistence of their opposition or the tests of God change their character, weaken their resolve to shape the distinctiveness of the Thessalonian church, or lessen their commitment to the gospel. This was a gospel worth starting with and staying with.

---

62. James D. G. Dunn, "Echoes of Intra-Jewish Polemic in Paul's Letter to the Galatians," *JBL* 112 (1993) 462.

63. Holloway, *"Peripateō* as a Thematic Marker for Pauline Ethics," 223-24.

REFLECTIONS

1. Among the images Paul uses in this section of the Thessalonian letter, that of the teacher/student relationship, deserves special attention. On a popular level, the value of teachers has been captured indelibly in such films as *To Sir, with Love, Mr. Holland's Opus,* and *Stand and Deliver.*

Long before Paul wrote 1 Thessalonians, the Greek world also knew the value of teachers. Homer introduced Mentor in the *Odyssey.* Aeschylus, the Athenian playwright, portrayed the legendary teacher Prometheus chained to a rock in *Prometheus Bound.* And Plato's *Apology* depicts Socrates as one who shared knowledge, not for pay, but out of a passionate commitment to teaching the truth.[64] Teachers in the Greek world and in the later Roman culture exercised a variety of roles, including that of psychagogy, the leading of the soul. Paul's ruminations on the teacher/student relationship reflect one of the standard rules for that relationship—namely, the practice of commending advice and aid suited to the particular disposition of each student. Central to this practice is a sense of the differing needs of each student. Thus Paul writes that the foundational leaders treated "each one of you like a father with his children" (2:11). Perhaps his later advice commending aid for different types of persons in the church (5:14) also indicates this pedagogical posture. Care for God's people today requires what Daniel O. Aleshire calls "the ministry of attending," the ministry of noticing carefully the development of individual believers so that "the Christian community of faith can help them learn a Christian way in the world and grow toward maturity in faith."[65] Not all believers are at the same place; not all grow at the same pace. But all deserve nurture and patience.

---

64. See Dona Gower, "Hero, Healer, and Martyr," *Parabola* 14 (1989) 46-49.
65. Daniel O. Aleshire, *Faithcare: Ministering to All God's People Through the Ages of Life* (Philadelphia: Westminster, 1988) 15.

---

2. Another promising image in this section is that of walking. "Walking" is a response to the calling of God, a walk defined neither by the individual nor by the society. The "walk worthy of God" is a walk that pleases God, a walk "in which God's own will rules, rather than selfish passions or greed."[66] It is a way of life not governed by our own sets of desires.

Nor is the walk governed by a set of desires routinized by polite societies and accepted by individuals to gain social prestige. Paul speaks about pleasing God, not people (2:4). He seeks not a transient "glory" from mortals, but the eternal "glory" into which God calls believers (2:12). The walk is a way of life in which one's prestige or worth comes not from one's kin and clan, but from one's alliance with God. What a measure of liberation is found in this walk. Here true prestige is not governed by the fads and fashions of society, not determined by the size of one's portfolio, and not hindered by the color of one's skin, the region of one's origins, or the pedigree of one's birth. Rather, the prestige of the walk is the kind we can assert simply from knowing that God has placed a claim on our lives.

66. Holloway, "*Peripateō* as a Thematic Marker for Pauline Ethics," 51.

1 Thessalonians 2:13-16, The Word's Relentless Power

NIV

[13]And we also thank God continually because, when you received the word of God, which you heard from us, you accepted it not as the word of men, but as it actually is, the word of God, which is at work in you who believe. [14]For you, brothers, became imitators of God's churches in Judea, which are in Christ Jesus: You suffered from your own countrymen the same things those churches suffered from the Jews, [15]who killed the Lord Jesus and the prophets and also drove us out. They displease God and are hostile to all men [16]in their effort to keep us from speaking to the Gentiles so that they may be saved. In this way they always heap up their sins to the limit. The wrath of God has come upon them at last.[a]

[a]16 Or *them fully*

NRSV

13We also constantly give thanks to God for this, that when you received the word of God that you heard from us, you accepted it not as a human word but as what it really is, God's word, which is also at work in you believers. [14]For you, brothers and sisters,[a] became imitators of the churches of God in Christ Jesus that are in Judea, for you suffered the same things from your own compatriots as they did from the Jews, [15]who killed both the Lord Jesus and the prophets,[b] and drove us out; they displease God and oppose everyone [16]by hindering us from speaking to the Gentiles so that they may be saved. Thus they have constantly been filling up the measure of their sins; but God's wrath has overtaken them at last.[c]

[a] Gk *brothers* [b]Other ancient authorities read *their own prophets*
[c]Or *completely* or *forever*

COMMENTARY

Given the focus on the word of the Lord or the gospel that characterized the two previous subunits, it is not surprising that Paul continues that theme in 2:13-16. Elaborating on the events of the foundational moments, Paul recalls the church's acceptance of the word of God for what it really was—not the words of humans, though it was communicated through human beings, but the word of God (v. 13*a*). Paul declares further that the same word is at work even now among the believers (v. 13*b*). Thus the word of God that could not be stopped and to which the foundational leaders remained committed is actively at work among the Thessalonians.

But how is this so? Paul's brief notice about the present work of the word is quickly followed by a longer, explanatory clause (vv. 14-16) that has been the subject of much controversy. Indeed, because of the apparently anti-Jewish tone of these verses, some interpreters have deemed vv. 14-16 to be an interpolation. The apparent theological difficulties of vv. 14-16 and the fact that v. 13 represents a second thanksgiving notice in this letter also has caused some scholars to see all of 2:13-16 as an interpolation, thus confusing, if not missing altogether, the real value of 2:13-16 in the letter.

A few words are in order, then, about the second thanksgiving notice in v. 13 and about the apparently anti-Jewish tone of vv. 14-16 before we can see the positive value of 2:13-16. In a letter in which one of the key themes is persistence, the appearance of a second thanksgiving notice is not unusual. Paul's repeated notices about thanksgiving throughout the letter (1:2-3; 2:13; 3:9-10) simply prepare the way for his request of the church to be thankful constantly (5:18). Furthermore, just as Paul earlier acknowledged his constant thanks to God ("We always give thanks to God," 1:2) for the church's steadfastness because of the power of the foundational leaders' word (1:5; cf. 2:1-12), so also he reminds his audience now of his continuous thanks ("We also constantly give thanks to God for this," 1:13) because of the church's acceptance of that same word as the word of God (2:13). There is not, then, an abrupt rupture between v. 12 and v. 13, as some commentators suggest. Just as vv. 1-12 imply that the inhospitable treatment meted out to Paul's leadership team in one city (Philippi) did not terminate their work among the Gentiles, so also vv. 13-16 imply, by analogy, the same effectiveness of the word in the church of the Thessalonians despite the inhospitable treatment of the foundational leaders by the church's neighbors.

As for the suggestion that 1 Thess 2:14-16 is a non-Pauline anti-Jewish interpolation, there is no manuscript support for this claim. Of course, some scholars think the expression "oppose everyone" (v. 15) reflects a typical slur made against Jewish people in the first century. Yet, whether Paul and the Thessalonians knew the negative ancient stereotype of the Jews as haters of non-Jewish people, a stereotype noted in Tacitus and in Josephus,[67] hardly matters because 1 Thess 2:14-16 is not directed toward all Jews—just

some. Obviously, Paul does not include himself in the lot. The prophets to whom he refers would themselves have been Jewish, but they, too, are not a part of the group against which Paul directs his polemic. According to Frank Gilliard the inclusion of a comma after "the Jews" in most English Bibles fails to indicate the way the rest of the Greek sentence restricts what is said about them. Paul's use of a participial phrase after "the Jews" reflects his customary use of a restrictive participial expression to qualify the meaning of the noun that precedes it. Thus Paul is not talking about *all* the Jews, just *some* Jews—those who opposed Jesus and his movement.[68]

If the passage is not directed against all the Jews, then any attempt to pinpoint "God's wrath" (v. 16) as being directed against all the Jews seems both speculative and misguided (although some interpreters still link God's wrath to the later destruction of the Temple or to the expulsion of the Jews from Rome in 49 CE or to the massacre of Jews in the temple court in 49 CE or to something else). And, if the passage is not directed against all the Jews, then it is also not in conflict with Romans 11, "where far from suggesting the final judgment of the Jews, [Paul] speaks concerning the continuing validity of God's covenant with them and indeed of their eventual salvation."[69]

Moreover, "in-house" Jewish debate was both active and vigorous in ancient times.[70] And Paul's expression "filling up the measure of their sins" is a typical lament "with which [some] Jews express[ed] their outrage at the faithlessness of other Jews."[71] It is not unreasonable to note, moreover, that members of certain minority groups within the Roman Empire would quickly quell the actions of other members of their own group at the slightest suggestion of subversive activity or if the actions outrightly could be deemed as treasonous by the imperial powers.

67. Tacitus *Histories* 5.5.2. Josephus *Against Apion* 2.121.

68. Frank Gilliard, "The Problem of the Anti-Semitic Comma between 1 Thessalonians 2:14 and 15," *NTS* 35 (1989) 481-502. Cf. W. D. Davies, "Paul and the People of Israel," *NTS* 24 (1977) 6-9; Willi Marxsen, *Der erste Brief an die Thessalonicher* (Zuerich: Theologischer Verlag, 1979) 149.

69. Donald Hagner, "Paul's Quarrel with Judaism," in *Anti-Semitism and Christianity: Issues of Polemic and Faith,* ed. Craig A. Evans and Donald A. Hagner (Minneapolis: Fortress, 1993) 131.

70. See, e.g., Josephus *Antiquities of the Jews* 1.15.91; Philo *Cherubim* 17. See Luke Timothy Johnson, "The New Testament's Anti-Jewish Slander and the Conventions of Ancient Polemic," *JBL* 108 (1989) 419-41; Hagner, "Paul's Quarrel with Judaism," 130-36.

71. Beverly R. Gaventa, *First and Second Thessalonians,* Interpretation (Louisville: John Knox, 1998) 37. As examples, Gaventa cites Dan 8:23; 2 Macc 6:14; Wis 19:3-5.

Yet what is often missed in readings of 2:14-16 is Paul's characterization of the relentlessness of those Jews who opposed the Judean churches. The litany of the opposition seems to go on and on until finally Paul concludes the list with the statement "they have constantly [πάντοτε *pantote*] been filling up the measure of their sins" (v. 16). The picture Paul draws is one of a group that appears to be unswerving in its efforts and obsessive in its pursuits.

With that description, three concerns seem critical for Paul. First, the description he gives is actually an analogy that depicts the character of the opposition in Thessalonica. Already Paul has mentioned the "persecution" (actually, the "great persecution") in which his Thessalonian church received the word (1:6) as well as the "great opposition" the foundational leaders faced in Thessalonica when they sought to declare the gospel (2:2). By analogy with the case of the Judean churches, what Paul now reveals is the constancy and relentlessness of that opposition in Thessalonica. That, of course, means that throughout the duration of the foundational visit, a time long enough for Paul to have received gifts "more than once" from the Philippians (Phil 4:16), his young church faced constant opposition. In fact, the end result of this opposition was the separation of the foundational leaders from the church, a topic Paul will take up explicitly in vv. 17-18.[72]

Second, the description also breathes with apocalyptic hope, as readers can see in v. 16*b,* the translation of which is also debated. Because 2:14-16 has often been read as a polemic against all Jews, some scholars have shied away from a translation of εἰς τέλος (*eis telos*) as "at last" or "forever" or "completely" (see the NRSV textual note to 2:16). Instead, preference is given to "until the end," which would correspond better with Rom 11:26. However, if readers interpret

the constancy of the aforementioned opposition as an indication of the apocalyptic worldview according to which the greater part of the old age's afflictions occur shortly before the end time (cf. Dan 12:1; Matt 24:9-14; Mark 13:19, 24), then "at last" or "finally" actually captures the apocalyptic urgency of the church's situation and conveys a word of assurance. In other words, Paul's reading of the times is that the greater volume of persecution that believers are now facing is an indicator of the imminence of the end. This interpretation, of course, requires that the verb that describes God's wrath be translated in a different way. Instead of rendering the expression as "God's wrath has overtaken [ἔφθασεν *ephthasen*] them at last," as in the NRSV, the text would read "God's wrath has drawn near [*ephthasen*] at last" (cf. Luke 11:20).[73]

Third, the description also speaks about the survival of the Thessalonian church despite constant opposition. What is often missed when considering this passage is that "the churches of God in Judea" (v. 14) evidently have survived. Even with the loss of their leaders—whether through death, as in the case of Christian prophets (e.g., Stephen and James the brother of John), or through separation, as with other Christian leaders like Paul, these churches did not disintegrate. Similarly, the church of Thessalonica, despite the absence of its leaders (as Paul will soon explicitly note, 3:6), still survives, a sign that God's word "is at work [right now] in you believers" (v. 13).

Thus after Paul gives a second thanksgiving report (v. 13*a*) and an acknowledgment of the auditors' acceptance of the foundational leaders' word (v. 13*b*), he then uses the diction of imitation to explain the ongoing effectiveness of the word on the church (vv. 14-16) and to amplify his earlier encomium about the church's endurance (1:1-10). In this case, however, Paul declares that the church became an imitator of the churches of God in Judea. What ties the church at Thessalonica to the churches of Judea, moreover, is the loss of its leaders, either through death or physical separation. So in 2:13-16, Paul describes what his church suffered throughout the duration of the foundational visit, especially the

---

72. While the order of the litany suggests opposition first to Jesus, then to the prophets (presumably Christian prophets because of the order), then to a group in which Paul includes himself, we are not given a specific timetable for the opposition of some Jews to Paul while he was with the Judean churches. From Acts, of course, some find opposition by Jewish persons to the Judean churches in Acts 8:1*bff.* and 11:19. If Paul indeed refers to this opposition, the irony is that he was driven out of Judea by an opposition of which he was originally a part. What seems clearer, however, is that Paul's language of being driven out from the churches of Judea is analogous to the same experience in Thessalonica and thus preparatory for 2:17. Even if the prophets are understood to be OT prophets on the order of Luke 13:31, the churches of Judea would still have lost those who were driven out with Paul.

73. I. H. Marshall, *1 and 2 Thessalonians* (Grand Rapids: Eerdmans, 1983) 80-81.

forced separation of its leaders from the believers (on the analogy of the Judean churches).

With 2:13-16, then, the first large unit of the letter (1:6–2:16) comes to a close. All three subunits highlight the effectiveness of the word of God on those who received it or on those who delivered it. All of 2:1-12 speaks of the word or gospel that Paul and his coworkers brought to the church (2:2-3, 5, 8-9). Both 1:6-10 and 2:13-16 speak of the word or gospel that the church heard. That word motivated its carriers and its receivers repeatedly to endure local hostility.

Thus Paul's first large unit does more than laud the church for its persistence. Implicitly, it indicates the resources for the church's persistence: the word or gospel and the leadership team's shaping and nurturing practices—its own persistence (vv. 1-2); its concern to please God, not others (vv. 3-8); its self-sufficiency (v. 9); its patience, evinced in Paul's metaphorical shift from "wet nurse" (v. 7) imagery to "father" imagery (vv. 11-12); its tailor-made psychagogy (v. 11); and its orientation toward a walk or way of life worthy of God (v. 12). In the next two large units, as we shall see, Paul will continue to give notice to these same resources for persistence.

REFLECTIONS

In his play *As You Like It,* Shakespeare wrote:

All the world's a stage,
And all the men and women merely players.
They have their exits and their entrances,
And one man in his time plays many parts.
(2.7.139)

On occasion, however, some characters or character groups play hidden roles off the observable stage of life. They never speak or move in the drama, but the audience knows that the story is not complete without them.

Because Christian anti-Semitism has repeatedly and regrettably clouded so much of the good that can be found in Christianity, many who read 1 Thess 2:13-16 fail to appreciate all of the characters implied in this brief drama of tensions. When fully appreciated, this section does not lend itself to the demonization of the Jews or of any other group. Paul's denunciation here of "some" Jews and "some" Gentiles, however, speaks about the ways in which strategies of containment work when people have to deal with the larger unspoken, but very real, forces of imperialism. Both Jews and the largely Greek population of Thessalonica lived under the shadow of Roman imperialism. And here and there some Jews and some Greeks exercised strategies of containment or control on those members of their own people who might be reckoned as subversive in the face of the Roman government.

Simplistic analyses of the imperial context of Paul's time thus lead many of us to overlook the other major character group in this drama: the Romans with their forces of imperialism. What this text should alert us to is the need to look for the hidden characters and forces that govern our culture and profoundly influence the way we think. The text suggests the need for us to "unmask the powers," Walter Wink's expression for exposing "the invisible, intangible interiority of collective enterprises, the invariant, determining forces of nature and society, or the archetypal images of the unconscious, all of which shape, nurture, and all too often cripple human existence."[74]

It is imperative that we ask ourselves: Do our responses to each other reflect greater fears and deeper anxieties that deserve scrutiny? Are we influenced by anxieties concerning our own survival? Our church's survival? All the world may be a stage, but many of the systems, ideas, and perspectives that influence us are standing in the wings.

74. Walter Wink, *Unmasking the Powers: The Invisible Forces That Determine Human Existence* (Philadelphia: Fortress, 1986) 173.

1 THESSALONIANS 2:17–3:13, CONCERN FOR THE CHURCH'S SURVIVAL AND MORAL TRAINING

OVERVIEW

After presenting a first large unit virtually on the earliest moments of the church's apocalyptic life (1:6–2:16), Paul now offers a second large unit that basically depicts a more recent period, from the departure of Paul's leadership team to the time of the letter's composition (2:17–3:13). Repetitive features suggest the configuration of this second large unit to be a series of three subunits. Two of the subunits are similar in that they treat the foundational leaders' desire to revisit the church (2:17-20; 3:9-13), while a central subunit indicates Timothy's role as an envoy between Paul and Silvanus, on the one hand, and the church of the Thessalonians, on the other hand (3:1-8).

The two outer subunits are similar to each other in form and diction. In form, both use rhetorical questions to echo the leadership team's joy about the community's expected (2:19) or present survival (2:20; 3:9). In diction, both subunits cite desired visits (2:17; 3:10), unsuccessful ones in the past (2:17), and a desired one in the future (3:10-11). Both mention as well a glorious apocalyptic visit or arrival: the parousia (2:19; 3:13), the present thought of which provides consolation for Paul's failed attempts to return to his church. The middle subunit (3:1-8) continues the theme of visits, but does so with two flashback sections on Timothy: one on his visit to the church (3:1-5) and another on his subsequent return to Paul (3:6-8). Altogether, the three subunits resound with the language of visits and the arrival of Jesus, the tenderest depictions of the foundational leaders' affection and their continuing concern about the church's ability to survive, and a vibrant example of Timothy's nurturing practices.

1 Thessalonians 2:17-20, Aborted Trips and the Parousia

NIV

[17]But, brothers, when we were torn away from you for a short time (in person, not in thought), out of our intense longing we made every effort to see you. [18]For we wanted to come to you—certainly I, Paul, did, again and again—but Satan stopped us. [19]For what is our hope, our joy, or the crown in which we will glory in the presence of our Lord Jesus when he comes? Is it not you? [20]Indeed, you are our glory and joy.

NRSV

[17]As for us, brothers and sisters,[a] when, for a short time, we were made orphans by being separated from you—in person, not in heart—we longed with great eagerness to see you face to face. [18]For we wanted to come to you—certainly I, Paul, wanted to again and again—but Satan blocked our way. [19]For what is our hope or joy or crown of boasting before our Lord Jesus at his coming? Is it not you? [20]Yes, you are our glory and joy!

[a] Gk brothers

COMMENTARY

With the first subunit (2:17-20), Paul explicitly notes the last local opposition that occurred during the foundational visit—namely, the abrupt forced separation of the leaders from the church. With language that expresses the depths of sorrow, Paul now describes the distress of this separation (v. 17) and laments the futility of his efforts to return (v. 18). He also neutralizes any possible discouragement about the aborted visits with a declaration of benefits accruing to another visit or arrival: the parousia, a future grand visit or arrival similar to that of Hellenistic kings and rulers (vv. 19-20).[75]

The account in the book of Acts seems to suggest that the departure of the leaders from the Thessalonian church was caused by Jewish agitation (Acts 17:5-9). However, Acts' reckoning of the events of Paul's work in Thessalonica is difficult to reconcile with Paul's own account in several ways. For one, as has already been noted (see the Introduction), Paul's Thessalonian converts included Jews and Gentiles according to Acts 17:1-4, but only Gentiles according to 1 Thess 1:9-10; 2:14-16. Second, although 1 Thessalonians seems to involve Timothy explicitly in the foundational work at Thessalonica (1:1; 3:1-2, 6), Acts directly mentions the difficulties Paul and Silas encountered in Philippi and Thessalonica but only directly notes Timothy when the three leaders are together in Beroea (Acts 17:14). Third, because the form of the word "alone" (μόνοι *monoi*, 3:1) is plural in Greek, Paul gives the impression that he and presumably Silvanus were in Athens when Timothy was sent to the Thessalonians. Acts gives the impression, however, that (after Beroea) Silvanus and Timothy did not join up with Paul until they arrived in Corinth (Acts 18:5).

However one seeks to reconcile these accounts, Paul seems less interested in naming the exact cause of the separation than in indicating the heavy toll it exacted on the entire leadership team and on his personal life. Having already noted the great anguish of the separation for the church (v.

14), Paul uses vv. 17-20 to show the effect of the separation from the vantage point of the foundational leaders. The expression "we were made orphans" sufficiently translates the Greek word that lies behind it (ἀπορφανισθέντες *aporphanisthentes*, v. 17); however, the NRSV adds "by being separated from you" (v. 17), although these words are not actually a part of the Greek text. Still, Paul's lament that his leadership team became orphans aptly catches the sense of deep grief caused by the separation.[76]

An indication of the depths of their grief is also shown in the way Paul heaps passionate phrases on top of one another to describe the attempts to return to Thessalonica. A literal translation of v. 17 would read: "As for us, brethren, when we were made orphans from you for a short time, in person [προσώπῳ *prosōpō*] not in heart, we even much more and with great longing made every effort to see your face [πρόσωπον *prosōpon*]."

As if the intensity of the leadership team's resolve is still not dramatized enough, however, Paul shifts from a description of the collective effects of the separation and recent endeavors to visit to his own personal strivings: "I, Paul . . . " (v. 18*b*). Shortly, as he continues to deal with the effects of the separation, Paul will similarly shift from the foundational leaders' inability to "bear" the separation to his own personal inability to do so (3:1, 5). For now, however, he seeks to expose the constancy of his effort to get back to the church. And constancy or persistence, as we have seen, is a recurring theme throughout the entire letter.

Exactly how often Paul tried to return is not known, for the expression "again and again" (lit., "once and twice [καὶ ἅπαξ καὶ δίς *kai hapax kai dis*]," v. 18*b*) connotes an "indefinite number of occasions"[77] (cf. Phil 4:16). Exactly what blocked his way is also not known, though some scholars speculate about a possible embargo or a physical malady.[78] What we do know, however,

---

75. Raymond Collins, *The Birth of the New Testament: The Origin and Development of the First Generation* (New York: Crossroad, 1993) 112.

76. Other writers in Paul's time (Seneca, e.g., in *Ad Helviam* 18.7) used the image of an orphan to describe feelings associated with exile.

77. I. H. Marshall, *1 and 2 Thessalonians* (Grand Rapids: Eerdmans, 1983) 86.

78. Ibid.

is that Paul's categorizing the obstruction as an effort of Satan is strategic on at least two levels.

On the one hand, this categorization reiterates Paul's apocalyptic ideas already noted in the letter. In his "already/not yet" apocalyptic understanding of reality, Satan is a deceiver who can take on the form of an angel of light, as can his envoys (2 Cor 2:11; 11:14). He is also a tempter (1 Cor 7:5; cf. 1 Thess 3:5) and one whom "God will shortly crush" (Rom 16:20). Thus, having already mentioned the "persecution" or "eschatological woes" (θλῖψις *thlipsis*, 1:6) in which the church received the word of God, Paul now highlights again the manifestations of the old age with a reference to the continuing hindrances of Satan. Once more, however, if the church recognizes that the intensity of the opposition described in vv. 14-16 is actually an indication of the imminence of God's wrath, the believers would likely recognize as well that Satan's repeated hindrances also signal the approaching end.

On the other hand, the categorization also anticipates Paul's next subunit, in which he will speak again in an oblique way about an evil force. In 3:5, Paul notes his former fear that the "tempter had tempted" his young church in the wake of his departure. Given that Satan was known as a tempter in Paul's apocalyptic worldview, it is likely that Paul is still speaking about the reality of the old age's pressure on believers (now with respect to the church). Indeed, Paul's use of the term "persecution" (θλίψεσιν *thlipsesin*, 3:3-4) also reinforces the apocalyptic context out of which Paul speaks. If he, indeed, is making the connection, he is also linking himself (and the other members of the leadership team) more solidly to his church. Both faced the pressures of the old age in the foundational moments of the work at Thessalonica; and the pressures continue.

Paul's reflections in vv. 17-20, however, do not end with his lament about the separation or his musings on Satan's hindrance. Because Satan's repeated hindrances would have signaled the imminence of the end to the Thessalonian addressees, Paul could not dwell on the hindrances alone. It is understandable why he would then launch out of the deep pathos of lamentation about the separation and aborted visits and shift the audi-

ence's thoughts to another visit or arrival, the parousia.

The word "parousia" has two essential meanings: "presence" (2 Macc 15:21; 3 Macc 3:17; 2 Cor 10:10; Phil 2:12) and "arrival" (Jdt 10:18; 2 Macc 8:12; 1 Cor 16:17; 2 Cor 7:6-7).[79] Howard notes that the word "came to have particular associations with the arrival of a central figure." The word indicated both "the physical act of arrival" and "the attendant circumstances in which the ruler was honored." It is generally believed that the early Christians adopted these "particular associations" to speak about Christ's coming. It is likely, moreover, that the term "would have evoked the image of the return of a triumphant conqueror in the Hellenistic world and the idea of a coronation on that occasion."[80]

For Paul, mentioning the parousia potentially had two results. First, with the imagery of a crown (v. 19), i.e., the laurel wreath won by an athletic victor, Paul could obliquely imply the success of his mission (cf. 1 Cor 9:25; Phil 4:1; 1 Thess 2:19). Presupposing the parousia as a time of mission assessment (cf. 1 Cor 4:10-15; 2 Cor 1:14), Paul makes the claim that the church will be his "crown of boasting" (cf. 1 Cor 9:25; Phil 4:1). That is, it will not disintegrate. The word of God that is still working in the believers will continue to do so (v. 13*b*), and the church will be the evidence of Paul's faithfulness to God in the call God assigned to him. Second, and related, because Paul and the Thessalonian believers will be together at the parousia, Paul is now neutralizing the present inability to get to them because of Satan's hindrances. Ultimately, he is suggesting that a reunion will occur between the foundational leaders and the church in spite of Satan's plots, even if that reunion must wait until his Lord's glorious parousia, the final blow to the manifestations of the old age. Indeed, he has joy (3:9) now as he thinks about the church in the light of that reunion. The church's joy was inspired by the Holy Spirit (1:6), God's pledge of all that is to come in the new age's consummation. Paul has joy as well as he thinks of that consummation. Satan has blocked his way, but not his joy.

79. Tracy Howard, "The Literary Unity of 1 Thessalonians 4:13-5:11," *Grace Theological Journal* 9 (1988) 176.
80. Collins, *The Birth of the New Testament,* 112.

REFLECTIONS

Joy comes in a number of forms. Some works of visual art evoke joy: the marvelous landscapes of Edward M. Bannister or the magnificent *Water Lilies* of Claude Monet. Some sights evoke joy: a view of the Mediterranean Sea from atop the Notre Dame de la Garde in Marseilles or the snow-capped peak of Mt. Ranier above Seattle's foggy mists. Some musical compositions or performances evoke sheer joy: Bach's Flute Concerto, Kathleen Battle's sweeping rendition of "Were You There When They Crucified My Lord?" or the voices of the three tenors, José Carreras, Placido Domingo, and Luciano Pavarotti.

Thefts, nature's path of destruction, and death, however, can deprive us of the beauty of these joys. Yet the joy of which Paul speaks has no favorite season beyond which it can be felt no more. It neither originates from nor depends on transient forces. It can be experienced by women and men who can claim it personally in their lives, but it is not an isolated, private joy. It is both a hope for concrete benefits in the future and a present reality.

This is the joy that breaks through the gloomiest of days to buoy the otherwise disheartened. This is the joy that comes not from changing circumstances, but from a constant presence in the believer's life, the Holy Spirit. This is the joy that arises out of sights that are sure but not yet fully seen or realized. This is the joy that can stir the heart of a man to write "It Is Well with My Soul" even after the loss of family members at sea, as if to transform incomprehensible sorrow through a tireless declaration of the believer's peace in God. This is the joy of bruised and berated black bards who defied their circumstances with the simplest, yet weightiest, of words: "This joy that I have, the world did not give it to me." This is the joy of Archbishop Romero, whose last letter before his assassination spoke of the "spirit of joy at being accorded the privilege of running the same risks as [the poor], as Jesus did by identifying with the causes of the dispossessed."[81] This is Paul's view of joy.

81. Oscar A. Romero, "Letter to Bishop Pedro Casaldaliga, March 24, 1980," in Jon Sobrino, *Archbishop Romero: Memories and Reflections,* trans. Robert R. Barr (Maryknoll, N.Y.: Orbis, 1990) 40.

1 Thessalonians 3:1-8, A Visit of Consolation in Hostile Times

NIV

3 So when we could stand it no longer, we thought it best to be left by ourselves in Athens. [2]We sent Timothy, who is our brother and God's fellow worker[a] in spreading the gospel of Christ, to strengthen and encourage you in your faith, [3]so that no one would be unsettled by these trials. You know quite well that we were destined for them. [4]In fact, when we were with you, we kept telling you that we would be persecuted. And it turned out that way, as you well know. [5]For this reason, when I could stand it no longer, I sent to find out about your faith. I was afraid that in some way the tempter might have tempted you and our efforts might have been useless.

a2 Some manuscripts brother and fellow worker; other manuscripts brother and God's servant

NRSV

3 Therefore when we could bear it no longer, we decided to be left alone in Athens; [2]and we sent Timothy, our brother and co-worker for God in proclaiming[a] the gospel of Christ, to strengthen and encourage you for the sake of your faith, [3]so that no one would be shaken by these persecutions. Indeed, you yourselves know that this is what we are destined for. [4]In fact, when we were with you, we told you beforehand that we were to suffer persecution; so it turned out, as you know. [5]For this reason, when I could bear it no longer, I sent to find out about your faith; I was afraid that somehow the tempter had tempted you and that our labor had been in vain.

a Gk lacks proclaiming

NIV

[6]But Timothy has just now come to us from you and has brought good news about your faith and love. He has told us that you always have pleasant memories of us and that you long to see us, just as we also long to see you. [7]Therefore, brothers, in all our distress and persecution we were encouraged about you because of your faith. [8]For now we really live, since you are standing firm in the Lord.

NRSV

6But Timothy has just now come to us from you, and has brought us the good news of your faith and love. He has told us also that you always remember us kindly and long to see us—just as we long to see you. [7]For this reason, brothers and sisters,[a] during all our distress and persecution we have been encouraged about you through your faith. [8]For we now live, if you continue to stand firm in the Lord.

[a] Gk brothers

COMMENTARY

Studies of the Thessalonian correspondence argue that the foundational leaders not only established the Thessalonian church and then gave it shape through the inculcation of a distinctive ethos, but also sought to nurture it. That is, the team sought to provide the church with sustenance for its ongoing growth. Examinations of the hortatory tradition reveal three of the basic strategies through which teachers nurtured their students: (1) the commissioning of an emissary, (2) the use of letters of exhortation, and (3) the commendation of mutual nurturing.[82]

Paul used all three of these strategies. The whole of 1 Thessalonians is a letter of exhortation. And within the letter Paul repeatedly instructs the Thessalonian believers to exhort (console, encourage, or admonish) one another (4:18; 5:11-14). Here, in 3:1-8, in the form of two flashbacks (vv. 1-5 and vv. 6-8), Paul reminds them of the work of his emissary Timothy.

With an initial flashback (vv. 1-5), Paul offers repeated remarks about Timothy's role as a proclaimer of the word and as one of the foundational leaders (vv. 1-3a, 5) and a parenthetical statement of the foundational team's forewarning about suffering (vv. 3b-4). Both the remarks and the statement are critical.

The remarks (vv. 1-3a, 5) have at least two functions. First, Paul's description of Timothy's visit reveals the nurturing role the latter played in his visit to the Thessalonians. That is, Timothy

was sent to "strengthen and to 'encourage'" (παρακαλέω *parakaleō*, v. 2), a role played by all the members of Paul's leadership team at their foundational visit in their "urging" (*parakaleō*; cf. 2:11) of the church. In that role, Timothy is described in the NRSV as "our brother and co-worker for God in . . . the gospel of Christ" (v. 2; cf. 2 Cor 6:2). While some manuscripts support the description of Timothy as "God's servant" or "our fellow-worker" or some combination of the two, most scholars accept the manuscript tradition that describes Timothy as God's coworker. The other manuscript traditions perhaps had problems conceiving of God as a coworker, but Paul has no problem perceiving the word that his team presents as the word of God (2:13). Thus, whatever role Timothy plays, God also was at work in it. Ultimately, God is the source of the church's nurturing.

Second, Paul's description of Timothy reveals the grave concern that the foundational leaders had for the stability of the church in the light of their acute separation. While Paul consistently praises the believers for their faith (1:3, 8; cf. 2:13), he also sends Timothy to find out about their faith (3:3, 5). Given the separation of the foundational leaders from the believers, he is concerned to know whether the church would be able to sustain itself without the nurturing presence of one or more members of his leadership team.

Paul's concern, however, is not narcissistic. It does not come from any self-aggrandizement on the part of the church's foundational leaders. Nor

82. Abraham J. Malherbe, *Paul and the Thessalonians: The Philosophic Tradition of Pastoral Care* (Philadelphia: Fortress, 1987) 61.

can it be chalked up simply to Paul's desire to visit all the churches that he established, although, in fact, he did have that desire. What is different about this church and what precipitates the grave concern here is the limited time the foundational leaders had with the believers. As Malherbe notes, "in no other letter does he write to people who had been Christians for so short a time and who were therefore especially in need of encouragement, preferably through personal contact."[83]

Because of the limited time he spent with the Thessalonian believers, Paul's fear was that the church might be "shaken" (σαίνομαι *sainomai*), or "unsettled emotionally" because of persecution,[84] with the result that his labor would be "in vain" (εἰς κενόν *eis kenon*), an expression he uses elsewhere to indicate his concern for the stability of his churches (Gal 2:2; Phil 2:16; cf. 1 Cor 15:58; Gal 4:11). Thus Timothy's role was to provide additional nurturing or moral training for the young church in the light of the team's grave concerns about its stability.

While Paul does not elaborate on the nature of the "persecutions" (θλίψεσιν *thlipsesin*, v. 3; cf. v. 4), here or elsewhere when he uses the expression it has been noted that he likely has in mind the eschatological woes that were thought to precede the approaching end. Although Paul has talked at length about the effect of the separation and aborted visits on all of the foundational leaders or on himself alone, it is not a foregone conclusion that he understood the persecutions to be those of the foundational leaders exclusively. The similarities previously noted about Satan's hindrances and the tempter's pressure on the church suggest, in fact, that the persecutions include whatever troubles the Thessalonians were experiencing as well.

Furthermore, with respect to the Thessalonians, Paul's use of the language of temptation ("the tempter had tempted," v. 5) leads some scholars to suggest that the persecutions or afflictions also included social alienation or pressures from the former networks out of which the church members came. That is, the basic Greek word πειράζω (*peirazō*) connotes both the idea of testing through suffering, as in the case of persecutions, and the idea of temptation through seduction. Thus the Thessalonian believers may have been seduced to return to their former families and friends, especially in the light of the fact that the foundational leaders had only a brief time to inculcate the values of the Christian life in them. Until the time of Timothy's visit no one had returned to help solidify them against the hostilities from which their church, since the very beginning, had seen no respite or escape.

The parenthetical statement on what the church knows and what the team has already shared with them (vv. 3b-4) implicitly reiterates the foundational leaders' consistency in their hortatory practices. A typical strategy in the hortatory tradition was a forewarning of coming troubles so that exhorted persons might ready themselves to meet them. Paul employs this strategy, but his discussion of the forewarning is strategically placed as a parenthesis between comments about Timothy's visit to the Thessalonians. As well, the parenthesis repeatedly acknowledges what the church already knows: "Indeed, you yourselves know . . . ; so it turned out, as you know." What Paul tells the Thessalonians in vv. 1-5, therefore, is a reminder of what he has already said. Because the imperfect form of a Greek verb conveys ongoing, continuous action in the past, Paul's use of the imperfect verbal form "told you beforehand" (προελέγομεν *proelegomen*, v. 4) in his comments on the forewarning suggests that the team had shared the apocalyptic commentary on persecutions continuously while they were with the church.[85] Thus the parenthesis dramatizes the foundational leaders' consistency. Of course, the emphasis on the leaders' consistency is probably just another way in which Paul invites his church to be consistent. Given the constancy of Satan's hindrances and the repeated instances of hostility since its birth, how could Paul's church do less?

With a second flashback (vv. 6-8), Paul relates the survival of the church (v. 6a), the believers' constant remembrance of their foundational leaders (v. 6b), and even the value of Timothy's "good news" to the other members of the foundational team (v. 7). Ever the exhorter in this letter, Paul again obliquely nudges the church toward persistence by linking the foundational team's very life to the believers' firm stand in the face of local opposition (v. 8).[86]

---

83. Ibid., 63.
84. Ibid., 65.

85. See I. H. Marshall, *1 and 2 Thessalonians* (Grand Rapids: Eerdmans, 1983) 92.
86. See Charles Wanamaker, *The Epistles to the Thessalonians,* NIGTC (Grand Rapids: Eerdmans, 1990) 136.

As Timothy had gone to the Thessalonians, he now returns to Paul and Silvanus. As he was sent to "encourage" the believers (v. 2), he now returns to Paul and Silvanus, bringing words that "encouraged" them (v. 7). Evidently all is fine because the news reveals the church's consistency and the mutuality of affection and support between the foundational team and the believers. Timothy's report indicates that the church "always" (πάντοτε *pantote*) remembers the foundational team (v. 6). Paul used the same word earlier to speak about the constancy of the foundational team's thanksgiving (1:2). Given the context of the hortatory tradition, the church's constant remembrance of the foundational team could also indicate the believers' commitment to the values that the foundational leaders had shared with them.

Timothy's report also indicates the deep mutuality between the church and the foundational leaders. Paul's earlier description of the foundational team included their longing for the Thessalonian believers and their desire to see them (2:17). Likewise, the church longed to see the foundational team (v. 6). Thus the separation appears to have been a mutually heartbreaking experience, and each group desired to be reunited fully with the other.

The mutuality, however, was not only one of affection, but one of support as well. Obviously, the foundational leaders' efforts to get to the church reveal their desire to support the Thessalonians through their difficulties, to provide nourishment for their maintenance. Yet Paul indicates that the report about the church helped the foundational team as well: "During all our distress and persecution [or endtime woes] we have been encouraged [or consoled] about you through your faith" (v. 7; cf. 2 Cor 7:3-7).

What is remarkable about this mutuality of support is that Paul implies that this same church that became a type for other believers (1:7)—a community whose faith was known everywhere (1:8)—actually had within it the ability to bring consolation or encouragement to others. It is little wonder, then, that he later commands the believers to encourage one another (4:18; 5:11). They had already been a source of encouragement to the foundational team, and, according to Paul, their encouragement of one another was not a new practice (5:11). If they could be a source of encouragement, that should be a sign that they had really committed themselves to the foundational team's teachings.

To encourage the believers even further (if not also to challenge them), Paul adds: "For now we live, if you continue to stand firm in the Lord" (v. 8). Paul often used the language of "standing firm" in his exhortations to his other churches (1 Cor 16:13; Gal 5:1; Phil 1:27; 4:1). But what did Paul mean by the expression "we live"? In part, Paul speaks here about the "quality of life, i.e., that Timothy's message allows the missionaries a fuller, less anxious life."[87] As well, the linking of the quality of the mission team's life to the steadfastness of the church is Paul's way of exhorting them to stand fast, to persist in the ways of the gospel he has shared with them.

87. Earl J. Richard, *First and Second Thessalonians,* Sacra Pagina (Collegeville, Minn.: Liturgical, 1995) 161.

REFLECTIONS

1. Readers will find much in this passage about the stresses of leadership, the importance of trustworthy people, the strategic value of teamwork, and the trials that can beset chuches. As for trust and teamwork, Timothy, Paul's trusted coworker, is pictured as a valued ally and an unselfish minister. Out of view of Paul and Silvanus, his elders, and working among the church members at Thessalonica, Timothy did not use the absence of his colleagues as an occasion for career advancement. He showed an acute perception of both the needs of those older, absent, anxious leaders and the needs of their solicitous church. Obviously, churches need comfort from time to time, but so do leaders. Leaders go through periods when they need to be on the receiving end, times when their leadership is particularly stressful, and they require rest, reassurance, and renewal. Timothy's work in Thessalonica helped the church and also helped to relieve Paul and Silvanus of anxiety about the Thessalonian Christians.

Timothy's unselfish spirit as a leader and team member is a worthy model of ministry in a time beset by the concerns of career building. He demonstrates the spirit of teamwork, showing how we can work trustingly with and for each other in fulfilling God's claim upon our lives.

2. It may be difficult for Christians who have never had to suffer for their beliefs to relate to the constant tests or afflictions that affected Paul and his church. If Paul's mention of "tests" is seen as an indication of a threat of apostasy, however, we may recognize his concern more clearly. Although we are not all tested directly by suffering for our faith, we are all familiar with being tempted because of our faith: tempted to ease up in our commitment, tempted to lose our convictions, tempted to relax our morality.

Dietrich Bonhoeffer, the German pastor and theologian who suffered imprisonment and made the ultimate sacrifice for his opposition to Nazism, argued in one of his writings that there is a relationship between these two types of tests. Bonhoeffer wrote: "Temptation to desire always includes the renunciation of the desire, that is to say, suffering. Temptation to suffering always includes the longing of freedom from suffering, that is to say, the desire. Thus the temptation of the flesh through desire and through suffering is at bottom one and the same."[88] Can it be that some of us face so few tests of suffering because we have given in too easily to so many tests of seduction?

88. Dietrich Bonhoeffer, *Creation and Fall, and Temptation: Two Biblical Studies* (New York: Macmillan, 1959) 118.

1 Thessalonians 3:9-13, An Expected Trip and the Parousia

NIV	NRSV
[9]How can we thank God enough for you in return for all the joy we have in the presence of our God because of you? [10]Night and day we pray most earnestly that we may see you again and supply what is lacking in your faith. [11]Now may our God and Father himself and our Lord Jesus clear the way for us to come to you. [12]May the Lord make your love increase and overflow for each other and for everyone else, just as ours does for you. [13]May he strengthen your hearts so that you will be blameless and holy in the presence of our God and Father when our Lord Jesus comes with all his holy ones.	[9]How can we thank God enough for you in return for all the joy that we feel before our God because of you? [10]Night and day we pray most earnestly that we may see you face to face and restore whatever is lacking in your faith. 11Now may our God and Father himself and our Lord Jesus direct our way to you. [12]And may the Lord make you increase and abound in love for one another and for all, just as we abound in love for you. [13]And may he so strengthen your hearts in holiness that you may be blameless before our God and Father at the coming of our Lord Jesus with all his saints.

COMMENTARY

A number of scholars suggest that the third subunit (3:9-13) of the second large unit (2:17–3:13) provides a brief summary of the argument's previous issues.[89] This is not an unreasonable assumption because Paul includes a wish-prayer

(3:11-13), and wish-prayers generally summarize foregoing material (cf. 1 Thess 5:23; Rom 15:5-6). Thus, as previously mentioned, 3:9-13 parallels 2:17-20. In addition, Paul's reference to the foundational team's love (3:12), particularly a love that focused on each person (as one could infer from Paul's description of the believers' love "for one another"), could remind the audience of their leaders' great care at the foundational visit (cf.

89. In agreement, see Robert Jewett, *The Thessalonian Correspondence: Pauline Rhetoric and Millenarian Piety*, Foundations and Facets (Philadelphia: Fortress, 1986) 140. Cf. Joseph O. Halloway, "*Peripateō* as a Thematic Marker for Pauline Ethics" (Ph.D. diss., Southwestern Baptist Theological Seminary, 1990) 37.

2:8). The foundational team's care was expressed for "each person," for Paul affirms that "we dealt with each one of you like a father with his children" (2:11).

Still, 1 Thess 3:9-13 is also a foreshadowing of the material that follows. As noted by form critics, its thanksgiving and prayer formulas point ahead to the life of love and holiness and to the letter's later interest in the parousia. So, since the subunit focuses on a complete or comprehensive love, the audience will not be surprised when eventually Paul commends a love for one another and to all (4:9-12). Also, since Paul prays that the believers' hearts will be strengthened in "holiness" (3:13), the auditors can expect Paul later to charge the church to exemplify "holiness" (4:4), a distinctive characteristic of God (cf. Isa 1:4; Jer 50:9; Ezek 39:7). And since Paul speaks of the parousia and the greatness with which it is associated (3:13), his readers will not find it striking for him to speak about the parousia and for him to comment on those who will be a part of Jesus' prestigious entourage (4:13–5:11).

This subsection, however, is critical for three other reasons. First, it reveals yet again the constancy of the foundational team. The team continues to give thanks even if here (3:9) they recognize that their thanksgiving to God is never enough compared to the joy they feel because of the church. As before, moreover, their constancy implicitly encourages the constancy of the church.

Second, this subsection also exposes the realism of the foundational team. Despite all the good they can say about the church, the foundational team's apocalyptic understanding of the realities of evil—of persecution, of Satan's blocking techniques, of the temptation (or seduction) for the believers to return to their former networks of support—leads them to pray for an opportunity to "restore what is lacking" in the church's faith (3:10). Paul does not state specifically what needs to be restored, and perhaps that would only be known when the foundational team's future visit was realized. What he does indicate, however, is that something is lacking. And given his apocalyptic understanding of reality, would not that always be the case until the parousia?

Third, Paul's brief comments on the parousia in conjunction with a wish-prayer for a reunion with the church emphasize the incredible strength the Thessalonian church could receive in thinking about the parousia. Paul is not sure whether he will get back to the church, although he prays for a chance to do so. He is certain, however, about the parousia's power to unite the people of God. So whether "all his saints" (NRSV) or "all his holy ones" (NIV) is the best translation of the Greek word that describes Jesus' entourage (ἅγιοι *hagioi*, 3:13), what Paul takes for granted is that the parousia will occur and that it will be a grand event of reunion. For an isolated church faced with continuous persecution, just knowing that they would be a part of that grand event would surely have brought them great encouragement. Satan would not have the last word.

Given the three subunits of the second large unit, how does the entire unit encourage the audience to maintain its apocalyptic way of life? Perhaps the believers are encouraged through Paul's emphasis on the persistence of both the foundational team and the church throughout hostilities and hindrances. The team's persistence was manifested through its embrace of the parousia as an event that neutralizes separation and through its persistent efforts to provide moral training for the church through Paul's acolyte, Timothy. Furthermore, the foundational leaders' persistence is evident in their continuous prayer to God (3:9-13). As for the church, its members evidently remain just as influenced by the apocalyptic word because Paul still hears something good about them. They continue to exhibit faith and love (3:6), and their remembrance of the foundational team is constant.

But what are the resources of persistence noted in the second large unit? They are, in fact, the very ones mentioned in the first large unit: the foundational team's earlier apocalyptic words and the consolatory or exhortatory practices of a specific leader, in this case Timothy. Paul continues to view the church's afflictions in the light of an apocalyptic prism. Yet, Timothy's presence is important as well. It is likely the case that Timothy secured the church with that apocalyptic word as he sought to strengthen and console the Thessalonian believers. With the word of God and the practices of moral training noted in two of the large units of Paul's letter, it is little wonder that the last large unit will feature the value of both the apocalyptic word and the practices of moral training. Paul's implicit emphasis on these resources anticipates the kinds of resources he will commend in 4:1–5:22 as he exhorts his church to persist in their distinctive way of life.

REFLECTIONS

Paul's love for the church spills over in this passage. Of course, the dearness of the church to Paul is found everywhere in the letter. Paul's metaphorical shift from wet nurse (2:7) to father (2:11-12) projects a friendly message, for the shift conveys the foundational leaders' continuous care for the converts from infancy onward. Paul praises the Thessalonians for their steadfastness (or their active and heroic constancy in the face of trials, 1:3) and for their continuous expressions of mutual support and comfort (4:1, 9; 5:11). A note of remembrance (1:3) registers Paul's admiration, and echoes of joy reverberate throughout the letter. Yet, only in 3:9-13—perhaps because Paul only now explicitly mentions the separation—do his deep affection and longing for the Thessalonian believers break through the surface to become a dominant theme as he confesses his intense desire to be present with them. Repeated hindrances follow repeated efforts to get to the church (2:17-18), and desperate agonizing over the church's survival leads to the dispatch of Timothy (3:1-5). Moreover, the separation is a mutually heartrending matter, for both Paul and the church long to see each other (2:17; 3:6, 10). And yet with all of the deep fondness and the relief that Timothy's report brings about the church's success, Paul, ever the pastor, speaks of his desire to "restore" or "supply" whatever is lacking in their faith (3:10).

These believers in Thessalonica are not like those in Corinth, with whom Paul would have a long and stormy relationship. Nor were they listening to outside agitators quibble about entrance requirements, as would be the case later among the Galatians. To the contrary, the church at Thessalonica was meritorious in many ways, moving from the rank of imitators to the rank of examples. Yet—for all the church's success—Paul's thanksgiving refrain is broken by a reminder that he wants not only to see the church, but also to supply whatever is still lacking in their faith (3:10).

Of the three thanksgiving reports, the other two simply laud the church for its success—for its active deployment of the triad of graces ("faith . . . love . . . hope," 1:3) or for its reception of the team's word as the word of God (2:13). But in the third one, Paul moves beyond an accounting of his joy before God for the church to a realism enriched by his apocalyptic vision. Again, Paul does not note exactly what is lacking. He just knows that something is.

This apocalyptic realism suggests that all is not yet complete. For Paul, as has been noted, manifestations of the old age still affect the believers who await Jesus' coming as the climactic event that will consummate the new age already begun with the death and resurrection of Jesus. Therefore, believers live between the "already" of what God has done through Jesus' death and resurrection and the "not yet" that awaits them.

This is hard realism for any church. As successful as a church may seem, something is still lacking because of the intrusions of the old age. As much light as the church may bring to others and as much good as it may do for the world, something is still lacking. Something inevitably needs the attention of those who lead the church, and God can be trusted to honor supplications on behalf of that need (cf. 3:11-13).

This realism bears witness to Paul's distinctive brand of apocalypticism—to the tension between the already and the not-yet of Paul's thought, as distilled from all of the undisputed letters. That same tension should rescue churches today from a one-sided view of salvation and its benefits. The value of the already dimension of God's work is that no one can make a claim to superiority based on previous entitlements outside of their lives in Christ. Whatever we are, we are by the grace of God already and always active in our lives. The value of the not-yet dimension of God's work, however, is that no one can claim perfection, as if the sanctification process is complete. Vestiges of the past still intrude, even if only in our memories, as if they are not dead, but only wounded and still seeking a toe-hold.[90] The goal for us, then, is to draw on the strength of the Holy Spirit, the seal or guarantee of the new age's consummation, and to wait with trust and diligence for the full transformation of our lives.

90. J. Paul Sampley, *Walking Between the Times: Paul's Moral Reasoning* (Minneapolis: Fortress, 1991) 10, 13.

1 THESSALONIANS 4:1–5:22, COMMENDING PERSISTENCE IN THE DISTINCTIVE LIFE

OVERVIEW

Having recalled the persistence of the church and the pastoral team at the foundational visit (1:6–2:16) and having recounted the recent events that occurred from the team's forced separation until the composition of the letter (2:17–3:13), Paul makes yet another temporal shift to urge the church to persist in its apocalyptic life in the face of local hostilities (4:1–5:22). Repetitive features in 4:1–5:22 suggest a large unit made up of three subunits: two units of explicit moral exhortation (4:1-12; 5:12-22) and a middle subunit with a direct focus on end-time events (4:13–5:11). Still, all of the material is exhortative, linking a number of imperatives to apocalyptic descriptions of the end time and describing for the church the distinctive life of love and holiness they must live before others as they wait with assurance for the parousia.

1 Thessalonians 4:1-12, Walking a Distinctive Life

NIV

4 Finally, brothers, we instructed you how to live in order to please God, as in fact you are living. Now we ask you and urge you in the Lord Jesus to do this more and more. ²For you know what instructions we gave you by the authority of the Lord Jesus.

³It is God's will that you should be sanctified: that you should avoid sexual immorality; ⁴that each of you should learn to control his own body[a] in a way that is holy and honorable, ⁵not in passionate lust like the heathen, who do not know God; ⁶and that in this matter no one should wrong his brother or take advantage of him. The Lord will punish men for all such sins, as we have already told you and warned you. ⁷For God did not call us to be impure, but to live a holy life. ⁸Therefore, he who rejects this instruction does not reject man but God, who gives you his Holy Spirit.

a4 Or learn to live with his own wife; or learn to acquire a wife

NRSV

4 Finally, brothers and sisters,[a] we ask and urge you in the Lord Jesus that, as you learned from us how you ought to live and to please God (as, in fact, you are doing), you should do so more and more. ²For you know what instructions we gave you through the Lord Jesus. ³For this is the will of God, your sanctification: that you abstain from fornication; ⁴that each one of you know how to control your own body[b] in holiness and honor, ⁵not with lustful passion, like the Gentiles who do not know God; ⁶that no one wrong or exploit a brother or sister[c] in this matter, because the Lord is an avenger in all these things, just as we have already told you beforehand and solemnly warned you. ⁷For God did not call us to impurity but in holiness. ⁸Therefore whoever rejects this rejects not human authority but God, who also gives his Holy Spirit to you.

a Gk brothers   b Or how to take a wife for himself   c Gk brother

NIV

[9]Now about brotherly love we do not need to write to you, for you yourselves have been taught by God to love each other. [10]And in fact, you do love all the brothers throughout Macedonia. Yet we urge you, brothers, to do so more and more.

[11]Make it your ambition to lead a quiet life, to mind your own business and to work with your hands, just as we told you, [12]so that your daily life may win the respect of outsiders and so that you will not be dependent on anybody.

NRSV

[9]Now concerning love of the brothers and sisters,[a] you do not need to have anyone write to you, for you yourselves have been taught by God to love one another; [10]and indeed you do love all the brothers and sisters[a] throughout Macedonia. But we urge you, beloved,[a] to do so more and more, [11]to aspire to live quietly, to mind your own affairs, and to work with your hands, as we directed you, [12]so that you may behave properly toward outsiders and be dependent on no one.

[a] Gk brothers

COMMENTARY

All of 4:1-12 is held together by the repetition of the word "walk" (περιπατέω *peripateō*; see the Commentary on 2:12) at the beginning and end of this subunit. The Greek term is translated by the NRSV as "live" (v. 1) and "behave" (v. 12). Within these verses, three integrated sections clarify the believer's distinctive walk. One section (vv. 1-2), introductory in nature, acknowledges the believers' apprehension of a distinctive walk that pleases God. Two other sections (vv. 3-8 and vv. 9-12) render specific details about that walk. In 4:3-8, three specific injunctions (vv. 3*b*-6*a*) and three specific motivations (vv. 6*b*-8) follow a maxim about the holiness of the community (v. 3*a*). In 4:9-12, Paul presents specific challenges about love (whether for each other or for other believers in Macedonia) and specific directives on behavior toward outsiders.[91]

4:1-2. Four features of these verses give them an introductory character. First, they begin with "finally" (λοιπόν *loipon*), a familiar transitional expression in Paul's writings (2 Cor 13:11; Phil 3:1). In the case of 1 Thessalonians, "finally" marks the last of three large units of Paul's overall proof section.

Second, these initial verses are couched as general statements of exhortation, leaving the specifics for later (in vv. 3-8 and vv. 9-12). It is doubtful that the specifics indicate a lack in the moral character of the church. Paul's previous affirmation of the church's model behavior (1:7) suggests the contrary. Furthermore, Paul repeatedly acknowledges the appropriate comportment that he already sees in the church (vv. 1, 9).

Third, these verses set the tone for all of the material in 4:1–5:22—namely, an emphasis on persistence, with echoes of earlier themes treated in the two previous large units. According to Paul's description of his leadership team at its foundational visit in Thessalonica, the team's aim was to please God, not human beings (2:4). The exhortations "to live [walk] and to please God" (4:1) are synonymous infinitive expressions for the same activity (in technical jargon, an example of a hendiadys). They express what should also be the goal of the church.

Paul's declaration that his urging was something the church "learned" (παρελάβετε *parelabete*, v. 1*b*) from the foundational team also resonates with Paul's earlier statement that the church "received" (παραλαβόντες *paralabontes*) the word they heard as the word of God, not of humans (2:13). Though not clearly indicated in the NRSV's rendering of v. 1, Paul's request for a persistence in the "walking" activity ("as in fact you are doing, you should do so more and more," v. 1*d*) echoes the language of his earlier wish-prayer when he prays for the church's love to abound (3:12). It is with little wonder, then, that Paul will highlight love in 4:9-10 and also request that the love of the church abound more and more (4:11).

---

91. Some scholars think Περὶ δε (*Peri de*, "and concerning") refers to a previous letter from the apostle. It is possible, however, simply to see *peri de* here and in 5:1 as a transitional marker. See the Commentary on 5:1.

Fourth, these initial verses also highlight the distinctiveness of the practices and perspectives Paul will recommend in the rest of this large unit. Like other teachers of the first century, Paul offered his assemblies a reformatory ethics—that is, an ethics of moral instruction. Paul notes the distinctiveness of his reformatory ethics, however, by repeatedly indicating the sphere in which he offers his moral instruction: "in the Lord Jesus" (v. 1) and "through the Lord Jesus" (v. 2). Thus, even if, as we shall see, Paul will draw on other traditions to shape and nurture the church, he will do so with the intention of building up a community whose origins and destiny lie in the relationship they have with the Lord Jesus. Indeed, throughout 4:1–5:22, Paul seeks to define the boundaries of his church apart from the larger culture.

4:3-8. The theme of "sanctification" (ἁγιασμός hagiasmos, v. 3) or "holiness" (hagiasmos vv. 4, 7) is the common thread that Paul weaves throughout these verses. Accordingly, Paul begins with a general maxim on sanctification (v. 3) before offering three specific injunctions about the holy life (vv. 4-6a) and three motivations for living the holy life as enjoined (vv. 6b-8).

Before clarifying the meaning of the three injunctions, it is important to note that they pertain to activity that stands in contrast to "the will of God," an expression that Paul (and other Jews) often used to speak about proper conduct (Rom 2:18; 12:2; 1 Esdr 9:9; 4 Macc 18:16). In general, Paul often noted certain improprieties as a way of defining the boundary lines of his communities.[92] Some actions were simply not permissible because they reflected the former practices of Gentile converts (1 Cor 5:1) or because they indicated the desires of the flesh—that is, selfishness (Gal 5:19)—as opposed to the fruit of the Spirit (5:22). Paul even argues that certain actions—immorality usually leading the list—are the behaviors of persons who will not inherit God's kingdom (Gal 5:19-21; cf. 1 Cor 5:11).

Only the first of the three injunctions is readily clear: that the church abstain from "fornication" or immorality (v. 3b). The meaning of the other two, however, is mired in debate because some of Paul's expressions are ambiguous.

In the second injunction, the NRSV translates "body" (v. 4) for the Greek noun σκεῦος (skeuos), but the textual note suggests that the word can also mean "a wife" (the translation favored by the RSV). This noun literally means a vessel like an earthen jar or pot (cf. Luke 8:16). Yet, it could also have metaphorical meanings. A clear illustration of its metaphorical potential is seen elsewhere in Paul when he describes the physical life on earth as "treasure in clay jars" (2 Cor 4:7). Some scholars think that in 1 Thessalonians the noun is a metaphorical euphemism for genitalia, hence the term "body." Others, however, prefer the term "wife" because 1 Pet 3:7, in the patriarchal spirit of the times, uses the noun skeuos to refer to the wife as the "weaker vessel" or "weaker sex" (NRSV).

How one translates the noun is also related to the verb that accompanies it. Some scholars render "to control" for the Greek infinitive κτᾶσθαι (ktasthai), while others favor "to take" or "to acquire" (the verb itself being capable of both translations). So is Paul referring to the control of the body (genitalia) or to the acquisition or possession of a wife? On the one hand, those who support the former may be influenced by political correctness—not wanting Paul to speak exclusively here to men who could take a wife or for Paul to speak of a wife as a possession. On the other hand, those who favor "to take a wife" actually weaken their translation by resorting to 1 Peter because that text implies that both the husband and the wife are vessels.

Despite these competing positions on the ambiguous terms, Paul's challenge for his church is clear: that the church operate in holiness (v. 4). Paul qualifies his directive by resorting to two well-known Jewish polemics against Gentiles: that they are sexually promiscuous (Wis 14:12-31; Philo *Allegorical Laws* 3:8) and that they are ignorant of God (Ps 79:6; Jer 10:25; Gal 4:8; Rom 1:28). Thus, both the first and the second injunctions are intended to accentuate the boundary lines of distinction between Paul and his church, on the one hand, and the larger society, on the other hand.

The ambiguity of the third injunction (v. 5) lies in the expression "matter" (πρᾶγμα pragma). Some scholars hold that all three injunctions speak about sexual behavior: against fornication (v. 3b);

---

92. J. Paul Sampley, *Walking Between the Times: Paul's Moral Reasoning* (Minneapolis: Fortress, 1991) 57.

against sexual activity outside an act of marriage, as if *skeuos* refers to a wife (vv. 4-5); and against any kind of sexual activity that would wrong the husband or father of the woman involved, as if *pragma* refers to one of the two previous injunctions (v. 6a).[93] Still others read *pragma* as a command about proper business practices.[94]

Whatever the meanings of the enigmatic expressions, the motivations are clear: (1) a previous warning about God's vengeance (v. 6b); (2) God's call to holiness, not impurity (v. 7); and (3) God's gift of the Holy Spirit (v. 8). The first motivation is one Paul must have mentioned before with some insistency. The word he uses to describe his previous challenge (διεμαρτυράμεθα *diemartyrametha*, "solemnly warned," v. 6) echoes what he says earlier in his reflections on foundational efforts to shape the church, for "pleading" (μαρτυρόμενοι *martyromenoi*, 2:12) was a critical part of the foundational leaders' tutelage of the church to lead (or to walk) the life worthy of God.

Obviously, to speak of the Lord as an avenger (v. 6) removes any notion of self-vindication among those wronged—a point well worth saying in a context in which Paul wanted his church to display comportment that could influence outsiders (v. 12). Paul here also likely has all three injunctions in mind, for he claims that the Lord is an avenger in "all these things" (v. 6). Furthermore, Paul here likely refers to "Lord" as "God," not Jesus, because the subsequent motivations refer to God. The idea of the Lord as an avenger, moreover, also indicates the possibility for believers to come under judgment despite their status as being saved.

The second motivation, God's call to holiness, not to impurity (v. 7), resounds the theme of holiness but likewise echoes the former talk of a God who "calls" persons into the church (2:12). Paul's observation about God's calling the church actually suggests an ongoing call for the sake of sanctification. Earlier, at the foundational moments and even now, Paul's goal was consistent. In fact, just as the foundational team did not

operate from "impure motives" (2:3) as it sought to declare the gospel to this church, so also the church cannot operate in "impurity" (4:7), for the life of holiness is one in which the chief aim is to "please" (2:4; 4:1) the God who entrusts special assignments (2:4) and calls believers (2:12).

The third motivation, God's gift of the Holy Spirit (v. 8), also focuses on God. God (as Lord) not only is responsible for judgment at the end of time (a time in which Paul thinks even believers will be assessed) but for the original call of believers into God's kingdom. God's continuous calling of the believers also equips them with what they need for the sanctified life, for growth and maturity—namely, the Holy Spirit. Rejection of the life of holiness, then, is not a rejection of human authority but of the very God who could help believers in the course of life, from their beginnings in the Lord until the moment of their full transformation at the parousia.

Altogether, then, vv. 3-8 are not a new commendation for this church. Paul had spoken earlier about the implication of God's call upon the believers' lives, and he continues to do so. The commendation, moreover, challenges the church to maintain a distinctive pattern of living—not as they once lived, but a life of holiness. As God's holy people and people whom God elected (1:4), the church has the responsibility of reflecting God's holiness as well.

4:9-12. These verses suggest the same emphasis on distinctive living—that is, on living a life distinct from that before conversion. The section begins with a *paralipsis* (a feigned statement) as Paul avers that he will not mention anything about the church's love for one another when, in fact, he does just that (v. 9a). Next, Paul indicates both the source (v. 9b) and the extent (v. 10a) of the church's love for the brothers and sisters. Then, Paul exhorts the church "to do so more and more" (i.e., to love) and to strive to perform three concrete practices (v. 11) with the goals of modeling and achieving self-sufficiency (v. 12).

Paul's remarks about "the love of brothers and sisters" use a term (φιλαδελφία *philadelphia*, v. 9) that initially focused on the love among siblings but that by Paul's day had widened in Christian assemblies to indicate the love among believers. When Paul turns to the source of this expanded form of love, his coinage "taught by God"

---

93. Jeffrey Weima, "How You Must Walk to Please God," in *The Thessalonian Correspondence,* ed. R. F. Collins (Leuven: University of Leuven Press, 1990) 109.

94. Walter Bauer, William F. Arndt, F. Wilbur Gingrich, and Frederick W. Danker, *A Greek-English Lexicon of the New Testament and Other Early Christian Literature,* 2nd ed. (Chicago: University of Chicago Press, 1979) 203-4.

(θεοδίδακτοί *theodidaktoi*, v. 9) is distinctive, for it is not found in Greek literature before it appears in his letters. In the estimation of some scholars, Paul's "taught by God" is also intended as a contrast to the Epicureans, who considered themselves "self-taught"; but there is no evidence that Paul had a reason (given what we know about the Thessalonian Christians) to distinguish his church specifically from the Epicureans. What does seem clear is that Paul is continuing to place the life of this church in the hands of God—noting God's vengeance, calling, giving of the Holy Spirit, and now God's teaching.

The source of the love clearly depicted, Paul then highlights the extent of the church's love and "urges" them to do so "more and more" (v. 10). It is little wonder that their love is extended to believers throughout Macedonia, for, given Paul's earlier hyperbole, their faith has gone out everywhere (1:8) and Paul hears about them from others (1:9). Elsewhere, Paul speaks of one thing counting: faith working through love (Gal 5:6). Timothy's report seems to support the young church's ability to work forth its faith in concrete practices of love, for he notes both their "faith and love" (3:6).

Yet, Paul challenges his young church to love even more (v. 10). He shows himself to be the consummate pastor here because he sees the good and praises it but recognizes room for improvement as well. It should be noted that the improvement he seeks is something the foundational team models (given the constancy of their care for the church) and the very thing for which they have prayed (3:11).

The usual recourse of interpretation for assessing the three concrete practices to which Paul next turns (vv. 11-12) is to appeal (explicitly or implicitly) to 2 Thess 3:6-12 as a framework for interpreting 1 Thess 4:11-12, as if the practices were commended to calm "apocalyptic fervor."[95] As long as the authorship of 2 Thessalonians remains a matter of debate, however, a more convincing argument that arises from 1 Thessalonians is that the practices resound to Paul's theme about the church's distinctive love or care for others.

Two pieces of evidence support this claim. First, if ancient auditors followed the progression of the love theme in vv. 9-12, from love for the members of the church (v. 9) to love for the believers throughout Macedonia (v. 10), it is not difficult to suppose that they would then expect a further extension of the love theme directed to others—that is, to unbelievers in vv. 11-12. Second, if 3:9-13 is a prefiguring of the rest of the letter, one could expect Paul, at some point in 4:1–5:28, to treat his desired wish that the community's love "increase" (περισσεύω *perisseuō*) "for one another and for all" (εἰς ἀλλήλους καὶ εἰς πάντας *eis allēlous kai eis pantas*, 3:12). With the reference to the "outsiders" (πρὸς τοὺς ἔξω *pros tous exō*) in 4:12, it appears that Paul has, in fact, specified in concrete ways how the church's love could "increase" (*perisseuō*, v. 10) to others beyond the believers.

With the guiding context of the love theme, then, the concrete practices are all ways of solidifying the church into an ideal community with the purpose of providing a model or good form for the outsiders.[96] Readers familiar with the imperatival infinitive "to aspire" (φιλοτιμεῖσθαι *philotimeisthai*, v. 11*a*) as a term to "describe a person ambitious for [political] fame through the offer of beneficence to a community" would recognize an ironic twist in Paul's logic because he actually recommends for the first concrete practice "a quiet life."[97] How is one to be ambitious but at the same time to seek a quiet life? Fame itself is not to be sought, but the community all together should seek to be distinctive—strikingly enough—by not aspiring to conventional forms of prestige.

Regarding Paul's admonition to "mind your own affairs," on the one hand, auditors familiar with the Platonic tradition could read the second (and related) concrete practice as a call away from public life to a smaller community or as a call to individuate one's contributions to the community to one's "own" natural gifts. On the other hand, this concrete practice could be more directly tied to the circumstances of the church. If the church faced local hostilities and alienation, the last thing they needed was to meddle in the affairs of the

---

95. For a sterling critique of this position, see Earl J. Richard, *First and Second Thessalonians*, Sacra Pagina (Collegeville, Minn.: Liturgical, 1995) 219ff.

96. Ibid., 220.

97. Abraham Smith, *Comfort One Another: Reconstructing the Rhetoric and Audience of 1 Thessalonians* (Louisville: Westminster, 1995) 40.

larger society. Indeed, given the imminence of the new age, such concerns would not be regarded as significant at all.

Given a context of local hostilities and alienation, moreover, auditors likely heard the expression "work with your hands" (v. 12) as a reference to the church's need to be self-sufficient. The pastoral team itself modeled self-sufficiency (2:9) in its foundational visit. Paul, in fact, notes that he is not saying anything new (4:11). Here, then, as elsewhere, Paul has already provided a model for the church in the concrete practices noted in the initial visit.

The aim of self-sufficiency, of course, is to "behave properly toward outsiders" (v. 12) or to provide a "good form" (εὐσχημόνως *euschēmonōs*). The early Christians, even if they drew boundaries around themselves, did not advocate "a need to go |completely| out of the world" before the parousia's consummation of the new age (cf. 1 Cor 5:10). Rather, they hoped to persuade outsiders to join them or to appreciate their conviction or to glorify the deity they represented through the model lives they lived before others. In 1 Peter, for example, believers are enjoined to allow their exemplary lives to influence others who may presently be the very cause of their suffering. In doing so, the believers both "silence the ignorance of the foolish" (1 Pet 2:15) and cause others eventually to "glorify God" (2:12). Perhaps, something similar lies behind Paul's reasoning in 1 Thessalonians as well (cf. 1 Cor 10:31-33).

Thus, in both 4:3-8 and 4:9-12, the theme is a distinctive walk, whether as a walk of holiness or as one of love for believers and outsiders. The distinctive life, moreover, is a life of consistency. The foundational leaders lived consistently before the Thessalonian church, and now Paul charges that church to continue the practices of their founding leaders with a similar consistency. If the church remained committed to its practices, perhaps the outsiders would be persuaded by their consistent quality of moral excellence and join them as believers in Paul's deity.

REFLECTIONS

1. We must be careful not to misunderstand Paul's emphasis on boundaries. If Christians are to be different from the larger society—and we are called to be different—our quest must not emanate from a will to retreat to remote corners of life. Our calling is not to isolate ourselves but to conduct ourselves as children of God. To be sure, there are those who become different—even unconventional—to make a personal statement. This may be symptomatic of something else, perhaps of poor self-esteem or of undue fear of losing one's individuality. In contrast, God's call to a life of holiness marks believers as different in healthy, unselfish, and strategic ways—and always for redemptive purposes.

Certainly, Paul does not define boundaries in 1 Thess 4:1-12 to commend parochialism of any sort. Rather, he challenges the Thessalonians to extend the limits of their love to all (1 Thess 4:9-12). We, too, are challenged to extend love to all, to transcend selfishness and short-sightedness. Insularity cripples spiritual growth and church outreach, and it may even give the impression that what we have is either too good for others or not worthy of their consideration.

2. A careful reading of 1 Thess 4:1-12 helps us to understand the comprehensive nature of Christian morality: its consideration for the individual, for others, and for God. Whatever the exact meaning of the passage, it is clear that Paul is addressing individuals, or "each of you" (4:4). At the same time, Paul goes further, addressing individuals in relation to others. The Christian life is not lived in personal isolation; unfortunately, too much Christian preaching has focused on individuals as if Christianity's goal was psychological fitness. Even the early Christian desert hermits withdrew to pray for the world. Yet, in the words of David Buttrick, "Most of our pulpits, Protestant and Catholic alike, have read scripture but then preached a psychological personalism for . . . decades, with sin as psychological dysfunction and salvation as inward good feeling. No wonder that American religion can be described as both 'gnosticism' and 'habits of the heart.' "[98]

Paul's consideration for the individual and for others is ultimately connected to consideration for God, the one who gives the Holy Spirit and the one who will issue vengeance upon those who exploit or violate others. Morality devoid of a consideration for God often leads to a static form of social relations, one that is ultimately not concerned with the wholeness of the entire universe. No wonder C. S. Lewis wrote, "Morality . . . seems to be concerned with three things. Firstly, with fair play and harmony between individuals. Secondly, with what might be called tidying up or harmonising the things inside each individual. Thirdly, with the general purpose of human life as a whole . . . what tune the conductor of the band [God] wants it to play."[99] If we miss the importance of these three elements, our lives will never rise above the din of society.

98. David Buttrick, *A Captive Voice: The Liberation of Preaching* (Louisville: Westminster/John Knox, 1994) 13-14.
99. C. S. Lewis, *Mere Christianity* (New York: Macmillan, 1943) 71.

1 Thessalonians 4:13–5:11, Maintaining the Apocalyptic Hope

NIV

[13]Brothers, we do not want you to be ignorant about those who fall asleep, or to grieve like the rest of men, who have no hope. [14]We believe that Jesus died and rose again and so we believe that God will bring with Jesus those who have fallen asleep in him. [15]According to the Lord's own word, we tell you that we who are still alive, who are left till the coming of the Lord, will certainly not precede those who have fallen asleep. [16]For the Lord himself will come down from heaven, with a loud command, with the voice of the archangel and with the trumpet call of God, and the dead in Christ will rise first. [17]After that, we who are still alive and are left will be caught up together with them in the clouds to meet the Lord in the air. And so we will be with the Lord forever. [18]Therefore encourage each other with these words.

5 Now, brothers, about times and dates we do not need to write to you, [2]for you know very well that the day of the Lord will come like a thief in the night. [3]While people are saying, "Peace and safety," destruction will come on them suddenly, as labor pains on a pregnant woman, and they will not escape.

[4]But you, brothers, are not in darkness so that this day should surprise you like a thief. [5]You are all sons of the light and sons of the day. We do not belong to the night or to the darkness. [6]So

NRSV

13But we do not want you to be uninformed, brothers and sisters,[a] about those who have died,[b] so that you may not grieve as others do who have no hope. [14]For since we believe that Jesus died and rose again, even so, through Jesus, God will bring with him those who have died.[b] [15]For this we declare to you by the word of the Lord, that we who are alive, who are left until the coming of the Lord, will by no means precede those who have died.[b] [16]For the Lord himself, with a cry of command, with the archangel's call and with the sound of God's trumpet, will descend from heaven, and the dead in Christ will rise first. [17]Then we who are alive, who are left, will be caught up in the clouds together with them to meet the Lord in the air; and so we will be with the Lord forever. [18]Therefore encourage one another with these words.

5 Now concerning the times and the seasons, brothers and sisters,[a] you do not need to have anything written to you. [2]For you yourselves know very well that the day of the Lord will come like a thief in the night. [3]When they say, "There is peace and security," then sudden destruction will come upon them, as labor pains come upon a pregnant woman, and there will be no escape! [4]But you, beloved,[a] are not in darkness, for that day to surprise you like a thief; [5]for you are all children of

[a] Gk *brothers*   [b] Gk *fallen asleep*

NIV

then, let us not be like others, who are asleep, but let us be alert and self-controlled. ⁷For those who sleep, sleep at night, and those who get drunk, get drunk at night. ⁸But since we belong to the day, let us be self-controlled, putting on faith and love as a breastplate, and the hope of salvation as a helmet. ⁹For God did not appoint us to suffer wrath but to receive salvation through our Lord Jesus Christ. ¹⁰He died for us so that, whether we are awake or asleep, we may live together with him. ¹¹Therefore encourage one another and build each other up, just as in fact you are doing.

NRSV

light and children of the day; we are not of the night or of darkness. ⁶So then let us not fall asleep as others do, but let us keep awake and be sober; ⁷for those who sleep sleep at night, and those who are drunk get drunk at night. ⁸But since we belong to the day, let us be sober, and put on the breastplate of faith and love, and for a helmet the hope of salvation. ⁹For God has destined us not for wrath but for obtaining salvation through our Lord Jesus Christ, ¹⁰who died for us, so that whether we are awake or asleep we may live with him. ¹¹Therefore encourage one another and build up each other, as indeed you are doing.

COMMENTARY

The second subunit (4:13–5:11) of the last large unit (4:1–5:22) has two discrete parts: an explicit consolatory section about the hope of believers in Jesus' parousia (4:13-18), and a section on the requisite vigilance of the believers as they await the day of the Lord (5:1-11). Both of these sections depict end-time events. Both also conclude with a call for mutual consolation within the church (4:18; 5:11). The letter's recurring theme of persistence in the apocalyptic hope and the ethical life that flows from it, moreover, seems to guide the interpretation of both sets of verses even in those places where Paul's descriptive diction is hard to decipher.

4:13-18. A careful reading of these verses would include the following division: (1) an opening statement on the distinction between the believers and others who have no hope (v. 13); (2) descriptions of the basis for the believers' hope (vv. 14-17*a*); (3) an acknowledgment of the permanent union of the believers with the Lord (v. 17*b*); and (4) a commendation toward mutual consolation (v. 18).[100]

Though some scholars think the expression "we do not want you to be uninformed" (v. 13) indicates that Paul here introduces new information (a supposition based on other examples of

the expression in Rom 1:13; 11:25; 1 Cor 10:1; 12:1; 2 Cor 1:8), the general exhortative character of 1 Thessalonians suggests that one need not infer the introduction of entirely new material,[101] as if the audience were totally unfamiliar with the subject of the resurrection itself.[102] Indeed, it is hard to imagine that Paul had talked about the resurrection of Jesus without talking about the resurrection of believers because Christ's resurrection, for Paul, was the very basis for his belief that the new age had dawned. And in Jewish thinking of the time, the new age was associated with the resurrection of believers.[103]

Instead, the expression could simply be a response to a grave need for consolation. Paul likely spoke to the church about the possibility of death even as he shared other afflictions that were manifestations of the old age (3:4). Death, albeit a traumatic manifestation, was still another instance of the old age's work. Yet, it is likely that the Thessalonians, despite hearing about the resurrection of the dead, honestly thought the parousia would come before any of their fellow believers died. Death having now visited them, Paul writes to console them about those who "sleep" (κοιμάομαι *koimaomai*, v. 13), Paul's euphemism

---

100. Other issues not demanding our full attention are as follows: (1) The word διά (*dia*, "through") in 4:14 likely goes with Jesus and not with the dead ones, and (2) modern interpreters—not Paul—seem to have generated interest on the place where the dead will be brought in 4:14.

101. See Charles Wanamaker, *The Epistles to the Thessalonians,* NIGTC (Grand Rapids: Eerdmans, 1990) 165.
102. So Richard, *First and Second Thessalonians,* 232-33.
103. Bart D. Ehrman, *The New Testament: An Historical Introduction to the Early Christian Writings,* 2nd ed. (New York; Oxford, 2000) 270.

for believers "who have died" (NRSV; cf. John 11:11-13; 1 Cor 7:39; 11:30).

As he consoles them, however, he also notes how different they are from those without the believers' hope. It is not accurate to say that others in Paul's world did not believe in the afterlife.[104] The hope that Paul has lies in the extraordinary power of the parousia as the consummation of the new age and the climactic conclusion to the old. That is, it has the power to raise the believers from the dead and to transform both the living and the risen into a lasting union with Christ (v. 17).

Paul's consolation includes two bases for the believers' hope, and both are related to Paul's apocalyptic understanding of the old and new ages. The first basis is expressed in a belief statement ("we believe that Jesus died and rose again," v. 14*a*) that is deemed to be a creedal formula. The belief statement is so considered because of its brevity and its description of the event as "Jesus rising" rather than Paul's customary language of "God raising Jesus" from the dead (Rom 4:24; 1 Cor 15:15; 2 Cor 4:14; Gal 1:1; 1 Thess 1:10).[105] From the creedal statement, Paul argues that God will secure the lives of believers who have died (v. 14*b*; cf. Rom 8:11). For Paul, as we have seen, Jesus' death and resurrection inaugurate the new age and sound a death knell to the old age.

A second basis for the believer's hope is the parousia, to which Paul turns after noting the death and resurrection of Jesus. Paul's description of the parousia here is introduced by the expression "by the word of the Lord" (v. 15). This expression need not indicate an actual word from Jesus (such as one would find in the later Synoptic and Johannine documents, which themselves depend on earlier traditions of Jesus' sayings).[106] Indeed, "Paul rarely explicitly identifies a saying as one of Jesus' (1 Cor 7:10)."[107] Relatedly, there is no way to know the origin of this "word of the Lord"—that is, to know whether Paul received it from an unknown medium (whether a post-Easter prophet or the church) or if "the word" is in fact an *agraphon*, an unwritten and thus unknown saying of Jesus—in the light of the fact that we may not have written testimony to all of Jesus' sayings. While scholars are able to see links between some of the written testimonies to the teachings of Jesus and Paul's own letters (cf. Matt 24:43; Luke 12:39-40; 1 Thess 5:2), Sampley has noted that "Paul's moral reflection did not follow a regular pattern of applying some teaching of Jesus to a problem at hand."[108] Gaventa has noted, moreover, that in the instance of 1 Thess 4:15, "nothing in the Gospels closely parallels the statements that follow [the expression "word of the Lord"] (although frequently Matt. 24:29-44 is invoked)."[109]

It seems more convincing, then, to suggest that Paul simply uses the expression "the word of the Lord" to give prophetic authority to words that he has already spoken in 4:14.[110] It is likely the case that Paul, like other hortatory guides in his age, gave his words authority by pointing to a higher authority deemed trustworthy by the readers.

Paul's description of the parousia (vv. 16-18), more richly symbolic than in the two previous allusions (2:19; 3:13), is a vivid yet terse apocalyptic drama that amplifies the value of Jesus' parousia. Against the backdrop of apocalyptic images like that of an "angel" (2 Esdr 4:36-37), the "trumpet of God" (*Pss Sol* 11:1; 2 Esdr 6:17-24), "[those] who are left" (Syriac Baruch 13:3; 76:2), and "clouds" (Dan 7:13), Paul portrays a group of brothers and sisters who will be united with each other and with the Lord imminently, powerfully, gloriously, and permanently.

The union will be imminent because Paul holds out the possibility that he will be one of those "who are left" (v. 17; but cf. 2 Cor 4:14). The union will be powerful because it will begin with "a cry of command" (v. 16), an image associated with a call to arms in a military battle. It will also be powerful because the dead believers (about whom the church now grieves) will live again (thus no longer subject to the powers of the old

104. See Plato *Gorgias* 52D.

105. Beverly R. Gaventa, *First and Second Thessalonians*, Interpretation (Louisville: John Knox, 1998) 64; F. F. Bruce, *1 & 2 Thessalonians*, WBC (Waco, Tex.: Word, 1982) 97.

106. For a critique of this position, see J. Delobel, "The Fate of the Dead According to 1 Thess 4 and 1 Cor 15," in *The Thessalonian Correspondence*, ed. Raymond F. Collins (Leuven: University of Leuven Press, 1990) 341.

107. J. Paul Sampley, *Walking Between the Times: Paul's Moral Reasoning* (Minneapolis: Fortress, 1991) 98.

108. Ibid., 98.

109. Gaventa, *First and Second Thessalonians*, 65.

110. Richard, *First and Second Thessalonians*, 240.

age). And it will likewise be powerful because those left "will be caught up" (lit., "will be snatched up," ἁρπαγησόμεθα *arpagēsometha*, v. 17), ironically a term often used to describe the action of death itself.[111] The union will be glorious not only because Paul uses the expression *parousia* (v. 15), which connoted (as previously shown) a grand affair, but it will be glorious as well because Paul uses the expression "meeting" (ἀπάντησις *apantēsis*), which at least connoted an entourage of citizens going out to meet a dignitary.[112]

The union, moreover, will be permanent as attested by the repetition of the preposition "with" (σύν *syn*, v. 17) and the result clause of v. 17*b*: "and so shall we be with the Lord forever." Paul envisions a reunion that can no longer be affected by the old age because, in fact, the parousia brings to an end all of the manifestations of the old age.

Paul closes his description of the parousia with a commendation to mutual consolation (v. 18). Thus here he speaks directly about some of the resources his church has for nurturing their lives together. Whether or not he can get to them, they have the power to console one another with the apocalyptic truths he has shared with them.

Before concluding this section, it is important to note that 1 Thess 4:13-18 should not be read in the light of 1 Corinthians 15. In part, given the audience-oriented perspective of this commentary, we should not read the Thessalonians passage in the light of the Corinthian passage because the church at Thessalonica would not have had 1 Corinthians 15 as a part of its repertoire for processing 1 Thess 4:13-18. In part, as well, 1 Corinthians 15 seems to have a different rhetorical interest from the one described for 1 Thess 4:13-18. While both texts note the death and resurrection of Jesus and appear to do so using pre-Pauline formulaic expressions, at least one of the rhetorical goals of 1 Corinthians 15 appears to be to challenge Corinthian enthusiasm or the overrealized eschatology within the Corinthian church through an insistence on the *future* resurrection of believers. Enthusiasm is not a problem in 1 Thessalonians. Furthermore, while the

word "then" (ἔπειτα *epeita*) in 1 Cor 15:23 indicates the sequence of resurrection from "Christ the first fruits" to "those who belong to Christ," or all believers, the same word in 1 Thess 4:17 suggests a sequence from the dead in Christ to the living faithful.[113]

Altogether then, 1 Thess 4:13-18 encourages the church in the midst of its grief to recognize the hope they have and how that hope distinguishes them from others. Their hope lies in an apocalyptic drama that speaks of the great power both of the death and resurrection of Jesus and of his parousia with respect to one of the fiercest manifestations of the old age: death. Whether the audience had the apocalyptic background to understand all of the particulars Paul mentioned about the parousia is uncertain.[114] What they did know, however, was that Jesus' death and resurrection and his parousia were instruments of God's power. With hope in these instruments, not only could they expect to see their loved ones again but also they could expect a grand and permanent reunion for all the believers. This hope—this distinctive hope—is a resource they can use even now to console each other.

5:1-11. Some interpreters see tensions between 5:1-11 and 4:13-18. That is, they presuppose that Paul's "Now concerning" (Περὶ δέ *Peri de*, 5:1; lit., "and/but concerning") transition implies a strong adversative contrast between the ideas of 4:13-18 and 5:1-11. Some think, therefore, that there is a contrast between a presumed timetable in 5:1-11 and a presumed timetable in 4:13-18, as if the day of the Lord occurs at a different time from the parousia. Yet, 1 Thess 5:1-11 does not support the contention that the day of the Lord follows *after* living believers are "caught up" at the Lord's coming, as noted in 4:13-18.[115] As Tracy Howard has argued, neither section gives a systematic chronological timetable, and both sections are exhortative in purpose and parallel in content.[116] Both commend a certain type of behavior in the light of eschatological matters. Both discuss the same event, the parousia

---

111. Plutarch uses the term "snatched up" several times in *Letter to Apollonius* 111C-D, 117B. See Abraham J. Malherbe, "Exhortation in First Thessalonians," *NovT* 25 (1983) 255-56.

112. Wanamaker, *The Epistles to the Thessalonians*, 175.

113. Bruce, *1 & 2 Thessalonians*, 101-2.

114. Beverly R. Gaventa, *First and Second Thessalonians*, Interpretation (Louisville: John Knox, 1998) 66.

115. On this view, see John F. Walvoord, *The Blessed Hope and the Tribulation: A Biblical and Historical Study of Posttribulation* (Grand Rapids: Zondervan, 1976) 115.

116. Tracy Howard, "The Literary Unity of 1 Thessalonians 4:13–5:11," *Grace Theological Journal* 9 (1988) 163-90.

(or the day of the Lord), and draw on various apocalyptic images to clarify the importance of that day for believers in the present.

Alternatively, again implying a strong contrast, some read 5:1-11 as if the church failed to understand Paul or as if the passage—though Pauline—postdates the other parts of the letter and reflects Paul's effort to quiet gnostic agitation.[117] To the contrary, the repetition of the expression "with" (*syn*) the Lord (4:17; 5:10) in both passages and the similar endings of both sections (4:18; 5:11) argue that the two are not radically distinct. Rather, they differ only in perspective. Each section uses a distinctive diction to characterize the consummation of the new age (either the parousia or the day of the Lord). The distinctive perspective of 1 Thess 5:1-11, however, is that here Paul reveals more of his thought about the *present* impact of vindication or judgment in the new age on believers. Paul's reference to the parousia now as the Day of the Lord simply highlights his shift to a focus on judgment. That is, the Day of the Lord (understood as YHWH's day) originally was the day of YHWH's vindication of the righteous and judgment of the unrighteous (cf. Joel 2:31; Amos 5:18; Mal 4:5). Thus, in this subunit, Paul will distinguish the believers from the unbelievers with respect to how believers can already celebrate their vindication.

In 5:1-11, Paul extends his previous discussion of the parousia and its distinguishing effects. Transitional markers divide the subunit into six small subsections: (1) vv. 1-2, the auditors' knowledge of the coming of the day of the Lord; (2) v. 3, the unbelievers' ignorance about the day of the Lord; (3) vv. 4-5, eschatological contrasts between believers and unbelievers; (4) vv. 6-8, requisite sobriety of believers; (5) vv. 9-10, justification for sobriety; and (6) v. 11, commendation toward mutual consolation and edification.

Paul's first move in this subunit is to use a well-known hendiadys, or a set of synonymous expressions ("times and seasons," 5:1; cf. Dan 2:21; 7:12; Wis 8:8) that by the first century CE (cf. Acts 1:7; 3:20-21) simply meant "a time of judgment" (not two separate kinds of times) in a *paralipsis* (a feigned statement).[118] That is, feign-

ing not to write about the time of judgment, he does just that. And while doing so, he notes the motivation for his reticence: The church already "know[s] very well" (5:2) the manner in which that time of judgment will come. The time of judgment will come in the surprising manner of a "thief at night," a well-known motif in apocalyptic traditions (5:2; cf. Luke 12:38-39; Rev 3:3).

Then, with a shift to a third-person style of writing and the use of the familiar apocalyptic diction of "labor pains" (5:3; cf. Ps 48:6; *1 Enoch* 62:4; Mark 13:8), Paul declares the destruction the day of the Lord will bring to the unbelievers whose lives were tethered exclusively to the present life. Given the auditors' familiarity with "peace and security" (5:3) as a propaganda slogan of the Roman imperial government (see the Introduction) moreover, the auditors likely recognized a pointed attack directed at the Roman Empire with which the Thessalonian outsiders had cast their lot of allegiance.

Shifting now again to the auditors (5:4), Paul next contrasts believers with unbelievers (5:4-5). Having already described unbelievers as persons capable of being surprised as if by a thief at night, Paul now presupposes that the "night" really represents a condition of unawareness or insensitivity. Thus he contrasts darkness and light imagery (or night and day imagery) as contrasting "spheres of existence."[119] Believers are not in a state of darkness (5:4) and do not have darkness as the source of their existence (5:5). Thus believers will not be surprised because they are "children of the day" (5:5), a Semitic expression that means that they belong to the realm of the day. By contrast, unbelievers are in darkness and have darkness as the source of their existence.

The imagery Paul uses here is that of eschatological battle, a familiar one in Jewish thought in Paul's time. Indeed, it is the imagery that the Qumran covenanters seized to portray the final eschatological battle.[120] With this imagery, Paul places the foundational team, along with the church, in an eschatological conflict, for he shifts from a second-person plural description of the church (all of you) to a first-person plural description ("we are not of the night or of darkness," 5:5).

117. Walter Schmithals, *The Apocalyptic Movement,* trans. John E. Steely (Nashville: Abingdon, 1975) 16-167.

118. See Charles Wanamaker, *The Epistles to the Thessalonians,* NIGTC (Grand Rapids: Eerdmans, 1990) 178.

119. Howard, "The Literary Unity of 1 Thessalonians 4:13–5:11," 172.

120. Helmut Koester, "From Paul's Eschatology to the Apocalyptic Schemata of 2 Thessalonians," in *The Thessalonian Correspondence,* ed. Raymond F. Collins (Leuven: University of Leuven Press, 1990) 451. See also 1QS 3:13–4:26; 1 QM 1:1, 3.

With another transitional marker, "so then" (ἄρα οὖν *ara oun*, 5:6), Paul's declaration of the distinction between believers and unbelievers now shifts to the behavior required of believers, who are children of the light and children of the day (5:6-8). Paul's distinction between children of the day and those of the night is not just about contrasting spheres of awareness or existence but also of contrasting spheres of action. The requisite behavior for believers, who are in a battle, is one of vigilance, an idea Paul conveys through a call for the foundational team and the church to be "awake" and "sober" (5:6). Both terms figure in eschatological thought as examples of vigilance (cf. Rom 13:11-13; 1 Cor 16:13), but Paul strengthens his request for requisite behavior with allusions to the direct opposites of "awake" and "sober," respectively, "asleep" and "drunk" (5:7). To do so, moreover, he returns to the imagery of the night but now cast as the time in which the inappropriate behaviors take place.

Seizing more battle imagery (5:8), Paul continues his call for sober behavior commensurate with those who belong to the day. In this case he reconfigures the earlier triad of faith, love, and hope (cf. 1:3) as the church's "weaponry for the eschatological battle."[121] It is important to realize, however, that the aorist, or past tense participle, translated in the NRSV as "[let us] put on" (ἐνδυσάμενοι *endysamenoi*, 5:8), as if it were present, should actually be translated as "already having put on." Thus the action of sobriety is an action that flows out of the fact that the believers are already clothed in battle gear.

Paul's shift to a justification for sobriety (5:9-10), then, is really an ultimate explanation for why the foundational leaders and the church are already garbed and thus should act in a manner befitting who they are in the eschatological battle. The ultimate explanation, of course, is based on God's initiative or election (5:9). Paul's discussion of the consequences of God's initiative rhetorically signals connections between 5:1-11 and 4:13-18. That is, although Paul initially used the word "sleep" (καθεύδω *katheudō*) to connote insensibility ("let us not fall asleep," 5:6), he now uses it to imply death (5:10), perhaps alluding to Dan 12:2 LXX and the subject of death in 1 Thess

4:13-18. As well, 5:10*b* (attached as it is to what some scholars call a pre-Pauline formula: "who died for us," 5:10*a*; cf. 4:14; Gal 1:4) seems to hark back to 1 Thess 4:17 because both speak of believers being "with the Lord."[122]

If that is the case, Paul's expression "whether we are awake or asleep" shifts now from the concern with vigilance and the contrast between being awake and being asleep to the contrast between being alive and being dead. For Paul, because of God's initiative and Jesus' death, a reunion with the Lord is possible for all believers, whether they are awake (alive) or asleep (dead).

Finally, as 5:1-11 draws to a close, Paul connects 4:13–5:11 to 5:12-22. On the one hand, he repeats 4:18 with its emphasis on mutual consolation. On the other hand, he anticipates the edification section of 5:12-22 with the expression "build up each other."[123]

Thus 5:1-11 seeks to continue the theme of the parousia with judgment as the perspective from which Paul now distinguishes the believers from the unbelievers.[124] The believers, moreover, are already "children of the day" because of the death of their Lord Jesus Christ on their behalf. Still, the full consummation of the new age has not yet occurred. So the church must be vigilant in its vision of a life influenced by that consummation and it must seek to offer consolation and individuated help to build one another up.

Throughout both sections (4:11-18; 5:1-11), Paul evinces the distinctiveness of the church—the distinctiveness of its hope or of its ethical life in the present as regulated by the events of the past (Jesus' death and resurrection) and the future (the parousia or day of the Lord). Like 4:1-12, then, the second subunit (4:13–5:11) of the last large unit (4:1–5:22) reinforces the idea of the church's distinctive apocalyptic life. For a church facing the painful ordeals of alienation, these words about a distinctive life likely provided a source of comfort. With little wonder it is, then, that Paul gives direct attention to his words at the closing of one of the sections: "Comfort one another with these words" (4:18).

---

121. Ibid., 451.

122. F. F. Bruce, *1 & 2 Thessalonians,* WBC (Waco, Tex.: Word, 1982) 113.
123. On the relationship between 5:11 and 5:12-22, see Abraham J. Malherbe, " 'Pastoral Care' in the Thessalonian Church," *NTS* 36 (1990) 388-89. Cf. Charles Wanamaker, *The Epistles to the Thessalonians,* NIGTC (Grand Rapids: Eerdmans, 1990) 191.
124. See Wanamaker, *The Epistles to the Thessalonians,* 177.

REFLECTIONS

When we read 1 Thess 4:13–5:11, we are prompted to think about end times, last things, and the ultimate destruction of the world as we know it. The proverbial "thief in the night" description of the day of the Lord of 1 Thessalonians (which is also mentioned in the Synoptics) appeared in medieval literature and continues to work its way in the thought of great texts today.[125] Julia Ward Howe's "Battle Hymn of the Republic" (1862) lyrically captures the 1 Thessalonians' end-time rhetoric about the Lord's coming with trumpets sounding forth (1 Thess 4:15-16). Paul's brief comments about believers being "caught up in the clouds" has become the basis for many books and for a degree of anxiety about a "rapture" of believers.

To be sure, these verses are saturated with apocalyptic imagery, that suggests an imminent end and final days. Yet Paul's apocalypticism inspired hope, gave comfort, and provided challenge to the socially alienated persons of his day. Reminders of God's provision for the absent (deceased) brothers and sisters in the future are powerful testaments to God's care for all believers in the present. Notices of permanent union with the Lord in the future are challenging statements about God's desire for believers to come together on earth right now, even though Martin Luther King, Jr.'s words are as true today as they were years ago: "At eleven o'clock on Sunday morning when we stand to sing 'In Christ there is no East or West,' " we stand in the most segregated hour of America."[126] Talk of eschatological battle is a serious invitation for us not to settle for easy "peace and security slogans" or other superficial changes that leave many people still confined to the margins of existence.

Thus, Paul's apocalyptic diction is not innocuous. It is radical and impinges on the quality of life lived in the present. In many ways, it is reminiscent of the apocalyptic spirit found in the Negro spirituals. Although the spirituals were noted for their otherworldly orientation, they also had this-worldly functions.[127]

The slave's world was full of trouble, storms, and hard times, as the songs "Soon I Will Be Done," "Been in the Storm So Long," and "I Been Rebuked and I Been Scorned" attest. These songs expressed longing and hope for another world. Among the this-worldly functions, however, were the building up of community solidarity and the practice of a veiled form of critique and communication.[128] With an eye toward the future and yet with a challenge for community solidarity in the present circumstances, the slaves sang "Walk Together Children." In "Swing Low, Sweet Chariot" and "Steal Away to Jesus," the slave likely engaged in covert communication, cryptically requesting or signaling the help of the "underground railroad" (sweet chariot) to get "home" (the northern states or Canada).

Thus, the spirituals included both "apocalyptic visions and heroic exploits of the Scripture," despite the tensions between the two.[129] On the one hand, the slaves spoke of a future day of judgment, as in "That Great Gittin' Up Morning," "Roll, Jordan, Roll," and "My Lord, What a Morning." On the other hand, they spoke of biblical heroes (e.g., David, Joshua, Moses, and Noah) whom God had delivered in this world.[130]

Both the future and the present were important for them. In sum, the spirituals confronted the slaves' sordid experiences, remythologized the biblical concepts to speak cryptically but encouragingly, and provided a source of comfort and challenge. Their apocalyptic strain, like Paul's apocalyptic vision, read the present reality in the light of the future expectation.

125. Dwight H. Purdy, "Thief in the Night," in *A Dictionary of Biblical Tradition in English Literature,* ed. David Lyle Jeffrey (Grand Rapids: Eerdmans, 1992) 763.

126. Martin Luther King, Jr., "Remaining Awake Through a Great Revolution," in *A Knock at Midnight: Inspiration from the Great Sermons of Reverend Martin Luther King, Jr,* ed. Clayborne Carson and Peter Holloran (New York: Warner, 2000) 209.

127. Frazier regards them as "essentially religious in sentiment and . . . otherworldly in outlook." See E. Franklin Frazier, *The Negro Church in America* (New York: Schocken, 1974) 19. On the spirituals as aids in transcending circumstances, see Lawrence Levine, *Black Culture and Black Consciousness: Afro-American Folk Thought from Slavery to Freedom* (Oxford: Oxford University Press, 1977) 19, 23.

128. On the spirituals as sources of communal bonding, especially through their antiphonal structure, see ibid., 33. On the spirituals as veiled communication, see ibid., 51.

129. Ibid., 41.

130. Ibid., 50.

1 Thessalonians 5:12-22, Nurturing Resources for the Distinctive Life

NIV

¹²Now we ask you, brothers, to respect those who work hard among you, who are over you in the Lord and who admonish you. ¹³Hold them in the highest regard in love because of their work. Live in peace with each other. ¹⁴And we urge you, brothers, warn those who are idle, encourage the timid, help the weak, be patient with everyone. ¹⁵Make sure that nobody pays back wrong for wrong, but always try to be kind to each other and to everyone else.

¹⁶Be joyful always; ¹⁷pray continually; ¹⁸give thanks in all circumstances, for this is God's will for you in Christ Jesus.

¹⁹Do not put out the Spirit's fire; ²⁰do not treat prophecies with contempt. ²¹Test everything. Hold on to the good. ²²Avoid every kind of evil.

NRSV

12But we appeal to you, brothers and sisters,[a] to respect those who labor among you, and have charge of you in the Lord and admonish you; ¹³esteem them very highly in love because of their work. Be at peace among yourselves. ¹⁴And we urge you, beloved,[a] to admonish the idlers, encourage the fainthearted, help the weak, be patient with all of them. ¹⁵See that none of you repays evil for evil, but always seek to do good to one another and to all. ¹⁶Rejoice always, ¹⁷pray without ceasing, ¹⁸give thanks in all circumstances; for this is the will of God in Christ Jesus for you. ¹⁹Do not quench the Spirit. ²⁰Do not despise the words of prophets,[b] ²¹but test everything; hold fast to what is good; ²²abstain from every form of evil.

[a] Gk brothers [b] Gk despise prophecies

COMMENTARY

The first (4:1-12) and second (4:13–5:11) subunits given, Paul now concludes his last large section with 5:12-22. A variety of markers aid the division of this material into three sections. First, the repetition of first-person plural verbs of exhortation, "we appeal" (ἐρωτῶμεν *erōtōmen*, v. 12) and "we urge" (παρακαλοῦμεν *parakaloumen*, v. 14), easily link the material in vv. 12 and 14 together. Likewise both vv. 12 and 14 include an address to the church ("Brothers and sisters"). Second, vv. 16-22 read like a series of terse imperatives all constructed with final verb formulations and interrupted in form only by the declarative sentence, "for this is the will of God in Christ Jesus for you" (v. 18*a*), as *Fig.* 19 suggests. Third, v. 15 seems to stand apart both from vv. 12-14 and vv. 16-22 because it is the only part of the section that uses the strong adversative transitional conjunction "but" (ἀλλά *alla*) and the only part imploring the church to direct its attention *inwardly* and *outwardly*. Fourth, if v. 15 constitutes a separate discrete part between vv. 12-14 and vv. 16-22, each of the

three discrete parts now formed would virtually end with an emphasis on "all" (or with a cognate form of the word πᾶς *pas*). That is, each discrete part would stress "all" persons in a particular group (vv. 12-14) or "all" outsiders (v. 15) or "all" or "every" form of evil (v. 22).

The markers shown, readers should be able to divide 5:12-22 into three discrete sections: (1) exhortations on the recognition of ongoing models of moral training within the church and on the practices of moral training within the church (vv. 12-14); (2) a caveat against seeking retribution with an admonition consistently to seek the good toward all believers and toward outsiders (v. 15); and (3) a series of terse imperatives on the proper dispositions toward circumstances or the nurturing resources accruing to the new age (vv. 16-22).

5:12-14. The first section describes moral training in the church from two perspectives. First, Paul addresses the church ("Brothers and sisters") on that which could build up the church (cf. 5:11). Using three participial expressions

---

Figure 19: A Diagram of 1 Thess 5:16-22

Always rejoice
Constantly pray
In all circumstances give thanks

For this is the will of God in Christ Jesus for you
The Spirit, do not quench.
Prophecy (or words of prophets), do not despise
Everything, test.
The good, hold fast
From every form of evil, abstain

("those who labor," "[those who] have charge," and "[those who] admonish"), Paul describes the ideal activities for aiding the community. Furthermore, the participle forms occur in the plural, as if Paul here speaks not about a single individual responsible for the activities or about single offices (which came later in the history of early Christianity) but about activities potentially practiced by several persons.[131] In addition, his final exhortation in vv. 12-14 commends the believers to have peace with one another.

Paul's injunction "to recognize" (εἰδέναι *eidenai*, v. 12*a*; the infinitive εἰδέναι [*eidenai*] should not be translated as "to respect") and "to esteem" (ἡγεῖσθαι *hēgeisthai*, v. 13) persons enaged in these edifying practices for their "work" (ἔργον *ergon*, v. 13) suggests that he favors those activities that are similar to the moral training practices mentioned earlier in the letter. Thus Paul's reference to "those who labor" (v. 12) recalls his use of "labor" (κόπος *kopos*) to describe the "labor" of the entire community (1:3), the "efforts" (or labor) of his foundational team (2:9), and his foundational "labor" as it was under attack by the tempter (3:5). Relatedly, Paul also used cognate forms of "work" (*ergon*) to describe the "work" of the entire community (1:3, 4:11), the "efforts" (ἐργαζόμενοι *ergazomenoi*) of the foundational

team (2:9), the "working" (ἐνεργεῖται *energeitai*) of God's word in the community (2:13), and the role of Timothy, God's "co-worker" (συνεργός *synergos*, 3:2; cf. 2 Cor 5:15–6:2).

Whatever the precise meanings of the words "labor" and "work," Paul's emphasis is on aid for the church—whether that aid comes from God, from the foundational leaders, or from the church itself. Thus "labor/work" is any form of aid that helps to make the church productive in its distinctive life. Because "work" and "labor" connote self-sufficiency in 2:9-12 and 4:11, moreover, it is possible that in 1 Thessalonians these expressions connote any efforts that could help the church maintain its self-sufficiency so as not to retreat to its former networks of support.

Second, Paul exhorts all of the church ("brothers and sisters") on the kinds of special needs that have to be addressed to build up one another in the church (cf. 5:11). As with the specific activities, the specific needs are relevant to the church's audience situation, especially as exposed by 2:1-12. Whatever the meaning of the terms ἀτάκτους (*ataktous*; NRSV, "idlers"), ὀλιγοψύχους (*oligopsychous*, "fainthearted"), and ἀσθενῶν (*asthenōn*, "weak"), the two commands to "admonish" (νουθετεῖτε *noutheteite*) and to "encourage" (παραμυθεῖσθε *paramytheisthe*), directed to the whole church, are used elsewhere in the letter. A cognate form of "admonish" is used in v. 12 to indicate the kind of activity the church should recognize and esteem. It can be inferred, then, that Paul continues to discuss moral training of some sort in v. 14 with a focus on how the church should look out for certain traits in the community. A cognate form of "encourage"

131. While many interpreters quickly turn to Paul's list of exhortations in Romans 12 as a context for analyzing the exhortations in 1 Thess 5:12-22, a key difference needs to be noted. When Paul uses προιστάμενος(*proistamenos*, "the leader") in Rom 12:8, the participle appears in a singular form, not the plural form as in 1 Thess 5:12. Following Malherbe, this commentary maintains that Paul refers not to a specific group of people in 5:12 as much as he refers to a specific group of activities that most of the church potentially could perform. See Abraham J. Malherbe, *Paul and the Thessalonians: The Philosophic Tradition of Pastoral Care* (Philadelphia: Fortress, 1987) 88.

was used earlier in 2:12 to indicate how the foundational leaders aided the church in its worthy walk. Both terms, then, are a part of Paul's moral training diction—that is, his language for efforts to make the church live out the new life to which God continuously calls them in the face of ongoing, difficult experiences.

We do not have any precise information about the specific needs of the church. Scholarly insistence that "idlers" is an appropriate translation of ἄτακτοι (ataktoi, v. 14) is misleading and likely based on construals of the audience situation in 2 Thessalonians (see the Introduction and the Commentary on 2 Thessalonians) where forms of the word appear again (3:6-7, 11). The term usually refers to those who "engage in anti-social conduct."[132] In the light of Paul's concern for the persistent worthy walk in the church, the expression ataktoi could simply refer to any type of person (of which there may be several) not in harmony with the mutual nurturing of the worthy walk.

Since "fainthearted" (ὀλιγοψύχους oligopsychous, v. 14; lit., "little-soul persons") never occurs again in Paul or elsewhere in the New Testament, it is difficult to know much about such people. The specific type of exhortation Paul recommends for them, however, is one of encouraging (or consoling), a type of exhortation that he has recommended for the entire congregation to offer each other (4:18; 5:11).

The identity of the "weak" (ἀσθενῶν asthenōn, v. 14) is also unclear though Paul elsewhere uses this word to describe persons with a deficiency of knowledge that renders them a limited measure of faith when compared to others (cf. 1 Cor 8:7-14). Whether this deficiency of knowledge is the issue for the "weak" in 1 Thessalonians is unclear, but Paul's term for the assistance they require ("help" or "support") is a need that anyone in the church could have had at one time or another.

Perhaps, then, all of these types—the "antisocial," the "fainthearted," and the "weak"—are persons who have to be exhorted by the church because they find it difficult at times either to engage in self-scrutiny or to take

on the otherwise communal role of nurturing.[133] It must be noted, however, that the three traits are not the same. In fact, Paul likely mentions all three to show the church how its nurturing must be individuated to the differing needs that may arise in the church.[134] Regardless of the differences, Paul commends patience toward all of them (v. 14).

In focus here in 5:12-14, then, is a comprehensive form of mutual nurturing, a form of edification in which the church looks to itself both for expressions of nurture and for the recognition of the needs that require nurture. That kind of mutual nurturing—itself a part of other alternative communities (like the Epicureans)—was vitally necessary if the church was to maintain its distinctive holy life with a strong commitment to its apocalyptic hope in the face of local hostilities.

5:15. The second section warns the church against retribution (cf. Prov 20:22; Matt 5:38-39, 43; Rom 12:17) but enjoins the persistent seeking of the good. Lest the previous exhortations appear simply as directions to an introverted group, Paul uses the exhortation in this verse to cover both inner and outer relations. Auditors here would likely remember 4:9-12, which also included a shift from the church to others, including outsiders. Furthermore, Paul exploits here the same expression ("to one another and to all" [εἰς ἀλλήλους καὶ εἰς πάντας [eis allēlous kai eis pantas]) used earlier (3:12) to describe the church's need to extend its love or care outward. The edification process, then, is not one of distinctiveness for its own sake. Rather, Paul is ever the mission-directed pastor, even in his comments to a beleagured church (cf. 4:12). He not only seeks edification within them, but also seeks to model appropriate behavior before outsiders who, in turn, will be influenced by the church's distinctive holy life.

5:16-22. The final section is sometimes labeled "Paul's shotgun paraenesis" because Paul quickly fires off one round of imperatives after another.[135] Scholars have noticed, moreover, that the first three imperatives (vv. 16-18) seem sepa-

---

132. Raymond Collins, *The Birth of the New Testament: The Origin and Development of the First Generation* (New York: Crossroad, 1993) 94.

133. On the unreadiness of some novices for self-scrutiny, see Seneca *Letters to Lucilius* 2.1.

134. Cf. Seneca *On Tranquility of Mind* 6.1-2.

135. Calvin Roetzel, "1 Thess 5:12-28: A Case Study," in *Society of Biblical Literature Annual Papers,* ed. Lane McGaughy (Chico, Calif.: Scholars Press, 1972), 375.

rated stylistically from the others because of constructions with initial adverbial expressions and because the adverbs are virtually synonymous (see *Fig. 19*, 730).[136] In addition, the first three imperatives would likely remind the auditors of other instances in which Paul modeled the very commands he now advances.

Earlier Paul spoke of the church's reception of the word with joy (1:6) in affliction as an imitation of the foundational team and of the Lord. Joy in the midst of affliction, then, is something Paul's team has modeled. A clearer example of this kind of joy emerges in the two parallel subunits of the second large unit, 2:17-20 and 3:9-13. In those instances, Paul's joy is based not on his present circumstance—separation from the church—but on present or future manifestations of the new age (cf. Phil 4:4-5). To tell the church to "rejoice always" (5:16) is to tell the church to exult in the new age's manifestations, whether the manifestations are already apparent or can be expected at the glorious parousia.

Similarly, Paul's command "to pray without ceasing" (v. 17) is modeled earlier in the letter. Paul speaks of "making prayers" constantly" (1:2), and his thanksgiving reports and wish-prayers are abundant. Paul has also used the expression "always" (ἀδιαλείπτως *adialeiptōs*) twice (1:2; 2:13) before 5:17. As with "joy," Paul's prayers or thanks for the church's success are gratitude to God for manifestations of the new age—either its effectiveness in the present because of the death of Jesus or its manifestations in the future consummation (e.g., in the community's blamelessness at the parousia, 3:13). What Paul commends in both instances in vv. 16-17, then, is a disposition of constant joy or prayer because of the present and imminent manifestations of the new age. Yet, because the consummation of the new age is not yet in effect, the church has to face local hostilities. But it does not have to face them without some resources—that is, without joy and prayer.

Obviously, the same is true for the third imperative of this set (v. 18*a*). To "give thanks in all circumstances" is both modeled by Paul (see the repeated thanksgiving notices) and a response to what God has done in Paul's apocalyptic

schema. What Paul has already modeled, then, becomes a command for the church as well.

It is little wonder that these three imperatives, all of which make an appeal for constancy, are followed by the declarative phrase "for this is the will of God in Christ Jesus for you" (v. 18*b*). Paul used the expression "will of God" earlier when he spoke about the sanctified life or the life of growing maturity (4:3). Furthermore, as noted before, "will of God" was often used in Jewish contexts as a descriptive term for proper activities.

In Greek, the last set of imperatives (vv. 19-22) all have a final verbal construction, as with the imperatives in vv. 16-18*a* (see *Fig. 19*, 730). The last ones, however, do not begin with adverbial constructions. According to several scholars, what holds the last set together is an emphasis on the Spirit. Perhaps! Another interpretation is to see the last set as more resources accruing to those who are a part of the new age, as the following paragraphs suggest.

Certainly the Holy Spirit functions as evidence of the new age. Earlier, when Paul shared with the community evidence of the new age in their lives (1:1-5), he spoke of the Holy Spirit, which elsewhere he designates as a pledge (or a first installment, 2 Cor 1:22). Whether one can prove that the church already knew about the Spirit's role as a pledge is not important for this argument. What is critical is that the Holy Spirit is mentioned early in the letter as evidence of the new age's presence in the church. Later, Paul speaks about the Holy Spirit as an agent of inspiration (1:6) and of the Holy Spirit as God's gift to the believers, who have been called not to live as they once lived but in the distinctive life of holiness (4:7-8). The exhortation "not to quench the Spirit" (v. 19), then, makes absolute sense for this audience's situation. In order to face the local hostilities and gain inspiration and guidance, the church needs to avail itself of the resource of the Holy Spirit.

Whether the next resource should be translated as "words of prophets" (as in NRSV, v. 20) or as the "gift of prophecy" is uncertain. For a church subject to local hostilities, however, what seems incontrovertible is the need for this resource (in either form) for the survival of the church. Likewise, the last resource, testing or discernment (v. 2; cf. 1 Cor 14:29), is also crucial. The church is exhorted to test everything and to seize (that

---

136. Charles Wanamaker, *The Epistles to the Thessalonians*, NIGTC (Grand Rapids: Eerdmans, 1990) 199-200.

which is determined by the church to be) the good. Should the test apply to the prophetic utterances? Many scholars think so. The range of the tests, however, is comprehensive. They are to test "everything." Furthermore, just as they seek the good, they are to avoid "every" form of evil. The import of this exhortation and the others, then, is to show the church that they have what they need for every decision and every deliberation. They need not go beyond their alternative community for the resources they need to survive. Indeed, with the forces of moral training, the appropriate dispositions and the basic resources, the church has a sufficient base for its survival even if Paul, Silvanus, and Timothy can never return.

Before moving on to the last unit of the letter (5:23-28), a few words are in order about all of the subunits of the last large unit. First, all of the subunits reinforce the distinctiveness of the church—in its life of holiness and love, in its hope and ethical behavior because of that hope, and in the nurturing force of its resources for moral training. Second, the emphasis of these subunits on the church's distinctiveness does not distract from Paul's abiding concern for outsiders who could be influenced by the distinctiveness of the church. Third, the subunits reiterate the value of the resources for persistence noted in the two previous large units—namely, the words and practices of leaders who inculcate moral training. The words of these leaders—whether in past teachings (4:1, 9; 5:1-2), in authorized words of comfort (cf. 4:13-18, esp. 4:14), or in maxims (5:16-22)—are available to help the church through its present crisis of alienation. In addition, the practices of the foundational leaders are held up as a model already at work in the church (5:12-15), whether in the form of admonition, encouragement, patience, or doing and seeking good rather than retribution. For a church facing local hostilities, these resources could help them continue in their new apocalyptic life, even if the foundational team could never get back to them again. Thus these resources are given to strengthen a church against the possibility of returning to their former way or walk of living.

REFLECTIONS

"Give thanks in all circumstances" (5:16 NRSV). In *every* circumstance? For *all* things? Most of us would want to adjust Paul's words, to qualify his exhortation. Perhaps we wish Paul to say "in *some* circumstances" or "in *some* things." That would be more acceptable for our own practical tastes, more suitable for our own set of realities. But in *every* circumstance? That has to be one of the most adventurous voyages of thought ever embarked on the rough waters of reason. And logically, it seems destined for shipwreck.

Paul certainly does not qualify the circumstances. He means "all." The two previous imperatives also have a comprehensive, unqualified character: "Rejoice always, praying without ceasing" (5:16-17 NRSV). Has Paul asked his church to do the impossible? Can a person face a fresh set of abuses every day and give thanks? Can a person rise above the psychic doubts left by years of abuse at the hands of a parent and give thanks? "Give thanks in everything"!?

Paul's words may lack qualification, but they do presuppose at least two basic truths. Because of these two truths, it is possible and necessary to give thanks in everything. The first truth is that worship of God is the context for *all* of life, not just the part we devote to God during our time in a sanctuary. In Karl Rahner's words, "Everyday life must become itself our prayer."[137] If all of life is worship for those who seek to do God's will, then thanks is a necessary and inevitable product. But we should note that Paul does not say thanks should be governed by circumstances. The thanks is governed by the life of worship. Whether good or bad be the lot, a life of worship (of seeking to please and honor God and of doing God's will) means perpetual thanksgiving.

---

137. Karl Rahner, *The Content of Faith: The Best of Karl Rahner's Theological Writings,* ed. Karl Lehmann and Albert Raffelt, trans. Harvey D. Egan, S.J. (New York: Crossroad, 1992) 511.

The second truth Paul presupposes is that life's depths, not solely its surfaces, must arrest our attention. Paul Tillich speaks of the "depth of existence" as the "ground of our historical life . . . the ultimate depth of history."[138] Tillich's words are not a call for residency near shallow waters, where thoughts are restricted to appearances near the shore. Yet, most of us live near such shallow waters. And we judge our lives by visible, surface, and indeed superficial determinants—that is, the occasional good things or bad things that happen to us.

Paul's (and Tillich's) challenge for us, however, is to move to a depth in which there are weightier truths that make it possible for us to give perpetual thanks. Paul's weightier truths are a part of his apocalyptic view of existence—his view of two ages (a new age and an old one), with Christ's death and resurrection securing us for salvation. From the depths of history, from which we get a comprehensive frame for life, we can defy circumstances (without ever glibly dismissing them). From the depths of life—a life "hidden with Christ in God" (Col 3:3)—we can take the onetime cross of shame and declare it to be God's choice over that which conventionally accrues honor (cf. 1 Corinthians 26–31). From the depths of life, one can join the poet James Russell Lowell and say:

Truth forever on the scaffold
Wrong forever on the throne
But that scaffold sways the future
and beyond the dim unknown
Standeth God within the shadows
Keeping watch above God's own.

138. Paul Tillich, *The Shaking of the Foundations* (New York: Scribner's, 1948) 58-59.

1 THESSALONIANS 5:23-28

THE PERORATION

NIV	NRSV
[23]May God himself, the God of peace, sanctify you through and through. May your whole spirit, soul and body be kept blameless at the coming of our Lord Jesus Christ. [24]The one who calls you is faithful and he will do it.	[23]May the God of peace himself sanctify you entirely; and may your spirit and soul and body be kept sound[a] and blameless at the coming of our Lord Jesus Christ. [24]The one who calls you is faithful, and he will do this.
[25]Brothers, pray for us. [26]Greet all the brothers with a holy kiss. [27]I charge you before the Lord to have this letter read to all the brothers.	[25]Beloved,[b] pray for us.
	[26]Greet all the brothers and sisters[c] with a holy kiss. [27]I solemnly command you by the Lord that this letter be read to all of them.[d]
[28]The grace of our Lord Jesus Christ be with you.	[28]The grace of our Lord Jesus Christ be with you.[e]

[a]Or *complete*   [b]Gk *Brothers*   [c]Gk *brothers*   [d]Gk *to all the brothers*   [e]Other ancient authorities add *Amen*

COMMENTARY

Given the letter's goal of encouraging a beleagured community, Paul writes the final lines (5:23-28) of his document. In epistolary analysis terms, all of these verses constitute the letter's closing. They include a peace benediction (v. 23), a concluding notice of encouragement, a brief series of exhortations (to pray a prayer of intercession, to greet one another with a kiss, and to read the letter to everyone), and a benediction.[139]

In terms of rhetorical analysis, the final section of a document is its peroration. Because the last large unit (4:1–5:22) ends at v. 22, v. 23 marks the beginning of 1 Thessalonians' peroration. Furthermore, with v. 23 as the beginning of the peroration, the entire letter is bound by a grace, peace (1:1), peace (v. 23), grace (v. 28) inclusio. The two intercessory prayers in 5:23 and 5:28 provide a nice final inclusio with both a notice of encouragement (v. 24) and exhortative material (vv. 24-25) occupying a central section. Assuming that the peroration includes all of 5:23-28, these final verses function in two ways. On the one hand, they stir the emotions; on the other hand, they summarize the contents of the letter.

Paul's use of an invocation at the beginning of the peroration gives his letter a closing emotional charge.[140] In addition, friendly terms and phrases in vv. 25-28 (e.g., "brothers and sisters," "greet with a holy kiss") bespeak an affectionate—even if exhortative—tone. The term "brothers" connotes the fictive kinship that Paul's team shared with the church of the Thessalonians and others as well. Furthermore, the "kiss" (cf. Rom 16:16; 1 Cor 16:20; 2 Cor 13:12), a symbol of "social union," also expressed the idea of a family.[141]

Just as the exordium (1:1-5) announced the letter's themes, so also the final verses (5:23-28) summarize some of those same themes. With final allusions to God's continuous calling (v. 24; cf. 1:4; 2:12; 4:7) and the parousia (v. 23; 2:19;

---

139. Cf. Jeffrey Weima, *Neglected Endings: The Significance of the Pauline Letter Closing* (Sheffield: JSOT, 1994) 176.

140. It is to be noted that Quintilian, a 1st century CE rhetor, regarded invocations as appropriate for the peroration of a speech. He asserts that the "invocation of the gods usually gives the impression that our speaker is conscious of the justice of his cause." Quintilian, *Institutio Oratoria,* trans. H. E. Butler and N. Heinemann, LCL (New York: Putnam, 1920–22).

141. Raymond Collins, *The Birth of the New Testament: The Origin and Development of the First Generation* (New York: Crossroad, 1993) 87.

3:13; 4:15), Paul highlights the apocalyptic hope in which the church is exhorted to persist.[142] As well, Paul's wish-prayer (v. 23) signals that the church must persevere not only in its hope but in the requisite actions of that hope as well. Indeed, Paul intimates one of those requisite actions: continuous prayer, with the inclusion of prayer forms (vv. 23, 28) and the request for prayer (v. 25; Rom 15:30; Phlm 22).

Because Paul spells out some of those requisite actions, the church hears a final time about the distinctive life to which it has been charged. Repetitive diction about sanctification or holiness in the wish-prayer and in one of the exhortations describes the distinctive life (vv. 23, 26). That diction and the hope for the church's blamelessness vividly remind the church of its distinctiveness as signaled earlier in 3:9-13. Moreover, with the repeated emphasis on concern for "all," Paul reminds the church that the distinctive life must be the goal of "all" of its members (v. 26). Thus, even if some are not present for the reading of the letter, the letter must be read to them as well.

Even the earlier emphasis on the effectiveness (or importance) of the writer's word or presence receives its due in the peroration. Given the role of Hellenistic letters as substitutes for a writer's presence, Paul's command that the letter be read aloud evokes his presence as often as the letter must be so read to reach all of the members of the church.[143]

It should be stated finally that the peroration reminds the church again of its resources for persistence—the words and moral training practices of its foundational leaders. Given its terse, striking character, 1 Thess 5:24 ("The one who calls you is faithful, and he will do this"; cf. 1 Cor 1:8-9) assumes the force of a maxim, as if to provide a basic truth through which the church can maintain its apocalyptic hopes. Also, the injunction to have the letter read conveys the authority of the words of the foundational leaders for all the members of the church. Paul's wish-prayer, moreover, exemplifies his persistence in prayer and reminds the church of the constant concern he has exhibited for them. If the church continues to emulate this concern for its members, they will continue to embody one of Paul's key moral training practices.

142. It must be noted, however, that Paul's trichotomous anthropology ("spirit and soul and body," 5:23) indicates not Paul's personal acceptance of the anthropology but the recognition (from the church's perspective) that "it is the whole human being who is to be found blameless at the parousia." See ibid., 158.

143. Cf. Seneca *Letters to Lucilius* 40.1.

REFLECTIONS

One of the recurring images of 1 Thessalonians, that of brothers and sisters, finds its way into the letter's peroration as well. As noted earlier, the term "brothers" occurs in Jewish literature (Deut 15:3).[144] In 1 Thessalonians, Paul uses the term repeatedly with a compensatory function. Given the local hostilities faced by the church, language of brotherhood compensates for the loss of former family networks. In addition, the term is one of solidarity, gathering together all believers who could claim Paul's God as their father (cf. 1:1). In Paul's final words, he writes to ensure that the believers embrace the solidarity they share. No one is to be left out: *All* the brothers and sisters are to be greeted with a holy kiss, and the letter is to be read to *all* the brothers and sisters.

Some aspects of ancient family life could prove beneficial for the church today if we better understood and appreciated the solidarity expressed in such families. All collateral relations in ancient families were important for the family's stability, but the most important was that between brothers. Brothers were considered to be "the main supports of the house and . . . the family's continuity and solidarity."[145] For the sake of the family's public image and as an

144. See Philo *On the Special Laws* 2.79-80; Josephus *Antiquities of the Jews* 10.20. See also Charles Wanamaker, *The Epistles to the Thessalonians,* NIGTC (Grand Rapids: Eerdmans, 1990) 77.

145. Cynthia Jordan Bannon, "Consors Mecum Temporum Illorum: Brothers in Republican Rome" (Ph.D. diss., University of Michigan, 1991) 75.

indication of family solidarity, brothers were expected to exhibit mutual trust, "emotional identification," self-sacrifice in the pursuit of common interests, and cooperation in the management and continuity of the family's property.[146] In addition, the ideal relations between brothers became the model for many of the relations that developed among the fictive kin of ancient clubs and associations. Thus, the ideal relations of blood brothers took on a metaphorical casting for the fictive kin, whether male or female, and whether near (in a particular city) or far (in another town).

Thinking of the church as a family with vital collateral relations of solidarity on the order of the ancient clubs and associations could prove helpful for the church today in several ways. First, the openness of the family is a breath of fresh air for our churches. The idea of family here, of course, is not that of a nuclear group with its issues of privacy and separation. Rather, the idea is more similar to the Latino experience of the extended family that, according to Justo González, is "a much wider group of people, of uncertain and ever-expandable limits."[147] Second, in a world of wariness and suspicion, the practice of mutual trust is a lost art that needs to be found again. Third, the demonstration of solidarity through emotional identification is a welcomed ideal that should replace mere toleration. Fourth, the ability to measure one's life by pursuits shared by a larger group is a wholesome counterforce to the pervasive dominance of rank individualism.

146. See ibid., 37, 52-53, 86, 98, 101.
147. Justo L. González, "In Quest of a Protestant Hispanic Ecclesiology," in *Teología en Conjunto: A Collaborative Hispanic Protestant Theology*, ed. Jose David Rodriguez and Loida I. Martell-Otero (Louisville: Westminster John Knox, 1997) 92.

THE SECOND LETTER TO THE THESSALONIANS

INTRODUCTION, COMMENTARY, AND REFLECTIONS
BY
ABRAHAM SMITH

THE SECOND LETTER TO THE

THESSALONIANS

INTRODUCTION

R eflecting his general concern for the church's stability in the face of mounting hostility from its neighbors and a more specific concern about an enthusiastic brand of apocalypticism, the writer of 2 Thessalonians crafts a letter to encourage the believers not to veer from his truth or traditions (2:15). That truth focuses on both the present and the future. Indeed, the present experiences of opposition are read in the light of traditions about the future, including the coming judgment at the parousia (1:5-10) and the apocalyptic events preceding the day of the Lord (2:1-12). Furthermore, the present works of the church are authorized when they stand in accordance with traditions that demand support for the image, care, and continuity of the whole church while it awaits its Lord's future revelation.

Like 1 Thessalonians, the letter falls within the hortatory tradition. It is a letter of exhortation not simply because it uses explicit hortatory appeals through imperatives, as in its requests for stability (2:15), prayer (3:1-2), and correct discipline (3:6-15). Like 1 Thessalonians and other letters of exhortation from the period, 2 Thessalonians uses other forms of exhortation: calls for imitation (3:7*a,* 9; cf. 1 Thess 1:6), reminders of a teacher's previous instruction (2:5, 15; 3:7*b*-10), and reminders of what recipients already know (2:6; 3:7; cf. 1 Thess 4:2; 5:2). Like 1 Thessalonians and unlike other letters of exhortation, however, 2 Thessalonians uses prayer forms with a hortatory intent as well (1:3-4; 2:13-14, 16-17; 3:5, 16; 1 Thess 1:2-5; 2:13; 3:9-13; 5:23).[1]

1. On the hortatory function of prayer forms, see Abraham J. Malherbe, *Paul and the Thessalonians* (Philadelphia: Fortress, 1987) 77.

❖　　　❖　　　❖　　　❖

For more discussion of the historical, theological, and literary background of 2 Thessalonians, see the Introduction to 1 Thessalonians. See also the annotated bibliography located there.

Outline of 2 Thessalonians

I. 2 Thessalonians 1:1-12, The Exordium

II. 2 Thessalonians 2:1–3:15, Maintaining the Traditions

> A. 2:1-17, Hortatory Appeals Against Apocalyptic Enthusiasm
>> 2:1-2, Do Not Be Shaken Up
>> 2:3-12, Do Not Be Deceived
>> 2:13-17, Reasons to Stand Firm and Hold On
> B. 3:1-15, Hortatory Appeals Against Irresponsible Behavior
>> 3:1-5, Doing What Is Commanded
>> 3:6-15, Doing What Is Responsible

III. 2 Thessalonians 3:16-18, The Peroration

NIV

1 Paul, Silas[a] and Timothy,

To the church of the Thessalonians in God our Father and the Lord Jesus Christ:

[2]Grace and peace to you from God the Father and the Lord Jesus Christ.

[3]We ought always to thank God for you, brothers, and rightly so, because your faith is growing more and more, and the love every one of you has for each other is increasing. [4]Therefore, among God's churches we boast about your perseverance and faith in all the persecutions and trials you are enduring.

[5]All this is evidence that God's judgment is right, and as a result you will be counted worthy of the kingdom of God, for which you are suffering. [6]God is just: He will pay back trouble to those who trouble you [7]and give relief to you who are troubled, and to us as well. This will happen when the Lord Jesus is revealed from heaven in blazing fire with his powerful angels. [8]He will punish those who do not know God and do not obey the gospel of our Lord Jesus. [9]They will be punished with everlasting destruction and shut out from the presence of the Lord and from the majesty of his power [10]on the day he comes to be glorified in his holy people and to be marveled at among all those who have believed. This includes you, because you believed our testimony to you.

[11]With this in mind, we constantly pray for you, that our God may count you worthy of his calling, and that by his power he may fulfill every good purpose of yours and every act prompted by your faith. [12]We pray this so that the name of our Lord Jesus may be glorified in you, and you in him, according to the grace of our God and the Lord Jesus Christ.[b]

[a]1 Greek *Silvanus*, a variant of *Silas*   [b]12 Or *God and Lord, Jesus Christ*

NRSV

1 Paul, Silvanus, and Timothy,

To the church of the Thessalonians in God our Father and the Lord Jesus Christ:

[2]Grace to you and peace from God our[a] Father and the Lord Jesus Christ.

[3]We must always give thanks to God for you, brothers and sisters,[b] as is right, because your faith is growing abundantly, and the love of everyone of you for one another is increasing. [4]Therefore we ourselves boast of you among the churches of God for your steadfastness and faith during all your persecutions and the afflictions that you are enduring.

[5]This is evidence of the righteous judgment of God, and is intended to make you worthy of the kingdom of God, for which you are also suffering. [6]For it is indeed just of God to repay with affliction those who afflict you, [7]and to give relief to the afflicted as well as to us, when the Lord Jesus is revealed from heaven with his mighty angels [8]in flaming fire, inflicting vengeance on those who do not know God and on those who do not obey the gospel of our Lord Jesus. [9]These will suffer the punishment of eternal destruction, separated from the presence of the Lord and from the glory of his might, [10]when he comes to be glorified by his saints and to be marveled at on that day among all who have believed, because our testimony to you was believed. [11]To this end we always pray for you, asking that our God will make you worthy of his call and will fulfill by his power every good resolve and work of faith, [12]so that the name of our Lord Jesus may be glorified in you, and you in him, according to the grace of our God and the Lord Jesus Christ.

[a]Other ancient authorities read *the*   [b]Gk *brothers*

COMMENTARY

In epistolary terms, 2 Thessalonians 1:1-12 includes both a prescript (vv. 1-2) and a prayer formula (vv. 3-12) of two parts—namely, a thanksgiving notice (vv. 3-10) and an intercessory prayer report (vv. 11-12). With its tripartite structure (sender, recipient, and superscription formulae), the prescript (vv. 1-2) is similar to the prescripts of the undisputed Pauline letters, although both 1 and 2 Thessalonians lack an elaborate superscription.[2] Even with respect to 1 Thessalonians, however, 2 Thessalonians' prescript has two noticeable additions: (1) the inclusion of the pronoun "our" to describe the Father and (2) the addition of the longer greetings ("from God our Father and the Lord Jesus Christ," v. 2). Indeed, the greeting's repetition of "God our Father and Lord Jesus Christ," already given in the writer's description of the recipients (v. 1*b*), appears awkward—except for the fact that this kind of greeting elaboration can be found in all of the undisputed Pauline letters aside from 1 Thessalonians (cf. Rom 1:7*b*; 1 Cor 1:3; 2 Cor 1:2; Gal 1:3; Phil 1:2; Phlm 3).[3]

Typical of other thanksgiving notices, the initial one in 2 Thessalonians renders an assessment of the church's progress (vv. 3-4). In addition, the thanksgiving notice presents a commentary on God's justice (vv. 5-10) to contextualize the church's suffering. A closing intercessory prayer report (vv. 11-12) follows to commend appropriate thinking and acting throughout the church's life, from inception to glorification.

In rhetorical terms, the audience could have actualized the first twelve verses in at least two ways. On the one hand, perhaps the auditors could hear the two sentences that immediately follow the prescript. One sentence is long and loose (vv. 3-10), reporting the writer's thanks to God for both the church's success despite suffering and for the justice of God that will bring relief to the persecuted on the day of their Lord's revelation and glorification. The other sentence is short (vv. 11-12), reporting the content (v. 11) and purpose (v. 12) of Paul's intercessory prayer

report. On the other hand, perhaps the auditors detected a framing pattern in the thanksgiving notice. That is, the explicit thanks in vv. 3-4 and the explicit intercessory prayer report in vv. 11-12 framed for the hearers a central section (vv. 5-10) on "apocalyptic retribution."[4]

In either case, the sonorous character of the intercessory prayer report (vv. 11-12), the use of the transitional expression "to this end" (v. 11), and the result clause with which the intercessory prayer report ends ("so that the name . . . ," v. 12) clearly mark v. 12 as the end of a unit of material. Furthermore, the repetition of the alliterative phrase "always . . . for you" (πάντοτε περὶ ὑμῶν *pantote peri hymōn*, vv. 3, 11) suggests that vv. 11-12 continue a unit that began at least with the thanksgiving notice of v. 3. Finally, the similar endings of v. 2 and v. 12 suggest that *all* of vv. 1-12 should be held together, not simply vv. 3-12. For our purposes, then, all of vv. 1-12 constitute a single unit with discrete sections: a prescript (vv. 1-2); a thanksgiving notice with its commentary (vv. 3-10), and an intercessory prayer report (vv. 11-12).

Many in the audience possibly heard all of the first twelve verses as an exordium. That is certainly the judgment of a number of scholars influenced by rhetorical criticism. Indeed, the prescript and the two sentences of vv. 1-12 together execute the twin goals of an exordium—namely, gaining goodwill and announcing the key issues of the document.[5]

However, some interpreters find it difficult to say that the initial thanksgiving of 2 Thessalonians was written to gain the audience's goodwill. For example, they point to the more effusive tone of friendship found in 1 Thessalonians or to the so-called obligatory thanks ("we must always give thanks") of the thanksgivings in vv. 3 and 13 as indications of the letter's coolness. Some interpreters even suspect that the obligatory thanks was a response to protests from a church that deemed itself far too unworthy to fit the claims of success

---

2. On "grace and peace" as a variation of a Jewish formula, see the commentary on 1 Thessalonians.

3. As the textual note for this verse attests, another manuscript tradition omits the pronoun "our."

4. Gerhard Krodel, *The Deutero-Pauline Letters: Ephesians, Colossians, 2 Thessalonians, 1–2 Timothy, Titus,* Proclamation Commentaries (Minneapolis: Fortress, 1993) 43.

5. Again, the exordium is the beginning part of a speech or argument. See Quintilian 3.8.59. Cf. Aristotle *Rhetoric* 3.13.12.

intimated in the thanksgiving in 1 Thess 1:2-5. It seems more convincing, however, to state that the writer uses the language of obligatory thanks—a vernacular that was not unusual for his day—to express truthfully his thanks to God because of the abundance and constancy of successes in the church.[6]

The writer speaks of the church's faith not simply as "growing," for which he could have simply used the Greek word αὐξάνω (*auxanō*), but as "growing abundantly" (ὑπεραυξάνω *hyperauxan*) to indicate an intensified type of growth (v. 3). Because the writer uses a present tense verbal form both to describe the growth of the church's faith and to indicate how the believers' love is "increasing" (πλεονάζει *pleonazei*, v. 3), he also indicates the endurance of the church's success: It is constant or ongoing. It should be noted as well that the writer qualifies the believers' love as the "love of everyone of you for one another." To note mutual love in the church, he could simply have written "love for one another" (as Paul did in 1 Thess 3:12; cf. 1 Thess 4:9). The expression here, one not found anywhere else in the NT, however, is emphatic. Thus the writer "must always give thanks" because he sees so many signs of success and at such a comprehensive level, all of which evoke feelings of thanks to God.

The argument about the writer's "coolness" set aside, the first twelve verses of the letter gain the goodwill of the audience in three salient ways: (1) by noting shared struggles and shared benefits, (2) by praising the church's model character, and (3) by expressing a passionate concern for the audience's suffering.[7]

As for the notices of shared struggles and shared benefits, the prescript, thanksgiving notice, and its attached commentary all accentuate important links between the Thessalonian church and the wider group of believers. In the epistolary prescript (vv. 1-2), the unifying pronoun "our" (ἡμῶν *hēmōn*) suggests that the writers and the letter's recipients share God as "our" Father.[8] It is a small step to move from the claim of God as "our" Father to the related one of the believers

as fictive "brothers" (and sisters), as expressed in the thanksgiving (v. 3). This section also implies shared bonds through the writer's assertion of boasting about the church to other churches of God (although they are not identified). The attached commentary (vv. 5-10) implies these bonds as well through the writer's insistence that the afflicted and the (implied) writer(s) ("us") will receive "relief" (or a cessation from suffering, v. 7). Likewise, the commentary section both places the church and the writer within the company of "all who have believed" (v. 10) and links them to all the believers who will marvel at the coming of the Lord. All of these connections would have had an endearing effect because ancient audiences were favorably disposed whenever they heard similarities shared between them and a speaker or writer.[9]

In remarking on the church's model character, the writer praises the believers for their progress in faith and steadfastness. Members of the audience would likely recognize this praise as the typical gesture of a teacher displaying deep concern for his students. Members of the audience who were familiar with 1 Thessalonians would likely discern as well the similar and yet nuanced laudatory remarks given in the initial thanksgiving of that letter. For example, the recipients of 1 Thessalonians received the word in spite of "persecution" (θλῖψις *thlipsis*, 1 Thess 1:6). Here, in 2 Thessalonians, the church is praised for its endurance of both "persecution" (διωγμός *diōgmos*, v. 4) and "affliction" (*thlipsis*, v. 4), with the latter word for "suffering" being the more general of the two.[10] Also, a trace of the triad of graces—faith, love, and hope—of 1 Thessalonians lingers in 2 Thessalonians (cf. 1 Thess 1:3), for the writer commends the continuing increase of the church's faith and love. Although hope is not directly mentioned in the thanksgiving of 2 Thessalonians, in contrast to the earlier letter, the writer still praises the steadfastness of the church despite the quantity and constancy of its suffering. The recognition of the believers' endurance and faith is enhanced by the writer's insistence that he boasts

---

6. See Philo *On Special Laws* 1.224.

7. On the *captatio benevolentiae* (captivation of goodwill) in an exordium, see Quintilian 3.8.6; Cicero *De Inventione* 1.15.20; and Aristotle *Rhetoric* 3.14.7.

8. On Silvanus and Timothy, see 1 Thess 1:1.

9. Aristotle *Rhetoric* 2.13.16.

10. The NRSV is not consistent in its translation of this word. It is translated as "persecution" in 1 Thessalonians, but as "affliction" in 2 Thessalonians. Perhaps this is so in anticipation of 1:6, in which it would appear odd to say "it is indeed just of God to repay with 'persecution' [θλῖψιν *thlipsin*] those who 'persecute' [θλίβουσιν *thlibousin*] you."

about them to the churches of God (v. 4; cf. 1 Cor 11:16). Some in the audience would likely remember Paul's similar praise of the Thessalonian church as a model for "all the believers in Macedonia and in Achaia" in 1 Thess 1:7. Obviously, the church—in the estimation of the writer—has continued as a model.

Expressing passionate concern for the church's suffering, the writer presents not (in his estimation) an inaccurate timetable (cf. 2:3-12), but an explicit apocalyptic schema that insists on retribution for the afflicters (1:6), "relief" for the church (1:7), and a dazzling display of power that will cause the church and other believers to marvel (1:10). This concern is also displayed in the intercessory prayer report (1:11-12) when the writer restates his constancy in praying for the Thessalonian believers (1:11) and clarifies the past and the present that guarantee the future relief from suffering that they can expect. The church's past lies in the "call" of God (1:11), a call that indicates God's election of the church even as it is connected to the glory of the Lord Jesus (1:12; 2:14). The writer's prayer for God to make the church worthy of God's call defines the earlier expression "make you worthy of the kingdom of God" (1:5). Both expressions are likely drawn from 1 Thess 2:12 ("that you lead a life worthy of God, who calls you into his own kingdom and glory"); and both, like 1 Thess 2:12, focus on the ongoing commitment that believers must have because of God's initiative. In the case of 2 Thess 1:11, however, the writer clarifies "worthy" by adding "fulfill by his power every good resolve and work of faith, so that the name of the Lord may be glorified in you, and you in him, according to the grace of our God and the Lord Jesus" (1:11b-12).

The first expression (v. 11b) indicates the role God will continue to play in the church members' lives as they await the future relief. Whether "every good resolve" is God's resolve or (as is more likely in the light of Rom 15:14; Gal 5:22) the church's resolve or desire or pleasure (εὐδοκία eudokia; cf. 2:12), the concern is for the completion of that resolve and of the "work of faith" (or the work that comes out of faith; cf. 1 Thess 1:3) that God will bring about. And whether "by his power" is an indication of the Holy Spirit, which for Paul brings about the products of transformation (see the Introduction to 1 Thessalonians; cf.

2 Thess 2:13), or simply an indication of the manner in which the completion will be accomplished (i.e., "powerfully"), the accomplishment is the same: The called of God are sustained in their commitment to God in every respect because of God.

The second expression (v. 12), cast as a result clause, indicates why the God who called this church will sustain its commitment: It is for a mutual glorification process that is also made possible by the grace of God. On the one hand, because of God's grace the name (or authority) of Jesus is glorified on the order of the glorification of the name of YHWH (in Isa 66:5 LXX) through the present lives of the church members (cf. 1:10). On the other hand, the church can expect a glorification as well (cf. 2:14) because of that same grace.

Both expressions, cast in this sonorous prayer report, would likely encourage the beleaguered church because the report places the believers solidly in the hands of God—from their inception through their ongoing commitment to God even to their glorification. They are not alone or on their own in the midst of their suffering. What God has done, is doing, and will do all assure them of the future relief they will receive.

Thus, despite what others detect as the "cooler" tone of this letter, its opening verses still function as a *captatio benevolentiae* (captivation of goodwill). With an accentuation of common bonds, with a commendation of the church's praiseworthy progress, and with an apocalyptic framework for interpreting the meaning of the afflictions, the writer captures the attention and the goodwill of the audience.

The first twelve verses also announce three significant issues in the letter.[11] First, the initial verses prepare the auditors to see the critical importance of belief in the writer's gospel or testimony. These verses repeatedly mention the church's faith: It is "growing abundantly" (v. 3); the writer boasts about it (v. 4); the church is a part of a larger group, all of whom "have believed" (v. 10); the church "believed" the writer's testimony (v. 10); and the writer prays that God will complete in the church "every . . . work of faith" (v. 11). Faith (or its absence) remains a

---

11. On the exordium's forecasting function, see Cicero *De Part. Or.* 27.97; Quintilian 3.8.10; cf. Aristotle *Rhetoric* 3.13.14.

crucial concern elsewhere in the letter. Some persons believed "what is false" and "have not believed the truth" (2:11-12). The church, the writer maintains, was chosen "for salvation through sanctification by the Spirit and through belief in the truth" (2:13). The writer recognizes, moreover, that "not all [presumably outsiders] have faith" (3:2) and that the church must "keep away from believers who are living in idleness [or better, disorder] and not according to the tradition that they received from us" (3:6). Even still, the errant ones are to be warned as "believers" (3:15).

The repetition of language about faith in the initial verses suggests a basis upon which the writer can exhort his church. On the one hand, because the church believed his testimony and on that basis acquired a fate distinct from the unbelievers (1:10), he can consider presumably dissident thought (2:3-12) and behavior (3:6-15)—whether within or outside the church—as falsehood that should not be believed or supported. As Menken notes, "Belief in the gospel is what distinguishes in the present the oppressed from the oppressors, and in the future the elect from the damned."[12] On the other hand, the writer can deem the truth as that which he already shared with the church (2:5, 15; 3:10).

Relatedly, a second issue signaled by the writer is that of standing firm. In several places throughout the letter the writer accentuates the need for the church to remain firm (2:15) and to be strengthened (2:17; 3:3). Toward that end, the "steadfastness of Christ" (whether read as the "steadfastness that Christ possessed" or as "steadfastness toward Christ") is held up as an example (3:5). Furthermore, repeated remarks about "traditions" (2:15; 3:6) or about the things told (2:5) or commanded (3:7-10) to the church at a previous visit have the effect here, as in the case of 1 Thessalonians, of emphasizing stability (see the Commentary on 1 Thess 4:1-12). Because 2:15 appears as a counterweight to 2:1-2, moreover, some scholars suggests that "standing firm" is accentuated as well through the antonymous expression "to be quickly shaken in mind" (2:2).[13]

12. Maarten J. J. Menken, *2 Thessalonians* (New York: Routledge, 1994) 92.
13. Jouette Bassler, "Peace in All Ways," in *Pauline Theology,* ed. Jouette Bassler (Minneapolis: Fortress, 1991) 1:78.

It is little wonder, then, that in the exordium the writer also commends the believers' steadfastness, which is the basis for his boasts to other churches of God (v. 4). Even the expression "enduring" (ἀνέχομαι *anechomai*), cast in the present tense (v. 4), implies the church's firm stance in the face of external difficulties up to the very moment of the letter's being written. With the intercessory prayer report (vv. 11-12), moreover, the scope of the church's commitment is clarified. The prayer report, as we have seen, implores God in the light of the initial call of the church and in the context of God's completion of "every resolve and work of faith" (v. 11). The scope of the believers' commitment extends beyond external difficulties to cover every aspect of their commitment to God. That is, the initial verses also prepare the audience for a commitment with respect to the specific internal issue raised in 3:6-15.

Third, these verses also signal God's continuing justice. Having commended the church for its endurance of persecutions and afflictions (v. 4), the writer next places its suffering in a more comprehensive apocalyptic context (vv. 5-10)—one that both defines or interprets the meaning of their suffering and contrasts the different fates of believers and unbelievers.

The interpretation of the suffering of the church is critical because a part of the audience's situation appears to be a potential unsettling from their foundational apocalyptic moorings due to an "enthusiastic" interpretation of their affliction. That is, some understood their suffering to mean that the "day of the Lord has already come" (2:1-2), presumably thinking that this had taken place in short order in the wake of their experience of suffering. This kind of thinking was quite possible in an apocalyptic mindset, for many an apocalyptic thinker viewed suffering as a part of the eschatological woes that were expected to take place shortly before the end time. Paul himself thought this way (see the Commentary on 1 Thess 3:1), although he never inferred that the day of the Lord had already arrived because of suffering.

As we shall shortly see, the writer's focus on the Lord as one yet to be revealed (v. 7) and to come (v. 10) works against an enthusiastic interpretation of present suffering. In fact, in the later discussion of the events to occur, the writer painstakingly renders a timetable that frustrates efforts to pinpoint the exact time of Jesus' revealing or coming (2:8).

Likewise, the contrast between the fates of believers and unbelievers is critical because the writer seeks to drive a wedge between believers who follow the writer's traditions (2:15) and unbelievers who "believe what is false" (2:11). Ultimately, of course, the distinction is critical also because there are requisite actions that follow right belief and adherence to the writer's traditions (3:6-15).

This comprehensive apocalyptic context as given in vv. 5-10, however, requires sustained reflection. Its value in demonstrating God's continuing justice is not fully appreciated without some specific comments about the rhetorical force of v. 5 and of vv. 6-10.

The Rhetorical Force of 2 Thessalonians 1:5. To help modern readers, translations of 1:3-10 divide this long and loose sentence into discrete sections. In doing so, however, a problem of ambiguity may escape readers who only have access to an English translation. In Greek, 2 Thess 1:5 actually begins with the word "evidence" (ἔνδειγμα *endeigma*), in front of which the NRSV has placed "This is" and the NIV has affixed "All this is." Even with the help given by these translations, however, the antecedent of "[the] evidence of the righteous judgment of God" is ambiguous. Presumably, the antecedent can be found in one or all of the clauses of 1:3-4, but which one (or which ones) remains uncertain.

Some interpreters think the antecedent of "evidence" is the church's suffering. The immediate response to this assertion, however, is, "How is the innocent suffering of Christians evidence of the righteousness of God?"[14] The proponents of this view respond that the justice of God in 2 Thessalonians is similar to the view of God's justice found in 2 Bar 13:8-10 and the *Pss Sol* 13:10-12. In those texts, the justice of God is seen in the afflictions of the righteous, who are punished for their sins in the present so that they will not be punished for them at the end of time.[15] But this theology of suffering perspective seems

unhelpful because it overlooks the fact that the writer does not speak here about the recipients' sins.[16] And would a writer who has spoken so wonderfully about a group so quickly explain their misery as a function of their sins anyway? Probably not!

An alternative position would be to see the antecedent of "evidence" as the ongoing endurance of the believers. That is, the evidence of God's righteous judgment is not their suffering, but that believers have been able successfully and constantly to withstand it. Thus, presupposing that some in the church think their continuous suffering is an indication of the end time, the writer initially focuses on how their endurance is evidence of the continuing righteous judgment of God. Then, drawing on the apocalyptic imagery of 1 Thess 2:12 ("that you lead a life worthy of God, who calls you into his own kingdom and glory"), the writer notes that their endurance (something actually granted rather than attained; see 1:11) in effect means that the believers are "counted worthy" or "made worthy" of the kingdom of God or of God's reign in the new age (1:5*b*). The church suffers for God's new order, but not in order to get into it. And the church's endurance is an indication of God's claim on their lives—that is, of God's previous call or election of them for salvation in that new order (cf. 1:10; 2:13).

The rhetorical force of 1:5, then, is to present an indication of God's righteous judgment in the ongoing present shortly before the long sentence of 1:3-10 continues with a more explicit apocalyptic scenario about God's justice in the future (1:6-10). Both parts reflect an apocalyptic view of reality, and both could prove encouraging, with 1:5 providing a shift from the present into the future.

The Rhetorical Force of 2 Thessalonians 1:6-10. Having described the present evidence of God's righteous judgment, the writer resumes the thought about God's justice, now looking toward the future, with a loose conditional ("If [or in this case, as shown below, Since] . . . then") statement (the statement is a loose construction because the expected transition "then" in the second clause has to be supplied). The statement has two parts: an initial

14. Bonnie Thurston, *Reading Colossians, Ephesians & 2 Thessalonians: A Literary and Theological Commentary* (New York: Crossroad, 1995) 171.

15. Jouette M. Bassler, "The Enigmatic Sign: 2 Thessalonians 1:5," *CBQ* 46 (1984) 501-6.

16. Beverly R. Gaventa, *First and Second Thessalonians,* Interpretation (Louisville: Westminster John Knox, 1998) 103.

clause that states what readers can take for granted (vv. 6-8) and a subsequent clause that applies more specifically the general principle of the initial clause (vv. 9-10).[17]

The initial clause (1:6-8) begins with the word "for" (εἴπερ *eiper*) or "since" because the type of Greek conditional statement used does not imply doubt but assumes with certainty that what follows is true. What is true and can be taken for granted by the recipients is that God is just in how God treats those who cause suffering and those who suffer (cf. Ps 7:10-13). With a play on words and an allusion to Isa 66:6, the writer notes God's retributive justice: God will "repay with affliction those who afflict you" (1:6). For the church and the writer ("us," 1:7), however, the promise is relief.

Yet it is clear from this initial clause that these things will happen "when the Lord Jesus is revealed," with "revealed" (ἀποκάλυψις *apokalypsis*) literally meaning "unveiled" (1:7). Thus the writer anticipates the issue of 2:1-8, for the Lord who will come (2:8) has not yet come. It is also clear from this clause that the justice of God will be meted out through Jesus with extraordinary force, consistency, and comprehensiveness.

The force is extraordinary because Jesus' unveiling from heaven will be accompanied by angels (1:7; cf. Zech 14:5; *1 Enoch* 1:9) and flaming fire (1:8; cf. Exod 3:2; Isa 66:15-16), both of which were identified with God in the OT but are now associated with Jesus. With respect to the angels, it is also clear in other NT texts that the early Christians expected Jesus to return with angels (Matt 13:49; 25:31).

The consistency is also extraordinary because precisely as a "just" (δίκαιος *dikaios*, 1:6) God "gives back" or "repays" (ἀνταπόδιδωμι *antapodidōmi*, 1:6) with affliction those who afflict, the writer envisions Jesus "giving" (διδόντος *didontos*) "vengeance" or "recompense" (ἐκδίκησις *ekdikēsis*) to those not aligned with the people of God (1:8). While God exacted vengeance in the OT (Deut 32:35: Ps 94:1), Jesus does so now, according to 2 Thessalonians; but the idea of this vengeance is that the recipients get back no more than what they deserve (cf. Rom 12:19). In either

case, vengeance is removed from the hands of "human beings who might act out of a spirit of retribution or vindictiveness rather than from motives of divine justice."[18]

The comprehensiveness is also extraordinary because the vengeance falls on all persons who have not aligned themselves with the people of God. Some scholars assume two groups as the recipients of the vengeance. One group, "those who do not know God" (1:8), is conventionally associated with the Gentiles (Ps 78:6; Jer 10:25). The expression "who do not know God" is found in 1 Thess 4:5, but the absence of the word for "Gentiles" (ἔθνη *ethnē*) in 2 Thessalonians suggests that this group is not necessarily limited to Gentiles alone. A second group, "those who do not obey the gospel of our Lord Jesus" (1:8), is conventionally limited exclusively to those Jews who did not accept the Christian gospel or, in Paul's words, "those who have not obeyed the gospel" (Rom 10:16 NRSV). If the two expressions are understood as synonymous, however, the latter group is also comprehensive.[19] This reckoning seems persuasive because a characteristic of 2 Thess 1:5-10 is the writer's transference of images related to God onto Jesus. In this case "those who do not know God" are the same as "those who have not obeyed the gospel of our Lord Jesus." Of course, within this comprehensive collection of persons receiving vengeance, the audience could place those who are afflicting the church (1:6) and, as we shall see, those who oppose the writer's attempt to spread the word of the Lord as well (3:1).

Having indicated what is taken for granted (that it is just for God to repay the afflicters and to grant rest to the afflicted), the writer's second clause (1:9-10) describes what that repayment entails and the benefits accruing to the believers. The repayment to be meted out includes suffering and separation. With an allusion to the aforementioned word "vengeance" (*ekdikēsis*, 1:8), the writer speaks of the afflicters as persons "who will suffer the punishment [δίκη *dikē*] of eternal destruction" (1:9). While some scholars think "destruction" (ὄλεγρος *olethros*, 1:9), a word Paul

---

17. For explicit details of the construction, see Earl J. Richard, *First and Second Thessalonians,* Sacra Pagina (Collegeville, Minn.: Liturgical, 1995) 305-10.

18. Thurston, *Reading Colossians, Ephesians and 2 Thessalonians,* 172.

19. F. F. Bruce, *1 and 2 Thessalonians,* WBC (Waco, Tex.: Word, 1982) 151-52.

used in 1 Thess 5:3, is simply an instant annihilation that is eternal (1:9) and thus irreversible, others argue that the description of the separation that follows only makes sense if an eternal (constant) ruination is intended.

Supporting the latter claim is the backdrop of 1 Thess 4:17, in which the believers are "with the Lord forever," in contrast to the afflicters, who, according to this perspective, are banished from the presence of the Lord forever. Of course, the translations "separated" (NRSV) and "shut out" (NIV) do not actually occur in the Greek, but the expression "from the presence of the Lord" (in both the NRSV and the NIV) implies spatial exclusion.

The separation is described with an allusion to the LXX form of Isa 2:10, which speaks of a coming judgment when persons will hide "away from the face of the terror of the Lord, and from the glory of his power." While Isaiah 2 speaks about God's judgment against idolaters and the arrogant, the writer of 2 Thessalonians sees Jesus as the agent of justice, as the one from whose presence and glory the afflicters will be excluded. Thus the writer, in this clause, continues the transference of images associated with God in the OT to Jesus.

The appearance of Jesus also brings benefits to the believers (1:10). While the afflicters act in this age, they take on a passive role at the judgment as they are afflicted, inflicted, or shuttled away. For believers, however, those who witness the Lord's coming will have the opportunity to play an active role at the end. The believers (of whom the writer's church is a part) will be able to respond to the coming of Jesus in association with "his holy ones" (τοῖς ἁγίοις αὐτου *tois hagiois autou;* translated as "saints" in the NRSV).

Because the likely background for 1:10 (Ps 88:8 LXX) views "his holy ones" as angels, there is uncertainty about whether the church is understood to be a part of "his holy ones." This problem is related to the translation of a similar expression in 1 Thess 3:13. For at least three reasons, however, some scholars (myself included) think the "holy ones" here include the believers. First, the glorification of the Lord by the "holy ones" in 1:10 possibly anticipates 1:12, where the writer speaks of the name of the Lord being "glorified in you." Second, the parallel nature of the two

expressions in 1:10 (both are infinitive clauses: "to be glorified by his saints" and "to be marveled at . . . among all who have believed") could mean that the two expressions are synonymous. Third, the characteristic transference of images once attributed to God but now to Jesus may also imply a transference of "the image of God with his angels . . . to Christ with his church."[20] However one resolves the ambiguity, the church is assuredly a part of the group characterized as "all who have believed" (1:10*b*) and, accordingly, will play an active role in marveling at Jesus.

The timing for the marveling at Jesus' appearance is set in the future, another anticipation of the problem of 2:2. Earlier, Jesus' appearance (1:7*b*) was described as the time when Jesus would be "revealed" (*apokalypsis*). Here it is depicted as the time when he "comes [ἔλθη *elthē*] . . . on that day." "That day," appearing in Greek at the end of this clause, alludes to the day of YHWH in Isa 2:11. Here, with the characteristic transference we have come to expect, however, "that day" is not the day of God, but the day of Jesus, and thus the expression anticipates the discussion of the day of the Lord in 2 Thess 2:2.

The rhetorical force of the two clauses of this conditional statement presuppose the justice of God in the future. The initial clause assumes that the justice of God is performed through the agency of Jesus, whose future revelation brings forth relief to believers, but vengeance to unbelievers. The second clause, building on the first one, elucidates the specific consequences of God's future justice—eternal separation for unbelievers and an opportunity to marvel at the powerful coming of Jesus for believers. This explicit apocalyptic framework is a word of encouragement both because the timing of the drama refutes the misinformation noted in 2:2 and because the dazzling display of Jesus' godlike power assures this church that the avenging Jesus is able to bring the relief promised.

With the rhetorical force of 2 Thess 1:5 and of 1:6-10 having been noted, a final word is necessary about the role of 1:5-10 as a whole in its contribution to the exordium's emphasis on the continuing justice of God. In connection with 1:11-12, vv. 5-10 comment not exclusively on the

---

20. Menken, *2 Thessalonians,* 91.

issue of God's present and future "justice," but as well on the church's "worthiness." Verses 11-12 resume the theme first mentioned in 1:5: that of the worthiness of the church. The correct interpretation of suffering, then, is a comprehensive apocalyptic one that acknowledges the present endurance, the future retribution, and the ultimate glorification that God has set into operation. The problem with the enthusiastic apocalyptic message is not just that the timetable is inaccurate, but that it does not sufficiently adumbrate the continuing justice of God (in its present and future dimensions). Further, it does not place the suffering of believers within the larger discourse of God's program of glorification, thereby leaving out the church's route to prestige or worth through association with its powerful Lord. The enthusiastic apocalyptic message is both pallid and narrow.

The comprehensive apocalyptic framework of 1:5-10 thus helps the church to see the great power of Jesus. For a church that no longer has its former networks of power and honor, the honor it brings to its Lord is one part of the glorification process, for the church (and all the saints) will "obtain the glory of our Lord Jesus" (2:14; cf. 1:12).

Altogether, then, the initial verses of 2 Thessalonians function as an exordium not only because they capture the goodwill of the auditors, but as well because they announce the critical issues that will be addressed in chapters 2 and 3. Thus the auditors would already know the letter's emphasis on the importance of belief in the writer's word, on standing firm or remaining committed, and on the vindication of the afflicted.

REFLECTIONS

The words of 2 Thess 1:11 about "good resolve and work of faith" call to mind two persons from our own time whose lives reflected these in vivid detail: Martin Luther King, Jr., and Mother Teresa. Few have found points of comparison between them. Mohandas Gandhi usually comes to mind when one casts about for a counterpart for King. For the fundamental philosophy of his movement, King adopted Gandhi's principles of nonviolent direct action, principles that Gandhi had used in overcoming the colonial power of British rule in India. Both were motivated by love as a powerful agent of social change. And, alas, both men met death at the hands of an assassin.

But King and the diminutive saint from Calcutta? Few would connect them. The exordium in 2 Thessalonians, however, provides a unique link that forces us to think about the paradigmatic lives of King and Mother Teresa at the same time. The link is the measure of worth or prestige.

How does one measure prestige? What counts as an index of honor? Is it keeping up with the latest fashions and fads of the day? Is it having limitless financial resources at our disposal? How do we measure worth? This is the backdrop of the exordium in 2 Thess 1:1-12. The Greeks and the Romans, at all levels of society, had an undying interest in social prestige. No wonder that we read in one of the ancient documents: "Glory drags along the obscure no less than the nobly-bound to her shining chariot."[21] But the writer of 2 Thessalonians speaks about glory or prestige as if it is something that God grants to those who seek to do good to others (1:11).

This is the measure of worth that was basic to the lives of Martin Luther King, Jr., and Mother Teresa. One died young; the other old. One was assassinated; the other lived a relatively long life. Both gave the world incredible examples of "good resolve and work[s] of faith" (1:11). King captured true worth in his sermon "The Drum Major Instinct," in which he asked not to be remembered for his Nobel Peace Prize, his numerous awards, or where he went to school. He asked, rather, to be remembered as someone who "tried to love and serve

21. Horace *Satires* 1.6.23-24.

humanity."[22] Mother Teresa may have been influenced by 2 Thessalonians when she prepared the following prayer:

> Make us worthy, Lord,
> to serve others throughout the world
> who live and die
> in poverty or hunger,
> Give them, through our hands, this day their daily
> bread, and by our understanding love,
> give peace and joy.[23]

22. Martin Luther King, Jr., "The Drum Major Instinct," in *I Have a Dream: Writings and Speeches That Changed the World,* ed. James M. Washington (New York: HarperCollins, 1992) 191.

23. Mother Teresa of Calcutta, "Make Us Worthy, Lord," in *A Gift for God: Prayers and Meditations* (New York: Harper & Row 1975) 71.

2 THESSALONIANS 2:1–3:15

MAINTAINING THE TRADITIONS

OVERVIEW

With its general concern for stability and its more specific concern about a misleading, enthusiastic brand of apocalypticism, the letter shifts from its exordium to a longer unit in which the writer encourages the church not to veer from the traditions they have received (2:15; 3:6). The unit (2:1–3:15) includes two sets of hortatory appeals: appeals to traditions against an apocalyptic enthusiasm (2:1-17) and appeals to traditions commending appropriate practical pursuits (3:1-15). A sequential analysis of 2:1–3:15 supports this contention, but two preliminary steps are in order. First, as in the case of the Commentary on 1 Thessalonians, it is important to note the various acoustic markers that clarify the broad strokes of the unit as discerned by epistolary analysis. Second, it is necessary to offer any other plausible arguments for the rhetorical delineation of 2:1–3:15. Those items in place, it will be possible to look sequentially and carefully at the discrete sections of verses that both constitute the two sets of hortatory appeals and advance the writer's argument about stability and the maintenance of traditions.

Epistolary analysis suggests the writer's inclusion of a thanksgiving report in 2:13-14 and wish-prayers in 2:16-17 and 3:5.[24] These prayer forms conventionally have the effect of summarizing previous material (as we have seen in the case of 1:11-12; cf. 1 Thess 3:11-13) or of anticipating subsequent material (again, note 1:11-12; cf. 1 Thess 1:3-5; 3:11-13). Thus, for example, 2:16-17 could be a conclusion to the material in 2:1-12.

Of course, determining the exact conclusion to 2:1-12 could appear confusing, for there are reasons to see 2:13-14, 2:15, or 2:16-17 as its conclusion. Like other prayer units, the thanksgiving in 2:13-14 is a fitting conclusion. We have already noticed how it is similar to the previous wish-prayer in 1:11-12, and its focus on constant thanks makes it obviously similar to the initial thanksgiving (1:3-4). Furthermore, it is directly related to 2:1-12 because it indicates that the fate of believers is different from that of the persons influenced by the delusion noted there since God chose (2:13) and called them (2:14). Yet 2:13-14 is quickly followed by "So then" (2:15), which also has the tone of a summation. Furthermore, in 2:15, the writer appears to contrast the traditions he had taught the church by word of mouth and letter with the enthusiastic agitation mentioned in 2:2. In addition, 2:16-17 is also a conclusion because it likewise indicates why the fate of believers is different from that of those under the delusion—namely, because God both loved them and gave them eternal consolation. It appears, therefore, that all three sections conclude 2:1-12 with 2:16-17 as its final conclusion because of its similarities with 1 Thess 3:11-13. That is, both 2 Thess 2:16-17 and 1 Thess 3:11-13 are wish-prayers, and both precede a transitional marker ("Finally," 2 Thess 3:1; 1 Thess 4:1).

Epistolary analysis also reveals the letter closing to begin at 3:16. According to Jeffrey Weima, the Pauline postscripts usually begin with a peace formula. Hence the peace formula of 3:16 (on the model of 1 Thess 5:23) marks the beginning of the closing unit (3:16-18) of 2 Thessalonians— that is, the peroration.[25]

If one accepts these benefits of the epistolary analysis along with some other specific rhetorical markers, it is possible to justify the delineation of 2:1–3:15 into two sets of appeals. Two pieces of evidence are crucial. First, the most obvious

---

24. See, e.g., Peter T. O'Brien, *Introductory Thanksgivings in the Letters of Paul* (Leiden: Brill, 1977) 184-93. Ibid., 193. Cf. Gordon P. Wiles, *Paul's Intercessory Prayers: The Significance of the Intercessory Prayer in the Letters of Paul* (Cambridge: Cambridge University Press, 1974) 32n. 2.

25. Jeffrey Weima, *Neglected Endings: The Significance of the Pauline Letter Closing* (Sheffield: JSOT, 1994) 187.

marker between the material in chaps. 2 and 3 is the transitional marker "finally" (λοιπόν *loipon*). In some of the undisputed Pauline letters, as has been noted, "finally" suggests either the last section of a letter (cf. 2 Cor 13:11; 1 Thess 4:1) or the last subsection of a unit (cf. Phil 3:1). In 2 Thess 3:1, "finally" probably marks the last large unit of the letter, although the repetition of cognate forms of "strengthen" (στηρίζω *stērizō*, 2:17; cf. 3:3) and "hearts" (καρδίας *kardias*, 2:17; 3:5) suggests a transitional role for 3:1-5.

Second, assuming the hortatory function of the writer's prayer reports and "finally" as a transitional marker, the rhetorical movement of the material in 2:1-17 appears to mirror that found in 3:1-15. On the one hand, consolatory exhortation couched in the solemn tones of prayer (2:13-17) appears to follow more explicit exhortations on the church's maintenance of its founding traditions (2:1-12) in 2:1-17. On the other hand, consolatory exhortation couched in solemn tones of prayer (3:1-5) appears to precede the more explicit exhortations on the church's maintenance of its founding traditions (3:6-15) in 3:1-15. Thus the transitional nature of 2:16-17, the delineation of 3:16-18 as a separate part of the letter, the transitional marker "finally" in 3:1, and the letter's reverse movements in 2:1-15 and 3:1-15 all suggest two separate large units for the proof section.

2 THESSALONIANS 2:1-17, HORTATORY APPEALS AGAINST APOCALYPTIC ENTHUSIASM

OVERVIEW

The first set of hortatory appeals easily divides into three parts: a brief initial section on the question of the parousia and the gathering of the believers (2:1-2); a longer section designed to refute the inaccurate information (2:3-12); and a set of concluding exhortations cast in the consolatory context of prayer (2:13-17). Of the three sections, both the initial and last ones are relatively straightforward. As we shall see, however, the middle section has been a source of puzzlement for centuries.

2 Thessalonians 2:1-2, Do Not Be Shaken Up

NIV

2 Concerning the coming of our Lord Jesus Christ and our being gathered to him, we ask you, brothers, ²not to become easily unsettled or alarmed by some prophecy, report or letter supposed to have come from us, saying that the day of the Lord has already come.

NRSV

2 As to the coming of our Lord Jesus Christ and our being gathered together to him, we beg you, brothers and sisters,[a] ²not to be quickly shaken in mind or alarmed, either by spirit or by word or by letter, as though from us, to the effect that the day of the Lord is already here.

[a] Gk *brothers*

COMMENTARY

These verses, though brief, are judged by some scholars to be a terse introduction to the material following it. That is, these verses help readers to anticipate the context, the scope, and the aim of the subsequent verses. The context of 2:1-2 and (by implication) the rest of 2:1-17 is apocalyptic, for messages about the day of the Lord (or about his coming) were prevalent in the apocalyptic material of the writer's age (cf. Mark 13).[26]

The scope of vv. 1-2 is not limited to Jesus' parousia alone. Given the earlier claims made about the glorification of Jesus and believers (1:11-12), it is little wonder that the initial verses of this set of hortatory appeals focus both on Jesus and the believers—that is, on the believers' "eschatological gathering."[27] Of course, this kind of gathering was once used to describe God's gathering of exiles (Isa 52:12; 2 Macc 2:18), but in NT times the idea was transferred to Jesus, who was expected by Christians to gather God's people together (cf. Matt 23:37; Mark 13:27; Luke 13:34).

With this double interest in Jesus and the believers, these initial verses reveal that the entire first set of exhortations say as much about the believers as they do about Jesus. Indeed, as we shall soon see, the force of all the material in 2:1-17 is really an argument about the founding traditions that show a radical difference between believers and unbelievers, on the one hand, and Jesus and a figure called the "lawless one" (2:3, 8) on the other hand.

The aim of vv. 1-2 and its subsequent material is to refute an unfounded claim that the day of the Lord had already "appeared" (v. 2). Since the word "appeared" (ἐνέστηκεν *enestēken*) can only mean "the day of the Lord has already occurred," and not "the day of the Lord is imminent," the refutation is aimed against a misleading notion that events associated with that day had already happened.[28]

While it may seem obvious to us that the day of the Lord had not come, it must be remembered that the readers and auditors of 2 Thessalonians would have lived during what Koester calls "the apocalyptic fervor of the second half of the first century."[29] Furthermore, it would not be difficult for them to assume the arrival of the events of the day because of the expectation that those events would follow in close proximity the believers' experience of great suffering.

With vv. 1-2, the refutation can only begin by casting about for possible sources of the confusion: (1) a spirit or perhaps someone claiming to speak a word of prophecy inspired by the Spirit (cf. 1 Thess 5:20); (2) a word, possibly a teaching of some sort, but in any case a word determined apart from the Spirit; or (3) a letter purporting to be from the writer. The subsequent verses will show, however, that the claim did not emanate from the writer, even if it seems "as though from us" (v. 2; cf. v. 15). No wonder that the writer begins, not with the unfounded claim itself, but with strong words of insistence ("we beg you," v. 1), a word order that is reversed in the NRSV and the NIV. No wonder as well that the writer will go on to pile up prayerful words of encouragement on top of each other in 2:13-17 to remind the church of its secure and continuous salvation because of God's claim on and benefactions for their lives.

With 2:1-2, moreover, the writer introduces his refutation, not with an explicit argument against the unfounded claim, but with a concern that the claim not cause the church (in the NRSV) "to be quickly shaken in mind or alarmed" (v. 2). A better translation that captures the nuancing of the Greek words of v. 2 is that the claim should not "shock the church suddenly" or "repeatedly agitate" them (v. 2).[30] Indeed, one translation for the first expression could be that the church not "be quickly shaken out of . . . [its] wits."[31] Envi-

---

26. For arguments against reading the context as a gnostic one, see Maarten J. J. Menken, *2 Thessalonians* (London: Routledge, 1994) 98. That Paul and the writer here viewed the day of the Lord and the parousia as the same event, see ibid., 99-100.

27. Charles Wanamaker, *The Epistles to the Thessalonians,* NIGTC (Grand Rapids: Eerdmans, 1990) 238. On the gathering schema in apocalyptic literature, see *Pss Sol* 17:26-28.

28. Cf. Beverly R. Gaventa, *First and Second Thessalonians,* Interpretation (Louisville: John Knox, 1998) 109.

29. Helmut Koester, "From Paul's Eschatology to the Apocalyptic Schemata of 2 Thessalonians," in *The Thessalonian Correspondence,* ed. Raymond F. Collins (Leuven: University of Leuven Press, 1990) 455.

30. On this reading, see Bonnie Thurston, *Reading Colossians, Ephesians and 2 Thessalonians: A Literary and Theological Commentary* (New York: Crossroad, 1995) 176.

31. F. F. Bruce, *1 & 2 Thessalonians,* WBC (Waco, Tex.: Word, 1982) 163.

sioned here is the idea that the church had been shaken at the very foundation and that the shaking—although it occurred only once, as is indicated by the kind of Greek verb the writer chose to describe the shock—had occurred easily. Furthermore, even if the shaking occurred once, the fallout of the shock had an enduring power. That is, the agitation it caused was ongoing. It appears that the agitation was similar to the kind that the Synoptic Gospels mention, for the writer and some of the synoptic gospel writers use forms of θροέω (*throeō*, "to agitate," 1 Thess 2:2; cf. Matt 24:6; Mark 13:7) to indicate a frenzied response to false claims on how the end-time events should be read. Finally, it must be noted that the precision with which the writer has spoken about the sudden shock and its enduring fallout reveals him to be a loving pastor. Here and elsewhere 2 Thessalonians is not a document by someone writing with a "cool" tone. Instead, it is the work of a loving pastor carefully warning his students against accepting false assumptions about reality.

REFLECTIONS

False claims exert a powerful force over the lives of people—precipitating needless panic, driving some to apostasy, and leading others to the precipice of despondency, if not over the cliff of despair. The writer of 2 Thess 2:1-2 also had to contend against false claims that had the potential to upset his church. One important lesson we can learn from him is that falsehood often comes wrapped in the same garb as truth. It seldom comes in the easily discernible guises of the fantastic, the iconoclastic, or the sophomoric. Rather, it moves with refined force. It comes in the name of science, declaring the depravity of some people and the superiority of those who would oppress and colonize them. It comes in the guise of a pastor's care, seeking personal gain and political grandstanding. It comes with the tone and touch of friendship, but it reveals private anguishes and intimate confidences spoken in closed chambers.

How, then, can we guard against falling prey to false claims that often appear as the truth—as a word, spirit, or letter "as though from us"? The answer is not to cave in to loveless logic or hateful science. Nor should we acquiesce to the fleecing of the faithful whether it emanates from the pulpit or the pew. And certainly we should not concede to a facile friendship with others who have not earned our trust through the tests of time. In all of these cases, rather, what is needed is an attitude of discernment, careful study, and relentless sifting of thought.

Christianity does not call us to be timid or gullible. It calls us, rather, to weigh every word, spirit, or letter carefully. Second Thessalonians shows us the great need for trained clergy and laity, for churches to make learning an everyday quest and a lifetime goal, and for all believers to take on that perennial pursuit first penned with precision in the Middle Ages by the great Anselm of Canterbury: "faith seeking understanding."

2 Thessalonians 2:3-12, Do Not Be Deceived

NIV

3Don't let anyone deceive you in any way, for ⌞that day will not come⌟ until the rebellion occurs and the man of lawlessness[a] is revealed, the man doomed to destruction. 4He will oppose and will exalt himself over everything that is called God or is worshiped, so that he sets himself up in God's temple, proclaiming himself to be God.

a3 Some manuscripts sin

NRSV

3Let no one deceive you in any way; for that day will not come unless the rebellion comes first and the lawless one[a] is revealed, the one destined for destruction.[b] 4He opposes and exalts himself above every so-called god or object of worship, so that he takes his seat in the temple of God, declaring himself to be God. 5Do you not remember that I

a Gk the man of lawlessness; other ancient authorities read the man of sin   b Gk the son of destruction

NIV

⁵Don't you remember that when I was with you I used to tell you these things? ⁶And now you know what is holding him back, so that he may be revealed at the proper time. ⁷For the secret power of lawlessness is already at work; but the one who now holds it back will continue to do so till he is taken out of the way. ⁸And then the lawless one will be revealed, whom the Lord Jesus will overthrow with the breath of his mouth and destroy by the splendor of his coming. ⁹The coming of the lawless one will be in accordance with the work of Satan displayed in all kinds of counterfeit miracles, signs and wonders, ¹⁰and in every sort of evil that deceives those who are perishing. They perish because they refused to love the truth and so be saved. ¹¹For this reason God sends them a powerful delusion so that they will believe the lie ¹²and so that all will be condemned who have not believed the truth but have delighted in wickedness.

NRSV

told you these things when I was still with you? ⁶And you know what is now restraining him, so that he may be revealed when his time comes. ⁷For the mystery of lawlessness is already at work, but only until the one who now restrains it is removed. ⁸And then the lawless one will be revealed, whom the Lord Jesus[a] will destroy[b] with the breath of his mouth, annihilating him by the manifestation of his coming. ⁹The coming of the lawless one is apparent in the working of Satan, who uses all power, signs, lying wonders, ¹⁰and every kind of wicked deception for those who are perishing, because they refused to love the truth and so be saved. ¹¹For this reason God sends them a powerful delusion, leading them to believe what is false, ¹²so that all who have not believed the truth but took pleasure in unrighteousness will be condemned.

[a]Other ancient authorities lack *Jesus*   [b]Other ancient authorities read *consume*

COMMENTARY

With 2:3-12, the writer treats the cosmic power dynamics of the realities of vengeance and vindication highlighted in 1:5-10 and assumed in 1:11-12. These verses do not skirt over the matter of the hostilities that the church faces or the consequences that its opponents must face. Rather, the verses describe in stark detail what will happen before and upon the coming of the Lord in accordance with what the writer has already said and on the basis of familiar apocalyptic traditions.

The stark detail, however, is not necessarily clear to modern interpreters. Descriptions of the material in vv. 3-12 range from "veiled and obscure" to "unconsciously vague."[32] One scholar suggests that the writer appears to "ransack the resources of apocalyptic thought to underscore his theme."[33] Perhaps, as we shall see, even veiled, vague, and unclear ransacking can have its purposes. For now, three concerns are relevant:

(1) a division of the material in vv. 3-12; (2) some explanations of ambiguous clauses in vv. 3-5 and 6-7; and (3) an argument about the sequential logic of the verses.

Regarding the division, the material breaks nicely into two sections. An initial section focuses on the coming of a mysterious figure called "the lawless one" (vv. 3-7). A subsequent section renders the source(s) and consequences of the lawless one's arrival (vv. 8-12).

As for the ambiguous clauses in vv. 3-5 and 6-7, the one in vv. 3-5 is an ellipsis. The words "that day will not come" (v. 3a) in the phrase "for that day will not come unless the rebellion comes first and the lawless one is revealed" (vv. 3a-b) are not found in the Greek, but are supplied by the NRSV to clarify what will not happen unless the rebellion comes first. Because the Greek sentence (vv. 3c-4) does not stop with its introduction of the lawless one, but winds on and on with more descriptions of this figure, the NRSV starts a new sentence at v. 4. Then the sentence is interrupted by a parenthetical clause about the writer's earlier words while he was with the

---

32. Respectively, see Thurston, *Reading Colossians, Ephesians and 2 Thessalonians,* 175; Koester, "From Paul's Eschatology to the Apocalyptic Schemata of 2 Thessalonians," 457.

33. Edgar Krentz, "Through a Lens," in *The Thessalonian Correspondence,* ed. Raymond F. Collins (Leuven: University of Leuven Press, 1990) 61-62.

church (v. 5), only to start again in v. 6. To note the interruption, the NRSV again begins a new sentence in v. 5.

In the case of vv. 6-7, there is ambiguity about the logic of using two different participial forms of the Greek verb "to restrain" (κατέχω *katechō*) to describe the restraint that is placed on the man of lawlessness. For one form, the NRSV gives the translation "what is now restraining" because that participle implies a thing rather than a person (v. 6). For the second, it gives the translation "the one who now restrains" because that participle implies the activity of a person (v. 7).[34] So scholars are not sure just what or who restrains the man of lawlessness. Is he restrained by a thing? By a person? And if only by one, why does the writer give both participles?

What we can know, however, is that because the restraint holds the man of lawlessness back, the day of the Lord has not occurred. In the reckoning of the writer, even though the "mystery of lawlessness" (perhaps a synonym for the activity of "those who do not know God," 1:8, or perhaps a cipher for the present persecutions) is already at work, the revelation or unveiling of the lawless one has not occurred (2:6). And until the restraint is removed, that revelation cannot occur. Furthermore, before the revelation, a rebellion (ἀποστασία *apostasia*, the word from which we get the English word "apostasy") must first occur (v. 3; cf. Matt 24:6-14; 1 Tim 4:1-14; 2 Tim 3:1-5; Jude 17-19). Then, with the revelation of the lawless one, the day of the Lord will come (v. 8).

With respect to the sequential logic, one must join the letter's first auditors, who would have heard vv. 3-12 as a refutation of the claim that the day of the Lord had appeared. To join them, however, requires that one note the force of the refutation, the intratextual context of the previous material, and the extratextual context that the auditors could have recalled in understanding the refutation.

Read apart from the preceding material, the force of much of the refutation is patently disturbing. That is, the writer's comprehensive schema suggests that the opposition will become more intense. As Krentz aptly notes: "The removal of that restraining person [or thing] will be the καιρός *kairos* [time] (2:6) for the ultimate revelation of ὁ ἄνθρωπος τῆς ἀνομίας (*ho anthrōpos tēs anomias* [lawless one]; 2:3), the nadir of apocalyptic misfortune."[35] How could the writer tell a group already facing external hostilities that the worst is yet to come? Would not his own words, at least until v. 8, cause the auditors to become "quickly shaken in mind or alarmed"? Precisely this is the reason why the preceding material of 1:5-12 had to be given first—to give the fuller drama of power in which the past and ongoing persecution should be set.

One must join the auditors, then, for an understanding of 2:3-12 that resonates with the preceding intratextual context given in 1:5-12. Given Jesus' own revelation as described in 1:7, the audience can expect the lawless one to have a revelation (2:3, 7). Indeed, the figure has a παρουσία (*parousia*, 2:9), as does Jesus (2:8). At least, therefore, as other scholars have noted, the audience could view the lawless one as a parody of Christ. Furthermore, the impression one gets of Jesus in 1:5-12 is that he comes as an agent of God who will inflict "vengeance on those who do not know God" (1:8). He does not seek glory, but both he (1:10) and his name (1:12) will be glorified. The picture of the lawless one, however, is that of a usurper: "He opposes and exalts himself above every so-called god or object of worship, so that he takes his seat in the temple of God, declaring himself to be God" (2:4). Unlike Jesus (1:8), the lawless one does not have a gospel, but seeks to deceive people who "refused to love the truth" (2:10). If the authority of God lies behind Jesus' action of vengeance (1:8), Satan lies behind the activity of the lawless one (2:9; cf. 1 Thess 2:18). If Jesus' coming will be marveled at by "all who have believed" (1:10), the coming of the lawless one (1:9) sets into play God's delusion of persons who will "believe what is false" (2:11). Even given the great might of the lawless one, a might expressed through all kinds of "power [a general word connoting miraculous ability], signs, lying wonders" (cf. Exod 7:3; Deut 6:22; Acts 2:22, 43), he is no match for Jesus.

On the one hand, the mouth of Jesus will put

---

34. For the most part, the commentary agrees with arguments given by Wanamaker on these verses. See Charles Wanamaker, *The Epistles to the Thessalonians*, NIGTC (Grand Rapids: Eerdmans, 1990) 249-57.

35. Krentz, "Through a Lens," 53.

an end to the lawless one. The image here reflects Isa 11:4 and other texts (cf. 4 Ezra 13:10; *1 Enoch* 62:2) in which the breath of God alone reduces enemies to nothing. On the other hand, the "manifestation" or epiphany (ἐπιφάνεια *epiphaneia*, 2:8) of Jesus' coming will reduce the effective work of the lawless one. The epiphany image here is Hellenistic. It is an image of the visit of a god to bring salvation or benefactions (cf. 1 Tim 6:14; 2 Tim 4:1, 8; Titus 2:13). Here, however, the visit brings both salvation and destruction.

In following the intratextual context and its contrasts between the lawless one and Jesus, readers probably will find it difficult to understand how God could be a deceiver. Robert Jewett offers a helpful explanation: "The phrases "having faith in" or "loving the truth" (vv. 2, 10) evoke the horizon of accepting or rejecting the gospel as the key to the judgment scheme in this apocalyptic theology."[36] Thus the delusion God brings is not the cause of the rejection of the gospel, but its result. The idea of God's sending a delusion, moreover, is not a unique expression. Elsewhere in biblical literature God grants the possibility for persons to be seduced or subjected to evil because of their failure to believe the truth about God (cf. Rom 1:18-32).

Another context important for joining the auditors is the extratextual context from which they could have understood their own plight in the light of the refutation given in 2:3-12. The commentary so far has deliberately not defined in explicit terms some of the key elements of the refutation—namely, the "lawless one" (vv. 3, 8), "what is now restraining" (v. 6), or the "the one who now restrains" (2:7). To gain even a provisional insight into these terms, one must be apprised of extratextual matters, both from the history of the subjugation of the Jewish subculture to which Paul and other early Christians belonged and from the larger political culture of the first century CE.

The "lawless man" or "man of lawlessness" is a Semitic expression that does not so much identify the figure as it describes his activity. This expression is qualified by the writer with yet a second Semitic expression, the "son of destruction" (v. 3).[37] Since this type of expression indicated the nature of a person or the realm to which a person belonged (cf. 1 Thess 5:4), the "son of destruction" also does not identify the figure, but aligns him with the cosmic forces of evil. He belongs to the realm of "destruction" (ἀπώλεια *apōleia*), and, indeed, his coming will be accompanied by deception "for those who are perishing" (ἀπόλλυμι *apollymi*, v. 10) or, as Richard has suggested, those "on the road to ruin."[38]

Beyond his aforementioned characterization as being against God and against Christ (though he is not called anti-Christ as in 1 John 2:18, 22; 4:3; 2 John 7), the figure could have connoted images of pseudo-prophets equipped with deceptive signs, as one finds in the synoptic apocalypses of the 70s and 80s CE.[39] Because the figure is associated with the Temple (presumably the Second Temple in Jerusalem) or is described as an "endtime tyrant," some scholars link him to the "king" in Dan 11:36-38 (i.e., Antiochus IV)[40] or to Roman figures, usually Pompey, who captured Jerusalem in 63 BCE,[41] or (better) Gaius Caligula, whose threat to set up statues of himself in Jerusalem in 40 CE almost succeeded.[42]

As noted earlier, both participles from the verb "to restrain" ("what is now restraining," v. 6; "the one who now restrains," v. 7) are interpretive hurdles. Some scholars wish to regard the first one in a positive way, as God[43] or as God's plan,[44] perhaps anticipating 2:8-12 where the writer will describe God as the ultimate source of the delusion promulgated by the lawless one and energized by Satan (cf. Rom 1:21-28). Notwithstanding God as the key designer of apocalyptic hopes in

---

36. Robert Jewett, "A Matrix of Grace: The Theology of 2 Thessalonians," in *Pauline Theology*, ed. Jouette Bassler (Minneapolis: Fortress, 1991) 1:67. Cf. Thurston, *Reading Colossians, Ephesians and 2 Thessalonians*, 180.

37. The identification of the "man of lawlessness" actually assumes an earlier text-critical problem—namely, whether one supports the textual variant "man of sin" or the variant "man of lawlessness." The former variant is widely attested, but not usually preferred because the figure of 2:6 is later identified specifically as the "lawless one" in 2:8. See Leon Morris, *The First and Second Epistles to the Thessalonians: The English Text with Introduction, Exposition and Notes* (Grand Rapids: Eerdmans, 1959) 21-22.

38. Earl J. Richard, *First and Second Thessalonians*, Sacra Pagina (Collegeville, Minn.: Liturgical, 1995) 327.

39. L. Hartman, "Eschatology of 2 Thessalonians" in *The Thessalonian Correspondence*, ed. Raymond F. Collins (Leuven: University of Leuven Press, 1990) 480; C. H. Giblin, "2 Thessalonians 2 Re-read," in ibid., 462.

40. Ibid., 462.

41. See *Pss Sol* 17:11-15.

42. See Josephus *The Jewish War* 2.184-185. See also Maarten J. J. Menken, *2 Thessalonians* (London: Routledge, 1994) 104-6.

43. Bonnie Thurston, *Reading Colossians, Ephesians and 2 Thessalonians: A Literary and Theological Commentary* (New York: Crossroad, 1995) 179; Hartman, "Eschatology of 2 Thessalonians," 481.

44. Menken, *2 Thessalonians*, 112.

vv. 8-12, others read the initial participle in a negative way, as tantamount to the "mystery (μυστήριον *mystērion*) of lawlessness."[45] Some scholars also read the second participle in a positive way, suggesting that it refers to an angel of God or even to God, though one wonders how God could be removed (v. 7). The problem with the positive formulations is that they do not explain the necessity of two different participles to express the idea that God's plan or someone representing God was restraining the appearance of the lawless one.[46]

If the second participle ("the one who now restrains") has a negative referent (v. 7), it could be a contemporary emperor. As Wanamaker notes, "Paul and his contemporaries intuitively recognized that the type of evil that defies God and seeks to usurp his position derives from corrupt and unjust social and political institutions such as imperial rule under Gaius Caesar."[47] Yet one need not specifically identify the referent. Perhaps the writer gives "veiled, deliberately mysterious reference to the restrainer, be it magistrate, governor, or emperor."[48] In the light of the

author's use of 1 Thessalonians, which highlights local hostility (v. 14) and the continuing hostilities in 2 Thessalonians, perhaps the author does not wish to limit the restrainer (whose removal will open up wide-scale rebellion and the revelation and deception of the lawless one) to a single figure. The problem is not a single instance of persecution. The problem is that the persecution that is already underway issues from many fronts.

The cryptic language, then, at least has the function of showing the varied character of the persecutions. In addition, as refutation, it makes it difficult for anyone to pinpoint the exact time of the future day of the Lord. With vv. 8-12 and their descriptions of the destruction of the lawless one and God's ultimate control, moreover, all of 2:3-12 functions as a source of encouragement for a beleaguered church. Indeed, the lawless one does not stand a chance. When he is revealed, he will exercise power and bring forth a deception. Yet, he will be destroyed or made inoperative by Jesus through "the breath of his mouth" (cf. Exod 15:8; 2 Sam 22:16). What the audience sees is that the power of the lawless one is no match for God's avenging agent.

45. Wanamaker, *The Epistles to the Thessalonians,* 253.
46. Ibid., 251.
47. Ibid., 248.
48. Gerhard Krodel, *The Deutero-Pauline Letters: Ephesians, Colossians, 2 Thessalonians, 1–2 Timothy, Titus* Proclamation Commentaries (Minneapolis: Fortress, 1993) 48.

REFLECTIONS

Despite the enigmatic character of 2:3-12 for us, the text likely breathed confidence into the lives of its original audience because it wove the plight of the church into a larger drama. Indeed, the text speaks even now to its readers and hearers with the challenge for us to respond to moments when life seems meaningless with a perspective that places life in a larger drama. There are persons who respond to moments of meaninglessness with a defeatist perspective. They look on the apparently hopeless individual scenes of life and wish to cry out with Lady Macbeth: "Out, out, brief candle! Life is but a walking shadow, a poor player that struts and frets his hour upon the stage, and then is heard no more; it is a tale told by an idiot, full of sound and fury, signifying nothing." Others respond to these moments through denial. They resort to hedonistic solutions—numbing shattered dreams with mood-altering chemicals, holding madness at bay through countless hours of computerized or televised virtual reality, delaying the arrival of despair through relentless and promiscuous sexual pursuits, or nursing the deep wounds of emptiness with the swabs of self-centered acquisition.

The writer of 2 Thessalonians recommends neither a perspective of defeatism nor one of denial. Rather, the writer takes on a defiant position. He places the sordid experiences of the church's suffering within the larger drama of what God is doing and will do in the world. The momentary scenes of meaninglessness may represent an act in the drama, but the drama is not a one-act play. There is a larger picture, a grand movement in which every scene fits. The full horizon has not been sketched in. There is more to come. This perspective allowed Martin Luther King, Jr., to peer down the telescope of time to find a moment in history—albeit dreamlike—unsullied by oppression and unsoiled by discrimination. It helped Gandhi to advocate *Satyagraha* (or a devotion to truth) against the Transvaal government in South Africa and later against British rule in India. It convinced Archbishop Romero to minister to the poor in El Salvador. And it inspired Nelson Mandela's stability and hope as he struggled against South Africa's entrenched system of apartheid. This perspective has given courage to untold numbers of those who fight against injustice with its remarkable message: Evil will be defeated!

2 Thessalonians 2:13-17, Reasons to Stand Firm and Hold On

NIV

¹³But we ought always to thank God for you, brothers loved by the Lord, because from the beginning God chose you*a* to be saved through the sanctifying work of the Spirit and through belief in the truth. ¹⁴He called you to this through our gospel, that you might share in the glory of our Lord Jesus Christ. ¹⁵So then, brothers, stand firm and hold to the teachings*b* we passed on to you, whether by word of mouth or by letter.

¹⁶May our Lord Jesus Christ himself and God our Father, who loved us and by his grace gave us eternal encouragement and good hope, ¹⁷encourage your hearts and strengthen you in every good deed and word.

a13 Some manuscripts *because God chose you as his firstfruits*
b15 Or *traditions*

NRSV

¹³But we must always give thanks to God for you, brothers and sisters*a* beloved by the Lord, because God chose you as the first fruits*b* for salvation through sanctification by the Spirit and through belief in the truth. ¹⁴For this purpose he called you through our proclamation of the good news,*c* so that you may obtain the glory of our Lord Jesus Christ. ¹⁵So then, brothers and sisters,*a* stand firm and hold fast to the traditions that you were taught by us, either by word of mouth or by our letter.

¹⁶Now may our Lord Jesus Christ himself and God our Father, who loved us and through grace gave us eternal comfort and good hope, ¹⁷comfort your hearts and strengthen them in every good work and word.

a Gk *brothers*   *b* Other ancient authorities read *from the beginning*
c Or *through our gospe*

COMMENTARY

As noted earlier, 2:13-17 is cast as a conclusion to 2:1-12. This exhortative material easily divides into two sets of prayers around a more central set of exhortations. Thus 2:13-17 includes a thanksgiving notice (vv. 13-14), a request to stand firm (v. 15), and a wish-prayer (vv. 16-17).

The material here also anticipates the next large unit (3:1-15), particularly, the initial verses (3:1-5), which are also set in a context of prayers. Both speak about God's love (2:16; 3:5). Both speak of hearts (2:17; 3:5) and of the strengthening of the church (2:17; 3:3). Both give attention to the issue of belief, either the belief of the

church (2:13) or others' lack of belief (3:2). Both also mention the writer's gospel (2:14) or the word of the Lord (3:1) and glory, either that obtained by the church (2:14) or by the word (3:1).

2:13-14. Like the thanksgiving in 1:3-4, the thanksgiving in these verses reflects the writer's obligation. Again, however, the obligation is not a challenge to a protest from the audience, but a genuine response to what God has done. The thanksgiving here also links God's call of the church to the writer's proclamation (v. 14). This is a critical link because the writer will later ask the church to stand firm and hold fast to traditions that he taught them (v. 15). It is also critical because a part of the audience's problem is its potential dissuasion from the writer's truth, even though the church came to belief through the writer. Little wonder it is, then, that the apocalyptic scenario given in vv. 3-12 is interrupted by a parenthesis in v. 5, in which the writer reminds the group that he had already told them the argument he was putting forth to refute the enthusiastic agitation. The inclusion of the initial words "But we" in this thanksgiving, moreover, sets up a contrast between the persons of doom noted in vv. 11-12 and the church. Those who are deceived will not be saved (v. 10), but the church was chosen for salvation (v. 13). The deceived ones are those who "refused to love the truth" (v. 10) and those who "have not believed the truth" (v. 12), but the church was chosen "through belief in the truth" (v. 13; cf. Deut 26:17-18 LXX).

It is also the case that this thanksgiving places the church's fate directly in God's hands—in what God has done, is doing, and will do. God's election of the church indicates God's past actions, and the election is evinced both through the words "God chose you" and through the description of the church as "beloved" (see 1 Thess 1:4). God's concern for the believers is also found in their present, ongoing life, for the expression "the Spirit" mentioned in v. 13 is not a human spirit, but the source by which the church gains its sanctification or maturity (cf. 1 Thess 4:3-8).

God's activity in the lives of the believers can be seen if further attention is given to the text-critical problem in v. 13. Although some scholars accept the variant "first fruits" (as in the NRSV) as closer to the original,[49] it should be noted that the Thessalonians were not the "first fruits" in the Macedonian ministry (the Philippians were). Other scholars, then, opt for the expression "from the beginning" as closer to the original.[50] Read this way, the passage continues to show God's control over events, now peering back into the unfathomable moments of creation (v. 13) and

eventually fastforwarding through time to speak about God's purpose in calling the church (to "obtain the glory of our Lord Jesus Christ," v. 14).

Thus, as noted earlier, the thanksgiving is one of the conclusions to the first set of hortatory appeals. After introducing the problem of the agitation and indicating the foundational traditions that refuted the enthusiastic message, the writer issues a word of prayer that reveals both the identity of the church (in contrast to those deceived by Satan) and the basis for that identity—namely, God's activity in their lives.

2:15. In the light of vv. 13-14, the writer asks the church in a positive form to do what he initially asked them to do in a negative form (v. 2). That is, if they stand fast and hold fast to the traditions that they already know (v. 6), they will not be shaken up. The writer's use of the word "traditions," however, is not simply to give a summation to the first set of hortatory appeals on maintaining the church's foundational traditions. It also prepares the audience for a similar discussion in the next set of hortatory appeals (cf. 3:6). In this case, the writer is refuting enthusiastic agitation. In the next large unit, the issue will be irresponsible behavior.

2:16-17. Even with the summation given in v. 15, the writer has not ended his hortatory appeals to return to the foundational traditions. And indeed, as already noted, this appeal will continue. In vv. 16-17, the writer gives a wish-prayer that both indicates the roles that the Lord Jesus and God have played in the church's lives and makes two appeals to God on the basis of those roles: a request for comfort and a request for strength or firming up of the hearts or inner beings of the church. Because this wish-prayer resembles the one in 1 Thess 3:11-13, the writer implicitly continues to make his point about maintaining the foundational traditions.

Thus in vv. 13-17 the writer offers comfort to the believers even as he exhorts them not to veer away from the apostolic traditions. Reminders that God chose them set the church apart from those deluded by Satan (v. 9). At the same time, the writer notes that salvation and glorification are related to the ongoing process of sanctification and a belief in the truth (vv. 13-14). With these reminders in place, he can emphatically admonish the church "to stand firm and hold fast to the

---

49. E.g., F. W. Hughes, *Early Christian Rhetoric and 2 Thessalonians* (Sheffield: JSOT, 1989) 61.

50. Charles Wanamaker, *The Epistles to the Thessalonians*, NIGTC (Grand Rapids: Eerdmans, 1990) 266; Bonnie Thurston, *Reading Colossians, Ephesians and 2 Thessalonians: A Literary and Theological Commentary* (New York: Crossroad, 1995) 183.

traditions" (v. 15) and close out the first set of exhortations with a word about the eternal comfort God gives (v. 16).

Altogether, the first set of exhortative appeals (vv. 1-17) includes three parts: (1) a statement of the problem (vv. 1-2); (2) a refutation of the delusion (vv. 3-12); and (3) a prayer collection that concludes the refutation and contrasts the fates of believers and unbelievers (vv. 13-17). The exhortations encourage the auditors to remain firm in the traditions already taught to them (a typical course in the hortatory tradition) and to avoid being shaken by traditions that do not accurately and comprehensively treat the reward of the righteous or the fate of those who refuse to believe.

REFLECTIONS

The writer of 2 Thessalonians speaks not only of God's comforting hearts, but (by implication) of God's strengthening them as well (2:17) The heart in ancient times referred to the inner convictions of a person. This is the strength for which the writer prayed and one that is sorely needed in our times. Our world is constantly bombarded by an emphasis on the outward, external appearance often to the exclusion of the internals. Nannie Helen Burroughs once said that maybe we have failed our children because we (as parents) have "been too bothered about the externals—clothes or money," but our young people need the internals and the eternals.[51] Indeed, when we read of inner-city youth willing to kill each other for the status that accrues to a designer jacket or fancy gym shoes, we must wonder if we have failed our children. And when sports figures are produced, packaged, and paraded as role models for the young by Madison Avenue with little regard for the violent behavior they promote in private or public spheres, we again must wonder if we have failed our children.

The focus on externals, however, extends beyond fashion trends. Consider the drug crisis in the world. So often countries focus on the outside in a quest to end drug use. Sure, something must be done to prohibit the traffic of drugs into or within a country. And those who deal this death rightly deserve prosecution and punishment. But it is also true that detox and rehabilitation centers must be available for those who are ready to resist these enslavers of the spirit. Yet even if drugs were eliminated totally from the planet, unless we grapple with the deeper cultural fixation on instant gratification, another evil will rise to take the place of drugs.

Or look at the almost exclusive attention that we place on the external physical self. Whole industries have developed to strengthen the physical body, to give us powerful physiques, carved and chiseled to aesthetic (or perhaps simply sensual) perfection. To be sure, proper care should be given to that which has been placed in our trust as God's stewards. But is a good physique everything? No, the life within must also be nourished. It must be fed and sustained to give us direction and stability. Lucie Campbell's great hymn of the church, "Something Within" (1919), is still appropriate:

> Something within that holds the reins.
> Something within that banishes pain.
> Something within I cannot explain.
> All that I know—there's something within.

51. Nannie Helen Burroughs, "Unload Your Uncle Toms," in *Black Women in White America: A Documentary History,* ed. Gerda Lerner (New York: Pantheon, 1972) 552.

2 THESSALONIANS 3:1-15, HORTATORY APPEALS AGAINST IRRESPONSIBLE BEHAVIOR

OVERVIEW

The second set of exhortations easily divides into two parts: (1) an initial section cast in the language of prayer (3:1-5) and (2) a longer section commending behavior requisite to the writer's tradition (3:6-15). Both sections reveal a concern for the church's stability. Both also encourage the church to turn to practical pursuits in accordance with the writer's commands.

2 Thessalonians 3:1-5, Doing What Is Commanded

NIV	NRSV
3 Finally, brothers, pray for us that the message of the Lord may spread rapidly and be honored, just as it was with you. ²And pray that we may be delivered from wicked and evil men, for not everyone has faith. ³But the Lord is faithful, and he will strengthen and protect you from the evil one. ⁴We have confidence in the Lord that you are doing and will continue to do the things we command. ⁵May the Lord direct your hearts into God's love and Christ's perseverance.	**3** Finally, brothers and sisters,[a] pray for us, so that the word of the Lord may spread rapidly and be glorified everywhere, just as it is among you, ²and that we may be rescued from wicked and evil people; for not all have faith. ³But the Lord is faithful; he will strengthen you and guard you from the evil one.[b] ⁴And we have confidence in the Lord concerning you, that you are doing and will go on doing the things that we command. ⁵May the Lord direct your hearts to the love of God and to the steadfastness of Christ.

[a] Gk brothers   [b] Or from evil

COMMENTARY

The use of the word "finally" signals here the beginning of the last large unit (cf. 1 Thess 4:1). The five verses may be divided into three sections: a command for prayer, vv. 1-2; statements of confidence and assurance about the church's constancy, vv. 3-4; and a wish-prayer, v. 5. In part, the verses prepare the audience for 3:6-15.[52] In part, they also continue the consolatory "prayer mode begun at 2:13."[53] And in part, they reiterate the theme of maintaining the foundational traditions through their allusions to 1 Thessalonians in form and diction.

3:1-2. The writer's prayer request is reminis-

cent of 1 Thess 5:25 ("Beloved, pray for us"), but details are given here of what the prayer should include. For a writer who has repeatedly written with parallels and doublets, a prayer request with two concerns is not unusual. One concern focuses on the word of the Lord, that it might "spread rapidly" or "run swiftly." While Paul often used athletic language to speak about his ministry (Rom 9:16; 1 Cor 9:24-27; Gal 2:2; 5:7; Phil 2:16), the emphasis here is on the running of the word. Thus most scholars see Ps 147:15 (LXX, "his word runs swiftly") as the background for this request, with the writer, in characteristic form, attributing the word to the Lord (Jesus) rather than to God.

The additional focus of the initial concern is that the word of the Lord might "be glorified everywhere" (v. 1). To demonstrate this additional

52. Maarten J. J. Menken, *2 Thessalonians* (London: Routledge, 1994) 125, reads 3:1-5 as preparation for the injunctions of 3:6-12.
53. Thurston, *Reading Colossians, Ephesians and 2 Thessalonians*, 185.

focus the writer speaks of the glorification of the word among his church's members. Whether the writer here indicates the past or present glorification is debated, but the word's glorification likely means its acceptance. Thus, given the context of opposition, the writer seeks to change others through their acceptance of the word of the Lord.

The second concern of the prayer request is more directly related to the writer. He may be a towering figure in the eyes of the church, but continuing use of first-person plural pronouns ("we" and "us") and the prayer request for deliverance from opposition suggest that he is not a lone hero. Furthermore, he *and* his church stand in opposition to others ("for not all have faith," v. 2), a somber, but realistic, recognition of the old age's presence and of the division of sides squared off against each other in the writer's apocalyptic perspective.[54]

3:3-4. In this passage the writer's consolatory statements of assurance about the Lord and the audience are reminiscent of 1 Thessalonians. God's faithfulness (1 Thess 5:24) now becomes the faithfulness of the Lord (Jesus, v. 3). And a wish-prayer for "strength" (1 Thess 3:13), already mentioned in the wish-prayer of 2 Thess 2:17, now becomes a statement of assurance (v. 3).

These verses, moreover, anticipate the content and tone of vv. 6-15. The writer's assurance that the church is "doing" (ποιεῖτε *poieite*) and will "do" (ποιήσετε *poiēsete*) the things he commands (v. 4) anticipates v. 13, a reminder to the church not to "be weary in doing [καλοποιοῦντες *kalopoiountes*] what is right." Also, the writer's tone of thoughtful concern for the larger church's battles with "the evil one" (τοῦ πονηροῦ *tou ponērou*; perhaps Satan, see Matt 13:19, 39; 1 John 2:13-14) or simply with "evil"—along with the earlier acknowledgment of the writer's own battles with πονηροὶ ἄνθρωποι (*ponēroi anthrōpoi*, "evil persons")—likely tips off the audience to the same kind of concern for thoughtfulness as noted in the example of useful work (vv. 7-9) given in the subsequent section. If so, at least one of the problems of those who live in "idleness" (as translated in the NRSV, v. 6) or "disorderliness" (ἀτάκτως *ataktōs*) is that their

work does not give aid or consideration to the larger church as it faces external difficulties. With the expression "in the Lord" (v. 4), moreover, the writer's tone of thoughtful consideration of others is no less one of authority. Later, when the writer issues commands (vv. 6, 12), he uses a similar expression to show the force or authority of his command.

3:5. In form, the wish-prayer in this verse is similar to 1 Thess 3:11-13. And it should not go unnoticed that the plenitude of prayer forms in 1 Thessalonians and the request for the church to pray without ceasing (1 Thess 5:17) and to give thanks in everything (1 Thess 5:18) probably influenced the writer's scattering of multiple prayers throughout 2 Thessalonians, including the ones in 3:1-5. In all of these ways, then, the writer continues to emphasize to the church the need to hold on to the foundational traditions.

More specifically, the wish-prayer here reiterates a concern for the "hearts" or inner convictions of the church (v. 5; cf. 2:17). Anticipating the thoughtfulness requested in the next section, however, the focus of the concern for the church's "hearts" here is on the "love of God" and the "steadfastness of Christ." While the Greek behind "love of God" could mean either God's kind of love or a love for God, the former is preferred because the writer does not elsewhere speak of a love for God. If hearts are directed to the love of God or God's kind of love, the church will have to show the constant concern for each other that God has demonstrated in loving (2:13) and sharing good gifts with this church (2:16). Likewise, while the Greek behind "steadfastness of Christ" could mean either Christ's own steadfastness or a steadfastness toward Christ, the former is preferred both because modeling is a key concern for the writer in anticipation of 3:6-15, and the writer has just stated his confidence that the church will "go on doing the things" he commands (v. 4).

Altogether, 3:1-5 provides a summary of the prayer mode begun earlier and a foreshadowing of the concern with proper conduct of the subsequent section. Its verses, while brief, give the second set of exhortations both a tone of proper regard for others and one of authority.

---

54. Cf. Menken, *2 Thessalonians*, 127.

REFLECTIONS

While the Greek words behind the "love of God" (3:5) are ambiguous, the writer's theme of mutuality is not. Even before he lifts himself up as a model of thoughtful concern for others in 3:6-15, he models mutuality through his request of prayer from others and his prayer for others. This mutuality rescues people from either a lone hero syndrome or a selfish pursuit syndrome, both of which wreak havoc on the world.

According to Bernard Brandon Scott, in the American context this "lone hero" type likely owes its origin to the early "settler" individuals who found themselves faced with the vastness of a supposedly open frontier and the freedom to shape it and mold it into submission.[55] Perhaps the myth is supported by Hollywood through its string of "Duke" (John Wayne) westerns and its urban "Dirty Harry" (Clint Eastwood) action films, which offer a variation on this theme.[56] Robert N. Bellah notes that this "mythic individualism" also can be traced to stories of flight from society, as in James Fennimore Cooper's *The Deerslayer* and Herman Melville's *Moby Dick,* and to detective stories about Sam Spade or Serpico.[57] Whatever its origin and force, it has camped in on the American psyche—among extremists who have given up on prevailing ideas of justice and who want to take matters into their own hands, for example.

The selfish pursuit type, however, is just as harmful and often more cunning. This type has not listened to Abraham Heschel's warnings against "arrogating to the self what is not its due."[58] Nor has this type heard Samuel Proctor's lament about preachers who take the selfish route in the name of good: "What a temptation it is for some preachers . . . to use . . . ameliorative, and even revolutionary, causes to promote themselves, to seize every photo opportunity, to manipulate the press, to elbow to the front of and center of every rostrum, to maneuver themselves into the focus of every television camera, and to leap to the front of every parade."[59]

For the writer of 2 Thessalonians, only mutuality and solidarity can provide the real sustenance for which these types unwittingly cry out. For the first type, the writer answers not with his own vengeance, but with the promotion of the truth as found in the word of the Lord. And for the second type, he responds with the challenge that our hearts, our inner convictions, need to be directed by a force that rises above our individual pursuits.

---

55. Bernard Brandon Scott, "Toward a Hermeneutics of the Solo Savior: Dirty Harry and Romans 5–8," in *Intersections: Post-Critical Studies in Preaching,* ed. Richard L. Eslinger (Grand Rapids: Eerdmans, 1994) 123-24.
56. Ibid., 124-56.
57. Robert N. Bellah et al., *Habits of the Heart: Individualism and Commitment in American Life* (Berkeley: University of California Press, 1985) 144-47.
58. Abraham J. Heschel, *God in Search of Man: A Philosophy of Judaism* (New York: Harper and Bros., 1966) 400.
59. Samuel D. Proctor, *The Certain Sound of the Trumpet: Crafting a Sermon of Authority* (Valley Forge: Judson, 1994) 135.

2 Thessalonians 3:6-15, Doing What Is Responsible

NIV	NRSV
⁶In the name of the Lord Jesus Christ, we command you, brothers, to keep away from every brother who is idle and does not live according to the teaching[a] you received from us. ⁷For you yourselves know how you ought to follow our example. We were not idle when we were with	6Now we command you, beloved,[a] in the name of our Lord Jesus Christ, to keep away from believers who are[b] living in idleness and not according to the tradition that they[c] received from us. ⁷For you yourselves know how you ought to
ᵃ6 Or *tradition*	ᵃ Gk *brothers* ᵇ Gk *from every brother who is* ᶜ Other ancient authorities read *you*

NIV

you, ⁸nor did we eat anyone's food without paying for it. On the contrary, we worked night and day, laboring and toiling so that we would not be a burden to any of you. ⁹We did this, not because we do not have the right to such help, but in order to make ourselves a model for you to follow. ¹⁰For even when we were with you, we gave you this rule: "If a man will not work, he shall not eat."

¹¹We hear that some among you are idle. They are not busy; they are busybodies. ¹²Such people we command and urge in the Lord Jesus Christ to settle down and earn the bread they eat. ¹³And as for you, brothers, never tire of doing what is right.

¹⁴If anyone does not obey our instruction in this letter, take special note of him. Do not associate with him, in order that he may feel ashamed. ¹⁵Yet do not regard him as an enemy, but warn him as a brother.

NRSV

imitate us; we were not idle when we were with you, ⁸and we did not eat anyone's bread without paying for it; but with toil and labor we worked night and day, so that we might not burden any of you. ⁹This was not because we do not have that right, but in order to give you an example to imitate. ¹⁰For even when we were with you, we gave you this command: Anyone unwilling to work should not eat. ¹¹For we hear that some of you are living in idleness, mere busybodies, not doing any work. ¹²Now such persons we command and exhort in the Lord Jesus Christ to do their work quietly and to earn their own living. ¹³Brothers and sisters,ᵃ do not be weary in doing what is right.

14Take note of those who do not obey what we say in this letter; have nothing to do with them, so that they may be ashamed. ¹⁵Do not regard them as enemies, but warn them as believers.ᵇ

ᵃ Gk Brothers   ᵇ Gk a brother

COMMENTARY

With the content and tone set by 3:1-5, the writer now directs his words both to the entire church (or to a group untouched by the disorderly behavior, vv. 6-10, 13-15) and to the erring ones (vv. 11-12).[60] As well, members of the audience recalling 1 Thessalonians would perhaps recognize with A. Van Aarde that vv. 6-12 are "the portion [of 2 Thessalonians] that has been most evidently taken over from 1 Thessalonians."[61] The language of exhortation "in the Lord" (v. 6; 1 Thess 4:1); imitation (vv. 7, 9; 1 Thess 1:6); disorderliness (vv. 6-7, 11; 1 Thess 5:14); useful work to avoid being a burden (vv. 8-9; 1 Thess 2:7-9); and quiet living (3:12; 1 Thess 4:11) clearly has its counterpart in 1 Thessalonians. Thus this section reinforces the theme of the maintenance of tradition.

3:6-10. This initial set of verses gives a specific command (v. 6) and a specific example drawn from the writer's previous visit and ongoing life while he was with the church (3:7-10).[62] On the one hand, the writer does not wish the church to be influenced by the conduct of those who depart from the writer's tradition (v. 6). Identification of the conduct is debated, with the NRSV describing the irresponsible behavior as "living in idleness" (ἀτάκτως ataktōs, v. 11). The basic idea of the behavior, however, is that of disorder.[63]

In using the word "tradition," moreover, the writer does not now mean something passed on to him from another, as Paul had used this word with respect to the transmitted truths about the resurrection (1 Cor 15:3) or the worship life (1 Cor 11:23). Rather, the tradition is "a specific practice of the apostles themselves."[64]

60. On the view that the addressees of the positive exhortations are not the entire church, see Jouette Bassler, "Peace in All Ways," in *Pauline Theology,* ed. Jouette Bassler (Minneapolis: Fortress, 1991) 1:79. It is clear, moreover, from v. 11 that the erring ones are an undefined quantity ("some") within the larger church.

61. A. Van Aarde, "The Struggle Against Heresy in the Thessalonian Correspondence and the Origin of the Apostolic Tradition," in *The Thessalonian Correspondence,* ed. Raymond F. Collins (Leuven: University of Leuven Press, 1990) 423.

62. As Wanamaker noted, the imperfect form of παρηγγέλλομεν (*parēngellomen*) should be translated as "we used to command" (3:10). See Charles Wanamaker, *The Epistles to the Thessalonians,* NIGTC (Grand Rapids: Eerdmans, 1990) 285.

63. Xenophon *Cyropaedia* 7.26; Thucydides *Histories* 3.108.

64. Beverly R. Gaventa, *First and Second Thessalonians,* Interpretation (Louisville: John Knox, 1998) 129.

On the other hand, the writer lifts up his own visit as a model for the church (vv. 7-10). In the course of doing so, he also draws on a Semitic idiom and a proverb. To "eat someone's bread" was an idiom meaning "to earn a living" (cf. Gen 3:19; 2 Kgs 9:7).[65] The expression "anyone unwilling to work should not eat" is not found in any of Paul's undisputed letters, but it resonates with a proverb found in Gen 3:19.[66] It is likely that the Semitic idiom and proverb, like the writer's example, would have reinforced the idea that the writer wished to emphasize traditions, either his own past example or the traditional wisdom of his heritage.

3:11-12. With the play on words in the exhortation directed to the erring ones, the writer clarifies the contrast between "the disorderly ones" (*ataktoi*) and his own "model" behavior. The erring ones are not "[really] working" (ἐργαζομένους *ergazomenous*) but "working around" (περιεργαζομένους *periergazomenous*, v. 11).[67] Furthermore, their activity stands in contrast to the action requested in 1 Thessalonians, a part of their traditions—namely, that of working quietly (1 Thess 4:11). What they do, in contrast to the model of the writer, does not aid the larger church, and thus they must be admonished "in the Lord Jesus Christ" (v. 12). The use of an antithesis between the model and anti-models

typically aids the moral guide (and in this case, the writer) in clarifying approved behavior.

3:13-15. The contrast in place and clarified, the writer next turns again to the larger church to stress its maintenance of good behavior and discipline. With the request that they not become "weary in doing what is right" (v. 13), he draws to a close with language reminiscent of the way he began this set of exhortations (cf. v. 4). The closing verses of the exhortation (vv. 14-15), moreover, invest the larger church with both the authority and the parameters for reforming the erring ones. On the one hand, the larger church has the authority to shame the erring ones because of the latter's deviation from the writer's word as given in the letter (v. 14). On the other hand, the parameters of the reform are clearly prescribed: The larger church must not regard the erring ones as enemies, but (as in 1 Thess 5:14) they must "warn" or "admonish" (νουθετέω *noutheteō*) them as believers (v. 15; cf. v. 6).[68]

The entire second set of exhortations, therefore, has the force of responding to the specific problem of irresponsible behavior based on deviation from the writer's traditions. The analyses of both sets of exhortations in 2:1–3:15 suggest, moreover, that the aim is to get the entire church not to turn back to its former family networks, but to trust that God will both vindicate their suffering and send God's avenging agent, Jesus, on their behalf.

---

65. Earl J. Richard, *First and Second Thessalonians,* Sacra Pagina (Collegeville, Minn.: Liturgical, 1995) 380.

66. Ibid., 381.

67. Cf. Demosthenes *Orations* 26.15; 32.28.

68. On 3:14-15 as a "clarification of v. 6," see Wanamaker, *The Epistles to the Thessalonians,* 288.

REFLECTIONS

In his famous "I Have a Dream" speech (1963), Martin Luther King, Jr., asked his government to live up to its economic promises, which had by then defaulted for many of its citizens.[69] He challenged the United States to act on its commitments to all of its people, to allow its deeds to match its ideals.

The same concern to match one's words with one's deeds was a serious consideration in the first century CE. In that age charlatans—not sages—acted in ways that did not match their words or thoughts.[70] Accordingly, the writer of 2 Thessalonians addresses not only the correct convictions or words that his church should espouse, but the correct actions as well. Indeed, a thread that runs throughout the textual fabric of the second set of exhortations is an emphasis on doing the right thing.

---

69. Martha Solomon, "Covenanted Rights: The Metaphoric Matrix of 'I Have a Dream,' " in *Martin Luther King, Jr., and the Sermonic Power of Public Discourse,* ed. Carolyn Calloway-Thomas and John Louis Lucaites (Tuscaloosa: University of Alabama Press, 1993) 77.

70. On the philosophical topos of the consistency of words and deeds, see Seneca *Epistle* 52.8-9; Philo *Life of Moses* 2.209-16; Epictetus *Discourses* 1:29-56; Dio Chrysostom *Oration* 4.28-39; 72.1; Maximus of Tyre *Discourse* 1.

Beyond the challenge for the church to match its deeds to its words, the writer challenges his readers not to "be weary in doing what is right" (3:13). Under the weight of opposition or because of the influence of false claims, even those who otherwise desire to do right could face fatigue if not disillusionment in their struggle. Even today susceptibility to burnout is a real possibility. Yet the writer's challenge for the people of God to continue doing what is right is clarion and clear. So when we see the homeless sleeping on the streets, let us not be weary in doing what is right. When persons infected by HIV or living with AIDS or other diseases cry out for assistance and for a cure, let us not be weary in doing what is right. When our children need us to rescue them from the throes of drug addiction or drug dealing, let us not be weary in doing what is right.

THE PERORATION

COMMENTARY

Given the letter's objective of encouraging a harassed church, how does the final section (3:16-18) contribute to the goals of a peroration—namely, to summarize the content of a document and to stir the emotions?

Its summarizing nature is clear to both epistolary and rhetorical analysts. Epistolary analysts not only see the peace wish in 3:16 as the beginning of the letter's closing, but they also suggest thematic functions for the letter's closing.[71] That is, they note how the letter's closing thematically reiterates two of the letter's earlier themes: (1) "conflict with the idlers" (or what this commentary has called persons acting disorderly or irresponsibly) and (2) "concern over Christ's return." For Weima, the writer addresses the "tensions and divisions caused by the idlers" in the double reference to peace in the benediction (v. 16), in the letter's repeated use of the word "all" (cf. vv. 16, 18), and in the letter's "autograph greeting and explanatory comment," which highlights the letter's authority for the "idlers." In addition, Weima suggests that the letter addresses the "concern over Christ's return" through its repeated references to the "Lord" (i.e., Jesus) in the "peace benediction" and "word of encouragement."[72]

Rhetorical criticism reveals other important links between the closing and the rest of the letter. Thurston notes how the letter closes as it opened "with a wish for peace (1:2)."[73] Similarly, Menken notes the letter's overall inclusio formed by the grace and peace formulae in the prescript and in the postscript.[74] Both Thurston and Menken also point out the similarities between the letter closings of 1 and 2 Thessalonians, particularly the similar peace wishes in 2 Thess 3:16 and 1 Thess 5:23 and the similar grace benedictions in 2 Thess 3:18 and 1 Thess 5:28.[75]

It should be stated as well that these last verses reiterate the themes noted in the exordium in at least three ways. First, the peroration's use of 1 Thessalonians reinforces both the theme about belief in the writer's gospel or testimony and the theme of standing firm. Second, the letter's pastoral insistence on restoration or reformation of the erring believers through an emphasis on "all" of the church implies the church's stability. That is, Paul's bare "The grace of our Lord Jesus Christ be with you" (1 Thess 5:28) is reinforced in 2 Thessalonians. In 2 Thessalonians, the writer has

---

71. Jeffrey Weima, *Neglected Endings: The Significance of the Pauline Letter Closing* (Sheffield: JSOT, 1994) 187-201.
72. Ibid., 189-90.

73. Bonnie Thurston, *Reading Colossians, Ephesians and 2 Thessalonians: A Literary and Theological Commentary* (New York: Crossroad, 1995) 194.
74. Maarten J. J. Menken, *2 Thessalonians* (London: Routledge, 1994) 54.
75. Ibid., 143. Thurston, *Reading Colossians, Ephesians and 2 Thessalonians,* 196.

both "The Lord be with all of you" (3:16) and "The grace of our Lord Jesus Christ be with all of you" (3:18). He does not want anyone to be left out, and thus he envisions that all will remain stable. Third, the insistence that the Lord of peace would give peace "at all times and in all ways" (v. 16) represents the defiance with which the letter has characterized the continuous justice of God. We must be careful here, however, not to miss the import of the peace the writer emphasizes through redundancy. As Jouette Bassler has noted, "The fundamental meaning of peace in the Greek tradition is precisely this notion of a state of rest following war, strife, or tribulation [θλῖψις *thlipsis*]."[76] Accordingly, this is the kind of peace brought by Augustus to the Roman government when he ended its civil wars. The writer here, however, does not speak of the peace of someone whose rule would pass on to another by death or other vicissitudes of life. This Lord has already been dramatized as a powerful avenging agent for God (throughout chaps. 1 and 2). Thus this Lord of peace can bring peace in all ways and at all times (cf. Rom 16:20; 2 Cor 13:11; Phil 4:9; 1 Thess 5:23).

Beyond its summarizing character, this peroration also would likely stir the emotions of the church. Certainly, as in the case of 1 Thessalonians, the prayer form that opens the peroration (v. 16; cf. 1 Thess 5:23) would give the letter closing an emotional charge. The repetition of peace in v. 16 also would stir the emotions of a church for whom hostilities had been a constant threat. Given that Jesus as Lord has been placed in the role of an avenger, the writer is likely suggesting that the peace that the believers have, and which they have always, comes from one who is actually able to give permanent peace because of the great power associated with his role as God's agent of vindication for believers. Furthermore, because the wish-prayer speaks of peace in all times and "in every way" (v. 16), the church could find assurance that they would not have to face the multiple and mounting threats alone.[77]

Given the summarizing and stirring character of this peroration, what should we make of the authentication remarks in v. 17? Some scholars suggest that these formulae are simply used to respond to an epistolary situation in which "the disorderly ones" need to be corrected with authority. Others see the letter's remarks on its authentication as an indication that Paul actually did not write this letter. Paul's letters often included his closing words in his own handwriting (as opposed to that of an amanuensis, 1 Cor 16:21; Gal 6:11) "but never in order to authenticate his letter and distinguish it from forgeries."[78] Some scholars have noted that the wording "every letter" is odd and presupposes the presence of a collection that one would not have if 2 Thessalonians is *Paul's* own imitation of 1 Thessalonians, his *first* letter. Some scholars have also noted the closing's lack of a typical Pauline personal tone, and instead, the closing's greater concern "to authenticate its message rather than to produce the style and content of Paul's greetings."[79] In my estimation, however, even the authentication remarks could help a beleaguered church needing to make sure that the beliefs and behavior it has endorsed are appropriate as it awaits its Lord's revelation.

---

76. Jouette Bassler, "Peace in All Ways," in *Pauline Theology*, ed. Jouette Bassler (Minneapolis: Fortress, 1991) 1:77. Cf. Plutarch *Advice on Public Life* 824D.

77. For the arguments supporting the variant "in every way" rather than "in every place," see Thurston, *Reading Colossians, Ephesians and 2 Thessalonians*, 194.

78. Gerhard Krodel, *The Deutero-Pauline Letters: Ephesians, Colossians, 2 Thessalonians, 1–2 Timothy, Titus*, Proclamation Commentaries (Minneapolis: Fortress, 1993) 56.

79. Thurston, *Reading Colossians, Ephesians and 2 Thessalonians*, 196.

REFLECTIONS

Peace in all ways and at all times! This is a daring thought, an almost audacious assumption about hitherto unexperienced dimensions of life. It is a frontal assault on nihilism, a movement of optimism made with a cosmic consciousness, as if one could summarize all of life in one sweeping statement for all of time and eternity.

Yet this is a statement the writer needed to make for a church that was a part of the Roman Empire. The Romans prided themselves on their "peace," the end of Rome's own civil strife and protection from all of its enemies. The writer's description of Jesus as the Lord of peace is an attempt to indicate his great power. Like the Romans, Jesus has incredible power—the power to vindicate believers and destroy evil. The difference between the Lord of peace and the great figures of the Roman Empire, however, is that the writer's Lord brings thorough or absolute peace: "Peace in all ways and at all times."

What a defiant logic! Yet it is the kind of profound thought that echoes throughout the writings of the early Christians. In his Lyman Beecher Lectures, Gardner Taylor gives an almost poetic description of this defiance:

> They [the early Christian preachers] had nothing but a word-of-mouth report, and what an incredibly wild word it was. The bearers were not too impressive in their own persons . . . What is more astonishing these men and women bore the most amazing tale ever spread . . . How dare they to face the Empire! What foolishness and madness!" But Taylor adds, "And then, incredibly enough, the Empire bent its knee and called the name of Jesus as Lord and Saviour.[80]

Thank God even today for this kind of peace! No condition escapes its compass, and no period evades its parameters. The peace is always available. This is an inviolate, irrevocable peace, not a partial or removable peace, strained by tensions with others or dismissed by new rulers who take over kingdoms. It knows no end. It furnishes freedom from anxiety eternally. Steady are its benefits, and confident are its claims. It is the great confidence of the church. And it says to us that there is not a millennium into which we can march or a new era into which we can advance when God is absent and the promises of God null and void. It was a word of hope for all those who despaired in this writer's day. And it can rekindle that hope in hearts today as well.

80. Gardner Taylor, *How Shall They Preach* (Elgin, Ill.: Progressive Baptist Publishing House, 1977) 47-50.

THE FIRST AND SECOND LETTERS
TO TIMOTHY AND
THE LETTER TO TITUS

INTRODUCTION, COMMENTARY, AND REFLECTIONS

BY

JAMES D. G. DUNN

THE FIRST AND SECOND LETTERS TO
TIMOTHY
AND THE LETTER TO
TITUS

INTRODUCTION

The Pastoral Epistles—1 and 2 Timothy and Titus—are among the most valued of New Testament writings. Yet the Pastorals are among the most discredited of NT writings. Why this paradox?

On the one hand, the Pastorals have been valued for a number of important reasons. They helped to establish the classic pattern of ministry and church structure (bishop, presybter, deacon), which was crucial in the triumph of the early Catholic Church over severe challenges from Marcionites and Gnosticism, and which has enabled the church to endure for nearly two millennia.[1] They helped to establish a pattern of "the truth," "the faith," and "sound teaching" as the yardstick and bulwark by which to judge and ward off false teaching and heresy.[2] And, less immediately obvious, they helped to secure the place of Paul within the NT canon; the more controversial aspects of his theology (e.g., seeming criticism of Peter in Galatians and a church order without bishops and elders in 1 Corinthians) were made more acceptable by the portrayal of Paul as founder of the tradition, ecclesiastical and dogmatic, by which the church lived and ordered its life.

1. According to the Muratorian Fragment (traditionally dated to about 200 CE), the letters were held "in honor in the catholic church for the ordering of ecclesiastical discipline" (18-20).

2. As its preface indicates, with its explicit reference to 1 Tim 1:4, Irenaeus wrote his great work, *Against Heresies* (late 2nd cent. CE), in the spirit of the Pastorals.

Recognition of this character of the letters lies behind their designation as "the Pastoral Epistles," common since the eighteenth century.[3]

On the other hand, the Pastorals have been widely disparaged for more than a century and a half. This is primarily because a majority consensus of scholarship has been convinced since then that the Pastorals were not written by Paul but by a later hand. Despite the same consensus that pseudonymity (false claim to authorship) was quite acceptable in those days, it has been difficult to escape the more negative modern judgment on pseudonymous writings: Can writings be so fully valued that misrepresent their hero so seriously? Bound up with this has been the particularly Protestant suspicion that the radicalism of the authentic Paul (the Paul of the undisputed Pauline letters)[4] has been compromised and blunted by the ecclesiastical orthodoxy of the Pastoral Epistles.

In the face of such a polarization of respected opinion, what is the modern reader of these letters to make of them? Before turning to the letters themselves, a number of issues need some clarification.

A SINGLE GROUP OR SEPARATE LETTERS?

The fashion has been to treat the three letters together, to talk of the theology or ecclesiology of the Pastorals, rather than of each letter separately. This can be misleading, since 2 Timothy has a significantly different scope. Most notably, the concerns for good order in church, household, and state that are such a feature of the other two letters are quite absent in 2 Timothy. Indeed, were it not for the other two, the personal character of 2 Timothy might have been sufficient within scholarly discussion to secure the authenticity of 2 Timothy on its own.[5] Tied in to this is the question of the order of the letters. In recent discussion, for example, Luke Johnson has placed 2 Timothy first.[6] On the other hand, Jerome Quinn tackled Titus first, its longer preface being treated as a preface to the whole three-letter corpus.[7] And both Gordon Fee and George Knight follow the order 1 Timothy, Titus, 2 Timothy.[8] The traditional order (1 Timothy, 2 Timothy, Titus), it should be remembered, was determined largely by length; the corpus of Pauline letters in the NT canon was laid out in decreasing length, and of the three 1 Timothy was the longest and Titus the shortest.

3. See P. N. Harrison, *The Problem of the Pastoral Epistles* (London: Oxford University Press, 1921) 13-16.

4. The undisputed Pauline letters are generally reckoned to be Romans, 1–2 Corinthians, Galatians, Philippians, 1 Thessalonians, and Philemon. Many would also include 2 Thessalonians and Colossians. Not many would add Ephesians.

5. See particularly M. Prior, *Paul the Letter-Writer and the Second Letter to Timothy,* JSNTSup 23 (Sheffield: JSOT, 1989). J. Murphy-O'Connor, "2 Timothy Contrasted with 1 Timothy and Titus," *Revue Biblique* 98 (1991) 403-18, discusses over thirty points on which 1 Timothy and Titus agree against 2 Timothy and vice versa, but overstates the disagreements.

6. L. T. Johnson, *Letters to Paul's Delegates: 1 Timothy, 2 Timothy, Titus,* The New Testament in Context (Valley Forge: Trinity Press International, 1996).

7. J. D. Quinn, *The Letter to Titus,* AB 35 (New York: Doubleday, 1990) 190-200. Titus seems to have been placed first of the three in the Muratonian Fragment—"To Titus one and to Timothy two" (17).

8. G. D. Fee, *1 and 2 Timothy, Titus,* New International Bible Commentary (Peabody, Mass.: Hendrickson, 1984; rev. ed. 1988); G. W. Knight, *The Pastoral Epistles: A Commentary on the Greek Text,* NIGTC (Grand Rapids: Eerdmans, 1992).

Overall, however, it does seem sensible to treat the three letters together. They are certainly closer to one another than they are to any other NT writings, including the undisputed letters of Paul. They share the same broad characteristic: Paul's counsel to two of his most important aides and coworkers. Indeed, 1 Timothy and Titus stand closely together. We need only compare 1 Tim 3:1-13 with Titus 1:5-9 (church officers), 1 Tim 5:1–6:2 with Titus 2:1-15 (good household management), and 1 Tim 2:1-2 with Titus 3:1-2 (civic authorities). But if 1 and 2 Timothy were written to the same person or situation we would not expect them to cover the same ground. More to the point is the similarity between the two letters to Timothy in terms of personal recollection (cf. 1 Tim 1:12-16 with 2 Tim 1:8-15; 1 Tim 1:20 with 2 Tim 2:17-18), personal commission (cf. 1 Tim 1:18 and 6:13 with 2 Tim 4:1; 1 Tim 4:14 with 2 Tim 1:6), and warnings against false teaching (cf. 1 Tim 1:3-7 and 4:1-3 with 2 Tim 3:1-5 and 4:1-4; 1 Tim 6:4, 20 with 2 Tim 2:14, 16, 23). And overall we find in all three letters the same high regard, as indicated by vocabulary and attitude, for "the faith"[9] and for piety/godliness,[10] and the same dismissive disparagement of alternatives.[11]

In view of the degree of cohesion between the letters, it does continue to make sense to treat them as a loose unit, sufficiently distinct as such within the NT canon. To attempt a closer analysis of their inter-relationship is unnecessary for this commentary. It is simplest, therefore, to treat them in their historic and canonical order. By analyzing each one in turn, however, we should be able to gain a clear enough sense of the emphases of each as well as of the whole. Since few people will read the complete corpus of three letters at a sitting, it is more important that we focus attention on the internal coherence and thrust of each section within the letters.

AUTHORSHIP

Given, then, that the Pastoral Epistles form a relatively closely knit group, we may assume that they were written by the same person. But who? The obvious answer, of course, is Paul the apostle, the author of the other ten letters that bear his name. After all, each of the three letters explicitly claims to be from Paul. But for most of the last 150 years the majority of NT specialists have been more impressed by the differences between the Pastorals and the undisputed letters. So what is the answer?

For the last 150 years or so the debate on authorship of the Pastorals has been rehearsed over and over again. Those who want to pursue it in detail can easily do so by consulting

9. "The faith"—1 Tim 1:19; 3:9, 13; 4:1, 6; 5:8; 6:10-12, 21; 2 Tim 1:13; 3:8; 4:7; Titus 1:1, 4, 13; 3:15. "Sound teaching/words"—1 Tim 1:10; 6:3; 2 Tim 1:13; 4:3; Titus 1:9; 2:1-2, 8. "Faithful saying"—1 Tim 1:15; 3:1; 4:9; 2 Tim 2:11; Titus 3:8. "The truth"—1 Tim 3:15; 4:3; 2 Tim 2:15, 18; 3:8; 4:4; Titus 1:14. "Knowledge of truth"—1 Tim 2:4; 2 Tim 3:7; Titus 1:1.

10. "Piety/godliness"—1 Tim 2:2; 3:16; 4:7-8; 5:4 (verb); 6:3, 5-6, 11; 2 Tim 3:5, 12 (adverb); Titus 1:1; 2:12 (adverb). "Good works/deeds"—1 Tim 2:10; 3:1; 5:10 (twice), 25; 6:18; 2 Tim 2:21; 3:17; Titus 1:16; 2:7, 14; 3:1, 8, 14.

11. 1 Tim 1:3-6; 4:1-3, 7; 6:3-5, 20; 2 Tim 2:16-17, 23; 3:15; 4:3-4; Titus 1:10, 15-16; 3:3, 9. "Myths"—1 Tim 1:4; 4:7; 2 Tim 4:4; Titus 1:14. "Empty/vain talk"—1 Tim 1:6; 6:20; 2 Tim 2:16; Titus 1:10.

any of the commentaries listed in the Bibliography (see especially the introductory paragraph there for the split in opinion between current commentaries). Here it will be sufficient to indicate the scope of the debate in broad terms, if only to alert readers to the features and factors that give the debate continued vitality. This seems to be the wiser course, since it is all too easy for this question to become the dominant one and for the value of the letters to be obscured by what in the end are questions of secondary importance.

The main features of the letters that continue to persuade the majority of specialists that they were not written by Paul are as follows:

(1) First is the distinctive vocabulary and style of the Pastorals. The most striking feature is the much higher proportion of *hapax legomena* (words occuring only once or only in the Pastorals) than in the other Paulines (between twice and four times as many as any other Pauline letter).[12] Style, of course, has an intangible quality, but it also leaves fingerprints in, for example, the choice of words, the use of conjunctions, and the structure of sentences; and in contrast to the typical liveliness of the earlier Pauline letters, the Pastorals seem consistently more prosaic.[13] These differences cannot be adequately explained by different subjects or different moods. The writer seems to be drawing from a different vocabulary pool, the writing to be of a different character. The perspective, in other words, seems to be at one remove from Paul, or one generation after Paul.

(2) The degree to which "faith" has been formalized into "the faith" (see footnote 9). The mood of the Pastorals is much less that of preaching faith than of preserving the faith, not so much of evangelism as of containment. In particular, it is notable that the most characteristic notes of Paul's gospel and theology appear in "faithful sayings" and formulae to be preserved (1 Tim 1:15; 2 Tim 1:9; 2:11-13; Titus 3:4-7). Clearly evident is the sense of a faith that was initially formulated by Paul and that has now to be passed on to future generations (esp. 2 Tim 1:12-14; 2:1-2).

(3) The threats to the gospel seem likewise to be different. Whereas the challenge from Christian Jews (usually designated "Judaizers") runs through the earlier Pauline correspondence (Romans 2–4; 2 Cor 2:14–4:6; 10–13; Galatians; Phil 3:2-11), all we hear in the Pastorals are at best echoes of that earlier dispute (1 Tim 1:7; Titus 1:10, 14). Notable again is the fact that the "faithful sayings" and formulae just mentioned lack the polemical thrust against Jewish Christians so characteristic of the earlier Paul. So, too, the degree of precision with which Paul aimed his counterthrusts, whether in matters of theology or those of praxis, enables the reader to gain a quite clear picture of the positions to which Paul objected. But in the Pastorals there is no such precision, and the dismissive fulminations generate much more heat than light.

(4) The degree of church structure seems more developed than anything in the earlier Paul. A distinctive office of "overseer (bishop)" has emerged (1 Tim 3:1; Titus 1:7), as also

12. See Harrison, *The Problem of the Pastoral Epistles,* 20-38. Despite qualifications, the basic contrast stands; see, e.g., Kelly, *The Pastoral Epistles,* 22-24.

13. Quinn, *The Letter to Titus,* 6, states that the "PE read in a calm, slow, colorless, monotonous fashion. Their tone is sententious, stern, didactic, sober, stiff, domesticated." Quinn is in danger of overstatement, but not by much.

that of "deacon (minister)" (1 Tim 3:8). These titles were already in use in Phil 1:1, but the concept of a formal office is more in evidence. Likewise, the office of "elder" appears in the Pauline corpus for the first time (1 Tim 5:17; Titus 1:5). It looks as though on this point the Pastorals share the hindsight perspective evident also in Luke's account of Paul's mission (Acts 14:23; 20:17), of which there is no trace in the earlier Pauline letters.[14] It may also be significant, then, that the only use of the term "charism," so central to Paul's concept of the body of Christ (Rom 12:6-8; 1 Corinthians 12), is limited to talk of Timothy's charism given through the laying on of hands in the past (1 Tim 4:14; 2 Tim 1:6).

(5) Finally, what might be described as a greater accommodation with the norms and structures of contemporary society should be mentioned. It is not simply the readiness to accept the political structures of the day (1 Tim 2:1-2; Titus 3:1); that was already true in Rom 13:1-7. It is, rather, the degree to which the contemporary ideal of good household order has become also a norm for the writer of 1 Timothy and Titus (1 Timothy 5; Titus 2) and, indeed, a norm for the good order of the church (1 Tim 2:11-15; 3:4-5, 12, 15; 5:14). This accommodation is evident also in the fact that virtues like "dignity, seriousness, respectfulness"[15] and "prudence, moderation"[16] are so strongly commended, not least because of the respect they commanded within the wider society.

These features have to be weighed alongside (or against) two others in particular. One has already been mentioned: the fact that all three letters explicitly claim to have been written by Paul (1 Tim 1:1; 2 Tim 1:1; Titus 1:1). Against the view that they were pseudonymous, and known to be so, is the universal acceptance of them from the earliest attributions as written by Paul himself (from at least 200 CE). The other is the strikingly personal character of several passages within the letters, particularly 2 Tim 4:6-21 and Titus 3:12-13. It is difficult to conceive of a later writer's having composed such passages except as an attempt to deceive his readers.

The issue of pseudonymity is a difficult one for us to grasp at this distance, especially when the importance of copyright and the wrongs of plagiarism have become such fundamental features of modern literary culture. Suffice it to say that the principles were not at all so clearly grasped or the conventions so firmly drawn in those days. Of particular importance here is the fact that, particularly within the Jewish literary tradition, there seem to have been other conventions that rather cut across the issue. One was the attribution of writings to heroes from the past; most readers will have at least heard of the cycle of writings attributed to Enoch (Gen 5:24).[17]

More to the point here is what we might call the concept of "living tradition." That is, within Israel's history we can readily discern several different streams of tradition, each

14. 1 Cor 16:15-18 and 1 Thess 5:12-13 seem to be calls to respect for those who have displayed leadership initiative rather than for those already appointed to recognized posts ("elders").

15. Six of the seven occurrences of σεμνός, σεμνότης (*semnos, semnotēs*) are in the Pastorals (1 Tim 2:2; 3:4, 8, 11; Titus 2:2, 7; otherwise only Phil 4:8).

16. Four of the six forms of the word σώφρων (*sōphrōn*) are found only in the Pastorals—1 Tim 2:9, 15; 3:2; 2 Tim 1:7; Titus 1:8; 2:2, 4-6, 12.

17. The document usually known as *1 Enoch* is itself a compilation of five books.

originating with an authoritative earlier figure, but elaborated and extended within the immediate circle of that figure's disciples and retained under the name of the originator of the tradition. The Pentateuch is generally recognized to have reached its final form in this way, and the present book of Isaiah to be the work of two or three generations. Just as David was remembered as the originator of a still-growing collection of psalms,[18] so also to Solomon was attributed a sequence of wisdom writings (most notably Proverbs and Ecclesiastes). A close comparison of the Gospels, even of the Synoptic Gospels alone, indicates that there was a basically similar elaboration and extension of the Jesus tradition within the Gospel format. John 21:24 attests to the activity of a circle around the Fourth Evangelist, who had at least some hand in the final form of John's Gospel. The Pastorals can be readily seen in similar terms. The point is that this practice was familiar and that attribution of the extended literary form to the originator of the form would not have been regarded as unacceptable or deceptive.[19]

There is a corollary to this that is often neglected but should certainly be given some attention. If pseudonymous practice of this or some similar sort was accepted at the time of the writing of the Pastorals (so that the issue of pseudonymity loses its ethical dimension), then it follows that the pseudonymous writing would be attributed to the originator only if it was deemed to be an appropriate elaboration or extension of the original.[20] That is to say, the very factors of style and content that have moved modern scholars to deny Pauline authorship to the Pastorals would *not* have been deemed sufficient by the first readers to deny the letters to Paul. The Pastorals would have been deemed authentically Pauline; therefore, their attribution to Paul would have caused no problem. Already, in this early judgment, the canonical definition of what was and what was not "Pauline" was being determined.

If the problem of pseudonymity may thus be defused, what about the other feature that counts so strongly for Pauline authorship: the personal notes? There are probably only two choices here. Either they carry with them the whole sweep of the Pastorals, despite their differences from the earlier Paulines, in which case we have to envision Paul writing later in his career, his style changed by experiences later in a ministry extended beyond the limit suggested by Acts.[21] Or these personal notes were, in fact, brief notes, most of them dispatched or even smuggled from Paul's last imprisonment, treasured by the churches that received them, and used as a basis for the Pauline elaborations that are the Pastorals.[22]

18. Several more psalms attributed to David are found in the Qumran Psalms Scroll.

19. A fuller discussion can be found in J. D. G. Dunn, "Pseudepigraphy," in *Dictionary of the Later New Testament and Its Developments,* ed. R. P. Martin and P. H. Davids (Downers Grove, Ill.: InterVarsity, 1997) 997-1084, which draws particularly on D. Meade, *Pseudonymity and Canon* (Tübingen: Mohr, 1986). For an alternative view see E. E. Ellis, "Pseudonymity and Canonicity of New Testament Documents," in M. J. Wilkins and T. Paige, eds., *Worship, Theology and Ministry in the Early Church,* ed. M. J. Wilkins and T. Paige, JSNTSup 87 (Sheffield: JSOT, 1992) 212-24.

20. Tertullian *Concerning Baptism* 17 reports that the reason why the *Acts of Paul* were not accepted as Pauline is that they attributed to the woman Thecla an authority (in teaching and baptizing) that ran counter to 1 Cor 14:34-35.

21. The differences cannot adequately be explained by the use of different secretaries; the differences of emphasis and ethos are so integral to the letters that they have to be attributed to the author of the letters.

22. See P. N. Harrison, *The Problem of the Pastoral Epistles* (London: Oxford University Press, 1921) 115-35. The newest variation is that of J. D. Miller, *The Pastoral Letters as Composite Documents,* SNTSMS 93 (Cambridge: Cambridge University Press, 1997). In contrast, L. R. Donelson, *Pseudepigraphy and Ethical Argument in the Pastoral Epistles* (Tübingen: J. C. B. Mohr [Siebeck], 1986) 54-65, sees the personal notes as evidence of current pseudepigraphical practice.

Whatever the current answer, it is important not to let the issue of authorship weigh too heavily in one's appreciation of and response to the Pastorals.[23] On the one hand, if they were written by Paul himself, then we have to speak of a "late Paul" and of the earlier undisputed letters as bearing witness to the "early Paul." Recognition of Pauline authorship must not allow us either to blur the different and distinctive perspective we find in the Pastorals or to homogenize a thirteen-letter Paul. On the other hand, if they were written during some period subsequent to Paul's death, that should not allow us to justify their being devalued and treated as sub-Pauline.[24] They are *also* Pauline and show how the Pauline churches perceived and evaluated their great founding apostle and the heritage he left with them. Either way, they are invaluable evidence of how Christianity and Christian theology faced the challenges of the second generation and/or post-Pauline period.

DATE AND RECIPIENTS

These considerations permit a much briefer resolution of other introductory questions. If the Pastorals were written late in Paul's life (cf. 2 Tim 4:16-18), then we have to envisage that Paul had been freed from his (first) imprisonment in Rome (Acts 28), and that he had deemed it more important to return to the Aegean than to pursue his earlier plans to go to Spain (Rom 15:23-24, 28).[25] This would explain such references as 1 Tim 1:3 and Titus 1:5 and allow us to date the letters in the mid-60s. If, however, the letters are pseudonymous, then a date sometime between the deaths of Paul (early 60s) and of Ignatius (c. 110s) seems appropriate. This is principally because the more developed ecclesiology of the Pastorals seems to be in the process of formation (see Commentary on 1 Tim 5:17 and Titus 1:7) and still some way from the monoepiscopacy that Ignatius promotes but also was able to assume.[26] Nor has the false teaching attacked in the Pastorals such clear shape as that attacked in the 110s by Ignatius (see below). Some have argued for a still later date, but the later the exercise the less likely that a pseudonymous writing would have been accepted as still genuinely Pauline. Most elect for a date in the late 80s or 90s of the first century. The possible points of contact with Acts, which have suggested to some that Luke was the author,[27] also point to the latter years of the first century.

If the letters were written by Paul, then the recipients were those specified—Timothy and Titus (see Commentary on 1 Tim 1:2 and Titus 1:4)—each serving as an apostolic delegate, Timothy in Ephesus (1 Tim 1:3) and Titus in Crete (Titus 1:5). If, on the other hand, the letters are post-Pauline, the naming of the recipients as Timothy and Titus may

23. As is the case, e.g., with Kelly, *Pastoral Epistles,* and Johnson, *Letters.*
24. Isaiah 40–55 is usually classified as Deutero-Isaiah, but who would even begin to think of these chapters as sub-Isaiah?
25. According to Eusebius *Church History* 2.22, "Tradition has it that after defending himself the apostle [Paul] was again sent on the ministry of preaching, and coming a second time to the same city, suffered martyrdom under Nero."
26. Particularly Ignatius *Smyrneans* 8.
27. See particularly S. G. Wilson, *Luke and the Pastoral Epistles* (London: SPCK, 1979).

The Eastern Mediterranean in Paul's Time

indicate either that they were indeed the recipients or that they were the inspiration behind the letters (What would Paul want to say to us were he still alive?),[28] or simply that the letters were from the close circle of Paul's coworkers or immediate successors. Either way, Timothy and Titus are clearly envisaged as Paul's representatives, functioning in a unique role between church founder and local leadership. At the same time, we should not confuse the letters' personal address with their function. Whatever their origin, they were not intended for the eyes and ears of Timothy and Titus alone. The plural form of the final "you" in each case indicates that these letters were intended to be read to the church as a whole and, therefore, to function as manuals of discipline for the benefit of whole congregations. As such, their value in effect bypasses the question of the historical status of Timothy and Titus, just as it outlasts the death of Paul.

WHO WERE THE FALSE TEACHERS?

The other great debate concerns the opponents regularly castigated in the letters. It is difficult, however, to gain a firm handle on them, and the general assumption that they formed a single front should certainly be put under question. Most of the attack on false teaching is, as already indicated, vague and imprecise, often using conventional vilification

28. See particularly R. Bauckham, "Pseudo-Apostolic Letters," *JBL* 107 (1988) 469-94.

of opponents, real or imagined.[29] There are only a few clear indications of concrete issues: 1 Tim 4:3, they forbid marriage and advocate abstinence from certain foods; 2 Tim 2:18, they claim that "the resurrection has already happened." These references, taken with the allusion to "knowledge [γνῶσις *gnōsis*] falsely so called" (1 Tim 6:20), could certainly be taken to imply an early form of Gnosticism, since all three features are present in the Gnostic systems of the later second century.

On the other hand, the references to those "desiring to be teachers of the law" (1 Tim 1:7) and to "those of the circumcision" (Titus 1:10) point to a Jewish dimension—that is, not just to Jewish elements in some syncretistic mix, but to people who prized a Jewish identity (see Commentary on Titus 1:10) and valued the principal Jewish identity marker (the law). The repeated references to "myths" (1 Tim 1:4; 4:7; 2 Tim 4:4; Titus 1:14) and to "genealogies" (1 Tim 1:4; Titus 3:9) in themselves could point in several directions, but the reference to "Jewish myths" (Titus 1:14) and the association of "genealogies" with "fights over the law" (Titus 3:9) again indicate an opposition more likely to be rooted in the local synagogues than anywhere else. The attempt to combine both sets of features into something like "Judaizing Gnosticism" (as many suggest)[30] is not very helpful, since "Judaizing" means "living as a Jew," and no gnostic system that we know of taught the need to Judaize.

As with other letters (notably 1 Corinthians), the older assumption that the threats addressed could be categorized simply in terms of religious or theological systems has been heavily qualified in more recent discussions. Social and financial pressures were obviously also a factor, particularly in 1 Timothy (1 Tim 2:9; 3:3, 8; 5:8, 17-19; 6:5-10, 17-19),[31] and the role of women in certain aspects of community life obviously worried the writer (1 Tim 2:9-15; 5:3-16).[32] In reading such passages we should recall how little we know of the situations envisaged and how much more complex they no doubt were than we can now appreciate. Straightforward transposition to contemporary situations of advice given in the Pastorals will rarely be wise.

THE THEOLOGY OF THE PASTORALS

The value of the Pastorals is reflected on at each stage throughout the following pages. Here we need simply to draw attention to the principal features.

(1) One is the strongly re-emphasized Jewish heritage. It is particularly clear in the insistence on affirming one of Israel's principal foundation pillars: the oneness of God

29. Documentation is provided by R. J. Karris, "The Background and Significance of the Polemic in the Pastoral Epistles," *JBL* 92 (1973) 549-64; A. J. Malherbe, "Medical Imagery in the Pastoral Epistles," *Paul and the Popular Philosophers* (Minneapolis: Fortress, 1989) 121-36.

30. The most recent variation is M. Goulder, "The Pastor's Wolves: Jewish Christian Visionaries Behind the Pastoral Epistles," *NovT* 38 (1996) 242-56.

31. See R. M. Kidd, *Wealth and Beneficence in the Pastoral Epistles: A "Bourgeois" Form of Early Christianity?* SBLDS 122 (Atlanta: Scholars Press, 1990).

32. See, e.g., A. Padgett, "Wealthy Women at Ephesus: 1 Timothy 2:8-15 in Social Context," *Int.* 41 (1987) 19-31.

(1 Tim 1:17; 2:5; 6:15-16). Other important features include the use of Israel's own self-identity: "the household of God, which is the church of the living God" (1 Tim 3:15 NRSV); "a people of his own" (Titus 2:14).[33] This is all the more important given that some opposition seems to have come from the synagogue. Here, in other words, we see not only early Christianity continuing to affirm its continuity and identity with its Jewish heritage, but also the importance to Pauline Christianity of that continuity and identity as integral to Christianity's own self-definition. It will be no accident that part of the same theology is the affirmation that God desires to save everyone (1 Tim 2:4, 6).

(2) The centrality of the christology and of "salvation" as the preeminent goal[34] is also clear, as the faithful sayings and creedal or hymnic formulae confirm (1 Tim 1:15; 2:4-6, 15; 3:16; 2 Tim 1:9-10; 2:11-13; Titus 3:4-7). The fact that God and Christ can equally be described as "Savior" (see Commentary on 1 Tim 1:1) is not an indication of confusion but of a recognition that Christ functions for God and that God has acted through Christ. The most careful formulations of the relationship between God and Christ are given in 1 Tim 2:4-6 and Titus 2:13-14, which should hardly be played off against each other. That salvation is a process working out between the two appearings of Christ[35] is a strong reaffirmation of a characteristically Pauline emphasis. Even if expressed primarily in traditional formulae, this gospel is still a matter of living faith[36] and may, indeed, have been freshly reformulated to present Christ as a more effective claimant to the title "Savior" than any emperor or other god.[37]

(3) The importance of faith clearly formulated and of the church well ordered has already been noted. Notable here is the affirmation of good household order as the model or criterion for good church order[38] and the concern for a proper respectability, or better, respect-worthiness as a measure of Christian conduct. One need not speculate about any influence of delay of parousia (of which there is no overt indication) to see in the Pastorals more helpful guidelines for churches confronted by a suspicious and dominant non-Christian society than in some of the earlier Paulines.

(4) Notable in this connection is the way in which theology and ethics are thoroughly integrated in the Pastorals—evident, not least, in the flow of argument in several passages (e.g., 1 Tim 2:1-6; 4:3-5; Titus 2:1-15; 3:1-7). Theology was not a mere clinging to old formulae; it issued directly in practical corollaries for daily living. Nor were ethics simply

33. The degree to which the Pastorals draw on the OT is not usually appreciated, but see M. Davies, *The Pastoral Epistles,* Epworth Commentaries (London: Epworth, 1996) 15-16.

34. "Save"—1 Tim 1:15; 2:4, 15; 4:16; 2 Tim 1:9; 4:18; Titus 3:5; "salvation"—2 Tim 2:10; 3:15; "Savior"—1 Tim 1:1; 2:3; 4:10; 2 Tim 1:10; Titus 1:3-4; 2:10, 13; 3:4, 6; "saving"—Titus 2:11.

35. First "appearing"—2 Tim 1:10; Titus 2:11; 3:4. Second "appearing"—1 Tim 6:14; 2 Tim 4:1, 8; Titus 2:13.

36. Often missed is the fact that the Pastorals speak more of "faith" (1 Tim 1:2, 4-5, 14, 19; 2:7, 15; 3:13; 4:12; 6:11; 2 Tim 1:5, 13; 2:22; 3:15; Titus 1:1, 4; 2:10; 3:15) than of "the faith."

37. For more detail see M. Dibelius and H. Conzelmann, *The Pastoral Epistles,* Hermeneia (Philadelphia: Fortress, 1972) 100-103; F. Young, *The Theology of the Pastoral Letters,* New Testament Theology (Cambridge: Cambridge University Press, 1994) 63-65.

38. So particularly D. C. Verner, *The Household of God: The Social World of the Pastoral Epistles,* SBLDS 71 (Chico, Calif.: Scholars Press, 1983).

a nervous conformity to bourgeois ideals; their rationale was deeply rooted in the gospel.[39] The importance of this observation for churches of all time can hardly be overemphasized.

(5) Not least of value is the enriching of the church's memory of Paul. Whether the portrait is Paul's own or the beginning of a modest hagiography, the fuller portrayal of Paul is certainly to be cherished—from his conversion (1 Tim 1:12-16), through his ministry (2 Tim 1:11-12; 3:10), to his final testimony of trust (2 Tim 4:6-8). This portrayal serves not least to establish and keep open the line of continuity and tradition begun with Paul and so helps to ensure that the Christianity that Paul did so much to shape and to spread remains in living communication with Paul, apostle to the Gentiles, model for the gospel preacher, and teacher of the church.[40]

39. See particularly P. H. Towner, *The Goal of Our Instruction: The Structure of Theology and Ethics,* JSNTSup 34 (Sheffield: Sheffield Academic, 1989).

40. See further M. C. de Boer, "Images of Paul in the Post-Apostolic Period," *CBQ* 42 (1980) 359-80.

BIBLIOGRAPHY

Two volumes stand as watersheds in the recent study of the Pastorals. P. N. Harrison's detailed analysis of the language of the letters, *The Problem of the Pastoral Epistles* (London: Oxford University Press, 1921), provides a definitive statement of the case for non-Pauline authorship. The still lively debate on the subject takes its starting point with Harrison, either in rebuttal (Guthrie, Kelly, Fee, Knight, Johnson) or as still more or less determinative (Barrett, Houlden, Hanson, Quinn, Bassler, Davies). Dibelius's commentary (2nd ed., 1931; revised by Conzelmann in 1955), with its presentation of a Christianity influenced by Hellenistic writings and emphasizing good citizenship, became equally a heritage both valued and disputed, but rarely ignored.

Commentaries:

Barrett, C. K. *The Pastoral Epistles.* New Clarendon Bible. Oxford: Clarendon, 1963. An excellent example of a brief treatment by one of the best NT commentators of the second half of the twentieth century.

Bassler, J. M. *1 Timothy, 2 Timothy, Titus.* ANTC. Nashville: Abingdon, 1996. A well-judged analysis, spiced with judicious use of background material and plenty of detail for further study and reflection.

Davies, M. *The Pastoral Epistles.* Epworth Commentaries. London: Epworth, 1996. Brief, but well informed.

Dibelius, M., and H. Conzelmann. *The Pastoral Epistles.* Hermeneia. Philadelphia: Fortress, 1972. The principal German commentary from the first three-quarters of the twentieth century.

Fee, G. D. *1 and 2 Timothy, Titus.* New International Biblical Commentary. Peabody, Mass.: Hendrickson, 1984; rev. ed. 1988. Useful treatment of the NIV text.

Guthrie, D. *The Pastoral Epistles: An Introduction and Commentary.* Tyndale New Testament Commentary. Leicester: InterVarsity Press, 1957. The first effective response to Harrison and a still-valuable exposition.

Hanson, A. T. *The Pastoral Epistles.* NCB. London: Marshall, Morgan & Scott, 1982. Insights variable, but Hanson was always his own man.

Houlden, J. L. *The Pastoral Epistles.* Pelican New Testament Commentaries. Harmondsworth: Penguin, 1976. Houlden has a good eye for questions of contemporary relevance and usefulness.

Johnson, L. T. *Letters to Paul's Delegates: 1 Timothy, 2 Timothy, Titus.* The New Testament in Context. Valley Forge: Trinity Press International, 1996. Johnson is one of today's most competent commentators, though the division of each passage into three sections (Notes on Translation, Literary Observations, Comment) makes it difficult to track down particular verses and leaves the Comment light on some important features of the text.

Kelly, J. N. D. *The Pastoral Epistles.* Black's New Testament Commentaries. London: A. & C. Black, 1963. The richness of Kelly's Patristic scholarship makes this a still very satisfying commentary to use.

Knight, G. W. *The Pastoral Epistles: A Commentary on the Greek Text.* NIGTC. Grand Rapids: Eerdmans, 1992. Heavy on detailed word and grammar study, though easy to lose sight of the woods for the trees.

Marshall, I. H. *The Pastoral Epistles.* ICC. Edinburgh: T. & T. Clark, 1999. The most recent detailed commentary; published too late to be used in what follows.

Quinn, J. D. *The Letter to Titus.* AB 35. New York: Doubleday, 1990. The fruit of nearly twenty-five years of study; full of rich detail.

Specialized Studies:

Davies, M. *The Pastoral Epistles.* New Testament Guides. Sheffield: Sheffield Academic, 1996. A valuable and up-to-date treatment of background, themes, and authorship.

Donelson, L. R. *Pseudepigraphy and Ethical Argument in the Pastoral Epistles.* Tübingen: J. C. B. Mohr (Siebeck), 1986. Argues for the deliberate use of pseudepigraphy to provide apostolic warrant for an orthodox ecclesiology and ethic.

Harrison, P. N. *The Problem of the Pastoral Epistles.* London: Oxford University Press, 1921. The most compelling statement of the case for post-Pauline authorship based on the language of the Pastorals.

Kidd, R. M. *Wealth and Beneficence in the Pastoral Epistles: A "Bourgeois" Form of Early Christianity?* SBLDS 122. Atlanta: Scholars Press, 1990. A study of the important social and cultural factors involved in the Pastorals.

MacDonald, D. T. *The Legend and the Apostle: The Battle for Paul in Story and Canon.* Philadelphia: Westminster, 1983. Argues that the Pastoral Epistles were written to contradict the image of Paul in popular legends.

Miller, J. D. *The Pastoral Letters as Composite Documents.* SNTSMS 93. Cambridge: Cambridge University Press, 1997. Argues that the Pastorals are composite documents based on brief, but genuine, Pauline notes written to Timothy and Titus.

Prior, M. *Paul the Letter-Writer and the Second Letter to Timothy.* JSNTSup 23. Sheffield: JSOT, 1989. The most thoroughgoing attempt to study 2 Timothy on its own as an authentic letter of Paul to Timothy.

Towner, P. H. *The Goal of Our Instruction: The Structure of Theology and Ethics.* JSNTSup 34. Sheffield: Sheffield Academic, 1989. Sees the overarching theological concern of the author as especially his emphasis on salvation as a present reality and the consequent task of the church.

Verner, D. C. *The Household of God: The Social World of the Pastoral Epistles.* SBLDS 71. Chico, Calif.: Scholars Press, 1983. Argues effectively that the hierarchical structure of the household provided the model for the structure of church authority.

Wilson, S. G. *Luke and the Pastoral Epistles.* London: SPCK, 1979. The most thoroughgoing attempt to argue that the real author of the Pastorals was Luke.

Young, F. *The Theology of the Pastoral Letters.* New Testament Theology. Cambridge: Cambridge University Press, 1994. Young's expertise in Patristic theology gives her a most insightful perspective.

OUTLINE OF THE PASTORALS

I. 1 Timothy 1:1–6:21

    A. 1:1-11, Address and Warning Against False Teachers

    B. 1:12-20, Paul's Example and Charge to Timothy

    C. 2:1-7, God's Concern Is for Everyone

    D. 2:8-15, The Role of Women Within This Strategy

    E. 3:1-16, Good Order in the Church

    F. 4:1-16, The Two Ways

    G. 5:1–6:2, On the Elderly, Widows, Elders, and Slaves

    H. 6:3-21, Putting Wealth in Its Place

II. 2 Timothy 1:1–4:22

    A. 1:1-7, Greetings and Personal Commendation

    B. 1:8-18, Paul's Own Testimony

    C. 2:1-26, Paul's Charge to Timothy

    D. 3:1-17, Lessons from Tradition

    E. 4:1-22, Paul's Final Charge and Requests to Timothy

III. Titus 1:1–3:15

    A. 1:1-4, Greetings and Reminder of Paul's Commission

    B. 1:5-16, The Church—Its Leadership and Enemies

    C. 2:1-15, Good Household Management and Its Theological Rationale

    D. 3:1-15, Of Grace and Works

1 TIMOTHY 1:1-11, ADDRESS AND WARNING
AGAINST FALSE TEACHERS

NIV

1 Paul, an apostle of Christ Jesus by the command of God our Savior and of Christ Jesus our hope,

²To Timothy my true son in the faith:

Grace, mercy and peace from God the Father and Christ Jesus our Lord.

³As I urged you when I went into Macedonia, stay there in Ephesus so that you may command certain men not to teach false doctrines any longer ⁴nor to devote themselves to myths and endless genealogies. These promote controversies rather than God's work—which is by faith. ⁵The goal of this command is love, which comes from a pure heart and a good conscience and a sincere faith. ⁶Some have wandered away from these and turned to meaningless talk. ⁷They want to be teachers of the law, but they do not know what they are talking about or what they so confidently affirm.

⁸We know that the law is good if one uses it properly. ⁹We also know that law[a] is made not for the righteous but for lawbreakers and rebels, the ungodly and sinful, the unholy and irreligious; for those who kill their fathers or mothers, for murderers, ¹⁰for adulterers and perverts, for slave traders and liars and perjurers—and for whatever else is contrary to the sound doctrine ¹¹that conforms to the glorious gospel of the blessed God, which he entrusted to me.

[a]9 Or *that the law*

NRSV

1 Paul, an apostle of Christ Jesus by the command of God our Savior and of Christ Jesus our hope,

²To Timothy, my loyal child in the faith:

Grace, mercy, and peace from God the Father and Christ Jesus our Lord.

³I urge you, as I did when I was on my way to Macedonia, to remain in Ephesus so that you may instruct certain people not to teach any different doctrine, ⁴and not to occupy themselves with myths and endless genealogies that promote speculations rather than the divine training[a] that is known by faith. ⁵But the aim of such instruction is love that comes from a pure heart, a good conscience, and sincere faith. ⁶Some people have deviated from these and turned to meaningless talk, ⁷desiring to be teachers of the law, without understanding either what they are saying or the things about which they make assertions.

⁸Now we know that the law is good, if one uses it legitimately. ⁹This means understanding that the law is laid down not for the innocent but for the lawless and disobedient, for the godless and sinful, for the unholy and profane, for those who kill their father or mother, for murderers, ¹⁰fornicators, sodomites, slave traders, liars, perjurers, and whatever else is contrary to the sound teaching ¹¹that conforms to the glorious gospel of the blessed God, which he entrusted to me.

[a] Or *plan*

COMMENTARY

The opening greeting (1:1-2) is quite typical of Paul's style. But unlike most of the earlier Pauline letters (and 2 Tim 1:3-5), there is no introductory thanksgiving or prayer for the readers. The letter begins, instead, with a forthright warning against other teachings regarded as false and dangerous (1:3-7). The writer evidently felt or intended his readers to feel that their faith was under threat. Most dangerous of all, some of their own number had already been caught up in this teaching and were being distracted from the faith. The theme continues into the next paragraph (1:8-11). Here the appeal is to the firm standard of the law as ruling out familiar categories of wrongdoing. But the thrust is in 1:10, where it becomes clear that the determinative standard of right and wrong is "the sound teaching."

1:1-2, The Greeting. The letter begins much as Paul would. He introduces himself and stresses his status as an apostle (v. 1). Fundamental to Paul's identity was the conviction, rooted already in his conversion (Gal 1:15-16), that he had been commissioned as an emissary ("apostle") of Messiah (Christ) Jesus, and in full accordance with God's intention (cf. 2 Tim 1:1). Typically Pauline is the association of Christ Jesus with God as equally the source of Paul's legitimacy as apostle (so also v. 2). The talk of Christ Jesus as "our hope" is reminiscent of Col 1:27 and recalls that Christian hope takes its character from the one hoped in rather than from any feelings of hopefulness (see also Commentary on Titus 1:2).

More distinctive, but also characteristic of the Pastorals, is the fuller description of God as Savior (also 2:3; 4:10; Titus 1:3; 2:10; 3:4), as characteristic, in fact, as the description of Christ Jesus as "Savior" (2 Tim 1:10; Titus 1:4; 2:13; 3:6), already touching on one of the central themes of the gospel according to the Pastorals (see Commentary on 1:15). A tension is thus set up: Are two salvations envisaged, or just one effected by both together or by one as the agent of the other? The point becomes steadily clearer through the subsequent references, but it is never fully clarified. The idea of God as "Savior" was, of course, familiar in the OT (e.g., Deut 32:15; Ps 27:1, 9; Isa 45:15, 21), and there were several "Savior" gods in Greco-Roman religion.[41] But the fact that "Savior" is used earlier in Paul only occasionally and only of Christ (Eph 5:23; Phil 3:20) suggests a distinctive development in the theology of the Pastorals.

The recipient, Timothy, was well known as Paul's chief lieutenant (v. 2). He had evidently been converted through Paul's ministry (Paul's child, cf. Acts 16:1-3; Phil 2:22), had been co-writer (or co-sender) of several of Paul's letters, and had acted as one of Paul's chief spokesmen in Thessalonica (1 Thess 3:2, 6) and Corinth (1 Cor 4:17; 16:10), as well as (by implication) here in Ephesus. The adjective describes literally a child born in wedlock, "legitimate," but its use here is probably figurative of the genuineness and mutual warmth of their relationship (Phil 2:20).

The typical Pauline greeting (v. 2) adapts the typical Greek "Greeting" (χαίρειν *chairein*) to the distinctive Christian "grace" (χάρις *charis*) and adds the typical Jewish "peace" (שלום *šālôm*, here translated as εἰρήνη *eirēnē*), rich in the sense of social well-being as well as individual tranquility. Here the Jewish character of the greeting is strengthened by adding "mercy" (ἔλεος *eleos*) the usual Greek translation of the strong Jewish term חסד (*ḥesed*), denoting God's "covenant love, loving kindness" (Exod 34:6-7), which had not been much used by Paul earlier (but note Rom 11:30-32; Gal 6:16).

1:3-11, Warning Against False Teachers. The indication that his mission in Ephesus was at Paul's explicit command (v. 3)[42] strengthens the line of command and the authority being asserted through Timothy. Characteristic of the initial polemic is the vagueness of the charge (vv. 3-7). It is "certain people" who are teaching otherwise (v. 3); the accusation is of preoccupation with "myths and endless genealogies," which simply promote "speculations" (v. 4); "some of them" have "turned away into fruitless talk" (v. 6).[43] "Myths" are a regular target (4:7; 2 Tim 4:4; Titus 1:14; otherwise only in 2 Pet 1:16), the term already familiar in the sense of "untrue story, fiction," as opposed to historical truth, and always used negatively in the NT. The basic meaning of "genealogy" (elsewhere only in Titus 3:9) is also clear enough. But more precise definition is not possible, the imprecision of the language having encouraged its own share of "speculation" and

---

41. "Savior" was also used of human benefactors. See F. W. Danker, *Benefactor: Epigraphic Study of a Greco-Roman and New Testament Semantic Field* (St. Louis: Clayton, 1982).

42. The awkwardness of the opening of v. 3 ("As I urged you . . ." the sentence being then left technically incomplete) may arise from the attempt to suggest that Timothy's commission derived from some time earlier, from Paul himself (cf. Acts 18:5; 19:22; 1 Cor 16:10-11; 1 Thess 3:2). Acts 20:25 implies that Paul never visited Ephesus again.

43. "Futile verbiage" (Kelly) "a wilderness of words" (NEB/REB).

"fruitless talk." Later gnostic speculation about series of emanations from the divine have often been cited, but talk of the law (v. 7) suggests a speculation fed by the Pentateuch's patriarchal narratives (see Titus 1:14, "Jewish myths"). Of course, the original readers might well have known who was in mind (some of Paul's earlier polemic is equally vague; see Rom 3:8; 2 Cor 3:1; Gal 1:7; 2:12). But such imprecision can be intentional, to include as many targets as necessary, on the principle "if the shoe fits. . . . "

The most specific detail is the desire of some to be teachers of the law, but their talk and confident pronouncements are dismissed for their lack of understanding (v. 7). The impression is thus given of people anxious to know the pedigree of their new faith, fascinated by the possible connections with great figures of the past (or divine beings) and searching the Torah for clues (the whole sequence of writings about Enoch were stimulated by the single verse Gen 5:24). To be noted is the fact that these were not opponents of the church in Ephesus but were involved with it, and evidently eager to learn more. The writer's fear (v. 6) is that through such speculation they will "miss the mark" (similarly 6:21; 2 Tim 2:18) and "turn away" (also 5:15; 6:20; 2 Tim 4:4) to false teaching.

Over against all this the writer sets "faith" (already in v. 2). Here the word evokes the characteristic Pauline sense of trust (in God or Christ), though subsequently it is "the faith" as an already well-established pattern of teaching to be believed that is in view (see footnote 9). It is this faith that gives a clearer understanding of God's "ordering" (οἰκονομία oikonomia) of salvation (v. 4); the word is often taken in the sense of "training" (NRSV), but the echo of Eph 3:9 suggests a carryover of Paul's earlier confidence that he had been given to know the mystery of God's purpose for Jew and Gentile (Rom 11:25-26; Col 1:26-27). It is this faith "unfeigned, without hypocrisy," together with a "clean heart" and a "good conscience," that will achieve the goal of "love" (v. 5).[44] Here the central emphasis of Paul is sustained: On the human side, it is faith alone that is decisive for salvation; undue elaboration of

that faith into speculative systems will usually mean a departure from that faith. At the same time, "clean heart" (v. 5; 2 Tim 2:22) and "good conscience" (vv. 5, 19) look like a single concept ("clean conscience," 3:9; 2 Tim 1:3), denoting a conscience instructed in a faith whose outline is already clearly drawn.

In an attempt to counter what he regards as abuse of the law, the writer reminds Timothy of its proper purpose. Where those warned against in v. 7 seem to have used also the narrative and other parts of the Torah (Pentateuch), the writer focuses exclusively on its function as law and implies that other use is unlawful (v. 8).[45] Echoing Rom 7:12, 16, he insists that the law is good and that its function is to define and warn off from lawless and undisciplined behavior (v. 9). There follows a list of those whom the law condemns for their behavior, initially in pairs, artistically contrived (the first five words all begin with "a"; cf. Rom 1:31), and using broad-brush terms ("lawless and undisciplined, godless and sinners, unholy and profane"). But then comes what seems to be a sequence of elaborations of the second table of the Ten Commandments: dishonoring parents, murder, adultery, theft, perjury. Today the most controversial of these is the putting of homosexual practice (v. 10; the term almost certainly comes from Lev 18:22; 20:13) under the prohibition of adultery; the teaching is consistent with Paul's views expressed earlier in Rom 1:26-27; 1 Cor 6:9-10.

With vv. 10-11 the criterion of "faith" is replaced by one of the most frequently recurring motifs in the Pastorals: "sound teaching" (v. 10; 2 Tim 4:3; Titus 1:9; 2:1), "sound words" (6:3; 2 Tim 1:13), "sound in faith" (Titus 1:13; 2:2). The image is of physical health, of being healthy, "sound in wind and limb."[46] This is linked, in turn, in a liturgically ringing phrase, with "the gospel of the glory of the blessed God" (see also 6:15). Over against the other teaching, marked by its speculations and fruitless talk, its misuse of

44. As in the earlier Paul (Rom 13:8-10; 1 Corinthians 13; Gal 5:22), "love" is the most highly prized of the Christian graces. See 1 Tim 1:14; 2:15; 4:12; 6:11; 2 Tim 1:7, 13; 2:22; 3:10; Titus 2:2-10.

45. The wordplay ("law," "lawfully") perhaps pulls the latter term away from its normal use. So it can possibly be translated as "correctly" (Barrett) or "appropriately" (Johnson). The NRSV's "legitimately" is probably best. See C. K. Barrett, *The Pastoral Epistles*, New Clarendon Bible (Oxford: Clarendon, 1963); L. T. Johnson, *Letters to Paul's Delegates: 1 Timothy, 2 Timothy, Titus*, The New Testament in Context (Valley Forge: Trinity Press International, 1996).

46. See further M. Dibelius and H. Conzelmann, *The Pastoral Epistles*, Hermeneia (Philadelphia: Fortress, 1972) 24-25. See also footnote 22.

the law and lack of discipline, is set the gospel, the faith that it promotes, the "sound teaching" that is its content, and the love that is its goal. Already there is a sense of a gospel and faith that is clearly defined (at least for the writer), and that provides a norm of "sound teaching." What is feared and attacked dismissively is teaching that fails to accord with this norm or goes beyond it needlessly.

REFLECTIONS

The situation addressed in these opening verses of 1 Timothy is one that can be well imagined early in the life of a new religious movement. The faith preached by Paul was not already well established or able to appeal to centuries of tradition behind it (as can be done by Christians today). Entirely to the contrary, it was one of those newcomer religious movements of which the more established religions will always be suspicious and speak dismissively. Acts 19:21-41 presents a vivid picture of the threat experienced in Ephesus by the ancient cult of Artemis, the city's established and famous religion.

This new faith in Jesus Christ was one of a number of new "sects" or "cults" (but finding the right word even to describe them is always difficult) that generally came from Egypt (particularly the cult of Isis) or from the East (particularly newly emerging Mithraism) and that were seeking to establish themselves in the major centers of the Roman Empire. For those moved by religious concerns or simply curious, there was a very active marketplace of possibilities. The more ancient a religion or its teaching could present itself to be, the more attractive it was to a culture that venerated the wisdom of age and of the ancients. The more divine its pedigree, or the pedigree it offered to inquirers, the more attractive it was to those anxious about their destiny or troubled by mortality.

The upshot is that many would be attracted to Christianity, without necessarily being committed to it; it was one option among many. Baptism could be regarded simply as the appropriate initiation into just one more cult. Attachment to Christianity would not necessarily dampen the religious questing and curiosity that had attracted them to it. Rather, Christianity's first statements of faith and its sacred book (Torah) could easily provide fresh matter (genealogies?) for fresh speculation. If the leaders of the Christian movement were to counter and contain such tendencies, it was necessary for them to develop clearer statements of faith and firmer patterns of acceptable behavior.

The situation has often been paralleled since then in the history of Christianity, in which more established patterns have been challenged both by movements of renewal within and by new teaching from without. The question church leaders have to face is how they can be open to renewal and fresh insight without losing hold on what continues to be fundamental. How can they attract the genuine seekers, the open-minded enquirers, without also encouraging an openness that might subvert their own foundations? How can they identify and affirm the fundamentals without turning their backs on the seekers after truth?

The strategy chosen by the writer of 1 Timothy is clear from this opening section. The gospel was already firmly drawn in outline, faith in Christ defined as "the sound teaching." What this faith consisted of will become clearer as he proceeds, but it is clear enough already that the "faith" gave him and his readers a firm foundation from which to engage with those other seekers, to warn them against more fanciful ideas. Here the dilemma is already clearly indicated, of a faith too little defined as to encourage fruitless discussion, or a faith too fully defined as to discourage growth in faith. Today one of the categories of conduct about whose lawlessness the writer was most confident (homosexual practice) has itself become a focus of debate. Today's Christian leaders have to determine whether its unacceptability is still part of the "sound teaching"—in particular whether current conduct should be guided more by the consistent emphasis in Pauline (and biblical) teaching, or by changing appreciation of the complexity of human sexuality. It is a test case in getting the balance right between the openness of "faith" and the more closed definition of "the faith."

1 TIMOTHY 1:12-20, PAUL'S EXAMPLE AND CHARGE TO TIMOTHY

NIV

[12]I thank Christ Jesus our Lord, who has given me strength, that he considered me faithful, appointing me to his service. [13]Even though I was once a blasphemer and a persecutor and a violent man, I was shown mercy because I acted in ignorance and unbelief. [14]The grace of our Lord was poured out on me abundantly, along with the faith and love that are in Christ Jesus.

[15]Here is a trustworthy saying that deserves full acceptance: Christ Jesus came into the world to save sinners—of whom I am the worst. [16]But for that very reason I was shown mercy so that in me, the worst of sinners, Christ Jesus might display his unlimited patience as an example for those who would believe on him and receive eternal life. [17]Now to the King eternal, immortal, invisible, the only God, be honor and glory for ever and ever. Amen.

[18]Timothy, my son, I give you this instruction in keeping with the prophecies once made about you, so that by following them you may fight the good fight, [19]holding on to faith and a good conscience. Some have rejected these and so have shipwrecked their faith. [20]Among them are Hymenaeus and Alexander, whom I have handed over to Satan to be taught not to blaspheme.

NRSV

[12]I am grateful to Christ Jesus our Lord, who has strengthened me, because he judged me faithful and appointed me to his service, [13]even though I was formerly a blasphemer, a persecutor, and a man of violence. But I received mercy because I had acted ignorantly in unbelief, [14]and the grace of our Lord overflowed for me with the faith and love that are in Christ Jesus. [15]The saying is sure and worthy of full acceptance, that Christ Jesus came into the world to save sinners—of whom I am the foremost. [16]But for that very reason I received mercy, so that in me, as the foremost, Jesus Christ might display the utmost patience, making me an example to those who would come to believe in him for eternal life. [17]To the King of the ages, immortal, invisible, the only God, be honor and glory forever and ever.[a] Amen.

[18]I am giving you these instructions, Timothy, my child, in accordance with the prophecies made earlier about you, so that by following them you may fight the good fight, [19]having faith and a good conscience. By rejecting conscience, certain persons have suffered shipwreck in the faith; [20]among them are Hymenaeus and Alexander, whom I have turned over to Satan, so that they may learn not to blaspheme.

[a] Gk to the ages of the ages

COMMENTARY

In effect the whole of the opening section (1:3-20) is Paul's charge to Timothy. The linking term is "charge/command/commission" (vv. 3, 5, 18); the theme is the wrong teaching (vv. 3-7, 10-11), which can shipwreck faith (vv. 19-20), but from which people can be delivered, as Paul himself had been delivered (vv. 13-16). Paul is thus set forward as the great paradigm: the one with whom the gospel had been entrusted (v. 11), which was the measure of the sound teaching (v. 10), and the one who displayed the effects of grace in fullest measure to serve as the paradigm for other believers (vv. 13-16). Whether this is Paul himself speaking or a somewhat idealized Paul, the effect is the same: to root the gospel firmly in the commission of Paul and in the one who commissioned him. Timothy can thus be still more clearly presented as the one who stands in that line of authentic gospel tradition (Christ → Paul → Timothy; v. 18), set over against the antithetical paradigms of Hymenaeus and Alexander (vv. 19-20).

1:12. The typical thanksgiving of Paul's letters (for those to whom he writes) is replaced by a thanksgiving for Paul himself. The thought is similar to what we often find in the earlier Paulines: Paul's consciousness of divine commissioning and enabling (cf., e.g., 1 Cor 15:8-10; Phil 4:13). But the talk of God's appointing him because of his (future?) faithfulness introduces a different note (cf. 1 Cor 4:2; 7:25), underlining the need felt by the writer to draw a firm equation between Paul's "faith alone" and faithfulness measured by loyalty to the more elaborated faith of his own generation.

1:13. The memory of Paul as persecutor is deeply rooted in all texts related to Paul (e.g., Acts 9:4-5; 1 Cor 15:9; Gal 1:3, 24). New is the thought of him as "blasphemer" (an ironic echo of Acts 26:11) and "violent, insolent" (an echo of Rom 1:30?). "Blaspheme" does not necessarily denote insult of Christ; the term can connote simply slanderous speech (cf. 6:4), though it is probably stronger here (v. 20; 6:1); even so, what is in view is probably the insult to God implicit in such a rejection of Christ (cf. v. 20). Notable here is both the emphasis on Paul's guilt and the excuse that he acted ignorantly. In this, too, Paul can serve as an example; the seriousness of such sin is sufficient proof that the person committing it was unaware of its full nature.

1:14. Equally strongly stressed is the mercy and overflowing grace of the Lord (presumably Jesus). The language here is archtypically Pauline: It was Paul who established the term "grace" (χάρις *charis*) in the Christian vocabulary (used 100 times in the Pauline corpus); the imagery of grace "multiplying" is Paul's (Rom 5:20; 6:1); and there is little that is more typical of Paul's thought than talk of "faith and love in Christ Jesus" (Col 1:4; 1 Thess 1:3; 2 Thess 1:3; Phlm 5), though this form of "faith in Christ" only occurs in the

later Paulines (cf. Col 1:4). In this not least Paul embodies what is most important about the gospel for which he was commissioned.

1:15-16. The point is made explicit in two ways here. First, the writer cites a "faithful saying and worthy of all acceptance" (v. 15). This is a formula he uses several times. In each case it seems to indicate an element of teaching that had become, or that the writer was trying to establish as, a more or less set formulation, encapsulating some gospel statement or principle regarding salvation or future life. In some cases, the identifying label comes before the saying (v. 15; 2 Tim 2:11), in others after it (3:1; 4:9; Titus 3:8). Here we can begin to see more clearly the content of the "sound teaching," by appeal to which the writer hoped to head off false teaching. In this case, the statement is as simple as it could be: the divine initiative embodied in Christ Jesus;[47] his mission to "save" (the key gospel term in the letters, v. 15; 2:4, 15; 4:16; 2 Tim 1:9; 4:18; Titus 3:5; "salvation," 2 Tim 2:10; 3:15); and the object "sinners," recalling a key term in Christian tradition, that summed up both the mission of Jesus (Mark 2:17; Luke 19:7-10) and the gospel for Paul (Gal 2:15-21).

Second, the point already made (vv. 13-14) is repeated for effect (vv. 15-16). Paul had been the worst of these "sinners," so that the mercy he received could serve as a model of the full sweep of God's patience toward those who were to believe subsequently. The overtone of the earlier talk of "sinner" as a term of condemnation used by those who judged the conduct of others to be unacceptable to God is not present here; as in Rom 5:19, the term simply means those who break or ignore God's law and are thus subject to God's judgment. This is the mercy of God that takes the initiative of grace not least to those who disdain God's directions for life (cf. 1 Cor 15:9-11).

1:17. As elsewhere (notably Rom 11:33-36), the thought of such undeserved mercy moves the writer to a paean of praise to such a God. It is the first of three passages in 1 Timothy that, very strikingly, affirm a strongly monotheistic faith (see

---

47. A rabbinic phrase describes human beings as "those who come into the world" and is probably reflected in John 1:9. So talk of Christ's coming into the world can be read as a description of his human existence (cf. 3:16), as in Rom 15:8 and Gal 4:4 (cf. Matt 1:21).

also 2:5; 6:15-16). The language is characteristically Jewish: "king of the ages"—time conceived as a sequence of ages (cf., e.g., Gal 1:5; Col 1:26). That God was "incorruptible" was generally assumed, but "invisible" was a more distinctively Jewish claim (John 1:18; Rom 1:20; Col 1:15; Heb 11:27; common in the Jewish philosopher Philo), the one who alone is God (John 5:44; Rom 3:30; 16:27; Jude 25; Rev 15:4; cf. 2 Kgs 19:15, 19; Ps 86:10; Isa 37:20; 2 Macc 1:24-25). As in the earlier Paul, the strong christological claims are held within a monotheistic framework.

1:18-20. Rounding off the section, the initial charge to Timothy (vv. 3, 5) is repeated in v. 18. It is reinforced by a fresh appeal to the personal relationship between Paul and Timothy (v. 2). The reader has been reminded of just who this Paul was and how weighty, therefore, is the authority embodied in the charge to his "son" Timothy. The point is reinforced still further by pointing out that the charge was in accordance with prophecies that had earlier referred to him; the precise meaning is unclear, but the same episode may be referred to in 4:14. In other words, Timothy's authority was based not only in his personal link with the great apostle, but also in a direct indication from God through prophecy.

Notable is the fact that the commission is described as "fighting the good warfare" (v. 18). The imagery was familiar in those days (cf. 1 Cor 9:7; 2 Cor 10:3-4; Eph 6:10-17), but here the context indicates that the reference was primarily to the need to fight to maintain the faith free from disabling distractions. To be noted is the fact that the metaphor envisages spiritual forces as the "enemies," not human beings; Paul does not encourage the idea of fighting against other people. The position from and for which the fighting is to be fought is once again given as "faith and a good conscience" (v. 19; see Commentary on 1:5).

Just as Paul had served as an example of "the faithful saying," so also others can serve as examples of what is being warned against. By rejecting conscience—that is, presumably, conscience in-

structed by those who had a clearer grasp of the faith—their faith had suffered shipwreck, a very vivid metaphor (v. 19) that Paul would certainly have appreciated (cf. 2 Cor 11:25). This third association of faith and conscience within a few verses (vv. 5, 19) drives home the point: Where faith and conscience are not in harmony, then shipwreck is likely.

Two cases in point are cited. Hymenaeus is mentioned only once elsewhere, in 2 Tim 2:17-18, where his (presumably the same) error is made explicit. He claimed that the resurrection had already taken place (see Commentary on 2 Tim 2:18). An Alexander is also mentioned in 2 Tim 4:14, but there is no hint that that Alexander ever came to faith (see Commentary on 2 Tim 4:14). If we generalize from Hymenaeus, however, the point of failure is clear: failure to hold to the understanding of resurrection on which Christian faith was based. Here we may have an example of how the faith was firming up, for whereas Paul simply argued against a denial of the resurrection of the dead (1 Cor 15:12), the writer here regards failure to hold to the belief expounded in 1 Corinthians 15 as tantamount to the shipwreck of faith in the resurrection.

The rather fearful-sounding final clause (v. 20) is almost certainly modeled on 1 Cor 5:5. In both cases some sort of excommunication (disfellowshipping) is probably intended; they would lose the protection of the "household of God" (cf. 1 Cor 5:9-13). In both cases, it is also important to recognize that the definite article is used—"the satan." In other words, the thought seems to be still of one who was ultimately God's agent and whose activities allowed by God were intended to test and prove those subjected to the satan's authority (Job 1–2; Zech 3:1-2). In both cases, then, handing over the individual to the power of the satan had in view that person's salvation (1 Cor 5:5) as well as discipline ("that they may learn"). The writer would certainly intend the reader to recall that Paul was the model of one who had learned not to "blaspheme" (v. 13).

REFLECTIONS

The use of examples from real life, the telling of how it worked out in someone else's experience, always makes a point far stronger than mere restatement. Here the writer follows in the train of psalmist and sage to cite the acts of God of time past. Just as the words and deeds of Jesus' own ministry were no doubt already being told and retold, so also the event of Paul's conversion was already gaining exemplary significance; in Acts it is recounted no less than three times. Similarly the sad tales of Balaam or Esau embody lessons for future generations, just as here do those of Hymenaeus and Alexander, both of whom and their fates were presumably known to the first readers.

In such circumstances there is always a temptation to add a flourish to the tale, to bring out the point being made more forcefully. Has that happened here? Where Paul described himself as "the least of the apostles, unfit to be called an apostle" (1 Cor 15:9), the writer here describes Paul as "first among sinners" (1:15). The motivation, presumably, is the same as when a Christian testimony describes pre-conversion life as plumbing the deepest depths of sin—that is, the more despairing the condition, the greater the grace that achieves redemption. There need be nothing dishonest or dishonorable in such hyperbole. A true mark of grace received is often a consciousness of the unworthiness of such grace, and without a degree of dramatic license there would be no art in storytelling. On the other hand, overstatement can easily slide into parody, and an element of unreality can enter that helps nobody.

Embedded within this testimony of Paul is the first "faithful saying," in which the gospel is summed up in eight words (in the Greek): "Christ Jesus came into the world to save sinners" (1:15). Evidently it was equally as important as the portrayal of Paul to be able to sum up the gospel in such simple terms. For those wanting greater precision, the formulation is overly simple and would hardly suffice for a theological analysis. But faith requires such slogan-like forms (like "Jesus is Lord") that can act as a unifying core, precisely by virtue of their degree of simplification or lack of sophistication; as such it can serve to anchor a wider range of faith seeking fuller definition (but not to be confused with "bumper sticker theology"). When even these do not provide that unifying core and anchor, then faith has, indeed, lost its identity.

Here, too, we may recall that the new Christian movement was still young. Its center was firmly fixed in the gospel of Jesus Christ, but its circumference was far from clear. The process of definition and boundary drawing required a firm hand; otherwise the identity of the new movement would be dissipated, and the movement itself might become just another scattering of elements in a wider syncretistic religiosity. Later generations may question some of these initial firm lines, but without them there would probably have been no lasting lines of definition from within which these questions could be posed.

At the same time, it should be again appreciated that the drawing of firm boundary lines cuts both ways in terms of evangelism and apostasy. Firmly drawn boundaries will exclude as well as retain. Permeable boundaries will leak as well as draw in. An open door allows people to exit as well as to enter. Is the former (exit) an inevitable corollary if the latter (enter) is to be successful? Arguably the most successful means of sustained local evangelism are groups that genuinely overlap the margins of a church. Perhaps, then, the loss of a Hymenaeus and an Alexander may be signs of a church's vitality!

1 TIMOTHY 2:1-7, GOD'S CONCERN IS FOR EVERYONE

NIV	NRSV
2 I urge, then, first of all, that requests, prayers, intercession and thanksgiving be made for everyone— [2]for kings and all those in	**2** First of all, then, I urge that supplications, prayers, intercessions, and thanksgivings be made for everyone, [2]for kings and all who are in

NIV

authority, that we may live peaceful and quiet lives in all godliness and holiness. ³This is good, and pleases God our Savior, ⁴who wants all men to be saved and to come to a knowledge of the truth. ⁵For there is one God and one mediator between God and men, the man Christ Jesus, ⁶who gave himself as a ransom for all men—the testimony given in its proper time. ⁷And for this purpose I was appointed a herald and an apostle—I am telling the truth, I am not lying—and a teacher of the true faith to the Gentiles.

NRSV

high positions, so that we may lead a quiet and peaceable life in all godliness and dignity. ³This is right and is acceptable in the sight of God our Savior, ⁴who desires everyone to be saved and to come to the knowledge of the truth. ⁵For

there is one God;
there is also one mediator between God
and humankind,
Christ Jesus, himself human,
⁶ who gave himself a ransom for all

—this was attested at the right time. ⁷For this I was appointed a herald and an apostle (I am telling the truth,[a] I am not lying), a teacher of the Gentiles in faith and truth.

[a] Other ancient authorities add *in Christ*

COMMENTARY

After the initial charge to Timothy, the primary emphasis seems to be to stress the breadth of concern that Christians could express (vv. 1-2), and precisely (v. 3) as a reflection of the breadth of God's concern (vv. 4-6). The key word here is "all"; prayers should be made for all (v. 1), particularly all in authority (v. 2), for God wants all to be saved (v. 4), and Christ Jesus gave himself as a ransom for all (v. 6). This, too, is the gospel that Paul had been appointed to preach (v. 7).

There could be several reasons why this emphasis was given such high prominence ("first of all," v. 1). (1) It set the gospel in still sharper contrast with the other teachings already attacked (1:3-7, 10-11, 19); by implication, their concern was more introverted and self-centered. (2) It developed an emphasis that had been integral to the gospel from the beginning: good news for all, sinner and not just righteous, Jew first but also Gentile ("all" is equally prominent in Romans). The emphasis, then, is not necessarily directed against a Gnostic elitism; the older Jewish "exclusivism" (Jews only) could equally be a target. (3) It made clear that the young Christian movement was not an anarchistic revolution, but was concerned rather to be a positive force in and for society. This last concern provides the link of continuity into the next section; good order in the

state leads naturally to thought of good order in the household (vv. 8-15; see also Titus 3:1-2).

2:1-2. Typical of the author is the heaping up of near synonyms—"supplications, prayers, intercessions and thanksgivings" (v. 1).[48] The whole range of prayer forms should be used to express Christian concern. And this concern should be for everyone (the Greek denotes all human beings, not just all "men"). The language, presumably, is not literally prescriptive, as though such prayer was practically possible (beyond the mere mouthing of "all"). Rather, it is indicative that Christian concern should exclude no one.

To be noted is the fact that the next requested prayer (for those in authority) is presented as a special case of this broader concern; the assumption is that good government is for the benefit of all, and that is why those in authority are to be prayed for (cf. Rom 13:1-7; 1 Pet 2:13-17). This, in fact, is spelled out in v. 2: The intention of such prayers is that we (Christians as part of society) might (be able to) lead a tranquil and quiet (again two near synonyms) life, in "all piety and dignity." These last terms are two of the key words in the Pastoral Epistles. The first, εὐσεβεία

48. It is unlikely that the last term, εὐχαριστία (*eucharistia*), has the Lord's supper (eucharist) particularly in mind (as Kelly, *The Pastoral Epistles,* 60). The typical usage is much broader. See 1 Cor 14:16; 2 Cor 4:15; 9:11-12; Eph 5:4; Phil 4:6; Col 2:7; 4:2; 1 Thess 3:9.

(*eusebeia*), occurs ten times (see footnote 10) and denotes religious obligation due to God—"piety," "godliness," even "religion."[49] The second, σεμνότης (*semnotēs*), which with its related adjective occurs six times (see footnote 16), has a range of meaning—"reverence," "dignity," "seriousness," "respectfulness," "holiness," "probity"—denoting the gravitas that a well-ordered religious life carries with it and that commands respect within the wider society.[50] Here is the other side of the universal concern being commended: that they themselves might be able to live in a way that wins the respect of all (cf. particularly 1 Thess 4:11-12).

Notable also are the echoes of older wisdom learned by those living under the yoke of foreign power: that prayers and offerings should be made for these rulers (Ezra 6:10; Jer 29:7; Bar 1:11-12; 1 Macc 7:33). In the often unfavorable realities of life, concern for others and self-interest need involve neither contradiction nor compromise.

2:3-4. Such concern for others and for rulers is not merely pragmatic policy but a theological necessity. It is fine and acceptable to God (the primary criterion), because "God our Savior" is not only "our Savior." There follows a statement that is as clear as any assertion of "Christian universalism": God wills the salvation of everyone. The God who wished to save Paul, "chief of sinners" (1:15), could hardly want anything less for everyone else (v. 4); the earlier Paul had spoken with equal boldness (Rom 11:32).

The traditional way of squaring this affirmation with the awareness of how few actually accept the gospel has been to distinguish between God's general will or desire and God's active determination of outcomes or permissive will in the face of human intransigence. But whatever the theological complications involved, it is important to recognize that the bottom line for the writer is God's concern for the salvation of everyone. The wholeness of the salvation in mind is indicated also in the complementary phrase "to come to knowledge of the truth" (v. 4), a phrase that

appears regularly in the Pastorals (e.g., v. 4; 4:3; 2 Tim 2:25; Titus 1:1). Salvation includes a knowing, both intellectual and existential, an awareness and acknowledgment of the reality of oneself and of the world.

2:5-6. The ground for this theological claim is given in another creedal fragment, one of the most striking in these or any Pauline letter (see also 1:15; 2:15; 3:16; 2 Tim 1:9-10; 2:11-13; Titus 3:4-7). The fact that God is one (the primary Jewish confession, *Shema*; Deut 6:4) leads inevitably to the conclusion that God is God of all (as in Rom 3:29-30) and, therefore, is concerned for all. But the point of the creed is to integrate the oneness of God with the singular role of Christ Jesus (as in 1 Cor 8:6). This is the second affirmation of traditional Jewish monotheism (1:17); however lofty the claims to be made for Christ, they are to be held within that frame of reference. In a formulation pushing toward universalism ("gave himself a ransom for all"), the limitation of effective mediation to Christ Jesus is not to exclude from salvation those who have not heard of Christ, but to affirm that effective salvation, wherever it is experienced, will be found to have been mediated through Christ. We may compare John 1:9 (the Word enlightens everyone) with John 14:6 (Jesus said, "No one comes to the Father except through me"). Particularly striking is the repeated antithesis between God and humankind: Christ comes from the side of human beings to act as mediator on their behalf with God (cf. 1:15). The thought is of a piece with Paul's earlier Adam christology: Christ is the second or last "man" who more than rectifies the damage done by the first (Rom 5:12-19; 1 Cor 15:21-22, 45-49).[51]

The second half of the creedal form echoes several earlier versions (Mark 10:45; Gal 1:4; 2:20; Eph 5:2, 25). The imagery is of something or someone given in place of others to secure their liberty (though 2 Tim 2:11 indicates that the imagery should not be overpressed). But the key linking word is again "all." The importance of the text is obvious for the old dispute about the scope of the atonement between Calvinists (atonement limited to the elect) and Arminians (atonement for all who will). Precisely what the final phrase

49. P. H. Towner, *The Goal of Our Instruction: The Structure of Theology and Ethics,* JSNTSup 34 (Sheffield: Sheffield Academic, 1989) 147-52, suggests that it functions as equivalent to the biblical phrase "the fear of the LORD," the knowledge of God that ensures reverence.

50. It is this passage that prompted Dibelius-Conzelmann's influential reflection on the Pastorals' advocacy of "the ideal of good Christian citizenship." See M. Dibelius and H. Conzelmann, *The Pastoral Epistles,* Hermeneia (Philadelphia: Fortress, 1972) 39-41.

51. For Adam christology, see J. D. G. Dunn, *The Theology of Paul the Apostle* (Grand Rapids: Eerdmans, 1998) §§9.1, 10.2, 11.4-5.

means ("the testimony for its own times") is unclear, but the following verse and similar language elsewhere (Rom 3:26; 2 Cor 6:2; Gal 4:4-5; Col 1:25-26) suggest a sense of the climactic character within the purpose of God, both of Christ's death and of Paul's commission to proclaim it.

2:7. For the third time the writer stresses Paul's sense of commission (see also 1:11-12). The verse has some curious features. It reinforces Paul's claim to apostleship (1:1) and the particular scope of his mission as to "the Gentiles" (cf. Rom 11:13). But nowhere else outside the Pastorals does Paul describe himself as a "herald" or "teacher" (the language is closely repeated in 2 Tim 1:11). And the double vow of sincerity (cf. Rom 9:1; Gal 1:20) is a little surprising here; it sounds rather as though a known Pauline affirmation is being used to strengthen the potentially more controversial formulation of the universalism of the preceding verses.

REFLECTIONS

Do we begin to see in this passage the lust for social acceptance that can so easily blunt the cutting edge of the gospel, at both the individual and the social level? To be seen as loyal to the state, as motivated by concern for the well-being of everyone can be politically astute and possibly even open the way to political and social influence. But the same process can also mean a blurring of principles and an accommodation with practices that previously would have been wholeheartedly condemned. So here the desire for a "quiet life" can easily be disparaged by those eager to turn the world upside down, and the prizing of "piety and dignity" can be denigrated as desire for a "respectability" that stifles necessary criticism and unavoidable controversy.

But such a line of reflection would be unjust to the writer of these letters. The situation envisaged was nothing like the modern Western democracy, where non-governmental organizations can exercise influence by freedom of speech and access to the media. It was, rather, the situation familiar to diaspora (and Palestinian) Jews for most of their history—the struggle to secure and maintain a foothold within a hostile environment, where political authorities would always tend to be suspicious of the little house groups whose legal status was at best ambiguous and be ready to act against them at short notice with little excuse (cf., e.g., Acts 18:2 with Rom 13:1-7). It was not yet a case of winning respectability, but of gaining basic respect. And only those whose "quiet and tranquility" have been little disturbed could begin to despise a desire for them as essential to any kind of security and prosperity in daily living. Here again, then, a sense of historical realism is necessary if such a passage is to be appreciated—not to mention a sense of empathy with little church groups struggling to survive in situations not so very different today.

Within this context a natural reaction is to become more secretive (like the ancient cults that celebrated secret mysteries) or to withdraw from the world to practice beliefs and principles as purely as possible (like the Qumran community, which withdrew to the Dead Sea). The first Christians chose the opposite alternative: to live within the world and for all their neighbors, high and low. That alternative inevitably involves some compromise with the principles and values governing the wider society, for where purity is possible only outside society, then "outside" has become an introverted self-concern cut off from wider community. But the theological imperative of "one God . . . and one mediator . . . who gave himself as a ransom for all" (2:5-6) left them no choice. The uncomfortable fact is that such universalism inevitably involves a fair degree of openness to the other and acceptance of the other in terms broader than one's own.

The problem with any theological system that turns its back on universalism, for no doubt good reasons of logic and self-reassurance, is that the resulting system postulates either a less generous God or a less omnipotent God than 1 Timothy envisions (cf. Rom 11:32). Here as elsewhere theological assertions need always to be qualified by the note of eschatological reserve. God's ultimate purpose is ultimate and, therefore, still unknown, as well as the divine means of achieving that purpose. All human judgment is subject to eschatological verification. At this point, theology must simply give way to wondering worship (as in Rom 11:33-36).

1 TIMOTHY 2:8-15, THE ROLE OF WOMEN WITHIN THIS STRATEGY

NIV

[8]I want men everywhere to lift up holy hands in prayer, without anger or disputing.

[9]I also want women to dress modestly, with decency and propriety, not with braided hair or gold or pearls or expensive clothes, [10]but with good deeds, appropriate for women who profess to worship God.

[11]A woman should learn in quietness and full submission. [12]I do not permit a woman to teach or to have authority over a man; she must be silent. [13]For Adam was formed first, then Eve. [14]And Adam was not the one deceived; it was the woman who was deceived and became a sinner. [15]But women[a] will be saved[b] through childbearing—if they continue in faith, love and holiness with propriety.

[a]15 Greek *she*   [b]15 Or *restored*

NRSV

[8]I desire, then, that in every place the men should pray, lifting up holy hands without anger or argument; [9]also that the women should dress themselves modestly and decently in suitable clothing, not with their hair braided, or with gold, pearls, or expensive clothes, [10]but with good works, as is proper for women who profess reverence for God. [11]Let a woman[a] learn in silence with full submission. [12]I permit no woman[a] to teach or to have authority over a man;[b] she is to keep silent. [13]For Adam was formed first, then Eve; [14]and Adam was not deceived, but the woman was deceived and became a transgressor. [15]Yet she will be saved through childbearing, provided they continue in faith and love and holiness, with modesty.

[a] Or *wife*   [b] Or *her husband*

COMMENTARY

The train of thought is clear enough, with v. 8 signaling the continuity. It is of a piece with this wider concern for the common good that the believing women should dress and act in ways that commended their religion (vv. 9-10). This evidently included also the way wives should comport themselves in the church's gatherings for worship, where the key word is ἡσυχία (*hēsychia*, vv. 11-12), the same word used in v. 2 to connote a quiet life; for wives to be given a teaching or authority role in respect of their husbands would also mean upsetting the social tranquility so prized earlier. The point is reinforced by a theological deduction drawn from the original creation story of Adam and Eve (vv. 13-15) and

is given added weight by being designated a "faithful saying" (3:1).[52]

2:8. The encouragement to pray is repeated, so that this verse forms a bracket with v. 1 and carries forward the logic behind the call to prayer into this paragraph also.[53] The verse confirms that a traditional manner of praying was with upraised hands (Ps 141:2), although talk of "holy hands" will be a carryover from the Jewish tradition of

52. Placing the label "Faithful is the saying" at the end of the saying is the practice also in 4:9 and Titus 3:8. The NIV and the NRSV, however, think that the label refers to what follows.

53. C. K. Barrett, *The Pastoral Epistles,* New Clarendon Bible (Oxford: Clarendon, 1963) 54, thinks that "in every place" means every "meeting-place" (cf. Mal 1:10-11; 1 Cor 1:2; 1 Thess 1:8). But since Christians met for fellowship and worship in members' homes, it is less likely that "place" had such a specific meaning.

ritual purification prior to prayer. If the final phrase is more than conventional, it is a reminder that motives for prayer can often be mixed and that prayer itself can often be used as a factional weapon—praying at or against another or praying for a party point (cf. Rom 14:1).

The limitation of the advice to "men" (v. 8) prefaces a sequence directed to "women" (vv. 9-15). Since the two words ἀνήρ (*anēr*) and γυνη (*gynē*) also mean "husband" and "wife," it is more than likely that the advice has in view the good functioning of what was generally recognized to be society's basic household unit, formed around husband and wife; the point is much clearer in the parallel instructions of 1 Pet 3:1-6. As in more detailed "household codes" (rules for household management) elsewhere (e.g., Eph 5:21–6:9; Col 3:18–4:1), the advice is part of an attempt to gain wider respect for the church by ensuring that the then conventional subjection of wife to husband is not disturbed by the greater freedoms brought by the gospel (cf. Gal 3:28). The context, it should be recalled, is that of worship (vv. 8, 11-12; cf. 1 Cor 11:2-16), but v. 10 suggests that the thought reaches beyond the subject of dress appropriate for prayer meetings.

2:9. The first concern is for women's/wives' dress and appearance. The writer calls on them to adorn themselves in orderly or respectable apparel with modesty or reverence and reasonableness or moderation, or in reference to women, decently or chastely (the last word denotes a classic Greek "virtue," often alluded to in the Pastorals; see 2:9, 15; 3:2; 2 Tim 1:7; Titus 1:8; 2:2, 4-6, 12). The piling up of near synonyms is noticeable. Warning is given against braided hair, gold (ornaments), pearls, and expensive clothing. The warning presupposes the presence of some wealth in the congregations being addressed and a tendency on the part of well-to-do women (often severely limited in their freedom of action, not least since legally they were always dependent on a male relative) to find satisfaction in costly attire (the tendency is illustrated in poems, paintings, and sculptures of the time). A religion that saw its end result in such terms would be no more than a club for social advancement.

2:10. In place of adornment should be "good deeds," such as befits women/wives who profess worship of God. The commendation of "good deeds" is frequent in the Pastorals (fourteen times; see footnote 10); the category is broad, but most societies would have a reasonable idea of what constituted "good deeds." As in the earlier Paulines (particularly Rom 14:6), the criterion of acceptable conduct is whether the one who so acts can worship God in doing so.

2:11-12. With these verses the instruction becomes more specific and focuses on the gatherings for worship. The thought is clearly determined by the attitude behind the household codes. In the ancient household the male head of the family, the *paterfamilias,* had all authority and power, and this was deemed to be essential for the good order of the household, itself the basic unit of city and state. In consequence, the proper relation of the wife to her husband was one of "submission" (ὑποταγη *hypotagē*); the same key word appears in non-Christian household codes,[54] as well as Christian (Eph 5:22; Col 3:18; 1 Pet 3:1, 5).

The possibility of confusion arose because the first churches all met in private homes. Consequently there was uncertainty as to whether the norms of behavior were those of household or of church. Probably in the early days of Christianity there were wives who, in exercise of prophetic or other gifts, had been seen to be teaching or exhorting their husbands (cf. 1 Cor 14:29-35). Conceivably, this may have been acceptable in church, but since church was also household, the practice was too easily understood to be subversive of the good order of the household and of the authority of the *paterfamilias.*[55] For a church concerned to be seen as supportive of what was good for society, the only solution was to conform church order to that of the well-ordered household (hence 3:4-5, 12) and to forbid wives to teach (διδάσκω *didaskō*) or to have authority (αὐθεντέω *authenteō;* the meaning could be stronger: "domineer") over their husbands.

2:13-14. However, as with vv. 5-6 (and Titus 2), the author wanted to root his counsel theologically. At this point there enters a disturbing tendentiousness, pushing a line. He not only argues from the prior creation of Adam (Gen 2:7,

---

54. E.g., Plutarch *Moralia* 142E.
55. The wife had authority within the household, principally over domestic arrangements (5:14; cf. Titus 2:4-5). But that did not affect the husband's supreme authority.

21-23), as in the more open 1 Cor 11:3, and he not only follows the Genesis account of Eve's initial deception (Gen 3:1-6), as in 2 Cor 11:3, but he also denies that Adam was deceived and puts the blame solely on the woman (Gen 3:13), in direct contrast to Paul's own earlier account of Adam's transgression (Rom 5:15-19; cf. Rom 7:11). Here the theology seems to be bending before social convention in spite of the biblical text referred to and the earlier Pauline use of it. (Would the "I" of Rom 7:11 be debarred from teaching authority by the same logic?) At the same time, however, the implication, supported by Gen 2:24, is that the relationship in view is still that of husband and wife, and not man and woman.

2:15. This verse confirms that notion, prompted no doubt by the punishment of the primal sin—for the woman/wife, labor pains in childbirth (Gen 3:16), which in those days could often be fatal. The implication is that childbearing is the means by which woman atones for her part in the primal sin, or, less negatively expressed, that labor pains are a sign of the out-of-jointedness of creation as a whole. In those days, childbearing was seen as woman's primary function, so that barrenness would be regarded typically as a cause of shame and rebuke (still reflected in the male tendency to blame failure to conceive on the wife). There have been attempts to refer "the childbearing" to the incarnation, but that thought seems to be far away at this point, and the qualification of the final clause implies that women endured the trauma of giving birth by their faith, love, and consecration, with moderation (the same word as in 2:9).[56] In designating the whole (or v. 15 alone) as a "faithful saying" (3:1), the author is appealing to and reinforcing a social tradition to which the early churches found it wiser to conform.

---

56. Alternatively, the plural "they" ("if they continue in . . .") could refer to the children thus born, and the reference would then include childrearing as well as giving birth. But that would seem to make the mother's salvation depend on her success in nurturing her children—that is, on the behavior of others, which is less likely. For a helpful discussion of 2:15, see S. E. Porter, "What Does It Mean to Be 'Saved by Childbirth' (1 Timothy 2:15)?" *JSNT* 49 (1993) 87-102.

REFLECTIONS

Few if any texts are more painful to modern sensitivities. The portrayal of women as effectively gagged in church, forbidden to exercise authority over men, and restricted to the role of childbearers, modest dressers, and doers of good deeds is about as remote from most twenty-first-century evaluations of women's roles in Western society, as one could imagine. What does one do with a text like this?

The tensions it sets up are partly relieved by the recognition that the focus of concern is not man and woman so much as husband and wife. It is not woman as woman who is to be subordinated to man as man, but woman as wife who is to be subordinated to man as husband. The freedom of the well-to-do unmarried woman or widow in business and in church would hardly be limitless, but would certainly be greater than that envisaged here (cf. Acts 18:26, Priscilla as instructor of Apollos; Rom 16:1-2, Phoebe as deacon and patron; Col 4:15, Nympha as host of the church in her house).

Still more to the point is the social context in which such instructions are given, including the norms and conventions of the time, and the consequently limited horizons and expectations of men and women of the time. Modern societies that only gave the vote to women within the last hundred years and that still connive at unequal opportunities for men and women should not be surprised that the earliest churches should be so conformist. The best minds of the day and the wisdom of the ancients all confirmed that the husband should have all legal authority and the wife should be subject to him. To challenge this then (nineteen centuries ahead of time!) would have been tantamount to calling marriage itself into question and would have been regarded as undermining the very foundations of society and state.

At the same time, recognition of the degree to which the counsel here was conditioned by the conventions of the time should caution against any attempt to transfer such directives directly into the different conditions of today's household—far less of church! To acknowledge the context-conditioned character of scripture teaching on relationships within marriage is not to deny authority to that teaching. Rather, it is to affirm the relevance of the teaching to the particular historical circumstances for which it was written. And it is to affirm that contemporary social teaching that does not take account of the (different) circumstances of today is that much less authoritative!

What emerges of lasting importance from this passage, therefore, is the concern to affirm the relationships that maintain the strength of marriage and the stability of the household. The perception of what these relationships are, and particularly of a wife's responsibility to and relation to her husband, have changed, though only in a radical way within the last hundred years. But arguably the principle of strong marriage and stable household remains fundamental to a Christianity that, like Jesus (Mark 10:7-8), looks back to Gen 2:24 as the most fundamental model for intimate human relationships. In this way, the force of the text can be recognized, while at the same time noting the time-conditioned character of its specific detail.

1 TIMOTHY 3:1-16, GOOD ORDER IN THE CHURCH

NIV

3 Here is a trustworthy saying: If anyone sets his heart on being an overseer,[a] he desires a noble task. [2]Now the overseer must be above reproach, the husband of but one wife, temperate, self-controlled, respectable, hospitable, able to teach, [3]not given to drunkenness, not violent but gentle, not quarrelsome, not a lover of money. [4]He must manage his own family well and see that his children obey him with proper respect. [5](If anyone does not know how to manage his own family, how can he take care of God's church?) [6]He must not be a recent convert, or he may become conceited and fall under the same judgment as the devil. [7]He must also have a good reputation with outsiders, so that he will not fall into disgrace and into the devil's trap.

[8]Deacons, likewise, are to be men worthy of respect, sincere, not indulging in much wine, and not pursuing dishonest gain. [9]They must keep hold of the deep truths of the faith with a clear conscience. [10]They must first be tested; and then if there is nothing against them, let them serve as deacons.

[11]In the same way, their wives[b] are to be women worthy of respect, not malicious talkers but temperate and trustworthy in everything.

[a]1 Traditionally *bishop*; also in verse 2   [b]11 Or *way, deaconesses*

NRSV

3 The saying is sure:[a] whoever aspires to the office of bishop[b] desires a noble task. [2]Now a bishop[c] must be above reproach, married only once,[d] temperate, sensible, respectable, hospitable, an apt teacher, [3]not a drunkard, not violent but gentle, not quarrelsome, and not a lover of money. [4]He must manage his own household well, keeping his children submissive and respectful in every way— [5]for if someone does not know how to manage his own household, how can he take care of God's church? [6]He must not be a recent convert, or he may be puffed up with conceit and fall into the condemnation of the devil. [7]Moreover, he must be well thought of by outsiders, so that he may not fall into disgrace and the snare of the devil.

[8]Deacons likewise must be serious, not double-tongued, not indulging in much wine, not greedy for money; [9]they must hold fast to the mystery of the faith with a clear conscience. [10]And let them first be tested; then, if they prove themselves blameless, let them serve as deacons. [11]Women[e] likewise must be serious, not slanderers, but temperate, faithful in all things. [12]Let deacons be

[a] Some interpreters place these words at the end of the previous paragraph. Other ancient authorities read *The saying is commonly accepted*   [b] Or *overseer*   [c] Or *an overseer*   [d] Gk *the husband of one wife*   [e] Or *Their wives*, or *Women deacons*

NIV

¹²A deacon must be the husband of but one wife and must manage his children and his household well. ¹³Those who have served well gain an excellent standing and great assurance in their faith in Christ Jesus.

¹⁴Although I hope to come to you soon, I am writing you these instructions so that, ¹⁵if I am delayed, you will know how people ought to conduct themselves in God's household, which is the church of the living God, the pillar and foundation of the truth. ¹⁶Beyond all question, the mystery of godliness is great:

He[a] appeared in a body,[b]
    was vindicated by the Spirit,
was seen by angels,
    was preached among the nations,
was believed on in the world,
    was taken up in glory.

a16 Some manuscripts God   b16 Or in the flesh

NRSV

married only once,[a] and let them manage their children and their households well; ¹³for those who serve well as deacons gain a good standing for themselves and great boldness in the faith that is in Christ Jesus.

14I hope to come to you soon, but I am writing these instructions to you so that, ¹⁵if I am delayed, you may know how one ought to behave in the household of God, which is the church of the living God, the pillar and bulwark of the truth. ¹⁶Without any doubt, the mystery of our religion is great:

He[b] was revealed in flesh,
    vindicated[c] in spirit,[d]
        seen by angels,
proclaimed among Gentiles,
    believed in throughout the world,
        taken up in glory.

a Gk be husbands of one wife   b Gk Who; other ancient authorities read God; others, Which   c Or justified   d Or by the Spirit

COMMENTARY

The concern for good order continues to direct the train of thought. Just as good order in the state (2:1-2) led into thoughts of good order in the household (2:9-15), so also that leads into thoughts of good order in the church (3:1-13). The transition would be all the more understandable for the author and his first readers, since, as already noted (see the Commentary on 2:11-12), the first churches all met in members' homes. Almost inevitably, therefore, the norms of good order within the home became the model for good order within the church and for the good order of their regular gatherings. This was already implicit in the restricted role allowed for wives (2:11-12), but the pattern now becomes explicit in the criteria for identifying those fit to take up the roles of overseer (3:4-5) and deacon (3:12).

The other criteria are an instructive mixture. Grosser acts or habits of intemperance (3:3, 8) would obviously rule someone out. Ability to teach (3:2) and clarity as to what "the mystery of the faith" consisted of (3:9) would also be expected, though at this point they are given little prominence. Hospitality (3:2) was widely recog-

nized as a desirable and commendable social tradition. More striking is the indication that remarriage was frowned on (3:2, 12) and the indication that commensurate standards of behavior were expected of the candidate's wife (3:11). Most striking of all is the other string of words that begin the curriculum vitae expected of the would-be overseer (3:2) and the criterion that brings the paragraph to a close (3:7). Here again prominence is given to the impression made on others, the public face of the church: "without reproach, temperate, moderate, respectable" (3:2; the last two words echoing those in 2:9); "having a good testimony from those outside" (3:7). We are already in a church for which the good opinion of the wider community was important (see also 5:14; 6:1; Titus 2:5, 8, 10).

The final paragraph (3:14-16) confirms both the concern for good order ("how to behave in . . . the church," 3:15) and the household as the model for that good order ("the household of God, which is the church," 3:15). Somewhat late in the day (cf. 2:4-6 and 2:13-14; but note 3:9), the author recalls that the most fundamental issue is that of truth (3:15) and that the whole depends on and is intended to serve the mystery of piety and its confession (3:16).

3:1-7, Overseers. The traditional verse division attached the "faithful saying" to the following instructions regarding overseers (v. 1), and this remains the majority opinion among commentators. But a reference back to a statement regarding salvation (2:15) makes better sense (see Commentary on 1:15), whereas use of the formula to boost the emerging ecclesiastical structure (v. 1) would be without parallel.[57] At the same time the aspiration (lit., stretching oneself or stretching out one's hand) for the role of overseer is commended as being one of the "fine/good works" to which believers should aspire. The singular need not imply that a single overseer in each place was meant.

The term ἐπισκοπή (*episkopē;* NRSV, "bishop"; NIV, "overseer") itself derives from the idea of a "visitation" to bring about good (e.g., Gen 50:24-25; Job 10:12; Wis 3:13; Luke 1:68, 78; 1 Pet 2:12), but already it had been extended to denote the regular function or office that had such oversight as its function (Num 4:16; Acts 1:20).[58] Ministries designated as "overseers" had already been in operation in Philippi (Phil 1:1); no hint is given regarding their function in that letter, though it is often assumed that they would have been financial officers (cf. Phil 4:10-18). Acts 20:28 envisages "overseers" as a function of "elders" appointed by Paul from the beginning (Acts 14:23), but most think Luke is at least giving greater formality to what had been much less clearly defined or designated ministries (cf. Titus 1:5-7). At any rate, whatever the precedents, vv. 2-7 are certainly the first clear attempt to define such ministry as an "office," with clearly identified conditions of candidature and some outline of responsibilities expected (hospitable, a good teacher and manager of the church as one would manage a household; cf Titus 1:7). Since the *paterfamilias* had such great authority, the model

of the household implies an analogous weight of authority being granted to the overseer.

With v. 2 a rule begins to be formulated: "it is necessary that . . ." (as in Titus 1:7 NRSV, "Now a bishop must be . . ."). The first criterion is that the overseer must be "blameless, without reproach"; the word ἀνεπίλημπτος (*anepilēmptos*) is used only in 1 Timothy, of widows (5:7) and of Timothy himself (6:14). More curious is the second: "the husband of but one wife," which can hardly be taken to imply that polygamy was otherwise acceptable (cf. 5:9; presumably there was no thought that a woman could be polygamous), presumably means that widowers who aspired to oversee could not marry again. The logic here is unclear (Marriage should be for life? see 5:11-12), but still today the rule is maintained within the Orthodox Church. The third criterion, "temperate" (νηφάλιος *nēphalios*, v. 11; Titus 2:2), may reflect the more particular sense of temperance in drinking (cf. v. 3), so "sober," "clear-headed," "self-controlled." The next two words echo those used of wives in 2:9, "moderate," "respectable" (σώφρων *sōphrōn*, κόσμιος *kosmios*), with the same implication of making a good impression on outsiders looking to criticize. "Hospitality" (φιλόξενος *philoxenos;* again in adjectival form in Titus 1:8 and as a verb in 1 Tim 5:10) was a much-approved social grace (Rom 12:13; Heb 13:2; 1 Pet 4:9); travelers abroad would regularly look to countrymen or fellow believers for bed and board, especially since the available inns were frequently dangerous and usually full of bedbugs. Almost surprising in a list of such social talents comes "skillfull in teaching" (elsewhere only in 2 Tim 2:24); the role of the overseer as the acceptable public face of the church was evidently of greater importance than his role as instructor in faith!

With v. 3 the checklist takes an almost surreal turn: not a "drunkard, addicted to wine," not a "bully, pugnacious" (both elsewhere only in Titus 1:7), but "gentle, yielding" and "peaceable," literally "without fighting" (both again in Titus 3:2), "not a lover of money, greedy" (otherwise only Heb 13:5). But we recall that these were still frontier days for many of these new churches; pugnacious and combative characters could commend themselves to positions of leadership; positions of relative power and responsibility could quickly be undermined by drink or financial ir-

---

57. However, the weakly attested variant—"This is a human/popular saying"—may have originated as a marginal note by a sarcastic scribe less enamored of the office of bishop.

58. There is no reason why the office should be derived from the Qumran *mebaqqer* as such, a popular suggestion in the early days following the discovery of the Dead Sea Scrolls. The comparable responsibilities (so far as they are indicated) are quite different. The emergence of such leadership is more or less a sociological inevitability, whatever the theological rationalization.

regularity (cf. 1 Cor 11:20-21). Paul himself was evidently suspected of financial irregularities (2 Cor 8:20-21; 12:14-18), and it would certainly not be the last time that a bishop acted as a bully.

With vv. 4-5 it becomes evident that the meeting of the church in households was becoming the church as a household. In a so far not very effective or clear job description (vv. 2-3), the role of *paterfamilias* in a properly ordered household was the most obvious role model for an overseer. The key term προΐστημι (*proistēmi*), used twice in the two verses (also in v. 12; 5:17; Titus 3:8, 14), means literally "place or stand before," with the double overtone of "give leadership to" and "take initiative on behalf of," so "be concerned about, care for." Either or both senses may be present in Rom 12:8 and 1 Thess 5:12; in v. 4 the initial thought is of firm leadership (linked to "keeping children in submission"), but in v. 5 "giving leadership to his own household" is set in parallel to "caring for God's church" (using a verb used elsewhere only in Luke 10:34-35). Again the idea of "keeping a child in submission" is jarring to modern ears but was in accordance with accepted parental wisdom well into the twentieth century ("Spare the rod and spoil the child"). Again, as with deacons in v. 8, their wives in v. 11, and earlier the wish for all (2:2), the desirable characteristic of such leadership is "dignity, respectfulness" (this last phrase probably continues the description of the overseer's attitude and conduct, not that of his children, as the NIV and the NRSV take it).

The leader must not be "a recent convert" (v. 6). The danger is that someone thus inexperienced would become conceited or be blinded by authority and act foolishly (the word νεόφυτος [*neophytos*] can have both meanings; it is used only in the Pastorals, here and in 6:4; 2 Tim 3:4), or that an untried convert could blind believers by his brilliant but superficial potential.[59] The counsel could be conventional wisdom, but suggests a young movement that had learned some harsh lessons; it would have been an attractive option in several circumstances to look to new converts of social standing and wealth to provide necessary leadership. To "fall into the condemnation of the

devil," perhaps, implies a reference to the pride that had brought down the kings of Babylon and Tyre (Isa 14:12-15; Ezekiel 28), and already applied to the fall of Satan.

Verse 7 is the most explicit appeal to the impression made on others by a church leader, with a repeated "it is necessary that" (as in v. 2). The criteria were not simply what pleased the church; the overseer had to be the sort of person who would command respect among nonbelievers, and who would match up to the criteria of what was generally acknowledged to be "good" standards and conduct (cf. 6:2). Otherwise he would be vulnerable to the reproach and the traps of the slanderer (διάβολος *diabolos;* lit., "devil," but here probably playing on the alternative sense of "slanderer," as more often in the Pastorals; see v. 11; 2 Tim 3:3; Titus 2:3). Where a leader does not measure up to the highest standards of public esteem, he is vulnerable to malicious gossip and attack.

3:8-13, Deacons. The term used in this case, διάκονος (*diakonos*), often retains overtones of its original sense, "waiter at table" (as in John 2:5, 9) and so "servant." Jesus could be so described (Rom 15:8), an echo presumably of such traditions as Mark 9:35; 10:43-45. It was initially used to identify the character of ministry, rather than the ministry as such (e.g., 1 Cor 3:5; 2 Cor 6:4; Col 1:7, 23, 25; 1 Tim 4:6). The sense of "waiting at tables" invites a reference to Acts 6:1-6, but the term is not actually used there. It had, however, already been used more as a title in Rom 16:1 and Phil 1:1. Here the process is taken a step further, and an office of deacon emerges, with similar criteria for candidature and again little indication of responsibilities expected to be borne.

The specific instruction again begins with the ruling (implied): "It is necessary that . . ." (v. 8). As with the overseers, the first criterion is "respectable, dignified, serious" (the adjective related to the noun first used in 2:2), but again we should recall that it was of major importance for these new little churches to gain wider respect within the cities where they lived and met. "Not double-tongued" is clear enough, though it is discouraging that such had to be among the first requirements. Even more so are the next two—"not addicted to much wine, not fond of dishonest

---

59. Lucian (2nd century) mocks Christians for being thus duped by the impressive sham Peregrinus, who, having started as a Cynic philosopher, was attracted for a time to Christianity, in which he quickly became a highly esteemed figure. See Lucian *Passing of Peregrinus* 11-13, 16.

gain/greedy for money." The instruction is much the same as that in v. 3 and Titus 1:7. What a range of possible candidates for these roles that such instruction had to be given!

The most distinctively theological criterion in the whole chapter appears in v. 9: "holding the mystery of the faith with a clean conscience." The term "mystery" (μυστήριον *mystērion*) had been Paul's way of speaking about the great revelation (given to him in particular) that Gentiles were to be included with Jews in the saving purposes of God (Rom 11:25; Eph 3:3-9; Col 1:26-27). Here it is linked with "the faith," now evidently understood as a fuller statement of what Christians were to believe (see footnote 9). So presumably the thought is either still of the gospel as a hidden mystery revealed in Christ (cf. v. 16), or it is becoming more like the later sense of "the faith" as ultimately mysterious and, therefore, requiring someone skilled in understanding and exposition to unveil it to initiates. Not that the deacons are necessarily to fill that role (but see v. 13); here it is sufficient that they hold to that mystery—that is, affirm their commitment to the faith despite its mysterious quality and do so wholeheartedly, without undue qualms of conscience (see Commentary on 1:5). Confidence of faith was thus established as a crucial characteristic of leadership from very early on.

Equally striking is the counsel that deacons should "first be tested," and only if proved "blameless" should they serve (v. 10). The need for such testing was from early on (1 Thess 5:21) required by Paul as a way of preventing abuse of charismatic ministry (cf. 1 Cor 12:10; 14:29). Here the principle is extended to more established ministries. What the testing consisted of is not indicated (Are vv. 8-12 such a checklist?), nor is it clear whether a sort of probationary period for would-be deacons is intended.

Another puzzle is whether we should translate v. 11 as "likewise women" or "likewise their wives." The former is certainly possible, in view of Rom 16:1, and need not clash with 2:12 if "deacon" was a post of administrative responsibility (as in a well-ordered household) but not teaching responsibility.[60] The latter would indicate an

early case of husbands' prospects for advancement being dependent on the behavior of their wives! Again the first word, σεμνός (*semnos*), is "respectable," "dignified," "serious" (as in v. 8). "Devils" (διαβόλους *diabolous*) should obviously be taken in its alternative sense of "slanderous." That they should be "temperate" was also required of overseers (v. 2). After such a list, "faithful in all things" comes closer to what might be found in an equivalent list today.

With v. 12 the criteria of "once married" and "experienced in good household management" again come to the fore (as in vv. 2, 4-5). Marriage and the household were seen as good testing grounds of leadership or ministry potential, and the degree to which administration of the church was being modeled on good household management is again evident.

Verse 13 gives the reason why the church had to be so choosy about its deacons—not least for their own sake: To serve well was to gain for oneself a "good step"—that is, presumably a step forward. The term βαθμὸν καλόν (*bathmon kalon*, "good or excellent standing") may indicate a step of advancement within "the mystery of the faith" (vv. 9, 16) or even a "stage or rank." The imagery, somewhat unnervingly, may be akin to a stage in further initiation into the deeper mysteries of a cult. But a further factor was that those who served well could have "much boldness or confidence in faith" (cf. 2 Cor 3:12; Eph 3:12), again described as "faith in Christ Jesus" (as in 1:14). Or perhaps we should translate it as "much openness [in speaking], frankness or plainness of speech" (cf. Eph 6:19). In that case, somewhat surprisingly (cf. Acts 6:2), deacons were thought to have an important teaching ministry, into the deeper mysteries of the faith (though it is worth noting that in Acts 6–8 the ministries of Stephen and Philip soon became much more focused on teaching and evangelism than on administration).

3:14-16, The Reason for These Instructions. The instructions were intended as a substitute for Paul's personal presence (vv. 14-15). Paul's record of delay and disappointment in his planned visits would have been well known (e.g., Rom 1:13; 2 Cor 1:15-18), so that the letter became his principal means of giving advice and guidance. His frustrations over sailing schedules, bad weather, and repeated unexpected demands on

---

60. The syntax favors the identification. See J. H. Stiefel, "Women Deacons in 1 Timothy: A Linguistic and Literary Look at 'Women Likewise . . .' (1 Tim 3.11)," *NTS* 41 (1995) 442-57. Writing in 112 CE, Pliny, governor of Bithynia, refers to two Christians as "maids who were called ministers/deacons." See Pliny *Letters* 10.96.

his time have thus brought unexpected benefit to subsequent generations and successors to the churches he founded. It was natural, then, that a letter should still function as the voice of the great, but absent, apostle.

The concern is that the recipients might know how it was "necessary" (δει *dei;* the same term as in v. 2 and implied in v. 8) for believers to conduct themselves within "the household of God" (v. 15). The phrase partly echoes the idea of the Temple as "the house of God" (reflected in 1 Pet 2:5). But in this case, the thought is almost certainly more of "house" as "household" = family (as the preceding usages in vv. 4-5, 12 surely indicate). The ambiguity of "church" meeting in a "house" (not dissimilar to the ambiguity of "house/Temple") reinforces the point, emerging throughout the chapter, that structures of good household management should provide the model for the ordering of the church.[61] In this case, it is "the household of God" that is in view; in this household, the real *paterfamilias* is God, from whom all authority ultimately derives and with whom all authority ultimately rests.

The ambiguity is carried forward into the next phrase (v. 15), where the echo of OT usage continues. "The church of Yahweh" was a familiar description of the assembly of Israel (e.g., Num 16:3; Deut 23:1-3, 8; Mic 2:5),[62] and "the living God" characterized the Jewish conviction that all other gods were dead idols (cf. 2 Cor 6:16; 1 Thess 1:9). "Pillar and foundation" sustains the image of a building and in the sequence of imagery would again probably evoke thought of the Temple (cf. Rev 3:12). It was a high claim for themselves that these little churches around the edge of the Mediterranean made for themselves: They were God's family, in direct continuity with the Israel of the one Lord God. It was this conviction that bolstered their claim to have "the truth" (see footnote 9), to have been given such a firm insight into and grasp of the true state of affairs.

This truth is then summed up in what appears to be a hymnic form, which encapsulates "the mystery" of God's purpose as it has been revealed to them in Christ (v. 16; see Commentary on 3:9). Here it is described as "the mystery of the piety," where εὐσέβεια (*eusebeia;* see Commentary on 2:2) seems to epitomize the new Christian religion as a whole. The parallel with the populist acclamation in Ephesus, "Great is Artemis of the Ephesians" (Acts 19:28, 34), raises the intriguing possibility that this was intended as a Christian parallel and as a response to the dominant piety of Ephesus.

The six lines cited are one of the clearest examples of an early Christian hymn:[63] Christ is not even mentioned—the referent of the familiar lines needs no fuller identification (there is no antecedent to the opening "who");[64] the lines are set out in parallel passive phrases with "in" and the dative (only the third line omits the "in"); and they are structured in antithetical couplets in which the nouns ("flesh/spirit," "angels/nations" [the term can be translated "Gentiles" (NRSV), but the NIV's "nations" is preferable], "world/glory") are more determinative than the verbs, only the first of which ("revealed") links into the theology elsewhere in the Pastorals (cf. 2 Tim 1:10; Titus 1:3). The epigrammatic form makes for some awkward sense, particularly the second line (lit., "justified in spirit"), but the antithesis is clearly between Christ's pre-Easter earthly existence and his post-Easter exaltation (cf. 1 Pet 3:18). To look for greater precision of meaning in such a tight epigrammatic structure would be most unwise. The other lines probably do not form a chronological account but simply juxtapose Christ's increasing missionary impact on earth with his triumphal reception in heaven. Here is the faith to be preached and believed, the truth on whose foundation the household of God was being built: It is Christ.

---

61. This is the key thematic text for D. C. Verner, *The Household of God: The Social World of the Pastoral Epistles,* SBLDS 71 (Chico, Calif.: Scholars Press, 1983) 107-11.

62. The Greek term ἐκκλησία (*ekklēsia*), in the NT usually translated "church," is used about 100 times in the LXX.

63. A fuller treatment may be found in R. H. Gundry, "The Form, Meaning, and Background of the Hymn Quoted in 1 Timothy 3:16," in *Apostolic History and the Gospel,* F. F. Bruce Festschrift, ed. W. W. Gasque and R. P. Martin (Grand Rapids: Eerdmans, 1970) 203 22.

64. The lack of identification prompted some scribes to tidy up the Greek, including the reading of "God" (θεός *theos*) instead of "who" (ὅς *hos*).

REFLECTIONS

The linking word in this chapter is *household.* Its effect is to set the church in a double relation—on the one hand to the well-ordered family, and on the other hand to the Israel of old. Both are fundamental to the church's identity, and awareness of that double identity is fundamental to the church's well-being.

On the one hand, it is important to note here how natural it is that family and church are not set in opposition to each other, or that one is not posed as a threat to the other. Such opposition seems to be implied in some of Jesus' statements (e.g., Mark 3:31-35; Luke 14:26), and the challenge to discipleship and the missionary call will often mean hard choices between priorities. But the hyperbole of Jesus' teaching should not be made a rule; not all people were to leave home and literally follow him. His commendation of the fifth command is unreserved (Mark 7:9-13), and the prodigal son's leaving home is an antitype of discipleship (Luke 15:11-32). Despite some misunderstanding, Paul's commendation of marriage and the priority he gives to children's welfare should be clear enough in 1 Cor 7:3-5, 12-14, 36-38 (so also 1 Tim 4:3).

Here, however, the point is still clearer: The well-ordered family is the pattern for the well-ordered church (see also 5:1-2, 4, 8); those who are not good and effective husbands and fathers (3:4-5, 12) should not be expected to provide good and effective leadership in the church. As with the issue of husbands and wives (2:11-15), we should not confuse the form of that good management, as it was then conceived, with the principle here expressed. The language of "submission" (2:11; 3:4) reflects the conventional wisdom of the day, not a divinely instituted order. The principle remains that the family structure (here only husbands and wives, parents and children, are in view) provides a positive analogy to the structure of the church (see also Reflections at 2:8-15). It should be added, however, that the traditional family structure is only an analogy and that this analogy does not give grounds, for example, for debarring single persons from positions of church leadership. Other analogies (e.g., shepherd, servant, gardener) that indicate otherwise can easily be called upon.

It also follows that models for discipleship that set church and family in antithesis should be regarded as suspect. It would be odd, indeed, if the basic unit of society (the family) were seen, as a structural unit, to be hostile to the church, as though the church were a revolutionary structure that overturned and replaced any other; individual cases of conflict do not overturn the more fundamental principle. If 1 Timothy 3 has continuing relevance, then, the family itself is to be seen as the primary force for nurturing of discipleship and the primary arena for discipleship, and as such it should be the proving ground for the church in discipline and order.[65]

What could be taken for granted, then, when the church met in a house and the relationships and ordering of the one blended into the other, needs to be restated in terms more meaningful to the mobile society and transient groupings of today. It would be a pity if all that resulted was negative criticism of one-parent families, divorces, families in which both parents pursued professional careers, as compared with an older ideal of family (as though that ideal had ever been fully realized); or if church fellowship was presented as a replacement for family (on the ground that some families are dysfunctional); or if the teaching was set aside because it did not apply equally to all church members. Discussion time would be better spent asking how far the positive principles implicit in this section can be safeguarded and promoted, given and within the changing circumstances of today.

The link implied by church—*ekklēsia*—the assembly of Israel, also needs fuller rethinking. For centuries the church has seen itself as replacing historic Israel, much as some have seen the church replacing the historic family unit. The long-term result has been centuries of

---

65. I am indebted here to my wife's thesis. See M. Dunn, "The Place of Family in Discipleship" (Ph.D. diss., Durham University, 1988).

anti-Semitism, culminating in the Holocaust. But now in the revulsion against that tragic history, Paul's attempt to hold together church and Israel (Gal 6:16), Gentile and Jewish believers as together constituting the called people of God (Rom 9:24-29; 11:17-24) is being heard afresh. That is what lies behind the merging of household into house of God, into pillar and foundation of God's Temple (3:15). It is only as the church understands itself in terms of Israel and in direct continuity with Israel (cf. Romans 9–11; Gal 6:16; see also Titus 2:14) that it can begin to understand itself, its Lord (Messiah Jesus), and three-quarters of its Bible (the OT)!

Within this alternate imagery it is striking that the functionaries named are not "priest" or "high priest," but "overseer" and "deacon." Continuity there may be, but not in the central office-bearers and functionaries of Israel's Temple. The functions, so far as they can be determined, are contained in the names themselves—to keep an eye out for good, to serve. To that extent, we may say that these functions are every bit as charismatic (engraced and enabled by God's Spirit) as those more explicitly so in Paul's earlier conception of church ministry (Rom 12:6-8; 1 Cor 12:4-11, 28). That is to say, they are ill-defined as to specific function, since their specific function was determined by the motivation expressed in their names.

Coordinate with that is the weight of the writer's concern in describing the criteria for candidates for such office—little or no anxiety about what we would call theological training or administrative expertise, but concern for character and for a life that would justifiably be respected by others. One may wonder at several items in these lists of criteria, but the priorities, particularly in recently formed groups, probably strange in character to their neighbors, are worth noting. Here again the church, and not least the much more established churches of the early twenty-first century, is bidden to pause and take fresh thought about such matters. Have character and motivation, for example, as criteria of function, become too lost to sight behind procedural rules and political considerations, as determinants for office?

1 TIMOTHY 4:1-16, THE TWO WAYS

NIV

4 The Spirit clearly says that in later times some will abandon the faith and follow deceiving spirits and things taught by demons. [2]Such teachings come through hypocritical liars, whose consciences have been seared as with a hot iron. [3]They forbid people to marry and order them to abstain from certain foods, which God created to be received with thanksgiving by those who believe and who know the truth. [4]For everything God created is good, and nothing is to be rejected if it is received with thanksgiving, [5]because it is consecrated by the word of God and prayer.

[6]If you point these things out to the brothers, you will be a good minister of Christ Jesus, brought up in the truths of the faith and of the good teaching that you have followed. [7]Have nothing to do with godless myths and old wives'

NRSV

4 Now the Spirit expressly says that in later[a] times some will renounce the faith by paying attention to deceitful spirits and teachings of demons, [2]through the hypocrisy of liars whose consciences are seared with a hot iron. [3]They forbid marriage and demand abstinence from foods, which God created to be received with thanksgiving by those who believe and know the truth. [4]For everything created by God is good, and nothing is to be rejected, provided it is received with thanksgiving; [5]for it is sanctified by God's word and by prayer.

[6]If you put these instructions before the brothers and sisters,[b] you will be a good servant[c] of Christ Jesus, nourished on the words of the faith and of the sound teaching that you have followed. [7]Have nothing to do with profane myths and old

[a] Or the last   [b] Gk brothers   [c] Or deacon

NIV

tales; rather, train yourself to be godly. [8]For physical training is of some value, but godliness has value for all things, holding promise for both the present life and the life to come.

[9]This is a trustworthy saying that deserves full acceptance [10](and for this we labor and strive), that we have put our hope in the living God, who is the Savior of all men, and especially of those who believe.

[11]Command and teach these things. [12]Don't let anyone look down on you because you are young, but set an example for the believers in speech, in life, in love, in faith and in purity. [13]Until I come, devote yourself to the public reading of Scripture, to preaching and to teaching. [14]Do not neglect your gift, which was given you through a prophetic message when the body of elders laid their hands on you.

[15]Be diligent in these matters; give yourself wholly to them, so that everyone may see your progress. [16]Watch your life and doctrine closely. Persevere in them, because if you do, you will save both yourself and your hearers.

NRSV

wives' tales. Train yourself in godliness, [8]for, while physical training is of some value, godliness is valuable in every way, holding promise for both the present life and the life to come. [9]The saying is sure and worthy of full acceptance. [10]For to this end we toil and struggle,[a] because we have our hope set on the living God, who is the Savior of all people, especially of those who believe.

[11]These are the things you must insist on and teach. [12]Let no one despise your youth, but set the believers an example in speech and conduct, in love, in faith, in purity. [13]Until I arrive, give attention to the public reading of scripture,[b] to exhorting, to teaching. [14]Do not neglect the gift that is in you, which was given to you through prophecy with the laying on of hands by the council of elders.[c] [15]Put these things into practice, devote yourself to them, so that all may see your progress. [16]Pay close attention to yourself and to your teaching; continue in these things, for in doing this you will save both yourself and your hearers.

[a] Other ancient authorities read *suffer reproach* [b] Gk *to the reading*
[c] Gk *by the presbytery*

COMMENTARY

Chapter 4 broadly follows a pattern of exhortation with ancient precedents, in Jewish tradition already quite elaborate in Deuteronomy 28–30. The speaker sets before his audience two paths, between which they have to choose, or two prospects, one of which will be realized, depending on how they respond to the speaker's challenge. The classic Christian examples are Matt 7:13-14 and the early second-century church manual, *Didache* 1–6. Here the indicative terms are "later times" and "depart from" (4:1); "follow" (4:6); "train yourself" (4:7-8); "promise of life" (4:8); "strive," "hope" (4:10); "progress" (4:15); and "you will save" (4:16). The first alternative is characterized by talk of "deceitful spirits" and "demons" (4:1); "hypocrisy of liars" and "seared conscience" (4:2); "godless and silly myths" (4:7); and, by implication, general slackness and lack of discipline (4:7-8, 10, 15). The second alternative, to which the writer wishes to point his hearers,

is characterized by "thanksgiving," "believing and knowing the truth" (4:3-4); "word of God and prayer" (4:5); "words of faith and of the good teaching" (4:6); "godliness" (4:7-8); "hope in God" and "believe" (4:10); "love, faith, purity" (4:12); "reading, encouraging, teaching" (4:13, 16); and "charism" (4:14). The contrast is stated sharply for effect, the former set out in pejorative terms, the latter in bland assertions; but sufficient detail is included to enable the reader to perceive that recognizable life-styles were in view.

4:1-5, The Wrong Way. The prospect of defection is held out as a certainty. It had been explicitly stated by the Spirit (v. 1). The reference is presumably either to the familiar scenario of immense suffering and persecution to be experienced by the faithful in the last days of the present age, or to a particular prophetic utterance elaborating the prospect in more detail. The prediction had been a feature in Jewish apocalyptic more or less since Dan 12:1-2. In Christian tradition, something similar is attributed to Jesus (Mark 13:5-6, 13, 19-22) and to Paul (Acts 20:29-30; 2 Thess 2:3-12), and the same foreboding is expressed in Revelation (e.g., Rev 2:5, 16; 14:9-12). The implication is that the writer understands his present as already "the last days."

The key word here, ἀφίστημι (aphistēmi), can be translated as "fall away," "become apostate," "desert" (NIV, "abandon"; NRSV, "renounce"), and is regularly used in the LXX of falling away from God (e.g., Deut 32:15; Jer 3:14; 1 Macc 1:15). There was a real choice to be made here, and given the volatility and lack of clear boundaries around the young churches, there would be considerable crossing of these boundaries, outward as well as inward (see Reflections on 1:1-11). The concern here, then, is to firm up the commitment and resolve of such recruits by painting the alternative in apocalyptic colors (cf. references to Daniel 12; Mark 13; 2 Thessalonians 2; and Revelation above).

The immediate contrast is between "the faith" and "deceitful spirits and teachings of demons." Presumably prophecies within or without the Christian assemblies are in view (cf. 2 Thess 2:2; 2 Pet 2:1; 1 John 4:1-3), promoting views that the writer saw as contrary to "the faith." The problem of false prophecy is an old one within the Judeo-Christian tradition (see, e.g., 1 Kings 22; Jeremiah 28; 1 Thess 5:19-22; Didache 11; Justin Dialogue with Trypho 82), though the earlier Paul was less disposed to attribute to false spirits and demons those prophecies that were to be rejected (see 1 Cor 10:20-21; 12:10). An example of such teaching supported by prophecy will be provided in 4:3, but it should be noted that the charismatic character of the earlier Pauline churches (1 Cor 14:26-32; 1 Thess 5:19-22) still persisted. The firmer structures of organization and formulation of "the faith" had presumably been found necessary, in part at least against the dangers of charismatic excess and false prophecy.

Verse 2 is a good example of polemical denigration. Those who depart from "the faith" for such reasons have simply succumbed to "the hypocritical preaching of liars whose own consciences have been seared" (lit., branded with a red-hot iron and thus desensitized).[66] The imagery evoked is vivid, but we should recall that it is coined by one who disagreed violently with the opinions expressed.

An example of such false teaching backed by prophetic utterance is the advocacy of an ascetic life-style: marriage forbidden and abstinence from certain foods advocated (v. 3). Similar issues had troubled the church in Corinth—regarding marriage (1 Cor 7:1)[67] and over the eating of meat offered to idols (1 Corinthians 8)—though in the latter case the principal problem was with those who thought it perfectly acceptable to eat such food (see Col 2:20-23). The advice here follows that in 1 Corinthians 7 and the theological logic of 1 Cor 10:25-26: Whatever has been created by God is good (Genesis 1).[68] The faithful, by definition, should know this truth, their consciences being instructed in the faith. The practical test is the same as in the nearest equivalent passage, Rom 14:6: Can the one who eats, acting in a way that seems overindulgent to others in the church, give thanks to God in doing so (v. 3)? The answer here is yes; the acceptability of a controversial life-style to God is more determinative than its acceptability to fellow church members.

The point is repeated in strong terms to reinforce it: "Everything created by God is fine and nothing need be rejected if it is received with thanksgiving, for then it is consecrated through the word of God and prayer" (vv. 4-5). That the rationale is essentially theological ("faith," "truth," "made by God," "word of God," "prayer"), and not simply freedom of the individual or liberty of opinion, should be noted.

4:6-10, The Right Way. The alternative is to be clearly taught by Timothy (v. 6). This is a primary responsibility of the "fine minister of Christ Jesus"; the term used is again διάκονος (diakonos, "minister," "one who serves"), underlining its still functional and not yet exclusively formal sense (as in 3:8-13; cf. 1:12; 2 Tim 4:5,

---

66. J. N. D. Kelly, The Pastoral Epistles, Black's New Testament Commentaries (London: A. & C. Black, 1963) 94-95, marginally prefers the sense "branded" as an owner would brand a slave—that is, by the "deceitful spirits" and "demons" of 4:2.

67. It is generally agreed that in 1 Cor 7:1b Paul quotes a letter he received from the Corinthians.

68. "A more powerful statement on the goodness of the created order would be hard to find," L. T. Johnson, Letters to Paul's Delegates: 1 Timothy, 2 Timothy, Titus, The New Testament in Context (Valley Forge: Trinity Press International, 1996) 164.

11; this was its more typical earlier use; cf. Rom 15:8; 1 Cor 3:5; 2 Cor 3:6; 6:4; 11:15, 23; Gal 2:17; 1 Thess 3:2). Here the idea of a way of discipleship comes more clearly to the fore, mingled with the earlier family imagery: Timothy has been "nourished, brought up"—that is, within "the household of God" (3:15)—and has "followed faithfully" (see Commentary on 2 Tim 3:10) "the words of the faith and the good teaching." The doubling up of two of the letters' most consistent terms to denote the body of teaching that had already been formulated as "Christian" (see footnote 9) makes clear the character and direction of the second alternative, the right way, being advocated. Again the impression is clearly given that within the relative amorphousness of the early Christian communities it soon became necessary to agree on and formulate more carefully defined statements of faith and more elaborate codes of acceptable conduct, presumably in order to give a sharper sense of Christian identity and a clearer boundary line over against wider society. In the Pastorals we see this process happening before our eyes.

In sharp contrast, the wrong-way alternative can be dismissed as "profane" (the same word appeared in the vice list in 1:9) and "old wives' tales [myths]" (v. 7), the latter phrase having the same disparaging overtone as today (see Commentary on 1:4). To avoid these requires strict self-discipline, which the writer clearly sees to be distinct from the asceticism of v. 3, in content, character, and goal.[69] The image now switches to the athlete's training (v. 8), an image much loved by Paul (1 Cor 9:24-25; Phil 3:13-14). If that is of some profit (as would be generally agreed), then training for "godliness" (the regular term of approbation in the Pastorals; see the Commentary on 2:2) is of profit for everything. The promise is not simply of the victor's wreath in the games, but of life both now and in the age to come (cf. 1:16; 6:12, 19; 2 Tim 1:1, 10; Titus 1:2; 3:7). The writer is so confident of the truth of his conviction that he designates it also a "faithful saying and worthy of all acceptance" (v. 9). Some think "the faithful saying" refers to what follows, but v. 8b has the more formulaic character (see the Commentary on 1:15).

With the age-old religious instinct to set this present life and its circumstances into a long-term context, the writer reaffirms the goal of godliness: a hope that looks for a salvation beyond the limits of current experience (v. 10). The thought is still of the discipline required: "for this cause we work hard and exert ourselves" (ἀγωνιζόμεθα, agōnizometha as in the agōn, "athletic contest").[70] "Hope," as almost always in the NT, is the confident Hebrew assurance, rather than the tentative Greek aspiration (cf. Rom 5:2-5; 8:24; Gal 5:5; Col 1:5), the Hebrew character of the thought reinforced by a further reference to "the living God" (see Commentary on 3:15) as the guarantor of the hope.

The hope arises out of the conviction that God is "Savior" (v. 10). Elsewhere in the Pastorals (see Commentary on 1:1), the thought is always of "our Savior," whether in reference to God or to Christ Jesus. But here the note of universalism, first loudly struck in 2:4-6 (see also Titus 2:11), is sounded again: "Savior of everyone." The additional phrase, "especially believers," sounds odd and has occasioned much discussion: Does it qualify the note of universalism? Presumably it is intended primarily to underline the confidence of the writer's hope: If God is Savior of everyone, then those of faith in God can be all the more confident that they will share in God's salvation.

4:11-16, Timothy as an Example. The role envisaged for Timothy becomes clearer: He receives instruction from Paul and passes it on with authority to instruct and to teach (v. 11). How someone should be described who commands overseers and deacons is not made clear. The writer is content to leave the impression, here and elsewhere, that Timothy is Paul's personal representative and emissary. So the authority with which Timothy teaches is that of Paul himself, not that of a distinct rank or office.

The reference to Timothy's youth (v. 12) is somewhat surprising. At first encounter he is described in terms suggesting a fair degree of maturity (a disciple well spoken of, Acts 16:1-2). Since then he had functioned as Paul's chief aide for the rest of Paul's ministry (see Commentary on 1:2). That is, if the Pastorals do come from a

---

69. It is unlikely that the "bodily training" was intended as a disparaging reference to the asceticism of 4:3. See J. M. Bassler, *1 Timothy, 2 Timothy, Titus,* ANTC (Nashville: Abingdon, 1996) 84. See also Kelly, *The Pastoral Epistles,* 100.

70. There is a variant reading: "suffer reproach." It is not very strongly attested, but since "exert ourselves" is more appropriate to the context, perhaps the former was replaced by the latter.

late phase of Paul's ministry, then Timothy would have been Paul's chief coworker for about fifteen years. To call someone already into his thirties a "youth" would be unusual, and after such a period of training and responsibility, was anyone who respected Paul likely to question Timothy's authority? If, alternatively, the letter was written later, as seems more likely, and if Timothy himself was still in view, then he would probably have been in his fifties at least. It looks, then, as though the writer is working with an image of Timothy drawn from the earlier letters of Paul. Timothy, in other words, may here function as a representative model of the youthful leader, like the younger member of Paul's mission team of earlier years, someone whose charism or natural ability brought him to the forefront despite his youth. In an era that venerated the wisdom of age, such a one might well be "despised" (1 Cor 16:11, a different word, written at least ten years earlier). And though Paul never uses the word in reference to himself (cf. Rom 2:4; 1 Cor 11:22), there certainly were those operating within his churches who had scorned him in the past (e.g., 2 Cor 10:10).

The best way of answering such attacks would be for Timothy to show himself as a model worthy to be copied (v. 12). On several occasions Paul had put himself forward as an example (1 Cor 4:16; 11:1; Phil 3:17); it is interesting to note that in the first of these, Timothy is sent to remind the Corinthians of Paul's example (1 Cor 4:17). So now it is Timothy who is to provide exemplary leadership "in speech, in conduct, in love, in faith, in purity," the last probably with the sexual sense of "chastity" (cf. 5:2). Little is more destructive of community than authority of status not matched by quality of life.

With the instruction of v. 13, whether an epistolary characterization or a real visit in prospect, the function of the letter as the voice of the absent Paul is underlined. Paul's letters were often written to signal an imminent visit or a visit delayed (see Commentary on 3:14-16). "Until I come" can serve as a piece of advice that endures. "Reading" probably means public, rather than private, reading. This would certainly refer to the Scriptures,[71] but also to writings worthy to be read

in church and probably already also readings of Christian documents—early collections of Jesus tradition and Paul's own letters (cf. Col 4:16; 2 Pet 3:15-16). It was in this way that their authority grew and spread. Worth noting is the implied content of a Christian assembly and its variety: the drawing upon ancient scriptural writings and newer writings of recognized worth; encouragement as well as teaching, presumably on the basis of the reading (see Luke 4:17-21; Acts 13:15).

Timothy's authority is underlined by reference back to what is considered a particular commissioning event (v. 14). It evidently had three elements: the giving of his "charism," that is, presumably, by the Spirit (1 Cor 12:4-7, 11); a "prophecy" (prophetic utterance; cf. 1:18); and "the laying on of hands by the presbytery." The event is referred to again in 2 Tim 1:6, and the nearest parallel is the commissioning of Barnabas and Saul by the leaders of the Antioch church at the behest of the Spirit, presumably through prophetic utterance (Acts 13:2-3; cf. Acts 14:23). The whole event, however, seems to be envisaged in more formal terms. The "charism" seems now to be conceived of as a permanent gift that Timothy can "neglect" (v. 14) or can "rekindle" (2 Tim 1:6), whereas Paul's earlier thought was more in terms of charism as the enactment of grace, coming to visible manifestation in a particular utterance or act (Rom 12:4-8; 1 Cor 12:4-11). The laying on of hands as an act of the presbytery (council of elders) sounds like a more formally conceived and structured act, though in 2 Tim 1:6 Paul refers only to his own action, and here the preposition "with" implies attendant circumstances rather than means ("through," as in 2 Tim 1:6; but see Commentary on 2 Tim 2:2). In v. 14, we appear to be on the way to a concept of "ordination" and of charism as "grace of office."

That commission ("these things") once given has to be thought about, carefully cultivated, and practiced (the first verb, μελετάω [meletaō], has this range of meaning); "these things" (v. 15) presumably embraces all that had been referred to in vv. 11-14. The charism that is not exercised will wither. "Be in them"; we might say, "Immerse yourself in them." The personal objective is "progress" in "these things"; the term "progress" (προκοπη prokopē) was popular in Stoic philosophy, and Paul had used it in Phil 1:25 (cf.

---

71. Kelly notes that "Public reading in the ancient world called for some technical accomplishment, for the words in the codex were not divided." See Kelly, *The Pastoral Epistles,* 105.

Phil 1:12). The advice complements that of 1 Tim 4:12.

The most important yardstick is "the teaching" (v. 16): "Stick with that." It is that which will ensure salvation both for Timothy and for those whom he instructs in the teaching. Here again we see a deep concern to mark out and delimit the terms of the gospel, the faith, and to forge an exclusive link between that teaching and salvation. Down that track lies the old slogan, "Outside the church no salvation," with both its strengths and its weaknesses. The strength is that the teaching does encapsulate what Christians have found from the start to contain the words of life. The weakness is that salvation can be thought to be conditional on adherence to a particular set of words, first framed to meet certain historical challenges and interpreted in a narrow and insensitive way.

REFLECTIONS

The advantage of the "two ways" imagery is twofold. In the first place, it emphasizes that there is a choice to be made and that this choice will entail what may be lasting consequences. The vision of endless freedom and an infinite pluralism of "good" possibilities cloaks an uncomfortable fact, summed up in the old aphorism: We are free to choose, but we are not free to choose the consequences of our choice. Freedom to choose a particular career or to experiment with drugs or to throw off sexual restraint sets in motion a sequence of consequences from which it is impossible to escape and which will be character shaping as well as life-style constraining. And these are simply illustrations of the potentially far more momentous choice in regard to religion and faith, if indeed it is the case that a fundamental reality of human beings is that they are also spiritual beings made by God and for relationship with God.

This does not mean that such a momentous choice once made need never be made again. The reality is that there will always be some people, initially drawn to choose the best way, who will "fall away" by paying too much attention to what the writer calls "deceitful spirits" (the problem of false prophecy) and "hypocritical preaching of liars" (teaching proffered for factional or personal motives). Here as in other spheres, the price of liberty is eternal vigilance. In this often disturbing reality of enticing alternatives and clashing opinions, it is often vital to have a clear grasp of the basic principles and values on which the religion, the godly life, is built. In the case of the Pastorals, this means "the words of the faith and of the sound teaching." Few can live out of a faith outline as brief as "God is one; Jesus is Lord" (cf. Rom 10:9; 1 Cor 8:6). Most need something more. It is the task of leadership to indicate and define what that more should be, drawing not least from the reading of Scripture and previous tradition (4:13).

The danger on the other side is that such a statement of "the faith and the teaching" can become overdefined and too prescriptive. Here it is important to note the way the writer takes a firm stand on a principle of liberty in regard to one of the most contentious issues for the early churches: whether certain foods were prohibited to believers. In earlier days it had been a make-or-break issue; the very definition and status of "Jew" and "Christian" hung on it (1 Macc 2:62-63; Rom 14:3-4). In the light of such tradition, a cautious respondent would have been tempted to counsel, "If it's offensive to others, don't." But in this instance the writer follows the line of Paul's advice: "If you can give thanks to God in what you do and for what you do, then it is a consecrated act acceptable to God" (see 4:4-5; cf. Rom 14:6). In other words, the make-or-break issues for one need not be so for others or for the church as a whole. Discerning the difference is what marks out mature leadership.

In the second place, the image of a "way" is a reminder that the Christian life is not to be conceived as something static. This is often the hidden implication of alternative metaphors like "position" and "viewpoint." But the first formal title for Christianity seems to have been "the way" (Acts 9:2; 18:25-26; 19:9, 23; 22:4; 24:14, 22). And Paul's favorite image for Christian conduct is "walk," itself reflecting the traditional Jewish image הלך (*hālāk*, "walk"), from which the term *halakhah* ("rules for conduct") is derived. Here the point is evoked particularly by talk of "following" (v. 6) and "progress" (v. 15). The point is that the Christian life involves movement, growth (nurture, v. 6), development. Too often in Christian mission so much attention is given to conversion that the equally important development toward maturity is neglected.

The writer makes clear that such growth and development depend on training and the discipline involved (vv. 7-8); they involve hard work and sweat-inducing exertion (v. 10); they require cultivation of the gift given and committed personal involvement (v. 15). Here again a choice once made has to be repeatedly reaffirmed and lived out.

The imagery also provides another angle on "the faith" and "the teaching." The Pastorals can be too easily disparaged for their reliance upon a faith and teaching already formulated and prescribed. But it would be more fair to see this emphasis as a stage on the way to greater maturity (of individual and church). That is to say, "the faith/teaching" actually refers to the process of giving Christian identity greater clarity of definition. It is not an endpoint ("the faith" finally defined), but "faith seeking understanding."

Such progress in faith need not mean a steadily lengthening list of "what we believe and do" (even the more prescriptive tendency of rabbinic Judaism allowed for plenty of dissenting opinions). What it should mean is a greater appreciation of how faith responds to and impacts upon an increasing range of alternative ideologies and practical issues, a process that in turn should provide guidelines (not straitjackets) for future responses and objectives. To "do theology" is not simply to learn about past doctrines and classic statements of faith. It means still more to think through the reality of a living faith and to bring that reality (not just formulae and statements about faith) into dialogue with alternative views of reality, resulting in fresh formulations of the faith. A faith that does not grow and develop condemns itself to wither and die. *Tertium non datur:* There is no third alternative!

1 TIMOTHY 5:1–6:2, ON THE ELDERLY, WIDOWS, ELDERS, AND SLAVES

NIV	NRSV
5 Do not rebuke an older man harshly, but exhort him as if he were your father. Treat younger men as brothers, ²older women as mothers, and younger women as sisters, with absolute purity. ³Give proper recognition to those widows who are really in need. ⁴But if a widow has children or grandchildren, these should learn first of all to put their religion into practice by caring for their own family and so repaying their parents and grandparents, for this is pleasing to God. ⁵The widow who is really in need and left all alone puts her hope in God and continues night and	**5** Do not speak harshly to an older man,ᵃ but speak to him as to a father, to younger men as brothers, ²to older women as mothers, to younger women as sisters—with absolute purity. 3Honor widows who are really widows. ⁴If a widow has children or grandchildren, they should first learn their religious duty to their own family and make some repayment to their parents; for this is pleasing in God's sight. ⁵The real widow, left alone, has set her hope on God and continues in supplications and prayers night and day; ⁶but the widowᵇ who lives for pleasure is dead even

ᵃ Or an elder, or *a presbyter*   *ᵇ Gk she*

NIV

day to pray and to ask God for help. ⁶But the widow who lives for pleasure is dead even while she lives. ⁷Give the people these instructions, too, so that no one may be open to blame. ⁸If anyone does not provide for his relatives, and especially for his immediate family, he has denied the faith and is worse than an unbeliever.

⁹No widow may be put on the list of widows unless she is over sixty, has been faithful to her husband,ᵃ ¹⁰and is well known for her good deeds, such as bringing up children, showing hospitality, washing the feet of the saints, helping those in trouble and devoting herself to all kinds of good deeds.

¹¹As for younger widows, do not put them on such a list. For when their sensual desires overcome their dedication to Christ, they want to marry. ¹²Thus they bring judgment on themselves, because they have broken their first pledge. ¹³Besides, they get into the habit of being idle and going about from house to house. And not only do they become idlers, but also gossips and busybodies, saying things they ought not to. ¹⁴So I counsel younger widows to marry, to have children, to manage their homes and to give the enemy no opportunity for slander. ¹⁵Some have in fact already turned away to follow Satan.

¹⁶If any woman who is a believer has widows in her family, she should help them and not let the church be burdened with them, so that the church can help those widows who are really in need.

¹⁷The elders who direct the affairs of the church well are worthy of double honor, especially those whose work is preaching and teaching. ¹⁸For the Scripture says, "Do not muzzle the ox while it is treading out the grain,"ᵇ and "The worker deserves his wages."ᶜ ¹⁹Do not entertain an accusation against an elder unless it is brought by two or three witnesses. ²⁰Those who sin are to be rebuked publicly, so that the others may take warning.

²¹I charge you, in the sight of God and Christ Jesus and the elect angels, to keep these instructions without partiality, and to do nothing out of favoritism.

ᵃ9 Or *has had but one husband*   ᵇ18 Deut. 25:4   ᶜ18 Luke 10:7

NRSV

while she lives. ⁷Give these commands as well, so that they may be above reproach. ⁸And whoever does not provide for relatives, and especially for family members, has denied the faith and is worse than an unbeliever.

9Let a widow be put on the list if she is not less than sixty years old and has been married only once;ᵃ ¹⁰she must be well attested for her good works, as one who has brought up children, shown hospitality, washed the saints' feet, helped the afflicted, and devoted herself to doing good in every way. ¹¹But refuse to put younger widows on the list; for when their sensual desires alienate them from Christ, they want to marry, ¹²and so they incur condemnation for having violated their first pledge. ¹³Besides that, they learn to be idle, gadding about from house to house; and they are not merely idle, but also gossips and busybodies, saying what they should not say. ¹⁴So I would have younger widows marry, bear children, and manage their households, so as to give the adversary no occasion to revile us. ¹⁵For some have already turned away to follow Satan. ¹⁶If any believing womanᵇ has relatives who are really widows, let her assist them; let the church not be burdened, so that it can assist those who are real widows.

17Let the elders who rule well be considered worthy of double honor,ᶜ especially those who labor in preaching and teaching; ¹⁸for the scripture says, "You shall not muzzle an ox while it is treading out the grain," and, "The laborer deserves to be paid." ¹⁹Never accept any accusation against an elder except on the evidence of two or three witnesses. ²⁰As for those who persist in sin, rebuke them in the presence of all, so that the rest also may stand in fear. ²¹In the presence of God and of Christ Jesus and of the elect angels, I warn you to keep these instructions without prejudice, doing nothing on the basis of partiality. ²²Do not ordainᵈ anyone hastily, and do not participate in the sins of others; keep yourself pure.

23No longer drink only water, but take a little wine for the sake of your stomach and your frequent ailments.

ᵃ Gk *the wife of one husband*   ᵇ Other ancient authorities read *believing man or woman;* others, *believing man*   ᶜ Or *compensation*
ᵈ Gk *Do not lay hands on*

NIV

²²Do not be hasty in the laying on of hands, and do not share in the sins of others. Keep yourself pure.

²³Stop drinking only water, and use a little wine because of your stomach and your frequent illnesses.

²⁴The sins of some men are obvious, reaching the place of judgment ahead of them; the sins of others trail behind them. ²⁵In the same way, good deeds are obvious, and even those that are not cannot be hidden.

6 All who are under the yoke of slavery should consider their masters worthy of full respect, so that God's name and our teaching may not be slandered. ²Those who have believing masters are not to show less respect for them because they are brothers. Instead, they are to serve them even better, because those who benefit from their service are believers, and dear to them. These are the things you are to teach and urge on them.

NRSV

24The sins of some people are conspicuous and precede them to judgment, while the sins of others follow them there. ²⁵So also good works are conspicuous; and even when they are not, they cannot remain hidden.

6 Let all who are under the yoke of slavery regard their masters as worthy of all honor, so that the name of God and the teaching may not be blasphemed. ²Those who have believing masters must not be disrespectful to them on the ground that they are members of the church;ᵃ rather they must serve them all the more, since those who benefit by their service are believers and beloved.ᵇ

ᵃ Gk are brothers   ᵇ Or since they are believers and beloved, who devote themselves to good deeds

COMMENTARY

The thought returns to one of the writer's principal preoccupations: the good ordering of the church. But whereas the previous instructions were posed in third-person terms (3:1-13), now the talk is more in second-person terms, of the responsibilities as primarily Timothy's. As someone still relatively young (4:12), a test of Timothy's leadership would be how he handled himself in regard to those whose age would ordinarily command respect, as well as to those closer to his own age (5:1-12). This train of thought leads to acknowledgment of the significant body of elderly widows who would naturally be part of or attracted to such a community (5:3-8), and in turn to the younger widows who would be no less prominent (5:9-16). The elderly presumably included the elders whose responsibilities under Timothy required still greater sensitivity on the part of Timothy (5:17-22). The following exhortations seem to arise from concern for Timothy's ability to handle the strain (5:23-25), and the concerns for good management are rounded off quite naturally with conventional advice to slaves, again in third-person terms (6:1-2).

5:1-2, On Old and Young. A fascinating feature of this section of 1 Timothy is the use of πρεσβύτερος (presbyteros) three times within a few verses (vv. 1, 17, 19), where in the first case the word clearly means "older man," while in the other two it should probably be translated "elder." The former meaning is put beyond dispute by the contrast with "younger men" (v. 1) and the complementary reference to "older women/younger women" (v. 2). Although mortality rates were much higher then than today, many men and women did live to ripe old age; v. 9 envisages "pensionable" age as sixty. The concern here is not simply Timothy's youth, but no doubt reflects the general high regard for age, as the repository of experience and of the wisdom that (usually) came with it. The fact that the first thought is that Timothy might "rebuke" such a senior member of the church says much for the authority invested in him as here envisaged. The contrasting image of a father ("encourage him as a father"), given all the authority a father had over his son, simply reinforces the authority being claimed.

The counsel had respect for the older members

primarily in view (vv. 3-10, 17-22); the reference to the younger men and women follows as a corollary (vv. 1-2). To be noted is the way in which the model of the family continues to provide guidelines. That the latter could also be used more generally for kinsfolk or fellow members of societies does not detract from the dominant family imagery here. Again, even more clearly than in 4:12, the writer recognizes that a still-young bachelor in a leadership role is likely to be vulnerable to thoughts of "impurity, unchastity" (see vv. 11-12).

5:3-8, Widows. A social feature of the time was the relatively high proportion of widows in any community. This was the result of a combination of factors. In particular, young girls beyond puberty were often married to much older men, and the mortality rate would often be high among men in military service. Unless well-to-do in her own right through inheritance, a widow's lack of legal status made her even more vulnerable; her legal (male) guardian might covet her wealth or abuse his authority.

Concern for the widow was a feature of Jewish legislation (e.g., Deut 14:29; 24:17-21; 26:12), and the prominence of widows in and around the early Christian churches is well enough indicated by the frequency of their mention in Luke–Acts (Luke 2:37; 4:25-26; 7:12; 18:3-5; 20:47; 21:2-3; Acts 6:1; 9:39-41). Their vulnerability made it all the more essential that a church that saw itself in direct continuity with the assembly of Israel (3:15) should take special measures to ensure that widows were properly cared for. Nothing is said explicitly, but the implication is that the churches would ordinarily administer some sort of social welfare fund (supplied by almsgiving; see Gal 2:10) on behalf of widows. The problem of caring adequately for widows arose already in the earliest days of the new movement (Acts 6:1) and had been dealt with in the same spirit as shown by Israel's ancient legislators (e.g., Deut 14:28-29; 24:19-21). Here it is clear that a formal register was already in operation (v. 9). The extensiveness of the treatment (vv. 3-16) may suggest that the policy was being clarified or extended, or even formulated for the first time.

The initial concern is that the communal funds be used only for those in genuine need—"real widows" (v. 3; the NIV's "really in need" in vv.

3, 5 says more than the Greek does). The term translated "honor" (τιμη *timē*) probably carries the connotation of "provide financial support for" (see also v. 17). The expectation was that a widow who had adult children or grandchildren should be looked after by them (v. 4). This is part of the basic "piety" that the writer both assumed and commended, as expected by and acceptable to God. Here "piety" is clearly defined by the fifth commandment (Exod 20:12), but the duty of children to parents was widely taught in the ancient world. A complementary consideration was the tradition of "favor" and "recompense" that governed acts of generosity by the gods or to a city, the honorific inscription as a way of returning the favor received. So provision for aged parents (here widowed mothers) is the "return" to be expected for their generosity in parenthood and upbringing. Here again it is to be noted how positive is the author's picture of the family; the family was expected to be the focus and model of care for the elderly.[72]

The "real" widow, in the sense of one who needs help not available to her from her immediate family, is the one "left alone" (v. 5). She has no one to hope in except God (an echo, perhaps, of Jer 49:11). Like Anna in Luke 2:37, she continues in prayer "night and day"—not, we may assume, simply out of a worry-free piety, but in her worry and distress the only one she can turn to is God (see Luke 18:2-7). The contrast is with the widow who has been left well off and can live luxuriously, in indulgence (v. 6).[73] The author's comment is dismissive and biting; such a one may be living it up, but she is so insensible to matters of true value that she is already as good as dead! It is Timothy's responsibility to make this plain to all widows (v. 7).

Significantly the thought returns to the responsibility of the family. It is the responsibility of the senior male member of a household to take forethought, to make provision for those in his care. Here we have a brief insight into the full sweep of responsibility of the *paterfamilias*. That respon-

---

72. See C. Osiek and D. Balch, *Families in the New Testament World: Households and House Churches* (Louisville: Westminster John Knox, 1997).

73. In *The Shepherd of Hermas* (mid 2nd cent. CE) the verb σπαταλάω (*spatalaō*) is used of sheep in rich pasture, perhaps in the sense "be frisky" (*Similitude* 6.1.6; 6.2.6). The only other NT occurrence, Jas 5:5, is more relevant.

sibility included all his near relatives, whether living in his own immediate household or not, on whose behalf he had been appointed guardian. But he had a special responsibility for members of his immediate household, and here it is particularly his wife who is in view. The writer gives this responsibility the highest rank. To fail in it was tantamount to denying the faith. Such a one was "worse than an unbeliever." The importance of family and of family responsibilities as part of Christian faith and discipleship, and of the integration (not antithesis) of family and church responsibilities could hardly be more strongly stressed.

5:9-16, Younger Widows. The writer clearly expects that the churches written to would have a register of widows (v. 9). It is clearly enrollment that is in view and not admission to an order of ministry, as in 3:1-13 and 5:22.[74] The first rules had already been outlined: (1) Husbands ought to make provision for their wives in case they were widowed (v. 8); and (2) for a widow with adult children or grandchildren, the primary responsibility for her care lay with them (v. 4). A third and fourth rule are immediately added: (3) She should not be less than sixty years old (v. 9); and (4) she should have been married only once,[75] the assumption being that a woman widowed twice would have been provided for twice over.

A final criterion is that she should be attested by her (presumably earlier record of) "good deeds," "every good deed"—the regular phrase used by the author to indicate the actions or activities that would generally be commended as good (v. 10). In this case, we could put a colon after "good deeds" and treat the following list as indicating the sort of deeds the author had in mind. The list gives a quick glimpse of the responsibilities a woman might be expected to carry out within a household at the time. She should "bring up [her] children," a responsibility usually (but not necessarily) completed by the time of puberty for the sons. (Did a childless wife help in

bringing up orphans?) She should welcome strangers, showing hospitality—again a reminder that the diaspora home played an important role in providing hospitality for kinsfolk and countrymen, and of the role of the woman in preparing or supervising preparation of meals (see Commentary on 3:2).

It is less clear whether "washing the feet of the saints" was conceived as a social courtesy or possibly a quasi-liturgical act (only the feet of the saints are mentioned). Either way, it is presumably significant that it is specified as a task undertaken by wives/widows. The humility expressed in the act is clearly implied in John 13:6-8. That this was expected of wives/widows as a regular act tells us something of the relatively low social status widows enjoyed. More conventional and less jarring is the image of the woman "helping" the afflicted, comforting those in pain, tending the cuts or bruises of any who had been roughed up.

The reason why younger widows should not be enrolled is then explained. Unfortunately the reason immediately given is very confusing (vv. 11-12). First, it uses a verb (καταστρηνιάω *katastrēniao*) that is otherwise unknown for this time. The verb is usually taken in the sense of "become wanton." How this governs the genitive phrase "[the] Christ," however, is unclear. Could it mean that they "feel sensuous impulses" in regard to Christ—that is, were they drawn to him sexually? Such a possibility, perhaps, should not be dismissed out of hand; the fact that in most churches the great majority of members are women presumably is not entirely to be divorced from the fact that the central figure of the Christian religion is male. But the phrase is usually taken in the sense "sensuous impulses that alienate them from Christ" (similarly NRSV and NIV).

The second puzzle is that they are condemned for wanting to marry, condemned for "rendering invalid their first faith." Does this refer to their Christian faith or to their first marriage? Either way, the writer's strong disapproval would presumably reflect his conviction that marriage should be for life—one life, one marriage (see Commentary on 3:2)—so that second marriage amounted to abandoning faith. But that would be odd in view of the subsequent advice that young widows should marry again (v. 14), unless the writer accepted this option unwillingly as a second

74. Johnson provides a valuable discussion of the recent suggestion that "widows" were an order of women who practiced active ministry. See L. T. Johnson, *Letters to Paul's Delegates: 1 Timothy, 2 Timothy, Titus,* The New Testament in Context (Valley Forge: Trinity Press International, 1996) 177-83.

75. The NIV's "faithful to her husband" introduces an implication ("unfaithfulness" in the sense usually understood in relation to marriage) not present in the text. See J. N. D. Kelly, *The Pastoral Epistles,* Black's New Testament Commentaries (London: A. & C. Black, 1963) 116.

best. Alternatively, is what was in view a "pledge" (NRSV, NIV) expected of widows when enrolled, as a commitment to the church or to Christ? That fits better with v. 14: the pledge of enrolled widowhood would then not have to be abandoned in the event of a second marriage. But then why the reference to their "*first* pledge"?[76] The lack of clarity here is disappointing, since properly understood the verses would tell us much about the writer's attitude toward marriage and (young) widows.

The other reason for what seems to be the writer's disapproval of young widows as a group is that they have nothing to do and fill their time in inappropriate ways (v. 13). The sketch is vivid: They learn to be "idle, lazy, unproductive"; they go from house to house, gossiping, talking nonsense, bringing unjustified charges against others;[77] they pay attention to things that do not concern them; they are meddlesome busybodies (cf. 2 Thess 3:11).[78] These sweeping generalizations either suggest someone who has had bad experiences with such women or are stereotypical criticisms of "flighty young widows."[79] To the extent that it is an accurate portrayal, it reflects the very awkward position in which the death of a husband would usually leave a young wife. If she had no children (as implied by the contrast in v. 14) and few independent means, she would often be an awkward appendage in the household of a relative. Lacking a clear responsibility and obvious function, they would find time heavy on their hands. In such circumstances the tendency to spend time with others in similar positions would be hard to resist. The fault, in other words, was as much society's for leaving young widows to lead such pointless lives.

The obvious solution was for the younger widow to remarry (v. 14). In that way she would have a fulfilling role and make good use of her time. Here again we are given a brief indication of what would generally be regarded as the wife's space and sphere of responsibility: primarily to bear children (cf. 2:15), though presumably some nurture is also implied (v. 10), and to manage her household—a clear enough, but still limited, sphere, subordinate to the overall authority of her husband (see Commentary on 2:11-12). The implication is that such responsibilities would keep the younger wife busy enough and give no occasion for abusive accusations, such as may underlie not only v. 13 but also vv. 11-12. "The opponent" could be superhuman (cf. 2 Thess 2:4; *1 Clem* 51:1; and note 5:15), but here is probably human. The reason why the writer was so sensitive at this point is probably because young widows were themselves particularly vulnerable to the kind of gossip in which suspicion and rumor thrive. But he was also conscious (v. 15) that the pattern of daily life indicated in v. 13 had resulted in some turning away (see the Commentary on 1:6) after the satan (see the Commentary on 1:20).

But if widows, younger or older, would not or could not remarry, the primary responsibility for looking after them lay with their relatives (v. 16). The female believer who "has widows" should "help them" (the same word used in 5:10) just as the male relatives should do. The fact that the writer puts the responsibility on the "believing woman"[80] again tells us something about the woman's sphere of influence. Women who were single or widowed and had independent means could take in relatives left on their own, and women who were married still had the possibility of bringing such relatives within the domestic arrangements for which they were responsible. Again we see the importance of the family and its network of relations as still carrying primary responsibility for needy members of the family and providing occasion to meet that need. In that way, the church would be spared the (financial) "burden" (a rather negative word) of caring for widows and would be able to direct its resources to "helping" (the same word again) "real widows"— that is, those not otherwise provided for by husband or family (vv. 4-5, 8).

---

76. That virgins are in view, whose "first pledge" was to remain celibate (J. M. Bassler, *1 Timothy, 2 Timothy, Titus,* ANTC [Nashville: Abingdon, 1996] 92-97) is unlikely. The support for the equation here of "widow" = "virgin" is slight (see Ignatius *Smyrneans* 13:1). In the key text (5:9) it is taken for granted that the widow had formerly been married, and the author has already denounced the forbidding of marriage as a demonic lie (4:1-3).

77. The noun φλύαροι (*phlyaroi*) is *hapax;* the fuller rendering indicated here is suggested by its cognate verb φλυαρέω (*phlyareō*), as in its only occurrence in the NT, 3 John 10.

78. The note of inquisitiveness in the third term (περίεργος *periergos*) may carry the further overtone of curiosity about magic (cf. its only other occurrence in the NT, Acts 19:19).

79. See D. T. MacDonald, *The Legend and the Apostle: The Battle for Paul in Story and Canon* (Philadelphia: Westminster, 1983) 76-77.

80. Some scribes evidently found the reference only to a believing woman surprising and added "believing man or," reflecting the assumption that such important decisions would usually be made by men.

5:17-25, Elders. In view of the earlier usage (vv. 1-2), how should we now translate πρεσβύτεροι (*presbyteroi*, v. 17)? "The older men" as a translation would hardly do enough justice to the responsibilities referred to them—leadership" (see Commentary on 3:4-5), "laboring hard[81] in word [preaching?] and teaching." In fact, the writer seems to be thinking in terms of a sort of sequence of narrowing circles: the *presbyteroi* in general; within them the *presbyteroi* who give good leadership; within them those who work hard in speaking and teaching. The most obvious way to read this is that the widest circle is that of "the older men" (v. 1), those who by age and experience would naturally be looked to for leadership in any community. Within that circle some would stand out as more natural or gifted leaders. They are worthy of "double honor"—that is, both the veneration for their age and the acknowledgment of their leadership (cf. 6:1-2)—or double support from the common fund (as v. 18 implies).[82] Within that narrower circle some would be recognized for their labors in speaking and teaching. Should we limit the more formal term "elder" only to the second circle (cf. 4:14)? In short, do we see here the term πρεσβύτερος (*presbyteros*), "older man," becoming the technical term *presbyteros*, "elder"?[83] At any rate, we should note that they were expected to minister in speaking and teaching and that these functions were not limited to apostles, prophets and teachers, overseers, or deacons.

In a sudden burst of scripture quotations, almost unique in the Pastorals (vv. 18-19; otherwise only 2 Tim 2:19; but see also 2 Tim 3:8, 16), the scriptural authorization is given for this commendation of elders (v. 18). The first text cited more or less exactly causes little surprise: "You shall not muzzle an ox when threshing the grain" (Deut 25:4). The same text (in slightly variant form) had already been cited in 1 Cor 9:9, and the precedent was established for referring it to the rights of the preacher to receive benefit (financial support) from those to whom he preached.

More striking is the fact that the second text, still under the heading of "scripture," seems to come from the tradition of Jesus' own teaching, where Jesus sends out his disciples in mission and encourages them to seek out and accept hospitality.[84] This is a very striking feature that must mean (a) that Jesus tradition circulated in the early churches before the Gospels as such were widely known and (b) that such tradition already had the status of "scripture"—that is, that the teaching of Jesus was prized as being of equivalent weight to the long-established scriptures of Israel (see also 6:3). The point is only slightly weakened if the Jesus tradition has been introduced here simply to elaborate the scriptural precept. It was evidently felt unnecessary to identify it as a saying of Jesus, probably suggesting that it would be well known as such and that its authority did not depend on explicit attribution. This single snatch of quotation, itself sandwiched within an isolated snatch of scripture quotation (vv. 18-19), can thus bear a substantial weight of inference about the use and value of Jesus tradition at this period.

Somewhat oddly, the advice turns abruptly to the question of disciplining an elder (v. 19)—a fact that strengthens the inference that this formal role was at an early stage of development and perhaps in danger of already falling into disrepute in Ephesus (hence the sustained emphasis in vv. 21-22, 24). Of course, any leadership role readily attracts criticism, though the actual advice here (v. 19) may reflect v. 13*b*, that unfounded accusations were arising out of gossip. Perhaps more to the point, however, is the complementary fact that the rest of the instruction focuses primarily on Timothy's authority in reference to elders, their discipline and appointment. Nothing like this is said of any other office in any Pauline letter (cf. 3:1-13); the implication again is of a lower-ranking function (under Timothy, himself under Paul),

---

81. In the earlier Paulines this is a term he used several times to connote the hard work that marks out someone whose leadership qualities should be recognized. See esp. 1 Cor 15:10; 16:16; 1 Thess 5:12; but note also Rom 16:6, 12.

82. The Greek word for "honor" (μισθός *misthos*) can also mean "price," and so here "honorarium" or "stipend." But was there already such a range and ranking of different ministries ("single stipend, double stipend") that the churches supported with a regular salary? Or is the good elder's stipend double that of the widow (5:3)? The elder of a village would usually be an honorific position.

83. The ambivalence in the reference of *presbyteros* (5:1, 17) puts a question mark against the argument, most recently by J. T. Burtchaell, *From Synagogue to Church: Public Services and Offices in the Earliest Christian Communities* (Cambridge: Cambridge University Press, 1992), that the structure of church organization was taken over from the synagogue. See also R. A. Campbell, *The Elders: Seniority Within Earliest Christianity* (Edinburgh: T. & T. Clark, 1994).

84. The wording is exactly that of Luke 10:7, slightly different from the parallel in Matt 10:10. The nearest OT texts are relatively remote: Num 18:31 and 2 Chr 15:7.

only beginning to take clearer and more recognized shape.

The first piece of counsel (v. 19) is a particular application of the traditional ruling that two or three witnesses were required if an accusation against a third party was to be sustained (Deut 19:15; cf. Matt 18:16; 2 Cor 13:1). Those who persisted in sin should be "reproved or corrected" (v. 20). The verb ἐλέγχω (elegchō) is used several times in the Pastorals (2 Tim 4:2; Titus 1:9, 13; 2:15), but here in context the more basic sense may be in mind: "bring to light," "expose." That is, a process seems to be in view: accusation investigated; if upheld, dealt with quietly; if conduct not discontinued, public exposure (cf. Matt 18:15-17). The purpose given is slightly disquieting—"in order that the rest might have fear"—but it is simply an application of the age-old rationale for punishment, that it should serve as an exemplary warning to others. In the context, "the others" must be other older men or elders.

A solemn charge follows: "before God, Christ Jesus and the elect angels" (v. 21; cf. Mark 13:32). As in *1 Enoch* 39:1, talk of the "elect" implies other angelic beings outside the sphere of God's favor. "The elect angels" presumably serve with God to form the heavenly court of judgment (cf. Job 1–2; Luke 12:8-9; 1 Cor 6:1-3). The charge is one that might be given, indeed perhaps was given, to a judge: to act "without prejudging the issue, without discrimination," and "not acting in accord with personal inclination, in a partisan way"; we are still in the ethos of the deuteronomic legislation (Deut 1:17; 16:19). Such is the role Timothy should expect to play and the authority he would have to exercise.

Timothy's responsibility in ensuring good order for the churches extends to commissioning and ordination (v. 22). It is not said that Timothy alone had this right or responsibility, but the impression is clearly given that a writ of authority is being passed down from Paul to Timothy to others that in itself would help to stabilize and give coherent identity to the churches in view. Such commissioning requires careful thought and perhaps also a period of probation (cf. 3:10); too hasty appointment could result in poor leadership.

The second piece of advice, in context, presumably reinforces the earlier advice: Failure to rebuke attested sin (vv. 19-20), partiality in judgment (v. 21), and overlooking shortcomings in a potential candidate (v. 22) would be to share in these sins. For the third time (also 4:12; 5:2), Timothy is urged to keep himself "pure, chaste" (similarly Titus 2:5).

The following sequence of exhortations (vv. 23-25) seems at first more disparate, but almost certainly they continue the line of thought. Timothy is envisaged as both somewhat ascetic (he drank only water) and as suffering from "frequent or numerous ailments or weaknesses" (v. 23). It is a pity that more detail is not given, since such brevity encouraged ill-informed speculation. But in context we can perhaps imagine an unduly serious young man whose heavy responsibilities caused him considerable stress, manifested in stomach cramps and other ailments. The counsel recognizes the value of wine as a relaxant, though perhaps also because it purified the drinking water.

Verses 24-25 read as a kind of proverbial afterthought following the advice of the previous paragraph. The meaning of the second half of v. 24 is somewhat obscure, but the two sentences are obviously set out in parallel.[85] Some sins are "clear, known to all"—and so can (should) be easily enough dealt with. But in other cases the sins themselves or their consequences only become visible later—judgment should never be hasty. In contrast, "good deeds" are also "clear, known to all"; but even those that are not cannot be hidden—perhaps an encouragement to persevere in good deeds not so far acknowledged within the community. Such apparently trite proverbs are not atypical of proverbial, including Jewish, wisdom (Proverbs 10–24 provides many examples).

6:1-2, Slaves. The only obvious reason for adding this piece of counsel is that advice regarding slaves was part of the regular code for good household management.[86] This became an established part of Christian paraenesis (i.e., practical

---

85. Johnson prefers to read v. 25*b* as "even deeds which are not good [rather than which are not obvious] cannot remain hidden," but that translation ignores the parallelism. See L. T. Johnson, *Letters to Paul's Delegates: 1 Timothy, 2 Timothy, Titus,* The New Testament in Context (Valley Forge: Trinity Press International, 1996) 186.

86. Slavery was an established fact of life in the ancient world. As many as one-third of the inhabitants of a city like Ephesus would have been slaves; even relatively modest households would have had one or more slaves.

instruction) with Col 3:18–4:1 (see also Eph 5:22–6:9; 1 Pet 2:18–3:7; Titus 2:1-10; *Did.* 4:9-11; Ignatius *Polycarp* 4:1–5:2; Polycarp *Philippians* 4:2-3). In this case it is almost a reflex reaction: No problem regarding slaves in Ephesus is envisaged[87] (cf. the relatively greater attention given in the other NT codes). The linking thought of "honor" (5:3, 17; 6:1) may be sufficient explanation. Otherwise, the teaching is fairly conventional. The writer did not think it necessary even to balance the counsel to slaves with corresponding counsel to masters (see Titus 2:9-10; 1 Pet 2:18-25; cf. Col 4:1; Eph 6:9). At the same time, the fact that slaves are addressed directly was unusual; even though slaves, they were full members of the Christian church and thus all the more, not less, responsible as such.

The advice is practical: Slaves should respect their (non-Christian) masters. A Christian slave who failed in his or her duty brought dishonor to God and to the teaching (6:1); note again that the good impression made on others is held up as a measure of Christian conduct (cf. Rom 2:24; 1 Thess 4:11-12; and see Commentary on 3:7). They should not disrespect their masters who were fellow Christians; on the contrary, as *brothers* they should be better *slaves* (cf. Phlm 15-16); in that way they would assist their masters to "devote themselves to doing good, benefactions" (6:2).[88]

---

87. Otherwise, e.g., G. D. Fee, *1 and 2 Timothy, Titus,* New International Biblical Commentary (Peabody, Mass.: Hendrickson, 1984; rev. ed. 1988) 136-37.

88. This rendering follows the NRSV margin. Most prefer to take the clause as referring to the benefit the masters gain from their slaves (so NIV, NRSV); but the term εὐεργεσία (*euergesia*) is more naturally taken as denoting the generous act of a benefactor (εὐεργέτης *euergetēs*).

REFLECTIONS

Still on the theme of the well-ordered congregation, two further testing areas are dealt with: how the church should treat its more vulnerable and needy members and how discipline should be handled.

The linking theme is the elderly. It is regrettable that in many societies and churches the "elders/elderly" no longer have the status and respect that were recognized to be their due in former generations. The reason why such status and respect were accorded is obvious: Knowledge was accumulated through years of experience, no doubt frequently being tested and proved; out of such knowledge grew wisdom. The elderly were repositories of accumulated wisdom and had a crucial function in the village or community in giving advice on the basis of that accumulated wisdom. The veneration still given to ancestors in a society like that of China is simply the extension of this insight, so fundamental in the good ordering of ancient society. But today there is a widespread assumption that such repositories of wisdom can be dispensed with; all we need is now contained in textbooks and computer disks.

The consequences are grave. For one thing, the elderly cease to have such a vital role in community; the very function for which they were valued has been taken from them; they become merely a burden and much less a blessing; they experience loneliness, along with loss of income, failing health, distance from family members and grandchildren, loss of friends. For developed countries, in which the retired are becoming a steadily larger proportion of the population, this is a fearful prospect, both for the societies and particularly for the less well-off retired people themselves. More hidden and, indeed, more serious is the loss of a sense of the character of and need for wisdom. Wisdom is being lost behind knowledge, and even knowledge is being submerged by mere information. It is imperative that knowledge, the ability to order and apply information, to discriminate between what is of relevance and what is not, should be given its proper place once again. But more important is that the still higher priority of wisdom, not least the wisdom of well-ordered human relations, be recovered. And then, we may hope, the vital role of the elderly as repositories and stewards of that wisdom may be restored, and with it more of the respect they are due.

Special attention is given in the text to widows. Somewhat surprisingly, they alone are mentioned of the four categories for whom welfare provision was specifically made in ancient Israel—widows, orphans, strangers, and the poor. The importance of hospitality toward strangers is taken for granted (5:10), but nothing is said of the other categories (though see 6:17-19). Presumably, we must assume that adequate provision was being made, not least through almsgiving, for others and that there were no problems needing to be addressed (cf. Jas 1:27). In terms of welfare provision, the only guidelines available to us relate to widows.

The principal point being made is that the primary responsibility belongs to the family: Children or grandchildren of a widow should make due return for all that had been done for them in childhood (5:4); the head of household is responsible to provide for needy relatives and particularly immediate kin (5:8); the woman of independent means should care for a needy relative who had been widowed (5:16). This responsibility is part of "the faith" (5:8); it should not be shifted to the church (5:16). Here again we see question marks to be lodged against more modern arguments that state or church can or should take over such family functions and responsibilities. Of course, in a more fragmented society in which families are often scattered, all kinds of support for caregivers may be needed and should be provided—by state and church; the loneliness of someone who cares for an aged parent with Alzheimer's, for example, is a burden that no one should be asked to bear alone. But the principle of the family as the primary network of supportive relationships is one that should not be lost. In contrast, the loss of family as the basic social unit, not least as the focus for nurture and the principal medium whereby the wisdom of the past is transferred through the generations, would be (is) disastrous for society.

The complementary notion of discipline is equally at threat—in this case the discipline required of younger widows (5:11-15) and in regard to elderly/elders from whom leadership was expected (5:19-22). Noteworthy is the fact that none of the matters in view in 1 Timothy 5 are items of doctrine or belief (cf. 1:19-20); the concern here is entirely over behavior. Contrast the laxer standards of postmodern society and the disparaging tone that now usually attaches to any talk of "good deeds." Here again a sense of "Christian character" needs to be recovered, of an ethos not narrowly defined by particular traditions of behavior, but illustrated as the writer does (5:10, 14, 17; 6:2), to bring out a more recognizable Christian identity by which claimants to the name "Christian" can measure themselves.

The threats to such Christian character will always include not only malicious gossip (5:13) and false accusation (5:19), but also accusations all too justified because of too hasty decisions (5:22) and irresponsible behavior (5:24). The wisdom and maturity of leadership will thus be evident in the way discipline is exercised. Good discipline will grow out of proper respect shown to others (5:1-2; 6:1-2), will thrive in a context where due responsibility is recognized (5:4, 8, 16) and undisciplined or unsocial behavior clearly criticized (5:6, 13, 24), and will be exercised by ignoring unsupported accusations (5:19), by forthright denunciation where that is needed (5:20), by maintaining strict impartiality overall (5:21), and by taking care in promoting people to leadership (5:22). Despite some unclarity (5:11-12) and suspicion that some criticisms are too sweeping and possibly even prejudiced (5:13), there is much here for any church council to reflect on.

So far as slavery is concerned (6:1-2), we should keep in mind that it was not at this time a moral issue (it took the slave trade to make it so). In the ancient world, slaves were simply the bottom rung of the economic ladder. We should not be surprised (or embarrassed), therefore, at the absence of any critique of slavery as such. The point of lasting note is that there are some basic circumstances of life that cannot be changed and that have to be accepted. The fruitful way forward is to work positively and creatively within them. The slave who constantly bemoaned his lot would benefit neither himself nor his master and would bring Christian teaching into disrepute. Even within such constraints there was opportunity to serve willingly and to honor the name of God. The teaching cannot be simply transferred to those at the bottom of the economic ladder today. The point is, rather, that where legitimate obligations exist, they should be carried out with goodwill and sincere dedication, as though to the master in heaven.

1 TIMOTHY 6:3-21, PUTTING WEALTH IN ITS PLACE

NIV

³If anyone teaches false doctrines and does not agree to the sound instruction of our Lord Jesus Christ and to godly teaching, ⁴he is conceited and understands nothing. He has an unhealthy interest in controversies and quarrels about words that result in envy, strife, malicious talk, evil suspicions ⁵and constant friction between men of corrupt mind, who have been robbed of the truth and who think that godliness is a means to financial gain.

⁶But godliness with contentment is great gain. ⁷For we brought nothing into the world, and we can take nothing out of it. ⁸But if we have food and clothing, we will be content with that. ⁹People who want to get rich fall into temptation and a trap and into many foolish and harmful desires that plunge men into ruin and destruction. ¹⁰For the love of money is a root of all kinds of evil. Some people, eager for money, have wandered from the faith and pierced themselves with many griefs.

¹¹But you, man of God, flee from all this, and pursue righteousness, godliness, faith, love, endurance and gentleness. ¹²Fight the good fight of the faith. Take hold of the eternal life to which you were called when you made your good confession in the presence of many witnesses. ¹³In the sight of God, who gives life to everything, and of Christ Jesus, who while testifying before Pontius Pilate made the good confession, I charge you ¹⁴to keep this command without spot or blame until the appearing of our Lord Jesus Christ, ¹⁵which God will bring about in his own time—God, the blessed and only Ruler, the King of kings and Lord of lords, ¹⁶who alone is immortal and who lives in unapproachable light, whom no one has seen or can see. To him be honor and might forever. Amen.

NRSV

Teach and urge these duties. ³Whoever teaches otherwise and does not agree with the sound words of our Lord Jesus Christ and the teaching that is in accordance with godliness, ⁴is conceited, understanding nothing, and has a morbid craving for controversy and for disputes about words. From these come envy, dissension, slander, base suspicions, ⁵and wrangling among those who are depraved in mind and bereft of the truth, imagining that godliness is a means of gain.[b] ⁶Of course, there is great gain in godliness combined with contentment; ⁷for we brought nothing into the world, so that[c] we can take nothing out of it; ⁸but if we have food and clothing, we will be content with these. ⁹But those who want to be rich fall into temptation and are trapped by many senseless and harmful desires that plunge people into ruin and destruction. ¹⁰For the love of money is a root of all kinds of evil, and in their eagerness to be rich some have wandered away from the faith and pierced themselves with many pains.

11But as for you, man of God, shun all this; pursue righteousness, godliness, faith, love, endurance, gentleness. ¹²Fight the good fight of the faith; take hold of the eternal life, to which you were called and for which you made[d] the good confession in the presence of many witnesses. ¹³In the presence of God, who gives life to all things, and of Christ Jesus, who in his testimony before Pontius Pilate made the good confession, I charge you ¹⁴to keep the commandment without spot or blame until the manifestation of our Lord Jesus Christ, ¹⁵which he will bring about at the right time—he who is the blessed and only Sovereign, the King of kings and Lord of lords. ¹⁶It is he alone who has immortality and dwells in unapproachable light, whom no one has ever seen or

[a] Other ancient authorities add *Withdraw yourself from such people*
[b] Other ancient authorities read *world—it is certain that*
[c] Gk *confessed*

NIV

¹⁷Command those who are rich in this present world not to be arrogant nor to put their hope in wealth, which is so uncertain, but to put their hope in God, who richly provides us with everything for our enjoyment. ¹⁸Command them to do good, to be rich in good deeds, and to be generous and willing to share. ¹⁹In this way they will lay up treasure for themselves as a firm foundation for the coming age, so that they may take hold of the life that is truly life.

²⁰Timothy, guard what has been entrusted to your care. Turn away from godless chatter and the opposing ideas of what is falsely called knowledge, ²¹which some have professed and in so doing have wandered from the faith.

Grace be with you.

NRSV

can see; to him be honor and eternal dominion. Amen.

17As for those who in the present age are rich, command them not to be haughty, or to set their hopes on the uncertainty of riches, but rather on God who richly provides us with everything for our enjoyment. ¹⁸They are to do good, to be rich in good works, generous, and ready to share, ¹⁹thus storing up for themselves the treasure of a good foundation for the future, so that they may take hold of the life that really is life.

20Timothy, guard what has been entrusted to you. Avoid the profane chatter and contradictions of what is falsely called knowledge; ²¹by professing it some have missed the mark as regards the faith.

Grace be with you.ᵃ

ᵃ The Greek word for *you* here is plural; in other ancient authorities it is singular. Other ancient authorities add *Amen*

COMMENTARY

Chapter 6 is evidently structured as a conclusion that balances the introductory chapter 1, with a similar warning against other teaching (1:3-10; 6:3-10), a similar charge to Timothy, and a benediction (1:12-18; 6:11-16), a final exemplary warning (1:19-20; 6:17-21a), and a brief farewell (6:21b; cf. 1:1-2). In the first paragraph, contrary teaching is scorned (6:3-5) and is set in contrast with a description of "godliness" in terms of "contentment," which in turn is contrasted to the dangers of coveting riches (6:6-10). The godliness Timothy should pursue has very different motivation and imagery—"the good fight," "the good confession," in reference to Christ Jesus and the only God (6:11-16). This middle paragraph is bracketed by a further warning to the rich (6:17-19) and a final swipe at the "knowledge" pedaled by others (6:20-21).

6:3-10, Godliness as Contentment. The last four (Greek) words of v. 2 look as though they sum up and conclude the main body of teaching (2:1–6:2). That teaching is evidently what the writer means by "sound words" and "the teaching which accords with piety" (6:3), two phrases that encapsulate the forms, values,

and standards that the writer so clearly cherished (see the Commentary on 1:10 and 2:2). The "sound words" are further identified as "of our Lord Jesus Christ" and may include reference to the church's store of Jesus tradition (see also 5:18). Anything opposed to this teaching is treated dismissively with a conventional vocabulary of vilification, which tells us next to nothing about the alternative teaching that is being attacked (6:4-5). Such a teacher is conceited or blinded (the same word as in 3:6); "he understands nothing"; "he is sick for controversy" (the same word appears in 2 Tim 2:23)[89] and "fighting over words" (the verb is used in 2 Tim 2:14) that produce "envy, strife, malicious talk, evil suspicions" (the equivalent verb is used in Acts 25:18) and constant irritations between people "wasted in mind" (cf. Rom 1:28) and "robbed of the truth" (cf. 2 Tim 4:4; Titus 1:14).

Only with the last phrase does a feature of substance emerge: "They think that godliness is a means to financial gain" (v. 5). In view are

89. The more usual translation is "morbid craving for controversy" (NRSV). Note the no-doubt deliberate contrast between other teaching as "sick" and the "sound/healthy" teaching (6:3) promoted by the author.

evidently those people, not uncommon in religious circles, who see their religious profession as a means of financial advantage (charging for their teaching) or of social advance.[90] This in itself is a reminder that the first Christian groups were not uniformly poor or successful in recruitment only among the disadvantaged. There were sufficient numbers of people of higher social status and some wealth for association with a church to provide such opportunities for "social climbing" (see also 2:9). But we should remember that the description is not necessarily unbiased.

In direct contrast, the real means of gain is "godliness with αὐτάρκεια [*autarkeia*]" (v. 6). The choice of this last word is striking (not least because the writer uses it to qualify or further define his favorite term, "godliness, piety"), for *autarkeia* was a favorite virtue of the Stoics and Cynics, the two main classical alternatives to Christianity.[91] It denoted "self-sufficiency," "contentment" and characterized an attitude that cherished simplicity and a life lived in acceptance of the hand dealt out by nature or fortune. Here perhaps more clearly than anywhere else in the Pastorals we can see a pattern of Christianity in which specific Christian teaching and virtues like love are integrated with already acknowledged virtues cherished by others (cf. particularly Phil 4:8, 11).

The elaboration of such "contentment" is given in what seems like a proverbial form that can be set out in four lines (vv. 7-8).[92] It is a classic statement of the contentment that finds value in life rather than possessions, and that looks for sufficiency rather than surfeit of food and clothing. It echoes a typically religious evaluation of possessions and wealth; in Jewish wisdom literature in particular the first two lines can be compared with Job 1:21 and Eccl 5:15, and the last two with Sir 29:21; nor should we forget Matt 6:25-34.

The point is elaborated in terms of the dangers of making the accumulation of wealth a goal to pursue (v. 9). The images are again conventional, but they resonate sufficiently with repeated examples in history for their force to be easily recognized: "falling into temptation," "snare," "senseless and harmful desires," "sink into ruin and destruction" (cf. Matt 7:13; Acts 8:20; Phil 3:19; 1 Thess 5:3). The warning is summed up in one of the most famous (and most misquoted) sayings in the Bible: "the root of all evils is the love of money" (v. 10; cf. Sir 27:1). It is directly to this craving that the writer attributes the fact that some "have wandered away or been led into error [the same word as in Mark 13:22] from the faith and have pierced themselves with many pains or woes." This is one of the most sustained critiques of desire for wealth in the NT, but it is easily paralleled by briefer allusions elsewhere (Mark 4:19; 10:25; Luke 1:53; 6:24; 12:15-21; 16:19-26; Jas 5:1-5; Rev 3:17-18). This emphasis undermines the argument that the Pastorals advocate a merely "bourgeois ethic."[93]

6:11-16, Timothy's Goal. The contrast with those described in vv. 9-10 is Timothy, "God's person"—an ancient title for a prophet (e.g., Deut 33:1; 1 Sam 2:27; 9:6-7; 1 Kgs 13:1; 17:18). His appropriate response is posed in the antithetical imagery of "fleeing from" and "pursuing after" (v. 11). Paul earlier used the same counsel of flight in regard to the two great *bêtes noires* that had repeatedly proved so disastrous in Israel's history: illicit sexual relations and idolatry (1 Cor 6:18; 10:14; cf. 2 Tim 2:22). Evidently some threats to piety are so subtle and so powerful that they can be dealt with only by running from them. The contrasting objects of pursuit are put in terms already classically Christian (cf. Titus 2:2, 12): righteousness, both of relationship with God (cf. Rom 9:30) and its social outworking (cf. 2 Cor 9:9-10); the writer's favorite "godliness," "piety"; "faith" merging into "faithfulness" (cf. Rom 14:22-23; Gal 5:22); "love," the highest Christian grace (see the Commentary on 1:5); "patience, endurance, fortitude," another much-prized grace (e.g., Rom 2:7; 5:3; 8:25); and "gentleness," a *hapax*, but understood at the time as a combination of "quietness" and "meekness," and less prized outside Christian circles.

---

90. On the different kinds of support teachers of the day could expect or hope for, see R. F. Hock, *The Social Context of Paul's Ministry: Tentmaking and Apostleship* (Philadelphia: Fortress, 1980).

91. Illustrations can be found in A. Malherbe, *Moral Exhortation: A Greco-Roman Sourcebook* (Philadelphia: Westminster, 1986) 40, 112-14, 120.

92. The NRSV's "so that" at the beginning of the second line attempts to make sense of what appears to be a redundant ὅτι (*hoti*), which can mean "that," but by itself would be most simply translated "because." Early scribes resolved the question by inserting a further word to read either "it is true that" or "it is clear that." The NIV, in effect, ignores the problem.

93. Dibelius-Conzelmann's commentary is notably light in this section and on 6:17-19. See M. Dibelius and H. Conzelmann, *The Pastoral Epistles,* Hermeneia (Philadelphia: Fortress, 1972).

"Fight the good fight" (v. 12) is the usual translation of the Greek in this passage, but the terms are broader. "Contest the good contest" does not read so well but is more accurate. The point is that maintaining "the faith" and living "the faith" require the energy and discipline of the good athlete (cf. 4:7). Eternal life is a gift of God's calling—a regular term for God's initiative in establishing the process of salvation (2 Tim 1:9; cf. Rom 4:17; 9:11, 24; 1 Cor 1:9; 1 Thess 5:24)—but they must "take hold of," "grasp" it. This is simply the outworking of the initial response to the divine "invitation" when Timothy "confessed the good confession" (see also v. 13), presumably at his baptism (cf. Rom 10:9-10) or ordination (4:14; 2 Tim 1:6), either way in public (see also 2 Tim 2:2).[94] Such emphasis on the complementarity of divine initiative and human commitment as characterizing the Christian life from first to last is characteristically Christian.

For the fourth time (v. 13; see also 1:3, 18; 5:21) the writer challenges Timothy in Paul's name, with the same solemnity as in 5:21. The epithets for God are honorific but have more immediate point. That God gives life to all things is the most basic statement of faith in God as Creator (cf. Neh 9:6; Wis 16:13; Rom 4:17; 1 Cor 15:22, 45; 1 Pet 3:18 19), but it is also the basis from which religious faith draws its strength. That Jesus "testified the good confession" is an unusual appeal within the NT letters (a reference back to Jesus as an example; cf. particularly 1 Pet 2:21-23), but it confirms how deeply embedded already within confessional faith was the memory of Christ's passion (including the name "Pontius Pilate").[95] "The good confession" evidently included public faithfulness to God in whatever was the commission given by God and not just a mouthing of a particular creed.

Verse 14 continues the imagery of a commission (here "commandment") that sums up the calling of God and its consequent responsibilities before God. That responsibility can be summed up in turn as "keeping" the commandment "with-out spot" (cf. Jas 1:27) or "blame" (cf. 3:2; 5:7). The negative imagery is not specified but complements the more positive imagery of vv. 11-12. The language here is a variation of a repeated aspiration in the Pauline letters (1 Cor 1:8; Eph 5:27; Phil 2:15-16; Col 1:22, 28; 1 Thess 3:13; 5:23; Jude 24). The endpoint in view is "the appearance of our Lord Jesus Christ," a regular referent in the Pastorals (see footnote 35); the term "epiphany" (ἐπιφάνεια *epiphaneia*) was commonly used in the religions of the time for the visible manifestation of a hidden deity.[96] That this will happen "in its own times" (the same phrase as in 2:6) may be partly a sign that the parousia was no longer expected imminently (cf. Rom 13:12; 1 Cor 7:29-31; Phil 4:5), but is principally an expression of confidence in God's ordering of the most significant events in human history.

As twice earlier (1:17; 2:4-6) the writer seems to take pains to set this faith with regard to Christ within a monotheistic framework (vv. 15-16). It is God who will "make known" this appearance of Christ "in its own times." The benediction that follows is, in effect, the more fundamental confession within which "the good confession" of Christ is to be integrated and understood. Its concepts and language are traditionally Jewish through and through, although they are usually shared with other religions. The "blessedness" of God (1:11) is particularly characteristic of the monotheistic faiths. That God was "alone" (vv. 15-16) is quintessentially Jewish (see Commentary on 1:17). "Ruler/sovereign" was an epithet used of God in early Judaism (Sir 46:5; 2 Macc 12:15). That God also was sovereign over all kings and masters is implicit in such passages as Psalm 2 and Dan 4:32 and explicit in 2 Macc 12:15 (cf. Deut 10:17; Ps 136:2-3); in Rev 17:14 the epithets are given to Christ (cf. Rom 10:12; 1 Cor 8:6). That God alone was immortal and invisible (v. 16) had already been affirmed in 1:17, but it is here elaborated, no doubt with allusion to such key precedents as Exod 33:20 and Isa 6:1-5.

6:17-21, Final Exhortations. It is striking that the writer should revert to his warnings about the hazards of wealth in this final paragraph (vv. 17-19). It is partly a stylistic feature (cf. the reversion

94. Others have suggested a public affirmation of faith made when put on trial, as with Jesus. But expectation of persecution by legal authorities is otherwise not in view in the Pastorals.

95. Kelly refers particularly to Acts 3:13; 4:27; 13:28 and to Ignatius *Magnesians* 11:1; *Trallians* 9:1; *Smyrneans* 1:2. See J. N. D. Kelly, *The Pastoral Epistles,* Black's New Testament Commentaries (London: A. & C. Black, 1963) 143.

96. For details see Dibelius and Conzelmann, *The Pastoral Epistles,* 104.

to the initial theme in 1:3, 18; 5:1, 17). But here, the fact that it takes the place that might otherwise have been given to pleasantries and future plans underlines the seriousness with which the writer regarded the danger. In this, too, it is parallel to the abrupt launch into the initial warnings of 1:3-11: The seriousness of the concern overrode normal literary conventions.

The warning is more specific than in vv. 9-10. Riches tend to make people proud and haughty (cf. Rom 11:20), encouraging the thought that wealth either gives superiority or can simply buy what is wanted. Wealth tends to give the rich a sense of security for the future that others do not have (v. 17). The writer pricks the balloon with his adjectives: rich "in the present age" (cf. 2 Tim 4:10; Titus 2:12),[97] the "uncertainty of" riches. The wise person trusts in God, who provides all that is necessary for enjoyment; the basic thought is the same as vv. 6-8. The rich, it should be noted, are condemned not for being rich but for indulging in the attitudes toward God and others that riches breed. Their safeguard is to use their wealth in doing good, sharing generously and liberally (cf. Rom 12:8); in both cases the point is made twice for emphasis (v. 18). In this way they will store up for themselves a good foundation for the future (v. 19, an odd mixture of echoes of Matt 6:20 and 1 Cor 3:14) and attain the same goal set before Timothy in v. 12. The final phrase is similar to the one used of widows in 5:3, 5, 16: "real life" in contrast with the insubstantial nature of a life consisting of or based on riches.

The other concern the writer wanted to leave with his reader(s) was the contrast between the sound teaching he has emphasized throughout and the inferior or dangerous alternatives being put before them (vv. 20-21). The parting image is of a παραθήκη (parathēkē)—that is, "a deposit or goods entrusted to someone else"—which is to be guarded (the same imagery recurs in 2 Tim 1:12, 14). The image is not elaborated here but presumably has in view "the faith" and "sound teaching" as summarized in such passages as 1:15 and 3:16 (see further on 2 Tim 1:12).

This is set in sharp contrast to a teaching that is given a slightly clearer identity (v. 20). We have already met the dismissive descriptions "profane" (1:9; 4:7) and "empty talk" (cf. 1:6). Greater promise of information is given by the *hapax* "antitheses, objections, contradictions" and "knowledge" (falsely so called). The latter has suggested to many that an early form of Gnosticism is in view, and the former has been seen by a few as a reference to a work of Marcion that evidently set the teachings of the OT and of Paul in sharp antithesis. But without that very late association (Marcion thrived in the middle of the 2nd cent.) both words could refer to a wide variety of teachings. "Knowledge" was clearly their word, but all philosophies and religions prized knowledge (cf. Rom 2:20; 1 Cor 8:1; Phil 3:8; Col 2:3). And "antitheses" sounds more like the writer's caricature. The only other thing we are told is that "some" by "promising or professing" this knowledge "had missed the mark" (the same word as in 1:6; 2 Tim 2:18) concerning the faith (cf. 1:19-20).

The final benediction is typically Pauline in its focus on grace, but it is surprisingly abrupt (cf. Col 4:18; 2 Tim 4:22). The plural "you" presumably indicates that the letter, despite being addressed to Timothy alone, would have been read aloud in a church gathering (as still more clearly in Phlm 3, 22, 25).

97. The writer is assuming the Jewish perspective on time: The present age will be followed by a future/new age. The same perspective lies behind most of the NT writings—e.g., Jesus' teaching on the kingdom of God (see particularly Mark 13) and Revelation.

REFLECTIONS

The dominant impression left by this chapter is the concern regarding the dangers of wealth and of the attitudes of mind and habits of life that acquisition and possession of wealth encourage (6:5, 9-10, 17). It echoes earlier warnings to similar effect (2:9; 3:3, 8; 5:13). The writer evidently saw here a serious threat to Christian character and community. No one who is wealthy relative to others, other Christians or other nations, can sit wholly comfortably under teaching like this. As with Jesus' words in the Sermon on the Mount (Matt 6:19-21) or to the wealthy young man (Mark 10:23-25) or the fierce denunciation of James (Jas 5:1-5), the only appropriate response has to be: Is this me/us? Have I/we fallen into this temptation and trap? An affirmative answer or troubled conscience can then look to 6:18 for the appropriate guidance.

At the same time, the teaching of the chapter undercuts any kind of "prosperity gospel." "Godliness," the principal summary word for the character of the religion commended by the Pastorals, is set in clear and sharp antithesis to any desire for riches (6:6-9). And any thought that godliness might be a means of gain is totally abhorrent to the writer (6:5). The contrast of a godliness content with the provision of fairly modest necessities is striking (6:6-8). The point should not be overplayed: The writer was equally clear that those with means should make proper provision for family and relatives (5:8, 16); the wealthy are not told to sell all their riches (6:18). But the idea that Christian profession ensured prosperity in the wealth of this age (6:17) would certainly be disowned and denounced by the writer as a false priority with faith-threatening and life-threatening consequences.

A second strong impression given by the chapter is the readiness of the writer to draw on ideals and ideas that were common to other philosophies and religions. Thus he makes use of ideas more familiar among Stoics and Cynics (6:6-8), of widely shared concerns about the perils of wealth (6:9-10, 17), of the religious technical term "epiphany" (6:14), and of conventional epithets for the deity (6:15-16). He trod a clear line between syncretism (where language begins to change and corrupt the central idea) and communication of ideas central to his faith (here particularly "piety" and belief in God as one). That line has to be maintained, hard though it be at times to distinguish the alternatives. The key, presumably, is not to become overly definitive and overly prescriptive, but to get the essential points and principles right and to ensure that they are not compromised in particular cases. Jesus showed the way in his teaching on the law (Mark 12:23-34; cf. Mark 2:23–3:5; 7:1-23).

A third strong impression with which one is left at the close of this letter is the writer's repeated assumption of and (by repetition) insistence on Israel's traditional monotheism. No New Testament writing is more persistent on that point (1:17; 2:4-6; 6:15-16; cf. John 5:44; 17:3). This emphasis needs to be borne in mind whenever the christology of the Pastorals is assessed (particularly Titus 2:13), for with its high evaluation of Christ, Christianity looked as though it was redefining its belief in God, that it was linking Jesus with God in such a way as to question its own monotheistic credentials. In other words, some might say, at this point Christianity did not avoid syncretism and began to speak in terms close to a kind of polytheism (two gods). It still seems that way to Jews and Muslims. And Christians with too casual talk of Jesus as God and a too simplistic concept of God as Trinity (often closer to tritheism) continue to feed that suspicion. It is important, therefore, that the emphasis of the writer here not be lost to sight: Christian faith is still governed by Israel's fundamental insight of God's oneness, and those who confess Christ and confess with Christ (6:13) make this a part of their confession that God is one (the Jewish *Shema*). Those who await the appearance of the Lord Jesus Christ (6:14) do so as believers that the Blessed One is alone sovereign (6:15) and alone has immortality (6:16).

2 TIMOTHY 1:1-7, GREETINGS AND PERSONAL COMMENDATION

NIV

1 Paul, an apostle of Christ Jesus by the will of God, according to the promise of life that is in Christ Jesus,

2To Timothy, my dear son:

Grace, mercy and peace from God the Father and Christ Jesus our Lord.

3I thank God, whom I serve, as my forefathers did, with a clear conscience, as night and day I constantly remember you in my prayers. 4Recalling your tears, I long to see you, so that I may be filled with joy. 5I have been reminded of your sincere faith, which first lived in your grandmother Lois and in your mother Eunice and, I am persuaded, now lives in you also. 6For this reason I remind you to fan into flame the gift of God, which is in you through the laying on of my hands. 7For God did not give us a spirit of timidity, but a spirit of power, of love and of self-discipline.

NRSV

1 Paul, an apostle of Christ Jesus by the will of God, for the sake of the promise of life that is in Christ Jesus,

2To Timothy, my beloved child:

Grace, mercy, and peace from God the Father and Christ Jesus our Lord.

3I am grateful to God—whom I worship with a clear conscience, as my ancestors did—when I remember you constantly in my prayers night and day. 4Recalling your tears, I long to see you so that I may be filled with joy. 5I am reminded of your sincere faith, a faith that lived first in your grandmother Lois and your mother Eunice and now, I am sure, lives in you. 6For this reason I remind you to rekindle the gift of God that is within you through the laying on of my hands; 7for God did not give us a spirit of cowardice, but rather a spirit of power and of love and of self-discipline.

COMMENTARY

The introduction to 2 Timothy is more typically Pauline than either of the other Pastoral Epistles. The self-identification is formulated in characteristic Pauline terms, with typically Pauline elaboration (1:1); the greeting (1:2) has the same variation as in 1 Tim 1:2. More striking is the fact that 1:3-7, unlike 1 Timothy and Titus, follows (with variations) the characteristic Pauline pattern of an initial thanksgiving and prayer for the recipients, assurance of desire to see them, and expression of confidence in their good faith (1:3-6; cf. particularly Rom 1:9-13; Phil 1:3-8). More distinctive of the Pastorals is the initial charge to Timothy (1:6-7).

1:1. If any title was grasped by Paul and more

or less insisted on, it was "apostle." Characteristic, too, was the conjunction of Christ Jesus and God in the determining of this identity: "apostle of Christ Jesus"; "through God's will" (1 Cor 1:1; 2 Cor 1:1; Gal 1:4; Eph 1:1; Col 1:1). That his commissioning by Christ should be in accordance with God's will was fundamental to both Paul's faith and his mission. The elaboration further specifies that his apostleship had in view the gospel (cf. Rom 1:1), here epitomized as "the promise of life that is in Christ Jesus" (cf. 1 Tim 4:8), again echoing strong Pauline themes: "promise" (e.g., Rom 4:13-16; Gal 3:14-29); "life" (e.g., Rom 5:17-21; 2 Cor 4:10-12); "in Christ," a favorite motif by which Paul indicated that the reality of the whole gospel and identity of believers as such was wholly bound up with Christ. The use of this motif in 2 Timothy (1:1, 9, 13; 2:1, 10; 3:12, 15) is more characteristically Pauline than in 1 Timothy (1 Tim 1:14; 3:13) and Titus (not used; though see the Commentary on 2:1).

1:2. The greeting is the same as in 1 Tim 1:1, except that Timothy is described as "beloved" rather than "legitimate, genuine." Paul used the term for fellow believers quite widely (e.g., Rom 1:7; 16:5, 8-9), but here it is the special relationship with Timothy (1 Cor 4:17) that is in view.

1:3. Paul's continuous resort to prayer is a feature of his letters (1 Cor 1:4; Phil 1:3-4; 1 Thess 1:2-3; the echo of Rom 1:8-9 is strong). However, the regularity of the pattern does not mean that the sentiments were merely conventional. Paul evidently lived his life as though in constant prayer dialogue with God. The reminder of his "service" serves a double purpose: The echo of its technical use (divine service in the Jerusalem Temple) strengthens the solemnity of the affirmation of regular prayer, and it implies continuity between Christian worship and the worship that had been focused in the Jerusalem Temple. The same point is reinforced by the reference to his "clean conscience" (a frequent motif in 1 Timothy; see 1 Tim 1:5). But the most striking feature is the assurance that Paul had thus served God "from my parents, ancestors," usually taken in the sense "as my parents, ancestors did." Either way the phrase underlines the conviction that the religion of his ancestors (not just the Judaism that he had previously practiced; see Gal 1:13-14) had sought to serve God in good faith and that Paul's apostolic ministry was in direct continuity with it. Since (pre-Christian) Judaism is regularly disparaged in Christian tradition (see Heb 8:13; or think of the bad overtones of the word "Pharisee" in English usage), the point is worth noting.

1:4. Paul's longing to see his readers is another characteristic theme of his letters (see Rom 1:11; Phil 1:8; 2:26; 1 Thess 3:6). The talk of "tears" (here of Timothy) underscores the emotional intensity of the longing (cf. Acts 20:19, 31; 2 Cor 2:4). The inverse proportion of apostolic suffering and its outcome is another Pauline theme (cf. Rom 8:17-25; 2 Cor 4:12-18; Phil 1:12-14). But somewhat oddly, this is the only mention of "joy" in the Pastorals.

1:5. In a clearly parallel way, the emphasis on the continuity of Paul's service with that of his forebears (v. 3) is balanced in this verse by the memory that both his mother and his grandmother were precursors of Timothy's faith. The reference may be to his Christian faith (Acts 16:1); already with Timothy we are in third-generation Christianity! Alternatively, since Timothy was already a young adult by the time the gospel reached Lystra (Acts 14:6-7; 16:1), the implication may be, rather, that this (Christian) faith was in direct continuity with the typical piety of a Jewish home (cf. 3:15). As in 1 Tim 1:5, "faith" that is "sincere, without hypocrisy" is what really matters.

1:6. This re-call to honored precedents of service and faith becomes in turn the basis for the initial "reminder" to Timothy—a less strong word than the injunctions of 1 Tim 1:3, 18; 5:21; 6:14, more in keeping with the overall friendlier tone of 2 Timothy. The exhortation is to the same effect as 1 Tim 4:14, only the image is more positive ("rekindle" as of a fire); the image is of a campfire kept going for days on end and requiring to be fanned into fresh flame every morning. Here as in 1 Tim 4:14 the impression is of a "charism," which is now "in" Timothy; that the word is used in this way and only of Timothy inevitably raises the question of whether the earlier charismatic theology of Paul has been formalized (cf. 1 Cor 12:7, 11; 14:1). Again, as in 1 Tim 4:14, Timothy's possession of the charism is attributed to "the laying on of hands," raising the same question (though cf. Acts 8:18). In this case, only Paul's hands are mentioned. If the reference is to the same event as in 1 Tim 4:14, as seems most likely, then the implication is presumably that the formality of the act was more important than the question of who participated in it (see the Commentary on 1 Tim 4:14).

1:7. The writer points to the Spirit as the source of the charism (as in 1 Cor 12:4). Timothy's exercising of his charism should be in accordance with the character of the Spirit—a Spirit not of "cowardice, timidity" but of "power" (cf. 1:8; 3:5), of "love" (see Commentary on 1 Tim 1:5), and of "good judgment, moderation" (a variation of the virtue commended in 1 Tim 2:9, 15; see Commentary on 1 Tim 2:9). The form is modeled on Rom 8:15 (though here the statement is generalized), but the echoes are of Mark 13:11 and 1 Cor 2:3-5.

REFLECTIONS

Here again we see a fine blend of epistolary conventions and Christian adaptation. The Christianity of Paul and the Pastorals did not seek to subvert or revolt against such conventions; nor did it want to create wholly new structures of social communication. Rather, it took the forms of the day and infused them with Christian spirit—"in Christ Jesus," "grace" (see the Commentary on 1 Tim 1:2).

Even more striking here is the theological emphasis on continuity with what had gone before: "apostle of Christ Jesus through God's will"; the grace of Christ in conjunction with the mercy of God (see Commentary on 1 Tim 1:2); Paul's service in the gospel (Rom 1:9) in continuity with the cultic worship of his forebears; the sincere faith of Timothy inherited from mother and grandmother; the charism in character with the Spirit given earlier. The emphasis is in marked contrast with a considerable portion of Christian history wherein Christianity has found it necessary to establish its own identity by denigrating the Judaism that preceded it—Christianity as "gospel" to Judaism's "law." Denigration of predecessors is an unlovely way to advance one's own claims at any time, but in the case of Christianity and the religion of Second Temple Judaism the continuity of theology and ethos is too integral to Christianity's own identity for such disparagement to be carried through without risk to Christianity itself. Given Christianity's debt to the religion of Israel (not least for its Scriptures and its Messiah), Christians should be the last persons to be anti-Semitic.

The continuity between Spirit first given and ongoing obligation was no less important for Paul; we need recall only Rom 8:23 and Gal 3:3. Maintaining the "first love" (Rev 2:4) can be easily sentimentalized and become an excuse for failure to grow in faith (see 1 Cor 3:1-2; Heb 5:11-14), but Paul would not have re-called his converts so often to the beginnings of their lives as Christians unless he saw the decisiveness of that first commitment and yielding to God as somehow paradigmatic for the life of the committed in dependence on God. The implication of Gal 3:3 is that the continuing and the ending need to be in the same spirit/Spirit as the beginning. How can the freshness of first love and devotion be maintained without becoming overformalized and entrapped in rules and procedures? Not a few are still looking for the church that can answer that question effectively!

2 TIMOTHY 1:8-18, PAUL'S OWN TESTIMONY

NIV	NRSV
[8]So do not be ashamed to testify about our Lord, or ashamed of me his prisoner. But join with me in suffering for the gospel, by the power of God, [9]who has saved us and called us to a holy life—not because of anything we have done but because of his own purpose and grace. This grace was given us in Christ Jesus before the beginning of time, [10]but it has now been revealed through the appearing of our Savior, Christ Jesus, who has destroyed death and has brought life and immortality to light through the gospel. [11]And of this gospel I was appointed a herald and an apostle	8Do not be ashamed, then, of the testimony about our Lord or of me his prisoner, but join with me in suffering for the gospel, relying on the power of God, [9]who saved us and called us with a holy calling, not according to our works but according to his own purpose and grace. This grace was given to us in Christ Jesus before the ages began, [10]but it has now been revealed through the appearing of our Savior Christ Jesus, who abolished death and brought life and immortality to light through the gospel. [11]For this gospel I was appointed a herald and an apostle and a

NIV

and a teacher. ¹²That is why I am suffering as I am. Yet I am not ashamed, because I know whom I have believed, and am convinced that he is able to guard what I have entrusted to him for that day.

¹³What you heard from me, keep as the pattern of sound teaching, with faith and love in Christ Jesus. ¹⁴Guard the good deposit that was entrusted to you—guard it with the help of the Holy Spirit who lives in us.

¹⁵You know that everyone in the province of Asia has deserted me, including Phygelus and Hermogenes.

¹⁶May the Lord show mercy to the household of Onesiphorus, because he often refreshed me and was not ashamed of my chains. ¹⁷On the contrary, when he was in Rome, he searched hard for me until he found me. ¹⁸May the Lord grant that he will find mercy from the Lord on that day! You know very well in how many ways he helped me in Ephesus.

NRSV

teacher,ᵃ ¹²and for this reason I suffer as I do. But I am not ashamed, for I know the one in whom I have put my trust, and I am sure that he is able to guard until that day what I have entrusted to him.ᵇ ¹³Hold to the standard of sound teaching that you have heard from me, in the faith and love that are in Christ Jesus. ¹⁴Guard the good treasure entrusted to you, with the help of the Holy Spirit living in us.

15You are aware that all who are in Asia have turned away from me, including Phygelus and Hermogenes. ¹⁶May the Lord grant mercy to the household of Onesiphorus, because he often refreshed me and was not ashamed of my chain; ¹⁷when he arrived in Rome, he eagerlyᶜ searched for me and found me ¹⁸—may the Lord grant that he will find mercy from the Lord on that day! And you know very well how much service he rendered in Ephesus.

ᵃ Other ancient authorities add *of the Gentiles*   ᵇ Or *what has been entrusted to me*   ᶜ Or *promptly*

COMMENTARY

Second Timothy stands out from the other two Pastoral Epistles as having more the form of a farewell address, with the characteristic hallmarks: reminder, warning, and charge (cf. Acts 20:18-35; 2 Peter). The actual "farewell" comes in 4:6-8, but 1:8-18 contains both charge (1:8-14) and reminder (1:15-18). The charge is further extended in 2:1-26 and 3:14–4:5, 9-21, and the reminder in 3:10-13, with 3:1-9 serving as the warning.

The appeal to the past is complemented by an appeal to Paul's own experience. The warrants for Timothy's ministry are the gospel entrusted to Paul (1:8-10), the ministry of Paul in discharging that trust (1:11-12), and the "sound words" that epitomize both (1:13-14). Equally paradigmatic for Timothy are the contrasting examples of those who abandoned Paul (1:15) as well as those who stood by him (1:16-18).

1:8. The appeal to Paul's own example parallels that in 1 Tim 1:12-20. But the distinctiveness of 2 Timothy within the Pastorals is heightened by the reference to Paul as a "prisoner" (only here

in the Pastorals; but cf. Eph 3:1; 4:1; Phlm 1, 9). Even more striking is the use of the distinctive feature of Pauline theology: a σύν- (*syn*-)compound ("suffer *with*"; used again in 2:3 and 2:11-12, but only in 2 Timothy). Talk of "being ashamed" recalls Rom 1:16 and becomes a linking motif in this section (1:8, 12, 16). That the gospel involves suffering is another characteristic theme of Paul (e.g., Rom 8:17-23; 2 Cor 4:7-18), as also is the conviction that such suffering can only be endured by God's enabling and that such weakness is the necessary complement to any experience of God's power (see 2 Cor 4:7; 12:9-10).

1:9-10. The gospel is then summarized in what appears to be another creedal-type of statement, which the author quotes. It is not called a "faithful saying" but is very similar to the "faithful saying" in Titus 3:4-7. As with that statement, it functions as a confession of God (not of Christ): The gospel is an account not so much of what Christ has done as of what God has done through Christ. The consistent aorist tenses (describing what has already been accomplished) need not imply a changed perspective from the earlier Paulines (where salvation is essentially a future good, the goal of the saving process; see, e.g., Rom 5:9-10; 1 Cor 1:18); note, after all, 2:10. It could, rather, be intended to emphasize the decisiveness of the divine action, seen, as it were, from its endpoint (cf. Rom 8:24, 30). The language picks up the key Pastoral image of "salvation" (see footnote 34) and the different image of an effective invitation (cf. 1 Tim 6:12). "Called with a holy calling" is Hebraic in form and echoes Israel's understanding of itself as "called to be saints" (as also particularly in Rom 1:7; 8:27-28). Once again the continuity of identity with God's earlier purpose, of Israel as defined by the call of God (cf. Rom 9:7-11, 24), is implicit.

"Not according to our works" is an equally strong echo of a central Pauline statement of the gospel (Rom 3:20, 28; Gal 2:16), but there is a significant shift of emphasis. The concept of "works" seems to have broadened out from a more specific "works of the law" (Paul was usually thinking of the things the law required and that distinguished Israel from other nations) to "our works," "anything we have done" (NIV, meaning any attempt to secure our own righteousness; cf. Eph 2:8; Titus 3:5). At any rate, the bulk of the weight is again placed on the divine initiative and purpose: in accordance with God's "own will and grace"; "given [as a gift] in Christ Jesus"; "before time immemorial." The "in Christ Jesus" refers to the embodiment of God's saving act both on the cross (cf. Gal 1:4; 1 Tim 2:6) and in the gift of saving grace (1 Cor 1:4). "Before times eternal" refers to the eternal purpose of God, not to Christ (or "us") as pre-existent (cf. 1 Pet 1:20).[98]

This eternally planned grace has now been manifested through the appearing of Christ Jesus our Savior (v. 10). Here are brought together two of the Pastorals' most distinctive themes: the title "Savior," used for the only time in 2 Timothy, but now of Christ (see the Commentary on 1 Tim 1:1); and the term "appearing" (ἐπιφάνεια epiphaneia), usually used of Christ's (second) coming (1 Tim 6:14; 2 Tim 4:1, 8; Titus 2:13), but here of his first (cf. the verb in Titus 2:11; 3:4). The fact that salvation and "Savior" are attributed indiscriminately to God and to Christ presumably indicates that for the author the saving action was one and the same; a more carefully described attribution is given in the formulations in 1:9 ("in Christ Jesus") and Titus 3:6 ("through Jesus Christ"), and the dual use of the technical term "epiphany" (see the Commentary on 1 Tim 6:14) presumably indicates that the author saw a direct continuity between the first and the second appearances of Christ as both the manifestation and the enactment of the divine purpose and grace (see also Commentary on Titus 2:13).

Not insignificant is the fact that the achievement of this first appearing is summarized (v. 10) in terms of the destruction of death (cf. Heb 2:14) and the bringing to light of life and immortality (cf. 1 Cor 15:53-54). The overcoming of death is usually the most important function of religion. No wonder, then, that the gospel focused so much on the resurrection of Christ; and no doubt it was the centrality of the resurrection of Christ that gave the gospel such effective power in the ancient world. "Light" and "life" are as attractive a combination of images as one could imagine (cf. John 1:4; Acts 26:23). Note also that "through the gospel" parallels "through the appearing of Christ": Just as Christ was the embodiment of God's saving purpose, so also the gospel is the medium through which that saving purpose comes to particular effect.

1:11. This verse is a way of making the point that the gospel just summarized was Paul's gospel. The reinforcement is twofold: The gospel thus affirmed by the writer goes back to Paul, bearing the stamp of his authority; and Paul in turn (and his emissary) are validated by the gospel he proclaimed. The verse, in effect, repeats 1 Tim 2:7, with the unusual titles for Paul of "herald"[99] and "teacher."[100] The two terms bracket and embrace the more typical Pauline self-designation "apostle": The gospel of the Pastorals goes back to Paul's proclamation; the "teaching" so insisted on by the author goes back to Paul the "teacher."

---

98. Despite J. N. D. Kelly, *The Pastoral Epistles,* Black's New Testament Commentaries (London: A. & C. Black, 1963) 163.

99. See Epictetus *Discourses* 3.22.69, where he speaks of the Cynic preacher as "the messenger, the scout, the herald of the gods."

100. Some MSS read "teacher of the Gentiles," influenced, no doubt, by 1 Tim 2:7.

1:12. In a well-rounded paragraph the writer returns to the theme of suffering and shame.[101] It is the same gospel that makes sense of Paul's suffering, particularly as a prisoner (v. 8). And over this gospel and the one it proclaims, Paul need not feel any cause for shame. As in Rom 1:16, which this verse echoes, there may well be a further echo of the Jesus tradition as contained in Mark 8:38 and Luke 9:26. The allusion is strengthened by the forward look once again "to that day." The image, then, is of a commission that others might well regard as a cause of shame: the proclamation of a crucified Christ (1 Cor 1:23). But the first appearing gives promise of a second, and the character and content of that first appearing—his words (Mark 8:38; Luke 9:26) and his death (1 Cor 1:23)—give sufficient ground that in the second appearing and the subsequent judgment belief in this Christ will be vindicated.

The theme of the faithfulness thus commended (v. 12) is summed up here and in v. 14 in the words παραθήκη (*parathēkē*), "deposit," "goods left in trust with someone else"—that is, presumably "the faith" (as in 1 Tim 6:20; see also on 1:13).[102] The image is rather static, and the complementary idea of "protecting" it (the same verb is used each time) encourages the picture of something retained and returned in the form in which it was first received. It is this image that probably above all gives the impression of a theology concerned more to preserve than to develop, a faith tied to earlier formulations and discouraged from seeking fresh expression. The Greek could be read as Paul's entrusting something to Christ (NIV, NRSV). And that makes good sense—entry upon the Christian life as a two way commitment, of convert to Christ (v. 12) and of Christ to convert (v. 14). But in context the parallel is more between Paul and Timothy: not being ashamed (vv. 8, 12), sharing the same suffering (vv. 8, 12). So here we expect the parallel: Paul's deposit, Timothy's deposit (vv. 12, 14). The result might seem rather odd: Paul's confidence is in *Christ's* ability to guard what had

been deposited with *Paul;* but that thought is itself very Pauline (e.g., Phil 4:13; Col 1:29).

1:13. Clearly Paul is being held up here as an example to be followed. This is precisely what the writer had said in 1 Tim 1:16, and he uses the same word here, the only two occurrences of the term in the NT. The implication is of a match between Paul's own life (as convert and apostle) and the gospel that converted him and that he preached. Both provide the "model/pattern/standard" in accordance with which others can both model and evaluate their own testimony and living. The "pattern" is here summed up in the familiar term "sound words" (ὑγιαινόντων λόγων *hygiainontōn logōn;* see footnote 9), presumably another way of saying the "gospel," another image for "the deposit." These, in turn, are correlated with the key Christian/Pauline terms "faith," "love," and "in Christ Jesus," as in 1 Tim 1:14.

1:14. In the parallel use of the *parathēkē* image (now "the fine deposit"),[103] it is Timothy who is to do the "guarding," as in 1 Tim 6:20. An important difference here (but no doubt assumed elsewhere) is that the indwelling Holy Spirit is the enabling power—the equivalent in v. 12 to Christ's guarding the deposit entrusted to Paul in v. 13. The Spirit does not appear much in the Pastorals; in fact, the Spirit hardly appears outside traditional formulations (1 Tim 3:16; Titus 3:5) or language modeled on an earlier distinctively Pauline formulation (2 Tim 1:7). First Timothy 4:1 could be regarded as an exception, but even that has the ring of an apocalyptic stereotype (the Spirit's predicting eschatological calamity and defection; see the Commentary on 1 Tim 4:1; cf. 2 Thess 2:2). Even 2 Tim 1:14 uses traditional Pauline language (cf. Rom 8:11: "the Spirit that dwells in you"). But the adaptation of the role of the indwelling Spirit to that of enabling Timothy to guard the deposit is distinctive of the Pastorals. We may compare the way Paul's much more liberal use of "charism" is limited now to a commissioning gift once given to Timothy (1 Tim 4:14; 2 Tim 1:6). Such features could be indicative of a changing pattern of experience of the Spirit and of the Spirit's engracing, but they could

---

101. It is important to realize that honor and shame were pivotal values in the first-century Mediterranean world. See B. J. Malina, *The New Testament World: Insights from Cultural Anthropology* (Atlanta: John Knox, 1981) chap. 2.

102. Not the charism: that has to be "fanned into flame, rekindled"; this has to be "guarded, kept safe."

103. Both the NIV and the NRSV blur the fact that the same phrase is used in 1:12 and 1:14, but the NRSV's translation "treasure" obscures the point still further.

also be indicative of a community that was trying to live out of the spiritual resources of the past, cherishing the pattern of sound words as those that encapsulated the gospel's experience of grace and ensured its continuance into the present and the future (cf. 2:1-2).

1:15. If Paul is the positive model for Timothy's responsibility, there are other models that come directly from Paul's own experience. As at the end of 1 Timothy 1, two negative examples are cited. The news that "all in Asia had turned away from or repudiated" Paul carries a shocking overtone. "Turn away from" (ἀποστρέφω *apostrephō*) is one of several words used in the Pastorals to describe defection or apostasy from "the truth" (4:4; Titus 1:14). But "*all* in Asia"—could that be so? Did all the churches in the large province of Asia (modern western Turkey) defect? That could hardly be true, in view of Revelation 2–3 and the letters of Ignatius. Alternatively, did all (or most of) the Christians of Asia abandon Paul in some crisis? Is there an allusion here to the episode hinted at in 2 Cor 1:8? Of course, there is an element of hyperbole in the language, but the sense of betrayal and isolation is very strong. We know nothing more of Phygelus and Hermogenes, who are mentioned only here, or of why they in particular should be mentioned. One possibility is that they were delegates from the Asian churches who had been sent to Rome to support Paul, but who in the event had abandoned him.[104]

1:16-18. In contrast stands Onesiphorus, who evidently lived in Ephesus; his household is mentioned again in 4:19. It is noticeable that his household gets the credit, as it were, for Onesiphorus's kindness. It is a small reminder that the head of the household, the *paterfamilias,* represented the household as a whole, so that his decisions and actions would carry the whole household with him. But it sounds as though the household acted as a team in Christian service (cf. 1 Cor 16:15). He is remembered for having often "refreshed" Paul (ἀναψύχω *anapsychō;* lit., "renewed his soul"), and in contrast to "all in Asia," he is an example of "not being ashamed" (the third time the word ἐπαισχύνομαι [*epaischynomai*] appears in the chap.: 1:8, 12, 16). The particular act of kindness is spelled out—implying that Paul's whereabouts (in detention?) in Rome were not always well known (v. 17)—as well as the memory of much service earlier in Ephesus (v. 18). The repeated prayer wish is that Onesiphorus and his household should receive (v. 16) or find mercy from the Lord on that day (v. 18).[105] The idiom is Hebraic (cf. Gen 6:8; 19:19; Exod 33:16; Luke 1:30; Heb 4:16; 10:25), but "the Lord" here is presumably Jesus Christ (cf. Jude 21).

---

104. Hermogenes and Onesiphorus, however, are subsequently drawn into what we would call the "novel" known as *The Acts of Paul and Thecla.* See D. T. MacDonald, *The Legend and the Apostle: The Battle for Paul in Story and Canon* (Philadelphia: Westminster, 1983) 59-62.

105. Had Onesiphorus died? If so we have the first example of a Christian prayer-wish for someone who had died. See Kelly, *The Pastoral Epistles,* 171. Unfortunately the text is too ambiguous on the point for us to be sure. See G. D. Fee, *1 and 2 Timothy, Titus,* New International Biblical Commentary (Peabody, Mass.: Hendrickson, 1984; rev. ed. 1988) 237.

REFLECTIONS

There are two prominent themes in this passage: First, the repeated talk of not being ashamed (1:8, 12, 16), and, second, the image of faith as a "deposit" (1:14; cf. 1:12).

First-century Mediterranean society can be described as an honor/shame culture. This would have been brought home to the first readers of these letters every day, since the public places of every city, and particularly the capital of a province (like Ephesus), were filled with statues and honorific plaques and inscriptions. Typically, these commemorated favors and benefactions were made by leading citizens to the city or state. Social ethos encouraged the seeking and deserving of such honor as a worthy motivation and goal. The converse was the shame that one properly felt at failing to act in accordance with the obligations or expectations of one's position in society. The honor/shame mind-set is well illustrated by Jesus' parable in Luke 14:7-11 (it was customary to seat people at a banquet in order of rank; in Greco-Roman society the quality of food would usually be better for those of higher rank). Paul had used the language of shame in reference to women acting against the social convention of the time in 1 Cor

11:6 and 14:35. We saw 1 Timothy using the language of honor in 1 Tim 5:3, 17, and 6:1; and 2 Timothy uses it in obviously familiar imagery in 2:20-21.

Today we can see operative similar motivations among the well-to-do, for example, in the financing of a new student center or laboratory on a university campus—where the honor of a building named after the donor is the return for the benefaction. Again, many social conditions today carry the stigma of shame—for example, single parents, the homeless, welfare dependency. But overall, honor and shame are less powerful factors in determining the ethos of present-day society. There is not such a broad consensus of what society has a right to expect from its members, such that failure to fulfill the expectation would bring a sense of shame. Social embarrassment tends to follow a much more subtle code than being held up to public censure and ridicule. Whether this is a good or bad thing would be an appropriate subject for discussion. Also worth discussing is the extent to which effective codes of honor and shame depend on the cohesiveness of society and the degree to which it shares common values, and whether there are cultural codes that Christians stand out against.

Notable here, then, is the fact that the primary determinant of and ground for shame in the Christian is failure to live in accordance with gospel expectations. According to the conventions of the day, one might well have been ashamed of a gospel that gave such prominence to one who had died the most shameful of deaths, crucifixion (1:12; 1 Cor 1:18 31), and of the fact that one of its leading proponents was a jailbird (1:8, 16). But the gospel radically transformed these values and codes, because it changed priorities and relationships. The sort of questions that may emerge from this line of reflection are whether concerns to protect the "good name of the family" are always Christianly based, or whether "dishonorable" discharge from military service should necessarily be always regarded as shameful.

The second theme is not unrelated. In this passage we see the most forceful expression of a tendency apparent throughout the Pastorals. It is signaled particularly by talk of "the faith" and "the sound teaching," as well as in the quotation of what had already become treasured formulations from earlier days (the "faithful sayings"). Here it is expressed in the quotation of a summary gospel statement (1:9-10), by reference to the "pattern of sound words" (1:13), and particularly by the (double) reference to "guarding the deposit" (of faith) once given. It is difficult to avoid the conclusion that the Pastorals see faith in more formal terms than had Paul, that a significant shift had taken place from believing "in" to believing "that," that the process of definition and creedal formation was already well advanced.

Such a process was, of course, inevitable, and the location of the Pastorals, with their talk of "sound teaching" and "faithful sayings," within the New Testament canon authenticates and validates that process. At the same time, it is good to recognize a danger in this process— the danger of losing the substance in the form, the danger of putting more weight on the "that" than on the "in," the danger of confusing the creedal affirmation with the faith that it affirms. It must always be remembered that words spoken by humans will never be adequate to express divine reality, that they can serve only as metaphors for and windows onto an ultimately inexpressible reality. As icons and images they can easily become idols. When humans reciting the creeds think that the words are the thing itself, then the icon has become the idol. This is not to say that the writer(s) of the Pastorals has fallen into this trap. There are sufficient indications of a faith still living and personal. But the Pastorals have been taken to encourage such a formalization, and if they are taken to epitomize Paulinism, that tendency may be reinforced. It is important, therefore, that the emphasis of the Pastorals at this point be recognized as complementary to the gospel according to the earlier Paulines and not as the whole or the definitive portrayal of Pauline Christianity.

2 TIMOTHY 2:1-26, PAUL'S CHARGE TO TIMOTHY

NIV

2 You then, my son, be strong in the grace that is in Christ Jesus. ²And the things you have heard me say in the presence of many witnesses entrust to reliable men who will also be qualified to teach others. ³Endure hardship with us like a good soldier of Christ Jesus. ⁴No one serving as a soldier gets involved in civilian affairs—he wants to please his commanding officer. ⁵Similarly, if anyone competes as an athlete, he does not receive the victor's crown unless he competes according to the rules. ⁶The hardworking farmer should be the first to receive a share of the crops. ⁷Reflect on what I am saying, for the Lord will give you insight into all this.

⁸Remember Jesus Christ, raised from the dead, descended from David. This is my gospel, ⁹for which I am suffering even to the point of being chained like a criminal. But God's word is not chained. ¹⁰Therefore I endure everything for the sake of the elect, that they too may obtain the salvation that is in Christ Jesus, with eternal glory.

¹¹Here is a trustworthy saying:
 If we died with him,
  we will also live with him;
¹²if we endure,
  we will also reign with him.
 If we disown him,
  he will also disown us;
¹³if we are faithless,
  he will remain faithful,
  for he cannot disown himself.

¹⁴Keep reminding them of these things. Warn them before God against quarreling about words; it is of no value, and only ruins those who listen. ¹⁵Do your best to present yourself to God as one approved, a workman who does not need to be ashamed and who correctly handles the word of truth. ¹⁶Avoid godless chatter, because those who indulge in it will become more and more ungodly. ¹⁷Their teaching will spread like gangrene. Among them are Hymenaeus and Philetus, ¹⁸who have wandered away from the truth. They say that the resurrection has already taken place, and they destroy the faith of some. ¹⁹Nevertheless, God's

NRSV

2 You then, my child, be strong in the grace that is in Christ Jesus; ²and what you have heard from me through many witnesses entrust to faithful people who will be able to teach others as well. ³Share in suffering like a good soldier of Christ Jesus. ⁴No one serving in the army gets entangled in everyday affairs; the soldier's aim is to please the enlisting officer. ⁵And in the case of an athlete, no one is crowned without competing according to the rules. ⁶It is the farmer who does the work who ought to have the first share of the crops. ⁷Think over what I say, for the Lord will give you understanding in all things.

8Remember Jesus Christ, raised from the dead, a descendant of David—that is my gospel, ⁹for which I suffer hardship, even to the point of being chained like a criminal. But the word of God is not chained. ¹⁰Therefore I endure everything for the sake of the elect, so that they may also obtain the salvation that is in Christ Jesus, with eternal glory. ¹¹The saying is sure:
 If we have died with him, we will also live
  with him;
¹² if we endure, we will also reign with him;
 if we deny him, he will also deny us;
¹³ if we are faithless, he remains faithful—
 for he cannot deny himself.

14Remind them of this, and warn them before God[a] that they are to avoid wrangling over words, which does no good but only ruins those who are listening. ¹⁵Do your best to present yourself to God as one approved by him, a worker who has no need to be ashamed, rightly explaining the word of truth. ¹⁶Avoid profane chatter, for it will lead people into more and more impiety, ¹⁷and their talk will spread like gangrene. Among them are Hymenaeus and Philetus, ¹⁸who have swerved from the truth by claiming that the resurrection has already taken place. They are upsetting the faith of some. ¹⁹But God's firm foundation stands, bearing this inscription: "The Lord knows those who are his," and, "Let everyone who calls on the name of the Lord turn away from wickedness."

[a] Other ancient authorities read the Lord

NIV

solid foundation stands firm, sealed with this inscription: "The Lord knows those who are his,"[a] and, "Everyone who confesses the name of the Lord must turn away from wickedness."

20In a large house there are articles not only of gold and silver, but also of wood and clay; some are for noble purposes and some for ignoble. 21If a man cleanses himself from the latter, he will be an instrument for noble purposes, made holy, useful to the Master and prepared to do any good work.

22Flee the evil desires of youth, and pursue righteousness, faith, love and peace, along with those who call on the Lord out of a pure heart. 23Don't have anything to do with foolish and stupid arguments, because you know they produce quarrels. 24And the Lord's servant must not quarrel; instead, he must be kind to everyone, able to teach, not resentful. 25Those who oppose him he must gently instruct, in the hope that God will grant them repentance leading them to a knowledge of the truth, 26and that they will come to their senses and escape from the trap of the devil, who has taken them captive to do his will.

[a]19 Num. 16:5 (see Septuagint)

NRSV

20In a large house there are utensils not only of gold and silver but also of wood and clay, some for special use, some for ordinary. 21All who cleanse themselves of the things I have mentioned[a] will become special utensils, dedicated and useful to the owner of the house, ready for every good work. 22Shun youthful passions and pursue righteousness, faith, love, and peace, along with those who call on the Lord from a pure heart. 23Have nothing to do with stupid and senseless controversies; you know that they breed quarrels. 24And the Lord's servant[b] must not be quarrelsome but kindly to everyone, an apt teacher, patient, 25correcting opponents with gentleness. God may perhaps grant that they will repent and come to know the truth, 26and that they may escape from the snare of the devil, having been held captive by him to do his will.[c]

[a] Gk of these things   [b] Gk slave   [c] Or by him, to do his (that is, God's) will

COMMENTARY

This chapter contains the most sustained of the charges put to Timothy or Titus in these letters. It begins with the commission to ensure an effective succession for the deposit (1:14) entrusted to Timothy (2:1-2), followed by a sequence of vivid reminders of the discipline required (2:3-7). This leads naturally into the thought of the suffering and endurance indicated in the gospel (2:8, 11-13) and certainly entailed by its service (2:9-10). Further imagery contrasts the good worker and the sound foundation (2:15, 19) with alternatives of catastrophe, profane and empty talk, gangrene (2:14, 16-18), and again the contrast of expensive pottery with cheap pottery (2:20-21), to underline the importance of faithful maintenance of and dedication to the faith. The final paragraph rounds off the exhortation with a scattering of personal advice (2:22-23) aimed at winning back those who have apostatized (2:24-26).

2:1-2, Be Strong. The sequence begins on a tender and very personal note: "my son" (v. 1). The first thought is the need for the strength that comes from without, from Christ (cf. Eph 6:10), as with Paul himself (4:17; see the Commentary on 1 Tim 1:12). Here, significantly, the focus of that strength is "grace" (χάρις charis), the word that more than any other in the Pauline letters sums up the initiative and action of God for and in human beings to rescue and remake them.[106] Typical of the Pastorals is the fact that it is here described as "the grace that is in Christ Jesus" (cf. 1:9), like the "faith and love that are in Christ Jesus" (1 Tim 1:14; 3:13; 2 Tim 1:13; 3:15), the "life which is in Christ Jesus" (1:1), the "salvation that is in Christ Jesus" (2:10). In these phrases,

106. See J. D. G. Dunn, *The Theology of Paul the Apostle* (Grand Rapids: Eerdmans, 1997) §13.2.

the "in Christ Jesus" describes less the immediacy of the individual's personal involvement with Christ (see, e.g., Rom 6:11; 8:1; 16:3; 1 Cor 1:2, 30) and more the assurance that Christ embodies all the gifts and graces that the gospel holds forth (see, e.g., Rom 3:24; 6:23; 8:2, 39; 1 Cor 1:4).

Verse 2 is the nearest we have in the NT to an idea of apostolic succession (cf. Heb 2:3-4)—or, better, of gospel succession (the verb "entrust" [παρατίθημι *paratithēmi*] is the natural correlate to "deposit" [παραθήκη *parathēkē*] in 1:12, 14). What is envisaged is not only the transmission from Paul to Timothy—a regular theme in the Pastorals (particularly 1:13 and 3:14, but implied in the very character of the letters) and here given added *gravitas* by the allusion to a solemn act of transmission "through" or "in the presence of" many witnesses.[107] In addition, however, two further stages in transmission are envisaged—from Timothy to "faithful people, who will be competent to teach others also"—four stages, we may even say four generations, in all. It is hard to avoid the sense that a much longer time span is now intended than in the earlier Paulines, with the faithful transmission of the established tradition as the uppermost thought.

2:3-7, Share in Suffering. The following images all emphasize the thought of discipline and hard work. But the opening exhortation (v. 3) gives particular prominence to the thought of shared suffering—that is, shared with other believers (1:8) and with Christ (2:11). The theme is archetypically Pauline (see the Commentary on 1:8) and underlines the conviction (itself born of experience) that faithful witness to the gospel would inevitably bring suffering in its train. Paul did not hesitate to use the image of the soldier (cf. Phil 2:25; Phlm 2), or to encourage the implication that service of the gospel was a real warfare (cf. Eph 6:10-18; 1 Thess 5:8; see also the Commentary on 1 Tim 1:18). But here the primary thought is of the single-mindedness of the good soldier (v. 4). The image assumes the established pattern of the professional conscript rather

than the older idea of the citizen militia and echoes the pride in which the successful army held its general. In this case, the enlisting officer (or general) was Paul.

Two other pictures from common experience underline the point (vv. 5-6). Those who lived in the Greek cities fringing the Aegean would be familiar with the great athletic contests held regularly; for example, the Isthmian Games hosted by Corinth every two years. It is not surprising that it was in his first letter to Corinth that Paul first made use of the image (1 Cor 9:24-25). There as here, it is the link between faithful application and the winner's crown that is emphasized. Since many successful military veterans retired to farm land granted them by the state, the two images (soldier and farmer) went naturally together (as in 1 Cor 9:7). The latter metaphor uses ideas that were important for Paul elsewhere: work hard (see the Commentary on 1 Tim 5:17); "share [in benefit]" (Rom 15:27; 1 Cor 9:10; 10:16-18; Gal 6:6; Phlm 6). For Paul the same rule applied to the community of faith and the service of the gospel. The imagery need not imply a regular stipend for ministry (but see the Commentary on 1 Tim 5:17).

The little homily on lessons from daily life is applied in good teacher fashion (v. 7): "Don't just hear my words, but think about them" (an echo of Prov 2:6). The same rule applies: The words heard required some hard thought; only then would they yield their richest fruit. The teacher is confident in the truth of the lesson given, but at the same time he acknowledges that "understanding" is a gift from the Lord. The Christian pupil listens with one ear cocked to hear the new insight God may bring even from an age-old lesson.

2:8-13, Remember Jesus Christ. The focus and reason for the hard work is the gospel of Jesus Christ (v. 8). The exhortation is unique in the Pauline letters; where Paul talks of "remembering," it is usually something else he has in mind (see Gal 2:10; Col 4:18; 1 Thess 1:3). But it strikes a warmer personal note than the image of guarding a deposit (1:12, 14). The present tense may be rendered, "Keep on remembering."

On this occasion the gospel is summarized in a form that strongly echoes what looks to be an already established confessional formula cited by

---

107. The διά (*dia*) could denote a further stage in the process of transmission: "through" Paul to many witnesses to Timothy. But that would run counter to the repeated impression of the directness of the link between Paul and Timothy. The preposition, therefore, is probably the *dia* of "attendant circumstances," denoting the presence and active approval or participation of the "many witnesses." Cf. the use of prepositions in 1 Tim 4:14 and 2 Tim 1:6. See also the Commentary on 1 Tim 4:14.

Paul in Rom 1:3-4. The two-liner focuses on the two earliest Christian claims that must have accounted for so much of the initial spread of the gospel among Jews: Jesus' qualification as the expected Davidic Messiah, and his having been raised from the dead. Evidently it was the importance of this double claim and the frequency with which it had to be asserted that established it as an early confession. In Paul's own ministry (among Gentiles) the Messianic claim was evidently less central because it was less controversial ("Christ" becomes more like a name than a title). It is the confession that this Jesus Christ had been "raised from the dead" that was more important and made the greater impact, as implied in the kerygmatic formula of 1 Cor 15:4, 12-17, 20 (note also the echoes in Rom 4:24-25; 6:4, 9; 7:4; 8:34; 2 Cor 5:15). "This is my gospel" (lit., "According to my gospel") echoes Rom 2:16 (and 16:25), not in the sense of being Paul's alone, but as indicating the gospel to which he had so tirelessly devoted himself. That the emphasis (for Gentiles as well as Jews, by faith alone) was characteristic, and to some extent distinctive, of Paul is balanced by the very basic nature of the gospel summary here.

Still in the mood of thinking about the physical consequences of Paul's commitment (vv. 3-6), the talk of resurrection from the dead prompts again the contrasting image of Paul in chains, like a criminal (v. 9). The thought is of a piece with the honor/shame contrast of 1:12. The linking preposition is usually translated as "for which," but the most obvious translation is "in which." The point presumably is, once again (see 1:8), that in Pauline theology suffering is not just a consequence of the gospel, but is itself part of the gospel—sharing in Christ's sufferings as the way in which and the means by which the resurrection from the dead comes to its full realization (see the discussion of v. 11). The contrast between his own imprisonment and ability to get about and the success of the gospel is one that gave delight to Paul elsewhere (Phil 1:7, 12-18).

Verse 10 simply elaborates the thought. Paul could endure his imprisonment and sufferings because they were in the service of the gospel. The gospel was the good news of Christ Jesus, in whom was salvation. The characterization of the beneficiaries as "the elect" was one of the terms Paul had carried over from his earlier Jewish self-understanding (e.g., Ps 105:6; Isa 42:1; 45:4; 65:9; Sir 47:22); it underpinned his claim that the salvation into which Gentiles were entering was the salvation promised to his own people by the God of Israel. The talk of "eternal glory" carries forward the honor/shame motif of the previous chapter and implicit in the contrasts of vv. 8-10: This glory comes not through great acts of heroism and civic honors, but through the rescue and wholeness offered by the gospel of the cross, proclaimed by a man in chains.

The theme is further elaborated by the fourth "faithful saying" (see the Commentary on 1 Tim 1:15) in vv. 11-13. Even more than the other gospel summaries (1 Tim 1:15; 2:6; 3:16; 2 Tim 1:9-10; Titus 3:4-7), it strikes a distinctively Pauline note, particularly at the beginning—so much so that it could be regarded as a formula or hymn crafted with the explicit purpose of keeping this emphasis of Paul's alive. The lines are obviously written to achieve effect by means of antithesis, but the theology is profound and the effect not merely rhetorical. The first-person plural "we" highlights the confessional nature of the sentiments.

The first line (v. 11) is almost a quotation of Rom 6:8, picking up Paul's distinctive *syn*-compound usage ("died *with,*" "live *with*"). The thought is sufficiently familiar that there is no need to specify who the "with" refers to: Christ.[108] It thus sums up the strong double insight of Paul: The way of life is through death, and that death can only be so transformed (to become the forecourt to life) if the death they die is the death of Christ (see Rom 6:3-11; Phil 3:8-11). The depth of this insight is profound and has rarely been adequately plumbed.[109]

The thought of "enduring" (v. 12) coordinates well with the first line, since the endurance of suffering is the most immediate implication (v. 10; cf. particularly Rom 8:23-25; 12:12; see also the formula used in Matt 10:22 and 24:13). The counterpart is a third *syn*-compound: "reigning with" (Christ). The thought is clearly of a piece

---

108. Some, however, prefer the thought of Timothy's being encouraged to share in Paul's sufferings. See J. M. Bassler, *1 Timothy, 2 Timothy, Titus,* ANTC (Nashville: Abingdon, 1996) 145-46.

109. It is inadequate, for example, to characterize Paul's language here in terms of "presenting Jesus as the supreme model for Christian behavior." See L. T. Johnson, *Letters to Paul's Delegates: 1 Timothy, 2 Timothy, Titus,* The New Testament in Context (Valley Forge: Trinity Press International, 1996) 67.

with v. 5, but it echoes the earlier Pauline language of Rom 5:17, 21, and 1 Cor 4:8.

The last three lines (vv. 12-13) are more coordinated, but create something of a puzzle. "If we deny him, he will also deny us" directly echoes one of Jesus' most disturbing sayings, in the form preserved in Matt 10:33. But there was a longer, more rooted tradition in Judaism that God remained faithful to the chosen people, even when they proved faithless time and time again (v. 13). It was a point that prophets like Second Isaiah and Hosea delighted in, and Paul had expressed himself clearly on the point in Rom 3:3-7, even before the lengthy exposition of Romans 9–11. The final line (v. 13) gives the reason for this confidence in classic theological terms: "He cannot deny himself." That is to say, the God here celebrated is the one committed to God's people (the foundational belief of Israel's covenant theology). This is the one God, a God faithful to creation (who wants all to be saved, 1 Tim 2:4) and to the chosen ones and concerned for their salvation, not arbitrary chance or blind fate. In this confidence, life can be lived confidently, whatever the suffering to be endured.

The problem is that lines three and four seem to run counter to each other: If denial of Christ brings denial by Christ in its train, how is it that unfaithfulness is not similarly punished? The answer will be partly that "denial" has a stronger tone of deliberate acting against and public renunciation, whereas "faithlessness" sounds more like failure to live up to one's profession. But it would surely be a mistake to press for any neat distinction. The point is presumably that the two lines serve different purposes: the first to warn the casual and to stiffen the resolve of the frightened, the second to comfort the broken and to give renewed hope to the despairing. However, it is of the nature of such epigrammatic summaries of Christian faith that they are open to different interpretations, intended to stimulate more than to teach.

2:14-21, Remind Them. The call to "remember" (v. 8) is matched by the call to "remind" ("keep reminding"). The exhortation begins (vv. 14-15) by picking up the gospel just summarized (vv. 8-13); by adding a further image (the unashamed worker), it effectively links the thought back to both the earlier images (vv. 3-7) and the

previous talk of being ashamed (1:8, 12, 16). All this provides a counter to alternatives again treated dismissively in another sequence of vilificatory imagery.

The other side of the faithful transmission of the gospel (vv. 1-2) is the encouragement of believers not to be distracted by arguments over mere words, verbal quibbles (v. 14; the same root [λογομαχέω *logomacheō*] as in 1 Tim 6:4 [λογομαχία *logomachia*]. Put like that, the warning has a much wider application than simply to teachers of what is obviously false doctrine. Even good and faithful believers can often stumble over particular terms or be distracted by attempts to overdefine or make the mistake of clinging to the word rather than to the substance (see Reflections at 1:8-18). But the sternness of the charge ("before God") indicates that the writer has in view a situation that, while it may have started in learned debate or word games, had now gone well beyond that, bringing "ruin," "destruction" (καταστροφή *katastrophē;* the word has given us the English term "catastrophe") to those who listened. What may have begun as debate about the meaning of "raised from the dead" (v. 8) had resulted in a teaching on the resurrection that had to be refuted (v. 18).

To counter the effects of ill-advised speculation, the teacher needs to be both approved by God and skilled in trade (v. 15). The first term ("approved" [δόκιμος *dokimos*]) has the connotation of "tried and tested" (cf. 2 Cor 10:18; 13:7), in contrast to "tried and failed" (3:8; 1 Cor 9:27; 2 Cor 13:5-7). The "unashamed workman" presumably is the one who has learned the trade well and who works consistently to good effect. The third image is of cutting a path straight across forested or rough country, so that travelers can go directly to their destination. So the thought presumably is either of cutting a straight path for the gospel or of leading the unwary through the thickets or uneven ground in the tradition that otherwise might cause them to lose their direction (given 2 Pet 3:16, the latter can hardly be dismissed). The gospel is sometimes described as "the word of salvation/righteousness/life"; here it is "the word of truth" (as in Eph 1:13; Col 1:5; Jas 1:18).

Alternatives are dismissed in familiar terms (v. 16): "profane" (1 Tim 1:9; 4:7; 6:20), "empty talk" (1 Tim 6:20), resulting in more and more "ungodliness" (Titus 2:12; the opposite of the Pastorals' favorite "piety," "godliness"). Their teaching will spread like gangrene (γάγγραινα gangraina, v. 17). Illustrative of the corrupting power of such teachers are Hymenaeus (mentioned already in 1 Tim 1:20) and Philetus (of whom we hear nothing more). And illustrative of the corrupting power of such teaching is their claim that "the resurrection has already happened" (v. 18).

What precisely is meant is unclear, but most infer a teaching that there was no future resurrection to look forward to (cf. 1 Cor 15:12). In this view, believers already shared in Christ's resurrection, and nothing more need be achieved so far as salvation was concerned. They already had resurrection life and would not die (cf. John 11:26).[110] If that is the case, we may further infer that Hymenaeus and Philetus set salvation and creation in antithesis (cf. 1 Tim 4:3), that salvation was seen as an escape from the body and from the material world, a denial that the created order would also participate in salvation (as Paul had taught, Rom 8:19-21). Whatever the precise teaching in view, the writer was convinced that in propounding it Hymenaeus and Philetus had "missed the mark, deviated from the truth" (ἀστοχέω astocheō; the same word as in 1 Tim 1:6; 6:21) and were "overturning, upsetting [as in Titus 1:11] the faith of some."

The counter and consoling thought is that "God's foundation is firm, solid, strong" (v. 19). The thought is probably prompted by Isa 28:16, a regularly cited text in early Christian apologetic (Rom 9:33; 10:11; 1 Pet 2:6; cf. Matt 21:42; Eph 2:20). In that case, the foundation is presumably Christ himself, or the gospel of his resurrection in particular (with the interpretation of it in 1 Corinthians 15 assumed). The image of a "seal" affixed to the foundation doubles the confidence-building imagery (see, e.g., 2 Cor 1:22; Eph 1:13; 4:30; Rev 7:2-8). The seal is identified with two scriptural quotations. The first is from Num 16:5, and with it an allusion to the classic case of presumption (Korah, Dathan, and Abiram) and its horrific outcome (Num 16:31-35; cf. Jude 11); those who were tempted to follow the teaching of Hymanaeus

and Philetus were confronted by as serious a choice. The second seems to be no particular text as such but an amalgamation or summary of repeated exhortations in Jewish Scripture and writings (see Num 16:26; Job 36:10; Ps 6:8; Isa 26:13; 52:11; Sir 17:26). As elsewhere in the NT, "the Lord" who is named or called upon will be thought of here as Christ, but with the ambiguity of continuity implied, as in the equivalent use made of Joel 2:32 in Acts 2:17-21 and Rom 10:11-13.

The image of a foundation suggests the further image of the house built upon it (v. 20) and of the different pottery found in a great house—gold and silver, wood and earthenware (cf. 1 Cor 3:12). The expense of the former indicates that they were intended for occasions where their value would be recognized, where they would bring honor and respect to their owners (all this can be indicated by the word "honor"). The cheapness of the latter indicates humdrum or hidden use in kitchens and privies, such as no one would boast of and would bring no honor to the owner—literally "dishonor," but in a relative sense. The NIV tries to maintain the contrast by translating the Greek as "noble/ignoble"; the NRSV's "special use/ordinary use" is not so successful. The contrast had already been made in Rom 9:21.

Unlike Rom 9:19-24, however, the author breaks away from the predestinarian mold that the image of the potter encouraged—pottery as made for a particular use—and only the potter could make it afresh (see Isa 45:9; Jer 18:1-6). In this case he envisages the common pot as being able to scour itself clean and to become useful in public display (v. 21). Even so, he quickly corrects himself by switching to the passive: "consecrated [that is, by the owner], useful to the master of the house, made ready/prepared for every good work." The readiness to go beyond the image and to adapt it to the situation imagined should be noted, as also the attempt to hold the balance between human responsibility and divine initiative.

2:22-26, Flee Youthful Lusts. As in 1 Tim 6:11 the final burst of advice to Timothy begins with the reminder that there are some forces that work through his own nature that he needs resolutely to shun (v. 22). Here most explicitly "de-

110. This is how the later gnostic texts understand resurrection. See *Treatise on the Resurrection* 49; *Gospel of Philip* 56.

sires" are in view, the term clearly used in its negative sense of "lusts"; the sexual connotation should not be ignored. Earlier on, Paul had indicated that he shared the Jewish tradition that untutored "desire" is the root of sin (Rom 7:7-11; cf. Jas 1:15). Again, as in 1 Tim 6:11, the contrast to "flee from" is "pursue," with three of the same goals in view (see the Commentary on 1 Tim 6:11), plus "peace." This, it is assumed, is the common goal of fellow believers. The phrase and its context give us, in effect, two definitions or identity markers of Christians: "those who call on the Lord" (see also Rom 10:12-14; 1 Cor 1:2)— but he adds, "from a clean heart" (cf. 1 Tim 1:5; Matt 5:8)—and those who make "righteousness, faith[fulness], love and peace" their goal. The formulaic character of the language should not be allowed to cloak the fact that the writer did not define Christianity purely in formal terms, as though only those who could recite the "faithful sayings," for example, were to be regarded as Christians. The emphasis in v. 22*b* may be compared with Rom 2:7, 10.

The complementary call to "refuse," "reject," "avoid" (v. 23) is hardly more illuminating than the other dismissive rebuttals—"stupid" (Titus 3:9); "uninstructed," "controversies" (1 Tim 6:4; Titus 3:9), which only "breed quarrels/disputes"

(Titus 3:9). The Lord's "slave/servant" ought to be quite the opposite (v. 24)—"not quarreling," but "gentle" (ἤπιος *ēpios*; the only other NT usage of this word, 1 Thess 2:7, evokes the image of the muse), "skillful in teaching" (1 Tim 3:2), "bearing evil without resentment." He will "correct his opponents with humility/considerateness" (cf. 1 Tim 3:3; Titus 3:2)—a fruit of the Spirit much prized by Paul (1 Cor 4:21; 2 Cor 10:1; Gal 5:23; 6:1; Eph 4:2; Col 3:12). The hope is that God may grant the repentance that will bring such people to the truth and make it possible for them to escape the snare of the devil (vv. 25-26; see also 1 Tim 3:7), in which they are held captive to do the devil's will.[111] Again we note the prejudicial language. But more to the point here is the mildness and pastoral sensitivity of the advice—in contrast to so much of the author's own dismissive language (1 Tim 1:4-7; 4:1-3, 7; 6:3-5, 20-21). Also to be noticed is the balance he attempts to maintain between human responsibility and the power experienced as operating from without, whether of God (v. 25) or of the devil (v. 26).

---

111. The Greek of the last clause is awkward, seeming to distinguish the one who captures from the one whose will is done. Hence the NRSV's margin: "may escape from the snare of the devil, having been held captive by him, to do his [that is, God's] will." Alternatively, both pronouns could be taken as referring to God: "snatched alive by God from the devil's snare, so that they can do God's will!" See Johnson, *Letters to Paul's Delegates*, 82.

REFLECTIONS

This passage is notable for several features. First we should note the variety, indeed, the kaleidoscope of images and metaphors on which it draws—soldier with commander, athlete with rule book, farmer with harvest, criminal in chains, catastrophe, worker, cutting a path, gangrene, foundation, seal, house, expensive and cheap pottery, snare. Such vivid imagery makes the attitude and message of the writer clear. Without metaphor and simile, parable and aphorism, communication is one-dimensional and rarely effective over a lengthy message. As Jesus knew well, it is the power of words to paint pictures, to enter the eye-gate as well as the ear-gate, that makes a speech memorable and effective. If that is so, then faith needs its metaphors as much as its creeds. The value of the metaphors in this chapter was presumably their relevance—they were drawn from the realities of everyday life as lived by both writer and readers. Presumably also it follows that contemporary attempts to convey the gospel have to draw on fresh metaphors. A metaphor that no longer "works" is a dead metaphor. It is like a dirty window; it needs to be cleaned or replaced.

Not least of importance here is the recognition that metaphorical speech is a richer way of communicating than is the teaching of algebraic or legal propositions. In metaphor the correlation between the word picture and its referent is not a simple one-to-one. The point of the metaphor is not simply to communicate data, but to tease the mind into fresh insights.

The metaphor is a better teacher than the proposition: The proposition can be learned; the metaphor has to be pondered. That is why the lack of correlation between the different metaphors is not a problem. Metaphors like those in 2 Timothy 2 are not intended to cover every inch of truth like a carpet without holes. Rather, they overlap; they jostle against each other; they point in different directions. They are not hard around the edges, like a box or a sword, where overlap and incompatibility would be a problem; they are fuzzy, like a range of different light sources illuminating their immediate vicinity. They do not give definition; they give illumination.

In this chapter in particular we see how the writer can use this kaleidoscope of images to say what might seem otherwise contradictory things—not just the more familiar thought that divine initiative of the Creator (potter) and human responsibility somehow go hand in hand (2:20-21, 24-26), but also the more subtle balance between thought of the secure foundation and the seal confirming the faithfulness of God, over against the responsibility to avoid godless chatter, to name the name of the Lord, and to depart from iniquity (2:16-19). And not least for the Pastorals, the still more delicate ability to distinguish between Hymenaeus and Philetus on the one hand, and those who might yet be drawn back to the truth, and to adopt the appropriate pastoral tactic (2:17-18, 24-26) on the other hand.

This complexity of a gospel, spoken of in metaphors as well as proclaimed, has to be borne in mind when taking on board the initial exhortation that stands as a headline for the chapter as a whole (2:1-2). Metaphor cannot be transposed directly into proposition without serious loss. And the tradition Timothy had received from Paul and that he had in turn passed on to teachers who would pass it on to still others is made up of both. A teacher who took the injunction of 2:1-2 to apply only to creedal statements would be doing only half his job. There is also the whole ethos that is encapsulated in, or better, caught by, the kaleidoscope of metaphors. The counsel to pastor as well as to denounce has to be considered as well. That is the other half of Timothy's job as envisaged in this chapter—not just the teacher, but also the pastor sensitive to the complexity of the gospel imagery and the need to remint fresh metaphors and images for different contexts and new challenges.

The second main line of reflection is the tremendous basis the chapter gives for a positive theology of suffering. It is not simply a matter of using imagery like that of the good soldier, the knowledgeable athlete, the hardworking farmer, with the overtones of energy expended in disciplined and effective ways (2:3-6). Such images are fine where such energy can be expended to such good effect. But the writer also evokes the image of Paul, the prisoner held in chains against his will and unable to act with any freedom (2:9). This, too, is part of the theology of suffering. So also, later on, the writer will use the much more negative and frightening images of corruption eating into live flesh (2:17) and the animal caught helpless in a snare, unable to escape its captor (2:26). There is a suffering that warns of a plight from which only God can deliver.

But all these are taken up in the restatement of one of Paul's most powerful theological motifs: that of sharing with Christ in his death and enduring with him in his passion (2:11-12). For the writer, as for Paul earlier, it is this identification with Christ, the sense of a whole life caught up into Christ's destiny, that in the end is the only thing that gives hope of making sense of even the worst suffering—suffering sometimes as a signal of danger, suffering at other times as a trial to be borne, suffering at still other times as the discipline required of the dedicated soldier, athlete, farmer. In the darkest moments of disaster or deep personal loss, such thoughts provide little comfort. But as the sages of Israel had long ago learned, it is in such ways that God seeks to wean us from the world and to have us grow up mature; we need only think of Job and the psalms of suffering (particularly Psalms 22; 69). It is *through* suffering that the resurrection becomes a reality (see Rom 8:17-23; 2 Cor 4:16–5:5; Phil 3:8-11).

2 TIMOTHY 3:1-17, LESSONS FROM TRADITION

NIV

3 But mark this: There will be terrible times in the last days. ²People will be lovers of themselves, lovers of money, boastful, proud, abusive, disobedient to their parents, ungrateful, unholy, ³without love, unforgiving, slanderous, without self-control, brutal, not lovers of the good, ⁴treacherous, rash, conceited, lovers of pleasure rather than lovers of God— ⁵having a form of godliness but denying its power. Have nothing to do with them.

⁶They are the kind who worm their way into homes and gain control over weak-willed women, who are loaded down with sins and are swayed by all kinds of evil desires, ⁷always learning but never able to acknowledge the truth. ⁸Just as Jannes and Jambres opposed Moses, so also these men oppose the truth—men of depraved minds, who, as far as the faith is concerned, are rejected. ⁹But they will not get very far because, as in the case of those men, their folly will be clear to everyone.

¹⁰You, however, know all about my teaching, my way of life, my purpose, faith, patience, love, endurance, ¹¹persecutions, sufferings—what kinds of things happened to me in Antioch, Iconium and Lystra, the persecutions I endured. Yet the Lord rescued me from all of them. ¹²In fact, everyone who wants to live a godly life in Christ Jesus will be persecuted, ¹³while evil men and impostors will go from bad to worse, deceiving and being deceived. ¹⁴But as for you, continue in what you have learned and have become convinced of, because you know those from whom you learned it, ¹⁵and how from infancy you have known the holy Scriptures, which are able to make you wise for salvation through faith in Christ Jesus. ¹⁶All Scripture is God-breathed and is useful for teaching, rebuking, correcting and training in righteousness, ¹⁷so that the man of God may be thoroughly equipped for every good work.

NRSV

3 You must understand this, that in the last days distressing times will come. ²For people will be lovers of themselves, lovers of money, boasters, arrogant, abusive, disobedient to their parents, ungrateful, unholy, ³inhuman, implacable, slanderers, profligates, brutes, haters of good, ⁴treacherous, reckless, swollen with conceit, lovers of pleasure rather than lovers of God, ⁵holding to the outward form of godliness but denying its power. Avoid them! ⁶For among them are those who make their way into households and captivate silly women, overwhelmed by their sins and swayed by all kinds of desires, ⁷who are always being instructed and can never arrive at a knowledge of the truth. ⁸As Jannes and Jambres opposed Moses, so these people, of corrupt mind and counterfeit faith, also oppose the truth. ⁹But they will not make much progress, because, as in the case of those two men,ᵃ their folly will become plain to everyone.

10Now you have observed my teaching, my conduct, my aim in life, my faith, my patience, my love, my steadfastness, ¹¹my persecutions, and my suffering the things that happened to me in Antioch, Iconium, and Lystra. What persecutions I endured! Yet the Lord rescued me from all of them. ¹²Indeed, all who want to live a godly life in Christ Jesus will be persecuted. ¹³But wicked people and impostors will go from bad to worse, deceiving others and being deceived. ¹⁴But as for you, continue in what you have learned and firmly believed, knowing from whom you learned it, ¹⁵and how from childhood you have known the sacred writings that are able to instruct you for salvation through faith in Christ Jesus. ¹⁶All scripture is inspired by God and isᵇ useful for teaching, for reproof, for correction, and for training in righteousness, ¹⁷so that everyone who belongs to God may be proficient, equipped for every good work.

ᵃ Gk lacks *two men*   ᵇ Or *Every scripture inspired by God is also*

COMMENTARY

Further warnings follow as to the sort of evil people who may be expected "in the last days" (3:1-5), a malaise that will affect the Christian communities and be actively spread within them (3:5-7). The implication is that Timothy should already know to expect such, since the expectation itself is traditional. But Scripture gives specific prototypes in Jannes and Jambres (3:8-9). In direct contrast is the memory of Paul's own steadfastness under severe trial (3:10-13). The inference that previous history provides such valuable lessons is confirmed by the final appeal to the role of inspired Scripture in giving instruction to safeguard against repetition of the one precedent and to promote the other (3:14-17).

3:1-9, People to Avoid. As in 1 Tim 4:1-5, the writer draws on the well-established expectation (Jewish and Christian) that the final days of this age will be marked by a crescendo of evil (v. 1; see the Commentary on 1 Tim 4:1). The first Christians evidently believed that Christ's resurrection and the giving of the Spirit (cf. Acts 2:17) had ushered in the final sequence of events that would climax in "the last day" of general resurrection and judgment (see John 6:39-40; 12:48). Despite the regular comment that the delay of the end was a problem for the writer, the expectation seems to be little different from other expressions of it (cf. Jude 18 and the still later 2 Pet 3:3). As in 1 Tim 4:1-5, the implication is that the writer saw these expectations already being fulfilled in the situations confronting the churches of his day. What he had in view in speaking of such "difficult times," "times of stress," is indicated in the following catalog.

What follows in vv. 2-5 is a typical example of a vice list, the sort of behavior that would generally be regarded as such and that would be abhorred by most right-thinking people (typical examples elsewhere in the NT include Rom 1:29-31; 1 Cor 6:9-10; Gal 5:19-21; 1 Tim 1:9-10). The list should not be taken as a prediction of particular evils but as indicative and representative of a society's ethos breaking down under stresses too great for the principles and values it claims to espouse.[112] It is worth following the writer's lead

in allowing the rapid array of character types that follow to build an impression of a type of society or community gone bad—"lovers of self/selfish," "lovers of money/avaricious" (Luke 16:14); "boasters/braggarts" (Rom 1:29); "arrogant/haughty" (Luke 1:51; Rom 1:30); "slanderous/blasphemers" (1 Tim 1:13); "disobedient to parents" (Rom 1:30); "ungrateful" (Luke 6:35); "unholy" (1 Tim 1:9); "unloving/lacking family affection" (Rom 1:31); "irreconcilable," "slanderers" (lit., "devils," as in 1 Tim 3:11; Titus 2:3); "without self-control/dissolute," "traitors/betrayers" (like Judas, Luke 6:16); "reckless/thoughtless" (Acts 19:36); "blinded or conceited" (1 Tim 3:6; 6:4); "lovers of pleasure rather than lovers of God."

The final description (v. 5) probably applies to all the preceding—"having the form of godliness [the Pastorals' favorite word; see footnote 10], but denying its power." The inference is clear: Those in view in the vice list of 3:2-4 are not outsiders; such people are also found within the church. The word used, "form" (μόρφωσις *morphōsis*), does not denote an appearance casually assumed or taken on to deceive, but a form that was appropriate to the reality—here the form that "godliness/piety" might well take (cf. Rom 2:20). The contrast, then, is with a godliness that really transforms a life and whose substance is displayed not simply in appearance but in useful service (2:21; cf. Titus 1:16). An example of the subtlety of the self-deception here warned against would be the self-assumptions criticized in Rom 2:17-24. Such people are to be avoided—an exhortation easier to give than to enact, given the subtlety of the self deceit just instanced.

The importance of this qualification becomes clearer in the light of the specific example given (vv. 6-7). Some of these people "creep into" or "worm their way into" households (the language is deliberately pejorative) and are successful in winning over those in the women's quarter. The picture is evidently drawn from experience, reflecting the fact that women were often effectively restricted within their households for large parts of the day and would often find time heavy on their hands; the door-to-door peddler of new religions and divergent sects has been a fact of life

---

112. The list shows some literary skill in its construction, particularly the almost unbroken sequence of eight words beginning with "a" in 3:2-3.

throughout Christian history and beyond (cf. 2 Cor 2:17). In the second century, Celsus made similar complaints regarding Christian evangelism.[113]

More disturbing for the modern reader are the disparaging terms with which the writer describes women who were enticed by such teaching (vv. 6-7). They are "little" women, a scornful diminutive, with the sense of "silly." They are filled up or overwhelmed by their sins, allowing themselves to be led astray by their desires, always trying to learn (cf. 1 Cor 14:35) and never able to come to a knowledge of the truth (cf. 1 Tim 2:4; Titus 1:1). There is a prejudice here, such as we see elsewhere in the Pastorals (particularly 1 Tim 4:7; 5:13), and it is difficult to know how much to discount for it, not least since it was one widely shared at the time.[114] At the same time, we should also recall the contrasting pictures of 1 Tim 5:10 and 2 Tim 1:5 and the disadvantaged state of the great majority of women, usually with little or no education and often hungry for knowledge, and so easy prey to the wandering teacher with good-looking credentials.

The description of such subversive teachers continues in familiar dismissive tones (v. 8): "they oppose the truth, people of corrupted mind, unfit, unapproved [the opposite of 2:15] concerning the faith." The writer is confident that he knows "the truth" and firmly grasps "the faith," but otherwise such description tells us more of his attitude to alternative renderings of that truth and faith (recall that they "have the form of godliness") than of the alternative renderings (cf. 1 Tim 6:3-5).

In this case, however, he can cite a parallel or precedent—that of Jannes and Jambres (vv. 8-9).[115] The reference is to the episode in Exodus 7, when the Egyptian magicians attempted to counter Moses first, unsuccessfully, in the contest of staves becoming snakes (Exod 7:11-12) and then, apparently more successfully, in the contest of turning water into blood (Exod 7:22). The episodes attracted some speculation in later Jewish circles, and the two names given here were evidently already given to these magicians;[116] this

is the way such traditions develop (cf. the story of the magi in Matthew 2, to whom later Western tradition gives the names of Balthasar, Melchior, and Gaspar). The reference to them, it should be noted, depends on the already developed tradition, since the brief account of Exodus 7 is inadequate in itself to support the suggestion that they were tricksters or deserving of comparison with those just described. The point, however, is that they represent an alternative religious standpoint, opposed to the truth and right of God (cf. Exod 9:27) and, therefore, can represent those against whom the writer warns here. More to the point, their failure in the face of the superior empowerment of Moses (note also Exod 9:11) provides an assurance that the truth of the faith will triumph in the end, exposing the folly of these other teachers in a similar way.

3:10-17, Precedents to Follow. Over against episodes in scriptural tradition such as that of Jannes and Jambres is set, not Moses, but Paul. Thus is picked up again an emphasis running through both letters to Timothy, where Paul is put forward, not only as Timothy's father and teacher in the faith, but also as a model for subsequent generations (1 Tim 1:12-16; 2:7; 2 Tim 1:11-12; 2:9-10; 3:10-12; 4:6-8). The point not to be missed here is that the reference to the traditions of Paul's mission work is sandwiched between references to the biblical precedent from Exodus 7 (3:8-9) and the fulsome affirmation of the role of Scripture (3:14-17). The implication is that the traditions of Paul (now preserved in Acts), like the traditions of Jesus' teaching (1 Tim 5:18, now preserved in the Gospels), already carry a paraenetical authority similar to that of the Hebrew (or Greek) Scriptures.

The appeal to Paul (vv. 10-11) is comprehensive: Timothy has "followed"—that is, he has "paid attention to" (precise translation is difficult, hence the NIV's "you have observed" and the NRSV's "you know all about"; it implies close attention to and learning from)—Paul's "teaching" (διδασκαλία *didaskalia*; one of the Pastorals' key terms), his way of life and conduct, his purpose and resolve (πρόθεσις *prothesis*; the same word as in 1:9), his faith or faithfulness (cf. 1 Tim 1:4-5; 4:12), his endurance or steadfastness (cf. 2 Cor 6:6; Gal 5:22), his love (see Commentary on 1 Tim 1:5), his patience (cf. 1 Tim 6:11; Titus 2:2),

---

113. See Origen *Against Celsus* 3:55.
114. See J. M. Bassler, *1 Timothy, 2 Timothy, Titus,* ANTC (Nashville: Abingdon, 1996) 161.
115. An equivalent episode from Christian history is that of Elymas, also described as a magician. See Acts 13:8.
116. See *Damascus Document* 5:18-19. For further detail, see M. Dibelius and H. Conzelmann, *The Pastoral Epistles,* Hermeneia (Philadelphia: Fortress, 1972) 117.

his persecutions, and his sufferings. The last two terms link in one of the dominant motifs in the preceding chapter (see 2:9-13) and introduce specific reminiscences of the hardships Paul endured in his mission. Clearly in view are the episodes vividly retold in Acts 13–14; even if this were a reminiscence between long-standing associates (see Acts 16:1), the fact that it is written with a view to a wider audience implies that such accounts of Paul's missionary work were familiar throughout the church founded by him. More to the point, Paul's history gave plenty of examples of the Lord's rescuing him from persecution—just the encouragement required for those enduring lesser troubles and pressures to stand firm. The language echoes Ps 34:19, evoking still earlier examples of steadfastness under trial and of God's deliverance.

The harsh reality is that such persecutions can be expected by "those who want to lead godly lives" (vv. 12-13; the adverb of his favorite "godliness" [εὐσέβεια *eusebeia*] is used here) in Christ Jesus (a usage that is closer to the earlier Pauline motif than others), while "wicked people and tricksters ["sorcerers" (γόητες *goētes*)] progress from bad to worse, deceiving and deceived." The recognition that followers of the crucified Christ were unlikely to escape persecution goes back to Jesus (particularly Matt 5:11; Mark 8:34). The use of *goetes* carries with it both the allusion to Jannes and Jambres (vv. 8-9) and the common suspicion that such "impostors" or "magicians" were more proficient at sleight of hand than they were mediums of supernatural power. At the same time, the recognition that such people can be self-deceived as well as deceivers, another common perception,[117] is a healthy qualification of the more regular cut-and-dried dismissal of contrary teaching. The contrast between the godly being persecuted and the wicked progressing in their wickedness is a variation on the regular theme in the psalms (e.g., Psalm 73), in which the righteous complain at the prosperity of the wicked.

The other secure guideline to wisdom and wholeness as recognized by God is the holy writings, which constituted Timothy's textbook from childhood (vv. 14-15); Timothy evidently owed much to his mother's and grandmother's teaching (see the Commentary on 1:5). Here we are reminded that the Torah, the Prophets, and the Writings provided the school curriculum for Jewish boys as well as Israel's law book and prayer book. Obviously implied is the continuity between Timothy's instruction from the Jewish Scriptures and his belief in Christ; it was because the two were so closely coordinated that Paul could defend and expound the gospel by referring to the Scriptures. So, too, the writer can take it for granted that the "holy writings" themselves are "able to make you wise for salvation through faith in Christ Jesus" (see 1 Tim 1:14; 3:13), without even referring to the gospel or to the teaching. Of course, the assumption is that the gospel is the outworking of Scripture, so that the wisdom, salvation, and faith held out in the gospel are continuous with that inculcated in the holy writings. That is also to say that the gospel's saving power is of a piece with the saving power of Scripture, or it is not the gospel.

The descriptions "sacred writings" (v. 15) and "every scripture" (v. 16) are obviously synonymous. Both terms, the latter singular as well as plural, had already been used by the Jewish philosopher Philo to refer more or less to what we call the Old Testament, the books of Moses in particular (see Rom 1:2). Their distinctive status is signaled by the striking term "God-breathed" (θεόπνευστος *theopneustos*), clearly indicating the writer's understanding of the process of inspiration (the word imagery is the same). To be noted is the fact that it is the scripture that is "God-breathed,"[118] and not merely the prophet who is "inspired," unless by that is meant inspired to speak particular words (cf. 2 Pet 1:20). It is for this reason that words of Scripture can be taken elsewhere in the NT to mean words spoken directly by God (explicit in Rom 9:15). This was the commonly understood phenomenon of prophetic inspiration—the speaking of words given not by the conscious mind but directly by the god possessing or the spirit inspiring.

At the same time, it is important to recognize

---

117. "Deceived deceivers" was a commonly used phrase. See Dibelius and Conzelmann, *The Pastoral Epistles*, 119. The Alexandrian Jewish philosopher Philo draws a similar deduction from Exodus 7. See Philo *Migration of Abraham* 83.

118. This expression could be translated as, "Every God-breathed scripture is also useful . . ."; but it would be unjustified to deduce from such a translation that the writer thought there were some "scriptures" that were *not* God-breathed.

that for the writer, the holy writings, Scripture, have a targeted purpose: "to make you wise for salvation" (v. 15); "useful/beneficial for teaching," for reproof,[119] for correction/improvement, for instruction/discipline (the regular term in Greek for "schooling" [ἐλεγμός *elegmos*]), that God's person (of whom Timothy was the type; see 1 Tim 6:11) might be capable/proficient (= able to meet all demands), "equipped for every good deed" (vv. 16-17). Presumably the two purposes are integrated: The purpose of Scripture is the purpose of good schooling—to produce the well-instructed and disciplined adult, proficient and well equipped in the graces and skills required for a positive role in church and society ("good work of every kind") and wise as to what makes for the wholeness of salvation. A similar rationale for Scripture and its continued usefulness is given in Rom 15:3-4 and 1 Cor 10:11.

119. The word used here, *elegmos*, is hapax (see Sir 21:6; 32:17), but it is a close synonym with ἐλεγχος (*elegchos*), which is a less well-attested variant reading (see Prov 1:25, 30).

REFLECTIONS

Talk of "the last days" always tends to be somewhat embarrassing for Christians. One reason why is that the first Christians seem to have concluded that the last days had already begun in the first coming and resurrection of Jesus, and that time would soon climax in the coming again of Jesus. But that second coming has not happened and is still awaited. Another reason is that at scattered intervals ever since there have been groups of Christians who read the signs of the times to conclude that the final end was nigh. And it was not. Such repeated disappointments should make us extremely cautious about reading the signs of the times in the same way. At the same time, Christians should not be so embarrassed at thinking of all time since Jesus as "the last days," for thereby they are affirming that the first coming of Jesus has altered forever the way Christians view time. They belong to a new age that regards the resurrection of Christ as its starting point and the coming again of Christ as its climax. To view reality from that perspective gives a fresh perspective on Christian relationships with God, with others, and with the world, and on Christian responsibility in these "last days."

The linking theme in this passage seems to be learning from tradition and being realistic in the lessons learned. Traditional views of the "last days" warn repeatedly of times of stress to come (3:1); all desiring to live a godly life in Christ should expect persecution (3:12). The gospel, in other words, gives no promise of a quiet life or of escape from hard times. But if this point is taken, then when hard times do come the insight is confirmed and the faith may be strengthened rather than weakened. Tradition can then serve one of its principal purposes by providing practical lessons and further insights from the accounts of faith under stress in earlier hard times. To that extent the fact that "the last days" seem to have stretched out interminably becomes less of a problem, for so far as the good having a hard time at the hands of the bad is concerned, "the last days" are no different in character from the former times, only perhaps in degree.

From the history of tradition we learn also that the gradations of deception are almost infinite. The distinction between having the form of godliness and denying its power (3:5) may be very fine; those idle people who are captivated by the plausible alternative may deserve more sympathy than denunciation (see 3:6-7). Jannes and Jambres have moved from being moderately successful magicians, in one case matching Moses' prowess, to the epitome of trickery and sorcery (3:8-9). The imagery is clear, but the talk of those who are deceivers but also deceived (3:13), of those who are "blinded," is a further reminder that lessons to be applied are rarely clear and simple and that the most testing challenge is not that of the evil person (here the otherwise sweeping denunciation of 3:2-4 can be less rather than more helpful), but the person who is wholly sincere but whose instruction or praxis is beginning to diverge onto a track of its own.

Here again the diverse history of tradition, both Scripture and the lives of great heroes of the faith like Paul, provides fruitful instruction to those who pay it due heed. In view of this, it is inexpressibly sad, and to our own disadvantage, that so many Christian denominations have lost a sense of the importance of their history, of the saints and sages, the heroes and martyrs, as well as the failures and mistakes, that the history of Christianity provides. Just as the New Testament writers affirmed that sacred history was "written down to instruct us" (1 Cor 10:11; cf. Heb 11), so also we today need to recall the great men and women, and the wicked deeds and policies carried out in the name of Christ, of the last twenty centuries who also are there to instruct us. A very valuable exercise for many a congregation would be to ask who they might consider appropriate to count among their own particular canon of saints and what might count among the cautionary tales of their past, and so to remind one another of the lessons that might be drawn from both.

The need to be realistic about expectations regarding the Scriptures is not least of importance. Too many focus the whole of the teaching of 3:15-17 on the important term "God-inspired," and proceed to miss the point by making deductions directly from that term for the value of Scripture in describing, for example, creation and history (often signaled over the past century by the label "inerrant"). But the text is clear: The sacredness of the writings is directed to the end of "making wise for salvation"; the point of Scripture's inspiration was that the Scriptures should be beneficial for teaching and equipping the student believer for effective living as a Christian. Since this text is the most explicit biblical statement of what Scripture is *for,* the fact that it targets the purpose of Scripture so explicitly, and with a clearly delimited scope, should be given more weight, both in the doctrine and in the use of Scripture. Too much time is misspent asking of Scripture what it was not designed to answer. Better that Scripture itself should instruct us as to what its purpose is.

2 TIMOTHY 4:1-22, PAUL'S FINAL CHARGE AND REQUESTS TO TIMOTHY

NIV

4 In the presence of God and of Christ Jesus, who will judge the living and the dead, and in view of his appearing and his kingdom, I give you this charge: ²Preach the Word; be prepared in season and out of season; correct, rebuke and encourage—with great patience and careful instruction. ³For the time will come when men will not put up with sound doctrine. Instead, to suit their own desires, they will gather around them a great number of teachers to say what their itching ears want to hear. ⁴They will turn their ears away from the truth and turn aside to myths. ⁵But you, keep your head in all situations, endure hardship, do the work of an evangelist, discharge all the duties of your ministry.

⁶For I am already being poured out like a drink offering, and the time has come for my departure.

NRSV

4 In the presence of God and of Christ Jesus, who is to judge the living and the dead, and in view of his appearing and his kingdom, I solemnly urge you: ²proclaim the message; be persistent whether the time is favorable or unfavorable; convince, rebuke, and encourage, with the utmost patience in teaching. ³For the time is coming when people will not put up with sound doctrine, but having itching ears, they will accumulate for themselves teachers to suit their own desires, ⁴and will turn away from listening to the truth and wander away to myths. ⁵As for you, always be sober, endure suffering, do the work of an evangelist, carry out your ministry fully.

6As for me, I am already being poured out as a libation, and the time of my departure has come. ⁷I have fought the good fight, I have finished the

NIV

[7]I have fought the good fight, I have finished the race, I have kept the faith. [8]Now there is in store for me the crown of righteousness, which the Lord, the righteous Judge, will award to me on that day—and not only to me, but also to all who have longed for his appearing.

[9]Do your best to come to me quickly, [10]for Demas, because he loved this world, has deserted me and has gone to Thessalonica. Crescens has gone to Galatia, and Titus to Dalmatia. [11]Only Luke is with me. Get Mark and bring him with you, because he is helpful to me in my ministry. [12]I sent Tychicus to Ephesus. [13]When you come, bring the cloak that I left with Carpus at Troas, and my scrolls, especially the parchments.

[14]Alexander the metalworker did me a great deal of harm. The Lord will repay him for what he has done. [15]You too should be on your guard against him, because he strongly opposed our message.

[16]At my first defense, no one came to my support, but everyone deserted me. May it not be held against them. [17]But the Lord stood at my side and gave me strength, so that through me the message might be fully proclaimed and all the Gentiles might hear it. And I was delivered from the lion's mouth. [18]The Lord will rescue me from every evil attack and will bring me safely to his heavenly kingdom. To him be glory for ever and ever. Amen.

[19]Greet Priscilla[a] and Aquila and the household of Onesiphorus. [20]Erastus stayed in Corinth, and I left Trophimus sick in Miletus. [21]Do your best to get here before winter. Eubulus greets you, and so do Pudens, Linus, Claudia and all the brothers.

[22]The Lord be with your spirit. Grace be with you.

a19 Greek *Prisca*, a variant of *Priscilla*

NRSV

race, I have kept the faith. [8]From now on there is reserved for me the crown of righteousness, which the Lord, the righteous judge, will give me on that day, and not only to me but also to all who have longed for his appearing.

[9]Do your best to come to me soon, [10]for Demas, in love with this present world, has deserted me and gone to Thessalonica; Crescens has gone to Galatia,[a] Titus to Dalmatia. [11]Only Luke is with me. Get Mark and bring him with you, for he is useful in my ministry. [12]I have sent Tychicus to Ephesus. [13]When you come, bring the cloak that I left with Carpus at Troas, also the books, and above all the parchments. [14]Alexander the coppersmith did me great harm; the Lord will pay him back for his deeds. [15]You also must beware of him, for he strongly opposed our message.

[16]At my first defense no one came to my support, but all deserted me. May it not be counted against them! [17]But the Lord stood by me and gave me strength, so that through me the message might be fully proclaimed and all the Gentiles might hear it. So I was rescued from the lion's mouth. [18]The Lord will rescue me from every evil attack and save me for his heavenly kingdom. To him be the glory forever and ever. Amen.

[19]Greet Prisca and Aquila, and the household of Onesiphorus. [20]Erastus remained in Corinth; Trophimus I left ill in Miletus. [21]Do your best to come before winter. Eubulus sends greetings to you, as do Pudens and Linus and Claudia and all the brothers and sisters.[b]

[22]The Lord be with your spirit. Grace be with you.[c]

a Other ancient authorities read *Gaul*   *b* Gk *all the brothers*   *c* The Greek word for *you* here is plural. Other ancient authorities add *Amen*

COMMENTARY

The poignant final charge to Timothy serves as a bracket in parallel to chap. 1. It recapitulates both the previous charges (4:1-2, 5) and the previous warnings about likely defection (4:3-4). As elsewhere, Paul, now in his own final lap, is held up as the example to follow (4:6-8). The final spattering of instructions really continues the portrayal of Paul's final testimony (4:9-18). More typical of the greetings characteristic of the closures of Paul's earlier letters is the final paragraph (4:19-21), with a brief double benediction (4:22).

4:1-5, Paul's Final Charge. The opening words (v. 1) repeat those of 1 Tim 5:21 and 2 Tim 2:14. As in the former case, Christ Jesus is linked with God as joint witnesses to and authorities behind the commission. This time, however, the thought is given a triple elaboration in respect of Christ: (1) Reference is made particularly to his coming role as judge of the living and the dead. That the risen and exalted Christ had been appointed to this role was early on affirmed within Christianity (cf. Acts 10:42; 2 Cor 5:10), though we should recall that in Jewish reflection other old-time heroes like Abel and Enoch were given similar roles, as indeed are disciples and saints in Matt 19:28 and 1 Cor 6:2. (2) This will follow on Christ's "epiphany/appearing" (ἐπιφάνεια *epiphaneia*). Here the word certainly has his "appearing" again (second coming) in view (see the Commentary on 1 Tim 6:14). (3) Most distinctive is the talk of "his kingdom." Although it sounds familiar in Christian ears, the thought is actually very infrequent in the NT (Matt 13:41; 25:31; Col 1:13), particularly as measured against the more regular talk of God's kingdom. Perhaps the idea is implied of a royal rulership bestowed by God on Christ (in line with the influential Ps 110:1), whose climax would be the return of the kingdom to God so that God might be all in all (as in 1 Cor 15:24-28). At any rate, the final charge to Timothy has a strong eschatological bias: The responsibility placed on Timothy is to be carried out in the light of the future kingdom and will be validated and vindicated only in the final judgment.

The charge focuses on Timothy's preaching and teaching ministry (v. 2). "The word" stands as summary for the "word of God" (1 Tim 4:5; 2 Tim 2:9; Titus 2:5), "the word of truth" (2:15), "the sure word" (Titus 1:9), as also the gospel, the "sound teaching," and so on (cf. Gal 6:6; Col 4:3). The second imperative has the sense of "stand by"—that is, "be ready," "be on hand"—for opportunities and crises as they arise, whether the time is opportune or not. As so often in the Pastorals, the command to "expose, convict, reprove" (1 Tim 5:20; note the parallel in Matt 18:15) is nearly doubled by the overlapping "rebuke/warn" (ἐπιτιμάω *epitimaō*; the word used by the Lukan parallel, Luke 17:3), but then balanced by the more positive "encourage/comfort"

(παρακαλέω *parakaleō*; as in 1 Tim 5:1; 6:2; Titus 2:15). Both (or all) should be aspects of the teaching, and both (or all) will require resilient "patience" (as in 3:10; cf. 2:24-25).

The need for such resoluteness is all the greater in view of what can be expected (vv. 3-4). Here is evident a clear sense that the "last days" (3:1) have still more unpleasant surprises to unfold (cf. 1 Tim 4:1); the eschatological horizon remains close (cf. Rom 13:11-12; 1 Cor 7:29-31; Phil 4:5) but still at some distance. A vivid little scenario is painted in three acts—the three stages of decline and defection. It begins with people "not putting up with, unwilling to listen to" (cf. Heb 13:22) "the sound teaching" (see the Commentary on 1 Tim 1:10). Instead, with "itching ears" (a well-known image for the curiosity that can be relieved only by scratching them with interesting and spicy bits of information), they "accumulate" teachers who appeal to their own interests and satisfy their desires. The outcome is that they "turn away" (1:15; Titus 1:14) from hearing "the truth" (see footnote 9) and "turn aside" (1 Tim 1:6; 5:15) to "the myths" (see the Commentary on 1 Tim 1:4). The writer uses his familiar praise and blame words, which tell us more of his attitude than of what it is he praises or blames. The double use of the image of "turning away/aside" provides a clear enough picture of how he conceived the errors he was concerned about.

Verse 5 in effect continues the commission of v. 2. "Be well-balanced, self-controlled" has been said elsewhere in complementary terms (e.g., 1:7; cf. 1 Pet 1:13). "Bear hardship patiently" uses the same word as in 2:9, evoking the same theological motif as in 2:3, 11-12. "Evangelist" (εὐαγγελιστής *euangelistēs*) was a recognized ministry, though it is less clear whether the term denoted a full-scale ministry, with the financial support that it would require (cf. Acts 21:8; Eph 4:11), or a function within a more diverse ministry (as here). "Your ministry" is obviously the more comprehensive term, with all the various functions implicit in it that 1 and 2 Timothy cover (the image is of a bowl or pitcher to be filled full).

4:6-8, Paul's Last Testimony. This is one of the most moving passages in the NT. Although the imagery is shared with (drawn directly from?) some of Paul's favorite imagery in his earlier letters,[120] it is hard to hear the passage as other than Paul's own words. Often neglected, however, is the way in which these verses act as a bracket with 1 Tim 1:15-16—the two letters held between Paul's own account of his beginning as a Christian and his imminent end. In fact, the various references back to Paul's ministry mean that the two letters effectively summarize his whole Christian life and ministry (1 Tim 1:15-16; 2 Tim 1:8, 11-13, 15-17; 2:2, 9-10; 3:10-11; 4:6-18). In other words, one of the purposes served by 1 and 2 Timothy seems to be to preserve the memory of the great apostle, illustrated by characteristic vignettes of his ministry. Whatever the origin of these passages, it is unlikely that this effect was unintended.

Paul drew on the imagery of priestly sacrifice (v. 6, "I am already being [or about to be] poured out as a libation/drink offering"; cf. Num 28:7) several times for his own ministry (see Rom 15:16). Here Paul himself is the sacrificial offering (σπένδω *spendō*; as in the other NT use of the verb, Phil 2:17). Clearly in view is Paul's death ("departure" [ἀνάλυσις *analysis*]; the verb is used in Phil 1:23), seen as imminent.

Equally characteristic of Paul is the imagery of the athletic contest or race (v. 7), but here again there seems to be almost a deliberate echo of 1 Cor 9:25-26, with the claim to have "completed the course" nicely answering to the sense of a race not yet finished in Phil 3:12-14 (not to mention 1 Tim 6:12). Precisely the same language is used in Paul's farewell speech in Acts 20:24. In context, since the metaphor runs on into v. 8, "I have kept the faith" should probably be understood as part of the same metaphor: I have competed as a good athlete, having kept the solemn promise or oath the athlete took at the beginning of the games to put out the utmost effort and to compete fairly (cf. 2:5).

That the imagery of 1 Cor 9:25 and Phil 3:14 was particularly in mind is suggested by the continuation of the metaphor in 4:8. The prize in view is "the crown of righteousness" (cf. Phil 4:1; 1 Thess 2:19), presumably the righteousness of final acquittal (cf. Gal 5:5); the precise language may have been suggested by the prospect of vindication held out to the suffering righteous in

Wis 5:15-16. In this case the imagery can be extended to the triumphal entry ("appearance") of the Lord of the games to take his throne on the final day of the games when the victors in the contests would be publicly honored—the day of judgment (as in 4:1).

That the final judgment would be "righteous," that absolute confidence could be placed in the fairness of the judge, was another fundamental conviction of Paul (Rom 3:3-6; cf. 2 Thess 1:5). And as with the use of "all" earlier (1 Tim 2:4-6), the open-endedness of the "all who have longed for his appearing" should not be lost to sight. The judgment of God may not be so closely correlated to the "sound teaching" as some may think. (Substance may be present without form, just as form is no proof of substance!) The God "who wants everyone to be saved" (1 Tim 2:4) may well recognize that "love of his appearing" is a more generous category than a narrow interpretation (which claims to be able, e.g., to specify the nature of that "appearing") allows. The mercy of God is always likely to be richer than even our best imaginings of it (cf. Rom 11:32-36).

4:9-18, Last Requests. The final exhortations, reminiscences, and personal requests are unique in the NT. They give the impression of a note-like communication, written under pressure of circumstances and time, where careful composition was impossible and the opportunity to communicate had to be seized. That it was a personal communication from the very last days of Paul's imprisonment, prior to his death (v. 6), is quite possible; it is just such a note that closely confined prisoners have managed to smuggle out in similar circumstances throughout history. If so, these could be the very last words penned by Paul—more poignant in the sense of abandonment and human aloneness than anything else he wrote, but confident in the Lord to the end.

Paul's close personal relationship with Timothy is a sustained feature of the letters (v. 9; cf. 1 Tim 1:2; 2 Tim 1:2). Little would bring more comfort to the failing Paul than to see and have Timothy with him for the last time. If this was a realistic request, it would take several months to fulfill, implying that Paul continued to hope for further delays before the second phase of his trial (v. 16); the end was not yet.

The plea is all the more affecting because of

120. The most obvious candidate would be Philippians, as the repeated references to Philippians in the Commentary might suggest.

Paul's loneliness, caused partly by desertion and partly by the need to maintain contact with some supervisory role in relation to other churches (v. 10). Demas we hear of earlier in both Col 4:14 and Phlm 24, in not particularly warm terms. Evidently he had not been particularly close to Paul, but his defection (the sixth specifically identified in these letters; see 1 Tim 1:20; 2 Tim 1:15; 2:17) seems to have been more hurtful personally than the others. The verb "forsake/abandon" (ἐγκαταλείπω *egkataleipō*) is the one used in Jesus' "cry of dereliction" on the cross (Mark 15:34). The reason given ("having loved the present age") is unspecific but evocative (see other references to "the present age," Rom 12:2; 1 Cor 1:20; 2:6-8; 1 Tim 6:17; Titus 2:12). Crescens we hear of only here; the reference to Galatia strengthens the likelihood that Paul continued to have good links with the most easterly of the churches that remained within his sphere of mission (see 1 Cor 16:1).[121] On Titus, see Titus 1:4; Dalmatia, southern Illyricum (see Rom 15:19), was roughly equivalent to present-day Croatia;[122] there is perhaps here an echo of 2 Cor 2:13.

Luke (v. 11) is associated with Demas in both Col 4:14 and Phlm 24. (Had he been brought into the Pauline circles by Luke?) The reference here supports the inference of the "we" passages in Acts 16:10-17; 20:5-15; 21:8-18; 27:1–28:16 that Luke (the author of Luke–Acts) was a very close companion of Paul, not least in the final phase of his career. Mark appears in the same contexts in Col 4:10 and Phlm 24; that two men to whom tradition attributed the writing of two of the four Gospels were close companions of Paul is as intriguing as any of the notes in this section. Mark is also associated with Peter (1 Pet 5:13) and in tradition is remembered as Peter's secretary whose Gospel was (based on) his own transcript of Peter's preaching. The positive affirmation of Mark ("he is useful to me for service") provides a pleasing sequel to the bruising breach recalled in Acts 15:36-40 (cf. the imagery of 2 Tim 2:21). The impression that Paul continued to exercise

pastoral oversight of his churches even while in prison is confirmed by v. 12. Next to Timothy and Titus, Tychicus was probably the most prominent of Paul's associate workers (note the commendatory epithets in Col 4:7 and Eph 6:21). According to Acts 20:4, Tychicus came from Asia, and in Eph 6:21-22 he is Paul's emissary to the region (or Ephesus in particular, as here). In Titus 3:12 he is to be sent to Crete.

The request for Paul's cloak, left with the otherwise unknown Carpus, and books, especially the parchments (v. 13), paints in a few strokes a graphic picture of Paul shivering in the winter nights and longing for reading material.[123] What would we give to know what these books were— quite possibly scrolls of particular biblical books (the word is used also, e.g., in Luke 4:17; John 20:30; Gal 3:10; Heb 10:7; Rev 22:7-19). And why were the parchments (μεμβράνα *membrana*) so special? Were there already biblical books in codex form? And were there already coherent collections (scrolls, codices) of Jesus tradition or even of (some of) Paul's own letters?[124]

The mention of Alexander (vv. 14-15) poses another intriguing puzzle. He is presumably not the same Alexander as in 1 Tim 1:20; this Alexander is remembered solely as an opponent. The suspicion that there is a mixed memory here of the episode in Acts 19 is given some support by the triple conjunction of Ephesus, a hostile metalworker (here coppersmith, but in Acts 19:24 the opponent is named as Demetrius, a silversmith), and the participation of an Alexander (a Jew) in the Ephesian riot (19:33; but he tries to calm the riot).[125] What the "great harm" was that he did to Paul is not otherwise indicated. At any rate, he is envisaged as still posing a threat to the Christian message (v. 15). The assurance that "the Lord will repay him according to his works" is not particularly vindictive; rather, it is an expression of the same confidence as at vv. 1 and 8 that

---

121. A reading with some support has "Gaul" instead of "Galatia." It is probably a scribal error, though supported by Kelly. Even the possibility that Paul had missionary links farther west and north than Rome itself is intriguing. See J. N. D. Kelly, *The Pastoral Epistles,* Black's New Testament Commentaries (London: A. & C. Black, 1963) 213.

122. On Dalmatia, see J. J. Wilkes, *Dalmatia* (Cambridge, Mass.: Harvard University Press, 1969); for Illyricum, see the "Index of Places," p. 554.

123. The φαιλόνης (*phailonēs*; Latin *penula*) was a heavy outer garment. It has been suggested that the *phailonēs* could mean a cloth for wrapping books or a case for containing them. But why would Paul mention this before the books and parchments?

124. It is possible that the word denotes "parchment notebooks." See C. H. Roberts and T. C. Skeat, *The Birth of the Codex* (London: British Academy, 1983) 15-23. Paul may have used and kept notebooks in drafting his letters. Parchment was expensive, but presumably scraps of parchment unsuitable for more elaborate or finished works were available for purchase.

125. Still another Alexander appears in the late 2nd-cent. tract *Acts of Paul and Thecla* 26-36.

God's judgment would be just (cf. Rom 2:6-16; 2 Cor 5:10), a confidence itself with deep scriptural roots (see Ps 62:12; Prov 24:12).

The sense of abandonment already prominent (v. 10) is reinforced by the pitiful complaint that in his first hearing (ἀπολογία *apologia,* "defense") no one had stood with him (v. 16), that all had abandoned him (the same word as used of Demas in v. 10). There need be no conflict here with v. 11 (Luke was with him). It is clear enough from the comings and goings indicated in vv. 10-12 that individuals came and went, often as much at Paul's behest as in accord with their own concerns and responsibilities. Nevertheless, the implication is clear that there were those who had been with him at the time and who had let him down. We gain something of the same flavor in Phil 1:15-17, and an echo of Jesus' abandonment (Mark 14:50; 15:34) may be deliberate. The thought that some Christians could have thus failed Paul is hardly encouraging, but Paul was a dominant personality who caused no little controversy within Christian circles. And we do not know how severe or serious was the outcome of the "first defense/hearing." The severity of Paul's state as indicated in this paragraph may also suggest that the hearing had gone badly and that Paul was being held in more restrictive captivity. The final prayer hope is less hostile than v. 14, but shows little desire for personal reconciliation (cf. Phil 1:18).

More characteristic of Paul is his unshakable confidence in his Lord (vv. 17-18). Unusual is the sense of the Lord's presence expressed in these terms ("stood beside me"), perhaps reflecting a sense of almost physical accompaniment, rather than Paul's more common mystical "in Christ" (but perhaps also reflecting the language and memory of Acts 23:11 and 27:23). More typical is the resulting sense of empowerment (see the Commentary on 1 Tim 1:12; 2 Tim 2:1). And still more characteristic is the conviction of a still-enduring commission to proclaim the gospel (here κήρυγμα *kērygma*) to all the Gentiles/nations (see the Commentary on 1 Tim 2:7).[126] This could still be fully discharged even in court

(cf. Acts 26), but also through and not just despite his sufferings and circumstances (see Phil 1:12-18). The recollection of Daniel's deliverance from the lions, a story no doubt well known in every Jewish household (Dan 6:22, 27; 1 Macc 2:60; Heb 11:33; see also Ps 22:21), implies that Paul's peril had been every bit as serious as Daniel's had been.

And it still was (v. 18), but the same confidence that had proved true for the past held firm for the future. The image of eschatological rescue is a variation on the more common (in the Pastorals) "save"; in the earlier Paulines we can compare Rom 7:24; 11:26; 1 Thess 1:10 (not forgetting Matt 6:13). Here the thought is of rescue from "every evil attack," a phrase general enough to include all the negative factors already mentioned (from abandonment to legal judgment). The thought is not of escaping such circumstances (being declared innocent), but of being rescued through them to Christ's heavenly kingdom (see the Commentary on 4:1), the image of an age and society where only justice and mercy prevail. In typically Jewish fashion, the thought inspires an appropriate benediction (1 Tim 1:17; 6:16; cf. Rom 1:25; 11:36; 16:27; Gal 1:5; Phil 4:20).

4:19-22, Final Greetings. It was Paul's practice to close his letters with a number of personal greetings (e.g., Rom 16:3-16). Not surprisingly, Prisca and Aquila are first named (v. 19). They were probably Paul's favorite hosts, active with Paul not so much as companions on his missionary journeys, as were those who everywhere used their houses for hospitality and church gatherings (see Acts 18:2-3; Rom 16:4-5; 1 Cor 16:5). The implication is that they ran, and as Christians continued to run, a successful business with branches in several cities and that Prisca (named first, as more often than not) was the more dominant partner. It is presumed here that they were back in Ephesus. The household of Onesiphorus we have already met (1:16-18).

The additional information on the whereabouts of other of Paul's associates comes in here (v. 20; note v. 10) rather oddly. The name "Erastus" has caused a ripple of excitement, since we know from an inscription in Corinth that there had been a prominent official of that name in Corinth about this time. But whether the Erastus of Acts 19:22 and the one here can be identified with the

---

126. J. Munck, *Paul and the Salvation of Mankind* (Richmond, Va.: John Knox, 1959) 332-34, suggested that when Paul stood before Nero, he would have understood (on the principle of the emperor's representative capacity) that he was fully proclaiming the gospel to "all the Gentiles."

Erastus of Rom 16:23 and then with the Erastus of the inscription is far from certain. According to Acts 20:4 and 21:29, Trophimus was from Ephesus; his presence with Paul in Jerusalem had been the trigger for the riot against Paul (Acts 21:27-30). Miletus was not too far from Ephesus (Acts 20:17) and was also a great seaport, a rival of Ephesus.

During the winter (November through March) sea travel virtually ceased (v. 21); hence, presumably, the request for speed (v. 9). The account in Acts 27:9-41 gives a good indication of the hazzards of winter travel. Of Eubulus, Pudens, Linus, and Claudia we know nothing more (the last three names are Latin), except, perhaps, the tradition first given by Irenaeus that Linus was Peter's successor as leader (bishop) of the Christian congregations in Rome.[127] Quite how the mention of these four, plus "all the brothers," squares with the sad plaint of v. 11 is hardly clear, but it may support the suggestion that vv. 9-18 and vv. 19-21 were quite different notes from Paul that were preserved separately.

The final benediction (v. 22) is a somewhat curious amalgam of Paul's more typical benedictions (cf. Rom 16:20; 1 Cor 16:23; Gal 6:18; Phil 4:23; 1 Thess 5:28; Phlm 25). As in 1 Tim 6:21, the "you" is plural.

127. Irenaeus *Against Heresies* III.3.3.

REFLECTIONS

The initial impact of this final section of 2 Timothy is the contrasting images of 4:1-5. On the one hand, there is the image of the committed preacher, teacher, and evangelist; on the other hand, the image of the kind of consituency or audience with which such a minister may well have to deal. The latter is particularly vivid; it conjures up the picture of interest groups, full of inquiry and eager to learn, but not finding their interest held by the church's preaching or teaching and seeking to satisfy their intellectual or spiritual curiosity in other arenas. What does a pastor do in such cases? Could it be that the preaching and teaching are not intellectually stimulating or spiritually satisfying? Could it be that the emphasis on "sound teaching" has become more emphatic on the "soundness" than on the "teaching"? Or are there more subtle and spiritually sophisticated approaches? The text gives no assurance that such situations (like those just envisaged) can be avoided. Pastors who find themselves asking such questions should not necessarily blame themselves—not necessarily. To ask such questions may be an essential stage in a congregation's growth toward maturity. At the same time, the balm that cures the itch (4:3) will probably not be the "sound teaching" itself, but the grace and skill with which it is explained and promoted (cf. 2:24-26).

The greater impact of this final chapter of 2 Timothy, however, is the portrayal of Paul, his final testimony and his last requests. It would be unfortunate if the value of the passage were restricted to the question of how it contributed to the debate on the authorship of the Pastorals. Whether it was penned by Paul or inserted into this part of the letter by a later writer, the effect is the same.

What we have in the first place is a moving self-testimony at the end of the career of one of the greatest of the world's movers and shakers—the Paul who effectively brought the gospel to Europe, who ensured its success as a universal religion, and who established in writing its theological character as a religion of grace and trust focused on the one God through the one Jesus Christ. We should allow the words of 4:6-8 to work on us in the way that the eulogy delivered at the funeral of a very fine person works on us—at the emotional level, to fire us not simply with admiration for that person, but with resolve to cherish the memory of that person and to allow it to influence and mold our own lives for the better.

This should be the value of Christian testimony, the value of "sharing" experience as well as faith in the way the earliest Methodist class meetings did so successfully. In these cases, "testimony" was not simply of one's conversion ("how I was saved"), but of one's continuing discipleship, of God's continuing dealings ("how I am being saved")—the low points as well as the high points. Such honest (not merely formal) testimony to the reality of grace in everyday life proved itself a powerful help to many a struggling Christian, both the testifier and the hearers. Sad to say, a society that has lost faith in priest and pastor now looks longingly to psychiatrist (or guru) for just that kind of role model and security in personal exposure. Sadder still, Christians often turn to that kind of help because they cannot find it in the fellowship of their own churches.

What we have in the second place is Paul's personal equivalent (4:9-18) of the psalms of complaint. What is so refreshing about even that final jumble of complaint and request is its honesty—the unashamed confession of reliance on others, the note of bitterness at betrayal, the concern for precious belongings that might seem trivial to others, the lament of the lonely. As with the honest prayer of the psalmist, Paul makes no attempt to impress or excuse; his relief at being able to pour it all out even in this intimate little note is almost tangible. When communication between Christians and in prayer can operate at that level, then real fellowship, healing, and wholeness can be experienced.

In the light of such honesty, the final expression of confidence (4:17-18) makes all the greater an impact. As again with the psalmist, it is the cathartic effect of such frank confession of human weakness that opens the one praying to the comforting and strengthening grace of God. It is a sad, but too often repeated, experience to be ignored, that the strength of Christ comes to its full expression only in the depth of human weakness. Prior to that, despite even best intentions, there is still the corrupting tendency to rely on one's own strength (abilities, success, family, and friends), to hold back from that complete reliance and trust that is faith. The lesson of this passage is that usually only *in extremis,* and only when that reality is accepted unconditionally, can there be that unconditional trust that remains confident in God through, as well as despite, everything.

TITUS 1:1-4, GREETINGS AND REMINDER OF PAUL'S COMMISSION

NIV

1 Paul, a servant of God and an apostle of Jesus Christ for the faith of God's elect and the knowledge of the truth that leads to godliness— [2] a faith and knowledge resting on the hope of eternal life, which God, who does not lie, promised before the beginning of time, [3] and at his appointed season he brought his word to light through the preaching entrusted to me by the command of God our Savior,

[4] To Titus, my true son in our common faith:

Grace and peace from God the Father and Christ Jesus our Savior.

NRSV

1 Paul, a servant[a] of God and an apostle of Jesus Christ, for the sake of the faith of God's elect and the knowledge of the truth that is in accordance with godliness, [2] in the hope of eternal life that God, who never lies, promised before the ages began— [3] in due time he revealed his word through the proclamation with which I have been entrusted by the command of God our Savior,

[4] To Titus, my loyal child in the faith we share:

Grace[b] and peace from God the Father and Christ Jesus our Savior.

[a] Gk *slave*   [b] Other ancient authorities read *Grace, mercy,*

COMMENTARY

The introduction takes the usual form of the writer's identifying first himself and then his recipients. In typical Pauline fashion, each element is elaborated with distinctive features (1:1-4a), possibly to give each letter its own personal quality. As with Rom 1:1-5 and Gal 1:1-2, the elaboration of Paul's authority and gospel (1:1-3) may indicate a sense that either or both were under some threat. The introduction concludes with the characteristic Pauline greeting (1:4b).

As in Rom 1:1 and Phil 1:1, Paul is described as "slave" (1:1), but whereas the normal usage is "slave of Jesus Christ," here it is "slave of God." This was language characteristic of Jewish worship (e.g., Neh 1:6, 11; Pss 19:11, 13; 27:9), and the great figures of Israel's history, particularly Moses and the prophets, were quite often referred to as Yahweh's slave (e.g., 2 Kgs 18:12; Ezra 9:11; Ps 105:26; Jer 7:25). The title, therefore, served several functions: It stressed the completeness of

commitment (a slave by definition belonged to someone else); it was honorific (the greater the master, the greater the slave's authority); and it underscored the sense of continuity with Christianity's Jewish heritage.

More typical of Paul's earlier usage is the description "apostle of Jesus Christ" (as in 1 Tim 1:1). Typical also is the double attribution of Paul's status and authority to both God and Christ. The distinctive elaboration here is the purpose given for his appointment as (slave and) apostle "for the faith of God's elect"—that is, presumably, to bring about and to bring to greater maturity Christian faith and knowledge. The preposition κατα (*kata*) is somewhat surprising here and could be translated "in accordance with," but usage indicating goal or purpose is attested (cf. 2 Cor 11:21). The concern for "faith" is similar to that in 1 Tim 1:4-5. For "elect," see the Commentary on 2 Tim 2:10. "Knowledge of the truth" is the same goal as in 1 Tim 2:4 (see also 2 Tim 3:7). As typical in the Pastorals, the measure and proof of this faith and knowledge are "godliness/piety" (see 1 Tim 6:3).

The third member of the characteristic Pauline triad, "hope" (along with faith and knowledge), is instinctively drawn in 1:2—as always in Paul with the full confidence of Jewish usage rather than the tentativeness of Greek and modern usage (i.e., "I hope, but have no confidence that it will be so"; see also 2:13; 3:7). Again the preposition (ἐπι *epi*) leaves the precise correlation of the phrase with its context unclear. The NRSV leaves the ambiguity unresolved; the NIV opts to relate it directly to the faith and knowledge just mentioned, but "faith and knowledge" are not repeated in the Greek. Here the confidence is rooted in God's promise and the degree to which it has already been fulfilled. Again it is a question of the evident continuity between a divine original purpose (see the Commentary on 2 Tim 1:9), as revealed through prophet and Scripture, and its due fulfillment (see the Commentary on 1 Tim 2:6) announced in the preaching of the gospel (1:3). It was a fundamental feature of Paul's self-consciousness that he had been given a special commission to make this message known (as in 1 Tim 1:11). The confidence of Christian hope was thus rooted in the coherence of a divine purpose unfolding in history and the immediacy of the encounter with the divine in human experience.

As was Timothy (1 Tim 1:2), Titus, too, is addressed as Paul's "genuine child in faith" (1:4), here described as their "common" or "shared" faith. Although we have no other testimony to that effect, the language presumably indicates that Titus had been converted through Paul's ministry (cf. 1 Cor 4:15-17; Gal 4:19; Phlm 10); from Gal 2:1-10 we learn at least that he was regarded as a typical product of Paul's mission to Gentiles. The phrase combines the thought of Titus's dependence on Paul and of their mutual interdependence in the faith (cf. 2 Cor 8:23). The greeting itself is the typical Pauline one: "grace and peace" (unlike 1 and 2 Timothy). Characteristic of the coordination and balance Paul maintained in his greetings between God and Christ is the way both God and Christ are described as "our Savior" within three or four lines (1:3-4; see the Commentary on 1 Tim 1:1).

REFLECTIONS

Whether written by Paul himself or not, the Pastoral Epistles confirm a Pauline pastoral tradition of adapting regular forms to particularize and personalize each of his letters. Here not only do we have the characteristic Pauline christianizing of the Greek and Jewish greetings ("grace and peace"; see the Commentary on 1 Tim 1:2) and the intimacy of the address ("loyal child"), but also the elaborate self-description of Paul. Given the importance of traditional forms for the author(s) of the Pastorals, this maintenance of the Pauline tradition of adaptation is worth noting. In the sphere of pastoral practice every person and every church is unique, and the distinctive needs in each case cannot be handled simply in accordance with some ready formula. The personal character of Paul's involvement with his churches no doubt added immeasurably to the authority of his letters.

The purpose of Paul's apostleship was the promotion of faith, knowledge, and hope. The terms can be varied or added to, but these three have a balance that should be ever sought in preaching and pastoral instruction: trust of heart and knowledge of head—the blend of intellectual appreciation and commitment with deep emotional roots; knowledge informed from the past; faith in God and in Christ here and now; and hope for the future. Where these are well integrated, we can begin to speak of maturity of believer and church.

TITUS 1:5-16, THE CHURCH—ITS LEADERSHIP AND ENEMIES

NIV

⁵The reason I left you in Crete was that you might straighten out what was left unfinished and appoint*a* elders in every town, as I directed you. ⁶An elder must be blameless, the husband of but one wife, a man whose children believe and are not open to the charge of being wild and disobedient. ⁷Since an overseer*b* is entrusted with God's work, he must be blameless—not overbearing, not quick-tempered, not given to drunkenness, not violent, not pursuing dishonest gain. ⁸Rather he must be hospitable, one who loves what is good, who is self-controlled, upright, holy and disciplined. ⁹He must hold firmly to the trustworthy message as it has been taught, so that he can encourage others by sound doctrine and refute those who oppose it.

¹⁰For there are many rebellious people, mere talkers and deceivers, especially those of the circumcision group. ¹¹They must be silenced, because they are ruining whole households by teaching things they ought not to teach—and that for the sake of dishonest gain. ¹²Even one of their own prophets has said, "Cretans are always liars, evil brutes, lazy gluttons." ¹³This testimony is true. Therefore, rebuke them sharply, so that they will be sound in the faith ¹⁴and will pay no attention to Jewish myths or to the commands of those who reject the truth. ¹⁵To the pure, all things are pure, but to those who are corrupted and do not believe, nothing is pure. In fact, both their minds and consciences are corrupted. ¹⁶They claim to know God, but by their actions they deny him. They are detestable, disobedient and unfit for doing anything good.

a5 Or ordain   *b7 Traditionally bishop*

NRSV

5I left you behind in Crete for this reason, so that you should put in order what remained to be done, and should appoint elders in every town, as I directed you: ⁶someone who is blameless, married only once,*a* whose children are believers, not accused of debauchery and not rebellious. ⁷For a bishop,*b* as God's steward, must be blameless; he must not be arrogant or quick-tempered or addicted to wine or violent or greedy for gain; ⁸but he must be hospitable, a lover of goodness, prudent, upright, devout, and self-controlled. ⁹He must have a firm grasp of the word that is trustworthy in accordance with the teaching, so that he may be able both to preach with sound doctrine and to refute those who contradict it.

10There are also many rebellious people, idle talkers and deceivers, especially those of the circumcision; ¹¹they must be silenced, since they are upsetting whole families by teaching for sordid gain what it is not right to teach. ¹²It was one of them, their very own prophet, who said,
"Cretans are always liars, vicious brutes,
          lazy gluttons."
¹³That testimony is true. For this reason rebuke them sharply, so that they may become sound in the faith, ¹⁴not paying attention to Jewish myths or to commandments of those who reject the truth. ¹⁵To the pure all things are pure, but to the corrupt and unbelieving nothing is pure. Their very minds and consciences are corrupted. ¹⁶They profess to know God, but they deny him by their actions. They are detestable, disobedient, unfit for any good work.

a Gk husband of one wife   *b Or an overseer*

COMMENTARY

The letter as a whole takes the form of a commission to Titus, and the typical thanksgiving (as in 2 Tim 1:3-4) is omitted. Notable is the fact that it begins with Titus's responsibility to appoint elders (1:5-6) and a summary description of the qualities looked for in an overseer (1:7-9). The emphasis is on the ability to refute false teaching (1:10-14). The description of such teachers is as dismissive as in the other two letters (1:10, 12, 15-16). But particular features suggest that Jewish or Jewish-Christian teaching is particularly in view (1:10, 14). That apart, the counsel here seems to summarize more lengthy instruction given particularly in 1 Timothy.

1:5-9, The Character of Christian Leadership. Just as Timothy had been left at Ephesus (1 Tim 1:3), so also Titus had been left in Crete (v. 5). We have no other indication of a Pauline mission to that island, unless the account of Paul's final journey (as in Acts 27:12) had been elaborated, perhaps along the lines of the related account of wintering in Malta (Acts 28:7-11).[128] The purpose of thus leaving Titus was that he might "set right" (ἐπιδιορθόω *epidiorthoō*; the only occurrence of this word in early Christian literature, but its meaning is clear enough) what remains or is "lacking/falls short" (as in 3:13). This is not to be taken to imply that Paul's mission was defective, but simply that when Paul left there were still things to be done, as he himself had indicated (v. 5).

Chief among these tasks, or the principal way of remedying defects, would be the appointment of "elders." Clearly in view are men similar to those referred to in 1 Tim 5:17-22; as there, presumably the thought is that among the ranks of the πρεσβύτεροι (*presbyteroi*, "older men") there will be some who should be accorded special authority as *presbyteroi* ("elders"). Although the language is different ("appoint"), the thought is no doubt the same as in 1 Tim 5:22 ("laying on of hands"). Notable is the echo of Acts 14:23 and the assumption that there was a church in almost every town. Like Timothy, Titus is expected to exercise an authority like that of Paul (cf. Acts 14:23), as one superior to the elders and overseers whose appointment is in view.

The qualities of the elder (v. 6) closely resemble those listed in regard to the overseers and deacons in 1 Tim 3:2-4, 10-12. They are to be "blameless" (1 Tim 3:10), once married (1 Tim 3:2, 12), have faithful children (1 Tim 3:4, 12), and should not be open to accusations of debauchery (cf. 1

Tim 3:3, 8) or lack of personal discipline (cf. 1 Tim 3:2-3). The lack of any mention of deacons here may indicate that the structures of leadership were developing in different ways in different places.

The linkage of thought into v. 7 ("for an overseer must . . .") strongly suggests that πρεσβύτερος (*presbyteros*) and ἐπίσκοπος (*episkopos*) were regarded as near synonyms (cf. Acts 20:17, 28). We may deduce that just as the elder was appointed from among the older men, so also the more specific role of overseer emerged from that of the elders. We are not yet at the stage where the overseer was a single figure, quite distinct in office and status from other leaders; bishop had not yet become distinct from presbyter/elder. At the same time, the function of the overseer is made clearer by the further description, "God's steward" (cf. 1 Cor 4:1-2); just as the steward administered an estate on its owner's behalf (cf. Gal 4:1-2), so also the overseer had to exercise oversight over God's estate (cf. 1 Tim 3:5) or household (cf. 1 Tim 3:15).

The qualities of the overseer (vv. 7-8) pick up from those already listed (v. 6): "blameless"; "not self-willed, stubborn, arrogant" (elsewhere in the NT only in 2 Pet 2:10); "not inclined to anger/quick-tempered"; "not addicted to wine" (1 Tim 3:3); "not a bully" (1 Tim 3:3); "not greedy for money" (1 Tim 3:8), but "hospitable" (1 Tim 3:2); "a lover of what is good" (a *hapax,* but common in honorific inscriptions of the time); "prudent/moderate" (1 Tim 3:2); "just," "holy," "self-controlled." Again it is worth noting that most of these qualities would have been regarded as virtues within religious or philosophical circles of the time; two in particular (moderate and just) belonged to the four cardinal virtues in Greek philosophy (prudence, justice, temperance, fortitude).

The more specific and distinctive Christian criteria emerge in v. 9 in the familiar language of the Pastorals: "holding to the faithful word in accord with the teaching" (see the Commentary on 1 Tim 1:15), "able to encourage in the sound teaching and to reprove/correct those who speak against it" (cf. 1 Tim 5:20). The doubling of the language reinforces the impression of a teaching, not necessarily greatly elaborated, but set out in clear formulations that had already become the

128. If, however, the letter was by Paul, then we would have to assume that Paul, following release from imprisonment in Rome, turned his attention back to the eastern Mediterranean (despite Rom 15:23-24, 28)—i.e., Crete, Ephesus, Troas, Macedonia, Nicopolos. Paul would have evangelized Crete at that time, leaving to Titus the organization of the young house churches on the island.

touchstones for the faith and soundness of profession (see the Commentary on 1 Tim 1:10). Without a clearer idea of what was being thus warned against, it is not possible to determine whether this was a faith-saving insistence on primary principles or merely a rather conservative unwillingness to allow alternative or exploratory formulations of the same basic faith.

1:10-16, The Character of False Teachers. Just as the description of the qualities of Christian leadership both emphasizes virtues that all would commend and highlights the importance of Christian teaching, so also the warning against false teaching both draws on the familiar rhetoric of vilification and opposes it to "the truth." Many are "lacking in personal discipline" (ἀνυπότακτοι *anypotaktoi*, v. 10; the same word as in 1:6; 1 Tim 1:9), "idle talkers" (cf. 1 Tim 1:6), "deceivers." Such terms tell us little or nothing about the teaching under attack. In view of the parallels with 1 Tim 4:1 and 2 Tim 3:1, the implication is that "the last days" are already upon them.

The next phrase, however, strikes a clearer note: "especially those of the circumcision" (v. 10). The phrase is the same as that in Acts 11:2; Gal 2:12;[129] and Col 4:11. It presumably, therefore, denotes Jews (only Jews regarded circumcision as a positive identity marker); but not Jews as such, rather Jews who, like Peter, Paul, and the others, had believed in Jesus as Messiah and continued to think as Jews—that is, they continued to assume that the way for Gentiles to share in Israel's covenant blessings (the Messiah!) was for them to be circumcised and become proselytes. Possibly this indicates that the letter had in view continuing opposition to the Pauline mission from (more) conservative Christian Jews (as in Galatians and Philippians 3). Or possibly this is simply a later picking up of a phrase that indicated opposition to Paul. This could mean, in turn, that the teaching generally resisted as false was that of conservative Jewish Christians or simply that such Christian Jews were one of several factions generally rubbished by the Pastorals. The alternative suggestion that circumcision was simply a Jewish element imported into a more amorphous syncretistic teaching is less likely; "those of the circumcision" indicates a group who espoused a distinctively Jewish identity; such people would not regard circumcision as a free-floating ritual easily combined with other, non-Jewish features.

This momentary illumination is lost again in the fierceness of the dismissal (v. 11). "Their mouths must be stopped"—the image of something being put into the mouth to prevent unwanted movement or speech is clear. That such an action was deemed possible suggests that those in view operated within the churches rather than from outside; but that may press the imagery too hard. "They upset [ἀνατρέπω *anatrepō;* the same word as in 2 Tim 2:18] whole households"; we are reminded of the importance put on the well-ordered household repeatedly in 1 Timothy (e.g., 1 Tim 2:11-15; 3:4-5, 12; 5:8, 10, 13-14), as again in Titus 2:1-10. "They teach for shameful gain what they ought not to teach" (cf. v. 7; 1 Tim 5:13); the distinction with teaching deserving of support (1 Tim 5:17-18) would again be clear by reference to the "teaching" itself.

The picture becomes rather more confused by use of the quotation from Epimenides (v. 12),[130] since it indicates that the opponents in view were themselves Cretans. There is evidence of several Jewish synagogues in Crete,[131] but the language here implies that such Jews could be regarded as native Cretans (cf. Acts 2:11). The quotation should not be regarded as a careful description, though Epimenides' low esteem for Cretans was widely shared;[132] it falls, rather, into the category of populist denigration, in which the inflated criticism primarily attests intercommunal rivalry or the reaction of a local boy made good looking back on his native place with a jaundiced eye (Epimenides was himself a Cretan). The fact that Epimenides is called a prophet reflects his reputation as a speaker of oracles;[133] it may mean that the writer understood the words to have been inspired (cf. John 11:51) or simply that he recog-

---

129. The correlation is interesting in view of Titus's involvement in the preceding incident see Gal 2:1-10.

130. For more information on Epimenides of Crete (6th–5th cents. BCE), see M. Dibelius and H. Conzelmann, *The Pastoral Epistles,* Hermeneia (Philadelphia: Fortress, 1972) 136.

131. Of some interest is a 4th-cent. epitaph from Crete that describes a woman named Sophia as both a "presbyter" and an ἀρχισυνάγωγος (*archisynagōgos,* "leader of the synagogue"). See B. J. Brooten, *Women Leaders in the Ancient Synagogue,* BJS 36 (Chico, Calif.: Scholars Press, 1982) 11-12.

132. Cretans were often called liars because they claimed to have the grave of Zeus on their island. See Dibelius and Conzelmann, *The Pastoral Epistles,* 137.

133. See, e.g., C. K. Barrett, *The Pastoral Epistles,* New Clarendon Bible (Oxford: Clarendon, 1963) 131. According to Plato, Epimenides predicted the failure of the Persian invasion. See Plato *Laws* 642D.

nized in the social commentary a true insight into Cretan character (v. 13*a*). At any rate, he finds in the citation justification for advising Titus to take a strong line with such people. "That they might be sound in the faith" confirms both that those in view were within the Christian community and that the author was working with a well-defined form of faith ("the faith") and with a model of "soundness" (see footnote 9).

That Christian Jews (in this instance, at least) in particular were thus being targeted is confirmed by the double description of the alternative teaching being warned against (v. 14). "Jewish myths" tells us little more than did 1 Tim 1:4 (see the Commentary on 1 Tim 1:4), except that the "myths" in view were Jewish—that is, presumably the sort of speculations about legendary figures of the past, such as Adam and Abel, Enoch and Abraham, whom we know of from the OT pseudepigrapha.[134] The second description, "commands of human beings," carries a strong echo of earlier Christian polemic against Jewish preoccupation with tradition (Matt 15:9/ Mark 5:7-8, 13; Col 2:22; cf. Gal 1:14). In the Greek, "those who turn away from the truth" (the same phrase as in 2 Tim 4:4) refers to the "human beings." The implication is either that the Cretans were enamored of teachings from elsewhere that, by the measure of "the truth," had already lost the way, or that the Cretan Christian Jews were themselves too caught up in such speculations and Jewish traditions and as a result had turned away from a truth whose focus and measure were Christ.

The attack on the false teachers continues to use Jewish categories. "To the pure all things are pure" (v. 15) echoes Paul's counsel in Rom 14:14 and 20. The imagery is that of the laws of clean and unclean, which were so fundamental to Jewish identity (cf. 1 Macc 1:62-63; Mark 7:1-23; Acts 10:14). In the context of the Temple (on which the purity laws centered), all things were indeed clean/pure; they had to be. So the worshiper, on entering the Temple duly purified, could be confident that nothing and no one

touched would render him or her impure. Paul had extended the principle: For the believer cleansed by faith (cf. Acts 15:9), the previous sharp distinction between sacred and secular had been broken down; all things given by God for human use (unclean food as well) could properly be regarded as clean (Rom 14:14, 20; cf. 1 Tim 4:4). The principle is that purity before God is primary: If God has accepted someone, the secondary human regulations about acceptable and unacceptable are irrelevant. In these circumstances, since God ignores such regulations, so can those accepted by God.

The opposite principle, which in fact underlays the laws of clean and unclean, is that impurity contaminates. "The corrupt" (μιαίνω *miainō*) uses a verb also drawn from the sphere of ceremonial impurity (as in John 18:28), though used here of moral defilement through sins and vices. Everything that such people touch is thereby rendered impure—here in particular their minds and conscience. If, indeed, the teachers under attack here were Christian Jews or those heavily influenced by Jewish tradition, the logic would likely have powerful effect.

The final dismissive attack is on their Christian profession (v. 16): "They profess to know God, but deny him by what they do." The thought is similar to that of 2 Tim 3:5. Is there a link to the claimed (higher) "knowledge" of 1 Tim 6:20? Not necessarily; the verb is different, and for Paul knowledge of God is the most fundamental description of true religion (Rom 1:21; 1 Cor 1:21; 1 Thess 4:5). It is not a higher knowledge of God that is disputed, but the basic claim to "know" God at all. Here, as in Matt 7:16, the fruit produced is evidence of the character of the tree; we might also note the echo of Ps 14:1. Implicit once again is the conviction that the writer's understanding of "godliness" is a measure of what is acceptable to God and what is not. The final clause reverts to vilification—"abominable," "detestable" (echoing the Jewish horror of idolatry; see Deut 29:17), "disobedient" (as in 3:3), "unfit [as in 2 Tim 3:8] for any good work."

134. See J. Charlesworth, ed., *The Old Testament Pseudepigrapha,* 2 vols. (Garden City, N.Y.: Doubleday, 1983–85).

REFLECTIONS

The sections of this paragraph are linked by the theme of development. Here we see more clearly than elsewhere how Christian ministry developed—how the role of overseer/bishop emerged from the broader role of presbyter/elder, just as that of elder had emerged from that of older man (1 Timothy 5). The development was natural. As Moses had realized centuries earlier (Exodus 18), heavy burdens of responsibility need to be defined and divided up; representative persons need to be appointed to represent both the unity and the diversity of the movement to each other. Thus the wisdom of age provided the obvious pool of leadership from which such representative roles could be drawn.

Interesting questions arise for those who regard the New Testament as canon—that is, as providing a rule for faith and life. Was this development once for all, so that its outcome (the increasing focus of representative ministry and authority in the bishop) should be regarded as determinative for all time? Or is the canonical force of a passage like this the character of ministry as *developing* to meet the emerging needs of the young churches? If the emergence of the episcopate was a natural development reflecting contemporary views of leadership (the older man as the elder, the overseer as steward of God's estate), to what extent should patterns of ministry continue to develop and to what extent should they draw on contemporary wisdom regarding management and leadership? We should not lightly turn our backs on the wisdom and lessons of the past; but neither should we assume that the church of tomorrow will take the same shape as the church of yesterday.

In the second half of the paragraph we are given an insight into the strains and tensions that were consequent on Christianity's development from within Judaism. The echoes of Jesus' critique of his contemporaries' overdependence on tradition (1:14-15) and of Paul's confrontation with "those of the circumcision" (1:10) are uncomfortable reminders that Christianity's claim on the heritage of Israel was neither so clear-cut as the Pastorals would imply nor so uncontested as the Pastorals confirm. The resulting dialogue between the heirs of Israel's heritage (Jews and Christians), "God's elect" (1:1), was not completed with the sweeping dismissal of 1:15-16. Rather, the testimony of the New Testament is that this dialogue is constitutive of Christianity's identity. Reflection on the significance of the patriarchal narratives ("Jewish myths"?) is not an exclusively Jewish preoccupation. And the Pastorals are the clearest evidence within the New Testament that tradition became a matter of defining importance for Christianity as much as for Judaism. Despite its vilificatory language (typical of the day), the Pastorals are themselves evidence of the ongoing dialogue on such matters. It is not the sentiments of the Pastorals that should be our guide here, but the reality of a faith wrestling with its heritage and with other claimants to that heritage.

One of the guidelines is given in the epigram, "To the pure all things are pure" (1:15). It is one of those epigrams that can be easily cheapened or abused. At one level, it can connote a naïveté that, lacking all worldly experience or wisdom, simply fails to recognize that which corrupts or contaminates. At another level, it is a reminder of the subtlety of the link between inner purity and ritual purity, which can neither be simply assumed nor lightly dismissed. Here it sums up the priority of purity with God, of acceptability in the presence of God. All who claim the heritage of Israel would affirm the first priority of "knowing God" (1:16), but the passage (and the precedents it echoes) is a reminder that that priority can become so hedged around with qualifications and further traditions or regulations as to lose its primacy. When acceptability before God is an insufficient criterion for acceptability between those who claim the same religious heritage, then we know that profession is being denied by deeds.

TITUS 2:1-15, GOOD HOUSEHOLD MANAGEMENT AND ITS THEOLOGICAL RATIONALE

NIV

2 You must teach what is in accord with sound doctrine. [2]Teach the older men to be temperate, worthy of respect, self-controlled, and sound in faith, in love and in endurance.

[3]Likewise, teach the older women to be reverent in the way they live, not to be slanderers or addicted to much wine, but to teach what is good. [4]Then they can train the younger women to love their husbands and children, [5]to be self-controlled and pure, to be busy at home, to be kind, and to be subject to their husbands, so that no one will malign the word of God.

[6]Similarly, encourage the young men to be self-controlled. [7]In everything set them an example by doing what is good. In your teaching show integrity, seriousness [8]and soundness of speech that cannot be condemned, so that those who oppose you may be ashamed because they have nothing bad to say about us.

[9]Teach slaves to be subject to their masters in everything, to try to please them, not to talk back to them, [10]and not to steal from them, but to show that they can be fully trusted, so that in every way they will make the teaching about God our Savior attractive.

[11]For the grace of God that brings salvation has appeared to all men. [12]It teaches us to say "No" to ungodliness and worldly passions, and to live self-controlled, upright and godly lives in this present age, [13]while we wait for the blessed hope—the glorious appearing of our great God and Savior, Jesus Christ, [14]who gave himself for us to redeem us from all wickedness and to purify for himself a people that are his very own, eager to do what is good.

[15]These, then, are the things you should teach. Encourage and rebuke with all authority. Do not let anyone despise you.

NRSV

2 But as for you, teach what is consistent with sound doctrine. [2]Tell the older men to be temperate, serious, prudent, and sound in faith, in love, and in endurance.

[3]Likewise, tell the older women to be reverent in behavior, not to be slanderers or slaves to drink; they are to teach what is good, [4]so that they may encourage the young women to love their husbands, to love their children, [5]to be self-controlled, chaste, good managers of the household, kind, being submissive to their husbands, so that the word of God may not be discredited.

[6]Likewise, urge the younger men to be self-controlled. [7]Show yourself in all respects a model of good works, and in your teaching show integrity, gravity, [8]and sound speech that cannot be censured; then any opponent will be put to shame, having nothing evil to say of us.

[9]Tell slaves to be submissive to their masters and to give satisfaction in every respect; they are not to talk back, [10]not to pilfer, but to show complete and perfect fidelity, so that in everything they may be an ornament to the doctrine of God our Savior.

[11]For the grace of God has appeared, bringing salvation to all,[a] [12]training us to renounce impiety and worldly[*] passions, and in the present age to live lives that are self-controlled, upright, and godly, [13]while we wait for the blessed hope and the manifestation of the glory of our great God and Savior,[b] Jesus Christ. [14]He it is who gave himself for us that he might redeem us from all iniquity and purify for himself a people of his own who are zealous for good deeds.

[15]Declare these things; exhort and reprove with all authority.[c] Let no one look down on you.

[a] Or has appeared to all, bringing salvation   [b] Or of the great God and our Savior   [c] Gk commandment

Commentary

2:1-10, The Well-Ordered Household. The letter to Titus shares with 1 Timothy a concern for good household management, no doubt both as a test of leadership (cf. 1:6) and as a model for good church management (as in 1 Tim 3:4-5, 12). In its compactness, the outline here comes closer to the model *Haustafel* (guidelines for good household management) found in Col 3:18–4:1 than does any other in that all the elements of the typical household of the time are present: wives, husbands, children (vv. 4-5), slaves, and masters (vv. 9-10). The slant of this passage, however, reflects the same distinctive concern displayed in 1 Timothy 5 over the older men and women (vv. 2-3) and places the responsibility for counseling wives on the older women (vv. 4-5). The responsibilities of younger men, and of Titus, are likewise inserted (vv. 6-8). Unusually, no word of counsel is given to the primary male member of the household: the husband, father and master (cf. Col 3:19, 21; 4:1). The implication may be that in the household of the church that role is to be filled by Titus. Unlike 1 Tim 5:3-6, there seems to be no problem regarding the rights and responsibilities of widows.

The focus now switches to Titus's own positive teaching (v. 1). He must speak "what is fitting, appropriate to sound teaching." Once again we note that there is a criterion and measure of acceptable teaching, what we might call the agreed syllabus of confessional claims and acceptable conduct.

Somewhat surprisingly, the first example of such teaching is the advice of how older men should conduct themselves (v. 2; the word here is not πρεσβύτερος [*presbyteros*] but πρεσβύτης [*presbytēs*], denoting a man aged in the 50s or 60s). Also somewhat surprising is the fact that the commendatory virtues listed are so similar to those used in 1 Timothy 3, particularly in reference to the overseer; the older men are to be temperate (as in 1 Tim 3:2, 11); respectable, dignified, serious (as in 1 Tim 3:8); prudent, moderate (as in 1:8 and 1 Tim 3:2); sound (like the teaching, v. 1) in faith (cf. 1 Tim 3:9), in love (cf. 2 Tim 1:13), and in patience (lit., "as to the faith, the love, the patience," where "the" indi-

cates "the well-known, characteristic"—i.e., themes familiar within the church's discourse; cf. 2 Tim 3:10). At the very least, the overlap confirms that the obvious place to look for leadership in the churches was from among the ranks of the older (more experienced, wiser) men.

As in 1 Tim 5:1-2, thought of responsibility toward the older men prompts a matching reflection on the role of older women (v. 3). What is striking here is the extent of the responsibility put upon them and the language used for them. Their "behavior/demeanor" should be "as befits a priest" (NIV and NRSV, "reverent"). The imagery would be surprising only if earliest Christianity had retained an office of priest and confined it to men. But Paul's language elsewhere indicates that he saw all ministry of the gospel as priestly in character (Rom 15:16; Phil 2:25); the "royal priesthood" of 1 Pet 2:9 was not gender related. So here, it evidently did not jar to associate the image of priest with the older women. They, too, could exercise a priestly ministry in serving the gospel (vv. 3-5; 1 Tim 5:3-10) or by their personal dedication (cf. Rom 12:1-2, the priestly task of offering their bodies as a sacrifice).

The following vices to be avoided give a more negative view of the women, but in fact accord with what was said regarding deacons in 1 Timothy 3: "not slanderers" (1 Tim 3:11), "not enslaved to much wine" (cf. 1 Tim 3:8). Perhaps most surprising of all, in view of 1 Tim 2:12, is the next criterion: They are to be "teachers of what is good." However, it becomes clear in vv. 4-5 that the teaching role of the older women is in reference to younger women. Nevertheless, the responsibility put upon the older women here is significantly larger than that envisaged in 1 Tim 5:5, 10. Here again the clear assumption is that the older person has a responsibility to pass on to the next generation the wisdom gained through the years.

The specific term σωφρονίζω (*sōphronizō*) can be translated quite strongly as "bring the younger women to their senses," but it may have the weaker sense of "encourage," "advise," "urge" (v. 4). Particularly in view is the role of the matriarch within the household: to encourage the wife of the household to "love her husband and love her children." That the wife's or the husband's mother should be given such respect within the household would be taken for granted; no hint is given of the pressures on the young wife under the authority of both her husband and her mother(-in-law), but they do not take much imaging.

Like the older men (v. 2) the younger women are to be encouraged to be prudent, moderate, perhaps here with the overtone of "chaste/modest/pure," like Timothy (1 Tim 5:22), "house-keepers" (οἰκουργούς *oikourgous*, "working at home."[135] More characteristic of the codes of good household management is the counsel that they should be "submissive" to their husbands (v. 5; see the Commentary on 1 Tim 2:11-12). As elsewhere the concern was lest the liberating message of the gospel might encourage Christian women to ignore or react against the patterns of sound household management and so bring the message of the gospel into disrepute as antisocial and destructive of the good order of society's basic unit (see 1 Tim 3:7).

If the responsibility for instructing the younger women was primarily that of the older women, the responsibility for instructing the younger men belongs to Titus himself (v. 6). They are to be "reasonable/sensible" (σώφρων *sōphrōn;* the same range of words denoting a highly prized virtue in Greek circles; both the NIV and the NRSV prefer "self-controlled"; the REB uses "temperate"). Titus has to present himself as a "model of good works" (v. 7, a favorite commendatory category in the Pastorals), in his teaching "incorrupt" (a *hapax,* but close in meaning to "sound"), "respectable," "dignified," "serious" (one of the Pastorals' favorite terms; see footnote 16), "sound" (the familiar term) in preaching that is "beyond reproach" (another *hapax*). The objective (but not the only one) is that "he who is opposed [another *hapax*] might be put to shame at having nothing bad to say about us" (v. 8). Worth noting, once again, is the concern for a good reputation and the assumption that behavior worthy of criti-

cism on the part of Titus would reflect badly on the whole community ("us").

As in other household codes, the responsibility of slaves to their masters is given final prominent place (vv. 9-10; see the Commentary on 1 Tim 6:1-2). The fact that the same term (ὑποτάσσω, *hypotassō,* "submit") is used for the attitude of the slave to the master as for that of wife to husband (v. 5) reflects the legal authority of the *paterfamilias.* At the same time, in both cases the writer is careful to specify that they are to be submissive to their *own* husbands/masters. What is in view is not the submissiveness of women or slaves as a class, but, once again, the good order of each individual household—it being taken for granted that such depended on the authority of the *paterfamilias* being properly recognized. As in 1 Tim 6:1-2, nothing is said of the responsibility of the master (cf. Col 4:1), but here that is paralleled by nothing's being said about the responsibility of the husband or the father. For some reason the writer restricts his counsel to one side of each of the three relationships that made up the typical household.

The goal of the slave should be to please the master; "in everything" could be linked to the first instruction, thus "submissive in everything" (NIV), or to the second, thus "well-pleasing in everything" (NRSV). Since the adjective "well-pleasing," "acceptable" (εὐάρεστος *euarestos*) is usually used in reference to God, we may assume that what is in view is the ideal slave (not one who pleases an evil master). He or she should not speak against or contradict the master (again assuming the ideal master; cf. 1 Tim 2:11-12). Nor should the ideal slave misappropriate or pilfer (νοσφίζω *nosphizō*) anything from the master (the same word is used in Acts 5:2-3). These last two words give a sharp insight into the temptations typically confronting the slave and to which, no doubt, many succumbed. The Christian alternative was to "show/demonstrate all faithfulness as good" (the NRSV takes the three words as a single phrase, "well-pleasing in everything"); the Christian slave should be the ideal slave. Such behavior would "adorn" (κοσμέω *kosmeō;* the same word as in 1 Tim 2:9) the teaching of the Savior in every way. Once again the concern is prominent that the Christian message should produce behavior that would commend it to others.

135. A few MSS read οἰκουρούς (*oikourous*) "staying at home," reflective of the common assumption that the home was the woman's proper place; the NRSV translates the "good" twice, both with *oikourgous,* "good managers of the household," and as "kind").

2:11-15, The Theological Rationale.

What follows, in effect, is another faithful saying—that is, a summary of the gospel (vv. 11-14). It focuses on the coherence between the two appearings of Christ (vv. 11, 13), between what has already been accomplished (vv. 11, 14) and the hope for what is yet to happen (v. 13). It is this correlation that provides the rationale for godly living in the present (v.12), as illustrated by the preceding paragraph. The exposition is completed with a repetition of the commission to Titus (v. 15), the section as a whole (vv. 1-15) being held together by the two bracketing exhortations (v. 1 and v. 15).

The opening of the theological affirmation (v. 11) is very similar to that of 2 Tim 1:9-10, with the common talk of the generous "grace/favor" of God and its saving manifestation (see the Commentary on 2 Tim 1:9-10). The language echoes traditional talk of God's self-revelation (as at Bethel in Gen 35:7 and in the Temple in 2 Macc 3:30). Christ is not mentioned as such, and, unusually, it is the adjective (rather than verb or noun) that is used: "bringing salvation" (σωτήριος *sōtērios*). But even if it is not clear enough here (see v. 14), the parallel between the two passages puts it beyond dispute that what is in view is the grace of God enacted in and through Christ in his first appearing.[136] As in 1 Tim 2:3-4 and 4:10, it is assumed that the purpose of God's gracious action in Christ is the salvation of *all*.

The immediate switch to first-person plural ("training us") is not a sudden diminution of that universal goal to the few who have responded. Rather, it is a reminder that the training of the few has in view the salvation of the whole (v. 12). Not that the few are envisaged as shock troops or as some elite squad charged to complete the saving purpose of God for all. Rather, the thought seems to be of the few as the first colony or circle of salvation, who by living as those on the way to complete salvation function as a representative sample of humanity, whose very lifestyle will be a witness to the quality of God's saving purpose. This is presumably why this final paragraph can function as the theological rationale

for the seemingly mundane household rules of vv. 1-10. It is divine grace expressed in the quality of basic human relationships that will be the most effective witness to the character of God's saving purpose.

For the same reason, the point of the earlier manifestation of God's grace can be put in such simple terms as "educating," training," "disciplining" (v. 12), the word παιδεύω (*paideuō*) embracing all that was involved in a good upbringing. The negative and positive goals of this education are both summed up in familiar Pastoral terms: "refusing/repudiating ungodliness" and "living a godly life in the present age." The former is elaborated in terms of worldly desires; there is a fine distinction involved here between κόσμιος (*kosmios*), denoting what society would respect (1 Tim 2:9), and κοσμικός (*kosmikos*), denoting what partook too much of the world in its opposition to God—that is, desires becoming lusts, desires for advancement and gain in the world. The latter is elaborated with the adverbial form of the term already used three times in the letter as an adjective (σώφρων *sōphrōn*), "soberly/moderately/displaying self-control," as well as with the adverbial form of its partner in 1:8 (δίκαιος *dikaios*), "justly." The appearance of three of the most highly prized virtues in Greek thought (piety, moderation, justice), following the classic Greek term for education, underlies the degree to which the Christianity of the Pastorals saw itself as complementary to the highest aspirations of Greek philosophical ethics.[137] The resulting picture is not very dynamic, but what is in view is the character of responsible living and relationships as the most potent forces of all.

What gives the community its dynamism is more the hope of what is to come; the community literally lives in hope of the appearance of Christ (v. 13). Indicative of the character of Christian hope is the fact that the word is used here for what is hoped for (cf. Col 1:5). Hope does not depend on human feelings of hopefulness, but on the one in whom that hope is invested. This is the second "appearing" in view, and, as with the first (v. 11), the theme of "salvation" (here "Savior") is linked with it (see the Commentary on 2 Tim 1:10). Clearly implied, then, is the thought

---

136. As in 3:4, the verb ἐπιφαίνω (*epiphainō*), "appear," is equivalent to the more regular noun, ἐπιφάνεια (*epiphaneia*), "epiphany," which in the Pastorals usually refers to the still-future coming of Christ (as in 2:13), with 2 Tim 2:10 being the sole exception.

137. See S. C. Mott, "Greek Ethics and Christian Conversion: The Philonic Background of Titus 2:10-14 and 3:3-7," *NovT* 20 (1978) 22-35.

that salvation is a process from first to second, begun by Christ's saving act in the first (v. 14) and climaxed by his appearing again. This also helps to clarify why the title "Savior" can be used equally of God and of Christ, for it is the saving purpose of God (v. 11) that is brought to effect in both appearings.

Verse 13 is particularly interesting for its christology, for the blessed hope is expressed as "the appearance of the glory of our great God and Savior Jesus Christ." The interest is not just in the further example of Christ being called "Savior" (see the Commentary on 1 Tim 1:1). It focuses more on the preceding phrase. Almost certainly what is in view is not a double appearance (of God and of Christ)—that would be a less obvious rendering of the Greek, and the formula "God and Savior" was common in inscriptions of the time.[138] The point is, rather, that Christ is described by the whole phrase: "our great God and Savior." In other words, here we have one of very few instances in the NT where Christ is called "God" (otherwise only John 1:1, 18; 20:28; Heb 1:8; and possibly Rom 9:5). This is how most understand the phrase.[139] But it is also possible that it is the still fuller phrase that should be taken in apposition to Jesus Christ: "the glory of our great God and Savior"—that is, Christ described as the visible manifestation of divine glory (as in John 12:41, referring to Isa 6:10).[140] Either way, the passage becomes a clear measure of the amazing significance already recognized in or attributed to Christ, that in Christ Christians realize that God, insofar as God may be known to human beings, had been manifested.

Just as the hope of the second appearing rests on the first, so also the recognition of Christ's divine significance rests on what he has already done (v. 14). The language of v. 14a is that of already well-established summaries of the gospel and is very similar to that of 1 Tim 2:6 (see the Commentary on 1 Tim 2:6). There is a strong echo of Ps 130:8: The Lord "will redeem Israel from all his iniquities." That the echo is deliberate is confirmed by the talk of God's cleansing "a chosen people, a people of his own" (the phrase used of Israel in Exod 19:5; Deut 7:6; 14:2; note also the echo of the great vision of Israel's restoration in Ezek 37:23). Clearly, then, the thought is of these little Christian communities in Crete fulfilling God's purpose for Israel. As Israel was pledged to live as God's people, so these Christians should be "zealous for good works." Given the hostility to "those of the circumcision" and to "Jewish myths" (1:10, 14), this positive assertion of the continuity of Israel in the Christian churches of Crete should be noted. And since the thought is of a piece with that of God as Savior of all (2:11), the implication presumably is that the churches, like Israel, formed a representative people, chosen with a view to benefit all, to be a light to the nations (Isa 49:1-16).

This, it should be noted again, is the rationale for the preceding instruction on good household management (vv. 1-10): Israel's obligation to be a people dedicated to God, living lives and maintaining households of positive benefit to neighbor and community. The repetition of the opening command (v. 1) in the final sentence (v. 15) underscores the integration of the whole chapter, with the "sound teaching" (v. 1) now documented both in its theological rationale (vv. 11-14) and in its practical outworking (vv. 2-10), and providing Titus with the terms of reference for both encouragement and reproof, as also the authority behind both (cf. 1 Tim 4:12).

138. However, Johnson and Davies prefer to read the text as "the glory/splendor of our great God and of our Savior Jesus Christ/Christ Jesus." See L. T. Johnson, *Letters to Paul's Delegates: 1 Timothy, 2 Timothy, Titus,* The New Testament in Context (Valley Forge: Trinity Press International, 1996) 238; M. Davies, *The Pastoral Epistles,* Epworth Commentaries (London: Epworth, 1996) 103. On "epiphany" as the appearance of deity see the Commentary on 1 Tim 6:14.

139. See M. J. Harris, "Titus 2:13 and the Deity of Christ," in *Pauline Studies: Essays Presented to F. F. Bruce,* ed. D. Hagner and M. J. Harris (Grand Rapids: Eerdmans, 1980) 262-77.

140. Favored by G. D. Fee, *1 and 2 Timothy, Titus,* New International Biblical Commentary (Peabody, Mass.: Hendrickson, 1984; rev. ed. 1988) 196.

REFLECTIONS

The logic of chapter 2 is indicated by the double bracket within which it operates. The first is the inclusio of 2:1 and 2:15, which rivets the whole chapter together. The detailed practicalities of 2:2-10 are thus held tightly together with the high theological reflection of 2:11-14. As the "for" at the beginning of 2:11 suggests, 2:11-14 provides the theological underpinning for the preceding instructions. Thus we can see that theology and ethics hang together and are mutually interdependent. In a highly pluralistic society, any ethical system needs to be justified; here such a justification is provided. Alternatively expressed, a theology is incomplete if it does not produce a coherent ethic. A theology may be profound and deeply challenging on its own account, but if it does not eventuate in a guide for right living, then there is something wrong with it. Here it is the humdrum ethics of family relationships—the responsibilities of the older members of the community, of the younger women and men, and of the slaves. For theology to come down to such a level is not a denigration of theology or an abandonment of its proper business; on the contrary, such practical ethical concern is a test of a theology's character and quality.

Any church, then, would be well advised to examine how its creedal affirmations correlate with its practical life-style and the social concerns of its people. Here the care taken that the life-style within the Christian household and family should accord with what was generally reckoned to be the best standards is to be noted. The respect of the wider community is something to be prized (2:5, 8, 10). At the same time, there are clearly indicated categories of behavior to be avoided—slander, excessive drink, disrespect for legitimate authority, dishonesty, impiety, and worldly lusts. The world does not set the agenda; the principles are provided by the theology.

The lesson to be derived from all this is not any slavish following of the precise advice given here, much of it conditioned to the values of the time. Rather, the lesson is that in the different circumstances of different times a similar strategy needs to be followed, an equivalent balance struck between what gains proper respect in the wider community and what is to be avoided, however acceptable to or even lauded by society's opinion formers. In some instances, the choice will be clear: Policies and practices that pander to our lower natures (what Paul calls the "flesh") are to be resisted (see Rom 8:5-8). Many would criticize the "prosperity gospel" at just this point (conformity to the world, Rom 12:2). But in other cases we will need to be ready to acknowledge and support what is "good," no matter who seeks to promote it (see Rom 2:7, 10). Luke 16:1-8 reminds us of how difficult it can be to recognize appropriate models of conduct. Here not least we need the gift of discernment to know (and do!) what is God's good and acceptable and perfect will (Rom 12:2; Phil 1:9-10; Col 1:9-10).

The second bracket shaping the chapter's theological rationale is that provided by the two appearances of Christ (2:11, 13), the first in the self-giving death as a ransom (2:14), the other as the appearing of divine glory (2:13). This reminds us of the character of the saving process "in the present age" between the two appearings—as a process begun, but not yet completed. This eschatological tension shapes all Christian ethics, indicating the starting point and resource for all conduct (God's grace and what God has done in Christ). But it also reminds us that all aspiration and conduct in the between-time will partake of the not yet incompleteness of God's "good work" (Phil 1:6), with its attendant failure and frustration. The relevance of this observation to the present chapter is the recognition that even good household management in first-century terms shared in the deficiences and inadequacies of the still-incomplete process of refashioning all too human beings into the body of Christ, but not yet measuring up to the full stature of Christ (Eph 4:13).

The bracketing of the two appearances of Christ also reinforces the strong sense that the little churches of Crete are in direct continuity with Israel of old and share in both Israel's privileges and Israel's responsibilities. Like Israel, they have been chosen to be "a people of his own" and in the time between Christ's appearances they should be "zealous for good works" (2:14). This provides a further resource for Christian ethics, not least in the ethical standards and principles of social welfare enshrined in Israel's Scriptures (e.g., Deuteronomy 24; Isa 1:12-17; Mic 6:6-8). But it also brings out other aspects of the eschatological tension: How are we to distinguish Israel's heritage from "Jewish myths" and "zeal for good works" from zeal for the law? How can an increasingly Gentile religion continue to affirm its destiny as Israel? And it sets up at the heart of Christianity that ambivalence between affirmation of God's choice of a people of God's own and affirmation of God's desire for the salvation of all (2:11). The question of how Christianity both affirms the Old Testament and appropriates that heritage without also denying it remains at the heart of Christian identity, a question that will not be finally resolved until that glorious appearing.

The reference to the double appearing helps as well to frame the Christian understanding of Christ and of God in/through Christ. Here an appreciation of the significance of Christ struggles to gain expression. It is not simply that he has acted on God's behalf; both Christ and God can be called "Savior" because it is the one salvation, one and the same grace of God. It is, rather, that in his appearing, here particularly his second appearing, Christ is spoken of as the manifestation of God in glory (2:13). The resulting tension between recognizing both "the man Christ Jesus" (1 Tim 2:5) and "the glory of our great God and Savior" (Titus 2:13), has been not only an awe-inspiring challenge but also an immensely fruitful dynamic at the heart of Christian theology. That Jesus, the man, the Jew of first-century Palestine, expresses and reveals the reality of God has been at the heart of all Christian thinking from the first. That his (re)appearing functions as a goal and motivation for a distinctively Christian way of living has been at the heart of all Christian ethics from the first. It is such depth and seriousness of theological reflection that lie behind and come to expression in the day-to-day ethic of Titus 2:1-10.

TITUS 3:1-15, OF GRACE AND WORKS

NIV

3 Remind the people to be subject to rulers and authorities, to be obedient, to be ready to do whatever is good, ²to slander no one, to be peaceable and considerate, and to show true humility toward all men.

³At one time we too were foolish, disobedient, deceived and enslaved by all kinds of passions and pleasures. We lived in malice and envy, being hated and hating one another. ⁴But when the kindness and love of God our Savior appeared, ⁵he saved us, not because of righteous things we had done, but because of his mercy. He saved us through the washing of rebirth and renewal by the Holy Spirit, ⁶whom he poured out on us generously through Jesus Christ our Savior, ⁷so that, having been justified by his grace, we might

NRSV

3 Remind them to be subject to rulers and authorities, to be obedient, to be ready for every good work, ²to speak evil of no one, to avoid quarreling, to be gentle, and to show every courtesy to everyone. ³For we ourselves were once foolish, disobedient, led astray, slaves to various passions and pleasures, passing our days in malice and envy, despicable, hating one another. ⁴But when the goodness and loving kindness of God our Savior appeared, ⁵he saved us, not because of any works of righteousness that we had done, but according to his mercy, through the water*a* of rebirth and renewal by the Holy Spirit. ⁶This Spirit he poured out on us richly

a Gk washing

NIV

become heirs having the hope of eternal life. [8]This is a trustworthy saying. And I want you to stress these things, so that those who have trusted in God may be careful to devote themselves to doing what is good. These things are excellent and profitable for everyone.

[9]But avoid foolish controversies and genealogies and arguments and quarrels about the law, because these are unprofitable and useless. [10]Warn a divisive person once, and then warn him a second time. After that, have nothing to do with him. [11]You may be sure that such a man is warped and sinful; he is self-condemned.

[12]As soon as I send Artemas or Tychicus to you, do your best to come to me at Nicopolis, because I have decided to winter there. [13]Do everything you can to help Zenas the lawyer and Apollos on their way and see that they have everything they need. [14]Our people must learn to devote themselves to doing what is good, in order that they may provide for daily necessities and not live unproductive lives.

[15]Everyone with me sends you greetings. Greet those who love us in the faith.

Grace be with you all.

NRSV

through Jesus Christ our Savior, [7]so that, having been justified by his grace, we might become heirs according to the hope of eternal life. [8]The saying is sure.

I desire that you insist on these things, so that those who have come to believe in God may be careful to devote themselves to good works; these things are excellent and profitable to everyone. [9]But avoid stupid controversies, genealogies, dissensions, and quarrels about the law, for they are unprofitable and worthless. [10]After a first and second admonition, have nothing more to do with anyone who causes divisions, [11]since you know that such a person is perverted and sinful, being self-condemned.

12When I send Artemas to you, or Tychicus, do your best to come to me at Nicopolis, for I have decided to spend the winter there. [13]Make every effort to send Zenas the lawyer and Apollos on their way, and see that they lack nothing. [14]And let people learn to devote themselves to good works in order to meet urgent needs, so that they may not be unproductive.

15All who are with me send greetings to you. Greet those who love us in the faith.

Grace be with all of you.[a]

[a] Other ancient authorities add *Amen*

COMMENTARY

Following the advice on good household management, reinforced by weighty theological consideration (2:1-15), the same pattern is followed with regard to wider responsibilities. Counsel on the attitudes Christians should adopt toward authorities and on relationships with the wider community (3:1-2) is likewise reinforced by a reminder of what their former lives were like (3:3) and by the fullest restatement of the gospel in the last of the faithful sayings (3:4-8a). This is followed by a brief summary repetition of the advice given earlier in the Pastorals to the good church leader—what to teach (3:8b), what to avoid (3:9), and the limits of effective church discipline (3:10-11). Personal instructions (3:12-13) are capped by a final reminder of the importance of "good works," the linking term in the passage (3:1, 5,

8, 14). The chapter closes with a final farewell (3:15).

3:1-8a, Living Within the World and Its Rationale. The concern that lay behind the advice on good household management (2:1-10)—that is, to demonstrate that Christian households were/should be a major contributory factor to the good order of the city and the state—becomes more explicit in these next exhortations (vv. 1-2). Christians should be "submissive" (ὑποτάσσω *hypotassō*) to the legitimate authorities. The term is the same as that used in 2:5 and 9, and the concern is the same: the need for believers to respect and live within the legal system of the day, to acknowledge by their submissiveness and obedience where authority and power lay in the ordering of the society of which they were a part.

The concern is the same as in Rom 13:1-7 and 1 Tim 2:1-2. In each case there is a sober appreciation of the realities of power in the ancient city and state and of the need to live within these realities. Here again it needs to be recalled that such small groups had no possibility of exercising political power on their own behalf. Since retreat into the desert was not yet conceived of as an option, the only alternative was to live within the system and within its terms. "Ready for every good work," however, indicates not a sullen acceptance of an unfavorable situation, but a keenness to identify and seize opportunities to do good whenever they arose. The "good works" are not identified, but the forward-looking, proactive attitude should be noted.

The concern for good relations with the wider community extends to practical advice (v. 2) on conduct with non-Christian neighbors in street and workplace (cf. the conjunction of 3:1-2 with Rom 12:9–13:10). There is to be no slanderous gossip (the same term as in 2:5), not quarrelsome but gentle (the same word contrast as in 1 Tim 3:3), showing all "gentleness, humility, courtesy, considerateness" (the same word is used in 2 Tim 2:25) to all. The picture is that of political weakness but of inner strength, of engagement with the wider community but displaying attractive qualities that would win the confidence of others and would, no doubt, provide opportunities for witness from time to time—though that would be a by-product of the policy, not its goal.

One encouragement to such positive engagement is the contrast with their pre-Christian attitudes and behavior (v. 3). The contrast is probably overdrawn (as is often the case in such before-and-after conversion contrasts; cf. such passages as 1 Cor 6:9-11; Col 3:5-10; 1 Pet 4:3). But even if v. 3 expresses a Christian perspective on non-Christian mores, it at least signifies how the early Christians perceived their lives before they came to faith—"foolish" (as in 1 Tim 6:9), "disobedient" (as in 1:16), "led astray, deceived" (as in 2 Tim 3:13), "enslaved to various lusts and pleasures" (similar to 1 Tim 6:9; 2 Tim 3:6), "spending our lives in malice/ill-will and envy/jealousy" (cf. 1 Tim 6:4), "hated and hating one another." The last three phrases in particular provide a vivid snapshot of the avaricious society of all times.

All this is a foil to the last and fullest of the faithful sayings (vv. 4-7; see the Commentary on 1 Tim 1:15), again an attempt to preserve important Pauline themes. As in 2:1-15, the praxis commended in vv. 1-2 is given theological underpinning by an appeal to first principles of the gospel. What has made the difference between former day-to-day living (v. 3) and what may now be expected (vv. 1-2) is the decisive intervention of the goodness (cf. Rom 2:4; 11:22) and loving kindness (φιλανθρωπία *philanthrōpia*) of God (v. 4). At once it should be noted that the saving action spoken of is entirely that of God; it is God who "saved us" and poured out on us the Spirit (vv. 5-6). Although both God and Christ are described as "our Savior" (vv. 4, 6), God is clearly understood as source and author, and Christ as agent of the divine action (cf. Eph 2:7).

Here again the verb ἐπιφαίνω (*epiphainō*, "appear") refers to the first appearance of divine grace (as in 2:11), but in this case the thought is not so immediately focused on the action of Christ as on the impact of saving grace in human experience.[141] In fact, what we have is one of the clearest statements in all the Bible that the implementation of God's saving purpose is wholly at the initiative of God—"not from works in righteousness which we have done, but according to his own mercy" (v. 5).

Several points call for comment here:

(1) It is not an anti-Jewish statement; the echo of Deut 9:5 is actually closer than that of, say, Rom 3:28. The principle of salvation by the initiative of divine grace is rooted in the original choice of a slave people to be God's people. The use of the term "mercy" (ἔλεος *eleos*) here is no accident, for, as we saw in 1 Tim 1:2, it is the usual Greek translation of the strong Hebrew term denoting God's "covenant love/loving kindness" (חסד *ḥesed*) so fundamental to Israel's self-understanding as God's chosen people (Exod 34:6-7).

(2) It is not a direct repetition of what Paul said; he spoke of righteousness as a gift from God (as in Rom 4:3) and of works of the law, not of righteous works. The more specific case made by Paul (that Gentile believers should not be required to take on a Jewish life-style/works) is broadened out into a restatement of the original principle behind God's saving act (as in Eph 2:8-9).

141. For the use of "saved" as denoting an act already achieved, see the Commentary on 2 Tim 1:9.

(3) It is not a disparagement of good works or of righteous deeds. That could hardly be the case in an author who commends good works so strongly (as consistently in this passage, see vv. 1, 8, 14; see also Eph 2:10). It is, rather, a reminder that neither human actions nor human goodness can provide an adequate basis for relationship with God, however good, however righteous. Only God can establish and sustain that relationship. Good works are necessary, but as the fruit, not the root, of the discipleship. Good works will be the inevitable expression (and proof) that the relationship is sound, not its basis. Getting and keeping that balance require constant watchfulness and honesty within the community of faith.

The implementation of God's saving act comes through three means (vv. 5b-6). (1) The "washing [or "bath"] of regeneration."[142] This may refer to spiritual cleansing (cf. 2:14) or to baptism or to both (cf. Eph 5:26). The absence of any mention of "faith" here (cf. Acts 15:9) is hardly significant in view of its prominence elsewhere in the letter (here vv. 8, 15). (2) "Renewal [ἀνακαίνωσις anakainōsis; the same word as in Rom 12:2] by the Holy Spirit." That the gift of the Spirit is the fundamental and decisive feature in conversion/initiation is a central feature in Pauline theology (see, e.g, Rom 8:9; Gal 3:2-3). Note that the two phrases are coordinated: The washing and the renewal form a kind of hendiadys (a single, complex idea) governed by the single preposition ("through"). The implication is either that the renewal by the Spirit happens in or through baptism or, more likely, that the spiritual cleansing is also renewal by the Spirit (cf. John 3:5; Acts 15:8-9; Heb 10:22). The echo of the Pentecost reference to Joel 2:28 (Acts 2:17, "poured out on us"; cf. Rom 5:5) implies that this initiating gift of the Spirit is the Pentecostal Spirit; the renewal is not only for personal salvation but also for witness. (3) "Jesus Christ our Savior."

This last phrase is given a double elaboration in v. 7: (a) "That we might be justified by his grace"—the saving goodness of God comes to expression in and as the saving grace of Christ, his redemptive death being primarily in view (cf. Rom 3:24). Note the taken-for-granted link between the act of the cross and the experience of saving grace subsequently in individual lives. Presumably it was because this experience came in the context of preaching on the cross and evinced the same character that the link was so much taken for granted. (b) "And become heirs in hope of eternal life" (see the Commentary on 1:2; cf. 1 Tim 1:16). The language echoes a familiar and central theme in Paul's theology. On the one hand, there is the theme of inheritance (absent in the rest of the Pastorals)—that is, of Christian believers as entering into a share of the inheritance promised to the seed of Abraham (Rom 4:13-14; Gal 3:29; cf. Col 1:12).[143] On the other hand, there is the idea that believers share with Christ both as son and heir to Abraham and as son and heir to God (Rom 8:17; Gal 4:7). The centrality and richness of the christology should not go unmarked: Christ embodies both the saving grace of God and the inheritance promised to Abraham and is the one through whom humans experience that grace.

3:8b-11, The Outworking of the Gospel.
As in Eph 2:8-10, the most immediate outcome for a life predicated on this gospel is "good works" (v. 8); once again, theology leads at once to praxis. Titus is to "speak confidently, insist" on the gospel expressed in such terms in order that transformed lives should result. Worth noting is the description of those for whom this gospel is the basis of life: "those who have believed [in] God" (the tense implies a commitment once made, determining a continuing orientation of life). The definition of a Christian need not always include reference to Christ. They are to be "intent upon/careful about" "engaging in/busying themselves with" good works (the same phrase in v. 14). "These things are excellent and profitable to fellow human beings"; again the wider impact of the gospel as reflected in Christian behavior comes at once to the fore. Here is a classic statement of the social gospel: It is sufficient rationale for Christian "good works" that they are fine in themselves and benefit others.

It would not be one of the Pastoral Epistles if

---

142. The word translated "regeneration" (παλιγγενεσία *palingenesia*) is unusual; the only other usage is Matt 19:28. But the imagery is expressed in other terms elsewhere, particularly in the Johannine writings; see John 1:13; 3:5; 1 John 2:29; 3:9; 4:7; 5:1, 4, 18; see also Jas 1:18; 1 Pet 1:3, 23. It is unclear here whether the word was intended to carry the eschatological overtones of Matt 19:28. Equally uncertain is the relevance of other use of rebirth imagery. See M. Dibelius and H. Conzelmann, *The Pastoral Epistles,* Hermeneia (Philadelphia: Fortress, 1972) 148-50.

143. Paul was not alone in broadening out the promise of the land (Canaan) to the idea of inheriting the earth (Rom 4:13; Sir 44:21) or the world to come (*2 Bar* 14:13; 51:3).

there was not a final swipe at competing teachings, dismissed, as usual, with a sequence of offhanded derogatory terms in v. 9: "stupid controversies" (as in 2 Tim 2:23), "genealogies" (see the Commentary on 1 Tim 1:4), "dissensions/strifes" (1 Tim 6:4), "fights over the law" (cf. 1 Tim 1:7-8), "unprofitable" and "futile/worthless." The reference to the law confirms the impression given in 1:10, 14 that Christian Jews are primarily in view. One of the issues, if not the issue, presumably was the continuation of the earlier question: To what extent do Gentile converts have to observe all of the law's injunctions?[144] Once again we see the tension between a claim to Jewish inheritance (implied in 3:7) and a denial that salvation required obedience to all the law.

Equally important in the final summary exhortation was the reminder of how persistent opponents should be dealt with (vv. 10-11). The initial phrase used could be translated "heretical person," but αἱρετικός (hairetikos; a hapax) does not have that more technical sense; rather, it denotes someone who persists in dissenting opinions, who promotes factions, or who causes actual divisions. Note once again, however, the clear implication that those in view are within rather than from outside the congregations; the implication of v. 9 is of tensions between Jewish and Gentile members of the same congregations. At an earlier point, Paul conceded that such factions had the value of demonstrating who the mature members of a congregation were (1 Cor 11:19). It is also worth noting that the closest parallel to the instruction given here is that regarding recalcitrant elders in 1 Tim 5:20; the discipline of withholding fellowship was already foreshadowed in 1 Cor 5:11 and 2 Thess 3:14-15. The logic of v. 11 is that persistence in such fractiousness is a sign that someone has turned from the way ("is perverted, warped") and continues to sin, and in consequence is self-condemned.

3:12-15, Final Instructions and Greetings. As typical of the Pauline letters, the final concern is with personal notes regarding travel plans (vv. 12-13). Whether these are derived from scrappy notes from Paul or indications of his own hand in the letter as a whole or suggest, rather, a later author drawing on knowledge of the Pauline letter may be less important than the reminder that these early congregations enjoyed, and to some extent depended on, a regular interchange of visitors. Of Artemas we know nothing more. Tychicus we have already met (see 2 Tim 4:12). The reference to Paul's intention to winter at Nicopolis (probably in Epirus, on the Greek coast, south of Corfu) certainly strengthens the view that the passage was penned by Paul himself, since that kind of personal detail is less likely to have been contrived. The same is true of the commendation of Zenas the lawyer (of whom, once again, we know nothing more) and Apollos. The latter was one of the most influential of the secondary figures of whom we hear in connection with Paul, having taught both in Ephesus (Acts 18:24-26) and particularly in Corinth to great effect (Acts 18:27-28; 1 Cor 1:12; 3:4-6, 22; 4:6; 16:12). The reference here confirms that there was no hostility between the two, as some of the 1 Corinthian references might suggest. The request here is for financial assistance in their travels (cf. Rom 15:24; 1 Cor 16:6, 11; 2 Cor 1:16).

The final exhortation, making a bracket with v. 1 (as in chap. 2), is to "apply themselves to good works" (v. 14). Somewhat surprisingly, at this last gasp, we are given a clue as to what constitutes such good works. The primary outcome will be that those who are looking for ways to do good will be the better ready to recognize and meet urgent needs[145] when they arise. Any society will need its emergency services; a Christian society will be forward in their provision. The secondary consequence will be that they live fruitful lives—fruitfulness here being understood not in terms of qualities of character (as in Gal 5:22-23) but in terms of actual help or benefit from one to another (see Eph 4:28-29).

As usual in the Pauline (as in most) letters the final word is one of greeting (v. 15; cf. 2 Tim 4:19-21). Interesting is the choice of the weaker term φιλέω (phileō, "love," "have affection for," "like") rather than the stronger ἀγαπάω (agapaō, "love [as Christ loved]"). Thus he tells them to

---

144. Justin Martyr indicates that there was still a range of views on the point among Jewish Christians in the middle of the second century. See Justin *Dialogue with Trypho* 47.

145. The phrase could signify "necessary needs" in the sense of the NIV's "daily necessities"; but the juxtaposition of two such close synonyms suggests, rather, that the two terms were intended to reinforce each other—"pressing needs." Cf. the sense of the noun ἀνάγκη (anagkē) as "distress," "calamity" in 1 Cor 7:26.

"greet those who have affection for us in faith." Otherwise it reinforces the typical Pauline connection between love and faith (as in 2:2). The final benediction is as that of the other two Pastorals, though here the "all" is a reminder that the letter would be read aloud at a gathering of the whole congregation.

REFLECTIONS

The linking theme here is "good works" (see also 1:1, 5, 8, 14). This term has had an uncomfortable history within Christian thought. On the one hand, it is associated with the attitude of those who try or hope to work for their passage to heaven. The problem has been that this attitude embraces a diverse spectrum of conditions and individuals—from the humble, perhaps unsophisticated believers, who instinctively feel that they must be able to show something for their life in its final reckoning, to the arrogant figures of political or financial power who naturally assume that the hard work or market manipulation that has gained them their prestige must count for something in the heavenly account books as in the obituaries of the quality newspapers. Do they all come under equal condemnation? The principle is clear and needs constant restatement: No human being on his or her own can achieve acceptability before God; no human society can bring about or emulate the kingdom of God. Without the initiative of God—as in creation, so in salvation—no one can hope to experience in any fullness that quality of existence and life that is encapsulated in the expressions "eternal life" and "heaven." To that end, all dependence on human works needs, indeed, to be warned against as the most subtle as well as the most blatant attempt of the creature to claim rights before the Creator. Religion begins from and with humility, and without such humility it never begins at all.

On the other hand, of the four references to "[good] works" in this chapter, three are positive and commendatory, and only one (3:5) is treated dismissively. The danger, then, is that the one is allowed to overshadow and devalue the three, that because of the danger of "good works" the disparagement of 3:5 is extended to the other three references. This is implied in the dismissive and mocking tone often used, even in Christian circles, of "good works" and "do-gooders." That is unfortunate in the extreme—if the balance of chapter 3 is any guide. Apart from anything else, it encourages the idea that religion—or to use the favorite term of the Pastorals, "godliness"—is expressed only in prayer and worship, in the activities of the church and of Sunday, and not those of home and workplace and leisure time, of Monday to Friday (not to mention Saturday). But clearly this is not the view of the Pastorals, as their repeated commendation of good works shows beyond dispute. Good works are evidently understood as the way "godliness" expresses itself precisely in the wider world, and without good works, godliness has been cut off at the root.

To be noted in this passage is the elaboration of the theme, both at beginning and at end (3:1-3, 14). In view, in the first place, is an ethos expressed in good citizenship, the refusal to share in slanderous gossip or to pick fights, and in gentleness and courtesy toward neighbors, toward fellow workers, and toward acquaintances (3:1-2). This is in contrast to the ethos that promotes the satisfaction of desire and pleasure as the greatest good and that expresses itself in malice, envy, intercommunal suspicion, and hatred (3:3). The importance of good works, in other words, is not just in the works themselves, but in the attitudes and priorities they express. In the second place, good works come to expression particularly in sensitivity to the needs of others and the readiness to help when crisis or emergency strikes, and generally in the image of a fruitful life (3:14).

The trick is in being able to distinguish between the two kinds of works—or rather, the two kinds of attitudes expressed in works. In the end, the negative term always comes back to a degree of self-centeredness: a concern to achieve, a concern for one's own dignity and prestige, a concern to justify and prove oneself. Like a worm at the center of an apple, that concern can undermine even the most Christian of activities; Paul had already warned against this in 1 Cor 13:1-3. The self-knowledge that can alert the doers of good works to their peril is not easily gained. Blessed is the Christian community in which friends and counselors can signal that alert before the condition becomes serious. The key factor is the recognition that the "good works" that gain the author's commendation are always those that spring from the goodness and loving kindness of God, which consciously take their beginning and inspiration from the grace of God in Christ and the outpoured Spirit. Here, too, it is only the genuine humility of the doer that prevents the good works urged upon believers from deteriorating into the works that prevent the grace of God in Christ from having its full effect in and through a human life.

THE LETTER TO PHILEMON

INTRODUCTION, COMMENTARY, AND REFLECTIONS
BY
CAIN HOPE FELDER

THE LETTER TO
PHILEMON

INTRODUCTION

T he Letter to Philemon is one of the seven letters that almost all biblical scholars hold were written by the apostle Paul. Having only twenty-five verses in its English rendering from the 335 words in the apostle's Greek original, Philemon is the shortest among the Pauline epistles. The textual integrity of the letter is complete (i.e., fully preserved) in twelve of the major uncial manuscripts, and there is a near-total word agreement among the Greek texts of the letter, with but few orthographical differences (in vv. 2, 6, 9, 12, 25).[1]

Most commentators agree that Philemon reflects Paul's spirit, theology, moral tone, language, and style, as do 1 Thessalonians, Galatians, 1 and 2 Corinthians, Romans, and Philippians, the six other undisputed letters. Ancient church tradition links the letter to Paul, and the major catalogs of the New Testament canon from the early centuries (e.g., the late second-century Muratorian Fragment and Bishop Athanasius's thirty-ninth Festal Letter to his clergy in 367 CE, among others) list it among Paul's writings.

DATE AND PLACE OF WRITING

The Letter to Philemon differs significantly from Paul's other writings in two ways. First, it is not addressed to a church but to specific persons. Second, it is a letter of mediation to foster reconciliation between two individuals to whom Paul bears common relation as

---

1. On the orthographical differences, see Bruce M. Metzger, *A Textual Commentary on the Greek New Testament* (London/New York: United Bible Societies, 1971) 657-58.

their spiritual leader: Philemon, a slavemaster, and Onesimus, a slave who fled Philemon's household but who has returned, concerned to make things right. This letter was Paul's plea for a renewed relationship between the two, but one on better terms than before in the light of their mutual faith as Christians.

Three options are usually set forth regarding the place from which Paul wrote the letter: Caesarea, Ephesus, or Rome. These are the places where Paul was imprisoned for considerable periods of time (although there were other occasions when he was taken into custody, as 2 Cor 11:23ff. reports). The dating of this letter depends in large measure on the location of its composition. If Paul wrote to Philemon from Rome, as seems most likely, then the letter was composed about 61 CE. If written during his imprisonment at Caesarea, the letter should be dated about 58 CE. If written from Ephesus, a date of 55 CE would be required.

The argument for Rome as the place of composition has particular merit. Since Philemon was the overseer of the Lycus Valley house churches at Colossae (see the map "Main Roadways of Asia Minor," 581), in Asia Minor, Onesimus, his slave, would most likely not have remained within a short distance from the household he had fled but would have found his way to Rome, where other runaway slaves from the provinces tended to seek refuge. Although Rome sought to protect slave owners' rights and even encouraged bounty for assistance in returning fugitive slaves to their owners, it is not certain that Onesimus was, in fact, a runaway at all or, if he was, that he had become one without just cause.

Those who suggest Ephesus as the place of origin for this letter cite Paul's request that Philemon prepare lodging for his visit (v. 22) as an indication that Paul must have been imprisoned nearby. In addition to this, Ephesus was a provincial capital whose proximity to Colossae made it a more convenient destination for a slave without resources. Against this argument, however, is the fact, based on Col 4:7-9, that Onesimus and Tychicus were commissioned by Paul to carry letters from him to Ephesus, Laodicea, and Colossae. As for Caesarea as the place of writing, it is the most improbable choice of the three because of the difficulty in aligning events surrounding Paul's imprisonment there (see Acts 23–25) and the contents of this letter to Philemon.

The circumstance occasioning the letter to Philemon has strong bearing on Col 4:7-9, which mentions Tychicus ("beloved brother, a faithful minister, and a fellow servant in the Lord," Col 4:7) as someone who will update the Colossian church members concerning Paul's situation. The same text refers to Onesimus as traveling with him; Paul there described Onesimus as "the faithful and beloved brother, who is one of you" (Col 4:9). It is also instructive, and doubtless indicative, that this mention of Onesimus occurs just after the segment in Colossians that details the subordination codes pertaining to slaves and masters (Col 3:22–4:1; it should be noted that the injunction in Col 4:1, advising those who owned slaves to "treat your slaves justly and fairly, for you know that you also have a Master in heaven" is a unique principle for such stock codes).

FOCUS

At first glance, the Letter to Philemon seems to focus almost entirely on the issue of slavery. Paul was imprisoned or under house arrest (vv. 9, 13, 23) as he wrote; nevertheless, he was able to provide refuge for the slave Onesimus, who for some reason had fled the household of his master, Philemon. Paul appeals to Philemon as a friend and fellow Christian to take Onesimus back and to receive him without penalty or prejudice, in view of the slave's conversion and new life in Christ, their common Lord. Thus the reference to Onesimus as a "beloved brother"; Onesimus had become a Christian in the interim between leaving Philemon's household and the time the letter was written. Paul's description of Onesimus as "my child, whose father I have become during my imprisonment" (v. 10) can be understood to mean that Paul was the primary human agent in helping Onesimus to become a Christian.

The view widely held across many centuries is that this is a fairly straightforward personal letter in which Paul petitions his friend Philemon to forgive and restore his runaway slave, who was both a fugitive and a thief. Now, various questions can be raised about why Onesimus left Philemon's household and why he sought out Paul. Had he been abused by Philemon? Had he, in leaving Philemon, caused him to undergo some financial loss? However, although Paul recognized Philemon's "claim" upon Onesimus, nothing in the letter provides warrant for the notion that Onesimus was a criminal fugitive who had stolen something from his master.

The central meaning and purpose of the Letter to Philemon concern the difference the transforming power of the gospel can make in the lives and relationships of believers, regardless of class or other distinctions. However, the way slavery has figured so prominently in modern history has obscured this deeper, more essential meaning and veiled the perennial significance of the letter. During the period of the European and American slave trade, many slave owners and other defenders of the system who laid claim to Christian leadership appealed to the Letter to Philemon to justify the racial stereotypes they held and the compliance they believed that Scripture requires from those under the slavery system. To be sure, the institution of slavery in the Roman Empire during the first century, the legal infrastructure that supported it, and the various moral judgments given in the New Testament regarding its legitimacy are issues that must be considered in reading the letter. However, close study of the text makes clear that Paul's primary focus is not on the institution of slavery but on the power of the gospel to transform human relationships and bring about reconciliation. There is no basis whatsoever for thinking of Onesimus as a progenitor of the African American slave, especially since the Roman Empire did not have a race-based policy for the institution of slavery, neither in the first century nor at any other time.[2] All things considered, the way Paul's letter to Philemon is viewed provides

2. See, among other pertinent studies, Frank M. Snowden, Jr., *Before Color Prejudice: The Ancient View of Blacks* (Cambridge, Mass.: Harvard University Press, 1963) 63-64, 69-71; W. L. Westermann, *The Slave Systems of Greek and Roman Antiquity* (Philadelphia: American Philosophical Society, 1955) esp. 102-9. For a helpful study on how scorn and rivalry were expressed among the diversified peoples unified under Roman imperialism, see A. N. Sherwin-White, *Racial Prejudice in Imperial Rome* (Cambridge: Cambridge University Press, 1970).

excellent opportunity for a case study about the ways in which a person's social location can serve as a tacit rationale for reading inappropriate values into the text, distorting the document's original intent.

Quite apart from the fact that it was the work of Paul, the inclusion of the letter to Philemon in the New Testament canon would be justified on the basis of its message about reconciliation. Lloyd Lewis draws attention to Paul's use of "family language" in the letter: "brother" (vv. 1, 7, 16, 20), "sister" (v. 2), "my child . . . whose father I have become" (v. 10), and the like. The frequency of use of the terms is so pronounced that the communal-family emphasis cannot be viewed as coincidental. Lewis highlights Paul's noble intent expressed in those terms of endearment; the apostle exposes "an unwillingness to canonize the social roles found in his environment."[3]

In addition to the many published studies that report traditional interpretations of the Letter to Philemon, new studies have appeared seeking to buttress older views or to supply fresh perspective on how the letter should be viewed and explained. Sarah C. Winter has suggested that the Letter to Philemon was primarily written to a church and was only formally addressed to Philemon as the congregational overseer. The references to the situation between Philemon and Onesimus are explained as not so much dealing with personal matters as framing a paradigm for changing master/slave relationships into new opportunities for manumission and shared fellowship.[4]

Perhaps the most dramatic departure from the traditional understanding of the Letter to Philemon of late is found in the work of Allen D. Callahan.[5] Callahan seeks to dispel the idea that Onesimus was a slave at all, suggesting rather that he and Philemon were estranged biological brothers whom Paul sought to reconcile. Despite flashes of keen insight, Callahan's heavy reliance on "silences of the text" and his literal interpretation of Paul's words about Onesimus as "a beloved brother . . . in the flesh and in the Lord" (v. 16) as indicating a blood kinship between Onesimus and Philemon move the interpretive center of the letter too far from the more common and ancient understanding of Onesimus as a runaway slave.

Eduard Lohse calls attention to the interpretive center of the Letter to Philemon in his majesterial commentary, citing Martin Luther's influential evaluation of the Pauline writing:

> This epistle gives us a masterful and tender illustration of Christian love. For here we see how St. Paul takes the part of poor Onesimus and, to the best of his ability, advocates his cause with his master. He acts exactly as if he were himself Onesimus, who had done wrong.

---

3. Lloyd A. Lewis, "An African American Appraisal of the Philemon-Paul-Onesimus Triangle," in *Stony the Road We Trod: African American Biblical Interpretation,* ed. Cain Hope Felder (Minneapolis: Fortress, 1991) 246.

4. S. C. Winter, "Methodical Observations of a New Interpretation of Paul's Letter to Philemon," *Union Seminary Quarterly Review* 39 (1984) 203-12. See also her study, "Paul's Letter to Philemon," *NTS* 33 (1987) 1-15.

5. Allen D. Callahan, *Embassy of Onesimus: The Letter of Paul to Philemon* (Valley Forge: Trinity Press International, 1997). See also Callahan's earlier article, "Paul's Epistle to Philemon: Toward an Alternative Argumentum," *HTR* 86:4 (1993) 357-76.

Yet, he does this not with force or compulsion, as lay within his rights; but empties himself of his rights in order to compel Philemon to waive his rights.[6]

Luther's observation conveys his view that Onesimus had done something wrong, yet exactly who in the letter is the injured party or real victim has remained open to debate. It is quite possible, for example, that Onesimus's only offense was leaving the household of a master—Philemon—who had abused him in some way. There is greater warrant for such a scenario than for viewing Onesimus as a lazy or dishonest servant—the view found in the folklore that circulated among the ruling classes of the modern Western world, especially those who championed and benefited from the institution of slavery.

While Paul's letter to Philemon does not focus on the issue of slavery, it certainly offers clues that help to clarify the apostle's moral stance on the issue. Paul was aware of the provisions in the Hebrew Bible that sanctioned some forms of slavery despite the abhorence of the Hebrews for the long period of their own bondage in Egypt. And, as a Roman citizen, he certainly knew the legal warrants for the system as practiced across the empire. He was astute enough to recognize that the role of a pronounced abolitionist would not only have been foolhardy for himself, despite his Roman citizenship, but it would also have been disastrous to the nascent Christian missionary movement. Such factors make all the more astonishing texts like Gal 5:1, "For freedom Christ has set us free. Stand firm, therefore, and do not submit again to a yoke of slavery"; or 1 Cor 7:21, which suggests that slaves should use every opportunity to gain manumission;[7] or 2 Cor 11:20-21, which castigates those who let others enslave them. These statements, rightly viewed, are hardly the words of someone who approves of the institution of slavery. On the contrary, they reflect an attitude consistent with the appeal made in the Letter to Philemon, making the words found there all the more poignant and significant, for Paul is also the one who brought Philemon into the faith.

6. Cited by Eduard Lohse, *Colossians and Philemon,* Hermeneia (Philadelphia: Fortress, 1971) 188.
7. See, however, on the history of interpretation of the Greek wording in 1 Cor 7:21, S. Scott Batchy, ΜΑΛΛΟΝ ΧΡΗΣΑΙ: *First-Century Slavery and the Interpretation of 1 Corinthians 7:21,* SBLDS 11 (Missoula, Mont.: Scholars Press, 1973).

BIBLIOGRAPHY

Commentaries:
Bruce, F. F. *The Epistles to the Colossians, to Philemon, and to the Ephesians.* NIGNT. Grand Rapids: Eerdmans, 1984. A scholarly, evangelical commentary.

Caird, George B. *Paul's Letters from Prison.* NCIB. Oxford: Oxford University Press, 1976. A classic commentary that explores the theological meaning and historical background of Paul's letters.

Dunn, James D. G. *The Epistles to the Colossians and to Philemon: A Commentary on the Greek Text.* NIGNT. Grand Rapids: Eerdmans, 1996. A scholarly commentary, particularly helpful for study of the Greek text.

Knox, John. "The Epistle to Philemon: Introduction and Exegesis." *Interpreter's Bible.* Vol. 10. Nashville: Abingdon, 1955. A classic commentary for preachers and teachers.

Lohse, Eduard. *Colossians and Philemon.* Hermeneia. Philadelphia: Fortress, 1971. A scholarly commentary, with extensive notes and references.

Metzger, Bruce M. *A Textual Commentary on the Greek New Testament.* New York: United Bible Societies, 1971. An excellent overview of the textual variants of the NT writings.

O'Brien, Peter T. *Colossians, Philemon.* WBC. Waco, Tex.: Word, 1982. A critical, scholarly, evangelical commentary.

Osiek, Carolyn. *Philippians, Philemon.* ANTC. Nashville: Abingdon, 2000. A concise, critical commentary, particularly valuable for its analysis of rhetorical strategies and social realities.

Other Specialized Studies:

Bartchy, S. Scott. ΜΑΛΛΟΝ ΧΡΗΣΑΙ: *First Century Slavery and the Interpretation of 1 Corinthians 7:21.* SBLDS. Missoula, Mont.: Scholars Press, 1973. A detailed, scholarly analysis.

Bruce, F. F. *Paul: Apostle of the Heart Set Free.* Grand Rapids: Eerdmans, 1997. A study of Paul's life and thought from an outstanding evangelical scholar.

Callahan, Allen D. "Paul's Epistle to Philemon: Toward an Alternative Argumentum." *HTR* 86:4 (1993). An intriguing reading of the Letter to Philemon.

———. *Embassy of Onesimus: The Letter of Paul to Philemon.* Valley Forge, Pa.: Trinity Press International, 1997. A comprehensive statement of the author's provocative reading of the Letter to Philemon.

Lewis, Lloyd A. "An African American Appraisal of the Philemon-Paul-Onesimus Triangle." In *Stony the Road We Trod: African American Biblical Interpretation.* Edited by Cain Hope Felder. Minneapolis: Augsburg Fortress, 1991. An analysis of the Letter to Philemon from a contemporary African American perspective.

Martin, Ralph P. *Reconciliation: A Study of Paul's Theology.* Atlanta: John Knox, 1981. A comprehensive examination of Pauline theology, emphasizing reconciliation.

Meeks, Wayne A. *The First Urban Christians: The Social World of the Apostle Paul.* New Haven: Yale University Press, 1983. A classic study of the social environment of the early Christian movement.

Sampley, J. Paul. *Pauline Partnership in Christ: Christian Community and Commitment in Light of Roman Law.* Philadelphia: Fortress, 1980. A study of partnership in Paul's missionary work and writing as influenced by concepts in Roman law.

Winter, S. C. "Methodical Observations of a New Interpretation of Paul's Letter to Philemon." *Union Seminary Quarterly Review* 39 (1984).

OUTLINE OF PHILEMON

I. Philemon 1-3, Opening Greetings

II. Philemon 4-7, Philemon Is Commended for His Faith and Charity

III. Philemon 8-20, Paul's Request Regarding Onesimus

IV. Philemon 21-22, Paul's Expectation to Visit

V. Philemon 23-25, Concluding Words and Benediction

OPENING GREETINGS

NIV

¹Paul, a prisoner of Christ Jesus, and Timothy our brother,

To Philemon our dear friend and fellow worker, ²to Apphia our sister, to Archippus our fellow soldier and to the church that meets in your home:

³Grace to you and peace from God our Father and the Lord Jesus Christ.

NRSV

1Paul, a prisoner of Christ Jesus, and Timothy our brother,ᵃ

To Philemon our dear friend and co-worker, ²to Apphia our sister,ᵇ to Archippus our fellow soldier, and to the church in your house:

3Grace to you and peace from God our Father and the Lord Jesus Christ.

ᵃ Gk *the brother*   ᵇ Gk *the sister*

COMMENTARY

Following the conventional forms of letter writing of his time, Paul names himself first as the one writing; then Timothy, a known close associate who was with him as he wrote. Finally he names the intended recipients: Philemon; Apphia and Archippus, two presumably key persons within Philemon's circle, possibly even family members; and the "church in [Philemon's] house." Paul describes himself as a "prisoner" (δέσμιος *desmios*, vv. 1, 9), which was his current situation, being in custody. However, he wanted it clearly understood that he did not view himself as a battle casualty but as an obedient servant to Jesus Christ. Thus the full self-designation "prisoner of Christ Jesus," which could also mean "prisoner for Christ Jesus" (as the Greek was rendered previously in the RSV).

Paul's self-description here as "prisoner of Christ Jesus" deviates from his more customary self-reference in the undisputed letters as an "apostle of Jesus Christ" (see 1 Cor 1:1; 2 Cor 1:1; Gal 1:1; etc.); in the deutero-Pauline Eph 3:1 we find his self-reference as "prisoner for Christ Jesus"; at Eph 4:1, "prisoner in the Lord"; and at 2 Tim 1:8, "me his prisoner." It is clear that Paul always associated his imprisonments with having been obedient to his Lord. Callahan has suggested that "perhaps Paul's failure to claim his apostolic credentials here, which he so readily flashes before those congregations he

has established personally, is better understood as a reflection of his rhetorical situation vis-à-vis churches in which his personal standing and relationship are less than certain."[8] Paul did sometimes assert his claims to apostolicity when his credentials were challenged by opponents; this is seen in his writing to the Corinthians and the Galatians. Yet it was not necessary for him to do so here; since he did not have to assert leadership priority in dealing with a house church that he did not plant, his apostleship is not being questioned. Paul is merely sending this particularly personal letter to Philemon, whom he addresses as his "dear friend and co-worker."

Philemon is not named elsewhere in the Pauline corpus or in the early Christian literature. Apart from his appearance by name in this letter, nothing more is known concerning him except that he was a slave owner, a head of a household, a leader of a church group that met within his properties, and, by inference, that he was engaged in some business that supported his status. (As for the name "Philemon," it was as common in the Greek-speaking culture as are "John" and "Joe" in English-speaking countries.)[9]

8. Allen D. Callahan, *Embassy of Onesimus: The Letter of Paul to Philemon* (Valley Forge: Trinity Press International, 1997) 23.
9. See *A Greek-English Lexicon of the New Testament and Other Early Christian Literature,* ed. Walter Bauer, William F. Arndt, F. Wilbur Gingrich, and Frederick W. Danker (Chicago: University of Chicago Press, 1979) 859.

Paul addressed Philemon as "dear friend" (ἀγαπητός *agapētos*, "beloved one"); the abstract adjective seems appropriate because he and Paul had known each other in some settings as coworkers in the furtherance of the gospel. Κοινωνία (*Koinōnia*), or "fellowship," exists between them, and Paul highlights this fact as he addresses his friend. Callahan suggests that this was Paul's way of preparing Philemon for the claim this letter would press upon him as he read it, "co-worker" being not only initially descriptive but finally prescriptive as well.

Apphia is traditionally assumed to have been Philemon's wife; that she was so is asserted by John Chrysostom (c. 344/354–407) in his first homily on the Letter to Philemon. Since Philemon is referred to as "beloved," some scribes added "the beloved" after her name as well in making copies of this letter, as many cursives (copies written in small cursive letters) reveal. As for Archippus, some commentators suggest that the person identified here by that name is the same person mentioned in Col 4:17. Indeed, many have promoted the view of Theodore of Mopsuestia (c. 350–428), influential Antiochene exegete and theologian, that the Archippus greeted here was a son of Philemon and Apphia. The paucity of information from that early period of church history has prompted the pressing of meager data into unwarranted and dubious constructions. Nevertheless, Paul's greeting—addressing them together with Philemon—indicates that both Apphia and Archippus were important figures in the house church headed by Philemon. Archippus is also addressed in loving terms, being greeted as "our fellow soldier" (συστρατιώτης *systratiōtēs*). F. F. Bruce has commented that "some personal association with Archippus in the work of the gospel is implied, but what it was is unknown to us."[10]

"The church in your house" is mentioned by way of extension. Paul acknowledges the work for which Philemon was responsible and shows concern for the welfare of the assembly. He was aware that Philemon and his family, so intimately related to the congregation for which Philemon had oversight, would appreciate a word that included the group's welfare. Moreover, Paul knew that the plea he was about to make to Philemon in this letter, no matter how it might be handled, would affect social relations within the assembly. So the formulaic close of the apostle's greetings, the implied prayer for continued "grace to you [plural] and peace from God our Father and the Lord Jesus Christ," is more than a simple expression of courtesy. The greetings and implied prayers found in Paul's correspondence always convey his pastoral concern.[11]

10. F. F. Bruce, *The Epistles to the Colossians, to Philemon, and to the Ephesians,* NICNT (Grand Rapids: Eerdmans, 1984) 206.
11. See Gordon P. Wiles, *Paul's Intercessory Prayers* (Cambridge: Cambridge University Press, 1974) esp. 217-18.

REFLECTIONS

1. A true soldier understands orders and obeys them, strengthened by trust in the cause and a disciplined will to fulfill a known duty. Paul understood himself as a soldier for Christ, a man under orders, so he had no shame in being a prisoner; he knew it was in the interest of the cause he served.

Imprisoned, with a Roman soldier always in his presence or within sight, Paul was reminded constantly of his own ties to authority. He viewed himself as a soldier sent out by his Lord under orders to deal with evil. Though confined for a time, he was content because he had been "captured" while "in battle." The soldier image must have been uppermost in his mind when, in greeting Philemon, Paul remembered his ties with Archippus (possibly Philemon's son) and greeted him as well, calling him "fellow soldier." Images from military life may not be as stimulating to the present generation as to those of the past, but it is not possible to understand the depth of Paul's commitment to Christ and his willingness to undergo his many periods of confinement in prison without taking into account the positive aspects of what it means to be "under orders" and to obey them despite the costs involved (cf. 2 Cor 9:16).

2. The church at Colossae, perhaps still in its early growth stage, was blessed by a hosting home where its members could meet. Stated church buildings would come only in the future (the third century, to be exact), but at that early time the nascent church realized itself and promoted its mission through gatherings in homes. The home was central to the tasks envisioned, the place where worship and learning could take place and fellowship could be experienced. Churches in our time have been discovering anew the importance of small-group life in teaching, in learning, and in community ministry.

With so much in our day that militates against quality time at home, there must be a commitment on the part of a family to provide space and time for church gatherings in the home setting. A church gains something vital when cells of believers can meet for prayer, Bible study, or fellowship in a home setting. Despite the conveniences afforded in other places available for congregational uses, it is in the home that openness beckons, love is promoted, unselfishness is modeled, intimacy deepens, encouragement is gained, and integrity is nurtured.

3. At the beginning of the third millennium, the phrase "church in your house" seems rather foreign; popular culture portrays the modern home as a secular institution. However, reflecting on that phrase takes us to the historical depths of church life—that is, the way particular congregations began and who assisted in their development. Many a vital church began when some person or family offered their dwelling place as a meeting site to help start a fellowship group. Providing space was a ministry that generated cooperation, cohesion, and growth—and that spawned other ministries.

A wise Christian fellowship will keep track of its life as it develops, teaching truths, marking trends, and charting timelines. And a caring church will honor those whose commitment encourages growth and ministry to happen. In modern consumer-oriented societies where so much is readily thrown away to make room for what is next, church leaders with vision will acquaint themselves and the other members of their congregation with information about their group's history, and they will inspire members to appreciate and add to that history through commitment to duties essential for a vital ministry.

PHILEMON IS COMMENDED FOR HIS FAITH AND CHARITY

NIV

⁴I always thank my God as I remember you in my prayers, ⁵because I hear about your faith in the Lord Jesus and your love for all the saints. ⁶I pray that you may be active in sharing your faith, so that you will have a full understanding of every good thing we have in Christ. ⁷Your love has given me great joy and encouragement, because you, brother, have refreshed the hearts of the saints.

NRSV

4When I remember you[a] in my prayers, I always thank my God ⁵because I hear of your love for all the saints and your faith toward the Lord Jesus. ⁶I pray that the sharing of your faith may become effective when you perceive all the good that we[b] may do for Christ. ⁷I have indeed received much joy and encouragement from your love, because the hearts of the saints have been refreshed through you, my brother.

[a] From verse 4 through verse 21, *you* is singular   [b] Other ancient authorities read *you* (plural)

COMMENTARY

Paul's pastoral concern involved him regularly in prayers for the churches under his care, for his coworkers, and for those converted under his ministry. Philemon, one of Paul's own converts (v. 19) as well as his "dear friend and co-worker," here learns about the prayers offered to God by Paul on his behalf. Those prayers are filled with thanksgiving over reports from others that Philemon shows "love for all the saints" and a contagious "faith toward the Lord Jesus" (v. 5). But they also include intercession, with the apostle asking God to help Philemon share his faith, informed by the knowledge of all the good ways in which this can be done and with an increased effectiveness that honors Christ, his Lord.

These words show us something more than a customary thanksgiving section of a letter: They reveal a specific commendation from Paul to Philemon. Although Paul wrote with particular instances of Philemon's charity in mind, many of which were shared with him by Epaphras (who is named in v. 23) and perhaps by Onesimus as well, no such details appear in this letter. Paul is impressed by Philemon's charitable disposition

and pays him tribute, acknowledging his deeds as having been done in love and inspired by his faith in the Lord Jesus. "Love" (ἀγάπη *agapē*) and "faith" (πίστις *pistis*) are highlighted here by Paul as they are in his other letters, but it is interesting that while "faith" is usually mentioned first elsewhere, "love" receives first mention here. It is likely that Paul was thinking strategically about the issue for which the letter was being sent, hoping that Philemon's charitable disposition would allow the forthcoming appeal regarding Onesimus to be received with understanding and acceptance.

Paul's words of tribute regarding Philemon's charity were not merely literary flourish or contrived flattery. They were an honest expression based on known facts regarding Philemon, knowledge gained, perhaps, from Paul's own previous experience with him, but surely from the good reports heard from others whose lives had been touched in helpful, meaningful ways by the man. Paul, therefore, adds a personal comment about his own emotion resulting from such good reports: "I have received much joy and encouragement from your love, because the hearts of the saints have been refreshed through you, my brother" (v. 7). Paul's words here are remarkably similar to those in 3 John 3, where John the Elder confesses his joy over reports about Gaius's "faithfulness to the truth, namely how you walk in the truth." Bruce has commented, "It is a pleasant coincidence that the two really personal letters in the NT should both be addressed to men so likeminded in their generosity."[12]

Paul's intercessory prayers for Philemon included concern regarding what the NIV translates as being "active in sharing your faith," but which the NRSV renders as "the sharing of your faith." All told, that "sharing" (κοινωνία *koinōnia*) would involve Philemon's witnessing to others about his faith as well as doing deeds that showed evidence of his faith. Generosity is the present focus, and that becomes clearly noted in v. 7 where Paul mentions how the "hearts of the saints have been refreshed [ἀναπέπαυται *anapepautai*, "calmed," "comforted," "relieved"]" through Philemon's charitable deeds. This commendation covers much about which we have no knowledge, but "the saints" did, and from personal experience.

While this much is certainly understood from the commendation in vv. 4-5, the grammatical construction of v. 6 leaves us perplexed by translation difficulties and many alternative exegetical possibilities. The Greek wording in v. 6 is awkward in its phrasing; the intended meaning of the crucial term *koinōnia*, especially linked with *pistis*, remains unclear. The differences between the NIV and the NRSV in translating the Greek are readily noted; other translation options can be observed by comparing additional renderings of v. 6 in English:

12. F. F. Bruce, *The Epistles to the Colossians, to Philemon, and to the Ephesians,* NICNT (Grand Rapids: Eerdmans, 1984) see 210n. 43.

The New English Bible: "My prayer is that your fellowship with us in our common faith may deepen the understanding of all the blessings that our union with Christ brings us [or "that bring us to Christ"]."

New American Standard: "And I pray that the fellowship of your faith may become effective through the knowledge of every good thing which is in you for Christ's sake."

The New King James Version: ". . . that the sharing of your faith may become effective by the acknowledgment of every good thing which is in you in Christ Jesus."

Good News: "My prayer is that our fellowship with you as believers will bring about a deeper understanding of every blessing which we have in our life in Christ."

Paul's use of *koinōnia,* linked in the context with the genitive πίστεως (*pisteōs*) and the possessive σου (*sou*), requires strict attention. While *koinōnia* primarily means "common participation" in something, as equal sharers, the question raised by linking that word in the verse with *pisteōs sou,* "your faith," is whether that "common participation" should be understood as objective—the fellowship or sharing that results from faith—or as subjective— one's experience of a commonly shared faith. If Paul intended the subjective meaning, then his prayer for Philemon was that God would make him increasingly knowledgeable and effective in the ways that good can be accomplished for, in, and through Christ. "To perceive (or understand) and appreciate all the good [ἐπιγνώσει παντὸς ἀγαθοῦ *epignōsei pantos agathou*]" no doubt refers ultimately to beneficial deeds and helpful relationships. As he wrote or dictated this passage of the letter, Paul was surely solicitous for Philemon to respond graciously to the request he was about to make on behalf of that leader's returning slave, Onesimus.

REFLECTIONS

1. Paul wrote with a quill dipped in the inkwell of grace. He offered thanksgiving to God for Philemon, and he confessed this to Philemon, thus complimenting him. Everyone has times of feeling misunderstood or unappreciated. And we are usually strengthened when appreciation for us is expressed or when good deeds we have done are acknowledged. At the same time, the person who expresses that appreciation is usually gladdened for having done so. While it may sometimes be vain to seek approval, the need for recognition is a basic human quality.

2. Paul knew of Philemon's social position and wealth. Paul did not commend him, however, for either his station or his possessions, but rather for his gracious and more just use of them. Not only had Philemon done good in "refreshing the hearts of the saints," but he also had done so in right ways and in the right spirit. The dignity of those who benefited from Philemon's largesse was not undermined but undergirded by the spirit he showed in sharing. No wonder Paul, like many others, no doubt, heard about Philemon's "love for all the saints." One is reminded of the line in William Shakespeare's *The Merchant of Venice:*

How far that little candle throws its beams!
So shines a good deed in a naughty world. (5.1.90)

Differences in status or financial condition should never get in the way of helping someone in distress, especially someone in the community of faith (see Gal 6:10). Christian love not only establishes new "familial" bonds, but also dictates timely action when needs are known.

PAUL'S REQUEST REGARDING ONESIMUS

NIV

⁸Therefore, although in Christ I could be bold and order you to do what you ought to do, ⁹yet I appeal to you on the basis of love. I then, as Paul—an old man and now also a prisoner of Christ Jesus— ¹⁰I appeal to you for my son Onesimus,ᵃ who became my son while I was in chains. ¹¹Formerly he was useless to you, but now he has become useful both to you and to me.

¹²I am sending him—who is my very heart—back to you. ¹³I would have liked to keep him with me so that he could take your place in helping me while I am in chains for the gospel. ¹⁴But I did not want to do anything without your consent, so that any favor you do will be spontaneous and not forced. ¹⁵Perhaps the reason he was separated from you for a little while was that you might have him back for good— ¹⁶no longer as a slave, but better than a slave, as a dear brother. He is very dear to me but even dearer to you, both as a man and as a brother in the Lord.

¹⁷So if you consider me a partner, welcome him as you would welcome me. ¹⁸If he has done you any wrong or owes you anything, charge it to me. ¹⁹I, Paul, am writing this with my own hand. I will pay it back—not to mention that you owe me your very self. ²⁰I do wish, brother, that I may have some benefit from you in the Lord; refresh my heart in Christ.

ᵃ10 Onesimus means useful.

NRSV

8For this reason, though I am bold enough in Christ to command you to do your duty, ⁹yet I would rather appeal to you on the basis of love—and I, Paul, do this as an old man, and now also as a prisoner of Christ Jesus.ᵃ ¹⁰I am appealing to you for my child, Onesimus, whose father I have become during my imprisonment. ¹¹Formerly he was useless to you, but now he is indeed usefulᵇ both to you and to me. ¹²I am sending him, that is, my own heart, back to you. ¹³I wanted to keep him with me, so that he might be of service to me in your place during my imprisonment for the gospel; ¹⁴but I preferred to do nothing without your consent, in order that your good deed might be voluntary and not something forced. ¹⁵Perhaps this is the reason he was separated from you for a while, so that you might have him back forever, ¹⁶no longer as a slave but more than a slave, a beloved brother—especially to me but how much more to you, both in the flesh and in the Lord.

17So if you consider me your partner, welcome him as you would welcome me. ¹⁸If he has wronged you in any way, or owes you anything, charge that to my account. ¹⁹I, Paul, am writing this with my own hand: I will repay it. I say nothing about your owing me even your own self. ²⁰Yes, brother, let me have this benefit from you in the Lord! Refresh my heart in Christ.

ᵃ Or as an ambassador of Christ Jesus, and now also his prisoner
ᵇ The name Onesimus means useful or (compare verse 20) beneficial

COMMENTARY

Having reiterated the basis for rapport between himself and Philemon (this being clear from the singular use of "you" in vv. 4-21), Paul now begins the primary message the letter is sent to convey. Thus the "therefore"

(διο dio), which here is translated "for this reason" (v. 8).

The intercession for Onesimus begins, couched in carefully chosen terms but offered in frankness: "I . . . appeal to you" (v. 9). Paul was aware that his situation as intercessor was legally defensible, Roman law having provided for cases of advocacy on behalf of runaway slaves who returned to their master. He also knew that he had a right to intercede on behalf of the now-converted runaway slave as Christ's apostle (thus the use of πρεσβύτης [*presbytēs*, "ambassador"]). Paul surprises us, however, by choosing not to appeal to Philemon from either position of authority. He makes his appeal for Onesimus "on the basis of love."

The appeal Paul is about to make is prefaced by a statement of relationship with Onesimus that notifies Philemon about a new fact concerning his runaway slave: "I am appealing to you for my child, Onesimus, whose father I have become during my imprisonment" (v. 10). John Knox commented that "this clearly means that Onesimus has become a believer in Christ under Paul's influence."[13] Peter T. O'Brien has suggested that:

This was the first news Philemon had received of his slave since he ran away and he might be expected to react negatively to the mention of his name. So with delicate tact Paul first establishes the central fact that Onesimus has become a Christian, converted during Paul's imprisonment.[14]

The situation of Onesimus as a runaway slave returning to face Philemon, his master, raises many questions. Why did Onesimus leave in the first place? Where did he go, and where could he expect refuge? If Onesimus had committed some crime, had Philemon published a reward notice regarding him? If so, then how widely would that reward notice have been circulated and known? If there was a reward notice, then Onesimus would have had increased need to remove himself as far from the master's arena of influence (Colossae) as resources and opportunity would allow. If he traveled as far from Colossae as Rome, then perhaps he came to Paul's notice through some encounter with Christians there, Onesimus having sought them out for whatever initial reasons.

But it is also possible that Onesimus went looking for Paul, aware of Paul's influence on Philemon. Paul could be an advocate for him in resolving his situation as a runaway slave. Roman law

regarding returning slaves did allow a friend of the master to advocate on the returning slave's behalf in the interest of his or her safety and well-being.[15]

There are still other questions. Had Philemon disappointed Onesimus, promising manumission and then delaying it? Had Onesimus reached thirty years of age, when freedom was sometimes granted to faithful and deserving slaves, and escaped because he had been denied it?[16]

There is all too little about Onesimus's situation that can be stated with certainty; too much is left for conjecture. But the little that is given in the Letter to Philemon is positive rather than negative. Onesimus has become converted, Paul's "child" (τέκνον *teknon*) in the faith (v. 10). He is now even more "useful" than before, since we must assume that he had served Philemon in some meaningful capacity before his decision to leave or escape Philemon's household. Paul's statement that "formerly he was useless [ἄχρηστος *achrēstos*] to you" (v. 11) could have been intended to cover only the period Onesimus was absent from Philemon and the problems associated with that absence, and, therefore, was not intended to mean that Onesimus was always a lazy or shiftless person. The notice that "now he is indeed useful [εὔχρηστος *euchrēstos*] both to you and to me" completes Paul's play on the meaning of the returning slave's name, Ὀνήσιμος (*Onēsimos*), which in Greek means "useful," "profitable." This name was common among slaves, either bestowed in tribute or perhaps as an incentive to usefulness and a master's profit. Now, as a converted person, Onesimus was more useful than ever.

Paul had no doubt benefited from that usefulness during the time Onesimus had been with him, thus his words "useful both to you and to me." Because of that usefulness, and having become fond of the slave, Paul would have kept Onesimus with him (see v. 13); but a reconciliation needed to occur between the runaway and

13. John Knox, "The Epistle to Philemon: Introduction and Exegesis," *Interpreter's Bible*, 12 vols. (Nashville: Abingdon, 1955) 10:567.

14. Peter T. O'Brien, *Colossians, Philemon,* WBC (Waco, Tex.: Word, 1982) 290.

15. See P. Lampe, "Keine 'Slavenlucht' des Onesimus," *ZNW* 76 (1985) 135-37. On reward notices about runaway slaves, see examples cited by C. F. D. Moule, *The Epistles of Paul the Apostle to the Colossians and to Philemon,* CGT (Cambridge: Cambridge University Press, 1957) 34-37.

16. See S. Scott Bartchy, ΜΑΛΛΟΝ ΧΡΗΣΑΙ: *First-Century Slavery and the Interpretation of 1 Corinthians 7:21,* SBLDS (Missoula, Mont.: Scholars Press, 1973) esp. 87-91. See also Francis Lyall, *Slaves, Citizens, Sons: Legal Metaphors in the Epistles* (Grand Rapids: Zondervan, 1984) esp. 39-45.

his master. The two, as Christians, needed to become friends—no longer one the master and the other a slave. So Paul writes: "I am sending him . . . back to you" (v. 12).

The appeal Paul makes, on the basis of love, not law, is for Philemon to receive Onesimus back "no longer as a slave but more than a slave, a beloved brother—especially to me but how much more to you, both in the flesh and in the Lord" (v. 16). Here is the substance of the appeal. Paul knew that this request might well test Philemon's heart, so Paul reveals his own emotion, confessing that Onesimus was linked with his heart: "I am sending him, that is, my own heart, back to you" (NIV, "[he] is my very heart").

Raymond E. Brown maintains that through appealing to Philemon's cooperativeness rather than censuring him, Paul challenged "a Christian slave owner to defy the conventions: To forgive and receive back into the household a runaway slave; to refuse financial reparation when it is offered, mindful of what one owes to Christ as proclaimed by Paul; to go farther in generosity by freeing the servant; and most important of all from a theological viewpoint to recognize in Onesimus a beloved brother and thus acknowledge his Christian transformation."[17]

Paul has already stated that he was not seeking to impose his own will (v. 14) or to use any authority he possessed (v. 8) to achieve the goal of his appeal; but some forcefulness is evident in his words in v. 17, when he invokes the rules of partnership: "So if you consider me your partner, welcome him as you would welcome me." Having earlier referred to himself as Christ's "ambassador" (*presbytēs*, v. 9), Paul here suggests that Philemon favorably honor his petition by accepting Onesimus with the same cordial diplomacy an envoy or ambassador expects and enjoys in representing the one who sends him or her. By introducing the concept of partnership, a mercantile image, Paul thereby invokes its terms, calling upon Philemon to honor all that partnership involves and implies: acceptance, trust, regard, divisions of responsibility in a common purpose, and equality of sharing (in profits and losses).[18] This

explains in part why Paul could so readily move forward to accept as his own any debts owed Philemon by Onesimus: "If he has wronged you in any way, or owes you anything, charge that to my account" (v. 18).

It must be noted from Paul's wording that he has allowed for the possibility of wrongdoing by Onesimus, but he does not mention that he knows of any. His "if" is probably more than rhetorical; it allows Philemon to reckon any damages due him, since only he would know of these. Like Paul's worthy greeting at the beginning of the letter, this gesture of willingness to assume responsibility for Onesimus, debts and all, was carried out in good faith. Paul was thus honoring the mutual dictates of partnership, and Philemon was being challenged to do the same. To authenticate that this was his own true pledge as Onesimus's guarantor, Paul did what was his custom when certifying his involvement in some special matter or action, signing his name in his own special way: "I, Paul, am writing this with my own hand: I will repay it" (v. 19*a*). (On Paul's custom of authenticating his presence and involvement in a letter, see 1 Cor 16:21; Gal 6:11; 2 Thess 3:17.)

Interestingly, if Colossians was written by Paul—and at about the same time as the letter to Philemon—Paul may have thought about the situation of Onesimus as he wrote the injunctions addressed in Col 3:22-25 to Christians who were slaves, particularly the warning Col 3:25: "For the wrongdoer will be paid back for whatever wrong has been done, and there is no partiality." But immediately thereafter, this stricture addressed to masters appears: "Masters, treat your slaves justly and fairly, for you know that you also have a Master in heaven" (Col 4:1). Although the injunctions to masters and slaves in some of Paul's letters reflect aspects of the social structure of the churches he addressed, it is natural to wonder whether in this case he had Onesimus and Philemon in mind. Given his stress on justice and fairness regarding slaves, one can reasonably argue that while Paul understood societal conventions and social groupings, he saw some of them ultimately as antithetical to Christian fulfillment through the κοινωνία (*koinōnia*) relationship made possible in Christ, as Col 3:11 and Gal 3:28 dramatically declare.

17. See Raymond E. Brown, *An Introduction to the New Testament,* ABRL (New York: Doubleday, 1997) 506.

18. On the terms of partnership in the Roman society, see Lyall, *Slaves, Citizens, Sons,* 143-45.

REFLECTIONS

1. Pastoral or ecclesiastical authority based on church law is often used as a warrant and resource in dealing with church problems. However, the more Christlike and creative approach calls for the spirit of persuasiveness, conditioned by love; and this usually yields a more peaceable and long-lasting harvest of harmony.

2. It is the work of divine grace to make "unprofitable" persons profitable. When apprehended by a sense that God's favor is being personally felt and known, every person can be changed into someone whose life offers profit (beneficial fruit) to God and to others. This is the triumph of Christ, his very reason for coming into the world; but it happens only through his "begetting" work in our lives.

Those who have been "born anew" must show others what that new birth means and can effect in everyday, practical terms. The highest and noblest service we believers can render is to reach beyond established barriers of human separation, social class, and ethnicity and touch the lives of persons who are considered "different" and "unprofitable" and, like Paul, help them in Christ to become "useful." However wasted anyone's life may seem to be, that person must never be written off. God's grace can intercept us, intervene in our particular situations, inspire hope in our hearts, and bring about needed change in our lives. There is a purpose for the life of each and all, and there is a service to be rendered by each of us in this world.

3. Written as a personal request, the Letter to Philemon could be considered a missive of "limited application." But in the light of the social problems of slavery and the repercussions of its existence and support in the centuries since Paul's day, the concern Paul expressed in this brief letter must be understood and valued as more than an ancient and isolated issue. The important theme in the letter was never highlighted in any of the great theological debates of the ancient church. Divine providence was at work in preserving this letter, for it speaks more forcefully in these later times to us, perhaps, than it did in the first century CE to Philemon, its initial primary reader.

Paul sent Onesimus, a runaway slave, back to his master, Philemon. Many modern readers bristle at Paul's action. They are influenced by modern notions of freedom and an abhorrence of all systems that delimit and circumscribe human dignity. Why did Paul not provide Onesimus with continued refuge? And why did he not overtly condemn the system of slavery within the Roman Empire at that time?

One explanation offered is that Paul did not view slavery as a wrongful institution. Being a Roman citizen, and hence someone who enjoyed the privileges associated with that social boon, he accepted the empire's customs and social systems as a given, and hence he felt no need, even as a Christian, to oppose slavery.

Another explanation put forward defends Paul's deed of returning Onesimus to Philemon by appealing to Paul's apocalyptic views as expressed in 1 Cor 7:29*a*, 31*b*. It suggests that because of Paul's view that "the appointed time has grown short" and that "the present form of this world is passing away," he was tolerant of the slavery system and content to live with it, informed by an interim-ethic. However, it must be pointed out that apocalyptic concerns have often served as a catalyst for radical action and protest, both within the Old Testament period and in New Testament times.

There is another more sensible way to answer the question, and it forms an explanation based on three pieces of evidence: this very letter to Philemon, Paul's steady emphasis on freedom in his writings, and a statement in 1 Cor 7:21. All of these passages underscore the personhood of slaves and thus grant us fresh perspective for viewing the socioeconomic arrangement of the master/slave relationship. When Paul made his plea to Philemon to "receive

[Onesimus, now converted] back no longer as a slave but more than a slave, a beloved brother" (v. 16), it should be forcefully clear that Paul wanted Philemon to honor their new tie as Christians *above and beyond* any legal demands. Their relationship was to be conditioned by love, not law, now that they were linked by faith, and not fealty.

Surely Paul must have sensed what this stipulation could mean in the long run and on an even wider scale, not only within but also beyond the household of Philemon. Paul's action here was that of a true ambassador, which is how he earlier described himself (v. 9). In returning Onesimus to Philemon, Paul used a form of diplomacy that appears to ignore one aspect of the slavery problem while offering his rationale for a new social arrangement that would in time effect a deeper concern and wider results.

4. In the *Declaration of Independence* of the United States, the first among the truths held and listed as "self-evident" are these: "that all men are created equal, that they are endowed by their Creator with certain unalienable rights." (Interestingly, at the time these truths were declared in writing, the Negro slave was not included, being viewed, rather, as but "three-fifths" of a person!) The full truth is this: Every person is unique and of worth because every person is made in the image of God; so human relations are fundamental and crucial. We who preach and teach must be leading examples and instruments of God's will in reaching out to people, in regarding each and all, in responding to acknowledged need, and in working steadily for the human good of all.

Unlike Paul's setting, which was dominated by Rome's monolithic, worldwide system of rule, our surroundings are smaller pockets of organized life within which our voices and votes and personal vision can have some impact. Paul was a significant actor within the world of his time, and his wit and will brought results far beyond his calculation and time. We who serve "the present age" must look to the same Lord for guidance in meeting the demands of our time and place. Paul was convinced that God's "plan for the fullness of time, [is] to gather up all things in [Christ]" (Eph 1:10). Our rightful work falls within that plan, and it is ours to serve our Lord with faith, courage, and commitment. While mindful that human servants can never bring in God's kingdom, we—like Paul—must work in this world with kingdom values informing and influencing our lives and deeds.

PAUL'S EXPECTATION TO VISIT

NIV

²¹Confident of your obedience, I write to you, knowing that you will do even more than I ask.

²²And one thing more: Prepare a guest room for me, because I hope to be restored to you in answer to your prayers.

NRSV

²¹Confident of your obedience, I am writing to you, knowing that you will do even more than I say.

22One thing more—prepare a guest room for me, for I am hoping through your prayers to be restored to you.

COMMENTARY

Paul was intent to do all within his power to reconcile Philemon and Onesimus. The apostle volunteered to remove any stumbling blocks to that desired end, and his letter spells out his role in the process. With Onesimus having been sent back to him, the rest would be up to Philemon. Paul asserted, doubtless for Philemon's encouragement, that he was "confident of [Philemon's] obedience" (v. 21), presumably to the dictates of Christian love, and that he expected Philemon to "do even more" than he had suggested.

Paul may have hoped that, once Philemon and Onesimus were reconciled, Onesimus might be released by Philemon to assist Paul in ministry. The slave was now "a beloved brother" who had proved to be "indeed useful"; his service was viewed by Paul as a possible further expression of Philemon's generosity (through Onesimus's manumission?). Onesimus could by mutual agreement be of service to Paul (in Philemon's place) during the apostle's imprisonment (see v. 13).

Paul expected eventually to be freed from prison and, therefore, expresses his hope to visit Philemon. Thus the second and last request made in the letter: "One thing more—prepare a guest room for me, for I am hoping through your prayers to be restored to you" (v. 22). The apostle was eager to visit Philemon and the believers at Colossae. This request reflects a more relaxed mood on Paul's part, but it also reflects his knowledge about Philemon's resources as a householder with the means to provide hospitality and support for guests at times of need. It is interesting that in reporting that he expects "to be restored to you," Paul returns to the plural for the first time since v. 3. This might well imply his recognition that Apphia—or even the entire membership of the house church—should also be informed of his plan to visit. Meanwhile, he lives in hope (ἐλπίζω *elpizō*) for this event, trusting their prayers, along with his own, to be fulfilled in God's time.

CONCLUDING WORDS AND BENEDICTION

23Epaphras, my fellow prisoner in Christ Jesus, sends you greetings. 24And so do Mark, Aristarchus, Demas and Luke, my fellow workers.

25The grace of the Lord Jesus Christ be with your spirit.

23Epaphras, my fellow prisoner in Christ Jesus, sends greetings to you,[a] 24and so do Mark, Aristarchus, Demas, and Luke, my fellow workers.

25The grace of the Lord Jesus Christ be with your spirit.[b]

[a] Here *you* is singular   [b] Other ancient authorities add *Amen*

COMMENTARY

The list of persons who sent greetings along with Paul is instructive, and their appearance in this letter provides a clue regarding the location of Philemon and his house church. Epaphras, mentioned first as Paul's "fellow prisoner in Christ Jesus" (v. 23), would surely have known Philemon at close range, since he was from Colossae (see Col 1:7 8; 4:12 13). Described as a "fellow prisoner," which should be understood literally, Epaphras was no doubt serving as a personal attendant to Paul, perhaps quartered with him along with the soldier holding authority over Paul. The kind of custody Paul experienced as a Roman citizen allowed him freedom to "conscript" volunteers to serve his outside interests while confined himself. It is possible that by adding "in Christ Jesus" to the description, Paul is really describing Epaphras as standing in close relation to him as a slave would be; a personal slave would have a freedom of access to an imprisoned "master" that others, even close friends, could not share.[19] Epaphras's role as a personal attendant, then, was something different in kind or extent than Timothy's, who is referred to as "our brother" (v. 1), while Mark, Aristarchus, Demas,

and Luke are described as "my fellow workers" (v. 23).

Mark, here, is the same John Mark of the book of Acts (see Acts 12:12, 25; 15:37, 39; Col 4:10; 2 Tim 4:11; 1 Pet 5:13), and it is likely that the Aristarchus mentioned here is the same person spoken of in Acts 19:29; 20:44; 27:2; and Col 4:10. If the view is accepted that the Letter to Philemon was written from Rome, then one can harmonize the data in Acts and Colossians to locate Aristarchus with Paul during Paul's imprisonment there, and thus relate Colossians and Philemon as having been written at about the same time. Demas, also mentioned elsewhere as being among Paul's circle of workers (Col 4:14; 2 Tim 4:10), joined Paul, Luke "the beloved physician" (Col 4:14), and the others in a statement of greeting to Philemon as Paul prepared to close the letter.

The letter required no final instructions. Its message had been shared, its appeal made, and a confidence expressed that its purpose would be honored. So Paul concluded the letter with his customary, brief, but earnest, benediction: "The grace of the Lord Jesus Christ be with your spirit" (v. 25). F. F. Bruce, in his commentary on this letter, asked: "Was Paul's request granted? Yes; otherwise the letter to Philemon would not have survived. That it survived at all is a matter calling

---

19. On this kind of privilege, see William M. Ramsay, *St. Paul the Traveller and the Roman Citizen* (Grand Rapids: Baker, 1965) esp. 310-12; see also Brian Rapske, *The Book of Acts and Paul in Roman Custody* (Grand Rapids: Eerdmans, 1994) 370-80.

for comment, but if Philemon had hardened his heart and refused to pardon and welcome Ones- imus, let alone send him back to Paul, he would certainly have suppressed the letter."[20]

20. F. F. Bruce, *The Epistles to the Colossians, to Philemon, and to the Ephesians*, NIGNT (Grand Rapids: Eerdmans, 1984) 200.

REFLECTIONS

A close look at the names of those who joined Paul in his final greeting to Philemon brings to view some treasured members of the apostle's circle. Those names, and the histories connected with them, also provide evidence of Paul's charisma as a person and as a leader.

Paul's personality involved something contagious that went far beyond any limitations to his physical appearance. Based on a legendary account of how he looked—the account being so plain and unflattering that the legend seems to embody some truth—Paul was "a man small of stature, with a balding head and crooked legs, in a good state of body, with eyebrows meeting and nose somewhat hooked, full of friendliness."[21] That phrase "full of friendliness" tells much about how Paul was known as a person and as a leader.

Three among those named were Gentile Christians: Epaphras, Demas, and Luke; the other two were Hebrews. The New Testament records both their distinctiveness and their unity. Most important, they were vital and valued members of Paul's circle. They were with him because Paul was a dynamic, creative leader.

What were some of Paul's leadership traits?

(1) Paul led as he was being led: "Be imitators of me, as I am of Christ" (1 Cor 11:1). Enthralled by his Lord, that supreme person Christ Jesus, Paul was forever busy listening for Christ's voice, forever seeking to fulfill the vision laid out for his life by his Lord. Paul not only knew the name "Jesus," but also *he experienced the risen Jesus.*

(2) Paul appreciated, recognized, and encouraged others. The many gracious compliments found in his letters are genuine, and not merely contrived. He was not making verbal backslaps with political ends in mind. Leaders of integrity, leaders who value people as persons, avoid the semblance of friendship.

(3) Paul always kept "the big picture" in view as he planned and worked. Even in this letter, something larger remains in view than the reconciling of Onesimus and Philemon, as essential as that was. Paul was eager to see the Christian enterprise move forward with greater effectiveness (see v. 6).

(4) Paul knew how, when, and to whom to delegate responsibilities. He needed to enlist the help of others, to be sure, but he also trusted their help and complimented those who gave it.

(5) Paul observed protocol, doing what he sensed to be right at the right time and in the right way.

(6) Paul had goals and sought to reach them through strategic means: prayer, planning, and the help of others, providing honest and honorable incentives to those who assisted him. The Letter to Philemon well illustrates this.

(7) Paul's leadership was characterized by the *servant-leader attitude.* He was not self-centered. He aspired to live what Martin Buber referred to in another connection as an "unexalted life."[22] "Christ will be exlated now as always in my body, whether by life or by death" (Phil 1:20*b*).

21. Cited from *New Testament Apocrypha*, vol. II: *Writings Relating to the Apostles, Apocalypses, and Related Subjects*, ed. Edgar Hennecke, Wilhelm Schneemelcher, Eng. trans. ed. Robert McLachlan Wilson (London: Lutterworth, 1965) 353-54. The assessment of the account as embodying "a very early tradition" is that of W. M. Ramsay, *The Church in the Roman Empire: Before* A.D. 170 (New York: G. P. Putnam's Sons, 1893) 32.

22. See Maurice Friedman, *Encounter on the Narrow Ridge: A Life of Martin Buber* (New York: Paragon House, 1991) 44.

These were some of the traits Paul's circle of friends were familiar with as they followed his lead. Small wonder, then, that he remained so influential and that his coterie of workers remained so loyal. Paul had that personal "power" about which Ralph Waldo Emerson commented in one of his essays: "Who shall set a limit to the influence of a human being? There are [leaders], who, by their sympathetic attractions, carry nations with them, and lead the activity of the human race."[23] While each of us has particular gifts with which to further the cause of Jesus Christ, we, too, would do well to follow Paul's lead as appropriate to our circumstances.

23. Ralph Waldo Emerson, "Power," in *Ralph Waldo Emerson: Essays and Lectures,* compiled by Joel Porter (New York: Library of America, 1983) 971.

TRANSLITERATION SCHEMA

HEBREW AND ARAMAIC TRANSLITERATION

Consonants:

א	=	’	ט	=	*ṭ*	פ or ף	=	*p*
ב	=	*b*	י	=	*y*	צ or ץ	=	*ṣ*
ג	=	*g*	כ or ך	=	*k*	ק	=	*q*
ד	=	*d*	ל	=	*l*	ר	=	*r*
ה	=	*h*	מ or ם	=	*m*	שׂ	=	*ś*
ו	=	*w*	נ or ן	=	*n*	שׁ	=	*š*
ז	=	*z*	ס	=	*s*	ת	=	*t*
ח	=	*ḥ*	ע	=	‘			

Masoretic Pointing:

Pure-long			Tone-long			Short			Composite		
הָ	=	*â*	ָ	=	*ā*	ַ	=	*a*	ֲ	=	*ă*
ֵי	=	*ê*	ֶ	=	*ē*	ֶ	=	*e*	ֱ or ֳ	=	*ĕ*
or ִי	=	*î*	ֵ			ִ	=	*i*			
or וֹ	=	*ô*	ֹ	=	*ō*	ָ	=	*o*	ֳ	=	*ŏ*
or וּ	=	*û*				ֻ	=	*u*			

GREEK TRANSLITERATION

α	=	*a*	ι	=	*i*	ρ	=	*r*
β	=	*b*	κ	=	*k*	σ or ς	=	*s*
γ	=	*g*	λ	=	*l*	τ	=	*t*
δ	=	*d*	μ	=	*m*	υ	=	*y*
ε	=	*e*	ν	=	*n*	φ	=	*ph*
ζ	=	*z*	ξ	=	*x*	χ	=	*ch*
η	=	*ē*	ο	=	*o*	ψ	=	*ps*
θ	=	*th*	π	=	*p*	ω	=	*ō*

Index of Maps, Charts, and Illustrations

INDEX OF EXCURSUSES

ABBREVIATIONS

BCE	Before the Common Era
CE	Common Era
c.	circa
cf.	compare
chap(s).	chapter(s)
d.	died
Dtr	deuteronomic historian
esp.	especially
fem.	feminine
HB	Hebrew Bible
lit.	literally
l(l).	line(s)
LXX	Septuagint
masc.	masculiine
MS(S)	manuscript(s)
MT	Masoretic Text
n.(n.)	note(s)
NT	New Testament
OL	Old Latin
OT	Old Testament
par.	parallel(s)
pl(s).	plate(s)
v(v).	verse(s)
Vg	Vulgate

Names of Biblical Books

Gen	Nah	1–4 Kgdms	John
Exod	Hab	Add Esth	Acts
Lev	Zeph	Bar	Rom
Num	Hag	Bel	1–2 Cor
Deut	Zech	1–2 Esdr	Gal
Josh	Mal	4 Ezra	Eph
Judg	Ps (Pss)	Jdt	Phil
1–2 Sam	Job	Ep Jer	Col
1–2 Kgs	Prov	1–4 Macc	1–2 Thess
Isa	Ruth	Pr Azar	1–2 Tim
Jer	Cant	Pr Man	Titus
Ezek	Eccl	Sir	Phlm
Hos	Lam	Sus	Heb
Joel	Esth	Tob	Jas
Amos	Dan	Wis	1–2 Pet
Obad	Ezra	Matt	1–3 John
Jonah	Neh	Mark	Jude
Mic	1–2 Chr	Luke	Rev

Names of Pseudepigrapical and Early Patristic Works

2 Apoc. Bar.	Syriac *Apocalypse of Baruch*
1-2-3 Enoch	Ethiopic, Slavonic, Hebrew *Enoch*
2 Enoch	Slavonic *Book of Enoch*
Apoc. Abr.	*Apocalypse of Abraham*

Apoc. Mos.	*Apocalypse of Moses*
Ascen. Isa.	*Ascension of Isaiah*
1-2 Clem.	*1-2 Clement*
Herm. Sim.	*Hermas, Similitude(s)*
Ign. *Magn.*	Ignatius, *Letter to the Magnesians*
Ign. *Smyrn.*	Ignatius, *Letter to the Smyrnaeans*
Jub.	*Jubilees*
POxy	B. P. Grenfell and A. S. Hunt (eds.), *Oxyrynchus Papyri*
Pss Sol	*Psalms of Solomon*
Sib. Or.	*Sibylline Oracles*
T. Benj.	*Testament of Benjamin*
T. Dan	*Testament of Dan*
T. Iss.	*Testament of Issachar*
T. Job	*Testament of Job*
T. Jud.	*Testament of Judah*
T. Levi	*Testament of Levi*
T. Naph.	*Testament of Naphtali*
T. Reub.	*Testament of Reuben*
T. Sim.	*Testament of Simeon*

Names of Dead Sea Scrolls and Related Texts

CD	Cairo text of the *Damascus Document*
Q	Qumran
1Q, 2Q, etc.	Numbered caves of Qumran, yielding written material; followed by abbreviation of biblical or apocryphal book
1Q28b	*Rule of the Blessings* (Qumran Cave 1)
1QH	*Thanksgiving Hymns* (Qumran Cave 1)
1QM	*War Scroll* (Qumran Cave 1)
1QpHab	*Pesher on Habakkuk* (Qumran Cave 1)
1QpPs	*Pesher on Psalms* (Qumran Cave 1)
1QS	*Rule of the Community* (Qumran Cave 1)
1QSa	*Rule of the Congregation* (Appendix a to 1QS)
1QSb	Appendix B (*Blessings*) to 1QS
4Q298	*Cryptic A: Words of the Sage to the Sons of Dawn* (Qumran Cave 4)
4Q416	*Sapiential Work A^b* (Qumran Cave 4)
4Q521	*Messianic Apocalypse* (Qumran Cave 4)
4QMMT	*Halakhic Letter* (Qumran Cave 4)
4QpNah	

Orders and Tractates in Mishnaic and Related Literature

Abot	*Abot*
Hag.	*Hagigah*
Ket.	*Ketubbot*

Other Rabbinic Works

Rab.	*Rabbah* (following abbreviation of biblical book: *Gen. Rab.* [with periods] = *Genesis Rabbah*

ABBREVIATIONS

$\mathfrak{P}^{46}$ Third-century Greek Papyrus manuscript of the Gospels

Names of Nag Hammadi Tractates

Ap. John	Apocryphon of John
Apoc. Adam	Apocalypse of Adam
Ep. Pet.	Letter of Peter to Philip
Exeg. Soul	Exegesis on the Soul
Gos. Phil.	Gospel of Philip
Gos. Truth	Gospel of Truth

Commonly Used Periodicals, Reference Works, and Serials

AB	Anchor Bible
ABD	D. N. Freedman (ed.), Anchor Bible Dictionary
AnBib	Analecta biblica
ANF	The Ante-Nicene Fathers
ANTC	Abingdon New Testament Commentaries
AusBR	Australian Biblical Review
BAGD	W. Bauer, W. F. Arndt, F. W. Gingrich (2nd ed.:, and F. W. Danker), Greek-English Lexicon of the New Testament
BDF	F. Blass, A. Debrunner, and R. W. Funk, A Greek Grammar of the New Testament
BEvT	Beitrage zur evanelischen Theologie
Bib	Biblica
CBQ	Catholic Biblical Quarterly
ConB	Coniectanea biblica
EvQ	Evangelical Quarterly
ExpTim	Expository Times
FRLANT	Forschungen zur Religion und Literatur des Alten und Neuen Testaments
HDR	Harvard Dissertations in Religion
HNT	Handbuch zum Neuen Testament
HTKNT	Herders theologischer Kommentar zum Neuen Testament
HTR	Harvard Theological Review
IB	Interpreter's Bible
ICC	International Critical Commentary
JAAR	Journal of the American Academy of Religion
JBL	Journal of Biblical Literature
JSNT	Journal for the Study of the New Testament
JSNTSup	Journal for the Study of the New Testament— Supplement Series
JThC	Journal for Theology and the Church
JTS	Journal of Theological Studies
LCL	Loeb Classical Library
NCB	New Century Bible
NIGTC	The New International Greek Testament Commentary
NIB	New Interpreter's Bible
NIV	New Internation Version
NovT	Novum Testamentum
NRSV	New Revised Standard Version
NTS	New Testament Studies
OBT	Overtures to Biblical Theology
PGM	K. Preisendanz (ed.), Papyri graecae magicae
RB	Revue biblique
SBLDS	SBL Dissertation Series
SBLMS	SBL Monograph Series
SBLRBS	SBL Resources for Biblical Study
SEÅ	Svensk exegetisk årsbok
SNTSMS	Society for New Testament Studies Monograph Series
TDNT	G.Kittel and G. Friedrich (eds.), Theological Dictionary of the New Testament
TynBul	Tyndale Bulletin

UBSGNT	United Bible Societies *Greek New Testament*
WBC	Word Biblical Commentary
WUNT	Wissenschaftliche Untersuchungen zum Neuen Testament
ZNW	*Zeitschrift für die neutestamentliche Wissenschaft*
ZThK	*Zeitschrift für Theologie und Kirche*